AF838334

INTERNATIONAL YEARBOOK OF INDUSTRIAL STATISTICS

2009

INTERNATIONAL YEARBOOK
OF
INDUSTRIAL STATISTICS
2009

UNITED NATIONS INDUSTRIAL DEVELOPMENT ORGANIZATION
VIENNA
2009

© United Nations Industrial Development Organization (UNIDO) 2009

All rights reserved. No part of this publication may be reproduced, stored in a retrieval system or transmitted in any form or by any means, electronic, mechanical or photocopying, recording, or otherwise without the prior permission of the publisher.

Published by
Edward Elgar Publishing Limited
The Lypiatts
15 Lansdown Road
Cheltenham
Glos GL50 2JA
UK

Edward Elgar Publishing, Inc.
The William Pratt House
9 Dewey Court
Northampton
Massachusetts 01060-3815
USA

A catalogue record for this book
is available from the British Library

The description and classification of countries and territories in this publication and the arrangement of the material do not imply the expression of any opinion whatsoever on the part of the Secretariat of the United Nations Industrial Development Organization concerning the legal status of any country, territory, city or area, or of its authorities, or concerning the delimitation of its frontiers or boundaries, or regarding its economic system or degree of development. The designation "country or area" covers countries, territories, cities and areas. The designation "region, country or area" extends the preceding one by including groupings of entities designated as "country or area". Designations such as "industrialized" and "developing" countries and "newly industrialized countries" are intended for statistical convenience and do not necessarily express a judgement about the stage reached by a particular country or area in the development process.

ISBN 978 1 84844 366 2

Printed and bound in Great Britain by MPG Books Ltd, Bodmin, Cornwall

Acknowledgements

The 2009 edition of the *International Yearbook of Industrial Statistics* was prepared by a team of statistical staff under the supervision of Shyam Upadhyaya, Chief Statistician of UNIDO. Overall IT support was provided by Valentin Todorov, who managed the integrated statistical databases and produced the final PDF/digital manuscript. Ömer Aksoycan, Brigitte Leutner, Rita Liang, Regina McFerren-Zenz and Véronique Pecenka were responsible for the collection of data and the compilation of the regional and country tables. Administrative support was provided to the team by Liliya Kirchberger. Anja Sedic joined the team at a later stage and contributed to the final verification of the tables in Part I.

Important contributions to the publication were made by a number of short-term staff and consultants. Nicolai Christov and Bernhard Karner assisted in the development and maintenance of the software infrastructure. Markus Fröhlich updated the GDP and manufacturing value added (MVA) database and produced recent year estimates, while Svetlin Tzolov collected the required data from different international sources. Kris Boudt provided methodological advice for improving nowcasting models and related statistical software applications.

The team members wish to express their sincere thanks to Ludovico Alcorta, Director of the Research and Statistics Branch of UNIDO, for his support during all stages of the preparation of this publication.

The co-operation of national statistical offices, the United Nations Statistics Division (UNSD), the Organisation for Economic Co-operation and Development (OECD), the World Bank and other international and regional agencies in providing the information that has served as the basis of the current publication is gratefully acknowledged.

Explanatory notes

Unless otherwise indicated, "manufacturing" includes the industry groups listed under major division D of the *International Standard Industrial Classification of All Economic Activities* [Statistical Papers, Series M, No.4/Rev.3 (United Nations publication, Sales No. E.90.XVII.II)]. It should be noted, however, that several countries have not made a switchover from their national industrial classification schemes that are based on, or related to, Revision 2 of the International Standard Industrial Classification of All Economic Activities (ISIC) [Statistical Papers, Series M, No.4/Rev.2 (United Nations publication, Sales No. E.68.XVII.8)] to those based on, or related to, Revision 3 of ISIC. In these instances, "manufacturing" refers to table category 3 in that classification.

ISIC code numbers are accompanied by a descriptive title (for example in the case of Revision 3 of ISIC, ISIC 2813: "Manufacture of steam generators, except central heating hot water boilers"). For considerations of space, however, the description is sometimes shortened (that is, ISIC 2813 may be described simply as "Steam generators"). For both Revisions 2 and 3 of ISIC, all 2-, 3- and 4-digit codes and their corresponding descriptive titles are listed in appendix II to the introduction.

In the presentation of several tables individual countries and areas are listed alphabetically, whenever appropriate, within two successive categories: industrialized countries and developing countries. Data relating to selected groups of countries are presented in part I. In addition to regional groupings, developing countries have been further classified into three income categories: developing countries with low income (less than $1,000 per capita gross domestic product in 2005 at current prices), those with middle income ($1,000 – $5,000) and those with high income (more than $5,000). This group has also been arranged in three development categories: newly industrialized countries (NICs), least developed countries and other developing countries. NICs category in this publication combines previous groupings of NICs and second generation NICs and few more countries selected on the basis of four variables: share in world MVA, MVA per capita, MVA share in GDP and the share of manufactured exports in total.

Hong Kong became the Hong Kong Special Administrative Region (SAR) of China on 1 July 1997. Macao became the Macao Special Administrative Region (SAR) of China on 20 December 1999. In the present publication, unless otherwise stated, data for China do not include data for Hong Kong SAR, for Macao SAR or for Taiwan Province of China, which are presented separately under China (Hong Kong SAR), China (Macao SAR) and China (Taiwan Province).

Countries and areas included in the groups are listed in appendix I to the introduction. Because of a lack of data, some countries could not be included in their respective groups in some tables.

Regardless of the year/period referred to, the country group European Union (EU) is related to the group consisting of the 27 countries shown under that country group in appendix I to the introduction. The abbreviation 'EU-15' refers to the European Union of 15 member countries before its enlargement in May 2004 (Austria, Belgium, Denmark, Finland, France, Germany, Greece, Ireland, Italy, Luxembourg, the Netherlands, Portugal, Spain, Sweden, United Kingdom). The abbreviation 'EU-12' refers to the 12 new member countries that acceded to the European Union after May 2004 (Bulgaria, the Czech Republic, Cyprus, Estonia, Hungary, Latvia, Lithuania, Malta, Poland, Romania, Slovakia and Slovenia).

In part I, references to dollars ($) are to United States dollars. National currencies have been converted to dollar equivalents by using period average exchange rates as published in *International Financial Statistics* (International Monetary Fund publication) and other sources.

Data converted to dollars by using current exchange rates are liable to be strongly influenced by fluctuations in exchange rates. Annual variations of data converted in that manner may not reflect movements in the national data.

In part II, for all member countries of the European Monetary Union (EMU), national data are expressed in Euros.

Unless otherwise noted, average annual growth rates are calculated from the data available for each year of a given period (for example, 2000-2005), using a semi-log regression over time. Growth rates are expressed in percentages.

Periods set off by a hyphen (for instance, 2000-2005) include the beginning and end years.

Apparent arithmetical discrepancies, such as percentages that do not add up to precise totals, result from the rounding of basic data or figures known to different degrees of precision.

Three dots (...) indicate that data are not available or are not separately reported.

A dash (-) indicates that an amount is nil or negligible.

The letter "x" designates the item applicable to a country when several options exist.

To avoid ambiguity, the letters "l", "o" and "O" are not used to designate footnotes.

The following abbreviations and acronyms are used:

ASEAN	Association of South-East Asian Nations
CACM	Central American Common Market
CARICOM	Caribbean Community
CEMAC	Central African Economic and Monetary Community
CEPGL	Economic Community of the Great Lakes Countries
CIS	Commonwealth of Independent States
ECOWAS	Economic Community of West African States
EMU	European Monetary Union
EU	European Union
EU-15	The 15 member countries of the EU before enlargement in May 2004
EU-12	The 12 new member countries that acceded to the EU after May 2004
GDP	gross domestic product
ISIC	International Standard Industrial Classification of All Economic Activities
LAIA	Latin American Integration Association
LDCs	least developed countries
MVA	manufacturing value added
n.e.c.	not elsewhere classified
n.e.s.	not elsewhere specified
NICs	newly industrialized countries
OECD	Organisation for Economic Co-operation and Development
OECS	Organization of Eastern Caribbean States
SAARC	South Asian Association for Regional Co-operation
UNIDO	United Nations Industrial Development Organization
UNSD	United Nations Statistics Division
VAT	value added tax

CONTENTS

Page

Page

PART II. COUNTRY TABLES [a/]

[a/] For information on the countries/areas that are not presented, please see page 181.

DATA AVAILABLE ON CD-ROM

UNIDO maintains several databases on industrial statistics, of which new sales versions are made available annually.

UNIDO INDSTAT4
Industrial Statistics
Database at the 4-digit
level of ISIC (Revision 2 and 3)

- **INDSTAT4-Rev.3** contains time series data on seven selected data items (number of establishments, total employment, female employment, wages and salaries paid to employees, output, value added and gross fixed capital formation) starting 1990 onwards. The data are arranged at the 3- and 4-digit level of ISIC (Revision 3) pertaining to the manufacturing sector, which comprises 151 manufacturing categories.

- **INDSTAT4-Rev.2** is available to the user to supplement INDSTAT4-Rev.3. The data refer to the seven variables and period 1981 onwards and are arranged according to ISIC (Revision 2) at the 4-digit level, which comprises 81 manufacturing industries.

- All value data are originally stored in national currency values at current prices. The system allows for data conversion from national currency into current U.S. dollars.

UNIDO IDSB
Industrial Demand-Supply
Balance Database at the 4-digit
level of ISIC (Revision 2 and 3)

- Time series (starting in 1990) for more than 75 countries on output, imports, exports and apparent consumption (all in current US dollars) at the 4-digit level of ISIC (Revision 3), supplemented with a similar database in accordance with ISIC (Revision 2).

Further details on above products may be obtained from:
Statistics Unit
Research and Statistics Branch, UNIDO
P.O. Box 300, A-1400 Vienna, Austria
Fax: +43-1-26026-6802
Email: stat@unido.org
INTERNET: http://www.unido.org

INTRODUCTION

This is the fifteenth issue of UNIDO's annual publication, the *International Yearbook of Industrial Statistics*. The *Yearbook* succeeded the *Handbook of Industrial Statistics* which was published biennially by UNIDO up to 1992. At the same time, it replaced the United Nations' *Industrial Statistics Yearbook,* volume I (General Industrial Statistics), which was discontinued after its 1991 edition published in 1993. These changes were in accordance with the recommendations of the United Nations Statistical Commission at its twenty-seventh session, namely that UNIDO, in collaboration with the Organisation for Economic Co-operation and Development (OECD), assumes responsibility for the collection and dissemination of world-wide general industrial statistics, effective 1994. The present *Yearbook* pertains to the manufacturing sector only.

The main purpose of the *Yearbook* is to provide statistical indicators to facilitate international comparisons relating to the manufacturing sector. The data presented were compiled bearing in mind the requirements of international comparability and the standards for this work promulgated by the United Nations. Concepts and definitions are drawn from the *International Recommendations for Industrial Statistics* [Statistical Papers, Series M, No.48/Rev.1 (United Nations publication, Sales No.E.83.XVII.8)] and the classification by industry follows Revision 2 or Revision 3 of ISIC.

The present *Yearbook* consists of two parts. Part I deals with the manufacturing sector as a whole (section 1.1) and with its divisions/branches (section 1.2). Statistical indicators are presented in terms of percentage distributions, cross-country averages, ratios and real growth rates that facilitate international comparison among selected country groups and/or countries. In the present publication data for manufacturing divisions/branches are arranged according to Revision 3 of ISIC at the two- or three-digit level. Part II consists of a series of country/area-specific tables showing detailed data on selected basic statistics that were reported by national statistical offices. Most countries have made a switchover from their national industrial classifications compatible with Revision 2 to those compatible with Revision 3 of ISIC. Consequently, data for those countries are presented in accordance with Revision 3 of ISIC. However, for some countries, data are still presented in accordance with Revision 2 of ISIC.

For the first time, part I of the Yearbook includes some graphical presentations followed by a brief description of the overall trend of world industrial growth.

Sources and methods

In section 1.1 of part I, manufacturing value added (MVA) was estimated in accordance with the national accounting concept, which represents the net contribution of the manufacturing sector to gross domestic product (GDP). The data on MVA and GDP were obtained from various national and international sources including the World Bank, OECD, the United Nations Statistics Division (UNSD), the International Monetary Fund and regional development banks. These sources were supplemented with estimates generated by UNIDO.

GDP and MVA data at constant prices refer to the year 2000, which was rebased from 1995 prior to the publication of the 2008 edition of the Yearbook. Due to the change in base year for constant prices there might be differences between the data shown in the present edition of the Yearbook and those shown in earlier editions. Figures with respect to population emanate from the 2006 revision of data compiled by the Population Division of the United Nations Secretariat.

The information in section 1.2 is drawn from the UNIDO Industrial Statistics Database, as well as data communicated to the United Nations by official national sources. With regard to the member countries of OECD, data were compiled by that organization. Information is solicited through a questionnaire issued jointly by the two organizations.

To facilitate the comparability of the data over time and across countries, UNIDO has supplemented originally reported data with information obtained from various other sources. The latter include: industrial censuses, statistics supplied by national and international organizations, unpublished data collected in the field by UNIDO as well as estimates made by the UNIDO secretariat.[1]

---

[1] UNIDO's procedures for estimation are described in *"UNIDO Industrial Statistics Database — Methodological Notes"* (IRD/R.11).

The indicators presented in tables 1.5 to 1.9 of section 1.2 were derived from estimates of value added at constant 2000 prices. For each country and industrial division, these value-added estimates were generated by applying production indexes to the 2000 value-added base weights, which in turn were generated by UNIDO from various national and international sources.

Except for index numbers of industrial production, the information for the countries and areas other than the OECD member countries, presented in part II, were compiled from (i) the 2006 edition of the UNIDO General Industrial Statistics Questionnaires completed by national statistical offices and (ii) relevant publications issued by national statistical offices. Information referring to OECD member countries is based on data compiled by OECD via questionnaires and incorporated in OECD's Information System on Industrial Statistics as well as in the UNIDO database. With respect to production indexes, data were supplied by UNSD that compiles these data regularly from national sources through the quarterly United Nations Index of Industrial Production Questionnaires.

In section 1.2 of part I and in part II, the measures generally used are census output and census value added. Thus, the costs of non-industrial services are included in value added, whereas the receipts for these services are excluded from output. For a quick reference, appendix III to this introduction provides notes on certain aspects of the data used, and it is recommended that the reader consult them when using the *Yearbook*. A detailed version appears in the individual country notes in part II, which also covers deviations from the standards applied. In general, these notes are also applicable to the estimates that supplement the officially reported data.

PART I. SUMMARY TABLES

Section 1.1: The manufacturing sector

Section 1.1 comprises tables 1.1 to 1.4. Table 1.1 shows the distribution of world MVA for various regions and groups of countries at constant 2000 prices as well as at current prices.

The reader should be aware that due to variation in official exchange rates the world distribution may change considerably, depending on the choice of the base year.

To maintain comparability over time, composition of each group of countries was kept the same throughout the period. In this connection, EU refers to the 27 countries that are listed in appendix I to this introduction. However, due to data limitations, several developing countries listed in appendix I are not included.

In tables 1.2 to 1.4, taking into account the large size of its economy, China is not included in the group classified according to income level or the group classified according to development level.

Table 1.2 shows the shares of selected groups of developing countries in MVA and in population of all developing countries. For the definitions of the income categories, see "Explanatory notes".

Table 1.3 shows real growth rates and index numbers (2000=100) of total and per-capita MVA as well as values of per-capita MVA for the latest year 2007 for individual countries and areas and for selected country groups. Data referring to country groups were based on cross-country aggregates of MVA in constant 2000 US dollars.

Table 1.4 shows the percentage shares of MVA in GDP estimated at both constant 2000 prices and current prices. The data are presented by individual countries and areas as well as by selected country groups. With respect to the selected country groups, common country samples were taken for both indicators and for all reference years.

Section 1.2: The manufacturing divisions/branches

Section 1.2 comprises tables 1.5 to 1.11. It focuses on the divisions/branches of the manufacturing sector. The ISIC (Revision 3) definition of manufacturing consists of 23 divisions reported in accordance with a two-digit code and 61 branches reported in accordance with a three-digit code.

In tables 1.5 to 1.9, Recycling (ISIC 37) had to be excluded from the presentation due to data limitations. Data for China and China (Taiwan Province) are UNIDO estimates. Furthermore, a number of estimates at the country level, especially for many developing countries, were also generated to enable regional aggregation or to derive world totals for the latest years.

Table 1.5 shows the world distribution of the respective value added of selected divisions among selected country groups.

Table 1.6 shows the shares of developing regions and the least developed countries in the value added of all developing countries in selected divisions.

Table 1.7 shows the world's leading producers in various industrial divisions as well as the leading developing countries and areas in terms of value added.

Table 1.8 shows the shares of individual divisions in total MVA by country grouping.

Table 1.9 shows real growth rates of value added of individual divisions, calculated for selected country groups. The reference periods are 2000-2005 and 2005-2007.

Table 1.10 presents the share of female employees in total employment in individual divisions. For some countries, employment refers to number of persons engaged instead of number of employees (see appendix III of the present introduction). Only a limited number of countries and areas have reported data on female employment at the division level.

Table 1.11 shows, for individual countries and areas, basic indicators that are characteristic of the manufacturing branches. Costs of input materials and utilities are calculated as output minus value added. Costs of labour refer to wages and salaries of employees only. Operating surplus is calculated as value added minus wages and salaries paid to employees.

Information concerning the following branches is excluded from table 1.11: Dressing & dyeing of fur; processing of fur (ISIC 1820); Reproduction of recorded media (ISIC 2230); Coke oven products (ISIC 2310); Refined petroleum products (ISIC 2320); Processing of nuclear fuel (ISIC 2330); Man-made fibres (ISIC 2430); Watches and clocks (ISIC 3330); Railway/tramway locomotives & rolling stock (ISIC 3520); Aircraft and spacecraft (ISIC 3530); Transport equipment n.e.c. (ISIC 359); Recycling of metal waste and scrap (ISIC 3710); Recycling of non-metal waste and scrap (ISIC 3720).

PART II. COUNTRY TABLES

Part II comprises country/area-specific tables presenting the following selected industrial statistics: number of establishments, number of employees (or, if not reported, number of persons engaged), wages and salaries paid to employees, output, value added, gross fixed capital formation and index numbers of industrial production. All value data are presented in current national currencies. The data on these items (except gross fixed capital formation and index numbers of industrial production) relate to the last four years for which data were reported. Gross fixed capital formation refers to the last two years for which data were reported. Index numbers of industrial production refer to the period 1995-2006.

Coverage of countries/areas

The countries/areas that are presented in part II are those which reported data during the current round of the UNIDO annual compilation programme of global industrial statistics. Those countries/areas, which reported data only in previous rounds of the UNIDO compilation programme, are not included in the present *Yearbook,* but were included in previous editions. At the beginning of part II, those countries/areas are listed together with a reference to the respective editions of the *Yearbook* in which their latest data were presented.

Industrial classification

The classification of industrial activity, set out in the tables, follows either Revision 2 or Revision 3 of ISIC, at the two-, three- and four-digit levels of ISIC depending on the individual country's data reporting scheme. Where information was not provided in this form, the estimates are shown in the most applicable ISIC category. Aggregates for total manufacturing are included. With regard to production indexes, data are arranged in accordance with the 2-digit level of Revision 3 of ISIC.

It should be noted that in several cases a figure presented for a 3-digit group does not agree with the sum of data given for the corresponding 4-digit categories. As far as possible, UNIDO resolved these discrepancies with the help of available supplementary information.

Reference unit

For most countries and areas represented, the data shown relate to the activity of "establishments" in the specified industries rather than any other type of industrial unit. In a few cases, however, the concepts of "kind-of-activity unit", "local unit" or "enterprise" are found. An "establishment" is ideally a unit that engages, under a single ownership or control, in one, or predominantly one, kind of activity at a single location; for example, workshop or factory. A "kind-of-activity unit" differs from the establishment in that there is no restriction with respect to the geographical area in which a given kind of activity is carried out by a single legal entity. A "local unit", on the other hand, comprises all activities carried out under a single ownership or control at a single location and differs from the establishment-type of unit in that there is no restriction on the range of these activities. An "enterprise" is a legal entity possessing the right to conduct business in its own name; for example, to enter into contracts, own property, incur liability for debts, and establish bank accounts. Specific information on the character of the units covered in the tables for each country is set out in the corresponding country note.

Reference period
The statistics in the tables relate, in general, to the calendar year. It should be noted, however, that in many cases where the basic reference period of the industrial inquiry is the calendar year, returns covering proximate fiscal years may be accepted for reporting purposes and the data for these years, incorporated in the calendar-year, aggregate without adjustment. In a few countries, fiscal years normally used for public accounting purposes have been adopted as the basic reference periods. In the case of fiscal-year coverage, the year indicated in the tables refers to the calendar year in which the major part of the fiscal year falls. In the case of fiscal years from 1 July to 30 June, the year referred to is normally the one in which the fiscal year ends.

Concepts and definitions of the items
The United Nations standards that have been applied in preparing the tables are set out below. All values are in national currency units and are at current prices unless otherwise indicated. For countries other than the OECD member countries, deviations from these concepts and definitions are described in the respective country notes. The country notes referring to OECD member countries are based on information presented in OECD's annual publication "Structural and Demographic Business Statistics 1996-2003".

(1) Number of persons engaged and number of employees
The number of persons engaged is defined as the total number of persons who worked in or for the establishment during the reference year. However, home workers are excluded. The concept covers working proprietors, active business partners and unpaid family workers as well as employees. The figures reported refer normally to the average number of persons engaged during the reference year, obtained as the sum of the "average number of employees" during the year and the total number of other persons engaged measured for a single period of the year. The category "employees" is intended to include all persons engaged other than working proprietors, active business partners and unpaid family workers. In this publication, preference has been given, whenever possible, to employees over persons engaged.

(2) Wages and salaries
Estimates of wages and salaries include all payments in cash or in kind made to "employees" during the reference year in relation to work done for the establishment. Payments include: (a) direct wages and salaries; (b) remuneration for time not worked; (c) bonuses and gratuities; (d) housing allowances and family allowances paid directly by the employer; and (e) payments in kind.

Compensation of employees is equivalent to wages and salaries plus employers' contributions on behalf of their employees paid to social security, pension and insurance schemes, as well as the benefits received by employees under these schemes and severance and termination pay.

(3) Output
The measure of output normally used in the tables is the census concept that covers only activities of an industrial nature. The value of census output in the case of estimates compiled on a production basis comprises: (a) the value of all products of the establishment; (b) the net change between the beginning and the end of the reference period in the value of work in progress and stocks of goods to be shipped in the same condition as received; (c) the value of industrial work done or industrial services rendered to others; (d) the value of goods shipped in the same condition as received less the amount paid for these goods; and (e) the value of fixed assets produced during the period by the unit for its own use. In the case of estimates compiled on a shipment basis, the net change in the value of stocks of finished goods between the beginning and the end of the reference period is also included.

Gross output is equivalent to census output plus the revenue from activities of a non-industrial nature. Valuation methods differ from country to country. An increasing number of countries are reporting at basic prices, which excludes taxes on commodity and includes commodity related subsidies. Other methods of reporting valuation are: (a) at factor costs, which excludes all indirect taxes falling on production and includes all current subsidies received in support of production activities; and (b) in producers' prices, which includes all indirect taxes except VAT, or any other deductible taxes and excludes all subsidies.

(4) Value added
The measure of value added normally used in the tables is the census concept, which is defined as the value of census output less the value of census input. Items covered in the latter include: (a) value of materials and supplies for production (including cost of all fuel and purchased electricity); and (b) cost of industrial services received (mainly payments for contract and commission work and repair and maintenance work). If input estimates are compiled on a "received" rather than on a "consumed" basis, the result is adjusted for the net change between the beginning and the end of the period in the value of stocks of materials, fuel and other supplies.

Total value added is the national accounting concept. It is ideally represented by the contribution of the establishments in each branch of activity to the gross domestic product. For the measure of total value added, the cost of non-industrial services is deducted and the receipts for non-industrial services are added to census value added. The estimates, whether in terms of census value added or total value added, are gross of depreciation and other provisions for capital consumption, unless otherwise stated. The valuation may be at factor costs, at basic prices or in producers' prices, depending on the treatment of indirect taxes and subsidies as described above.

(5) Gross fixed capital formation

Estimates refer to the value of purchases and own-account construction of fixed assets during the reference year less the value of corresponding sales. The fixed assets covered are those (whether new or used) with a productive life of one year or more. These assets, which are intended for the use of the establishment, include fixed assets made by the establishment's own labour force for its own use. Major additions, alterations and improvements to existing assets that extend their normal economic life or raise their productivity are also included. New fixed assets include all those that have not been previously used in the country. Thus, newly imported fixed assets are considered new whether or not used before they were imported. Used fixed assets include all those that have been previously used within the country.

Transactions in fixed assets include: (a) cost of land purchased and land improvement; (b) buildings and structures; and (c) machinery and equipment. Countries that have started implementation of recent recommendations for industrial statistics might have extended the coverage of fixed assets to products of research and development, computer software and database and other intellectual property products.

Assets acquired from others are valued at purchasers' prices, which cover all costs directly connected with the acquisition and installation of the items for use. In principle, assets produced on own account are also valued in this manner. However, it may frequently be necessary to value such own-account production at explicit cost, including any imputations that may be required in respect of the employed own-account labour.

Assets produced by one establishment of a multi-establishment enterprise, for the use of another establishment of the same enterprise, should be valued by the receiving establishment as though purchased from outside the enterprise. Sales of assets should be valued at the actual amounts realized rather than at book values.

(6) Index numbers of industrial production

The indexes in the tables are compiled from national indexes that are calculated by use of the Laspeyres formula. The comparison base year is 2000. However, if different base years are used in any countries, the national indexes are converted to the comparison base year.

APPENDIX I
LIST OF COUNTRIES AND AREAS INCLUDED IN SELECTED GROUPINGS
INDUSTRIALIZED COUNTRIES

CIS

Armenia
Azerbaijan
Belarus
Georgia
Kazakhstan
Kyrgyzstan
Republic of Moldova
Russian Federation
Tajikistan
Turkmenistan
Ukraine
Uzbekistan

EU

Austria
Belgium
Bulgaria
Cyprus
Czech Republic
Denmark
Estonia
Finland
France
Germany
Greece
Hungary
Ireland
Italy
Latvia
Lithuania
Luxembourg
Malta
Netherlands
Poland
Portugal
Romania
Slovakia
Slovenia
Spain
Sweden
United Kingdom

Other Europe

Iceland
Norway
Switzerland

East Asia

Japan
Republic of Korea
Singapore

North America

Canada
United States of America

Others

Australia
Israel
New Zealand
South Africa

APPENDIX I

(continued)

LIST OF COUNTRIES AND AREAS INCLUDED IN SELECTED GROUPINGS

DEVELOPING COUNTRY GROUPING BY REGION

North Africa

Algeria
Egypt
Libyan Arab Jamahiriya
Morocco
Sudan
Tunisia

Central Africa

Angola
Burundi
Cameroon
Central African Republic
Chad
Congo
Democratic Rep. of the Congo
Equatorial Guinea
Gabon
Rwanda
Sao Tome and Principe

Western Africa (ECOWAS)

Benin
Burkina Faso
Cape Verde
Côte d'Ivoire
Gambia
Ghana
Guinea
Guinea-Bissau
Liberia
Mali
Mauritania
Niger
Nigeria
Senegal
Sierra Leone
Togo

Eastern and Southern Africa

Botswana
Comoros
Djibouti
Eritrea
Ethiopia
Kenya
Lesotho
Madagascar
Malawi
Mauritius
Mozambique
Namibia
Réunion
Seychelles
Somalia
Swaziland
Uganda
United Republic of Tanzania
Zambia
Zimbabwe

Europe

Albania
Bosnia and Herzegovina
Croatia
Montenegro
Serbia
The former Yugoslav Rep. of Macedonia
Turkey

Asia

Afghanistan
Bahrain
Bangladesh
Bhutan
Brunei Darussalam
Cambodia
China
China (Hong Kong SAR)
China (Macao SAR)
China (Taiwan Province)
Cook Islands
Democratic People's Rep. of Korea
Fiji
French Polynesia
Guam
India
Indonesia
Iran (Islamic Republic of)
Iraq
Jordan
Kiribati
Kuwait
Lao People's Dem. Rep.
Lebanon
Malaysia
Maldives
Marshall Islands
Micronesia (Federated States of)
Mongolia
Myanmar
Nepal
New Caledonia
Occupied Palestinian Territory
Oman
Pakistan
Palau
Papua New Guinea
Philippines
Qatar
Samoa
Saudi Arabia
Solomon Islands
Sri Lanka
Syrian Arab Republic
Thailand
Timor-Leste
Tonga
Tuvalu
United Arab Emirates
Vanuatu
Viet Nam
Yemen

Latin America

Anguilla
Antigua and Barbuda
Argentina
Aruba
Bahamas
Barbados
Belize
Bermuda
Bolivia
Brazil
British Virgin Islands
Chile
Colombia
Costa Rica
Cuba
Dominica
Dominican Republic
Ecuador
El Salvador
French Guiana
Grenada
Guadeloupe
Guatemala
Guyana
Haiti
Honduras
Jamaica
Martinique
Mexico
Montserrat
Netherlands Antilles
Nicaragua
Panama
Paraguay
Peru
Puerto Rico
Saint Kitts and Nevis
Saint Lucia
Saint Vincent and the Grenadines
Suriname
Trinidad and Tobago
United States Virgin Islands
Uruguay
Venezuela (Bolivarian Republic of)

(continued)

APPENDIX I
LIST OF COUNTRIES AND AREAS INCLUDED IN SELECTED GROUPINGS
DEVELOPING COUNTRY GROUPING BY INCOME

Low income

Afghanistan
Bangladesh
Benin
Bhutan
Burkina Faso
Burundi
Cambodia
Central African Republic
Chad
Comoros
Côte d'Ivoire
Democratic People's Rep. of Korea
Democratic Rep. of the Congo
Djibouti
Eritrea
Ethiopia
Gambia
Ghana
Guinea
Guinea-Bissau
Haiti
India
Kenya
Kiribati
Lao People's Dem. Rep.
Lesotho
Liberia
Madagascar
Malawi
Mali
Mauritania
Mongolia
Mozambique
Myanmar
Nepal
Nicaragua
Niger
Nigeria
Pakistan
Papua New Guinea
Rwanda
Sao Tome and Principe
Senegal
Sierra Leone
Solomon Islands
Somalia
Sudan
Timor-Leste
Togo
Uganda
United Republic of Tanzania
Viet Nam
Yemen
Zambia
Zimbabwe

Middle income

Albania
Algeria
Angola
Argentina
Belize
Bolivia
Bosnia and Herzegovina
Brazil
Cameroon
Cape Verde
China
Colombia
Congo
Costa Rica
Cuba
Dominica
Dominican Republic
Ecuador
Egypt
El Salvador
Equatorial Guinea
Fiji
Guatemala
Guyana
Honduras
Indonesia
Iran (Islamic Republic of)
Iraq
Jamaica
Jordan
Maldives
Marshall Islands
Micronesia (Federated States of)
Montenegro
Morocco
Namibia
Occupied Palestinian Territory
Panama
Paraguay
Peru
Philippines
Saint Vincent and the Grenadines
Samoa
Serbia
Sri Lanka
Suriname
Swaziland
Syrian Arab Republic
Thailand
The former Yugoslav Rep. of Macedonia
Tonga
Tunisia
Turkey
Tuvalu
Uruguay
Vanuatu

High income

Anguilla
Antigua and Barbuda
Aruba
Bahamas
Bahrain
Barbados
Bermuda
Botswana
British Virgin Islands
Brunei Darussalam
Chile
China (Hong Kong SAR)
China (Macao SAR)
China (Taiwan Province)
Cook Islands
Croatia
French Guiana
French Polynesia
Gabon
Grenada
Guadeloupe
Guam
Kuwait
Lebanon
Libyan Arab Jamahiriya
Malaysia
Martinique
Mauritius
Mexico
Montserrat
Netherlands Antilles
New Caledonia
Oman
Palau
Puerto Rico
Qatar
Réunion
Saint Kitts and Nevis
Saint Lucia
Saudi Arabia
Seychelles
Trinidad and Tobago
United Arab Emirates
United States Virgin Islands
Venezuela (Bolivarian Republic of)

(continued)

APPENDIX I
LIST OF COUNTRIES AND AREAS INCLUDED IN SELECTED GROUPINGS
DEVELOPING COUNTRY GROUPING BY DEVELOPMENT

Least developed countries

Afganistan
Angola
Bangladesh
Benin
Bhutan
Burkina Faso
Burundi
Cambodia
Cape Verde
Central African Republic
Chad
Comoros
Democratic Rep. of the Congo
Djibouti
Equatorial Guinea
Eritrea
Ethiopia
Gambia
Guinea
Guinea-Bissau
Haiti
Kiribati
Lao People's Dem. Rep.
Lesotho
Liberia
Madagascar
Malawi
Maldives
Mali
Mauritania
Mozambique
Myanmar
Nepal
Niger
Rwanda
Samoa
Sao Tome and Principe
Senegal
Sierra Leone
Solomon Islands
Somalia
Sudan
Timor-Leste
Togo
Tuvalu
Uganda
United Republic of Tanzania
Vanuatu
Yemen
Zambia

NICs

Argentina
Brazil
Chile
China (Hong Kong SAR)
China (Taiwan Province)
Colombia
Egypt
India
Indonesia
Malaysia
Mexico
Morocco
Philippines
Thailand
Tunisia
Turkey
Uruguay

China

Other developing countries

Albania
Algeria
Anguilla
Antigua and Barbuda
Aruba
Bahamas
Bahrain
Barbados
Belize
Bermuda
Bolivia
Bosnia and Herzegovina
Botswana
British Virgin Islands
Brunei Darussalam
Cameroon
China (Macao SAR)
Congo
Cook Islands
Costa Rica
Côte d'Ivoire
Croatia
Cuba
Democratic People's Rep. of Korea
Dominica
Dominican Republic
Ecuador
El Salvador
Fiji
French Guiana
French Polynesia
Gabon
Ghana
Grenada
Guadeloupe
Guam
Guatemala
Guyana
Honduras
Iran (Islamic Republic of)
Iraq
Jamaica
Jordan
Kenya
Kuwait
Lebanon
Libyan Arab Jamahiriya
Marshall Islands
Martinique
Mauritius
Micronesia (Federated States of)
Mongolia
Montenegro
Montserrat
Namibia
Netherlands Antilles
New Caledonia
Nicaragua
Nigeria
Occupied Palestinian Territory
Oman
Pakistan
Palau
Panama
Papua New Guinea
Paraguay
Peru
Puerto Rico
Qatar
Réunion
Saint Kitts and Nevis
Saint Lucia
Saint Vincent and the Grenadines
Saudi Arabia
Serbia
Seychelles
Sri Lanka
Suriname
Swaziland
Syrian Arab Republic
The former Yugoslav Rep. of Macedonia
Tonga
Trinidad and Tobago
United Arab Emirates
United States Virgin Islands
Venezuela (Bolivarian Republic of)
Viet Nam
Zimbabwe

(continued)

APPENDIX I
LIST OF COUNTRIES AND AREAS INCLUDED IN SELECTED GROUPINGS
OTHER DEVELOPING COUNTRY GROUPINGS

Andean Group

Bolivia
Colombia
Ecuador
Peru
Venezuela (Bolivarian Republic of)

ASEAN

Brunei Darussalam
Cambodia
Indonesia
Lao People's Dem. Rep.
Malaysia
Myanmar
Philippines
Singapore
Thailand
Viet Nam

CACM

Costa Rica
El Salvador
Guatemala
Honduras
Nicaragua

CARICOM

Antigua and Barbuda
Bahamas
Barbados
Belize
Dominica
Grenada
Guyana
Haiti
Jamaica
Montserrat
Saint Kitts and Nevis
Saint Lucia
Saint Vincent and the Grenadines
Suriname
Trinidad and Tobago

CEMAC

Cameroon
Central African Republic
Chad
Congo
Equatorial Guinea
Gabon

CEPGL

Burundi
Democratic Rep. of the Congo
Rwanda

LAIA

Argentina
Bolivia
Brazil
Chile
Colombia
Cuba
Ecuador
Mexico
Paraguay
Peru
Uruguay
Venezuela (Bolivarian Republic of)

OECS

Anguilla
Antigua and Barbuda
British Virgin Islands
Dominica
Grenada
Montserrat
Saint Kitts and Nevis
Saint Lucia
Saint Vincent and the Grenadines

SAARC

Afghanistan
Bangladesh
Bhutan
India
Maldives
Nepal
Pakistan
Sri Lanka

APPENDIX II

DETAILED DESCRIPTION OF INTERNATIONAL STANDARD INDUSTRIAL CLASSIFICATION OF ALL ECONOMIC ACTIVITIES (ISIC) - REVISION 2 AND 3

ISIC REVISION 2

ISIC		Description
3		**MANUFACTURING**
311/2		**Food manufacturing**
	3111	Slaughtering, preparing and preserving meat
	3112	Manufacture of dairy products
	3113	Canning and preserving of fruits and vegetables
	3114	Canning, preserving and processing of fish, crustacea and similar foods
	3115	Manufacture of vegetable and animal oils and fats
	3116	Grain mill products
	3117	Manufacture of bakery products
	3118	Sugar factories and refineries
	3119	Manufacture of cocoa, chocolate and sugar confectionery
	3121	Manufacture of food products not elsewhere classified
	3122	Manufacture of prepared animal feeds
313		**Beverage industries**
	3131	Distilling, rectifying and blending spirits
	3132	Wine industries
	3133	Malt liquors and malt
	3134	Soft drinks and carbonated waters industries
314	**3140**	**Tobacco manufactures**
321		**Manufacture of textiles**
	3211	Spinning, weaving and finishing textiles
	3212	Manufacture of made-up textile goods except wearing apparel
	3213	Knitting mills
	3214	Manufacture of carpets and rugs
	3215	Cordage, rope and twine industries
	3219	Manufacture of textiles not elsewhere classified
322	**3220**	**Manufacture of wearing apparel, except footwear**
323		**Manufacture of leather and products of leather, leather substitutes and fur, except footwear and wearing apparel**
	3231	Tanneries and leather finishing
	3232	Fur dressing and dyeing industries
	3233	Manufacture of products of leather and leather substitutes, except footwear and wearing apparel
324	**3240**	**Manufacture of footwear, except vulcanized or moulded rubber or plastic footwear**

ISIC REVISION 2 (continued)

ISIC		Description
331		**Manufacture of wood and wood and cork products, except furniture**
	3311	Sawmills, planing and other wood mills
	3312	Manufacture of wooden and cane containers and small cane ware
	3319	Manufacture of wood and cork products not elsewhere classified
332	**3320**	**Manufacture of furniture and fixtures, except primarily of metal**
341		**Manufacture of paper and paper products**
	3411	Manufacture of pulp, paper and paperboard
	3412	Manufacture of containers and boxes of paper and paperboard
	3419	Manufacture of pulp, paper and paperboard articles not elsewhere classified
342	**3420**	**Printing, publishing and allied industries**
351		**Manufacture of industrial chemicals**
	3511	Manufacture of basic industrial chemicals except fertilizers
	3512	Manufacture of fertilizers and pesticides
	3513	Manufacture of synthetic resins, plastic materials and man-made fibres except glass
352		**Manufacture of other chemical products**
	3521	Manufacture of paints, varnishes and lacquers
	3522	Manufacture of drugs and medicines
	3523	Manufacture of soap and cleaning preparations, perfumes, cosmetics and other toilet preparations
	3529	Manufacture of chemical products not elsewhere classified
353	**3530**	**Petroleum refineries**
354	**3540**	**Manufacture of miscellaneous products of petroleum and coal**
355		**Manufacture of rubber products**
	3551	Tyre and tube industries
	3559	Manufacture of rubber products not elsewhere classified
356	**3560**	**Manufacture of plastic products not elsewhere classified**
361	**3610**	**Manufacture of pottery, china and earthenware**
362	**3620**	**Manufacture of glass and glass products**
369		**Manufacture of other non-metallic mineral products**
	3691	Manufacture of structural clay products
	3692	Manufacture of cement, lime and plaster
	3699	Manufacture of non-metallic mineral products not elsewhere classified
371	**3710**	**Iron and steel basic industries**

ISIC REVISION 2 (continued)

ISIC		Description
372	**3720**	**Non-ferrous metal basic industries**
381		**Manufacture of fabricated metal products, except machinery and equipment**
	3811	Manufacture of cutlery, hand tools and general hardware
	3812	Manufacture of furniture and fixtures primarily of metal
	3813	Manufacture of structural metal products
	3819	Manufacture of fabricated metal products except machinery and equipment not elsewhere classified
382		**Manufacture of machinery except electrical**
	3821	Manufacture of engines and turbines
	3822	Manufacture of agricultural machinery and equipment
	3823	Manufacture of metal and wood working machinery
	3824	Manufacture of special industrial machinery and equipment except metal and wood working machinery
	3825	Manufacture of office, computing and accounting machinery
	3829	Machinery and equipment except electrical not elsewhere classified
383		**Manufacture of electrical machinery, apparatus, appliances and supplies**
	3831	Manufacture of electrical industrial machinery and apparatus
	3832	Manufacture of radio, television and communication equipment and apparatus
	3833	Manufacture of electrical appliances and housewares
	3839	Manufacture of electrical apparatus and supplies not elsewhere classified
384		**Manufacture of transport equipment**
	3841	Ship building and repairing
	3842	Manufacture of railroad equipment
	3843	Manufacture of motor vehicles
	3844	Manufacture of motorcycles and bicycles
	3845	Manufacture of aircraft
	3849	Manufacture of transport equipment not elsewhere classified
385		**Manufacture of professional and scientific, and measuring and controlling equipment not elsewhere classified, and of photographic and optical goods**
	3851	Manufacture of professional and scientific, and measuring and controlling equipment, not elsewhere classified
	3852	Manufacture of photographic and optical goods
	3853	Manufacture of watches and clocks
390		**Other manufacturing industries**
	3901	Manufacture of jewellery and related articles
	3902	Manufacture of musical instruments
	3903	Manufacture of sporting and athletic goods
	3909	Manufacturing industries not elsewhere classified

ISIC REVISION 3

ISIC		Description
D		**MANUFACTURING**
DIVISION 15		MANUFACTURE OF FOOD PRODUCTS AND BEVERAGES
151		**Production, processing and preservation of meat, fish, fruit, vegetables, oils and fats**
	1511	Production, processing and preserving of meat and meat products
	1512	Processing and preserving of fish and fish products
	1513	Processing and preserving of fruit and vegetables
	1514	Manufacture of vegetable and animal oils and fats
152	**1520**	**Manufacture of dairy products**
153		**Manufacture of grain mill products, starches and starch products, and prepared animal feeds**
	1531	Manufacture of grain mill products
	1532	Manufacture of starches and starch products
	1533	Manufacture of prepared animal feeds
154		**Manufacture of other food products**
	1541	Manufacture of bakery products
	1542	Manufacture of sugar
	1543	Manufacture of cocoa, chocolate and sugar confectionery
	1544	Manufacture of macaroni, noodles, couscous and similar farinaceous products
	1549	Manufacture of other food products n.e.c.
155		**Manufacture of beverages**
	1551	Distilling, rectifying and blending of spirits; ethyl alcohol production from fermented materials
	1552	Manufacture of wines
	1553	Manufacture of malt liquors and malt
	1554	Manufacture of soft drinks; production of mineral waters
DIVISION 16		MANUFACTURE OF TOBACCO PRODUCTS
160	**1600**	**Manufacture of tobacco products**
DIVISION 17		MANUFACTURE OF TEXTILES
171		**Spinning, weaving and finishing of textiles**
	1711	Preparation and spinning of textile fibres; weaving of textiles
	1712	Finishing of textiles
172		**Manufacture of other textiles**
	1721	Manufacture of made-up textile articles, except apparel
	1722	Manufacture of carpets and rugs
	1723	Manufacture of cordage, rope, twine and netting
	1729	Manufacture of other textiles n.e.c.

ISIC REVISION 3 (continued)

ISIC		Description
173	**1730**	**Manufacture of knitted and crocheted fabrics and articles**
DIVISION 18		MANUFACTURE OF WEARING APPAREL; DRESSING AND DYEING OF FUR
181	**1810**	**Manufacture of wearing apparel, except fur apparel**
182	**1820**	**Dressing and dyeing of fur; manufacture of articles of fur**
DIVISION 19		TANNING AND DRESSING OF LEATHER; MANUFACTURE OF LUGGAGE, HANDBAGS, SADDLERY, HARNESS AND FOOTWEAR
191		**Tanning and dressing of leather; manufacture of luggage, handbags, saddlery and harness**
	1911	Tanning and dressing of leather
	1912	Manufacture of luggage, handbags and the like, saddlery and harness
192	**1920**	**Manufacture of footwear**
DIVISION 20		MANUFACTURE OF WOOD AND OF PRODUCTS OF WOOD AND CORK, EXCEPT FURNITURE; MANUFACTURE OF ARTICLES OF STRAW AND PLAITING MATERIALS
201	**2010**	**Sawmilling and planing of wood**
202		**Manufacture of products of wood, cork, straw and plaiting materials**
	2021	Manufacture of veneer sheets; manufacture of plywood, laminboard, particle board and other panels and boards
	2022	Manufacture of builders' carpentry and joinery
	2023	Manufacture of wooden containers
	2029	Manufacture of other products of wood; manufacture of articles of cork, straw and plaiting materials
DIVISION 21		MANUFACTURE OF PAPER AND PAPER PRODUCTS
210		**Manufacture of paper and paper products**
	2101	Manufacture of pulp, paper and paperboard
	2102	Manufacture of corrugated paper and paperboard and of containers of paper and paperboard
	2109	Manufacture of other articles of paper and paperboard
DIVISION 22		PUBLISHING, PRINTING AND REPRODUCTION OF RECORDED MEDIA
221		**Publishing**
	2211	Publishing of books, brochures, musical books and other publications
	2212	Publishing of newspapers, journals and periodicals
	2213	Publishing of recorded media
	2219	Other publishing

ISIC REVISION 3 (continued)

ISIC		Description
222		**Printing and service activities related to printing**
	2221	Printing
	2222	Service activities related to printing
223	**2230**	**Reproduction of recorded media**
DIVISION 23		MANUFACTURE OF COKE, REFINED PETROLEUM PRODUCTS AND NUCLEAR FUEL
231	**2310**	**Manufacture of coke oven products**
232	**2320**	**Manufacture of refined petroleum products**
233	**2330**	**Processing of nuclear fuel**
DIVISION 24		MANUFACTURE OF CHEMICALS AND CHEMICAL PRODUCTS
241		**Manufacture of basic chemicals**
	2411	Manufacture of basic chemicals, except fertilizers and nitrogen compounds
	2412	Manufacture of fertilizers and nitrogen compounds
	2413	Manufacture of plastics in primary forms and of synthetic rubber
242		**Manufacture of other chemical products**
	2421	Manufacture of pesticides and other agro-chemical products
	2422	Manufacture of paints, varnishes and similar coatings, printing ink and mastics
	2423	Manufacture of pharmaceuticals, medicinal chemicals and botanical products
	2424	Manufacture of soap and detergents, cleaning and polishing preparations, perfumes and toilet preparations
	2429	Manufacture of other chemical products n.e.c.
243	**2430**	**Manufacture of man-made fibres**
DIVISION 25		MANUFACTURE OF RUBBER AND PLASTICS PRODUCTS
251		**Manufacture of rubber products**
	2511	Manufacture of rubber tyres and tubes; retreading and rebuilding of rubber tyres
	2519	Manufacture of other rubber products
252	**2520**	**Manufacture of plastics products**
DIVISION 26		MANUFACTURE OF OTHER NON-METALLIC MINERAL PRODUCTS
261	**2610**	**Manufacture of glass and glass products**

ISIC REVISION 3 (continued)

ISIC		Description
269		**Manufacture of non-metallic mineral products n.e.c.**
	2691	Manufacture of non-structural non-refractory ceramic ware
	2692	Manufacture of refractory ceramic products
	2693	Manufacture of structural non-refractory clay and ceramic products
	2694	Manufacture of cement, lime and plaster
	2695	Manufacture of articles of concrete, cement and plaster
	2696	Cutting, shaping and finishing of stone
	2699	Manufacture of other non-metallic mineral products n.e.c.
DIVISION 27		MANUFACTURE OF BASIC METALS
271	**2710**	**Manufacture of basic iron and steel**
272	**2720**	**Manufacture of basic precious and non-ferrous metals**
273		**Casting of metals**
	2731	Casting of iron and steel
	2732	Casting of non-ferrous metals
DIVISION 28		MANUFACTURE OF FABRICATED METAL PRODUCTS, EXCEPT MACHINERY AND EQUIPMENT
281		**Manufacture of structural metal products, tanks, reservoirs and steam generators**
	2811	Manufacture of structural metal products
	2812	Manufacture of tanks, reservoirs and containers of metal
	2813	Manufacture of steam generators, except central heating hot water boilers
289		**Manufacture of other fabricated metal products; metal working service activities**
	2891	Forging, pressing, stamping and roll-forming of metal; powder metallurgy
	2892	Treatment and coating of metals; general mechanical engineering on a fee or contract basis
	2893	Manufacture of cutlery, hand tools and general hardware
	2899	Manufacture of other fabricated metal products n.e.c.
DIVISION 29		MANUFACTURE OF MACHINERY AND EQUIPMENT N.E.C.
291		**Manufacture of general purpose machinery**
	2911	Manufacture of engines and turbines, except aircraft, vehicle and cycle engines
	2912	Manufacture of pumps, compressors, taps and valves
	2913	Manufacture of bearings, gears, gearing and driving elements
	2914	Manufacture of ovens, furnaces and furnace burners
	2915	Manufacture of lifting and handling equipment
	2919	Manufacture of other general purpose machinery

ISIC REVISION 3 (continued)

ISIC		Description
292		**Manufacture of special purpose machinery**
	2921	Manufacture of agricultural and forestry machinery
	2922	Manufacture of machine-tools
	2923	Manufacture of machinery for metallurgy
	2924	Manufacture of machinery for mining, quarrying and construction
	2925	Manufacture of machinery for food, beverage and tobacco processing
	2926	Manufacture of machinery for textile, apparel and leather production
	2927	Manufacture of weapons and ammunition
	2929	Manufacture of other special purpose machinery
293	**2930**	**Manufacture of domestic appliances n.e.c.**
DIVISION 30		MANUFACTURE OF OFFICE, ACCOUNTING AND COMPUTING MACHINERY
300	**3000**	**Manufacture of office, accounting and computing machinery**
DIVISION 31		MANUFACTURE OF ELECTRICAL MACHINERY AND APPARATUS N.E.C.
311	**3110**	**Manufacture of electric motors, generators and transformers**
312	**3120**	**Manufacture of electricity distribution and control apparatus**
313	**3130**	**Manufacture of insulated wire and cable**
314	**3140**	**Manufacture of accumulators, primary cells and primary batteries**
315	**3150**	**Manufacture of electric lamps and lighting equipment**
319	**3190**	**Manufacture of other electrical equipment n.e.c.**
DIVISION 32		MANUFACTURE OF RADIO, TELEVISION AND COMMUNICATION EQUIPMENT AND APPARATUS
321	**3210**	**Manufacture of electronic valves and tubes and other electronic components**
322	**3220**	**Manufacture of television and radio transmitters and apparatus for line telephony and line telegraphy**
323	**3230**	**Manufacture of television and radio receivers, sound or video recording or reproducing apparatus, and associated goods**
DIVISION 33		MANUFACTURE OF MEDICAL, PRECISION AND OPTICAL INSTRUMENTS, WATCHES AND CLOCKS
331		**Manufacture of medical appliances and instruments and appliances for measuring, checking, testing, navigating and other purposes, except optical instruments**
	3311	Manufacture of medical and surgical equipment and orthopaedic appliances
	3312	Manufacture of instruments and appliances for measuring, checking, testing, navigating and other purposes, except industrial process control equipment
	3313	Manufacture of industrial process control equipment

ISIC REVISION 3 (continued)

ISIC		Description
332	**3320**	**Manufacture of optical instruments and photographic equipment**
333	**3330**	**Manufacture of watches and clocks**
DIVISION 34		MANUFACTURE OF MOTOR VEHICLES, TRAILERS AND SEMI-TRAILERS
341	**3410**	**Manufacture of motor vehicles**
342	**3420**	**Manufacture of bodies (coachwork) for motor vehicles; manufacture of trailers and semi-trailers**
343	**3430**	**Manufacture of parts and accessories for motor vehicles and their engines**
DIVISION 35		MANUFACTURE OF OTHER TRANSPORT EQUIPMENT
351		**Building and repairing of ships and boats**
	3511	Building and repairing of ships
	3512	Building and repairing of pleasure and sporting boats
352	**3520**	**Manufacture of railway and tramway locomotives and rolling stock**
353	**3530**	**Manufacture of aircraft and spacecraft**
359		**Manufacture of transport equipment n.e.c.**
	3591	Manufacture of motorcycles
	3592	Manufacture of bicycles and invalid carriages
	3599	Manufacture of other transport equipment n.e.c.
DIVISION 36		MANUFACTURE OF FURNITURE; MANUFACTURING N.E.C.
361	**3610**	**Manufacture of furniture**
369		**Manufacturing n.e.c.**
	3691	Manufacture of jewellery and related articles
	3692	Manufacture of musical instruments
	3693	Manufacture of sports goods
	3694	Manufacture of games and toys
	3699	Other manufacturing n.e.c.
DIVISION 37		RECYCLING
371	**3710**	**Recycling of metal waste and scrap**
372	**3720**	**Recycling of non-metal waste and scrap**

Appendix III

DESCRIPTION OF DATA USED IN SECTION 1.2

Country or area	Value added				Output				Employment			Country or area
	Factor values	Producers' prices	Unspecified	Mixed	Factor values	Producers' prices	Unspecified	Mixed	Persons engaged	Employees	Mixed	
Afghanistan										X		Afghanistan
Albania		X				X				X		Albania
Argentina		X				X				X		Argentina
Armenia						X				X		Armenia
Aruba										X		Aruba
Australia			X				X		X			Australia
Austria				X			X				X	Austria
Azerbaijan	X							X		X		Azerbaijan
Bahamas				X				X		X		Bahamas
Bangladesh	X				X					X		Bangladesh
Belgium	X						X			X		Belgium
Bermuda									X			Bermuda
Bolivia		X				X				X		Bolivia
Botswana			X				X			X		Botswana
Brazil	X				X				X			Brazil
Bulgaria		X				X				X		Bulgaria
Cambodia		X				X					X	Cambodia
Canada		X				X				X		Canada
Cape Verde							X		X			Cape Verde
Chile		X				X				X		Chile
China (Macao SAR)		X				X			X			China (Macao SAR)
Colombia	X				X					X		Colombia
Cook Islands			X				X			X		Cook Islands
Croatia										X		Croatia
Cyprus		X				X				X		Cyprus
Czech Republic				X			X			X		Czech Republic
Denmark				X			X				X	Denmark
Dominican Republic										X		Dominican Republic
Ecuador		X				X				X		Ecuador
Egypt	X				X						X	Egypt
Eritrea		X				X				X		Eritrea
Estonia			X				X			X		Estonia
Ethiopia		X				X				X		Ethiopia
Fiji		X				X				X		Fiji
Finland				X			X				X	Finland
France	X						X			X		France
Gambia		X				X				X		Gambia
Georgia			X				X		X			Georgia
Germany	X							X			X	Germany
Ghana		X				X				X		Ghana
Greece	X							X		X		Greece
Guatemala									X			Guatemala
Haiti							X			X		Haiti

Appendix III
(continued)

DESCRIPTION OF DATA USED IN SECTION 1.2

Country or area	Value added				Output				Employment			Country or area
	Factor values	Producers' prices	Unspecified	Mixed	Factor values	Producers' prices	Unspecified	Mixed	Persons engaged	Employees	Mixed	
Hungary				X			X			X		Hungary
Iceland			X				X			X		Iceland
India		X				X			X			India
Indonesia	X					X				X		Indonesia
Iran (Islamic Republic of)		X				X				X		Iran (Islamic Republic of)
Iraq	X						X			X		Iraq
Ireland	X							X		X		Ireland
Israel				X				X			X	Israel
Italy				X			X			X		Italy
Japan			X				X			X		Japan
Jordan		X				X					X	Jordan
Kazakhstan							X			X		Kazakhstan
Kenya			X				X			X		Kenya
Kyrgyzstan			X			X					X	Kyrgyzstan
Lao People's Dem. Rep.		X				X				X		Lao People's Dem. Rep.
Latvia	X				X					X		Latvia
Lebanon			X				X			X		Lebanon
Lesotho										X		Lesotho
Lithuania	X							X		X		Lithuania
Luxembourg	X						X			X		Luxembourg
Madagascar				X				X		X		Madagascar
Malawi		X				X				X		Malawi
Malaysia		X				X				X		Malaysia
Maldives									X			Maldives
Malta		X				X				X		Malta
Mauritius		X				X				X		Mauritius
Mexico				X				X			X	Mexico
Mongolia		X				X			X			Mongolia
Morocco	X				X					X		Morocco
Nepal		X				X				X		Nepal
Netherlands	X						X			X		Netherlands
Netherlands Antilles		X				X				X		Netherlands Antilles
New Zealand			X				X			X		New Zealand
Niger		X				X				X		Niger
Nigeria						X			X			Nigeria
Norway			X				X			X		Norway
Oman			X				X			X		Oman
Panama		X				X				X		Panama
Papua New Guinea				X				X		X		Papua New Guinea
Paraguay			X				X			X		Paraguay
Peru				X				X	X			Peru
Philippines		X				X				X		Philippines
Poland				X			X			X		Poland

Appendix III
(continued)

DESCRIPTION OF DATA USED IN SECTION 1.2

Country or area	Value added				Output				Employment			Country or area
	Factor values	Producers' prices	Unspecified	Mixed	Factor values	Producers' prices	Unspecified	Mixed	Persons engaged	Employees	Mixed	
Portugal	X						X			X		Portugal
Qatar		X				X				X		Qatar
Republic of Korea			X				X			X		Republic of Korea
Republic of Moldova			X			X				X		Republic of Moldova
Romania				X				X		X		Romania
Russian Federation			X			X				X		Russian Federation
Rwanda		X				X				X		Rwanda
Saudi Arabia			X				X				X	Saudi Arabia
Senegal		X					X			X		Senegal
Serbia			X				X					Serbia
Sierra Leone						X			X			Sierra Leone
Singapore				X				X			X	Singapore
Slovakia				X			X			X		Slovakia
Slovenia	X						X			X		Slovenia
South Africa			X				X			X		South Africa
Spain				X			X			X		Spain
Sri Lanka		X				X				X		Sri Lanka
Sudan		X				X				X		Sudan
Suriname			X			X				X		Suriname
Sweden	X							X		X		Sweden
Switzerland	X						X		X			Switzerland
Syrian Arab Republic			X				X			X		Syrian Arab Republic
Tajikistan							X			X		Tajikistan
Thailand		X				X				X		Thailand
The f. Yugosl. Rep. of Macedonia			X				X			X		The f. Yugosl. Rep. of Macedonia
Tonga						X					X	Tonga
Trinidad and Tobago				X				X		X		Trinidad and Tobago
Turkey			X				X			X		Turkey
Turkmenistan							X		X			Turkmenistan
Uganda			X				X			X		Uganda
Ukraine		X						X		X		Ukraine
United Kingdom	X						X			X		United Kingdom
United States of America			X				X			X		United States of America
Uruguay		X				X			X			Uruguay
Viet Nam		X						X		X		Viet Nam
Yemen			X				X			X		Yemen
Zimbabwe	X				X					X		Zimbabwe

Part I
SUMMARY TABLES

Section 1.1
THE MANUFACTURING SECTOR

Major trends of growth and distribution of manufacturing in the world

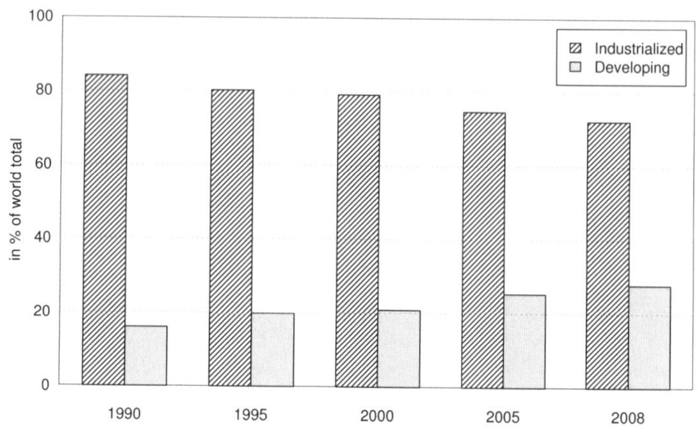

Figure 1: Share of country groups in the world MVA at constant 2000 prices.

Industrialized countries play the dominant role in the manufacturing industry, with a nearly three-quarters share in total world MVA. However, the share of developing countries is rising. According to recent estimates for 2008, developing countries now produce almost 30 per cent of world MVA, compared to 16 per cent in 1990. The increasing share of developing world vis-à-vis industrialized countries is also explained by the shift of location of manufacturing, especially assembling of final products, from industrialized countries to developing countries.

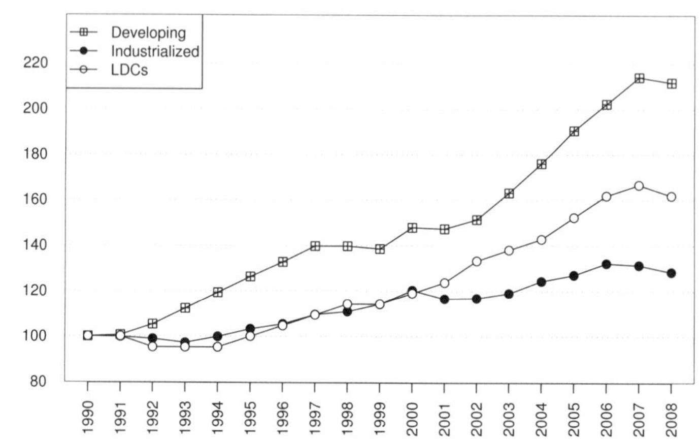

Figure 2: Growth of MVA per-capita by development groups at constant 2000 prices, 1990=100.

The increasing role of developing countries in world industry has been achieved thanks to their relatively higher growth in recent years. The phenomenon has been impressive, as well, in relation to the size of developing countries' population. MVA per capita in developing countries doubled in 2006, compared to 1990, while the industrialized world achieved merely 30 per cent increase. According to recent UNIDO estimates, MVA per capita in LDCs rose by 60 per cent in 2008, compared to that for 1990.

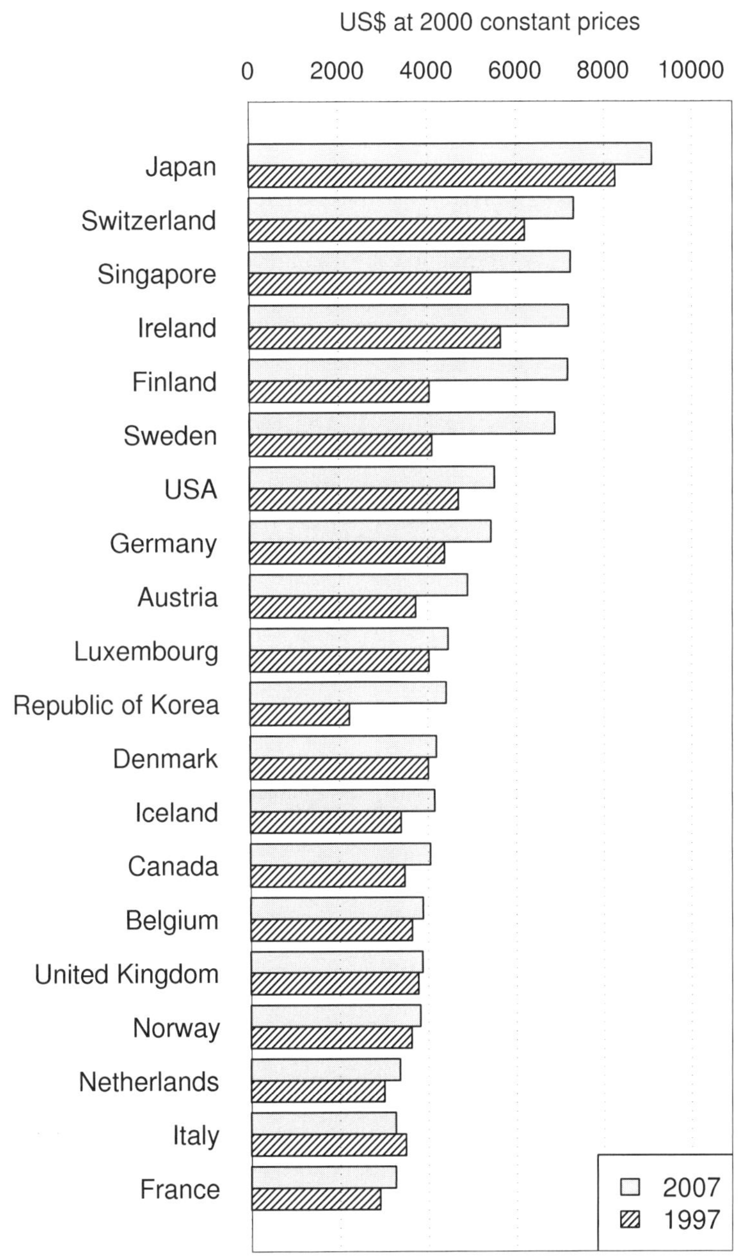

Figure 3: Leading industrialized countries by MVA per capita.

Japan remains the world's most industrialized country in terms of MVA per capita. Although in most of the industrialized countries, the share of manufacturing is decreasing, due to the increasing role of service sectors and outsourcing of production activities abroad mainly to developing countries, manufacturing still accounts for more than 20 per cent of GDP of Japan, compared to the 17 per cent average for all industrialized countries (see Table 1.4). The figure reveals some remarkable changes among other industrialized countries in the last ten years. Thanks to the greater role of production of ICT goods in manufacturing, countries with relatively smaller economies such as Singapore, Ireland, and Finland have achieved significant increases in MVA per capita. As a result, they have outperformed relatively larger economies such as the United States, Germany, Canada and France. MVA per capita has remained almost stagnant in other major industrialized countries such as the United Kingdom and Italy.

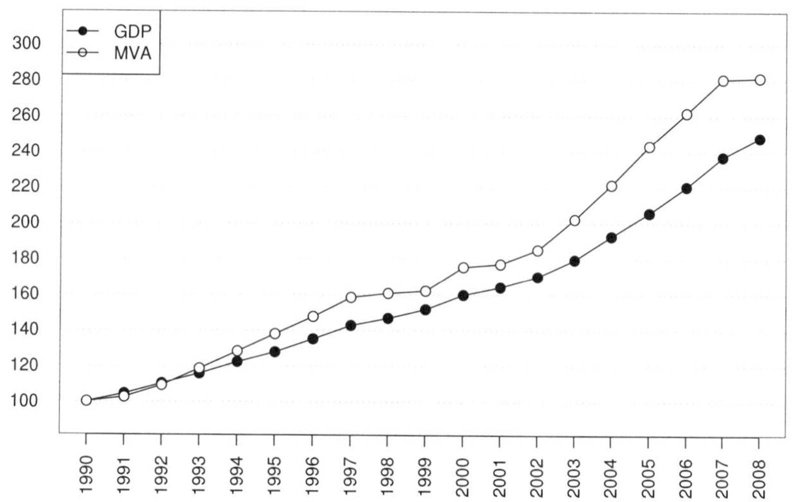

Figure 4: GDP and MVA growth of developing countries at constant 2000 prices, 1990=100.

For developing countries, manufacturing has been the major source of overall economic growth. Industrial production grew faster than all other sectors, which resulted in a higher growth rate of MVA than GDP in all years since 1990. According to recent UNIDO estimates, developing countries' MVA nearly tripled in 2007 from 1990. The figure indicates the increasing growth trend of manufacturing compared to the economy as a whole. The contribution of the manufacturing sector to GDP of developing countries has exceeded that of industrialized countries (see Table 1.4).

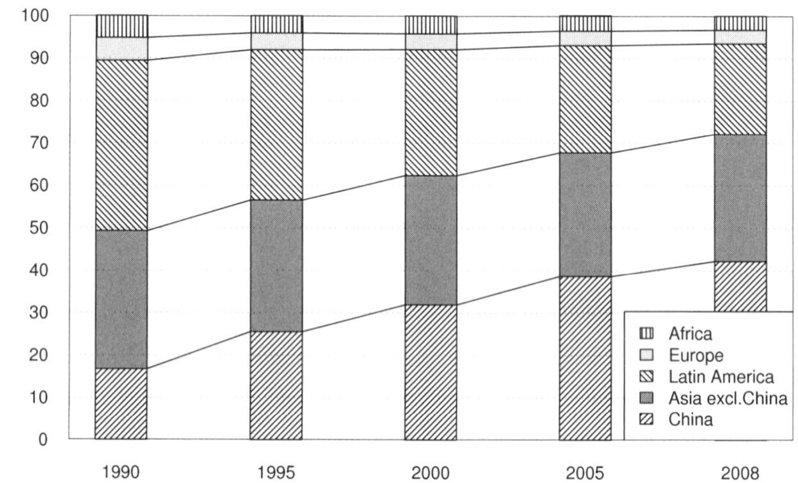

Figure 5: Distribution of total MVA of developing countries by region at constant 2000 prices.

Among developing countries, those in Asia account for nearly three-fourths of total MVA, of which China alone produces 42 per cent of MVA of all developing countries. Due to the increasing share of Asian countries, the contribution of Latin America to the total MVA of the developing world declined to 21 per cent in 2008, compared to 40 in 1990. The share of Africa slightly decreased, remaining less than five per cent during all these years. Other developing countries, which are mostly comprised of those in South-East Europe, account for less than five per cent of the developing world's MVA.

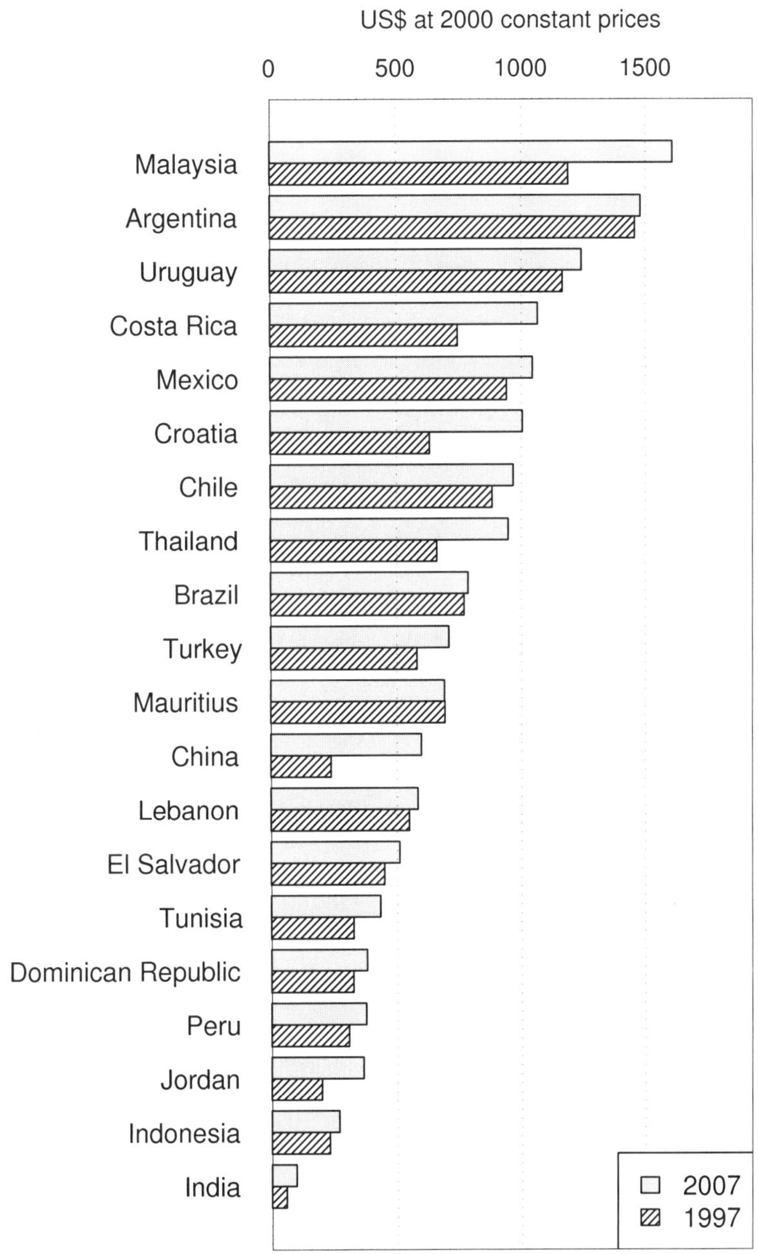

Figure 6: Leading developing economies by MVA per capita.

Malaysia is the most industrialized country in the developing world (excluding predominantly oil-producing countries), based on MVA per capita. The majority of other developing countries with higher MVA per capita are in Latin America. Argentina has nearly same MVA per capita as Malaysia, however, industrialization of Malaysia has been much faster. In the last ten years, its MVA per capita has increased by more than 35 per cent, compared to 1.6 per cent in Argentina. In relation to population size, Costa Rica produced more than Mexico and Chile, while Brazil did not gain much during this period. Among other Asian countries, Thailand and China significantly increased their MVA per capita in the last ten years. China's MVA per capita increased by 2.5 times but was still only 63 per cent of the level achieved by Thailand in 2007. Africa is represented by the relatively small economies of Mauritius and Tunisia. Large developing economies such as Indonesia and India were not among the top 20 countries, but they are represented in the chart for reference purposes.

Table 1.1

DISTRIBUTION OF WORLD MVA, 1995-2008

Year	Industrialized countries							Developing countries							
		Europe						Regional groups				Development groups			
	CIS	EU-15	EU-12	Other	East Asia	North America	Others	Africa	Latin America	Asia	Europe	NICs	Least developed countries	China	Others
	Percentage share in world total MVA (at constant 2000 prices)														
1995	1.3	25.7	1.2	1.2	22.6	26.4	1.8	0.8	7.0	11.2	0.8	11.6	0.2	5.1	2.9
1996	1.2	24.8	1.3	1.2	22.8	26.5	1.7	0.8	7.0	11.9	0.8	11.8	0.3	5.4	3.0
1997	1.2	24.5	1.3	1.2	22.3	26.9	1.7	0.8	7.2	12.1	0.8	11.9	0.2	5.7	3.1
1998	1.0	24.8	1.3	1.2	20.8	28.3	1.7	0.8	7.0	12.2	0.9	11.5	0.2	6.1	3.1
1999	1.1	24.6	1.3	1.1	20.6	29.1	1.7	0.9	6.2	12.7	0.7	10.8	0.2	6.4	3.1
2000	1.1	24.3	1.3	1.1	20.6	29.0	1.7	0.9	6.2	13.0	0.8	10.9	0.3	6.7	3.0
2001	1.3	24.9	1.4	1.2	20.0	28.0	1.7	0.9	6.0	13.9	0.7	10.6	0.3	7.4	3.2
2002	1.2	24.4	1.4	1.1	19.7	28.3	1.7	1.0	5.6	14.8	0.8	10.6	0.4	8.0	3.2
2003	1.4	23.5	1.4	1.1	20.0	27.6	1.7	0.9	5.7	15.9	0.8	10.9	0.3	8.9	3.2
2004	1.4	22.5	1.5	1.1	20.1	27.7	1.6	0.9	6.0	16.3	0.9	11.3	0.4	9.1	3.3
2005	1.4	21.8	1.5	1.1	19.9	27.4	1.5	0.9	6.4	17.2	0.9	11.8	0.4	9.8	3.4
2006 a/	1.4	21.5	1.6	1.1	20.3	26.7	1.5	0.9	6.3	17.8	0.9	11.9	0.4	10.2	3.4
2007 b/	1.4	21.3	1.6	1.1	20.0	25.7	1.6	0.9	6.4	19.2	0.8	12.3	0.3	11.2	3.5
2008 b/	1.4	21.2	1.7	1.0	19.9	25.4	1.6	0.9	5.9	20.1	0.9	12.5	0.4	11.8	3.1
	Percentage share in world total MVA (at current prices)														
2000	1.1	24.3	1.3	1.1	20.6	29.0	1.7	0.9	6.2	13.0	0.8	10.9	0.3	6.7	3.0
2001	1.4	25.1	1.4	1.2	18.2	28.9	1.6	1.0	6.3	14.2	0.7	10.8	0.3	7.7	3.4
2002	1.4	25.9	1.6	1.3	17.2	28.5	1.7	1.0	5.5	15.1	0.8	10.6	0.3	8.2	3.3
2003	1.7	27.5	1.7	1.3	17.0	26.1	1.9	0.9	5.2	15.7	1.0	10.5	0.4	8.7	3.2
2004	2.0	27.7	1.9	1.4	16.9	24.7	2.0	0.8	5.4	16.1	1.1	10.8	0.3	9.0	3.3
2005	2.5	26.3	2.0	1.3	15.9	24.6	2.0	0.8	5.9	17.5	1.2	11.5	0.3	10.1	3.5
2006 a/	2.9	25.8	2.2	1.3	14.7	23.8	1.9	0.9	6.1	19.2	1.2	12.1	0.4	11.3	3.6

a/ Provisional.
b/ Estimate.

Table 1.2 DISTRIBUTION OF MVA AND POPULATION AMONG SELECTED GROUPS OF DEVELOPING COUNTRIES, SELECTED YEARS

(Percentage)

Country group	MVA at constant 2000 prices					MVA at current prices					Population				
	1995	2000	2005	2007 b/	2008 b/	2002	2003	2004	2005	2006 a/	1995	2000	2005	2007	2008
Low Income	9.1	8.9	9.0	9.4	10.0	9.6	9.8	9.9	9.9	9.7	44.5	45.6	46.7	47.1	47.3
Middle income (excl. China)	40.0	32.3	30.3	28.4	27.9	28.4	28.9	29.4	29.5	29.7	22.8	22.7	22.6	22.6	22.6
China	25.5	31.9	38.6	41.1	42.3	36.5	38.2	38.4	39.6	41.1	27.6	26.6	25.6	25.2	25.0
High income	25.4	26.9	22.1	21.1	19.8	25.5	23.1	22.3	21.0	19.5	5.1	5.1	5.1	5.1	5.1
Developing Countries	100.0	100.0	100.0	100.0	100.0	100.0	100.0	100.0	100.0	100.0	100.0	100.0	100.0	100.0	100.0
NICs	58.5	52.1	46.7	44.8	45.1	47.3	46.2	46.0	45.2	44.2	41.6	41.7	41.8	41.8	41.8
Least developed countries	1.3	1.4	1.4	1.5	1.5	1.5	1.6	1.6	1.5	1.5	13.6	14.2	14.9	15.2	15.4
China	25.5	31.9	38.6	41.1	42.3	36.5	38.2	38.4	39.6	41.1	27.6	26.6	25.6	25.2	25.0
Other developing countries	14.7	14.6	13.3	12.6	11.1	14.7	14.0	14.0	13.7	13.2	17.2	17.5	17.7	17.8	17.8
Developing Countries	100.0	100.0	100.0	100.0	100.0	100.0	100.0	100.0	100.0	100.0	100.0	100.0	100.0	100.0	100.0
Africa	4.1	4.2	3.6	3.3	3.3	4.2	3.9	3.6	3.3	3.2	15.5	16.2	17.0	17.3	17.5
Latin America	35.4	29.7	25.2	23.3	21.3	24.7	23.0	23.2	23.1	22.4	11.0	10.9	10.8	10.8	10.8
Asia	56.5	62.3	67.8	70.2	72.2	67.5	69.0	68.7	68.9	69.9	71.5	70.9	70.3	70.0	69.8
Europe	4.0	3.8	3.4	3.2	3.2	3.6	4.1	4.5	4.7	4.5	2.0	2.0	1.9	1.9	1.9
Developing Countries	100.0	100.0	100.0	100.0	100.0	100.0	100.0	100.0	100.0	100.0	100.0	100.0	100.0	100.0	100.0

a/ Provisional.
b/ Estimate.

Table 1.3

ANNUAL GROWTH OF MVA, 2000-2007 AND PER-CAPITA MVA, 2007[a/]

Country group or country/area	Total MVA						Per-capita MVA						
	Growth rate (percentage)		Index (2000 = 100)				Growth rate (percentage)		Index (2000 = 100)				Value (dollars)
	2000-2005	2005-2007	2004	2005	2006[b/]	2007[c/]	2000-2005	2005-2007	2004	2005	2006[b/]	2007[c/]	2007[c/]
Industrialized Countries	1.8	2.1	105	108	113	112	1.4	1.7	103	106	110	109	3712
CIS	6.9	4.9	131	137	143	150	7.1	5.0	133	138	145	152	362
Armenia	9.1	-1.4	140	150	148	146	9.6	-1.1	142	153	152	150	203
Azerbaijan	9.1	2.2	142	149	161	155	8.5	1.5	139	145	156	149	51
Belarus	11.3	5.9	149	170	187	191	11.9	6.5	152	174	193	198	678
Georgia	6.3	12.1	120	133	156	167	7.5	13.1	126	141	166	180	143
Kazakhstan	9.0	7.2	145	156	168	179	8.6	6.5	144	153	164	174	350
Kyrgyzstan	0.7	-8.9	117	97	85	81	-0.3	-9.8	112	93	80	75	38
Republic of Moldova	8.3	-6.9	146	150	135	130	9.7	-5.9	154	160	146	142	63
Russian Federation	5.9	3.8	127	130	136	140	6.4	4.3	129	133	140	145	502
Tajikistan	10.3	5.7	154	164	177	183	9.0	4.2	147	154	165	168	82
Turkmenistan	3.1	8.4	110	122	133	144	1.6	6.9	104	114	122	130	421
Ukraine	12.8	8.9	169	174	183	206	13.7	9.7	175	181	192	218	228
Uzbekistan	1.8	18.3	109	111	113	155	0.4	16.6	103	103	104	140	64
EU	0.8	2.4	103	105	109	110	0.5	2.2	102	103	107	107	3286
Austria	1.3	3.9	105	108	117	116	0.8	3.4	103	105	114	113	4904
Belgium	0.4	0.2	102	102	104	102	-0.1	-0.1	101	100	102	100	3878
Bulgaria	5.4	4.3	121	129	144	141	6.1	5.0	124	134	150	147	365
Cyprus	0.8	1.4	104	103	104	106	-0.4	0.2	99	97	96	97	1007
Czech Republic	5.6	8.3	118	132	151	155	5.6	8.3	118	133	151	156	2101
Denmark	-0.4	1.6	98	99	105	102	-0.7	1.4	96	98	103	100	4190
Estonia	10.0	10.5	146	165	186	201	10.4	10.9	149	168	190	206	1350
Finland	4.0	5.5	117	122	136	136	3.7	5.2	116	120	134	133	7178
France	1.0	-0.2	104	105	107	105	0.4	-0.7	102	102	103	101	3244
Germany	1.2	3.3	104	107	113	114	1.1	3.3	103	107	113	114	5430
Greece	1.2	3.0	104	111	116	118	0.9	2.8	103	110	114	116	1418
Hungary	6.1	5.2	121	135	150	149	6.3	5.5	122	136	153	152	1432
Ireland	-1.4	5.7	98	96	96	107	-3.1	3.8	91	88	86	95	7199
Italy	-1.7	0.6	94	92	95	93	-2.0	0.4	93	90	94	91	3247
Latvia	7.4	5.7	136	144	153	161	8.1	6.3	139	148	159	168	679
Lithuania	10.5	7.1	152	164	176	189	11.0	7.7	154	168	181	195	1092
Luxembourg	0.8	0.2	103	101	105	102	-0.1	-0.8	99	97	99	95	4461
Malta	-3.8	3.1	77	78	78	83	-4.5	2.6	75	76	75	80	1562
Netherlands	0.1	1.0	100	101	103	103	-0.4	0.7	98	98	100	100	3344
Poland	6.2	7.2	125	130	146	149	6.3	7.4	126	131	147	151	1107
Portugal	0.1	1.6	100	102	103	105	-0.5	1.1	98	99	99	101	1658
Romania	5.9	6.6	128	133	140	151	6.4	7.0	131	136	144	156	572

a/ At constant 2000 prices.
b/ Provisional.
c/ Estimate.

Table 1.3
(continued)

ANNUAL GROWTH OF MVA, 2000-2007 AND PER-CAPITA MVA, 2007[a/]

Country group or country/area	Total MVA						Per-capita MVA						
	Growth rate (percentage)		Index (2000 = 100)				Growth rate (percentage)		Index (2000 = 100)				Value (dollars)
	2000-2005	2005-2007	2004	2005	2006[b/]	2007[c/]	2000-2005	2005-2007	2004	2005	2006[b/]	2007[c/]	2007[c/]
Slovakia	9.9	6.5	137	167	185	190	9.9	6.4	137	167	185	189	1572
Slovenia	4.2	4.8	119	122	131	134	4.0	4.7	118	121	130	133	2981
Spain	0.7	0.4	104	104	107	105	-0.9	-0.6	98	97	98	95	2319
Sweden	4.9	4.2	118	124	130	134	4.5	3.8	117	121	127	131	6883
United Kingdom	-0.4	2.9	98	97	96	103	-0.9	2.4	96	95	94	100	3864
Other Europe	1.5	3.5	106	109	115	117	1.0	3.0	103	106	112	113	5921
Iceland	2.4	3.8	114	114	123	123	1.4	3.0	109	108	116	114	4149
Norway	2.4	1.1	108	112	117	114	1.7	0.4	105	108	112	109	3814
Switzerland	1.2	4.3	105	108	114	118	0.7	3.9	103	106	111	114	7315
East Asia	2.6	3.6	107	110	118	118	2.3	3.4	106	109	117	117	7809
Japan	1.9	2.9	104	106	114	113	1.7	2.9	103	106	113	112	9108
Republic of Korea	7.0	7.4	129	138	150	159	6.5	7.0	126	135	146	154	4416
Singapore	5.2	4.6	112	123	137	135	3.7	3.3	106	114	126	122	7243
North America	2.0	0.3	105	108	111	109	1.0	-0.7	101	103	104	101	5368
Canada	-0.1	2.4	97	98	97	103	-1.1	1.4	93	93	92	96	4051
United States of America	2.2	0.1	106	109	112	109	1.2	-0.9	101	103	106	102	5509
Others	1.2	4.2	104	106	111	115	0.0	3.3	99	100	103	106	1379
Australia	1.1	4.0	106	105	108	114	-0.1	2.9	101	99	100	105	2530
Israel	-0.8	8.6	90	93	104	110	-2.7	6.7	83	85	92	97	3073
New Zealand	2.6	3.7	113	111	117	120	1.3	2.6	108	105	109	110	2361
South Africa	2.5	1.8	109	115	120	119	1.4	1.1	105	109	113	111	562
Developing Countries	7.1	7.4	126	139	149	160	5.5	5.9	119	129	137	145	366
Afghanistan	16.5	13.6	182	217	253	280	12.1	9.2	156	180	201	214	40
Albania	4.5	2.6	102	140	155	148	4.0	2.0	100	137	151	142	173
Algeria	2.4	4.0	109	113	118	122	0.9	2.4	103	105	107	110	139
Angola	13.4	22.7	154	192	278	289	10.1	19.3	137	166	234	236	45
Antigua and Barbuda	2.3	1.9	110	111	115	115	0.7	0.7	103	103	105	104	176
Argentina	3.7	4.1	107	115	125	125	2.7	3.1	103	110	118	116	1479
Aruba	0.6	1.8	102	102	102	106	-2.1	1.3	91	89	88	92	738
Bahamas	4.6	2.4	126	128	126	135	3.3	1.2	120	121	117	123	812
Bahrain	9.3	5.3	128	160	181	177	6.9	3.3	117	143	159	153	2400

a/ At constant 2000 prices.
b/ Provisional.
c/ Estimate.

Table 1.3
(continued)

ANNUAL GROWTH OF MVA, 2000-2007 AND PER-CAPITA MVA, 2007[a/]

Country group or country/area	Total MVA						Per-capita MVA						
	Growth rate (percentage)		Index (2000 = 100)				Growth rate (percentage)		Index (2000 = 100)				Value (dollars)
	2000-2005	2005-2007	2004	2005	2006 b/	2007 c/	2000-2005	2005-2007	2004	2005	2006 b/	2007 c/	2007 c/
Bangladesh	6.7	5.4	129	139	154	155	4.7	3.6	119	127	138	136	67
Barbados	2.5	-4.3	93	119	110	109	2.1	-4.6	91	116	108	106	494
Belize	3.0	15.5	113	114	154	152	0.6	13.1	103	101	134	129	421
Benin	2.7	1.9	113	118	114	123	-0.5	-1.2	99	101	94	98	27
Bermuda	-5.0	10.5	78	78	94	95	-5.3	9.6	77	77	92	92	976
Bhutan	4.7	-0.1	119	123	127	123	1.9	-1.7	107	108	109	105	68
Bolivia	3.1	4.1	113	116	125	125	1.0	2.2	104	105	111	110	146
Bosnia and Herzegovina	6.9	6.2	129	138	149	156	6.2	6.0	125	133	144	150	185
Botswana	2.1	0.7	108	110	111	112	0.9	-0.5	103	104	103	103	150
Brazil	8.7	3.8	114	146	148	157	7.2	2.5	108	136	136	143	787
Brunei Darussalam	1.8	-0.1	109	107	108	107	-0.6	-2.1	99	95	94	91	2521
Burkina Faso	6.6	8.2	119	126	130	147	3.2	5.0	105	107	107	118	40
Burundi	3.6	5.0	113	119	125	131	0.2	0.9	100	101	102	103	8
Cambodia	14.0	13.1	174	191	224	244	12.0	11.1	162	175	202	216	99
Cameroon	5.3	3.2	127	132	138	141	2.9	1.1	116	118	120	120	147
Cape Verde	7.5	0.5	125	137	139	139	5.0	-1.7	114	122	121	118	129
Central African Republic	-1.3	6.9	92	98	104	112	-2.9	5.0	87	90	94	100	16
Chad	7.1	3.3	129	151	178	161	3.3	0.3	111	126	144	127	18
Chile	3.9	-0.1	113	121	124	121	2.7	-1.1	108	114	116	112	967
China	11.1	10.9	150	168	185	206	10.4	10.2	146	162	177	197	598
China (Hong Kong SAR)	-5.7	0.3	75	76	78	77	-6.8	-0.7	71	72	73	71	924
China (Macao SAR)	-5.0	29.8	80	72	102	122	-6.3	28.7	75	67	94	111	1284
China (Taiwan Province)	5.4	8.9	117	125	134	148	5.0	8.5	114	122	131	144	4932
Colombia	4.1	4.5	116	121	134	132	2.6	3.2	109	112	123	119	349
Comoros	1.7	-1.2	107	110	107	108	-1.0	-3.6	96	96	92	90	12
Congo	12.8	6.4	172	187	201	211	10.1	4.1	157	166	175	179	63
Costa Rica	3.9	5.0	106	117	130	129	1.9	3.3	98	107	116	114	1065
Côte d'Ivoire	-3.3	-3.3	84	88	82	83	-4.9	-5.0	79	81	74	73	97
Croatia	5.5	4.1	123	130	136	141	5.2	4.1	122	129	135	140	1004
Cuba	-5.0	11.5	85	81	82	101	-5.2	11.5	85	80	81	99	408
Democratic People's Rep. of Korea	1.5	0.3	105	110	110	110	0.9	0.0	102	107	107	106	87
Democratic Rep. of the Congo	4.8	8.7	107	117	127	139	1.7	5.3	96	101	106	112	5
Djibouti	3.2	3.3	114	117	120	125	1.3	1.4	105	106	107	109	19
Dominica	-1.5	7.2	88	89	102	102	-1.5	8.0	88	89	102	104	307
Dominican Republic	0.7	3.5	99	104	112	112	-0.9	2.0	93	96	102	100	380
Ecuador	4.5	4.4	116	127	138	138	3.3	3.3	111	120	128	128	225
Egypt	2.9	3.2	110	118	125	126	1.1	1.4	103	108	112	111	299
El Salvador	2.3	1.4	111	112	116	115	0.8	0.0	104	104	106	104	510

a/ At constant 2000 prices.
b/ Provisional.
c/ Estimate.

Table 1.3
(continued)

ANNUAL GROWTH OF MVA, 2000-2007 AND PER-CAPITA MVA, 2007[a/]

Country group or country/area	Total MVA						Per-capita MVA						
	Growth rate (percentage)		Index (2000 = 100)				Growth rate (percentage)		Index (2000 = 100)				Value (dollars)
	2000-2005	2005-2007	2004	2005	2006 b/	2007 c/	2000-2005	2005-2007	2004	2005	2006 b/	2007 c/	2007 c/
Equatorial Guinea	61.8	10.9	1358	1815	1850	2230	58.0	8.3	1237	1616	1608	1896	768
Eritrea	5.7	3.0	128	132	136	140	1.4	-0.5	108	107	106	106	19
Ethiopia	3.6	7.0	113	122	131	139	1.0	4.4	102	107	113	116	7
Fiji	2.1	3.6	127	108	115	116	1.4	2.9	123	104	111	110	284
French Polynesia	1.0	1.9	101	108	109	112	-0.6	0.6	94	99	99	100	949
Gabon	4.2	1.1	121	129	127	131	2.3	-0.5	112	118	114	117	186
Gambia	3.9	3.7	118	119	123	128	0.7	0.9	104	102	103	104	15
Ghana	4.6	5.0	119	125	131	137	2.2	2.9	109	111	115	118	26
Grenada	-3.8	0.3	75	87	88	88	-4.8	-0.2	71	83	83	83	212
Guatemala	1.5	1.9	105	108	112	112	-1.0	-0.6	95	96	97	94	214
Guinea	1.9	6.1	110	112	118	126	0.1	4.0	103	102	105	110	16
Guinea-Bissau	3.5	2.2	117	122	129	127	0.4	-0.8	103	105	108	103	16
Guyana	0.8	3.2	113	101	108	107	0.7	3.3	112	100	108	107	70
Haiti	0.1	2.4	99	101	102	106	-1.5	0.8	93	93	93	95	34
Honduras	4.2	3.1	118	124	130	131	2.2	1.1	109	112	115	115	187
India	6.9	12.3	127	138	155	174	5.2	10.6	119	128	141	156	98
Indonesia	5.2	3.4	122	127	133	136	3.8	2.2	116	119	123	125	269
Iran (Islamic Republic of)	10.2	6.5	153	160	169	182	9.1	5.2	147	153	159	169	338
Jamaica	0.1	-2.3	102	100	98	96	-0.6	-2.8	99	97	94	92	360
Jordan	11.1	6.4	156	168	184	190	8.0	3.0	139	145	154	154	365
Kenya	3.3	4.3	111	116	124	126	0.6	1.5	100	102	106	105	44
Kiribati	1.6	-0.6	108	108	108	107	-0.2	-2.2	101	99	97	94	4
Kuwait	11.4	6.5	150	157	171	178	7.2	3.6	128	130	137	139	1627
Lao People's Dem. Rep.	10.4	9.6	151	165	180	198	8.6	7.8	142	152	163	177	99
Lebanon	5.6	-3.7	127	128	117	119	4.3	-4.8	121	121	109	110	584
Lesotho	3.3	7.5	124	114	126	131	2.3	6.7	119	108	119	123	86
Liberia	5.4	5.1	113	119	106	131	3.2	0.7	103	106	91	107	19
Libyan Arab Jamahiriya	-4.7	2.7	80	81	83	85	-6.6	0.7	73	73	73	74	230
Madagascar	1.0	0.9	104	107	109	109	-1.8	-1.8	93	93	92	89	24
Malawi	0.1	4.6	89	95	101	105	-2.5	2.0	80	84	87	87	15
Malaysia	5.2	8.6	117	123	132	145	3.2	6.7	108	112	117	127	1609
Maldives	4.4	5.5	131	118	126	131	2.8	3.6	123	109	115	117	193
Mali	5.7	5.6	120	122	123	136	2.6	2.4	107	105	103	110	9
Marshall Islands	0.0	0.0	100	100	100	100	-1.8	-1.7	93	91	90	88	91
Mauritania	-4.1	4.6	82	73	81	80	-6.9	1.9	73	63	68	65	23
Mauritius	0.6	-4.6	107	104	104	95	-0.4	-5.4	103	100	98	89	692
Mexico	0.1	2.1	98	99	104	104	-0.8	1.0	95	95	99	97	1044
Micronesia, Federated States of	0.1	-0.2	99	100	100	100	-0.5	-0.7	98	98	96	96	26

a/ At constant 2000 prices.
b/ Provisional.
c/ Estimate.

Table 1.3
(continued)

ANNUAL GROWTH OF MVA, 2000-2007 AND PER-CAPITA MVA, 2007[a/]

Country group or country/area	Total MVA						Per-capita MVA						
	Growth rate (percentage)		Index (2000 = 100)				Growth rate (percentage)		Index (2000 = 100)				Value (dollars)
	2000-2005	2005-2007	2004	2005	2006 b/	2007 c/	2000-2005	2005-2007	2004	2005	2006 b/	2007 c/	2007 c/
Mongolia	9.8	22.5	191	154	174	231	8.8	21.4	184	147	165	217	39
Montenegro	-16.9	11.6	44	43	54	54	-15.1	12.5	47	47	60	60	188
Morocco	3.4	3.5	115	119	124	128	2.3	2.3	110	113	116	118	235
Mozambique	14.2	5.7	186	202	209	226	11.4	3.6	169	179	182	192	48
Myanmar	18.9	11.0	206	215	248	265	17.8	10.1	198	206	236	249	28
Namibia	5.3	-2.3	125	128	117	122	3.8	-3.6	118	119	107	111	201
Nepal	0.1	1.8	100	103	105	107	-1.9	-0.2	92	93	93	92	18
New Caledonia	0.0	0.3	85	89	91	90	-1.6	-1.4	79	82	83	80	678
Nicaragua	4.9	3.4	121	129	135	137	3.5	2.1	114	120	125	125	145
Niger	4.0	2.6	119	120	122	126	0.4	-1.0	104	100	99	98	11
Nigeria	8.8	5.5	139	151	165	167	6.1	3.0	126	133	142	141	19
Occupied Palestinian Territory	-6.1	2.1	73	73	75	76	-9.4	-1.2	63	61	61	59	103
Oman	8.5	7.1	148	163	186	187	7.7	5.3	143	156	176	173	775
Pakistan	9.5	5.6	139	161	177	179	7.5	3.7	129	147	159	158	110
Panama	-1.5	1.8	90	93	97	96	-3.3	0.1	84	85	87	85	316
Papua New Guinea	2.0	4.5	99	109	114	119	-0.4	2.3	89	96	99	101	54
Paraguay	0.9	1.7	102	104	108	108	-1.1	-0.1	94	95	96	94	193
Peru	4.9	4.2	118	126	137	137	3.6	3.0	112	118	127	126	376
Philippines	4.4	2.0	117	124	129	129	2.2	0.1	108	111	114	112	247
Qatar	9.4	11.2	143	161	179	200	3.9	8.2	116	125	134	147	2293
Rwanda	1.4	9.7	103	115	130	138	-0.9	6.9	93	101	112	116	29
Saint Lucia	4.3	1.8	116	123	127	128	3.2	0.5	112	117	119	119	226
Samoa	3.4	-1.6	125	121	112	117	2.6	-2.4	121	116	107	111	214
Sao Tome and Principe	6.5	8.7	138	138	150	162	4.6	7.0	128	126	135	144	45
Saudi Arabia	5.8	4.1	124	132	141	143	3.1	1.7	112	116	121	121	1055
Senegal	3.2	-2.9	118	116	109	110	0.5	-5.3	107	102	93	92	54
Serbia	-0.8	5.5	96	96	101	107	-0.3	5.5	98	98	104	110	209
Seychelles	-5.2	-0.1	81	79	77	79	-6.3	-0.7	77	74	73	73	1069
Sierra Leone	7.2	-0.8	127	158	145	155	2.6	-3.2	107	128	114	120	6
Solomon Islands	0.1	6.2	89	93	99	105	-2.4	3.6	80	82	85	88	31
Somalia	2.7	4.1	114	114	119	124	-0.3	1.0	101	98	99	100	15
Sri Lanka	2.9	3.4	107	114	120	121	2.5	2.9	105	111	117	118	155
St. Kitts and Nevis	0.8	-5.7	106	106	96	95	-0.5	-6.7	99	100	89	87	558
St. Vincent and the Grenadines	1.2	3.7	103	105	112	113	0.7	3.3	101	103	108	110	161
Sudan	8.4	5.8	130	143	156	160	6.2	3.5	120	130	138	139	42
Suriname	14.7	5.7	166	170	174	190	13.8	5.0	161	164	167	181	303
Swaziland	1.8	1.5	107	109	111	112	0.6	0.8	102	102	104	104	340
Syrian Arab Republic	16.5	4.9	193	217	235	239	13.4	2.2	173	190	200	198	154

a/ At constant 2000 prices.
b/ Provisional.
c/ Estimate.

Table 1.3
(continued)

ANNUAL GROWTH OF MVA, 2000-2007 AND PER-CAPITA MVA, 2007[a/]

Country group or country/area	Total MVA						Per-capita MVA						
	Growth rate (percentage)		Index (2000 = 100)				Growth rate (percentage)		Index (2000 = 100)				Value (dollars)
	2000-2005	2005-2007	2004	2005	2006[b/]	2007[c/]	2000-2005	2005-2007	2004	2005	2006[b/]	2007[c/]	2007[c/]
Thailand	7.2	3.6	130	137	145	147	6.4	2.8	126	132	139	139	947
The f. Yugosl. Rep. of Macedonia	0.4	-0.6	99	100	102	99	0.1	-0.7	98	99	101	97	301
Timor-Leste	3.8	-3.2	128	129	97	121	-1.7	-6.9	103	99	71	86	9
Togo	7.5	-0.3	133	143	122	142	4.4	-2.9	119	124	102	117	24
Tonga	3.0	-5.0	113	115	115	104	2.8	-5.5	112	114	113	102	69
Trinidad and Tobago	9.0	6.6	139	155	173	176	8.6	6.3	137	152	170	172	760
Tunisia	3.0	3.6	115	117	122	126	1.9	2.5	110	111	114	117	433
Turkey	6.4	3.9	121	129	138	139	5.0	2.6	115	120	127	126	710
Uganda	5.8	0.8	122	136	138	139	2.5	-2.4	107	116	114	111	24
United Arab Emirates	8.5	9.1	131	149	163	177	3.5	5.6	108	118	125	132	3835
United Republic of Tanzania	8.0	2.6	134	146	156	153	5.3	0.1	121	128	134	128	24
Uruguay	2.3	3.6	101	111	120	119	2.3	3.3	100	110	120	118	1241
Vanuatu	-1.0	1.7	89	95	97	98	-3.5	-0.8	81	84	83	83	46
Venezuela (Bolivarian Republic of)	0.6	7.2	99	106	116	122	-1.2	5.4	92	97	104	108	959
Viet Nam	11.5	10.4	153	173	195	212	9.9	8.9	144	161	179	191	140
Yemen	3.9	3.3	115	124	131	133	0.8	0.3	102	107	109	108	29
Zambia	5.4	3.5	124	129	136	138	3.5	1.6	115	117	122	121	38
Zimbabwe	-12.0	-1.8	64	53	57	51	-12.6	-2.6	62	51	54	49	39
Developing countries (excl.China)	4.9	5.2	115	125	133	138	3.1	3.4	108	115	120	123	288
Low Income	7.0	9.8	128	140	155	169	5.0	7.7	118	127	138	148	73
Middle income (excl. China)	5.9	3.9	117	130	137	140	4.4	2.5	111	121	126	127	459
High income	2.9	5.0	108	114	120	126	1.6	3.7	103	107	111	114	1506
Africa	3.1	3.4	112	118	124	126	0.7	0.9	102	105	107	107	70
Central Africa	7.2	6.8	133	146	160	166	4.2	3.7	119	127	135	136	38
Eastern and southern Africa	2.7	2.1	111	115	119	119	0.1	-0.4	101	101	102	100	31
North Africa	2.8	3.5	111	116	123	125	1.1	1.7	103	107	111	111	215
Western Africa (ECOWAS)	3.1	2.1	111	117	118	122	0.5	-0.4	100	103	101	102	27
Asia	8.8	9.3	137	151	164	180	7.5	8.0	130	141	152	165	367
Europe	5.9	3.9	120	127	136	137	4.8	2.9	115	121	128	128	624
Latin America	3.6	3.2	106	118	123	126	2.3	1.9	101	110	114	115	789
Andean Group	2.6	5.6	108	115	125	128	1.1	4.2	102	107	115	116	462
ASEAN	5.9	4.8	123	130	139	143	4.5	3.4	116	121	128	130	413
CACM	3.0	3.0	109	115	122	122	1.0	1.1	101	104	109	107	355
CARICOM	3.4	2.3	113	118	123	124	2.2	1.1	108	111	114	114	195
CEMAC	7.2	4.0	136	146	153	158	4.4	1.7	123	129	132	133	98
CEPGL	3.1	8.7	106	116	128	137	0.1	5.3	95	100	107	111	8

a/ At constant 2000 prices.
b/ Provisional.
c/ Estimate.

Table 1.3
(continued)

ANNUAL GROWTH OF MVA, 2000-2007 AND PER-CAPITA MVA, 2007 [a/]

Country group or country/area	Total MVA						Per-capita MVA						
	Growth rate (percentage)		Index (2000 = 100)				Growth rate (percentage)		Index (2000 = 100)				Value (dollars)
	2000-2005	2005-2007	2004	2005	2006 [b/]	2007 [c/]	2000-2005	2005-2007	2004	2005	2006 [b/]	2007 [c/]	2007 [c/]
LAIA	3.8	3.5	106	119	124	127	2.5	2.3	101	112	115	117	809
OECS	0.7	0.9	99	104	106	106	-0.2	0.2	96	100	101	100	240
SAARC	7.1	10.6	128	141	157	172	5.3	8.9	120	129	142	153	95
Least developed countries	7.4	6.2	132	142	155	161	4.8	3.7	120	126	134	136	35
African LDCs	6.9	5.9	128	140	150	156	4.0	3.0	115	122	127	129	22
NICs	4.9	5.3	114	124	132	138	3.4	3.8	107	115	121	124	393
World	3.0	3.4	110	114	120	122	1.8	2.2	104	108	112	112	1061

a/ At constant 2000 prices.
b/ Provisional.
c/ Estimate.

Table 1.4

SHARE OF MVA IN GDP, SELECTED YEARS
(Percentage)

Country group or country/area	At constant 2000 prices						At current prices					
	1995	2000	2004	2005	2006 a/	2007 b/	2001	2002	2003	2004	2005	2006 a/
Industrialized Countries	17.4	17.8	17.3	17.3	17.5	17.0	16.7	16.2	15.9	15.8	15.7	15.6
CIS	18.9	18.9	19.2	18.7	18.2	17.6	18.3	17.1	18.3	17.5	18.6	18.2
Armenia	25.0	21.9	19.6	18.4	16.1	13.9	20.1	18.9	19.3	19.2	19.1	15.4
Azerbaijan	9.2	5.3	5.0	4.2	3.4	2.6	6.2	7.4	8.6	8.3	6.5	5.3
Belarus	22.9	27.0	30.8	32.0	32.0	30.2	26.6	26.0	26.7	28.6	29.0	28.1
Georgia	7.9	12.2	11.3	11.4	12.2	11.7	12.2	12.8	13.0	12.2	12.1	11.1
Kazakhstan	15.7	16.5	16.1	15.7	15.3	15.0	16.4	14.5	14.2	13.3	12.0	11.6
Kyrgyzstan	13.4	18.1	17.6	14.6	12.4	10.9	17.6	13.0	13.3	15.3	12.9	11.3
Republic of Moldova	16.3	14.2	15.9	15.1	13.2	12.1	15.8	14.9	15.5	14.5	13.3	12.0
Russian Federation	19.9	19.6	19.6	19.0	18.5	17.7	18.5	17.0	18.5	17.5	19.2	18.8
Tajikistan	33.6	30.8	32.3	32.3	32.6	31.3	31.1	30.9	28.0	21.6	21.0	16.8
Turkmenistan	56.2	35.0	34.2	34.7	34.6	34.5	36.7	34.3	34.8	34.2	34.7	34.6
Ukraine	13.3	16.3	19.5	19.6	19.2	20.1	17.4	17.9	18.6	18.6	17.3	17.9
Uzbekistan	9.7	8.3	7.4	7.0	6.7	8.6	8.3	8.1	8.0	8.8	8.1	9.8
EU	17.5	17.5	16.8	16.7	16.9	16.6	17.0	16.4	15.9	15.7	15.4	15.5
Austria	17.0	18.2	18.1	18.2	19.3	18.5	18.2	17.9	17.5	17.4	17.4	18.0
Belgium	16.8	17.1	16.5	16.2	16.1	15.3	16.5	16.2	15.6	15.5	15.2	14.9
Bulgaria	21.9	15.7	15.7	15.7	16.5	15.2	15.5	14.9	15.2	14.7	14.6	15.1
Cyprus	10.5	8.7	8.0	7.7	7.4	7.3	8.4	8.2	7.9	7.9	7.6	7.2
Czech Republic	20.1	24.3	25.3	26.7	28.7	27.7	23.9	23.0	22.4	24.1	23.8	24.4
Denmark	14.7	13.9	13.1	12.9	13.2	12.7	13.6	13.5	12.9	12.4	12.0	12.4
Estonia	15.1	15.9	17.3	17.6	17.9	18.1	16.5	16.1	15.8	15.2	14.7	14.7
Finland	19.1	22.9	24.3	24.6	26.0	24.9	22.5	21.8	20.9	20.4	20.0	20.4
France	14.0	14.3	14.0	13.9	13.9	13.3	13.8	13.2	12.7	12.2	11.7	11.0
Germany	20.5	20.7	21.0	21.4	22.1	21.7	20.6	20.2	20.1	20.4	21.0	21.2
Greece	9.8	9.3	8.1	8.4	8.3	8.2	9.4	9.3	8.8	8.2	8.7	9.1
Hungary	15.6	20.1	20.5	21.9	23.5	23.0	19.2	18.5	18.8	18.9	19.0	19.5
Ireland	27.9	30.0	24.0	22.3	21.1	22.5	29.2	29.4	25.5	23.5	21.7	20.2
Italy	19.9	18.7	17.1	16.6	16.9	16.3	18.3	17.9	17.2	16.9	16.4	16.2
Latvia	12.7	12.3	12.4	11.9	11.3	10.8	12.5	12.3	11.9	11.8	11.1	10.4
Lithuania	15.2	17.2	19.3	19.4	19.3	19.0	17.7	16.7	17.3	18.9	18.9	15.9
Luxembourg	10.7	10.1	9.3	8.8	8.6	8.0	9.9	9.2	8.7	8.4	7.9	7.6
Malta	18.8	19.6	14.9	14.7	14.2	14.6	16.3	16.0	16.7	14.9	14.7	14.2
Netherlands	14.4	13.9	13.4	13.2	13.1	12.6	13.1	12.7	12.6	12.7	12.5	11.9
Poland	14.5	16.5	18.3	18.4	19.4	18.7	15.0	14.6	15.6	17.0	16.4	16.5
Portugal	15.1	14.9	14.5	14.6	14.6	14.6	14.6	14.2	13.6	13.2	12.7	12.3
Romania	19.2	21.9	22.2	22.1	21.7	22.0	23.0	22.6	20.8	20.9	21.1	20.7

a/ Provisional.
b/ Estimate.

Table 1.4
(continued)

SHARE OF MVA IN GDP, SELECTED YEARS
(Percentage)

Country group or country/area	At constant 2000 prices						At current prices					
	1995	2000	2004	2005	2006 a/	2007 b/	2001	2002	2003	2004	2005	2006 a/
Slovakia	21.3	22.0	25.4	29.3	30.0	27.8	22.9	20.3	21.2	21.0	20.7	19.8
Slovenia	21.7	23.0	24.0	23.8	24.2	23.4	23.2	22.6	22.9	22.2	21.4	21.5
Spain	16.6	16.8	15.4	15.0	14.8	14.0	16.4	15.7	15.0	14.5	13.9	13.6
Sweden	15.8	19.3	20.9	21.3	21.5	21.6	18.0	17.7	17.2	17.3	17.1	21.5
United Kingdom	17.4	15.8	14.0	13.6	13.1	13.6	15.0	14.0	13.0	12.5	12.1	12.8
Other Europe	15.9	14.9	14.9	15.1	15.4	15.1	15.3	15.0	14.8	14.6	14.2	14.3
Iceland	11.9	11.7	11.6	10.9	11.5	11.0	13.7	11.7	11.3	10.7	8.4	10.2
Norway	10.4	9.3	9.3	9.3	9.5	9.0	9.4	9.4	9.3	9.1	8.5	8.4
Switzerland	19.4	18.9	19.1	19.4	19.9	19.8	19.4	19.0	18.7	18.6	19.1	19.6
East Asia	22.0	22.6	22.7	22.9	24.0	23.4	21.3	21.0	21.3	21.8	21.7	22.1
Japan	21.9	22.2	22.0	22.1	23.1	22.4	20.9	20.6	21.0	21.2	21.0	21.4
Republic of Korea	22.1	26.1	28.1	28.9	29.8	30.2	24.4	23.7	23.3	25.5	25.3	24.7
Singapore	25.2	25.7	25.3	26.0	26.9	24.5	22.9	24.2	24.0	26.5	26.5	27.6
North America	14.8	15.9	15.3	15.3	15.3	14.6	14.6	14.3	13.7	13.6	13.6	13.4
Canada	16.2	17.9	15.8	15.5	14.9	15.3	16.7	16.4	15.4	15.1	15.6	15.4
United States of America	14.6	15.8	15.3	15.3	15.3	14.6	14.5	14.1	13.6	13.5	13.4	13.2
Others	14.3	13.7	12.6	12.4	12.5	12.5	13.0	13.1	13.0	12.6	12.1	12.1
Australia	12.6	11.5	10.7	10.3	10.3	10.5	11.0	11.4	11.3	10.7	10.1	10.2
Israel	15.1	16.0	13.7	13.5	14.3	14.5	14.2	13.6	13.7	13.7	13.2	13.9
New Zealand	16.9	15.7	15.3	14.7	15.2	15.1	15.2	15.0	13.6	13.8	14.2	14.2
South Africa	17.5	17.3	16.4	16.4	16.4	15.4	17.3	17.9	17.6	17.0	16.6	16.1
Developing Countries	19.3	19.7	20.6	21.2	21.3	21.2	19.7	20.1	20.4	20.4	20.3	20.5
Afghanistan	4.6	14.4	11.9	12.5	13.5	13.3	17.5	14.8	14.8	15.4	14.4	15.1
Albania	9.6	10.2	8.4	11.0	11.6	10.4	9.3	8.8	10.9	11.8	11.0	11.6
Algeria	8.4	7.0	6.4	6.3	6.3	6.3	7.3	7.2	6.6	6.0	5.3	5.0
Angola	2.9	2.9	3.3	3.4	4.1	3.6	3.9	3.7	3.9	4.0	3.5	4.3
Antigua and Barbuda	2.0	2.0	1.9	1.8	1.7	1.6	1.9	2.0	2.0	1.8	1.7	1.6
Argentina	17.9	16.5	17.5	17.2	17.3	15.8	16.1	20.3	22.5	22.3	21.4	20.6
Aruba	2.6	3.9	3.8	3.7	3.7	3.8	3.9	3.9	3.9	3.8	3.8	3.7
Bahamas	3.0	4.0	4.9	4.9	4.6	4.8	4.4	4.3	4.2	3.9	4.0	3.9
Bahrain	13.6	12.8	13.1	15.2	16.2	14.9	13.4	13.1	12.5	11.8	10.9	11.2

a/ Provisional.
b/ Estimate.

Table 1.4
(continued)

SHARE OF MVA IN GDP, SELECTED YEARS
(Percentage)

Country group or country/area	At constant 2000 prices						At current prices					
	1995	2000	2004	2005	2006 a/	2007 b/	2001	2002	2003	2004	2005	2006 a/
Bangladesh	14.4	14.7	15.4	15.7	16.3	15.4	15.1	15.3	15.2	15.5	15.9	16.6
Barbados	6.0	5.3	4.7	5.8	5.2	4.9	5.0	5.3	5.4	5.6	5.8	5.2
Belize	9.7	9.6	8.5	8.4	10.8	10.5	8.9	8.3	7.8	7.8	7.8	10.6
Benin	8.4	8.8	8.4	8.6	7.9	8.2	9.2	8.6	8.5	7.6	7.5	7.5
Bermuda	2.5	2.5	1.7	1.6	1.9	1.8	2.2	2.1	1.7	1.8	1.6	1.9
Bhutan	8.5	8.1	7.1	6.9	6.5	5.4	8.1	7.4	7.2	7.3	7.0	7.1
Bolivia	13.7	13.2	13.4	13.2	13.7	13.1	13.3	13.0	12.8	12.5	11.6	11.5
Bosnia and Herzegovina	13.0	8.8	9.3	9.5	9.7	9.5	8.7	8.5	8.7	9.4	9.3	9.6
Botswana	4.9	4.1	3.5	3.5	3.4	3.3	3.9	3.9	3.9	3.7	3.4	3.3
Brazil	21.4	14.9	15.3	19.0	18.6	18.7	14.7	14.5	15.6	16.5	15.9	15.8
Brunei Darussalam	14.5	15.4	15.2	14.8	14.2	14.0	15.7	15.7	15.3	13.3	12.3	10.5
Burkina Faso	13.0	15.3	14.4	14.3	13.8	14.7	12.2	13.3	13.3	14.1	13.6	12.6
Burundi	8.0	7.7	7.9	8.2	8.2	8.3	7.9	7.6	7.6	7.6	8.0	8.2
Cambodia	8.8	16.0	20.3	19.6	20.8	20.5	16.8	17.6	18.2	18.9	17.8	18.6
Cameroon	17.2	19.3	20.8	21.2	21.4	21.0	19.3	19.1	18.7	17.9	17.0	16.8
Cape Verde	9.3	9.3	10.2	10.0	9.5	8.9	5.8	6.1	8.0	7.2	7.6	4.8
Central African Republic	7.6	6.6	6.5	6.7	6.8	7.1	6.5	6.6	6.6	6.7	7.0	7.1
Chad	9.0	8.6	6.0	6.5	7.6	6.9	9.2	9.1	7.7	5.0	4.6	5.2
Chile	19.6	17.6	17.2	17.3	17.0	15.8	18.4	18.4	16.4	15.9	14.8	12.8
China	30.5	32.1	33.6	34.1	33.9	33.9	31.6	31.4	32.8	32.4	33.5	34.5
China (Hong Kong SAR)	7.6	5.1	3.4	3.2	3.1	2.8	4.6	4.0	3.6	3.4	3.3	3.1
China (Macao SAR)	7.1	8.6	4.1	3.5	4.3	4.0	7.0	5.9	5.0	4.0	3.4	3.1
China (Taiwan Province)	23.8	23.8	24.6	25.3	25.9	27.0	22.7	23.7	23.7	23.7	23.2	22.9
Colombia	16.3	14.6	15.0	14.9	15.5	14.2	14.4	14.3	14.6	15.0	14.9	15.0
Comoros	4.7	4.5	4.4	4.4	4.2	4.2	4.6	4.4	4.4	4.4	4.4	4.2
Congo	4.4	3.5	5.2	5.3	5.3	5.6	4.5	5.3	6.5	6.3	5.4	4.9
Costa Rica	20.1	23.1	21.2	22.2	22.6	21.0	19.8	19.5	19.2	19.7	19.7	19.5
Côte d'Ivoire	18.8	21.7	18.5	19.2	17.7	17.5	21.0	19.5	17.8	18.6	19.3	18.3
Croatia	17.7	17.6	17.9	18.1	18.1	17.8	17.5	16.3	16.4	16.7	17.4	17.2
Cuba	13.0	14.0	10.4	8.8	8.0	9.1	13.0	11.6	9.3	8.2	7.2	7.0
Democratic People's Rep. of Korea	21.2	17.7	17.0	17.1	17.4	17.2	18.1	18.0	18.5	18.5	19.0	19.5
Democratic Rep. of the Congo	5.8	4.8	4.5	4.6	4.7	4.9	4.8	5.3	5.3	6.1	6.4	6.2
Djibouti	2.5	2.3	2.3	2.3	2.2	2.3	2.3	2.3	2.3	2.3	2.3	2.2
Dominica	7.3	7.4	5.5	5.4	6.0	5.9	6.3	6.5	6.6	6.6	6.5	6.0
Dominican Republic	18.0	16.8	15.3	14.8	14.3	13.2	16.1	15.7	15.6	15.5	15.1	14.0
Ecuador	13.8	13.6	12.9	13.3	13.9	13.6	11.7	10.4	9.6	8.8	8.9	9.0
Egypt	15.6	18.0	17.3	17.7	17.6	16.5	17.7	18.3	17.1	16.9	16.3	15.6
El Salvador	21.2	23.1	23.5	23.2	22.9	21.8	23.1	23.1	22.5	22.1	21.1	20.6

a/ Provisional.
b/ Estimate.

Table 1.4
(continued)

SHARE OF MVA IN GDP, SELECTED YEARS
(Percentage)

Country group or country/area	At constant 2000 prices						At current prices					
	1995	2000	2004	2005	2006 a/	2007 b/	2001	2002	2003	2004	2005	2006 a/
Equatorial Guinea	5.4	1.4	6.5	8.1	8.7	9.6	5.8	6.3	6.4	5.9	7.6	8.5
Eritrea	8.6	10.4	11.2	11.4	11.9	12.1	10.0	10.5	10.5	10.1	7.5	8.0
Ethiopia	5.5	5.3	5.0	4.9	4.9	4.8	5.5	5.5	5.3	5.0	4.9	4.9
Fiji	11.2	12.2	13.8	11.7	12.1	12.5	13.6	12.9	11.7	12.7	11.1	12.5
French Polynesia	6.4	6.5	5.9	6.1	6.0	6.0	6.4	6.4	6.0	5.9	6.1	6.0
Gabon	2.9	3.7	4.2	4.4	4.3	4.2	4.6	4.8	4.7	4.6	4.1	4.1
Gambia	5.6	4.8	4.9	4.7	4.7	4.5	4.6	5.1	4.8	4.8	4.7	4.6
Ghana	8.9	9.0	8.9	8.8	8.7	8.6	9.0	9.0	9.0	8.7	8.7	8.5
Grenada	5.3	6.2	4.8	5.0	5.0	4.8	6.0	5.7	5.1	4.5	4.7	4.8
Guatemala	14.1	13.2	12.7	12.6	12.5	11.8	13.0	12.8	12.7	12.7	12.6	12.5
Guinea	3.6	3.7	3.7	3.6	3.7	3.9	3.8	3.8	3.6	3.5	3.5	3.5
Guinea-Bissau	14.6	9.7	11.8	11.9	12.1	11.7	9.9	9.9	9.7	8.8	8.6	7.1
Guyana	8.0	6.8	7.2	6.6	6.8	6.4	7.1	7.6	7.9	8.1	6.6	6.1
Haiti	13.2	8.0	8.3	8.3	8.2	8.2	7.2	7.1	7.3	5.5	5.0	4.4
Honduras	15.9	17.0	17.5	17.7	17.5	16.6	17.7	18.2	18.2	18.0	17.9	17.7
India	15.1	14.3	14.2	14.1	14.5	14.9	13.8	14.1	14.1	14.5	14.6	14.8
Indonesia	25.1	27.7	28.4	28.1	27.8	26.8	30.8	30.4	28.3	28.1	27.7	28.0
Iran (Islamic Republic of)	10.5	13.1	15.9	16.0	16.1	16.4	13.2	11.3	11.1	11.1	11.6	11.6
Jamaica	14.6	12.7	12.1	11.7	11.1	10.8	12.8	12.5	12.3	12.6	12.6	11.6
Jordan	12.3	13.5	16.7	16.8	17.4	17.0	13.5	14.5	15.0	16.2	16.3	17.0
Kenya	11.5	10.3	10.2	10.1	10.1	9.6	9.8	9.8	9.7	9.9	10.3	10.2
Kiribati	0.9	0.7	0.8	0.8	0.7	0.7	0.7	0.6	0.7	0.7	0.7	0.7
Kuwait	7.8	6.9	8.1	7.8	8.0	8.0	6.3	7.8	7.9	8.3	7.4	7.9
Lao People's Dem. Rep.	14.0	16.9	20.2	20.5	20.8	21.2	17.7	18.9	18.9	20.1	20.4	20.7
Lebanon	14.4	11.9	12.6	12.6	11.5	11.2	12.2	11.5	11.8	11.7	11.7	9.8
Lesotho	14.9	15.4	17.1	15.2	15.6	15.6	16.3	18.7	18.1	16.2	15.5	15.9
Liberia	4.1	9.4	14.1	14.2	11.8	13.3	7.1	5.7	7.3	12.8	12.4	9.9
Libyan Arab Jamahiriya	5.2	4.8	3.5	3.3	3.2	3.1	4.6	3.2	2.4	1.8	1.4	1.8
Madagascar	10.9	11.1	10.8	10.6	10.3	9.6	11.5	11.8	12.6	12.9	12.8	12.2
Malawi	14.0	11.6	10.1	10.6	10.4	10.0	10.5	11.0	12.1	11.8	12.3	12.1
Malaysia	27.7	32.6	32.3	32.4	32.8	33.9	30.4	30.5	31.1	30.4	29.8	29.8
Maldives	7.2	7.2	7.1	6.7	5.8	5.6	7.4	8.0	7.7	7.3	6.7	5.7
Mali	6.1	3.5	3.3	3.2	3.0	3.3	2.9	2.9	2.6	3.1	2.9	2.8
Marshall Islands	2.6	4.8	4.3	4.2	4.1	3.9	4.6	4.3	4.2	4.8	4.5	4.2
Mauritania	6.6	8.3	5.9	5.0	5.0	4.8	6.1	5.6	5.5	5.4	4.6	5.0
Mauritius	20.6	20.5	18.7	17.5	16.8	14.8	20.6	20.4	19.3	18.4	17.6	16.7
Mexico	16.5	18.4	17.0	16.8	16.8	16.2	17.7	17.0	16.3	16.3	15.9	16.2
Micronesia, Federated States of	1.4	1.4	1.3	1.3	1.3	1.3	1.4	1.4	1.3	1.3	1.3	1.3

a/ Provisional.
b/ Estimate.

Table 1.4
(continued)

SHARE OF MVA IN GDP, SELECTED YEARS
(Percentage)

Country group or country/area	At constant 2000 prices						At current prices					
	1995	2000	2004	2005	2006 a/	2007 b/	2001	2002	2003	2004	2005	2006 a/
Mongolia	8.3	4.1	6.1	4.6	4.8	5.8	5.2	4.1	4.3	3.5	3.7	3.5
Montenegro	27.7	22.2	9.0	8.5	9.2	8.5	19.5	10.9	10.4	10.3	10.1	10.0
Morocco	16.4	15.5	14.3	14.6	14.0	14.0	14.5	14.6	15.4	14.9	15.5	14.7
Mozambique	6.4	10.6	14.2	14.3	13.7	13.8	12.4	12.7	15.0	16.0	14.0	14.0
Myanmar	6.5	7.2	9.1	8.4	8.6	8.7	7.8	9.2	9.8	11.6	10.2	10.5
Namibia	11.1	10.0	10.4	10.1	9.0	9.1	9.4	10.0	11.4	11.0	10.2	12.6
Nepal	8.2	8.8	7.7	7.7	7.6	7.5	8.7	8.2	7.9	7.8	7.6	7.4
New Caledonia	3.0	6.8	5.7	5.9	6.1	5.9	5.0	5.5	6.6	5.7	5.9	6.1
Nicaragua	15.0	15.1	16.2	16.6	16.8	16.5	16.5	17.9	16.9	17.0	16.5	16.2
Niger	6.4	6.8	7.1	6.6	6.5	6.3	6.6	6.6	6.6	7.0	6.2	6.1
Nigeria	4.0	3.6	4.1	4.1	4.3	4.1	3.8	4.4	3.9	3.7	3.2	3.3
Occupied Palestinian Territory	18.4	13.4	11.2	10.6	10.8	10.9	14.0	14.4	12.9	13.7	12.8	13.1
Oman	4.8	5.4	6.8	7.0	7.5	7.1	8.3	7.7	8.2	8.3	8.1	10.2
Pakistan	13.7	13.7	16.0	17.2	17.7	16.9	14.4	14.4	14.9	16.0	17.5	18.3
Palau	0.9	1.4	0.4	0.4	0.4	0.4	1.4	1.5	0.4	0.4	0.4	...
Panama	12.1	9.5	7.4	7.1	6.9	6.1	8.8	7.9	7.1	7.2	6.8	7.0
Papua New Guinea	7.6	8.4	7.9	8.4	8.6	8.4	7.0	6.3	6.1	6.3	5.8	5.5
Paraguay	15.3	15.5	14.3	14.2	14.1	13.2	15.9	15.0	15.0	14.2	12.4	11.8
Peru	15.1	14.4	14.8	14.8	14.9	13.7	14.7	14.7	14.3	14.9	14.9	14.9
Philippines	23.1	22.2	22.0	22.1	21.9	20.4	22.9	23.1	23.3	23.0	23.3	22.9
Puerto Rico	36.0	38.3	37.2	38.2	37.3	37.6	39.9	38.6	38.4	38.0	38.7	38.4
Qatar	6.7	5.4	5.6	6.0	6.0	5.9	6.1	7.2	7.6	10.4	8.4	7.7
Rwanda	13.5	11.3	9.5	10.0	10.8	10.8	11.7	11.2	8.9	8.0	8.2	8.5
Saint Lucia	5.2	4.4	4.8	4.7	4.7	4.6	4.4	3.9	4.2	4.1	4.4	4.7
Samoa	18.2	14.8	15.7	14.4	13.0	13.0	16.0	15.8	16.3	15.9	14.7	13.9
Sao Tome and Principe	7.3	5.9	6.9	6.5	6.6	6.7	5.7	5.7	5.9	6.8	6.4	5.9
Saudi Arabia	8.2	9.7	10.5	10.6	10.8	10.6	10.1	10.3	10.7	10.2	9.4	9.5
Senegal	13.7	12.9	12.8	12.0	10.9	10.5	14.9	15.1	14.4	14.4	13.2	12.0
Serbia	20.1	21.5	17.0	16.0	16.0	15.7	19.2	15.7	13.9	14.4	14.3	14.4
Seychelles	13.9	19.2	17.1	16.6	15.4	14.9	18.0	18.3	16.4	16.8	16.0	15.2
Sierra Leone	5.5	3.3	2.4	2.8	2.4	2.4	2.8	3.1	3.5	3.0	2.8	2.5
Solomon Islands	3.6	5.0	4.3	4.3	4.3	4.3	5.3	5.3	5.5	5.5	5.5	5.5
Somalia	4.8	5.6	5.7	5.6	5.7	5.7	5.7	5.7	5.7	5.7	5.6	5.6
Sri Lanka	13.7	15.1	14.1	14.1	13.8	13.1	14.1	14.0	13.8	13.6	13.1	12.3
St. Kitts and Nevis	7.6	9.0	8.4	8.0	6.9	6.5	8.9	7.9	8.7	8.3	8.0	6.9
St. Vincent and the Grenadines	7.5	5.1	4.6	4.6	4.5	4.3	5.7	5.6	4.8	4.8	5.3	5.0
Sudan	5.4	8.2	8.5	8.6	8.4	7.8	7.6	7.8	7.2	6.8	6.4	5.8
Suriname	6.3	8.2	10.8	10.5	10.2	10.5	10.8	7.4	6.6	6.2	5.4	4.6
Swaziland	26.0	24.9	24.3	24.1	24.2	23.5	25.0	23.8	22.7	22.4	21.7	22.5

a/ Provisional.
b/ Estimate.

Table 1.4
(continued)

SHARE OF MVA IN GDP, SELECTED YEARS
(Percentage)

Country group or country/area	At constant 2000 prices						At current prices					
	1995	2000	2004	2005	2006 a/	2007 b/	2001	2002	2003	2004	2005	2006 a/
Syrian Arab Republic	13.8	6.7	10.9	11.8	12.1	11.9	8.1	7.7	7.9	10.0	9.0	8.0
Thailand	30.0	33.6	35.7	35.9	36.3	35.0	33.4	33.7	34.8	34.5	34.8	35.0
The f. Yugosl. Rep. of Macedonia	17.9	17.3	16.6	16.1	16.0	14.7	16.9	15.5	15.8	15.0	15.5	15.8
Timor-Leste	4.2	2.8	3.4	3.4	2.6	2.8	3.0	3.2	3.4	3.4	3.4	2.6
Togo	8.5	8.4	10.1	10.7	8.8	10.0	8.9	9.1	9.3	9.4	10.1	8.6
Tonga	3.7	4.5	4.6	4.6	4.5	4.1	4.2	3.9	3.8	3.9	3.2	2.9
Trinidad and Tobago	5.9	7.1	7.0	7.2	7.2	7.0	7.4	8.0	6.4	6.7	6.3	5.7
Tunisia	18.5	18.2	17.6	17.2	17.0	16.5	18.5	18.6	17.9	17.7	17.5	17.4
Turkey	19.2	19.2	20.2	20.0	20.2	19.4	20.6	20.1	20.0	20.4	20.8	21.1
Uganda	6.6	8.9	8.8	9.2	8.8	8.2	8.8	9.2	8.6	8.4	8.5	8.3
United Arab Emirates	8.5	13.4	12.9	13.6	13.6	13.7	13.8	13.8	13.0	13.1	14.5	14.1
United Republic of Tanzania	6.5	6.9	7.2	7.3	7.4	6.8	6.8	6.8	6.7	6.4	6.3	6.4
Uruguay	18.5	16.9	17.3	17.9	18.1	16.7	16.3	17.5	18.6	21.3	22.5	23.2
Vanuatu	5.1	4.4	4.0	4.0	3.8	3.6	3.8	3.6	3.6	3.6	3.6	3.4
Venezuela (Bolivarian Republic of)	14.9	18.5	17.9	17.4	17.1	16.7	17.0	16.4	17.1	16.5	13.7	11.9
Viet Nam	15.2	18.6	21.4	22.4	23.3	23.3	19.8	20.6	20.5	20.3	20.6	21.3
Yemen	4.6	5.2	5.2	5.3	5.4	5.3	5.3	5.2	4.7	5.0	4.9	5.3
Zambia	9.7	10.2	10.5	10.4	10.3	9.8	9.8	10.4	10.9	10.9	10.7	10.4
Zimbabwe	15.1	13.6	10.8	9.5	10.7	10.3	13.2	12.0	12.3	10.8	9.5	10.4
Developing countries (excl.China)	17.2	16.7	16.7	17.1	17.1	16.8	16.5	16.6	16.5	16.6	16.1	16.0
Low Income	13.1	13.0	13.3	13.5	13.8	13.9	12.9	13.1	13.1	13.4	13.3	13.5
Middle income (excl. China)	19.4	17.5	18.1	19.1	19.0	18.3	17.6	18.1	18.3	18.4	17.9	18.0
High income	16.0	17.2	16.6	16.6	16.6	16.5	16.8	16.8	16.4	16.2	15.4	15.0
Africa	11.0	11.2	10.6	10.6	10.5	10.1	11.1	11.2	10.4	9.8	9.0	8.6
Central Africa	7.9	8.4	8.8	8.8	9.0	8.5	8.9	8.8	8.8	8.1	7.2	7.1
Eastern and southern Africa	10.2	10.0	9.6	9.4	9.3	8.8	10.0	10.2	10.1	9.8	9.5	9.5
North Africa	13.2	13.1	12.3	12.4	12.3	11.8	13.0	13.2	12.2	11.3	10.5	10.0
Western Africa (ECOWAS)	7.4	7.5	7.1	7.0	6.7	6.7	7.4	7.9	7.3	7.2	6.4	6.0
Asia	21.1	22.6	24.0	24.4	24.6	24.8	22.7	22.9	23.5	23.4	23.7	24.4
Europe	18.9	18.8	19.4	19.2	19.4	18.7	19.5	18.8	18.7	19.1	19.6	19.8
Latin America	18.6	17.0	16.6	17.6	17.4	16.9	16.8	16.7	16.8	16.9	16.3	16.0
Andean Group	15.3	16.1	15.9	15.7	15.9	15.1	15.3	14.7	14.7	14.8	13.8	13.2
ASEAN	25.5	27.7	28.3	28.4	28.6	27.6	27.9	28.2	28.0	28.1	27.9	28.1
CACM	17.6	18.6	18.2	18.4	18.5	17.5	17.8	17.7	17.3	17.3	16.9	16.6
CARICOM	8.9	7.9	7.8	7.8	7.6	7.4	8.0	7.9	7.3	7.3	7.1	6.5
CEMAC	10.1	11.1	11.9	12.2	12.6	12.5	11.7	11.9	11.8	10.6	9.7	9.7

a/ Provisional.
b/ Estimate.

Table 1.4
(continued)

SHARE OF MVA IN GDP, SELECTED YEARS
(Percentage)

Country group or country/area	At constant 2000 prices						At current prices					
	1995	2000	2004	2005	2006 a/	2007 b/	2001	2002	2003	2004	2005	2006 a/
CEPGL	7.2	6.8	6.2	6.4	6.7	6.8	6.7	6.8	6.2	6.6	6.9	6.8
LAIA	18.3	16.5	16.2	17.3	17.1	16.6	16.1	16.0	16.1	16.4	15.8	15.6
OECS	5.2	5.0	4.5	4.5	4.3	4.1	4.9	4.6	4.6	4.4	4.5	4.3
SAARC	14.7	14.2	14.4	14.5	14.9	15.0	14.0	14.1	14.2	14.7	14.9	15.1
Least developed countries	9.1	9.8	10.2	10.2	10.4	10.0	10.0	10.0	10.0	9.9	9.4	9.2
African LDCs	6.7	7.3	7.5	7.5	7.5	7.2	7.4	7.4	7.4	7.2	6.8	6.7
NICs	19.3	18.2	18.3	18.9	18.9	18.6	18.0	18.4	18.5	18.7	18.3	18.4
World	17.7	18.1	18.0	18.1	18.4	18.0	17.3	16.9	16.7	16.7	16.6	16.7

a/ Provisional.
b/ Estimate.

Section 1.2

THE MANUFACTURING DIVISIONS / BRANCHES

Table 1.5

DISTRIBUTION OF WORLD VALUE ADDED, SELECTED DIVISIONS AND YEARS[a/]
(Percentage)

ISIC Division	Year	Industrialized countries								Developing countries			World
				Europe									
		All countries	CIS	EU-15	EU-12	Other	East Asia	North America	Others	All countries	NICs	Others[b/]	
15 Food and beverages	2000	70.0	1.8	25.0	2.1	0.8	20.2	17.3	2.8	30.0	16.6	13.4	100.0
	2005	63.4	2.2	22.9	2.1	0.7	16.9	15.9	2.6	36.6	16.5	20.2	100.0
	2007	62.1	2.5	22.3	2.2	0.6	15.9	16.0	2.6	37.9	16.8	21.1	100.0
16 Tobacco products	2000	40.4	0.9	11.5	1.3	2.4	11.7	11.0	1.6	59.6	19.7	39.9	100.0
	2005	30.5	0.9	7.2	0.8	2.3	10.0	8.0	1.3	69.5	15.3	54.2	100.0
	2007	27.2	0.9	6.0	0.8	2.7	9.6	6.0	1.3	72.8	13.5	59.2	100.0
17 Textiles	2000	54.0	1.2	24.3	1.7	0.5	11.3	13.5	1.5	46.0	22.0	24.0	100.0
	2005	39.3	1.3	17.6	1.6	0.3	6.9	10.5	1.0	60.7	18.7	42.1	100.0
	2007	35.5	1.5	16.5	1.6	0.3	6.3	8.4	0.9	64.5	18.8	45.7	100.0
18 Wearing apparel, fur	2000	63.9	1.1	20.8	3.2	0.5	19.4	17.3	1.6	36.1	17.9	18.2	100.0
	2005	44.6	1.3	15.6	3.1	0.5	12.4	10.3	1.4	55.4	20.4	35.0	100.0
	2007	40.8	1.3	14.8	2.7	0.9	10.7	9.1	1.3	59.2	20.2	39.0	100.0
19 Leather, leather products and footwear	2000	54.2	0.9	30.1	2.7	0.3	9.4	9.5	1.3	45.8	21.6	24.2	100.0
	2005	35.6	1.2	19.4	2.2	0.1	6.1	5.6	1.0	64.4	20.0	44.4	100.0
	2007	32.8	1.3	18.0	2.4	0.1	5.2	4.8	0.9	67.2	18.5	48.8	100.0
20 Wood products (excl. furniture)	2000	84.3	0.9	25.8	2.7	3.2	10.2	38.9	2.6	15.7	10.6	5.1	100.0
	2005	79.8	1.2	23.9	3.2	3.0	7.4	38.5	2.6	20.2	10.6	9.6	100.0
	2007	78.9	1.4	25.5	3.8	3.3	7.2	35.1	2.6	21.1	9.9	11.2	100.0
21 Paper and paper products	2000	83.0	1.1	25.4	1.0	1.0	20.0	30.3	4.2	17.0	10.1	6.9	100.0
	2005	76.6	1.5	24.5	1.2	0.8	18.4	26.1	4.1	23.4	10.3	13.1	100.0
	2007	74.2	1.6	24.7	1.4	0.7	18.0	24.0	3.8	25.8	10.6	15.2	100.0
22 Printing and publishing	2000	90.9	0.3	33.2	1.4	1.8	23.1	29.8	1.3	9.1	5.7	3.4	100.0
	2005	87.7	0.5	33.1	1.7	1.6	22.1	27.3	1.4	12.3	6.5	5.8	100.0
	2007	86.4	0.5	32.4	1.8	1.6	23.2	25.5	1.4	13.6	6.9	6.7	100.0
23 Coke,refined petroleum products,nuclear fuel	2000	58.8	1.4	10.6	1.4	1.0	32.4	11.1	0.9	41.2	23.1	18.1	100.0
	2005	52.0	1.5	8.9	1.3	0.8	27.5	11.2	0.7	48.0	24.3	23.8	100.0
	2007	48.5	1.6	8.5	1.3	0.9	25.9	9.6	0.7	51.5	25.5	26.0	100.0
24 Chemicals and chemical products	2000	75.9	1.1	28.0	1.0	1.9	17.8	24.7	1.5	24.1	13.3	10.7	100.0
	2005	70.4	1.1	26.3	1.0	2.1	15.3	23.2	1.4	29.6	13.5	16.1	100.0
	2007	68.8	1.1	25.6	1.2	2.4	14.9	22.3	1.4	31.2	13.9	17.2	100.0

a/ At constant 2000 prices.
b/ Including China.

Table 1.5
(continued)

DISTRIBUTION OF WORLD VALUE ADDED, SELECTED DIVISIONS AND YEARS[a/]
(Percentage)

ISIC Division	Year	Industrialized countries								Developing countries			World
				Europe									
		All countries	CIS	EU-15	EU-12	Other	East Asia	North America	Others	All countries	NICs	Others[b/]	
25 Rubber and plastics products	2000	74.7	0.7	33.7	1.6	0.9	9.9	25.8	2.1	25.3	14.0	11.3	100.0
	2005	66.0	0.9	29.1	2.2	0.8	8.8	22.2	2.0	34.0	14.6	19.4	100.0
	2007	63.9	1.2	28.4	2.7	0.8	8.5	20.4	1.9	36.1	13.7	22.4	100.0
26 Non-metallic mineral products	2000	70.9	1.8	30.4	2.4	1.1	18.9	14.4	1.8	29.1	14.4	14.8	100.0
	2005	61.9	2.2	26.0	2.5	1.4	14.5	13.3	2.0	38.1	14.6	23.5	100.0
	2007	61.0	2.7	25.2	3.0	1.4	14.1	12.6	2.1	39.0	14.9	24.0	100.0
27 Basic metals	2000	72.6	3.7	19.0	1.3	2.2	26.8	16.7	2.8	27.4	11.8	15.7	100.0
	2005	53.6	3.3	13.6	1.0	1.3	20.6	11.7	2.1	46.4	10.5	35.9	100.0
	2007	50.0	3.2	12.8	1.0	1.2	19.3	10.5	2.0	50.0	10.9	39.1	100.0
28 Fabricated metal products	2000	85.0	0.7	35.2	1.6	1.3	18.6	25.5	2.1	15.0	9.5	5.5	100.0
	2005	79.7	1.2	34.7	2.3	1.2	15.1	23.1	2.2	20.3	9.5	10.7	100.0
	2007	78.8	1.3	35.0	2.8	1.2	13.6	22.6	2.3	21.2	9.3	11.9	100.0
29 Machinery and equipment n.e.c.	2000	85.9	1.2	32.7	1.4	1.7	25.8	22.2	0.9	14.1	6.3	7.8	100.0
	2005	76.5	1.5	29.1	1.9	1.3	23.8	18.0	0.9	23.5	6.8	16.7	100.0
	2007	75.8	1.7	29.5	2.3	1.4	23.5	16.6	0.9	24.2	6.9	17.2	100.0
30 Office, accounting and computing machinery	2000	91.4	0.0	14.4	0.2	0.7	17.9	55.8	2.4	8.6	6.2	2.4	100.0
	2005	87.4	0.2	9.9	0.3	0.3	18.0	56.9	1.8	12.6	8.1	4.5	100.0
	2007	87.8	0.1	9.1	0.3	0.2	15.6	60.9	1.6	12.2	8.2	4.0	100.0
31 Electrical machinery and apparatus	2000	77.8	0.7	27.3	1.3	0.7	26.5	20.6	0.7	22.2	8.3	13.9	100.0
	2005	63.2	0.9	22.1	1.9	0.5	23.5	13.7	0.6	36.8	9.2	27.6	100.0
	2007	58.9	0.9	20.4	1.9	0.6	22.9	11.6	0.6	41.1	8.5	32.6	100.0
32 Radio,television and communication equipment	2000	89.4	0.2	7.7	0.2	0.2	18.0	62.6	0.5	10.6	6.3	4.3	100.0
	2005	88.1	0.1	4.5	0.3	0.1	15.0	67.8	0.4	11.9	4.8	7.0	100.0
	2007	87.2	0.1	3.9	0.2	0.0	14.1	68.6	0.3	12.8	5.4	7.4	100.0
33 Medical, precision and optical instruments	2000	91.1	1.5	30.8	1.2	2.3	14.6	38.7	2.0	8.9	5.4	3.5	100.0
	2005	88.3	4.3	27.6	1.4	1.9	11.9	39.5	1.7	11.7	5.8	5.9	100.0
	2007	87.7	4.6	27.4	1.7	2.0	12.2	38.1	1.7	12.3	5.7	6.6	100.0
34 Motor vehicles, trailers, semi-trailers	2000	88.8	0.7	31.2	0.8	0.1	27.9	27.0	1.2	11.2	10.0	1.1	100.0
	2005	86.1	0.8	29.5	1.2	0.1	28.7	24.6	1.3	13.9	11.2	2.6	100.0
	2007	85.2	0.9	29.4	1.6	0.1	30.5	21.4	1.3	14.8	11.5	3.3	100.0

a/ At constant 2000 prices.
b/ Including China.

Table 1.5
(continued)

DISTRIBUTION OF WORLD VALUE ADDED, SELECTED DIVISIONS AND YEARS[a/]
(Percentage)

ISIC Division	Year	Industrialized countries								Developing countries			World
				Europe									
		All countries	CIS	EU-15	EU-12	Other	East Asia	North America	Others	All countries	NICs	Others[b/]	
35 Other transport equipment	2000	70.9	1.8	23.4	1.2	1.4	11.0	30.5	1.6	29.1	10.4	18.7	100.0
	2005	55.8	1.6	17.1	1.1	1.0	11.0	22.8	1.2	44.2	12.2	32.0	100.0
	2007	51.3	1.7	15.4	1.1	1.1	9.2	21.8	1.0	48.7	11.3	37.4	100.0
36 Furniture; manufacturing n.e.c.	2000	82.5	0.8	23.6	1.9	0.9	30.8	22.9	1.6	17.5	8.3	9.2	100.0
	2005	68.9	1.1	19.1	2.5	0.7	21.5	22.5	1.5	31.1	7.6	23.5	100.0
	2007	69.4	1.2	18.0	2.7	0.7	24.5	20.9	1.4	30.6	7.2	23.4	100.0

a/ At constant 2000 prices.
b/ Including China.

Table 1.6

DISTRIBUTION OF VALUE ADDED OF SELECTED DIVISIONS AMONG DEVELOPING REGIONS, 2000 AND 2007[a/]

(Percentage)

ISIC Division	Developing regions												Least developed countries	
	North Africa		Sub-saharan Africa		Latin America		Asia[b/]		Europe		All countries			
	2000	2007	2000	2007	2000	2007	2000	2007	2000	2007	2000	2007	2000	2007
15 Food and beverages	3.6	1.8	3.0	2.3	43.0	31.1	47.4	62.5	3.0	2.3	100.0	100.0	2.5	2.0
16 Tobacco products	3.0	1.6	1.8	1.2	17.4	9.5	75.2	86.2	2.6	1.5	100.0	100.0	3.5	3.2
17 Textiles	4.5	2.5	1.6	1.2	17.1	10.6	71.1	82.3	5.7	3.4	100.0	100.0	3.3	4.3
18 Wearing apparel, fur	4.8	3.7	1.9	1.0	24.7	14.5	63.3	77.9	5.3	2.9	100.0	100.0	4.3	4.5
19 Leather, leather products and footwear	3.4	2.0	1.4	1.1	28.2	18.3	65.2	77.6	1.8	1.0	100.0	100.0	2.7	3.0
20 Wood products (excl. furniture)	3.9	2.3	3.9	1.5	45.8	35.0	44.0	58.8	2.4	2.4	100.0	100.0	1.2	1.0
21 Paper and paper products	2.1	2.0	1.7	1.1	36.1	26.5	57.6	68.2	2.5	2.2	100.0	100.0	1.0	0.6
22 Printing and publishing	3.0	5.1	2.4	2.1	44.2	33.9	47.0	54.9	3.4	4.0	100.0	100.0	1.6	1.5
23 Coke,refined petroleum products,nuclear fuel	2.6	3.6	0.7	0.6	35.5	24.5	58.9	69.6	2.3	1.7	100.0	100.0	0.5	0.4
24 Chemicals and chemical products	3.9	3.6	0.8	0.6	39.1	25.9	53.4	67.5	2.8	2.4	100.0	100.0	1.3	1.2
25 Rubber and plastics products	1.5	0.8	0.8	0.7	30.9	20.2	63.2	75.1	3.6	3.2	100.0	100.0	0.6	0.5
26 Non-metallic mineral products	5.4	5.8	1.2	1.0	28.6	21.1	60.2	68.3	4.6	3.8	100.0	100.0	1.1	1.2
27 Basic metals	2.0	0.9	0.5	0.3	24.5	11.0	68.9	85.5	4.1	2.3	100.0	100.0	0.4	0.2
28 Fabricated metal products	2.6	2.1	1.7	1.5	35.0	24.4	57.8	68.9	2.9	3.1	100.0	100.0	0.8	0.7
29 Machinery and equipment n.e.c.	1.8	0.8	0.2	0.2	26.5	15.2	67.7	80.5	3.8	3.3	100.0	100.0	0.2	0.2
30 Office, accounting and computing machinery	1.1	0.5	0.2	0.2	31.8	17.3	66.0	81.3	0.9	0.7	100.0	100.0	0.3	0.1
31 Electrical machinery and apparatus	1.6	0.9	0.3	0.1	20.3	9.4	75.6	88.4	2.2	1.2	100.0	100.0	0.3	0.1
32 Radio,television and communication equipment	0.2	0.1	0.1	0.0	9.4	3.9	87.9	94.1	2.4	1.9	100.0	100.0	0.2	0.1
33 Medical, precision and optical instruments	0.8	0.6	0.2	0.2	48.2	33.4	49.8	65.3	1.0	0.5	100.0	100.0	0.2	0.1
34 Motor vehicles, trailers, semi-trailers	2.9	1.2	0.7	0.7	57.5	41.2	33.5	50.2	5.4	6.7	100.0	100.0	0.4	0.3
35 Other transport equipment	0.5	0.1	0.3	0.2	21.8	15.5	76.8	83.9	0.6	0.3	100.0	100.0	0.4	0.1
36 Furniture; manufacturing n.e.c.	0.9	0.5	1.5	1.0	29.1	14.5	65.8	82.7	2.7	1.3	100.0	100.0	0.9	0.6

a/ At constant 2000 prices.
b/ Including China.

Table 1.7

LEADING PRODUCERS IN SELECTED DIVISIONS, 2000 AND 2007

World leading countries				Leading developing countries			
2000		2007		2000		2007	
Country or area	Share a/ (percentage)	Country or area	Share a/ (percentage)	Country or area	Share b/ (percentage)	Country or area	Share b/ (percentage)
Food and beverages (ISIC 15)							
Japan	18.7	Japan	14.6	China	21.3	China	37.7
United States of America	14.9	China	14.3	Mexico	12.5	Mexico	8.7
China	6.4	United States of America	13.7	Brazil	9.3	Brazil	6.9
Germany	4.9	Germany	4.4	Indonesia	6.3	Indonesia	6.3
United Kingdom	4.5	United Kingdom	3.8	Argentina	6.0	Argentina	4.7
France	4.2	France	3.6	Thailand	4.0	Thailand	4.0
Mexico	3.7	Mexico	3.3	India	3.1	India	3.1
Italy	3.3	Italy	2.9	Turkey	2.6	Turkey	2.0
Brazil	2.8	Brazil	2.6	Venezuela (Bolivarian Republic of)	2.2	Venezuela (Bolivarian Republic of)	1.7
Canada	2.3	Indonesia	2.4	China (Taiwan Province)	2.0	Chile	1.6
Spain	2.3	Canada	2.3	Puerto Rico	2.0	Iran (Islamic Republic of)	1.6
Indonesia	1.9	Spain	2.1	Colombia	1.8	Colombia	1.3
Argentina	1.8	Argentina	1.8	Chile	1.7	Viet Nam	1.3
Australia	1.7	Russian Federation	1.7	Iran (Islamic Republic of)	1.7	China (Taiwan Province)	1.2
Republic of Korea	1.4	Thailand	1.5	Philippines	1.7	Malaysia	1.2
Sum of above	**74.8**	**Sum of above**	**75.0**	**Sum of above**	**78.2**	**Sum of above**	**83.3**
Tobacco products (ISIC 16)							
China	30.7	China	51.4	China	51.5	China	70.6
Japan	10.6	Japan	8.5	Indonesia	10.0	Indonesia	6.5
United States of America	9.4	United States of America	5.5	Argentina	5.4	Argentina	2.8
Indonesia	6.0	Indonesia	4.7	Brazil	2.6	Bangladesh	1.9
Argentina	3.2	Switzerland	2.6	Thailand	2.2	Mexico	1.3
United Kingdom	2.7	Argentina	2.0	Turkey	2.1	Pakistan	1.3
Germany	2.4	Bangladesh	1.4	Mexico	2.0	Thailand	1.3
Switzerland	2.3	Netherlands	1.3	Pakistan	1.9	Turkey	1.3
Netherlands	1.8	United Kingdom	1.3	Bangladesh	1.8	India	1.2
Canada	1.6	Republic of Korea	1.0	India	1.8	Chile	1.1
Brazil	1.5	Germany	0.9	China (Taiwan Province)	1.7	Viet Nam	1.1
Thailand	1.3	India	0.9	Dominican Republic	1.5	Venezuela (Bolivarian Republic of)	1.0
Turkey	1.3	Mexico	0.9	Chile	1.4	Brazil	0.9
Mexico	1.2	Pakistan	0.9	Philippines	1.4	China (Taiwan Province)	0.8
Bangladesh	1.1	Thailand	0.9	Venezuela (Bolivarian Republic of)	1.3	Dominican Republic	0.6
Sum of above	**77.1**	**Sum of above**	**84.2**	**Sum of above**	**88.6**	**Sum of above**	**93.7**

a/ In world total value added at constant 2000 prices.
b/ In total value added of developing countries at constant 2000 prices.

Table 1.7

LEADING PRODUCERS IN SELECTED DIVISIONS, 2000 AND 2007

World leading countries				Leading developing countries			
2000		2007		2000		2007	
Country or area	Share a/ (percentage)	Country or area	Share a/ (percentage)	Country or area	Share b/ (percentage)	Country or area	Share b/ (percentage)
Textiles (ISIC 17)							
China	17.2	China	36.7	China	37.4	China	56.9
United States of America	12.0	United States of America	7.5	India	7.4	India	6.5
Italy	8.9	Italy	6.1	Mexico	6.0	Pakistan	3.5
Japan	7.0	India	4.2	Turkey	5.5	Turkey	3.3
Republic of Korea	4.3	Japan	4.0	Brazil	5.0	Brazil	3.2
India	3.4	Pakistan	2.3	China (Taiwan Province)	4.9	Bangladesh	3.0
United Kingdom	3.4	Germany	2.2	Indonesia	4.6	Mexico	3.0
Germany	3.0	Republic of Korea	2.2	Thailand	3.8	Thailand	2.9
Mexico	2.8	Brazil	2.1	Pakistan	3.3	Indonesia	2.1
France	2.7	Turkey	2.1	Egypt	3.0	China (Taiwan Province)	1.9
Turkey	2.5	United Kingdom	2.1	Bangladesh	2.2	Egypt	1.5
Brazil	2.3	Mexico	2.0	Iran (Islamic Republic of)	2.1	Argentina	1.4
China (Taiwan Province)	2.2	Bangladesh	1.9	Argentina	2.0	Iran (Islamic Republic of)	1.3
Indonesia	2.1	Thailand	1.9	China (Hong Kong SAR)	1.3	Peru	0.8
Thailand	1.8	France	1.5	Morocco	1.0	Morocco	0.7
Sum of above	**75.6**	**Sum of above**	**78.8**	**Sum of above**	**89.5**	**Sum of above**	**92.0**
Wearing apparel, fur (ISIC 18)							
Japan	18.0	China	28.7	China	28.6	China	48.5
United States of America	15.2	Japan	9.2	Thailand	10.1	Thailand	8.9
China	10.3	United States of America	7.9	Brazil	6.6	Indonesia	4.2
Italy	7.9	Italy	7.4	Mexico	5.2	Brazil	3.3
Thailand	3.6	Thailand	5.3	Turkey	4.7	Bangladesh	2.9
United Kingdom	3.0	Indonesia	2.5	Indonesia	3.7	Viet Nam	2.8
France	2.7	United Kingdom	2.1	Argentina	2.9	Mexico	2.7
Brazil	2.4	Brazil	2.0	Bangladesh	2.9	Turkey	2.6
Canada	2.1	Bangladesh	1.7	Iran (Islamic Republic of)	2.6	Argentina	2.1
Germany	1.9	Viet Nam	1.7	Colombia	2.5	Egypt	2.1
Mexico	1.9	Mexico	1.6	China (Hong Kong SAR)	2.1	Colombia	1.8
Spain	1.7	Turkey	1.6	Philippines	2.1	Philippines	1.7
Turkey	1.7	Republic of Korea	1.4	China (Taiwan Province)	2.0	Puerto Rico	1.4
Republic of Korea	1.4	Egypt	1.3	Puerto Rico	2.0	Peru	1.3
Indonesia	1.3	Argentina	1.2	Egypt	1.8	Iran (Islamic Republic of)	1.2
Sum of above	**75.1**	**Sum of above**	**75.6**	**Sum of above**	**79.8**	**Sum of above**	**87.5**

a/ In world total value added at constant 2000 prices.
b/ In total value added of developing countries at constant 2000 prices.

Table 1.7

LEADING PRODUCERS IN SELECTED DIVISIONS, 2000 AND 2007

World leading countries				Leading developing countries			
2000		2007		2000		2007	
Country or area	Share a/ (percentage)	Country or area	Share a/ (percentage)	Country or area	Share b/ (percentage)	Country or area	Share b/ (percentage)
Leather, leather products and footwear (ISIC 19)							
China	16.3	China	39.1	China	35.6	China	58.2
Italy	13.9	Italy	7.7	Thailand	8.7	Argentina	6.3
United States of America	8.7	United States of America	4.5	Argentina	7.7	Viet Nam	4.1
Japan	6.1	Argentina	4.2	Brazil	6.9	Thailand	4.1
Thailand	4.0	Japan	3.5	Mexico	6.3	Mexico	3.9
Spain	3.6	Thailand	2.8	India	4.4	Brazil	3.3
Argentina	3.5	Viet Nam	2.7	Indonesia	3.8	India	3.0
France	3.3	Mexico	2.6	Saudi Arabia	2.5	Saudi Arabia	2.1
Republic of Korea	3.2	Brazil	2.2	Viet Nam	2.4	Bangladesh	2.0
Brazil	3.1	India	2.0	Colombia	2.0	Colombia	1.5
Mexico	2.9	Finland	1.7	Iran (Islamic Republic of)	1.8	Indonesia	1.4
United Kingdom	2.7	France	1.7	Bangladesh	1.6	Puerto Rico	0.9
Germany	2.2	Spain	1.7	Puerto Rico	1.4	Morocco	0.8
India	2.0	Republic of Korea	1.6	Turkey	1.4	Turkey	0.8
Portugal	1.9	Germany	1.4	China (Taiwan Province)	1.2	Pakistan	0.7
Sum of above	**77.4**	**Sum of above**	**79.4**	**Sum of above**	**87.7**	**Sum of above**	**93.1**
Wood products (excl. furniture) (ISIC 20)							
United States of America	31.5	United States of America	28.4	Brazil	25.0	China	42.0
Japan	9.3	China	8.9	China	18.3	Brazil	17.7
Canada	7.4	Canada	6.7	Indonesia	10.1	Argentina	7.7
Germany	5.8	Japan	6.3	Argentina	7.9	Malaysia	4.9
Italy	5.1	Germany	5.4	Mexico	6.5	Mexico	4.0
Brazil	3.9	Italy	5.0	Malaysia	6.1	Indonesia	3.6
France	3.2	Brazil	3.7	Chile	2.5	Chile	2.4
China	2.9	France	3.1	China (Taiwan Province)	1.9	Turkey	1.9
Switzerland	2.6	Switzerland	2.7	Morocco	1.6	Saudi Arabia	1.3
United Kingdom	2.4	United Kingdom	2.3	Turkey	1.6	United Arab Emirates	1.2
Spain	1.9	Austria	2.0	Côte d'Ivoire	1.5	Thailand	1.1
Sweden	1.8	Sweden	2.0	Saudi Arabia	1.3	Morocco	0.9
Indonesia	1.6	Poland	1.7	Thailand	1.0	Viet Nam	0.9
Australia	1.5	Argentina	1.6	United Arab Emirates	1.0	Tunisia	0.9
Austria	1.5	Spain	1.6	Tunisia	1.0	Iran (Islamic Republic of)	0.8
Sum of above	**82.4**	**Sum of above**	**81.4**	**Sum of above**	**87.3**	**Sum of above**	**91.3**

a/ In world total value added at constant 2000 prices.
b/ In total value added of developing countries at constant 2000 prices.

Table 1.7

LEADING PRODUCERS IN SELECTED DIVISIONS, 2000 AND 2007

World leading countries				Leading developing countries			
2000		2007		2000		2007	
Country or area	Share a/ (percentage)	Country or area	Share a/ (percentage)	Country or area	Share b/ (percentage)	Country or area	Share b/ (percentage)
Paper and paper products (ISIC 21)							
United States of America	25.1	United States of America	20.1	China	29.4	China	50.0
Japan	17.6	Japan	15.5	Brazil	11.3	Brazil	8.2
Canada	5.2	China	12.9	Mexico	8.2	Mexico	4.8
China	5.0	Germany	4.8	Indonesia	7.7	Chile	4.5
Germany	4.5	Canada	3.9	Argentina	5.3	India	4.4
United Kingdom	3.6	United Kingdom	3.3	China (Taiwan Province)	5.1	Argentina	3.6
France	3.2	Finland	2.8	India	4.9	China (Taiwan Province)	3.2
Australia	3.0	France	2.8	Chile	4.5	Indonesia	2.8
Finland	2.9	Australia	2.6	Thailand	2.9	Thailand	2.2
Italy	2.7	Italy	2.6	Turkey	2.1	Malaysia	1.9
Sweden	2.6	Sweden	2.5	Malaysia	1.9	Turkey	1.8
Brazil	1.9	Brazil	2.1	Colombia	1.8	Colombia	1.3
Spain	1.9	Spain	1.9	Venezuela (Bolivarian Republic of)	1.7	Venezuela (Bolivarian Republic of)	1.2
Republic of Korea	1.8	Republic of Korea	1.8	Philippines	1.2	Peru	1.1
Mexico	1.4	Russian Federation	1.5	Peru	0.9	Morocco	0.9
Sum of above	**82.4**	**Sum of above**	**81.1**	**Sum of above**	**88.9**	**Sum of above**	**91.9**
Printing and publishing (ISIC 22)							
United States of America	26.9	United States of America	22.2	China	17.7	China	28.2
Japan	21.6	Japan	21.9	Argentina	11.6	Argentina	8.9
United Kingdom	8.2	Germany	7.1	Mexico	11.6	Mexico	7.7
Germany	7.8	United Kingdom	7.0	Brazil	9.9	Brazil	6.8
France	4.0	China	3.8	China (Hong Kong SAR)	6.5	India	5.5
Italy	3.4	France	3.5	India	4.7	Egypt	4.6
Canada	2.9	Canada	3.3	China (Taiwan Province)	3.4	China (Hong Kong SAR)	4.3
Netherlands	2.0	Italy	3.3	United Arab Emirates	2.6	United Arab Emirates	3.1
Spain	2.0	Ireland	2.4	Egypt	2.5	China (Taiwan Province)	2.8
China	1.6	Spain	2.4	Malaysia	2.4	Croatia	2.4
Sweden	1.2	Netherlands	1.8	Venezuela (Bolivarian Republic of)	1.9	Venezuela (Bolivarian Republic of)	2.4
Argentina	1.1	Argentina	1.2	Turkey	1.7	Malaysia	2.3
Ireland	1.1	Sweden	1.1	Colombia	1.6	Indonesia	1.9
Republic of Korea	1.1	Mexico	1.0	Indonesia	1.6	Peru	1.5
Mexico	1.1	Poland	1.0	Thailand	1.6	Turkey	1.4
Sum of above	**86.0**	**Sum of above**	**83.0**	**Sum of above**	**81.3**	**Sum of above**	**83.8**

a/ In world total value added at constant 2000 prices.
b/ In total value added of developing countries at constant 2000 prices.

Table 1.7

LEADING PRODUCERS IN SELECTED DIVISIONS, 2000 AND 2007

World leading countries				Leading developing countries			
2000		2007		2000		2007	
Country or area	Share a/ (percentage)	Country or area	Share a/ (percentage)	Country or area	Share b/ (percentage)	Country or area	Share b/ (percentage)
Coke,refined petroleum products,nuclear fuel (ISIC 23)							
Japan	28.1	Japan	22.1	China	18.5	China	30.6
United States of America	10.7	China	15.7	Brazil	17.0	Brazil	11.7
China	7.6	United States of America	8.8	Saudi Arabia	9.5	China (Taiwan Province)	8.1
Brazil	7.0	Brazil	6.0	China (Taiwan Province)	7.1	Indonesia	7.7
France	3.9	China (Taiwan Province)	4.1	Indonesia	5.4	Saudi Arabia	7.6
Saudi Arabia	3.9	Indonesia	4.0	Venezuela (Bolivarian Republic of)	4.9	India	3.6
China (Taiwan Province)	2.9	Saudi Arabia	3.9	Argentina	4.8	Venezuela (Bolivarian Republic of)	3.4
Republic of Korea	2.7	France	3.0	India	4.1	Argentina	3.2
Indonesia	2.2	Republic of Korea	2.1	Thailand	3.5	Malaysia	2.9
Argentina	2.0	India	1.8	Mexico	3.3	Thailand	2.7
Venezuela (Bolivarian Republic of)	2.0	Venezuela (Bolivarian Republic of)	1.8	Malaysia	2.9	Egypt	2.4
United Kingdom	1.8	Argentina	1.7	Kuwait	1.9	Mexico	2.1
India	1.7	Singapore	1.6	Turkey	1.9	Kuwait	1.6
Singapore	1.6	Malaysia	1.5	Philippines	1.5	Turkey	1.5
Thailand	1.4	Thailand	1.4	Iran (Islamic Republic of)	1.4	Philippines	1.2
Sum of above	**79.5**	**Sum of above**	**79.5**	**Sum of above**	**87.7**	**Sum of above**	**90.3**
Chemicals and chemical products (ISIC 24)							
United States of America	22.7	United States of America	20.7	China	24.2	China	40.0
Japan	15.3	China	12.5	India	11.0	India	11.3
Germany	7.4	Japan	12.2	Brazil	9.9	Brazil	6.2
China	5.8	Germany	6.8	Puerto Rico	9.5	Puerto Rico	6.0
United Kingdom	4.9	United Kingdom	4.2	Mexico	8.1	China (Taiwan Province)	4.9
France	3.8	France	3.5	China (Taiwan Province)	5.6	Mexico	4.9
Italy	3.1	India	3.5	Argentina	4.4	Indonesia	3.4
India	2.6	Republic of Korea	2.5	Egypt	2.8	Argentina	3.0
Brazil	2.4	Italy	2.3	Indonesia	2.5	Egypt	2.8
Republic of Korea	2.4	Ireland	2.2	Turkey	2.5	Turkey	2.3
Puerto Rico	2.3	Switzerland	2.1	Venezuela (Bolivarian Republic of)	2.0	Venezuela (Bolivarian Republic of)	1.6
Canada	2.0	Brazil	1.9	Iran (Islamic Republic of)	1.7	Iran (Islamic Republic of)	1.5
Mexico	2.0	Puerto Rico	1.9	Malaysia	1.7	Malaysia	1.5
Ireland	1.8	Netherlands	1.8	Thailand	1.6	Thailand	1.5
Spain	1.7	Canada	1.6	Chile	1.4	Chile	1.3
Sum of above	**80.2**	**Sum of above**	**79.7**	**Sum of above**	**88.9**	**Sum of above**	**92.2**

a/ In world total value added at constant 2000 prices.
b/ In total value added of developing countries at constant 2000 prices.

Table 1.7

LEADING PRODUCERS IN SELECTED DIVISIONS, 2000 AND 2007

World leading countries				Leading developing countries			
2000		2007		2000		2007	
Country or area	Share a/ (percentage)	Country or area	Share a/ (percentage)	Country or area	Share b/ (percentage)	Country or area	Share b/ (percentage)
Rubber and plastics products (ISIC 25)							
United States of America	22.6	China	18.3	China	30.7	China	50.6
Germany	10.3	United States of America	17.8	Brazil	10.4	Brazil	6.0
China	7.8	Germany	9.5	China (Taiwan Province)	8.2	China (Taiwan Province)	4.2
Japan	6.8	Japan	5.3	Mexico	6.3	Argentina	4.1
United Kingdom	5.9	United Kingdom	4.2	Argentina	5.7	India	3.8
France	4.7	France	3.9	Indonesia	5.1	Malaysia	3.7
Italy	4.7	Italy	3.5	Malaysia	4.3	Indonesia	3.6
Canada	3.2	Republic of Korea	3.1	Saudi Arabia	3.8	Mexico	3.5
Republic of Korea	3.0	Canada	2.6	India	3.5	Saudi Arabia	3.0
Spain	2.9	Spain	2.6	Turkey	3.3	Turkey	3.0
Brazil	2.6	Brazil	2.2	Thailand	2.9	Thailand	2.2
China (Taiwan Province)	2.1	Argentina	1.5	Venezuela (Bolivarian Republic of)	1.7	Venezuela (Bolivarian Republic of)	1.7
Mexico	1.6	China (Taiwan Province)	1.5	Chile	1.6	Chile	1.3
Argentina	1.4	Poland	1.5	Colombia	1.2	Colombia	1.0
Indonesia	1.3	India	1.4	Puerto Rico	1.0	Viet Nam	0.9
Sum of above	**80.9**	**Sum of above**	**78.9**	**Sum of above**	**89.7**	**Sum of above**	**92.6**
Non-metallic mineral products (ISIC 26)							
Japan	16.5	China	16.1	China	29.9	China	41.3
United States of America	12.7	Japan	11.8	Brazil	9.6	Brazil	6.4
China	8.7	United States of America	10.8	Mexico	9.6	Mexico	6.4
Germany	6.9	Germany	5.4	India	6.1	India	5.5
Italy	6.2	Italy	4.9	Turkey	4.2	Egypt	3.9
France	4.1	France	3.4	China (Taiwan Province)	4.1	Turkey	3.3
United Kingdom	3.7	United Kingdom	3.3	Saudi Arabia	3.5	Saudi Arabia	3.1
Spain	3.5	Spain	3.1	Egypt	2.9	China (Taiwan Province)	2.4
Brazil	2.8	Brazil	2.5	Thailand	2.6	Thailand	2.4
Mexico	2.8	Mexico	2.5	Iran (Islamic Republic of)	2.2	United Arab Emirates	2.4
Republic of Korea	2.4	Republic of Korea	2.2	United Arab Emirates	2.2	Iran (Islamic Republic of)	2.3
India	1.8	Russian Federation	2.2	Malaysia	2.1	Venezuela (Bolivarian Republic of)	2.0
Canada	1.7	India	2.1	Venezuela (Bolivarian Republic of)	2.1	Pakistan	1.8
Russian Federation	1.6	Canada	1.8	Argentina	1.8	Malaysia	1.7
Australia	1.2	Egypt	1.5	Indonesia	1.6	Argentina	1.6
Sum of above	**76.6**	**Sum of above**	**73.6**	**Sum of above**	**84.5**	**Sum of above**	**86.5**

a/ In world total value added at constant 2000 prices.
b/ In total value added of developing countries at constant 2000 prices.

Table 1.7

LEADING PRODUCERS IN SELECTED DIVISIONS, 2000 AND 2007

World leading countries				Leading developing countries			
2000		2007		2000		2007	
Country or area	Share a/ (percentage)	Country or area	Share a/ (percentage)	Country or area	Share b/ (percentage)	Country or area	Share b/ (percentage)
Basic metals (ISIC 27)							
Japan	22.7	China	36.3	China	46.2	China	72.6
United States of America	13.8	Japan	15.9	India	8.1	India	5.9
China	12.7	United States of America	8.7	Mexico	7.6	Mexico	2.8
Germany	5.7	Germany	4.3	China (Taiwan Province)	7.1	Brazil	2.7
Republic of Korea	3.7	Republic of Korea	3.0	Brazil	6.3	China (Taiwan Province)	2.7
Canada	2.9	India	2.9	Turkey	3.9	Turkey	2.3
United Kingdom	2.8	Russian Federation	2.3	Venezuela (Bolivarian Republic of)	3.7	Venezuela (Bolivarian Republic of)	1.6
Russian Federation	2.7	Canada	1.9	Argentina	2.2	Iran (Islamic Republic of)	1.4
Italy	2.3	Italy	1.6	Iran (Islamic Republic of)	2.2	Chile	1.2
India	2.2	United Kingdom	1.6	Chile	2.0	Colombia	1.2
France	2.1	China (Taiwan Province)	1.4	Egypt	1.5	Argentina	1.0
Mexico	2.1	Mexico	1.4	Colombia	1.4	Egypt	0.7
China (Taiwan Province)	1.9	Spain	1.4	Malaysia	1.0	United Arab Emirates	0.6
Spain	1.9	Brazil	1.3	United Arab Emirates	0.9	Malaysia	0.4
Brazil	1.7	Australia	1.2	Philippines	0.7	Pakistan	0.4
Sum of above	**81.2**	**Sum of above**	**85.2**	**Sum of above**	**94.8**	**Sum of above**	**97.5**
Fabricated metal products (ISIC 28)							
United States of America	22.6	United States of America	19.9	China	24.9	China	44.6
Japan	16.2	Japan	11.4	Brazil	16.1	Brazil	11.3
Germany	9.9	Germany	10.4	Mexico	10.5	Mexico	6.6
Italy	6.2	China	9.4	Indonesia	9.8	Indonesia	5.7
France	5.7	Italy	5.8	China (Taiwan Province)	8.3	China (Taiwan Province)	4.9
United Kingdom	5.1	France	5.3	India	4.5	India	2.7
China	3.7	United Kingdom	4.8	Argentina	3.2	Turkey	2.5
Canada	2.9	Canada	2.7	Thailand	2.3	Malaysia	2.3
Brazil	2.4	Brazil	2.4	Turkey	2.3	Argentina	2.2
Spain	2.3	Spain	2.3	Iran (Islamic Republic of)	1.8	Iran (Islamic Republic of)	2.1
Republic of Korea	1.9	Republic of Korea	1.8	Malaysia	1.8	Thailand	2.1
Mexico	1.6	Austria	1.4	Venezuela (Bolivarian Republic of)	1.4	Venezuela (Bolivarian Republic of)	1.2
Indonesia	1.5	Mexico	1.4	Chile	1.0	Viet Nam	0.8
China (Taiwan Province)	1.3	Poland	1.3	Egypt	0.9	United Arab Emirates	0.8
Netherlands	1.3	Indonesia	1.2	United Arab Emirates	0.8	Egypt	0.8
Sum of above	**84.6**	**Sum of above**	**81.5**	**Sum of above**	**89.6**	**Sum of above**	**90.6**

a/ In world total value added at constant 2000 prices.
b/ In total value added of developing countries at constant 2000 prices.

Table 1.7

LEADING PRODUCERS IN SELECTED DIVISIONS, 2000 AND 2007

World leading countries				Leading developing countries			
2000		2007		2000		2007	
Country or area	Share a/ (percentage)	Country or area	Share a/ (percentage)	Country or area	Share b/ (percentage)	Country or area	Share b/ (percentage)
Machinery and equipment n.e.c. (ISIC 29)							
Japan	22.4	Japan	19.5	China	46.3	China	65.8
United States of America	20.3	China	15.9	Brazil	9.5	Brazil	6.5
Germany	12.8	United States of America	15.0	Mexico	7.6	India	5.6
China	6.5	Germany	12.0	India	7.3	Mexico	3.3
Italy	5.7	Italy	4.4	China (Taiwan Province)	5.3	Turkey	3.1
United Kingdom	4.0	United Kingdom	3.4	Turkey	3.6	China (Taiwan Province)	3.0
France	3.2	France	2.8	Venezuela (Bolivarian Republic of)	3.1	Argentina	2.3
Republic of Korea	2.5	Republic of Korea	2.8	Argentina	2.9	Thailand	2.1
Canada	1.9	Canada	1.7	Thailand	2.6	Venezuela (Bolivarian Republic of)	1.4
Spain	1.5	Brazil	1.6	Malaysia	1.6	Iran (Islamic Republic of)	1.0
Sweden	1.4	Russian Federation	1.5	Puerto Rico	1.4	Indonesia	0.8
Switzerland	1.4	India	1.4	Egypt	1.4	Puerto Rico	0.7
Brazil	1.3	Sweden	1.4	Iran (Islamic Republic of)	1.2	Egypt	0.6
Mexico	1.1	Spain	1.3	China (Hong Kong SAR)	0.7	Malaysia	0.5
Russian Federation	1.1	Austria	1.2	Pakistan	0.7	Pakistan	0.5
Sum of above	**87.1**	**Sum of above**	**85.9**	**Sum of above**	**95.2**	**Sum of above**	**97.2**
Office, accounting and computing machinery (ISIC 30)							
United States of America	54.1	United States of America	60.2	China	18.6	Thailand	38.6
Japan	15.1	Japan	10.6	Thailand	17.4	China	26.5
United Kingdom	6.3	Germany	5.6	Mexico	17.2	Brazil	9.4
Germany	4.5	Republic of Korea	4.7	Brazil	13.7	Mexico	7.6
Republic of Korea	2.5	Thailand	4.7	Malaysia	10.4	Philippines	3.5
Israel	2.3	China	3.2	Philippines	6.3	Malaysia	2.9
Canada	1.7	United Kingdom	1.8	Saudi Arabia	4.3	Saudi Arabia	2.7
China	1.6	Israel	1.6	United Arab Emirates	2.7	India	2.6
Mexico	1.5	Brazil	1.1	China (Hong Kong SAR)	1.7	United Arab Emirates	2.1
Thailand	1.5	Ireland	0.9	India	1.7	Indonesia	0.7
Brazil	1.2	Mexico	0.9	Indonesia	1.2	Turkey	0.7
Ireland	1.2	Canada	0.7	China (Taiwan Province)	1.0	China (Taiwan Province)	0.5
France	1.0	Philippines	0.4	Turkey	0.8	Viet Nam	0.5
Malaysia	0.9	France	0.3	Egypt	0.8	Egypt	0.5
Switzerland	0.7	India	0.3	Costa Rica	0.4	China (Hong Kong SAR)	0.4
Sum of above	**96.1**	**Sum of above**	**97.0**	**Sum of above**	**98.2**	**Sum of above**	**99.2**

a/ In world total value added at constant 2000 prices.
b/ In total value added of developing countries at constant 2000 prices.

Table 1.7

LEADING PRODUCERS IN SELECTED DIVISIONS, 2000 AND 2007

World leading countries				Leading developing countries			
2000		2007		2000		2007	
Country or area	Share a/ (percentage)	Country or area	Share a/ (percentage)	Country or area	Share b/ (percentage)	Country or area	Share b/ (percentage)
Electrical machinery and apparatus (ISIC 31)							
Japan	21.6	China	30.8	China	55.0	China	74.9
United States of America	19.4	Japan	19.0	Brazil	7.9	India	7.5
China	12.2	United States of America	11.1	India	7.1	Brazil	4.9
Germany	12.1	Germany	10.1	Mexico	6.2	Mexico	2.2
Italy	3.5	India	3.1	China (Taiwan Province)	4.9	China (Taiwan Province)	1.6
United Kingdom	3.3	France	2.2	Puerto Rico	3.4	Puerto Rico	1.3
France	3.2	Singapore	2.1	Turkey	1.9	Iran (Islamic Republic of)	1.1
Singapore	2.7	Brazil	2.0	Malaysia	1.8	Turkey	1.1
Republic of Korea	2.1	United Kingdom	1.9	Indonesia	1.5	Malaysia	1.0
Brazil	1.7	Italy	1.8	Argentina	1.3	Viet Nam	0.6
India	1.6	Republic of Korea	1.8	Philippines	1.1	Thailand	0.6
Spain	1.6	Spain	1.5	Thailand	1.1	Argentina	0.5
Mexico	1.4	Mexico	0.9	Egypt	1.0	Egypt	0.5
Canada	1.2	Czech Republic	0.8	Iran (Islamic Republic of)	0.7	Pakistan	0.3
China (Taiwan Province)	1.1	Russian Federation	0.8	Venezuela (Bolivarian Republic of)	0.6	United Arab Emirates	0.3
Sum of above	**88.7**	**Sum of above**	**89.9**	**Sum of above**	**95.5**	**Sum of above**	**98.4**
Radio,television and communication equipment (ISIC 32)							
United States of America	61.8	United States of America	68.5	China	38.6	China	56.3
Japan	15.1	Japan	10.0	China (Taiwan Province)	27.7	China (Taiwan Province)	26.8
China	4.1	China	7.2	Malaysia	8.4	Malaysia	4.4
China (Taiwan Province)	2.9	Republic of Korea	4.1	Brazil	4.4	Brazil	1.9
Republic of Korea	2.9	China (Taiwan Province)	3.4	Mexico	4.0	Philippines	1.9
United Kingdom	2.0	Germany	1.5	Philippines	3.8	Thailand	1.9
Germany	1.4	Malaysia	0.6	Thailand	3.4	Turkey	1.9
Canada	0.9	Finland	0.5	Turkey	2.3	Mexico	1.6
Malaysia	0.9	United Kingdom	0.5	India	2.0	India	0.7
France	0.8	France	0.3	China (Hong Kong SAR)	1.9	Indonesia	0.6
Finland	0.7	Brazil	0.2	Indonesia	0.9	China (Hong Kong SAR)	0.4
Italy	0.7	Israel	0.2	Argentina	0.6	Iran (Islamic Republic of)	0.3
Brazil	0.5	Italy	0.2	Pakistan	0.3	Argentina	0.2
Netherlands	0.5	Mexico	0.2	United Arab Emirates	0.3	Pakistan	0.2
Israel	0.4	Netherlands	0.2	Iran (Islamic Republic of)	0.2	Viet Nam	0.2
Sum of above	**95.6**	**Sum of above**	**97.6**	**Sum of above**	**98.8**	**Sum of above**	**99.3**

a/ In world total value added at constant 2000 prices.
b/ In total value added of developing countries at constant 2000 prices.

Table 1.7

LEADING PRODUCERS IN SELECTED DIVISIONS, 2000 AND 2007

World leading countries				Leading developing countries			
2000		2007		2000		2007	
Country or area	Share a/ (percentage)	Country or area	Share a/ (percentage)	Country or area	Share b/ (percentage)	Country or area	Share b/ (percentage)
Medical, precision and optical instruments (ISIC 33)							
United States of America	37.2	United States of America	35.8	Brazil	23.9	China	41.0
Japan	13.2	Japan	11.0	China	20.3	Brazil	19.6
Germany	11.1	Germany	10.3	Puerto Rico	12.4	Puerto Rico	6.9
France	5.3	China	5.1	Mexico	7.7	India	5.6
United Kingdom	5.1	France	4.8	China (Taiwan Province)	6.0	China (Taiwan Province)	5.4
Italy	3.7	Russian Federation	4.4	India	4.8	Mexico	4.1
Brazil	2.1	United Kingdom	4.3	Thailand	4.5	Thailand	3.5
Switzerland	2.0	Brazil	2.4	United Arab Emirates	3.5	United Arab Emirates	3.2
China	1.8	Italy	2.4	Malaysia	3.1	Malaysia	2.0
Canada	1.5	Canada	2.3	China (Hong Kong SAR)	2.7	Philippines	1.5
Israel	1.5	Switzerland	1.8	Philippines	2.2	Argentina	1.2
Russian Federation	1.4	Ireland	1.5	Argentina	1.9	Indonesia	1.1
Republic of Korea	1.3	Israel	1.2	Indonesia	1.6	China (Hong Kong SAR)	0.8
Puerto Rico	1.1	Sweden	1.1	Venezuela (Bolivarian Republic of)	0.9	Colombia	0.6
Sweden	1.1	Republic of Korea	1.0	Colombia	0.8	Iran (Islamic Republic of)	0.6
Sum of above	**89.4**	**Sum of above**	**89.4**	**Sum of above**	**96.3**	**Sum of above**	**97.1**
Motor vehicles, trailers, semi-trailers (ISIC 34)							
Japan	24.9	Japan	26.4	Mexico	40.0	Mexico	24.1
United States of America	24.1	United States of America	18.5	Brazil	10.6	Iran (Islamic Republic of)	13.8
Germany	15.2	Germany	15.5	India	8.4	India	10.9
Mexico	4.5	Mexico	3.6	Argentina	5.4	Brazil	10.4
France	4.1	France	3.3	Turkey	5.3	Thailand	8.9
United Kingdom	3.6	Republic of Korea	3.3	China (Taiwan Province)	5.2	Turkey	6.6
Canada	2.9	United Kingdom	3.1	Thailand	4.7	Argentina	5.0
Republic of Korea	2.7	Canada	2.9	Indonesia	4.5	China	4.0
Spain	2.7	Spain	2.1	Iran (Islamic Republic of)	3.3	Indonesia	4.0
Italy	2.0	Iran (Islamic Republic of)	2.0	Egypt	2.0	China (Taiwan Province)	3.4
Sweden	1.6	Sweden	1.8	China	1.9	Malaysia	1.3
Brazil	1.2	India	1.6	Malaysia	1.7	United Arab Emirates	1.2
India	0.9	Brazil	1.5	United Arab Emirates	1.2	Colombia	1.0
Belgium	0.8	Italy	1.3	Philippines	1.1	Viet Nam	0.9
Australia	0.7	Thailand	1.3	Saudi Arabia	0.7	Philippines	0.7
Sum of above	**91.9**	**Sum of above**	**88.2**	**Sum of above**	**96.0**	**Sum of above**	**96.2**

a/ In world total value added at constant 2000 prices.
b/ In total value added of developing countries at constant 2000 prices.

Table 1.7

LEADING PRODUCERS IN SELECTED DIVISIONS, 2000 AND 2007

World leading countries				Leading developing countries			
2000		2007		2000		2007	
Country or area	Share a/ (percentage)	Country or area	Share a/ (percentage)	Country or area	Share b/ (percentage)	Country or area	Share b/ (percentage)
Other transport equipment (ISIC 35)							
United States of America	26.4	China	35.9	China	60.1	China	73.7
China	17.4	United States of America	19.0	Brazil	17.5	Brazil	13.7
Japan	7.6	Brazil	6.7	India	7.4	India	4.8
United Kingdom	6.5	Japan	5.6	China (Taiwan Province)	3.3	China (Taiwan Province)	1.4
Brazil	5.1	United Kingdom	4.2	Mexico	2.8	Mexico	1.0
France	4.4	France	3.5	United Arab Emirates	1.1	United Arab Emirates	0.7
Canada	4.0	Republic of Korea	3.4	Thailand	0.9	Viet Nam	0.6
Italy	3.9	Canada	2.8	China (Hong Kong SAR)	0.8	Thailand	0.6
Germany	3.6	Germany	2.8	Malaysia	0.8	Iran (Islamic Republic of)	0.5
Republic of Korea	3.2	India	2.4	Pakistan	0.7	Pakistan	0.5
India	2.2	Italy	1.9	Viet Nam	0.5	Malaysia	0.4
Spain	1.7	Norway	1.0	Argentina	0.4	Argentina	0.2
Russian Federation	1.6	Russian Federation	1.0	Philippines	0.4	Colombia	0.2
Norway	1.2	Spain	1.0	Egypt	0.4	Croatia	0.2
China (Taiwan Province)	1.0	China (Taiwan Province)	0.7	Chile	0.3	China (Hong Kong SAR)	0.2
Sum of above	**89.8**	**Sum of above**	**91.9**	**Sum of above**	**97.4**	**Sum of above**	**98.7**
Furniture; manufacturing n.e.c. (ISIC 36)							
Japan	29.6	Japan	23.7	China	39.7	China	67.5
United States of America	19.9	China	20.7	Thailand	10.3	Thailand	5.4
China	6.9	United States of America	18.2	Mexico	9.7	Mexico	4.6
Italy	4.9	Italy	3.6	Brazil	8.5	Brazil	4.4
Germany	4.8	Germany	3.5	China (Taiwan Province)	4.8	Argentina	1.8
United Kingdom	3.9	United Kingdom	3.0	Argentina	4.6	Malaysia	1.6
Canada	3.0	Canada	2.7	Malaysia	2.4	China (Taiwan Province)	1.3
France	2.8	France	2.0	Turkey	2.2	Viet Nam	1.1
Netherlands	1.8	Spain	1.6	United Arab Emirates	1.3	United Arab Emirates	1.0
Spain	1.8	Thailand	1.6	Philippines	1.1	Turkey	1.0
Thailand	1.8	Netherlands	1.5	Saudi Arabia	1.1	Philippines	0.8
Mexico	1.7	Brazil	1.4	Dominican Republic	0.9	Peru	0.7
Brazil	1.5	Mexico	1.4	El Salvador	0.9	Saudi Arabia	0.7
Republic of Korea	1.2	Poland	1.1	China (Hong Kong SAR)	0.9	India	0.6
Austria	1.1	Austria	0.9	Peru	0.9	Nigeria	0.6
Sum of above	**86.7**	**Sum of above**	**86.9**	**Sum of above**	**89.3**	**Sum of above**	**93.1**

a/ In world total value added at constant 2000 prices.
b/ In total value added of developing countries at constant 2000 prices.

Table 1.8

STRUCTURE OF MVA IN SELECTED COUNTRY GROUPS, SELECTED YEARS[a/]

(Percentage)

ISIC Division	Year	Industrialized countries							Developing countries			
			Europe									
		CIS	EU-15	EU-12	Other	East Asia	North America	All countries	NICs	Least developed countries	Others[b/]	All countries
15 Food and beverages	2000	16.9	10.8	16.6	7.3	10.2	6.2	9.2	15.4	27.4	13.6	14.8
	2005	17.5	11.4	14.8	6.8	9.6	5.5	8.8	15.1	25.0	11.5	13.0
	2007	17.1	10.8	13.7	6.2	8.6	4.8	8.0	14.3	22.7	10.3	11.9
16 Tobacco products	2000	0.9	0.5	1.1	2.3	0.6	0.4	0.5	1.9	7.9	4.2	3.0
	2005	0.8	0.4	0.7	2.8	0.7	0.3	0.5	1.5	8.7	3.4	2.7
	2007	0.7	0.4	0.6	3.1	0.6	0.3	0.4	1.4	8.1	3.4	2.7
17 Textiles	2000	2.9	2.7	3.4	1.1	1.4	1.2	1.8	5.2	14.2	6.1	5.7
	2005	2.5	2.1	2.6	0.8	1.0	0.9	1.3	4.1	16.8	5.6	5.1
	2007	2.5	1.9	2.2	0.8	0.8	0.6	1.1	3.8	19.6	5.1	4.8
18 Wearing apparel, fur	2000	1.9	1.6	4.7	0.8	1.8	1.1	1.5	3.1	10.5	3.3	3.3
	2005	1.5	1.1	3.1	0.9	1.0	0.5	0.9	2.7	10.3	2.8	2.8
	2007	1.3	1.0	2.4	1.3	0.8	0.4	0.8	2.5	11.5	2.7	2.7
19 Leather, leather products and footwear	2000	0.6	0.8	1.5	0.2	0.4	0.2	0.4	1.4	3.1	1.7	1.5
	2005	0.5	0.5	1.0	0.1	0.2	0.1	0.3	1.1	3.5	1.5	1.4
	2007	0.5	0.5	0.9	0.1	0.2	0.1	0.2	1.0	3.7	1.4	1.3
20 Wood products (excl. furniture)	2000	1.6	2.1	4.0	5.6	1.0	2.6	2.1	1.8	1.3	1.0	1.4
	2005	1.6	2.0	3.9	5.7	0.8	2.3	1.9	1.7	1.0	1.0	1.3
	2007	1.5	2.0	3.7	5.3	0.6	1.7	1.6	1.4	1.0	0.9	1.1
21 Paper and paper products	2000	3.1	3.1	2.3	2.7	2.8	3.1	3.1	2.6	1.8	2.0	2.4
	2005	3.1	3.1	2.3	2.3	2.7	2.3	2.8	2.4	1.3	2.0	2.2
	2007	2.9	3.1	2.1	1.8	2.5	1.9	2.5	2.3	1.1	2.0	2.1
22 Printing and publishing	2000	1.2	6.1	4.8	7.5	5.0	4.6	5.1	2.3	2.3	1.5	1.9
	2005	1.3	5.9	4.3	6.5	4.5	3.4	4.4	2.1	2.2	1.2	1.6
	2007	1.4	5.5	3.8	5.8	4.3	2.7	3.9	2.0	2.2	1.1	1.5

a/ Percentage shares of individual divisions in total MVA at constant 2000 prices.
b/ Including China.

Table 1.8
(continued)

STRUCTURE OF MVA IN SELECTED COUNTRY GROUPS, SELECTED YEARS[a/]
(Percentage)

ISIC Division	Year	Industrialized countries							Developing countries			
			Europe									
		CIS	EU-15	EU-12	Other	East Asia	North America	All countries	NICs	Least developed countries	Others[b/]	All countries
23 Coke,refined petroleum products,nuclear fuel	2000	4.9	1.6	3.8	3.4	5.7	1.4	2.7	7.5	2.9	6.8	7.1
	2005	4.3	1.6	3.3	3.5	5.6	1.4	2.6	8.1	2.5	5.0	6.2
	2007	3.9	1.5	2.8	3.5	4.9	1.0	2.2	7.7	2.3	4.7	5.8
24 Chemicals and chemical products	2000	9.5	11.1	7.2	16.6	8.3	8.2	9.2	11.4	10.9	10.4	10.9
	2005	8.3	12.4	7.1	21.8	8.2	7.6	9.3	11.7	10.9	8.8	10.0
	2007	7.7	12.2	6.9	23.4	7.8	6.6	8.6	11.6	10.9	8.4	9.6
25 Rubber and plastics products	2000	2.1	4.4	3.8	2.6	1.5	2.8	3.0	3.9	1.7	3.6	3.7
	2005	2.1	4.3	4.8	2.7	1.5	2.3	2.8	4.0	1.6	3.4	3.6
	2007	2.6	4.3	5.0	2.6	1.4	1.9	2.6	3.6	1.6	3.5	3.5
26 Non-metallic mineral products	2000	6.4	4.7	6.7	3.8	3.4	1.8	3.4	4.8	4.3	5.6	5.2
	2005	6.1	4.5	6.2	5.3	2.9	1.6	3.0	4.7	5.1	4.8	4.7
	2007	6.7	4.4	6.5	4.7	2.7	1.4	2.8	4.5	4.7	4.3	4.4
27 Basic metals	2000	17.4	4.0	5.0	10.1	6.6	2.9	4.7	5.3	1.9	8.2	6.6
	2005	15.0	3.9	4.3	8.3	6.7	2.3	4.3	5.5	2.1	12.2	9.5
	2007	14.0	3.9	3.7	7.7	6.4	2.0	4.0	5.7	2.2	12.3	9.8
28 Fabricated metal products	2000	3.6	8.4	6.9	6.9	5.2	5.1	6.2	4.9	2.6	3.2	4.1
	2005	4.6	8.6	7.9	6.8	4.2	4.0	5.5	4.3	2.6	3.1	3.6
	2007	4.6	8.7	8.7	6.6	3.8	3.5	5.2	4.1	2.2	3.1	3.4
29 Machinery and equipment n.e.c.	2000	8.5	10.1	8.1	11.4	9.3	5.7	8.2	4.2	0.8	6.1	5.0
	2005	8.7	10.5	9.4	10.2	9.8	4.5	7.7	4.5	1.1	7.1	6.0
	2007	9.4	11.2	10.6	10.7	9.9	3.9	7.6	4.6	1.2	6.8	5.9
30 Office, accounting and computing machinery	2000	0.2	1.7	0.4	2.0	2.5	5.6	3.4	1.6	0.3	0.7	1.2
	2005	0.3	1.4	0.6	0.9	2.9	5.6	3.5	2.1	0.3	0.8	1.3
	2007	0.3	1.6	0.6	0.7	3.0	6.6	4.1	2.5	0.2	0.7	1.4

a/ Percentage shares of individual divisions in total MVA at constant 2000 prices.
b/ Including China.

Table 1.8
(continued)

STRUCTURE OF MVA IN SELECTED COUNTRY GROUPS, SELECTED YEARS[a/]
(Percentage)

ISIC Division	Year	Industrialized countries							Developing countries			
			Europe									
		CIS	EU-15	EU-12	Other	East Asia	North America	All countries	NICs	Least developed countries	Others[b/]	All countries
31 Electrical machinery and apparatus	2000	2.7	4.9	4.5	2.7	5.6	3.1	4.3	3.2	1.2	6.2	4.6
	2005	2.9	4.8	5.9	2.3	5.8	2.1	3.8	3.7	0.9	7.1	5.7
	2007	3.3	5.1	6.1	2.9	6.3	1.8	3.9	3.7	0.8	8.5	6.6
32 Radio,television and communication equipment	2000	1.4	4.4	2.0	2.0	11.9	29.5	15.4	7.7	0.9	6.0	6.8
	2005	1.5	3.8	2.8	1.5	14.6	40.2	21.1	7.6	0.8	7.1	7.2
	2007	1.4	4.3	3.3	1.4	17.4	47.7	25.8	10.6	0.8	8.6	9.3
33 Medical, precision and optical instruments	2000	2.9	2.7	1.8	4.4	1.5	2.8	2.4	1.0	0.1	0.8	0.9
	2005	7.2	2.9	2.0	4.4	1.4	2.9	2.6	1.1	0.1	0.7	0.9
	2007	7.2	3.0	2.4	4.6	1.5	2.6	2.5	1.1	0.1	0.7	0.8
34 Motor vehicles, trailers, semi-trailers	2000	4.5	8.5	3.9	0.5	8.9	6.2	7.5	5.9	1.0	0.8	3.5
	2005	3.8	9.3	5.3	0.5	10.3	5.4	7.6	6.5	0.8	1.0	3.1
	2007	4.3	9.2	6.4	0.4	10.6	4.2	7.1	6.3	0.8	1.1	3.0
35 Other transport equipment	2000	4.5	2.5	2.5	3.3	1.4	2.8	2.4	2.4	1.0	5.1	3.6
	2005	3.8	2.6	2.3	3.4	1.9	2.4	2.4	3.4	0.8	5.7	4.7
	2007	4.1	2.6	2.3	3.9	1.7	2.3	2.3	3.3	0.7	6.6	5.3
36 Furniture; manufacturing n.e.c.	2000	2.3	3.3	5.0	2.8	5.0	2.7	3.5	2.5	1.9	3.1	2.8
	2005	2.6	2.9	5.4	2.5	3.7	2.4	2.9	2.1	1.6	4.2	3.4
	2007	2.6	2.8	5.3	2.5	4.2	2.0	2.8	2.0	1.6	3.8	3.1
D Total manufacturing	2000	100.0	100.0	100.0	100.0	100.0	100.0	100.0	100.0	100.0	100.0	100.0
	2005	100.0	100.0	100.0	100.0	100.0	100.0	100.0	100.0	100.0	100.0	100.0
	2007	100.0	100.0	100.0	100.0	100.0	100.0	100.0	100.0	100.0	100.0	100.0

a/ Percentage shares of individual divisions in total MVA at constant 2000 prices.
b/ Including China.

Table 1.9

ANNUAL GROWTH OF VALUE ADDED OF DIVISIONS, SELECTED COUNTRY GROUPS, 2000-2005 AND 2005-2007[a/]

(Percentage)

ISIC Division	Industrialized countries excluding CIS		CIS		Developing countries					
					NICs		Least developed countries		Others[b/]	
	2000-2005	2005-2007	2000-2005	2005-2007	2000-2005	2005-2007	2000-2005	2005-2007	2000-2005	2005-2007
15 Food and beverages	1.1	1.3	8.1	8.1	3.2	3.7	4.7	1.2	13.0	5.0
16 Tobacco products	-0.9	-0.5	4.4	0.9	-1.1	-0.8	8.7	2.2	11.9	10.5
17 Textiles	-4.4	-3.4	3.9	7.6	-0.7	2.5	9.9	14.7	14.6	5.9
18 Wearing apparel, fur	-8.9	-1.0	1.1	3.0	1.3	3.0	5.9	12.4	11.9	9.2
19 Leather, leather products and footwear	-8.0	0.2	6.2	10.6	-0.4	0.7	8.2	8.2	13.6	10.0
20 Wood products (excl. furniture)	0.9	-2.0	8.0	7.3	3.0	-4.4	-0.8	9.0	15.6	6.9
21 Paper and paper products	0.3	0.4	7.0	5.2	2.7	3.8	0.5	-3.5	16.1	10.4
22 Printing and publishing	-1.0	0.7	9.8	12.0	3.1	4.4	6.1	5.1	11.2	9.1
23 Coke,refined petroleum products,nuclear fuel	1.4	-2.0	4.3	5.1	4.9	4.2	3.8	3.3	10.6	6.4
24 Chemicals and chemical products	2.6	2.8	4.7	5.1	4.5	5.9	6.8	6.2	13.5	7.7
25 Rubber and plastics products	0.9	2.8	7.8	20.6	4.8	1.5	4.7	5.8	15.5	12.6
26 Non-metallic mineral products	0.0	2.1	6.8	13.6	3.2	4.6	9.5	2.0	13.5	4.5
27 Basic metals	0.9	2.7	4.7	5.6	5.3	8.4	8.6	6.6	28.6	11.2
28 Fabricated metal products	-0.3	3.7	12.0	8.6	1.3	3.1	6.8	-3.1	15.4	9.9
29 Machinery and equipment n.e.c.	1.2	6.0	8.8	13.5	6.2	7.9	12.0	12.8	21.7	8.3
30 Office, accounting and computing machinery	2.5	15.2	26.8	14.2	10.0	15.9	4.8	-0.9	19.8	8.1
31 Electrical machinery and apparatus	0.4	7.2	9.6	15.0	6.9	7.2	0.9	-1.0	21.3	20.8
32 Radio,television and communication equipment	9.7	18.1	8.6	5.9	3.7	26.3	5.1	5.6	22.4	21.4
33 Medical, precision and optical instruments	2.9	5.5	29.4	9.8	6.4	5.5	5.8	4.8	17.3	12.0
34 Motor vehicles, trailers, semi-trailers	3.1	3.0	4.3	16.0	6.4	4.8	2.7	4.8	26.0	16.7
35 Other transport equipment	1.3	5.2	7.3	14.1	10.9	5.9	1.8	0.8	20.8	19.2
36 Furniture; manufacturing n.e.c.	-1.5	5.0	10.1	9.3	0.4	1.8	2.4	5.8	25.9	4.3

a/ At constant 2000 prices.
b/ Including China.

Table 1.9
(continued)

ANNUAL GROWTH OF VALUE ADDED OF DIVISIONS, SELECTED COUNTRY GROUPS, 2000-2005 AND 2005-2007[a/]

(Percentage)

ISIC Division	Developing countries											
	All countries		North Africa		Sub-Saharan Africa		Latin America		Asia[b/]		Europe	
	2000-2005	2005-2007	2000-2005	2005-2007	2000-2005	2005-2007	2000-2005	2005-2007	2000-2005	2005-2007	2000-2005	2005-2007
15 Food and beverages	7.8	4.4	-5.7	3.3	3.4	0.0	3.5	-1.9	12.3	8.2	3.2	4.4
16 Tobacco products	8.1	7.9	-3.4	2.2	1.1	4.7	-1.1	0.5	10.6	9.0	-2.4	4.3
17 Textiles	8.2	5.2	-1.6	0.6	0.3	5.8	0.1	1.6	10.9	6.1	0.4	0.5
18 Wearing apparel, fur	7.0	7.1	0.3	8.6	-3.2	0.8	-1.3	0.6	10.7	8.8	-1.1	-1.4
19 Leather, leather products and footwear	7.8	7.1	-0.9	-0.5	7.2	-5.0	2.1	0.6	10.4	9.3	-1.6	8.4
20 Wood products (excl. furniture)	7.6	1.1	-1.4	-2.1	-2.4	-20.3	3.9	-2.0	12.3	3.8	6.0	8.5
21 Paper and paper products	8.9	7.4	7.4	9.8	2.1	-1.0	3.2	5.0	12.2	8.6	7.0	4.5
22 Printing and publishing	6.3	6.6	13.3	20.1	4.9	2.7	2.2	3.4	8.9	7.7	10.7	7.4
23 Coke,refined petroleum products,nuclear fuel	7.5	5.3	3.8	35.1	6.8	3.7	1.4	1.1	10.9	5.9	2.2	1.7
24 Chemicals and chemical products	8.8	6.8	6.5	1.5	2.5	5.3	1.9	1.9	13.2	9.2	6.9	7.5
25 Rubber and plastics products	10.1	8.0	5.7	-8.6	4.9	5.6	2.4	3.9	13.3	9.8	11.5	-0.9
26 Non-metallic mineral products	8.8	4.5	5.7	15.1	5.8	1.5	2.1	4.4	12.0	3.9	6.1	2.4
27 Basic metals	20.5	10.5	2.4	13.7	4.6	1.9	4.5	3.9	25.6	11.5	7.5	11.1
28 Fabricated metal products	7.3	6.7	0.0	12.4	5.3	2.1	1.0	3.6	10.9	7.4	5.8	15.5
29 Machinery and equipment n.e.c.	15.8	8.2	0.6	0.5	4.3	0.3	3.1	7.4	20.0	8.3	13.3	13.0
30 Office, accounting and computing machinery	13.0	13.1	3.5	-0.3	4.3	-1.8	3.3	4.0	16.9	15.5	10.9	19.0
31 Electrical machinery and apparatus	16.6	17.5	6.0	9.9	2.6	-7.6	2.3	6.8	20.1	19.0	2.6	18.6
32 Radio,television and communication equipment	12.6	23.4	3.6	8.1	-0.7	-12.0	0.9	1.3	13.4	25.5	21.6	-3.7
33 Medical, precision and optical instruments	11.2	8.8	0.7	11.4	9.4	14.0	4.9	3.2	16.4	12.2	4.2	-6.2
34 Motor vehicles, trailers, semi-trailers	9.0	7.1	-8.3	0.6	6.9	5.0	1.4	6.6	18.2	7.5	19.4	9.9
35 Other transport equipment	17.5	15.6	-11.3	7.0	13.5	9.5	11.8	7.9	19.3	17.3	2.3	10.3
36 Furniture; manufacturing n.e.c.	16.1	3.7	-4.1	11.4	5.7	4.8	-0.7	5.4	22.1	3.5	-0.5	-2.5

a/ At constant 2000 prices.
b/ Including China.

Table 1.10

SHARE OF FEMALES IN TOTAL EMPLOYMENT BY DIVISION, SELECTED YEARS
(Percentage)

ISIC Division	Azerbaijan		Bulgaria		Chile		Croatia		Cyprus	
	2000	2006	2000	2006	2001	2006	2000	2006	2000	2006
15 Food and beverages	32.3	32.1	47.4	50.4	27.6	31.0	41.8	42.6	42.8	46.3
16 Tobacco products	23.2	15.8	52.7	48.4	10.1	10.9	45.9	42.9	51.3	45.4
17 Textiles	52.0	50.2	68.0	69.8	30.6	35.1	68.8	74.0	68.9	58.8
18 Wearing apparel, fur	54.4	61.4	88.6	88.6	64.7	64.7	87.0	87.1	95.6	86.5
19 Leather, leather products and footwear	48.3	51.1	76.9	84.7	29.1	28.8	78.5	80.0	59.4	56.7
20 Wood products (excl. furniture)	18.4	14.0	32.5	27.2	6.6	6.6	30.6	29.0	13.3	9.2
21 Paper and paper products	26.8	34.6	48.4	45.7	8.7	9.5	35.8	31.1	44.9	42.6
22 Printing and publishing	40.1	29.5	54.8	54.0	19.6	18.2	47.7	48.8	46.7	47.1
23 Coke,refined petroleum products,nuclear fuel	42.7	36.4	32.8	...	6.7	5.9	26.4	31.2	8.2	16.9
24 Chemicals and chemical products	40.1	37.2	46.0	47.2	25.3	25.6	39.5	39.5	45.8	52.8
25 Rubber and plastics products	34.6	15.6	48.7	37.9	13.5	12.4	35.0	29.0	30.4	29.1
26 Non-metallic mineral products	26.4	18.1	33.5	25.3	10.5	6.6	21.9	20.4	14.1	13.4
27 Basic metals	34.5	19.9	28.6	23.1	3.9	7.4	16.0	17.2	18.0	15.4
28 Fabricated metal products	21.9	17.4	30.0	24.2	8.8	7.4	19.5	13.7	14.9	14.2
29 Machinery and equipment n.e.c.	26.6	26.1	32.2	27.4	6.7	7.1	17.3	15.5	15.5	17.2
30 Office, accounting and computing machinery	52.9	31.8	48.0	51.3	...	14.3	28.7	27.0	...	...
31 Electrical machinery and apparatus	34.2	26.4	44.1	47.8	17.4	15.8	38.6	32.1	25.4	26.9
32 Radio,television and communication equipment	27.8	33.5	36.8	54.1	20.5	18.5	45.3	45.6	...	43.5
33 Medical, precision and optical instruments	39.8	22.8	49.5	48.1	23.9	26.3	39.4	42.6	51.6	56.5
34 Motor vehicles, trailers, semi-trailers	30.9	13.5	24.3	22.7	6.9	7.4	28.5	35.4	24.5	34.1
35 Other transport equipment	14.8	12.8	23.0	17.7	9.7	9.6	12.0	9.9	4.0	16.3
36 Furniture; manufacturing n.e.c.	17.7	15.2	40.7	33.3	17.1	15.7	34.3	32.3	26.8	33.3
37 Recycling	20.7	15.4	24.1	22.9	...	...	22.5	23.9	10.2	13.3
D Total manufacturing	35.0	29.2	51.3	51.5	21.3	21.8	41.4	37.6	37.8	35.9

Table 1.10

SHARE OF FEMALES IN TOTAL EMPLOYMENT BY DIVISION, SELECTED YEARS
(Percentage)

ISIC Division	Ecuador		Eritrea		Ethiopia		India		Indonesia	
	2002	2005	2000	2006	2000	2006	2000	2004	2000	2005
15 Food and beverages	26.9	30.7	45.3	48.4	18.8	18.8	16.4	17.7	39.8	39.1
16 Tobacco products	14.9	21.1	30.9	28.9	40.3	43.7	21.2	24.6	82.5	81.2
17 Textiles	26.1	23.2	80.2	78.7	36.7	47.2	7.8	11.9	50.8	49.4
18 Wearing apparel, fur	72.7	71.5	65.0	74.8	61.5	62.4	51.3	44.5	78.3	79.4
19 Leather, leather products and footwear	20.0	23.3	55.3	59.5	29.5	27.6	22.4	22.1	71.6	70.5
20 Wood products (excl. furniture)	11.2	9.8	0.0	0.0	17.6	12.5	9.2	6.6	36.0	37.2
21 Paper and paper products	21.2	23.7	31.9	54.9	26.7	29.5	5.3	4.9	21.7	21.4
22 Printing and publishing	32.6	37.1	47.0	46.3	40.0	43.8	3.7	3.6	31.1	31.7
23 Coke,refined petroleum products,nuclear fuel	15.8	16.6	0.0	0.0	0.0	0.0	2.0	1.4	12.2	15.2
24 Chemicals and chemical products	29.1	32.5	24.6	47.0	28.4	33.9	11.4	10.9	34.9	34.8
25 Rubber and plastics products	14.5	13.5	58.7	71.2	24.8	36.8	5.1	5.2	36.1	38.6
26 Non-metallic mineral products	14.7	16.1	14.2	24.0	13.5	16.4	5.6	4.6	...	23.4
27 Basic metals	8.5	8.3	32.0	41.2	11.6	12.3	0.9	0.6	8.8	7.1
28 Fabricated metal products	10.2	10.1	21.9	27.0	14.6	34.0	1.4	1.5	25.4	29.9
29 Machinery and equipment n.e.c.	13.4	12.1	...	40.5	6.8	9.4	1.0	1.3	19.1	25.8
30 Office, accounting and computing machinery	0.0	0.0	0.0	0.0	0.0	0.0	8.4	7.1	31.2	59.8
31 Electrical machinery and apparatus	13.8	13.8	12.5	0.0	11.1	30.4	5.8	5.7	44.4	47.6
32 Radio,television and communication equipment	8.3	12.0	0.0	0.0	0.0	0.0	17.0	13.4	70.2	68.1
33 Medical, precision and optical instruments	25.0	28.9	46.5	...	0.0	0.0	13.4	11.9	65.7	61.3
34 Motor vehicles, trailers, semi-trailers	8.5	8.8	32.3	20.0	8.6	11.4	1.9	1.9	10.7	9.5
35 Other transport equipment	24.1	14.7	0.0	0.0	0.0	0.0	1.1	1.2	11.4	11.5
36 Furniture; manufacturing n.e.c.	24.2	26.0	16.3	23.0	14.3	12.4	12.4	12.4	43.5	41.0
37 Recycling	0.0	0.0	0.0	0.0	0.0	0.0	4.5	5.7	47.1	38.9
D Total manufacturing	24.6	27.4	46.0	47.7	26.6	29.5	10.9	11.8	47.9	47.0

Table 1.10

SHARE OF FEMALES IN TOTAL EMPLOYMENT BY DIVISION, SELECTED YEARS
(Percentage)

ISIC Division	Iran (Islamic Republic of)		Jordan		Kyrgyzstan		Lithuania		Malaysia	
	2000	2005	2000	2006	2000	2006	2000	2006	2000	2005
15 Food and beverages	9.3	12.8	7.7	7.4	48.4	38.9	...	58.6	33.2	32.8
16 Tobacco products	6.4	7.5	6.7	12.2	36.6	41.3	...	27.5	58.7	52.0
17 Textiles	7.2	10.4	19.6	23.2	63.6	87.9	...	72.3	41.6	42.0
18 Wearing apparel, fur	37.9	42.7	70.3	47.2	16.7	40.3	...	89.4	74.2	70.4
19 Leather, leather products and footwear	4.9	6.5	6.0	7.0	81.0	46.3	...	65.3	46.6	46.0
20 Wood products (excl. furniture)	2.4	1.8	0.1	0.3	6.2	1.1	...	24.2	33.6	31.7
21 Paper and paper products	6.9	12.6	14.4	11.1	41.1	42.4	...	44.6	33.2	29.8
22 Printing and publishing	7.4	10.3	9.9	12.9	...	28.0	...	58.2	40.4	37.4
23 Coke,refined petroleum products,nuclear fuel	2.3	3.6	2.3	2.2	31.1	38.9	...	27.3	26.5	12.9
24 Chemicals and chemical products	10.6	12.7	18.9	17.3	32.9	27.2	...	40.1	28.9	28.6
25 Rubber and plastics products	6.6	9.1	8.1	5.8	36.7	36.3	...	30.6	45.3	42.3
26 Non-metallic mineral products	4.8	5.8	1.3	1.6	24.0	31.2	...	25.9	21.1	19.7
27 Basic metals	1.9	2.7	1.9	1.3	25.0	9.5	...	22.8	19.1	16.6
28 Fabricated metal products	3.6	5.5	3.3	1.1	23.7	32.9	...	18.9	28.9	25.1
29 Machinery and equipment n.e.c.	4.2	6.1	4.5	3.6	19.5	34.5	...	27.5	27.9	25.7
30 Office, accounting and computing machinery	22.5	27.6	0.0	0.0	69.7	0.0	...	26.6	67.3	59.0
31 Electrical machinery and apparatus	12.5	18.5	9.2	8.7	44.2	47.3	...	66.7	59.4	54.6
32 Radio,television and communication equipment	21.0	21.8	0.0	0.0	62.4	40.6	...	53.6	67.5	67.0
33 Medical, precision and optical instruments	22.5	24.5	32.7	15.0	39.2	27.0	...	51.4	69.1	67.4
34 Motor vehicles, trailers, semi-trailers	4.1	5.4	5.6	6.0	16.1	37.6	...	13.5	23.5	20.5
35 Other transport equipment	2.4	4.3	0.0	3.3	3.2	0.0	...	19.6	12.3	18.9
36 Furniture; manufacturing n.e.c.	8.8	7.3	6.9	4.5	39.3	30.3	...	39.3	34.7	26.5
37 Recycling	0.0	14.5	0.0	0.0	15.0	0.0	...	19.7	26.3	17.5
D Total manufacturing	6.8	9.0	16.9	12.3	38.2	36.9	...	48.0	46.2	41.6

Table 1.10

SHARE OF FEMALES IN TOTAL EMPLOYMENT BY DIVISION, SELECTED YEARS
(Percentage)

ISIC Division	Oman		Panama		Philippines		Sri Lanka		Viet Nam	
	2000	2006	2000	2005	2001	2005	2000	2006	2001	2006
15 Food and beverages	4.8	8.3	22.4	23.6	31.8	36.0	...	42.0	56.7	56.0
16 Tobacco products	0.0	0.0	0.0	...	48.0	36.0	...	64.4	51.4	48.3
17 Textiles	7.0	8.1	57.0	41.0	57.1	48.1	...	58.6	69.0	69.3
18 Wearing apparel, fur	62.7	49.2	80.1	78.7	79.0	75.8	...	77.2	81.1	83.1
19 Leather, leather products and footwear	16.4	20.9	21.5	31.9	59.2	53.0	...	60.0	81.3	83.1
20 Wood products (excl. furniture)	1.1	1.8	5.7	11.1	20.6	24.2	...	32.0	45.0	50.7
21 Paper and paper products	2.5	10.3	14.7	14.1	31.8	25.6	...	9.1	36.8	37.3
22 Printing and publishing	6.2	8.5	25.7	34.4	37.2	37.7	...	30.0	42.2	42.4
23 Coke,refined petroleum products,nuclear fuel	5.6	8.6	6.6	...	21.6	23.5	...	14.9	19.1	...
24 Chemicals and chemical products	4.0	6.7	33.6	35.0	30.8	33.9	...	28.6	44.1	39.5
25 Rubber and plastics products	4.7	3.5	15.1	12.4	36.0	37.9	...	37.2	43.3	45.7
26 Non-metallic mineral products	1.1	1.6	6.6	10.0	20.9	22.7	...	30.2	33.7	31.6
27 Basic metals	1.1	1.8	4.7	7.6	16.7	16.6	...	5.1	21.0	20.5
28 Fabricated metal products	1.3	2.4	7.5	17.0	27.5	29.2	...	48.1	23.5	25.8
29 Machinery and equipment n.e.c.	6.5	7.2	...	13.8	34.9	38.3	...	5.5	26.2	22.5
30 Office, accounting and computing machinery	18.4	...	...	...	76.6	73.2	...	88.7	54.1	78.3
31 Electrical machinery and apparatus	1.4	1.4	...	11.7	64.5	59.4	...	25.7	59.5	67.0
32 Radio,television and communication equipment	0.0	0.0	...	...	73.9	71.9	...	74.4	50.9	60.6
33 Medical, precision and optical instruments	7.3	6.6	...	31.0	74.4	68.6	...	20.0	41.7	64.5
34 Motor vehicles, trailers, semi-trailers	0.0	1.8	...	11.6	22.4	35.7	...	16.0	21.6	36.2
35 Other transport equipment	0.0	0.0	...	6.0	14.5	16.9	...	37.8	23.0	21.0
36 Furniture; manufacturing n.e.c.	2.7	4.9	...	14.5	38.1	37.3	...	43.6	52.3	50.7
37 Recycling	0.0	0.0	...	...	32.9	39.1	...	30.0	40.6	37.2
D Total manufacturing	13.9	6.5	24.0	23.6	50.2	50.0	...	52.2	57.8	59.2

Table 1.11

SELECTED CHARACTERISTICS OF BRANCHES, SELECTED YEARS AND COUNTRIES

Country or area	Latest year	Processed meat,fish,fruit,vegetables,fats (ISIC 151)												
		Value added per employee (current 1000 dollars)		Wages and salaries per employee (current 1000 dollars)		Percentage in output [a/]								
						Costs of input materials and utilities			Costs of labour			Operating surplus		
	(LY)	2000	LY	2000	LY	2000	2003	LY	2000	2003	LY	2000	2003	LY
Industrialized Countries														
CIS														
Azerbaijan	2006	...	12.0	0.2	0.9	...	75.8	87.5	3.2	1.2	0.9	...	23.0	11.6
Georgia	2006	3.4	2.6	0.2	1.3	71.0	87.7	88.6	1.7	2.8	5.6	27.3	9.4	5.9
Kyrgyzstan	2005	...	2.1	0.2	0.7	...	50.6	78.6	3.1	3.4	6.6	...	46.0	14.8
Republic of Moldova	2006	...	...	0.4	1.4	...	...	...	6.4	5.1	6.5	...	...	...
Russian Federation	2006	...	19.4	0.8	3.7	...	77.8	69.6	8.4	7.2	5.8	...	15.0	24.7
EU-15														
Austria	2005	43.4	64.4	20.6	30.7	72.8	...	74.1	12.9	...	12.4	14.3	...	13.5
Belgium	2005	49.7	78.8	22.5	34.9	83.1	84.0	83.4	7.7	7.1	7.4	9.3	8.9	9.3
Denmark	2005	...	77.5	...	51.4	...	...	77.7	...	...	14.8	...	...	7.5
Germany	2005	27.6	44.1	16.3	24.6	79.1	78.7	81.0	12.3	11.9	10.6	8.6	9.4	8.4
Greece	2004	...	46.0	...	19.2	...	...	72.9	...	...	11.3	...	...	15.8
Ireland	2005	35.0	59.3	17.7	31.8	82.4	81.3	79.7	8.9	10.7	10.9	8.7	8.1	9.4
Netherlands	2004	49.8	82.4	24.5	41.7	84.0	83.3	84.2	7.9	8.3	8.0	8.1	8.4	7.8
Portugal	2005	...	26.9	7.8	12.7	...	81.6	82.1	7.8	8.1	8.5	...	10.3	9.5
Spain	2005	28.7	52.4	13.7	22.4	82.5	81.7	81.7	8.3	8.1	7.8	9.1	10.1	10.5
United Kingdom	2004	...	58.0	...	30.4	...	72.1	73.1	...	14.6	14.1	...	13.3	12.8
EU-12														
Bulgaria	2006	1.9	6.0	0.9	1.8	87.8	86.5	86.2	5.8	4.6	4.1	6.4	8.9	9.7
Cyprus	2006	24.5	44.1	12.0	20.2	81.8	80.7	81.5	9.0	9.3	8.5	9.3	10.0	10.0
Estonia	2005	5.6	12.7	2.8	6.2	76.5	78.6	79.9	11.7	11.1	9.8	11.8	10.3	10.4
Hungary	2005	8.9	17.3	3.6	8.3	81.2	80.7	81.7	7.6	9.0	8.8	11.1	10.3	9.5
Latvia	2006	5.5	9.6	2.2	3.8	70.5	80.8	77.1	11.8	9.7	9.2	17.8	9.6	13.7
Lithuania	2006	3.4	7.6	1.8	4.2	83.7	85.6	85.2	8.5	8.5	8.1	7.8	5.9	6.7
Malta	2005	35.9	68.2	10.4	14.7	65.0	65.4	54.4	10.1	10.3	9.8	24.9	24.2	35.8
Poland	2005	...	13.1	...	5.9	...	82.2	84.2	...	7.8	7.2	...	10.0	8.7
Romania	2006	...	9.0	...	4.6	64.2	86.1	86.2	...	6.5	7.0	...	7.4	6.9
Other Europe														
Norway	2004	46.8	67.0	28.2	44.7	79.3	79.9	82.9	12.5	13.1	11.4	8.3	7.0	5.7

a/ At current prices.

Table 1.11
(continued)

SELECTED CHARACTERISTICS OF BRANCHES, SELECTED YEARS AND COUNTRIES

Processed meat,fish,fruit,vegetables,fats (ISIC 151)														
Country or area	Latest year	Value added per employee (current 1000 dollars)		Wages and salaries per employee (current 1000 dollars)		Percentage in output [a/]								
						Costs of input materials and utilities			Costs of labour			Operating surplus		
	(LY)	2000	LY	2000	LY	2000	2003	LY	2000	2003	LY	2000	2003	LY
Other Countries														
Australia	2005	53.7	54.6	20.3	...	64.3	77.1	78.1	13.5	...	...	22.3	...	...
Israel	2005	35.3	31.4	23.9	22.9	78.3	77.2	83.6	14.7	14.0	12.0	7.1	8.8	4.4
Japan	2005	67.6	64.1	16.4	15.8	68.2	68.5	69.4	7.7	7.7	7.5	24.1	23.8	23.0
Republic of Korea	2006	40.9	61.6	10.5	17.5	65.3	68.0	69.4	8.9	9.4	8.7	25.7	22.6	21.9
Singapore	2006	27.3	35.1	15.3	16.8	80.8	80.9	80.0	10.7	11.5	9.6	8.4	7.6	10.4
United States of America	2005	92.4	127.8	25.2	29.0	66.4	64.1	63.9	9.2	8.8	8.2	24.4	27.1	27.9
Developing Countries														
Albania	2006	2.6	6.8	0.7	2.2	76.6	81.1	78.7	6.1	5.1	6.8	17.3	13.9	14.5
Brazil	2005	18.0	27.0	4.1	4.4	74.2	66.3	67.5	5.9	4.4	5.3	19.9	29.4	27.1
Chile	2006	...	45.5	...	8.4	...	61.5	58.0	...	8.4	7.8	...	30.1	34.2
Colombia	2005	24.6	35.0	3.7	4.4	67.0	72.4	70.4	5.0	3.6	3.7	28.0	24.0	25.9
Ecuador	2005	...	14.9	...	3.8	...	73.5	75.4	...	6.1	6.3	...	20.4	18.3
Ethiopia	2006	3.5	2.8	0.7	0.9	58.1	55.3	66.7	7.8	9.9	11.1	34.1	34.8	22.2
Fiji	2004	...	9.1	...	4.8	...	80.7	83.2	...	11.6	9.0	...	7.6	7.9
India	2004	4.1	4.7	0.8	1.0	92.7	94.5	94.2	1.4	1.1	1.2	5.9	4.4	4.7
Indonesia	2005	7.1	15.1	0.8	1.4	74.1	76.9	71.7	3.0	2.8	2.7	22.9	20.4	25.6
Iran (Islamic Republic of)	2005	38.6	13.9	9.1	3.5	72.0	73.8	74.7	6.6	6.0	6.4	21.4	20.2	18.9
Jordan	2006	9.7	26.9	3.5	4.2	79.1	74.9	75.1	7.6	5.3	3.9	13.3	19.8	21.0
Madagascar	2006	...	0.4	...	0.2	...	66.7	68.5	...	11.4	15.7	...	21.9	15.7
Malaysia	2005	18.3	19.6	4.1	5.0	87.5	90.0	91.1	2.8	2.0	2.3	9.7	8.0	6.7
Morocco	2005	8.5	12.6	3.4	5.9	73.1	80.3	81.7	10.9	8.1	8.6	16.0	11.6	9.7
Oman	2006	20.6	18.8	6.0	6.4	67.1	67.9	75.3	9.6	9.0	8.4	23.3	23.1	16.3
Philippines	2005	...	10.4	...	3.1	...	76.7	80.8	...	4.8	5.7	...	18.5	13.5
Qatar	2006	9.4	25.0	6.3	7.5	86.3	76.0	67.2	9.2	10.2	9.8	4.5	13.7	23.0
Sri Lanka	2006	...	16.9	...	0.9	...	...	69.1	...	...	1.7	...	...	29.1
Trinidad and Tobago	2004	18.0	...	5.5	...	79.3	85.5	83.1	6.3	10.5	12.3	14.4	4.0	4.6
Uruguay	2005	15.1	10.9	8.1	5.1	82.4	86.9	86.9	9.4	5.8	6.2	8.2	7.3	6.9

a/ At current prices.

Table 1.11

SELECTED CHARACTERISTICS OF BRANCHES, SELECTED YEARS AND COUNTRIES

Dairy products (ISIC 1520)														
Country or area	Latest year	Value added per employee (current 1000 dollars)		Wages and salaries per employee (current 1000 dollars)		Percentage in output [a]								
						Costs of input materials and utilities			Costs of labour			Operating surplus		
	(LY)	2000	LY	2000	LY	2000	2003	LY	2000	2003	LY	2000	2003	LY
Industrialized Countries														
CIS														
Georgia	2006	...	4.0	...	1.8	...	71.1	74.0	...	7.0	12.0	...	21.9	14.0
Kyrgyzstan	2005	...	3.8	0.4	1.2	...	80.9	77.5	7.2	6.3	7.0	...	12.8	15.5
Republic of Moldova	2006	...	...	0.7	1.6	...	...	...	5.2	8.5	9.0	...	...	...
Russian Federation	2006	...	9.6	0.8	3.4	...	80.1	79.2	5.6	7.4	7.3	...	12.6	13.5
EU-15														
Austria	2005	51.7	89.2	28.2	39.4	84.7	81.5	81.1	8.4	8.2	8.3	6.9	10.3	10.5
Belgium	2005	46.9	83.3	26.9	39.3	88.2	85.0	85.0	6.8	7.0	7.1	5.0	8.1	8.0
Finland	2005	40.6	75.9	24.4	41.1	85.8	83.9	82.4	8.5	9.2	9.5	5.7	6.9	8.1
France	2005	42.9	63.5	21.5	33.5	86.1	86.5	86.3	7.0	6.9	7.2	6.9	6.6	6.5
Germany	2005	60.0	87.0	29.2	43.2	85.8	85.5	86.9	6.9	7.5	6.5	7.3	7.0	6.6
Greece	2004	...	60.7	...	23.3	...	...	73.9	...	...	10.0	...	...	16.1
Ireland	2005	75.8	107.4	26.1	46.0	78.8	79.1	81.1	7.3	8.7	8.1	13.9	12.2	10.8
Italy	2005	49.6	84.0	20.1	30.2	81.3	81.2	82.6	7.6	7.0	6.3	11.1	11.8	11.2
Netherlands	2005	66.2	104.4	31.7	55.4	86.5	87.8	86.7	6.5	6.2	7.0	7.1	6.0	6.2
Portugal	2005	26.4	51.1	9.7	16.8	83.5	80.8	80.8	6.0	6.4	6.3	10.5	12.8	12.9
Spain	2005	47.2	80.1	19.3	30.9	80.3	79.6	80.6	8.1	7.7	7.5	11.6	12.7	11.9
Sweden	2005	33.1	71.5	27.2	35.9	87.1	...	79.4	10.6	...	10.3	2.3	...	10.2
United Kingdom	2005	53.5	68.3	26.6	38.9	78.3	77.6	81.1	10.8	9.7	10.7	10.9	12.6	8.1
EU-12														
Bulgaria	2006	2.4	6.9	1.0	2.2	84.1	85.1	81.5	6.4	6.6	5.8	9.5	8.3	12.7
Cyprus	2006	27.2	44.2	13.4	24.9	71.8	70.5	68.6	13.9	16.3	17.7	14.4	13.2	13.7
Czech Republic	2004	9.1	15.3	3.6	6.7	87.2	89.4	87.9	5.0	5.5	5.3	7.8	5.1	6.8
Estonia	2006	6.9	20.5	3.6	8.9	84.5	83.2	83.6	8.1	7.6	7.1	7.4	9.2	9.2
Hungary	2005	12.0	23.1	4.1	10.3	83.5	79.8	82.1	5.6	7.2	8.0	10.9	13.0	9.9
Latvia	2006	8.4	16.0	3.2	6.5	70.6	76.9	81.1	11.0	8.2	7.6	18.4	14.9	11.3
Lithuania	2006	5.0	18.6	2.9	6.4	81.1	77.9	77.5	11.1	10.2	7.7	7.9	12.0	14.8
Malta	2005	20.2	36.7	10.5	16.3	81.3	81.7	76.5	9.7	11.3	10.4	9.0	7.0	13.1
Poland	2005	8.0	19.6	...	8.1	84.3	80.5	83.5	...	8.3	6.8	...	11.2	9.7
Romania	2006	...	10.0	...	5.0	68.8	81.5	82.2	...	10.0	8.9	...	8.5	8.9
Slovakia	2005	5.9	10.2	3.1	7.1	90.3	92.0	92.7	5.1	5.3	5.1	4.6	2.6	2.2
Other Europe														
Norway	2004	54.1	71.4	32.8	49.0	78.6	73.9	78.2	13.0	14.7	14.9	8.4	11.4	6.9

a/ At current prices.

Table 1.11
(continued)

SELECTED CHARACTERISTICS OF BRANCHES, SELECTED YEARS AND COUNTRIES

Dairy products (ISIC 1520)														
Country or area	Latest year	Value added per employee (current 1000 dollars)		Wages and salaries per employee (current 1000 dollars)		Percentage in output [a/]								
						Costs of input materials and utilities			Costs of labour			Operating surplus		
	(LY)	2000	LY	2000	LY	2000	2003	LY	2000	2003	LY	2000	2003	LY
Other Countries														
Israel	2005	55.1	48.9	31.3	29.2	69.9	71.3	73.0	17.1	17.4	16.1	13.0	11.3	10.9
Japan	2005	158.5	161.7	35.9	33.2	68.7	69.6	70.2	7.1	6.4	6.1	24.2	24.0	23.7
Republic of Korea	2006	137.6	248.0	16.6	31.2	60.0	61.4	56.9	4.8	5.4	5.4	35.2	33.2	37.7
United States of America	2005	152.0	198.6	34.7	41.6	67.0	66.5	67.0	7.5	7.4	6.9	25.5	26.1	26.1
Developing Countries														
Albania	2006	8.1	13.0	0.9	1.9	65.3	73.2	75.6	4.1	3.0	3.5	30.6	23.7	20.8
Brazil	2005	29.5	26.6	5.3	4.9	63.2	66.1	70.0	6.6	5.3	5.5	30.2	28.6	24.5
Chile	2006	...	67.2	...	11.3	...	62.6	62.7	...	6.1	6.2	...	31.3	31.0
Colombia	2005	35.4	46.1	4.4	5.2	64.5	65.1	66.8	4.4	4.1	3.7	31.2	30.8	29.5
Ecuador	2005	14.7	24.9	2.6	5.6	74.3	76.5	79.7	4.5	7.6	4.6	21.2	15.9	15.7
Eritrea	2006	1.3	4.0	0.8	1.1	68.9	88.6	80.8	17.8	3.1	5.2	13.3	8.3	14.0
Ethiopia	2006	3.2	7.3	0.4	0.9	53.1	54.1	56.0	6.4	8.7	5.2	40.6	37.2	38.8
Fiji	2004	...	11.2	...	4.4	...	89.8	88.3	...	5.5	4.6	...	4.7	7.2
India	2004	6.6	6.7	1.8	2.1	87.1	88.6	89.4	3.6	3.5	3.3	9.3	7.9	7.3
Indonesia	2005	...	24.5	...	2.6	...	62.3	72.8	...	4.2	2.9	...	33.5	24.3
Iran (Islamic Republic of)	2005	37.7	20.5	10.8	4.1	81.6	78.1	74.1	5.3	5.1	5.2	13.2	16.8	20.7
Jordan	2006	8.1	5.1	3.0	1.8	75.5	78.0	79.2	9.0	8.5	7.2	15.6	13.6	13.6
Madagascar	2006	...	0.3	...	0.1	...	71.9	73.5	...	3.3	4.6	...	24.8	22.0
Malaysia	2005	33.4	31.0	7.5	11.8	73.2	74.2	80.8	6.1	7.1	7.3	20.8	18.6	11.9
Morocco	2005	17.3	23.4	6.6	9.5	75.6	72.9	77.0	9.3	9.4	9.3	15.0	17.7	13.6
Oman	2006	27.9	24.1	6.4	5.2	71.4	67.4	80.7	6.6	3.3	4.1	22.0	29.4	15.2
Peru	2006	...	13.3	...	3.3	...	73.4	73.4	...	6.4	6.6	...	20.2	20.0
Philippines	2005	...	41.0	...	10.7	...	64.3	81.3	...	5.0	4.9	...	30.7	13.9
Qatar	2006	21.2	16.3	4.8	4.7	47.4	57.5	56.2	11.9	14.1	12.6	40.7	28.4	31.2
Sri Lanka	2006	...	25.8	...	1.1	...	...	50.3	...	...	2.1	...	...	47.6
Trinidad and Tobago	2004	30.4	...	14.1	...	58.9	54.1	54.4	19.1	20.4	19.5	22.0	25.5	26.1
Uruguay	2005	26.4	17.1	16.7	8.2	74.7	77.9	81.4	16.1	9.3	8.9	9.3	12.8	9.7

a/ At current prices.

Table 1.11

SELECTED CHARACTERISTICS OF BRANCHES, SELECTED YEARS AND COUNTRIES

Grain mill products; starches; animal feeds (ISIC 153)

Country or area	Latest year	Value added per employee (current 1000 dollars)		Wages and salaries per employee (current 1000 dollars)		Percentage in output [a]								
						Costs of input materials and utilities			Costs of labour			Operating surplus		
	(LY)	2000	LY	2000	LY	2000	2003	LY	2000	2003	LY	2000	2003	LY
Industrialized Countries														
CIS														
Azerbaijan	2006	...	17.8	0.3	0.7	...	75.8	87.5	2.5	0.2	0.5	...	24.0	12.0
Georgia	2006	1.8	5.7	0.5	1.2	83.5	87.7	86.4	4.1	3.4	2.8	12.4	8.9	10.8
Kyrgyzstan	2006	...	...	0.3	0.5	...	...	...	1.2	6.7	2.7	...	...	...
Republic of Moldova	2005	...	...	0.3	0.8	...	...	...	8.4	10.7	20.0	...	...	...
Russian Federation	2006	...	11.1	0.8	3.2	...	79.2	76.8	5.9	6.3	6.6	...	14.6	16.6
EU-15														
Austria	2005	49.2	84.3	24.6	35.9	74.2	74.9	74.0	12.9	10.8	11.1	12.9	14.3	14.9
Belgium	2005	75.5	107.4	31.8	48.1	85.9	88.1	87.7	5.9	5.1	5.5	8.1	6.8	6.8
Finland	2005	57.2	97.6	26.1	43.4	83.7	83.4	79.7	7.5	6.9	9.0	8.9	9.7	11.3
France	2005	55.4	86.7	24.2	39.8	82.1	81.9	81.3	7.8	8.3	8.6	10.1	9.9	10.1
Germany	2005	66.9	87.7	28.7	39.7	77.0	78.5	78.3	9.9	9.7	9.8	13.1	11.7	11.9
Greece	2004	...	53.2	...	22.0	...	...	76.5	...	...	9.7	...	...	13.8
Ireland	2005	54.2	87.2	23.5	40.5	81.1	79.8	79.3	8.2	8.0	9.6	10.7	12.2	11.1
Italy	2005	59.3	97.9	20.3	34.5	87.9	86.9	85.9	4.1	4.6	5.0	7.9	8.5	9.1
Netherlands	2005	59.4	116.4	29.7	53.6	86.8	82.8	83.8	6.6	7.6	7.5	6.6	9.6	8.7
Portugal	2005	27.2	43.8	10.4	16.3	86.7	84.9	83.6	5.1	5.7	6.1	8.2	9.4	10.3
Spain	2005	47.9	73.7	18.1	29.5	86.6	86.3	86.9	5.1	5.0	5.3	8.3	8.7	7.9
Sweden	2005	...	86.4	...	36.0	...	...	80.3	...	...	8.2	...	...	11.5
United Kingdom	2005	76.3	112.7	34.3	48.7	75.0	73.8	73.0	11.3	10.8	11.7	13.8	15.3	15.3
EU-12														
Bulgaria	2006	3.6	9.5	1.2	2.5	84.1	84.4	82.2	5.2	4.4	4.7	10.7	11.3	13.1
Cyprus	2006	26.6	44.8	12.6	21.9	81.8	78.9	81.6	8.6	9.8	9.0	9.5	11.3	9.4
Czech Republic	2004	11.3	21.6	4.1	7.6	81.6	80.7	80.6	6.7	7.4	6.8	11.7	11.9	12.6
Estonia	2005	6.5	23.0	2.6	7.3	70.3	81.8	79.3	12.1	6.4	6.5	17.6	11.9	14.2
Hungary	2005	14.7	32.4	4.0	11.0	77.5	76.0	74.9	6.2	7.3	8.5	16.3	16.7	16.6
Latvia	2006	11.2	8.4	4.1	7.1	71.9	77.7	90.7	10.2	9.1	7.8	17.8	13.2	1.4
Lithuania	2006	7.8	22.7	3.0	7.7	81.0	81.4	82.9	7.4	5.3	5.8	11.6	13.3	11.3
Malta	2005	35.1	40.8	12.9	15.5	82.0	81.9	80.5	6.6	7.8	7.4	11.3	10.3	12.1
Poland	2005	...	34.2	...	9.6	...	80.4	78.5	...	5.8	6.0	...	13.8	15.5
Romania	2006	...	6.2	...	4.2	72.7	88.7	85.7	...	6.4	9.5	...	4.9	4.7
Slovakia	2005	6.3	19.8	3.2	7.6	86.2	79.7	82.2	7.1	6.6	6.9	6.8	13.6	11.0
Other Europe														
Norway	2004	...	124.8	...	55.1	...	...	81.3	...	...	8.3	...	...	10.4

a/ At current prices.

Table 1.11
(continued)

SELECTED CHARACTERISTICS OF BRANCHES, SELECTED YEARS AND COUNTRIES

Grain mill products; starches; animal feeds (ISIC 153)

Country or area	Latest year	Value added per employee (current 1000 dollars)		Wages and salaries per employee (current 1000 dollars)		Percentage in output [a]								
						Costs of input materials and utilities			Costs of labour			Operating surplus		
	(LY)	2000	LY	2000	LY	2000	2003	LY	2000	2003	LY	2000	2003	LY
Other Countries														
Australia	2005	111.6	84.1	22.6	...	59.3	78.2	74.8	8.2	...	...	32.5	...	...
Israel	2005	67.5	66.5	28.2	30.0	81.0	82.6	86.8	7.9	7.1	6.0	11.1	10.3	7.3
Japan	2005	142.8	146.7	24.2	22.0	79.1	80.4	81.2	3.5	3.0	2.8	17.3	16.6	16.0
Republic of Korea	2006	125.6	171.1	16.2	27.7	73.5	76.9	73.5	3.4	3.7	4.3	23.0	19.4	22.2
Singapore	2006	33.4	34.2	24.3	27.9	78.1	83.8	84.1	15.9	14.1	12.9	6.0	2.1	2.9
United States of America	2005	222.9	365.2	36.9	46.4	57.1	54.1	54.0	7.1	6.5	5.9	35.8	39.4	40.2
Developing Countries														
Brazil	2005	27.2	37.1	5.2	6.0	70.8	68.3	68.1	5.6	4.3	5.1	23.6	27.4	26.8
Chile	2006	...	59.4	...	12.0	...	73.8	78.9	...	6.2	4.3	...	20.0	16.9
Colombia	2005	28.4	48.2	3.8	5.2	80.5	80.6	77.7	2.6	2.4	2.4	16.9	17.0	19.9
Ecuador	2005	11.0	39.6	1.7	4.7	85.8	80.1	70.6	2.2	3.6	3.5	12.0	16.3	25.9
Eritrea	2006	2.6	...	0.8	1.1	92.5	...	...	2.3	3.2	5.6	5.2	...	...
Ethiopia	2006	3.5	3.0	0.7	0.7	80.7	74.1	79.8	3.9	5.2	4.5	15.4	20.7	15.6
India	2004	2.0	2.4	0.5	0.7	92.1	93.2	92.9	2.1	1.9	1.9	5.8	4.9	5.2
Indonesia	2005	6.3	6.4	0.6	1.3	76.5	80.3	85.5	2.1	3.2	2.9	21.3	16.5	11.6
Iran (Islamic Republic of)	2005	36.3	13.9	7.9	3.5	56.2	60.0	64.2	9.5	10.3	8.9	34.2	29.7	26.9
Jordan	2006	15.7	11.2	4.4	4.3	89.1	86.0	87.0	3.0	2.5	4.9	7.8	11.4	8.0
Madagascar	2006	...	...	...	0.1	...	...	...	...	10.7	14.7	...	...	...
Malaysia	2005	20.1	17.6	4.8	6.5	83.0	85.2	87.8	4.1	4.7	4.5	12.9	10.1	7.7
Morocco	2005	13.4	22.0	4.3	6.1	90.7	90.4	88.9	3.0	3.1	3.0	6.3	6.6	8.0
Oman	2006	58.9	48.7	13.7	14.4	76.0	78.9	80.8	5.6	5.3	5.7	18.4	15.9	13.5
Philippines	2005	...	19.4	...	2.2	...	87.0	81.0	...	2.4	2.1	...	10.7	16.9
Qatar	2006	18.7	...	9.7	9.5	68.3	...	...	16.5	23.3	18.6	15.2	...	...
Sri Lanka	2006	...	5.9	...	0.9	...	...	68.0	...	...	4.9	...	...	27.0
Trinidad and Tobago	2004	36.2	...	12.0	...	80.2	75.0	77.0	6.5	9.3	8.6	13.2	15.7	14.5
Uruguay	2005	25.6	14.1	12.3	5.4	78.0	81.7	84.0	10.5	4.8	6.1	11.4	13.5	9.9

a/ At current prices.

Table 1.11

SELECTED CHARACTERISTICS OF BRANCHES, SELECTED YEARS AND COUNTRIES

Country or area	Latest year (LY)	Other food products (ISIC 154): Value added per employee (current 1000 dollars)		Wages and salaries per employee (current 1000 dollars)		Percentage in output[a/]: Costs of input materials and utilities			Costs of labour			Operating surplus		
		2000	LY	2000	LY	2000	2003	LY	2000	2003	LY	2000	2003	LY
Industrialized Countries														
CIS														
Azerbaijan	2006	...	5.7	0.1	0.7	...	75.8	87.5	0.4	0.5	1.6	...	23.7	11.0
Georgia	2006	0.7	2.3	0.4	0.7	83.3	78.9	82.7	8.2	4.2	5.5	8.5	17.0	11.8
Kyrgyzstan	2005	...	3.5	0.6	0.8	...	79.7	74.9	5.0	4.5	6.0	...	15.8	19.1
Republic of Moldova	2006	...	...	0.6	1.6	...	...	...	9.7	11.5	10.6	...	...	...
Russian Federation	2006	...	10.2	1.0	3.6	...	71.6	67.9	9.8	11.2	11.4	...	17.3	20.7
EU-15														
Austria	2005	33.9	49.7	18.8	28.2	55.9	55.5	58.0	24.4	23.3	23.8	19.7	21.2	18.2
Belgium	2005	43.1	71.7	18.9	30.0	71.6	71.5	72.5	12.5	12.3	11.5	15.9	16.3	16.0
Denmark	2005	39.5	57.9	22.8	36.8	62.1	62.2	64.3	21.9	23.4	22.7	16.0	14.4	13.0
Finland	2004	34.0	65.5	20.6	34.1	68.7	63.3	62.3	19.0	18.9	19.6	12.3	17.7	18.1
France	2005	37.8	53.8	16.6	25.5	67.2	67.7	68.0	14.4	15.2	15.2	18.4	17.1	16.8
Germany	2005	27.1	41.5	15.9	23.0	67.6	65.3	65.9	19.0	19.6	18.9	13.3	15.1	15.2
Greece	2004	...	50.9	...	19.1	...	...	64.9	...	...	13.2	...	...	21.9
Italy	2005	46.7	63.6	16.4	24.0	70.3	69.2	71.2	10.4	11.1	10.9	19.2	19.7	18.0
Luxembourg	2005	31.2	44.3	17.9	31.8	49.7	48.2	47.7	28.8	34.9	37.5	21.5	16.9	14.8
Netherlands	2005	45.1	83.5	20.8	34.0	67.9	69.4	68.6	14.7	13.7	12.8	17.3	17.0	18.6
Portugal	2005	13.8	21.8	6.6	10.6	65.8	63.5	64.2	16.3	17.1	17.4	17.9	19.4	18.4
Spain	2005	28.3	49.4	13.8	23.2	64.6	65.7	65.6	17.3	16.3	16.1	18.1	18.0	18.2
Sweden	2005	45.5	63.0	22.7	31.2	63.7	...	64.9	18.1	...	17.4	18.2	...	17.7
United Kingdom	2005	52.5	90.9	23.6	34.4	59.6	56.3	54.4	18.1	18.3	17.3	22.3	25.4	28.3
EU-12														
Bulgaria	2006	2.1	4.7	1.0	2.0	80.9	80.5	78.3	8.8	9.3	9.1	10.3	10.1	12.6
Cyprus	2005	17.9	26.3	9.5	15.9	54.3	52.7	51.9	24.2	26.1	29.1	21.5	21.1	19.0
Czech Republic	2004	7.6	15.0	3.4	6.0	72.7	70.2	70.1	12.0	12.7	11.9	15.3	17.1	18.0
Estonia	2006	5.7	11.4	2.8	6.6	66.3	63.6	67.6	16.6	18.4	18.8	17.0	18.0	13.6
Hungary	2005	7.5	15.6	3.1	6.5	72.9	70.0	69.7	11.1	12.9	12.7	16.0	17.0	17.6
Latvia	2006	5.2	12.6	2.6	4.6	70.5	67.5	62.4	14.8	13.6	13.6	14.6	18.8	23.9
Lithuania	2006	4.2	8.9	2.3	4.6	72.1	70.2	69.9	15.4	14.1	15.5	12.5	15.7	14.7
Malta	2005	18.7	20.6	7.9	10.2	55.4	58.9	60.9	18.8	21.4	19.3	25.8	19.7	19.7
Poland	2005	10.8	18.5	...	6.1	69.7	71.8	69.4	...	11.3	10.1	...	16.9	20.4
Romania	2006	...	6.8	...	3.7	62.5	83.0	79.6	...	9.8	11.0	...	7.2	9.5
Slovakia	2005	4.9	12.3	2.8	5.6	78.9	73.9	75.1	12.2	11.5	11.4	8.9	14.6	13.5
Other Europe														
Norway	2004	44.7	73.1	24.3	38.2	55.5	54.5	56.6	24.2	23.5	22.6	20.3	22.0	20.8

a/ At current prices.

Table 1.11
(continued)

SELECTED CHARACTERISTICS OF BRANCHES, SELECTED YEARS AND COUNTRIES

Other food products (ISIC 154)														
Country or area	Latest year	Value added per employee (current 1000 dollars)		Wages and salaries per employee (current 1000 dollars)		Percentage in output [a/]								
						Costs of input materials and utilities			Costs of labour			Operating surplus		
	(LY)	2000	LY	2000	LY	2000	2003	LY	2000	2003	LY	2000	2003	LY
Other Countries														
Israel	2005	29.8	28.3	19.5	19.5	59.7	60.8	65.5	26.3	25.7	23.8	14.0	13.5	10.7
Japan	2005	74.0	72.1	19.6	18.6	55.0	54.8	56.2	11.9	11.7	11.3	33.1	33.5	32.5
Republic of Korea	2006	71.3	89.5	12.8	20.4	50.4	55.0	56.2	8.9	9.6	10.0	40.7	35.5	33.8
United States of America	2005	140.8	166.4	30.8	34.0	41.0	40.5	41.6	12.9	12.8	11.9	46.1	46.7	46.4
Developing Countries														
Brazil	2005	14.7	18.5	3.8	4.3	58.2	57.5	55.9	10.7	10.1	10.4	31.1	32.4	33.7
Chile	2006	...	43.0	...	8.3	...	55.5	46.9	...	9.7	10.3	...	34.8	42.8
Colombia	2005	26.9	42.8	4.1	5.2	60.2	60.5	63.3	6.0	4.9	4.4	33.8	34.6	32.3
Ecuador	2005	10.9	10.5	2.5	4.1	75.5	68.9	71.3	5.5	11.2	11.4	19.0	19.9	17.4
Eritrea	2006	2.7	2.7	0.8	0.7	67.2	76.2	74.9	9.6	5.4	6.2	23.2	18.4	18.9
Ethiopia	2006	10.1	7.1	0.9	1.1	35.6	29.5	57.8	5.5	7.6	6.7	58.8	63.0	35.5
Fiji	2004	...	7.0	...	5.3	...	69.9	83.0	...	14.6	12.9	...	15.5	4.1
India	2004	2.8	3.2	0.9	1.0	81.3	83.1	81.0	5.9	6.2	5.7	12.8	10.7	13.3
Indonesia	2005	3.4	5.4	0.8	1.0	64.8	59.6	59.8	8.7	7.0	7.4	26.5	33.3	32.8
Iran (Islamic Republic of)	2005	22.4	10.0	9.4	3.7	67.7	67.6	64.3	13.5	12.5	13.2	18.8	19.9	22.5
Jordan	2006	5.8	6.8	2.4	2.5	72.0	69.3	71.2	11.5	10.6	10.4	16.4	20.1	18.4
Madagascar	2006	...	3.9	...	0.2	...	19.5	23.9	...	2.1	3.0	...	78.4	73.2
Malaysia	2005	12.2	11.5	3.7	4.7	71.0	69.5	76.5	8.7	10.0	9.6	20.2	20.5	13.9
Morocco	2005	11.0	18.7	5.1	8.4	71.8	72.9	67.7	13.0	12.6	14.6	15.1	14.5	17.7
Oman	2005	13.8	17.9	5.0	5.8	54.8	53.5	60.1	16.4	16.8	13.1	28.8	29.7	26.8
Qatar	2006	11.0	33.2	4.1	9.2	52.0	51.8	46.6	18.1	18.3	14.8	29.9	29.9	38.6
Sri Lanka	2006	...	4.9	...	0.7	...	...	57.6	...	...	6.4	...	...	36.0
Trinidad and Tobago	2004	15.1	...	12.3	...	81.3	...	73.1	15.3	...	15.4	3.4	...	11.5
Uruguay	2005	31.0	18.3	10.6	3.4	55.3	55.7	50.1	15.3	10.1	9.3	29.4	34.3	40.7

a/ At current prices.

Table 1.11

SELECTED CHARACTERISTICS OF BRANCHES, SELECTED YEARS AND COUNTRIES

Country or area	Latest year	Beverages (ISIC 155)												
		Value added per employee (current 1000 dollars)		Wages and salaries per employee (current 1000 dollars)		Percentage in output a/								
						Costs of input materials and utilities			Costs of labour			Operating surplus		
	(LY)	2000	LY	2000	LY	2000	2003	LY	2000	2003	LY	2000	2003	LY
Industrialized Countries														
CIS														
Azerbaijan	2006	...	2.9	0.8	1.8	...	75.8	87.5	10.4	9.5	8.0	...	14.7	4.5
Georgia	2006	2.6	6.0	0.7	2.1	71.3	73.6	75.1	7.8	5.3	8.8	20.9	21.2	16.1
Kyrgyzstan	2005	...	3.0	0.4	0.9	...	72.8	68.2	6.7	9.6	9.3	...	17.6	22.5
Republic of Moldova	2006	...	...	0.6	1.1	...	...	...	4.8	5.1	7.5	...	...	...
Russian Federation	2006	...	34.2	1.5	5.5	...	63.0	61.1	7.9	6.7	6.2	...	30.3	32.7
EU-15														
Austria	2005	61.7	102.9	30.3	44.3	64.5	62.7	63.5	17.4	16.1	15.7	18.1	21.1	20.8
Belgium	2005	75.0	135.3	30.5	46.8	71.0	69.8	69.8	11.8	11.0	10.4	17.2	19.2	19.8
Denmark	2005	68.9	104.8	32.4	56.4	67.0	73.0	69.8	15.5	11.8	16.2	17.5	15.2	14.0
Finland	2005	...	110.1	...	47.6	...	66.0	67.4	...	13.0	14.1	...	20.9	18.5
France	2005	93.9	132.4	28.8	44.6	72.6	74.6	75.3	8.4	8.2	8.3	19.0	17.3	16.4
Germany	2005	62.1	89.2	30.8	43.9	72.2	71.7	71.4	13.7	13.7	14.0	14.0	14.5	14.5
Greece	2004	...	90.5	...	31.4	...	...	60.7	...	...	13.6	...	...	25.7
Italy	2005	68.8	94.6	21.2	35.1	79.1	82.0	81.6	6.4	6.3	6.8	14.4	11.7	11.6
Luxembourg	2005	74.4	114.0	27.4	41.5	59.4	63.8	64.1	15.0	14.2	13.1	25.6	22.0	22.9
Netherlands	2005	116.4	160.9	34.0	54.4	66.3	71.0	71.1	9.8	9.7	9.8	23.8	19.3	19.1
Portugal	2005	38.4	51.9	11.8	18.5	73.1	75.1	73.9	8.3	8.5	9.3	18.6	16.5	16.8
Spain	2005	72.2	108.7	23.6	35.7	71.7	70.8	72.3	9.2	9.7	9.1	19.1	19.5	18.6
Sweden	2005	81.8	121.0	28.6	39.6	66.9	...	66.1	11.6	...	11.1	21.5	...	22.8
United Kingdom	2005	112.0	139.0	34.4	56.6	67.5	70.1	71.9	10.0	11.2	11.4	22.5	18.7	16.7
EU-12														
Bulgaria	2006	4.8	9.4	1.5	3.0	79.0	79.4	77.1	6.5	7.1	7.4	14.5	13.4	15.5
Cyprus	2006	48.2	60.6	15.6	29.9	57.7	61.5	55.6	13.7	19.1	21.9	28.6	19.5	22.5
Czech Republic	2004	...	39.2	...	9.5	...	67.1	67.0	...	7.4	8.0	...	25.6	25.0
Estonia	2006	13.9	37.1	4.9	11.3	73.8	69.0	68.4	9.2	10.3	9.6	16.9	20.7	22.0
Hungary	2005	14.1	31.5	5.3	11.8	76.3	73.8	76.3	9.0	8.4	8.9	14.8	17.8	14.9
Latvia	2006	18.4	22.7	4.8	8.2	52.5	54.3	77.7	12.4	9.3	8.1	35.1	36.3	14.2
Lithuania	2006	11.8	31.3	4.1	8.5	63.3	66.2	68.9	12.9	10.6	8.4	23.9	23.2	22.7
Poland	2005	57.3	133.2	...	12.1	42.8	43.2	40.5	...	6.0	5.4	...	50.8	54.1
Romania	2006	...	22.8	...	7.6	66.4	76.9	75.6	...	7.5	8.1	...	15.6	16.3
Slovakia	2005	7.3	20.8	3.3	7.5	81.9	76.8	76.6	8.3	9.1	8.5	9.8	14.1	14.9
Other Europe														
Norway	2004	123.4	241.1	33.0	52.0	41.2	36.0	35.4	15.7	13.7	13.9	43.1	50.3	50.6

a/ At current prices.

Table 1.11
(continued)

SELECTED CHARACTERISTICS OF BRANCHES, SELECTED YEARS AND COUNTRIES

Country or area	Latest year	Value added per employee (current 1000 dollars)		Wages and salaries per employee (current 1000 dollars)		Percentage in output [a/] Costs of input materials and utilities			Costs of labour			Operating surplus		
Beverages (ISIC 155)	(LY)	2000	LY	2000	LY	2000	2003	LY	2000	2003	LY	2000	2003	LY
Other Countries														
Australia	2005	149.6	133.3	22.3	...	49.6	65.5	63.9	7.5	...	...	42.9	...	...
Japan	2005	300.2	290.5	31.2	29.6	63.8	63.6	64.4	3.8	3.5	3.6	32.4	32.9	32.0
Republic of Korea	2006	193.2	304.5	16.1	30.8	39.0	45.1	42.0	5.1	5.1	5.9	55.9	49.8	52.1
United States of America	2005	219.6	351.2	39.7	46.7	53.4	48.7	46.3	8.4	7.7	7.1	38.2	43.5	46.5
Developing Countries														
Albania	2006	3.9	12.2	1.3	3.0	65.9	74.5	73.6	11.7	5.5	6.4	22.5	20.1	20.0
Botswana	2006	36.0	44.1	0.4	0.3	75.5	72.2	72.6	0.2	...	0.2	24.3	...	27.2
Brazil	2005	40.5	41.0	6.1	6.3	48.1	54.7	48.8	7.8	7.6	7.9	44.0	37.7	43.3
Chile	2006	...	107.2	...	48.2	...	46.1	48.4	...	6.9	23.2	...	47.1	28.4
Colombia	2005	71.5	192.0	5.9	7.7	34.1	33.1	31.3	5.4	3.6	2.8	60.5	63.3	65.9
Ecuador	2005	23.8	63.7	2.1	5.7	61.6	64.2	42.7	3.3	8.1	5.1	35.1	27.8	52.2
Eritrea	2006	18.5	18.0	1.4	1.2	36.8	38.3	37.9	4.7	2.9	4.3	58.5	58.8	57.8
Ethiopia	2006	10.5	12.4	1.0	1.9	28.6	30.3	44.8	6.9	9.4	8.2	64.5	60.3	47.0
India	2004	6.0	6.2	1.4	1.6	77.5	74.3	81.8	5.2	4.8	4.7	17.4	20.9	13.5
Indonesia	2005	7.4	9.6	0.9	1.4	51.6	45.5	51.7	5.6	6.5	7.0	42.8	48.0	41.4
Iran (Islamic Republic of)	2005	44.5	15.6	12.3	4.8	49.6	55.0	59.3	14.0	15.5	12.4	36.4	29.4	28.3
Jordan	2006	24.8	28.6	4.2	4.9	46.2	50.1	51.3	9.2	9.1	8.4	44.6	40.8	40.3
Madagascar	2006	...	8.4	...	0.4	...	56.5	59.5	...	1.6	2.1	...	41.9	38.4
Malaysia	2005	29.6	55.5	6.1	6.9	67.4	70.4	58.6	6.7	9.5	5.1	25.9	20.1	36.3
Morocco	2005	45.3	75.3	7.8	17.1	48.2	46.1	44.2	9.0	12.8	12.6	42.8	41.1	43.1
Oman	2006	12.2	24.6	6.4	8.2	78.2	65.2	61.2	11.4	13.5	12.9	10.3	21.3	26.0
Philippines	2005	...	35.4	...	5.2	...	57.8	59.8	...	5.4	5.9	...	36.7	34.3
Qatar	2006	18.7	14.2	6.2	5.8	60.4	63.3	63.6	13.1	14.7	14.9	26.5	22.0	21.6
Sri Lanka	2006	...	11.1	...	1.1	...	...	31.1	...	...	6.8	...	...	62.1
Trinidad and Tobago	2004	37.6	...	8.3	...	57.9	51.6	52.3	9.2	11.9	14.3	32.9	36.5	33.3
Uruguay	2005	71.1	54.5	23.1	10.2	46.0	58.7	53.9	17.5	9.5	8.6	36.5	31.9	37.4

a/ At current prices.

Table 1.11

SELECTED CHARACTERISTICS OF BRANCHES, SELECTED YEARS AND COUNTRIES

Tobacco products (ISIC 1600)														
Country or area	Latest year	Value added per employee (current 1000 dollars)		Wages and salaries per employee (current 1000 dollars)		Percentage in output a/								
						Costs of input materials and utilities			Costs of labour			Operating surplus		
	(LY)	2000	LY	2000	LY	2000	2003	LY	2000	2003	LY	2000	2003	LY
Industrialized Countries														
CIS														
Azerbaijan	2006	...	3.3	0.8	2.3	...	75.8	87.5	5.7	6.5	8.5	...	17.7	4.0
Georgia	2006	...	14.5	...	4.3	...	94.3	82.6	...	3.8	5.2	...	1.9	12.3
Kyrgyzstan	2005	...	11.3	0.7	2.8	...	74.4	68.9	5.1	6.7	7.6	...	19.0	23.4
Republic of Moldova	2006	...	3.1	1.6	2.1	...	84.7	78.7	10.0	10.9	14.4	...	4.4	6.8
Russian Federation	2006	...	90.7	3.3	11.2	...	63.0	64.2	4.3	3.9	4.4	...	33.1	31.4
EU-15														
Austria	2005	127.3	84.3	44.5	74.0	59.6	...	76.9	14.1	...	20.3	26.3	...	2.8
Belgium	2005	75.4	152.8	24.6	45.0	86.7	85.9	82.9	4.3	4.1	5.0	8.9	10.0	12.1
Germany	2005	133.4	167.1	41.7	67.3	87.2	89.4	89.3	4.0	4.2	4.3	8.8	6.4	6.4
Greece	2004	...	116.1	...	40.1	...	...	56.3	...	...	15.1	...	...	28.6
Netherlands	2004	...	444.1	...	56.7	70.7	68.2	68.2	3.6	3.7	4.1	25.7	28.1	27.7
Portugal	2005	...	187.0	16.9	31.8	...	55.7	56.4	8.0	7.3	7.4	...	36.9	36.2
Spain	2005	72.5	124.2	25.5	43.7	59.9	58.7	52.6	14.1	13.4	16.7	26.0	27.9	30.7
United Kingdom	2004	...	456.0	...	83.0	...	86.2	85.8	...	3.1	2.6	...	10.6	11.6
EU-12														
Bulgaria	2006	8.4	14.6	2.6	6.2	66.2	73.6	68.0	10.5	11.9	13.6	23.3	14.4	18.5
Cyprus	2005	277.0	494.1	19.8	36.9	31.8	25.1	22.1	4.9	5.3	5.8	63.3	69.6	72.1
Hungary	2005	39.0	70.7	8.7	29.7	66.6	87.4	90.1	7.5	3.3	4.2	25.9	9.2	5.8
Lithuania	2006	32.8	70.4	9.4	18.4	79.3	64.9	77.9	5.9	9.8	5.8	14.8	25.3	16.3
Poland	2005	175.1	517.3	...	15.9	26.0	21.5	17.7	...	2.8	2.5	...	75.7	79.7
Romania	2006	14.0	30.4	2.5	16.6	70.5	92.8	93.5	5.2	3.6	3.5	24.2	3.6	2.9
Other Europe														
Norway	2004	...	1991.9	...	58.3	...	...	8.1	...	...	2.7	...	...	89.2

a/ At current prices.

Table 1.11
(continued)

SELECTED CHARACTERISTICS OF BRANCHES, SELECTED YEARS AND COUNTRIES

Tobacco products (ISIC 1600)														
Country or area	Latest year	Value added per employee (current 1000 dollars)		Wages and salaries per employee (current 1000 dollars)		Percentage in output a/								
						Costs of input materials and utilities			Costs of labour			Operating surplus		
	(LY)	2000	LY	2000	LY	2000	2003	LY	2000	2003	LY	2000	2003	LY
Other Countries														
Australia	2005	347.2	455.6	38.3	...	28.9	42.9	28.8	7.8	...	...	63.3	...	...
Japan	2005	950.3	1303.3	66.2	63.7	76.3	82.0	79.3	1.7	1.2	1.0	22.1	16.7	19.7
Republic of Korea	2006	675.7	752.3	32.8	44.9	35.8	34.6	44.3	3.1	3.2	3.3	61.1	62.2	52.4
Developing Countries														
Albania	2006	3.2	4.7	1.2	2.7	66.5	75.5	84.2	12.3	10.4	9.3	21.2	14.1	6.5
Brazil	2005	76.0	60.3	10.2	9.9	42.5	51.9	58.2	7.7	6.1	6.8	49.7	42.0	35.0
Colombia	2005	97.3	122.0	5.3	8.0	42.5	50.1	41.7	3.1	2.9	3.8	54.4	47.0	54.5
Ecuador	2005	20.5	35.9	3.9	10.0	64.9	67.6	69.8	6.7	8.1	8.4	28.4	24.3	21.8
Eritrea	2006	67.8	78.8	2.6	5.3	49.2	26.3	39.2	1.9	1.3	4.1	48.9	72.5	56.7
Ethiopia	2006	25.8	39.8	1.4	3.5	30.9	37.4	37.1	3.8	5.3	5.5	65.4	57.2	57.4
India	2004	1.9	2.4	0.4	0.5	64.7	58.2	57.5	7.4	7.8	8.0	27.9	34.0	34.5
Indonesia	2005	7.5	15.2	0.6	0.9	56.2	27.5	32.5	3.6	4.6	3.8	40.2	67.9	63.7
Iran (Islamic Republic of)	2005	41.3	17.5	15.1	4.0	37.1	54.2	48.2	23.0	39.4	11.7	39.9	6.5	40.1
Jordan	2006	197.7	180.4	6.3	5.7	29.3	38.4	36.0	2.3	2.3	2.0	68.4	59.3	62.0
Madagascar	2006	...	0.6	...	0.1	...	24.0	29.2	...	12.5	17.8	...	63.5	53.0
Malaysia	2005	8.9	16.6	2.7	7.5	78.8	73.0	78.5	6.4	8.7	9.7	14.7	18.3	11.8
Philippines	2005	...	39.7	...	4.0	...	52.7	65.8	...	4.2	3.4	...	43.1	30.7
Saudi Arabia	2006	...	11.5	...	5.1	...	...	75.3	...	...	10.9	...	...	13.8
Sri Lanka	2006	...	112.7	...	3.2	...	...	7.3	...	...	2.6	...	...	90.1
Trinidad and Tobago	2004	162.0	...	16.6	...	24.9	26.7	25.7	7.7	6.2	7.6	67.4	67.1	66.7
Uruguay	2005	311.4	269.0	34.7	26.2	30.6	37.0	26.3	7.7	7.9	7.2	61.6	55.1	66.5
Yemen	2006	55.2	29.6	4.0	0.9	42.1	41.8	57.9	4.2	1.7	1.2	53.7	56.5	40.9

a/ At current prices.

Table 1.11

SELECTED CHARACTERISTICS OF BRANCHES, SELECTED YEARS AND COUNTRIES

Spinning, weaving and finishing of textiles (ISIC 171)															
Country or area	Latest year	Value added per employee (current 1000 dollars)		Wages and salaries per employee (current 1000 dollars)		Percentage in output a/									
						Costs of input materials and utilities			Costs of labour			Operating surplus			
	(LY)	2000	LY	2000	LY	2000	2003	LY	2000	2003	LY	2000	2003	LY
Industrialized Countries															
CIS															
Azerbaijan	2006	...	1.3	0.2	0.8	...	70.7	82.6	9.2	7.5	10.7	...	21.8	6.6
Kyrgyzstan	2005	...	1.7	0.2	0.6	...	88.5	67.3	3.9	9.9	12.0	...	1.6	20.7
Russian Federation	2006	...	7.2	0.6	2.3	...	78.9	72.0	16.4	9.8	8.9	...	11.3	19.1
EU-15															
Austria	2005	41.1	53.1	24.6	35.8	63.5	63.9	68.9	21.8	21.1	21.0	14.7	15.1	10.1
Belgium	2005	44.8	53.0	20.7	29.1	68.8	70.6	72.6	14.4	14.9	15.0	16.8	14.5	12.3
Denmark	2005	...	65.9	...	43.8	...	58.6	62.4	...	26.9	25.0	...	14.6	12.6
Finland	2005	34.4	49.5	19.7	32.0	65.3	67.4	63.0	19.8	18.3	23.9	14.9	14.3	13.0
France	2005	33.7	44.4	19.1	30.5	74.8	77.1	76.6	14.3	14.7	16.1	10.9	8.1	7.3
Germany	2005	36.9	51.1	24.6	35.1	66.2	68.8	68.3	22.5	22.0	21.7	11.3	9.2	10.0
Greece	2004	...	35.5	...	20.5	...	...	67.2	...	...	18.9	...	...	13.8
Italy	2005	41.2	54.1	17.5	26.4	68.6	70.6	72.2	13.3	14.1	13.6	18.1	15.3	14.3
Netherlands	2005	46.1	70.4	25.7	41.2	64.8	...	65.5	19.6	...	20.1	15.6	...	14.3
Portugal	2005	14.2	18.5	7.2	11.5	68.5	68.4	69.1	15.9	17.6	19.2	15.6	14.0	11.7
Spain	2005	27.5	40.0	14.2	25.1	69.0	68.5	71.5	16.0	18.0	17.9	15.0	13.6	10.7
Sweden	2005	36.4	47.2	19.6	30.9	66.2	...	69.3	18.2	...	20.1	15.6	...	10.6
United Kingdom	2005	38.8	43.8	24.8	33.5	63.1	59.4	68.1	23.6	24.5	24.4	13.3	16.1	7.5
EU-12															
Bulgaria	2006	1.8	7.9	1.0	2.3	75.7	78.2	78.6	13.4	8.6	6.3	10.9	13.2	15.2
Cyprus	2006	19.8	36.5	10.0	17.9	54.5	55.4	56.8	23.1	29.0	21.2	22.4	15.6	22.0
Czech Republic	2004	7.1	11.8	3.2	5.7	71.4	...	70.4	12.9	...	14.2	15.7	...	15.3
Estonia	2006	6.5	8.8	2.7	5.4	75.7	67.3	66.2	10.2	17.4	20.7	14.1	15.4	13.1
Hungary	2005	5.9	14.3	2.9	7.1	69.5	...	65.0	14.9	...	17.5	15.6	...	17.5
Latvia	2006	5.1	7.9	3.0	4.9	59.6	65.9	76.0	23.8	17.0	14.9	16.6	17.1	9.1
Lithuania	2006	3.6	8.3	2.7	5.2	69.8	71.0	66.1	22.9	18.9	21.3	7.2	10.1	12.6
Malta	2005	45.6	51.0	14.0	16.6	49.5	...	43.9	15.5	...	18.3	34.9	...	37.7
Poland	2005	7.1	12.9	...	6.1	65.4	70.7	67.8	...	15.2	15.2	...	14.1	17.0
Romania	2006	...	6.9	...	4.6	...	68.9	75.5	...	19.0	16.2	...	12.1	8.3
Slovakia	2004	3.1	6.3	2.3	4.9	76.2	75.8	78.0	17.6	18.7	17.2	6.2	5.5	4.8
Other Europe															
Norway	2004	34.2	58.3	24.8	37.5	60.8	...	58.5	28.5	...	26.6	10.7	...	14.8

a/ At current prices.

Table 1.11
(continued)

SELECTED CHARACTERISTICS OF BRANCHES, SELECTED YEARS AND COUNTRIES

Spinning, weaving and finishing of textiles (ISIC 171)														
Country or area	Latest year	Value added per employee (current 1000 dollars)		Wages and salaries per employee (current 1000 dollars)		Percentage in output[a/]								
						Costs of input materials and utilities			Costs of labour			Operating surplus		
	(LY)	2000	LY	2000	LY	2000	2003	LY	2000	2003	LY	2000	2003	LY
Other Countries														
Australia	2005	47.4	48.5	23.5	...	57.5	68.3	64.5	21.1	...	...	21.4	...	...
Japan	2005	64.8	60.9	20.1	17.9	55.4	53.7	55.4	13.8	12.7	13.1	30.8	33.6	31.5
Republic of Korea	2006	44.6	58.5	13.1	20.8	56.9	58.2	60.7	12.6	14.6	14.0	30.5	27.1	25.3
Singapore	2006	38.8	33.0	17.9	20.1	74.7	82.3	81.9	11.7	10.9	11.0	13.6	6.8	7.1
United States of America	2005	61.2	82.6	26.4	29.7	59.8	59.2	59.3	17.3	16.5	14.6	22.9	24.3	26.0
Developing Countries														
Brazil	2005	15.0	14.5	4.1	4.7	58.1	64.5	61.6	11.4	10.7	12.3	30.5	24.8	26.1
Chile	2006	...	19.1	...	8.4	...	67.6	62.9	...	17.3	16.3	...	15.1	20.8
Colombia	2005	16.9	21.4	3.9	4.7	52.6	58.0	58.1	11.0	9.6	9.3	36.4	32.4	32.7
Ecuador	2005	9.4	13.4	1.3	4.1	70.5	67.6	64.2	4.0	11.4	10.8	25.5	21.1	24.9
Eritrea	2006	1.2	2.0	0.3	0.8	59.7	51.2	55.7	10.2	30.6	18.1	30.1	18.2	26.3
Ethiopia	2006	1.2	1.2	0.6	0.7	61.9	67.7	75.1	18.2	14.9	14.0	19.9	17.5	10.9
India	2004	2.9	3.5	1.1	1.2	81.4	81.9	82.4	7.1	6.5	6.2	11.5	11.6	11.4
Indonesia	2005	4.6	4.9	0.7	0.9	66.5	68.5	73.6	4.9	6.0	5.1	28.5	25.5	21.3
Iran (Islamic Republic of)	2005	16.1	7.5	8.5	3.5	62.7	64.7	64.2	19.7	19.4	16.9	17.6	15.9	18.9
Jordan	2006	19.9	23.4	4.3	6.5	57.5	53.7	57.1	9.3	7.3	11.8	33.2	38.9	31.1
Madagascar	2006	...	...	...	0.1	...	...	...	...	21.5	32.9	...	...	...
Malaysia	2005	17.3	10.6	4.3	5.1	69.2	77.0	83.8	7.7	9.4	7.8	23.1	13.6	8.4
Morocco	2005	8.5	9.6	3.8	5.1	64.0	70.5	70.4	16.0	14.9	15.6	20.0	14.6	14.0
Oman	2006	25.1	15.7	9.8	8.2	53.1	56.3	57.0	18.3	23.8	22.6	28.6	19.8	20.5
Philippines	2005	...	4.2	...	2.0	...	77.5	78.2	...	9.5	10.5	...	13.1	11.3
Sri Lanka	2006	...	5.4	...	0.6	...	...	38.6	...	...	6.9	...	...	54.5
Trinidad and Tobago	2004	16.1	...	7.5	...	43.3	57.5	68.0	26.3	9.9	21.6	30.4	32.6	10.4
Uruguay	2005	21.5	11.6	11.3	5.9	71.5	72.4	78.0	15.0	6.9	11.1	13.5	20.7	10.8

a/ At current prices.

Table 1.11

SELECTED CHARACTERISTICS OF BRANCHES, SELECTED YEARS AND COUNTRIES

Other textiles (ISIC 172)														
Country or area	Latest year	Value added per employee (current 1000 dollars)		Wages and salaries per employee (current 1000 dollars)		Percentage in output [a/]								
						Costs of input materials and utilities			Costs of labour			Operating surplus		
	(LY)	2000	LY	2000	LY	2000	2003	LY	2000	2003	LY	2000	2003	LY
Industrialized Countries														
CIS														
Azerbaijan	2006	...	0.2	0.1	0.2	...	70.7	82.6	25.9	17.6	14.1	...	11.7	3.3
Georgia	2006	0.4	4.9	0.2	0.4	90.1	83.3	57.4	5.7	1.1	3.6	4.2	15.6	39.0
Kyrgyzstan	2005	...	4.6	0.3	0.4	...	88.2	55.6	7.3	5.8	3.5	...	6.0	40.9
Russian Federation	2006	...	...	0.4	2.4	...	...	...	63.2	...	...	...	...	...
EU-15														
Austria	2005	44.6	65.0	20.7	32.8	55.4	62.1	60.1	20.6	19.0	20.1	23.9	18.9	19.8
Belgium	2005	44.9	61.8	20.6	32.3	74.9	74.0	75.4	11.5	12.2	12.8	13.6	13.8	11.7
Denmark	2005	41.1	70.3	26.5	44.6	65.1	62.9	63.8	22.6	23.6	23.0	12.4	13.5	13.3
Finland	2005	51.4	74.7	23.1	37.0	57.1	58.6	58.8	19.3	20.6	20.4	23.7	20.7	20.8
France	2005	34.2	49.7	18.7	29.7	69.9	69.2	69.6	16.5	17.7	18.2	13.6	13.1	12.2
Germany	2005	36.7	57.6	21.7	34.4	65.9	65.3	65.2	20.1	21.7	20.8	13.9	13.0	14.0
Greece	2004	...	39.3	...	16.5	...	...	62.0	...	...	16.0	...	...	22.0
Italy	2005	41.5	56.4	14.8	23.2	73.7	73.6	72.6	9.4	11.0	11.3	16.9	15.4	16.1
Netherlands	2005	50.7	76.4	26.8	40.7	69.0	71.3	70.3	16.4	16.2	15.8	14.6	12.5	13.9
Portugal	2005	12.6	16.9	6.5	9.5	66.5	66.8	66.8	17.3	18.5	18.7	16.2	14.8	14.5
Spain	2005	24.8	36.4	12.5	20.5	68.4	69.4	70.4	15.8	17.2	16.7	15.7	13.3	12.9
Sweden	2005	45.5	62.8	22.7	32.9	61.6	...	60.9	19.1	...	20.5	19.2	...	18.6
United Kingdom	2005	35.3	55.6	21.4	31.1	60.0	59.2	59.3	24.2	22.6	22.8	15.8	18.2	17.9
EU-12														
Bulgaria	2006	1.7	4.1	1.0	1.8	72.6	73.1	75.5	15.6	11.3	10.4	11.8	15.6	14.1
Cyprus	2006	14.9	31.5	7.9	16.6	60.7	62.2	52.4	20.8	21.1	25.1	18.5	16.7	22.5
Czech Republic	2004	6.7	14.4	3.1	5.5	69.7	67.2	66.8	13.9	13.1	12.7	16.4	19.7	20.4
Estonia	2006	5.2	14.4	2.9	6.7	76.1	70.6	72.3	13.3	11.8	13.0	10.6	17.6	14.7
Hungary	2005	5.1	9.7	2.6	5.4	73.0	69.9	55.6	13.7	20.8	24.8	13.3	9.3	19.6
Latvia	2006	4.2	9.0	2.5	3.8	66.9	66.6	65.3	19.5	14.7	14.7	13.6	18.7	20.0
Lithuania	2006	6.8	9.9	2.6	4.8	79.8	71.0	71.3	7.8	13.7	13.8	12.4	15.3	14.9
Malta	2005	11.3	16.4	6.6	10.3	56.9	...	55.2	25.2	...	28.1	17.9	...	16.7
Poland	2005	9.9	14.2	...	6.0	63.3	67.4	69.1	...	13.2	12.9	...	19.5	17.9
Romania	2006	...	5.5	...	3.5	...	63.2	65.9	...	21.8	21.4	...	15.0	12.6
Slovakia	2005	3.0	9.5	2.3	5.1	69.5	68.0	67.5	23.7	19.7	17.3	6.9	12.2	15.2
Other Europe														
Norway	2004	39.9	59.5	25.8	39.9	61.9	59.5	62.8	24.6	26.8	24.9	13.5	13.6	12.3

a/ At current prices.

Table 1.11
(continued)

SELECTED CHARACTERISTICS OF BRANCHES, SELECTED YEARS AND COUNTRIES

Other textiles (ISIC 172)

Country or area	Latest year	Value added per employee (current 1000 dollars)		Wages and salaries per employee (current 1000 dollars)		Percentage in output[a] — Costs of input materials and utilities			Costs of labour			Operating surplus		
	(LY)	2000	LY	2000	LY	2000	2003	LY	2000	2003	LY	2000	2003	LY
Other Countries														
Australia	2005	42.7	46.5	16.0	...	51.1	67.3	64.0	18.3	...	...	30.6	...	...
Israel	2005	26.6	46.9	19.5	23.5	63.8	68.2	70.4	26.5	22.0	14.8	9.7	9.8	14.8
Japan	2005	64.1	64.9	13.9	14.2	58.2	58.1	59.0	9.1	8.7	9.0	32.7	33.3	32.0
Republic of Korea	2006	41.7	68.1	12.0	20.7	57.8	59.6	64.4	12.2	13.2	10.8	30.0	27.2	24.8
United States of America	2005	67.0	100.9	26.6	31.6	58.2	54.3	57.8	16.6	15.5	13.2	25.2	30.2	29.0
Developing Countries														
Brazil	2005	13.9	13.9	4.2	4.3	56.2	57.7	57.8	13.4	12.7	13.2	30.5	29.6	29.1
Chile	2006	...	23.3	...	8.6	...	59.5	59.6	...	16.2	15.0	...	24.3	25.4
Colombia	2005	17.4	24.3	3.1	4.5	53.1	54.3	56.2	8.5	7.8	8.1	38.4	37.9	35.7
Ecuador	2005	8.8	8.2	0.9	2.5	60.8	68.4	74.4	3.9	7.9	7.8	35.3	23.7	17.8
India	2004	3.5	3.9	0.9	1.1	78.2	81.9	82.0	5.5	5.3	5.3	16.4	12.8	12.7
Indonesia	2005	2.8	3.2	0.6	0.9	64.5	61.7	69.9	7.8	9.3	8.4	27.7	29.0	21.7
Iran (Islamic Republic of)	2005	15.1	8.5	6.2	3.1	69.1	66.3	67.8	12.6	11.0	11.6	18.3	22.6	20.6
Jordan	2006	10.0	10.5	2.9	2.7	58.1	55.1	59.3	12.3	12.5	10.4	29.6	32.4	30.3
Madagascar	2006	...	0.1	...	0.1	...	57.8	51.9	...	23.3	35.6	...	18.9	12.5
Malaysia	2005	8.6	7.9	3.5	4.7	63.9	60.7	69.3	14.6	17.9	18.1	21.5	21.3	12.5
Morocco	2005	5.3	6.4	3.0	3.6	67.2	62.6	66.4	18.7	20.4	18.8	14.1	17.0	14.8
Oman	2006	...	20.8	...	6.6	...	...	56.2	...	...	13.8	...	...	30.0
Qatar	2006	14.0	13.3	4.7	5.8	40.0	40.1	50.5	20.0	20.0	21.5	40.0	39.8	28.0
Sri Lanka	2006	...	1.8	...	0.9	...	...	44.7	...	...	26.6	...	...	28.7
Trinidad and Tobago	2004	8.7	...	6.0	...	58.5	48.8	56.9	28.7	37.2	33.3	12.8	14.0	9.8
Uruguay	2005	12.3	7.3	8.4	3.1	61.6	62.7	67.9	26.4	15.3	13.8	12.1	22.0	18.4

a/ At current prices.

Table 1.11

SELECTED CHARACTERISTICS OF BRANCHES, SELECTED YEARS AND COUNTRIES

Country or area	Latest year (LY)	Value added per employee (current 1000 dollars)		Wages and salaries per employee (current 1000 dollars)		Percentage in output [a]								
						Costs of input materials and utilities			Costs of labour			Operating surplus		
		2000	LY	2000	LY	2000	2003	LY	2000	2003	LY	2000	2003	LY
Knitted and crocheted fabrics and articles (ISIC 1730)														
Industrialized Countries														
CIS														
Azerbaijan	2006	...	1.5	0.3	0.6	...	70.7	82.6	26.2	17.3	7.0	...	12.0	10.4
Kyrgyzstan	2006	...	...	0.2	0.9	...	...	...	22.7	16.3	20.7	...	...	...
Russian Federation	2006	...	...	0.7	2.4	...	...	...	1.0	...	...	...	...	...
EU-15														
Austria	2005	36.6	52.9	22.2	33.6	72.4	65.9	58.1	16.8	19.8	26.7	10.8	14.3	15.3
Belgium	2005	30.8	45.4	14.7	26.3	61.3	64.2	72.1	18.5	19.3	16.2	20.2	16.5	11.7
Denmark	2005	...	66.1	...	47.0	...	73.0	70.9	...	19.7	20.7	...	7.2	8.4
Finland	2005	28.8	42.6	17.9	27.1	59.2	59.6	57.7	25.4	24.8	26.9	15.4	15.6	15.4
France	2005	31.0	48.1	18.3	28.2	66.0	68.1	67.7	20.1	18.2	18.9	13.9	13.7	13.4
Germany	2005	33.8	51.9	20.2	31.3	64.3	62.7	64.9	21.4	22.0	21.1	14.4	15.3	13.9
Greece	2004	...	39.2	...	17.5	...	...	67.0	...	...	14.7	...	...	18.3
Ireland	2005	14.2	15.6	9.5	11.2	54.3	60.3	63.2	30.4	33.3	26.3	15.2	6.3	10.5
Italy	2005	33.6	48.3	12.9	20.9	73.7	74.4	73.7	10.1	11.4	11.4	16.2	14.3	14.9
Netherlands	2005	33.9	46.7	17.7	32.3	65.0	...	64.9	18.2	...	24.3	16.8	...	10.8
Portugal	2005	11.4	15.8	6.3	9.6	72.7	72.5	72.1	14.9	15.8	17.0	12.4	11.7	10.9
Spain	2005	21.9	34.6	12.0	19.7	68.4	67.6	71.5	17.3	18.4	16.2	14.3	14.0	12.3
Sweden	2005	37.2	61.3	19.6	32.7	65.4	...	66.4	18.2	...	17.9	16.4	...	15.7
United Kingdom	2005	31.9	35.1	22.9	27.3	59.2	60.6	61.0	29.4	25.4	30.3	11.4	14.0	8.7
EU-12														
Bulgaria	2006	2.0	4.6	1.0	2.2	60.8	64.1	64.6	20.5	16.1	16.5	18.7	19.8	18.8
Cyprus	2006	11.9	23.4	8.4	13.2	59.0	58.1	53.8	28.9	24.0	26.0	12.1	17.9	20.2
Czech Republic	2004	4.9	8.3	2.8	4.8	67.0	...	65.4	18.7	...	20.0	14.3	...	14.6
Estonia	2005	2.9	7.5	1.8	4.6	53.6	59.8	57.9	29.0	21.6	25.6	17.4	18.6	16.5
Hungary	2005	3.8	7.8	2.0	4.4	64.2	62.5	38.9	18.8	23.4	34.5	17.0	14.1	26.6
Latvia	2006	7.6	9.1	3.1	4.8	52.4	57.5	67.8	19.7	21.3	17.1	28.0	21.2	15.1
Lithuania	2006	4.0	6.7	2.4	3.9	62.2	59.1	62.0	22.6	22.7	22.2	15.2	18.3	15.8
Poland	2005	7.5	11.0	...	5.4	59.9	68.7	68.8	...	14.7	15.2	...	16.6	16.0
Romania	2006	...	5.1	...	4.0	...	56.8	57.8	...	28.3	33.2	...	14.8	9.1
Slovakia	2004	...	6.3	...	3.9	...	53.7	57.9	...	29.1	26.0	...	17.2	16.1
Other Europe														
Norway	2004	30.9	44.8	22.6	34.3	55.4	...	61.0	32.6	...	29.9	12.0	...	9.1

a/ At current prices.

Table 1.11
(continued)

SELECTED CHARACTERISTICS OF BRANCHES, SELECTED YEARS AND COUNTRIES

Knitted and crocheted fabrics and articles (ISIC 1730)														
Country or area	Latest year	Value added per employee (current 1000 dollars)		Wages and salaries per employee (current 1000 dollars)		Percentage in output a/								
						Costs of input materials and utilities			Costs of labour			Operating surplus		
	(LY)	2000	LY	2000	LY	2000	2003	LY	2000	2003	LY	2000	2003	LY
Other Countries														
Israel	2005	21.4	30.0	16.6	23.5	64.9	66.4	68.0	27.3	27.3	25.0	7.8	6.3	6.9
Japan	2005	43.1	42.5	12.5	11.1	57.8	55.8	56.8	12.2	10.9	11.2	30.0	33.3	32.0
Republic of Korea	2006	41.8	71.4	11.9	20.4	61.4	63.4	63.8	11.0	10.3	10.4	27.6	26.3	25.8
Singapore	2006	26.4	17.4	13.8	13.3	80.3	80.0	81.3	10.3	11.8	14.3	9.4	8.2	4.4
United States of America	2005	47.3	74.6	21.4	27.0	54.5	52.9	52.3	20.6	19.8	17.2	24.9	27.3	30.4
Developing Countries														
Brazil	2005	14.8	12.5	3.7	4.2	60.5	65.0	63.4	9.7	10.7	12.3	29.7	24.3	24.4
Chile	2006	...	18.5	...	7.8	...	57.9	57.2	...	18.9	18.0	...	23.2	24.8
Colombia	2005	14.9	20.5	3.6	4.7	57.5	60.5	59.5	10.4	10.8	9.3	32.1	28.6	31.2
Ecuador	2005	7.0	8.7	1.0	3.6	64.5	65.9	69.4	5.3	11.4	12.6	30.2	22.7	18.0
Eritrea	2006	2.1	2.9	0.7	0.9	51.1	30.5	39.5	15.2	19.8	17.8	33.7	49.6	42.7
Ethiopia	2006	0.7	1.8	0.3	0.4	47.1	53.5	51.4	20.3	8.4	11.3	32.6	38.0	37.3
India	2004	3.5	2.7	0.8	0.9	81.8	81.4	82.2	4.1	6.3	6.2	14.1	12.2	11.5
Indonesia	2005	2.0	5.2	0.7	1.2	66.8	67.6	59.3	10.9	10.8	9.6	22.4	21.5	31.2
Iran (Islamic Republic of)	2005	17.6	5.7	8.2	2.8	55.4	60.2	67.3	20.7	10.9	16.0	23.9	28.9	16.7
Jordan	2006	2.4	4.6	1.8	2.6	76.7	53.3	56.5	18.1	22.5	24.1	5.2	24.2	19.4
Madagascar	2006	...	0.1	...	0.1	...	33.7	24.3	...	46.5	71.1	...	19.8	4.6
Malaysia	2005	10.5	6.7	3.7	4.0	67.5	66.1	77.5	11.6	14.8	13.3	20.9	19.2	9.2
Morocco	2005	4.1	4.5	2.5	3.3	69.7	69.0	68.2	18.3	18.3	23.1	12.0	12.6	8.7
Sri Lanka	2006	...	9.0	...	1.2	...	...	31.1	...	...	8.8	...	...	60.1
Trinidad and Tobago	2006	6.5	...	...	...	68.6	75.0	70.0	...	...	...	...	...	...
Uruguay	2005	10.4	5.8	5.9	2.7	49.7	56.1	54.2	28.4	19.2	20.9	21.9	24.7	24.8

a/ At current prices.

Table 1.11

SELECTED CHARACTERISTICS OF BRANCHES, SELECTED YEARS AND COUNTRIES

Wearing apparel, except fur apparel (ISIC 1810)

Country or area	Latest year	Value added per employee (current 1000 dollars)		Wages and salaries per employee (current 1000 dollars)		Percentage in output a/								
						Costs of input materials and utilities			Costs of labour			Operating surplus		
	(LY)	2000	LY	2000	LY	2000	2003	LY	2000	2003	LY	2000	2003	LY
Industrialized Countries														
CIS														
Azerbaijan	2006	...	1.3	0.1	0.5	...	70.7	82.6	11.4	6.2	7.1	...	23.1	10.3
Georgia	2006	0.3	1.9	0.2	1.2	60.5	...	56.5	24.8	...	27.0	14.7	...	16.5
Kyrgyzstan	2005	...	4.6	0.2	0.3	...	79.4	73.8	6.3	10.2	1.6	...	10.4	24.6
Russian Federation	2006	...	6.4	0.5	2.1	...	67.8	57.4	21.4	10.8	13.8	...	21.4	28.8
EU-15														
Belgium	2005	...	53.5	...	24.6	...	81.6	73.8	...	10.9	12.1	...	7.4	14.2
Denmark	2005	41.6	67.6	27.4	43.1	71.7	73.1	76.3	18.6	18.1	15.1	9.7	8.8	8.6
Finland	2005	28.0	50.7	17.6	29.2	64.5	60.3	58.5	22.3	23.1	23.9	13.3	16.7	17.6
France	2005	28.6	55.8	17.1	30.2	72.6	...	70.2	16.4	...	16.1	11.0	...	13.7
Germany	2005	33.8	58.2	20.8	33.5	73.2	72.5	74.3	16.5	15.8	14.8	10.3	11.7	10.9
Greece	2004	...	31.3	...	14.8	...	...	66.3	...	...	15.9	...	...	17.7
Ireland	2005	...	66.2	...	30.7	...	...	49.3	...	...	23.5	...	...	27.2
Italy	2005	31.4	42.7	12.7	19.5	70.7	73.9	74.2	11.9	12.0	11.8	17.4	14.1	14.0
Portugal	2004	8.7	14.1	5.4	8.6	64.3	63.9	64.6	22.2	22.8	21.6	13.5	13.2	13.8
Spain	2005	18.0	28.9	9.8	18.3	67.5	66.9	71.1	17.7	17.7	18.3	14.8	15.4	10.6
Sweden	2005	40.7	72.0	18.9	32.0	66.0	...	71.7	15.8	...	12.6	18.2	...	15.7
United Kingdom	2005	...	70.4	...	28.0	...	...	54.1	...	...	18.2	...	...	27.7
EU-12														
Bulgaria	2006	1.4	3.0	0.8	1.6	53.7	61.2	61.7	26.1	20.4	19.8	20.3	18.4	18.5
Cyprus	2006	15.7	23.8	7.8	15.4	60.5	57.1	60.2	19.7	22.1	25.9	19.8	20.7	14.0
Czech Republic	2004	4.6	10.0	2.3	5.1	57.8	58.1	52.4	21.4	22.5	24.4	20.8	19.4	23.2
Estonia	2004	4.1	7.2	2.4	4.4	53.8	56.8	53.9	27.1	27.6	28.3	19.1	15.6	17.8
Hungary	2005	3.8	7.9	2.2	4.7	56.2	63.6	63.2	24.9	21.8	21.8	18.9	14.6	15.1
Latvia	2006	3.4	7.1	2.0	3.7	50.2	49.3	53.9	28.7	26.1	23.7	21.1	24.6	22.4
Lithuania	2006	3.0	6.3	1.8	3.9	42.1	53.0	56.4	34.6	26.9	26.7	23.3	20.1	16.9
Malta	2005	...	23.0	...	14.7	...	69.5	61.7	...	28.0	24.4	...	2.5	13.9
Poland	2005	5.4	6.8	...	4.1	49.5	59.6	57.4	...	24.0	25.9	...	16.5	16.6
Romania	2006	...	4.4	...	3.5	54.2	53.5	57.4	...	32.0	34.0	...	14.5	8.6
Slovakia	2005	2.5	5.5	2.0	4.0	62.2	51.4	54.8	31.3	32.3	32.6	6.5	16.3	12.6
Other Europe														
Norway	2004	34.2	65.8	22.2	35.4	60.2	65.2	58.1	25.9	20.5	22.5	13.9	14.3	19.4

a/ At current prices.

Table 1.11
(continued)

SELECTED CHARACTERISTICS OF BRANCHES, SELECTED YEARS AND COUNTRIES

Country or area	Latest year	Wearing apparel, except fur apparel (ISIC 1810)												
		Value added per employee (current 1000 dollars)		Wages and salaries per employee (current 1000 dollars)		Percentage in output[a/]								
						Costs of input materials and utilities			Costs of labour			Operating surplus		
	(LY)	2000	LY	2000	LY	2000	2003	LY	2000	2003	LY	2000	2003	LY
Other Countries														
Israel	2005	20.8	19.4	15.0	13.3	63.3	61.3	65.2	26.5	20.6	23.8	10.2	18.1	10.9
Japan	2005	36.8	34.1	10.8	10.2	47.6	47.7	48.5	15.4	15.3	15.4	37.0	37.1	36.1
Republic of Korea	2006	27.6	66.5	10.4	17.8	52.5	53.8	49.7	17.9	15.7	13.5	29.6	30.5	36.8
Singapore	2006	16.8	17.1	11.0	12.3	76.7	75.4	67.2	15.3	20.1	23.6	8.0	4.5	9.3
United States of America	2005	56.5	72.2	20.1	24.1	54.0	49.6	48.4	16.3	15.9	17.2	29.7	34.4	34.3
Developing Countries														
Chile	2006	...	22.6	...	8.8	...	63.3	58.7	...	15.7	16.1	...	21.1	25.2
Colombia	2005	9.6	14.7	2.3	3.0	49.9	53.7	52.7	11.7	10.4	9.5	38.4	35.9	37.7
Ecuador	2005	3.2	8.5	0.8	2.7	67.1	...	56.1	7.8	...	13.8	25.1	...	30.2
Eritrea	2006	1.8	1.6	0.7	0.6	35.9	47.8	66.7	26.8	30.8	12.8	37.3	21.4	20.5
Ethiopia	2006	0.9	0.9	0.5	0.7	55.8	40.7	61.9	24.3	29.4	31.6	19.9	29.8	6.5
Fiji	2004	...	5.6	...	3.9	...	68.6	68.5	...	22.5	21.9	...	8.9	9.5
India	2004	2.5	2.5	0.8	1.0	77.9	77.9	78.8	6.9	9.3	8.8	15.1	12.8	12.4
Indonesia	2005	2.2	2.7	0.8	1.0	63.2	60.0	67.9	12.7	13.2	12.1	24.2	26.8	20.0
Iran (Islamic Republic of)	2005	12.1	7.6	6.4	2.7	61.7	56.2	56.4	20.2	20.8	15.7	18.1	23.1	28.0
Jordan	2006	4.0	12.4	1.7	2.4	36.3	40.9	46.2	27.5	13.9	10.5	36.2	45.2	43.3
Madagascar	2006	...	0.3	...	0.2	...	56.4	50.2	...	18.4	28.2	...	25.2	21.6
Malaysia	2004	5.9	6.2	3.2	3.8	67.7	67.7	68.0	17.3	19.2	19.5	15.0	13.1	12.5
Morocco	2005	3.5	4.6	2.3	3.4	58.1	55.5	56.9	28.4	30.1	31.1	13.5	14.4	12.0
Oman	2006	6.0	5.0	2.8	3.3	63.1	53.4	54.7	17.3	22.8	30.0	19.7	23.8	15.4
Sri Lanka	2006	...	5.2	...	1.1	...	...	42.9	...	...	11.7	...	...	45.4
Trinidad and Tobago	2006	6.3	...	4.0	...	61.4	60.0	60.4	24.9	19.0	24.9	13.7	21.0	14.7
Uruguay	2005	9.7	6.5	5.8	2.9	62.3	63.1	59.0	22.7	16.6	18.4	15.0	20.3	22.5

a/ At current prices.

Table 1.11

SELECTED CHARACTERISTICS OF BRANCHES, SELECTED YEARS AND COUNTRIES

Tanning, dressing and processing of leather (ISIC 191)

Country or area	Latest year (LY)	Value added per employee (current 1000 dollars)		Wages and salaries per employee (current 1000 dollars)		Percentage in output [a/]: Costs of input materials and utilities			Costs of labour			Operating surplus		
		2000	LY	2000	LY	2000	2003	LY	2000	2003	LY	2000	2003	LY
Industrialized Countries														
CIS														
Azerbaijan	2006	...	2.9	0.0	0.5	...	71.0	70.9	1.3	5.2	5.0	...	23.8	24.1
Georgia	2006	...	2.0	...	0.6	...	83.5	62.3	...	11.2	12.4	...	5.3	25.3
Kyrgyzstan	2005	...	1.1	0.4	0.7	...	79.7	84.7	13.9	6.0	9.3	...	14.3	6.0
Russian Federation	2006	...	26.4	0.7	3.0	...	74.5	62.8	6.5	4.8	4.2	...	20.7	33.0
EU-15														
Austria	2005	32.5	46.2	15.9	26.7	78.2	...	76.3	10.6	...	13.7	11.1	...	10.0
Finland	2005	38.3	56.5	18.7	26.6	65.8	69.9	64.6	16.8	16.5	16.7	17.5	13.6	18.8
France	2005	37.1	58.2	17.8	28.2	59.4	58.3	58.4	19.4	20.3	20.1	21.2	21.4	21.4
Germany	2005	31.0	48.6	20.9	27.8	70.1	71.1	69.1	20.2	17.1	17.7	9.7	11.8	13.3
Greece	2004	...	36.1	...	17.3	...	...	65.3	...	...	16.7	...	...	18.1
Italy	2005	40.8	56.1	15.1	24.1	80.3	80.7	79.7	7.3	8.3	8.7	12.4	11.0	11.6
Netherlands	2005	46.0	65.7	24.4	36.3	74.7	74.2	73.6	13.4	14.4	14.6	11.9	11.4	11.8
Spain	2005	24.3	36.3	12.9	21.3	74.6	73.1	69.6	13.5	16.5	17.9	11.9	10.3	12.5
Sweden	2005	42.2	54.6	21.3	30.3	68.8	...	69.3	15.7	...	17.1	15.4	...	13.6
United Kingdom	2005	43.0	66.7	19.5	29.5	61.6	65.3	62.3	17.4	16.9	16.7	21.0	17.7	21.1
EU-12														
Bulgaria	2005	2.2	2.7	1.0	1.6	78.4	64.4	77.4	10.3	9.0	13.1	11.2	26.6	9.5
Cyprus	2006	18.0	38.1	10.3	15.9	51.2	48.9	47.2	27.9	38.1	22.0	20.8	13.1	30.8
Czech Republic	2004	5.1	10.1	2.9	5.2	67.3	64.8	63.3	18.3	20.1	19.0	14.3	15.1	17.7
Estonia	2006	3.1	7.4	2.1	4.7	67.2	59.3	61.4	21.5	23.4	24.4	11.3	17.3	14.1
Hungary	2005	...	8.6	...	6.7	...	60.0	75.8	...	25.7	18.8	...	14.3	5.3
Latvia	2006	4.1	5.7	1.3	2.8	52.2	66.4	73.6	15.3	17.2	13.2	32.5	16.4	13.2
Lithuania	2006	5.4	10.4	2.3	3.5	83.3	75.2	59.6	7.2	11.9	13.7	9.5	13.0	26.7
Malta	2005	10.0	14.3	8.1	11.8	61.8	60.5	61.1	31.1	31.4	32.0	7.1	8.1	6.9
Poland	2005	7.1	9.9	...	5.0	67.5	74.5	69.6	...	14.0	15.5	...	11.5	14.9
Romania	2006	...	5.2	...	3.8	...	67.9	65.0	...	18.9	25.9	...	13.2	9.1
Other Europe														
Norway	2004	...	59.5	...	43.1	...	75.1	69.6	...	21.2	22.0	...	3.7	8.4

a/ At current prices.

Table 1.11
(continued)

SELECTED CHARACTERISTICS OF BRANCHES, SELECTED YEARS AND COUNTRIES

Country or area	Latest year	Value added per employee (current 1000 dollars)		Wages and salaries per employee (current 1000 dollars)		Percentage in output a/								
		Tanning, dressing and processing of leather (ISIC 191)				Costs of input materials and utilities			Costs of labour			Operating surplus		
	(LY)	2000	LY	2000	LY	2000	2003	LY	2000	2003	LY	2000	2003	LY
Other Countries														
Japan	2005	67.6	68.6	13.8	14.4	58.8	59.6	61.0	8.4	7.8	8.2	32.8	32.6	30.8
Republic of Korea	2006	50.4	73.5	13.4	21.7	67.0	68.9	65.5	8.8	9.6	10.2	24.2	21.5	24.3
Singapore	2006	30.3	31.7	13.8	19.1	78.0	76.0	76.9	10.0	14.4	14.0	12.0	9.5	9.2
South Africa	2006	6.8	13.7	4.3	5.8	84.5	84.7	82.8	9.8	10.1	7.3	5.7	5.2	9.9
United States of America	2005	73.9	83.3	25.2	30.4	52.2	53.1	54.6	16.3	16.6	16.6	31.5	30.2	28.8
Developing Countries														
Botswana	2006	15.2	26.8	...	19.5	69.9	70.4	70.1	...	...	21.8	...	...	8.1
Brazil	2005	8.8	12.2	3.2	3.7	73.4	71.2	69.5	9.6	7.1	9.3	17.0	21.6	21.3
Chile	2006	...	25.6	...	9.0	...	68.2	68.9	...	12.1	11.0	...	19.7	20.2
Colombia	2005	10.7	16.4	2.6	3.3	58.8	58.9	57.5	10.2	8.1	8.6	31.0	33.1	33.9
Ecuador	2005	5.4	7.8	0.9	2.9	74.1	75.0	72.2	4.2	8.3	10.4	21.7	16.7	17.4
Eritrea	2006	2.8	1.9	0.9	1.0	69.4	75.0	80.2	10.4	11.1	10.3	20.3	14.0	9.5
Ethiopia	2006	3.6	4.0	1.1	1.3	72.3	81.0	80.7	8.4	6.0	6.4	19.4	13.0	12.9
India	2004	1.9	2.5	0.8	0.9	90.1	90.1	89.1	4.1	3.7	4.0	5.8	6.1	7.0
Indonesia	2005	3.0	6.4	0.6	1.0	66.8	64.4	79.5	6.9	7.6	3.1	26.3	28.0	17.4
Iran (Islamic Republic of)	2005	28.2	14.2	6.4	2.7	70.8	77.9	65.6	6.6	4.8	6.6	22.6	17.4	27.8
Jordan	2006	10.1	3.8	4.5	3.3	66.9	69.9	74.7	14.6	18.9	21.9	18.5	11.2	3.4
Madagascar	2005	...	0.1	...	0.0	...	39.0	32.4	...	18.1	25.2	...	42.9	42.5
Malaysia	2005	6.1	7.0	3.4	4.1	71.9	67.4	74.6	15.7	18.3	14.8	12.5	14.3	10.5
Morocco	2005	5.8	6.8	3.0	4.4	75.7	69.4	64.7	12.5	18.3	22.7	11.9	12.3	12.6
Peru	2006	...	1.8	...	0.9	...	77.8	78.2	...	9.9	11.0	...	12.3	10.8
Uruguay	2005	40.8	16.9	12.9	5.8	80.3	80.7	79.4	6.2	4.9	7.0	13.5	14.3	13.6

a/ At current prices.

Table 1.11

SELECTED CHARACTERISTICS OF BRANCHES, SELECTED YEARS AND COUNTRIES

Footwear (ISIC 1920)

Country or area	Latest year	Value added per employee (current 1000 dollars)		Wages and salaries per employee (current 1000 dollars)		Percentage in output a/								
						Costs of input materials and utilities			Costs of labour			Operating surplus		
	(LY)	2000	LY	2000	LY	2000	2003	LY	2000	2003	LY	2000	2003	LY
Industrialized Countries														
CIS														
Azerbaijan	2006	...	2.0	0.2	0.8	...	71.0	70.9	14.1	8.0	11.0	...	21.0	18.0
Georgia	2006	...	0.8	...	0.5	...	88.6	87.3	...	6.0	7.3	...	5.4	5.4
Kyrgyzstan	2005	...	1.5	0.3	0.4	...	...	67.7	11.1	...	7.5	...	...	24.9
Russian Federation	2006	...	...	0.6	2.3	...	...	...	17.8	...	...	...	...	...
EU-15														
Austria	2005	31.3	68.6	17.5	32.5	66.8	62.6	65.5	18.6	21.0	16.3	14.6	16.4	18.2
Finland	2005	31.3	47.8	17.2	28.4	58.1	59.4	60.4	23.1	24.1	23.5	18.8	16.5	16.1
France	2005	26.2	39.7	16.6	25.5	65.8	68.0	66.4	21.6	21.3	21.6	12.6	10.7	12.0
Germany	2005	34.9	59.0	21.0	31.3	71.7	71.2	72.7	17.0	16.1	14.5	11.3	12.7	12.8
Greece	2004	...	37.6	...	16.8	...	...	58.5	...	...	18.6	...	...	22.9
Italy	2005	29.6	43.7	12.6	20.9	73.9	74.8	75.8	11.1	12.3	11.6	15.0	12.9	12.6
Netherlands	2005	29.6	92.1	18.3	47.6	65.6	58.6	63.5	21.2	22.8	18.9	13.1	18.6	17.6
Portugal	2005	9.3	14.1	5.8	8.6	70.7	69.5	68.3	18.2	18.9	19.2	11.1	11.6	12.5
Spain	2005	17.0	27.3	9.5	15.9	74.9	74.7	75.3	14.1	14.1	14.4	11.0	11.1	10.3
Sweden	2005	31.9	51.4	19.9	27.7	69.9	...	67.4	18.7	...	17.6	11.4	...	15.0
United Kingdom	2005	46.7	47.2	23.6	26.4	49.2	50.8	56.9	25.7	22.0	24.1	25.1	27.3	19.0
EU-12														
Bulgaria	2005	1.2	2.3	0.8	1.3	61.3	69.0	68.0	24.4	16.9	18.1	14.4	14.1	13.9
Cyprus	2006	17.4	28.3	10.0	16.0	55.8	55.2	48.4	25.4	29.2	29.1	18.8	15.5	22.5
Czech Republic	2004	3.8	7.3	2.6	4.8	65.6	65.0	60.5	23.1	23.6	25.8	11.3	11.4	13.7
Estonia	2006	5.4	9.7	2.9	6.2	68.3	...	53.7	16.9	...	29.6	14.9	...	16.7
Hungary	2005	3.9	8.6	2.3	5.0	56.6	56.5	52.9	25.6	30.3	27.3	17.7	13.2	19.8
Latvia	2006	...	6.2	...	3.0	...	53.6	58.1	...	26.7	20.1	...	19.8	21.9
Lithuania	2006	...	8.1	...	4.5	...	63.0	58.3	...	25.0	23.1	...	12.1	18.6
Malta	2005	15.7	17.6	9.1	13.5	68.6	67.6	66.9	18.3	21.4	25.5	13.1	11.0	7.6
Poland	2005	5.6	10.5	...	4.8	66.0	66.6	67.3	...	18.1	15.1	...	15.3	17.7
Romania	2006	...	4.5	...	3.6	...	57.6	62.3	...	29.6	29.8	...	12.7	7.9
Slovakia	2005	2.6	8.0	2.1	4.4	74.1	76.1	72.9	20.8	14.8	14.9	5.1	9.2	12.2
Other Europe														
Norway	2004	...	46.3	...	34.3	...	63.0	63.0	...	27.4	27.4	...	9.6	9.6

a/ At current prices.

Table 1.11
(continued)

SELECTED CHARACTERISTICS OF BRANCHES, SELECTED YEARS AND COUNTRIES

Footwear (ISIC 1920)														
Country or area	Latest year	Value added per employee (current 1000 dollars)		Wages and salaries per employee (current 1000 dollars)		Percentage in output [a/]								
						Costs of input materials and utilities			Costs of labour			Operating surplus		
	(LY)	2000	LY	2000	LY	2000	2003	LY	2000	2003	LY	2000	2003	LY
Other Countries														
Israel	2005	24.8	27.7	18.0	19.1	66.9	66.5	64.4	24.1	21.5	24.6	9.0	12.0	11.0
Japan	2005	51.9	52.2	15.0	14.6	60.9	59.6	60.5	11.3	10.2	11.0	27.8	30.1	28.4
Republic of Korea	2006	28.7	54.0	11.0	18.6	55.5	55.9	56.8	17.0	16.0	14.9	27.5	28.2	28.3
Singapore	2006	28.6	16.2	19.2	10.7	62.0	75.9	82.9	25.5	22.2	11.2	12.5	1.9	5.9
South Africa	2006	7.9	12.1	3.2	5.8	74.3	75.1	74.6	10.5	15.3	12.0	15.2	9.6	13.3
United States of America	2005	56.0	67.4	22.9	28.1	54.7	50.2	47.8	18.5	21.9	21.7	26.8	27.9	30.4
Developing Countries														
Brazil	2005	8.0	8.0	2.6	3.2	55.9	56.2	54.2	14.6	15.6	18.2	29.6	28.2	27.6
Chile	2006	...	26.8	...	8.5	...	54.5	55.2	...	21.0	14.2	...	24.5	30.6
Colombia	2005	9.4	13.2	2.3	2.8	53.8	55.8	54.3	11.5	9.6	9.8	34.7	34.6	35.9
Ecuador	2005	4.4	10.2	1.0	3.2	75.3	71.9	69.1	5.6	10.9	9.8	19.1	17.2	21.0
Eritrea	2006	2.0	3.4	0.6	0.8	57.0	61.2	55.1	13.1	13.0	9.9	29.9	25.8	34.9
Ethiopia	2006	2.6	3.0	0.7	0.8	64.0	60.0	65.4	10.1	11.4	9.2	25.9	28.6	25.5
Fiji	2004	...	5.9	...	5.0	...	72.2	54.4	...	20.2	38.6	...	7.6	6.9
India	2004	2.4	2.4	0.8	0.9	83.0	81.5	84.7	5.7	6.8	6.1	11.3	11.7	9.2
Indonesia	2005	2.6	3.5	0.8	1.3	58.7	60.0	60.8	12.7	8.3	14.9	28.6	31.6	24.3
Iran (Islamic Republic of)	2005	9.9	6.2	7.2	2.7	61.7	60.7	66.4	27.8	14.4	14.5	10.5	25.0	19.0
Jordan	2006	5.9	8.4	2.7	1.2	73.2	62.6	62.8	12.4	14.4	5.6	14.3	23.0	31.7
Madagascar	2006	...	0.5	...	0.2	...	45.4	45.8	...	14.7	21.6	...	39.9	32.6
Malaysia	2005	4.6	7.4	2.9	4.5	67.3	62.8	69.1	20.6	20.6	18.9	12.1	16.6	11.9
Morocco	2005	4.0	5.5	2.8	3.8	60.3	60.9	60.0	27.0	26.5	28.0	12.6	12.7	12.0
Oman	2006	12.3	19.7	5.0	5.1	49.8	58.7	56.6	20.4	20.4	11.2	29.8	20.9	32.1
Peru	2006	...	0.3	...	0.3	...	64.2	64.4	...	20.4	26.3	...	15.5	9.2
Qatar	2006	...	6.1	...	5.8	...	...	79.5	...	...	19.5	...	...	1.1
Sri Lanka	2006	...	3.1	...	1.0	...	...	57.2	...	...	14.4	...	...	28.4
Trinidad and Tobago	2006	7.3	...	3.8	...	53.6	38.3	53.8	24.2	18.3	23.1	22.2	43.3	23.1
Uruguay	2005	14.1	6.0	5.5	2.9	66.1	69.1	65.8	13.2	15.1	16.5	20.7	15.9	17.7

a/ At current prices.

Table 1.11

SELECTED CHARACTERISTICS OF BRANCHES, SELECTED YEARS AND COUNTRIES

Sawmilling and planing of wood (ISIC 2010)														
Country or area	Latest year	Value added per employee (current 1000 dollars)		Wages and salaries per employee (current 1000 dollars)		Percentage in output [a]								
						Costs of input materials and utilities			Costs of labour			Operating surplus		
	(LY)	2000	LY	2000	LY	2000	2003	LY	2000	2003	LY	2000	2003	LY
Industrialized Countries														
CIS														
Georgia	2006	0.5	1.9	0.2	0.6	71.1	66.1	63.7	13.2	11.2	10.8	15.7	22.7	25.5
Russian Federation	2006	...	11.0	0.8	2.8	...	65.0	59.4	16.5	20.5	10.2	...	14.6	30.4
EU-15														
Austria	2005	55.6	73.0	21.2	34.0	72.3	74.3	75.7	10.6	10.9	11.3	17.1	14.8	13.0
Belgium	2005	40.2	72.3	18.4	29.4	78.1	78.9	78.1	10.1	10.0	8.9	11.9	11.1	13.0
Denmark	2005	41.8	61.1	26.2	38.8	67.1	65.2	66.4	20.6	23.3	21.4	12.3	11.5	12.2
Finland	2005	51.8	64.6	22.5	35.9	80.2	82.8	84.2	8.6	8.7	8.8	11.2	8.5	7.0
France	2005	34.6	49.7	17.7	28.1	67.8	67.6	68.8	16.5	18.5	17.7	15.7	13.9	13.5
Germany	2005	38.5	62.0	18.8	30.2	72.7	74.2	74.2	13.3	14.3	12.6	13.9	11.6	13.3
Greece	2004	...	34.4	...	17.2	...	...	64.7	...	...	17.6	...	...	17.6
Ireland	2005	46.7	103.1	21.7	36.9	73.5	65.9	69.9	12.3	11.6	10.8	14.2	22.4	19.3
Italy	2005	37.5	64.4	13.5	22.1	73.2	71.4	70.7	9.7	9.8	10.0	17.1	18.8	19.2
Netherlands	2005	56.2	70.7	26.6	38.9	70.6	...	64.9	13.9	...	19.3	15.5	...	15.8
Portugal	2005	12.4	19.5	6.2	9.7	73.8	71.8	72.7	13.2	15.5	13.5	13.0	12.6	13.7
Spain	2005	23.9	40.3	11.5	19.7	73.7	74.3	71.2	12.7	13.6	14.1	13.6	12.2	14.8
Sweden	2005	51.7	72.3	23.9	35.2	79.6	...	81.5	9.5	...	9.0	11.0	...	9.5
United Kingdom	2005	38.0	76.7	19.3	33.9	59.7	64.5	60.0	20.5	15.8	17.7	19.9	19.7	22.3
EU-12														
Bulgaria	2006	1.1	4.1	0.7	1.4	86.2	82.4	79.6	8.9	7.6	6.9	4.9	9.9	13.5
Cyprus	2006	15.3	27.7	9.3	12.1	59.8	62.7	53.9	24.3	24.3	20.1	15.9	13.0	25.9
Czech Republic	2004	5.5	16.2	3.1	5.6	82.3	77.6	75.7	10.0	7.9	8.5	7.7	14.4	15.8
Estonia	2006	6.9	20.0	2.6	7.2	78.5	78.2	79.0	8.0	7.8	7.6	13.5	14.0	13.4
Hungary	2005	4.6	8.4	2.0	4.3	71.1	71.3	74.0	12.9	14.8	13.2	16.1	13.9	12.8
Latvia	2006	5.1	13.4	1.7	4.0	68.0	72.3	73.6	10.6	7.8	7.8	21.4	19.9	18.6
Lithuania	2006	3.1	7.4	1.7	3.7	76.3	76.5	76.1	12.9	10.2	12.2	10.8	13.4	11.7
Poland	2005	6.7	11.8	...	4.9	72.5	73.1	73.9	...	12.9	10.7	...	14.0	15.4
Romania	2006	...	5.4	...	2.8	...	78.0	80.9	...	10.2	9.7	...	11.7	9.3
Slovakia	2005	3.7	8.0	2.3	4.5	74.5	78.8	76.4	15.6	15.3	13.1	9.9	6.0	10.5
Other Europe														
Norway	2004	51.5	65.5	27.6	40.8	69.9	74.4	78.2	16.1	17.9	13.6	14.0	7.7	8.2

a/ At current prices.

Table 1.11
(continued)

SELECTED CHARACTERISTICS OF BRANCHES, SELECTED YEARS AND COUNTRIES

Sawmilling and planing of wood (ISIC 2010)														
Country or area	Latest year	Value added per employee (current 1000 dollars)		Wages and salaries per employee (current 1000 dollars)		Percentage in output a/								
						Costs of input materials and utilities			Costs of labour			Operating surplus		
	(LY)	2000	LY	2000	LY	2000	2003	LY	2000	2003	LY	2000	2003	LY
Other Countries														
Japan	2005	63.4	60.0	6.9	7.3	63.8	62.8	64.8	3.9	4.2	4.3	32.3	33.0	30.9
Republic of Korea	2006	44.3	66.3	12.2	20.0	60.1	65.5	68.1	11.0	11.9	9.6	28.9	22.6	22.3
Singapore	2004	35.6	27.2	22.5	16.8	58.6	51.5	61.3	26.2	28.3	23.9	15.3	20.3	14.8
United States of America	2005	60.5	103.9	27.0	36.8	69.7	67.9	66.6	13.5	13.3	11.8	16.8	18.8	21.6
Developing Countries														
Brazil	2005	6.4	11.3	2.3	3.3	47.2	51.3	51.3	18.5	13.5	14.1	34.3	35.2	34.6
Chile	2006	...	49.8	...	7.1	...	63.5	61.1	...	5.8	5.5	...	30.7	33.4
Colombia	2005	10.3	14.4	3.1	3.9	74.4	52.7	65.6	7.7	17.5	9.3	17.9	29.7	25.1
Ecuador	2005	6.5	8.2	1.4	3.3	62.9	66.7	79.9	8.0	12.5	8.2	29.1	20.8	11.9
Fiji	2004	...	13.5	...	8.6	...	74.9	77.7	...	12.4	14.3	...	12.7	8.1
India	2004	1.0	0.9	0.4	0.5	87.3	91.0	96.1	4.9	4.0	2.2	7.8	5.0	1.7
Indonesia	2005	2.2	2.5	0.6	0.6	61.9	72.6	76.4	9.6	4.1	5.9	28.4	23.4	17.7
Iran (Islamic Republic of)	2005	12.8	5.2	8.0	4.1	50.7	32.3	40.5	30.6	45.9	47.6	18.7	21.7	11.9
Jordan	2006	10.7	4.3	2.2	2.4	74.2	67.1	81.9	5.2	7.5	10.4	20.6	25.4	7.7
Madagascar	2006	...	0.1	...	0.0	...	54.8	54.6	...	15.6	22.2	...	29.6	23.2
Malaysia	2005	7.6	7.1	3.1	4.0	72.4	72.5	79.3	11.2	13.3	11.7	16.4	14.2	9.0
Morocco	2005	7.7	10.3	3.5	3.8	84.7	86.9	85.8	7.0	4.5	5.2	8.3	8.6	9.0
Qatar	2006	16.7	9.9	1.2	1.9	36.4	32.5	40.7	4.6	20.0	11.1	59.0	47.5	48.1
Sri Lanka	2006	...	4.6	...	1.1	...	...	24.4	...	...	18.1	...	...	57.5
Trinidad and Tobago	2004	5.1	...	2.0	...	69.2	70.6	64.6	12.2	17.2	21.5	18.6	12.1	14.0
Uruguay	2005	22.7	19.6	8.6	5.1	66.5	63.7	79.1	12.7	3.8	5.4	20.7	32.5	15.5

a/ At current prices.

Table 1.11

SELECTED CHARACTERISTICS OF BRANCHES, SELECTED YEARS AND COUNTRIES

	Products of wood, cork, straw, etc. (ISIC 202)													
Country or area	Latest year	Value added per employee (current 1000 dollars)		Wages and salaries per employee (current 1000 dollars)		Percentage in output [a]								
						Costs of input materials and utilities			Costs of labour			Operating surplus		
	(LY)	2000	LY	2000	LY	2000	2003	LY	2000	2003	LY	2000	2003	LY
Industrialized Countries														
CIS														
Azerbaijan	2006	...	1.8	0.1	1.0	...	68.4	82.0	7.2	8.2	10.5	...	23.4	7.5
Georgia	2006	0.6	1.8	0.2	0.6	65.6	...	66.2	11.3	12.8	12.5	23.1	...	21.4
Russian Federation	2006	...	10.5	0.6	3.3	...	62.8	59.7	24.2	13.9	12.4	...	23.2	27.8
EU-15														
Austria	2005	36.7	61.8	21.6	33.5	64.9	64.7	65.9	20.7	19.3	18.5	14.4	16.0	15.6
Belgium	2005	55.5	90.6	20.7	33.3	72.8	72.0	72.0	10.2	9.4	10.3	17.0	18.5	17.8
Denmark	2005	40.5	65.7	28.1	43.6	60.9	61.9	61.3	27.1	27.2	25.7	12.0	10.9	13.1
Finland	2005	39.8	58.5	21.3	33.4	65.8	71.2	71.2	18.3	16.4	16.4	16.0	12.4	12.4
France	2005	35.3	53.7	17.9	28.4	71.0	72.2	69.8	14.7	15.0	16.0	14.3	12.7	14.2
Germany	2005	35.1	53.2	23.6	31.5	64.5	65.8	68.4	23.8	20.2	18.7	11.7	14.0	12.8
Greece	2004	...	40.7	...	15.5	...	...	65.0	...	...	13.4	...	...	21.7
Ireland	2005	34.1	65.9	18.5	33.4	71.1	70.0	64.6	15.7	17.8	17.9	13.2	12.3	17.4
Italy	2005	39.6	57.3	13.6	21.9	68.7	70.2	69.7	10.7	11.1	11.6	20.6	18.7	18.7
Netherlands	2005	44.3	67.1	23.7	37.3	65.4	64.8	66.3	18.5	20.2	18.7	16.1	15.0	15.0
Portugal	2005	16.0	22.9	7.2	10.8	77.8	76.1	74.6	10.1	11.0	12.0	12.1	13.0	13.4
Spain	2005	23.9	40.3	11.8	20.9	71.4	70.5	70.1	14.1	15.2	15.5	14.4	14.3	14.4
Sweden	2005	43.2	62.8	22.3	31.9	68.1	...	67.7	16.5	...	16.4	15.4	...	15.9
United Kingdom	2005	43.5	66.5	22.6	32.4	61.3	60.6	59.0	20.1	20.0	20.0	18.7	19.4	21.0
EU-12														
Bulgaria	2006	2.0	6.8	1.0	2.2	80.7	81.2	74.1	9.2	9.1	8.5	10.1	9.7	17.4
Cyprus	2006	20.9	37.8	10.8	22.0	56.3	57.9	58.8	22.7	20.7	24.0	21.0	21.4	17.3
Czech Republic	2004	7.0	18.1	3.0	5.5	73.7	68.1	68.2	11.5	9.9	9.7	14.9	22.0	22.1
Estonia	2006	6.2	16.9	2.8	7.9	70.5	68.4	69.3	13.6	13.7	14.3	16.0	17.9	16.4
Hungary	2005	5.6	11.9	2.4	5.7	72.1	72.7	71.1	12.0	13.2	13.8	15.9	14.1	15.1
Latvia	2006	7.9	12.3	3.5	5.9	60.0	70.0	76.6	17.9	14.3	11.2	22.1	15.7	12.1
Lithuania	2006	3.6	10.3	2.1	5.0	69.8	71.7	69.5	17.3	14.5	14.8	12.9	13.8	15.7
Malta	2005	17.5	21.1	5.8	10.5	49.0	56.0	58.5	16.9	21.6	20.7	34.2	22.4	20.7
Poland	2005	11.6	17.0	...	5.5	67.6	70.7	72.7	...	10.1	8.8	...	19.3	18.5
Romania	2006	...	6.8	...	3.8	...	74.5	79.9	...	12.5	11.2	...	12.9	8.9
Slovakia	2005	4.6	13.4	2.5	5.4	77.2	79.9	76.5	12.3	10.4	9.4	10.5	9.7	14.1
Other Europe														
Norway	2004	40.0	64.6	27.3	42.4	66.4	66.8	64.3	22.9	23.1	23.4	10.7	10.1	12.3

a/ At current prices.

Table 1.11
(continued)

SELECTED CHARACTERISTICS OF BRANCHES, SELECTED YEARS AND COUNTRIES

Products of wood, cork, straw, etc. (ISIC 202)														
Country or area	Latest year	Value added per employee (current 1000 dollars)		Wages and salaries per employee (current 1000 dollars)		Percentage in output [a]								
						Costs of input materials and utilities			Costs of labour			Operating surplus		
	(LY)	2000	LY	2000	LY	2000	2003	LY	2000	2003	LY	2000	2003	LY
Other Countries														
Israel	2005	30.1	21.9	23.0	18.3	64.8	65.1	71.1	27.0	23.3	24.1	8.2	11.6	4.7
Japan	2005	69.1	69.1	13.3	12.8	60.1	60.2	61.1	7.7	7.4	7.2	32.2	32.4	31.7
Republic of Korea	2006	46.6	65.7	13.3	22.5	59.2	64.1	64.9	11.7	11.8	12.0	29.2	24.1	23.1
Singapore	2006	25.6	22.1	15.9	16.1	76.5	78.0	79.4	14.6	16.0	15.0	8.9	6.0	5.6
United States of America	2005	61.5	78.0	27.1	32.2	56.3	55.3	57.3	19.3	19.0	17.6	24.4	25.6	25.1
Developing Countries														
Brazil	2005	9.7	13.3	3.0	3.9	49.6	51.2	56.9	15.5	12.6	12.8	34.8	36.2	30.3
Chile	2006	...	55.9	...	10.8	...	58.0	53.1	...	9.4	9.1	...	32.7	37.8
Colombia	2005	19.1	25.5	3.1	3.8	46.1	50.7	53.5	8.8	7.5	7.0	45.0	41.8	39.6
Ecuador	2005	9.4	24.2	1.6	4.3	67.0	61.0	53.5	5.6	8.0	8.3	27.4	31.0	38.2
India	2004	1.9	2.5	0.7	0.9	82.2	84.7	85.1	6.5	5.0	5.1	11.4	10.3	9.8
Indonesia	2005	4.2	5.8	0.8	1.3	63.7	58.6	62.6	6.9	8.0	8.5	29.3	33.4	28.9
Iran (Islamic Republic of)	2005	22.8	11.8	9.7	4.1	54.2	55.8	57.0	19.6	17.0	15.1	26.2	27.2	27.9
Jordan	2006	5.3	4.8	2.3	1.0	66.8	61.7	58.4	14.3	10.0	9.0	18.9	28.3	32.6
Madagascar	2006	...	0.2	...	0.1	...	29.3	28.8	...	25.1	35.7	...	45.7	35.5
Malaysia	2005	8.9	8.5	2.6	3.4	67.8	67.5	75.8	9.5	10.7	9.7	22.6	21.9	14.5
Morocco	2005	7.6	8.9	3.2	5.2	66.3	72.1	74.8	14.2	15.2	14.7	19.5	12.7	10.5
Oman	2006	10.5	33.4	4.4	5.2	49.0	54.1	37.6	21.2	25.3	9.7	29.8	20.6	52.6
Qatar	2006	11.2	11.3	4.2	4.2	45.4	41.6	34.9	20.3	20.7	23.9	34.3	37.7	41.2
Sri Lanka	2006	...	2.0	...	0.7	...	...	37.3	...	...	23.1	...	...	39.6
Uruguay	2005	8.5	4.9	5.5	2.8	53.2	64.1	65.9	30.6	19.2	19.7	16.2	16.7	14.4

a/ At current prices.

Table 1.11

SELECTED CHARACTERISTICS OF BRANCHES, SELECTED YEARS AND COUNTRIES

Paper and paper products (ISIC 210)

Country or area	Latest year	Value added per employee (current 1000 dollars)		Wages and salaries per employee (current 1000 dollars)		Percentage in output [a/]								
						Costs of input materials and utilities			Costs of labour			Operating surplus		
	(LY)	2000	LY	2000	LY	2000	2003	LY	2000	2003	LY	2000	2003	LY
Industrialized Countries														
CIS														
Azerbaijan	2006	...	5.9	0.1	1.0	...	61.6	69.6	5.2	2.5	5.2	...	35.9	25.2
Georgia	2006	1.1	2.8	0.5	1.3	60.2	81.9	76.6	16.7	7.3	10.5	23.1	10.8	12.9
Kyrgyzstan	2006	...	...	0.3	1.0	...	...	...	9.4	19.5	10.0	...	...	...
Republic of Moldova	2006	...	3.7	0.5	1.8	...	84.9	85.2	10.6	8.6	7.3	...	6.6	7.5
Russian Federation	2006	...	18.2	1.6	5.0	...	69.1	69.8	7.8	10.6	8.3	...	20.3	21.9
EU-15														
Austria	2005	87.6	109.5	32.3	48.3	67.2	65.9	68.6	12.1	14.0	13.9	20.7	20.0	17.6
Belgium	2005	70.2	91.3	28.9	43.5	71.2	73.8	76.0	11.9	11.5	11.4	17.0	14.7	12.6
Denmark	2005	55.9	77.9	34.1	54.7	64.0	62.2	66.0	22.0	23.6	23.8	14.0	14.2	10.1
Finland	2005	123.7	111.4	32.0	49.6	64.4	73.8	75.3	9.2	11.2	11.0	26.4	15.0	13.7
France	2005	50.1	64.9	24.3	37.6	75.2	72.8	75.3	12.0	13.9	14.3	12.8	13.3	10.4
Germany	2005	57.3	81.2	30.5	44.5	68.8	68.4	69.7	16.6	17.5	16.6	14.6	14.1	13.7
Greece	2004	...	51.0	...	23.6	...	...	67.8	...	...	14.9	...	...	17.3
Ireland	2005	56.2	79.1	26.1	45.2	61.9	57.8	60.9	17.7	19.1	22.3	20.4	23.1	16.8
Italy	2005	54.1	73.4	20.0	30.4	75.2	75.2	75.9	9.1	9.9	10.0	15.6	14.9	14.2
Netherlands	2005	58.1	90.0	29.4	47.6	70.4	68.8	71.1	15.0	16.0	15.3	14.6	15.2	13.6
Portugal	2005	62.1	71.4	13.2	21.1	59.7	69.1	68.7	8.6	9.0	9.3	31.8	21.9	22.0
Spain	2005	51.3	74.6	19.6	32.7	70.3	70.7	70.8	11.4	12.4	12.8	18.4	16.9	16.4
Sweden	2005	105.3	109.5	28.6	43.3	62.7	...	72.7	10.2	...	10.8	27.2	...	16.5
United Kingdom	2005	62.5	67.8	32.5	43.3	64.9	67.5	74.1	18.3	18.6	16.5	16.9	14.0	9.4
EU-12														
Bulgaria	2006	1.7	7.1	1.2	2.5	83.9	82.3	78.6	11.3	8.2	7.5	4.8	9.5	13.9
Cyprus	2006	22.8	35.9	11.8	20.2	63.3	62.2	63.0	18.9	18.8	20.9	17.7	19.0	16.2
Czech Republic	2004	17.5	26.0	4.3	7.8	72.9	74.5	74.2	6.6	8.0	7.7	20.5	17.5	18.1
Estonia	2006	12.0	22.6	4.1	9.3	72.0	72.7	75.6	9.7	10.1	10.1	18.4	17.2	14.3
Hungary	2005	14.2	19.0	4.9	8.6	78.3	71.4	71.2	7.5	11.5	13.0	14.1	17.1	15.8
Latvia	2006	8.9	17.3	2.9	6.5	67.8	71.7	70.9	10.4	9.2	10.9	21.8	19.1	18.2
Lithuania	2006	6.0	16.2	3.2	6.9	72.8	76.2	76.3	14.5	9.2	10.1	12.6	14.5	13.6
Malta	2005	20.1	25.7	11.2	15.4	62.0	62.8	63.8	21.1	23.3	21.8	16.9	13.9	14.4
Poland	2005	16.4	31.5	...	8.7	74.7	72.1	72.0	...	7.9	7.7	...	20.0	20.3
Romania	2006	8.0	8.5	1.2	5.2	64.4	80.6	81.3	5.2	9.8	11.4	30.4	9.6	7.3
Slovakia	2005	16.0	30.9	3.6	8.5	73.1	76.5	78.6	6.1	6.4	5.9	20.8	17.1	15.6
Other Europe														
Norway	2004	102.5	91.9	38.7	53.5	58.4	69.6	73.7	15.7	17.5	15.3	25.9	12.8	11.0

a/ At current prices.

Table 1.11
(continued)

SELECTED CHARACTERISTICS OF BRANCHES, SELECTED YEARS AND COUNTRIES

Paper and paper products (ISIC 210)														
Country or area	Latest year	Value added per employee (current 1000 dollars)		Wages and salaries per employee (current 1000 dollars)		Percentage in output [a/]								
						Costs of input materials and utilities			Costs of labour			Operating surplus		
	(LY)	2000	LY	2000	LY	2000	2003	LY	2000	2003	LY	2000	2003	LY
Other Countries														
Israel	2005	44.2	33.4	27.6	22.4	64.4	67.6	71.6	22.3	19.6	19.1	13.4	12.8	9.3
Japan	2005	114.8	118.1	29.1	27.7	62.5	62.5	63.6	9.5	8.9	8.5	28.0	28.6	27.9
New Zealand	2006	49.2	86.9	...	42.8	66.8	68.3	71.6	...	14.7	14.0	...	17.0	14.4
Republic of Korea	2006	79.7	97.2	16.0	25.8	63.5	61.9	64.2	7.3	9.0	9.5	29.2	29.1	26.3
Singapore	2006	43.3	36.2	19.0	21.6	60.5	77.0	74.2	17.4	16.4	15.4	22.1	6.6	10.4
South Africa	2006	23.3	39.2	10.2	7.1	75.4	76.2	78.2	10.7	12.8	4.0	13.9	11.0	17.9
United States of America	2005	141.8	176.7	41.0	48.2	52.6	51.6	53.4	13.7	13.9	12.7	33.7	34.5	33.9
Developing Countries														
Brazil	2005	45.8	45.2	7.8	8.8	46.8	50.5	54.2	9.0	7.9	8.9	44.2	41.6	36.9
Chile	2006	...	...	...	15.9	...	50.3	47.2	...	5.9	5.8	...	43.8	47.0
Colombia	2005	37.2	46.9	5.6	6.9	57.2	61.1	62.1	6.4	5.4	5.6	36.4	33.4	32.3
Ecuador	2005	15.1	15.0	2.4	5.0	82.8	53.4	82.9	2.7	3.7	5.7	14.5	42.9	11.3
Eritrea	2006	2.4	2.9	0.7	0.8	58.4	58.2	44.7	12.6	8.7	14.8	29.0	33.0	40.5
Ethiopia	2006	3.5	6.2	0.8	1.4	57.8	63.7	58.4	9.5	9.8	9.1	32.8	26.5	32.5
Fiji	2004	...	16.6	...	5.3	...	70.5	73.0	...	9.7	8.7	...	19.8	18.3
India	2004	5.7	5.5	1.3	1.6	75.5	79.1	80.4	5.7	5.8	5.6	18.9	15.1	14.0
Indonesia	2005	9.4	20.8	1.0	2.4	77.0	59.7	64.6	2.4	5.2	4.0	20.6	35.1	31.3
Iran (Islamic Republic of)	2005	41.0	14.6	12.0	4.8	63.5	65.2	64.5	10.7	13.0	11.7	25.9	21.8	23.8
Jordan	2006	14.4	18.2	3.9	4.0	69.8	66.7	67.1	8.1	7.5	7.2	22.1	25.8	25.7
Malaysia	2005	16.9	12.9	4.4	5.6	68.2	69.2	77.4	8.3	10.9	9.9	23.6	20.0	12.8
Morocco	2005	22.4	23.8	6.0	8.8	65.6	70.0	69.8	9.2	9.6	11.1	25.2	20.4	19.0
Oman	2006	18.1	22.4	6.6	7.1	63.1	63.8	69.3	13.5	14.4	9.7	23.4	21.7	21.0
Peru	2006	...	61.8	...	5.1	...	62.7	62.4	...	5.0	3.1	...	32.3	34.4
Philippines	2005	...	8.3	...	2.4	...	73.2	80.7	...	7.3	5.7	...	19.6	13.6
Qatar	2006	13.1	44.6	6.0	5.1	66.2	66.2	72.3	15.5	15.5	3.2	18.3	18.3	24.6
Saudi Arabia	2006	...	47.0	...	9.5	...	...	61.8	...	...	7.7	...	...	30.5
Sri Lanka	2006	...	7.1	...	1.7	...	...	70.7	...	...	7.1	...	...	22.2
Trinidad and Tobago	2004	16.6	...	5.5	...	69.0	64.4	66.9	10.3	10.6	10.7	20.7	25.0	22.4
Uruguay	2005	34.5	20.5	13.8	7.7	61.7	64.7	71.9	15.4	10.6	10.6	22.9	24.7	17.5
Yemen	2006	6.5	10.9	1.1	1.1	63.7	61.4	76.0	6.2	6.1	2.4	30.1	32.5	21.6

a/ At current prices.

Table 1.11

SELECTED CHARACTERISTICS OF BRANCHES, SELECTED YEARS AND COUNTRIES

Publishing (ISIC 221)														
Country or area	Latest year	Value added per employee (current 1000 dollars)		Wages and salaries per employee (current 1000 dollars)		Percentage in output[a/]								
						Costs of input materials and utilities			Costs of labour			Operating surplus		
	(LY)	2000	LY	2000	LY	2000	2003	LY	2000	2003	LY	2000	2003	LY
Industrialized Countries														
CIS														
Azerbaijan	2006	...	4.7	0.5	1.0	...	61.6	69.6	22.9	7.7	6.2	...	30.7	24.3
Georgia	2006	0.8	4.6	0.4	1.3	63.2	76.4	57.5	21.2	15.6	12.0	15.5	8.1	30.5
Kyrgyzstan	2006	...	...	0.7	0.9	...	...	...	36.2	26.9	27.5	...	...	...
Russian Federation	2006	...	16.1	1.4	5.2	...	48.3	46.6	...	21.4	17.1	...	30.3	36.3
EU-15														
Austria	2005	74.5	104.7	35.9	49.1	62.0	65.6	64.0	18.3	17.7	16.9	19.7	16.8	19.1
Belgium	2005	69.4	110.6	31.7	52.1	69.1	67.0	67.7	14.1	15.7	15.2	16.8	17.2	17.1
Denmark	2005	31.8	64.2	22.7	41.5	57.9	60.3	54.8	30.1	29.3	29.3	12.0	10.5	16.0
Finland	2005	49.3	78.9	26.7	43.5	59.6	62.2	60.8	21.9	20.8	21.6	18.5	17.0	17.6
France	2005	61.9	91.9	33.0	50.6	68.5	68.3	67.7	16.8	17.5	17.8	14.7	14.2	14.5
Germany	2005	52.7	65.3	28.0	36.9	62.4	63.4	62.9	20.1	22.7	21.0	17.6	13.9	16.1
Greece	2004	...	70.3	...	25.7	...	...	56.9	...	...	15.7	...	...	27.3
Ireland	2005	71.6	99.7	30.0	49.4	41.8	40.7	45.7	24.3	25.3	26.9	33.9	34.0	27.4
Italy	2005	88.4	135.4	33.1	51.4	68.9	69.4	70.2	11.6	12.1	11.3	19.4	18.5	18.5
Luxembourg	2005	...	91.4	...	58.9	...	...	40.8	...	...	38.2	...	...	21.1
Netherlands	2005	73.0	98.3	32.7	47.5	57.3	58.0	62.7	19.1	19.8	18.0	23.6	22.2	19.3
Portugal	2005	31.5	44.5	15.9	24.2	67.4	64.4	65.0	16.5	21.3	19.0	16.1	14.3	15.9
Spain	2005	56.5	89.5	24.4	38.8	59.6	60.6	60.2	17.5	17.7	17.2	22.9	21.7	22.5
Sweden	2005	49.8	67.4	27.8	37.9	67.7	...	70.3	18.0	...	16.7	14.3	...	13.0
United Kingdom	2005	74.2	105.4	35.6	48.9	56.7	54.0	52.1	20.8	22.3	22.3	22.6	23.7	25.7
EU-12														
Bulgaria	2006	5.6	10.4	1.3	3.1	72.3	74.7	72.8	6.6	8.4	8.2	21.1	17.0	19.0
Cyprus	2006	30.5	45.9	17.0	27.2	55.7	54.8	54.1	24.6	28.9	27.2	19.6	16.3	18.7
Czech Republic	2004	12.5	24.8	5.2	10.6	75.8	68.7	69.1	10.1	12.3	13.3	14.1	19.0	17.7
Estonia	2006	7.9	21.0	5.1	12.1	64.7	58.8	58.8	22.6	23.2	23.8	12.6	18.0	17.4
Hungary	2005	16.9	30.4	4.7	13.5	71.5	70.6	69.7	7.9	12.5	13.5	20.6	16.9	16.9
Latvia	2006	9.7	17.8	4.0	8.0	31.3	54.4	53.2	28.2	21.2	21.0	40.5	24.4	25.8
Lithuania	2006	6.7	11.4	4.0	6.3	62.1	62.2	70.5	22.4	18.9	16.4	15.4	18.9	13.1
Malta	2005	27.1	27.0	11.0	15.0	35.0	37.4	35.8	26.5	38.2	35.6	38.6	24.3	28.6
Poland	2005	27.4	38.9	...	13.9	55.1	61.1	55.8	...	16.2	15.8	...	22.7	28.3
Romania	2006	...	10.9	...	5.4	...	74.9	71.6	...	14.2	14.2	...	10.9	14.2
Slovakia	2005	6.6	22.0	3.7	8.8	69.8	68.1	64.9	16.9	13.0	14.0	13.4	19.0	21.1
Other Europe														
Norway	2004	46.3	82.2	30.2	51.8	56.6	54.7	55.8	28.3	28.4	27.9	15.1	16.9	16.4

a/ At current prices.

Table 1.11
(continued)

SELECTED CHARACTERISTICS OF BRANCHES, SELECTED YEARS AND COUNTRIES

Publishing (ISIC 221)													
Country or area	Latest year	Value added per employee (current 1000 dollars)		Wages and salaries per employee (current 1000 dollars)		Percentage in output [a]							
						Costs of input materials and utilities			Costs of labour			Operating surplus	
	(LY)	2000	LY	2000	LY	2000	2003	LY	2000	2003	LY	2000	2003	LY
Other Countries														
Israel	2005	37.4	29.6	25.9	21.3	59.7	59.7	54.1	27.9	27.9	33.0	12.4	12.4	12.8
Republic of Korea	2006	75.2	99.1	17.6	27.8	38.6	37.7	39.2	14.4	17.2	17.0	47.1	45.1	43.7
Developing Countries														
Brazil	2005	31.7	33.9	8.8	8.9	36.0	37.0	35.0	17.8	16.0	17.0	46.2	47.0	48.0
Chile	2006	...	35.0	...	13.8	...	53.7	57.6	...	19.3	16.7	...	26.9	25.7
Colombia	2005	21.3	40.9	4.5	6.8	41.7	34.8	30.6	12.4	11.1	11.6	45.9	54.0	57.8
Ecuador	2005	5.5	21.8	2.1	8.4	71.1	60.0	55.6	11.4	14.2	17.1	17.6	25.8	27.3
Fiji	2004	...	19.3	...	5.7	...	40.3	57.7	...	21.5	12.5	...	38.2	29.8
India	2004	7.6	9.9	2.5	3.3	70.5	64.5	69.9	9.7	10.8	10.2	19.8	24.6	19.9
Indonesia	2005	14.6	11.1	0.9	2.2	46.6	51.1	63.9	3.2	14.6	7.2	50.3	34.3	28.9
Iran (Islamic Republic of)	2005	30.6	9.6	9.2	5.1	44.5	50.1	47.8	16.7	24.0	27.6	38.8	25.9	24.6
Jordan	2006	17.1	27.9	6.4	8.3	44.3	43.2	43.0	20.6	17.4	16.9	35.0	39.4	40.1
Madagascar	2006	...	0.2	...	0.1	...	70.8	68.7	...	25.3	25.4	...	3.9	5.9
Malaysia	2005	22.3	19.7	6.7	9.7	50.7	50.6	64.6	14.7	18.1	17.4	34.5	31.3	18.0
Morocco	2005	10.8	12.1	6.2	7.2	52.1	58.8	53.2	27.4	26.8	27.7	20.6	14.3	19.1
Oman	2006	18.3	9.3	7.6	8.5	28.7	35.0	79.8	29.8	23.0	18.5	41.5	42.0	1.8
Philippines	2005	...	9.0	...	4.0	...	75.3	68.4	...	14.0	14.0	...	10.7	17.6
Sri Lanka	2006	...	2.2	...	1.0	...	...	73.6	...	...	12.0	...	...	14.4
Trinidad and Tobago	2004	22.3	...	10.7	...	48.9	45.7	45.8	24.6	23.1	20.9	26.6	31.3	33.3
Uruguay	2005	31.8	14.6	15.6	6.5	50.9	57.5	56.8	24.1	18.0	19.1	25.1	24.6	24.1

a/ At current prices.

Table 1.11

SELECTED CHARACTERISTICS OF BRANCHES, SELECTED YEARS AND COUNTRIES

Printing and related service activities (ISIC 222)

Country or area	Latest year	Value added per employee (current 1000 dollars)		Wages and salaries per employee (current 1000 dollars)		Percentage in output[a/]								
						Costs of input materials and utilities			Costs of labour			Operating surplus		
	(LY)	2000	LY	2000	LY	2000	2003	LY	2000	2003	LY	2000	2003	LY
Industrialized Countries														
CIS														
Azerbaijan	2006	...	3.5	0.5	1.1	...	61.6	69.6	12.2	4.9	9.7	...	33.5	20.8
Georgia	2006	0.9	5.2	0.3	1.1	69.7	75.9	62.0	12.2	6.2	8.0	18.1	17.9	30.0
Kyrgyzstan	2006	...	...	0.5	1.1	...	...	...	21.3	18.3	19.7	...	...	...
Russian Federation	2006	...	11.5	1.1	4.3	...	59.7	63.5	17.7	16.9	13.6	...	23.4	22.9
EU-15														
Austria	2005	53.9	80.4	30.0	44.0	51.2	53.7	53.9	27.2	26.4	25.2	21.6	19.8	20.9
Belgium	2005	53.7	83.9	24.9	38.7	63.1	64.7	63.7	17.1	17.2	16.8	19.8	18.0	19.6
Denmark	2005	47.8	76.7	32.7	49.7	55.5	54.3	57.4	30.5	32.1	27.6	14.0	13.6	15.0
Finland	2005	46.5	72.7	24.3	39.6	57.1	59.0	59.3	22.4	23.2	22.2	20.5	17.8	18.5
France	2005	38.6	56.5	22.7	34.4	62.9	63.0	64.1	21.8	22.4	21.9	15.3	14.6	14.0
Germany	2005	45.7	67.1	26.4	40.0	54.2	57.6	58.5	26.5	26.5	24.7	19.4	16.0	16.7
Greece	2004	...	105.5	...	22.2	...	...	54.5	...	...	9.6	...	...	35.9
Ireland	2005	43.2	87.3	22.7	44.2	52.1	54.2	46.3	25.2	28.9	27.2	22.7	16.8	26.5
Italy	2005	43.2	63.7	18.2	27.9	64.5	65.3	65.2	15.0	14.7	15.3	20.5	20.1	19.5
Luxembourg	2005	60.3	72.7	30.4	41.1	44.3	49.0	53.4	28.1	30.5	26.4	27.5	20.5	20.3
Netherlands	2005	49.2	72.7	25.6	42.4	57.9	59.7	60.4	22.0	23.1	23.1	20.1	17.2	16.5
Portugal	2005	21.4	28.7	9.9	13.8	55.8	54.2	55.3	20.5	22.1	21.5	23.7	23.7	23.1
Spain	2005	32.4	51.5	16.8	27.0	60.6	58.6	58.8	20.4	20.9	21.6	19.0	20.5	19.5
Sweden	2005	46.4	62.8	25.0	35.7	61.9	...	63.2	20.5	...	20.9	17.6	...	15.9
United Kingdom	2005	56.7	73.2	31.4	39.0	51.0	49.6	50.4	27.2	28.1	26.4	21.8	22.3	23.2
EU-12														
Bulgaria	2006	4.0	8.7	1.6	2.5	69.7	71.8	70.0	12.2	9.8	8.7	18.2	18.4	21.2
Cyprus	2006	25.5	38.9	12.6	21.3	49.5	51.0	56.6	25.0	26.9	23.8	25.5	22.1	19.6
Czech Republic	2004	...	22.5	...	7.3	...	64.5	62.1	...	12.7	12.3	...	22.9	25.6
Estonia	2006	9.8	24.2	4.5	10.0	63.6	63.3	63.0	16.7	16.3	15.4	19.7	20.4	21.7
Hungary	2005	8.1	17.5	3.3	7.7	69.7	65.3	65.0	12.5	15.5	15.5	17.8	19.2	19.5
Latvia	2006	10.2	14.0	3.4	5.3	43.7	55.7	73.4	18.7	12.0	10.2	37.6	32.2	16.4
Lithuania	2006	6.3	14.8	2.8	5.9	65.3	65.5	66.8	15.3	12.5	13.3	19.4	22.0	19.9
Malta	2005	29.5	64.3	12.0	19.5	54.1	66.0	38.4	18.7	19.0	18.7	27.1	15.0	42.9
Poland	2005	16.2	24.7	...	7.8	64.2	70.1	64.8	...	11.1	11.1	...	18.8	24.1
Romania	2006	...	13.9	...	5.9	...	64.0	64.9	...	11.0	14.9	...	25.1	20.2
Slovakia	2005	7.4	17.5	3.7	7.7	74.0	72.8	72.1	13.2	9.9	12.3	12.8	17.4	15.5
Other Europe														
Norway	2004	52.8	80.7	35.2	49.5	59.0	58.3	58.5	27.3	26.9	25.5	13.7	14.8	16.0

a/ At current prices.

Table 1.11
(continued)

SELECTED CHARACTERISTICS OF BRANCHES, SELECTED YEARS AND COUNTRIES

Printing and related service activities (ISIC 222)															
Country or area	Latest year	Value added per employee (current 1000 dollars)		Wages and salaries per employee (current 1000 dollars)		Percentage in output [a/]									
						Costs of input materials and utilities			Costs of labour			Operating surplus			
	(LY)	2000	LY	2000	LY	2000	2003	LY	2000	2003	LY	2000	2003	LY	
Other Countries															
Japan	2005	87.6	89.2	23.4	23.2	53.8	53.4	53.6	12.3	11.8	12.1	33.8	34.8	34.4	
Republic of Korea	2006	38.3	62.3	13.2	22.8	50.9	49.2	48.6	17.0	19.1	18.8	32.2	31.7	32.6	
Singapore	2006	48.4	48.3	22.7	25.8	50.5	53.2	54.1	23.3	25.9	24.5	26.3	20.9	21.4	
United States of America	2005	77.7	91.7	34.6	38.8	39.5	38.6	39.3	26.9	27.3	25.6	33.6	34.1	35.1	
Developing Countries															
Brazil	2005	15.3	18.3	4.9	4.9	39.1	43.6	42.6	19.5	18.8	15.4	41.4	37.7	42.0	
Chile	2006	...	33.2	...	13.8	...	56.1	59.2	...	17.4	17.0	...	26.5	23.8	
Colombia	2005	18.1	25.1	4.0	5.2	59.2	56.2	55.0	9.1	8.6	9.4	31.6	35.2	35.6	
Ecuador	2005	7.2	13.1	1.8	4.6	69.6	65.3	64.1	7.5	9.7	12.7	22.9	25.0	23.2	
Eritrea	2006	3.2	5.1	1.1	1.3	55.6	44.7	55.8	15.0	11.7	11.1	29.5	43.6	33.1	
Ethiopia	2006	3.6	3.9	0.9	1.2	46.6	45.6	61.7	13.7	13.8	11.5	39.7	40.7	26.7	
Fiji	2004	...	13.6	...	7.5	...	58.8	66.2	...	20.8	18.6	...	20.4	15.2	
India	2004	3.8	4.1	1.1	1.3	70.7	73.6	76.7	8.7	8.6	7.6	20.7	17.7	15.7	
Indonesia	2005	2.9	6.5	0.6	1.7	33.6	65.2	71.1	12.5	11.7	7.3	54.0	23.1	21.6	
Iran (Islamic Republic of)	2005	17.1	9.4	7.4	3.3	54.1	60.1	62.6	19.9	16.2	13.0	26.1	23.7	24.4	
Jordan	2006	9.2	9.5	3.4	3.6	64.8	60.3	63.6	13.0	13.0	13.8	22.2	26.7	22.6	
Madagascar	2006	...	0.5	...	0.4	...	66.5	64.1	...	21.1	28.1	...	12.4	7.8	
Malaysia	2005	11.3	10.9	4.6	5.8	59.8	58.2	66.7	16.4	20.4	17.8	23.8	21.5	15.4	
Morocco	2005	7.6	11.7	4.0	6.9	64.7	66.6	67.2	18.5	19.0	19.5	16.8	14.4	13.3	
Oman	2006	12.8	18.2	5.3	6.0	51.2	31.1	50.4	20.1	28.8	16.5	28.7	40.1	33.1	
Sri Lanka	2006	...	8.3	...	1.3	...	...	66.9	...	...	5.3	...	...	27.8	
Trinidad and Tobago	2004	13.6	...	7.2	...	61.3	54.8	59.5	20.4	20.9	21.7	18.3	24.4	18.8	

a/ At current prices.

Table 1.11 SELECTED CHARACTERISTICS OF BRANCHES, SELECTED YEARS AND COUNTRIES

Country or area	Latest year	Basic chemicals (ISIC 241)												
		Value added per employee (current 1000 dollars)		Wages and salaries per employee (current 1000 dollars)		Percentage in output [a/]								
						Costs of input materials and utilities			Costs of labour			Operating surplus		
	(LY)	2000	LY	2000	LY	2000	2003	LY	2000	2003	LY	2000	2003	LY
Industrialized Countries														
CIS														
Azerbaijan	2006	...	5.6	0.7	2.1	...	79.3	76.7	10.9	6.4	8.8	...	14.3	14.5
Georgia	2006	1.5	10.5	0.9	2.6	54.8	72.3	61.9	27.3	21.9	9.3	17.9	5.8	28.8
Kyrgyzstan	2005	...	2.1	0.4	1.1	...	...	74.4	27.9	...	12.8	...	...	12.7
Russian Federation	2006	...	28.2	1.3	5.5	...	66.4	71.6	10.7	6.1	5.5	...	27.4	22.8
EU-15														
Austria	2005	112.9	135.1	40.1	57.3	69.2	72.7	76.5	11.0	11.1	10.0	19.9	16.2	13.5
Belgium	2005	129.1	213.5	42.2	71.2	74.2	76.4	76.5	8.4	8.9	7.8	17.3	14.7	15.7
Denmark	2005	90.7	158.6	45.5	71.2	64.0	62.4	52.1	18.0	19.6	21.5	17.9	18.0	26.4
Finland	2005	103.1	148.7	32.1	53.9	70.5	71.6	74.5	9.2	10.2	9.2	20.3	18.2	16.2
France	2005	84.5	104.3	31.6	49.5	78.7	81.2	82.2	8.0	9.5	8.4	13.3	9.3	9.3
Germany	2005	83.8	139.9	43.4	67.1	68.4	68.4	69.6	16.4	17.4	14.6	15.2	14.3	15.8
Greece	2004	...	72.3	...	35.3	...	...	77.6	...	...	10.9	...	...	11.5
Italy	2005	71.9	96.0	25.9	40.8	80.6	83.7	85.2	7.0	7.8	6.3	12.4	8.4	8.5
Netherlands	2005	137.0	315.9	42.5	70.3	80.4	78.4	79.8	6.1	6.4	4.5	13.6	15.1	15.7
Portugal	2004	57.4	93.7	18.2	29.9	79.0	80.0	79.3	6.7	7.6	6.6	14.3	12.4	14.1
Spain	2005	87.7	131.5	27.3	43.4	74.1	75.7	76.9	8.1	9.2	7.6	17.9	15.1	15.5
Sweden	2005	84.6	137.5	30.6	50.6	71.9	...	72.4	10.2	...	10.2	18.0	...	17.4
United Kingdom	2005	82.5	128.1	44.5	57.7	74.9	73.1	76.6	13.5	12.2	10.6	11.6	14.6	12.9
EU-12														
Bulgaria	2006	6.7	16.9	2.3	4.6	80.7	78.9	81.5	6.7	5.5	5.0	12.7	15.6	13.5
Cyprus	2004	35.1	57.4	16.4	24.7	50.9	52.3	44.8	22.9	26.3	23.7	26.2	21.4	31.5
Czech Republic	2004	20.9	41.6	5.1	9.3	75.9	75.9	76.1	5.8	6.5	5.4	18.3	17.7	18.5
Estonia	2006	4.9	29.0	3.5	9.0	89.4	76.1	78.5	7.6	8.1	6.7	3.0	15.8	14.8
Hungary	2005	24.4	56.1	5.8	16.1	77.1	76.2	80.9	5.5	7.6	5.5	17.4	16.2	13.6
Latvia	2006	5.6	8.8	2.5	3.2	60.7	69.1	76.1	17.5	10.8	8.6	21.7	20.1	15.3
Lithuania	2006	6.6	39.9	5.6	13.0	91.9	84.2	83.6	6.8	6.1	5.3	1.3	9.8	11.0
Poland	2005	21.5	45.5	...	11.6	71.1	75.6	75.5	...	6.9	6.2	...	17.4	18.2
Romania	2006	...	12.8	...	8.1	82.4	84.3	84.5	...	11.9	9.8	...	3.8	5.6
Slovakia	2005	11.7	27.6	3.8	9.2	79.0	84.0	80.6	6.9	8.0	6.5	14.2	8.0	13.0
Other Europe														
Norway	2004	158.6	188.3	88.5	71.6	63.5	69.4	69.2	20.4	12.9	11.7	16.1	17.7	19.1

a/ At current prices.

Table 1.11
(continued)

SELECTED CHARACTERISTICS OF BRANCHES, SELECTED YEARS AND COUNTRIES

Basic chemicals (ISIC 241)														
Country or area	Latest year	Value added per employee (current 1000 dollars)		Wages and salaries per employee (current 1000 dollars)		Percentage in output a/								
						Costs of input materials and utilities			Costs of labour			Operating surplus		
	(LY)	2000	LY	2000	LY	2000	2003	LY	2000	2003	LY	2000	2003	LY
Other Countries														
Japan	2005	293.8	320.2	54.1	53.0	57.3	62.6	66.9	7.9	6.5	5.5	34.8	30.8	27.6
Republic of Korea	2006	179.7	247.4	23.9	41.4	69.9	71.0	78.2	4.0	4.2	3.7	26.1	24.8	18.2
United States of America	2005	231.8	434.8	52.8	64.6	61.5	62.2	58.7	8.8	8.7	6.1	29.7	29.1	35.2
Developing Countries														
Brazil	2005	82.0	94.1	13.4	14.9	68.6	70.0	71.3	5.1	4.1	4.5	26.3	26.0	24.1
Colombia	2005	66.1	99.1	6.9	8.7	62.3	63.0	68.6	3.9	3.1	2.8	33.8	33.9	28.6
Ecuador	2005	32.1	40.8	3.0	8.7	74.4	76.1	69.0	2.4	5.6	6.6	23.2	18.3	24.4
Eritrea	2006	2.4	6.8	1.4	1.3	63.4	36.2	26.3	21.9	12.0	13.9	14.6	51.9	59.8
India	2004	17.0	25.0	2.5	3.4	78.2	78.9	79.1	3.2	3.2	2.8	18.6	17.9	18.1
Indonesia	2005	22.8	42.0	2.5	4.7	62.9	54.1	63.1	4.1	4.3	4.2	33.0	41.7	32.7
Iran (Islamic Republic of)	2005	272.6	91.3	18.7	6.9	26.0	46.2	50.5	5.1	5.6	3.8	68.9	48.2	45.7
Jordan	2006	30.4	45.7	7.9	9.1	80.8	78.6	69.8	5.0	5.1	6.0	14.2	16.3	24.2
Madagascar	2006	...	1.6	...	0.6	...	44.4	37.6	...	14.5	22.0	...	41.0	40.4
Malaysia	2005	79.7	117.1	9.1	14.3	68.2	68.2	72.8	3.6	3.8	3.3	28.2	28.0	23.9
Morocco	2005	31.7	57.4	11.5	22.7	68.6	69.9	72.6	11.4	13.3	10.8	20.0	16.8	16.6
Oman	2006	44.3	240.1	7.4	14.5	46.7	55.2	26.8	8.9	8.1	4.4	44.4	36.7	68.8
Peru	2006	...	79.3	...	16.4	...	54.6	54.3	...	13.3	9.4	...	32.1	36.2
Philippines	2005	...	13.7	...	2.9	...	60.6	82.6	...	4.0	3.7	...	35.3	13.7
Qatar	2006	152.5	249.1	22.9	29.7	23.0	20.1	30.8	11.6	11.8	8.3	65.5	68.1	60.9
Sri Lanka	2006	...	30.5	...	3.5	...	...	49.1	...	...	5.9	...	...	45.0
Trinidad and Tobago	2004	250.3	...	21.8	...	57.4	57.9	53.9	3.7	3.9	3.9	38.9	38.2	42.2
Uruguay	2005	47.5	44.3	22.3	15.0	69.3	71.2	78.2	14.4	7.0	7.4	16.3	21.8	14.4

a/ At current prices.

Table 1.11

SELECTED CHARACTERISTICS OF BRANCHES, SELECTED YEARS AND COUNTRIES

Other chemicals (ISIC 242)														
Country or area	Latest year	Value added per employee (current 1000 dollars)		Wages and salaries per employee (current 1000 dollars)		Percentage in output [a]								
						Costs of input materials and utilities			Costs of labour			Operating surplus		
	(LY)	2000	LY	2000	LY	2000	2003	LY	2000	2003	LY	2000	2003	LY
Industrialized Countries														
CIS														
Azerbaijan	2006	...	2.2	0.3	1.2	...	79.3	76.7	2.1	13.0	13.4	...	7.7	9.9
Georgia	2006	1.4	5.9	0.4	1.7	64.0	72.2	58.8	9.8	8.7	11.6	26.2	19.1	29.6
Kyrgyzstan	2005	...	1.1	0.3	0.3	...	...	83.0	12.7	8.3	4.8	...	...	12.2
Russian Federation	2006	...	13.9	1.0	4.7	...	66.3	67.2	6.0	11.3	11.1	...	22.4	21.7
EU-15														
Austria	2005	74.5	133.3	34.0	49.0	60.7	...	53.5	18.0	...	17.1	21.4	...	29.4
Belgium	2005	115.1	188.4	38.9	61.4	60.9	...	61.7	13.2	...	12.5	25.9	...	25.8
France	2005	78.8	121.3	33.1	50.2	72.8	72.8	71.2	11.4	11.1	11.9	15.8	16.2	16.9
Germany	2005	66.3	112.9	37.5	56.2	65.8	65.3	63.9	19.4	18.8	17.9	14.9	15.9	18.1
Greece	2004	...	63.9	...	26.3	...	...	64.0	...	...	14.8	...	...	21.2
Italy	2005	77.1	106.3	29.1	44.2	70.0	72.2	73.1	11.3	10.8	11.2	18.7	17.0	15.7
Netherlands	2005	78.1	123.0	33.2	53.0	73.8	...	68.2	11.1	...	13.7	15.1	...	18.1
Spain	2005	57.6	88.3	26.0	41.7	68.5	70.3	71.2	14.2	13.7	13.6	17.3	16.0	15.2
Sweden	2005	...	211.2	...	47.9	...	...	51.6	...	...	11.0	...	...	37.4
United Kingdom	2005	...	144.4	...	55.9	...	61.1	56.3	...	17.5	16.9	...	21.5	26.8
EU-12														
Bulgaria	2006	5.6	12.7	1.6	3.5	69.6	71.7	71.4	8.9	8.6	7.8	21.5	19.7	20.8
Cyprus	2006	34.9	49.1	13.6	22.3	60.9	61.8	59.4	15.3	18.4	18.4	23.8	19.7	22.2
Estonia	2006	13.8	38.5	4.1	11.4	67.5	69.4	75.6	9.6	8.5	7.2	23.0	22.1	17.2
Hungary	2005	...	67.9	...	19.2	...	53.4	53.3	...	12.8	13.2	...	33.8	33.5
Latvia	2006	9.6	22.7	3.5	8.2	53.5	53.4	53.8	17.0	17.6	16.7	29.6	29.0	29.4
Lithuania	2006	4.5	16.3	3.4	7.0	70.3	77.8	71.4	22.2	14.8	12.3	7.5	7.4	16.2
Malta	2005	23.1	37.3	10.7	18.6	67.7	51.2	65.7	15.0	21.9	17.2	17.3	27.0	17.2
Poland	2005	...	43.2	...	12.3	...	65.5	64.2	...	11.1	10.2	...	23.3	25.6
Romania	2006	...	19.9	...	8.5	60.1	71.0	70.5	...	11.8	12.6	...	17.2	16.9
Slovakia	2005	8.5	18.5	3.8	8.5	81.6	77.2	77.1	8.2	9.9	10.5	10.2	12.8	12.4
Other Europe														
Norway	2004	88.5	144.1	41.4	64.6	63.8	59.2	55.6	16.9	19.8	19.9	19.3	21.0	24.5

a/ At current prices.

Table 1.11
(continued)

SELECTED CHARACTERISTICS OF BRANCHES, SELECTED YEARS AND COUNTRIES

Other chemicals (ISIC 242)

Country or area	Latest year	Value added per employee (current 1000 dollars)		Wages and salaries per employee (current 1000 dollars)		Percentage in output [a/]: Costs of input materials and utilities			Costs of labour			Operating surplus		
	(LY)	2000	LY	2000	LY	2000	2003	LY	2000	2003	LY	2000	2003	LY
Other Countries														
Israel	2005	61.7	128.7	34.7	41.4	63.9	62.2	60.6	20.3	15.5	12.7	15.8	22.3	26.7
Japan	2005	302.3	322.0	46.8	45.2	47.0	43.6	45.4	8.2	7.7	7.7	44.8	48.7	46.9
Republic of Korea	2006	109.2	185.2	17.2	28.5	50.6	47.1	48.8	7.8	8.1	7.9	41.6	44.8	43.4
South Africa	2006	19.3	56.0	11.6	11.3	78.1	78.6	76.1	13.1	10.0	4.8	8.8	11.4	19.1
United States of America	2005	284.8	433.8	47.7	58.5	37.9	33.6	34.5	10.4	10.0	8.8	51.7	56.4	56.6
Developing Countries														
Brazil	2005	44.0	51.5	10.7	12.6	51.5	56.2	55.5	11.8	10.1	10.9	36.7	33.7	33.6
Chile	2006	...	69.0	...	19.0	...	49.5	48.4	...	14.6	14.2	...	35.9	37.3
Colombia	2005	50.3	56.7	6.1	7.7	47.2	47.9	49.3	6.4	6.6	6.9	46.3	45.5	43.8
Ecuador	2005	37.0	26.6	2.6	6.0	50.2	72.7	68.2	3.4	6.6	7.1	46.3	20.7	24.7
Eritrea	2006	5.2	6.9	0.7	1.1	49.7	60.0	61.5	6.4	4.7	6.0	43.8	35.4	32.5
Ethiopia	2006	6.1	6.5	0.8	1.2	62.3	60.7	71.4	5.1	6.4	5.2	32.5	32.9	23.4
India	2004	6.7	10.3	1.5	2.0	75.2	72.6	72.3	5.4	5.1	5.3	19.4	22.3	22.4
Indonesia	2005	8.6	14.1	1.6	2.1	60.2	55.5	54.6	7.3	6.9	6.8	32.5	37.6	38.6
Iran (Islamic Republic of)	2005	45.0	18.1	10.6	4.9	62.4	61.4	63.2	8.9	9.3	9.9	28.7	29.3	26.9
Jordan	2006	18.6	23.8	4.9	6.9	61.1	61.9	63.7	10.3	9.9	10.5	28.6	28.2	25.8
Madagascar	2006	...	0.2	...	0.1	...	30.4	22.6	...	36.5	55.0	...	33.0	22.5
Malaysia	2005	22.5	24.3	6.2	8.1	70.6	68.0	76.3	8.1	8.6	7.9	21.3	23.4	15.8
Morocco	2005	22.6	33.0	10.1	14.3	67.2	58.6	54.1	14.7	19.1	19.9	18.1	22.3	26.0
Oman	2006	38.9	36.0	7.8	8.7	63.7	62.8	62.4	7.3	7.9	9.1	29.0	29.4	28.5
Peru	2006	...	41.5	...	8.1	...	58.6	58.8	...	10.7	8.1	...	30.7	33.1
Qatar	2006	25.7	51.2	8.5	8.9	62.3	63.9	39.9	12.5	11.5	10.4	25.1	24.5	49.7
Sri Lanka	2006	...	22.5	...	2.2	...	...	68.2	...	...	3.0	...	...	28.8
Trinidad and Tobago	2004	8.9	...	4.9	...	78.2	61.7	45.1	12.0	17.4	14.8	9.7	20.9	40.1
Uruguay	2005	37.0	22.6	21.4	9.9	60.4	60.6	63.7	22.9	14.7	15.9	16.7	24.7	20.4

a/ At current prices.

Table 1.11

SELECTED CHARACTERISTICS OF BRANCHES, SELECTED YEARS AND COUNTRIES

Rubber products (ISIC 251)

Country or area	Latest year	Value added per employee (current 1000 dollars)		Wages and salaries per employee (current 1000 dollars)		Percentage in output a/								
						Costs of input materials and utilities			Costs of labour			Operating surplus		
	(LY)	2000	LY	2000	LY	2000	2003	LY	2000	2003	LY	2000	2003	LY
Industrialized Countries														
CIS														
Georgia	2005	1.1	2.0	0.5	0.6	69.4	81.9	79.4	13.5	5.8	6.0	17.0	12.3	14.6
Russian Federation	2006	...	29.6	1.0	4.0	...	76.0	73.8	8.8	6.1	3.5	...	17.9	22.6
EU-15														
Austria	2005	53.3	88.3	29.2	44.9	56.9	56.0	62.5	23.6	20.2	19.1	19.5	23.8	18.4
Belgium	2005	57.8	130.6	26.6	48.2	66.5	78.4	70.1	15.4	10.8	11.0	18.1	10.8	18.9
Denmark	2005	43.6	61.2	32.6	50.0	60.2	62.0	66.5	29.8	29.7	27.3	10.0	8.3	6.1
Finland	2005	58.9	108.9	27.3	43.4	53.9	51.1	55.6	21.3	19.4	17.7	24.7	29.5	26.7
France	2005	43.0	63.6	23.8	35.2	63.6	65.2	67.4	20.1	19.5	18.1	16.3	15.3	14.6
Germany	2005	49.5	75.4	31.3	45.4	59.1	60.7	62.2	25.8	23.7	22.8	15.1	15.6	15.0
Greece	2004	...	70.7	...	25.2	...	...	60.0	...	...	14.3	...	...	25.7
Ireland	2005	28.9	74.6	20.2	36.5	64.2	56.5	51.6	25.0	24.3	23.7	10.8	19.1	24.7
Italy	2005	45.6	65.4	20.6	32.6	66.5	70.0	71.3	15.1	14.5	14.3	18.4	15.5	14.4
Luxembourg	2005	65.8	91.3	47.9	62.7	54.7	57.3	65.6	32.9	25.6	23.7	12.3	17.1	10.8
Netherlands	2005	52.8	79.9	28.2	41.1	59.4	59.3	63.0	21.7	24.0	19.0	18.9	16.7	18.0
Portugal	2005	...	33.2	10.7	16.0	...	57.6	73.4	13.5	14.1	12.8	...	28.3	13.8
Spain	2005	46.0	67.5	21.5	34.6	58.8	62.1	64.6	19.3	20.2	18.2	21.9	17.7	17.3
Sweden	2005	46.9	66.7	22.6	37.5	61.8	...	65.0	18.4	...	19.7	19.8	...	15.3
United Kingdom	2005	49.0	84.5	31.5	46.0	55.8	50.6	59.0	28.3	23.4	22.3	15.8	25.9	18.7
EU-12														
Bulgaria	2006	2.5	5.2	1.2	2.4	74.7	77.2	81.6	12.6	10.0	8.5	12.7	12.7	9.9
Cyprus	2006	17.3	35.9	9.7	17.0	56.9	66.7	57.0	24.1	22.2	20.4	19.0	11.1	22.6
Czech Republic	2004	14.6	28.2	4.8	8.2	69.9	75.9	77.0	9.9	6.9	6.7	20.2	17.1	16.3
Estonia	2006	8.9	15.5	3.8	7.5	64.8	62.8	63.2	15.0	17.7	17.9	20.2	19.5	19.0
Hungary	2005	11.1	24.7	4.9	11.8	72.5	70.1	68.4	12.1	15.5	15.1	15.4	14.4	16.5
Latvia	2006	4.9	18.5	2.2	6.6	53.8	65.5	69.4	21.0	10.4	11.0	25.2	24.1	19.6
Lithuania	2006	2.0	10.5	1.9	5.0	80.7	65.4	68.9	18.4	16.0	14.9	1.0	18.6	16.2
Malta	2005	35.6	35.7	16.1	18.8	35.2	36.6	41.4	29.2	33.9	30.8	35.5	29.5	27.8
Poland	2005	14.3	26.3	...	9.2	65.2	67.0	69.4	...	11.2	10.7	...	21.7	19.9
Romania	2006	...	12.2	...	6.3	69.3	79.5	79.2	...	10.0	10.8	...	10.5	10.0
Slovakia	2005	10.7	29.3	4.5	9.8	74.8	73.7	75.7	10.6	9.1	8.1	14.5	17.2	16.2
Other Europe														
Norway	2004	41.9	73.9	27.7	50.0	57.8	54.7	50.6	27.9	33.8	33.4	14.3	11.5	16.0

a/ At current prices.

Table 1.11
(continued)

SELECTED CHARACTERISTICS OF BRANCHES, SELECTED YEARS AND COUNTRIES

Rubber products (ISIC 251)														
Country or area	Latest year	Value added per employee (current 1000 dollars)		Wages and salaries per employee (current 1000 dollars)		Percentage in output [a]								
						Costs of input materials and utilities			Costs of labour			Operating surplus		
	(LY)	2000	LY	2000	LY	2000	2003	LY	2000	2003	LY	2000	2003	LY
Other Countries														
Australia	2005	57.8	65.2	27.8	...	45.5	64.3	60.9	26.2	...	...	28.3	...	...
Israel	2005	35.9	37.9	30.7	26.2	61.7	64.0	67.2	32.7	27.0	22.7	5.6	9.0	10.1
Japan	2005	109.3	110.8	34.0	33.2	53.4	54.0	56.0	14.5	13.5	13.2	32.1	32.5	30.8
Republic of Korea	2006	61.6	105.0	16.0	28.2	53.4	54.0	55.4	12.1	12.1	12.0	34.4	33.9	32.7
Singapore	2006	36.8	52.8	19.1	25.1	69.9	60.9	59.9	15.6	21.5	19.0	14.5	17.6	21.0
South Africa	2006	17.2	28.1	9.4	12.7	74.1	74.1	75.5	14.2	21.6	11.1	11.7	4.3	13.5
United States of America	2005	89.1	110.3	35.4	42.8	47.8	47.8	52.4	20.7	20.3	18.5	31.5	31.9	29.1
Developing Countries														
Brazil	2005	23.6	29.0	6.9	7.7	54.2	54.4	56.7	13.4	11.8	11.5	32.4	33.8	31.8
Chile	2006	...	45.4	...	16.1	...	55.7	62.9	...	12.6	13.2	...	31.7	24.0
Colombia	2005	23.4	28.1	6.2	7.7	57.2	57.7	63.5	11.4	9.6	10.0	31.4	32.7	26.5
Ecuador	2005	17.3	15.1	3.5	6.3	74.7	76.6	77.4	5.2	14.1	9.5	20.2	9.4	13.2
Eritrea	2006	1.4	14.7	0.7	1.2	71.5	69.2	74.7	13.4	5.4	2.1	15.1	25.4	23.2
Ethiopia	2006	11.9	14.9	1.5	2.0	51.2	46.1	43.0	5.9	7.8	7.5	42.8	46.0	49.5
India	2004	6.1	7.2	1.4	1.8	74.6	78.0	79.5	5.9	5.5	5.1	19.5	16.5	15.4
Indonesia	2005	4.2	8.0	1.0	1.2	74.4	...	82.1	5.9	...	2.8	19.7	...	15.1
Iran (Islamic Republic of)	2005	41.0	20.5	11.4	5.2	60.0	63.7	55.7	11.1	14.2	11.3	28.9	22.1	32.9
Jordan	2006	7.6	7.7	3.2	3.1	58.9	56.8	72.2	17.5	13.1	11.3	23.6	30.0	16.4
Madagascar	2006	...	...	...	0.1	...	...	...	...	16.3	19.2	...	...	...
Malaysia	2005	12.5	11.3	3.6	4.9	67.9	75.3	81.4	9.2	9.3	8.0	22.9	15.4	10.5
Morocco	2005	20.2	12.6	12.4	8.9	61.9	63.4	47.4	23.4	24.0	37.1	14.7	12.6	15.5
Oman	2006	8.0	44.2	5.9	5.2	66.1	60.7	31.8	25.2	16.3	8.0	8.7	23.0	60.2
Philippines	2005	...	8.7	...	3.0	...	64.8	72.7	...	12.6	9.5	...	22.7	17.8
Qatar	2006	...	...	...	...	...	...	12.5	...	...	5.5	...	...	82.0
Sri Lanka	2006	...	5.9	...	1.0	...	...	49.3	...	...	8.8	...	...	41.9
Trinidad and Tobago	2004	13.7	...	6.6	...	45.3	63.8	75.3	26.2	12.2	7.9	28.5	24.0	16.8
Uruguay	2005	15.0	5.7	13.7	3.3	67.9	69.7	59.8	29.2	18.8	23.4	2.9	11.4	16.8

a/ At current prices.

Table 1.11

SELECTED CHARACTERISTICS OF BRANCHES, SELECTED YEARS AND COUNTRIES

Plastic products (ISIC 2520)

Country or area	Latest year	Value added per employee (current 1000 dollars)		Wages and salaries per employee (current 1000 dollars)		Percentage in output [a/]								
						Costs of input materials and utilities			Costs of labour			Operating surplus		
	(LY)	2000	LY	2000	LY	2000	2003	LY	2000	2003	LY	2000	2003	LY
Industrialized Countries														
CIS														
Azerbaijan	2006	...	3.7	...	1.0	...	79.3	80.2	...	2.0	5.1	...	18.7	14.8
Georgia	2006	0.9	4.9	0.5	2.4	84.8	90.2	71.6	9.1	3.2	14.0	6.1	6.6	14.4
Kyrgyzstan	2005	...	3.0	0.4	0.5	...	79.6	84.4	4.6	4.7	2.5	...	15.8	13.1
EU-15														
Austria	2005	47.0	72.7	25.6	38.7	62.6	60.2	61.8	20.4	21.0	20.3	17.0	18.8	17.9
Belgium	2005	62.2	94.3	28.4	43.6	70.7	69.9	73.4	13.4	14.0	12.3	15.9	16.2	14.3
Denmark	2005	47.1	81.9	29.8	49.8	57.3	57.4	59.6	27.0	26.9	24.6	15.6	15.7	15.8
Finland	2005	49.8	73.1	23.1	38.6	59.9	60.7	64.6	18.6	19.8	18.7	21.4	19.5	16.7
France	2005	40.2	58.8	20.9	32.6	69.5	69.8	71.2	15.8	16.4	15.9	14.7	13.8	12.9
Germany	2005	44.4	66.1	26.4	38.7	62.7	62.9	64.8	22.2	22.0	20.6	15.1	15.1	14.6
Greece	2004	...	50.0	...	19.6	...	...	62.6	...	...	14.6	...	...	22.7
Ireland	2005	43.2	68.0	19.9	36.3	62.9	63.6	63.4	17.1	20.5	19.6	20.0	15.9	17.1
Italy	2005	45.4	64.6	17.7	27.8	70.8	72.5	74.3	11.4	11.3	11.1	17.8	16.2	14.7
Luxembourg	2005	81.1	77.9	39.0	51.8	64.8	67.2	73.1	16.9	16.7	17.9	18.3	16.1	9.0
Netherlands	2005	49.6	76.8	25.7	40.9	68.0	66.7	69.4	16.5	17.8	16.3	15.5	15.5	14.3
Portugal	2005	21.4	32.1	9.7	15.2	71.2	68.3	72.4	13.1	14.4	13.1	15.7	17.3	14.6
Spain	2005	34.4	57.5	16.5	28.1	68.7	68.6	71.0	15.0	15.2	14.2	16.3	16.2	14.8
Sweden	2005	48.8	70.6	24.1	35.6	63.4	...	65.6	18.0	...	17.3	18.5	...	17.0
United Kingdom	2005	46.4	66.9	25.4	37.3	60.2	62.1	62.6	21.8	21.9	20.9	18.0	16.0	16.6
EU-12														
Bulgaria	2006	2.4	7.1	1.1	1.9	77.5	76.5	79.9	10.0	7.3	5.3	12.5	16.2	14.9
Cyprus	2006	22.1	39.3	12.4	22.3	58.5	53.6	59.4	23.2	25.8	23.0	18.2	20.6	17.6
Czech Republic	2004	9.6	17.9	3.9	7.1	74.1	69.3	72.4	10.4	11.3	11.0	15.5	19.3	16.6
Estonia	2006	7.6	19.1	3.2	8.6	72.9	73.9	74.9	11.6	10.8	11.4	15.6	15.4	13.8
Hungary	2005	10.7	21.7	3.6	8.9	73.3	69.2	71.1	9.1	11.5	11.9	17.7	19.3	17.0
Latvia	2006	8.4	12.6	1.9	5.2	68.4	71.9	78.0	7.1	8.2	9.1	24.5	19.9	12.9
Lithuania	2006	6.0	20.8	2.4	6.2	76.8	79.7	74.2	9.5	6.6	7.6	13.8	13.7	18.2
Malta	2005	18.3	28.9	10.5	15.5	48.5	45.9	50.0	29.5	32.1	26.8	22.1	22.1	23.2
Poland	2005	12.2	21.4	...	6.8	71.3	71.6	72.8	...	9.5	8.7	...	18.9	18.6
Romania	2006	...	10.3	...	4.7	63.2	75.8	80.7	...	9.3	8.8	...	15.0	10.5
Slovakia	2005	6.1	16.0	3.4	6.6	81.7	76.7	78.5	10.0	9.3	8.9	8.3	14.1	12.6
Other Europe														
Norway	2004	45.2	71.4	31.2	46.7	64.1	63.9	66.5	24.8	23.8	21.9	11.1	12.3	11.6

a/ At current prices.

Table 1.11
(continued)

SELECTED CHARACTERISTICS OF BRANCHES, SELECTED YEARS AND COUNTRIES

Plastic products (ISIC 2520)														
Country or area	Latest year	Value added per employee (current 1000 dollars)		Wages and salaries per employee (current 1000 dollars)		Percentage in output a/								
						Costs of input materials and utilities			Costs of labour			Operating surplus		
	(LY)	2000	LY	2000	LY	2000	2003	LY	2000	2003	LY	2000	2003	LY
Other Countries														
Israel	2005	39.8	48.0	24.3	26.4	63.9	65.1	70.0	22.1	19.4	16.5	14.0	15.6	13.5
Japan	2005	92.0	100.2	24.1	24.2	59.4	59.0	59.7	10.6	10.3	9.7	29.9	30.6	30.6
Republic of Korea	2006	47.9	76.8	13.4	22.5	60.5	62.0	63.5	11.1	11.7	10.7	28.5	26.3	25.8
Singapore	2006	28.8	31.6	15.6	19.5	67.3	65.3	69.3	17.7	19.7	18.9	15.0	15.0	11.8
South Africa	2006	12.2	36.4	7.8	8.0	67.9	66.8	65.4	20.7	9.9	7.6	11.4	23.3	27.0
United States of America	2005	85.7	108.5	31.4	36.3	48.7	47.9	51.8	18.8	18.1	16.1	32.5	34.0	32.1
Developing Countries														
Brazil	2005	16.5	19.5	5.2	5.7	63.6	63.9	62.9	11.5	10.6	10.9	24.9	25.4	26.2
Chile	2006	...	40.1	...	11.4	...	60.4	61.9	...	12.4	10.9	...	27.2	27.3
Colombia	2005	20.7	31.9	3.8	4.9	57.7	60.3	60.3	7.9	6.9	6.1	34.4	32.8	33.5
Ecuador	2005	13.8	18.8	1.8	4.8	69.9	64.2	72.9	3.9	6.2	6.9	26.2	29.6	20.2
Eritrea	2006	6.5	2.3	0.9	0.6	31.7	62.1	60.8	9.3	8.3	10.4	59.0	29.6	28.8
Ethiopia	2006	4.3	5.7	0.7	0.7	58.9	55.0	61.4	7.0	6.9	4.9	34.2	38.1	33.7
Fiji	2004	...	19.8	...	4.5	...	...	...	...	...	...	...	...	...
India	2004	4.5	6.2	1.0	1.3	82.2	82.1	84.4	4.0	3.8	3.4	13.8	14.1	12.2
Indonesia	2005	3.9	6.0	0.7	1.5	65.2	61.5	66.9	6.5	10.7	8.1	28.4	27.8	25.0
Iran (Islamic Republic of)	2005	24.4	11.9	8.2	3.3	66.7	67.6	70.0	11.2	10.3	8.4	22.1	22.0	21.6
Jordan	2006	9.3	16.0	3.0	3.5	69.6	64.4	68.4	9.9	8.7	7.0	20.5	26.9	24.7
Madagascar	2006	...	0.3	...	0.2	...	70.7	70.5	...	14.0	16.5	...	15.3	13.0
Malaysia	2005	11.1	10.8	3.7	5.0	66.0	65.3	74.6	11.4	11.6	11.7	22.6	23.1	13.8
Morocco	2005	8.9	12.0	4.2	6.0	69.9	71.4	74.7	14.2	13.8	12.5	15.9	14.8	12.8
Oman	2006	18.1	17.9	5.2	6.0	62.0	60.8	75.0	11.0	11.0	8.4	27.0	28.2	16.7
Philippines	2005	...	7.1	...	2.0	...	70.3	70.8	...	10.7	8.3	...	19.0	20.9
Qatar	2006	14.4	41.3	5.6	6.1	48.5	48.6	32.2	20.1	20.1	10.0	31.4	31.3	57.7
Sri Lanka	2006	...	17.1	...	1.4	...	...	38.0	...	...	5.0	...	...	57.0
Trinidad and Tobago	2004	10.5	...	5.2	...	69.0	71.3	55.4	15.4	16.6	15.2	15.6	12.1	29.3
Uruguay	2005	20.8	19.3	10.3	5.5	68.7	67.9	69.9	15.4	9.7	8.5	15.8	22.4	21.6

a/ At current prices.

Table 1.11

SELECTED CHARACTERISTICS OF BRANCHES, SELECTED YEARS AND COUNTRIES

Glass and glass products (ISIC 2610)

Country or area	Latest year	Value added per employee (current 1000 dollars)		Wages and salaries per employee (current 1000 dollars)		Percentage in output a/								
						Costs of input materials and utilities			Costs of labour			Operating surplus		
	(LY)	2000	LY	2000	LY	2000	2003	LY	2000	2003	LY	2000	2003	LY
Industrialized Countries														
CIS														
Azerbaijan	2006	...	1.3	0.2	0.5	...	79.3	67.0	25.1	17.3	14.3	...	3.4	18.7
Georgia	2006	1.6	13.4	0.6	3.0	69.8	46.9	66.6	10.7	4.5	7.6	19.4	48.7	25.8
Kyrgyzstan	2005	...	6.3	...	1.6	...	50.9	65.9	...	7.6	8.9	...	41.5	25.2
Russian Federation	2006	...	15.3	0.9	4.0	...	61.3	60.5	16.2	18.2	10.2	...	20.5	29.3
EU-15														
Austria	2005	60.1	98.9	26.1	41.2	41.6	41.5	38.7	25.3	30.7	25.5	33.1	27.8	35.8
Belgium	2005	61.4	90.5	30.6	46.1	65.7	72.1	72.3	17.1	14.4	14.1	17.2	13.4	13.6
Denmark	2005	42.8	75.1	28.0	46.2	58.9	59.2	60.0	26.9	27.2	24.6	14.2	13.7	15.4
Finland	2005	47.9	100.9	24.5	42.1	56.2	57.8	50.4	22.5	23.4	20.7	21.4	18.8	28.9
France	2005	47.7	66.2	24.5	37.1	62.9	62.6	64.6	19.0	19.9	19.8	18.1	17.5	15.6
Germany	2005	48.9	69.2	27.4	41.5	59.4	60.3	62.3	22.8	23.9	22.6	17.8	15.8	15.1
Greece	2004	...	59.8	...	24.7	...	...	54.3	...	...	18.9	...	...	26.8
Ireland	2005	61.5	60.8	26.4	38.1	42.3	55.6	58.9	24.7	24.7	25.8	32.9	19.7	15.3
Italy	2005	50.1	66.4	19.1	29.5	65.7	67.1	67.0	13.1	13.0	14.7	21.2	19.9	18.3
Netherlands	2005	64.4	82.8	30.2	45.8	63.0	59.5	63.7	17.3	20.5	20.1	19.7	20.0	16.2
Portugal	2004	26.6	47.9	11.3	17.9	59.7	60.8	60.7	17.2	16.5	14.7	23.1	22.7	24.6
Spain	2005	45.2	66.0	19.0	29.3	59.8	61.3	60.8	16.9	17.4	17.4	23.3	21.3	21.8
Sweden	2005	42.0	70.7	23.1	36.3	62.6	...	66.2	20.6	...	17.4	16.9	...	16.5
United Kingdom	2005	54.1	73.7	28.5	40.4	56.1	54.9	56.4	23.1	22.1	23.9	20.8	23.0	19.7
EU-12														
Bulgaria	2006	2.1	20.7	1.4	3.4	80.0	70.7	66.0	13.2	8.6	5.5	6.8	20.7	28.5
Cyprus	2006	19.0	36.9	8.7	18.8	60.5	59.6	56.5	18.0	20.1	22.2	21.5	20.3	21.3
Czech Republic	2004	12.6	21.6	4.1	7.3	59.7	60.6	61.3	13.2	13.5	13.1	27.0	25.9	25.6
Estonia	2006	15.8	32.9	5.2	12.0	67.7	66.3	69.1	10.7	10.3	11.2	21.6	23.4	19.6
Hungary	2005	10.9	23.1	3.6	8.9	58.4	66.7	65.3	13.6	14.2	13.3	28.0	19.1	21.3
Latvia	2006	5.1	13.6	2.5	7.0	60.0	78.3	72.7	19.5	18.4	14.0	20.6	3.3	13.3
Lithuania	2006	6.3	14.5	3.8	6.9	67.7	71.9	74.8	19.5	13.3	12.0	12.8	14.8	13.2
Malta	2005	17.5	26.1	7.5	13.2	51.7	53.0	54.7	20.7	24.6	22.8	27.6	22.4	22.5
Poland	2005	11.1	22.0	...	7.4	58.6	60.4	60.0	...	14.7	13.4	...	24.9	26.6
Romania	2006	...	5.6	...	4.7	51.3	65.3	78.7	...	24.9	17.9	...	9.8	3.4
Slovakia	2005	7.6	17.7	3.4	6.9	67.5	70.4	67.0	14.6	12.7	12.9	17.9	16.9	20.1
Other Europe														
Norway	2004	53.0	78.0	32.4	49.3	57.0	61.0	59.8	26.3	27.0	25.4	16.8	12.0	14.8

a/ At current prices.

Table 1.11
(continued)

SELECTED CHARACTERISTICS OF BRANCHES, SELECTED YEARS AND COUNTRIES

Glass and glass products (ISIC 2610)														
Country or area	Latest year	Value added per employee (current 1000 dollars)		Wages and salaries per employee (current 1000 dollars)		Percentage in output [a]								
						Costs of input materials and utilities			Costs of labour			Operating surplus		
	(LY)	2000	LY	2000	LY	2000	2003	LY	2000	2003	LY	2000	2003	LY
Other Countries														
Japan	2005	148.4	173.7	39.4	39.1	49.4	48.0	49.0	13.4	12.4	11.5	37.1	39.6	39.6
New Zealand	2006	...	64.5	...	26.1	...	55.6	54.1	...	18.9	18.6	...	25.6	27.3
Republic of Korea	2006	113.8	151.5	18.9	28.8	41.5	47.8	52.2	9.7	10.5	9.1	48.8	41.8	38.7
Singapore	2006	73.2	58.2	18.1	19.8	57.8	55.6	59.1	10.5	12.5	13.9	31.8	31.9	27.0
South Africa	2006	19.6	50.2	14.3	8.2	65.4	66.2	64.6	25.2	7.9	5.8	9.4	25.8	29.7
United States of America	2005	112.5	125.1	36.3	41.2	39.0	43.3	45.8	19.7	18.9	17.9	41.3	37.7	36.3
Developing Countries														
Brazil	2005	31.2	38.5	8.5	8.2	50.2	49.8	47.5	13.6	11.1	11.2	36.2	39.0	41.2
Chile	2006	...	72.2	...	16.0	...	41.1	38.6	...	11.6	13.6	...	47.3	47.8
Colombia	2005	36.4	48.1	5.3	6.2	41.4	48.4	49.6	8.5	6.6	6.5	50.1	45.0	43.9
Ecuador	2005	11.8	35.3	3.7	4.5	80.0	57.1	55.5	6.3	11.4	5.6	13.7	31.4	38.9
Eritrea	2006	...	2.3	...	0.9	...	67.9	77.7	...	15.8	8.5	...	16.3	13.7
Ethiopia	2006	3.6	9.2	0.8	1.5	31.0	29.3	48.3	15.0	26.8	8.6	54.0	43.9	43.0
Fiji	2004	...	21.5	...	14.6	...	69.5	79.6	...	11.3	13.9	...	19.2	6.5
India	2004	4.2	7.3	1.3	1.5	73.4	71.9	71.2	7.9	6.9	6.0	18.7	21.2	22.7
Indonesia	2005	...	15.3	...	1.6	...	48.2	52.1	...	11.2	5.2	...	40.6	42.8
Iran (Islamic Republic of)	2005	34.0	10.9	9.3	4.1	49.1	50.1	57.5	13.9	13.9	16.0	37.0	36.0	26.5
Jordan	2006	7.8	11.7	3.2	3.5	63.7	56.6	58.1	14.8	17.9	12.6	21.5	25.5	29.2
Malaysia	2005	41.9	23.9	5.9	8.4	50.8	57.0	70.0	7.0	10.4	10.6	42.2	32.6	19.4
Morocco	2005	15.2	19.5	4.7	8.3	46.0	54.0	54.7	16.8	19.7	19.2	37.2	26.2	26.1
Oman	2006	18.3	18.5	6.8	6.2	53.7	53.7	69.0	17.2	11.0	10.4	29.2	35.3	20.6
Philippines	2005	...	18.7	...	4.9	...	65.6	63.3	...	11.0	9.6	...	23.4	27.1
Qatar	2006	7.5	15.5	4.0	6.3	45.7	50.0	49.1	29.4	25.8	20.6	24.9	24.3	30.3
Trinidad and Tobago	2004	33.5	...	13.5	...	41.5	41.5	55.7	23.7	52.1	21.3	34.8	6.5	23.0
Uruguay	2005	19.0	7.9	10.0	4.7	70.3	71.2	68.2	15.7	14.0	18.8	14.0	14.8	13.0

a/ At current prices.

Table 1.11

SELECTED CHARACTERISTICS OF BRANCHES, SELECTED YEARS AND COUNTRIES

Non-metallic mineral products n.e.c. (ISIC 269)														
Country or area	Latest year	Value added per employee (current 1000 dollars)		Wages and salaries per employee (current 1000 dollars)		Percentage in output a/								
						Costs of input materials and utilities			Costs of labour			Operating surplus		
	(LY)	2000	LY	2000	LY	2000	2003	LY	2000	2003	LY	2000	2003	LY
Industrialized Countries														
CIS														
Azerbaijan	2006	...	10.1	0.7	1.9	...	65.8	67.1	25.6	7.9	6.3	...	26.3	26.7
Georgia	2006	1.4	4.2	0.6	1.5	69.9	...	75.0	13.8	...	9.0	16.3	...	16.0
Russian Federation	2006	...	12.5	0.9	4.5	...	65.6	63.6	13.0	18.2	13.0	...	16.2	23.5
EU-15														
Austria	2005	57.3	87.9	30.3	44.2	58.8	58.2	60.5	21.8	21.1	19.9	19.4	20.7	19.7
Belgium	2005	61.9	93.6	26.0	41.5	67.2	66.8	68.1	13.8	13.9	14.2	19.0	19.3	17.8
Denmark	2005	54.8	89.0	31.2	54.1	56.3	57.1	58.5	24.9	27.4	25.2	18.8	15.5	16.3
Finland	2005	59.0	88.7	23.9	39.0	61.2	62.3	62.6	15.7	17.0	16.5	23.1	20.7	21.0
France	2005	48.9	81.3	22.9	35.4	67.9	68.2	68.4	15.0	14.9	13.8	17.1	16.9	17.9
Germany	2005	48.7	66.8	27.6	39.9	60.7	62.5	64.2	22.3	23.1	21.4	17.1	14.4	14.4
Greece	2004	...	72.2	...	27.1	...	...	60.2	...	...	15.0	...	...	24.9
Ireland	2005	66.0	125.6	23.5	44.1	57.4	57.3	59.9	15.1	15.0	14.1	27.5	27.7	26.0
Italy	2005	50.1	73.5	18.4	29.0	66.6	67.3	70.3	12.3	11.7	11.7	21.1	21.0	18.0
Netherlands	2005	67.0	90.3	28.6	44.5	61.2	62.1	65.6	16.6	18.0	16.9	22.3	20.0	17.5
Portugal	2004	24.5	33.1	8.8	14.0	58.9	61.4	63.4	14.7	16.0	15.5	26.4	22.7	21.2
Spain	2005	42.5	72.6	16.9	28.3	62.4	64.9	65.2	15.0	14.4	13.6	22.6	20.7	21.2
Sweden	2005	53.1	80.0	25.4	37.8	63.7	...	65.0	17.4	...	16.5	18.9	...	18.5
United Kingdom	2005	52.2	88.1	25.4	40.5	56.4	56.8	55.7	21.2	19.8	20.4	22.3	23.4	23.9
EU-12														
Bulgaria	2006	3.3	15.1	1.4	2.8	75.8	72.1	71.2	10.2	8.1	5.3	14.0	19.8	23.5
Cyprus	2006	37.6	75.4	15.2	28.3	59.4	63.3	63.9	16.4	15.2	13.5	24.1	21.5	22.5
Estonia	2006	11.2	39.7	4.0	12.1	57.8	53.3	52.7	15.1	15.9	14.5	27.1	30.8	32.8
Hungary	2005	13.8	30.9	4.4	10.5	62.0	62.0	64.9	12.1	12.3	11.9	25.9	25.7	23.3
Latvia	2006	7.4	28.8	3.0	7.3	63.8	58.2	66.8	14.5	9.7	8.4	21.7	32.1	24.8
Lithuania	2006	3.5	21.5	2.6	7.0	73.4	65.8	62.1	20.1	15.2	12.4	6.5	19.0	25.5
Malta	2005	18.4	26.2	8.2	12.0	58.6	61.8	63.9	18.4	18.4	16.6	23.1	19.8	19.5
Poland	2005	...	29.8	...	8.4	...	62.6	62.4	...	11.4	10.6	...	25.9	26.9
Romania	2006	...	19.5	...	6.5	61.5	65.9	67.0	...	14.1	10.9	...	20.0	22.1
Slovakia	2005	7.8	22.9	3.4	8.0	72.8	68.7	69.8	12.0	11.1	10.5	15.2	20.2	19.7
Other Europe														
Norway	2004	65.1	89.5	33.8	53.5	59.7	64.3	65.5	20.9	22.1	20.7	19.4	13.6	13.9

a/ At current prices.

Table 1.11
(continued)

SELECTED CHARACTERISTICS OF BRANCHES, SELECTED YEARS AND COUNTRIES

Non-metallic mineral products n.e.c. (ISIC 269)

Country or area	Latest year	Value added per employee (current 1000 dollars)		Wages and salaries per employee (current 1000 dollars)		Percentage in output [a/] Costs of input materials and utilities			Costs of labour			Operating surplus		
	(LY)	2000	LY	2000	LY	2000	2003	LY	2000	2003	LY	2000	2003	LY
Other Countries														
Japan	2005	103.8	110.5	20.2	19.4	52.0	50.1	52.3	9.3	8.8	8.4	38.7	41.2	39.3
New Zealand	2006	...	67.9	...	29.1	...	61.2	63.1	...	17.0	15.8	...	21.8	21.1
Republic of Korea	2006	83.2	127.4	14.9	25.9	53.3	56.0	56.9	8.4	7.8	8.8	38.4	36.1	34.3
Singapore	2006	28.4	38.8	17.9	20.7	81.3	78.4	79.9	11.7	12.2	10.7	6.9	9.4	9.4
South Africa	2006	16.0	22.3	7.1	6.5	66.2	66.8	67.5	15.0	15.9	9.4	18.8	17.3	23.1
United States of America	2005	107.3	150.2	35.0	41.7	46.9	46.1	45.8	17.3	16.7	15.0	35.7	37.1	39.1
Developing Countries														
Brazil	2005	16.2	18.2	3.9	4.7	46.7	47.4	51.8	12.7	10.9	12.5	40.6	41.7	35.8
Chile	2006	...	87.5	...	14.5	...	55.7	54.8	...	9.2	7.5	...	35.1	37.7
Colombia	2005	42.4	55.8	4.4	5.2	37.5	34.5	43.5	6.5	4.9	5.2	56.0	60.5	51.3
Ecuador	2005	25.7	39.8	3.1	5.1	61.5	63.4	57.5	4.7	6.0	5.5	33.8	30.6	37.1
Eritrea	2006	1.8	2.5	0.7	1.0	62.4	64.5	67.5	14.6	11.6	12.6	23.0	23.9	19.9
Ethiopia	2006	5.2	8.9	0.8	1.1	50.5	49.3	53.4	7.7	6.8	5.7	41.8	43.9	40.8
India	2004	5.1	6.3	1.1	1.1	69.3	73.6	70.5	6.4	5.9	5.3	24.4	20.6	24.2
Indonesia	2005	...	11.3	...	1.8	...	50.0	47.3	...	10.6	8.3	...	39.4	44.4
Iran (Islamic Republic of)	2005	30.9	16.5	9.1	4.3	44.4	42.0	42.0	16.4	15.9	15.1	39.2	42.1	42.9
Jordan	2006	14.8	25.0	3.9	3.6	52.8	50.3	51.6	12.5	8.5	7.0	34.7	41.2	41.5
Malaysia	2005	17.9	16.1	4.5	6.4	62.0	58.2	72.1	9.7	10.7	11.1	28.4	31.1	16.8
Morocco	2005	14.0	22.7	4.0	5.9	50.8	55.5	58.4	14.1	11.6	10.8	35.1	32.8	30.8
Oman	2006	21.8	45.9	5.5	6.8	43.5	40.5	33.2	14.2	13.4	9.8	42.3	46.1	57.0
Philippines	2005	...	18.4	...	3.4	...	63.7	67.7	...	7.5	6.0	...	28.8	26.3
Qatar	2006	18.0	45.1	5.4	5.6	59.8	59.4	53.6	12.2	9.8	5.8	28.0	30.7	40.6
Sri Lanka	2006	...	4.0	...	1.3	...	...	71.3	...	...	9.0	...	...	19.7
Trinidad and Tobago	2004	30.3	...	10.9	...	50.0	49.0	39.4	17.9	19.2	17.2	32.0	31.8	43.4
Uruguay	2005	23.1	16.6	15.2	7.2	60.2	62.1	62.4	26.3	18.8	16.4	13.5	19.1	21.2

a/ At current prices.

Table 1.11

SELECTED CHARACTERISTICS OF BRANCHES, SELECTED YEARS AND COUNTRIES

Basic iron and steel (ISIC 2710)														
Country or area	Latest year	Value added per employee (current 1000 dollars)		Wages and salaries per employee (current 1000 dollars)		Percentage in output a/								
						Costs of input materials and utilities			Costs of labour			Operating surplus		
	(LY)	2000	LY	2000	LY	2000	2003	LY	2000	2003	LY	2000	2003	LY
Industrialized Countries														
CIS														
Azerbaijan	2006	...	5.6	0.2	2.5	...	62.6	80.3	30.7	11.4	8.9	...	26.0	10.8
Georgia	2006	0.3	4.8	0.2	1.7	86.5	79.0	85.3	8.7	10.6	5.2	4.8	10.4	9.5
Russian Federation	2006	...	34.1	1.5	6.1	...	70.5	69.7	8.5	7.3	5.4	...	22.2	24.9
EU-15														
Austria	2005	67.7	143.0	34.5	54.0	62.5	66.4	68.9	19.1	16.0	11.7	18.4	17.6	19.3
Belgium	2005	73.9	145.2	33.4	55.3	74.1	77.4	76.3	11.7	11.9	9.1	14.2	10.6	14.7
Denmark	2005	44.0	85.4	31.8	50.3	68.4	76.6	76.6	22.8	18.5	13.8	8.8	4.9	9.6
Finland	2005	...	140.8	...	49.3	...	74.8	75.2	...	10.6	8.7	...	14.6	16.1
France	2005	66.0	102.4	28.0	41.1	74.7	77.8	77.7	10.8	11.2	8.9	14.6	11.0	13.3
Germany	2005	60.0	114.8	33.3	50.7	71.3	72.5	73.8	15.9	15.6	11.6	12.8	11.9	14.6
Greece	2004	...	83.7	...	29.0	...	...	82.0	...	...	6.2	...	...	11.8
Ireland	2005	43.7	75.5	24.9	37.3	68.1	63.3	59.3	18.1	22.9	20.1	13.7	13.8	20.6
Italy	2005	56.6	101.5	22.2	34.4	79.3	82.1	81.7	8.1	7.9	6.2	12.6	10.0	12.1
Netherlands	2005	84.7	...	34.0	...	62.8	...	64.1	15.0	...	14.1	22.3	...	21.7
Portugal	2005	40.5	72.2	13.1	20.6	82.3	83.1	86.4	5.7	4.9	3.9	12.0	12.0	9.7
Spain	2005	70.3	112.4	24.4	40.2	74.2	78.4	78.8	8.9	9.7	7.6	16.8	12.0	13.6
Sweden	2005	69.9	112.6	29.2	41.0	68.1	...	76.9	13.3	...	8.4	18.6	...	14.7
United Kingdom	2005	51.6	75.8	36.1	52.5	75.6	84.4	82.9	17.1	15.6	11.9	7.3	0.1	5.2
EU-12														
Bulgaria	2006	5.1	12.6	2.1	5.5	82.0	87.0	87.7	7.5	6.7	5.4	10.6	6.3	6.9
Czech Republic	2004	11.3	...	4.9	9.4	79.2	79.1	...	9.0	7.7	5.2	11.7	13.2	...
Hungary	2005	10.8	33.1	5.2	14.4	86.0	82.9	82.1	6.7	8.6	7.7	7.3	8.4	10.1
Lithuania	2006	7.1	8.6	3.9	4.9	77.5	85.4	76.7	12.4	7.3	13.3	10.1	7.3	10.0
Malta	2005	...	18.1	...	13.1	...	...	56.6	...	...	31.4	...	...	11.9
Poland	2005	15.6	41.5	...	11.1	76.7	83.0	78.4	...	7.7	5.8	...	9.2	15.8
Romania	2006	...	18.6	...	9.2	79.0	78.3	82.3	...	12.0	8.8	...	9.7	8.9
Slovakia	2005	10.8	43.2	4.6	11.9	79.6	...	71.0	8.6	...	8.0	11.8	...	21.0
Other Europe														
Norway	2004	73.1	185.9	38.1	59.7	73.6	73.8	68.8	13.7	13.7	10.0	12.7	12.6	21.2

a/ At current prices.

Table 1.11
(continued)

SELECTED CHARACTERISTICS OF BRANCHES, SELECTED YEARS AND COUNTRIES

Country or area	Latest year	Basic iron and steel (ISIC 2710)												
		Value added per employee (current 1000 dollars)		Wages and salaries per employee (current 1000 dollars)		Percentage in output [a]								
						Costs of input materials and utilities			Costs of labour			Operating surplus		
	(LY)	2000	LY	2000	LY	2000	2003	LY	2000	2003	LY	2000	2003	LY
Other Countries														
Israel	2005	71.6	47.5	33.4	31.8	71.4	73.2	86.3	13.4	15.3	9.2	15.3	11.5	4.5
Japan	2005	193.8	352.0	48.6	51.1	65.6	65.2	63.8	8.6	6.8	5.2	25.8	28.0	30.9
Republic of Korea	2006	146.8	274.2	20.2	38.6	67.7	66.9	68.7	4.4	4.5	4.4	27.9	28.5	26.9
United States of America	2005	125.8	249.5	46.1	56.4	61.2	63.0	60.3	14.2	12.9	9.0	24.6	24.1	30.7
Developing Countries														
Brazil	2005	61.6	114.9	10.7	13.5	55.1	55.8	56.5	7.8	5.8	5.1	37.1	38.4	38.4
Chile	2006	...	88.7	...	20.6	...	56.5	63.9	...	8.5	8.4	...	35.1	27.7
Colombia	2005	49.5	129.9	5.6	7.2	50.3	47.6	50.3	5.6	3.9	2.8	44.0	48.5	46.9
Ecuador	2005	17.6	31.8	1.8	6.3	83.9	86.5	81.2	1.6	4.7	3.7	14.5	8.9	15.0
Eritrea	2006	15.1	1.7	0.9	1.2	49.3	63.8	73.9	3.1	1.5	18.9	47.6	34.7	7.2
Ethiopia	2006	8.3	16.6	1.2	1.7	66.1	53.7	77.7	5.0	5.1	2.2	28.9	41.1	20.0
Fiji	2004	...	22.0	...	4.3	...	81.4	87.4	...	6.2	2.5	...	12.4	10.1
India	2004	7.9	25.5	2.5	2.9	80.7	77.2	75.4	6.2	4.5	2.8	13.2	18.3	21.8
Indonesia	2005	16.7	21.9	2.5	4.3	77.0	79.5	87.6	3.4	3.4	2.4	19.6	17.1	9.9
Iran (Islamic Republic of)	2005	94.7	70.8	17.9	7.4	58.4	56.0	53.1	7.9	7.1	4.9	33.8	36.9	42.0
Jordan	2006	35.4	58.0	4.2	5.8	60.7	64.4	67.3	4.7	4.6	3.3	34.7	31.0	29.5
Malaysia	2005	14.7	21.2	5.5	7.6	86.3	76.4	89.4	5.1	4.9	3.8	8.6	18.6	6.8
Morocco	2005	25.7	62.3	5.8	11.2	77.8	77.4	80.7	5.0	3.7	3.5	17.1	19.0	15.8
Oman	2006	14.1	54.7	3.5	6.9	88.2	83.3	84.2	2.9	3.1	2.0	8.8	13.5	13.8
Peru	2006	...	72.7	...	11.2	...	60.9	61.0	...	12.0	6.0	...	27.1	33.0
Philippines	2005	...	13.6	...	2.6	...	80.2	82.7	...	4.5	3.3	...	15.3	14.0
Qatar	2006	...	...	20.1	28.9	36.1	36.2	33.4	7.7	5.7	4.7	56.2	58.1	61.9
Trinidad and Tobago	2004	18.2	...	12.5	...	91.0	87.0	61.4	6.2	5.6	4.2	2.8	7.4	34.4

a/ At current prices.

Table 1.11

SELECTED CHARACTERISTICS OF BRANCHES, SELECTED YEARS AND COUNTRIES

Country or area	Latest year	Value added per employee (current 1000 dollars)		Wages and salaries per employee (current 1000 dollars)		Percentage in output a/								
						Costs of input materials and utilities			Costs of labour			Operating surplus		
	(LY)	2000	LY	2000	LY	2000	2003	LY	2000	2003	LY	2000	2003	LY
Basic precious and non-ferrous metals (ISIC 2720)														
Industrialized Countries														
CIS														
Azerbaijan	2006	...	12.8	...	2.7	...	62.6	80.3	...	6.8	4.2	...	30.6	15.5
Kyrgyzstan	2005	...	38.8	0.4	9.0	...	69.4	65.1	1.0	2.5	8.0	...	28.1	26.8
Russian Federation	2006	...	89.1	2.9	7.5	...	69.8	58.9	10.0	8.1	3.5	...	22.1	37.6
EU-15														
Austria	2005	61.3	118.7	30.5	48.3	79.4	77.9	76.1	10.3	11.2	9.7	10.4	10.9	14.1
Belgium	2005	84.9	99.3	32.9	51.7	82.4	82.5	87.7	6.8	8.9	6.4	10.8	8.6	5.9
Denmark	2005	47.0	74.4	32.8	51.2	74.3	73.9	74.1	17.9	16.7	17.8	7.8	9.4	8.0
Finland	2005	94.1	149.3	27.8	48.0	80.7	83.3	82.6	5.7	7.1	5.6	13.6	9.6	11.8
France	2005	70.3	96.8	27.8	43.1	81.4	82.9	81.6	7.4	9.5	8.2	11.3	7.6	10.2
Germany	2005	66.4	88.9	35.1	53.9	77.0	77.1	80.6	12.2	13.9	11.8	10.8	9.0	7.7
Greece	2004	...	84.9	...	28.6	...	...	75.9	...	...	8.1	...	...	16.0
Ireland	2005	42.7	97.2	29.0	54.4	75.0	73.6	76.4	17.0	15.4	13.2	8.0	11.0	10.4
Italy	2005	64.2	74.9	22.7	33.8	83.5	84.0	86.6	5.8	6.9	6.0	10.7	9.1	7.3
Netherlands	2005	67.4	96.4	31.4	51.4	75.4	74.9	78.9	11.4	13.6	11.2	13.1	11.5	9.8
Portugal	2005	28.8	32.5	11.0	17.7	73.6	77.4	80.7	10.1	11.2	10.5	16.3	11.4	8.8
Spain	2005	77.8	103.3	23.8	36.5	78.7	83.6	82.8	6.5	7.9	6.1	14.8	8.5	11.1
Sweden	2005	67.8	105.4	28.5	40.8	77.4	...	80.5	9.5	...	7.6	13.1	...	11.9
United Kingdom	2005	69.0	104.2	33.6	47.3	75.7	77.0	76.8	11.8	13.5	10.5	12.4	9.5	12.7
EU-12														
Bulgaria	2006	8.5	57.1	2.6	6.0	83.7	92.7	89.1	5.1	4.9	1.1	11.2	2.5	9.7
Czech Republic	2004	13.2	27.2	4.9	9.0	83.3	80.4	80.7	6.2	6.7	6.4	10.6	13.0	12.9
Hungary	2005	23.0	46.3	6.8	18.0	81.3	79.3	78.6	5.6	8.6	8.3	13.1	12.1	13.1
Lithuania	2006	3.4	19.2	1.6	3.3	76.1	71.7	76.8	11.1	17.4	3.9	12.8	10.9	19.3
Poland	2005	15.3	28.7	...	10.8	79.8	78.9	81.0	...	8.7	7.2	...	12.4	11.8
Romania	2006	...	33.4	...	10.2	83.8	81.9	75.2	...	9.9	7.6	...	8.2	17.2
Slovakia	2005	20.1	45.9	4.0	9.2	75.6	81.1	80.1	4.9	5.7	4.0	19.5	13.3	15.9
Other Europe														
Norway	2004	152.0	178.8	41.7	72.9	73.1	74.9	68.8	7.4	10.5	12.7	19.5	14.5	18.5

a/ At current prices.

Table 1.11
(continued)

SELECTED CHARACTERISTICS OF BRANCHES, SELECTED YEARS AND COUNTRIES

Basic precious and non-ferrous metals (ISIC 2720)														
Country or area	Latest year	Value added per employee (current 1000 dollars)		Wages and salaries per employee (current 1000 dollars)		Percentage in output [a/]								
						Costs of input materials and utilities			Costs of labour			Operating surplus		
	(LY)	2000	LY	2000	LY	2000	2003	LY	2000	2003	LY	2000	2003	LY
Other Countries														
Israel	2005	31.2	41.1	25.0	27.6	80.4	78.3	81.8	15.7	15.8	12.2	3.9	5.9	6.0
Japan	2005	150.7	186.8	44.5	43.3	73.3	75.9	73.9	7.9	7.0	6.1	18.8	17.2	20.0
Republic of Korea	2006	92.0	193.2	17.0	30.1	75.3	77.6	80.8	4.6	4.9	3.0	20.1	17.6	16.2
South Africa	2006	71.9	74.4	11.3	10.1	68.5	66.3	62.7	5.0	4.8	5.1	26.5	28.9	32.3
United States of America	2005	114.9	170.7	39.0	48.2	67.1	65.6	70.1	11.2	11.4	8.4	21.7	23.0	21.5
Developing Countries														
Brazil	2005	61.3	70.1	9.3	11.4	55.3	60.0	63.1	6.8	6.0	6.0	37.9	33.9	30.9
Colombia	2005	31.3	52.4	5.0	5.6	77.3	84.2	82.7	3.6	1.6	1.9	19.0	14.2	15.5
Ecuador	2005	...	38.6	...	5.2	...	81.0	76.6	...	5.2	3.2	...	13.8	20.3
India	2004	11.9	26.6	2.0	2.8	76.8	81.5	79.5	3.9	3.1	2.2	19.2	15.4	18.3
Indonesia	2005	18.8	31.2	1.8	3.5	63.9	66.0	68.2	3.4	4.6	3.6	32.7	29.4	28.2
Iran (Islamic Republic of)	2005	107.0	43.9	19.6	8.8	54.0	62.0	65.0	8.4	9.1	7.0	37.5	28.9	28.1
Jordan	2006	16.0	37.9	3.7	4.0	64.8	57.8	57.7	8.0	6.4	4.4	27.1	35.8	37.9
Madagascar	2006	...	0.3	...	0.1	...	...	83.8	...	4.8	6.8	...	...	9.4
Malaysia	2005	27.4	21.5	5.8	8.3	77.0	80.9	88.7	4.8	5.6	4.4	18.1	13.5	7.0
Morocco	2005	13.6	48.9	4.1	10.1	81.1	78.5	61.6	5.7	10.0	8.0	13.2	11.5	30.4
Oman	2006	38.6	28.3	11.4	12.6	50.3	56.4	73.9	14.6	16.3	11.6	35.0	27.3	14.5
Peru	2006	...	186.5	...	15.9	...	86.5	86.6	...	2.9	1.1	...	10.6	12.3
Philippines	2005	...	33.7	...	3.8	...	88.8	89.8	...	1.4	1.1	...	9.8	9.0
Sri Lanka	2006	...	13.9	...	1.9	...	...	67.0	...	...	4.6	...	...	28.5

a/ At current prices.

Table 1.11

SELECTED CHARACTERISTICS OF BRANCHES, SELECTED YEARS AND COUNTRIES

Casting of metals (ISIC 273)														
Country or area	Latest year	Value added per employee (current 1000 dollars)		Wages and salaries per employee (current 1000 dollars)		Percentage in output [a]								
						Costs of input materials and utilities			Costs of labour			Operating surplus		
	(LY)	2000	LY	2000	LY	2000	2003	LY	2000	2003	LY	2000	2003	LY
Industrialized Countries														
CIS														
Azerbaijan	2006	...	2.5	0.3	1.1	...	62.5	80.3	40.5	29.1	8.2	...	8.4	11.4
EU-15														
Austria	2005	47.5	74.2	26.5	45.9	56.7	58.8	61.6	24.1	24.3	23.7	19.1	16.8	14.6
Belgium	2005	47.3	68.1	27.1	41.2	64.2	62.5	68.0	20.5	20.7	19.3	15.3	16.8	12.6
Denmark	2005	39.0	52.6	28.1	46.0	51.1	55.1	62.4	35.2	32.5	32.8	13.7	12.4	4.7
Finland	2005	...	63.1	...	39.3	...	57.2	59.4	...	26.0	25.3	...	16.8	15.3
France	2005	34.2	50.0	20.2	30.9	65.5	65.9	67.4	20.4	21.7	20.1	14.1	12.4	12.4
Germany	2005	44.2	76.6	29.2	45.2	57.3	57.0	59.9	28.2	27.4	23.7	14.5	15.7	16.4
Greece	2004	...	56.0	...	17.8	...	...	60.7	...	...	12.5	...	...	26.8
Ireland	2005	62.7	79.4	19.3	26.5	60.6	42.9	50.0	12.1	28.6	16.7	27.3	28.6	33.3
Italy	2005	45.1	65.0	19.6	30.8	70.4	73.0	73.5	12.8	13.0	12.6	16.7	14.0	14.0
Netherlands	2005	43.1	...	25.5	...	64.3	...	69.0	21.1	...	19.5	14.6	...	11.5
Portugal	2005	19.7	26.9	9.5	15.0	59.4	58.6	63.0	19.5	23.7	20.7	21.1	17.7	16.3
Spain	2005	37.4	63.6	19.4	31.7	65.6	65.3	68.1	17.9	18.9	15.9	16.6	15.8	16.0
Sweden	2005	50.0	58.4	24.0	33.6	55.6	...	61.4	21.3	...	22.2	23.1	...	16.4
United Kingdom	2005	45.0	60.4	26.7	37.4	52.9	58.7	56.0	27.9	28.9	27.2	19.2	12.4	16.8
EU-12														
Bulgaria	2006	1.9	5.4	1.1	2.4	73.1	70.4	75.0	15.4	16.4	11.3	11.5	13.2	13.7
Czech Republic	2004	7.6	14.0	3.9	7.1	69.0	69.2	70.8	15.9	16.6	14.9	15.1	14.2	14.4
Estonia	2006	...	11.7	...	6.2	...	63.3	62.9	...	19.5	19.4	...	17.2	17.7
Hungary	2005	8.5	18.8	3.8	9.0	66.4	65.9	67.8	15.1	16.6	15.4	18.5	17.6	16.8
Lithuania	2006	3.3	10.9	3.1	6.6	65.2	62.0	59.4	32.6	28.1	24.7	2.2	9.9	15.9
Poland	2005	7.5	16.2	...	7.8	66.7	67.9	67.6	...	17.0	15.6	...	15.1	16.8
Romania	2006	...	6.8	...	5.0	65.2	77.9	82.3	...	20.2	12.8	...	1.8	4.8
Slovakia	2005	4.5	15.9	3.5	6.9	78.3	...	71.1	16.7	...	12.6	4.9	...	16.3
Other Europe														
Norway	2004	44.5	58.6	32.3	47.8	52.9	56.9	62.7	34.2	33.3	30.5	12.9	9.8	6.9

a/ At current prices.

Table 1.11
(continued)

SELECTED CHARACTERISTICS OF BRANCHES, SELECTED YEARS AND COUNTRIES

Casting of metals (ISIC 273)

Country or area	Latest year	Value added per employee (current 1000 dollars)		Wages and salaries per employee (current 1000 dollars)		Percentage in output a/								
						Costs of input materials and utilities			Costs of labour			Operating surplus		
	(LY)	2000	LY	2000	LY	2000	2003	LY	2000	2003	LY	2000	2003	LY
Other Countries														
Israel	2005	...	43.2	...	30.5	...	45.7	63.9	...	41.3	25.4	...	12.9	10.7
Japan	2005	90.0	103.6	31.3	31.6	54.1	55.1	57.0	15.9	14.8	13.1	29.9	30.1	29.9
Republic of Korea	2006	46.8	86.4	15.4	25.4	53.1	57.0	65.4	15.5	14.9	10.2	31.5	28.1	24.4
United States of America	2005	78.3	101.9	35.3	42.4	41.2	43.9	46.2	26.5	25.9	22.4	32.3	30.3	31.4
Developing Countries														
Brazil	2005	9.3	15.6	4.2	5.7	52.3	54.9	58.1	21.3	16.1	15.1	26.4	28.9	26.7
Colombia	2004	9.9	9.9	2.6	1.8	41.4	...	53.7	15.2	...	8.3	43.4	...	38.0
Ecuador	2005	3.4	15.9	0.6	3.2	41.1	...	47.5	10.2	...	10.6	48.7	...	41.9
India	2004	2.5	4.2	1.2	1.5	81.2	82.2	83.5	9.3	6.9	5.7	9.6	10.8	10.8
Indonesia	2005	12.5	34.9	1.3	1.8	71.2	57.1	49.3	3.0	7.4	2.6	25.8	35.5	48.0
Iran (Islamic Republic of)	2005	21.8	10.8	10.4	4.5	55.4	51.4	58.2	21.2	19.5	17.4	23.4	29.1	24.4
Jordan	2006	3.3	16.5	3.1	1.8	73.5	61.7	51.7	25.6	26.6	5.3	0.9	11.7	43.0
Malaysia	2005	15.3	13.2	4.9	6.4	74.4	75.2	83.1	8.2	9.3	8.2	17.4	15.5	8.7
Morocco	2005	5.4	7.2	4.1	4.2	31.2	61.4	66.7	52.5	32.5	19.5	16.3	6.0	13.8
Oman	2006	...	16.9	...	6.9	...	39.3	56.6	...	19.2	17.8	...	41.5	25.7
Philippines	2005	...	12.5	...	2.3	...	70.8	71.2	...	6.9	5.4	...	22.4	23.4
Qatar	2006	23.8	18.8	9.6	6.0	29.9	30.6	73.8	28.3	28.3	8.4	41.8	41.2	17.9
Sri Lanka	2006	...	14.9	...	3.8	...	...	47.2	...	...	13.5	...	...	39.3

a/ At current prices.

Table 1.11

SELECTED CHARACTERISTICS OF BRANCHES, SELECTED YEARS AND COUNTRIES

Struct.metal products;tanks;steam generators (ISIC 281)

Country or area	Latest year	Value added per employee (current 1000 dollars)		Wages and salaries per employee (current 1000 dollars)		Percentage in output a/								
						Costs of input materials and utilities			Costs of labour			Operating surplus		
	(LY)	2000	LY	2000	LY	2000	2003	LY	2000	2003	LY	2000	2003	LY
Industrialized Countries														
CIS														
Azerbaijan	2006	...	2.9	0.7	2.6	...	62.6	80.3	17.3	11.9	17.4	...	25.5	2.2
Georgia	2006	0.6	2.8	0.4	1.5	77.0	73.8	71.5	15.7	13.0	15.4	7.3	13.2	13.2
Kyrgyzstan	2006	...	...	0.3	0.8	...	...	...	9.3	21.6	15.5	...	...	...
Russian Federation	2006	...	9.6	1.0	4.3	...	65.5	70.0	9.9	19.4	13.4	...	15.1	16.7
EU-15														
Austria	2005	44.5	66.7	25.1	39.5	58.2	58.7	62.7	23.6	22.8	22.1	18.2	18.5	15.2
Belgium	2005	45.6	66.1	23.8	36.9	65.8	66.3	67.8	17.8	18.3	18.0	16.4	15.4	14.2
Denmark	2004	40.6	66.8	30.6	50.8	60.8	...	57.8	29.5	...	32.1	9.7	...	10.1
Finland	2005	42.6	67.3	23.7	38.0	67.8	67.6	63.9	18.0	19.4	20.4	14.3	13.0	15.7
France	2005	39.7	58.2	21.4	32.9	63.8	64.8	64.8	19.6	21.0	19.9	16.7	14.2	15.3
Germany	2005	38.7	58.1	25.9	37.5	63.3	62.4	63.5	24.5	24.6	23.5	12.2	13.1	13.0
Greece	2004	...	73.1	...	18.0	...	...	64.2	...	...	8.8	...	...	26.9
Ireland	2005	39.9	57.5	20.1	37.6	63.2	67.3	65.9	18.6	22.1	22.3	18.3	10.7	11.8
Italy	2005	38.3	56.4	16.0	24.4	69.5	68.9	70.2	12.7	13.6	12.9	17.7	17.5	16.9
Netherlands	2005	43.1	70.1	25.9	43.4	68.2	...	70.0	19.1	...	18.6	12.7	...	11.4
Portugal	2005	15.2	24.2	8.2	12.5	70.1	69.0	68.4	16.2	18.4	16.3	13.7	12.6	15.3
Spain	2005	26.3	42.8	14.2	23.1	66.9	63.2	66.6	17.8	20.1	18.0	15.3	16.7	15.3
Sweden	2005	45.8	63.3	24.8	33.8	65.6	...	68.5	18.6	...	16.8	15.8	...	14.7
United Kingdom	2005	48.0	67.8	32.5	40.6	62.6	57.5	63.7	25.3	23.3	21.7	12.0	19.2	14.5
EU-12														
Bulgaria	2006	1.7	6.1	1.1	2.1	75.3	79.2	79.7	16.6	9.5	7.0	8.1	11.3	13.4
Cyprus	2006	20.9	42.8	10.5	22.0	65.3	63.3	64.2	17.4	17.1	18.4	17.4	19.6	17.4
Czech Republic	2004	8.4	14.0	4.2	7.0	72.8	...	75.7	13.5	...	12.2	13.7	...	12.1
Estonia	2005	5.8	14.5	3.4	7.3	72.8	73.4	74.1	15.8	14.3	13.0	11.4	12.4	12.8
Hungary	2005	8.2	16.9	3.4	7.7	65.4	67.8	69.5	14.4	15.4	13.8	20.3	16.8	16.7
Latvia	2006	5.5	14.7	2.1	5.5	60.6	65.0	70.4	15.2	13.7	11.1	24.3	21.3	18.5
Lithuania	2006	4.5	14.4	2.2	6.7	69.5	71.5	69.4	14.7	13.4	14.2	15.8	15.2	16.4
Malta	2005	14.6	21.7	7.4	11.6	62.9	60.8	64.6	18.9	22.0	18.9	18.2	17.3	16.5
Poland	2005	10.7	19.0	...	7.8	67.6	66.4	65.6	...	14.3	14.1	...	19.4	20.3
Romania	2006	...	8.7	...	5.4	...	71.6	73.6	...	18.6	16.4	...	9.7	10.0
Slovakia	2004	4.8	14.7	3.3	6.2	78.7	73.1	73.7	14.6	12.3	11.2	6.7	14.6	15.1
Other Europe														
Norway	2004	40.2	66.6	31.2	47.4	60.0	60.2	61.0	31.0	30.1	27.7	8.9	9.6	11.3

a/ At current prices.

Table 1.11
(continued)

SELECTED CHARACTERISTICS OF BRANCHES, SELECTED YEARS AND COUNTRIES

Struct.metal products;tanks;steam generators (ISIC 281)														
Country or area	Latest year	Value added per employee (current 1000 dollars)		Wages and salaries per employee (current 1000 dollars)		Percentage in output[a/]								
						Costs of input materials and utilities			Costs of labour			Operating surplus		
	(LY)	2000	LY	2000	LY	2000	2003	LY	2000	2003	LY	2000	2003	LY
Other Countries														
Australia	2005	46.7	58.4	19.7	...	54.2	66.6	65.3	19.4	...	...	26.5	...	...
Israel	2005	28.6	30.5	22.7	19.9	67.1	63.3	69.9	26.0	26.9	19.6	6.9	9.8	10.5
Japan	2005	100.2	95.8	23.4	20.3	58.9	56.0	60.2	9.6	9.3	8.4	31.5	34.7	31.4
Republic of Korea	2006	50.9	82.0	16.9	26.5	61.5	65.2	67.8	12.8	12.7	10.4	25.7	22.2	21.8
Singapore	2006	20.4	23.1	14.0	15.8	72.6	70.4	69.6	18.8	21.3	20.7	8.6	8.4	9.7
United States of America	2005	79.9	103.0	33.9	39.5	49.1	47.7	50.5	21.6	22.2	19.0	29.3	30.1	30.5
Developing Countries														
Brazil	2005	10.6	15.8	4.2	5.3	53.8	53.8	55.0	18.4	18.1	15.0	27.8	28.2	30.0
Chile	2006	...	18.3	...	8.1	...	58.7	59.1	...	16.4	18.1	...	25.0	22.7
Colombia	2005	13.2	22.3	3.1	3.9	56.5	60.6	65.3	10.1	7.0	6.1	33.4	32.4	28.6
Ecuador	2005	7.2	12.3	1.1	3.8	64.8	72.6	70.7	5.5	9.7	9.1	29.7	17.7	20.2
Eritrea	2006	5.7	6.2	1.0	1.3	52.2	63.0	49.3	8.8	9.4	10.4	39.0	27.6	40.3
Ethiopia	2006	1.9	2.6	0.5	0.6	58.0	60.7	68.7	11.4	10.6	6.9	30.6	28.8	24.4
India	2004	3.3	5.0	1.8	1.8	79.0	79.3	82.3	11.8	7.7	6.4	9.3	13.0	11.3
Indonesia	2005	15.2	14.2	1.6	1.8	60.1	49.9	48.0	4.1	9.8	6.4	35.9	40.4	45.6
Iran (Islamic Republic of)	2005	33.2	11.7	14.2	4.1	52.9	51.2	63.3	20.2	15.0	13.0	26.9	33.8	23.7
Jordan	2006	6.4	6.2	2.3	1.7	59.9	65.3	67.7	14.7	10.0	9.1	25.4	24.7	23.2
Madagascar	2006	...	...	...	0.2	...	...	...	...	5.0	7.3	...	...	...
Malaysia	2005	11.0	9.9	4.4	5.3	68.7	67.2	73.9	12.4	15.2	13.9	18.8	17.6	12.2
Morocco	2005	7.2	11.5	4.2	6.8	56.5	69.5	75.3	25.5	18.3	14.6	18.0	12.3	10.1
Oman	2006	9.3	15.8	6.0	5.6	51.5	40.5	54.9	31.4	24.0	16.0	17.2	35.5	29.1
Sri Lanka	2006	...	1.7	...	0.7	...	...	59.4	...	...	17.6	...	...	23.0
Trinidad and Tobago	2004	17.2	...	14.2	...	64.8	53.5	60.9	28.9	34.6	14.5	6.3	11.9	24.6
Uruguay	2005	16.0	12.5	10.7	4.7	59.7	66.2	68.5	26.9	11.4	11.9	13.4	22.4	19.6

a/ At current prices.

Table 1.11

SELECTED CHARACTERISTICS OF BRANCHES, SELECTED YEARS AND COUNTRIES

Other metal products; metal working services (ISIC 289)

Country or area	Latest year	Value added per employee (current 1000 dollars)		Wages and salaries per employee (current 1000 dollars)		Percentage in output a/								
						Costs of input materials and utilities			Costs of labour			Operating surplus		
	(LY)	2000	LY	2000	LY	2000	2003	LY	2000	2003	LY	2000	2003	LY
Industrialized Countries														
CIS														
Azerbaijan	2006	...	2.9	0.3	2.6	...	46.0	80.3	30.1	25.2	17.3	...	28.8	2.4
Georgia	2006	0.8	2.6	0.4	1.3	56.7	63.4	77.4	22.9	19.8	11.1	20.4	16.8	11.4
Kyrgyzstan	2006	...	...	0.3	0.9	...	...	...	18.2	12.9	13.1	...	...	...
Russian Federation	2006	...	5.3	0.8	3.7	...	68.2	74.7	5.9	16.2	17.9	...	15.6	7.4
EU-15														
Austria	2005	47.7	79.3	25.1	39.3	54.7	54.4	55.7	23.8	22.7	21.9	21.5	22.9	22.3
Belgium	2005	49.4	76.0	24.2	37.2	63.4	64.3	67.0	17.9	17.8	16.1	18.7	17.9	16.8
Denmark	2004	43.4	71.0	28.2	45.2	54.1	...	52.6	29.8	...	30.2	16.1	...	17.2
Finland	2005	45.9	67.7	22.5	35.0	51.7	53.6	56.0	23.7	24.7	22.7	24.6	21.7	21.3
France	2005	39.6	59.1	21.3	33.3	61.2	62.2	63.0	20.9	22.0	20.8	17.9	15.8	16.1
Germany	2005	45.1	65.2	27.2	38.4	55.4	55.6	58.8	26.9	26.9	24.3	17.7	17.5	16.9
Greece	2004	...	67.9	...	19.5	...	...	63.2	...	...	10.6	...	...	26.3
Ireland	2005	40.4	55.5	20.6	36.3	54.2	56.5	60.1	23.3	24.8	26.2	22.5	18.7	13.8
Italy	2005	44.7	65.1	16.7	27.3	63.0	62.9	66.7	13.8	15.3	14.0	23.2	21.8	19.3
Netherlands	2005	46.5	77.7	24.6	42.3	60.6	...	63.3	20.8	...	20.0	18.6	...	16.7
Portugal	2005	16.6	23.4	8.0	11.3	64.4	62.7	63.7	17.2	17.9	17.6	18.4	19.4	18.7
Spain	2005	34.1	55.9	17.2	29.1	61.7	61.9	64.0	19.2	20.2	18.8	19.0	17.9	17.3
Sweden	2005	42.6	72.1	22.6	34.5	56.9	...	58.8	22.9	...	19.7	20.3	...	21.5
United Kingdom	2005	48.8	67.5	27.4	36.1	48.9	49.7	50.1	28.7	28.4	26.7	22.4	21.9	23.2
EU-12														
Bulgaria	2006	2.4	6.5	1.0	2.2	75.8	71.6	72.9	10.3	10.8	9.2	13.8	17.6	17.9
Cyprus	2006	23.7	43.2	11.1	23.1	54.0	51.1	53.0	21.7	21.9	25.1	24.3	27.0	21.9
Czech Republic	2004	8.7	20.0	3.8	7.0	68.8	...	64.7	13.5	...	12.3	17.6	...	23.0
Estonia	2005	7.1	15.8	3.3	7.3	70.0	65.8	74.0	13.9	13.8	11.9	16.1	20.3	14.1
Hungary	2005	8.3	17.3	3.4	7.9	64.3	66.9	68.6	14.6	15.1	14.3	21.1	18.0	17.1
Latvia	2006	6.3	11.7	2.2	4.8	53.3	64.6	67.4	16.3	16.2	13.5	30.3	19.2	19.1
Lithuania	2006	3.1	9.8	2.2	5.5	64.2	65.5	75.6	25.2	18.2	13.8	10.6	16.3	10.6
Malta	2005	26.3	39.2	10.5	17.7	53.5	61.5	58.7	18.5	21.4	18.6	28.0	17.1	22.7
Poland	2005	12.5	19.3	...	6.8	61.0	68.9	67.9	...	12.3	11.3	...	18.9	20.8
Romania	2006	...	8.6	...	5.6	...	67.5	72.7	...	19.5	18.0	...	13.0	9.3
Slovakia	2004	5.9	12.1	3.1	6.0	71.5	67.1	70.1	14.9	16.1	15.0	13.6	16.8	14.9
Other Europe														
Norway	2004	46.8	72.6	30.6	48.1	56.7	55.7	57.2	28.3	30.3	28.4	15.0	13.9	14.4

a/ At current prices.

Table 1.11
(continued)

SELECTED CHARACTERISTICS OF BRANCHES, SELECTED YEARS AND COUNTRIES

Country or area	Latest year (LY)	Value added per employee (current 1000 dollars) 2000	Value added per employee (current 1000 dollars) LY	Wages and salaries per employee (current 1000 dollars) 2000	Wages and salaries per employee (current 1000 dollars) LY	Percentage in output a/: Costs of input materials and utilities 2000	Costs of input materials and utilities 2003	Costs of input materials and utilities LY	Costs of labour 2000	Costs of labour 2003	Costs of labour LY	Operating surplus 2000	Operating surplus 2003	Operating surplus LY
	Other metal products; metal working services (ISIC 289)													
Other Countries														
Israel	2005	47.5	46.4	27.2	22.7	50.4	52.4	55.7	28.5	25.8	21.7	21.2	21.8	22.6
Japan	2005	85.9	90.8	23.4	23.7	53.1	53.5	54.4	12.8	12.5	11.9	34.1	34.0	33.7
Republic of Korea	2006	42.4	68.1	13.6	23.0	52.0	54.9	57.0	15.4	16.4	14.5	32.6	28.7	28.5
Singapore	2006	35.4	39.6	18.0	21.5	71.9	71.6	75.1	14.3	16.2	13.5	13.8	12.2	11.4
United States of America	2005	80.9	100.6	35.1	40.9	42.2	42.6	44.7	25.0	24.4	22.5	32.7	33.1	32.8
Developing Countries														
Brazil	2005	16.2	22.4	5.3	6.1	54.2	57.0	54.7	14.9	12.7	12.4	30.9	30.3	33.0
Chile	2006	...	36.8	...	12.6	...	56.8	63.5	...	14.9	12.5	...	28.2	24.1
Colombia	2005	19.6	23.7	4.0	4.5	49.6	56.6	60.2	10.3	8.4	7.5	40.0	35.0	32.2
Ecuador	2005	24.3	22.2	2.6	7.0	59.6	60.5	71.3	4.4	8.1	9.1	36.0	31.4	19.7
Ethiopia	2006	2.8	4.6	0.8	1.1	53.7	58.0	65.0	13.0	13.1	8.7	33.3	28.9	26.3
India	2004	3.8	4.6	1.1	1.4	77.8	81.3	82.1	6.6	5.6	5.5	15.6	13.1	12.4
Indonesia	2005	6.0	5.9	1.0	1.2	62.2	61.9	68.3	6.4	8.2	6.7	31.3	29.9	25.1
Iran (Islamic Republic of)	2005	27.1	12.2	9.0	3.8	57.1	64.8	64.9	14.2	13.5	11.0	28.7	21.7	24.1
Jordan	2006	10.0	17.3	3.0	2.3	66.9	62.1	60.4	10.0	9.2	5.3	23.1	28.7	34.2
Madagascar	2006	...	0.3	...	0.1	...	51.6	49.1	...	8.1	11.9	...	40.3	39.1
Malaysia	2005	14.6	13.4	4.5	5.9	72.2	72.9	79.3	8.7	9.5	9.1	19.1	17.6	11.6
Morocco	2005	9.1	14.5	4.9	6.5	65.9	70.3	73.6	18.5	15.2	11.9	15.7	14.6	14.5
Oman	2006	14.5	25.5	4.7	7.2	48.9	61.1	55.4	16.4	12.2	12.7	34.7	26.7	31.9
Sri Lanka	2006	...	2.0	...	1.0	...	...	45.3	...	...	25.5	...	...	29.3
Trinidad and Tobago	2004	6.8	...	4.9	...	61.1	53.8	83.7	28.0	11.7	11.0	10.9	34.5	5.3
Uruguay	2005	19.3	13.4	12.2	4.4	70.0	64.5	60.8	19.0	12.9	12.7	10.9	22.7	26.4

a/ At current prices.

Table 1.11

SELECTED CHARACTERISTICS OF BRANCHES, SELECTED YEARS AND COUNTRIES

Country or area	Latest year	General purpose machinery (ISIC 291)													
		Value added per employee (current 1000 dollars)		Wages and salaries per employee (current 1000 dollars)		Percentage in output a/									
						Costs of input materials and utilities			Costs of labour			Operating surplus			
	(LY)	2000	LY	2000	LY	2000	2003	LY	2000	2003	LY	2000	2003	LY
Industrialized Countries															
CIS															
Azerbaijan	2006	...	3.9	0.6	1.5	...	46.0	54.4	28.8	13.3	17.3	...	40.7	28.3
Georgia	2006	2.9	8.9	1.0	4.2	40.6	45.5	38.3	20.6	24.7	28.9	38.9	29.8	32.8
Kyrgyzstan	2006	...	...	0.2	0.5	...	...	...	21.7	12.7	5.1	...	...	...
Russian Federation	2006	...	5.1	0.7	5.0	...	59.3	64.5	43.4	34.0	34.8	...	6.7	0.8
EU-15															
Austria	2005	53.4	92.8	29.8	47.9	60.8	58.4	61.6	21.9	21.8	19.8	17.3	19.8	18.6
Belgium	2005	63.4	98.9	28.9	45.7	65.9	69.7	71.7	15.5	15.2	13.0	18.5	15.0	15.2
Denmark	2005	46.1	75.2	33.2	55.5	58.6	59.8	61.2	29.8	29.2	28.6	11.6	11.0	10.1
Finland	2005	50.5	85.2	27.3	44.6	70.8	71.6	71.4	15.8	17.5	15.0	13.4	10.9	13.6
France	2005	44.2	72.4	24.4	38.6	67.4	66.8	66.5	18.0	18.4	17.9	14.6	14.9	15.7
Germany	2005	50.5	82.4	34.0	51.6	60.1	60.7	62.1	26.9	26.5	23.7	13.1	12.7	14.2
Greece	2004	...	47.3	...	20.1	...	...	52.9	...	...	20.0	...	...	27.1
Ireland	2005	52.5	97.9	23.9	41.3	60.1	65.0	61.0	18.2	18.9	16.4	21.8	16.1	22.5
Italy	2005	49.2	78.1	20.0	34.0	68.1	69.4	69.5	12.9	13.6	13.3	18.9	17.0	17.2
Netherlands	2005	46.8	81.4	27.4	46.8	64.9	63.4	65.6	20.6	21.6	19.8	14.5	15.0	14.6
Portugal	2005	20.3	30.4	10.2	15.1	67.9	65.6	67.9	16.2	17.3	15.9	15.9	17.1	16.2
Spain	2005	37.1	60.6	19.4	32.5	64.5	64.2	65.2	18.6	19.3	18.6	16.9	16.5	16.1
Sweden	2005	56.1	82.9	28.3	42.0	63.5	...	67.4	18.4	...	16.5	18.1	...	16.1
United Kingdom	2005	50.1	78.1	31.6	45.3	61.1	59.0	60.0	24.6	24.7	23.2	14.4	16.3	16.8
EU-12															
Bulgaria	2006	2.8	7.0	1.4	3.2	69.3	72.1	75.6	15.9	13.5	11.0	14.8	14.4	13.3
Cyprus	2006	22.4	37.9	11.8	21.5	59.5	59.1	56.5	21.3	25.0	24.7	19.1	15.9	18.8
Czech Republic	2004	8.7	17.5	4.5	8.1	67.3	68.8	71.0	16.9	14.7	13.5	15.8	16.5	15.5
Estonia	2006	4.6	18.0	3.4	9.8	71.7	61.9	66.0	21.0	20.2	18.4	7.2	17.9	15.6
Hungary	2005	8.6	21.0	4.1	10.7	62.7	68.5	68.0	17.9	15.6	16.3	19.4	15.9	15.7
Latvia	2006	5.3	13.5	2.5	6.1	61.0	61.8	66.2	18.7	14.9	15.2	20.4	23.2	18.6
Lithuania	2006	3.1	14.4	2.9	7.0	63.6	63.9	63.1	34.0	23.1	17.8	2.4	13.0	19.1
Malta	2005	17.9	31.4	8.2	14.3	67.5	56.2	72.5	14.9	25.8	12.6	17.6	18.0	15.0
Poland	2005	11.2	22.1	...	9.2	60.3	61.4	63.6	...	17.6	15.2	...	21.0	21.2
Romania	2006	...	8.1	...	6.7	60.6	67.2	69.3	...	28.1	25.3	...	4.7	5.4
Slovakia	2005	5.2	20.0	3.2	7.9	75.7	72.1	70.2	15.0	11.0	11.7	9.3	16.9	18.1
Other Europe															
Norway	2004	49.2	92.0	34.6	60.4	68.5	66.6	67.4	22.1	20.5	21.4	9.3	13.0	11.2

a/ At current prices.

Table 1.11
(continued)

SELECTED CHARACTERISTICS OF BRANCHES, SELECTED YEARS AND COUNTRIES

General purpose machinery (ISIC 291)

Country or area	Latest year	Value added per employee (current 1000 dollars)		Wages and salaries per employee (current 1000 dollars)		Percentage in output [a]								
						Costs of input materials and utilities			Costs of labour			Operating surplus		
	(LY)	2000	LY	2000	LY	2000	2003	LY	2000	2003	LY	2000	2003	LY
Other Countries														
Israel	2005	42.0	45.8	37.3	38.3	61.6	60.0	64.9	34.0	34.2	29.4	4.3	5.8	5.7
Japan	2005	103.7	120.2	35.6	35.8	63.3	59.2	60.4	12.6	12.8	11.8	24.1	28.0	27.8
Republic of Korea	2006	57.5	97.0	16.1	26.9	59.9	60.5	63.3	11.2	11.4	10.2	28.9	28.1	26.5
Singapore	2006	37.2	57.5	19.6	26.2	67.7	62.4	66.7	17.0	18.7	15.1	15.3	19.0	18.1
United States of America	2005	103.8	134.3	39.6	45.5	50.7	49.5	52.5	18.8	17.4	16.1	30.5	33.1	31.4
Developing Countries														
Brazil	2005	23.5	28.2	7.8	9.0	50.8	55.7	58.8	16.4	13.3	13.1	32.8	31.0	28.1
Chile	2006	...	24.7	...	10.9	...	47.2	56.3	...	23.9	19.3	...	28.8	24.4
Colombia	2005	14.8	22.2	3.5	4.3	48.8	53.3	52.8	12.2	9.4	9.1	39.0	37.4	38.1
Ecuador	2005	5.7	12.6	0.9	4.1	69.2	65.5	68.0	5.0	6.9	10.3	25.8	27.6	21.8
Eritrea	2006	...	18.8	...	0.9	...	67.3	26.5	...	2.5	3.5	...	30.3	70.1
Ethiopia	2006	1.2	13.3	0.3	1.0	53.0	51.3	79.4	13.5	8.8	1.5	33.4	39.9	19.1
India	2004	6.0	8.0	2.2	2.5	73.8	75.6	76.7	9.5	8.1	7.2	16.7	16.3	16.1
Indonesia	2005	5.3	12.2	1.4	1.6	57.3	58.9	67.9	11.2	5.6	4.1	31.5	35.5	28.0
Iran (Islamic Republic of)	2005	28.6	11.4	9.9	4.4	59.6	58.3	64.1	14.0	15.5	13.7	26.3	26.2	22.2
Jordan	2006	8.7	14.7	3.8	4.8	68.3	66.3	68.7	13.7	13.8	10.2	18.0	19.9	21.1
Madagascar	2006	...	...	...	0.4	...	...	...	...	15.7	21.2	...	...	...
Malaysia	2005	21.7	19.6	5.5	8.0	69.2	66.9	79.4	7.8	10.8	8.5	23.0	22.4	12.2
Morocco	2005	8.4	11.8	5.4	6.7	63.3	59.6	65.2	23.6	24.2	19.9	13.1	16.2	14.9
Oman	2006	21.0	67.5	7.1	7.6	59.8	65.4	47.7	13.5	12.4	5.9	26.7	22.2	46.4
Sri Lanka	2006	...	3.0	...	0.6	...	...	52.4	...	...	9.9	...	...	37.7
Uruguay	2005	13.3	13.0	13.1	7.8	...	48.5	50.1	...	25.6	29.8	...	25.9	20.1

a/ At current prices.

Table 1.11

SELECTED CHARACTERISTICS OF BRANCHES, SELECTED YEARS AND COUNTRIES

Special purpose machinery (ISIC 292)

Country or area	Latest year	Value added per employee (current 1000 dollars)		Wages and salaries per employee (current 1000 dollars)		Percentage in output a/								
						Costs of input materials and utilities			Costs of labour			Operating surplus		
	(LY)	2000	LY	2000	LY	2000	2003	LY	2000	2003	LY	2000	2003	LY
Industrialized Countries														
CIS														
Azerbaijan	2006	...	4.1	0.7	1.3	...	46.0	54.4	16.2	14.7	14.1	...	39.3	31.5
Georgia	2006	...	4.8	...	2.3	...	...	80.5	...	...	9.3	...	...	10.2
Russian Federation	2006	...	...	0.9	...	...	62.8	66.2	19.5	...	...	...	...	...
EU-15														
Austria	2005	51.2	86.7	29.5	47.9	61.5	63.8	63.0	22.2	21.0	20.4	16.3	15.2	16.6
Belgium	2005	55.9	81.6	28.5	44.0	70.6	66.5	63.8	15.0	19.4	19.5	14.4	14.2	16.7
Denmark	2004	...	68.3	...	52.6	...	61.9	59.2	...	30.4	31.4	...	7.7	9.4
Finland	2005	51.3	75.7	27.7	44.0	67.3	69.6	70.2	17.6	18.9	17.3	15.1	11.5	12.5
France	2005	45.9	67.0	25.2	39.6	68.4	68.1	69.5	17.3	18.5	18.0	14.3	13.4	12.5
Germany	2005	50.3	75.2	33.5	49.0	62.0	62.8	64.6	25.3	25.6	23.1	12.7	11.7	12.3
Greece	2004	...	40.9	...	23.6	...	...	59.2	...	...	23.5	...	...	17.3
Ireland	2005	34.9	60.3	20.9	36.0	60.3	58.5	60.3	23.8	25.5	23.7	15.9	16.0	16.0
Italy	2005	49.4	70.3	21.4	34.3	70.3	71.0	71.5	12.9	14.1	13.9	16.8	14.9	14.6
Netherlands	2005	...	92.1	...	50.2	65.0	73.1	69.1	15.7	19.2	16.8	19.3	7.7	14.1
Portugal	2005	20.8	26.6	10.8	14.8	58.7	56.8	58.3	21.4	25.4	23.2	19.9	17.8	18.5
Spain	2005	35.6	53.6	19.0	30.2	63.2	64.9	63.1	19.6	21.0	20.8	17.2	14.1	16.1
Sweden	2005	54.4	85.1	27.5	40.5	67.0	...	68.4	16.7	...	15.1	16.3	...	16.6
United Kingdom	2005	53.7	82.9	32.6	45.3	61.8	63.3	65.3	23.2	21.9	19.0	15.1	14.8	15.7
EU-12														
Bulgaria	2006	2.1	5.8	1.3	2.6	62.9	66.2	67.0	22.2	18.3	14.9	14.9	15.6	18.1
Cyprus	2006	23.1	46.2	10.6	25.2	51.5	55.9	57.7	22.3	21.6	23.1	26.2	22.6	19.3
Czech Republic	2004	8.1	15.9	4.1	7.9	64.0	66.5	67.2	18.3	17.0	16.3	17.7	16.5	16.5
Estonia	2005	6.2	17.6	3.4	8.4	61.8	62.9	64.7	21.0	17.3	16.8	17.3	19.8	18.5
Hungary	2005	8.4	19.9	4.1	10.4	64.0	67.4	68.5	17.6	17.8	16.4	18.4	14.7	15.1
Latvia	2006	5.3	9.8	2.4	5.2	41.3	52.2	59.0	26.7	22.6	22.0	32.0	25.2	19.0
Lithuania	2006	4.2	13.6	2.9	6.8	56.4	61.5	51.7	30.2	22.7	24.1	13.4	15.9	24.2
Malta	2005	27.6	41.8	11.7	17.3	31.9	54.1	53.8	28.9	17.7	19.2	39.1	28.2	27.0
Poland	2005	9.4	20.1	...	8.3	57.3	62.2	63.5	...	19.0	15.2	...	18.8	21.4
Romania	2006	...	6.6	...	6.2	56.9	...	69.0	...	...	29.2	...	...	1.8
Slovakia	2005	3.6	12.9	3.2	7.4	75.7	69.7	67.9	21.7	19.5	18.4	2.7	10.8	13.7
Other Europe														
Norway	2004	50.1	75.8	36.4	55.3	60.2	63.1	64.7	29.0	26.9	25.7	10.9	10.1	9.5

a/ At current prices.

Table 1.11
(continued)

SELECTED CHARACTERISTICS OF BRANCHES, SELECTED YEARS AND COUNTRIES

Special purpose machinery (ISIC 292)														
Country or area	Latest year	Value added per employee (current 1000 dollars)		Wages and salaries per employee (current 1000 dollars)		Percentage in output [a]								
						Costs of input materials and utilities			Costs of labour			Operating surplus		
	(LY)	2000	LY	2000	LY	2000	2003	LY	2000	2003	LY	2000	2003	LY
Other Countries														
Israel	2005	63.8	58.4	39.7	39.3	63.5	69.6	72.8	22.7	26.2	18.3	13.8	4.2	8.9
Japan	2005	105.1	121.7	31.0	30.8	57.3	59.8	61.1	12.6	11.5	9.8	30.1	28.7	29.1
Republic of Korea	2006	53.2	93.3	16.3	27.2	56.3	59.4	62.2	13.4	13.5	11.0	30.3	27.1	26.8
Singapore	2006	42.4	47.9	20.5	25.4	63.0	67.9	73.3	17.8	18.9	14.2	19.2	13.1	12.5
United States of America	2005	110.9	141.4	42.4	48.5	50.1	50.8	52.0	19.1	19.5	16.5	30.8	29.7	31.5
Developing Countries														
Brazil	2005	20.4	26.0	7.1	8.4	53.2	54.7	56.8	16.3	13.0	13.9	30.5	32.3	29.3
Chile	2006	...	39.6	...	17.2	...	54.9	53.3	...	19.5	20.4	...	25.6	26.4
Colombia	2005	9.9	19.8	3.0	4.2	51.5	47.9	49.1	14.5	10.3	10.8	34.0	41.8	40.0
Ethiopia	2006	1.3	2.6	0.6	0.7	52.3	...	41.9	22.2	...	15.9	25.5	...	42.2
India	2004	5.4	7.8	1.9	2.3	75.1	77.2	79.3	8.6	7.6	6.2	16.3	15.2	14.5
Indonesia	2005	6.2	9.4	1.2	2.2	60.2	69.4	41.0	7.7	10.7	13.8	32.1	19.9	45.1
Iran (Islamic Republic of)	2005	24.1	15.4	11.1	5.1	55.3	60.1	59.6	20.5	14.3	13.4	24.1	25.6	27.0
Jordan	2006	5.7	12.8	2.4	3.1	65.9	62.8	66.8	14.4	9.1	8.1	19.7	28.1	25.1
Madagascar	2006	...	1.0	...	0.2	...	16.0	7.2	...	12.0	16.3	...	72.0	76.4
Malaysia	2005	14.0	15.0	5.3	7.4	62.2	63.8	72.4	14.4	15.8	13.5	23.4	20.4	14.1
Morocco	2005	7.1	10.6	3.5	6.4	62.0	39.8	53.2	18.8	31.4	28.2	19.2	28.8	18.6
Oman	2006	37.9	48.8	9.1	13.7	27.1	15.0	21.8	17.5	24.4	22.1	55.4	60.5	56.2
Sri Lanka	2006	...	1.1	...	0.6	...	...	61.4	...	...	22.3	...	...	16.3
Uruguay	2005	51.3	14.8	19.7	4.3	76.2	69.9	60.8	9.1	12.1	11.3	14.7	18.0	27.9

a/ At current prices.

Table 1.11

SELECTED CHARACTERISTICS OF BRANCHES, SELECTED YEARS AND COUNTRIES

Domestic appliances n.e.c. (ISIC 2930)														
Country or area	Latest year	Value added per employee (current 1000 dollars)		Wages and salaries per employee (current 1000 dollars)		Percentage in output [a]								
						Costs of input materials and utilities			Costs of labour			Operating surplus		
	(LY)	2000	LY	2000	LY	2000	2003	LY	2000	2003	LY	2000	2003	LY
Industrialized Countries														
CIS														
Azerbaijan	2006	...	1.1	0.1	0.5	...	46.0	54.4	34.4	36.4	22.2	...	17.6	23.4
Georgia	2006	0.5	0.9	0.3	0.1	76.8	73.1	69.5	15.9	7.4	4.8	7.4	19.6	25.7
Kyrgyzstan	2005	...	0.6	0.5	0.5	...	71.6	67.2	49.1	22.7	25.2	...	5.7	7.6
Russian Federation	2006	...	7.7	0.9	4.0	...	59.3	74.6	12.4	9.6	13.2	...	31.1	12.1
EU-15														
Austria	2005	48.6	91.1	26.2	39.7	58.6	55.5	58.4	22.4	18.3	18.1	19.0	26.2	23.5
Belgium	2005	44.1	70.3	22.3	36.8	62.9	65.3	64.6	18.7	19.5	18.6	18.4	15.2	16.9
Denmark	2004	...	70.7	...	50.4	...	73.4	68.4	...	16.8	22.5	...	9.8	9.1
Finland	2005	41.8	65.2	23.8	34.7	67.8	63.3	62.6	18.3	19.6	19.9	13.8	17.0	17.5
France	2005	43.7	65.8	24.5	35.2	72.3	69.4	70.4	15.5	15.1	15.8	12.2	15.5	13.7
Germany	2005	51.7	74.9	33.6	51.0	63.4	62.0	64.2	23.9	25.0	24.4	12.8	13.0	11.4
Greece	2004	...	54.6	...	22.5	...	...	61.0	...	...	16.0	...	...	23.0
Ireland	2005	36.8	59.6	18.6	36.7	58.8	55.3	61.8	20.8	13.5	23.5	20.4	31.3	14.7
Italy	2005	45.3	58.4	19.5	29.9	72.9	76.0	77.4	11.7	11.9	11.5	15.4	12.1	11.0
Netherlands	2005	...	72.0	...	38.2	61.0	66.0	65.0	19.1	17.4	18.5	19.9	16.6	16.4
Portugal	2005	23.8	38.7	9.4	13.4	72.4	70.4	68.7	10.9	10.7	10.8	16.7	18.8	20.5
Spain	2005	35.4	71.6	18.6	31.4	71.8	71.3	69.0	14.8	14.4	13.6	13.4	14.4	17.4
Sweden	2005	38.6	57.6	24.7	39.5	67.6	...	72.8	20.8	...	18.7	11.7	...	8.6
United Kingdom	2005	45.0	57.8	25.3	40.3	63.1	62.7	72.1	20.8	19.8	19.4	16.1	17.5	8.5
EU-12														
Bulgaria	2006	...	9.0	...	3.1	...	78.0	78.3	...	7.1	7.5	...	14.8	14.2
Cyprus	2006	18.0	43.6	10.2	20.2	58.6	66.4	64.1	23.4	19.0	16.6	17.9	14.6	19.3
Czech Republic	2004	7.6	16.2	3.8	6.8	70.4	69.5	73.5	14.8	11.9	11.1	14.8	18.6	15.3
Hungary	2005	9.5	21.4	3.7	8.8	76.2	75.0	76.5	9.3	10.1	9.7	14.5	15.0	13.8
Latvia	2006	1.1	15.3	...	10.5	...	61.9	51.0	...	16.4	33.7	...	21.7	15.2
Lithuania	2006	4.1	10.8	2.7	6.3	74.6	75.4	79.7	16.9	10.7	11.8	8.5	13.9	8.4
Malta	2005	22.6	19.3	8.8	12.8	76.4	62.8	57.5	9.2	25.0	28.2	14.4	12.2	14.3
Poland	2005	9.7	28.7	...	8.5	70.4	72.7	77.1	...	9.0	6.8	...	18.3	16.1
Romania	2006	...	11.4	...	5.6	56.9	73.8	79.3	...	9.5	10.2	...	16.6	10.6
Slovakia	2004	...	8.7	...	5.8	...	86.7	93.5	...	4.6	4.3	...	8.7	2.1
Other Europe														
Norway	2004	105.6	54.0	68.7	40.1	56.8	56.9	64.1	28.1	26.0	26.6	15.1	17.1	9.2

a/ At current prices.

Table 1.11
(continued)

SELECTED CHARACTERISTICS OF BRANCHES, SELECTED YEARS AND COUNTRIES

Domestic appliances n.e.c. (ISIC 2930)

Country or area	Latest year	Value added per employee (current 1000 dollars)		Wages and salaries per employee (current 1000 dollars)		Percentage in output[a/] Costs of input materials and utilities			Costs of labour			Operating surplus		
	(LY)	2000	LY	2000	LY	2000	2003	LY	2000	2003	LY	2000	2003	LY
Other Countries														
Japan	2005	131.3	149.2	36.0	35.2	60.2	59.7	59.8	10.9	10.0	9.5	28.9	30.3	30.7
Republic of Korea	2006	71.3	111.4	14.9	25.5	62.0	67.7	67.0	8.0	8.5	7.5	30.0	23.9	25.5
Singapore	2006	40.4	47.5	25.6	16.7	76.0	59.8	60.7	15.2	18.5	13.8	8.8	21.7	25.5
United States of America	2005	101.8	136.3	32.6	35.1	56.2	55.2	57.4	14.0	12.0	11.0	29.8	32.8	31.6
Developing Countries														
Brazil	2005	28.1	30.1	7.6	8.1	57.9	61.1	64.4	11.4	10.5	9.5	30.7	28.5	26.0
Chile	2006	...	37.8	...	12.0	...	64.1	64.9	...	11.1	11.2	...	24.8	23.9
Colombia	2005	17.1	25.0	3.8	4.8	60.5	60.6	63.9	8.8	8.0	7.0	30.7	31.4	29.1
Ecuador	2005	4.7	15.6	1.4	4.6	80.4	72.8	69.2	6.0	10.4	9.1	13.6	16.8	21.6
India	2004	6.3	6.3	1.6	1.8	76.8	83.7	85.2	6.0	4.9	4.3	17.2	11.4	10.6
Indonesia	2005	7.0	6.6	1.0	1.4	67.8	80.6	45.3	4.8	9.3	11.7	27.5	10.1	43.1
Iran (Islamic Republic of)	2005	39.2	11.0	10.2	4.1	60.5	67.0	68.1	10.3	12.6	12.0	29.2	20.4	19.8
Jordan	2006	10.6	18.7	3.6	4.1	64.8	65.3	61.9	12.0	12.5	8.4	23.2	22.1	29.7
Malaysia	2005	15.7	21.7	6.2	6.9	77.2	79.1	84.8	8.9	8.7	4.8	13.9	12.2	10.3
Morocco	2005	10.4	20.8	4.8	10.0	77.1	70.6	73.8	10.6	15.7	12.6	12.3	13.7	13.6
Oman	2006	18.7	14.3	6.7	3.4	49.4	83.6	78.8	18.1	15.9	5.1	32.5	0.5	16.2
Qatar	2006	9.4	39.1	9.4	11.4	68.4	...	5.6	31.5	...	27.5	0.1	...	66.9
Sri Lanka	2006	...	11.4	...	1.1	...	...	40.2	...	...	6.0	...	...	53.7
Trinidad and Tobago	2004	...	...	7.6	...	...	73.5	39.2	11.7	8.8	25.9	...	17.7	34.9
Uruguay	2005	21.4	15.9	12.2	5.5	59.7	63.1	50.8	23.1	21.6	17.0	17.2	15.2	32.2

a/ At current prices.

Table 1.11

SELECTED CHARACTERISTICS OF BRANCHES, SELECTED YEARS AND COUNTRIES

Office, accounting and computing machinery (ISIC 3000)

Country or area	Latest year	Value added per employee (current 1000 dollars)		Wages and salaries per employee (current 1000 dollars)		Percentage in output [a/]								
						Costs of input materials and utilities			Costs of labour			Operating surplus		
	(LY)	2000	LY	2000	LY	2000	2003	LY	2000	2003	LY	2000	2003	LY
Industrialized Countries														
CIS														
Azerbaijan	2006	...	12.9	0.2	0.9	...	...	57.4	48.0	...	3.1	...	...	39.6
Kyrgyzstan	2005	...	0.9	0.3	0.6	...	...	80.9	6.4	...	11.9	...	...	7.2
Republic of Moldova	2006	...	2.5	0.3	1.3	...	79.5	55.4	19.7	9.4	23.1	...	11.2	21.4
Russian Federation	2006	...	16.1	0.7	4.2	...	60.1	73.7	4.5	23.0	6.9	...	16.9	19.4
EU-15														
Austria	2005	61.0	75.9	23.8	41.6	82.5	92.1	75.0	6.8	5.9	13.7	10.6	2.0	11.3
Belgium	2005	56.7	93.1	29.9	40.2	65.7	71.5	77.1	18.1	12.4	9.9	16.2	16.2	13.0
Denmark	2005	56.6	105.8	36.5	60.8	61.6	64.3	63.8	24.8	20.7	20.8	13.6	15.0	15.4
Finland	2005	...	61.9	25.8	45.0	...	76.7	78.0	14.2	13.9	16.0	...	9.5	6.0
France	2005	70.7	69.9	42.7	41.6	77.0	75.4	76.2	13.9	12.6	14.2	9.1	12.0	9.7
Germany	2005	81.8	113.0	44.5	62.1	74.7	72.2	71.8	13.7	16.0	15.5	11.5	11.8	12.7
Greece	2004	...	173.2	...	28.9	...	...	50.0	...	...	8.3	...	...	41.7
Ireland	2005	116.2	194.4	23.2	45.5	86.7	92.2	88.7	2.7	2.8	2.6	10.6	5.1	8.7
Italy	2005	46.2	59.1	22.4	31.8	82.4	79.8	81.4	8.5	10.4	10.0	9.1	9.8	8.6
Netherlands	2005	69.7	...	36.6	...	79.4	77.4	72.2	10.8	18.2	18.2	9.8	4.4	9.6
Portugal	2005	32.5	31.9	14.1	18.2	80.6	80.1	68.2	8.4	10.8	18.2	11.0	9.1	13.6
Spain	2005	68.8	62.2	32.5	29.7	79.3	79.7	74.3	9.8	13.4	12.3	10.9	6.9	13.4
Sweden	2005	46.8	68.6	29.2	40.1	69.0	...	67.2	19.3	...	19.2	11.6	...	13.6
United Kingdom	2005	61.0	84.2	38.4	45.7	83.4	67.2	67.8	10.4	11.5	17.5	6.1	21.3	14.7
EU-12														
Bulgaria	2006	2.6	9.1	1.3	2.8	82.7	91.8	77.8	8.6	7.3	6.7	8.7	1.0	15.5
Czech Republic	2004	8.2	17.0	4.1	7.4	85.6	97.0	95.3	7.2	1.9	2.0	7.2	1.1	2.6
Estonia	2006	11.0	22.0	4.2	10.2	84.6	85.8	86.4	5.8	7.6	6.3	9.5	6.6	7.3
Hungary	2005	19.2	69.5	4.1	11.3	91.2	71.8	81.8	1.9	5.0	3.0	6.9	23.1	15.2
Latvia	2006	13.8	52.7	2.2	8.9	79.1	80.1	73.0	3.4	7.2	4.6	17.5	12.8	22.5
Lithuania	2006	2.4	12.3	1.9	5.2	87.0	62.0	76.4	10.6	11.9	10.0	2.5	26.2	13.6
Poland	2005	22.1	22.1	...	8.9	61.8	73.9	77.8	...	10.5	8.9	...	15.6	13.3
Romania	2005	...	11.4	...	3.9	70.9	...	88.6	...	...	3.9	...	...	7.5
Slovakia	2005	5.7	32.1	3.4	7.7	71.1	...	93.1	17.4	...	1.7	11.5	...	5.2
Other Europe														
Norway	2004	...	106.2	...	70.2	...	...	69.1	...	...	20.5	...	...	10.5

a/ At current prices.

Table 1.11
(continued)

SELECTED CHARACTERISTICS OF BRANCHES, SELECTED YEARS AND COUNTRIES

Office, accounting and computing machinery (ISIC 3000)

Country or area	Latest year	Value added per employee (current 1000 dollars)		Wages and salaries per employee (current 1000 dollars)		Percentage in output[a]								
						Costs of input materials and utilities			Costs of labour			Operating surplus		
	(LY)	2000	LY	2000	LY	2000	2003	LY	2000	2003	LY	2000	2003	LY
Other Countries														
Australia	2005	53.0	53.6	27.9	...	80.4	68.8	69.3	10.3	...	...	9.3	...	...
Japan	2005	110.0	128.5	43.5	43.5	78.9	78.3	75.3	8.4	8.7	8.4	12.8	13.0	16.3
Republic of Korea	2006	128.1	134.1	18.9	27.4	72.7	73.5	61.5	4.0	5.4	7.9	23.3	21.0	30.7
Singapore	2006	100.8	101.8	18.6	24.7	85.4	86.0	83.2	2.7	3.4	4.1	11.9	10.6	12.7
United States of America	2005	214.1	350.4	52.5	61.6	60.3	55.4	46.6	9.8	12.5	9.4	30.0	32.1	44.0
Developing Countries														
Brazil	2005	74.6	40.6	13.6	10.6	64.5	64.7	69.1	6.4	7.9	8.1	29.0	27.4	22.8
China (Macao SAR)	2005	29.8	32.2	8.7	14.3	76.5	75.9	85.7	6.8	12.7	6.4	16.7	11.4	8.0
Chile	2006	...	15.8	...	9.7	...	42.4	49.1	...	41.2	31.3	...	16.5	19.5
India	2004	10.8	12.8	2.5	3.2	80.2	71.7	77.1	4.6	4.3	5.7	15.2	24.0	17.3
Indonesia	2005	3.1	18.0	0.9	0.8	40.0	31.3	63.4	17.6	24.5	1.7	42.4	44.2	34.9
Iran (Islamic Republic of)	2005	47.7	14.4	8.7	4.4	54.8	67.4	48.9	8.3	11.8	15.6	37.0	20.9	35.6
Malaysia	2005	20.6	27.8	4.8	7.2	85.8	87.3	86.7	3.3	2.4	3.4	10.9	10.4	9.8
Morocco	2005	12.4	18.1	7.5	13.2	53.9	75.0	83.0	27.8	0.0	12.4	18.2	25.0	4.6
Philippines	2005	...	11.9	...	2.7	...	88.6	85.5	...	3.3	3.3	...	8.1	11.1
Saudi Arabia	2006	...	13.6	...	3.3	...	...	61.5	...	...	9.2	...	...	29.2
Sri Lanka	2006	...	5.1	...	0.9	...	...	58.1	...	...	7.0	...	...	34.8
Uruguay	2005	13.7	22.7	3.8	16.1	81.7	...	82.6	5.0	...	12.3	13.3	...	5.0

a/ At current prices.

Table 1.11

SELECTED CHARACTERISTICS OF BRANCHES, SELECTED YEARS AND COUNTRIES

Electric motors, generators and transformers (ISIC 3110)

Country or area	Latest year	Value added per employee (current 1000 dollars)		Wages and salaries per employee (current 1000 dollars)		Percentage in output [a/]								
						Costs of input materials and utilities			Costs of labour			Operating surplus		
	(LY)	2000	LY	2000	LY	2000	2003	LY	2000	2003	LY	2000	2003	LY
Industrialized Countries														
CIS														
Azerbaijan	2006	...	7.9	0.4	1.2	...	62.4	57.4	9.8	5.0	6.3	...	32.6	36.3
Georgia	2006	0.7	3.9	0.5	2.5	70.0	59.6	50.0	19.7	24.8	32.1	10.3	15.6	17.9
Kyrgyzstan	2006	...	...	0.3	0.9	...	...	...	36.3	29.6	24.4	...	...	...
EU-15														
Austria	2005	63.4	88.7	31.8	50.6	65.7	73.8	73.4	17.2	17.3	15.2	17.1	8.9	11.4
Belgium	2005	62.2	92.5	29.6	49.4	62.2	64.9	70.1	18.0	21.4	15.9	19.8	13.7	13.9
Finland	2005	60.8	90.0	28.3	45.8	68.5	66.1	67.8	14.7	19.5	16.4	16.9	14.4	15.9
France	2005	43.0	67.2	23.0	36.9	66.4	65.7	67.3	17.9	19.6	18.0	15.7	14.7	14.7
Germany	2005	47.2	71.5	29.3	44.5	66.4	67.8	67.8	20.8	21.3	20.0	12.7	11.0	12.2
Greece	2004	...	59.3	...	25.1	...	...	63.1	...	...	15.6	...	...	21.3
Italy	2005	40.2	67.1	17.0	28.6	65.1	71.8	71.6	14.8	13.1	12.1	20.1	15.1	16.3
Netherlands	2005	49.7	82.5	25.9	46.3	67.2	65.5	61.1	17.1	20.3	21.8	15.7	14.2	17.1
Spain	2005	46.2	60.3	23.1	35.9	77.7	75.3	84.6	11.1	12.6	9.1	11.2	12.1	6.2
Sweden	2005	47.6	79.0	28.0	43.4	68.0	...	74.1	18.8	...	14.2	13.1	...	11.7
United Kingdom	2005	66.6	76.8	29.3	37.0	60.5	71.3	66.9	17.4	21.5	15.9	22.1	7.3	17.1
EU-12														
Bulgaria	2006	2.0	6.5	1.2	2.7	72.3	76.4	75.5	16.1	13.0	10.1	11.6	10.6	14.5
Cyprus	2006	15.6	40.5	9.3	22.1	43.9	46.1	47.3	33.5	36.0	28.7	22.5	17.9	24.0
Czech Republic	2004	9.8	21.1	3.7	7.2	71.4	61.5	65.6	10.8	12.2	11.7	17.9	26.2	22.7
Estonia	2006	8.7	26.6	4.0	11.9	66.8	56.0	72.3	15.3	19.6	12.4	17.9	24.4	15.3
Hungary	2005	7.6	16.3	4.5	9.7	65.2	69.9	74.3	20.4	18.0	15.3	14.3	12.1	10.5
Latvia	2006	4.2	19.7	2.0	8.6	77.0	65.9	66.5	11.0	10.6	14.6	12.0	23.4	18.9
Lithuania	2006	...	8.5	...	5.5	...	75.9	68.7	...	19.5	20.4	...	4.6	10.9
Malta	2005	12.8	19.6	8.8	15.2	42.7	48.2	50.0	39.2	43.9	38.8	18.1	7.9	11.3
Poland	2005	10.3	18.5	...	8.8	64.6	66.9	69.1	...	16.5	14.7	...	16.6	16.2
Romania	2006	...	6.5	...	5.6	...	66.7	77.6	...	22.3	19.2	...	10.9	3.2
Slovakia	2005	7.1	20.4	3.1	7.4	81.8	81.8	80.2	7.8	8.6	7.2	10.4	9.6	12.6
Other Europe														
Norway	2004	59.7	66.6	39.0	58.0	61.8	68.8	72.7	24.9	25.4	23.8	13.3	5.8	3.5

a/ At current prices.

Table 1.11
(continued)

SELECTED CHARACTERISTICS OF BRANCHES, SELECTED YEARS AND COUNTRIES

Electric motors, generators and transformers (ISIC 3110)

Country or area	Latest year	Value added per employee (current 1000 dollars)		Wages and salaries per employee (current 1000 dollars)		Percentage in output [a]								
						Costs of input materials and utilities			Costs of labour			Operating surplus		
	(LY)	2000	LY	2000	LY	2000	2003	LY	2000	2003	LY	2000	2003	LY
Other Countries														
Israel	2005	37.9	46.2	28.1	30.3	58.4	61.3	59.9	30.8	17.2	26.2	10.8	21.5	13.9
Japan	2005	79.1	88.8	32.8	33.8	63.4	62.7	63.0	15.2	14.8	14.1	21.4	22.5	22.9
Republic of Korea	2006	44.8	72.2	13.8	24.6	64.0	67.0	66.7	11.1	11.7	11.4	24.9	21.3	22.0
Singapore	2006	44.6	49.0	21.0	22.6	76.3	78.8	83.0	11.2	9.2	7.9	12.5	12.0	9.2
United States of America	2005	80.2	109.2	30.1	38.3	47.1	47.1	50.8	19.9	19.1	17.3	33.1	33.7	32.0
Developing Countries														
Brazil	2005	22.0	27.2	7.8	8.7	53.8	55.3	57.8	16.3	17.4	13.6	29.9	27.3	28.7
Chile	2006	...	56.9	...	15.0	...	61.8	51.8	...	15.9	12.7	...	22.3	35.4
Colombia	2005	12.2	19.7	6.0	8.0	59.2	63.0	62.8	20.0	17.6	15.2	20.7	19.4	22.1
Ecuador	2005	8.0	13.7	1.3	4.3	71.4	71.4	75.9	4.7	...	7.6	23.8	...	16.5
Fiji	2004	...	20.8	...	0.9	...	61.6	16.6	...	15.8	3.6	...	22.6	79.8
India	2004	5.6	10.2	3.1	2.8	75.6	76.4	79.1	13.3	6.4	5.8	11.1	17.1	15.1
Indonesia	2005	12.8	13.2	1.0	1.9	31.3	58.4	61.3	5.5	7.8	5.7	63.2	33.8	33.0
Iran (Islamic Republic of)	2005	33.1	20.1	12.1	4.9	66.5	61.2	59.8	12.2	15.0	9.8	21.3	23.8	30.5
Jordan	2006	22.3	15.5	5.1	5.4	78.1	73.5	86.9	5.0	6.0	4.5	16.9	20.6	8.5
Malaysia	2005	8.6	8.0	3.2	5.0	73.3	72.8	81.4	10.0	15.0	11.5	16.7	12.2	7.0
Morocco	2005	9.8	8.7	5.9	7.2	58.2	73.6	70.3	25.0	15.8	24.4	16.8	10.6	5.3
Sri Lanka	2006	...	3.7	...	1.0	...	...	61.9	...	...	10.6	...	...	27.5

a/ At current prices.

Table 1.11

SELECTED CHARACTERISTICS OF BRANCHES, SELECTED YEARS AND COUNTRIES

Electricity distribution & control apparatus (ISIC 3120)														
Country or area	Latest year	Value added per employee (current 1000 dollars)		Wages and salaries per employee (current 1000 dollars)		Percentage in output[a/]								
						Costs of input materials and utilities			Costs of labour			Operating surplus		
	(LY)	2000	LY	2000	LY	2000	2003	LY	2000	2003	LY	2000	2003	LY
Industrialized Countries														
CIS														
Azerbaijan	2006	...	6.1	1.0	1.6	...	62.4	57.4	41.9	13.3	11.0	...	24.3	31.7
Georgia	2005	0.4	0.8	0.3	0.6	85.9	...	73.0	10.9	12.9	21.3	3.2	...	5.7
Kyrgyzstan	2006	...	...	0.1	0.7	...	...	...	75.1	13.5	9.9	...	...	...
EU-15														
Austria	2005	50.0	81.9	26.5	43.7	55.4	60.8	58.9	23.7	22.8	21.9	21.0	16.4	19.2
Belgium	2005	61.9	71.6	33.4	45.3	63.3	65.2	63.1	19.8	20.9	23.4	16.9	13.9	13.5
Denmark	2005	47.5	82.9	31.0	49.3	53.4	56.7	61.2	30.4	29.0	23.1	16.2	14.3	15.8
Finland	2005	45.2	63.2	24.3	37.0	62.5	63.3	66.3	20.2	21.6	19.8	17.3	15.1	14.0
France	2005	50.1	72.5	25.8	39.4	65.2	68.5	71.0	18.0	19.1	15.8	16.8	12.4	13.2
Germany	2005	62.0	77.9	40.4	60.0	58.9	63.4	65.8	26.8	27.5	26.3	14.3	9.1	7.9
Greece	2004	...	39.7	...	19.4	...	...	62.2	...	...	18.5	...	...	19.3
Ireland	2005	71.2	51.9	19.8	40.6	53.8	...	69.0	12.9	...	24.2	33.4	...	6.7
Italy	2005	49.4	74.7	21.1	32.9	65.0	65.8	65.2	15.0	14.7	15.4	20.1	19.5	19.5
Netherlands	2005	54.4	95.1	31.7	47.0	63.4	58.5	60.0	21.3	21.3	19.8	15.2	20.2	20.2
Portugal	2005	...	30.8	...	13.6	...	...	63.4	...	...	16.1	...	...	20.5
Spain	2005	44.5	72.4	19.9	33.1	60.4	58.5	60.3	17.7	19.4	18.2	21.9	22.1	21.5
Sweden	2005	51.4	84.4	26.3	40.3	66.7	...	59.4	17.1	...	19.4	16.2	...	21.2
United Kingdom	2005	47.5	70.4	29.9	38.6	57.4	58.5	56.8	26.9	25.7	23.7	15.7	15.8	19.5
EU-12														
Bulgaria	2006	2.5	6.7	1.2	2.7	68.7	70.4	71.4	15.0	14.6	11.5	16.3	15.1	17.0
Cyprus	2006	25.2	42.9	12.2	23.0	56.2	56.1	63.9	21.2	23.2	19.3	22.6	20.6	16.8
Czech Republic	2004	9.9	17.8	4.5	7.9	71.5	68.2	71.2	12.9	14.2	12.7	15.6	17.7	16.1
Estonia	2006	8.3	23.1	4.5	9.9	61.2	68.3	75.7	21.1	12.9	10.4	17.7	18.8	13.9
Hungary	2005	9.9	21.4	4.2	9.5	68.7	68.9	69.2	13.3	11.5	13.6	18.0	19.6	17.1
Latvia	2006	9.7	19.4	3.5	8.1	42.4	58.9	64.3	21.1	16.5	15.0	36.5	24.6	20.7
Lithuania	2006	8.8	10.7	3.4	5.7	64.4	74.2	68.7	13.6	15.8	16.7	21.9	10.0	14.5
Malta	2005	15.0	59.1	11.8	19.0	76.4	70.9	69.6	18.6	11.9	9.8	5.0	17.3	20.6
Poland	2005	11.9	20.4	...	8.6	61.0	63.6	63.0	...	17.1	15.6	...	19.4	21.3
Romania	2005	...	8.2	...	5.1	...	67.3	70.7	...	18.8	18.1	...	13.9	11.2
Slovakia	2005	5.2	12.5	3.2	6.6	77.7	74.9	76.0	13.8	13.9	12.8	8.5	11.3	11.2
Other Europe														
Norway	2004	43.5	88.9	27.3	50.9	56.7	55.6	53.2	27.2	28.2	26.8	16.1	16.1	20.0

a/ At current prices.

Table 1.11
(continued)

SELECTED CHARACTERISTICS OF BRANCHES, SELECTED YEARS AND COUNTRIES

Electricity distribution & control apparatus (ISIC 3120)														
Country or area	Latest year	Value added per employee (current 1000 dollars)		Wages and salaries per employee (current 1000 dollars)		Percentage in output[a/]								
						Costs of input materials and utilities			Costs of labour			Operating surplus		
	(LY)	2000	LY	2000	LY	2000	2003	LY	2000	2003	LY	2000	2003	LY
Other Countries														
Japan	2005	93.0	89.4	35.1	32.9	59.7	61.5	64.0	15.2	13.7	13.2	25.1	24.8	22.7
Republic of Korea	2006	53.0	82.8	14.7	24.8	58.1	59.8	63.8	11.7	12.3	10.8	30.3	27.9	25.3
Singapore	2006	33.0	39.3	18.9	22.3	66.3	69.2	80.8	19.3	20.2	10.9	14.5	10.6	8.3
United States of America	2005	108.2	129.6	36.9	44.5	43.2	41.1	44.5	19.4	20.7	19.1	37.5	38.3	36.4
Developing Countries														
Brazil	2005	26.0	31.3	9.4	10.5	44.5	51.5	49.0	20.1	16.6	17.2	35.4	32.0	33.8
Chile	2006	...	33.2	...	11.7	...	57.7	59.4	...	14.4	14.4	...	27.9	26.2
Colombia	2005	12.0	24.1	3.6	4.8	54.5	50.7	52.8	13.7	13.1	9.4	31.8	36.1	37.8
Ecuador	2005	5.9	9.4	1.8	2.6	66.2	63.6	74.9	10.1	18.2	6.9	23.7	18.2	18.2
India	2004	5.6	8.6	2.2	2.5	75.0	74.8	74.9	10.0	8.7	7.4	15.0	16.5	17.7
Indonesia	2005	5.3	9.7	1.2	1.6	62.6	48.1	51.3	8.7	14.1	7.9	28.7	37.9	40.8
Iran (Islamic Republic of)	2005	30.3	12.9	10.4	3.9	50.7	56.8	51.6	17.0	14.5	14.8	32.4	28.8	33.7
Jordan	2006	7.6	10.5	2.9	3.2	48.3	63.8	63.1	19.8	9.8	11.3	32.0	26.4	25.6
Malaysia	2005	12.7	11.8	4.4	6.1	70.2	70.9	76.8	10.3	10.5	12.1	19.5	18.6	11.2
Morocco	2005	10.0	16.5	5.6	9.1	50.7	50.5	47.3	27.9	28.1	29.0	21.4	21.4	23.7
Oman	2006	21.8	33.2	8.8	8.1	62.1	74.3	70.4	15.4	17.6	7.2	22.5	8.1	22.4
Qatar	2006	...	53.3	...	9.3	...	...	71.6	...	...	5.0	...	...	23.5

a/ At current prices.

Table 1.11

SELECTED CHARACTERISTICS OF BRANCHES, SELECTED YEARS AND COUNTRIES

Country or area	Latest year	Insulated wire and cable (ISIC 3130)												
		Value added per employee (current 1000 dollars)		Wages and salaries per employee (current 1000 dollars)		Percentage in output [a]								
						Costs of input materials and utilities			Costs of labour			Operating surplus		
	(LY)	2000	LY	2000	LY	2000	2003	LY	2000	2003	LY	2000	2003	LY
Industrialized Countries														
CIS														
Azerbaijan	2006	...	3.3	0.2	0.7	...	62.4	57.4	66.6	8.5	9.3	...	29.1	33.3
Georgia	2005	0.5	2.4	0.3	0.5	84.2	...	84.3	10.1	...	3.1	5.8	...	12.5
Russian Federation	2006	...	17.2	1.3	5.1	...	...	82.1	7.0	...	5.3	...	...	12.6
EU-15														
Austria	2005	50.3	78.9	29.4	40.7	61.0	69.5	72.7	22.8	18.4	14.1	16.2	12.1	13.2
Belgium	2005	52.0	80.9	28.5	46.8	74.4	72.9	76.9	14.1	17.7	13.4	11.6	9.4	9.7
Denmark	2005	...	90.4	...	53.2	...	...	67.2	...	...	19.3	...	...	13.5
Finland	2005	45.2	69.3	25.1	40.1	76.0	74.3	77.8	13.3	16.6	12.9	10.7	9.1	9.3
France	2005	55.0	63.7	26.1	39.4	72.7	72.4	75.8	13.0	19.9	15.0	14.4	7.7	9.2
Germany	2005	47.0	68.4	29.0	43.5	70.5	72.4	73.8	18.2	19.6	16.7	11.3	8.0	9.5
Greece	2004	...	51.0	...	25.5	...	...	82.7	...	...	8.7	...	...	8.7
Italy	2005	43.3	60.0	21.6	32.3	81.2	81.1	85.0	9.4	10.0	8.1	9.5	8.9	6.9
Netherlands	2005	66.1	87.6	29.6	55.2	64.6	61.8	74.1	15.8	21.4	16.3	19.6	16.8	9.6
Portugal	2005	27.1	46.8	12.4	20.5	79.5	79.7	83.5	9.4	9.5	7.2	11.1	10.9	9.3
Spain	2005	39.0	72.5	18.7	34.8	76.4	75.7	80.0	11.4	13.7	9.6	12.3	10.6	10.4
Sweden	2005	67.7	80.4	28.8	38.9	69.6	...	75.1	12.9	...	12.0	17.5	...	12.8
United Kingdom	2005	53.9	64.9	24.1	37.5	61.4	64.5	71.1	17.2	21.6	16.7	21.3	13.9	12.2
EU-12														
Bulgaria	2006	5.8	16.6	1.8	3.4	82.1	84.3	84.2	5.7	5.8	3.2	12.3	9.9	12.5
Czech Republic	2004	10.5	14.8	3.9	6.6	74.4	76.7	78.4	9.6	11.1	9.6	16.0	12.2	12.0
Estonia	2006	...	12.7	...	6.5	...	69.3	80.0	...	12.3	10.2	...	18.3	9.8
Hungary	2005	8.9	17.1	3.8	8.4	67.3	76.4	82.3	14.0	10.9	8.7	18.7	12.7	9.0
Lithuania	2006	5.4	22.3	2.7	6.3	76.0	71.2	79.8	11.7	10.4	5.7	12.2	18.3	14.4
Poland	2005	18.4	28.5	...	8.2	74.1	75.0	80.9	...	7.1	5.5	...	17.9	13.6
Romania	2006	...	20.5	...	6.5	...	78.1	80.6	...	10.5	6.1	...	11.4	13.3
Slovakia	2005	4.4	11.1	2.8	5.8	82.7	76.7	70.8	11.1	13.9	15.3	6.3	9.4	13.9
Other Europe														
Norway	2004	56.4	124.0	44.1	65.4	73.3	57.7	66.4	20.8	23.0	17.7	5.8	19.3	15.9

a/ At current prices.

Table 1.11
(continued)

SELECTED CHARACTERISTICS OF BRANCHES, SELECTED YEARS AND COUNTRIES

Insulated wire and cable (ISIC 3130)

Country or area	Latest year	Value added per employee (current 1000 dollars)		Wages and salaries per employee (current 1000 dollars)		Percentage in output [a]								
						Costs of input materials and utilities			Costs of labour			Operating surplus		
	(LY)	2000	LY	2000	LY	2000	2003	LY	2000	2003	LY	2000	2003	LY
Other Countries														
Japan	2005	120.5	125.5	44.8	43.0	68.9	73.1	75.2	11.6	10.4	8.5	19.5	16.5	16.3
Republic of Korea	2006	88.4	151.9	16.4	26.6	65.5	72.6	68.9	6.4	7.9	5.5	28.1	19.5	25.6
Singapore	2006	44.7	69.1	21.7	24.2	71.2	63.2	70.0	14.0	15.9	10.5	14.9	20.9	19.5
United States of America	2005	136.0	130.9	37.1	42.7	58.5	58.2	65.5	11.4	14.8	11.3	30.2	27.0	23.2
Developing Countries														
Brazil	2005	25.5	32.4	7.3	7.8	71.3	72.2	72.5	8.3	8.0	6.6	20.4	19.8	20.8
Chile	2006	...	93.8	...	22.2	...	77.8	89.1	...	11.7	2.6	...	10.5	8.3
Colombia	2005	48.5	76.8	6.1	7.1	67.7	69.7	70.3	4.1	4.1	2.7	28.2	26.2	26.9
Ecuador	2005	9.3	22.1	1.8	5.2	83.1	85.3	83.5	3.3	5.9	3.9	13.6	8.8	12.7
India	2004	8.1	5.9	1.7	1.8	83.0	89.4	89.1	3.5	3.6	3.3	13.6	7.0	7.5
Indonesia	2005	6.1	5.5	1.2	1.6	69.2	66.5	75.1	6.2	11.9	7.4	24.6	21.7	17.4
Iran (Islamic Republic of)	2005	40.3	25.7	10.8	4.8	71.4	71.3	67.9	7.7	7.0	6.0	20.9	21.7	26.1
Jordan	2006	23.9	27.0	4.3	3.2	76.6	76.9	78.4	4.2	3.5	2.6	19.2	19.7	19.0
Malaysia	2005	14.6	13.0	4.8	5.9	78.8	74.4	83.4	6.9	11.3	7.5	14.3	14.3	9.1
Morocco	2005	22.4	34.6	6.9	12.0	71.8	73.8	79.6	8.7	6.4	7.1	19.5	19.9	13.4
Oman	2006	53.7	33.4	7.9	10.1	70.6	85.1	94.8	4.3	4.2	1.6	25.1	10.7	3.6
Philippines	2005	...	5.7	...	2.4	...	80.4	83.7	...	9.2	7.0	...	10.5	9.3
Trinidad and Tobago	2004	...	...	...	...	...	68.1	55.5	...	11.0	8.4	...	20.9	36.1

a/ At current prices.

Table 1.11

SELECTED CHARACTERISTICS OF BRANCHES, SELECTED YEARS AND COUNTRIES

Accumulators, primary cells and batteries (ISIC 3140)

Country or area	Latest year	Value added per employee (current 1000 dollars)		Wages and salaries per employee (current 1000 dollars)		Percentage in output a/								
						Costs of input materials and utilities			Costs of labour			Operating surplus		
	(LY)	2000	LY	2000	LY	2000	2003	LY	2000	2003	LY	2000	2003	LY
Industrialized Countries														
CIS														
Azerbaijan	2006	...	2.3	0.3	0.9	...	62.4	57.3	33.2	24.7	17.9	...	12.9	24.7
Georgia	2005	0.1	1.2	0.0	0.6	69.9	...	80.7	9.3	...	8.9	20.8	...	10.4
Kyrgyzstan	2006	...	...	0.3	0.4	...	...	...	12.1	10.3	21.7	...	...	...
Russian Federation	2006	...	...	1.1	3.9	...	...	...	11.0	...	...	...	...	...
EU-15														
Austria	2005	64.4	84.5	31.3	48.3	64.7	56.8	67.8	17.1	20.4	18.4	18.1	22.7	13.8
Belgium	2005	69.8	115.1	29.9	48.9	69.5	57.5	48.9	13.1	17.7	21.7	17.4	24.8	29.4
Denmark	2005	...	47.6	...	35.7	...	...	81.8	...	...	13.6	...	...	4.5
France	2005	33.3	53.0	21.8	35.2	74.2	71.2	71.9	16.8	18.0	18.7	9.0	10.8	9.4
Germany	2005	41.0	77.3	33.0	52.3	71.8	61.8	72.9	22.7	23.4	18.3	5.5	14.8	8.8
Greece	2004	...	60.1	...	18.3	...	...	64.1	...	...	10.9	...	...	25.0
Ireland	2005	34.1	89.6	20.5	33.6	70.6	...	50.0	17.6	...	18.8	11.8	...	31.3
Italy	2005	42.3	57.3	21.5	33.2	73.6	75.3	80.3	13.4	14.3	11.4	13.0	10.4	8.3
Netherlands	2005	50.4	142.5	23.6	58.3	72.0	62.3	59.3	13.1	14.4	16.7	14.9	23.4	24.1
Spain	2005	49.0	68.3	22.9	33.5	68.0	67.9	71.0	15.0	14.7	14.2	17.1	17.4	14.7
United Kingdom	2005	54.7	63.7	28.5	39.3	62.6	71.5	64.0	19.5	18.4	22.2	17.9	10.1	13.8
EU-12														
Bulgaria	2006	4.4	12.1	1.7	3.9	71.7	67.2	73.9	10.6	10.9	8.5	17.7	21.9	17.6
Czech Republic	2004	8.4	17.6	3.4	8.1	75.7	71.3	...	9.9	12.7	...	14.5	16.1	...
Hungary	2005	13.1	31.1	3.8	10.3	81.7	69.7	88.4	5.3	3.0	3.8	13.0	27.4	7.8
Lithuania	2006	...	26.5	...	11.8	...	62.5	60.9	...	15.8	17.4	...	21.7	21.6
Poland	2005	15.5	37.3	...	12.0	74.7	67.9	76.0	...	9.3	7.7	...	22.9	16.3
Romania	2004	...	11.7	...	5.4	...	70.6	73.7	...	10.9	12.1	...	18.5	14.2
Slovakia	2005	9.4	9.0	3.7	7.2	73.9	86.2	82.4	10.3	13.8	14.1	15.8	0.0	3.5

a/ At current prices.

Table 1.11
(continued)

SELECTED CHARACTERISTICS OF BRANCHES, SELECTED YEARS AND COUNTRIES

Accumulators, primary cells and batteries (ISIC 3140)														
Country or area	Latest year	Value added per employee (current 1000 dollars)		Wages and salaries per employee (current 1000 dollars)		Percentage in output a/								
						Costs of input materials and utilities			Costs of labour			Operating surplus		
	(LY)	2000	LY	2000	LY	2000	2003	LY	2000	2003	LY	2000	2003	LY
Other Countries														
Japan	2005	143.1	132.8	46.2	48.6	66.6	68.0	71.7	10.8	11.4	10.4	22.6	20.6	18.0
Republic of Korea	2006	62.2	98.5	16.4	30.3	65.2	60.5	64.8	9.2	12.0	10.8	25.6	27.5	24.4
Singapore	2006	80.2	84.3	23.5	31.0	52.5	57.4	63.2	13.9	14.6	13.5	33.6	28.0	23.3
United States of America	2005	128.8	124.5	37.7	43.0	48.3	50.5	53.1	15.1	15.8	16.2	36.6	33.7	30.7
Developing Countries														
Brazil	2005	19.7	23.3	7.3	7.9	68.2	65.9	63.2	11.8	12.8	12.5	20.0	21.4	24.2
Chile	2004	...	31.4	...	10.0	...	57.1	63.1	...	10.6	11.8	...	32.3	25.2
Colombia	2005	72.5	49.3	4.2	6.0	41.0	48.1	60.0	3.4	4.1	4.8	55.5	47.8	35.1
Ecuador	2005	10.1	20.3	3.2	5.8	79.5	66.7	68.4	6.5	...	9.0	13.9	...	22.7
Fiji	2004	...	5.2	...	2.7	...	69.6	70.3	...	14.0	15.2	...	16.4	14.5
India	2004	7.8	10.5	1.6	2.0	68.7	71.8	70.9	6.3	6.5	5.6	25.0	21.7	23.5
Indonesia	2005	52.4	24.0	1.9	1.8	59.7	73.3	66.4	1.4	4.7	2.5	38.9	21.9	31.1
Iran (Islamic Republic of)	2005	62.8	15.0	9.1	6.3	52.6	55.1	58.8	6.9	13.1	17.2	40.5	31.8	24.0
Madagascar	2006	...	1.6	...	0.5	...	64.2	57.8	...	9.4	14.0	...	26.3	28.2
Malaysia	2005	15.2	16.3	4.7	7.0	63.9	67.0	73.4	11.3	11.4	11.4	24.9	21.7	15.2
Morocco	2005	13.0	16.8	7.7	8.2	60.2	70.8	64.4	23.5	14.2	17.4	16.3	15.0	18.1
Oman	2006	21.4	22.6	6.0	5.5	62.8	63.6	71.4	10.4	12.0	7.0	26.8	24.4	21.7
Trinidad and Tobago	2004	...	...	...	...	...	74.0	71.9	...	17.4	7.1	...	8.6	21.0

a/ At current prices.

Table 1.11

SELECTED CHARACTERISTICS OF BRANCHES, SELECTED YEARS AND COUNTRIES

Lighting equipment and electric lamps (ISIC 3150)

Country or area	Latest year	Value added per employee (current 1000 dollars)		Wages and salaries per employee (current 1000 dollars)		Percentage in output a/								
						Costs of input materials and utilities			Costs of labour			Operating surplus		
	(LY)	2000	LY	2000	LY	2000	2003	LY	2000	2003	LY	2000	2003	LY
Industrialized Countries														
CIS														
Azerbaijan	2005	...	0.6	0.1	0.5	...	...	62.1	56.4	...	31.0	...	...	6.9
Georgia	2006	...	12.5	...	3.8	...	...	55.8	...	...	13.6	...	...	30.6
Kyrgyzstan	2006	...	...	0.5	1.2	...	...	...	12.7	17.7	23.6	...	...	...
Russian Federation	2006	...	...	0.7	2.9	...	...	...	12.5	...	...	...	...	...
EU-15														
Austria	2005	60.7	64.2	28.5	41.9	50.5	52.3	55.7	23.2	28.6	28.9	26.3	19.1	15.4
Belgium	2005	61.9	77.4	25.4	37.6	53.6	59.6	60.4	19.0	20.7	19.2	27.4	19.7	20.4
Denmark	2005	43.4	53.2	27.8	45.5	60.8	65.4	65.9	25.1	27.5	29.2	14.1	7.1	4.9
Finland	2005	48.6	84.8	23.6	37.7	62.2	61.8	59.1	18.4	18.5	18.2	19.5	19.7	22.7
France	2005	36.6	60.9	19.7	35.0	64.1	63.0	63.6	19.3	20.5	20.9	16.6	16.6	15.5
Germany	2005	45.3	72.4	27.3	44.4	53.9	53.7	57.0	27.9	28.8	26.4	18.3	17.6	16.6
Greece	2004	...	52.0	...	17.3	...	...	62.0	...	...	12.7	...	...	25.3
Ireland	2005	35.8	75.7	16.8	43.3	56.4	60.0	57.6	20.5	25.0	24.2	23.1	15.0	18.2
Italy	2005	40.7	66.5	16.8	28.0	69.2	68.5	69.5	12.7	12.2	12.8	18.0	19.2	17.7
Netherlands	2005	37.6	67.3	21.3	40.6	70.3	65.7	66.7	16.8	18.8	20.1	12.9	15.4	13.2
Portugal	2005	...	24.5	8.0	12.6	...	64.8	62.2	20.7	21.2	19.5	...	14.0	18.3
Spain	2005	28.3	46.1	15.5	27.1	67.8	68.0	69.1	17.6	17.5	18.2	14.5	14.5	12.7
United Kingdom	2005	41.5	71.4	25.8	37.5	61.0	59.4	53.1	24.3	26.1	24.7	14.7	14.5	22.3
EU-12														
Bulgaria	2006	1.7	6.7	0.9	1.7	80.6	82.6	77.9	9.8	5.5	5.5	9.5	11.9	16.6
Czech Republic	2004	6.8	15.3	3.4	6.7	71.5	72.2	...	14.1	11.2	...	14.4	16.6	...
Estonia	2005	...	11.7	...	5.4	...	46.6	64.5	...	30.4	16.4	...	23.0	19.1
Hungary	2005	11.3	75.8	4.3	11.5	68.4	58.1	42.5	12.0	10.6	8.7	19.6	31.3	48.7
Lithuania	2006	3.5	18.6	2.4	5.8	59.8	76.9	79.4	27.8	13.7	6.4	12.4	9.4	14.2
Malta	2005	23.0	21.0	11.2	10.4	40.3	56.7	58.8	29.0	26.5	20.4	30.7	16.8	20.9
Poland	2005	10.5	28.0	...	7.6	70.4	62.6	64.1	...	10.7	9.7	...	26.7	26.2
Romania	2006	...	10.3	...	5.8	...	53.2	68.9	...	14.9	17.6	...	31.9	13.5
Slovakia	2005	4.2	17.4	2.8	6.7	79.7	73.2	73.3	13.7	12.2	10.3	6.6	14.6	16.4
Other Europe														
Norway	2004	41.0	73.2	32.5	51.9	63.6	...	62.0	28.9	...	26.9	7.6	...	11.1

a/ At current prices.

Table 1.11
(continued)

SELECTED CHARACTERISTICS OF BRANCHES, SELECTED YEARS AND COUNTRIES

Lighting equipment and electric lamps (ISIC 3150)														
Country or area	Latest year	Value added per employee (current 1000 dollars)		Wages and salaries per employee (current 1000 dollars)		Percentage in output [a]								
						Costs of input materials and utilities			Costs of labour			Operating surplus		
	(LY)	2000	LY	2000	LY	2000	2003	LY	2000	2003	LY	2000	2003	LY
Other Countries														
Japan	2005	108.2	123.1	36.3	36.8	59.6	60.2	60.6	13.6	12.4	11.8	26.8	27.4	27.6
Republic of Korea	2006	37.5	74.6	12.4	22.8	56.1	59.4	58.5	14.5	13.6	12.7	29.4	27.0	28.8
Singapore	2006	18.5	29.6	16.0	23.7	73.9	72.2	74.5	22.7	23.1	20.4	3.5	4.7	5.1
United States of America	2005	99.9	96.8	31.6	39.1	43.5	43.5	44.2	17.9	18.1	22.5	38.6	38.5	33.3
Developing Countries														
Brazil	2005	16.1	14.3	6.5	9.2	49.5	52.8	57.1	20.5	21.3	27.6	30.0	25.9	15.4
Chile	2006	...	29.4	...	11.6	...	66.2	68.7	...	13.3	12.4	...	20.5	18.9
Colombia	2005	13.8	16.3	3.4	4.6	51.0	55.9	62.6	12.1	9.9	10.5	36.8	34.2	26.9
India	2004	4.4	5.1	1.3	1.5	72.7	74.5	77.1	7.8	7.2	7.0	19.5	18.3	15.9
Indonesia	2005	7.5	9.4	1.2	1.1	51.5	63.3	66.7	7.9	16.2	3.9	40.6	20.5	29.4
Iran (Islamic Republic of)	2005	26.4	9.0	9.6	3.4	56.2	54.9	54.8	15.9	16.9	17.2	27.9	28.2	28.0
Jordan	2006	21.0	21.5	4.3	4.2	46.6	51.9	51.9	10.9	12.7	9.5	42.5	35.4	38.6
Malaysia	2005	20.4	16.6	5.0	7.5	63.4	67.2	80.1	8.9	9.8	9.0	27.7	23.0	10.9
Morocco	2005	7.6	8.8	5.0	5.9	56.9	60.2	66.4	28.2	23.4	22.3	14.9	16.4	11.3
Oman	2006	16.1	13.3	4.2	7.1	62.8	41.1	60.7	9.7	12.6	20.8	27.5	46.3	18.5

a/ At current prices.

Table 1.11

SELECTED CHARACTERISTICS OF BRANCHES, SELECTED YEARS AND COUNTRIES

Other electrical equipment n.e.c. (ISIC 3190)														
Country or area	Latest year	Value added per employee (current 1000 dollars)		Wages and salaries per employee (current 1000 dollars)		Percentage in output [a]								
						Costs of input materials and utilities			Costs of labour			Operating surplus		
	(LY)	2000	LY	2000	LY	2000	2003	LY	2000	2003	LY	2000	2003	LY
Industrialized Countries														
CIS														
Azerbaijan	2006	...	2.4	0.2	1.5	...	62.4	57.3	29.8	35.0	25.9	...	2.6	16.8
Georgia	2006	0.9	1.3	0.4	0.4	73.5	71.7	51.5	10.1	5.7	14.6	16.4	22.6	33.8
Kyrgyzstan	2006	...	...	0.1	0.6	...	...	...	15.0	38.3	26.9	...	...	...
Russian Federation	2006	...	8.7	0.9	4.3	...	...	70.6	12.2	...	14.6	...	...	14.9
EU-15														
Austria	2005	56.2	88.7	22.6	41.4	55.9	55.6	64.3	17.7	18.1	16.7	26.4	26.3	19.1
Belgium	2005	56.4	80.8	28.8	44.7	62.2	66.8	65.7	19.3	21.2	19.0	18.5	12.0	15.3
Denmark	2005	42.6	66.5	28.8	46.3	58.4	63.0	65.2	28.1	26.6	24.2	13.5	10.4	10.6
Finland	2005	40.2	77.9	21.4	39.2	68.0	62.7	62.1	17.0	19.4	19.1	15.0	17.9	18.8
France	2005	42.6	70.1	24.3	40.2	71.1	70.5	68.3	16.5	16.8	18.2	12.4	12.6	13.5
Germany	2005	51.6	76.3	30.5	49.9	61.9	63.2	65.0	22.5	23.5	22.9	15.6	13.3	12.1
Greece	2004	...	62.1	...	17.7	...	...	61.8	...	...	10.9	...	...	27.3
Ireland	2005	39.9	71.2	19.0	32.0	69.2	63.5	79.5	14.6	13.3	9.2	16.2	23.1	11.3
Italy	2005	40.7	63.8	18.5	28.3	70.3	66.5	67.8	13.5	15.9	14.3	16.2	17.6	17.9
Luxembourg	2005	37.2	56.5	26.2	40.4	55.2	...	58.8	31.6	...	29.4	13.2	...	11.8
Netherlands	2005	55.8	89.1	27.4	52.7	65.0	62.8	66.9	17.2	18.8	19.6	17.8	18.4	13.5
Portugal	2005	14.0	20.4	8.8	15.3	68.8	71.6	74.6	19.7	17.2	19.1	11.5	11.2	6.3
Spain	2005	35.7	67.6	18.4	32.9	65.4	66.2	67.4	17.8	16.7	15.8	16.7	17.1	16.7
Sweden	2005	45.3	74.6	24.3	38.8	69.1	...	67.2	16.6	...	17.0	14.3	...	15.7
United Kingdom	2005	52.0	69.0	30.8	40.5	56.3	61.5	62.4	25.9	23.1	22.0	17.8	15.3	15.5
EU-12														
Bulgaria	2006	2.4	7.1	1.0	1.8	68.4	78.4	79.7	14.0	6.7	5.3	17.6	15.0	15.0
Czech Republic	2004	8.3	15.8	3.7	7.1	69.3	68.0	71.4	13.8	13.7	12.8	16.9	18.3	15.8
Estonia	2006	6.5	14.6	3.7	8.6	59.2	...	46.1	23.0	...	31.7	17.9	...	22.2
Hungary	2005	14.2	20.8	4.3	9.9	86.6	70.6	73.1	4.1	13.3	12.8	9.3	16.1	14.1
Lithuania	2006	...	19.9	...	5.8	...	75.4	62.5	...	8.8	10.9	...	15.7	26.6
Malta	2005	31.5	48.8	14.1	22.4	50.0	49.8	46.5	22.3	26.1	24.6	27.6	24.1	28.9
Poland	2005	12.5	18.9	...	7.5	61.7	68.2	69.7	...	13.2	11.9	...	18.7	18.4
Romania	2006	...	6.9	...	5.4	...	67.1	74.8	...	21.5	19.5	...	11.5	5.7
Slovakia	2005	4.0	11.0	2.9	5.5	67.8	70.4	72.7	22.7	16.1	13.7	9.5	13.6	13.6
Other Europe														
Norway	2004	45.3	83.5	33.8	54.6	67.1	58.2	59.9	24.6	26.3	26.2	8.3	15.4	13.9

a/ At current prices.

Table 1.11
(continued)

SELECTED CHARACTERISTICS OF BRANCHES, SELECTED YEARS AND COUNTRIES

Other electrical equipment n.e.c. (ISIC 3190)														
Country or area	Latest year	Value added per employee (current 1000 dollars)		Wages and salaries per employee (current 1000 dollars)		Percentage in output [a/]								
						Costs of input materials and utilities			Costs of labour			Operating surplus		
	(LY)	2000	LY	2000	LY	2000	2003	LY	2000	2003	LY	2000	2003	LY
Other Countries														
Japan	2005	86.8	99.8	33.5	34.7	70.9	66.6	67.0	11.2	13.0	11.5	17.9	20.3	21.6
Republic of Korea	2006	46.6	78.2	13.2	25.1	59.6	64.2	68.3	11.5	10.8	10.1	28.9	25.0	21.5
Singapore	2006	26.5	52.4	22.3	25.5	82.4	69.6	65.2	14.7	22.0	17.0	2.8	8.3	17.8
United States of America	2005	108.4	130.9	39.3	46.1	50.6	47.4	50.7	17.9	17.6	17.3	31.5	35.0	31.9
Developing Countries														
Brazil	2005	21.0	22.9	6.4	7.3	54.8	58.1	59.2	13.8	13.3	13.0	31.4	28.6	27.8
Chile	2006	...	24.7	...	9.7	...	46.0	50.7	...	25.1	19.3	...	28.9	30.0
Colombia	2005	10.8	26.3	2.5	3.6	44.6	49.6	52.4	12.9	13.4	6.6	42.5	36.9	41.0
India	2004	4.5	6.7	1.4	1.6	78.4	78.0	78.9	6.7	6.6	5.1	14.9	15.4	15.9
Indonesia	2005	1.5	12.6	0.7	3.1	62.6	80.8	44.7	16.7	6.5	13.6	20.7	12.8	41.7
Iran (Islamic Republic of)	2005	18.2	18.4	6.5	4.2	67.0	74.8	65.6	11.9	6.2	7.9	21.1	19.0	26.5
Malaysia	2005	11.3	10.3	3.7	4.7	62.2	57.5	70.4	12.4	15.2	13.4	25.4	27.3	16.2
Morocco	2005	7.2	9.7	3.9	5.6	75.1	77.3	78.6	13.4	11.3	12.3	11.5	11.4	9.1
Sri Lanka	2006	...	20.8	...	2.3	...	...	51.6	...	...	5.4	...	...	43.0

a/ At current prices.

Table 1.11

SELECTED CHARACTERISTICS OF BRANCHES, SELECTED YEARS AND COUNTRIES

Electronic valves, tubes, etc. (ISIC 3210)

Country or area	Latest year	Value added per employee (current 1000 dollars)		Wages and salaries per employee (current 1000 dollars)		Percentage in output a/								
						Costs of input materials and utilities			Costs of labour			Operating surplus		
	(LY)	2000	LY	2000	LY	2000	2003	LY	2000	2003	LY	2000	2003	LY
Industrialized Countries														
CIS														
Azerbaijan	2006	...	2.1	0.2	0.6	...	62.4	57.4	26.6	30.5	13.0	...	7.1	29.7
Kyrgyzstan	2006	...	...	0.3	1.4	...	...	...	27.6	19.6	17.0	...	...	...
EU-15														
Austria	2005	67.1	104.5	26.3	51.5	56.6	56.6	58.3	17.0	20.3	20.6	26.4	23.2	21.2
Belgium	2005	77.6	109.7	32.2	51.9	69.3	56.8	59.3	12.7	19.2	19.3	18.0	23.9	21.4
Denmark	2005	39.7	68.8	26.5	46.5	56.7	58.7	58.3	28.9	25.8	28.2	14.4	15.5	13.5
Finland	2005	45.5	49.7	22.1	36.0	58.0	66.4	70.5	20.4	22.4	21.4	21.6	11.2	8.1
France	2005	56.6	75.0	26.3	40.9	73.1	66.9	65.8	12.5	19.5	18.7	14.4	13.6	15.5
Germany	2005	76.2	93.6	34.2	53.6	62.7	67.3	67.1	16.7	20.5	18.8	20.6	12.2	14.0
Greece	2004	...	44.3	...	16.1	...	...	47.6	...	...	19.0	...	...	33.3
Italy	2005	68.6	72.9	22.0	32.5	59.8	60.7	60.0	12.9	16.2	17.9	27.3	23.0	22.2
Netherlands	2005	44.8	83.0	24.5	50.9	68.7	67.7	63.9	17.1	23.7	22.1	14.2	8.6	13.9
Portugal	2004	34.9	54.3	10.9	17.1	73.9	86.8	87.3	8.2	4.6	4.0	17.9	8.6	8.7
Spain	2005	42.5	47.2	19.7	27.8	59.5	69.9	66.8	18.8	21.7	19.5	21.7	8.4	13.7
Sweden	2004	55.4	54.1	27.4	37.3	66.8	...	72.4	16.4	...	19.0	16.8	...	8.6
United Kingdom	2005	73.3	81.0	33.7	43.6	58.4	67.4	64.9	19.1	18.4	18.9	22.5	14.1	16.2
EU-12														
Bulgaria	2006	2.3	6.9	1.2	2.5	77.1	70.7	73.6	12.4	10.1	9.4	10.5	19.3	17.0
Czech Republic	2004	8.5	19.1	3.5	6.9	59.3	67.2	77.7	16.7	12.5	8.1	24.0	20.3	14.2
Estonia	2006	7.0	17.1	3.1	7.7	56.9	78.7	75.6	19.4	10.1	11.1	23.8	11.2	13.4
Hungary	2005	9.0	39.7	4.1	10.4	76.2	84.5	71.4	10.9	7.5	7.5	12.9	8.0	21.1
Latvia	2006	6.9	9.2	2.3	4.1	43.2	59.5	44.3	19.0	19.7	24.5	37.8	20.8	31.2
Malta	2005	92.7	53.6	15.0	21.0	83.4	85.7	88.0	2.7	4.8	4.7	13.9	9.5	7.3
Poland	2005	9.4	11.7	...	7.5	58.8	72.3	70.8	...	14.0	18.6	...	13.7	10.6
Romania	2006	...	10.5	...	7.8	...	38.5	53.6	...	31.1	34.4	...	30.5	12.0
Slovakia	2005	3.2	9.4	2.9	6.2	86.5	80.7	86.5	12.2	7.0	8.9	1.2	12.3	4.6
Other Europe														
Norway	2004	47.6	73.6	34.4	53.0	70.0	64.9	67.5	21.6	24.0	23.4	8.3	11.1	9.1

a/ At current prices.

Table 1.11
(continued)

SELECTED CHARACTERISTICS OF BRANCHES, SELECTED YEARS AND COUNTRIES

Electronic valves, tubes, etc. (ISIC 3210)

Country or area	Latest year	Value added per employee (current 1000 dollars)		Wages and salaries per employee (current 1000 dollars)		Percentage in output [a]								
						Costs of input materials and utilities			Costs of labour			Operating surplus		
	(LY)	2000	LY	2000	LY	2000	2003	LY	2000	2003	LY	2000	2003	LY
Other Countries														
Israel	2005	129.5	58.8	32.5	34.1	33.7	44.8	53.0	16.7	24.1	27.3	49.7	31.1	19.7
Japan	2005	139.7	151.7	43.7	45.2	62.6	62.6	61.7	11.7	11.7	11.4	25.7	25.7	26.9
Republic of Korea	2006	142.4	186.7	19.9	31.9	41.7	48.6	50.8	8.1	8.2	8.4	50.1	43.2	40.8
Singapore	2006	102.4	120.3	23.3	28.4	72.2	76.5	73.8	6.3	7.0	6.2	21.5	16.5	20.0
United States of America	2005	193.5	248.9	47.6	53.9	36.8	35.7	31.5	15.5	16.0	14.8	47.7	48.2	53.6
Developing Countries														
Brazil	2005	23.8	22.7	7.3	7.2	61.0	64.9	66.0	12.0	10.1	10.7	27.0	25.1	23.2
Chile	2006	...	19.6	...	13.0	...	44.5	34.4	...	26.2	43.4	...	29.3	22.2
Colombia	2005	8.3	7.8	2.7	3.0	52.8	55.9	58.0	15.2	16.9	16.5	32.1	27.3	25.5
India	2004	7.2	8.5	1.9	2.6	71.1	70.9	72.2	7.8	7.8	8.3	21.1	21.3	19.5
Indonesia	2005	15.6	9.6	1.5	2.1	61.5	60.2	48.6	3.8	5.3	11.5	34.7	34.5	40.0
Iran (Islamic Republic of)	2005	28.3	9.9	6.8	3.7	55.9	77.4	64.1	10.5	7.2	13.3	33.6	15.4	22.6
Malaysia	2005	25.7	18.6	5.3	7.0	74.8	76.5	84.0	5.2	6.1	6.0	20.0	17.3	10.0
Morocco	2005	8.7	13.9	5.6	9.9	64.1	50.0	48.9	23.3	36.7	36.2	12.6	13.4	14.9
Sri Lanka	2006	...	2.5	...	0.9	...	...	28.5	...	...	24.2	...	...	47.3

a/ At current prices.

Table 1.11

SELECTED CHARACTERISTICS OF BRANCHES, SELECTED YEARS AND COUNTRIES

TV/radio transmitters; line comm. apparatus (ISIC 3220)

Country or area	Latest year	Value added per employee (current 1000 dollars)		Wages and salaries per employee (current 1000 dollars)		Percentage in output[a]								
						Costs of input materials and utilities			Costs of labour			Operating surplus		
	(LY)	2000	LY	2000	LY	2000	2003	LY	2000	2003	LY	2000	2003	LY
Industrialized Countries														
CIS														
Kyrgyzstan	2005	...	12.6	0.2	0.5	...	...	66.0	21.7	13.2	1.3	...	...	32.7
EU-15														
Austria	2005	77.6	127.6	46.9	70.4	56.7	62.7	59.1	26.2	27.3	22.6	17.1	10.0	18.3
Belgium	2005	97.4	144.3	43.4	73.1	65.7	56.8	67.9	15.3	25.8	16.3	19.0	17.4	15.8
Denmark	2005	39.7	109.0	28.1	66.0	76.7	74.9	52.5	16.5	16.4	28.8	6.8	8.7	18.7
Finland	2005	164.9	200.1	31.2	61.0	67.7	56.7	70.2	6.1	9.4	9.1	26.2	34.0	20.7
France	2005	64.9	83.1	33.4	54.1	76.0	76.8	75.8	12.3	19.3	15.7	11.6	3.9	8.4
Germany	2005	51.9	92.4	41.8	60.0	72.9	70.6	73.6	21.9	23.1	17.1	5.3	6.3	9.3
Greece	2004	...	67.3	...	29.7	...	...	50.8	...	...	21.7	...	...	27.5
Ireland	2005	106.9	130.5	26.5	34.4	68.5	81.1	78.6	7.8	10.0	5.6	23.7	8.9	15.8
Italy	2005	57.2	68.0	26.3	37.1	79.3	68.3	71.0	9.5	15.5	15.8	11.2	16.2	13.2
Netherlands	2005	...	75.3	...	38.4	71.1	62.9	63.6	23.8	19.7	18.6	5.1	17.5	17.9
Portugal	2004	41.7	86.7	22.1	38.2	74.0	73.7	72.3	13.8	12.5	12.2	12.2	13.7	15.5
Spain	2005	53.9	55.1	33.8	31.9	70.5	64.9	70.3	18.5	17.4	17.2	11.0	17.7	12.5
United Kingdom	2005	97.2	67.5	42.3	59.6	66.2	71.1	77.0	14.7	24.2	20.3	19.1	4.7	2.7
EU-12														
Bulgaria	2006	2.9	12.9	1.6	2.7	63.6	71.6	58.0	20.5	6.1	8.9	15.9	22.3	33.1
Czech Republic	2004	13.9	38.3	6.0	11.9	73.9	...	...	11.1	...	...	14.9	...	...
Hungary	2005	21.3	38.8	6.0	15.9	65.6	73.0	78.1	9.7	11.4	9.0	24.8	15.6	13.0
Latvia	2006	4.8	41.5	2.1	11.4	57.5	53.8	53.1	18.8	13.2	12.9	23.7	33.0	34.0
Lithuania	2006	11.2	27.2	5.6	9.4	59.3	83.0	64.2	20.4	8.5	12.4	20.3	8.6	23.4
Poland	2005	18.6	25.4	...	10.3	76.5	73.0	78.3	...	10.3	8.8	...	16.7	12.9
Romania	2006	...	26.4	...	14.0	...	67.5	76.4	...	16.2	12.5	...	16.3	11.1
Slovakia	2005	5.7	8.2	3.3	7.7	71.3	71.4	74.4	16.9	17.4	23.9	11.9	11.2	1.7
Other Europe														
Norway	2004	93.1	124.8	53.2	81.1	65.2	68.3	68.5	19.9	20.2	20.5	14.9	11.5	11.0

a/ At current prices.

Table 1.11
(continued)

SELECTED CHARACTERISTICS OF BRANCHES, SELECTED YEARS AND COUNTRIES

TV/radio transmitters; line comm. apparatus (ISIC 3220)														
Country or area	Latest year	Value added per employee (current 1000 dollars)		Wages and salaries per employee (current 1000 dollars)		Percentage in output a/								
						Costs of input materials and utilities			Costs of labour			Operating surplus		
	(LY)	2000	LY	2000	LY	2000	2003	LY	2000	2003	LY	2000	2003	LY
Other Countries														
Israel	2005	133.2	92.9	63.2	54.4	54.4	64.4	61.1	21.6	26.8	22.7	23.9	8.8	16.1
Japan	2005	213.5	175.0	48.0	48.4	66.1	74.6	72.6	7.6	7.3	7.6	26.3	18.0	19.9
Republic of Korea	2006	105.5	218.6	15.1	27.8	70.1	64.9	59.7	4.3	4.4	5.1	25.6	30.7	35.2
Singapore	2006	94.8	182.9	32.2	27.8	79.6	...	71.5	6.9	...	4.3	13.4	...	24.1
United States of America	2005	258.4	269.3	67.8	64.6	47.5	50.0	45.3	13.8	14.8	13.1	38.8	35.1	41.6
Developing Countries														
Brazil	2005	87.3	80.6	13.0	15.9	61.3	69.8	71.6	5.8	5.3	5.6	32.9	24.9	22.8
Chile	2004	...	13.8	...	11.9	...	52.3	54.9	...	37.6	39.1	...	10.1	6.1
Colombia	2005	27.0	32.3	4.3	6.2	42.2	57.8	62.1	9.2	9.0	7.2	48.6	33.2	30.7
Ecuador	2005	5.6	12.0	1.5	5.4	59.7	...	54.1	10.6	...	20.5	29.8	...	25.4
India	2004	5.0	10.2	2.3	3.0	80.8	81.6	76.5	8.8	8.2	6.8	10.3	10.2	16.7
Indonesia	2005	9.1	13.4	1.1	1.6	51.8	59.7	62.6	5.9	6.4	4.3	42.3	33.9	33.1
Iran (Islamic Republic of)	2005	51.7	20.1	10.9	6.0	51.0	65.4	55.3	10.3	10.0	13.3	38.7	24.7	31.5
Malaysia	2005	33.0	24.5	4.8	6.9	76.4	81.4	88.2	3.4	3.7	3.3	20.2	14.9	8.5

a/ At current prices.

Table 1.11

SELECTED CHARACTERISTICS OF BRANCHES, SELECTED YEARS AND COUNTRIES

TV and radio receivers and associated goods (ISIC 3230)

Country or area	Latest year	Value added per employee (current 1000 dollars)		Wages and salaries per employee (current 1000 dollars)		Percentage in output [a/]								
						Costs of input materials and utilities			Costs of labour			Operating surplus		
	(LY)	2000	LY	2000	LY	2000	2003	LY	2000	2003	LY	2000	2003	LY
Industrialized Countries														
CIS														
Azerbaijan	2006	...	4.3	0.5	1.1	...	62.4	57.5	...	16.7	10.8	...	20.9	31.7
Kyrgyzstan	2006	...	...	0.2	0.5	...	...	...	9.2	69.2	6.3	...	...	...
EU-15														
Austria	2005	60.3	75.6	33.8	47.0	74.5	56.7	57.5	14.3	25.9	26.4	11.2	17.4	16.0
Belgium	2005	81.8	130.4	30.7	50.6	76.9	64.9	66.1	8.7	13.8	13.1	14.4	21.3	20.7
Denmark	2005	35.3	70.2	25.3	43.5	67.2	66.6	67.5	23.5	20.7	20.1	9.2	12.7	12.4
Finland	2005	54.1	60.4	26.6	42.3	64.8	69.2	66.7	17.3	22.7	23.3	17.9	8.1	10.0
France	2005	38.1	74.6	22.8	45.5	82.4	78.2	74.9	10.5	14.0	15.3	7.1	7.8	9.8
Germany	2005	53.7	87.6	33.8	49.6	69.0	70.1	66.1	19.6	19.1	19.2	11.5	10.8	14.7
Greece	2004	...	48.4	...	16.1	...	...	52.0	...	...	16.0	...	...	32.0
Italy	2005	39.7	46.3	17.8	27.6	74.8	76.2	74.1	11.3	13.4	15.4	13.9	10.4	10.5
Portugal	2005	25.8	52.0	11.7	18.6	83.6	80.8	81.2	7.4	6.7	6.7	9.0	12.5	12.1
Spain	2005	30.9	63.5	19.5	37.4	86.4	85.0	83.8	8.6	8.8	9.6	5.0	6.2	6.7
Sweden	2005	52.0	70.6	27.2	37.6	78.2	...	74.0	11.4	...	13.9	10.4	...	12.1
United Kingdom	2005	47.8	61.8	27.3	39.8	73.4	70.9	72.2	15.1	16.6	17.9	11.4	12.5	9.9
EU-12														
Bulgaria	2006	2.7	4.3	1.2	3.5	58.3	...	80.0	19.4	15.5	16.1	22.3	...	3.9
Czech Republic	2004	12.7	17.7	3.7	6.9	...	...	...	...	...	...	...	...	...
Hungary	2005	12.6	36.4	4.2	10.6	90.5	89.9	91.0	3.2	2.4	2.6	6.3	7.7	6.4
Latvia	2006	2.8	10.3	2.5	4.5	53.7	68.9	50.5	40.2	14.9	21.6	6.1	16.2	28.0
Lithuania	2006	4.5	9.8	2.8	6.3	76.9	80.4	88.8	14.4	9.6	7.1	8.7	10.0	4.1
Malta	2004	59.5	89.3	12.4	18.4	57.2	...	81.0	8.9	...	3.9	33.9	...	15.1
Poland	2005	8.5	35.5	...	11.1	90.3	79.1	85.5	...	5.7	4.5	...	15.2	10.0
Romania	2006	...	10.7	...	5.7	...	82.6	83.6	...	6.4	8.7	...	11.0	7.7
Slovakia	2005	5.0	13.8	2.9	6.6	80.2	78.0	88.2	11.6	8.2	5.6	8.2	13.8	6.2
Other Europe														
Norway	2004	63.6	89.9	36.0	46.6	78.5	...	61.7	12.1	...	19.8	9.3	...	18.4

a/ At current prices.

Table 1.11
(continued)

SELECTED CHARACTERISTICS OF BRANCHES, SELECTED YEARS AND COUNTRIES

TV and radio receivers and associated goods (ISIC 3230)

Country or area	Latest year	Value added per employee (current 1000 dollars)		Wages and salaries per employee (current 1000 dollars)		Percentage in output [a/]								
						Costs of input materials and utilities			Costs of labour			Operating surplus		
	(LY)	2000	LY	2000	LY	2000	2003	LY	2000	2003	LY	2000	2003	LY
Other Countries														
Israel	2005	...	60.2	...	59.2	...	66.7	64.2	...	31.2	35.2	...	2.1	0.6
Japan	2005	105.5	135.8	35.6	39.0	67.6	69.5	69.4	10.9	9.1	8.8	21.5	21.4	21.8
Republic of Korea	2006	50.2	104.7	13.5	33.5	68.3	70.6	59.8	8.5	8.4	12.9	23.2	21.0	27.3
Singapore	2006	33.0	33.5	20.6	28.1	86.5	84.9	84.1	8.4	8.5	13.3	5.1	6.6	2.6
United States of America	2005	66.5	161.7	20.1	43.4	64.9	63.1	70.1	10.6	11.5	8.0	24.5	25.4	21.9
Developing Countries														
Brazil	2005	44.1	50.6	7.9	8.2	68.2	72.5	68.7	5.7	5.5	5.1	26.1	22.0	26.2
Chile	2004	...	13.5	...	5.4	...	62.5	61.5	...	21.9	15.5	...	15.6	23.0
Colombia	2005	9.1	11.9	2.4	3.6	61.9	60.2	60.6	9.9	7.2	11.9	28.3	32.6	27.5
India	2004	10.7	14.2	1.7	3.1	86.1	88.0	90.2	2.2	2.0	2.1	11.7	10.0	7.7
Indonesia	2005	6.5	15.3	1.2	2.1	76.4	60.1	34.6	4.3	4.7	9.0	19.3	35.3	56.5
Iran (Islamic Republic of)	2005	63.0	19.8	13.7	4.8	67.3	74.2	68.0	7.1	7.4	7.9	25.6	18.5	24.2
Malaysia	2005	12.8	14.3	4.3	7.3	87.2	85.9	90.1	4.3	5.5	5.0	8.4	8.6	4.9
Morocco	2005	4.5	8.3	3.2	5.5	76.2	78.9	62.5	16.9	21.1	25.0	6.9	0.0	12.5
Philippines	2005	...	10.7	...	2.0	...	87.8	81.9	...	5.1	3.3	...	7.1	14.7
Sri Lanka	2006	...	3.0	...	1.0	...	...	70.5	...	...	10.0	...	...	19.5

a/ At current prices.

Table 1.11

SELECTED CHARACTERISTICS OF BRANCHES, SELECTED YEARS AND COUNTRIES

Medical, measuring, testing appliances, etc. (ISIC 331)														
Country or area	Latest year (LY)	Value added per employee (current 1000 dollars)		Wages and salaries per employee (current 1000 dollars)		Percentage in output [a/]								
						Costs of input materials and utilities			Costs of labour			Operating surplus		
		2000	LY	2000	LY	2000	2003	LY	2000	2003	LY	2000	2003	LY
Industrialized Countries														
CIS														
Azerbaijan	2006	...	1.3	0.3	1.2	...	62.4	57.3	31.0	24.0	37.7	...	13.6	5.0
Georgia	2006	0.2	2.5	0.1	0.9	65.1	50.7	53.1	21.4	18.5	17.4	13.4	30.8	29.5
Kyrgyzstan	2006	...	...	0.5	1.3	...	...	...	17.6	15.1	42.6	...	...	...
Russian Federation	2006	...	9.6	0.7	4.7	...	...	55.4	16.6	...	21.8	...	...	22.7
EU-15														
Austria	2005	41.7	79.5	23.2	39.0	47.9	48.2	46.1	28.9	27.3	26.4	23.1	24.5	27.5
Belgium	2005	58.9	88.2	25.5	43.7	63.4	69.5	67.1	15.8	17.4	16.3	20.7	13.2	16.6
Denmark	2005	56.4	103.5	34.0	56.8	53.6	51.1	51.9	28.0	27.2	26.4	18.4	21.7	21.7
Finland	2005	56.2	91.3	26.9	46.2	56.6	61.1	59.6	20.8	20.2	20.4	22.6	18.6	19.9
France	2005	51.2	79.9	28.2	44.3	63.4	65.3	61.5	20.1	19.5	21.3	16.5	15.1	17.2
Germany	2005	47.9	71.5	29.7	41.4	53.6	53.6	53.1	28.7	28.3	27.1	17.7	18.1	19.8
Greece	2004	...	75.0	...	18.5	...	...	52.0	...	...	11.9	...	...	36.2
Italy	2005	52.1	81.4	21.7	34.1	60.5	63.7	63.0	16.4	15.9	15.5	23.0	20.4	21.5
Luxembourg	2004	...	53.7	...	32.6	...	...	52.8	...	...	28.7	...	...	18.5
Netherlands	2004	54.4	74.6	29.2	42.7	57.5	59.4	58.1	22.8	22.1	24.0	19.7	18.5	17.9
Portugal	2005	21.1	29.0	10.8	15.0	61.6	67.8	66.8	19.7	17.8	17.1	18.7	14.4	16.0
Spain	2005	42.7	52.9	21.1	28.6	60.6	60.2	61.4	19.5	20.1	20.9	19.9	19.7	17.7
Sweden	2005	56.1	106.6	30.0	45.1	64.4	...	57.1	19.1	...	18.2	16.5	...	24.8
United Kingdom	2005	58.3	97.4	31.5	42.8	54.0	50.7	48.7	24.9	24.8	22.5	21.1	24.5	28.8
EU-12														
Bulgaria	2006	1.8	7.8	1.0	2.7	66.7	74.6	69.5	19.0	10.4	10.7	14.3	15.1	19.8
Cyprus	2006	20.9	42.7	10.5	24.3	38.6	39.2	36.2	30.8	33.1	36.4	30.6	27.6	27.5
Czech Republic	2004	10.0	18.1	4.2	7.8	68.1	63.0	68.7	13.5	14.3	13.5	18.5	22.7	17.8
Estonia	2006	7.6	18.6	3.6	10.2	68.7	67.9	71.4	14.6	17.4	15.7	16.7	14.7	12.9
Hungary	2005	7.4	21.0	4.1	9.4	67.5	57.5	56.8	17.9	18.9	19.3	14.6	23.6	23.9
Latvia	2006	6.6	15.1	2.6	5.3	58.6	65.4	55.8	16.6	15.0	15.6	24.9	19.6	28.6
Lithuania	2006	5.5	15.1	3.0	6.6	62.6	60.3	59.8	20.1	17.6	17.6	17.2	22.2	22.6
Malta	2005	34.7	23.1	13.2	13.3	52.2	58.0	58.2	18.2	17.4	24.1	29.6	24.7	17.7
Poland	2005	17.1	22.3	...	8.5	46.4	55.8	57.7	...	19.0	16.2	...	25.2	26.1
Romania	2006	...	12.4	...	6.8	...	63.8	68.1	...	17.3	17.4	...	18.9	14.5
Slovakia	2004	8.5	13.6	3.8	7.0	71.9	68.1	68.5	12.5	15.7	16.2	15.6	16.1	15.3
Other Europe														
Norway	2004	58.6	93.1	44.4	64.9	65.3	62.3	62.3	26.3	26.4	26.3	8.4	11.3	11.4

a/ At current prices.

Table 1.11
(continued)

SELECTED CHARACTERISTICS OF BRANCHES, SELECTED YEARS AND COUNTRIES

Medical, measuring, testing appliances, etc. (ISIC 331)														
Country or area	Latest year	Value added per employee (current 1000 dollars)		Wages and salaries per employee (current 1000 dollars)		Percentage in output [a]								
						Costs of input materials and utilities			Costs of labour			Operating surplus		
	(LY)	2000	LY	2000	LY	2000	2003	LY	2000	2003	LY	2000	2003	LY
Other Countries														
Japan	2005	112.8	127.1	36.6	35.7	47.6	54.1	54.8	17.0	13.8	12.7	35.4	32.1	32.5
Republic of Korea	2006	52.6	72.5	13.9	23.9	52.9	53.5	55.4	12.4	14.9	14.7	34.6	31.6	29.8
Singapore	2006	99.4	91.5	21.4	27.5	53.8	55.3	61.4	9.9	9.5	11.6	36.2	35.2	27.0
United States of America	2005	125.1	178.4	45.5	58.3	34.7	32.1	33.5	23.7	23.7	21.7	41.5	44.2	44.8
Developing Countries														
Brazil	2005	24.1	26.5	7.0	8.2	41.6	49.4	45.5	17.0	16.9	16.8	41.4	33.7	37.6
Chile	2006	...	27.6	...	15.7	...	65.3	72.0	...	12.8	16.0	...	21.9	12.0
Colombia	2005	13.4	20.8	3.3	4.5	49.5	52.6	53.3	12.3	8.7	10.1	38.2	38.7	36.6
Ecuador	2005	2.3	7.7	0.9	3.8	66.9	...	55.7	12.6	...	21.8	20.5	...	22.5
India	2004	5.8	9.9	1.8	2.6	73.6	72.8	74.1	8.2	7.9	6.9	18.2	19.4	19.0
Indonesia	2005	5.3	5.2	1.3	2.0	47.9	62.3	73.6	12.8	28.9	10.0	39.3	8.8	16.4
Iran (Islamic Republic of)	2005	20.9	9.5	8.3	3.2	60.1	56.5	51.7	15.9	17.4	16.4	24.0	26.1	31.9
Jordan	2006	6.0	9.2	3.1	3.3	62.8	56.6	60.3	19.1	16.9	14.4	18.1	26.5	25.3
Malaysia	2005	11.8	17.3	4.8	7.0	72.0	66.7	73.7	11.3	14.5	10.7	16.7	18.8	15.6
Morocco	2005	10.2	14.6	5.0	6.3	74.7	65.1	74.0	12.3	13.7	11.2	13.0	21.2	14.8

a/ At current prices.

Table 1.11

SELECTED CHARACTERISTICS OF BRANCHES, SELECTED YEARS AND COUNTRIES

Country or area	Latest year (LY)	Optical instruments & photographic equipment (ISIC 3320): Value added per employee (current 1000 dollars) 2000	LY	Wages and salaries per employee (current 1000 dollars) 2000	LY	Percentage in output [a/]: Costs of input materials and utilities 2000	2003	LY	Costs of labour 2000	2003	LY	Operating surplus 2000	2003	LY
Industrialized Countries														
CIS														
Azerbaijan	2006	...	1.1	0.1	0.3	...	62.1	56.7	33.3	28.6	10.0	...	9.3	33.3
Kyrgyzstan	2006	...	...	0.2	1.1	...	...	...	29.1	11.4	13.6	...	...	...
Russian Federation	2006	...	8.7	0.8	4.3	...	...	56.6	26.9	...	21.4	...	...	22.0
EU-15														
Austria	2005	46.3	91.9	24.4	42.3	46.9	45.7	46.9	28.0	24.5	24.5	25.1	29.8	28.7
Belgium	2005	46.8	83.8	28.5	39.1	72.1	61.7	65.9	17.0	19.6	15.9	10.9	18.7	18.2
Denmark	2005	122.9	104.0	32.6	60.2	45.7	...	56.4	14.4	...	25.3	39.9	...	18.4
France	2005	42.1	73.7	22.6	38.9	58.9	60.3	59.7	22.1	22.7	21.3	19.1	17.0	19.0
Germany	2005	51.1	76.8	31.2	46.1	54.9	55.3	56.0	27.5	27.7	26.4	17.5	16.9	17.6
Greece	2004	...	72.8	...	16.6	...	...	37.1	...	...	14.3	...	...	48.6
Ireland	2005	...	222.5	...	40.4	...	...	33.5	...	...	12.1	...	...	54.5
Italy	2005	51.7	69.9	16.7	28.4	62.5	63.8	62.4	12.1	15.0	15.3	25.4	21.3	22.3
Netherlands	2004	74.3	71.9	27.1	36.0	49.9	58.9	56.0	18.2	22.2	22.0	31.8	18.9	22.0
Portugal	2005	23.3	39.1	10.3	16.5	59.4	63.4	61.2	18.0	15.8	16.4	22.6	20.9	22.4
Spain	2005	34.8	67.4	19.9	30.3	60.9	63.4	59.6	22.4	19.2	18.1	16.7	17.4	22.3
Sweden	2005	55.9	103.6	33.0	43.5	64.7	...	58.8	20.9	...	17.3	14.4	...	23.9
United Kingdom	2005	40.1	70.7	28.3	35.9	52.4	54.8	53.7	33.6	29.1	23.5	14.0	16.2	22.8
EU-12														
Bulgaria	2006	2.3	6.4	1.4	2.7	58.8	73.9	69.2	25.0	13.3	13.1	16.2	12.8	17.6
Cyprus	2006	21.5	30.6	9.2	16.6	61.2	55.8	50.0	16.5	18.3	27.0	22.3	25.9	22.9
Czech Republic	2004	7.0	15.5	3.4	6.7	55.5	42.3	57.2	21.5	24.1	18.4	23.1	33.6	24.3
Estonia	2004	...	...	...	...	...	...	68.5	...	...	22.2	...	...	9.3
Hungary	2005	7.1	19.8	3.4	9.2	63.6	53.7	55.0	17.7	19.3	21.0	18.7	27.0	24.0
Latvia	2006	10.5	17.9	2.7	10.2	39.1	41.9	58.1	15.7	19.0	23.8	45.2	39.1	18.1
Lithuania	2006	12.9	29.8	5.5	13.8	63.1	57.8	59.0	15.7	23.5	18.9	21.2	18.6	22.0
Poland	2005	14.3	24.0	...	7.4	59.0	59.7	57.1	...	15.2	13.3	...	25.1	29.7
Romania	2004	...	6.4	...	3.7	...	48.0	51.3	...	30.1	28.2	...	21.9	20.5
Other Europe														
Norway	2004	37.5	70.2	30.1	49.4	59.0	...	53.7	32.9	...	32.6	8.1	...	13.7

a/ At current prices.

Table 1.11
(continued)

SELECTED CHARACTERISTICS OF BRANCHES, SELECTED YEARS AND COUNTRIES

Country or area	Latest year	Optical instruments & photographic equipment (ISIC 3320)												
		Value added per employee (current 1000 dollars)		Wages and salaries per employee (current 1000 dollars)		Percentage in output a/								
						Costs of input materials and utilities			Costs of labour			Operating surplus		
	(LY)	2000	LY	2000	LY	2000	2003	LY	2000	2003	LY	2000	2003	LY
Other Countries														
Israel	2005	80.6	82.1	52.5	59.5	48.8	58.0	57.6	33.3	34.1	30.7	17.8	7.9	11.7
Japan	2005	75.1	80.1	29.4	30.4	61.0	62.7	62.4	15.3	14.1	14.3	23.8	23.1	23.4
Republic of Korea	2006	36.5	73.1	11.4	23.0	50.6	50.8	66.1	15.4	17.3	10.7	34.0	31.9	23.2
United States of America	2005	126.0	152.5	34.8	49.7	33.7	38.9	38.8	18.3	21.0	19.9	48.0	40.1	41.3
Developing Countries														
Brazil	2005	17.2	19.5	5.0	4.9	44.6	37.8	40.6	15.9	13.8	14.9	39.5	48.4	44.5
Chile	2006	...	14.6	...	13.3	...	47.8	57.3	...	28.3	38.9	...	23.9	3.8
Colombia	2005	15.1	18.2	3.2	3.7	42.0	49.0	34.3	12.5	12.3	13.1	45.5	38.7	52.6
Ecuador	2005	4.0	13.7	1.2	3.9	57.0	80.0	72.1	12.9	...	7.9	30.0	...	19.9
India	2004	7.2	17.6	1.9	1.9	61.0	68.4	49.1	10.1	7.7	5.6	28.9	24.0	45.3
Indonesia	2005	10.3	3.7	1.0	2.1	40.6	77.8	68.7	5.5	10.7	17.9	53.9	11.5	13.4
Iran (Islamic Republic of)	2005	13.8	21.1	8.0	3.9	62.9	53.2	49.8	21.5	23.9	9.3	15.7	23.0	40.9
Malaysia	2005	10.2	12.4	4.6	5.5	82.5	82.7	85.1	8.0	8.3	6.6	9.5	9.0	8.3
Morocco	2005	7.9	4.8	4.9	3.2	48.3	57.1	50.0	31.9	42.9	33.3	19.8	0.0	16.7
Oman	2006	58.3	71.5	17.6	19.5	54.5	56.8	55.9	13.7	11.4	12.0	31.8	31.8	32.1
Sri Lanka	2006	...	1.8	...	0.5	...	...	10.3	...	...	22.9	...	...	66.8

a/ At current prices.

Table 1.11

SELECTED CHARACTERISTICS OF BRANCHES, SELECTED YEARS AND COUNTRIES

Motor vehicles (ISIC 3410)

Country or area	Latest year (LY)	Value added per employee (current 1000 dollars)		Wages and salaries per employee (current 1000 dollars)		Percentage in output a/: Costs of input materials and utilities			Percentage in output a/: Costs of labour			Percentage in output a/: Operating surplus		
		2000	LY	2000	LY	2000	2003	LY	2000	2003	LY	2000	2003	LY
Industrialized Countries														
CIS														
Azerbaijan	2006	...	34.1	0.2	0.4	...	...	45.1	5.2	...	0.7	...	...	54.2
Kyrgyzstan	2006	...	...	0.5	0.7	...	...	...	31.8	45.4	55.2	...	...	...
EU-15														
Austria	2005	65.8	132.8	31.6	49.1	76.0	79.6	81.8	11.5	9.0	6.7	12.5	11.4	11.4
Belgium	2005	58.2	88.1	31.2	45.7	81.3	81.1	83.4	10.0	9.2	8.6	8.7	9.8	8.0
Finland	2005	44.5	69.9	25.4	40.9	59.1	67.8	71.1	23.4	21.1	16.9	17.6	11.1	12.0
France	2005	71.9	94.2	28.6	46.2	86.9	92.8	85.1	5.2	3.6	7.3	7.9	3.7	7.6
Germany	2005	53.1	94.3	41.6	65.9	80.6	75.9	79.4	15.2	15.2	14.4	4.2	8.8	6.2
Greece	2004	...	62.1	...	27.4	...	...	70.3	...	...	13.1	...	...	16.6
Ireland	2005	...	188.7	...	34.3	...	66.2	60.7	...	8.5	7.1	...	25.4	32.1
Italy	2005	41.2	51.8	21.3	31.7	86.0	91.3	88.7	7.2	6.3	6.9	6.8	2.4	4.4
Netherlands	2005	79.6	190.4	31.1	54.7	79.5	75.2	74.9	8.0	8.6	7.2	12.5	16.2	17.9
Portugal	2005	58.0	56.3	14.0	23.3	79.6	86.2	84.7	4.9	5.5	6.3	15.5	8.3	8.9
Spain	2005	52.6	76.3	24.3	37.2	85.1	85.4	86.5	6.9	6.5	6.6	8.0	8.1	6.9
Sweden	2005	90.4	90.2	29.7	42.5	72.7	...	83.4	9.0	...	7.8	18.3	...	8.8
United Kingdom	2005	51.2	89.2	39.3	55.0	84.9	83.4	83.8	11.6	10.3	10.0	3.5	6.3	6.2
EU-12														
Bulgaria	2004	2.7	3.2	1.1	1.7	54.5	...	66.7	19.3	22.2	17.7	26.2	...	15.6
Estonia	2006	...	32.2	...	16.2	...	69.0	62.3	...	22.1	18.9	...	8.8	18.7
Hungary	2005	79.1	114.3	6.7	18.5	82.5	84.4	85.4	1.5	2.4	2.4	16.0	13.3	12.2
Lithuania	2006	1.0	8.0	1.8	4.8	...	76.5	87.7	...	20.2	7.5	...	3.4	4.9
Poland	2005	19.1	60.3	...	11.9	86.4	83.7	84.9	...	3.7	3.0	...	12.6	12.2
Romania	2004	...	9.8	...	5.7	...	85.4	86.1	...	11.5	8.1	...	3.1	5.9

a/ At current prices.

Table 1.11
(continued)

SELECTED CHARACTERISTICS OF BRANCHES, SELECTED YEARS AND COUNTRIES

Motor vehicles (ISIC 3410)														
Country or area	Latest year	Value added per employee (current 1000 dollars)		Wages and salaries per employee (current 1000 dollars)		Percentage in output[a/]								
						Costs of input materials and utilities			Costs of labour			Operating surplus		
	(LY)	2000	LY	2000	LY	2000	2003	LY	2000	2003	LY	2000	2003	LY
Other Countries														
Japan	2005	242.0	359.3	66.4	67.1	77.7	74.3	74.1	6.1	5.2	4.8	16.2	20.4	21.1
Republic of Korea	2006	142.4	251.0	27.0	54.9	61.8	61.9	66.9	7.2	7.1	7.2	30.9	31.0	25.8
United States of America	2005	190.0	245.6	51.3	59.2	72.8	69.1	71.9	7.3	6.7	6.8	19.8	24.2	21.3
Developing Countries														
Brazil	2005	53.6	76.5	16.0	17.2	67.2	70.4	71.6	9.8	8.0	6.4	23.0	21.6	22.1
Colombia	2005	41.3	88.6	9.5	10.2	79.6	81.5	79.0	4.7	3.0	2.4	15.7	15.4	18.6
Ecuador	2005	18.1	25.0	3.0	4.8	91.0	89.4	91.7	1.5	2.0	1.6	7.5	8.6	6.7
Eritrea	2006	1.3	2.5	0.7	0.9	63.8	65.0	51.5	18.4	18.4	17.8	17.8	16.6	30.7
India	2004	9.7	31.2	3.5	4.7	86.0	81.1	89.1	5.0	3.8	1.6	9.0	15.1	9.2
Indonesia	2005	67.4	188.5	2.4	7.2	54.4	15.8	13.6	1.6	4.1	3.3	44.0	80.1	83.2
Iran (Islamic Republic of)	2005	128.0	59.5	23.0	9.6	65.8	73.2	76.7	6.1	3.9	3.8	28.0	22.9	19.5
Malaysia	2005	32.4	25.2	6.0	7.8	83.8	71.6	87.1	3.0	3.8	4.0	13.2	24.7	8.9
Morocco	2005	23.7	38.1	8.8	15.5	69.9	61.8	70.9	11.2	13.9	11.8	19.0	24.3	17.2
Oman	2006	...	13.4	...	3.9	...	...	12.5	...	...	25.4	...	...	62.2

a/ At current prices.

Table 1.11

SELECTED CHARACTERISTICS OF BRANCHES, SELECTED YEARS AND COUNTRIES

Automobile bodies, trailers & semi-trailers (ISIC 3420)

Country or area	Latest year	Value added per employee (current 1000 dollars)		Wages and salaries per employee (current 1000 dollars)		Percentage in output [a]								
						Costs of input materials and utilities			Costs of labour			Operating surplus		
	(LY)	2000	LY	2000	LY	2000	2003	LY	2000	2003	LY	2000	2003	LY
Industrialized Countries														
CIS														
Azerbaijan	2006	...	0.0	...	1.9	...	51.6	...	...	...	...	...	...	...
Kyrgyzstan	2004	...	...	0.4	0.2	...	...	...	25.0	...	4.8	...	...	...
EU-15														
Austria	2005	41.1	60.8	21.3	35.8	65.0	66.9	68.5	18.1	20.4	18.5	16.9	12.7	12.9
Belgium	2005	43.7	69.0	23.4	34.3	73.9	75.3	78.0	14.0	13.1	11.0	12.1	11.6	11.1
Denmark	2004	44.6	70.1	30.9	49.7	72.4	...	72.0	19.1	...	19.8	8.5	...	8.2
Finland	2005	41.3	61.0	23.5	36.5	65.3	65.7	67.1	19.7	20.7	19.7	15.0	13.7	13.2
France	2005	34.9	52.2	19.9	30.2	71.1	70.1	71.2	16.5	17.8	16.7	12.4	12.0	12.1
Germany	2005	40.4	63.5	26.6	37.8	71.0	72.6	75.1	19.1	17.8	14.8	9.9	9.6	10.1
Greece	2004	...	63.1	...	16.9	...	...	61.0	...	...	10.5	...	...	28.6
Ireland	2005	...	61.6	...	33.9	...	74.1	69.2	...	19.8	16.9	...	6.2	13.8
Italy	2005	36.8	53.0	19.1	29.7	75.5	73.9	76.2	12.7	14.2	13.3	11.8	11.8	10.4
Netherlands	2005	35.4	59.4	23.0	38.4	72.5	71.2	74.0	17.8	19.2	16.8	9.6	9.6	9.2
Portugal	2005	13.8	21.2	8.0	15.4	68.9	72.2	74.2	18.0	20.9	18.7	13.1	7.0	7.1
Spain	2005	31.6	48.3	15.5	26.1	73.9	73.3	75.9	12.8	13.4	13.0	13.3	13.3	11.1
Sweden	2005	45.5	82.3	24.2	37.4	68.3	...	66.3	16.9	...	15.3	14.8	...	18.4
United Kingdom	2005	40.9	67.3	27.2	35.9	70.2	70.0	67.2	19.8	19.4	17.5	10.0	10.6	15.3
EU-12														
Bulgaria	2006	1.4	5.0	1.0	2.3	71.4	72.7	77.8	20.0	13.0	10.3	8.6	14.3	12.0
Cyprus	2006	...	42.2	...	25.3	...	74.2	59.8	...	15.2	24.2	...	10.6	16.1
Estonia	2006	...	17.5	...	9.4	...	72.0	71.6	...	14.0	15.2	...	14.0	13.2
Hungary	2005	12.0	28.0	4.6	13.9	78.8	72.8	74.8	8.1	9.0	12.5	13.1	18.2	12.7
Latvia	2006	5.0	13.5	1.7	5.6	57.6	76.8	82.9	14.5	8.5	7.0	27.9	14.6	10.1
Lithuania	2006	4.1	27.1	2.4	8.3	86.2	82.9	82.4	7.9	4.4	5.4	5.9	12.7	12.2
Malta	2005	20.7	32.3	7.7	10.9	49.6	48.2	29.4	18.7	21.3	23.9	31.7	30.5	46.7
Poland	2005	8.2	15.2	...	6.9	74.6	77.3	78.5	...	11.1	9.8	...	11.6	11.7
Romania	2004	...	4.8	...	3.4	...	75.1	79.4	...	21.6	14.6	...	3.3	5.9
Other Europe														
Norway	2004	43.2	59.8	30.3	43.7	67.8	67.2	71.8	22.6	25.0	20.6	9.7	7.8	7.6

a/ At current prices.

Table 1.11
(continued)

SELECTED CHARACTERISTICS OF BRANCHES, SELECTED YEARS AND COUNTRIES

Automobile bodies, trailers & semi-trailers (ISIC 3420)														
Country or area	Latest year	Value added per employee (current 1000 dollars)		Wages and salaries per employee (current 1000 dollars)		Percentage in output [a/]								
						Costs of input materials and utilities			Costs of labour			Operating surplus		
	(LY)	2000	LY	2000	LY	2000	2003	LY	2000	2003	LY	2000	2003	LY
Other Countries														
Japan	2005	111.8	101.0	55.4	57.9	78.3	82.0	84.2	10.8	8.4	9.0	11.0	9.6	6.7
Republic of Korea	2006	41.5	79.4	15.8	24.4	79.7	69.2	64.2	7.7	9.0	11.0	12.5	21.9	24.8
United States of America	2005	57.3	72.8	27.4	34.1	61.3	59.5	65.1	18.5	19.9	16.3	20.2	20.6	18.5
Developing Countries														
Brazil	2005	16.9	19.8	6.0	7.1	60.2	62.4	66.2	14.1	13.3	12.1	25.7	24.3	21.6
Chile	2006	...	34.5	...	11.0	...	57.8	62.3	...	15.8	12.0	...	26.4	25.8
Colombia	2005	13.5	23.0	3.2	4.0	59.4	61.7	66.6	9.5	7.2	5.8	31.0	31.1	27.6
Ecuador	2005	1.6	5.6	0.8	2.9	81.5	68.4	76.7	8.8	10.5	11.8	9.7	21.1	11.4
Ethiopia	2006	19.0	9.0	1.1	2.0	72.6	69.2	73.8	1.5	7.8	5.7	25.8	23.0	20.5
Fiji	2004	...	10.8	...	6.7	...	71.3	69.9	...	7.2	18.7	...	21.5	11.5
India	2004	1.8	2.8	1.2	1.2	80.9	83.6	83.3	12.8	8.3	7.4	6.3	8.1	9.2
Indonesia	2005	2.6	5.0	0.6	1.1	45.6	56.9	42.7	12.7	7.6	12.6	41.7	35.5	44.7
Iran (Islamic Republic of)	2005	13.8	10.5	5.7	4.4	61.7	70.5	72.8	15.8	10.8	11.4	22.5	18.6	15.8
Jordan	2006	14.6	13.3	4.0	4.0	67.8	63.9	66.3	8.8	9.9	10.2	23.4	26.3	23.5
Malaysia	2005	13.7	21.0	4.3	6.1	64.3	75.3	67.9	11.2	11.6	9.3	24.5	13.1	22.9
Morocco	2005	6.1	8.7	5.1	4.8	81.3	80.3	78.7	15.6	7.9	11.7	3.1	11.9	9.6
Qatar	2006	...	6.0	...	4.5	...	...	50.0	...	...	37.5	...	...	12.5
Trinidad and Tobago	2004	7.4	...	5.3	...	75.9	83.1	81.3	17.2	13.3	12.1	6.9	3.6	6.6

a/ At current prices.

Table 1.11

SELECTED CHARACTERISTICS OF BRANCHES, SELECTED YEARS AND COUNTRIES

Parts/accessories for automobiles (ISIC 3430)														
Country or area	Latest year	Value added per employee (current 1000 dollars)		Wages and salaries per employee (current 1000 dollars)		Percentage in output a/								
						Costs of input materials and utilities			Costs of labour			Operating surplus		
	(LY)	2000	LY	2000	LY	2000	2003	LY	2000	2003	LY	2000	2003	LY
Industrialized Countries														
CIS														
Azerbaijan	2006	...	3.0	0.3	1.4	...	51.6	45.2	67.8	4.7	24.5	...	43.7	30.3
Georgia	2006	0.2	2.6	0.1	1.1	67.4	68.8	71.7	11.6	12.6	11.6	20.9	18.6	16.7
Kyrgyzstan	2006	...	...	0.2	0.9	...	...	...	10.6	15.7	14.7	...	...	...
EU-15														
Austria	2005	71.9	103.4	26.9	43.6	65.3	69.1	70.7	13.0	14.3	12.4	21.7	16.6	17.0
Belgium	2005	54.1	93.5	26.3	42.4	72.9	70.0	75.7	13.2	12.9	11.0	13.9	17.1	13.3
Denmark	2005	42.7	70.0	31.5	48.3	55.6	...	59.1	32.8	...	28.2	11.6	...	12.7
Finland	2005	41.8	81.4	23.3	39.1	61.3	58.5	62.1	21.5	21.2	18.2	17.1	20.3	19.7
France	2005	45.6	72.2	24.4	39.2	76.2	76.6	74.6	12.8	11.6	13.8	11.0	11.7	11.6
Germany	2005	52.7	79.5	34.5	54.0	65.4	67.8	68.9	22.7	21.8	21.1	11.9	10.3	10.0
Greece	2004	...	58.4	...	15.6	...	...	50.0	...	...	13.3	...	...	36.7
Ireland	2005	43.5	74.6	21.4	34.7	67.1	64.7	67.9	16.1	17.4	14.9	16.7	17.9	17.2
Italy	2005	42.3	62.1	20.0	32.2	72.6	72.9	75.1	12.9	12.7	12.9	14.4	14.4	12.0
Netherlands	2005	40.8	76.1	25.9	44.8	69.4	67.4	71.4	19.4	19.6	16.9	11.2	13.0	11.7
Portugal	2005	21.0	37.7	9.5	17.1	74.3	74.2	76.8	11.7	10.4	10.5	14.1	15.4	12.7
Spain	2005	41.6	63.2	20.3	32.3	70.9	72.7	74.2	14.2	13.6	13.2	14.9	13.7	12.6
Sweden	2005	48.4	71.0	25.3	37.4	68.7	...	73.3	16.3	...	14.1	15.0	...	12.6
United Kingdom	2005	45.5	68.8	31.0	43.5	64.9	70.2	70.3	23.9	20.1	18.8	11.2	9.7	10.9
EU-12														
Bulgaria	2006	2.6	7.1	1.3	2.5	62.1	72.2	75.8	18.7	16.8	8.6	19.2	11.0	15.5
Cyprus	2006	17.5	30.5	10.1	17.4	55.2	54.8	56.8	26.0	25.4	24.7	18.8	19.8	18.5
Czech Republic	2004	...	27.9	...	8.6	...	75.6	75.7	...	7.9	7.5	...	16.4	16.8
Estonia	2006	...	26.6	...	10.4	...	68.9	68.8	...	10.4	12.2	...	20.7	19.0
Hungary	2005	17.0	33.8	4.6	11.6	69.1	71.6	73.8	8.4	10.5	9.0	22.5	17.9	17.3
Latvia	2006	1.8	15.1	0.9	8.5	64.3	63.1	78.0	17.2	12.8	12.4	18.5	24.1	9.6
Lithuania	2006	...	6.5	...	4.4	...	65.0	72.8	...	20.4	18.4	...	14.6	8.9
Malta	2005	14.6	9.0	7.8	5.2	41.0	56.2	76.6	31.6	36.9	13.6	27.5	6.9	9.8
Poland	2005	10.8	27.9	...	8.5	73.6	73.4	72.7	...	9.1	8.3	...	17.5	19.0
Romania	2006	...	9.7	...	6.4	...	68.0	77.1	...	17.7	15.1	...	14.3	7.8
Slovakia	2005	8.9	20.4	3.4	7.9	67.9	87.4	83.5	12.2	6.1	6.4	19.9	6.5	10.1
Other Europe														
Norway	2004	51.9	86.9	35.2	55.3	60.8	60.9	60.8	26.6	25.4	24.9	12.6	13.7	14.2

a/ At current prices.

Table 1.11
(continued)

SELECTED CHARACTERISTICS OF BRANCHES, SELECTED YEARS AND COUNTRIES

Parts/accessories for automobiles (ISIC 3430)														
Country or area	Latest year	Value added per employee (current 1000 dollars)		Wages and salaries per employee (current 1000 dollars)		Percentage in output [a/]								
						Costs of input materials and utilities			Costs of labour			Operating surplus		
	(LY)	2000	LY	2000	LY	2000	2003	LY	2000	2003	LY	2000	2003	LY
Other Countries														
Japan	2005	97.6	115.1	42.0	43.6	69.6	68.4	69.8	13.1	11.8	11.4	17.3	19.9	18.8
Republic of Korea	2006	55.8	100.3	15.7	27.8	61.2	62.6	66.5	10.9	11.3	9.3	27.9	26.0	24.2
United States of America	2005	103.9	129.3	44.1	49.2	56.8	56.4	59.0	18.3	16.9	15.6	24.9	26.7	25.4
Developing Countries														
Brazil	2005	25.6	32.9	8.2	9.8	55.7	58.3	63.9	14.2	11.9	10.7	30.1	29.8	25.4
Chile	2006	...	15.5	...	9.7	...	48.9	54.0	...	29.2	28.8	...	21.9	17.2
Colombia	2005	13.5	29.1	3.1	4.3	52.5	50.6	54.8	10.9	10.2	6.7	36.6	39.2	38.5
Ecuador	2005	5.5	11.4	1.2	3.6	67.9	58.3	80.9	7.0	16.7	6.1	25.1	25.0	13.0
Eritrea	2006	2.3	5.3	1.2	2.0	55.3	29.5	57.9	23.1	15.3	16.1	21.7	55.3	26.0
Ethiopia	2006	7.2	2.8	0.6	0.6	17.3	36.8	53.5	6.7	28.8	9.1	76.0	34.4	37.5
India	2004	5.7	8.4	1.8	2.2	74.3	75.3	76.8	8.0	6.5	6.1	17.7	18.2	17.1
Indonesia	2005	20.7	13.1	1.9	2.0	46.2	56.4	73.0	4.8	8.0	4.1	48.9	35.6	23.0
Iran (Islamic Republic of)	2005	35.9	14.2	10.3	4.3	66.2	68.3	69.0	9.7	11.2	9.4	24.1	20.5	21.6
Jordan	2006	5.0	8.3	3.0	3.5	77.6	66.7	65.4	13.7	12.6	14.4	8.8	20.8	20.2
Malaysia	2005	14.0	13.1	4.0	5.9	65.2	68.5	75.7	9.8	10.4	11.0	24.9	21.1	13.3
Morocco	2005	9.0	11.6	4.6	6.4	66.6	66.9	67.3	17.2	17.8	18.1	16.2	15.3	14.6
Oman	2006	7.9	10.6	3.6	4.9	24.9	...	47.9	34.6	...	24.0	40.5	...	28.1
Qatar	2006	5.8	31.8	3.1	7.0	41.3	50.0	36.8	31.9	29.9	13.9	26.8	20.1	49.3
Sri Lanka	2006	...	4.5	...	1.8	...	...	55.5	...	...	17.4	...	...	27.1

a/ At current prices.

Table 1.11

SELECTED CHARACTERISTICS OF BRANCHES, SELECTED YEARS AND COUNTRIES

Building and repairing of ships and boats (ISIC 351)														
Country or area	Latest year	Value added per employee (current 1000 dollars)		Wages and salaries per employee (current 1000 dollars)		Percentage in output [a/]								
						Costs of input materials and utilities			Costs of labour			Operating surplus		
	(LY)	2000	LY	2000	LY	2000	2003	LY	2000	2003	LY	2000	2003	LY
Industrialized Countries														
CIS														
Azerbaijan	2006	...	22.9	2.4	5.2	...	51.6	45.1	15.5	16.9	12.5	...	31.5	42.4
EU-15														
Austria	2005	47.1	64.5	26.0	32.3	55.6	48.4	56.1	24.5	22.7	22.0	19.9	28.9	22.0
Belgium	2005	42.6	64.8	24.9	36.1	60.7	64.4	69.4	23.0	20.8	17.1	16.3	14.8	13.6
Finland	2005	29.9	60.4	23.8	36.7	79.1	69.4	73.0	16.7	15.6	16.4	4.3	15.0	10.6
France	2005	44.8	65.2	21.2	32.6	76.3	73.4	68.1	11.2	14.7	16.0	12.5	12.0	15.9
Germany	2005	41.3	67.7	30.5	48.0	75.2	77.3	76.5	18.3	15.4	16.7	6.5	7.2	6.8
Greece	2004	...	43.6	...	23.9	...	...	67.5	...	...	17.8	...	...	14.7
Ireland	2005	28.9	57.7	21.0	35.5	56.0	60.5	55.2	32.0	26.3	27.6	12.0	13.2	17.2
Italy	2005	43.1	71.6	18.2	29.0	70.3	73.8	73.5	12.6	12.2	10.7	17.2	13.9	15.8
Netherlands	2005	46.5	86.9	27.7	51.6	75.7	79.0	75.1	14.5	15.8	14.8	9.8	5.2	10.1
Portugal	2005	18.4	26.7	12.7	15.7	63.3	73.5	68.4	25.4	21.1	18.7	11.3	5.4	13.0
Spain	2005	23.6	46.1	18.7	32.7	72.8	72.2	72.4	21.5	19.7	19.6	5.7	8.1	8.0
Sweden	2005	47.3	42.3	24.6	35.3	65.0	...	75.9	18.2	...	20.1	16.8	...	4.0
United Kingdom	2005	51.0	56.1	30.1	42.9	54.1	59.4	62.5	27.1	31.4	28.7	18.8	9.2	8.8
EU-12														
Bulgaria	2006	4.3	10.4	1.8	4.6	73.5	74.5	66.5	11.1	13.5	14.7	15.3	12.0	18.9
Cyprus	2006	22.5	40.6	12.4	20.5	51.0	47.0	52.0	27.1	24.8	24.2	22.0	28.2	23.8
Czech Republic	2004	...	10.7	...	6.4	...	...	75.2	...	...	14.8	...	...	10.0
Estonia	2005	8.8	14.7	3.3	8.9	59.9	68.0	75.2	15.0	15.6	14.9	25.0	16.4	9.8
Hungary	2005	6.8	12.3	2.5	6.2	51.1	66.3	60.7	17.8	18.3	19.6	31.1	15.4	19.6
Latvia	2006	8.2	13.2	3.3	5.8	57.9	72.2	71.6	17.1	16.0	12.4	25.0	11.8	16.0
Lithuania	2006	5.9	16.0	4.1	9.0	54.7	56.9	61.1	31.6	28.2	21.9	13.7	14.9	16.9
Poland	2005	10.4	20.2	...	10.6	76.8	78.6	70.4	...	18.8	15.5	...	2.6	14.1
Slovakia	2004	...	13.2	...	5.6	...	77.5	73.5	...	15.3	11.1	...	7.2	15.3
Other Europe														
Norway	2004	49.7	80.2	37.9	64.3	67.3	67.5	68.6	24.9	24.8	25.2	7.8	7.7	6.2

a/ At current prices.

Table 1.11
(continued)

SELECTED CHARACTERISTICS OF BRANCHES, SELECTED YEARS AND COUNTRIES

Building and repairing of ships and boats (ISIC 351)														
Country or area	Latest year	Value added per employee (current 1000 dollars)		Wages and salaries per employee (current 1000 dollars)		Percentage in output [a]								
						Costs of input materials and utilities			Costs of labour			Operating surplus		
	(LY)	2000	LY	2000	LY	2000	2003	LY	2000	2003	LY	2000	2003	LY
Other Countries														
Australia	2005	44.3	51.8	18.7	...	56.7	66.0	63.8	18.2	...	...	25.1	...	...
Japan	2005	135.5	133.7	38.4	37.1	64.8	63.1	70.0	10.0	8.9	8.3	25.2	28.0	21.7
Republic of Korea	2006	79.7	123.0	24.3	42.2	56.5	62.9	67.2	13.3	13.8	11.3	30.2	23.3	21.6
Singapore	2006	21.6	27.5	14.4	15.6	66.8	68.0	73.5	22.1	22.2	15.0	11.1	9.8	11.5
United States of America	2005	68.1	96.6	34.1	39.9	49.1	42.8	46.8	25.5	23.6	22.0	25.4	33.7	31.2
Developing Countries														
Brazil	2005	15.2	19.5	4.7	7.8	53.5	52.1	61.9	14.5	16.6	15.2	32.0	31.3	22.9
Chile	2006	...	26.2	...	12.5	...	38.3	56.6	...	28.0	20.8	...	33.8	22.6
Colombia	2005	23.5	57.9	3.7	3.9	20.8	25.6	30.6	12.4	6.1	4.7	66.8	68.3	64.6
India	2004	2.6	4.7	1.9	2.4	88.9	85.8	79.2	8.0	9.4	10.6	3.0	4.9	10.2
Indonesia	2005	7.0	19.4	1.1	2.3	76.6	41.8	41.3	3.7	6.6	7.0	19.7	51.5	51.6
Iran (Islamic Republic of)	2005	25.2	34.1	12.3	5.3	46.4	33.2	53.9	26.2	6.9	7.2	27.4	59.9	38.9
Jordan	2006	16.5	19.5	6.1	14.4	50.0	41.1	56.5	18.6	13.0	32.1	31.4	45.9	11.4
Madagascar	2006	...	0.4	...	0.3	...	67.9	63.7	...	22.2	31.7	...	9.8	4.6
Malaysia	2005	14.1	15.1	7.4	7.8	62.5	58.5	80.6	19.7	18.8	10.0	17.8	22.7	9.4
Morocco	2005	9.4	13.9	6.7	10.0	53.6	49.2	55.4	33.0	36.5	32.1	13.4	14.3	12.4
Qatar	2006	19.9	...	10.3	...	35.6	35.7	37.0	33.3	32.1	28.3	31.1	32.1	34.7
Sri Lanka	2006	...	2.1	...	1.6	...	...	44.8	...	...	42.8	...	...	12.3
Trinidad and Tobago	2004	...	...	6.6	...	...	85.8	48.7	6.9	8.2	35.9	...	5.9	15.4
Uruguay	2005	18.8	14.7	11.3	7.1	47.0	58.5	53.8	32.0	22.9	22.3	21.0	18.6	23.9

a/ At current prices.

Table 1.11

SELECTED CHARACTERISTICS OF BRANCHES, SELECTED YEARS AND COUNTRIES

Furniture (ISIC 3610)

Country or area	Latest year	Value added per employee (current 1000 dollars)		Wages and salaries per employee (current 1000 dollars)		Percentage in output [a/]								
						Costs of input materials and utilities			Costs of labour			Operating surplus		
	(LY)	2000	LY	2000	LY	2000	2003	LY	2000	2003	LY	2000	2003	LY
Industrialized Countries														
CIS														
Azerbaijan	2006	...	2.9	0.1	0.7	...	81.4	74.7	4.0	3.4	5.9	...	15.2	19.4
Georgia	2006	0.4	2.3	0.2	0.9	67.5	74.4	73.3	12.8	11.5	10.8	19.7	14.1	15.9
Kyrgyzstan	2005	...	0.8	0.3	0.5	...	...	83.3	5.5	...	9.5	...	...	7.2
Russian Federation	2006	...	9.3	0.7	3.0	...	65.5	64.3	8.9	9.8	11.7	...	24.7	23.9
EU-15														
Austria	2005	34.3	48.8	18.9	29.8	49.0	54.3	58.4	28.1	28.5	25.4	22.9	17.2	16.2
Belgium	2005	39.2	60.7	19.2	29.9	70.7	72.3	72.5	14.4	14.3	13.5	14.9	13.4	13.9
Denmark	2005	40.5	70.8	26.7	44.6	63.9	61.4	62.4	23.8	25.2	23.7	12.3	13.4	13.9
Finland	2005	37.0	54.9	20.1	33.3	60.3	62.4	65.8	21.6	23.0	20.8	18.1	14.6	13.4
France	2005	33.2	49.6	18.6	29.8	68.0	69.6	71.0	18.0	17.8	17.4	14.0	12.5	11.6
Germany	2005	38.9	56.4	25.3	36.1	65.8	66.5	67.9	22.2	23.3	20.5	11.9	10.2	11.6
Greece	2004	...	41.6	...	15.6	...	...	56.5	...	...	16.3	...	...	27.2
Ireland	2004	29.0	54.3	16.7	30.9	62.0	61.1	59.1	21.9	23.1	23.3	16.2	15.8	17.6
Italy	2005	38.9	52.6	14.7	22.7	72.8	72.3	73.0	10.3	12.9	11.6	16.9	14.8	15.4
Luxembourg	2005	31.7	59.9	20.1	39.9	48.6	50.0	52.6	32.6	27.8	31.6	18.8	22.2	15.8
Netherlands	2005	40.2	60.9	22.0	36.1	64.5	63.6	66.2	19.4	21.6	20.0	16.1	14.8	13.8
Portugal	2005	11.3	15.9	6.1	9.0	66.4	68.7	68.2	18.0	17.7	18.1	15.6	13.6	13.8
Spain	2005	23.2	37.5	12.7	21.3	67.5	66.7	67.2	17.8	19.5	18.7	14.7	13.8	14.2
Sweden	2005	33.5	56.7	20.9	31.1	65.1	...	71.1	21.8	...	15.8	13.1	...	13.1
United Kingdom	2005	36.4	59.1	21.1	34.3	59.2	61.5	61.1	23.7	24.5	22.6	17.1	14.0	16.4
EU-12														
Bulgaria	2006	1.6	4.4	0.8	1.7	73.7	75.3	73.6	13.3	10.9	10.4	13.0	13.7	16.0
Cyprus	2006	20.8	34.7	10.6	19.9	51.9	53.6	53.2	24.4	25.8	26.8	23.7	20.6	20.0
Czech Republic	2004	6.9	14.6	3.5	6.1	76.7	72.8	72.1	11.6	11.9	11.6	11.7	15.3	16.3
Estonia	2006	5.4	13.3	2.8	7.4	68.3	70.0	70.3	16.7	17.2	16.5	15.0	12.8	13.2
Hungary	2005	4.6	10.1	2.3	5.6	70.0	71.4	70.1	15.1	16.6	16.7	14.9	12.1	13.2
Latvia	2006	5.2	9.9	2.0	4.5	58.7	62.5	65.3	15.9	17.1	15.6	25.4	20.4	19.0
Lithuania	2006	3.8	8.7	2.2	5.3	69.2	68.9	72.0	17.7	15.8	16.9	13.1	15.3	11.1
Malta	2005	15.0	23.7	7.4	11.9	49.3	53.5	53.2	25.2	30.4	23.5	25.6	16.1	23.2
Poland	2005	7.8	13.7	...	5.6	71.6	71.4	72.0	...	11.9	11.5	...	16.7	16.5
Romania	2006	...	5.7	...	3.9	52.7	69.8	74.8	...	19.1	17.3	...	11.1	7.9
Slovakia	2005	3.7	14.7	2.6	6.3	85.9	86.8	79.7	10.2	6.9	8.6	3.9	6.3	11.6
Other Europe														
Norway	2004	40.6	68.7	27.2	43.0	63.1	62.4	61.8	24.7	25.2	23.9	12.2	12.4	14.3

a/ At current prices.

Table 1.11
(continued)

SELECTED CHARACTERISTICS OF BRANCHES, SELECTED YEARS AND COUNTRIES

Furniture (ISIC 3610)														
Country or area	Latest year	Value added per employee (current 1000 dollars)		Wages and salaries per employee (current 1000 dollars)		Percentage in output [a/]								
						Costs of input materials and utilities			Costs of labour			Operating surplus		
	(LY)	2000	LY	2000	LY	2000	2003	LY	2000	2003	LY	2000	2003	LY
Other Countries														
Israel	2005	28.3	28.4	22.2	17.5	63.4	64.2	66.0	28.7	19.5	21.0	7.9	16.4	13.0
Japan	2005	72.3	72.0	19.5	18.5	56.0	56.4	57.1	11.8	11.0	11.0	32.2	32.6	31.9
Republic of Korea	2006	43.6	71.4	12.5	22.0	57.4	63.8	64.9	12.2	12.5	10.8	30.4	23.8	24.3
Singapore	2006	21.2	18.8	15.2	14.1	72.2	70.7	70.1	19.8	23.0	22.4	7.9	6.3	7.5
South Africa	2006	7.1	14.3	5.2	5.4	75.3	75.6	72.2	18.0	15.2	10.5	6.7	9.2	17.2
United States of America	2005	67.9	88.4	28.4	33.5	48.2	47.4	50.1	21.7	20.3	18.9	30.2	32.4	31.0
Developing Countries														
Brazil	2005	8.7	9.7	3.2	3.7	62.5	61.5	62.8	14.1	13.7	14.2	23.5	24.8	23.0
Chile	2006	...	20.1	...	8.0	...	59.6	56.0	...	16.7	17.5	...	23.6	26.5
Colombia	2005	10.4	18.8	2.6	3.5	50.5	53.4	53.7	12.1	9.8	8.5	37.4	36.8	37.7
Ecuador	2005	7.0	12.1	1.1	3.6	68.4	68.5	72.1	5.1	10.5	8.3	26.6	21.0	19.6
Eritrea	2006	3.5	4.2	1.3	1.2	54.1	55.3	52.8	16.7	9.4	13.7	29.2	35.3	33.5
Ethiopia	2006	1.9	2.4	0.7	0.7	51.9	56.1	58.8	17.1	13.4	12.2	31.1	30.5	29.0
Fiji	2004	...	11.3	...	5.4	...	70.3	72.1	...	13.8	13.5	...	15.9	14.4
India	2004	4.0	4.8	1.6	1.9	81.8	80.4	81.8	7.2	7.1	7.3	11.0	12.5	10.8
Indonesia	2005	1.8	2.3	0.6	0.9	61.1	58.9	61.5	13.7	12.8	14.9	25.2	28.3	23.6
Iran (Islamic Republic of)	2005	17.1	11.5	7.4	4.1	50.9	55.5	53.5	21.2	15.7	16.4	27.9	28.8	30.1
Jordan	2006	5.6	6.1	2.2	2.2	62.0	58.7	58.0	15.2	13.4	15.5	22.8	27.9	26.5
Madagascar	2006	...	0.2	...	0.2	...	51.0	52.2	...	29.4	40.6	...	19.6	7.2
Malaysia	2005	8.2	7.3	3.2	4.1	68.2	70.0	76.4	12.2	13.9	13.1	19.6	16.1	10.4
Morocco	2005	10.8	13.2	5.8	8.4	48.5	66.2	67.6	27.7	24.3	20.7	23.9	9.4	11.8
Oman	2006	14.4	24.4	4.8	5.0	44.8	45.2	44.8	18.3	14.3	11.3	36.9	40.4	43.9
Philippines	2005	...	4.1	...	1.8	...	67.5	72.6	...	13.9	11.8	...	18.5	15.6
Qatar	2006	11.0	21.4	4.8	5.9	42.2	40.5	50.1	25.4	23.5	13.7	32.3	36.0	36.2
Sri Lanka	2006	...	4.7	...	0.8	...	...	58.2	...	...	6.8	...	...	35.0
Uruguay	2005	17.8	8.6	9.2	4.3	70.1	68.2	75.6	15.4	9.5	12.1	14.4	22.3	12.4

a/ At current prices.

Table 1.11

SELECTED CHARACTERISTICS OF BRANCHES, SELECTED YEARS AND COUNTRIES

Manufacturing n.e.c. (ISIC 369)														
Country or area	Latest year	Value added per employee (current 1000 dollars)		Wages and salaries per employee (current 1000 dollars)		Percentage in output a/								
						Costs of input materials and utilities			Costs of labour			Operating surplus		
	(LY)	2000	LY	2000	LY	2000	2003	LY	2000	2003	LY	2000	2003	LY
Industrialized Countries														
CIS														
Azerbaijan	2006	...	2.8	0.2	0.8	...	81.4	74.7	6.6	13.7	7.1	...	4.9	18.3
Georgia	2006	...	2.9	...	1.8	...	...	60.2	...	...	24.5	...	...	15.3
Kyrgyzstan	2006	...	...	0.2	0.2	...	...	...	10.1	...	13.3	...	...	...
Russian Federation	2006	...	17.0	0.8	4.0	...	51.4	65.0	12.7	5.4	8.2	...	43.1	26.8
EU-15														
Austria	2005	48.0	80.4	23.3	38.4	59.3	64.7	62.6	19.8	18.2	17.9	21.0	17.0	19.5
Belgium	2005	42.0	67.1	19.0	27.0	77.6	78.7	80.8	10.1	10.3	7.7	12.3	11.0	11.5
Denmark	2005	...	62.1	...	47.8	...	...	71.7	...	...	21.8	...	...	6.5
Finland	2005	43.8	69.4	20.5	34.7	56.4	60.1	60.1	20.4	21.1	19.9	23.2	18.8	19.9
France	2005	37.1	60.5	20.1	33.0	68.4	66.8	65.5	17.1	17.9	18.8	14.5	15.3	15.7
Germany	2005	35.3	58.0	21.8	31.9	57.0	56.9	57.1	26.6	25.1	23.6	16.4	18.0	19.3
Italy	2005	37.9	55.2	14.4	22.8	74.6	73.0	74.7	9.7	10.7	10.5	15.8	16.3	14.9
Luxembourg	2005	38.7	74.2	23.5	37.1	76.5	62.5	50.0	14.3	25.0	25.0	9.3	12.5	25.0
Netherlands	2005	46.9	78.4	21.4	45.0	62.9	64.7	66.0	16.9	17.6	19.5	20.2	17.8	14.5
Portugal	2005	14.3	18.5	7.5	10.2	70.3	67.6	70.8	15.6	17.0	16.1	14.2	15.5	13.1
Spain	2005	28.4	43.6	14.1	23.4	64.5	65.1	66.9	17.7	18.5	17.8	17.8	16.5	15.3
United Kingdom	2005	46.4	65.2	19.7	28.6	56.9	57.0	56.4	18.3	19.5	19.1	24.8	23.5	24.5
EU-12														
Cyprus	2006	20.5	31.4	8.9	17.7	63.3	58.8	55.0	15.8	20.9	25.4	20.9	20.3	19.6
Czech Republic	2004	6.6	13.6	3.0	5.5	64.5	62.0	61.9	16.2	15.6	15.4	19.3	22.4	22.7
Estonia	2006	5.4	16.7	2.8	6.8	67.2	61.7	58.6	16.9	18.6	16.8	15.9	19.7	24.6
Hungary	2005	4.4	13.8	2.3	5.6	65.4	59.6	59.9	17.7	19.7	16.1	16.9	20.7	24.0
Latvia	2006	5.0	10.0	2.3	4.1	40.3	47.3	57.4	27.8	23.4	17.5	31.9	29.3	25.1
Lithuania	2006	2.8	10.7	1.9	5.1	62.8	57.6	59.9	24.9	22.1	19.2	12.3	20.4	20.9
Malta	2005	39.9	51.7	12.4	19.2	56.9	53.6	48.4	13.4	18.7	19.1	29.7	27.7	32.5
Poland	2005	8.9	12.4	...	4.7	66.3	68.6	70.3	...	12.7	11.3	...	18.7	18.4
Romania	2006	...	6.0	...	3.8	57.7	60.8	70.1	...	21.8	18.7	...	17.4	11.2
Slovakia	2005	3.9	11.4	2.5	5.4	70.9	75.0	64.2	18.4	17.8	17.0	10.7	7.2	18.8
Other Europe														
Norway	2004	44.6	69.1	29.1	42.9	51.6	54.8	56.7	31.6	30.7	26.8	16.8	14.5	16.4

a/ At current prices.

Table 1.11
(continued)

SELECTED CHARACTERISTICS OF BRANCHES, SELECTED YEARS AND COUNTRIES

Manufacturing n.e.c. (ISIC 369)														
Country or area	Latest year	Value added per employee (current 1000 dollars)		Wages and salaries per employee (current 1000 dollars)		Percentage in output [a]								
						Costs of input materials and utilities			Costs of labour			Operating surplus		
	(LY)	2000	LY	2000	LY	2000	2003	LY	2000	2003	LY	2000	2003	LY
Other Countries														
Israel	2005	26.9	29.8	19.1	18.1	70.0	75.7	70.1	21.4	14.2	18.2	8.7	10.0	11.7
Japan	2005	86.4	86.0	19.4	19.2	60.3	62.9	61.6	8.9	8.0	8.6	30.8	29.1	29.8
Republic of Korea	2006	37.0	53.8	12.4	20.0	55.4	56.6	57.4	14.9	15.8	15.9	29.6	27.6	26.8
Singapore	2006	38.1	25.9	17.7	18.4	71.0	71.5	82.4	13.4	15.7	12.5	15.6	12.8	5.1
United States of America	2005	77.0	115.9	29.7	36.7	46.2	43.9	42.6	20.8	21.2	18.2	33.0	34.9	39.2
Developing Countries														
Brazil	2005	13.6	13.8	4.0	4.5	42.4	46.5	44.4	16.8	16.7	18.2	40.8	36.8	37.4
Chile	2006	...	40.0	...	11.1	...	52.1	50.4	...	17.4	13.8	...	30.5	35.8
Colombia	2005	20.0	26.4	3.8	4.5	51.7	55.3	60.4	9.2	7.1	6.8	39.1	37.6	32.8
Ecuador	2005	5.4	12.1	1.2	4.1	63.8	59.4	60.0	7.9	9.4	13.6	28.4	31.3	26.5
India	2004	4.4	5.4	1.1	1.5	81.5	88.5	87.5	4.8	3.7	3.5	13.7	7.8	9.0
Indonesia	2005	2.6	4.3	0.7	0.9	57.9	60.5	61.9	10.7	18.6	7.9	31.4	20.9	30.2
Iran (Islamic Republic of)	2005	19.0	7.3	7.4	3.1	62.7	61.6	60.9	14.5	15.2	16.4	22.8	23.2	22.7
Jordan	2006	4.8	9.7	2.9	2.1	49.5	66.6	66.6	30.7	9.7	7.2	19.8	23.7	26.2
Madagascar	2006	...	2.4	...	0.6	...	60.4	61.3	...	7.2	10.0	...	32.4	28.7
Malaysia	2005	9.3	9.1	3.7	5.3	67.9	67.9	79.4	12.6	15.5	12.1	19.5	16.6	8.4
Morocco	2005	11.3	10.6	6.4	5.9	61.9	72.6	72.2	21.6	14.6	15.6	16.5	12.8	12.3
Oman	2006	12.6	22.2	4.9	6.3	83.3	...	51.9	6.5	...	13.7	10.2	...	34.4
Peru	2006	...	6.4	...	1.4	...	59.1	57.5	...	10.8	9.5	...	30.0	33.0
Philippines	2005	...	3.9	...	2.0	...	67.2	66.8	...	16.0	16.7	...	16.8	16.5
Qatar	2006	...	13.6	...	9.0	...	...	...	...	...	...	...	...	...
Sri Lanka	2006	...	2.4	...	0.9	...	...	46.2	...	...	19.8	...	...	34.0
Trinidad and Tobago	2004	12.3	...	5.9	...	69.9	63.4	69.2	14.4	24.3	13.0	15.7	12.3	17.9
Uruguay	2005	14.1	6.8	8.6	3.4	52.9	58.5	55.6	28.7	25.7	22.0	18.4	15.8	22.4

a/ At current prices.

Part II

COUNTRY TABLES

Countries/areas for which data were presented in previous editions of the *Yearbook* but not in part II of the current edition

Country/area	Latest edition in which data were presented	Country/area	Latest edition in which data were presented	Country/area	Latest edition in which data were presented
Afghanistan	2005	Dominican Republic	2000	Nepal	2005
Algeria	2001	Ecuador	2008	Niger	2006
Angola	1997	Egypt	2005	Nigeria	2007
Argentina	2007	El Salvador	2001	Pakistan	2001
Aruba	2004	Gabon	1998	Papua New Guinea	2006
Australia	2008	Gambia	1999	Paraguay	2008
Bahamas	2004	Ghana	2007	Rwanda	2002
Bahrain	1996	Grenada	1999	Saint Lucia	2001
Bangladesh	2004	Haiti	2001	Saint Vincent and the Grenadines	2004
Barbados	2001	Honduras	1999	Senegal	2005
Belize	1995	Iceland	2008	Serbia and Montenegro	2005
Benin	2003	India	2008	Sierra Leone	2008
Bolivia	2006	Iraq	2001	Solomon Islands	1999
Bosnia and Herzegovina	1999	Kuwait	2005	Sudan	2006
Burkina Faso	2001	Lao People's Democratic Republic	2002	Suriname	2007
Burundi	1995	Lebanon	2002	Swaziland	1999
Cambodia	2004	Liechtenstein	1998	Switzerland	2008
Cameroon	2006	Malawi	2004	Tajikistan	2005
Canada	2006	Maldives	2004	Thailand	2003
Cape Verde	2000	Malta	2008	Tonga	2007
Central African Republic	1998	Mauritius	2008	Turkey	2006
Chad	1998	Mexico	2004	Turkmenistan	2003
Colombia	2008	Mongolia	2003	United Republic of Tanzania	2002
Costa Rica	2008	Mozambique	2003	Venezuela (Bolivarian Republic of)	2002
Côte d'Ivoire	2000	Myanmar	2005	Zambia	1997
Czech Republic	2008	Namibia	1998	Zimbabwe	2003

Albania

Supplier of information:
Institute of Statistics, Tirana.

Basic source of data:
Annual census/exhaustive survey; sample survey.

Major deviations from ISIC (Revision 3):
The data presented in ISIC (Revision 3) were originally classified according to NACE (Revision 1).

Reference period:
Calendar year.

Scope:
All registered enterprises.

Method of data collection:
Direct interview in the field.

Type of enumeration:
Enterprises with five or more employees are completely enumerated; enterprises with less than five employees are sampled.

Adjusted for non-response:
Yes.

Concepts and definitions of variables:
Output includes deductible subsidies and indirect taxes.
Value added excludes net change between the beginning and end of the year in the stocks of fuels and materials and supplies (deductible).
Output and Value added are valued at basic prices (including related subsidies).

Related national publications:
General Results of Annual Structural Survey of Economic Enterprises, published by Directorate of Statistics, Ministry of Economy, Tirana.

Albania

ISIC Revision 3		Number of enterprises					Number of employees					Wages and salaries paid to employees				
			(number)					(number)					(millions of Albanian Leks)			
ISIC	Industry	Note	2003	2004	2005	2006	Note	2003	2004	2005	2006	Note	2003	2004	2005	2006
151	Processed meat,fish,fruit,vegetables,fats		73	87	148	90		1344	1372	1651	1654		199.1	226.3	291.1	353.0
1511	Processing/preserving of meat	a/	37	46	93	43	a/	968	946	1215	1285	a/	135.2	154.2	215.5	265.4
1512	Processing/preserving of fish	a/	...	...	...	...	a/	...	...	...	...	a/	...	...	...	...
1513	Processing/preserving of fruit & vegetables		15	16	33	17		76	89	110	63		12.5	18.0	18.2	18.0
1514	Vegetable and animal oils and fats		21	25	22	30		300	337	326	306		51.4	54.2	57.4	69.7
1520	Dairy products		131	237	206	249		91	185	406	355		12.6	27.1	62.4	65.3
153	Grain mill products; starches; animal feeds	b/	1060	1099	1369	1402	b/	1620	1952	2090	2277	b/	256.9	317.2	370.0	452.8
1531	Grain mill products		...	...	...	...		...	...	...	...		...	...	...	...
1532	Starches and starch products		...	...	...	...		...	...	...	...		...	...	...	...
1533	Prepared animal feeds		...	...	...	...		...	...	...	...		...	...	...	...
154	Other food products	b/	...	...	...	...	b/	...	...	...	...	b/	...	...	...	...
1541	Bakery products		...	...	...	...		...	...	...	...		...	...	...	...
1542	Sugar		...	...	...	...		...	...	...	...		...	...	...	...
1543	Cocoa, chocolate and sugar confectionery		...	...	...	...		...	...	...	...		...	...	...	...
1544	Macaroni, noodles & similar products		...	...	...	...		...	...	...	...		...	...	...	...
1549	Other food products n.e.c.		...	...	...	...		...	...	...	...		...	...	...	...
155	Beverages		124	157	126	149		910	1090	1083	1217		221.9	272.4	306.4	353.5
1551	Distilling, rectifying & blending of spirits		...	...	...	...		...	...	...	...		...	...	...	...
1552	Wines		...	...	...	...		...	...	...	...		...	...	...	...
1553	Malt liquors and malt		...	...	...	...		...	...	...	...		...	...	...	...
1554	Soft drinks; mineral waters		...	...	...	...		...	...	...	...		...	...	...	...
1600	Tobacco products		10	7	4	5		374	253	240	188		60.9	46.4	47.2	50.5
171	Spinning, weaving and finishing of textiles	c/	390	438	564	606	c/	10479	10213	10018	9807	c/	1678.7	1711.7	1723.9	1832.5
1711	Textile fibre preparation; textile weaving		...	...	...	...		...	...	...	...		...	...	...	...
1712	Finishing of textiles		...	...	...	...		...	...	...	...		...	...	...	...
172	Other textiles	c/	...	...	...	...	c/	...	...	...	...	c/	...	...	...	...
1721	Made-up textile articles, except apparel		...	...	...	...		...	...	...	...		...	...	...	...
1722	Carpets and rugs		...	...	...	...		...	...	...	...		...	...	...	...
1723	Cordage, rope, twine and netting		...	...	...	...		...	...	...	...		...	...	...	...
1729	Other textiles n.e.c.		...	...	...	...		...	...	...	...		...	...	...	...
1730	Knitted and crocheted fabrics and articles	c/	...	...	...	...	c/	...	...	...	...	c/	...	...	...	...
1810	Wearing apparel, except fur apparel	c/	...	...	...	...	c/	...	...	...	...	c/	...	...	...	...
1820	Dressing & dyeing of fur; processing of fur	c/	...	...	...	...	c/	...	...	...	...	c/	...	...	...	...
191	Tanning, dressing and processing of leather	d/	96	92	95	99	d/	7717	7417	7413	8605	d/	1591.0	1588.9	1557.5	1839.2
1911	Tanning and dressing of leather		...	...	...	...		...	...	...	...		...	...	...	...
1912	Luggage, handbags, etc.; saddlery & harness		...	...	...	...		...	...	...	...		...	...	...	...
1920	Footwear	d/	...	...	...	...	d/	...	...	...	...	d/	...	...	...	...
2010	Sawmilling and planing of wood	e/	357	475	364	490	e/	740	783	547	803	e/	114.6	130.0	98.5	150.8
202	Products of wood, cork, straw, etc.	e/	...	...	...	...	e/	...	...	...	...	e/	...	...	...	...
2021	Veneer sheets, plywood, particle board, etc.		...	...	...	...		...	...	...	...		...	...	...	...
2022	Builders' carpentry and joinery		...	...	...	...		...	...	...	...		...	...	...	...
2023	Wooden containers		...	...	...	...		...	...	...	...		...	...	...	...
2029	Other wood products; articles of cork/straw		...	...	...	...		...	...	...	...		...	...	...	...
210	Paper and paper products	f/	127	236	233	257	f/	1366	2113	1833	1878	f/	253.2	393.0	366.9	407.0
2101	Pulp, paper and paperboard		...	...	...	...		...	...	...	...		...	...	...	...
2102	Corrugated paper and paperboard		...	...	...	...		...	...	...	...		...	...	...	...
2109	Other articles of paper and paperboard		...	...	...	...		...	...	...	...		...	...	...	...
221	Publishing	f/	...	...	...	...	f/	...	...	...	...	f/	...	...	...	...
2211	Publishing of books and other publications		...	...	...	...		...	...	...	...		...	...	...	...
2212	Publishing of newspapers, journals, etc.		...	...	...	...		...	...	...	...		...	...	...	...
2213	Publishing of recorded media		...	...	...	...		...	...	...	...		...	...	...	...
2219	Other publishing		...	...	...	...		...	...	...	...		...	...	...	...

222	Printing and related service activities	f/	...	...	...	...	f/	...	...	...	...	f/	...	...	...	...
2221	Printing		...	...	...	...		...	...	...	...		...	...	...	...
2222	Service activities related to printing		...	...	...	...		...	...	...	...		...	...	...	...
2230	Reproduction of recorded media	f/	...	...	...	...	f/	...	...	...	...	f/	...	...	...	...
2310	Coke oven products		4g/	3g/	...h/	...h/		3407g/	1900g/	...h/	...h/		1939.0g/	1181.5g/	...h/	...h/
2320	Refined petroleum products		...g/	...g/	...h/	...h/		...g/	...g/	...h/	...h/		...g/	...g/	...h/	...h/
2330	Processing of nuclear fuel		...g/	...g/	...h/	...h/		...g/	...g/	...h/	...h/		...g/	...g/	...h/	...h/
241	Basic chemicals		111i/	112i/	125h/	154h/		1151i/	1446i/	3423h/	3440h/		199.1i/	256.7i/	1584.4h/	1697.2h/
2411	Basic chemicals, except fertilizers		...	...	...	...		...	...	...	...		...	...	...	...
2412	Fertilizers and nitrogen compounds		...	...	...	...		...	...	...	...		...	...	...	...
2413	Plastics in primary forms; synthetic rubber		...	...	...	...		...	...	...	...		...	...	...	...
242	Other chemicals		...i/	...i/	...h/	...h/		...i/	...i/	...h/	...h/		...i/	...i/	...h/	...h/
2421	Pesticides and other agro-chemical products		...	...	...	...		...	...	...	...		...	...	...	...
2422	Paints, varnishes, printing ink and mastics		...	...	...	...		...	...	...	...		...	...	...	...
2423	Pharmaceuticals, medicinal chemicals, etc.		...	...	...	...		...	...	...	...		...	...	...	...
2424	Soap, cleaning & cosmetic preparations		...	...	...	...		...	...	...	...		...	...	...	...
2429	Other chemical products n.e.c.		...	...	...	...		...	...	...	...		...	...	...	...
2430	Man-made fibres		...i/	...i/	...h/	...h/		...i/	...i/	...h/	...h/		...i/	...i/	...h/	...h/
251	Rubber products		...i/	...i/	...h/	...h/		...i/	...i/	...h/	...h/		...i/	...i/	...h/	...h/
2511	Rubber tyres and tubes		...	...	...	...		...	...	...	...		...	...	...	...
2519	Other rubber products		...	...	...	...		...	...	...	...		...	...	...	...
2520	Plastic products		...i/	...i/	...h/	...h/		...i/	...i/	...h/	...h/		...i/	...i/	...h/	...h/
2610	Glass and glass products	j/	338	399	419	407	j/	3281	3217	3277	3535	j/	1062.5	973.2	1097.6	1212.3
269	Non-metallic mineral products n.e.c.	j/	...	...	...	...	j/	...	...	...	...	j/	...	...	...	...
2691	Pottery, china and earthenware		...	...	...	...		...	...	...	...		...	...	...	...
2692	Refractory ceramic products		...	...	...	...		...	...	...	...		...	...	...	...
2693	Struct.non-refractory clay; ceramic products		...	...	...	...		...	...	...	...		...	...	...	...
2694	Cement, lime and plaster		...	...	...	...		...	...	...	...		...	...	...	...
2695	Articles of concrete, cement and plaster		...	...	...	...		...	...	...	...		...	...	...	...
2696	Cutting, shaping & finishing of stone		...	...	...	...		...	...	...	...		...	...	...	...
2699	Other non-metallic mineral products n.e.c.		...	...	...	...		...	...	...	...		...	...	...	...
2710	Basic iron and steel	k/	488	649	792	1107	k/	2565	4083	3999	5586	k/	699.1	1377.3	1379.0	1789.1
2720	Basic precious and non-ferrous metals	k/	...	...	...	...	k/	...	...	...	...	k/	...	...	...	...
273	Casting of metals	k/	...	...	...	...	k/	...	...	...	...	k/	...	...	...	...
2731	Casting of iron and steel		...	...	...	...		...	...	...	...		...	...	...	...
2732	Casting of non-ferrous metals		...	...	...	...		...	...	...	...		...	...	...	...
281	Struct.metal products;tanks;steam generators	k/	...	...	...	...	k/	...	...	...	...	k/	...	...	...	...
2811	Structural metal products		...	...	...	...		...	...	...	...		...	...	...	...
2812	Tanks, reservoirs and containers of metal		...	...	...	...		...	...	...	...		...	...	...	...
2813	Steam generators		...	...	...	...		...	...	...	...		...	...	...	...
289	Other metal products; metal working services	k/	...	...	...	...	k/	...	...	...	...	k/	...	...	...	...
2891	Metal forging/pressing/stamping/roll-forming		...	...	...	...		...	...	...	...		...	...	...	...
2892	Treatment & coating of metals		...	...	...	...		...	...	...	...		...	...	...	...
2893	Cutlery, hand tools and general hardware		...	...	...	...		...	...	...	...		...	...	...	...
2899	Other fabricated metal products n.e.c.		...	...	...	...		...	...	...	...		...	...	...	...
291	General purpose machinery	k/	...	...	...	...	k/	...	...	...	...	k/	...	...	...	...
2911	Engines & turbines (not for transport equipment)		...	...	...	...		...	...	...	...		...	...	...	...
2912	Pumps, compressors, taps and valves		...	...	...	...		...	...	...	...		...	...	...	...
2913	Bearings, gears, gearing & driving elements		...	...	...	...		...	...	...	...		...	...	...	...
2914	Ovens, furnaces and furnace burners		...	...	...	...		...	...	...	...		...	...	...	...
2915	Lifting and handling equipment		...	...	...	...		...	...	...	...		...	...	...	...
2919	Other general purpose machinery		...	...	...	...		...	...	...	...		...	...	...	...
292	Special purpose machinery	k/	...	...	...	...	k/	...	...	...	...	k/	...	...	...	...
2921	Agricultural and forestry machinery		...	...	...	...		...	...	...	...		...	...	...	...
2922	Machine tools		...	...	...	...		...	...	...	...		...	...	...	...
2923	Machinery for metallurgy		...	...	...	...		...	...	...	...		...	...	...	...
2924	Machinery for mining & construction		...	...	...	...		...	...	...	...		...	...	...	...
2925	Food/beverage/tobacco processing machinery		...	...	...	...		...	...	...	...		...	...	...	...
2926	Machinery for textile, apparel and leather		...	...	...	...		...	...	...	...		...	...	...	...
2927	Weapons and ammunition		...	...	...	...		...	...	...	...		...	...	...	...
2929	Other special purpose machinery		...	...	...	...		...	...	...	...		...	...	...	...

continued

Albania

ISIC Revision 3			Number of enterprises					Number of employees					Wages and salaries paid to employees			
			(number)					(number)					(millions of Albanian Leks)			
ISIC	Industry	Note	2003	2004	2005	2006	Note	2003	2004	2005	2006	Note	2003	2004	2005	2006
2930	Domestic appliances n.e.c.	k/	...	...	...	...	k/	...	...	...	...	k/	...	...	...	...
3000	Office, accounting and computing machinery		25m/	26m/	34n/	28n/		766m/	741m/	687n/	845n/		198.2m/	260.7m/	236.5n/	309.8n/
3110	Electric motors, generators and transformers		...m/	...m/	...n/	...n/		...m/	...m/	...n/	...n/		...m/	...m/	...n/	...n/
3120	Electricity distribution & control apparatus		...m/	...m/	...n/	...n/		...m/	...m/	...n/	...n/		...m/	...m/	...n/	...n/
3130	Insulated wire and cable		...m/	...m/	...n/	...n/		...m/	...m/	...n/	...n/		...m/	...m/	...n/	...n/
3140	Accumulators, primary cells and batteries		...m/	...m/	...n/	...n/		...m/	...m/	...n/	...n/		...m/	...m/	...n/	...n/
3150	Lighting equipment and electric lamps		...m/	...m/	...n/	...n/		...m/	...m/	...n/	...n/		...m/	...m/	...n/	...n/
3190	Other electrical equipment n.e.c.		...m/	...m/	...n/	...n/		...m/	...m/	...n/	...n/		...m/	...m/	...n/	...n/
3210	Electronic valves, tubes, etc.		...	...	...n/	...n/		...	...	...n/	...n/		...	...	...n/	...n/
3220	TV/radio transmitters; line comm. apparatus		...	...	...n/	...n/		...	...	...n/	...n/		...	...	...n/	...n/
3230	TV and radio receivers and associated goods		...	...	...n/	...n/		...	...	...n/	...n/		...	...	...n/	...n/
331	Medical, measuring, testing appliances, etc.		...	...	...n/	...n/		...	...	...n/	...n/		...	...	...n/	...n/
3311	Medical, surgical and orthopaedic equipment		...	...	...	...		...	...	...	...		...	...	...	...
3312	Measuring/testing/navigating appliances,etc.		...	...	...	...		...	...	...	...		...	...	...	...
3313	Industrial process control equipment		...	...	...	...		...	...	...	...		...	...	...	...
3320	Optical instruments & photographic equipment		...	...	...n/	...n/		...	...	...n/	...n/		...	...	...n/	...n/
3330	Watches and clocks		...	...	...n/	...n/		...	...	...n/	...n/		...	...	...n/	...n/
3410	Motor vehicles		...	...	...n/	...n/		...	...	...n/	...n/		...	...	...n/	...n/
3420	Automobile bodies, trailers & semi-trailers		...	...	...n/	...n/		...	...	...n/	...n/		...	...	...n/	...n/
3430	Parts/accessories for automobiles		...	...	...n/	...n/		...	...	...n/	...n/		...	...	...n/	...n/
351	Building and repairing of ships and boats		...	...	...n/	...n/		...	...	...n/	...n/		...	...	...n/	...n/
3511	Building and repairing of ships		...	...	...	...		...	...	...	...		...	...	...	...
3512	Building/repairing of pleasure/sport. boats		...	...	...	...		...	...	...	...		...	...	...	...
3520	Railway/tramway locomotives & rolling stock		...	...	...n/	...n/		...	...	...n/	...n/		...	...	...n/	...n/
3530	Aircraft and spacecraft		...	...	...n/	...n/		...	...	...n/	...n/		...	...	...n/	...n/
359	Transport equipment n.e.c.		...	...	...n/	...n/		...	...	...n/	...n/		...	...	...n/	...n/
3591	Motorcycles		...	...	...	...		...	...	...	...		...	...	...	...
3592	Bicycles and invalid carriages		...	...	...	...		...	...	...	...		...	...	...	...
3599	Other transport equipment n.e.c.		...	...	...	...		...	...	...	...		...	...	...	...
3610	Furniture	p/	393	400	578	703	p/	1219	1400	1940	1888	p/	216.5	242.4	349.6	386.5
369	Manufacturing n.e.c.	p/	...	...	...	...	p/	...	...	...	...	p/	...	...	...	...
3691	Jewellery and related articles		...	...	...	...		...	...	...	...		...	...	...	...
3692	Musical instruments		...	...	...	...		...	...	...	...		...	...	...	...
3693	Sports goods		...	...	...	...		...	...	...	...		...	...	...	...
3694	Games and toys		...	...	...	...		...	...	...	...		...	...	...	...
3699	Other manufacturing n.e.c.		...	...	...	...		...	...	...	...		...	...	...	...
3710	Recycling of metal waste and scrap		...	...	3q/	5q/		...	...	99q/	41q/		...	...	15.5q/	17.4q/
3720	Recycling of non-metal waste and scrap		...	...	...q/	...q/		...	...	...q/	...q/		...	...	...q/	...q/
D	Total manufacturing	r/	3727	4417	5060	5751	r/	37030	38165	38706	42119	r/	8703.2	9004.8	9486.4	10917.0

a/ 1511 includes 1512.
b/ 153 includes 154.
c/ 171 includes 172, 1730, 1810 and 1820.
d/ 191 includes 1920.
e/ 2010 includes 202.
f/ 210 includes 221, 222 and 2230.
g/ 2310 includes 2320 and 2330.
h/ 241 includes 2310, 2320, 2330, 242, 2430, 251 and 2520.
i/ 241 includes 242, 2430, 251 and 2520.
j/ 2610 includes 269.

k/ 2710 includes 2720, 273, 281, 289, 291, 292 and 2930.
m/ 3000 includes 3110, 3120, 3130, 3140, 3150 and 3190.
n/ 3000 includes 31, 32, 33, 34 and 35.
p/ 3610 includes 369.
q/ 3710 includes 3720.
r/ Sum of available data.

Albania

ISIC Revision 3		Output in producers' prices					Value added in producers' prices					Gross fixed capital formation		
			(millions of Albanian Leks)					(millions of Albanian Leks)					(millions of Albanian Leks)	
ISIC	Industry	Note	2003	2004	2005	2006	Note	2003	2004	2005	2006	Note	2005	2006
151	Processed meat,fish,fruit,vegetables,fats		3921.8	4203.2	4997.5	5197.6		742.6	820.0	1025.6	1109.2		625.8	413.0
1511	Processing/preserving of meat	a/	1291.4	1810.4	2485.8	2516.2	a/	377.9	534.1	703.2	767.1	a/	572.6	349.5
1512	Processing/preserving of fish	a/	...	...	...	...	a/	...	...	...	...	a/	...	...
1513	Processing/preserving of fruit & vegetables		120.8	155.2	161.5	98.6		20.0	2.3	52.8	27.2		19.4	29.3
1514	Vegetable and animal oils and fats		2509.6	2237.5	2350.3	2582.9		344.6	283.6	269.6	315.0		33.8	34.2
1520	Dairy products		419.2	837.6	2162.8	1859.1		112.2	190.0	828.7	453.0		833.0	220.9
153	Grain mill products; starches; animal feeds	b/	6129.5	7824.5	8345.7	9469.0	b/	1405.8	1433.1	1721.5	2005.2	b/	402.3	591.9
1531	Grain mill products		...	...	...	...		...	...	...	...		...	...
1532	Starches and starch products		...	...	...	...		...	...	...	...		...	...
1533	Prepared animal feeds		...	...	...	...		...	...	...	...		...	...
154	Other food products	b/	...	...	...	...	b/	...	...	...	...	b/	...	...
1541	Bakery products		...	...	...	...		...	...	...	...		...	...
1542	Sugar		...	...	...	...		...	...	...	...		...	...
1543	Cocoa, chocolate and sugar confectionery		...	...	...	...		...	...	...	...		...	...
1544	Macaroni, noodles & similar products		...	...	...	...		...	...	...	...		...	...
1549	Other food products n.e.c.		...	...	...	...		...	...	...	...		...	...
155	Beverages		4067.8	4638.1	5178.7	5506.1		1039.1	1315.9	1465.5	1453.0		2347.8	2303.0
1551	Distilling, rectifying & blending of spirits		...	...	...	...		...	...	...	...		...	...
1552	Wines		...	...	...	...		...	...	...	...		...	...
1553	Malt liquors and malt		...	...	...	...		...	...	...	...		...	...
1554	Soft drinks; mineral waters		...	...	...	...		...	...	...	...		...	...
1600	Tobacco products		586.5	264.8	560.4	545.3		143.7	-13.1	140.2	86.0		23.6	0.2
171	Spinning, weaving and finishing of textiles	c/	6795.6	6360.2	6525.3	7578.0	c/	3429.5	3005.9	3321.5	3640.3	c/	595.8	623.0
1711	Textile fibre preparation; textile weaving		...	...	...	...		...	...	...	...		...	...
1712	Finishing of textiles		...	...	...	...		...	...	...	...		...	...
172	Other textiles	c/	...	...	...	...	c/	...	...	...	...	c/	...	...
1721	Made-up textile articles, except apparel		...	...	...	...		...	...	...	...		...	...
1722	Carpets and rugs		...	...	...	...		...	...	...	...		...	...
1723	Cordage, rope, twine and netting		...	...	...	...		...	...	...	...		...	...
1729	Other textiles n.e.c.		...	...	...	...		...	...	...	...		...	...
1730	Knitted and crocheted fabrics and articles	c/	...	...	...	...	c/	...	...	...	...	c/	...	...
1810	Wearing apparel, except fur apparel	c/	...	...	...	...	c/	...	...	...	...	c/	...	...
1820	Dressing & dyeing of fur; processing of fur	c/	...	...	...	...	c/	...	...	...	...	c/	...	...
191	Tanning, dressing and processing of leather	d/	6610.9	6331.9	6398.6	7124.4	d/	2827.4	2994.0	2914.0	3204.3	d/	509.4	631.6
1911	Tanning and dressing of leather		...	...	...	...		...	...	...	...		...	...
1912	Luggage, handbags, etc.; saddlery & harness		...	...	...	...		...	...	...	...		...	...
1920	Footwear	d/	...	...	...	...	d/	...	...	...	...	d/	...	...
2010	Sawmilling and planing of wood	e/	1620.1	2083.5	1306.5	2067.9	e/	384.8	551.1	380.8	653.4	e/	77.9	162.2
202	Products of wood, cork, straw, etc.	e/	...	...	...	...	e/	...	...	...	...	e/	...	...
2021	Veneer sheets, plywood, particle board, etc.		...	...	...	...		...	...	...	...		...	...
2022	Builders' carpentry and joinery		...	...	...	...		...	...	...	...		...	...
2023	Wooden containers		...	...	...	...		...	...	...	...		...	...
2029	Other wood products; articles of cork/straw		...	...	...	...		...	...	...	...		...	...
210	Paper and paper products	f/	2544.0	4038.6	4077.9	3639.4	f/	695.6	1266.2	1211.2	1252.3	f/	465.6	396.6
2101	Pulp, paper and paperboard		...	...	...	...		...	...	...	...		...	...
2102	Corrugated paper and paperboard		...	...	...	...		...	...	...	...		...	...
2109	Other articles of paper and paperboard		...	...	...	...		...	...	...	...		...	...
221	Publishing	f/	...	...	...	...	f/	...	...	...	...	f/	...	...
2211	Publishing of books and other publications		...	...	...	...		...	...	...	...		...	...
2212	Publishing of newspapers, journals, etc.		...	...	...	...		...	...	...	...		...	...
2213	Publishing of recorded media		...	...	...	...		...	...	...	...		...	...
2219	Other publishing		...	...	...	...		...	...	...	...		...	...

continued

Albania

ISIC Revision 3		Output in producers' prices					Value added in producers' prices					Gross fixed capital formation		
			(millions of Albanian Leks)					(millions of Albanian Leks)					(millions of Albanian Leks)	
ISIC	Industry	Note	2003	2004	2005	2006	Note	2003	2004	2005	2006	Note	2005	2006
222	Printing and related service activities	f/	...	...	...	...	f/	...	...	...	...	f/	...	...
2221	Printing		...	...	...	...		...	...	...	...		...	...
2222	Service activities related to printing		...	...	...	...		...	...	...	...		...	...
2230	Reproduction of recorded media	f/	...	...	...	...	f/	...	...	...	...	f/	...	...
2310	Coke oven products		16158.2g/	10940.6g/	...h/	...h/		1607.8g/	2143.9g/	...h/	...h/		...h/	...h/
2320	Refined petroleum products		...g/	...g/	...h/	...h/		...g/	...g/	...h/	...h/		...h/	...h/
2330	Processing of nuclear fuel		...g/	...g/	...h/	...h/		...g/	...g/	...h/	...h/		...h/	...h/
241	Basic chemicals		3359.8i/	4596.1i/	16266.5h/	20268.0h/		731.2i/	1043.4i/	3370.5h/	5299.5h/		3847.6h/	1147.5h/
2411	Basic chemicals, except fertilizers		...	...	...	...		...	...	...	...		...	...
2412	Fertilizers and nitrogen compounds		...	...	...	...		...	...	...	...		...	...
2413	Plastics in primary forms; synthetic rubber		...	...	...	...		...	...	...	...		...	...
242	Other chemicals		...i/	...i/	...h/	...h/		...i/	...i/	...h/	...h/		...h/	...h/
2421	Pesticides and other agro-chemical products		...	...	...	...		...	...	...	...		...	...
2422	Paints, varnishes, printing ink and mastics		...	...	...	...		...	...	...	...		...	...
2423	Pharmaceuticals, medicinal chemicals, etc.		...	...	...	...		...	...	...	...		...	...
2424	Soap, cleaning & cosmetic preparations		...	...	...	...		...	...	...	...		...	...
2429	Other chemical products n.e.c.		...	...	...	...		...	...	...	...		...	...
2430	Man-made fibres		...i/	...i/	...h/	...h/		...i/	...i/	...h/	...h/		...h/	...h/
251	Rubber products		...i/	...i/	...h/	...h/		...i/	...i/	...h/	...h/		...h/	...h/
2511	Rubber tyres and tubes		...	...	...	...		...	...	...	...		...	...
2519	Other rubber products		...	...	...	...		...	...	...	...		...	...
2520	Plastic products		...i/	...i/	...h/	...h/		...i/	...i/	...h/	...h/		...h/	...h/
2610	Glass and glass products	j/	12924.4	13334.1	15800.9	21126.0	j/	2937.2	2881.3	3128.6	4710.0	j/	8583.8	3887.8
269	Non-metallic mineral products n.e.c.	j/	...	...	...	...	j/	...	...	...	...	j/	...	...
2691	Pottery, china and earthenware		...	...	...	...		...	...	...	...		...	...
2692	Refractory ceramic products		...	...	...	...		...	...	...	...		...	...
2693	Struct.non-refractory clay; ceramic products		...	...	...	...		...	...	...	...		...	...
2694	Cement, lime and plaster		...	...	...	...		...	...	...	...		...	...
2695	Articles of concrete, cement and plaster		...	...	...	...		...	...	...	...		...	...
2696	Cutting, shaping & finishing of stone		...	...	...	...		...	...	...	...		...	...
2699	Other non-metallic mineral products n.e.c.		...	...	...	...		...	...	...	...		...	...
2710	Basic iron and steel	k/	9671.4	14732.5	15697.4	19476.8	k/	1899.2	3208.7	2863.1	4521.4	k/	849.2	1567.5
2720	Basic precious and non-ferrous metals	k/	...	...	...	...	k/	...	...	...	...	k/	...	...
273	Casting of metals	k/	...	...	...	...	k/	...	...	...	...	k/	...	...
2731	Casting of iron and steel		...	...	...	...		...	...	...	...		...	...
2732	Casting of non-ferrous metals		...	...	...	...		...	...	...	...		...	...
281	Struct.metal products;tanks;steam generators	k/	...	...	...	...	k/	...	...	...	...	k/	...	...
2811	Structural metal products		...	...	...	...		...	...	...	...		...	...
2812	Tanks, reservoirs and containers of metal		...	...	...	...		...	...	...	...		...	...
2813	Steam generators		...	...	...	...		...	...	...	...		...	...
289	Other metal products; metal working services	k/	...	...	...	...	k/	...	...	...	...	k/	...	...
2891	Metal forging/pressing/stamping/roll-forming		...	...	...	...		...	...	...	...		...	...
2892	Treatment & coating of metals		...	...	...	...		...	...	...	...		...	...
2893	Cutlery, hand tools and general hardware		...	...	...	...		...	...	...	...		...	...
2899	Other fabricated metal products n.e.c.		...	...	...	...		...	...	...	...		...	...
291	General purpose machinery	k/	...	...	...	...	k/	...	...	...	...	k/	...	...
2911	Engines & turbines (not for transport equipment)		...	...	...	...		...	...	...	...		...	...
2912	Pumps, compressors, taps and valves		...	...	...	...		...	...	...	...		...	...
2913	Bearings, gears, gearing & driving elements		...	...	...	...		...	...	...	...		...	...
2914	Ovens, furnaces and furnace burners		...	...	...	...		...	...	...	...		...	...
2915	Lifting and handling equipment		...	...	...	...		...	...	...	...		...	...
2919	Other general purpose machinery		...	...	...	...		...	...	...	...		...	...

292	Special purpose machinery	k/	...	...	...	...	k/	...	...	...	...	k/	...	...
2921	Agricultural and forestry machinery		...	...	...	...		...	...	...	...		...	...
2922	Machine tools		...	...	...	...		...	...	...	...		...	...
2923	Machinery for metallurgy		...	...	...	...		...	...	...	...		...	...
2924	Machinery for mining & construction		...	...	...	...		...	...	...	...		...	...
2925	Food/beverage/tobacco processing machinery		...	...	...	...		...	...	...	...		...	...
2926	Machinery for textile, apparel and leather		...	...	...	...		...	...	...	...		...	...
2927	Weapons and ammunition		...	...	...	...		...	...	...	...		...	...
2929	Other special purpose machinery		...	...	...	...		...	...	...	...		...	...
2930	Domestic appliances n.e.c.	k/	...	...	...	...	k/	...	...	...	...	k/	...	...
3000	Office, accounting and computing machinery		907.8m/	1571.8m/	1589.2n/	1785.2n/		510.3m/	944.3m/	783.0n/	906.1n/		105.4n/	84.5n/
3110	Electric motors, generators and transformers		...m/	...m/	...n/	...n/		...m/	...m/	...n/	...n/		...n/	...n/
3120	Electricity distribution & control apparatus		...m/	...m/	...n/	...n/		...m/	...m/	...n/	...n/		...n/	...n/
3130	Insulated wire and cable		...m/	...m/	...n/	...n/		...m/	...m/	...n/	...n/		...n/	...n/
3140	Accumulators, primary cells and batteries		...m/	...m/	...n/	...n/		...m/	...m/	...n/	...n/		...n/	...n/
3150	Lighting equipment and electric lamps		...m/	...m/	...n/	...n/		...m/	...m/	...n/	...n/		...n/	...n/
3190	Other electrical equipment n.e.c.		...m/	...m/	...n/	...n/		...m/	...m/	...n/	...n/		...n/	...n/
3210	Electronic valves, tubes, etc.		...	...	...n/	...n/		...	...	...n/	...n/		...n/	...n/
3220	TV/radio transmitters; line comm. apparatus		...	...	...n/	...n/		...	...	...n/	...n/		...n/	...n/
3230	TV and radio receivers and associated goods		...	...	...n/	...n/		...	...	...n/	...n/		...n/	...n/
331	Medical, measuring, testing appliances, etc.		...	...	...n/	...n/		...	...	...n/	...n/		...n/	...n/
3311	Medical, surgical and orthopaedic equipment		...	...	...	...		...	...	...	...		...	...
3312	Measuring/testing/navigating appliances,etc.		...	...	...	...		...	...	...	...		...	...
3313	Industrial process control equipment		...	...	...	...		...	...	...	...		...	...
3320	Optical instruments & photographic equipment		...	...	...n/	...n/		...	...	...n/	...n/		...n/	...n/
3330	Watches and clocks		...	...	...n/	...n/		...	...	...n/	...n/		...n/	...n/
3410	Motor vehicles		...	...	...n/	...n/		...	...	...n/	...n/		...n/	...n/
3420	Automobile bodies, trailers & semi-trailers		...	...	...n/	...n/		...	...	...n/	...n/		...n/	...n/
3430	Parts/accessories for automobiles		...	...	...n/	...n/		...	...	...n/	...n/		...n/	...n/
351	Building and repairing of ships and boats		...	...	...n/	...n/		...	...	...n/	...n/		...n/	...n/
3511	Building and repairing of ships		...	...	...	...		...	...	...	...		...	...
3512	Building/repairing of pleasure/sport. boats		...	...	...	...		...	...	...	...		...	...
3520	Railway/tramway locomotives & rolling stock		...	...	...n/	...n/		...	...	...n/	...n/		...n/	...n/
3530	Aircraft and spacecraft		...	...	...n/	...n/		...	...	...n/	...n/		...n/	...n/
359	Transport equipment n.e.c.		...	...	...n/	...n/		...	...	...n/	...n/		...n/	...n/
3591	Motorcycles		...	...	...	...		...	...	...	...		...	...
3592	Bicycles and invalid carriages		...	...	...	...		...	...	...	...		...	...
3599	Other transport equipment n.e.c.		...	...	...	...		...	...	...	...		...	...
3610	Furniture	p/	3976.9	3499.0	4124.3	4668.8	p/	826.9	816.4	1265.5	1399.6	p/	260.6	226.1
369	Manufacturing n.e.c.	p/	...	...	...	...	p/	...	...	...	...	p/	...	...
3691	Jewellery and related articles		...	...	...	...		...	...	...	...		...	...
3692	Musical instruments		...	...	...	...		...	...	...	...		...	...
3693	Sports goods		...	...	...	...		...	...	...	...		...	...
3694	Games and toys		...	...	...	...		...	...	...	...		...	...
3699	Other manufacturing n.e.c.		...	...	...	...		...	...	...	...		...	...
3710	Recycling of metal waste and scrap		...	...	49.0q/	30.9q/		...	...	35.6q/	9.0q/		1.3q/	0.4q/
3720	Recycling of non-metal waste and scrap		...	...	...q/	...q/		...	...	...q/	...q/		...q/	...q/
D	Total manufacturing	r/	79693.9	85256.3	93080.7	110342.4	r/	19293.1	22601.2	24455.2	30702.4	r/	19529.2	12256.3

a/ 1511 includes 1512.
b/ 153 includes 154.
c/ 171 includes 172, 1730, 1810 and 1820.
d/ 191 includes 1920.
e/ 2010 includes 202.
f/ 210 includes 221, 222 and 2230.
g/ 2310 includes 2320 and 2330.
h/ 241 includes 2310, 2320, 2330, 242, 2430, 251 and 2520.
i/ 241 includes 242, 2430, 251 and 2520.
j/ 2610 includes 269.

k/ 2710 includes 2720, 273, 281, 289, 291, 292 and 2930.
m/ 3000 includes 3110, 3120, 3130, 3140, 3150 and 3190.
n/ 3000 includes 31, 32, 33, 34 and 35.
p/ 3610 includes 369.
q/ 3710 includes 3720.
r/ Sum of available data.

Albania

ISIC Revision 3			Index numbers of industrial production											
			(2000=100)											
ISIC	Industry	Note	1995	1996	1997	1998	1999	2000	2001	2002	2003	2004	2005	2006
15	Food and beverages		...	...	...	...	...	...	...	...	...	...	...	...
16	Tobacco products		...	...	...	...	...	...	...	...	...	...	...	...
17	Textiles		...	...	...	...	...	...	...	...	...	...	...	...
18	Wearing apparel, fur		...	...	...	...	...	...	...	...	...	...	...	...
19	Leather, leather products and footwear		...	...	...	...	...	...	...	...	...	...	...	...
20	Wood products (excl. furniture)		...	...	...	...	...	...	...	...	...	...	...	...
21	Paper and paper products		...	...	...	...	...	...	...	...	...	...	...	...
22	Printing and publishing		...	...	...	...	...	...	...	...	...	...	...	...
23	Coke,refined petroleum products,nuclear fuel		...	...	...	...	...	...	...	...	...	...	...	...
24	Chemicals and chemical products		...	...	...	...	...	...	...	...	...	...	...	...
25	Rubber and plastics products		...	...	...	...	...	...	...	...	...	...	...	...
26	Non-metallic mineral products		...	...	...	...	...	...	...	...	...	...	...	...
27	Basic metals		...	...	...	...	...	...	...	...	...	...	...	...
28	Fabricated metal products		...	...	...	...	...	...	...	...	...	...	...	...
29	Machinery and equipment n.e.c.		...	...	...	...	...	...	...	...	...	...	...	...
30	Office, accounting and computing machinery		...	...	...	...	...	...	...	...	...	...	...	...
31	Electrical machinery and apparatus		...	...	...	...	...	...	...	...	...	...	...	...
32	Radio,television and communication equipment		...	...	...	...	...	...	...	...	...	...	...	...
33	Medical, precision and optical instruments		...	...	...	...	...	...	...	...	...	...	...	...
34	Motor vehicles, trailers, semi-trailers		...	...	...	...	...	...	...	...	...	...	...	...
35	Other transport equipment		...	...	...	...	...	...	...	...	...	...	...	...
36	Furniture; manufacturing n.e.c.		...	...	...	...	...	...	...	...	...	...	...	...
37	Recycling		...	...	...	...	...	...	...	...	...	...	...	...
D	Total manufacturing		86	70	64	59	67	100	67	76	82	92	126	...

Armenia

Supplier of information:
National Statistical Service of the Republic of Armenia, Yerevan.

Basic source of data:
Annual survey; administrative source.

Major deviations from ISIC (Revision 3):
The data presented in ISIC (Revision 3) were originally classified according to NACE (Revision 1).

Reference period:
Calendar year.

Scope:
All registered establishments.

Method of data collection:
Field enumeration.

Type of enumeration:
Not reported.

Adjusted for non-response:
Yes.

Concepts and definitions of variables:
Wages and salaries excludes payments in kind.
Output includes value of sale of all products and value of industrial work done or industrial services rendered to others.

Related national publications:
The Statistical Yearbook of Armenia, published by the National Statistical Service of the Republic of Armenia, Yerevan.

Armenia

ISIC Revision 3		Number of establishments					Number of employees					Wages and salaries paid to employees				
			(number)					(number)					(millions of Armenian Drams)			
ISIC	Industry	Note	2003	2004	2005	2006	Note	2003	2004	2005	2006	Note	2003	2004	2005	2006
151	Processed meat,fish,fruit,vegetables,fats		86	87	94	100		...	...	...	...		...	...	...	...
1511	Processing/preserving of meat		56	57	62	71		...	...	...	...		...	...	...	...
1512	Processing/preserving of fish		2	3	4	4		...	...	...	...		...	...	...	...
1513	Processing/preserving of fruit & vegetables		25	24	24	22		...	...	...	...		...	...	...	...
1514	Vegetable and animal oils and fats		3	3	4	3		...	...	...	...		...	...	...	...
1520	Dairy products		74	76	75	74		...	...	...	...		...	...	...	...
153	Grain mill products; starches; animal feeds		44	43	43	41		...	...	...	...		...	...	...	...
1531	Grain mill products		44	43	43	41		...	...	...	...		...	...	...	...
1532	Starches and starch products		-	-	-	-		...	...	...	...		...	...	...	...
1533	Prepared animal feeds		...	-	-	-		...	...	...	...		...	...	...	...
154	Other food products		460	480	473	477		...	...	...	...		...	...	...	...
1541	Bakery products		378	391	383	386		...	...	...	...		...	...	...	...
1542	Sugar		-	1	1	1		...	...	...	...		...	...	...	...
1543	Cocoa, chocolate and sugar confectionery		16	17	19	17		...	...	...	...		...	...	...	...
1544	Macaroni, noodles & similar products		20	27	24	23		...	...	...	...		...	...	...	...
1549	Other food products n.e.c.		46	44	46	50		...	...	...	...		...	...	...	...
155	Beverages		136	131	127	127		...	...	...	...		...	...	...	...
1551	Distilling, rectifying & blending of spirits		45	35	30	29		...	...	...	...		...	...	...	...
1552	Wines		24	27	28	25		...	...	...	...		...	...	...	...
1553	Malt liquors and malt		4	4	5	5		...	...	...	...		...	...	...	...
1554	Soft drinks; mineral waters		63	65	64	68		...	...	...	...		...	...	...	...
1600	Tobacco products		7	7	7	4		...	...	...	...		...	...	...	...
171	Spinning, weaving and finishing of textiles		7	6	7	5		...	...	...	...		...	...	...	...
1711	Textile fibre preparation; textile weaving		7	6	7	5		...	...	...	...		...	...	...	...
1712	Finishing of textiles		-	-	-	-		...	...	...	...		...	...	...	...
172	Other textiles		37	35	33	29		...	...	...	...		...	...	...	...
1721	Made-up textile articles, except apparel		4	2	1	-		...	...	...	...		...	...	...	...
1722	Carpets and rugs		27	28	28	25		...	...	...	...		...	...	...	...
1723	Cordage, rope, twine and netting		-	-	-	-		...	...	...	...		...	...	...	...
1729	Other textiles n.e.c.		6	5	4	4		...	...	...	...		...	...	...	...
1730	Knitted and crocheted fabrics and articles		21	20	18	15		...	...	...	...		...	...	...	...
1810	Wearing apparel, except fur apparel		52	56	57	56		...	...	...	...		...	...	...	...
1820	Dressing & dyeing of fur; processing of fur		1	2	2	1		...	...	...	...		...	...	...	...
191	Tanning, dressing and processing of leather		10	10	11	13		...	...	...	...		...	...	...	...
1911	Tanning and dressing of leather		5	5	5	5		...	...	...	...		...	...	...	...
1912	Luggage, handbags, etc.; saddlery & harness		5	5	6	8		...	...	...	...		...	...	...	...
1920	Footwear		31	33	36	31		...	...	...	...		...	...	...	...
2010	Sawmilling and planing of wood		17	18	20	29		...	...	...	...		...	...	...	...
202	Products of wood, cork, straw, etc.		44	44	56	58		...	...	...	...		...	...	...	...
2021	Veneer sheets, plywood, particle board, etc.		2	1	2	2		...	...	...	...		...	...	...	...
2022	Builders' carpentry and joinery		35	33	43	46		...	...	...	...		...	...	...	...
2023	Wooden containers		1	2	2	2		...	...	...	...		...	...	...	...
2029	Other wood products; articles of cork/straw		6	8	9	8		...	...	...	...		...	...	...	...
210	Paper and paper products		21	27	30	29		...	...	...	...		...	...	...	...
2101	Pulp, paper and paperboard		1	1	2	2		...	...	...	...		...	...	...	...
2102	Corrugated paper and paperboard		9	8	10	9		...	...	...	...		...	...	...	...
2109	Other articles of paper and paperboard		11	18	18	18		...	...	...	...		...	...	...	...
221	Publishing		93	116	125	135		...	...	...	...		...	...	...	...
2211	Publishing of books and other publications		48	49	49	48		...	...	...	...		...	...	...	...
2212	Publishing of newspapers, journals, etc.		30	53	59	68		...	...	...	...		...	...	...	...
2213	Publishing of recorded media		1	1	2	1		...	...	...	...		...	...	...	...
2219	Other publishing		14	13	15	18		...	...	...	...		...	...	...	...

222	Printing and related service activities	86	98	97	100	...	...	...	...	...	...	...	...
2221	Printing	69	75	71	70	...	...	...	...	...	...	...	...
2222	Service activities related to printing	17	23	26	30	...	...	...	...	...	...	...	...
2230	Reproduction of recorded media	...	1	1	4	...	...	...	...	...	...	...	...
2310	Coke oven products	-	-	-	-	...	...	...	...	...	...	...	...
2320	Refined petroleum products	-	-	-	-	...	...	...	...	...	...	...	...
2330	Processing of nuclear fuel	-	-	-	-	...	...	...	...	...	...	...	...
241	Basic chemicals	12	15	14	14	...	...	...	...	...	...	...	...
2411	Basic chemicals, except fertilizers	8	10	10	10	...	...	...	...	...	...	...	...
2412	Fertilizers and nitrogen compounds	2	2	1	1	...	...	...	...	...	...	...	...
2413	Plastics in primary forms; synthetic rubber	2	3	3	3	...	...	...	...	...	...	...	...
242	Other chemicals	38	43	45	52	...	...	...	...	...	...	...	...
2421	Pesticides and other agro-chemical products	-	-	-	-	...	...	...	...	...	...	...	...
2422	Paints, varnishes, printing ink and mastics	8	10	12	11	...	...	...	...	...	...	...	...
2423	Pharmaceuticals, medicinal chemicals, etc.	18	18	17	19	...	...	...	...	...	...	...	...
2424	Soap, cleaning & cosmetic preparations	9	12	14	16	...	...	...	...	...	...	...	...
2429	Other chemical products n.e.c.	3	3	2	6	...	...	...	...	...	...	...	...
2430	Man-made fibres	-	-	-	-	...	...	...	...	...	...	...	...
251	Rubber products	8	8	10	10	...	...	...	...	...	...	...	...
2511	Rubber tyres and tubes	1	1	1	1	...	...	...	...	...	...	...	...
2519	Other rubber products	7	7	9	9	...	...	...	...	...	...	...	...
2520	Plastic products	45	53	64	60	...	...	...	...	...	...	...	...
2610	Glass and glass products	8	9	10	7	...	...	...	...	...	...	...	...
269	Non-metallic mineral products n.e.c.	146	166	169	177	...	...	...	...	...	...	...	...
2691	Pottery, china and earthenware	7	7	6	4	...	...	...	...	...	...	...	...
2692	Refractory ceramic products	3	3	2	3	...	...	...	...	...	...	...	...
2693	Struct.non-refractory clay; ceramic products	3	3	4	3	...	...	...	...	...	...	...	...
2694	Cement, lime and plaster	7	8	7	6	...	...	...	...	...	...	...	...
2695	Articles of concrete, cement and plaster	55	67	63	72	...	...	...	...	...	...	...	...
2696	Cutting, shaping & finishing of stone	65	70	80	81	...	...	...	...	...	...	...	...
2699	Other non-metallic mineral products n.e.c.	6	8	7	8	...	...	...	...	...	...	...	...
2710	Basic iron and steel	1	4	4	5	...	...	...	...	...	...	...	...
2720	Basic precious and non-ferrous metals	7	6	6	6	...	...	...	...	...	...	...	...
273	Casting of metals	3	2	5	5	...	...	...	...	...	...	...	...
2731	Casting of iron and steel	3	1	4	5	...	...	...	...	...	...	...	...
2732	Casting of non-ferrous metals	-	1	1	-	...	...	...	...	...	...	...	...
281	Struct.metal products;tanks;steam generators	43	62	76	104	...	...	...	...	...	...	...	...
2811	Structural metal products	40	57	73	102	...	...	...	...	...	...	...	...
2812	Tanks, reservoirs and containers of metal	3	5	3	2	...	...	...	...	...	...	...	...
2813	Steam generators	-	-	-	-	...	...	...	...	...	...	...	...
289	Other metal products; metal working services	47	50	51	57	...	...	...	...	...	...	...	...
2891	Metal forging/pressing/stamping/roll-forming	18	16	16	15	...	...	...	...	...	...	...	...
2892	Treatment & coating of metals	2	3	4	7	...	...	...	...	...	...	...	...
2893	Cutlery, hand tools and general hardware	9	9	9	9	...	...	...	...	...	...	...	...
2899	Other fabricated metal products n.e.c.	18	22	22	26	...	...	...	...	...	...	...	...
291	General purpose machinery	27	24	23	22	...	...	...	...	...	...	...	...
2911	Engines & turbines (not for transport equipment)	7	7	6	5	...	...	...	...	...	...	...	...
2912	Pumps, compressors, taps and valves	6	4	4	4	...	...	...	...	...	...	...	...
2913	Bearings, gears, gearing & driving elements	3	3	3	3	...	...	...	...	...	...	...	...
2914	Ovens, furnaces and furnace burners	2	2	2	2	...	...	...	...	...	...	...	...
2915	Lifting and handling equipment	2	2	1	1	...	...	...	...	...	...	...	...
2919	Other general purpose machinery	7	6	7	7	...	...	...	...	...	...	...	...
292	Special purpose machinery	42	40	42	43	...	...	...	...	...	...	...	...
2921	Agricultural and forestry machinery	1	1	2	2	...	...	...	...	...	...	...	...
2922	Machine tools	23	22	21	21	...	...	...	...	...	...	...	...
2923	Machinery for metallurgy	-	-	-	-	...	...	...	...	...	...	...	...
2924	Machinery for mining & construction	2	1	2	2	...	...	...	...	...	...	...	...
2925	Food/beverage/tobacco processing machinery	2	2	3	3	...	...	...	...	...	...	...	...
2926	Machinery for textile, apparel and leather	1	1	1	1	...	...	...	...	...	...	...	...
2927	Weapons and ammunition	-	-	-	-	...	...	...	...	...	...	...	...
2929	Other special purpose machinery	13	13	13	14	...	...	...	...	...	...	...	...

continued

Armenia

ISIC Revision 3		Number of establishments					Number of employees					Wages and salaries paid to employees				
			(number)					(number)					(millions of Armenian Drams)			
ISIC	Industry	Note	2003	2004	2005	2006	Note	2003	2004	2005	2006	Note	2003	2004	2005	2006
2930	Domestic appliances n.e.c.		21	20	19	19		...	...	...	...		...	...	...	...
3000	Office, accounting and computing machinery		8	7	7	6		...	...	...	...		...	...	...	...
3110	Electric motors, generators and transformers		9	10	11	11		...	...	...	...		...	...	...	...
3120	Electricity distribution & control apparatus		13	15	14	13		...	...	...	...		...	...	...	...
3130	Insulated wire and cable		10	10	8	7		...	...	...	...		...	...	...	...
3140	Accumulators, primary cells and batteries		1	1	1	1		...	...	...	...		...	...	...	...
3150	Lighting equipment and electric lamps		5	5	5	4		...	...	...	...		...	...	...	...
3190	Other electrical equipment n.e.c.		11	12	12	13		...	...	...	...		...	...	...	...
3210	Electronic valves, tubes, etc.		4	4	4	4		...	...	...	...		...	...	...	...
3220	TV/radio transmitters; line comm. apparatus		3	3	2	2		...	...	...	...		...	...	...	...
3230	TV and radio receivers and associated goods		11	8	8	7		...	...	...	...		...	...	...	...
331	Medical, measuring, testing appliances, etc.		25	22	21	19		...	...	...	...		...	...	...	...
3311	Medical, surgical and orthopaedic equipment		6	6	5	5		...	...	...	...		...	...	...	...
3312	Measuring/testing/navigating appliances,etc.		15	12	12	11		...	...	...	...		...	...	...	...
3313	Industrial process control equipment		4	4	4	3		...	...	...	...		...	...	...	...
3320	Optical instruments & photographic equipment		...	1	2	2		...	...	...	...		...	...	...	...
3330	Watches and clocks		7	5	5	5		...	...	...	...		...	...	...	...
3410	Motor vehicles		1	1	1	-		...	...	...	...		...	...	...	...
3420	Automobile bodies, trailers & semi-trailers		-	-	-	-		...	...	...	...		...	...	...	...
3430	Parts/accessories for automobiles		3	1	1	2		...	...	...	...		...	...	...	...
351	Building and repairing of ships and boats		-	-	-	-		...	...	...	...		...	...	...	...
3511	Building and repairing of ships		-	-	-	-		...	...	...	...		...	...	...	...
3512	Building/repairing of pleasure/sport. boats		-	-	-	-		...	...	...	...		...	...	...	...
3520	Railway/tramway locomotives & rolling stock		1	1	1	1		...	...	...	...		...	...	...	...
3530	Aircraft and spacecraft		-	-	-	-		...	...	...	...		...	...	...	...
359	Transport equipment n.e.c.		2	2	2	2		...	...	...	...		...	...	...	...
3591	Motorcycles		-	-	-	-		...	...	...	...		...	...	...	...
3592	Bicycles and invalid carriages		1	1	1	1		...	...	...	...		...	...	...	...
3599	Other transport equipment n.e.c.		1	1	1	1		...	...	...	...		...	...	...	...
3610	Furniture		40	61	87	93		...	...	...	...		...	...	...	...
369	Manufacturing n.e.c.		60	68	64	63		...	...	...	...		...	...	...	...
3691	Jewellery and related articles		37	46	46	44		...	...	...	...		...	...	...	...
3692	Musical instruments		-	-	-	-		...	...	...	...		...	...	...	...
3693	Sports goods		-	1	1	1		...	...	...	...		...	...	...	...
3694	Games and toys		2	1	1	-		...	...	...	...		...	...	...	...
3699	Other manufacturing n.e.c.		21	20	16	18		...	...	...	...		...	...	...	...
3710	Recycling of metal waste and scrap		4	3	3	3		...	...	...	...		...	...	...	...
3720	Recycling of non-metal waste and scrap		-	-	-	-		...	...	...	...		...	...	...	...
D	Total manufacturing		1893	2033	2109	2167		110100	106900	109500	106300		41881	48191	54536	61490

Armenia

ISIC	Industry	Note	Output in producers' prices (millions of Armenian Drams) 2003	2004	2005	2006	Note	Value added (millions of Armenian Drams) 2003	2004	2005	2006	Note	Gross fixed capital formation (millions of Armenian Drams) 2005	2006
151	Processed meat,fish,fruit,vegetables,fats		11028	8956	11195	12599		...	...	...	...		...	...
1511	Processing/preserving of meat		4494	4846	5372	5098		...	...	...	...		...	...
1512	Processing/preserving of fish		187	123	131	21		...	...	...	...		...	...
1513	Processing/preserving of fruit & vegetables		6168	3932	5522	6571		...	...	...	...		...	...
1514	Vegetable and animal oils and fats		179	55	170	909		...	...	...	...		...	...
1520	Dairy products		6274	7818	16588	17975		...	...	...	...		...	...
153	Grain mill products; starches; animal feeds		10615	21162	16660	17303		...	...	...	...		...	...
1531	Grain mill products		10615	21162	16660	17303		...	...	...	...		...	...
1532	Starches and starch products		-	-	-	-		...	...	...	...		...	...
1533	Prepared animal feeds		...	-	-	-		...	...	...	...		...	...
154	Other food products		58842	75470	82112	85364		...	...	...	...		...	...
1541	Bakery products		54442	67816	70796	70666		...	...	...	...		...	...
1542	Sugar		-	143	297	309		...	...	...	...		...	...
1543	Cocoa, chocolate and sugar confectionery		259	254	3592	6166		...	...	...	...		...	...
1544	Macaroni, noodles & similar products		178	727	760	832		...	...	...	...		...	...
1549	Other food products n.e.c.		3963	6530	6667	7391		...	...	...	...		...	...
155	Beverages		59042	53472	58912	56561		...	...	...	...		...	...
1551	Distilling, rectifying & blending of spirits		42787	33322	36868	30701		...	...	...	...		...	...
1552	Wines		4545	7343	8943	10412		...	...	...	...		...	...
1553	Malt liquors and malt		3942	4672	4158	4583		...	...	...	...		...	...
1554	Soft drinks; mineral waters		7768	8135	8943	10865		...	...	...	...		...	...
1600	Tobacco products		14253	14798	15009	14767		...	...	...	...		...	...
171	Spinning, weaving and finishing of textiles		285	189	202	320		...	...	...	...		...	...
1711	Textile fibre preparation; textile weaving		285	189	202	320		...	...	...	...		...	...
1712	Finishing of textiles		-	-	-	-		...	...	...	...		...	...
172	Other textiles		995	1166	1013	1148		...	...	...	...		...	...
1721	Made-up textile articles, except apparel		15	...	...	-		...	...	...	...		...	...
1722	Carpets and rugs		730	998	965	1126		...	...	...	...		...	...
1723	Cordage, rope, twine and netting		-	-	-	-		...	...	...	...		...	...
1729	Other textiles n.e.c.		250	168	48	22		...	...	...	...		...	...
1730	Knitted and crocheted fabrics and articles		971	1544	1085	1312		...	...	...	...		...	...
1810	Wearing apparel, except fur apparel		2154	2184	2074	2307		...	...	...	...		...	...
1820	Dressing & dyeing of fur; processing of fur		47	51	70	35		...	...	...	...		...	...
191	Tanning, dressing and processing of leather		170	119	118	235		...	...	...	...		...	...
1911	Tanning and dressing of leather		92	80	82	84		...	...	...	...		...	...
1912	Luggage, handbags, etc.; saddlery & harness		78	39	36	151		...	...	...	...		...	...
1920	Footwear		181	215	215	283		...	...	...	...		...	...
2010	Sawmilling and planing of wood		903	842	429	417		...	...	...	...		...	...
202	Products of wood, cork, straw, etc.		1030	901	763	1016		...	...	...	...		...	...
2021	Veneer sheets, plywood, particle board, etc.		2	3	14	17		...	...	...	...		...	...
2022	Builders' carpentry and joinery		908	753	597	892		...	...	...	...		...	...
2023	Wooden containers		29	24	37	12		...	...	...	...		...	...
2029	Other wood products; articles of cork/straw		91	121	115	95		...	...	...	...		...	...
210	Paper and paper products		1166	1460	1505	1895		...	...	...	...		...	...
2101	Pulp, paper and paperboard		13	12	28	27		...	...	...	...		...	...
2102	Corrugated paper and paperboard		985	1115	1175	1436		...	...	...	...		...	...
2109	Other articles of paper and paperboard		168	333	302	432		...	...	...	...		...	...
221	Publishing		3428	4267	4951	5127		...	...	...	...		...	...
2211	Publishing of books and other publications		2137	2623	2708	2902		...	...	...	...		...	...
2212	Publishing of newspapers, journals, etc.		989	1284	1826	1729		...	...	...	...		...	...
2213	Publishing of recorded media		35	63	35	46		...	...	...	...		...	...
2219	Other publishing		267	297	382	450		...	...	...	...		...	...

continued

Armenia

ISIC Revision 3		Output in producers' prices					Value added					Gross fixed capital formation		
			(millions of Armenian Drams)					(millions of Armenian Drams)					(millions of Armenian Drams)	
ISIC	Industry	Note	2003	2004	2005	2006	Note	2003	2004	2005	2006	Note	2005	2006
222	Printing and related service activities		2832	2852	3312	4465		...	...	...	...		...	...
2221	Printing		2329	2258	2462	3407		...	...	...	...		...	...
2222	Service activities related to printing		503	594	850	1058		...	...	...	...		...	...
2230	Reproduction of recorded media		...	1	...	37		...	...	...	...		...	...
2310	Coke oven products		-	-	-	-		...	...	...	...		...	...
2320	Refined petroleum products		-	-	-	-		...	...	...	...		...	...
2330	Processing of nuclear fuel		-	-	-	-		...	...	...	...		...	...
241	Basic chemicals		4012	6889	10897	7905		...	...	...	...		...	...
2411	Basic chemicals, except fertilizers		1022	1119	488	720		...	...	...	...		...	...
2412	Fertilizers and nitrogen compounds		17	1	1	1		...	...	...	...		...	...
2413	Plastics in primary forms; synthetic rubber		2973	5769	10408	7184		...	...	...	...		...	...
242	Other chemicals		3028	3662	4744	6588		...	...	...	...		...	...
2421	Pesticides and other agro-chemical products		-	-	-	-		...	...	...	...		...	...
2422	Paints, varnishes, printing ink and mastics		969	1280	2432	3169		...	...	...	...		...	...
2423	Pharmaceuticals, medicinal chemicals, etc.		1683	1909	1875	2318		...	...	...	...		...	...
2424	Soap, cleaning & cosmetic preparations		373	448	429	1029		...	...	...	...		...	...
2429	Other chemical products n.e.c.		3	25	8	72		...	...	...	...		...	...
2430	Man-made fibres		-	-	-	-		...	...	...	...		...	...
251	Rubber products		395	510	479	171		...	...	...	...		...	...
2511	Rubber tyres and tubes		134	217	227	10		...	...	...	...		...	...
2519	Other rubber products		261	293	252	161		...	...	...	...		...	...
2520	Plastic products		1405	2181	3630	3714		...	...	...	...		...	...
2610	Glass and glass products		1069	1204	1717	2169		...	...	...	...		...	...
269	Non-metallic mineral products n.e.c.		12896	16807	22328	29225		...	...	...	...		...	...
2691	Pottery, china and earthenware		204	191	36	48		...	...	...	...		...	...
2692	Refractory ceramic products		26	30	39	77		...	...	...	...		...	...
2693	Struct.non-refractory clay; ceramic products		304	151	297	263		...	...	...	...		...	...
2694	Cement, lime and plaster		7530	10884	14585	19661		...	...	...	...		...	...
2695	Articles of concrete, cement and plaster		3781	4357	5535	7393		...	...	...	...		...	...
2696	Cutting, shaping & finishing of stone		869	1059	1629	1570		...	...	...	...		...	...
2699	Other non-metallic mineral products n.e.c.		182	135	207	213		...	...	...	...		...	...
2710	Basic iron and steel		54	37697	99910	72266		...	...	...	...		...	...
2720	Basic precious and non-ferrous metals		45100	29384	23370	33356		...	...	...	...		...	...
273	Casting of metals		1291	108	2912	3616		...	...	...	...		...	...
2731	Casting of iron and steel		1291	108	2912	3616		...	...	...	...		...	...
2732	Casting of non-ferrous metals		-	...	...	-		...	...	...	...		...	...
281	Struct.metal products;tanks;steam generators		2201	3365	3739	6567		...	...	...	...		...	...
2811	Structural metal products		1813	2469	3689	6567		...	...	...	...		...	...
2812	Tanks, reservoirs and containers of metal		388	896	50	-		...	...	...	...		...	...
2813	Steam generators		-	-	-	-		...	...	...	...		...	...
289	Other metal products; metal working services		1723	1676	2780	3514		...	...	...	...		...	...
2891	Metal forging/pressing/stamping/roll-forming		792	911	1089	791		...	...	...	...		...	...
2892	Treatment & coating of metals		31	40	547	1190		...	...	...	...		...	...
2893	Cutlery, hand tools and general hardware		653	362	358	383		...	...	...	...		...	...
2899	Other fabricated metal products n.e.c.		247	363	786	1150		...	...	...	...		...	...
291	General purpose machinery		1749	1878	1537	1651		...	...	...	...		...	...
2911	Engines & turbines (not for transport equipment)		855	731	1013	1101		...	...	...	...		...	...
2912	Pumps, compressors, taps and valves		130	150	108	257		...	...	...	...		...	...
2913	Bearings, gears, gearing & driving elements		19	23	25	26		...	...	...	...		...	...
2914	Ovens, furnaces and furnace burners		11	11	36	4		...	...	...	...		...	...
2915	Lifting and handling equipment		417	525	...	1		...	...	...	...		...	...
2919	Other general purpose machinery		317	438	355	262		...	...	...	...		...	...

292	Special purpose machinery	3267	4933	4768	5419	...	...	...	...	...	...
2921	Agricultural and forestry machinery	1	1	78	20	...	...	...	...	...	...
2922	Machine tools	1864	2819	3028	2493	...	...	...	...	...	...
2923	Machinery for metallurgy	-	-	-	-	...	...	...	...	...	...
2924	Machinery for mining & construction	17	12	670	858	...	...	...	...	...	...
2925	Food/beverage/tobacco processing machinery	19	22	68	54	...	...	...	...	...	...
2926	Machinery for textile, apparel and leather	7	19	1	-	...	...	...	...	...	...
2927	Weapons and ammunition	-	-	-	-	...	...	...	...	...	...
2929	Other special purpose machinery	1359	2060	923	1994	...	...	...	...	...	...
2930	Domestic appliances n.e.c.	805	708	322	491	...	...	...	...	...	...
3000	Office, accounting and computing machinery	745	1018	695	634	...	...	...	...	...	...
3110	Electric motors, generators and transformers	1213	1353	1291	1973	...	...	...	...	...	...
3120	Electricity distribution & control apparatus	969	1418	1548	1725	...	...	...	...	...	...
3130	Insulated wire and cable	373	355	569	702	...	...	...	...	...	...
3140	Accumulators, primary cells and batteries	119	130	200	-	...	...	...	...	...	...
3150	Lighting equipment and electric lamps	695	688	487	121	...	...	...	...	...	...
3190	Other electrical equipment n.e.c.	496	550	518	583	...	...	...	...	...	...
3210	Electronic valves, tubes, etc.	103	47	59	12	...	...	...	...	...	...
3220	TV/radio transmitters; line comm. apparatus	63	103	130	115	...	...	...	...	...	...
3230	TV and radio receivers and associated goods	660	324	409	559	...	...	...	...	...	...
331	Medical, measuring, testing appliances, etc.	2247	1857	2192	2502	...	...	...	...	...	...
3311	Medical, surgical and orthopaedic equipment	340	498	580	732	...	...	...	...	...	...
3312	Measuring/testing/navigating appliances,etc.	1552	841	1276	1364	...	...	...	...	...	...
3313	Industrial process control equipment	355	518	336	406	...	...	...	...	...	...
3320	Optical instruments & photographic equipment	...	28	51	54	...	...	...	...	...	...
3330	Watches and clocks	818	1265	1013	609	...	...	...	...	...	...
3410	Motor vehicles	10	19	50	-	...	...	...	...	...	...
3420	Automobile bodies, trailers & semi-trailers	-	-	-	-	...	...	...	...	...	...
3430	Parts/accessories for automobiles	...	...	...	52	...	...	...	...	...	...
351	Building and repairing of ships and boats	-	-	-	-	...	...	...	...	...	...
3511	Building and repairing of ships	-	-	-	-	...	...	...	...	...	...
3512	Building/repairing of pleasure/sport. boats	-	-	-	-	...	...	...	...	...	...
3520	Railway/tramway locomotives & rolling stock	143	645	227	230	...	...	...	...	...	...
3530	Aircraft and spacecraft	-	-	-	-	...	...	...	...	...	...
359	Transport equipment n.e.c.	22	20	11	2	...	...	...	...	...	...
3591	Motorcycles	-	-	-	-	...	...	...	...	...	...
3592	Bicycles and invalid carriages	5	3	2	2	...	...	...	...	...	...
3599	Other transport equipment n.e.c.	17	17	9	-	...	...	...	...	...	...
3610	Furniture	1188	1593	2023	2778	...	...	...	...	...	...
369	Manufacturing n.e.c.	22250	16807	13529	6680	...	...	...	...	...	...
3691	Jewellery and related articles	22032	16462	13278	6507	...	...	...	...	...	...
3692	Musical instruments	-	-	-	-	...	...	...	...	...	...
3693	Sports goods	-	174	79	14	...	...	...	...	...	...
3694	Games and toys	2	...	...	-	...	...	...	...	...	...
3699	Other manufacturing n.e.c.	216	171	172	159	...	...	...	...	...	...
3710	Recycling of metal waste and scrap	13	13	15	11	...	...	...	...	...	...
3720	Recycling of non-metal waste and scrap	-	-	-	-	...	...	...	...	...	...
D	Total manufacturing	285338	336704	424363	419161	...	...	...	...	...	...

Austria

Supplier of information:
Statistics Austria, Vienna.
Industrial statistics for the OECD countries are compiled by the OECD secretariat, which supplies them to UNIDO.

Basic source of data:
Structural Census.

Major deviations from ISIC (Revision 3):
None reported.

Reference period:
Calendar year.

Scope:
All enterprises.

Method of data collection:
Not reported.

Type of enumeration:
Not reported.

Adjusted for non-response:
Not reported.

Concepts and definitions of variables:
Number of enterprises refers to the smallest legal unit which may consist of one or more establishments. The definitions correspond to those referred to by the EU-Council regulation on statistical units.
Number of employees refers to persons employed on 31 December.
Wages and salaries includes employers' contributions to social security schemes and pension funds.
Output is gross output valued in producers' prices, including all indirect taxes except value added tax and all subsidies.
Value added is based on the national accounts concept. Input estimates are on a consumed basis.
Gross fixed capital formation is investment expenditure defined as the value of purchases of fixed assets, including own-account construction of assets. The value of sales of fixed assets is not deducted. "Fixed assets" are those with a productive life of at least one year, including assets made by a unit's labour force; additions, alterations, and repairs to existing assets; new assets, whether yet in use or not; and used assets. The valuation is at full cost including delivered price, cost of installation, fees and taxes (except value added tax).

Related national publications:
Structural Census, 1999, published by Statistics Austria, Vienna.

Austria

ISIC Revision 3		Number of enterprises					Number of employees					Wages and salaries paid to employees				
			(number)					(number)					(millions of Euros)			
ISIC	Industry	Note	2002	2003	2004	2005	Note	2002	2003	2004	2005	Note	2002	2003	2004	2005
151	Processed meat,fish,fruit,vegetables,fats		1370	1373	1345	1291		...	...	...	19727		...	...	...	487.0
1511	Processing/preserving of meat		1217	1214	1183	1138		16018	16336	15995	16022		333.6	351.6	349.3	359.0
1512	Processing/preserving of fish		6	5	5	5		216	...	...	265		4.6	...	...	6.0
1513	Processing/preserving of fruit & vegetables		107	116	115	106		3514	3351	3591	2994		111.4	111.3	119.7	106.0
1514	Vegetable and animal oils and fats		40	38	42	42		...	426	446	446		...	15.3	15.3	15.0
1520	Dairy products		133	151	157	169		4561	4632	4671	4673		137.9	141.6	144.5	148.0
153	Grain mill products; starches; animal feeds		207	223	222	206		2561	2573	3123	3084		69.1	67.0	89.2	89.0
1531	Grain mill products		147	158	158	152		...	1204	1276	...		...	32.6	35.9	...
1532	Starches and starch products		2	4	4	3		...	49	530	...		...	0.3	16.8	...
1533	Prepared animal feeds		58	61	60	51		1384	1320	1317	1240		36.4	34.1	36.5	34.0
154	Other food products		2363	2334	2297	2164		36684	36612	36852	36333		762.7	785.9	824.6	823.0
1541	Bakery products		2202	2162	2130	2001		29364	29148	29228	29028		538.5	555.4	562.5	564.0
1542	Sugar		1	1	3	3		...	...	...	...		...	...	...	...
1543	Cocoa, chocolate and sugar confectionery		28	28	29	25		2015	2020	2362	2272		56.1	53.9	98.8	86.0
1544	Macaroni, noodles & similar products		43	49	46	46		433	507	538	579		9.4	11.6	12.3	14.0
1549	Other food products n.e.c.		89	94	89	89		...	...	...	...		...	...	...	...
155	Beverages		292	302	306	304		9135	8861	8564	8414		306.5	312.2	306.7	300.0
1551	Distilling, rectifying & blending of spirits		105	111	109	111		656	661	652	...		14.8	17.0	16.9	...
1552	Wines		61	58	62	63		...	...	...	523		...	...	...	15.0
1553	Malt liquors and malt		53	59	60	60		...	...	...	...		...	...	...	...
1554	Soft drinks; mineral waters		73	74	75	70		3351	3218	3091	3054		105.2	108.1	99.7	101.0
1600	Tobacco products		1	1	1	1		...	...	...	1092		...	...	...	65.0
171	Spinning, weaving and finishing of textiles		169	165	162	161		7537	6699	6332	5766		212.2	180.1	177.0	166.0
1711	Textile fibre preparation; textile weaving		85	80	77	74		5400	4974	4854	4451		146.8	132.4	136.9	129.0
1712	Finishing of textiles		84	85	85	87		2137	1725	1478	1315		65.4	47.7	40.1	37.0
172	Other textiles		615	624	607	557		7826	7593	6936	6414		191.5	188.5	177.8	169.0
1721	Made-up textile articles, except apparel		138	145	137	133		2686	2535	2493	2488		62.7	60.2	59.9	61.0
1722	Carpets and rugs		43	42	36	28		348	362	335	172		8.2	8.7	8.6	4.0
1723	Cordage, rope, twine and netting		21	23	24	24		372	364	367	368		11.2	11.4	11.4	12.0
1729	Other textiles n.e.c.		413	414	410	372		4420	4332	3741	3386		109.4	108.3	97.9	92.0
1730	Knitted and crocheted fabrics and articles		91	85	74	72		3687	3216	2403	2329		93.9	67.9	63.3	63.0
1810	Wearing apparel, except fur apparel		969	951	909	815	a/	9579	8771	7979	7397	a/	180.2	171.1	157.0	150.0
1820	Dressing & dyeing of fur; processing of fur		84	88	86	82	a/	...	...	...	...	a/	...	...	...	...
191	Tanning, dressing and processing of leather		121	115	111	105		...	...	...	2612		...	...	...	56.0
1911	Tanning and dressing of leather		42	43	44	33		2224	2309	2236	2252		38.2	42.8	43.2	47.0
1912	Luggage, handbags, etc.; saddlery & harness		79	72	67	72		...	...	...	360		...	...	...	10.0
1920	Footwear		103	105	101	102		3624	2937	2564	2030		76.1	66.1	65.1	53.0
2010	Sawmilling and planing of wood		1203	1212	1194	1135		9936	10152	10488	10747		237.3	257.9	271.8	294.0
202	Products of wood, cork, straw, etc.		2117	2291	2312	2271		24964	24663	24649	24018		601.1	626.7	655.4	647.0
2021	Veneer sheets, plywood, particle board, etc.		26	28	29	27		4688	4694	4653	4622		153.8	158.5	165.5	171.0
2022	Builders' carpentry and joinery		1515	1678	1707	1729		17640	17495	17433	16839		396.7	416.8	433.0	420.0
2023	Wooden containers		123	127	123	123		886	875	900	924		16.0	17.4	19.0	20.0
2029	Other wood products; articles of cork/straw		453	458	453	392		1750	1599	1663	1633		34.6	34.0	37.9	37.0
210	Paper and paper products		158	151	150	144		17666	17763	17792	17852		646.3	672.2	690.6	694.0
2101	Pulp, paper and paperboard		40	41	37	35		8662	8652	8632	7811		351.9	356.5	361.5	327.0
2102	Corrugated paper and paperboard		71	67	70	67		5639	5600	5593	6471		175.5	183.5	198.0	234.0
2109	Other articles of paper and paperboard		47	43	43	42		3365	3511	3567	3570		118.9	132.2	131.1	133.0
221	Publishing		809	926	949	1034		9133	8892	8761	8252		328.1	336.6	335.2	326.0
2211	Publishing of books and other publications		328	385	402	439		1849	1909	2069	1779		52.8	60.5	65.6	56.0
2212	Publishing of newspapers, journals, etc.		348	382	380	416		7042	6751	6433	6231		268.5	269.7	262.9	264.0
2213	Publishing of recorded media		51	78	90	102		55	41	53	65		2.7	0.9	1.1	1.0
2219	Other publishing		82	81	77	77		187	191	206	177		4.0	5.5	5.5	5.0

222	Printing and related service activities	1088	1095	1070	1032	16066	15196	14572	14270	554.6	533.4	512.7	505.0
2221	Printing	831	827	793	758	13671	13101	12674	12497	486.7	471.1	457.3	452.0
2222	Service activities related to printing	257	268	277	274	2395	2095	1898	1773	67.8	62.4	55.4	52.0
2230	Reproduction of recorded media	17	22	21	19	1456	1351	1381	1369	47.0	46.4	51.0	51.0
2310	Coke oven products	-	-	-	-	-	-	-	-	-	-	-	-
2320	Refined petroleum products	9	7	7	4	...	...	...	...	...	...	...	...
2330	Processing of nuclear fuel	-	-	-	-	-	-	-	-	-	-	-	-
241	Basic chemicals	94	95	86	92	6424	6525	6395	6425	273.7	285.1	292.9	296.0
2411	Basic chemicals, except fertilizers	54	53	49	52	...	...	...	...	...	...	...	...
2412	Fertilizers and nitrogen compounds	10	9	9	9	866	899	873	925	39.3	39.6	42.8	42.0
2413	Plastics in primary forms; synthetic rubber	30	33	28	31	...	...	...	...	...	...	...	...
242	Other chemicals	313	323	329	341	16598	...	17420	17152	619.6	...	668.0	676.0
2421	Pesticides and other agro-chemical products	5	3	7	7	92	...	210	224	4.4	...	9.1	10.0
2422	Paints, varnishes, printing ink and mastics	51	47	48	44	3154	3171	3174	3072	106.7	112.1	117.0	110.0
2423	Pharmaceuticals, medicinal chemicals, etc.	83	92	94	95	9258	9483	9965	9549	364.0	392.2	403.7	406.0
2424	Soap, cleaning & cosmetic preparations	109	109	110	118	2267	2279	2363	2554	74.7	78.5	73.2	81.0
2429	Other chemical products n.e.c.	65	72	70	77	1827	1656	1708	1753	69.8	63.7	65.0	69.0
2430	Man-made fibres	5	5	5	5	2771	...	2789	2763	115.4	...	122.5	125.0
251	Rubber products	48	50	46	48	3794	3283	3274	3267	128.8	111.8	118.8	118.0
2511	Rubber tyres and tubes	10	10	10	10	...	...	...	569	...	...	...	20.0
2519	Other rubber products	38	40	36	38	2617	2619	2623	2698	87.4	89.6	94.2	98.0
2520	Plastic products	563	567	573	577	25134	24046	24261	23941	721.2	714.7	741.6	745.0
2610	Glass and glass products	195	199	205	201	10536	10518	10389	10633	334.8	368.4	336.5	352.0
269	Non-metallic mineral products n.e.c.	1170	1239	1254	1256	24718	24719	24462	23894	820.0	847.0	863.0	849.0
2691	Pottery, china and earthenware	233	254	238	230	...	...	...	...	...	...	...	...
2692	Refractory ceramic products	15	15	14	13	2030	2064	2125	1764	86.1	89.4	95.1	78.0
2693	Struct.non-refractory clay; ceramic products	29	29	29	28	...	...	...	...	...	...	...	...
2694	Cement, lime and plaster	11	12	14	14	...	...	...	...	...	...	...	...
2695	Articles of concrete, cement and plaster	333	348	355	348	11568	11850	11718	11564	384.1	402.1	411.2	409.0
2696	Cutting, shaping & finishing of stone	485	509	530	544	3461	3375	3203	3199	85.2	85.9	84.2	84.0
2699	Other non-metallic mineral products n.e.c.	64	72	74	79	3248	3275	3247	3177	114.7	120.1	121.9	122.0
2710	Basic iron and steel	51	55	55	50	19682	19473	19802	20208	747.4	733.9	777.0	878.0
2720	Basic precious and non-ferrous metals	50	52	52	51	6446	6342	6468	6766	229.2	236.9	244.6	263.0
273	Casting of metals	60	61	59	61	5967	6442	6002	6152	191.6	214.7	208.6	227.0
2731	Casting of iron and steel	20	22	21	21	1581	...	...	...	52.2	...	...	...
2732	Casting of non-ferrous metals	40	39	38	40	4386	...	...	...	139.4	...	...	...
281	Struct.metal products;tanks;steam generators	1188	1236	1262	1317	28665	28266	28153	27780	820.2	849.1	872.6	882.0
2811	Structural metal products	1122	1165	1188	1240	23462	22682	22721	22304	648.5	645.9	669.0	669.0
2812	Tanks, reservoirs and containers of metal	51	55	59	62	3716	3636	3464	3398	124.4	129.7	127.8	131.0
2813	Steam generators	15	16	15	15	1487	1948	1968	2078	47.3	73.5	75.8	82.0
289	Other metal products; metal working services	2510	2724	2783	2819	36740	37536	37984	38985	1049.2	1114.7	1205.7	1231.0
2891	Metal forging/pressing/stamping/roll-forming	570	608	611	604	5379	5658	5797	5879	147.3	173.0	180.6	181.0
2892	Treatment & coating of metals	556	627	674	681	8471	9127	8971	9160	226.9	253.5	267.2	275.0
2893	Cutlery, hand tools and general hardware	870	967	984	1014	13820	14137	14736	15281	413.0	442.6	487.6	509.0
2899	Other fabricated metal products n.e.c.	514	522	514	520	9070	8614	8480	8665	262.0	245.6	270.3	266.0
291	General purpose machinery	795	839	847	875	32791	33183	32029	32374	1123.5	1179.1	1209.3	1247.0
2911	Engines & turbines (not for transport equipment)	22	23	22	23	509	497	617	672	18.8	20.3	26.7	32.0
2912	Pumps, compressors, taps and valves	122	128	128	137	5866	6076	6108	6296	206.6	215.1	230.0	247.0
2913	Bearings, gears, gearing & driving elements	41	45	46	43	2878	2902	3059	3105	98.0	108.1	118.4	125.0
2914	Ovens, furnaces and furnace burners	47	54	49	52	1924	1945	1892	2010	63.0	62.8	70.0	74.0
2915	Lifting and handling equipment	169	181	187	194	10417	10548	10272	10514	395.0	412.2	423.7	429.0
2919	Other general purpose machinery	394	408	415	426	11197	11215	10081	9777	342.1	360.6	340.4	342.0
292	Special purpose machinery	1229	1267	1285	1297	41127	41760	41324	41826	1362.4	1459.1	1535.9	1610.0
2921	Agricultural and forestry machinery	478	476	475	470	6791	7613	6616	6534	186.1	246.2	204.5	208.0
2922	Machine tools	154	179	188	205	6892	6624	6671	6907	225.3	216.3	241.5	260.0
2923	Machinery for metallurgy	13	17	20	17	455	523	815	748	17.2	20.5	33.0	30.0
2924	Machinery for mining & construction	69	77	76	75	3998	4109	4220	4299	140.7	146.9	164.5	171.0
2925	Food/beverage/tobacco processing machinery	112	105	108	109	2003	1871	1914	1868	65.3	63.5	65.5	66.0
2926	Machinery for textile, apparel and leather	36	37	40	35	1541	1491	1499	1472	53.8	56.0	60.9	63.0
2927	Weapons and ammunition	38	41	39	39	1248	1198	1108	1107	42.6	45.7	42.9	43.0
2929	Other special purpose machinery	329	335	339	347	18199	18331	18481	18891	631.4	664.0	723.0	769.0

continued

Austria

ISIC Revision 3		Number of enterprises					Number of employees					Wages and salaries paid to employees				
			(number)					(number)					(millions of Euros)			
ISIC	Industry	Note	2002	2003	2004	2005	Note	2002	2003	2004	2005	Note	2002	2003	2004	2005
2930	Domestic appliances n.e.c.		100	109	101	101		4499	4343	4235	4041		123.4	123.6	129.3	129.0
3000	Office, accounting and computing machinery		54	65	67	64		1333	1336	1209	1196		35.2	43.0	36.1	40.0
3110	Electric motors, generators and transformers		119	120	130	138		7411	6044	6988	7096		270.5	228.7	279.6	289.0
3120	Electricity distribution & control apparatus		165	183	173	170		8433	8514	8248	8200		275.8	282.4	275.1	288.0
3130	Insulated wire and cable		25	23	23	23		1980	1647	1516	1465		60.2	50.0	48.3	48.0
3140	Accumulators, primary cells and batteries		7	9	9	11		672	734	659	412		22.9	27.3	28.1	16.0
3150	Lighting equipment and electric lamps		86	92	92	92		2656	2628	2546	2615		87.2	86.8	83.0	88.0
3190	Other electrical equipment n.e.c.		136	141	142	150		7165	7480	6954	7275		223.0	246.4	212.6	242.0
3210	Electronic valves, tubes, etc.		81	83	86	88		10253	9506	9833	9994		357.5	348.4	392.4	414.0
3220	TV/radio transmitters; line comm. apparatus		58	69	77	91		14023	14487	14000	13930		731.4	793.9	768.7	789.0
3230	TV and radio receivers and associated goods		56	59	58	55		2802	1577	1580	1481		99.5	55.8	56.5	56.0
331	Medical, measuring, testing appliances, etc.		1088	1142	1197	1241		11495	11981	12376	12574		297.6	347.4	363.4	394.0
3311	Medical, surgical and orthopaedic equipment		800	836	876	896		6335	6622	6986	6976		137.0	167.0	170.0	182.0
3312	Measuring/testing/navigating appliances,etc.		260	268	282	287		4357	4342	4446	4648		130.0	139.0	152.0	166.0
3313	Industrial process control equipment		28	38	39	58		803	1017	944	950		31.0	42.0	41.0	45.0
3320	Optical instruments & photographic equipment		160	164	167	159		3088	3011	2535	2408		84.9	97.0	84.8	82.0
3330	Watches and clocks		33	41	43	43		128	131	131	115		4.2	4.2	4.0	4.0
3410	Motor vehicles		26	29	26	28		14587	15471	16987	16744		570.3	622.3	682.9	661.0
3420	Automobile bodies, trailers & semi-trailers		143	159	168	161		3045	3005	2971	3088		77.5	82.2	85.6	89.0
3430	Parts/accessories for automobiles		68	75	77	78		10512	10969	13121	13325		328.4	358.8	436.3	467.0
351	Building and repairing of ships and boats		48	54	52	56		342	360	342	347		9.5	9.4	9.0	9.0
3511	Building and repairing of ships		6	8	6	6		105	120	102	102		3.8	4.2	3.7	4.0
3512	Building/repairing of pleasure/sport. boats		42	46	46	50		237	240	240	245		5.7	5.2	5.3	6.0
3520	Railway/tramway locomotives & rolling stock		9	10	10	10		4640	4943	4929	...		204.6	234.8	234.2	...
3530	Aircraft and spacecraft		30	36	40	39		352	374	420	560		11.5	13.0	12.9	18.0
359	Transport equipment n.e.c.		9	14	13	16		1018	1223	1368	...		27.1	34.5	40.1	...
3591	Motorcycles		2	4	3	5		...	...	...	...		...	...	...	...
3592	Bicycles and invalid carriages		7	10	10	10		...	...	...	...		...	...	...	...
3599	Other transport equipment n.e.c.		-	-	-	1		-	-	-	...		-	-	-	...
3610	Furniture		3656	3697	3675	3655		33106	31577	31100	29840		687.6	700.1	722.3	715.0
369	Manufacturing n.e.c.		1112	1152	1133	1105		11091	10511	10220	9592		290.2	287.0	294.6	296.0
3691	Jewellery and related articles		454	446	435	428		891	787	794	804		21.3	20.9	21.2	21.0
3692	Musical instruments		209	231	234	229		760	772	733	713		17.2	19.7	18.7	19.0
3693	Sports goods		67	78	82	85		4642	4396	4336	4378		135.9	135.2	139.4	150.0
3694	Games and toys		98	111	109	102		2018	2009	1967	1530		52.5	52.9	58.0	52.0
3699	Other manufacturing n.e.c.		284	286	273	261		2780	2547	2390	2167		63.3	58.3	57.3	55.0
3710	Recycling of metal waste and scrap		62	66	68	70		538	452	461	500		16.0	13.2	14.0	16.0
3720	Recycling of non-metal waste and scrap		51	56	60	72		438	497	522	523		11.1	12.9	14.1	15.0
D	Total manufacturing		27572	28581	28609	28374		609318	601612	598730	598185		18716.1	19251.3	19756.4	20300.0

a/ 1810 includes 1820.

Austria

ISIC Revision 3		Output					Value added in factor values					Gross fixed capital formation		
			(millions of Euros)					(millions of Euros)					(millions of Euros)	
ISIC	Industry	Note	2002	2003	2004	2005	Note	2002	2003	2004	2005	Note	2004	2005
151	Processed meat,fish,fruit,vegetables,fats		...	...	...	3941		...	...	...	1021		...	131
1511	Processing/preserving of meat		2404	2456	2482	2665		642	698	666	672		94	99
1512	Processing/preserving of fish		25	...	...	35		10	...	...	15		...	2
1513	Processing/preserving of fruit & vegetables		1089	1144	1110	1064		315	318	294	299		38	26
1514	Vegetable and animal oils and fats		...	153	167	178		...	28	28	35		4	4
1520	Dairy products		1639	1719	1746	1774		246	318	322	335		73	59
153	Grain mill products; starches; animal feeds		606	619	819	804		144	155	206	209		41	40
1531	Grain mill products		...	281	295	...		...	74	75	...		15	...
1532	Starches and starch products		...	1	153	...		...	-	38	...		6	...
1533	Prepared animal feeds		348	336	372	347		71	81	93	90		20	15
154	Other food products		3252	3370	3645	3459		1420	1499	1548	1453		217	175
1541	Bakery products		1706	1747	1771	1813		948	982	974	970		151	126
1542	Sugar		...	...	...	...		...	...	...	...		...	...
1543	Cocoa, chocolate and sugar confectionery		336	344	676	509		100	109	209	160		21	15
1544	Macaroni, noodles & similar products		55	67	72	80		21	30	28	31		5	4
1549	Other food products n.e.c.		...	...	...	...		...	...	...	...		...	...
155	Beverages		1920	1934	1883	1906		695	721	692	696		133	136
1551	Distilling, rectifying & blending of spirits		143	141	129	...		32	35	35	...		5	...
1552	Wines		...	...	...	112		...	...	...	32		...	9
1553	Malt liquors and malt		...	...	...	...		...	...	...	...		...	...
1554	Soft drinks; mineral waters		729	712	691	727		251	251	245	230		36	60
1600	Tobacco products		...	...	...	320		...	...	...	74		...	17
171	Spinning, weaving and finishing of textiles		975	854	891	791		348	309	290	246		31	27
1711	Textile fibre preparation; textile weaving		756	690	754	665		252	239	231	195		29	24
1712	Finishing of textiles		219	164	137	127		97	70	59	51		2	4
172	Other textiles		978	991	895	839		401	376	356	335		29	34
1721	Made-up textile articles, except apparel		319	345	337	339		110	103	114	105		7	10
1722	Carpets and rugs		43	45	44	12		15	16	14	6		1	1
1723	Cordage, rope, twine and netting		61	63	64	69		20	22	26	25		1	2
1729	Other textiles n.e.c.		555	539	449	419		256	235	202	199		19	21
1730	Knitted and crocheted fabrics and articles		630	343	247	236		156	117	101	99		5	4
1810	Wearing apparel, except fur apparel	a/	824	799	755	723	a/	286	257	273	283	a/	13	8
1820	Dressing & dyeing of fur; processing of fur	a/	...	...	...	...	a/	...	...	...	...	a/	...	...
191	Tanning, dressing and processing of leather		...	...	...	410		...	...	...	97		...	5
1911	Tanning and dressing of leather		434	450	444	369		62	78	93	81		15	4
1912	Luggage, handbags, etc.; saddlery & harness		...	...	...	42		...	...	...	16		...	1
1920	Footwear		387	315	331	325		144	118	120	112		5	4
2010	Sawmilling and planing of wood		2224	2371	2555	2602		607	609	646	631		176	137
202	Products of wood, cork, straw, etc.		3063	3248	3443	3501		1112	1147	1210	1194		146	191
2021	Veneer sheets, plywood, particle board, etc.		1035	1105	1211	1327		287	285	317	358		41	86
2022	Builders' carpentry and joinery		1789	1921	1988	1923		711	767	791	732		91	93
2023	Wooden containers		84	82	90	100		34	30	33	39		3	4
2029	Other wood products; articles of cork/straw		156	140	155	151		81	66	69	65		11	9
210	Paper and paper products		4960	4790	4847	5001		1756	1633	1597	1572		402	279
2101	Pulp, paper and paperboard		3252	3055	3089	2972		1049	954	902	804		285	154
2102	Corrugated paper and paperboard		1075	1076	1101	1330		436	397	412	478		65	75
2109	Other articles of paper and paperboard		633	659	657	699		271	281	284	291		52	50
221	Publishing		1784	1906	1900	1928		613	657	657	695		20	35
2211	Publishing of books and other publications		248	284	311	303		94	120	141	151		4	7
2212	Publishing of newspapers, journals, etc.		1472	1581	1545	1580		506	521	501	528		15	27
2213	Publishing of recorded media		36	11	13	14		4	4	4	5		-	-
2219	Other publishing		29	31	31	31		10	12	11	11		1	1

continued

Austria

ISIC Revision 3		Output					Value added in factor values					Gross fixed capital formation		
			(millions of Euros)					(millions of Euros)					(millions of Euros)	
ISIC	Industry	Note	2002	2003	2004	2005	Note	2002	2003	2004	2005	Note	2004	2005
222	Printing and related service activities		2066	2020	2017	2001		974	934	923	923		108	94
2221	Printing		1873	1838	1849	1840		862	825	826	832		96	85
2222	Service activities related to printing		193	182	168	160		113	109	97	91		11	9
2230	Reproduction of recorded media		437	502	491	468		216	245	244	217		20	11
2310	Coke oven products		-	-	-	-		-	-	-	-		-	-
2320	Refined petroleum products		...	...	...	...		...	...	...	...		...	...
2330	Processing of nuclear fuel		-	-	-	-		-	-	-	-		-	-
241	Basic chemicals		2593	2578	2818	2967		734	703	721	698		102	146
2411	Basic chemicals, except fertilizers		...	...	...	...		...	...	...	...		...	...
2412	Fertilizers and nitrogen compounds		320	342	327	380		119	122	101	110		15	18
2413	Plastics in primary forms; synthetic rubber		...	...	...	...		...	...	...	...		...	...
242	Other chemicals		3482	...	3590	3957		1332	...	1501	1839		225	148
2421	Pesticides and other agro-chemical products		54	...	83	119		17	...	31	60		4	3
2422	Paints, varnishes, printing ink and mastics		494	509	534	512		175	185	204	204		16	15
2423	Pharmaceuticals, medicinal chemicals, etc.		2134	2335	2084	2369		855	1077	925	1217		172	94
2424	Soap, cleaning & cosmetic preparations		410	461	479	511		135	139	191	198		17	19
2429	Other chemical products n.e.c.		390	377	410	446		149	147	150	159		17	18
2430	Man-made fibres		614	...	635	661		255	...	254	267		133	65
251	Rubber products		568	553	587	619		256	243	238	232		19	31
2511	Rubber tyres and tubes		...	...	...	169		...	...	...	42		...	1
2519	Other rubber products		389	401	436	450		193	194	193	190		16	30
2520	Plastic products		3665	3404	3662	3667		1413	1356	1441	1400		217	241
2610	Glass and glass products		1217	1202	1270	1380		674	703	749	846		83	140
269	Non-metallic mineral products n.e.c.		3776	4007	4195	4274		1575	1676	1718	1689		249	247
2691	Pottery, china and earthenware		...	...	...	...		...	...	...	...		...	...
2692	Refractory ceramic products		349	385	382	314		159	184	173	121		11	15
2693	Struct.non-refractory clay; ceramic products		...	...	...	...		...	...	...	...		...	...
2694	Cement, lime and plaster		...	...	...	...		...	...	...	...		...	...
2695	Articles of concrete, cement and plaster		1868	2005	2114	2187		717	763	786	801		151	133
2696	Cutting, shaping & finishing of stone		290	300	303	302		148	149	154	155		11	12
2699	Other non-metallic mineral products n.e.c.		610	643	683	718		236	253	271	295		23	25
2710	Basic iron and steel		4444	4600	5552	7477		1527	1546	1809	2323		401	418
2720	Basic precious and non-ferrous metals		2167	2114	2263	2708		489	468	511	646		66	109
273	Casting of metals		794	883	903	956		326	364	357	367		66	60
2731	Casting of iron and steel		217	...	...	...		87	...	...	...		...	...
2732	Casting of non-ferrous metals		577	...	...	...		240	...	...	...		...	...
281	Struct.metal products;tanks;steam generators		3557	3730	3889	3999		1479	1540	1590	1491		139	141
2811	Structural metal products		2957	2969	3042	3106		1214	1248	1245	1163		117	112
2812	Tanks, reservoirs and containers of metal		441	470	496	568		203	202	217	231		18	18
2813	Steam generators		160	291	352	326		62	90	128	97		4	11
289	Other metal products; metal working services		4570	4900	5209	5618		2096	2235	2390	2486		333	334
2891	Metal forging/pressing/stamping/roll-forming		669	860	947	1027		281	397	337	352		56	57
2892	Treatment & coating of metals		1031	1165	1023	1066		448	508	516	524		78	74
2893	Cutlery, hand tools and general hardware		1640	1691	1906	2194		856	847	979	1101		145	152
2899	Other fabricated metal products n.e.c.		1229	1185	1334	1330		511	482	558	509		55	51
291	General purpose machinery		5220	5404	5644	6299		2120	2250	2205	2416		168	183
2911	Engines & turbines (not for transport equipment)		63	78	123	171		38	45	50	54		4	7
2912	Pumps, compressors, taps and valves		801	924	1018	1112		355	426	427	449		53	53
2913	Bearings, gears, gearing & driving elements		452	461	549	610		230	210	254	286		32	38
2914	Ovens, furnaces and furnace burners		260	275	316	404		110	123	127	163		9	11
2915	Lifting and handling equipment		2071	2031	2208	2550		746	789	769	887		31	41
2919	Other general purpose machinery		1574	1634	1432	1451		641	657	579	578		39	34

292	Special purpose machinery	6319	6951	7218	7880	2416	2519	2568	2916	296	270
2921	Agricultural and forestry machinery	1173	1407	1203	1276	344	353	391	405	32	27
2922	Machine tools	913	903	973	1125	381	379	413	472	51	59
2923	Machinery for metallurgy	59	67	110	106	29	35	57	53	4	7
2924	Machinery for mining & construction	708	792	924	1025	273	301	294	345	44	39
2925	Food/beverage/tobacco processing machinery	271	294	250	279	124	139	107	126	8	6
2926	Machinery for textile, apparel and leather	156	183	194	201	74	83	92	98	5	5
2927	Weapons and ammunition	238	263	261	251	75	58	82	103	10	24
2929	Other special purpose machinery	2802	3044	3305	3616	1116	1170	1132	1314	142	104
2930	Domestic appliances n.e.c.	606	677	653	711	244	301	262	296	28	34
3000	Office, accounting and computing machinery	764	726	576	292	107	57	42	73	3	2
3110	Electric motors, generators and transformers	1283	1319	1634	1903	332	346	489	506	34	40
3120	Electricity distribution & control apparatus	1090	1241	1225	1314	463	486	516	540	36	37
3130	Insulated wire and cable	290	272	299	341	88	83	85	93	6	9
3140	Accumulators, primary cells and batteries	129	134	134	87	54	58	56	28	4	3
3150	Lighting equipment and electric lamps	310	303	306	305	134	145	145	135	8	9
3190	Other electrical equipment n.e.c.	1332	1359	1331	1452	630	603	512	519	56	55
3210	Electronic valves, tubes, etc.	1830	1720	1931	2013	731	747	870	840	141	173
3220	TV/radio transmitters; line comm. apparatus	3034	2908	3329	3498	1053	1085	1297	1429	136	71
3230	TV and radio receivers and associated goods	671	216	249	212	164	93	90	90	15	6
331	Medical, measuring, testing appliances, etc.	1107	1274	1417	1493	574	660	728	804	41	53
3311	Medical, surgical and orthopaedic equipment	470	549	672	718	285	323	369	422	19	20
3312	Measuring/testing/navigating appliances,etc.	529	583	615	657	242	262	284	324	20	32
3313	Industrial process control equipment	109	142	130	117	47	75	75	57	2	2
3320	Optical instruments & photographic equipment	377	397	374	335	196	215	211	178	17	17
3330	Watches and clocks	15	15	16	16	7	7	8	7	-	-
3410	Motor vehicles	6378	6929	9454	9845	1316	1411	1570	1788	285	280
3420	Automobile bodies, trailers & semi-trailers	401	403	437	480	154	133	147	151	16	15
3430	Parts/accessories for automobiles	2541	2506	3555	3779	766	774	1050	1108	281	167
351	Building and repairing of ships and boats	44	42	37	41	25	21	19	18	1	1
3511	Building and repairing of ships	13	14	11	13	6	9	6	6	-	-
3512	Building/repairing of pleasure/sport. boats	31	27	26	28	19	13	13	13	1	1
3520	Railway/tramway locomotives & rolling stock	1738	1886	1815	...	365	415	203	...	23	...
3530	Aircraft and spacecraft	45	38	55	96	19	18	22	42	4	3
359	Transport equipment n.e.c.	334	428	476	...	89	79	95	...	16	...
3591	Motorcycles	...	...	...	...	...	...	...	...	...	...
3592	Bicycles and invalid carriages	...	...	...	...	...	...	...	...	...	...
3599	Other transport equipment n.e.c.	-	-	-	...	-	-	-	...	-	...
3610	Furniture	2540	2457	2810	2814	1243	1124	1158	1171	94	85
369	Manufacturing n.e.c.	1854	1575	1604	1658	856	556	581	620	71	76
3691	Jewellery and related articles	536	271	236	219	330	58	36	57	10	4
3692	Musical instruments	60	59	64	54	36	35	37	30	3	1
3693	Sports goods	704	696	755	729	251	240	266	246	31	30
3694	Games and toys	284	338	340	442	114	128	135	179	21	32
3699	Other manufacturing n.e.c.	270	211	210	214	125	95	107	109	7	8
3710	Recycling of metal waste and scrap	144	143	203	211	41	45	54	54	9	11
3720	Recycling of non-metal waste and scrap	64	71	89	103	24	31	39	40	7	8
D	Total manufacturing	107073	108581	117393	124492	37516	37876	39364	41601	5613	5318

a/ 1810 includes 1820.

Austria

ISIC Revision 3			Index numbers of industrial production											
			(2000=100)											
ISIC	Industry	Note	1995	1996	1997	1998	1999	2000	2001	2002	2003	2004	2005	2006
15	Food and beverages		83	83	90	94	97	100	101	103	103	104	107	112
16	Tobacco products		68	77	80	88	95	100	109	142	153	152	144	147
17	Textiles		100	98	103	106	100	100	97	100	99	87	80	80
18	Wearing apparel, fur		164	145	128	129	111	100	89	87	88	86	82	87
19	Leather, leather products and footwear		100	92	97	100	99	100	111	97	87	89	93	68
20	Wood products (excl. furniture)		70	72	80	84	92	100	100	101	111	119	124	136
21	Paper and paper products		85	80	87	90	94	100	98	102	104	112	112	116
22	Printing and publishing		70	75	78	90	95	100	102	102	108	109	111	116
23	Coke,refined petroleum products,nuclear fuel		90	94	96	96	90	100	104	67	69	89	93	108
24	Chemicals and chemical products		76	76	78	87	94	100	105	111	115	117	131	138
25	Rubber and plastics products		79	79	81	88	91	100	103	101	102	104	105	114
26	Non-metallic mineral products		97	95	98	97	98	100	104	102	106	109	109	114
27	Basic metals		79	76	88	91	90	100	106	107	108	117	122	131
28	Fabricated metal products		73	71	82	90	95	100	105	104	114	128	137	152
29	Machinery and equipment n.e.c.		73	77	78	88	91	100	105	112	113	125	133	152
30	Office, accounting and computing machinery		21	23	25	31	65	100	163	174	178	162	102	82
31	Electrical machinery and apparatus		36	40	44	62	78	100	96	99	100	104	116	126
32	Radio,television and communication equipment		74	74	77	81	86	100	89	78	71	82	89	90
33	Medical, precision and optical instruments		59	61	69	75	93	100	105	110	106	114	118	124
34	Motor vehicles, trailers, semi-trailers		51	54	64	72	84	100	106	101	105	134	138	146
35	Other transport equipment		83	76	80	103	105	100	103	137	173	160	169	169
36	Furniture; manufacturing n.e.c.		76	77	81	84	86	100	102	95	92	97	96	104
37	Recycling		94	95	85	122	104	100	81	124	100	134	153	206
D	Total manufacturing		73	73	79	86	91	100	102	102	104	112	117	125

Azerbaijan

Supplier of information:
State Statistical Committee of the Republic of Azerbaijan, Baku.

Basic source of data:
Annual survey.

Major deviations from ISIC (Revision 3):
None reported.

Reference period:
Calendar year.

Scope:
All enterprises.

Method of data collection:
Mail questionnaires.

Type of enumeration:
Complete enumeration.

Adjusted for non-response:
No.

Concepts and definitions of variables:
Wages and salaries excludes housing and family allowances paid directly by the employer and payments in kind.

Related national publications:
Statistical Yearbook "Industry of Azerbaijan", published by State Statistical Committee of the Republic of Azerbaijan, Baku.

ISIC Revision 3		Number of enterprises					Number of employees					Wages and salaries paid to employees				
			(number)					(number)					(thousands of Azerbaijan Manats)			
ISIC	Industry	Note	2003	2004	2005	2006	Note	2003	2004	2005	2006	Note	2003	2004	2005	2006
151	Processed meat,fish,fruit,vegetables,fats		116	111	109	108		3100	3360	3956	3499		1048	1322	2420	2727
1511	Processing/preserving of meat		43	40	35	30		566	634	746	606		95	174	551	397
1512	Processing/preserving of fish		12	12	14	12		967	989	1047	769		336	339	579	524
1513	Processing/preserving of fruit & vegetables		55	53	54	60		999	1130	1579	1511		305	433	879	1153
1514	Vegetable and animal oils and fats		6	6	6	6		568	607	584	613		311	376	411	653
1520	Dairy products		45	60	48	31		523	570	718	860		83	334	379	595
153	Grain mill products; starches; animal feeds		91	93	91	84		2155	2467	2282	2118		475	772	1169	1312
1531	Grain mill products		88	91	89	82		2026	2419	2264	2111		469	759	1158	1310
1532	Starches and starch products	a/	3	2	2	2	a/	129	48	18	7	a/	6	13	11	2
1533	Prepared animal feeds	a/	...	...	...	...	a/	...	...	...	...	a/	...	...	...	...
154	Other food products		266	264	288	268		3172	5009	6027	7323		745	1553	2710	4641
1541	Bakery products		212	220	242	221		2243	3538	3892	4354		423	1068	1766	2915
1542	Sugar		14	9	7	8		85	158	352	646		59	123	275	582
1543	Cocoa, chocolate and sugar confectionery		20	16	19	18		423	727	1273	1519		89	139	383	606
1544	Macaroni, noodles & similar products		4	7	7	8		54	100	119	244		9	25	58	164
1549	Other food products n.e.c.		16	12	13	13		367	486	391	560		165	198	228	376
155	Beverages		110	108	108	105		3358	4120	4310	4755		3305	4403	5821	7773
1551	Distilling, rectifying & blending of spirits		6	7	5	6		757	767	930	1050		230	249	468	620
1552	Wines		29	24	24	24		1316	1349	1479	1517		936	1090	1336	1549
1553	Malt liquors and malt		12	12	13	14		269	377	426	511		896	1198	1773	2421
1554	Soft drinks; mineral waters		63	65	66	61		1016	1627	1475	1677		1243	1866	2244	3182
1600	Tobacco products		10	11	12	11		1108	1131	1165	1132		1858	1947	2198	2306
171	Spinning, weaving and finishing of textiles		54	43	40	41		6484	6431	7045	7597		1479	2296	3788	5314
1711	Textile fibre preparation; textile weaving		54	43	40	41		6484	6431	7045	7597		1479	2296	3788	5314
1712	Finishing of textiles		-	-	-	-		-	-	-	-		-	-	-	-
172	Other textiles		41	41	48	50		3267	3453	2989	2880		168	241	278	453
1721	Made-up textile articles, except apparel		15	12	13	13		301	379	184	152		30	48	49	85
1722	Carpets and rugs		20	23	29	30		2861	2997	2720	2495		121	174	200	259
1723	Cordage, rope, twine and netting		1	1	2	1		7	11	5	11		1	4	5	5
1729	Other textiles n.e.c.		5	5	4	6		98	66	80	222		16	15	24	103
1730	Knitted and crocheted fabrics and articles		29	28	30	30		1039	943	784	626		416	323	481	344
1810	Wearing apparel, except fur apparel		69	62	67	75		2235	2096	2088	2073		553	413	756	1011
1820	Dressing & dyeing of fur; processing of fur		2	2	2	-		205	10	5	-		63	1	...	-
191	Tanning, dressing and processing of leather		10	10	13	13		906	693	582	437		61	202	342	191
1911	Tanning and dressing of leather		8	7	10	10		713	638	517	378		51	185	312	164
1912	Luggage, handbags, etc.; saddlery & harness		2	3	3	3		193	55	65	59		10	17	30	27
1920	Footwear		16	15	16	17		547	450	438	496		158	167	196	337
2010	Sawmilling and planing of wood		8	9	7	7		136	177	127	147		24	64	62	109
202	Products of wood, cork, straw, etc.		63	58	67	70		843	1290	1048	1346		151	326	656	1230
2021	Veneer sheets, plywood, particle board, etc.		1	1	1	2		151	150	6	6		4	8	1	3
2022	Builders' carpentry and joinery		49	50	57	59		605	1032	927	1001		135	285	584	682
2023	Wooden containers		4	2	3	3		38	63	16	109		1	23	5	288
2029	Other wood products; articles of cork/straw		9	5	6	6		49	45	99	230		10	10	66	257
210	Paper and paper products		13	13	14	17		208	203	275	318		68	92	138	289
2101	Pulp, paper and paperboard		1	-	...	...		24	-	1	3		8	-	...	2
2102	Corrugated paper and paperboard		6	6	...	...		109	124	154	164		52	77	...	210
2109	Other articles of paper and paperboard		6	7	...	...		75	79	120	151		9	15	...	77
221	Publishing		42	45	51	49		823	886	717	738		451	515	595	632
2211	Publishing of books and other publications		18	17	22	21		427	403	462	460		356	379	510	478
2212	Publishing of newspapers, journals, etc.		16	16	16	14		328	415	185	153		67	112	65	88
2213	Publishing of recorded media		-	2	1	1		-	9	1	5		-	8	...	2
2219	Other publishing		8	10	12	13		68	59	69	120		29	16	20	58

222	Printing and related service activities	93	103	122	131	1151	1307	1338	1469	532	838	1065	1451
2221	Printing	82	86	101	108	1041	1178	1179	1299	487	774	960	1318
2222	Service activities related to printing	11	17	21	23	110	129	159	170	45	64	105	132
2230	Reproduction of recorded media	4	3	6	8	62	74	68	95	15	23	37	61
2310	Coke oven products	-	-	-	-	-	-	-	-	-	-	-	-
2320	Refined petroleum products	9	7	7	5	6430	6748	6724	6508	7635	9971	12705	18074
2330	Processing of nuclear fuel	-	-	-	-	-	-	-	-	-	-	-	-
241	Basic chemicals	41	38	45	45	8514	8607	8152	7937	8166	10245	11408	14981
2411	Basic chemicals, except fertilizers	30	27	33	33	3241	3552	3419	2931	3483	4384	5223	5594
2412	Fertilizers and nitrogen compounds	1	1	1	1	446	409	376	346	185	214	249	273
2413	Plastics in primary forms; synthetic rubber	10	10	11	11	4827	4646	4357	4660	4498	5647	5936	9114
242	Other chemicals	51	53	59	60	2966	2798	2868	2928	1316	1673	2188	3251
2421	Pesticides and other agro-chemical products	1	1	1	2	33	34	32	33	8	15	18	23
2422	Paints, varnishes, printing ink and mastics	21	22	25	22	174	223	233	260	51	79	110	146
2423	Pharmaceuticals, medicinal chemicals, etc.	7	7	9	10	182	198	164	204	50	59	64	99
2424	Soap, cleaning & cosmetic preparations	16	17	18	21	807	809	800	786	102	145	310	324
2429	Other chemical products n.e.c.	6	6	6	5	1770	1534	1639	1645	1105	1375	1686	2659
2430	Man-made fibres	-	-	-	-	-	-	-	-	-	-	-	-
251	Rubber products	6	10	6	8	289	293	269	237	84	132	157	230
2511	Rubber tyres and tubes	1	5	1	1	92	97	71	60	31	49	57	146
2519	Other rubber products	5	5	5	7	197	196	198	177	53	83	100	84
2520	Plastic products	69	72	81	82	962	1338	1525	1638	235	654	906	1398
2610	Glass and glass products	25	22	22	24	787	743	764	785	183	211	310	385
269	Non-metallic mineral products n.e.c.	165	186	205	229	4530	5178	5830	5931	5257	6409	7832	10198
2691	Pottery, china and earthenware	7	6	7	7	954	908	926	119	38	37	86	72
2692	Refractory ceramic products	-	1	1	2	-	16	11	97	-	8	2	36
2693	Struct.non-refractory clay; ceramic products	23	35	30	37	836	1154	1405	1900	277	513	944	1373
2694	Cement, lime and plaster	13	16	23	27	688	848	994	1230	3802	4446	4611	5931
2695	Articles of concrete, cement and plaster	68	73	81	95	1582	1767	1957	2037	1056	1273	1761	2420
2696	Cutting, shaping & finishing of stone	52	53	61	59	443	472	459	514	74	127	278	326
2699	Other non-metallic mineral products n.e.c.	2	2	2	2	27	13	78	34	10	5	150	39
2710	Basic iron and steel	9	11	10	12	4841	4743	4971	4805	5654	7791	9640	10800
2720	Basic precious and non-ferrous metals	10	12	13	13	3808	3816	3441	3689	3992	5277	6305	9028
273	Casting of metals	8	9	11	11	385	827	1294	1346	135	390	767	1286
2731	Casting of iron and steel	5	6	7	7	326	776	1269	1276	125	380	759	1193
2732	Casting of non-ferrous metals	3	3	4	4	59	51	25	70	10	10	8	93
281	Struct.metal products;tanks;steam generators	54	47	47	53	2062	2223	2225	2350	2189	2302	3114	5389
2811	Structural metal products	50	43	44	47	2051	2196	2191	2312	2188	2289	3082	5358
2812	Tanks, reservoirs and containers of metal	4	4	3	6	11	27	34	38	1	13	32	32
2813	Steam generators	-	-	-	-	-	-	-	-	-	-	-	-
289	Other metal products; metal working services	28	24	28	31	1169	1488	1522	1543	5845	5119	3785	3568
2891	Metal forging/pressing/stamping/roll-forming	6	6	7	8	470	608	868	866	188	215	500	730
2892	Treatment & coating of metals	7	4	5	6	348	345	233	193	5527	4744	2942	2393
2893	Cutlery, hand tools and general hardware	3	3	3	3	141	169	160	139	43	67	87	130
2899	Other fabricated metal products n.e.c.	12	11	13	14	210	366	261	345	87	93	256	315
291	General purpose machinery	36	34	35	44	4482	5186	4807	4889	2642	4111	4902	6471
2911	Engines & turbines (not for transport equipment)	3	3	3	5	758	789	733	709	82	148	190	239
2912	Pumps, compressors, taps and valves	13	14	14	18	2193	2880	2359	2438	1313	2320	2502	3387
2913	Bearings, gears, gearing & driving elements	1	1	1	1	110	167	108	112	80	94	110	147
2914	Ovens, furnaces and furnace burners	2	2	1	2	211	30	151	97	26	56	315	384
2915	Lifting and handling equipment	6	4	4	6	145	246	233	334	44	127	159	235
2919	Other general purpose machinery	11	10	12	12	1065	1074	1223	1199	1097	1366	1626	2079
292	Special purpose machinery	28	29	29	33	3902	2518	2454	2445	2772	1853	2159	2791
2921	Agricultural and forestry machinery	10	11	12	13	683	346	354	391	231	145	174	277
2922	Machine tools	6	5	4	7	96	83	70	74	26	32	34	48
2923	Machinery for metallurgy	1	1	1	1	151	143	131	116	84	85	99	118
2924	Machinery for mining & construction	6	7	7	7	973	818	812	800	722	449	558	783
2925	Food/beverage/tobacco processing machinery	2	2	2	2	20	22	19	16	7	19	5	8
2926	Machinery for textile, apparel and leather	-	-	-	-	-	-	-	-	-	-	-	-
2927	Weapons and ammunition	-	-	-	-	-	-	-	-	-	-	-	-
2929	Other special purpose machinery	3	3	3	3	1978	1106	1068	1048	1702	1123	1289	1578

continued

Azerbaijan

ISIC Revision 3		Number of enterprises					Number of employees					Wages and salaries paid to employees			
			(number)					(number)					(thousands of Azerbaijan Manats)		
ISIC	Industry	Note	2003	2004	2005	2006	Note	2003	2004	2005	2006	Note	2003	2004	2005	2006
2930	Domestic appliances n.e.c.		14	13	13	13		2767	1969	1857	1384		470	415	556	640
3000	Office, accounting and computing machinery		3	4	5	7		434	400	314	267		44	90	173	221
3110	Electric motors, generators and transformers		16	16	19	19		618	660	649	721		163	354	502	756
3120	Electricity distribution & control apparatus		4	5	6	6		274	309	359	333		186	270	499	470
3130	Insulated wire and cable		8	8	8	11		316	349	358	342		37	122	181	219
3140	Accumulators, primary cells and batteries		8	5	6	7		115	122	182	227		37	49	215	192
3150	Lighting equipment and electric lamps		1	1	1	1		510	34	21	...		48	10	9	...
3190	Other electrical equipment n.e.c.		4	5	3	3		338	262	263	192		115	144	196	254
3210	Electronic valves, tubes, etc.		5	4	5	4		192	182	293	319		125	131	131	183
3220	TV/radio transmitters; line comm. apparatus		5	4	4	3		619	610	563	533		184	234	235	285
3230	TV and radio receivers and associated goods		4	3	2	2		66	36	34	35		20	8	32	34
331	Medical, measuring, testing appliances, etc.		16	12	16	17		1993	1614	1477	1390		749	869	1068	1431
3311	Medical, surgical and orthopaedic equipment		8	7	8	7		369	412	428	409		155	216	306	432
3312	Measuring/testing/navigating appliances,etc.		5	4	6	7		1608	1187	1032	898		580	648	753	778
3313	Industrial process control equipment		3	1	2	3		16	15	17	83		14	5	9	221
3320	Optical instruments & photographic equipment		2	1	1	1		20	19	20	13		4	5	4	3
3330	Watches and clocks		-	-	-	-		-	-	-	-		-	-	-	-
3410	Motor vehicles		2	1	1	2		41	29	24	71		13	7	9	26
3420	Automobile bodies, trailers & semi-trailers		1	1	1	-		...	309	339	325		...	358	437	540
3430	Parts/accessories for automobiles		7	6	4	4		90	193	243	182		33	100	162	220
351	Building and repairing of ships and boats		21	22	25	28		3426	3410	3841	3879		11458	10773	15959	18028
3511	Building and repairing of ships		21	22	25	28		3426	3410	3841	3879		11458	10773	15959	18028
3512	Building/repairing of pleasure/sport. boats		-	-	-	-		-	-	-	-		-	-	-	-
3520	Railway/tramway locomotives & rolling stock		4	6	6	6		4114	4459	4511	4545		3017	4316	5368	6550
3530	Aircraft and spacecraft		3	3	3	3		513	517	493	491		1023	1050	1072	1818
359	Transport equipment n.e.c.		-	-	-	-		-	-	-	-		-	-	-	-
3591	Motorcycles		-	-	-	-		-	-	-	-		-	-	-	-
3592	Bicycles and invalid carriages		-	-	-	-		-	-	-	-		-	-	-	-
3599	Other transport equipment n.e.c.		-	-	-	-		-	-	-	-		-	-	-	-
3610	Furniture		62	70	77	90		1137	1952	1817	1922		180	683	1277	1141
369	Manufacturing n.e.c.		52	55	68	61		804	1036	1129	1034		348	430	541	727
3691	Jewellery and related articles		18	18	19	17		550	590	565	565		306	319	318	384
3692	Musical instruments		2	2	3	2		10	6	6	4		...	...	2	2
3693	Sports goods		-	-	-	-		-	-	-	-		-	-	-	-
3694	Games and toys		1	1	1	1		45	38	5	2		...	...	2	1
3699	Other manufacturing n.e.c.		31	34	45	41		199	402	553	463		40	108	219	340
3710	Recycling of metal waste and scrap		5	5	9	10		246	89	50	171		331	130	24	314
3720	Recycling of non-metal waste and scrap		7	8	7	5		215	331	136	127		151	296	102	125
D	Total manufacturing		1875	1891	2027	2068		95297	100067	101781	103443		76494	92814	118021	152803

a/ 1532 includes 1533.

Azerbaijan

ISIC Revision 3		Output in factor values					Value added in factor values					Gross fixed capital formation		
			(millions of Azerbaijan Manats)					(millions of Azerbaijan Manats)					(millions of Azerbaijan Manats)	
ISIC	Industry	Note	2003	2004	2005	2006	Note	2003	2004	2005	2006	Note	2005	2006
151	Processed meat,fish,fruit,vegetables,fats		86.5	254.0	301.7	299.7		20.9	59.7	54.0	37.6		19.1	8.8
1511	Processing/preserving of meat		38.0	208.4	218.4	222.3		9.2	49.0	39.1	27.9		1.1	-
1512	Processing/preserving of fish		2.3	3.1	6.3	1.2		0.6	0.7	1.1	0.1		3.0	0.1
1513	Processing/preserving of fruit & vegetables		29.4	26.8	57.0	56.7		7.1	6.3	10.2	7.1		4.8	8.7
1514	Vegetable and animal oils and fats		16.7	15.7	20.0	19.6		4.0	3.7	3.6	2.5		10.2	-
1520	Dairy products		486.6	284.2	288.0	291.5		117.8	66.8	51.5	36.5		0.9	0.6
153	Grain mill products; starches; animal feeds		225.8	267.9	255.1	268.1		54.7	63.0	45.6	33.6		4.7	3.0
1531	Grain mill products		50.7	267.8	255.1	268.1		12.3	62.9	45.6	33.6		4.7	3.0
1532	Starches and starch products	a/	175.1	0.1	-	-		42.4a/	-a/	-a/	...	a/	-	-
1533	Prepared animal feeds	a/	...	...	...	...		...a/	...a/	...a/	...	a/	...	...
154	Other food products		160.1	180.5	249.8	295.0		38.7	42.4	44.7	37.0		11.2	77.6
1541	Bakery products		150.4	162.7	221.6	231.4		36.4	38.2	39.7	29.0		8.9	-
1542	Sugar		0.1	7.9	12.9	49.3		-	1.9	2.3	6.2		0.7	76.8
1543	Cocoa, chocolate and sugar confectionery		1.3	2.4	7.5	4.8		0.3	0.6	1.3	0.6		1.3	-
1544	Macaroni, noodles & similar products		0.2	0.7	0.6	0.9		-	0.2	0.1	0.1		0.3	0.3
1549	Other food products n.e.c.		8.1	6.8	7.1	8.6		2.0	1.6	1.3	1.1		-	0.4
155	Beverages		34.9	49.8	72.5	97.0		8.4	11.7	13.0	12.2		10.1	48.5
1551	Distilling, rectifying & blending of spirits		2.6	2.9	4.3	6.0		0.6	0.7	0.8	0.8		-	2.3
1552	Wines		6.9	9.3	10.9	17.6		1.7	2.2	2.0	2.2		2.9	35.1
1553	Malt liquors and malt		6.7	10.1	15.7	20.1		1.6	2.4	2.8	2.5		0.8	1.7
1554	Soft drinks; mineral waters		18.7	27.5	41.6	53.3		4.5	6.5	7.4	6.7		6.4	9.5
1600	Tobacco products		28.7	21.0	30.5	27.0		6.9	4.9	5.5	3.4		8.2	0.2
171	Spinning, weaving and finishing of textiles		19.7	18.0	32.5	49.5		5.8	5.2	5.0	8.6		4.7	21.8
1711	Textile fibre preparation; textile weaving		19.7	18.0	32.5	49.5		5.8	5.2	5.0	8.6		4.7	21.8
1712	Finishing of textiles		-	-	-	-		-	-	-	-		-	-
172	Other textiles		1.0	1.5	2.2	3.2		0.3	0.5	0.3	0.6		0.1	-
1721	Made-up textile articles, except apparel		0.4	0.4	0.5	0.6		0.1	0.1	0.1	0.1		-	-
1722	Carpets and rugs		0.3	0.8	1.4	1.2		0.1	0.2	0.2	0.2		-	-
1723	Cordage, rope, twine and netting		-	-	0.1	-		-	-	-	-		-	-
1729	Other textiles n.e.c.		0.2	0.4	0.3	1.4		0.1	0.1	-	0.2		0.1	-
1730	Knitted and crocheted fabrics and articles		2.4	3.7	7.0	4.9		0.7	1.1	1.1	0.9		-	0.4
1810	Wearing apparel, except fur apparel		8.9	6.3	9.4	14.3		2.6	1.8	1.4	2.5		0.7	-
1820	Dressing & dyeing of fur; processing of fur		1.2	-	-	-		0.3	-	-	-		-	-
191	Tanning, dressing and processing of leather		1.2	3.6	3.0	3.8		0.3	0.9	0.6	1.1		0.4	0.1
1911	Tanning and dressing of leather		0.9	3.3	2.7	3.5		0.3	0.8	0.5	1.0		0.4	0.1
1912	Luggage, handbags, etc.; saddlery & harness		0.2	0.3	0.3	0.4		0.1	0.1	0.1	0.1		-	-
1920	Footwear		2.0	1.1	1.4	3.1		0.6	0.3	0.3	0.9		0.1	0.3
2010	Sawmilling and planing of wood		0.1	0.3	0.2	0.5		-	0.1	-	0.1		0.1	0.4
202	Products of wood, cork, straw, etc.		1.8	4.3	9.4	11.7		0.6	1.3	2.1	2.1		-	1.0
2021	Veneer sheets, plywood, particle board, etc.		-	-	-	0.1		-	-	-	-		-	-
2022	Builders' carpentry and joinery		1.8	3.7	8.8	8.7		0.6	1.1	1.9	1.6		-	1.0
2023	Wooden containers		-	0.5	-	1.3		-	0.1	-	0.2		-	-
2029	Other wood products; articles of cork/straw		0.1	0.1	0.6	1.6		-	-	0.1	0.3		-	-
210	Paper and paper products		2.7	2.3	3.1	5.5		1.0	0.8	0.6	1.7		1.3	1.4
2101	Pulp, paper and paperboard		0.9	-	-	...		0.3	-	...	...		-	-
2102	Corrugated paper and paperboard		1.6	2.0	2.7	...		0.6	0.7	...	...		0.8	1.4
2109	Other articles of paper and paperboard		0.2	0.2	0.4	...		0.1	0.1	...	...		0.5	-
221	Publishing		5.9	5.0	9.0	10.3		2.3	1.8	1.8	3.1		1.5	2.3
2211	Publishing of books and other publications		3.6	2.5	7.6	6.1		1.4	0.9	1.5	1.9		1.5	2.3
2212	Publishing of newspapers, journals, etc.		1.9	2.0	0.9	3.4		0.7	0.7	0.2	1.0		-	-
2213	Publishing of recorded media		-	0.1	-	-		-	-	-	-		-	-
2219	Other publishing		0.3	0.4	0.5	0.7		0.1	0.1	0.1	-		-	-

continued

Azerbaijan

ISIC Revision 3		Output in factor values					Value added in factor values					Gross fixed capital formation		
			(millions of Azerbaijan Manats)					(millions of Azerbaijan Manats)					(millions of Azerbaijan Manats)	
ISIC	Industry	Note	2003	2004	2005	2006	Note	2003	2004	2005	2006	Note	2005	2006
222	Printing and related service activities		10.9	13.2	13.2	15.0		4.2	4.7	2.7	4.6		1.9	1.1
2221	Printing		10.5	12.4	12.4	13.6		4.0	4.4	2.5	4.2		1.9	1.1
2222	Service activities related to printing		0.4	0.8	0.8	1.3		0.2	0.3	0.2	0.4		-	-
2230	Reproduction of recorded media		0.3	0.5	0.9	1.1		0.1	0.2	0.2	0.3		-	-
2310	Coke oven products		-	-	-	-		-	-	-	-		-	-
2320	Refined petroleum products		634.3	709.7	836.8	1821.2		183.9	201.6	243.2	565.8		20.4	25.4
2330	Processing of nuclear fuel		-	-	-	-		-	-	-	-		-	-
241	Basic chemicals		127.5	165.2	174.5	170.4		26.4	33.2	48.6	39.7		5.0	2.4
2411	Basic chemicals, except fertilizers		71.3	67.0	76.5	47.7		14.7	13.5	21.3	11.1		5.0	1.2
2412	Fertilizers and nitrogen compounds		0.9	0.8	0.5	0.6		0.2	0.2	0.1	0.1		-	-
2413	Plastics in primary forms; synthetic rubber		55.4	97.3	97.5	122.1		11.5	19.6	27.2	28.5		-	1.3
242	Other chemicals		10.1	15.0	24.5	24.3		2.1	3.0	6.8	5.7		0.1	3.2
2421	Pesticides and other agro-chemical products		-	-	-	0.1		-	-	-	-		-	-
2422	Paints, varnishes, printing ink and mastics		0.7	1.2	1.5	1.3		0.1	0.3	0.4	0.3		-	0.3
2423	Pharmaceuticals, medicinal chemicals, etc.		0.9	0.9	0.7	1.2		0.2	0.2	0.2	0.3		-	0.2
2424	Soap, cleaning & cosmetic preparations		1.3	1.3	1.5	1.5		0.3	0.3	0.4	0.4		0.1	1.9
2429	Other chemical products n.e.c.		7.2	11.5	20.7	20.1		1.5	2.3	5.8	4.7		-	0.8
2430	Man-made fibres		-	-	-	-		-	-	-	-		-	-
251	Rubber products		0.1	0.3	0.3	0.2		-	0.1	0.1	-		-	-
2511	Rubber tyres and tubes		-	0.1	0.1	-		-	-	-	-		-	-
2519	Other rubber products		0.1	0.3	0.2	0.2		-	0.1	-	-		-	-
2520	Plastic products		11.9	19.5	23.2	27.5		2.5	4.1	5.4	5.5		2.7	5.2
2610	Glass and glass products		1.1	1.3	1.9	2.7		0.2	0.3	0.5	0.9		0.4	-
269	Non-metallic mineral products n.e.c.		66.6	105.0	133.5	162.5		22.8	34.8	32.3	53.5		13.2	30.5
2691	Pottery, china and earthenware		0.2	0.2	1.3	0.3		0.1	0.1	0.3	0.1		1.9	-
2692	Refractory ceramic products		-	0.1	0.1	0.2		-	-	-	0.1		-	0.3
2693	Struct.non-refractory clay; ceramic products		5.0	6.8	8.3	11.2		1.7	2.2	2.0	3.7		-	16.7
2694	Cement, lime and plaster		46.3	69.6	82.6	95.0		15.8	23.1	20.0	31.3		9.9	4.6
2695	Articles of concrete, cement and plaster		14.1	26.9	39.0	52.6		4.8	8.9	9.4	17.3		1.5	8.3
2696	Cutting, shaping & finishing of stone		0.7	1.4	2.1	2.9		0.2	0.5	0.5	1.0		-	0.6
2699	Other non-metallic mineral products n.e.c.		0.2	-	0.1	0.2		0.1	-	-	0.1		-	-
2710	Basic iron and steel		49.4	88.9	107.9	121.6		18.5	32.7	28.1	23.9		14.5	1.9
2720	Basic precious and non-ferrous metals		58.9	98.0	143.7	214.5		22.0	36.1	37.4	42.2		1.7	-
273	Casting of metals		0.5	5.8	20.4	15.6		0.2	2.1	5.3	3.1		0.1	0.4
2731	Casting of iron and steel		0.5	5.8	20.3	14.7		0.2	2.1	5.3	2.9		0.1	0.2
2732	Casting of non-ferrous metals		-	-	0.1	0.9		-	-	-	0.2		-	0.2
281	Struct.metal products;tanks;steam generators		18.4	20.1	23.3	30.9		6.9	7.4	6.1	6.1		1.7	1.9
2811	Structural metal products		18.4	20.1	23.2	30.8		6.9	7.4	6.0	6.1		1.0	1.9
2812	Tanks, reservoirs and containers of metal		-	-	0.1	0.1		-	-	-	-		0.7	-
2813	Steam generators		-	-	-	-		-	-	-	-		-	-
289	Other metal products; metal working services		23.2	33.0	33.0	20.7		12.5	15.5	8.6	4.1		2.8	7.7
2891	Metal forging/pressing/stamping/roll-forming		2.9	6.8	10.1	11.1		1.6	3.2	2.6	2.2		2.5	2.9
2892	Treatment & coating of metals		19.9	24.1	18.5	0.2		10.7	11.4	4.8	-		-	1.2
2893	Cutlery, hand tools and general hardware		0.3	0.3	0.2	0.5		0.2	0.2	0.1	0.1		-	1.1
2899	Other fabricated metal products n.e.c.		0.1	1.7	4.2	8.9		0.1	0.8	1.1	1.7		0.3	2.5
291	General purpose machinery		19.9	31.1	22.0	37.4		10.7	14.6	7.0	17.0		4.1	1.8
2911	Engines & turbines (not for transport equipment)		3.7	13.5	1.7	0.9		2.0	6.3	0.5	0.4		0.1	0.4
2912	Pumps, compressors, taps and valves		10.7	10.5	11.2	17.4		5.8	4.9	3.5	7.9		1.1	-
2913	Bearings, gears, gearing & driving elements		0.3	0.4	0.4	0.7		0.1	0.2	0.1	0.3		-	-
2914	Ovens, furnaces and furnace burners		0.1	-	-	0.1		-	-	-	0.1		1.8	0.1
2915	Lifting and handling equipment		0.7	1.0	1.5	7.4		0.4	0.5	0.5	3.4		-	0.5
2919	Other general purpose machinery		4.5	5.7	7.2	10.9		2.5	2.7	2.3	5.0		1.1	0.8

292	Special purpose machinery	18.8	13.0	11.9	19.8	10.2	6.1	3.8	9.0	1.0	0.3
2921	Agricultural and forestry machinery	1.6	1.2	1.5	2.7	0.8	0.5	0.5	1.2	0.7	-
2922	Machine tools	0.2	0.3	0.1	0.4	0.1	0.1	-	0.2	-	-
2923	Machinery for metallurgy	0.4	0.3	0.3	0.5	0.2	0.1	0.1	0.2	-	-
2924	Machinery for mining & construction	4.6	3.5	4.4	7.5	2.5	1.6	1.4	3.4	-	0.2
2925	Food/beverage/tobacco processing machinery	-	-	0.1	0.2	-	-	-	0.1	-	-
2926	Machinery for textile, apparel and leather	-	-	-	-	-	-	-	-	-	-
2927	Weapons and ammunition	-	-	-	-	-	-	-	-	-	-
2929	Other special purpose machinery	12.0	7.7	5.6	8.6	6.5	3.6	1.8	3.9	0.3	0.1
2930	Domestic appliances n.e.c.	1.3	1.9	2.7	2.9	0.7	0.9	0.9	1.3	-	-
3000	Office, accounting and computing machinery	0.1	0.3	2.8	7.2	-	0.1	1.1	3.1	1.1	-
3110	Electric motors, generators and transformers	3.2	3.7	6.4	12.0	1.2	1.3	2.4	5.1	-	0.2
3120	Electricity distribution & control apparatus	1.4	2.2	3.5	4.3	0.5	0.8	1.3	1.8	0.5	0.2
3130	Insulated wire and cable	0.4	2.4	4.2	2.3	0.2	0.8	1.6	1.0	0.3	0.2
3140	Accumulators, primary cells and batteries	0.2	0.2	1.3	1.1	0.1	0.1	0.5	0.5	4.3	0.2
3150	Lighting equipment and electric lamps	0.1	-	-	...	-	-	-	...	-	-
3190	Other electrical equipment n.e.c.	0.3	0.5	0.6	1.0	0.1	0.2	0.2	0.4	-	-
3210	Electronic valves, tubes, etc.	0.4	0.3	1.2	1.4	0.2	0.1	0.5	0.6	-	0.5
3220	TV/radio transmitters; line comm. apparatus	0.6	0.6	0.5	0.6	0.2	0.2	0.2	0.2	-	-
3230	TV and radio receivers and associated goods	0.1	0.1	0.2	0.3	-	-	0.1	0.1	-	-
331	Medical, measuring, testing appliances, etc.	3.1	3.3	5.3	3.8	1.2	1.1	2.0	1.6	1.6	0.2
3311	Medical, surgical and orthopaedic equipment	1.1	1.4	2.5	1.6	0.4	0.5	0.9	0.7	0.3	0.2
3312	Measuring/testing/navigating appliances,etc.	1.7	1.8	2.6	1.4	0.7	0.6	1.0	0.6	1.3	-
3313	Industrial process control equipment	0.3	0.1	0.2	0.7	0.1	-	0.1	0.3	-	0.1
3320	Optical instruments & photographic equipment	-	-	-	-	-	-	-	-	-	-
3330	Watches and clocks	-	-	-	-	-	-	-	-	-	-
3410	Motor vehicles	-	-	-	3.9	-	-	-	2.2	-	3.1
3420	Automobile bodies, trailers & semi-trailers	1.5	1.9	2.2	-	0.7	0.9	1.7	-	-	-
3430	Parts/accessories for automobiles	0.7	0.6	3.0	0.9	0.3	0.3	2.3	0.5	-	1.8
351	Building and repairing of ships and boats	67.7	62.0	139.2	144.4	32.7	28.9	108.0	79.3	7.3	0.9
3511	Building and repairing of ships	67.7	62.0	139.2	144.4	32.7	28.9	108.0	79.3	7.3	0.9
3512	Building/repairing of pleasure/sport. boats	-	-	-	-	-	-	-	-	-	-
3520	Railway/tramway locomotives & rolling stock	4.6	13.6	13.4	16.0	2.2	6.4	10.4	8.8	0.7	0.2
3530	Aircraft and spacecraft	4.3	5.4	7.4	8.6	2.1	2.5	5.7	4.7	0.2	15.6
359	Transport equipment n.e.c.	-	-	-	-	-	-	-	-	-	-
3591	Motorcycles	-	-	-	-	-	-	-	-	-	-
3592	Bicycles and invalid carriages	-	-	-	-	-	-	-	-	-	-
3599	Other transport equipment n.e.c.	-	-	-	-	-	-	-	-	-	-
3610	Furniture	5.3	12.4	17.5	19.4	1.0	2.1	5.0	4.9	2.1	1.7
369	Manufacturing n.e.c.	2.5	7.6	16.0	10.3	0.5	1.3	4.6	2.6	5.2	2.1
3691	Jewellery and related articles	0.5	0.8	...	0.8	0.1	0.1	...	0.2	-	-
3692	Musical instruments	...	...	...	0.1	...	...	...	-	-	-
3693	Sports goods	-	-	-	-	-	-	-	-	-	-
3694	Games and toys	...	...	...	-	...	...	...	-	-	-
3699	Other manufacturing n.e.c.	2.0	6.8	...	9.4	0.4	1.2	...	2.4	5.2	2.1
3710	Recycling of metal waste and scrap	0.7	0.1	0.2	0.4	0.1	-	0.1	0.1	-	-
3720	Recycling of non-metal waste and scrap	0.2	0.8	0.9	0.8	-	0.1	0.3	0.2	-	-
D	Total manufacturing	2220.0	2543.4	3074.2	4312.2	629.4	707.0	812.4	1082.2	156.2	275.1

a/ 1532 includes 1533.

Azerbaijan

ISIC Revision 3			Index numbers of industrial production											
			(2000=100)											
ISIC	Industry	Note	1995	1996	1997	1998	1999	2000	2001	2002	2003	2004	2005	2006
15	Food and beverages	a/	...	...	...	...	...	100	114	113	119	119	126	132
16	Tobacco products	a/	...	...	...	...	...	...	...	...	...	...	...	...
17	Textiles	b/	...	...	...	...	...	100	88	96	107	112	166	145
18	Wearing apparel, fur	b/	...	...	...	...	...	...	...	...	...	...	...	...
19	Leather, leather products and footwear		...	...	...	...	...	100	52	92	67	72	74	59
20	Wood products (excl. furniture)		...	...	...	...	...	100	83	104	101	101	84	83
21	Paper and paper products	c/	...	...	...	...	...	100	93	89	134	106	96	106
22	Printing and publishing	c/	...	...	...	...	...	...	...	...	...	...	...	...
23	Coke,refined petroleum products,nuclear fuel		...	...	...	...	...	100	75	76	79	87	99	101
24	Chemicals and chemical products		...	...	...	...	...	100	86	121	130	163	166	189
25	Rubber and plastics products		...	...	...	...	...	100	53	46	59	75	77	62
26	Non-metallic mineral products		...	...	...	...	...	100	186	260	307	466	589	601
27	Basic metals	d/	...	...	...	...	...	100	142	203	539	958	1277	1395
28	Fabricated metal products	d/	...	...	...	...	...	...	...	...	...	...	...	...
29	Machinery and equipment n.e.c.	e/	...	...	...	...	...	100	105	79	86	61	56	88
30	Office, accounting and computing machinery	e/	...	...	...	...	...	...	...	...	...	...	...	...
31	Electrical machinery and apparatus	e/	...	...	...	...	...	...	...	...	...	...	...	...
32	Radio,television and communication equipment	e/	...	...	...	...	...	...	...	...	...	...	...	...
33	Medical, precision and optical instruments	e/	...	...	...	...	...	...	...	...	...	...	...	...
34	Motor vehicles, trailers, semi-trailers	e/	...	...	...	...	...	...	...	...	...	...	...	...
35	Other transport equipment	e/	...	...	...	...	...	...	...	...	...	...	...	...
36	Furniture; manufacturing n.e.c.		...	...	...	...	...	...	...	...	...	...	...	...
37	Recycling		...	...	...	...	...	...	...	...	...	...	...	...
D	Total manufacturing		119	107	108	95	87	100	103	109	128	141	163	175

a/ 15 includes 16.
b/ 17 includes 18.
c/ 21 includes 22.
d/ 27 includes 28.
e/ 29 includes 30, 31, 32, 33, 34 and 35.

Belgium

Supplier of information:
National Institute of Statistics (Institut National de Statistique), Brussels.
Industrial statistics for the OECD countries are compiled by the OECD secretariat, which supplies them to UNIDO.

Basic source of data:
Annual survey.

Major deviations from ISIC (Revision 3):
Data have been converted from national NACE-related classification system to ISIC (Revision 3).

Reference period:
Calendar year.

Scope:
All registered enterprises.

Method of data collection:
Not reported.

Type of enumeration:
All enterprises with 20 or more employees and/or turnover of more than eight million euros are surveyed every year; smaller enterprises are selected via a sample and grossed up to the entire industry.

Adjusted for non-response:
Not reported.

Concepts and definitions of variables:
No deviations from the standard UN concepts and definitions are reported.

Related national publications:
None reported.

Belgium

ISIC Revision 3		Number of enterprises					Number of employees					Wages and salaries paid to employees				
			(number)					(number)					(millions of Euros)			
ISIC	Industry	Note	2002	2003	2004	2005	Note	2002	2003	2004	2005	Note	2002	2003	2004	2005
151	Processed meat,fish,fruit,vegetables,fats		...	958	1165	997		...	23628	23482	23549		...	632.4	662.0	661.0
1511	Processing/preserving of meat		...	764	967	782		...	14040	14001	13983		...	354.1	368.1	363.0
1512	Processing/preserving of fish		...	53	52	62		...	1429	1400	1467		...	37.6	37.8	40.0
1513	Processing/preserving of fruit & vegetables		...	126	130	137		...	6830	6765	6846		...	188.2	195.5	204.0
1514	Vegetable and animal oils and fats		...	15	16	16		...	1329	1316	1253		...	52.5	60.6	55.0
1520	Dairy products		...	382	444	381		...	7032	7273	6746		...	214.9	225.2	213.0
153	Grain mill products; starches; animal feeds		...	300	323	315		...	5722	5789	5872		...	210.1	215.8	227.0
1531	Grain mill products		...	...	...	...		...	...	...	...		...	...	...	...
1532	Starches and starch products		...	...	...	...		...	...	...	...		...	...	...	...
1533	Prepared animal feeds		...	173	205	203		...	3226	3260	3248		...	110.1	109.9	112.0
154	Other food products		...	5999	6041	5755		...	41086	42134	41311		...	941.2	970.6	996.0
1541	Bakery products		...	5323	5317	5073		...	25096	26100	24894		...	423.0	427.4	416.0
1542	Sugar		...	11	9	9		...	1556	1385	1393		...	64.3	63.4	59.0
1543	Cocoa, chocolate and sugar confectionery		...	402	407	323		...	8315	8311	8150		...	250.3	268.2	273.0
1544	Macaroni, noodles & similar products		...	39	42	40		...	1202	1207	1250		...	36.6	37.8	40.0
1549	Other food products n.e.c.		...	223	266	310		...	4915	5131	5624		...	167.0	173.9	208.0
155	Beverages		...	197	214	223		...	10889	10983	10533		...	393.7	408.2	396.0
1551	Distilling, rectifying & blending of spirits		...	...	...	...		...	...	...	...		...	...	...	...
1552	Wines		...	...	...	...		...	...	...	...		...	...	...	...
1553	Malt liquors and malt		...	113	125	128		...	6592	6251	6102		...	248.8	243.7	239.0
1554	Soft drinks; mineral waters		...	29	34	30		...	3836	4325	3988		...	130.9	152.6	143.0
1600	Tobacco products		...	29	29	32		...	2250	1967	1880		...	69.6	78.1	68.0
171	Spinning, weaving and finishing of textiles		...	552	566	549		...	14623	13733	12730		...	343.4	328.6	298.0
1711	Textile fibre preparation; textile weaving		...	404	415	390		...	11937	11280	10358		...	273.5	266.9	238.0
1712	Finishing of textiles		...	148	151	159		...	2686	2453	2372		...	69.9	61.7	59.0
172	Other textiles		...	838	841	827		...	20533	19486	18607		...	508.2	489.2	483.0
1721	Made-up textile articles, except apparel		...	483	478	475		...	4844	4718	4326		...	112.4	100.1	100.0
1722	Carpets and rugs		...	184	188	182		...	11559	11548	11294		...	286.3	298.8	297.0
1723	Cordage, rope, twine and netting		...	19	18	19		...	224	220	219		...	4.3	4.3	5.0
1729	Other textiles n.e.c.		...	...	...	...		...	...	...	...		...	...	...	...
1730	Knitted and crocheted fabrics and articles		...	100	97	86		...	1924	1668	1371		...	31.8	31.2	29.0
1810	Wearing apparel, except fur apparel		...	1014	1084	985		...	7779	6533	6280		...	182.8	120.3	124.0
1820	Dressing & dyeing of fur; processing of fur		...	35	36	32		...	294	292	281		...	5.4	5.2	5.0
191	Tanning, dressing and processing of leather		...	...	...	...		...	...	...	...		...	...	...	...
1911	Tanning and dressing of leather		...	15	15	15		...	183	191	173		...	4.2	4.7	4.0
1912	Luggage, handbags, etc.; saddlery & harness		...	...	...	...		...	...	...	...		...	...	...	...
1920	Footwear		...	...	...	...		...	...	...	...		...	...	...	...
2010	Sawmilling and planing of wood		...	289	286	291		...	2258	2159	2115		...	47.0	49.2	50.0
202	Products of wood, cork, straw, etc.		...	1349	1375	1406		...	10072	10457	10771		...	261.8	274.1	288.0
2021	Veneer sheets, plywood, particle board, etc.		...	66	73	72		...	3149	3461	3473		...	104.7	113.2	120.0
2022	Builders' carpentry and joinery		...	885	902	937		...	4879	5040	5412		...	113.9	117.9	126.0
2023	Wooden containers		...	112	112	112		...	1166	1122	1110		...	25.3	25.2	25.0
2029	Other wood products; articles of cork/straw		...	286	288	285		...	878	834	776		...	17.9	17.8	17.0
210	Paper and paper products		...	307	314	310		...	14719	15372	15130		...	498.7	519.4	529.0
2101	Pulp, paper and paperboard		...	...	63	64		...	...	5346	5203		...	...	209.9	214.0
2102	Corrugated paper and paperboard		...	145	146	139		...	5542	5462	5534		...	164.5	163.0	167.0
2109	Other articles of paper and paperboard		...	...	105	107		...	...	4564	4393		...	...	146.5	148.0
221	Publishing		...	1085	1160	1176		...	9557	9937	10003		...	381.9	404.5	419.0
2211	Publishing of books and other publications		...	301	363	353		...	2820	2952	2749		...	118.8	130.1	122.0
2212	Publishing of newspapers, journals, etc.		...	378	384	400		...	6205	6461	6803		...	247.5	261.7	285.0
2213	Publishing of recorded media		...	196	164	174		...	100	80	66		...	4.4	1.8	2.0
2219	Other publishing		...	211	249	249		...	431	444	385		...	11.1	10.8	10.0

222	Printing and related service activities	...	3748	3810	3965	...	20067	19585	19284	...	617.0	612.2	600.0
2221	Printing	...	2131	2092	2077	...	16587	16109	15650	...	517.3	517.7	497.0
2222	Service activities related to printing	...	1617	1718	1888	...	3481	3476	3634	...	99.7	94.5	103.0
2230	Reproduction of recorded media	...	77	98	112	...	245	230	203	...	6.6	6.2	6.0
2310	Coke oven products	...	...	...	...	...	...	...	...	...	...	...	...
2320	Refined petroleum products	...	25	20	16	...	4005	4097	4084	...	401.9	438.6	447.0
2330	Processing of nuclear fuel	...	...	...	...	...	...	...	...	...	...	...	...
241	Basic chemicals	...	210	229	238	...	26685	25649	25623	...	1390.7	1388.2	1466.0
2411	Basic chemicals, except fertilizers	...	122	135	129	...	19206	18202	17981	...	1002.7	981.4	1028.0
2412	Fertilizers and nitrogen compounds	...	29	34	35	...	657	678	687	...	28.7	29.8	30.0
2413	Plastics in primary forms; synthetic rubber	...	59	60	74	...	6821	6769	6955	...	359.4	376.9	407.0
242	Other chemicals	...	...	529	548	...	...	40227	39484	...	...	1923.3	1949.0
2421	Pesticides and other agro-chemical products	...	...	14	14	...	...	1254	554	...	...	56.5	30.0
2422	Paints, varnishes, printing ink and mastics	...	105	108	110	...	4322	4240	4208	...	183.3	200.9	196.0
2423	Pharmaceuticals, medicinal chemicals, etc.	...	115	116	122	...	20022	19898	19890	...	973.7	959.9	1015.0
2424	Soap, cleaning & cosmetic preparations	...	154	168	171	...	5868	5928	5976	...	207.6	211.9	215.0
2429	Other chemical products n.e.c.	...	118	123	131	...	9199	8907	8856	...	514.5	494.1	492.0
2430	Man-made fibres	...	...	26	26	...	...	2261	2108	...	...	69.3	71.0
251	Rubber products	...	84	93	88	...	3461	3416	3456	...	140.4	124.8	134.0
2511	Rubber tyres and tubes	...	...	...	...	...	...	...	...	...	...	...	...
2519	Other rubber products	...	63	69	69	...	2281	2218	2321	...	92.7	83.9	93.0
2520	Plastic products	...	651	696	693	...	23476	22962	22151	...	780.0	775.1	777.0
2610	Glass and glass products	...	182	268	195	...	10714	10460	10032	...	369.7	366.6	372.0
269	Non-metallic mineral products n.e.c.	...	1298	1260	1276	...	21109	21030	21447	...	654.2	662.8	716.0
2691	Pottery, china and earthenware	...	...	...	...	...	...	...	...	...	...	...	...
2692	Refractory ceramic products	...	21	22	23	...	643	583	597	...	20.0	19.6	21.0
2693	Struct.non-refractory clay; ceramic products	...	65	87	86	...	1973	1715	1843	...	59.9	55.3	62.0
2694	Cement, lime and plaster	...	9	8	7	...	2811	3047	2693	...	125.2	137.5	130.0
2695	Articles of concrete, cement and plaster	...	425	429	450	...	11321	11572	11938	...	337.8	339.0	376.0
2696	Cutting, shaping & finishing of stone	...	668	604	622	...	2573	2461	2485	...	51.7	55.2	61.0
2699	Other non-metallic mineral products n.e.c.	...	41	43	44	...	1024	1016	1346	...	37.1	35.9	49.0
2710	Basic iron and steel	...	163	167	161	...	23766	23402	23440	...	1015.0	1017.0	1043.0
2720	Basic precious and non-ferrous metals	...	70	73	77	...	9283	8778	8788	...	356.4	343.3	365.0
273	Casting of metals	...	92	90	88	...	2927	2878	2866	...	92.4	95.3	95.0
2731	Casting of iron and steel	...	44	42	40	...	1943	1898	1889	...	61.7	61.7	61.0
2732	Casting of non-ferrous metals	...	48	48	48	...	984	980	977	...	30.7	33.6	34.0
281	Struct.metal products;tanks;steam generators	...	2163	2306	2247	...	29862	30711	31271	...	846.1	915.9	928.0
2811	Structural metal products	...	1836	1960	1896	...	20409	22083	22026	...	557.9	633.7	634.0
2812	Tanks, reservoirs and containers of metal	...	176	184	177	...	5924	5411	5361	...	179.0	169.0	175.0
2813	Steam generators	...	151	162	174	...	3529	3217	3884	...	109.2	113.2	119.0
289	Other metal products; metal working services	...	3719	3968	3794	...	30151	28723	29295	...	842.6	852.5	876.0
2891	Metal forging/pressing/stamping/roll-forming	...	457	620	578	...	1693	1826	1762	...	43.2	51.7	51.0
2892	Treatment & coating of metals	...	2360	2406	2395	...	17854	16519	17478	...	472.3	474.0	505.0
2893	Cutlery, hand tools and general hardware	...	342	471	337	...	3338	3184	3181	...	100.2	97.0	98.0
2899	Other fabricated metal products n.e.c.	...	560	471	484	...	7266	7194	6874	...	226.9	229.8	222.0
291	General purpose machinery	...	778	836	943	...	19999	20015	20777	...	699.3	714.8	763.0
2911	Engines & turbines (not for transport equipment)	...	23	...	...	...	831	...	...	...	40.9	...	...
2912	Pumps, compressors, taps and valves	...	73	...	...	...	4146	...	...	...	154.1	...	...
2913	Bearings, gears, gearing & driving elements	...	46	48	50	...	2188	2135	2482	...	79.2	79.6	92.0
2914	Ovens, furnaces and furnace burners	...	16	21	19	...	388	275	281	...	12.1	10.2	10.0
2915	Lifting and handling equipment	...	185	204	202	...	4582	4649	4547	...	154.0	158.4	160.0
2919	Other general purpose machinery	...	435	464	564	...	7865	7930	8223	...	259.2	263.3	279.0
292	Special purpose machinery	...	823	897	1041	...	19369	19205	19380	...	652.9	663.9	685.0
2921	Agricultural and forestry machinery	...	301	313	399	...	4130	3352	3741	...	133.6	108.2	129.0
2922	Machine tools	...	129	157	131	...	1690	1694	1546	...	51.5	51.9	51.0
2923	Machinery for metallurgy	...	13	15	16	...	299	276	198	...	10.6	13.3	8.0
2924	Machinery for mining & construction	...	50	54	54	...	4621	4926	5173	...	156.6	170.7	183.0
2925	Food/beverage/tobacco processing machinery	...	97	104	112	...	909	925	1064	...	24.9	26.4	33.0
2926	Machinery for textile, apparel and leather	...	56	60	58	...	2876	2814	2889	...	94.9	96.5	98.0
2927	Weapons and ammunition	...	31	36	29	...	1439	1500	1483	...	53.6	58.1	59.0
2929	Other special purpose machinery	...	...	...	...	...	...	...	...	...	...	...	...

continued

Belgium

ISIC Revision 3		Number of enterprises					Number of employees					Wages and salaries paid to employees				
			(number)					(number)					(millions of Euros)			
ISIC	Industry	Note	2002	2003	2004	2005	Note	2002	2003	2004	2005	Note	2002	2003	2004	2005
2930	Domestic appliances n.e.c.		...	67	89	76		...	1458	1465	1486		...	39.9	41.4	44.0
3000	Office, accounting and computing machinery		...	102	113	120		...	647	747	681		...	23.7	24.7	22.0
3110	Electric motors, generators and transformers		...	162	173	166		...	3143	2734	2822		...	110.8	100.4	112.0
3120	Electricity distribution & control apparatus		...	104	107	104		...	7812	6901	5019		...	307.6	240.9	183.0
3130	Insulated wire and cable		...	25	27	26		...	1535	1437	2045		...	52.2	51.1	77.0
3140	Accumulators, primary cells and batteries		...	7	7	7		...	1390	1313	1297		...	53.7	49.9	51.0
3150	Lighting equipment and electric lamps		...	186	186	225		...	3243	2620	2779		...	94.0	77.7	84.0
3190	Other electrical equipment n.e.c.		...	156	168	184		...	3585	3913	3926		...	139.1	141.3	141.0
3210	Electronic valves, tubes, etc.		...	79	82	79		...	5196	4530	4240		...	204.5	188.4	177.0
3220	TV/radio transmitters; line comm. apparatus		...	25	32	32		...	5581	6678	6550		...	367.8	437.3	385.0
3230	TV and radio receivers and associated goods		...	115	114	118		...	6072	6075	6198		...	259.8	265.5	252.0
331	Medical, measuring, testing appliances, etc.		...	1327	1363	1367		...	6465	6642	6258		...	209.6	223.2	220.0
3311	Medical, surgical and orthopaedic equipment		...	1160	1189	1162		...	3273	3533	3203		...	92.5	103.6	96.0
3312	Measuring/testing/navigating appliances,etc.		...	84	90	113		...	2211	2183	2170		...	83.3	87.8	92.0
3313	Industrial process control equipment		...	83	84	92		...	981	926	885		...	33.8	31.8	32.0
3320	Optical instruments & photographic equipment		...	55	63	68		...	484	483	445		...	14.7	15.1	14.0
3330	Watches and clocks		...	22	22	24		...	176	178	172		...	5.6	5.6	6.0
3410	Motor vehicles		...	26	26	32		...	31751	29316	28866		...	1101.0	1093.3	1060.0
3420	Automobile bodies, trailers & semi-trailers		...	268	280	282		...	6494	6650	6850		...	183.2	193.6	189.0
3430	Parts/accessories for automobiles		...	134	146	139		...	10677	11252	11210		...	335.0	374.0	382.0
351	Building and repairing of ships and boats		...	154	168	170		...	1499	1561	1515		...	41.6	44.0	44.0
3511	Building and repairing of ships		...	116	124	126		...	1324	1352	1316		...	37.3	38.9	39.0
3512	Building/repairing of pleasure/sport. boats		...	37	44	44		...	175	209	199		...	4.3	5.1	5.0
3520	Railway/tramway locomotives & rolling stock		...	...	...	...		...	...	...	...		...	...	...	...
3530	Aircraft and spacecraft		...	46	53	56		...	6379	6392	6255		...	226.8	234.4	235.0
359	Transport equipment n.e.c.		...	...	...	...		...	...	...	...		...	...	...	...
3591	Motorcycles		...	4	4	5		...	4	4	4		...	0.1	0.1	-
3592	Bicycles and invalid carriages		...	...	...	...		...	...	...	...		...	...	...	...
3599	Other transport equipment n.e.c.		...	...	...	...		...	...	...	...		...	...	...	...
3610	Furniture		...	2914	2460	2399		...	18269	17695	16684		...	396.7	418.0	401.0
369	Manufacturing n.e.c.		...	1389	1281	1393		...	4296	4081	3874		...	94.1	95.3	84.0
3691	Jewellery and related articles		...	720	699	730		...	2023	1858	2073		...	39.5	39.8	42.0
3692	Musical instruments		...	104	107	115		...	100	112	121		...	1.6	2.0	2.0
3693	Sports goods		...	31	30	39		...	174	155	146		...	4.0	3.2	3.0
3694	Games and toys		...	60	63	71		...	683	705	358		...	20.0	20.6	10.0
3699	Other manufacturing n.e.c.		...	474	382	438		...	1316	1251	1176		...	29.0	29.7	27.0
3710	Recycling of metal waste and scrap		...	140	151	157		...	1227	1181	1424		...	34.7	34.8	43.0
3720	Recycling of non-metal waste and scrap		...	314	220	237		...	2207	2123	2294		...	49.0	52.4	59.0
D	Total manufacturing		...	36089	36904	36571		...	595009	585582	578031		...	20120.0	20322.1	20496.0

Belgium

ISIC Revision 3		Output					Value added in factor values					Gross fixed capital formation		
			(millions of Euros)					(millions of Euros)					(millions of Euros)	
ISIC	Industry	Note	2002	2003	2004	2005	Note	2002	2003	2004	2005	Note	2004	2005
151	Processed meat,fish,fruit,vegetables,fats		...	8889.7	8769.6	8985.0		...	1423.5	1459.7	1493.0		235.2	243.0
1511	Processing/preserving of meat		...	4502.2	4633.7	4796.0		...	755.7	778.5	797.0		124.8	116.0
1512	Processing/preserving of fish		...	441.5	426.8	500.0		...	95.4	86.0	89.0		14.2	8.0
1513	Processing/preserving of fruit & vegetables		...	2063.2	2144.6	2212.0		...	456.2	475.2	487.0		76.8	107.0
1514	Vegetable and animal oils and fats		...	1882.8	1564.5	1478.0		...	116.2	120.0	121.0		19.4	13.0
1520	Dairy products		...	3090.9	3180.9	3006.0		...	464.8	477.5	452.0		67.2	88.0
153	Grain mill products; starches; animal feeds		...	4147.1	4332.1	4121.0		...	493.5	498.7	507.0		86.3	87.0
1531	Grain mill products		...	...	...	...		...	...	...	...		...	...
1532	Starches and starch products		...	...	...	...		...	...	...	...		...	...
1533	Prepared animal feeds		...	2286.9	2326.5	2151.0		...	240.4	244.0	242.0		51.3	54.0
154	Other food products		...	7672.1	8247.2	8667.0		...	2189.1	2297.5	2381.0		368.3	452.0
1541	Bakery products		...	2512.7	2682.5	2740.0		...	927.2	952.8	965.0		174.1	255.0
1542	Sugar		...	1070.4	1003.3	929.0		...	250.4	260.9	253.0		12.3	42.0
1543	Cocoa, chocolate and sugar confectionery		...	2333.1	2730.7	2814.0		...	559.2	620.2	600.0		94.8	63.0
1544	Macaroni, noodles & similar products		...	309.6	326.5	360.0		...	74.4	81.8	87.0		26.2	16.0
1549	Other food products n.e.c.		...	1446.2	1504.1	1823.0		...	377.9	381.8	477.0		60.7	76.0
155	Beverages		...	3584.6	3808.7	3797.0		...	1081.3	1132.4	1146.0		345.5	284.0
1551	Distilling, rectifying & blending of spirits		...	...	...	...		...	...	...	...		...	...
1552	Wines		...	...	...	...		...	...	...	...		...	...
1553	Malt liquors and malt		...	2055.1	2037.1	2054.0		...	722.0	712.4	752.0		240.6	206.0
1554	Soft drinks; mineral waters		...	1367.2	1643.2	1597.0		...	334.1	397.3	369.0		97.6	73.0
1600	Tobacco products		...	1687.5	1548.6	1351.0		...	238.7	235.0	231.0		20.0	22.0
171	Spinning, weaving and finishing of textiles		...	2304.4	2222.6	1984.0		...	678.0	635.7	543.0		63.9	65.0
1711	Textile fibre preparation; textile weaving		...	1834.2	1793.6	1595.0		...	544.3	519.1	433.0		53.3	54.0
1712	Finishing of textiles		...	470.2	429.0	388.0		...	133.7	116.6	110.0		10.6	10.0
172	Other textiles		...	4150.4	3851.5	3766.0		...	1080.7	978.2	925.0		117.8	94.0
1721	Made-up textile articles, except apparel		...	840.2	653.2	681.0		...	240.2	174.2	194.0		18.5	20.0
1722	Carpets and rugs		...	2370.7	2479.6	2380.0		...	594.8	613.1	557.0		78.8	56.0
1723	Cordage, rope, twine and netting		...	34.2	33.3	40.0		...	9.3	8.9	9.0		1.4	1.0
1729	Other textiles n.e.c.		...	...	...	...		...	...	...	...		...	...
1730	Knitted and crocheted fabrics and articles		...	165.0	176.3	179.0		...	59.1	59.9	50.0		14.1	6.0
1810	Wearing apparel, except fur apparel		...	1671.7	991.8	1029.0		...	307.0	251.2	270.0		26.0	25.0
1820	Dressing & dyeing of fur; processing of fur		...	25.7	27.5	22.0		...	8.8	8.8	8.0		0.8	-
191	Tanning, dressing and processing of leather		...	...	...	...		...	...	...	...		...	...
1911	Tanning and dressing of leather		...	47.9	51.5	36.0		...	7.7	9.4	7.0		0.9	1.0
1912	Luggage, handbags, etc.; saddlery & harness		...	...	...	...		...	...	...	...		...	...
1920	Footwear		...	...	...	...		...	...	...	...		...	...
2010	Sawmilling and planing of wood		...	471.0	534.6	561.0		...	99.4	106.9	123.0		29.8	17.0
202	Products of wood, cork, straw, etc.		...	2778.4	2750.9	2800.0		...	776.6	773.2	785.0		159.9	199.0
2021	Veneer sheets, plywood, particle board, etc.		...	1500.3	1466.5	1415.0		...	430.3	423.0	414.0		90.0	138.0
2022	Builders' carpentry and joinery		...	904.9	896.2	992.0		...	253.7	257.5	278.0		54.9	51.0
2023	Wooden containers		...	274.0	285.7	285.0		...	54.0	54.5	57.0		12.2	6.0
2029	Other wood products; articles of cork/straw		...	99.2	102.5	108.0		...	38.6	38.2	36.0		2.8	4.0
210	Paper and paper products		...	4330.1	4442.2	4626.0		...	1134.6	1139.3	1111.0		149.8	171.0
2101	Pulp, paper and paperboard		...	...	1914.3	1894.0		...	...	374.0	371.0		49.6	66.0
2102	Corrugated paper and paperboard		...	1139.0	1130.5	1114.0		...	347.7	337.5	331.0		55.7	67.0
2109	Other articles of paper and paperboard		...	...	1397.4	1619.0		...	...	427.8	410.0		44.6	38.0
221	Publishing		...	2426.2	2772.4	2757.0		...	800.2	845.3	890.0		50.1	52.0
2211	Publishing of books and other publications		...	744.6	850.4	822.0		...	299.5	327.2	350.0		15.6	17.0
2212	Publishing of newspapers, journals, etc.		...	1572.6	1800.4	1813.0		...	466.0	490.2	507.0		26.6	30.0
2213	Publishing of recorded media		...	29.6	33.7	41.0		...	12.0	4.8	10.0		0.4	2.0
2219	Other publishing		...	79.5	87.9	81.0		...	22.7	23.1	23.0		7.5	3.0

continued

Belgium

ISIC Revision 3		Output					Value added in factor values					Gross fixed capital formation		
			(millions of Euros)					(millions of Euros)					(millions of Euros)	
ISIC	Industry	Note	2002	2003	2004	2005	Note	2002	2003	2004	2005	Note	2004	2005
222	Printing and related service activities		...	3578.9	3508.7	3581.0		...	1262.0	1307.8	1301.0		224.0	227.0
2221	Printing		...	3103.4	3024.1	3022.0		...	1054.2	1087.3	1073.0		173.2	187.0
2222	Service activities related to printing		...	475.5	484.5	559.0		...	207.9	220.4	229.0		50.7	39.0
2230	Reproduction of recorded media		...	36.7	39.7	38.0		...	12.4	13.2	12.0		3.3	7.0
2310	Coke oven products		...	...	...	...		...	...	...	...		...	...
2320	Refined petroleum products		...	15301.6	19740.8	27187.0		...	1077.0	1553.4	1797.0		141.1	79.0
2330	Processing of nuclear fuel		...	...	...	...		...	...	...	...		...	...
241	Basic chemicals		...	15621.8	17486.9	18719.0		...	3682.0	3873.9	4399.0		332.7	438.0
2411	Basic chemicals, except fertilizers		...	11179.7	12514.5	13120.0		...	2709.3	2880.4	3266.0		228.5	314.0
2412	Fertilizers and nitrogen compounds		...	310.2	332.3	365.0		...	68.4	81.7	86.0		19.1	5.0
2413	Plastics in primary forms; synthetic rubber		...	4131.9	4640.2	5234.0		...	904.2	911.7	1047.0		85.2	119.0
242	Other chemicals		...	...	15647.2	15599.0		...	...	5634.2	5981.0		372.6	436.0
2421	Pesticides and other agro-chemical products		...	...	447.7	161.0		...	...	92.8	59.0		2.1	7.0
2422	Paints, varnishes, printing ink and mastics		...	1615.2	1677.7	1723.0		...	364.6	400.8	433.0		28.3	37.0
2423	Pharmaceuticals, medicinal chemicals, etc.		...	8707.1	8677.1	9072.0		...	3657.8	3662.7	4014.0		221.0	282.0
2424	Soap, cleaning & cosmetic preparations		...	1812.5	1914.5	1796.0		...	493.0	482.7	475.0		48.4	46.0
2429	Other chemical products n.e.c.		...	2780.3	2930.2	2847.0		...	1108.1	995.2	1000.0		72.8	65.0
2430	Man-made fibres		...	...	583.1	591.0		...	...	141.6	132.0		15.6	23.0
251	Rubber products		...	1303.8	1043.7	1214.0		...	281.0	321.3	363.0		26.5	41.0
2511	Rubber tyres and tubes		...	...	...	...		...	...	...	...		...	...
2519	Other rubber products		...	722.5	618.0	741.0		...	185.2	177.1	202.0		12.0	31.0
2520	Plastic products		...	5587.7	5980.8	6309.0		...	1682.9	1722.0	1680.0		187.0	192.0
2610	Glass and glass products		...	2564.2	2570.2	2631.0		...	714.3	720.0	730.0		55.2	54.0
269	Non-metallic mineral products n.e.c.		...	4694.2	4773.3	5055.0		...	1558.5	1607.6	1614.0		219.2	297.0
2691	Pottery, china and earthenware		...	...	...	...		...	...	...	...		...	...
2692	Refractory ceramic products		...	103.7	104.0	100.0		...	33.2	34.1	34.0		2.3	3.0
2693	Struct.non-refractory clay; ceramic products		...	366.9	363.4	368.0		...	139.2	144.0	159.0		29.6	70.0
2694	Cement, lime and plaster		...	1000.4	1073.4	1028.0		...	420.4	447.8	388.0		33.3	37.0
2695	Articles of concrete, cement and plaster		...	2373.3	2314.5	2632.0		...	711.4	717.1	775.0		110.4	126.0
2696	Cutting, shaping & finishing of stone		...	433.8	500.0	419.0		...	126.3	136.2	123.0		27.7	30.0
2699	Other non-metallic mineral products n.e.c.		...	303.5	313.4	419.0		...	76.2	84.0	97.0		7.2	23.0
2710	Basic iron and steel		...	8505.4	11012.2	11524.0		...	1918.5	2477.9	2736.0		204.7	105.0
2720	Basic precious and non-ferrous metals		...	3994.1	3631.6	5701.0		...	700.7	752.7	702.0		72.5	76.0
273	Casting of metals		...	446.0	487.1	491.0		...	167.3	164.5	157.0		17.0	11.0
2731	Casting of iron and steel		...	292.1	309.5	314.0		...	105.3	104.4	107.0		13.1	7.0
2732	Casting of non-ferrous metals		...	153.9	177.7	177.0		...	62.1	60.1	50.0		3.9	3.0
281	Struct.metal products;tanks;steam generators		...	4634.5	5032.3	5158.0		...	1560.9	1636.5	1661.0		179.5	217.0
2811	Structural metal products		...	3206.7	3621.1	3693.0		...	1034.8	1130.1	1157.0		132.5	110.0
2812	Tanks, reservoirs and containers of metal		...	894.5	863.7	941.0		...	322.1	308.9	315.0		26.5	95.0
2813	Steam generators		...	533.3	547.5	524.0		...	204.0	197.5	189.0		20.5	12.0
289	Other metal products; metal working services		...	4725.4	5181.3	5426.0		...	1688.1	1727.9	1790.0		233.3	258.0
2891	Metal forging/pressing/stamping/roll-forming		...	303.4	401.8	404.0		...	89.2	108.2	100.0		11.8	20.0
2892	Treatment & coating of metals		...	2441.8	2705.9	2775.0		...	964.4	971.6	1029.0		145.6	149.0
2893	Cutlery, hand tools and general hardware		...	472.0	487.1	492.0		...	180.4	183.6	184.0		28.4	30.0
2899	Other fabricated metal products n.e.c.		...	1508.2	1586.5	1756.0		...	454.1	464.5	477.0		47.5	60.0
291	General purpose machinery		...	4589.6	5135.9	5847.0		...	1388.5	1474.1	1653.0		222.3	138.0
2911	Engines & turbines (not for transport equipment)		...	528.3	...	...		...	72.6	...	...		...	...
2912	Pumps, compressors, taps and valves		...	1309.0	...	...		...	413.8	...	...		...	...
2913	Bearings, gears, gearing & driving elements		...	377.7	358.6	483.0		...	134.2	138.6	170.0		76.2	26.0
2914	Ovens, furnaces and furnace burners		...	51.4	47.3	50.0		...	18.7	19.9	20.0		0.8	1.0
2915	Lifting and handling equipment		...	748.2	828.9	869.0		...	266.4	295.4	298.0		76.2	37.0
2919	Other general purpose machinery		...	1575.1	1923.1	2292.0		...	482.7	483.3	576.0		37.9	47.0

292	Special purpose machinery	...	3372.1	3292.3	3510.0	...	1130.7	1193.1	1271.0	105.2	112.0
2921	Agricultural and forestry machinery	...	805.6	618.4	833.0	...	214.9	194.6	243.0	10.2	41.0
2922	Machine tools	...	286.6	330.1	302.0	...	88.4	94.7	89.0	10.9	11.0
2923	Machinery for metallurgy	...	48.8	45.5	31.0	...	15.2	15.8	14.0	1.5	5.0
2924	Machinery for mining & construction	...	482.1	532.3	595.0	...	278.8	300.8	315.0	32.6	4.0
2925	Food/beverage/tobacco processing machinery	...	133.3	152.4	187.0	...	45.7	50.4	65.0	5.9	9.0
2926	Machinery for textile, apparel and leather	...	736.3	712.9	717.0	...	169.7	187.3	201.0	18.7	20.0
2927	Weapons and ammunition	...	297.1	264.9	258.0	...	103.8	112.2	115.0	7.3	6.0
2929	Other special purpose machinery	...	...	...	...	...	...	...	...	...	...
2930	Domestic appliances n.e.c.	...	204.4	212.4	237.0	...	70.9	78.5	84.0	7.3	6.0
3000	Office, accounting and computing machinery	...	191.6	203.8	223.0	...	54.7	53.3	51.0	4.9	5.0
3110	Electric motors, generators and transformers	...	517.8	567.6	703.0	...	181.8	187.6	210.0	9.2	7.0
3120	Electricity distribution & control apparatus	...	1470.2	1121.2	783.0	...	512.2	385.1	289.0	15.7	9.0
3130	Insulated wire and cable	...	294.8	324.7	576.0	...	79.9	83.5	133.0	2.4	4.0
3140	Accumulators, primary cells and batteries	...	304.2	268.1	235.0	...	129.2	124.4	120.0	2.3	8.0
3150	Lighting equipment and electric lamps	...	453.8	380.3	437.0	...	183.2	154.4	173.0	6.2	14.0
3190	Other electrical equipment n.e.c.	...	656.3	739.5	743.0	...	218.1	254.9	255.0	15.7	19.0
3210	Electronic valves, tubes, etc.	...	1063.3	963.6	919.0	...	458.9	407.2	374.0	27.3	35.0
3220	TV/radio transmitters; line comm. apparatus	...	1425.1	2319.5	2368.0	...	615.2	756.1	760.0	13.0	23.0
3230	TV and radio receivers and associated goods	...	1880.3	1925.6	1920.0	...	660.9	635.9	650.0	39.2	21.0
331	Medical, measuring, testing appliances, etc.	...	1206.5	1335.8	1351.0	...	368.3	427.4	444.0	48.3	28.0
3311	Medical, surgical and orthopaedic equipment	...	562.4	624.9	541.0	...	165.0	199.2	193.0	28.7	19.0
3312	Measuring/testing/navigating appliances,etc.	...	488.2	509.8	631.0	...	146.5	162.8	193.0	13.6	6.0
3313	Industrial process control equipment	...	155.9	201.1	179.0	...	56.8	65.4	57.0	6.0	3.0
3320	Optical instruments & photographic equipment	...	75.0	83.4	88.0	...	28.7	32.0	30.0	1.2	3.0
3330	Watches and clocks	...	22.0	25.2	26.0	...	9.0	8.6	10.0	0.3	-
3410	Motor vehicles	...	12029.6	12812.0	12344.0	...	2275.0	2004.5	2044.0	229.1	360.0
3420	Automobile bodies, trailers & semi-trailers	...	1400.4	1631.6	1724.0	...	345.5	360.4	380.0	31.5	45.0
3430	Parts/accessories for automobiles	...	2596.7	3222.8	3470.0	...	778.7	867.3	843.0	77.8	62.0
351	Building and repairing of ships and boats	...	200.3	217.7	258.0	...	71.3	75.1	79.0	6.5	6.0
3511	Building and repairing of ships	...	176.3	190.5	228.0	...	63.9	66.3	71.0	3.2	5.0
3512	Building/repairing of pleasure/sport. boats	...	24.0	27.2	30.0	...	7.4	8.9	8.0	3.4	2.0
3520	Railway/tramway locomotives & rolling stock	...	...	...	...	...	...	...	...	...	...
3530	Aircraft and spacecraft	...	983.0	1055.3	1167.0	...	425.9	476.2	505.0	39.8	26.0
359	Transport equipment n.e.c.	...	...	...	...	...	...	...	...	...	...
3591	Motorcycles	...	0.4	0.4	-	...	0.2	0.2	-	-	-
3592	Bicycles and invalid carriages	...	...	...	...	...	...	...	...	...	...
3599	Other transport equipment n.e.c.	...	...	...	...	...	...	...	...	...	...
3610	Furniture	...	2780.5	2962.0	2965.0	...	770.5	834.7	814.0	234.4	81.0
369	Manufacturing n.e.c.	...	913.0	1090.8	1090.0	...	194.9	215.2	209.0	28.1	26.0
3691	Jewellery and related articles	...	553.7	733.4	728.0	...	70.0	90.6	109.0	10.7	13.0
3692	Musical instruments	...	10.8	12.6	15.0	...	4.4	4.9	6.0	1.3	2.0
3693	Sports goods	...	16.4	13.6	17.0	...	8.1	6.8	7.0	0.3	-
3694	Games and toys	...	111.1	106.1	71.0	...	49.9	43.3	27.0	7.7	2.0
3699	Other manufacturing n.e.c.	...	221.0	225.1	259.0	...	62.5	69.6	62.0	8.1	9.0
3710	Recycling of metal waste and scrap	...	807.9	1135.2	1178.0	...	103.6	125.7	139.0	27.0	36.0
3720	Recycling of non-metal waste and scrap	...	508.2	728.0	867.0	...	148.0	161.8	199.0	36.2	84.0
D	Total manufacturing	...	176863.0	189564.0	203136.0	...	45700.9	46461.2	48132.0	5272.4	5446.0

Belgium

ISIC Revision 3			Index numbers of industrial production											
			(2000=100)											
ISIC	Industry	Note	1995	1996	1997	1998	1999	2000	2001	2002	2003	2004	2005	2006
15	Food and beverages		91	93	97	100	96	100	104	111	115	121	123	128
16	Tobacco products		148	105	112	116	109	100	96	51	52	59	53	53
17	Textiles		88	87	95	95	94	100	97	95	92	96	91	98
18	Wearing apparel, fur		324	240	204	171	119	100	90	76	64	57	53	52
19	Leather, leather products and footwear		163	165	167	174	168	100	92	78	80	94	93	113
20	Wood products (excl. furniture)		76	75	81	84	89	100	101	110	111	113	111	120
21	Paper and paper products		73	73	81	86	91	100	98	103	107	112	106	106
22	Printing and publishing		86	86	88	93	99	100	97	96	97	100	101	106
23	Coke,refined petroleum products,nuclear fuel		89	100	99	99	100	100	106	114	113	106	93	86
24	Chemicals and chemical products		72	75	83	84	90	100	97	106	113	120	114	118
25	Rubber and plastics products		78	78	85	88	93	100	97	94	99	104	107	116
26	Non-metallic mineral products		90	86	90	89	93	100	98	100	101	105	103	110
27	Basic metals		94	91	92	95	95	100	89	89	92	84	70	72
28	Fabricated metal products		76	81	86	91	96	100	103	104	105	109	107	117
29	Machinery and equipment n.e.c.		97	96	100	103	95	100	99	103	102	111	116	129
30	Office, accounting and computing machinery		41	49	54	59	57	100	93	76	55	49	60	63
31	Electrical machinery and apparatus		61	64	71	76	84	100	98	95	92	99	100	110
32	Radio,television and communication equipment		63	63	68	77	75	100	90	71	74	73	67	65
33	Medical, precision and optical instruments		93	84	90	104	98	100	105	113	115	131	126	144
34	Motor vehicles, trailers, semi-trailers		115	114	111	116	112	100	118	108	101	113	117	122
35	Other transport equipment		84	81	91	92	112	100	98	99	72	82	93	91
36	Furniture; manufacturing n.e.c.		108	100	96	97	95	100	95	86	71	66	63	62
37	Recycling		72	83	90	93	96	100	100	95	84	81	78	80
D	Total manufacturing		86	86	91	93	94	100	100	101	101	106	104	109

Bermuda

Supplier of information:
Department of Statistics, Hamilton.

Basic source of data:
Employment survey.

Major deviations from ISIC (Revision 3):
None reported.

Reference period:
Calendar year.

Scope:
All economically active establishments.

Method of data collection:
Mail questionnaires; online survey.

Type of enumeration:
Complete enumeration.

Adjusted for non-response:
Yes.

Concepts and definitions of variables:
Number of persons engaged is the average of a reference week around the middle of the year.

Related national publications:
The Employment Briefs, published by the Department of Statistics, Hamilton.

Bermuda

ISIC Revision 3		Number of establishments					Number of persons engaged					Wages and salaries				
			(number)					(number)					(Bermudan Dollars)			
ISIC	Industry	Note	2003	2004	2005	2006	Note	2003	2004	2005	2006	Note	2003	2004	2005	2006
151	Processed meat,fish,fruit,vegetables,fats		...	...	...	...		...	...	...	...		...	...	...	...
1511	Processing/preserving of meat		2	2	2	-		2	2	2	-		...	...	...	...
1512	Processing/preserving of fish		...	...	...	...		...	...	...	...		...	...	...	...
1513	Processing/preserving of fruit & vegetables		...	...	...	...		...	...	...	...		...	...	...	...
1514	Vegetable and animal oils and fats		...	...	...	...		...	...	...	...		...	...	...	...
1520	Dairy products		1	1	1	2		18	16	16	22		...	...	...	...
153	Grain mill products; starches; animal feeds		...	...	...	...		...	...	...	...		...	...	...	...
1531	Grain mill products		...	...	...	...		...	...	...	...		...	...	...	...
1532	Starches and starch products		...	...	...	...		...	...	...	...		...	...	...	...
1533	Prepared animal feeds		...	...	...	...		...	...	...	...		...	...	...	...
154	Other food products		...	...	...	...		...	...	...	...		...	...	...	...
1541	Bakery products		11	11	10	10		113	82	81	73		...	...	...	...
1542	Sugar		...	...	...	...		...	...	...	...		...	...	...	...
1543	Cocoa, chocolate and sugar confectionery		...	...	...	...		...	...	...	...		...	...	...	...
1544	Macaroni, noodles & similar products		...	...	...	...		...	...	...	...		...	...	...	...
1549	Other food products n.e.c.		...	...	...	...		...	...	...	...		...	...	...	...
155	Beverages		...	...	...	...		...	...	...	...		...	...	...	...
1551	Distilling, rectifying & blending of spirits		...	...	...	...		...	...	...	...		...	...	...	...
1552	Wines		...	...	...	...		...	...	...	...		...	...	...	...
1553	Malt liquors and malt		...	...	...	...		...	...	...	...		...	...	...	...
1554	Soft drinks; mineral waters		3	1	1	1		100	108	110	115		...	...	...	...
1600	Tobacco products		...	...	...	...		...	...	...	...		...	...	...	...
171	Spinning, weaving and finishing of textiles		...	...	...	...		...	...	...	...		...	...	...	...
1711	Textile fibre preparation; textile weaving		...	...	...	...		...	...	...	...		...	...	...	...
1712	Finishing of textiles		...	...	...	...		...	...	...	...		...	...	...	...
172	Other textiles		...	...	...	...		...	...	...	...		...	...	...	...
1721	Made-up textile articles, except apparel		4	4	4	4		15	12	14	15		...	...	...	...
1722	Carpets and rugs		...	...	...	...		...	...	...	...		...	...	...	...
1723	Cordage, rope, twine and netting		...	...	...	...		...	...	...	...		...	...	...	...
1729	Other textiles n.e.c.		...	1	1	1		...	6	5	4		...	...	...	...
1730	Knitted and crocheted fabrics and articles		...	...	...	...		...	...	...	...		...	...	...	...
1810	Wearing apparel, except fur apparel		12	9	-	7		17	15	-	12		...	...	...	...
1820	Dressing & dyeing of fur; processing of fur		...	...	...	...		...	...	...	...		...	...	...	...
191	Tanning, dressing and processing of leather		...	...	...	...		...	...	...	...		...	...	...	...
1911	Tanning and dressing of leather		...	...	...	...		...	...	...	...		...	...	...	...
1912	Luggage, handbags, etc.; saddlery & harness		...	...	...	...		...	...	...	...		...	...	...	...
1920	Footwear		...	...	...	...		...	...	...	...		...	...	...	...
2010	Sawmilling and planing of wood		1	1	1	1		2	2	4	5		...	...	...	...
202	Products of wood, cork, straw, etc.		14	13	10	10		25	28	24	24		...	...	...	...
2021	Veneer sheets, plywood, particle board, etc.		...	...	...	...		...	...	...	...		...	...	...	...
2022	Builders' carpentry and joinery		2	2	2	1		6	7	7	6		...	...	...	...
2023	Wooden containers		...	...	...	...		...	...	...	...		...	...	...	...
2029	Other wood products; articles of cork/straw		...	...	...	...		...	...	...	...		...	...	...	...
210	Paper and paper products		...	...	...	...		...	...	...	...		...	...	...	...
2101	Pulp, paper and paperboard		...	...	...	...		...	...	...	...		...	...	...	...
2102	Corrugated paper and paperboard		...	...	...	...		...	...	...	...		...	...	...	...
2109	Other articles of paper and paperboard		...	...	...	...		...	...	...	...		...	...	...	...
221	Publishing		...	...	...	...		...	...	...	...		...	...	...	...
2211	Publishing of books and other publications		4	7	8	8		10	13	15	18		...	...	...	...
2212	Publishing of newspapers, journals, etc.		3	3	3	3		204	202	203	194		...	...	...	...
2213	Publishing of recorded media		...	...	...	...		...	...	...	...		...	...	...	...
2219	Other publishing		6	5	6	6		18	14	16	12		...	...	...	...

222	Printing and related service activities	12	11	11	11	138	126	118	97	...	...	...	...
2221	Printing	...	...	...	...	...	...	...	...	...	...	...	...
2222	Service activities related to printing	...	...	...	...	...	...	...	...	...	...	...	...
2230	Reproduction of recorded media	...	...	...	...	...	...	...	...	...	...	...	...
2310	Coke oven products	...	...	...	...	...	...	...	...	...	...	...	...
2320	Refined petroleum products	...	...	...	...	...	...	...	...	...	...	...	...
2330	Processing of nuclear fuel	...	...	...	...	...	...	...	...	...	...	...	...
241	Basic chemicals	...	...	1	...	...	...	4	...	...	...	...	...
2411	Basic chemicals, except fertilizers	...	...	...	...	...	...	...	...	...	...	...	...
2412	Fertilizers and nitrogen compounds	...	...	...	...	...	...	...	...	...	...	...	...
2413	Plastics in primary forms; synthetic rubber	...	...	...	...	...	...	...	...	...	...	...	...
242	Other chemicals	...	...	...	...	...	...	...	...	...	...	...	...
2421	Pesticides and other agro-chemical products	...	...	...	...	...	...	...	...	...	...	...	...
2422	Paints, varnishes, printing ink and mastics	2	2	2	2	19	20	17	16	...	...	...	...
2423	Pharmaceuticals, medicinal chemicals, etc.	...	...	...	...	...	...	...	...	...	...	...	...
2424	Soap, cleaning & cosmetic preparations	2	2	1	1	12	8	2	4	...	...	...	...
2429	Other chemical products n.e.c.	...	...	...	...	...	...	...	...	...	...	...	...
2430	Man-made fibres	...	...	...	...	...	...	...	...	...	...	...	...
251	Rubber products	...	...	...	...	...	...	...	...	...	...	...	...
2511	Rubber tyres and tubes	...	...	...	...	...	...	...	...	...	...	...	...
2519	Other rubber products	...	...	...	...	...	...	...	...	...	...	...	...
2520	Plastic products	2	2	2	2	5	7	7	7	...	...	...	...
2610	Glass and glass products	3	2	2	2	18	10	10	16	...	...	...	...
269	Non-metallic mineral products n.e.c.	...	...	...	...	...	...	...	...	...	...	...	...
2691	Pottery, china and earthenware	...	...	...	...	...	...	...	...	...	...	...	...
2692	Refractory ceramic products	...	...	...	...	...	...	...	...	...	...	...	...
2693	Struct.non-refractory clay; ceramic products	...	1	1	-	...	1	1	-	...	...	...	...
2694	Cement, lime and plaster	...	...	...	...	...	...	...	...	...	...	...	...
2695	Articles of concrete, cement and plaster	2	3	3	3	109	110	109	102	...	...	...	...
2696	Cutting, shaping & finishing of stone	1	1	1	-	1	1	1	-	...	...	...	...
2699	Other non-metallic mineral products n.e.c.	...	...	...	...	...	...	...	...	...	...	...	...
2710	Basic iron and steel	...	...	...	...	...	...	...	...	...	...	...	...
2720	Basic precious and non-ferrous metals	...	...	...	...	...	...	...	...	...	...	...	...
273	Casting of metals	...	...	...	...	...	...	...	...	...	...	...	...
2731	Casting of iron and steel	...	...	...	...	...	...	...	...	...	...	...	...
2732	Casting of non-ferrous metals	...	...	...	...	...	...	...	...	...	...	...	...
281	Struct.metal products;tanks;steam generators	2	2	3	3	7	8	10	9	...	...	...	...
2811	Structural metal products	...	...	...	...	...	...	...	...	...	...	...	...
2812	Tanks, reservoirs and containers of metal	...	...	...	...	...	...	...	...	...	...	...	...
2813	Steam generators	...	...	...	...	...	...	...	...	...	...	...	...
289	Other metal products; metal working services	18	18	19	22	35	39	38	39	...	...	...	...
2891	Metal forging/pressing/stamping/roll-forming	...	...	...	...	...	...	...	...	...	...	...	...
2892	Treatment & coating of metals	...	...	...	...	...	...	...	...	...	...	...	...
2893	Cutlery, hand tools and general hardware	...	...	...	...	...	...	...	...	...	...	...	...
2899	Other fabricated metal products n.e.c.	...	...	...	...	...	...	...	...	...	...	...	...
291	General purpose machinery	...	...	...	...	...	...	...	...	...	...	...	...
2911	Engines & turbines (not for transport equipment)	...	...	...	...	...	...	...	...	...	...	...	...
2912	Pumps, compressors, taps and valves	...	...	...	...	...	...	...	...	...	...	...	...
2913	Bearings, gears, gearing & driving elements	...	...	...	...	...	...	...	...	...	...	...	...
2914	Ovens, furnaces and furnace burners	...	...	...	...	...	...	...	...	...	...	...	...
2915	Lifting and handling equipment	...	...	...	...	...	...	...	...	...	...	...	...
2919	Other general purpose machinery	...	...	...	...	...	...	...	...	...	...	...	...
292	Special purpose machinery	...	...	...	...	...	...	...	...	...	...	...	...
2921	Agricultural and forestry machinery	...	...	...	...	...	...	...	...	...	...	...	...
2922	Machine tools	...	...	...	...	...	...	...	...	...	...	...	...
2923	Machinery for metallurgy	...	...	...	...	...	...	...	...	...	...	...	...
2924	Machinery for mining & construction	...	...	...	...	...	...	...	...	...	...	...	...
2925	Food/beverage/tobacco processing machinery	...	...	...	...	...	...	...	...	...	...	...	...
2926	Machinery for textile, apparel and leather	...	...	...	...	...	...	...	...	...	...	...	...
2927	Weapons and ammunition	...	...	...	...	...	...	...	...	...	...	...	...
2929	Other special purpose machinery	...	...	...	...	...	...	...	...	...	...	...	...

continued

Bermuda

ISIC Revision 3		Number of establishments					Number of persons engaged					Wages and salaries				
			(number)					(number)					(Bermudan Dollars)			
ISIC	Industry	Note	2003	2004	2005	2006	Note	2003	2004	2005	2006	Note	2003	2004	2005	2006
2930	Domestic appliances n.e.c.		1	2	2	1		2	3	3	1		...	...	...	...
3000	Office, accounting and computing machinery		...	...	...	...		...	...	...	...		...	...	...	...
3110	Electric motors, generators and transformers		...	...	...	...		...	...	...	...		...	...	...	...
3120	Electricity distribution & control apparatus		1	1	-	1		4	4	-	6		...	...	...	...
3130	Insulated wire and cable		...	...	...	...		...	...	...	...		...	...	...	...
3140	Accumulators, primary cells and batteries		...	...	...	...		...	...	...	...		...	...	...	...
3150	Lighting equipment and electric lamps		...	...	...	...		...	...	...	...		...	...	...	...
3190	Other electrical equipment n.e.c.		...	...	...	...		...	...	...	...		...	...	...	...
3210	Electronic valves, tubes, etc.		...	...	...	...		...	...	...	...		...	...	...	...
3220	TV/radio transmitters; line comm. apparatus		...	...	...	...		...	...	...	...		...	...	...	...
3230	TV and radio receivers and associated goods		...	...	...	...		...	...	...	...		...	...	...	...
331	Medical, measuring, testing appliances, etc.		...	...	...	...		...	...	...	...		...	...	...	...
3311	Medical, surgical and orthopaedic equipment		...	...	...	...		...	...	...	...		...	...	...	...
3312	Measuring/testing/navigating appliances,etc.		...	...	...	...		...	...	...	...		...	...	...	...
3313	Industrial process control equipment		...	...	...	...		...	...	...	...		...	...	...	...
3320	Optical instruments & photographic equipment		...	...	...	...		...	...	...	...		...	...	...	...
3330	Watches and clocks		...	...	...	...		...	...	...	...		...	...	...	...
3410	Motor vehicles		...	...	...	...		...	...	...	...		...	...	...	...
3420	Automobile bodies, trailers & semi-trailers		...	...	...	...		...	...	...	...		...	...	...	...
3430	Parts/accessories for automobiles		...	...	...	...		...	...	...	...		...	...	...	...
351	Building and repairing of ships and boats		30	25	27	30		70	57	59	62		...	...	...	...
3511	Building and repairing of ships		...	...	...	...		...	...	...	...		...	...	...	...
3512	Building/repairing of pleasure/sport. boats		...	...	...	...		...	...	...	...		...	...	...	...
3520	Railway/tramway locomotives & rolling stock		...	...	...	...		...	...	...	...		...	...	...	...
3530	Aircraft and spacecraft		...	...	...	...		...	...	...	...		...	...	...	...
359	Transport equipment n.e.c.		...	...	...	...		...	...	...	...		...	...	...	...
3591	Motorcycles		...	...	...	...		...	...	...	...		...	...	...	...
3592	Bicycles and invalid carriages		...	...	...	...		...	...	...	...		...	...	...	...
3599	Other transport equipment n.e.c.		...	...	...	...		...	...	...	...		...	...	...	...
3610	Furniture		38	36	36	35		116	104	107	102		...	...	...	...
369	Manufacturing n.e.c.		5	4	4	3		10	7	6	4		...	...	...	...
3691	Jewellery and related articles		...	...	...	...		...	...	...	...		...	...	...	...
3692	Musical instruments		...	...	...	...		...	...	...	...		...	...	...	...
3693	Sports goods		...	...	...	...		...	...	...	...		...	...	...	...
3694	Games and toys		...	...	...	...		...	...	...	...		...	...	...	...
3699	Other manufacturing n.e.c.		...	...	...	...		...	...	...	...		...	...	...	...
3710	Recycling of metal waste and scrap		...	...	...	...		...	...	...	...		...	...	...	...
3720	Recycling of non-metal waste and scrap		...	...	9	...		...	...	14	...		...	...	...	...
D	Total manufacturing		183	172	173	170		1078	1012	1003	965		...	...	...	...

Botswana

Supplier of information:
Central Statistics Office, Gaborone.

Basic source of data:
Survey of employment and employees (biannual); census of production and distribution (annual).

Major deviations from ISIC (Revision 3):
None reported.

Reference period:
Fiscal year ending 30 June of the year indicated.

Scope:
Licensed establishments with one or more paid employees.

Method of data collection:
Mail questionnaires.

Type of enumeration:
Not reported.

Adjusted for non-response:
Yes.

Concepts and definitions of variables:
Wages and salaries refers only to direct wages and salaries.

Related national publications:
Statistical Bulletin (quarterly); Employment Survey Report (annual); National Accounts of Botswana (annual), all published by the Central Statistics Office, Gaborone.

ISIC Revision 3		Number of establishments					Number of employees					Wages and salaries paid to employees				
			(number)					(number)					(thousands of Botswana Pula)			
ISIC	Industry	Note	2003	2004	2005	2006	Note	2003	2004	2005	2006	Note	2003	2004	2005	2006
151	Processed meat,fish,fruit,vegetables,fats		...	...	...	...		...	...	...	...		...	...	...	...
1511	Processing/preserving of meat		11	11	11	...		1847	1586	1466	1431		4170	4850	4700	5189
1512	Processing/preserving of fish		...	...	...	...		...	...	...	...		...	...	...	...
1513	Processing/preserving of fruit & vegetables		...	...	...	...		...	...	...	...		...	...	...	...
1514	Vegetable and animal oils and fats		...	...	...	...		...	...	...	...		...	...	...	...
1520	Dairy products		24	23	26	...		316	377	494	461		460	550	600	1927
153	Grain mill products; starches; animal feeds		38	36	34	...		1392	1608	2353	2604		1820	2400	3400	1668
1531	Grain mill products		...	...	...	...		...	...	...	...		...	...	...	...
1532	Starches and starch products		...	...	...	...		...	...	...	...		...	...	...	...
1533	Prepared animal feeds		...	...	...	...		...	...	...	...		...	...	...	...
154	Other food products		...	...	...	...		...	...	...	...		...	...	...	...
1541	Bakery products		105	103	106	...		2016	2339	1645	4372		1760	2320	1500	1173
1542	Sugar		...	...	...	...	a/	386	276	294	467		...	...	...	2491a/
1543	Cocoa, chocolate and sugar confectionery		...	...	...	...	a/	...	...	...	...		...	...	...	...a/
1544	Macaroni, noodles & similar products		...	...	...	...	a/	...	...	...	...		...	...	...	...a/
1549	Other food products n.e.c.		43	...	41	...	a/	...	...	...	...		...	...	...	...a/
155	Beverages		10	10	11	...		863	806	1098	1167		...	...	...	2133
1551	Distilling, rectifying & blending of spirits		...	...	...	...		...	...	...	...		...	...	...	...
1552	Wines		...	...	...	...		...	...	...	...		...	...	...	...
1553	Malt liquors and malt		...	...	...	...		...	...	...	...		...	...	...	...
1554	Soft drinks; mineral waters		...	...	...	...		...	...	...	...		...	...	...	...
1600	Tobacco products		...	...	...	...		...	...	...	...		...	...	...	...
171	Spinning, weaving and finishing of textiles		85b/	84b/	86b/	...	b/	2791	3315	2702	1923	b/	2000	3000	2100	890
1711	Textile fibre preparation; textile weaving		...	...	...	...		...	...	...	...		...	...	...	...
1712	Finishing of textiles		...	...	...	...		...	...	...	...		...	...	...	...
172	Other textiles		...b/	...b/	...b/	...	b/	...	...	...	...	b/	...	...	...	...
1721	Made-up textile articles, except apparel		...	...	...	...		...	...	...	...		...	...	...	...
1722	Carpets and rugs		...	...	...	...		...	...	...	...		...	...	...	...
1723	Cordage, rope, twine and netting		...	...	...	...		...	...	...	...		...	...	...	...
1729	Other textiles n.e.c.		...	...	...	...		...	...	...	...		...	...	...	...
1730	Knitted and crocheted fabrics and articles		...b/	...b/	...b/	...	b/	...	...	...	...	b/	...	...	...	...
1810	Wearing apparel, except fur apparel		233	229	236	...	c/	8344	8463	7319	4389	c/	4940	7060	5300	840
1820	Dressing & dyeing of fur; processing of fur		...	...	...	...	c/	...	...	...	...	c/	...	...	...	...
191	Tanning, dressing and processing of leather		11	10	11	...		25	...	19	39		...	...	...	4448
1911	Tanning and dressing of leather		...	...	...	...		...	...	...	...		...	...	...	...
1912	Luggage, handbags, etc.; saddlery & harness		...	...	...	...		...	...	...	...		...	...	...	...
1920	Footwear		7	7	7	...		607	542	540	557		400	390	400	683
2010	Sawmilling and planing of wood		29d/	29d/	30d/	...	d/	690	452	537	490	d/	710	450	600	1129
202	Products of wood, cork, straw, etc.		...d/	...d/	...d/	...	d/	...	...	...	...	d/	...	...	...	...
2021	Veneer sheets, plywood, particle board, etc.		...	...	...	...		...	...	...	...		...	...	...	...
2022	Builders' carpentry and joinery		...	...	...	...		...	...	...	...		...	...	...	...
2023	Wooden containers		...	...	...	...		...	...	...	...		...	...	...	...
2029	Other wood products; articles of cork/straw		...	...	...	...		...	...	...	...		...	...	...	...
210	Paper and paper products		33	30	28	...		367	333	289	428		490	450	300	1988
2101	Pulp, paper and paperboard		...	...	...	...		...	...	...	...		...	...	...	...
2102	Corrugated paper and paperboard		...	...	...	...		...	...	...	...		...	...	...	...
2109	Other articles of paper and paperboard		...	...	...	...		...	...	...	...		...	...	...	...
221	Publishing		91e/	89e/	94e/	...	e/	1143	1922	1617	1216	e/	1810	4280	5400	2084
2211	Publishing of books and other publications		...	...	...	...		...	...	...	...		...	...	...	...
2212	Publishing of newspapers, journals, etc.		...	...	...	...		...	...	...	...		...	...	...	...
2213	Publishing of recorded media		...	...	...	...		...	...	...	...		...	...	...	...
2219	Other publishing		...	...	...	...		...	...	...	...		...	...	...	...

222	Printing and related service activities	...e/	...e/	...e/	...	e/	...	...	...	...	e/	...	...	...	...
2221	Printing	...	...	...	...		...	...	...	...		...	...	...	...
2222	Service activities related to printing	...	...	...	...		...	...	...	...		...	...	...	...
2230	Reproduction of recorded media	...	...	...	...		...	...	...	...		...	...	...	...
2310	Coke oven products	...	...	...	...		...	...	...	...		...	...	...	...
2320	Refined petroleum products	...	...	...	...		...	...	...	...		...	...	...	...
2330	Processing of nuclear fuel	...	...	...	...		...	...	...	...		...	...	...	...
241	Basic chemicals	60f/	58f/	57f/	...	f/	666	680	677	1183	f/	1320	1890	1900	2649
2411	Basic chemicals, except fertilizers	...	...	...	...		...	...	...	...		...	...	...	...
2412	Fertilizers and nitrogen compounds	...	...	...	...		...	...	...	...		...	...	...	...
2413	Plastics in primary forms; synthetic rubber	...	...	...	...		...	...	...	...		...	...	...	...
242	Other chemicals	...f/	...f/	...f/	...	f/	...	...	...	...	f/	...	...	...	...
2421	Pesticides and other agro-chemical products	...	...	...	...		...	...	...	...		...	...	...	...
2422	Paints, varnishes, printing ink and mastics	...	...	...	...		...	...	...	...		...	...	...	...
2423	Pharmaceuticals, medicinal chemicals, etc.	...	...	...	...		...	...	...	...		...	...	...	...
2424	Soap, cleaning & cosmetic preparations	...	...	...	...		...	...	...	...		...	...	...	...
2429	Other chemical products n.e.c.	...	...	...	...		...	...	...	...		...	...	...	...
2430	Man-made fibres	...f/	...f/	...f/	...	f/	...	...	...	...	f/	...	...	...	...
251	Rubber products	22g/	20g/	20g/	...	g/	896	1555	1189	482	g/	4620	1130	3500	2509
2511	Rubber tyres and tubes	...	...	...	...		...	...	...	...		...	...	...	...
2519	Other rubber products	...	...	...	...		...	...	...	...		...	...	...	...
2520	Plastic products	...g/	...g/	...g/	...	g/	...	...	...	...	g/	...	...	...	...
2610	Glass and glass products	108h/	103h/	108h/	...	h/	2122	2798	2616	2363	h/	2770	3360	12400	1324
269	Non-metallic mineral products n.e.c.	...h/	...h/	...h/	...	h/	...	...	...	...	h/	...	...	...	...
2691	Pottery, china and earthenware	...	...	...	...		...	...	...	...		...	...	...	...
2692	Refractory ceramic products	...	...	...	...		...	...	...	...		...	...	...	...
2693	Struct.non-refractory clay; ceramic products	...	...	...	...		...	...	...	...		...	...	...	...
2694	Cement, lime and plaster	...	...	...	...		...	...	...	100		...	...	...	6774
2695	Articles of concrete, cement and plaster	...	...	...	...		...	...	...	...		...	...	...	...
2696	Cutting, shaping & finishing of stone	...	...	...	...		...	...	...	...		...	...	...	...
2699	Other non-metallic mineral products n.e.c.	...	...	...	...		...	...	...	...		...	...	...	...
2710	Basic iron and steel	5i/	5i/	5i/	...	i/	294	83	83	83	i/	210	80	100	928
2720	Basic precious and non-ferrous metals	...i/	...i/	...i/	...	i/	...	...	...	...	i/	...	...	...	...
273	Casting of metals	...i/	...i/	...i/	...	i/	...	...	...	...	i/	...	...	...	...
2731	Casting of iron and steel	...	...	...	...		...	...	...	...		...	...	...	...
2732	Casting of non-ferrous metals	...	...	...	...		...	...	...	...		...	...	...	...
281	Struct.metal products;tanks;steam generators	...	...	...	...		...	...	...	...		...	...	...	...
2811	Structural metal products	190j/	186j/	181j/	...	j/	2976	5115	3092	2904	j/	3110	8290	3400	2317
2812	Tanks, reservoirs and containers of metal	...	...	...	...		...	...	...	...		...	...	...	...
2813	Steam generators	...	...	...	...		...	...	...	...		...	...	...	...
289	Other metal products; metal working services	...j/	...j/	...j/	...	j/	...	...	...	...	j/	...	...	...	...
2891	Metal forging/pressing/stamping/roll-forming	...	...	...	...		...	...	...	...		...	...	...	...
2892	Treatment & coating of metals	...	...	...	...		...	...	...	...		...	...	...	...
2893	Cutlery, hand tools and general hardware	...	...	...	...		...	...	...	...		...	...	...	...
2899	Other fabricated metal products n.e.c.	...	...	...	...		...	...	...	...		...	...	...	...
291	General purpose machinery	23k/	20k/	23k/	...	k/	325	652	1036	754	k/	650	1180	1900	1768
2911	Engines & turbines (not for transport equipment)	...	...	...	...		...	...	...	...		...	...	...	...
2912	Pumps, compressors, taps and valves	...	...	...	...		...	...	...	...		...	...	...	...
2913	Bearings, gears, gearing & driving elements	...	...	...	...		...	...	...	...		...	...	...	...
2914	Ovens, furnaces and furnace burners	...	...	...	...		...	...	...	...		...	...	...	...
2915	Lifting and handling equipment	...	...	...	...		...	...	...	...		...	...	...	...
2919	Other general purpose machinery	...	...	...	...		...	...	...	...		...	...	...	...
292	Special purpose machinery	...k/	...k/	...k/	...	k/	...	...	...	...	k/	...	...	...	...
2921	Agricultural and forestry machinery	...	...	...	...		...	...	...	...		...	...	...	...
2922	Machine tools	...	...	...	...		...	...	...	...		...	...	...	...
2923	Machinery for metallurgy	...	...	...	...		...	...	...	...		...	...	...	...
2924	Machinery for mining & construction	...	...	...	...		...	...	...	...		...	...	...	...
2925	Food/beverage/tobacco processing machinery	...	...	...	...		...	...	...	...		...	...	...	...
2926	Machinery for textile, apparel and leather	...	...	...	...		...	...	...	...		...	...	...	...
2927	Weapons and ammunition	...	...	...	...		...	...	...	...		...	...	...	...
2929	Other special purpose machinery	...	...	...	...		...	...	...	...		...	...	...	...

continued

Botswana

ISIC Revision 3		Number of establishments					Number of employees					Wages and salaries paid to employees				
			(number)					(number)					(thousands of Botswana Pula)			
ISIC	Industry	Note	2003	2004	2005	2006	Note	2003	2004	2005	2006	Note	2003	2004	2005	2006
2930	Domestic appliances n.e.c.		...k/	...k/	...k/	...	k/	...	...	...	...	k/	...	...	...	...
3000	Office, accounting and computing machinery		2	2	7	...		...	...	...	180		...	...	...	4353
3110	Electric motors, generators and transformers		...	...	...	...		...	...	...	...		160	40	...	4649
3120	Electricity distribution & control apparatus		...	...	...	...		...	...	...	...		...	...	...	...
3130	Insulated wire and cable		...	...	...	...		...	...	...	...		...	...	...	...
3140	Accumulators, primary cells and batteries		...	...	...	...		...	...	...	...		...	...	...	...
3150	Lighting equipment and electric lamps		...	...	...	...		...	...	...	...		...	...	...	...
3190	Other electrical equipment n.e.c.		4	4	4	...		...	...	...	...		...	...	...	...
3210	Electronic valves, tubes, etc.		...	...	...	...		...	...	...	...		30	30	...	...
3220	TV/radio transmitters; line comm. apparatus		...	...	...	...		...	...	...	16		...	...	...	4649
3230	TV and radio receivers and associated goods		2	2	2	...		...	...	...	...		...	...	...	...
331	Medical, measuring, testing appliances, etc.		2m/	2m/	4m/	...		9m/	...	...	130m/		20m/	260m/	...	2551m/
3311	Medical, surgical and orthopaedic equipment		...	...	...	...		...	...	...	...		...	...	...	...
3312	Measuring/testing/navigating appliances,etc.		...	...	...	...		...	...	...	...		...	...	...	...
3313	Industrial process control equipment		...	...	...	...		...	...	...	...		...	...	...	...
3320	Optical instruments & photographic equipment		...m/	...m/	...m/	...		...m/	...	...	...m/		...m/	...m/	...	...m/
3330	Watches and clocks		...m/	...m/	...m/	...		...m/	...	...	...m/		...m/	...m/	...	...m/
3410	Motor vehicles		18n/	18n/	17n/	...	n/	198	282	325	83	n/	410	380	600	2648
3420	Automobile bodies, trailers & semi-trailers		...n/	...n/	...n/	...	n/	...	...	...	...	n/	...	...	...	...
3430	Parts/accessories for automobiles		...n/	...n/	...n/	...	n/	...	...	...	...	n/	...	...	...	...
351	Building and repairing of ships and boats		...	...	...	...		...	...	...	...		...	...	...	...
3511	Building and repairing of ships		...	...	...	...		...	...	...	...		...	...	...	...
3512	Building/repairing of pleasure/sport. boats		...	...	...	...		...	...	...	...		...	...	...	...
3520	Railway/tramway locomotives & rolling stock		...	...	...	...		...	...	...	...		...	...	...	...
3530	Aircraft and spacecraft		...	...	...	...		...	...	...	...		...	...	...	...
359	Transport equipment n.e.c.		2	2	2	...		...	...	...	...		...	...	...	...
3591	Motorcycles		...	...	...	...		...	...	...	...		...	...	...	...
3592	Bicycles and invalid carriages		...	...	...	...		...	...	...	...		...	...	...	...
3599	Other transport equipment n.e.c.		...	...	...	...		...	...	...	10		...	...	...	964
3610	Furniture		72	70	72	...		699	1409	1440	5515		910	1600	1800	750
369	Manufacturing n.e.c.		70	67	67	...		547	661	670	377		810	870	800	...
3691	Jewellery and related articles		10	10	8	...		476	416	445	803		320	280	300	1845
3692	Musical instruments		...	...	...	...		...	...	...	...		...	...	...	...
3693	Sports goods		...	...	...	...		...	...	...	...		...	...	...	...
3694	Games and toys		...	...	...	...		...	...	...	...		...	...	...	...
3699	Other manufacturing n.e.c.		...	...	...	...		...	...	...	...		...	...	...	688
3710	Recycling of metal waste and scrap		3	3	3	...		...	...	...	...		...	...	...	...
3720	Recycling of non-metal waste and scrap		...	...	...	...		...	...	...	...		...	...	...	...
D	Total manufacturing		1313	1272	1301	...		30169	35254	31946	34533		...	...	...	...

a/ 1542 includes 1543, 1544 and 1549.
b/ 171 includes 172 and 1730.
c/ 1810 includes 1820.
d/ 2010 includes 202.
e/ 221 includes 222.
f/ 241 includes 242 and 2430.
g/ 251 includes 2520.
h/ 2610 includes 269.
i/ 2710 includes 2720 and 273.
j/ 2811 includes 289.
k/ 291 includes 292 and 2930.
m/ 331 includes 3320 and 3330.
n/ 3410 includes 3420 and 3430.

Botswana

ISIC Revision 3		Output					Value added					Gross fixed capital formation		
			(millions of Botswana Pula)					(millions of Botswana Pula)					(millions of Botswana Pula)	
ISIC	Industry	Note	2003	2004	2005	2006	Note	2003	2004	2005	2006	Note	2005	2006
151	Processed meat,fish,fruit,vegetables,fats		...	...	...	...		...	...	...	...		...	...
1511	Processing/preserving of meat		384.6	432.3	471.2	509.0		95.5	102.6	111.7	120.8		...	...
1512	Processing/preserving of fish		...	...	...	...		...	...	...	...		...	...
1513	Processing/preserving of fruit & vegetables		...	...	...	...		...	...	...	...		...	...
1514	Vegetable and animal oils and fats		...	...	...	...		...	...	...	...		...	...
1520	Dairy products		...	...	...	...		...	...	...	...		...	...
153	Grain mill products; starches; animal feeds		...	...	...	...		...	...	...	...		...	...
1531	Grain mill products		...	...	...	...		...	...	...	...		...	...
1532	Starches and starch products		...	...	...	...		...	...	...	...		...	...
1533	Prepared animal feeds		...	...	...	...		...	...	...	...		...	...
154	Other food products		...	...	...	...		...	...	...	...		...	...
1541	Bakery products		...	...	...	...		...	...	...	...		...	...
1542	Sugar		...	...	...	...		...	...	...	...		...	...
1543	Cocoa, chocolate and sugar confectionery		...	...	...	...		...	...	...	...		...	...
1544	Macaroni, noodles & similar products		...	...	...	...		...	...	...	...		...	...
1549	Other food products n.e.c.		...	...	...	...		...	...	...	...		...	...
155	Beverages		794.9	851.6	1054.6	1094.9		221.0	233.0	288.4	300.2		...	...
1551	Distilling, rectifying & blending of spirits		...	...	...	...		...	...	...	...		...	...
1552	Wines		...	...	...	...		...	...	...	...		...	...
1553	Malt liquors and malt		...	...	...	...		...	...	...	...		...	...
1554	Soft drinks; mineral waters		...	...	...	...		...	...	...	...		...	...
1600	Tobacco products		...	...	...	...		...	...	...	...		...	...
171	Spinning, weaving and finishing of textiles	a/	221.2	208.6	248.9	297.0	a/	64.3	55.8	69.1	81.7		...	...
1711	Textile fibre preparation; textile weaving		...	...	...	...		...	...	...	...		...	...
1712	Finishing of textiles		...	...	...	...		...	...	...	...		...	...
172	Other textiles	a/	...	...	...	...	a/	...	...	...	...		...	...
1721	Made-up textile articles, except apparel		...	...	...	...		...	...	...	...		...	...
1722	Carpets and rugs		...	...	...	...		...	...	...	...		...	...
1723	Cordage, rope, twine and netting		...	...	...	...		...	...	...	...		...	...
1729	Other textiles n.e.c.		...	...	...	...		...	...	...	...		...	...
1730	Knitted and crocheted fabrics and articles	a/	...	...	...	...	a/	...	...	...	...		...	...
1810	Wearing apparel, except fur apparel		...	...	...	...		...	...	...	...		...	...
1820	Dressing & dyeing of fur; processing of fur		...	...	...	...		...	...	...	...		...	...
191	Tanning, dressing and processing of leather		20.6	18.3	12.9	20.4		6.1	7.6	3.8	6.1		...	...
1911	Tanning and dressing of leather		...	...	...	...		...	...	...	...		...	...
1912	Luggage, handbags, etc.; saddlery & harness		...	...	...	...		...	...	...	...		...	...
1920	Footwear		...	...	...	...		...	...	...	...		...	...
2010	Sawmilling and planing of wood		...	...	...	...		...	...	...	...		...	...
202	Products of wood, cork, straw, etc.		...	...	...	...		...	...	...	...		...	...
2021	Veneer sheets, plywood, particle board, etc.		...	...	...	...		...	...	...	...		...	...
2022	Builders' carpentry and joinery		...	...	...	...		...	...	...	...		...	...
2023	Wooden containers		...	...	...	...		...	...	...	...		...	...
2029	Other wood products; articles of cork/straw		...	...	...	...		...	...	...	...		...	...
210	Paper and paper products		...	...	...	...		...	...	...	...		...	...
2101	Pulp, paper and paperboard		...	...	...	...		...	...	...	...		...	...
2102	Corrugated paper and paperboard		...	...	...	...		...	...	...	...		...	...
2109	Other articles of paper and paperboard		...	...	...	...		...	...	...	...		...	...
221	Publishing		...	...	...	...		...	...	...	...		...	...
2211	Publishing of books and other publications		...	...	...	...		...	...	...	...		...	...
2212	Publishing of newspapers, journals, etc.		...	...	...	...		...	...	...	...		...	...
2213	Publishing of recorded media		...	...	...	...		...	...	...	...		...	...
2219	Other publishing		...	...	...	...		...	...	...	...		...	...

continued

Botswana

ISIC Revision 3		Output					Value added					Gross fixed capital formation		
			(millions of Botswana Pula)					(millions of Botswana Pula)					(millions of Botswana Pula)	
ISIC	Industry	Note	2003	2004	2005	2006	Note	2003	2004	2005	2006	Note	2005	2006
222	Printing and related service activities		...	...	...	...		...	...	...	...		...	...
2221	Printing		...	...	...	...		...	...	...	...		...	...
2222	Service activities related to printing		...	...	...	...		...	...	...	...		...	...
2230	Reproduction of recorded media		...	...	...	...		...	...	...	...		...	...
2310	Coke oven products		...	...	...	...		...	...	...	...		...	...
2320	Refined petroleum products		...	...	...	...		...	...	...	...		...	...
2330	Processing of nuclear fuel		...	...	...	...		...	...	...	...		...	...
241	Basic chemicals		...	...	...	...		...	...	...	...		...	...
2411	Basic chemicals, except fertilizers		...	...	...	...		...	...	...	...		...	...
2412	Fertilizers and nitrogen compounds		...	...	...	...		...	...	...	...		...	...
2413	Plastics in primary forms; synthetic rubber		...	...	...	...		...	...	...	...		...	...
242	Other chemicals		...	...	...	...		...	...	...	...		...	...
2421	Pesticides and other agro-chemical products		...	...	...	...		...	...	...	...		...	...
2422	Paints, varnishes, printing ink and mastics		...	...	...	...		...	...	...	...		...	...
2423	Pharmaceuticals, medicinal chemicals, etc.		...	...	...	...		...	...	...	...		...	...
2424	Soap, cleaning & cosmetic preparations		...	...	...	...		...	...	...	...		...	...
2429	Other chemical products n.e.c.		...	...	...	...		...	...	...	...		...	...
2430	Man-made fibres		...	...	...	...		...	...	...	...		...	...
251	Rubber products		...	...	...	...		...	...	...	...		...	...
2511	Rubber tyres and tubes		...	...	...	...		...	...	...	...		...	...
2519	Other rubber products		...	...	...	...		...	...	...	...		...	...
2520	Plastic products		...	...	...	...		...	...	...	...		...	...
2610	Glass and glass products		...	...	...	...		...	...	...	...		...	...
269	Non-metallic mineral products n.e.c.		...	...	...	...		...	...	...	...		...	...
2691	Pottery, china and earthenware		...	...	...	...		...	...	...	...		...	...
2692	Refractory ceramic products		...	...	...	...		...	...	...	...		...	...
2693	Struct.non-refractory clay; ceramic products		...	...	...	...		...	...	...	...		...	...
2694	Cement, lime and plaster		...	...	...	...		...	...	...	...		...	...
2695	Articles of concrete, cement and plaster		...	...	...	...		...	...	...	...		...	...
2696	Cutting, shaping & finishing of stone		...	...	...	...		...	...	...	...		...	...
2699	Other non-metallic mineral products n.e.c.		...	...	...	...		...	...	...	...		...	...
2710	Basic iron and steel		...	...	...	...		...	...	...	...		...	...
2720	Basic precious and non-ferrous metals		...	...	...	...		...	...	...	...		...	...
273	Casting of metals		...	...	...	...		...	...	...	...		...	...
2731	Casting of iron and steel		...	...	...	...		...	...	...	...		...	...
2732	Casting of non-ferrous metals		...	...	...	...		...	...	...	...		...	...
281	Struct.metal products;tanks;steam generators		...	...	...	...		...	...	...	...		...	...
2811	Structural metal products		...	...	...	...		...	...	...	...		...	...
2812	Tanks, reservoirs and containers of metal		...	...	...	...		...	...	...	...		...	...
2813	Steam generators		...	...	...	...		...	...	...	...		...	...
289	Other metal products; metal working services		...	...	...	...		...	...	...	...		...	...
2891	Metal forging/pressing/stamping/roll-forming		...	...	...	...		...	...	...	...		...	...
2892	Treatment & coating of metals		...	...	...	...		...	...	...	...		...	...
2893	Cutlery, hand tools and general hardware		...	...	...	...		...	...	...	...		...	...
2899	Other fabricated metal products n.e.c.		...	...	...	...		...	...	...	...		...	...
291	General purpose machinery		...	...	...	...		...	...	...	...		...	...
2911	Engines & turbines (not for transport equipment)		...	...	...	...		...	...	...	...		...	...
2912	Pumps, compressors, taps and valves		...	...	...	...		...	...	...	...		...	...
2913	Bearings, gears, gearing & driving elements		...	...	...	...		...	...	...	...		...	...
2914	Ovens, furnaces and furnace burners		...	...	...	...		...	...	...	...		...	...
2915	Lifting and handling equipment		...	...	...	...		...	...	...	...		...	...
2919	Other general purpose machinery		...	...	...	...		...	...	...	...		...	...

292	Special purpose machinery	...	...	...	...	...	...	...	...	...	...
2921	Agricultural and forestry machinery	...	...	...	...	...	...	...	...	...	...
2922	Machine tools	...	...	...	...	...	...	...	...	...	...
2923	Machinery for metallurgy	...	...	...	...	...	...	...	...	...	...
2924	Machinery for mining & construction	...	...	...	...	...	...	...	...	...	...
2925	Food/beverage/tobacco processing machinery	...	...	...	...	...	...	...	...	...	...
2926	Machinery for textile, apparel and leather	...	...	...	...	...	...	...	...	...	...
2927	Weapons and ammunition	...	...	...	...	...	...	...	...	...	...
2929	Other special purpose machinery	...	...	...	...	...	...	...	...	...	...
2930	Domestic appliances n.e.c.	...	...	...	...	...	...	...	...	...	...
3000	Office, accounting and computing machinery	...	...	...	...	...	...	...	...	...	...
3110	Electric motors, generators and transformers	...	...	...	...	...	...	...	...	...	...
3120	Electricity distribution & control apparatus	...	...	...	...	...	...	...	...	...	...
3130	Insulated wire and cable	...	...	...	...	...	...	...	...	...	...
3140	Accumulators, primary cells and batteries	...	...	...	...	...	...	...	...	...	...
3150	Lighting equipment and electric lamps	...	...	...	...	...	...	...	...	...	...
3190	Other electrical equipment n.e.c.	...	...	...	...	...	...	...	...	...	...
3210	Electronic valves, tubes, etc.	...	...	...	...	...	...	...	...	...	...
3220	TV/radio transmitters; line comm. apparatus	...	...	...	...	...	...	...	...	...	...
3230	TV and radio receivers and associated goods	...	...	...	...	...	...	...	...	...	...
331	Medical, measuring, testing appliances, etc.	...	...	...	...	...	...	...	...	...	...
3311	Medical, surgical and orthopaedic equipment	...	...	...	...	...	...	...	...	...	...
3312	Measuring/testing/navigating appliances,etc.	...	...	...	...	...	...	...	...	...	...
3313	Industrial process control equipment	...	...	...	...	...	...	...	...	...	...
3320	Optical instruments & photographic equipment	...	...	...	...	...	...	...	...	...	...
3330	Watches and clocks	...	...	...	...	...	...	...	...	...	...
3410	Motor vehicles	...	...	...	...	...	...	...	...	...	...
3420	Automobile bodies, trailers & semi-trailers	...	...	...	...	...	...	...	...	...	...
3430	Parts/accessories for automobiles	...	...	...	...	...	...	...	...	...	...
351	Building and repairing of ships and boats	...	...	...	...	...	...	...	...	...	...
3511	Building and repairing of ships	...	...	...	...	...	...	...	...	...	...
3512	Building/repairing of pleasure/sport. boats	...	...	...	...	...	...	...	...	...	...
3520	Railway/tramway locomotives & rolling stock	...	...	...	...	...	...	...	...	...	...
3530	Aircraft and spacecraft	...	...	...	...	...	...	...	...	...	...
359	Transport equipment n.e.c.	...	...	...	...	...	...	...	...	...	...
3591	Motorcycles	...	...	...	...	...	...	...	...	...	...
3592	Bicycles and invalid carriages	...	...	...	...	...	...	...	...	...	...
3599	Other transport equipment n.e.c.	4893.4	5348.4	5798.1	6316.5	...	...	...	...	...	...
3610	Furniture	...	...	...	...	...	...	...	...	...	...
369	Manufacturing n.e.c.	...	...	...	...	1166.8	1248.5	1299.5	1402.8	...	...
3691	Jewellery and related articles	...	...	...	...	...	...	...	...	...	...
3692	Musical instruments	...	...	...	...	...	...	...	...	...	...
3693	Sports goods	...	...	...	...	...	...	...	...	...	...
3694	Games and toys	...	...	...	...	...	...	...	...	...	...
3699	Other manufacturing n.e.c.	...	...	...	...	...	...	...	...	...	...
3710	Recycling of metal waste and scrap	...	...	...	...	...	...	...	...	...	...
3720	Recycling of non-metal waste and scrap	...	...	...	...	...	...	...	...	...	...
D	Total manufacturing	6314.7	6859.2	7585.7	8237.8	1553.7	1647.5	1772.5	1911.6	...	...

a/ 171 includes 172 and 1730.

Brazil

Supplier of information:
Fundação Instituto Brasileiro de Geografía e Estatística (IBGE), Rio de Janeiro.

Basic source of data:
Annual sample survey.

Major deviations from ISIC (Revision 3):
None reported.

Reference period:
Calendar year.

Scope:
Local units with five or more persons engaged.

Method of data collection:
Data are collected by enumerators using specially designed questionnaires.

Type of enumeration:
Complete enumeration of local units with 30 or more persons engaged; stratified random samples for local units with 5 to 29 persons engaged.

Adjusted for non-response:
Yes.

Concepts and definitions of variables:
Number of establishments refers to local units.
Wages and salaries includes employers' contribution paid to social security, pension and insurance scheme as well as the benefits received by employees under these schemes and severance and termination pay.
Output excludes value of goods shipped in the same condition as received less the amount paid for these goods.

Related national publications:
Annual Industrial Survey - Enterprise Issue, published by Fundação Instituto Brasileiro de Geografía e Estatística (IBGE), Rio de Janeiro.

Brazil

ISIC Revision 3		Number of establishments					Number of persons engaged					Wages and salaries paid to employees				
			(number)					(thousands)					(millions of Brazilian Reais)			
ISIC	Industry	Note	2002	2003	2004	2005	Note	2002	2003	2004	2005	Note	2002	2003	2004	2005
151	Processed meat,fish,fruit,vegetables,fats		3508	3769	4066	4105		308.6	356.0	420.5	440.5		2617.7	3194.7	3962.9	4767.8
1511	Processing/preserving of meat		...	...	...	...		...	...	...	...		...	...	...	...
1512	Processing/preserving of fish		...	...	...	...		...	...	...	...		...	...	...	...
1513	Processing/preserving of fruit & vegetables		...	...	...	...		...	...	...	...		...	...	...	...
1514	Vegetable and animal oils and fats		...	...	...	...		...	...	...	...		...	...	...	...
1520	Dairy products		3400	3506	3553	3290		81.5	78.2	81.7	86.9		930.1	816.1	911.9	1035.9
153	Grain mill products; starches; animal feeds		2501	2866	2807	2809		84.1	88.1	94.7	92.7		981.5	1055.3	1193.1	1345.4
1531	Grain mill products		...	...	...	...		...	...	...	...		...	...	...	...
1532	Starches and starch products		...	...	...	...		...	...	...	...		...	...	...	...
1533	Prepared animal feeds		...	...	...	...		...	...	...	...		...	...	...	...
154	Other food products		12583	12346	13693	14095		445.2	492.8	532.1	559.4		3609.6	4519.8	5210.4	5920.8
1541	Bakery products		...	...	...	...		...	...	...	...		...	...	...	...
1542	Sugar		...	...	...	...		...	...	...	...		...	...	...	...
1543	Cocoa, chocolate and sugar confectionery		...	...	...	...		...	...	...	...		...	...	...	...
1544	Macaroni, noodles & similar products		...	...	...	...		...	...	...	...		...	...	...	...
1549	Other food products n.e.c.		...	...	...	...		...	...	...	...		...	...	...	...
155	Beverages		1729	1658	1704	1657		137.8	154.7	159.9	174.9		1741.8	2107.0	2289.7	2694.5
1551	Distilling, rectifying & blending of spirits		...	...	...	...		...	...	...	...		...	...	...	...
1552	Wines		...	...	...	...		...	...	...	...		...	...	...	...
1553	Malt liquors and malt		...	...	...	...		...	...	...	...		...	...	...	...
1554	Soft drinks; mineral waters		...	...	...	...		...	...	...	...		...	...	...	...
1600	Tobacco products		213	179	197	228		16.1	13.1	19.1	22.5		333.0	363.9	495.3	540.1
171	Spinning, weaving and finishing of textiles		1958	1937	2099	2144		148.6	151.9	159.7	157.0		1320.5	1488.8	1658.7	1780.1
1711	Textile fibre preparation; textile weaving		...	...	...	...		...	...	...	...		...	...	...	...
1712	Finishing of textiles		...	...	...	...		...	...	...	...		...	...	...	...
172	Other textiles		2267	2748	2934	2845		99.2	104.2	110.7	114.0		854.8	962.9	1101.1	1200.6
1721	Made-up textile articles, except apparel		...	...	...	...		...	...	...	...		...	...	...	...
1722	Carpets and rugs		...	...	...	...		...	...	...	...		...	...	...	...
1723	Cordage, rope, twine and netting		...	...	...	...		...	...	...	...		...	...	...	...
1729	Other textiles n.e.c.		...	...	...	...		...	...	...	...		...	...	...	...
1730	Knitted and crocheted fabrics and articles		845	802	1054	1343		28.6	27.8	31.8	32.3		218.8	228.3	293.0	328.0
1810	Wearing apparel, except fur apparel	a/	19096	19901	20005	20314	a/	429.7	433.7	486.8	484.9	a/	2177.1	2506.4	2876.7	3280.9
1820	Dressing & dyeing of fur; processing of fur	a/	...	...	...	...	a/	...	...	...	...	a/	...	...	...	...
191	Tanning, dressing and processing of leather		2197	1806	1976	1983		68.7	71.0	74.1	74.1		436.8	541.6	610.1	666.8
1911	Tanning and dressing of leather		...	...	...	...		...	...	...	...		...	...	...	...
1912	Luggage, handbags, etc.; saddlery & harness		...	...	...	...		...	...	...	...		...	...	...	...
1920	Footwear		4338	4543	4914	5087		294.8	344.4	377.1	314.2		1741.4	2357.3	2672.5	2439.8
2010	Sawmilling and planing of wood		4035	3988	4472	4154		95.5	104.3	117.7	96.3		513.5	622.6	771.7	765.1
202	Products of wood, cork, straw, etc.		4338	4461	4232	4345		123.2	137.7	139.4	130.5		799.0	1077.0	1192.0	1251.1
2021	Veneer sheets, plywood, particle board, etc.		...	...	...	...		...	...	...	...		...	...	...	...
2022	Builders' carpentry and joinery		...	...	...	...		...	...	...	...		...	...	...	...
2023	Wooden containers		...	...	...	...		...	...	...	...		...	...	...	...
2029	Other wood products; articles of cork/straw		...	...	...	...		...	...	...	...		...	...	...	...
210	Paper and paper products		3155	2951	3076	3075		147.9	150.3	156.0	153.4		2344.8	2791.6	3098.9	3282.1
2101	Pulp, paper and paperboard		...	...	...	...		...	...	...	...		...	...	...	...
2102	Corrugated paper and paperboard		...	...	...	...		...	...	...	...		...	...	...	...
2109	Other articles of paper and paperboard		...	...	...	...		...	...	...	...		...	...	...	...
221	Publishing		4280	4037	4005	4586		127.4	129.6	125.3	127.2		2254.0	2394.4	2676.6	2744.4
2211	Publishing of books and other publications		...	...	...	...		...	...	...	...		...	...	...	...
2212	Publishing of newspapers, journals, etc.		...	...	...	...		...	...	...	...		...	...	...	...
2213	Publishing of recorded media		...	...	...	...		...	...	...	...		...	...	...	...
2219	Other publishing		...	...	...	...		...	...	...	...		...	...	...	...

222	Printing and related service activities	3913	4241	4901	4469	54.7	59.5	68.6	64.2	544.0	633.9	802.4	768.2
2221	Printing	...	...	...	...	...	...	...	...	...	...	...	...
2222	Service activities related to printing	...	...	...	...	...	...	...	...	...	...	...	...
2230	Reproduction of recorded media	89	81	77	80	6.8	6.2	5.6	5.5	155.9	151.4	161.3	147.1
2310	Coke oven products	3	3	4	4	0.1	0.1	0.3	0.2	1.2	1.6	2.5	3.4
2320	Refined petroleum products	104	137	174	168	25.4	25.5	27.4	27.8	1373.1	1826.7	2217.0	2516.6
2330	Processing of nuclear fuel	4	4	6	6	0.7	0.7	0.8	0.7	27.2	33.0	34.6	34.6
241	Basic chemicals	1645	1649	1818	2050	79.9	87.2	92.7	96.6	2271.2	2633.5	3160.5	3507.9
2411	Basic chemicals, except fertilizers	...	...	...	...	...	...	...	...	...	...	...	...
2412	Fertilizers and nitrogen compounds	...	...	...	...	...	...	...	...	...	...	...	...
2413	Plastics in primary forms; synthetic rubber	...	...	...	...	...	...	...	...	...	...	...	...
242	Other chemicals	4717	5064	4922	5168	216.6	234.1	234.6	237.3	4940.6	5919.6	6513.2	7261.2
2421	Pesticides and other agro-chemical products	...	...	...	...	...	...	...	...	...	...	...	...
2422	Paints, varnishes, printing ink and mastics	...	...	...	...	...	...	...	...	...	...	...	...
2423	Pharmaceuticals, medicinal chemicals, etc.	...	...	...	...	...	...	...	...	...	...	...	...
2424	Soap, cleaning & cosmetic preparations	...	...	...	...	...	...	...	...	...	...	...	...
2429	Other chemical products n.e.c.	...	...	...	...	...	...	...	...	...	...	...	...
2430	Man-made fibres	56	50	51	47	6.4	6.5	7.1	5.9	147.6	120.1	148.0	159.9
251	Rubber products	1658	1772	1798	1906	72.0	100.3	83.5	86.5	1055.3	1745.7	1517.0	1624.8
2511	Rubber tyres and tubes	...	...	...	...	...	...	...	...	...	...	...	...
2519	Other rubber products	...	...	...	...	...	...	...	...	...	...	...	...
2520	Plastic products	5513	5853	6124	6163	203.3	222.9	233.8	249.4	2202.7	2640.3	3019.0	3465.7
2610	Glass and glass products	438	471	533	431	27.1	27.7	32.0	30.1	423.9	501.5	595.7	603.6
269	Non-metallic mineral products n.e.c.	12113	12449	12682	12375	265.5	264.9	274.3	274.8	2234.8	2574.6	2878.3	3152.1
2691	Pottery, china and earthenware	...	...	...	...	...	...	...	...	...	...	...	...
2692	Refractory ceramic products	...	...	...	...	...	...	...	...	...	...	...	...
2693	Struct.non-refractory clay; ceramic products	...	...	...	...	...	...	...	...	...	...	...	...
2694	Cement, lime and plaster	...	...	...	...	...	...	...	...	...	...	...	...
2695	Articles of concrete, cement and plaster	...	...	...	...	...	...	...	...	...	...	...	...
2696	Cutting, shaping & finishing of stone	...	...	...	...	...	...	...	...	...	...	...	...
2699	Other non-metallic mineral products n.e.c.	...	...	...	...	...	...	...	...	...	...	...	...
2710	Basic iron and steel	739	988	833	929	99.7	106.8	114.3	112.8	2487.9	2833.2	3462.0	3700.8
2720	Basic precious and non-ferrous metals	640	549	646	798	40.5	42.5	44.7	44.1	833.5	1039.2	1210.0	1218.4
273	Casting of metals	918	840	815	1078	26.0	28.5	30.7	37.1	247.5	328.7	372.0	510.7
2731	Casting of iron and steel	...	...	...	...	...	...	...	...	...	...	...	...
2732	Casting of non-ferrous metals	...	...	...	...	...	...	...	...	...	...	...	...
281	Struct.metal products;tanks;steam generators	4009	4003	4669	4632	88.9	85.0	92.2	95.5	827.4	898.8	1016.6	1221.9
2811	Structural metal products	...	...	...	...	...	...	...	...	...	...	...	...
2812	Tanks, reservoirs and containers of metal	...	...	...	...	...	...	...	...	...	...	...	...
2813	Steam generators	...	...	...	...	...	...	...	...	...	...	...	...
289	Other metal products; metal working services	9253	9174	9828	10912	236.5	239.5	269.6	285.5	2688.9	3020.0	3648.2	4252.6
2891	Metal forging/pressing/stamping/roll-forming	...	...	...	...	...	...	...	...	...	...	...	...
2892	Treatment & coating of metals	...	...	...	...	...	...	...	...	...	...	...	...
2893	Cutlery, hand tools and general hardware	...	...	...	...	...	...	...	...	...	...	...	...
2899	Other fabricated metal products n.e.c.	...	...	...	...	...	...	...	...	...	...	...	...
291	General purpose machinery	3939	3669	4062	3710	162.4	150.6	169.4	160.8	2654.8	2665.0	3319.9	3509.8
2911	Engines & turbines (not for transport equipment)	...	...	...	...	...	...	...	...	...	...	...	...
2912	Pumps, compressors, taps and valves	...	...	...	...	...	...	...	...	...	...	...	...
2913	Bearings, gears, gearing & driving elements	...	...	...	...	...	...	...	...	...	...	...	...
2914	Ovens, furnaces and furnace burners	...	...	...	...	...	...	...	...	...	...	...	...
2915	Lifting and handling equipment	...	...	...	...	...	...	...	...	...	...	...	...
2919	Other general purpose machinery	...	...	...	...	...	...	...	...	...	...	...	...
292	Special purpose machinery	3783	4678	4745	5217	148.0	196.3	203.9	205.7	2235.8	3217.5	3731.1	4188.5
2921	Agricultural and forestry machinery	...	...	...	...	...	...	...	...	...	...	...	...
2922	Machine tools	...	...	...	...	...	...	...	...	...	...	...	...
2923	Machinery for metallurgy	...	...	...	...	...	...	...	...	...	...	...	...
2924	Machinery for mining & construction	...	...	...	...	...	...	...	...	...	...	...	...
2925	Food/beverage/tobacco processing machinery	...	...	...	...	...	...	...	...	...	...	...	...
2926	Machinery for textile, apparel and leather	...	...	...	...	...	...	...	...	...	...	...	...
2927	Weapons and ammunition	...	...	...	...	...	...	...	...	...	...	...	...
2929	Other special purpose machinery	...	...	...	...	...	...	...	...	...	...	...	...

continued

Brazil

ISIC Revision 3		Number of establishments					Number of persons engaged					Wages and salaries paid to employees				
			(number)					(thousands)					(millions of Brazilian Reais)			
ISIC	Industry	Note	2002	2003	2004	2005	Note	2002	2003	2004	2005	Note	2002	2003	2004	2005
2930	Domestic appliances n.e.c.		426	501	311	298		42.7	45.9	43.7	41.9		657.7	758.5	785.0	823.5
3000	Office, accounting and computing machinery		365	427	417	439		15.7	19.9	21.7	27.8		439.3	538.5	634.6	721.2
3110	Electric motors, generators and transformers		603	642	629	667		32.8	35.1	39.2	42.6		566.9	705.3	763.9	904.9
3120	Electricity distribution & control apparatus		491	551	569	559		28.6	32.5	27.6	28.9		445.8	720.7	629.2	742.0
3130	Insulated wire and cable		285	284	297	292		15.1	18.7	20.0	20.4		230.8	280.6	314.9	387.1
3140	Accumulators, primary cells and batteries		129	117	112	111		7.9	7.8	7.9	8.5		120.3	130.2	133.6	164.8
3150	Lighting equipment and electric lamps		596	539	556	516		16.4	16.2	16.1	15.0		249.7	284.1	305.9	335.9
3190	Other electrical equipment n.e.c.		749	685	841	928		44.6	42.9	50.0	53.1		648.5	656.7	831.2	946.1
3210	Electronic valves, tubes, etc.		485	430	402	477		24.3	22.4	22.4	25.0		327.4	335.5	342.8	436.0
3220	TV/radio transmitters; line comm. apparatus		357	308	354	334		22.9	20.1	33.6	31.6		903.6	732.6	1062.4	1223.1
3230	TV and radio receivers and associated goods		222	212	250	213		24.0	23.0	27.8	24.8		406.8	414.9	500.4	497.3
331	Medical, measuring, testing appliances, etc.		1149	1222	1320	1310		43.4	47.9	47.8	50.2		656.8	777.0	889.5	1001.0
3311	Medical, surgical and orthopaedic equipment		...	...	...	...		...	...	...	...		...	...	...	...
3312	Measuring/testing/navigating appliances,etc.		...	...	...	...		...	...	...	...		...	...	...	...
3313	Industrial process control equipment		...	...	...	...		...	...	...	...		...	...	...	...
3320	Optical instruments & photographic equipment		236	232	230	243		8.8	9.3	9.7	9.0		90.0	93.3	103.0	107.7
3330	Watches and clocks		86	88	74	74		3.2	3.2	2.9	3.0		45.3	44.4	52.4	54.6
3410	Motor vehicles		819	910	934	897		98.9	100.6	105.4	110.0		3398.8	4043.6	4185.0	4593.5
3420	Automobile bodies, trailers & semi-trailers		750	777	787	771		35.9	38.9	44.3	42.6		466.0	585.2	654.5	739.2
3430	Parts/accessories for automobiles		1614	1612	1632	1687		156.5	198.7	205.5	213.4		2728.8	3967.1	4469.4	5075.1
351	Building and repairing of ships and boats		288	360	322	337		14.9	20.7	22.2	24.1		191.9	343.5	461.7	455.4
3511	Building and repairing of ships		...	...	...	...		...	...	...	...		...	...	...	...
3512	Building/repairing of pleasure/sport. boats		...	...	...	...		...	...	...	...		...	...	...	...
3520	Railway/tramway locomotives & rolling stock		67	79	76	99		6.0	8.5	11.1	12.5		99.2	158.1	182.2	268.7
3530	Aircraft and spacecraft		119	159	160	167		14.7	19.6	22.5	23.5		607.3	752.5	1053.7	1084.7
359	Transport equipment n.e.c.		336	321	366	380		19.7	20.5	26.8	26.3		256.2	354.1	527.8	556.7
3591	Motorcycles		...	...	...	...		...	...	...	...		...	...	...	...
3592	Bicycles and invalid carriages		...	...	...	...		...	...	...	...		...	...	...	...
3599	Other transport equipment n.e.c.		...	...	...	...		...	...	...	...		...	...	...	...
3610	Furniture		8570	8747	8487	9296		204.9	198.1	201.4	205.5		1392.8	1523.1	1679.3	1854.0
369	Manufacturing n.e.c.		3093	3787	3778	3605		78.4	84.5	87.4	85.6		684.2	797.9	942.2	943.6
3691	Jewellery and related articles		...	...	...	...		...	...	...	...		...	...	...	...
3692	Musical instruments		...	...	...	...		...	...	...	...		...	...	...	...
3693	Sports goods		...	...	...	...		...	...	...	...		...	...	...	...
3694	Games and toys		...	...	...	...		...	...	...	...		...	...	...	...
3699	Other manufacturing n.e.c.		...	...	...	...		...	...	...	...		...	...	...	...
3710	Recycling of metal waste and scrap		109	148	138	186		2.8	4.1	4.1	4.7		32.7	47.8	55.8	68.8
3720	Recycling of non-metal waste and scrap		324	392	508	595		5.7	7.8	9.7	11.1		29.1	40.6	58.7	82.0
D	Total manufacturing		146246	150706	157025	160684		5366.3	5769.6	6182.6	6222.5		65903.7	78898.0	90442.9	99957.5

a/ 1810 includes 1820.

Brazil

ISIC Revision 3			Output in factor values					Value added in factor values					Gross fixed capital formation	
			(millions of Brazilian Reais)					(millions of Brazilian Reais)					(millions of Brazilian Reais)	
ISIC	Industry	Note	2002	2003	2004	2005	Note	2002	2003	2004	2005	Note	2004	2005
151	Processed meat,fish,fruit,vegetables,fats		57516	73416	91282	89134		17237	24767	27689	28959		...	...
1511	Processing/preserving of meat		...	...	...	...		...	...	...	...		...	...
1512	Processing/preserving of fish		...	...	...	...		...	...	...	...		...	...
1513	Processing/preserving of fruit & vegetables		...	...	...	...		...	...	...	...		...	...
1514	Vegetable and animal oils and fats		...	...	...	...		...	...	...	...		...	...
1520	Dairy products		12413	15285	16644	18765		4209	5181	5093	5627		...	...
153	Grain mill products; starches; animal feeds		21911	24465	27601	26224		6298	7747	8099	8366		...	...
1531	Grain mill products		...	...	...	...		...	...	...	...		...	...
1532	Starches and starch products		...	...	...	...		...	...	...	...		...	...
1533	Prepared animal feeds		...	...	...	...		...	...	...	...		...	...
154	Other food products		39097	44946	48688	57167		16544	19089	21122	25191		...	...
1541	Bakery products		...	...	...	...		...	...	...	...		...	...
1542	Sugar		...	...	...	...		...	...	...	...		...	...
1543	Cocoa, chocolate and sugar confectionery		...	...	...	...		...	...	...	...		...	...
1544	Macaroni, noodles & similar products		...	...	...	...		...	...	...	...		...	...
1549	Other food products n.e.c.		...	...	...	...		...	...	...	...		...	...
155	Beverages		23509	27647	29423	34139		11443	12524	14082	17465		...	...
1551	Distilling, rectifying & blending of spirits		...	...	...	...		...	...	...	...		...	...
1552	Wines		...	...	...	...		...	...	...	...		...	...
1553	Malt liquors and malt		...	...	...	...		...	...	...	...		...	...
1554	Soft drinks; mineral waters		...	...	...	...		...	...	...	...		...	...
1600	Tobacco products		5522	5938	8210	7916		2821	2857	3432	3308		...	...
171	Spinning, weaving and finishing of textiles		11437	13864	15064	14455		4501	4926	5680	5546		...	...
1711	Textile fibre preparation; textile weaving		...	...	...	...		...	...	...	...		...	...
1712	Finishing of textiles		...	...	...	...		...	...	...	...		...	...
172	Other textiles		6608	7589	9023	9127		3002	3207	3769	3853		...	...
1721	Made-up textile articles, except apparel		...	...	...	...		...	...	...	...		...	...
1722	Carpets and rugs		...	...	...	...		...	...	...	...		...	...
1723	Cordage, rope, twine and netting		...	...	...	...		...	...	...	...		...	...
1729	Other textiles n.e.c.		...	...	...	...		...	...	...	...		...	...
1730	Knitted and crocheted fabrics and articles		2064	2125	2941	2676		748	744	967	980		...	...
1810	Wearing apparel, except fur apparel	a/	10989	12169	13747	16755	a/	5027	5517	6331	7045		...	...
1820	Dressing & dyeing of fur; processing of fur	a/	...	...	...	...	a/	...	...	...	...		...	...
191	Tanning, dressing and processing of leather		6047	7587	8108	7184		1784	2183	2314	2195		...	...
1911	Tanning and dressing of leather		...	...	...	...		...	...	...	...		...	...
1912	Luggage, handbags, etc.; saddlery & harness		...	...	...	...		...	...	...	...		...	...
1920	Footwear		11666	15124	16195	13429		5397	6624	7295	6147		...	...
2010	Sawmilling and planing of wood		3434	4615	5531	5424		1895	2245	2798	2639		...	...
202	Products of wood, cork, straw, etc.		6160	8566	10355	9809		3043	4179	4864	4225		...	...
2021	Veneer sheets, plywood, particle board, etc.		...	...	...	...		...	...	...	...		...	...
2022	Builders' carpentry and joinery		...	...	...	...		...	...	...	...		...	...
2023	Wooden containers		...	...	...	...		...	...	...	...		...	...
2029	Other wood products; articles of cork/straw		...	...	...	...		...	...	...	...		...	...
210	Paper and paper products		28718	35527	37063	36836		15033	17574	18373	16874		...	...
2101	Pulp, paper and paperboard		...	...	...	...		...	...	...	...		...	...
2102	Corrugated paper and paperboard		...	...	...	...		...	...	...	...		...	...
2109	Other articles of paper and paperboard		...	...	...	...		...	...	...	...		...	...
221	Publishing		12989	14972	15619	16174		8219	9428	10052	10509		...	...
2211	Publishing of books and other publications		...	...	...	...		...	...	...	...		...	...
2212	Publishing of newspapers, journals, etc.		...	...	...	...		...	...	...	...		...	...
2213	Publishing of recorded media		...	...	...	...		...	...	...	...		...	...
2219	Other publishing		...	...	...	...		...	...	...	...		...	...

continued

Brazil

ISIC Revision 3		Output in factor values					Value added in factor values					Gross fixed capital formation		
			(millions of Brazilian Reais)					(millions of Brazilian Reais)					(millions of Brazilian Reais)	
ISIC	Industry	Note	2002	2003	2004	2005	Note	2002	2003	2004	2005	Note	2004	2005
222	Printing and related service activities		2572	3379	4423	4979		1497	1907	2601	2859		...	...
2221	Printing		...	...	...	...		...	...	...	...		...	...
2222	Service activities related to printing		...	...	...	...		...	...	...	...		...	...
2230	Reproduction of recorded media		1823	1680	2222	2168		1077	1063	1370	1301		...	...
2310	Coke oven products		24	41	77	90		10	13	32	36		...	...
2320	Refined petroleum products		46255	61271	73202	85753		30112	41349	45427	57195		...	...
2330	Processing of nuclear fuel		86	80	66	110		29	32	27	38		...	...
241	Basic chemicals		47998	64597	81987	77107		15171	19409	24098	22128		...	...
2411	Basic chemicals, except fertilizers		...	...	...	...		...	...	...	...		...	...
2412	Fertilizers and nitrogen compounds		...	...	...	...		...	...	...	...		...	...
2413	Plastics in primary forms; synthetic rubber		...	...	...	...		...	...	...	...		...	...
242	Other chemicals		48176	58778	68002	66853		22016	25735	28670	29747		...	...
2421	Pesticides and other agro-chemical products		...	...	...	...		...	...	...	...		...	...
2422	Paints, varnishes, printing ink and mastics		...	...	...	...		...	...	...	...		...	...
2423	Pharmaceuticals, medicinal chemicals, etc.		...	...	...	...		...	...	...	...		...	...
2424	Soap, cleaning & cosmetic preparations		...	...	...	...		...	...	...	...		...	...
2429	Other chemical products n.e.c.		...	...	...	...		...	...	...	...		...	...
2430	Man-made fibres		1681	1614	2516	1901		490	644	772	799		...	...
251	Rubber products		8504	14826	13873	14096		3754	6758	5999	6107		...	...
2511	Rubber tyres and tubes		...	...	...	...		...	...	...	...		...	...
2519	Other rubber products		...	...	...	...		...	...	...	...		...	...
2520	Plastic products		18520	24805	28646	31873		7169	8946	10421	11828		...	...
2610	Glass and glass products		3846	4506	5362	5366		2026	2260	2903	2816		...	...
269	Non-metallic mineral products n.e.c.		19740	23519	25078	25286		11042	12374	12714	12193		...	...
2691	Pottery, china and earthenware		...	...	...	...		...	...	...	...		...	...
2692	Refractory ceramic products		...	...	...	...		...	...	...	...		...	...
2693	Struct.non-refractory clay; ceramic products		...	...	...	...		...	...	...	...		...	...
2694	Cement, lime and plaster		...	...	...	...		...	...	...	...		...	...
2695	Articles of concrete, cement and plaster		...	...	...	...		...	...	...	...		...	...
2696	Cutting, shaping & finishing of stone		...	...	...	...		...	...	...	...		...	...
2699	Other non-metallic mineral products n.e.c.		...	...	...	...		...	...	...	...		...	...
2710	Basic iron and steel		37025	48729	69772	72540		16715	21525	33091	31572		...	...
2720	Basic precious and non-ferrous metals		14313	17198	21625	20393		5668	6876	9009	7525		...	...
273	Casting of metals		1303	2037	2663	3372		614	919	1114	1412		...	...
2731	Casting of iron and steel		...	...	...	...		...	...	...	...		...	...
2732	Casting of non-ferrous metals		...	...	...	...		...	...	...	...		...	...
281	Struct.metal products;tanks;steam generators		4823	4976	6076	8136		2137	2300	2650	3662		...	...
2811	Structural metal products		...	...	...	...		...	...	...	...		...	...
2812	Tanks, reservoirs and containers of metal		...	...	...	...		...	...	...	...		...	...
2813	Steam generators		...	...	...	...		...	...	...	...		...	...
289	Other metal products; metal working services		18670	23717	28432	34380		8967	10195	12993	15581		...	...
2891	Metal forging/pressing/stamping/roll-forming		...	...	...	...		...	...	...	...		...	...
2892	Treatment & coating of metals		...	...	...	...		...	...	...	...		...	...
2893	Cutlery, hand tools and general hardware		...	...	...	...		...	...	...	...		...	...
2899	Other fabricated metal products n.e.c.		...	...	...	...		...	...	...	...		...	...
291	General purpose machinery		18007	20061	24608	26784		8413	8888	10580	11030		...	...
2911	Engines & turbines (not for transport equipment)		...	...	...	...		...	...	...	...		...	...
2912	Pumps, compressors, taps and valves		...	...	...	...		...	...	...	...		...	...
2913	Bearings, gears, gearing & driving elements		...	...	...	...		...	...	...	...		...	...
2914	Ovens, furnaces and furnace burners		...	...	...	...		...	...	...	...		...	...
2915	Lifting and handling equipment		...	...	...	...		...	...	...	...		...	...
2919	Other general purpose machinery		...	...	...	...		...	...	...	...		...	...

292	Special purpose machinery	17429	24845	31670	30088	8051	11245	14215	13002	...	...
2921	Agricultural and forestry machinery	...	...	...	...	...	...	...	...	...	...
2922	Machine tools	...	...	...	...	...	...	...	...	...	...
2923	Machinery for metallurgy	...	...	...	...	...	...	...	...	...	...
2924	Machinery for mining & construction	...	...	...	...	...	...	...	...	...	...
2925	Food/beverage/tobacco processing machinery	...	...	...	...	...	...	...	...	...	...
2926	Machinery for textile, apparel and leather	...	...	...	...	...	...	...	...	...	...
2927	Weapons and ammunition	...	...	...	...	...	...	...	...	...	...
2929	Other special purpose machinery	...	...	...	...	...	...	...	...	...	...
2930	Domestic appliances n.e.c.	7465	7256	8421	8624	3328	2825	3098	3068	...	...
3000	Office, accounting and computing machinery	6120	6817	7115	8898	2357	2408	2208	2749	...	...
3110	Electric motors, generators and transformers	4145	4043	5017	6673	1884	1808	2166	2817	...	...
3120	Electricity distribution & control apparatus	3173	4354	3976	4323	1397	2112	1888	2204	...	...
3130	Insulated wire and cable	2691	3497	4886	5841	731	972	1321	1604	...	...
3140	Accumulators, primary cells and batteries	927	1021	1115	1314	461	348	396	483	...	...
3150	Lighting equipment and electric lamps	1022	1335	1317	1219	475	630	600	523	...	...
3190	Other electrical equipment n.e.c.	4879	4937	6218	7254	2217	2067	2773	2963	...	...
3210	Electronic valves, tubes, etc.	3683	3338	3574	4065	1447	1173	1529	1381	...	...
3220	TV/radio transmitters; line comm. apparatus	13216	13876	23409	21839	5022	4191	6745	6197	...	...
3230	TV and radio receivers and associated goods	7624	7501	9831	9774	2496	2065	2888	3056	...	...
331	Medical, measuring, testing appliances, etc.	4256	4601	5278	5941	2165	2327	2815	3235	...	...
3311	Medical, surgical and orthopaedic equipment	...	...	...	...	...	...	...	...	...	...
3312	Measuring/testing/navigating appliances,etc.	...	...	...	...	...	...	...	...	...	...
3313	Industrial process control equipment	...	...	...	...	...	...	...	...	...	...
3320	Optical instruments & photographic equipment	638	674	741	723	344	420	438	429	...	...
3330	Watches and clocks	445	417	386	408	239	221	228	256	...	...
3410	Motor vehicles	40028	50731	62193	72078	13034	15000	18310	20490	...	...
3420	Automobile bodies, trailers & semi-trailers	3501	4403	5675	6095	1415	1657	2010	2059	...	...
3430	Parts/accessories for automobiles	21007	33219	42581	47359	9228	13859	16815	17089	...	...
351	Building and repairing of ships and boats	1259	2064	4425	2998	581	990	1268	1141	...	...
3511	Building and repairing of ships	...	...	...	...	...	...	...	...	...	...
3512	Building/repairing of pleasure/sport. boats	...	...	...	...	...	...	...	...	...	...
3520	Railway/tramway locomotives & rolling stock	733	948	1364	2353	361	520	719	1156	...	...
3530	Aircraft and spacecraft	8412	8497	11764	10310	4632	3962	5139	3514	...	...
359	Transport equipment n.e.c.	4561	5721	7641	8600	1463	1675	2572	2626	...	...
3591	Motorcycles	...	...	...	...	...	...	...	...	...	...
3592	Bicycles and invalid carriages	...	...	...	...	...	...	...	...	...	...
3599	Other transport equipment n.e.c.	...	...	...	...	...	...	...	...	...	...
3610	Furniture	9818	11087	12356	13087	3966	4269	4663	4863	...	...
369	Manufacturing n.e.c.	4083	4783	5209	5179	2243	2559	2812	2879	...	...
3691	Jewellery and related articles	...	...	...	...	...	...	...	...	...	...
3692	Musical instruments	...	...	...	...	...	...	...	...	...	...
3693	Sports goods	...	...	...	...	...	...	...	...	...	...
3694	Games and toys	...	...	...	...	...	...	...	...	...	...
3699	Other manufacturing n.e.c.	...	...	...	...	...	...	...	...	...	...
3710	Recycling of metal waste and scrap	177	264	318	543	128	171	182	236	...	...
3720	Recycling of non-metal waste and scrap	154	177	295	505	73	89	142	290	...	...
D	Total manufacturing	724894	900056	1080903	1132491	313848	379544	444369	467070	...	...

a/ 1810 includes 1820.

Brazil

ISIC Revision 3			Index numbers of industrial production											
			(2000=100)											
ISIC	Industry	Note	1995	1996	1997	1998	1999	2000	2001	2002	2003	2004	2005	2006
15	Food and beverages		93	97	98	99	102	100	104	105	103	107	109	113
16	Tobacco products		110	124	151	117	108	100	95	57	54	64	63	66
17	Textiles		112	106	99	92	94	100	95	95	91	100	98	99
18	Wearing apparel, fur		107	101	95	96	92	100	90	96	84	85	81	77
19	Leather, leather products and footwear		121	123	115	101	99	100	96	95	85	87	85	82
20	Wood products (excl. furniture)		94	95	97	91	97	100	100	104	110	118	113	105
21	Paper and paper products		85	88	90	90	96	100	100	103	110	119	122	125
22	Printing and publishing		107	104	100	103	91	100	89	94	94	92	102	104
23	Coke,refined petroleum products,nuclear fuel		87	94	97	102	102	100	104	101	99	101	103	105
24	Chemicals and chemical products		85	86	91	93	96	100	94	93	94	100	102	103
25	Rubber and plastics products		95	100	104	98	96	100	95	96	92	99	98	100
26	Non-metallic mineral products		89	94	102	101	98	100	98	97	93	98	101	103
27	Basic metals		88	90	96	93	91	100	100	104	110	114	112	115
28	Fabricated metal products		104	99	103	99	98	100	102	105	99	109	109	108
29	Machinery and equipment n.e.c.		94	87	93	89	84	100	104	107	113	131	129	134
30	Office, accounting and computing machinery		...	...	...	...	...	...	...	...	...	...	...	...
31	Electrical machinery and apparatus		87	87	96	97	90	100	120	119	121	130	140	152
32	Radio,television and communication equipment		130	142	133	93	75	100	97	86	87	102	117	117
33	Medical, precision and optical instruments		...	...	...	...	...	...	...	...	...	...	...	...
34	Motor vehicles, trailers, semi-trailers		99	101	115	93	84	100	100	98	102	133	142	144
35	Other transport equipment		69	61	58	74	82	100	124	151	165	182	192	196
36	Furniture; manufacturing n.e.c.		...	...	...	...	...	...	...	...	...	...	...	...
37	Recycling		...	...	...	...	...	...	...	...	...	...	...	...
D	Total manufacturing		95	96	99	96	94	100	101	102	102	110	113	116

Bulgaria

Supplier of information:
National Statistical Institute of the Republic of Bulgaria, Sofia.

Basic source of data:
Census; survey.

Major deviations from ISIC (Revision 3):
Data have been converted from NACE (Revision 2.2) to ISIC (Revision 3).

Reference period:
Calendar year.

Scope:
All enterprises.

Method of data collection:
Mail and electronic questionnaires.

Type of enumeration:
Complete enumeration.

Adjusted for non-response:
Yes.

Concepts and definitions of variables:
<u>Output</u> refers to gross output.

Related national publications:
Statistical Yearbook of the Republic of Bulgaria, published by the National Statistical Institute of the Republic of Bulgaria, Sofia.

Bulgaria

ISIC Revision 3		Number of enterprises					Number of employees					Wages and salaries paid to employees				
			(number)					(number)					(millions of Bulgarian Leva)			
ISIC	Industry	Note	2003	2004	2005	2006	Note	2003	2004	2005	2006	Note	2003	2004	2005	2006
151	Processed meat,fish,fruit,vegetables,fats		1074	1118	1032	994		25133	25650	27411	29193		53.3	57.4	69.5	81.0
1511	Processing/preserving of meat		...	...	599	534		...	...	15278	16014		...	...	36.7	42.0
1512	Processing/preserving of fish		...	...	35	36		...	...	918	1184		...	...	2.0	2.8
1513	Processing/preserving of fruit & vegetables		...	...	311	335		...	...	8492	9030		...	...	22.6	26.5
1514	Vegetable and animal oils and fats		...	...	87	89		...	...	2723	2965		...	...	8.2	9.6
1520	Dairy products		456	454	411	356		7073	7722	7554	8042		17.7	20.7	23.3	27.3
153	Grain mill products; starches; animal feeds		399	394	337	318		6811	6295	5798	5492		18.7	18.8	19.7	21.3
1531	Grain mill products		...	...	236	208		...	...	...	...		...	...	...	...
1532	Starches and starch products		...	...	3	3		...	...	...	...		...	...	...	...
1533	Prepared animal feeds		...	...	98	107		...	...	1640	1725		...	...	5.2	6.3
154	Other food products		3556	3448	3313	3137		37472	38333	40148	42031		84.7	95.4	112.2	130.0
1541	Bakery products		...	...	2965	2774		...	...	29844	31407		...	...	72.7	83.9
1542	Sugar		...	...	6	8		...	...	1825	1922		...	...	6.8	8.2
1543	Cocoa, chocolate and sugar confectionery		...	...	103	98		...	...	4786	4826		...	...	21.7	25.5
1544	Macaroni, noodles & similar products		...	...	38	34		...	...	564	544		...	...	1.2	1.4
1549	Other food products n.e.c.		...	...	201	223		...	...	3129	3332		...	...	9.8	11.0
155	Beverages		890	920	844	824		16733	16941	17144	17380		58.3	64.3	71.5	81.8
1551	Distilling, rectifying & blending of spirits		...	...	272	312		...	...	2587	2637		...	...	5.7	6.5
1552	Wines		...	...	116	124		...	...	5520	6027		...	...	18.4	20.8
1553	Malt liquors and malt		...	...	12	12		...	...	3158	2830		...	...	20.7	23.1
1554	Soft drinks; mineral waters		...	...	444	376		...	...	5879	5886		...	...	26.8	31.5
1600	Tobacco products		33	34	34	33		10268	8512	7336	6207		65.5	62.2	62.8	59.7
171	Spinning, weaving and finishing of textiles		183	186	175	180		15977	14894	13283	12540		41.5	43.2	41.6	45.2
1711	Textile fibre preparation; textile weaving		...	...	151	150		...	...	12970	12100		...	...	40.5	43.7
1712	Finishing of textiles		...	...	24	30		...	...	313	440		...	...	1.1	1.5
172	Other textiles		324	353	361	393		5710	6362	5894	6049		12.2	15.3	15.1	16.6
1721	Made-up textile articles, except apparel		...	...	184	198		...	...	3037	3336		...	...	7.3	8.7
1722	Carpets and rugs		...	...	23	25		...	...	995	1030		...	...	3.0	3.3
1723	Cordage, rope, twine and netting		...	...	23	24		...	...	215	189		...	...	0.5	0.5
1729	Other textiles n.e.c.		...	...	131	146		...	...	1647	1494		...	...	4.3	4.1
1730	Knitted and crocheted fabrics and articles		255	253	271	271		12710	13484	13791	14525		30.9	34.4	42.3	49.1
1810	Wearing apparel, except fur apparel		4120	4567	4482	4526		138086	143910	135692	133235		258.0	291.7	297.9	326.5
1820	Dressing & dyeing of fur; processing of fur		46	39	38	33		647	549	335	329		1.1	1.0	0.7	0.7
191	Tanning, dressing and processing of leather		124	121	114	117		2650	2477	2815	...		6.6	5.9	7.0	...
1911	Tanning and dressing of leather		...	...	24	27		...	...	783	...		...	...	2.1	...
1912	Luggage, handbags, etc.; saddlery & harness		...	...	90	90		...	...	2032	2079		...	...	4.8	5.9
1920	Footwear		357	384	388	394		17640	16850	16100	...		31.1	32.0	32.8	...
2010	Sawmilling and planing of wood		835	912	906	953		6127	6746	7016	7274		10.0	11.6	13.6	15.6
202	Products of wood, cork, straw, etc.		1033	1021	1091	1054		9704	10367	11021	10691		25.2	28.5	34.0	37.1
2021	Veneer sheets, plywood, particle board, etc.		...	...	52	46		...	...	4225	3830		...	...	19.3	20.9
2022	Builders' carpentry and joinery		...	...	426	395		...	...	3005	3089		...	...	6.7	7.6
2023	Wooden containers		...	...	171	167		...	...	1206	1367		...	...	2.4	2.8
2029	Other wood products; articles of cork/straw		...	...	442	446		...	...	2585	2405		...	...	5.7	5.8
210	Paper and paper products		380	410	430	424		12158	11850	11032	10325		37.7	38.1	38.5	40.2
2101	Pulp, paper and paperboard		...	...	29	23		...	...	3388	2827		...	...	18.4	17.6
2102	Corrugated paper and paperboard		...	...	202	208		...	...	4742	4614		...	...	12.3	14.2
2109	Other articles of paper and paperboard		...	...	199	193		...	...	2902	2884		...	...	7.8	8.5
221	Publishing		671	670	663	664		4605	5253	5610	6064		18.5	21.5	25.0	29.5
2211	Publishing of books and other publications		...	...	238	234		...	...	1188	1124		...	...	4.9	5.3
2212	Publishing of newspapers, journals, etc.		...	...	319	323		...	...	3911	4385		...	...	18.6	22.4
2213	Publishing of recorded media		...	...	21	18		...	...	...	260		...	...	...	0.5
2219	Other publishing		...	...	85	89		...	...	...	295		...	...	...	1.3

222	Printing and related service activities	818	815	857	914	7858	8438	8584	9324	26.8	28.6	32.0	37.1
2221	Printing	...	...	585	632	...	...	7819	8556	...	...	30.2	35.2
2222	Service activities related to printing	...	...	272	282	...	...	765	768	...	...	1.8	1.8
2230	Reproduction of recorded media	17	17	23	28	240	257	101	139	0.6	0.7	0.5	0.7
2310	Coke oven products	...	...	...	...	...	...	...	...	...	...	...	...
2320	Refined petroleum products	15	19	19	16	8054	...	...	...	...	...	...	...
2330	Processing of nuclear fuel	...	...	...	...	...	...	...	...	...	...	...	...
241	Basic chemicals	149	141	154	144	5732	5253	4996	5122	31.7	31.7	33.3	36.6
2411	Basic chemicals, except fertilizers	...	...	120	112	...	...	2540	2593	...	...	19.9	21.8
2412	Fertilizers and nitrogen compounds	...	...	17	18	...	...	2375	2439	...	...	13.1	14.5
2413	Plastics in primary forms; synthetic rubber	...	...	17	14	...	...	81	90	...	...	0.2	0.2
242	Other chemicals	461	470	453	466	19347	18218	17870	18172	80.1	78.2	84.7	97.9
2421	Pesticides and other agro-chemical products	...	...	14	15	...	...	370	420	...	...	1.3	1.7
2422	Paints, varnishes, printing ink and mastics	...	...	68	72	...	...	1970	2306	...	...	8.1	10.7
2423	Pharmaceuticals, medicinal chemicals, etc.	...	...	59	61	...	...	8117	8196	...	...	48.9	56.0
2424	Soap, cleaning & cosmetic preparations	...	...	174	171	...	...	4997	4870	...	...	16.2	18.6
2429	Other chemical products n.e.c.	...	...	138	147	...	...	2416	2380	...	...	10.1	10.9
2430	Man-made fibres	...	...	...	3	334	...	...	...	...	...	...	...
251	Rubber products	254	260	243	227	3465	3477	3417	3432	10.1	10.6	11.3	12.9
2511	Rubber tyres and tubes	...	...	89	78	...	...	912	885	...	...	2.9	3.0
2519	Other rubber products	...	...	154	149	...	...	2505	2547	...	...	8.4	9.9
2520	Plastic products	929	1013	1085	1291	14944	14450	15905	18864	36.5	37.5	43.6	54.9
2610	Glass and glass products	80	89	81	107	3217	3145	4272	4377	12.6	13.0	18.1	22.9
269	Non-metallic mineral products n.e.c.	808	911	952	1081	18588	19709	21515	23444	65.7	72.9	84.1	101.3
2691	Pottery, china and earthenware	...	...	132	163	...	...	3083	3094	...	...	16.4	17.9
2692	Refractory ceramic products	...	...	17	17	...	...	745	690	...	...	2.8	3.1
2693	Struct.non-refractory clay; ceramic products	...	...	58	53	...	...	4247	4457	...	...	11.6	13.8
2694	Cement, lime and plaster	...	...	58	56	...	...	2407	2468	...	...	18.7	21.3
2695	Articles of concrete, cement and plaster	...	...	412	460	...	...	7927	9438	...	...	26.3	35.4
2696	Cutting, shaping & finishing of stone	...	...	195	236	...	...	1859	1946	...	...	4.6	5.2
2699	Other non-metallic mineral products n.e.c.	...	...	80	96	...	...	1247	1351	...	...	3.8	4.6
2710	Basic iron and steel	37	35	37	43	13289	12163	11743	11917	80.5	84.8	86.7	102.9
2720	Basic precious and non-ferrous metals	37	50	51	53	5222	5063	5222	5204	36.5	40.1	44.2	48.5
273	Casting of metals	131	142	137	139	4686	4769	4882	4908	13.3	14.2	16.3	18.6
2731	Casting of iron and steel	...	...	92	90	...	...	3924	4032	...	...	13.2	15.4
2732	Casting of non-ferrous metals	...	...	45	49	...	...	958	876	...	...	3.0	3.2
281	Struct.metal products;tanks;steam generators	920	1042	1189	1371	12639	13496	14875	16740	32.9	36.7	42.9	54.2
2811	Structural metal products	...	...	1077	1251	...	...	10936	12674	...	...	29.9	38.9
2812	Tanks, reservoirs and containers of metal	...	...	84	88	...	...	2182	2285	...	...	6.6	8.3
2813	Steam generators	...	...	28	32	...	...	1757	1781	...	...	6.4	7.1
289	Other metal products; metal working services	1999	2093	2237	2347	18018	18666	19453	21116	45.0	51.1	60.5	73.0
2891	Metal forging/pressing/stamping/roll-forming	...	...	60	56	...	...	768	784	...	...	2.7	2.6
2892	Treatment & coating of metals	...	...	1255	1337	...	...	5268	5831	...	...	16.3	21.2
2893	Cutlery, hand tools and general hardware	...	...	218	209	...	...	3325	3419	...	...	12.2	14.2
2899	Other fabricated metal products n.e.c.	...	...	704	745	...	...	10092	11082	...	...	29.3	35.0
291	General purpose machinery	1005	971	995	1012	23067	22776	23905	26361	85.4	94.1	104.8	129.8
2911	Engines & turbines (not for transport equipment)	...	...	23	18	...	...	2879	2981	...	...	11.6	13.4
2912	Pumps, compressors, taps and valves	...	...	112	98	...	...	9098	9185	...	...	51.0	58.9
2913	Bearings, gears, gearing & driving elements	...	...	26	31	...	...	2162	2186	...	...	7.9	9.7
2914	Ovens, furnaces and furnace burners	...	...	19	18	...	...	176	191	...	...	0.5	0.8
2915	Lifting and handling equipment	...	...	542	552	...	...	6585	7851	...	...	23.9	32.0
2919	Other general purpose machinery	...	...	273	295	...	...	3005	3967	...	...	9.8	15.0
292	Special purpose machinery	794	802	806	801	37894	36510	36386	35859	121.9	125.1	139.0	147.1
2921	Agricultural and forestry machinery	...	...	112	104	...	...	2477	1695	...	...	8.4	5.9
2922	Machine tools	...	...	191	185	...	...	6704	6713	...	...	25.8	29.1
2923	Machinery for metallurgy	...	...	17	18	...	...	1874	2428	...	...	8.2	10.5
2924	Machinery for mining & construction	...	...	66	69	...	...	3107	3074	...	...	14.8	16.9
2925	Food/beverage/tobacco processing machinery	...	...	133	135	...	...	2941	3003	...	...	10.0	11.5
2926	Machinery for textile, apparel and leather	...	...	37	41	...	...	267	523	...	...	0.7	1.4
2927	Weapons and ammunition	...	...	31	29	...	...	14774	14102	...	...	55.9	54.9
2929	Other special purpose machinery	...	...	219	220	...	...	4242	4321	...	...	15.3	17.0

continued

Bulgaria

ISIC Revision 3		Number of enterprises					Number of employees					Wages and salaries paid to employees				
			(number)					(number)					(millions of Bulgarian Leva)			
ISIC	Industry	Note	2003	2004	2005	2006	Note	2003	2004	2005	2006	Note	2003	2004	2005	2006
2930	Domestic appliances n.e.c.		99	110	100	101		4060	4230	4504	5267		13.0	15.1	18.3	25.6
3000	Office, accounting and computing machinery		103	99	82	75		1532	1763	2271	1967		5.3	6.7	8.8	8.5
3110	Electric motors, generators and transformers		165	167	161	148		5194	4942	4871	5127		15.9	17.2	19.3	21.3
3120	Electricity distribution & control apparatus		171	179	158	171		4823	4992	4461	4794		15.7	17.0	16.9	20.2
3130	Insulated wire and cable		11	13	13	15		1195	1230	1227	1891		5.1	5.3	6.4	10.1
3140	Accumulators, primary cells and batteries		15	15	15	15		1950	1799	1835	1909		7.3	7.5	9.5	11.7
3150	Lighting equipment and electric lamps		87	77	73	73		1246	1352	1477	1433		2.5	2.9	3.4	3.7
3190	Other electrical equipment n.e.c.		194	192	169	163		3804	3892	4421	5532		9.0	9.5	12.7	15.8
3210	Electronic valves, tubes, etc.		66	62	57	63		2518	2754	3020	3064		7.6	8.4	10.4	11.7
3220	TV/radio transmitters; line comm. apparatus		123	121	116	104		2772	2598	1754	1689		13.2	11.8	6.8	7.2
3230	TV and radio receivers and associated goods		33	33	34	36		438	423	447	591		1.7	1.9	2.3	3.2
331	Medical, measuring, testing appliances, etc.		796	815	810	829		3968	4530	4272	4706		11.8	14.2	15.6	19.9
3311	Medical, surgical and orthopaedic equipment		...	...	619	639		...	...	1765	1858		...	...	5.1	6.0
3312	Measuring/testing/navigating appliances,etc.		...	...	148	143		...	...	2117	2370		...	...	8.7	11.0
3313	Industrial process control equipment		...	...	43	47		...	...	390	478		...	...	1.9	3.0
3320	Optical instruments & photographic equipment		41	46	33	30		1158	1051	1182	1207		3.1	3.5	4.4	5.1
3330	Watches and clocks		10	12	9	4		38	40	40	40		0.1	0.1	0.1	0.1
3410	Motor vehicles		6	7	3	3		153	197	...	...		0.4	0.5	...	...
3420	Automobile bodies, trailers & semi-trailers		21	18	18	20		600	546	525	516		1.4	1.5	1.6	1.8
3430	Parts/accessories for automobiles		96	95	93	85		2034	1960	2201	2001		6.1	6.3	7.9	7.9
351	Building and repairing of ships and boats		284	281	274	255		5481	6276	6088	6940		24.9	30.2	36.7	49.4
3511	Building and repairing of ships		...	...	262	242		...	...	6008	6861		...	...	36.4	49.1
3512	Building/repairing of pleasure/sport. boats		...	...	12	13		...	...	80	79		...	...	0.3	0.3
3520	Railway/tramway locomotives & rolling stock		19	20	19	18		3383	3032	2874	2810		10.4	11.9	14.5	16.6
3530	Aircraft and spacecraft		4	4	5	6		42	163	143	168		0.1	0.7	0.7	1.0
359	Transport equipment n.e.c.		18	20	22	25		720	720	768	955		1.3	1.4	1.7	2.1
3591	Motorcycles		...	...	-	-		...	...	-	-		...	...	-	-
3592	Bicycles and invalid carriages		...	...	13	18		...	...	697	897		...	...	1.6	2.0
3599	Other transport equipment n.e.c.		...	...	9	7		...	...	71	58		...	...	0.1	0.1
3610	Furniture		1369	1512	1608	1714		18979	21687	23458	25298		39.5	48.4	59.0	68.2
369	Manufacturing n.e.c.		...	...	...	581		5211	...	...	...		11.9	...	...	...
3691	Jewellery and related articles		...	...	233	243		...	...	670	746		...	...	2.1	2.6
3692	Musical instruments		...	...	...	21		...	...	...	...		...	...	...	...
3693	Sports goods		...	...	28	22		...	...	677	707		...	...	3.5	3.8
3694	Games and toys		...	...	52	50		...	...	2087	2655		...	...	4.4	6.5
3699	Other manufacturing n.e.c.		...	...	260	245		...	...	2201	2249		...	...	6.2	6.8
3710	Recycling of metal waste and scrap		26	32	37	32		429	...	...	847		1.1	...	...	2.5
3720	Recycling of non-metal waste and scrap		20	25	27	30		121	158	282	364		0.2	0.3	0.6	0.9
D	Total manufacturing		27603	28730	28740	29310		597947	606767	606660	626452		1724.0	1864.0	2054.7	2355.6

Bulgaria

ISIC	Industry	Note	Output 2003	Output 2004	Output 2005	Output 2006	Note	Value added 2003	Value added 2004	Value added 2005	Value added 2006	Note	GFCF 2005	GFCF 2006
ISIC Revision 3			Output in producers' prices (millions of Bulgarian Leva)					Value added in producers' prices (millions of Bulgarian Leva)					Gross fixed capital formation (millions of Bulgarian Leva)	
151	Processed meat,fish,fruit,vegetables,fats		1147	1344	1678	1959		155	184	226	271		93	207
1511	Processing/preserving of meat		...	...	1027	1194		...	...	129	143		60	116
1512	Processing/preserving of fish		...	...	33	48		...	...	6	9		1	4
1513	Processing/preserving of fruit & vegetables		...	...	378	442		...	...	57	82		15	63
1514	Vegetable and animal oils and fats		...	...	240	275		...	...	34	37		17	24
1520	Dairy products		269	333	380	470		40	50	63	87		53	36
153	Grain mill products; starches; animal feeds		429	455	387	456		67	56	71	81		76	18
1531	Grain mill products		...	...	...	...		...	...	...	...		13	8
1532	Starches and starch products		...	...	...	...		...	...	...	...		...	6
1533	Prepared animal feeds		...	...	120	147		...	...	16	20		...	4
154	Other food products		910	1052	1195	1422		177	213	261	309		113	102
1541	Bakery products		...	...	581	668		...	...	145	167		68	77
1542	Sugar		...	...	172	209		...	...	23	24		...	5
1543	Cocoa, chocolate and sugar confectionery		...	...	287	366		...	...	61	79		23	3
1544	Macaroni, noodles & similar products		...	...	13	16		...	...	3	4		...	5
1549	Other food products n.e.c.		...	...	142	163		...	...	29	35		16	12
155	Beverages		817	916	1001	1109		168	209	241	254		68	124
1551	Distilling, rectifying & blending of spirits		...	...	101	67		...	...	24	11		18	26
1552	Wines		...	...	305	348		...	...	43	51		30	21
1553	Malt liquors and malt		...	...	248	296		...	...	54	72		-17	17
1554	Soft drinks; mineral waters		...	...	347	398		...	...	120	120		37	60
1600	Tobacco products		550	572	582	440		145	150	195	141		18	28
171	Spinning, weaving and finishing of textiles		481	567	635	723		105	146	154	155		24	12
1711	Textile fibre preparation; textile weaving		...	...	626	712		...	...	151	151		23	11
1712	Finishing of textiles		...	...	9	11		...	...	3	4		1	1
172	Other textiles		108	147	140	159		29	38	35	39		20	5
1721	Made-up textile articles, except apparel		...	...	74	92		...	...	15	19		12	-1
1722	Carpets and rugs		...	...	28	29		...	...	...	...		...	3
1723	Cordage, rope, twine and netting		...	...	3	3		...	...	...	...		-	-
1729	Other textiles n.e.c.		...	...	35	35		...	...	10	10		...	3
1730	Knitted and crocheted fabrics and articles		192	216	251	297		69	77	91	105		26	25
1810	Wearing apparel, except fur apparel		1264	1421	1447	1649		491	566	556	632		76	84
1820	Dressing & dyeing of fur; processing of fur		15	6	6	5		2	1	1	1		-	-
191	Tanning, dressing and processing of leather		73	44	53	...		26	12	12	...		3	-
1911	Tanning and dressing of leather		...	...	18	...		...	...	3	...		1	-1
1912	Luggage, handbags, etc.; saddlery & harness		...	...	35	46		...	...	9	11		2	1
1920	Footwear		184	166	181	...		57	56	58	...		5	9
2010	Sawmilling and planing of wood		131	176	190	225		23	34	35	46		14	18
202	Products of wood, cork, straw, etc.		277	360	400	436		52	90	99	113		38	21
2021	Veneer sheets, plywood, particle board, etc.		...	...	268	288		...	...	63	71		26	11
2022	Builders' carpentry and joinery		...	...	55	62		...	...	16	18		4	5
2023	Wooden containers		...	...	28	35		...	...	7	8		2	3
2029	Other wood products; articles of cork/straw		...	...	49	51		...	...	13	16		6	2
210	Paper and paper products		458	492	545	538		81	92	108	115		44	37
2101	Pulp, paper and paperboard		...	...	264	231		...	...	50	51		20	22
2102	Corrugated paper and paperboard		...	...	170	185		...	...	34	39		16	9
2109	Other articles of paper and paperboard		...	...	111	122		...	...	24	25		8	6
221	Publishing		221	242	305	360		56	62	77	98		7	15
2211	Publishing of books and other publications		...	...	63	80		...	...	8	20		1	2
2212	Publishing of newspapers, journals, etc.		...	...	224	258		...	...	62	72		5	10
2213	Publishing of recorded media		...	...	...	9		...	...	...	...		1	...
2219	Other publishing		...	...	...	13		...	...	...	...		-	...

continued

Bulgaria

ISIC Revision 3		Output in producers' prices					Value added in producers' prices					Gross fixed capital formation		
			(millions of Bulgarian Leva)					(millions of Bulgarian Leva)					(millions of Bulgarian Leva)	
ISIC	Industry	Note	2003	2004	2005	2006	Note	2003	2004	2005	2006	Note	2005	2006
222	Printing and related service activities		273	314	354	424		77	94	107	127		53	61
2221	Printing		...	...	328	393		...	...	99	118		48	55
2222	Service activities related to printing		...	...	26	31		...	...	8	9		5	6
2230	Reproduction of recorded media		6	11	9	18		3	7	4	8		...	2
2310	Coke oven products		...	...	...	...		...	...	...	...		...	...
2320	Refined petroleum products		...	...	...	...		...	...	...	...		...	...
2330	Processing of nuclear fuel		...	...	...	...		...	...	...	...		...	...
241	Basic chemicals		574	605	719	729		121	105	118	135		63	-169
2411	Basic chemicals, except fertilizers		...	...	339	381		...	...	78	124		51	37
2412	Fertilizers and nitrogen compounds		...	...	372	340		...	...	...	10		12	...
2413	Plastics in primary forms; synthetic rubber		...	...	8	8		...	...	...	1		-	...
242	Other chemicals		929	946	1100	1260		263	266	320	360		69	81
2421	Pesticides and other agro-chemical products		...	...	19	24		...	...	4	6		2	...
2422	Paints, varnishes, printing ink and mastics		...	...	169	218		...	...	32	39		8	11
2423	Pharmaceuticals, medicinal chemicals, etc.		...	...	479	504		...	...	189	197		55	43
2424	Soap, cleaning & cosmetic preparations		...	...	255	316		...	...	48	67		3	...
2429	Other chemical products n.e.c.		...	...	178	198		...	...	47	51		1	13
2430	Man-made fibres		...	...	...	...		...	...	...	...		...	...
251	Rubber products		101	112	122	152		23	24	24	28		17	27
2511	Rubber tyres and tubes		...	...	36	40		...	...	5	6		...	...
2519	Other rubber products		...	...	86	112		...	...	19	22		...	...
2520	Plastic products		497	606	812	1043		117	123	158	210		108	112
2610	Glass and glass products		147	188	244	415		43	62	72	141		111	242
269	Non-metallic mineral products n.e.c.		809	1054	1443	1914		226	311	405	552		139	263
2691	Pottery, china and earthenware		...	...	120	125		...	...	36	39		16	6
2692	Refractory ceramic products		...	...	17	21		...	...	6	7		3	-1
2693	Struct.non-refractory clay; ceramic products		...	...	140	179		...	...	43	67		18	30
2694	Cement, lime and plaster		...	...	469	589		...	...	186	224		21	72
2695	Articles of concrete, cement and plaster		...	...	558	815		...	...	98	157		64	137
2696	Cutting, shaping & finishing of stone		...	...	40	57		...	...	12	18		5	5
2699	Other non-metallic mineral products n.e.c.		...	...	99	128		...	...	24	40		12	14
2710	Basic iron and steel		1201	1770	1536	1904		156	360	204	235		13	129
2720	Basic precious and non-ferrous metals		751	1763	2495	4259		55	124	255	463		322	7
273	Casting of metals		81	103	130	164		24	28	32	41		20	9
2731	Casting of iron and steel		...	...	108	130		...	...	27	33		18	8
2732	Casting of non-ferrous metals		...	...	22	34		...	...	5	8		2	1
281	Struct.metal products;tanks;steam generators		346	485	578	777		72	96	110	158		34	51
2811	Structural metal products		...	...	476	644		...	...	86	125		30	45
2812	Tanks, reservoirs and containers of metal		...	...	73	95		...	...	14	21		2	5
2813	Steam generators		...	...	29	38		...	...	10	12		2	1
289	Other metal products; metal working services		415	507	615	794		118	140	175	215		75	68
2891	Metal forging/pressing/stamping/roll-forming		...	...	21	23		...	...	7	7		-	2
2892	Treatment & coating of metals		...	...	147	200		...	...	50	68		13	19
2893	Cutlery, hand tools and general hardware		...	...	81	95		...	...	34	35		13	10
2899	Other fabricated metal products n.e.c.		...	...	366	476		...	...	84	105		49	37
291	General purpose machinery		630	754	876	1178		176	200	229	287		52	103
2911	Engines & turbines (not for transport equipment)		...	...	100	103		...	...	23	27		6	6
2912	Pumps, compressors, taps and valves		...	...	390	488		...	...	125	136		20	33
2913	Bearings, gears, gearing & driving elements		...	...	44	57		...	...	4	8		7	6
2914	Ovens, furnaces and furnace burners		...	...	7	14		...	...	1	3		-	1
2915	Lifting and handling equipment		...	...	218	331		...	...	47	71		11	47
2919	Other general purpose machinery		...	...	117	185		...	...	29	42		8	10

292	Special purpose machinery	668	788	945	985	226	238	308	325	61	37
2921	Agricultural and forestry machinery	...	...	59	37	...	...	18	11	6	2
2922	Machine tools	...	...	206	224	...	...	54	63	15	17
2923	Machinery for metallurgy	...	...	56	91	...	...	19	36	-	-16
2924	Machinery for mining & construction	...	...	86	118	...	...	30	34	3	9
2925	Food/beverage/tobacco processing machinery	...	...	124	121	...	...	33	29	4	6
2926	Machinery for textile, apparel and leather	...	...	4	9	...	...	2	4	-	-
2927	Weapons and ammunition	...	...	292	255	...	...	112	104	19	-3
2929	Other special purpose machinery	...	...	118	130	...	...	40	44	14	22
2930	Domestic appliances n.e.c.	182	213	268	341	40	47	58	74	8	18
3000	Office, accounting and computing machinery	73	117	143	126	6	23	31	28	5	4
3110	Electric motors, generators and transformers	123	128	165	212	29	33	49	52	6	7
3120	Electricity distribution & control apparatus	108	117	123	175	32	37	38	50	6	11
3130	Insulated wire and cable	89	98	165	311	14	10	31	49	...	7
3140	Accumulators, primary cells and batteries	67	79	104	138	22	24	27	36	9	14
3150	Lighting equipment and electric lamps	46	52	60	68	8	10	13	15	5	6
3190	Other electrical equipment n.e.c.	134	138	213	301	29	33	41	61	14	11
3210	Electronic valves, tubes, etc.	75	71	110	125	22	21	29	33	1	5
3220	TV/radio transmitters; line comm. apparatus	215	119	162	81	61	51	92	34	-1	7
3230	TV and radio receivers and associated goods	11	13	12	20	...	3	3	4	-	3
331	Medical, measuring, testing appliances, etc.	114	146	150	187	29	39	46	57	7	9
3311	Medical, surgical and orthopaedic equipment	...	...	43	46	...	...	14	16	1	3
3312	Measuring/testing/navigating appliances,etc.	...	...	78	100	...	...	24	28	5	2
3313	Industrial process control equipment	...	...	29	41	...	...	8	13	1	4
3320	Optical instruments & photographic equipment	23	28	28	39	6	8	8	12	-	-5
3330	Watches and clocks	2	3	2	4	...	...	1	1	...	...
3410	Motor vehicles	2	3	...	...	...	1	...	...	...	...
3420	Automobile bodies, trailers & semi-trailers	11	11	13	18	3	3	3	4	-	1
3430	Parts/accessories for automobiles	36	45	75	91	10	15	20	22	2	2
351	Building and repairing of ships and boats	184	239	256	337	47	73	87	113	12	30
3511	Building and repairing of ships	...	...	255	335	...	...	87	112	12	30
3512	Building/repairing of pleasure/sport. boats	...	...	1	2	...	...	...	1	-	-
3520	Railway/tramway locomotives & rolling stock	62	75	112	140	19	20	28	27	5	4
3530	Aircraft and spacecraft	1	3	2	3	...	...	...	1	...	...
359	Transport equipment n.e.c.	40	45	52	71	5	6	7	11	2	4
3591	Motorcycles	...	...	-	-	...	...	...	-	-	-
3592	Bicycles and invalid carriages	...	...	50	70	...	...	7	11	2	4
3599	Other transport equipment n.e.c.	...	...	2	1	...	...	...	...	-	-
3610	Furniture	361	481	569	656	89	115	145	173	53	60
369	Manufacturing n.e.c.	100	...	...	...	32	...	...	...	3	13
3691	Jewellery and related articles	...	...	14	19	...	...	6	7	-	1
3692	Musical instruments	...	...	...	...	...	...	...	...	-	-
3693	Sports goods	...	...	27	31	...	...	8	9	1	1
3694	Games and toys	...	...	27	50	...	...	10	19	3	7
3699	Other manufacturing n.e.c.	...	...	49	57	...	...	15	16	-1	4
3710	Recycling of metal waste and scrap	76	...	...	382	4	...	...	46	-2	12
3720	Recycling of non-metal waste and scrap	7	8	12	12	...	...	1	4	3	3
D	Total manufacturing	19794	24351	29410	36176	4094	5270	6211	6933	2047	2115

Bulgaria

ISIC Revision 3			Index numbers of industrial production (2000=100)											
ISIC	Industry	Note	1995	1996	1997	1998	1999	2000	2001	2002	2003	2004	2005	2006
15	Food and beverages		133	130	100	101	101	100	98	101	121	142	151	158
16	Tobacco products		154	182	117	132	101	100	91	85	95	102	102	76
17	Textiles		162	169	152	130	95	100	98	127	188	222	225	252
18	Wearing apparel, fur		87	106	81	89	84	100	117	142	174	198	190	209
19	Leather, leather products and footwear		180	201	147	116	94	100	101	121	145	155	164	187
20	Wood products (excl. furniture)		97	95	90	81	97	100	99	123	158	191	209	240
21	Paper and paper products		175	165	138	125	101	100	86	105	148	185	197	196
22	Printing and publishing		184	162	91	90	89	100	94	88	90	92	109	107
23	Coke,refined petroleum products,nuclear fuel		...	...	...	...	...	...	...	...	...	...	...	...
24	Chemicals and chemical products		146	173	136	103	87	100	101	95	105	105	117	117
25	Rubber and plastics products		135	129	101	98	93	100	103	104	151	179	187	188
26	Non-metallic mineral products		142	164	126	114	104	100	98	113	133	171	196	240
27	Basic metals		124	127	124	102	86	100	84	90	113	192	206	220
28	Fabricated metal products		167	128	117	106	95	100	111	125	132	188	223	279
29	Machinery and equipment n.e.c.		118	117	119	113	102	100	107	127	141	188	213	223
30	Office, accounting and computing machinery		100	140	115	89	78	100	67	113	66	68	54	60
31	Electrical machinery and apparatus		130	142	106	93	91	100	101	101	123	149	180	222
32	Radio,television and communication equipment		104	66	54	64	65	100	169	266	310	187	230	130
33	Medical, precision and optical instruments		138	124	105	116	109	100	88	124	131	152	139	159
34	Motor vehicles, trailers, semi-trailers		301	257	205	151	94	100	95	66	77	58	73	73
35	Other transport equipment		190	185	151	180	110	100	106	105	136	145	196	245
36	Furniture; manufacturing n.e.c.		118	115	77	95	102	100	109	130	190	270	254	311
37	Recycling		...	...	...	...	...	...	...	...	...	...	...	...
D	Total manufacturing		134	140	113	100	93	100	101	109	129	157	169	182

Chile

Supplier of information:
Instituto Nacional de Estadísticas, Santiago

Basic source of data:
Monthly survey on registered establishments.

Major deviations from ISIC (Revision 3):
None reported.

Reference period:
Calendar year.

Scope:
All establishments.

Method of data collection:
Data are collected through on-line survey (self entry), fax and e-mail.

Type of enumeration:
Complete enumeration.

Adjusted for non-response:
Yes.

Concepts and definitions of variables:
Number of employees includes full and part time employees.
Wages and salaries refers to direct wages and salaries.

Related national publications:
Anuario de la Industria Manufacturera, published by the Instituto Nacional de Estadísticas, Santiago.

Chile

ISIC Revision 3		Number of establishments					Number of employees					Wages and salaries paid to employees				
			(number)					(number)					(millions of Chilean Pesos)			
ISIC	Industry	Note	2003	2004	2005	2006a/	Note	2003	2004	2005	2006a/	Note	2003	2004	2005	2006a/
151	Processed meat,fish,fruit,vegetables,fats		392	422	452	434		56886	61116	74961	70912		235357	259378	327439	316085
1511	Processing/preserving of meat		113	123	147	133		10071	11698	18452	16929		49450	57895	100733	88570
1512	Processing/preserving of fish		162	176	177	175		31916	32775	36686	34292		132899	136415	156338	144375
1513	Processing/preserving of fruit & vegetables		88	93	108	105		11750	13690	18230	18102		37733	45981	53413	65762
1514	Vegetable and animal oils and fats		29	30	20	21		3149	2953	1593	1589		15274	19087	16955	17379
1520	Dairy products		65	63	65	65		7005	6275	8100	7943		39479	35011	47165	47436
153	Grain mill products; starches; animal feeds		153	152	146	141		9870	10685	6564	6684		47977	57196	38252	42443
1531	Grain mill products		107	103	116	111		3658	3448	4073	3984		19685	21174	23493	24402
1532	Starches and starch products		13	14	...	...		1629	1924	...	...		7336	9443	...	...
1533	Prepared animal feeds		33	35	30	30		4583	5313	2491	2700		20956	26579	14759	18041
154	Other food products		843	848	808	753		32449	31531	30392	26762		137279	128891	127363	118477
1541	Bakery products		735	736	710	660		20607	20156	20073	17777		75436	68229	69498	62596
1542	Sugar		12	15	...	...		1258	1419	...	...		6165	7313	...	...
1543	Cocoa, chocolate and sugar confectionery		37	33	34	31		4939	4233	3421	1922		21034	17438	16887	12001
1544	Macaroni, noodles & similar products		9	7	3	3		1406	1441	1435	1486		9218	7984	7547	7891
1549	Other food products n.e.c.	b/	50	57	61	59	b/	4239	4282	5463	5577	b/	25427	27926	33431	35990
155	Beverages		157	201	203	206		14797	14926	15955	17322		102426	105177	118819	442927
1551	Distilling, rectifying & blending of spirits		20	17	12	19		2110	1435	724	1027		10329	8425	5836	7392
1552	Wines		86	128	140	134		6959	7520	9433	10235		36828	38116	48948	371386
1553	Malt liquors and malt	c/	...	...	...	...	c/	...	...	...	...	c/	...	...	...	...
1554	Soft drinks; mineral waters	c/	51	56	51	53	c/	5728	5971	5798	6060	c/	55269	58635	64036	64150
1600	Tobacco products	b/	...	...	...	...	b/	...	...	...	...	b/	...	...	...	...
171	Spinning, weaving and finishing of textiles		70	71	69	64		6305	6136	5358	4958		29612	27560	23351	22113
1711	Textile fibre preparation; textile weaving		70	71	69	64		6305	6136	5358	4958		29612	27560	23351	22113
1712	Finishing of textiles		...	...	...	...		...	...	...	...		...	...	...	...
172	Other textiles		137	137	125	119		4370	4124	4555	4280		18733	17543	18561	19621
1721	Made-up textile articles, except apparel		50	52	51	51		1890	1694	2305	2138		6506	6418	7417	8483
1722	Carpets and rugs		16	14	12	9		527	442	411	392		2959	2412	2819	3070
1723	Cordage, rope, twine and netting		26	23	11	11		900	967	590	574		3905	4167	2740	3022
1729	Other textiles n.e.c.		45	48	51	48		1053	1021	1249	1176		5364	4546	5584	5046
1730	Knitted and crocheted fabrics and articles		65	60	56	49		2470	2666	2618	2578		10916	10700	11184	10664
1810	Wearing apparel, except fur apparel		282	283	264	245		15128	15756	15362	15089		56879	62580	66962	70326
1820	Dressing & dyeing of fur; processing of fur		...	...	...	...		...	...	...	...		...	...	...	...
191	Tanning, dressing and processing of leather		41	43	39	38		2046	2373	1500	1413		8639	9872	6567	6770
1911	Tanning and dressing of leather		23	26	25	24		1151	1352	1059	1033		5331	6282	4852	5019
1912	Luggage, handbags, etc.; saddlery & harness		18	17	14	14		895	1021	441	380		3307	3590	1715	1751
1920	Footwear		105	102	83	77		6736	6589	5767	5413		26699	27007	24020	24427
2010	Sawmilling and planing of wood		228	226	240	228		14161	14286	17872	16484		52027	54681	63916	61797
202	Products of wood, cork, straw, etc.		126	136	122	114		8161	8850	7721	9091		36465	38708	38629	52183
2021	Veneer sheets, plywood, particle board, etc.		27	29	30	28		3231	3150	3548	3579		18114	17457	21835	26580
2022	Builders' carpentry and joinery		39	36	33	33		1533	2072	1938	3449		7953	9699	8585	17190
2023	Wooden containers		25	29	27	25		1876	2150	1599	1592		5599	6461	5565	6172
2029	Other wood products; articles of cork/straw		35	42	32	28		1521	1478	636	471		4799	5090	2644	2240
210	Paper and paper products		159	169	166	158		12493	12935	13570	14006		96419	105550	113800	117986
2101	Pulp, paper and paperboard		33	34	30	28		4489	4545	4775	4606		43980	46947	51762	50911
2102	Corrugated paper and paperboard		65	71	78	74		4972	5152	5665	5808		31388	35350	39981	42520
2109	Other articles of paper and paperboard		61	64	58	56		3032	3238	3130	3592		21051	23253	22056	24555
221	Publishing		179	183	182	178		6880	6376	6230	5837		46932	41357	42200	42710
2211	Publishing of books and other publications		69	74	74	72		2724	3037	3069	3301		17146	16541	17611	23126
2212	Publishing of newspapers, journals, etc.		39	39	38	36		2737	1913	1668	1405		21474	15724	15468	13891
2213	Publishing of recorded media		3	3	...	...		162	144	...	...		2017	1915	...	...
2219	Other publishing		68	67	70	70		1257	1282	1493	1131		6295	7177	9121	5693

222	Printing and related service activities		92	92	94	84		3343	3575	3598	3309		20026	22431	26308	24241
2221	Printing		86	86	87	78		3242	3472	3487	3236		19618	22022	25792	23942
2222	Service activities related to printing		6	6	7	6		101	103	111	73		408	409	517	299
2230	Reproduction of recorded media		4	6	3	3		198	256	218	224		1604	1353	1402	1384
2310	Coke oven products		...	...	...	...		...	...	...	...		...	...	...	...
2320	Refined petroleum products	d/	...	...	...	...	d/	...	...	...	...	d/	...	...	...	...
2330	Processing of nuclear fuel		...	...	...	...		...	...	...	...		...	...	...	...
241	Basic chemicals		98	100	104	106		9248	9457	9579	10129		122671	136970	144149	167610
2411	Basic chemicals, except fertilizers	d/	81	80	81	80	d/	6486	6783	6840	7378	d/	98256	109242	119468	139076
2412	Fertilizers and nitrogen compounds		3	6	7	7		1903	1869	2120	2002		15703	19307	17197	16974
2413	Plastics in primary forms; synthetic rubber		14	14	16	19		859	805	619	749		8713	8421	7485	11561
242	Other chemicals		215	219	229	209		18865	18699	21654	20087		175289	184190	207887	202911
2421	Pesticides and other agro-chemical products		5	4	3	4		295	338	174	264		2120	2116	1164	2028
2422	Paints, varnishes, printing ink and mastics		36	34	33	30		3021	3041	2958	2947		24316	25664	25967	26597
2423	Pharmaceuticals, medicinal chemicals, etc.		43	39	49	48		6768	6492	7790	8142		58089	63345	72009	79138
2424	Soap, cleaning & cosmetic preparations		56	62	67	58		4985	5505	6811	5712		56010	58610	68814	63562
2429	Other chemical products n.e.c.		75	80	77	69		3796	3323	3921	3022		34754	34455	39932	31586
2430	Man-made fibres		8	8	...	...		595	594	...	...		4131	4322	...	...
251	Rubber products		58	59	56	52		3560	3627	3634	3264		28635	29629	27852	27856
2511	Rubber tyres and tubes		27	31	30	22		2028	2098	2058	1606		17139	18162	17134	14157
2519	Other rubber products		31	28	26	30		1532	1529	1576	1658		11496	11467	10718	13699
2520	Plastic products		282	300	294	292		14350	14375	15696	16948		79195	81603	89791	102811
2610	Glass and glass products		36	39	36	37		2283	2709	2665	2681		16286	18267	19585	22688
269	Non-metallic mineral products n.e.c.		230	229	238	249		10383	9874	10698	10584		68144	69263	74900	81214
2691	Pottery, china and earthenware		13	10	8	8		1117	881	803	811		6696	7130	4410	4778
2692	Refractory ceramic products		15	12	9	21		1182	905	1321	1309		7044	5489	5847	9574
2693	Struct.non-refractory clay; ceramic products		12	16	15	15		962	1073	1053	1123		7757	7175	8150	9241
2694	Cement, lime and plaster		24	22	22	22		1340	1300	1298	1238		16210	15788	18346	18631
2695	Articles of concrete, cement and plaster		137	145	159	158		4360	4523	5103	5008		23759	25978	30688	31195
2696	Cutting, shaping & finishing of stone		8	4	4	4		152	99	108	126		593	439	546	630
2699	Other non-metallic mineral products n.e.c.		21	20	21	21		1270	1093	1012	969		6086	7265	6913	7165
2710	Basic iron and steel		54	61	67	70		6271	6908	7622	8051		66153	75053	84615	88126
2720	Basic precious and non-ferrous metals		70	89	92	89		15108	19002	18912	19841		237748	328280	388696	371859
273	Casting of metals		...	...	...	...		...	...	...	...		...	...	...	...
2731	Casting of iron and steel		...	...	...	...		...	...	...	...		...	...	...	...
2732	Casting of non-ferrous metals		...	...	...	...		...	...	...	...		...	...	...	...
281	Struct.metal products;tanks;steam generators		198	206	212	223		8109	9887	13106	14752		37788	43582	59941	63443
2811	Structural metal products		159	164	176	185		6205	7796	11590	13273		29231	34728	53547	56237
2812	Tanks, reservoirs and containers of metal		29	31	28	30		1755	1923	1361	1367		7940	8082	5994	6716
2813	Steam generators		10	11	8	8		149	168	155	112		617	772	400	490
289	Other metal products; metal working services		197	210	198	180		9469	10112	9744	8989		57056	62297	61524	59958
2891	Metal forging/pressing/stamping/roll-forming		8	10	4	4		374	433	84	82		1538	2074	322	344
2892	Treatment & coating of metals		12	12	10	10		471	628	560	569		1703	2387	2216	2342
2893	Cutlery, hand tools and general hardware		7	8	9	7		404	325	665	406		1605	1763	4414	2617
2899	Other fabricated metal products n.e.c.		170	180	175	159		8220	8726	8435	7932		52209	56074	54572	54655
291	General purpose machinery		115	121	118	101		4424	4559	5160	4844		23343	25916	27279	27927
2911	Engines & turbines (not for transport equipment)		...	...	...	...		...	...	...	...		...	...	...	...
2912	Pumps, compressors, taps and valves		22	26	28	25		1046	1476	1755	1807		5666	8382	8625	8172
2913	Bearings, gears, gearing & driving elements		16	18	8	6		359	287	142	130		1043	1005	601	604
2914	Ovens, furnaces and furnace burners		9	11	3	3		473	444	68	74		3936	3613	416	401
2915	Lifting and handling equipment		28	25	20	15		1302	1168	721	608		6631	6042	4728	4255
2919	Other general purpose machinery		40	41	59	52		1244	1184	2474	2225		6066	6874	12910	14496
292	Special purpose machinery		176	187	185	187		8500	8481	7903	8152		65626	71447	71783	74564
2921	Agricultural and forestry machinery		40	45	49	50		1716	1818	2112	2383		14681	16915	15997	15267
2922	Machine tools		26	29	16	15		2002	1745	275	231		23597	24864	1277	1148
2923	Machinery for metallurgy		11	13	19	23		211	317	514	755		826	1865	3270	4649
2924	Machinery for mining & construction		35	34	52	49		1907	1960	3484	3379		13063	13671	42868	45529
2925	Food/beverage/tobacco processing machinery		31	32	20	17		1437	1310	502	535		7220	7335	2599	2812
2926	Machinery for textile, apparel and leather		12	6	4	4		309	227	104	53		1683	862	617	275
2927	Weapons and ammunition		4	9	...	...		532	714	...	...		2620	3933	...	...
2929	Other special purpose machinery		17	19	25	29		386	390	912	816		1936	2001	5154	4885

continued

Chile

ISIC Revision 3		Number of establishments					Number of employees					Wages and salaries paid to employees			
			(number)					(number)					(millions of Chilean Pesos)		
ISIC	Industry	Note	2003	2004	2005	2006a/	Note	2003	2004	2005	2006a/	Note	2003	2004	2005	2006a/
2930	Domestic appliances n.e.c.		27	27	26	27		2384	2615	2765	3056		13800	15462	15961	19466
3000	Office, accounting and computing machinery		3	3	3	3		95	98	86	98		705	728	467	505
3110	Electric motors, generators and transformers		10	11	13	12		862	887	903	898		5249	5605	6879	7165
3120	Electricity distribution & control apparatus		26	28	29	24		1058	1267	1311	1234		6009	8173	8316	7689
3130	Insulated wire and cable		6	6	4	5		325	295	262	428		1346	1193	911	5029
3140	Accumulators, primary cells and batteries		3	3	...	...		32	29	...	...		138	177	...	...
3150	Lighting equipment and electric lamps		25	24	22	17		935	906	806	718		4451	4589	4840	4418
3190	Other electrical equipment n.e.c.		16	19	17	15		310	352	321	281		1345	1585	1633	1439
3210	Electronic valves, tubes, etc.		6	6	6	4		97	102	95	65		537	643	560	448
3220	TV/radio transmitters; line comm. apparatus		3	3	...	...		103	108	...	...		778	786	...	...
3230	TV and radio receivers and associated goods		3	3	...	...		57	86	...	...		364	284	...	...
331	Medical, measuring, testing appliances, etc.		24	23	24	24		734	795	815	901		5059	6209	6347	7521
3311	Medical, surgical and orthopaedic equipment		14	11	12	12		267	226	224	265		1237	1120	1103	1478
3312	Measuring/testing/navigating appliances,etc.		10	12	12	12		467	569	591	636		3822	5088	5243	6042
3313	Industrial process control equipment		...	...	...	...		...	...	...	...		...	...	...	...
3320	Optical instruments & photographic equipment		7	7	7	7		575	594	539	540		3350	3416	3566	3808
3330	Watches and clocks		3	3	3	3		52	47	193	191		124	121	508	514
3410	Motor vehicles		11	12	26	26		740	644	1055	904		6966	6864	9667	8014
3420	Automobile bodies, trailers & semi-trailers		30	28	23	19		1165	951	890	857		4935	4242	4490	4983
3430	Parts/accessories for automobiles		42	44	43	43		1429	1480	1472	1184		8193	8397	8616	6077
351	Building and repairing of ships and boats		26	30	30	30		3709	3924	4102	3982		20901	21514	25207	26460
3511	Building and repairing of ships		26	30	30	30		3709	3924	4102	3982		20901	21514	25207	26460
3512	Building/repairing of pleasure/sport. boats		...	...	...	...		...	...	...	...		...	...	...	...
3520	Railway/tramway locomotives & rolling stock		...	...	...	...		...	...	...	...		...	...	...	...
3530	Aircraft and spacecraft		3	3	3	3		1404	1398	1515	1487		8042	7977	8758	9542
359	Transport equipment n.e.c.		19	22	20	18		1056	958	609	476		5833	4327	3078	1795
3591	Motorcycles		...	...	...	...		...	...	...	...		...	...	...	...
3592	Bicycles and invalid carriages		9	12	8	8		524	707	300	302		3061	3306	1094	1238
3599	Other transport equipment n.e.c.		10	10	12	10		532	251	309	174		2771	1020	1983	557
3610	Furniture		193	216	205	188		8939	10544	11480	9829		32982	39797	43486	41722
369	Manufacturing n.e.c.		58	60	60	47		2228	2297	2267	1651		11097	9949	12202	9727
3691	Jewellery and related articles		9	13	13	11		375	445	391	322		1947	1920	2213	1695
3692	Musical instruments		6	6	3	3		83	89	18	19		241	281	65	69
3693	Sports goods		9	9	7	3		143	146	98	65		609	660	506	453
3694	Games and toys		8	6	8	6		226	163	314	151		661	473	954	471
3699	Other manufacturing n.e.c.		26	26	29	24		1401	1454	1446	1094		7638	6615	8464	7039
3710	Recycling of metal waste and scrap		...	...	...	...		...	...	...	...		...	...	...	...
3720	Recycling of non-metal waste and scrap		...	...	...	...		...	...	...	...		...	...	...	...
D	Total manufacturing		5379	5603	5510	5266		342752	357116	378200	369407		2091741	2287849	2519431	2878880

a/ Preliminary data.
b/ 1549 includes 1600.
c/ 1554 includes 1553.
d/ 2411 includes 2320.

Chile

ISIC Revision 3		Output in producers' prices					Value added in producers' prices					Gross fixed capital formation		
			(millions of Chilean Pesos)					(millions of Chilean Pesos)					(millions of Chilean Pesos)	
ISIC	Industry	Note	2003	2004	2005	2006a/	Note	2003	2004	2005	2006a/	Note	2005	2006a/
151	Processed meat,fish,fruit,vegetables,fats		2803633	3160225	3851403	4073964		1079938	1154675	1473539	1710960		173419	241595
1511	Processing/preserving of meat		655526	837894	1400758	1350129		186675	247285	466724	464974		59348	94260
1512	Processing/preserving of fish		1548245	1630623	1735118	1963670		665238	643732	703548	897853		94811	106767
1513	Processing/preserving of fruit & vegetables		404841	497374	541571	556454		148900	186208	223787	251675		20267	31638
1514	Vegetable and animal oils and fats		195021	194334	173956	203711		79125	77450	79480	96459		-1006	8930
1520	Dairy products		648655	584343	793995	759835		242410	200701	272199	283059		27342	39274
153	Grain mill products; starches; animal feeds		774205	953096	828982	997940		203075	239253	178122	210651		28953	12307
1531	Grain mill products		368070	350141	372304	380117		92824	85434	98833	101404		20820	10298
1532	Starches and starch products		38087	57226	...	...		15002	30366	...	...		...	...
1533	Prepared animal feeds		368047	545728	456678	617824		95249	123452	79290	109247		8133	2009
154	Other food products		1411986	1365984	1220722	1150378		629014	758298	588518	610607		38779	47357
1541	Bakery products		486944	437619	433594	350272		229736	215835	208518	162700		20116	7846
1542	Sugar		141381	125635	...	...		61728	37618	...	...		...	...
1543	Cocoa, chocolate and sugar confectionery		287513	296229	108592	79325		67637	241299	55293	56434		7751	775
1544	Macaroni, noodles & similar products		107989	108654	109327	113422		56558	46775	46291	59211		-2321	4093
1549	Other food products n.e.c.	b/	388159	397847	569209	607359	b/	213355	216771	278417	332261	b/	13233	34643
155	Beverages		1493532	1536891	1629872	1907361		805547	851245	840550	984737		85823	100449
1551	Distilling, rectifying & blending of spirits		73766	51164	48517	92528		36333	16242	16066	49049		1210	1828
1552	Wines		614438	661996	721616	828079		296391	333345	325962	348995		58435	52973
1553	Malt liquors and malt	c/	...	...	...	...	c/	...	...	...	...	c/	...	...
1554	Soft drinks; mineral waters	c/	805328	823731	859739	986753	c/	472823	501659	498522	586693	c/	26178	45648
1600	Tobacco products	b/	...	...	...	...	b/	...	...	...	...	b/	...	...
171	Spinning, weaving and finishing of textiles		170927	172803	139666	135445		55360	60491	53731	50252		4978	1302
1711	Textile fibre preparation; textile weaving		170927	172803	139666	135445		55360	60491	53731	50252		4978	1302
1712	Finishing of textiles		...	...	...	...		...	...	...	...		...	...
172	Other textiles		115786	116292	124316	131207		46886	45032	44357	52943		1132	5704
1721	Made-up textile articles, except apparel		44978	39327	51827	57833		19035	14950	17962	24336		382	1803
1722	Carpets and rugs		25930	26959	28127	29888		8581	8324	7795	10217		-277	1657
1723	Cordage, rope, twine and netting		18538	23620	18509	21499		7161	10280	6782	7581		821	1296
1729	Other textiles n.e.c.		26340	26386	25854	21987		12110	11477	11818	10809		207	948
1730	Knitted and crocheted fabrics and articles		57775	56844	56985	59190		24306	27057	25025	25314		2259	-130
1810	Wearing apparel, except fur apparel		363435	389118	402321	437381		133394	152211	167245	180457		12273	19813
1820	Dressing & dyeing of fur; processing of fur		...	...	...	...		...	...	...	...		...	...
191	Tanning, dressing and processing of leather		71459	86269	59613	61608		22693	29433	20252	19184		1096	1333
1911	Tanning and dressing of leather		53023	62966	47436	47602		13495	17848	14207	13641		1083	469
1912	Luggage, handbags, etc.; saddlery & harness		18436	23303	12177	14006		9198	11585	6045	5543		13	864
1920	Footwear		127129	167266	152629	171641		57898	80091	68597	76941		4019	217
2010	Sawmilling and planing of wood		900769	1033985	1039993	1120121		328974	405263	378046	435601		76100	39305
202	Products of wood, cork, straw, etc.		389947	452084	445973	574979		163837	198801	191458	269459		17916	54008
2021	Veneer sheets, plywood, particle board, etc.		261146	296199	312037	399213		110775	136091	129721	189764		12789	47692
2022	Builders' carpentry and joinery		54719	77216	74150	119840		24782	33821	40941	59754		3717	4642
2023	Wooden containers		38196	40623	36782	34805		16263	15110	15688	14412		1385	886
2029	Other wood products; articles of cork/straw		35886	38045	23004	21121		12017	13778	5108	5529		24	788
210	Paper and paper products		1637470	1811190	1839727	2036686		813650	928202	959593	1074732		111288	104061
2101	Pulp, paper and paperboard		1043717	1176977	1196240	1331627		557395	641699	680433	775136		63883	66476
2102	Corrugated paper and paperboard		337493	359169	386811	376167		133523	138845	131391	129209		22479	16180
2109	Other articles of paper and paperboard		256261	275044	256676	328892		122732	147658	147770	170387		24925	21404
221	Publishing		242810	259699	239122	256049		112341	117364	91631	108476		15629	19171
2211	Publishing of books and other publications		88084	92337	98580	141443		47722	43354	44848	61359		6690	6919
2212	Publishing of newspapers, journals, etc.		105169	112568	87903	82842		40057	46248	22105	28209		8088	10052
2213	Publishing of recorded media		9996	10341	...	...		4239	3162	...	...		...	...
2219	Other publishing		39560	44453	52638	31764		20324	24601	24678	18908		852	2199

continued

Chile

ISIC Revision 3		Output in producers' prices (millions of Chilean Pesos)					Value added in producers' prices (millions of Chilean Pesos)					Gross fixed capital formation (millions of Chilean Pesos)	
ISIC	Industry	Note	2003	2004	2005	2006a/	Note	2003	2004	2005	2006a/	Note	2005	2006a/
222	Printing and related service activities		115162	137265	145182	142849		50524	63186	68154	58215		7661	3694
2221	Printing		113733	135736	143788	142024		49735	62260	67279	57727		7634	3693
2222	Service activities related to printing		1430	1529	1395	825		789	927	874	488		27	1
2230	Reproduction of recorded media		5712	6520	5551	5438		3203	4344	2370	2330		425	184
2310	Coke oven products		...	...	...	...		...	...	...	...		...	...
2320	Refined petroleum products	d/	...	...	...	...	d/	...	...	...	...	d/	...	...
2330	Processing of nuclear fuel		...	...	...	...		...	...	...	...		...	...
241	Basic chemicals		5403777	5786730	9116130	8122006		2029115	2097987	3622108	2830271		319871	346066
2411	Basic chemicals, except fertilizers	d/	4979792	5306905	8414374	7421609	d/	1817199	1848914	3228432	2482859	d/	222431	241548
2412	Fertilizers and nitrogen compounds		247112	284904	492678	451882		146689	179772	329768	275643		96668	97389
2413	Plastics in primary forms; synthetic rubber		176874	194921	209079	248516		65227	69301	63908	71769		772	7129
242	Other chemicals		1200633	1286970	1447115	1425072		605859	695311	750262	734981		49250	34582
2421	Pesticides and other agro-chemical products		8651	12256	10920	38203		5356	6181	4132	18149		278	810
2422	Paints, varnishes, printing ink and mastics		168276	165195	192292	182810		63667	60855	62487	67007		3066	3261
2423	Pharmaceuticals, medicinal chemicals, etc.		323500	362399	417726	445148		200837	241375	275771	280230		32342	19906
2424	Soap, cleaning & cosmetic preparations		391739	416135	474008	475015		195900	244817	278669	264967		8397	5942
2429	Other chemical products n.e.c.		308466	330985	352169	283896		140099	142082	129201	104628		5167	4663
2430	Man-made fibres		17991	19938	...	...		7749	7919	...	...		...	...
251	Rubber products		227716	228933	252233	211468		100774	85212	78202	78527		8140	7513
2511	Rubber tyres and tubes		152299	163759	188575	131640		73574	59067	53389	42982		6654	5411
2519	Other rubber products		75417	65174	63658	79829		27201	26145	24813	35545		1485	2102
2520	Plastic products		638703	715784	867785	943780		252613	281025	324335	360011		56622	50637
2610	Glass and glass products		140631	159022	174230	167212		82767	101904	96593	102668		14000	49841
269	Non-metallic mineral products n.e.c.		739035	823907	939298	1086058		327619	358375	400674	491085		31642	48366
2691	Pottery, china and earthenware		31363	29814	32700	38492		16197	18258	18314	21443		818	8523
2692	Refractory ceramic products		38963	38753	40352	157548		11591	12576	17212	106923		4215	10090
2693	Struct.non-refractory clay; ceramic products		40859	39068	41364	46009		22889	17385	15112	14965		1827	3410
2694	Cement, lime and plaster		275422	286592	309522	312887		141410	138932	152215	145909		11897	12083
2695	Articles of concrete, cement and plaster		286386	345611	415173	429254		111860	136704	160313	166366		11309	9803
2696	Cutting, shaping & finishing of stone		2686	1799	2063	2499		1144	833	986	1281		12	90
2699	Other non-metallic mineral products n.e.c.		63356	82269	98124	99370		22527	33687	36523	34198		1564	4368
2710	Basic iron and steel		782054	1015386	914234	1048821		340336	446977	342726	378791		17470	25507
2720	Basic precious and non-ferrous metals		7068670	14967410	17228725	23465920		2192670	7441620	9102898	14202807		537052	1563017
273	Casting of metals		...	...	...	...		...	...	...	...		...	...
2731	Casting of iron and steel		...	...	...	...		...	...	...	...		...	...
2732	Casting of non-ferrous metals		...	...	...	...		...	...	...	...		...	...
281	Struct.metal products;tanks;steam generators		230983	277194	352578	350153		95483	120596	136819	143038		15245	14206
2811	Structural metal products		179203	214425	307009	295287		71996	93106	117961	123638		13453	11310
2812	Tanks, reservoirs and containers of metal		45519	54252	38824	47723		20532	24704	14275	14973		1769	2900
2813	Steam generators		6262	8517	6744	7142		2954	2786	4583	4426		23	-5
289	Other metal products; metal working services		381731	472150	498282	480468		164855	173792	162310	175525		17412	14481
2891	Metal forging/pressing/stamping/roll-forming		6263	8142	1923	2300		3270	4059	1024	1392		29	-37
2892	Treatment & coating of metals		6067	9403	9699	11950		4020	6004	5534	5364		157	261
2893	Cutlery, hand tools and general hardware		8143	11535	19192	9269		4362	3807	10017	4832		193	264
2899	Other fabricated metal products n.e.c.		361257	443070	467468	456948		153203	159922	145734	163937		17033	13993
291	General purpose machinery		97497	111803	142921	144822		51437	56836	59921	63320		2317	2907
2911	Engines & turbines (not for transport equipment)		...	...	...	...		...	...	...	...		...	...
2912	Pumps, compressors, taps and valves		24039	35363	49219	36954		12356	18516	15797	16279		826	720
2913	Bearings, gears, gearing & driving elements		3864	4127	2416	2120		2283	2461	1621	1440		123	51
2914	Ovens, furnaces and furnace burners		15314	16252	1308	1040		10683	9729	746	704		-	20
2915	Lifting and handling equipment		25730	23888	21328	24248		11833	10505	8784	10687		697	87
2919	Other general purpose machinery		28550	32172	68651	80460		14282	15625	32973	34210		671	2029

292	Special purpose machinery	336580	376038	410742	366188	151665	160891	180139	171117	10171	6426
2921	Agricultural and forestry machinery	50754	61331	78852	80049	22382	31527	46194	34872	4568	1018
2922	Machine tools	158947	168854	4675	4046	61336	65081	2463	2190	2	71
2923	Machinery for metallurgy	3981	12559	13442	18094	2223	4721	6761	10408	238	443
2924	Machinery for mining & construction	64128	74739	273028	235644	33701	33505	110698	111512	3701	4788
2925	Food/beverage/tobacco processing machinery	29222	23478	14951	11610	15168	12177	6092	5131	708	-238
2926	Machinery for textile, apparel and leather	11565	7476	7573	994	5984	2792	2418	523	278	10
2927	Weapons and ammunition	11039	20869	...	...	6639	6657	...	...	...	...
2929	Other special purpose machinery	6945	6731	18221	15751	4234	4431	5513	6482	677	334
2930	Domestic appliances n.e.c.	124305	143864	158104	174566	44625	52043	56672	61256	2533	3386
3000	Office, accounting and computing machinery	1714	1994	1172	1612	987	1025	656	820	11	19
3110	Electric motors, generators and transformers	33017	38822	48277	56296	12611	11702	22612	27108	-1247	786
3120	Electricity distribution & control apparatus	41611	43755	55717	53465	17619	19540	19819	21716	973	1208
3130	Insulated wire and cable	11495	15688	7684	195081	2552	2679	2418	21299	649	2416
3140	Accumulators, primary cells and batteries	1303	1503	...	...	559	555	...	...	...	...
3150	Lighting equipment and electric lamps	33448	33088	31408	35748	11300	8407	11054	11186	144	692
3190	Other electrical equipment n.e.c.	5361	7212	7736	7477	2895	3986	4035	3686	34	-201
3210	Electronic valves, tubes, etc.	2048	1993	1731	1033	1138	1146	955	677	-236	40
3220	TV/radio transmitters; line comm. apparatus	2067	2013	...	...	987	909	...	...	...	...
3230	TV and radio receivers and associated goods	1662	1835	...	...	623	706	...	...	...	...
331	Medical, measuring, testing appliances, etc.	39519	40073	45229	47049	13715	14314	13706	13180	2540	31
3311	Medical, surgical and orthopaedic equipment	4108	3381	4416	7052	2455	2124	2542	4034	70	64
3312	Measuring/testing/navigating appliances,etc.	35411	36692	40813	39997	11260	12190	11164	9146	2470	-33
3313	Industrial process control equipment	...	...	...	...	...	...	...	...	...	...
3320	Optical instruments & photographic equipment	11826	10520	10684	9794	6179	5459	5948	4179	884	255
3330	Watches and clocks	411	282	1703	1753	204	185	1102	1083	-	30
3410	Motor vehicles	217543	218147	251129	233635	28733	54233	77632	51458	486	431
3420	Automobile bodies, trailers & semi-trailers	31222	27408	32844	41577	13173	11844	11728	15694	786	1276
3430	Parts/accessories for automobiles	28096	32676	31986	21125	14356	16509	16339	9712	780	490
351	Building and repairing of ships and boats	74700	80929	131523	127388	46113	39014	62944	55243	5035	4712
3511	Building and repairing of ships	74700	80929	131523	127388	46113	39014	62944	55243	5035	4712
3512	Building/repairing of pleasure/sport. boats	...	...	...	...	...	...	...	...	...	...
3520	Railway/tramway locomotives & rolling stock	...	...	...	...	...	...	...	...	...	...
3530	Aircraft and spacecraft	26133	26512	24914	17701	11196	15065	9779	7502	1464	841
359	Transport equipment n.e.c.	46738	22954	22549	15663	28512	5892	7928	7566	545	31
3591	Motorcycles	...	...	...	...	...	...	...	...	...	...
3592	Bicycles and invalid carriages	22976	18434	8870	12672	9460	4624	2973	6242	154	23
3599	Other transport equipment n.e.c.	23762	4520	13679	2992	19052	1268	4955	1324	391	8
3610	Furniture	197086	230787	228805	238265	79528	88151	101847	104873	6507	5203
369	Manufacturing n.e.c.	63894	62554	69904	70499	30581	31710	34671	34986	582	-247
3691	Jewellery and related articles	13550	14894	14693	26977	4298	5914	1986	9432	101	320
3692	Musical instruments	1126	983	354	319	506	530	112	102	-20	6
3693	Sports goods	5252	4997	4480	4522	1689	1926	1529	1506	32	28
3694	Games and toys	5319	2123	5305	2288	2651	1165	2577	1074	117	1
3699	Other manufacturing n.e.c.	38647	39558	45072	36392	21436	22175	28467	22872	352	-602
3710	Recycling of metal waste and scrap	...	...	...	...	...	...	...	...	...	...
3720	Recycling of non-metal waste and scrap	...	...	...	...	...	...	...	...	...	...
D	Total manufacturing	29591592	39575747	46483423	53183771	11544182	17729165	21142219	26339283	1710751	2874591

a/ Preliminary data.
b/ 1549 includes 1600.
c/ 1554 includes 1553.
d/ 2411 includes 2320.

Chile

ISIC Revision 3			Index numbers of industrial production											
			(2000=100)											
ISIC	Industry	Note	1995	1996	1997	1998	1999	2000	2001	2002	2003	2004	2005	2006
15	Food and beverages		104	104	102	96	98	100	105	109	113	121	127	141
16	Tobacco products		79	84	91	94	96	100	96	100	100	107	120	131
17	Textiles		130	132	127	113	97	100	94	86	106	127	133	117
18	Wearing apparel, fur		189	179	152	117	105	100	79	75	75	77	67	61
19	Leather, leather products and footwear		...	...	...	...	...	...	...	...	...	...	...	...
20	Wood products (excl. furniture)		93	96	97	90	91	100	98	113	124	134	138	144
21	Paper and paper products		92	93	91	93	96	100	102	111	120	126	127	128
22	Printing and publishing		145	143	151	137	127	100	112	112	123	139	140	135
23	Coke,refined petroleum products,nuclear fuel		...	...	...	...	...	...	...	...	...	...	...	...
24	Chemicals and chemical products		...	...	...	...	...	...	...	...	...	...	...	...
25	Rubber and plastics products		...	...	...	...	...	...	...	...	...	...	...	...
26	Non-metallic mineral products		...	...	...	...	...	...	...	...	...	...	...	...
27	Basic metals		...	...	...	...	...	...	...	...	...	...	...	...
28	Fabricated metal products		93	99	107	106	99	100	104	100	102	105	106	112
29	Machinery and equipment n.e.c.		98	90	106	100	99	100	117	106	108	121	131	136
30	Office, accounting and computing machinery		...	...	...	...	...	...	...	...	...	...	...	...
31	Electrical machinery and apparatus		104	108	114	106	92	100	78	68	67	81	119	93
32	Radio,television and communication equipment		...	...	...	...	...	...	...	...	...	...	...	...
33	Medical, precision and optical instruments		125	136	150	139	88	100	86	83	149	164	195	182
34	Motor vehicles, trailers, semi-trailers		86	87	104	86	71	100	81	84	63	56	61	40
35	Other transport equipment		...	...	...	...	...	...	...	...	...	...	...	...
36	Furniture; manufacturing n.e.c.		...	...	...	...	...	...	...	...	...	...	...	...
37	Recycling		...	...	...	...	...	...	...	...	...	...	...	...
D	Total manufacturing		89	91	96	97	97	100	101	104	109	118	124	128

China

Supplier of information:
National Bureau of Statistics, Beijing.

Basic source of data:
Annual report.

Major deviations from ISIC (Revision 2):
None reported.

Reference period:
Calendar year.

Scope:
All state-owned industrial enterprises and non-state-owned industrial enterprises with annual sales higher than 5 million yuan.

Method of data collection:
Not reported.

Type of enumeration:
Not reported.

Adjusted for non-response:
Not reported.

Concepts and definitions of variables:
No deviations from the standard UN concepts and definitions are reported.

Related national publications:
Statistical Yearbook of China (annual), published by the National Bureau of Statistics, Beijing.

China

ISIC Revision 2		Number of enterprises					Number of employees					Wages and salaries				
			(number)					(thousands)					(billions of Chinese Yuan)			
ISIC	Industry	Note	2003	2004	2005	2006	Note	2003	2004	2005	2006	Note	2003	2004	2005	2006
311/2	Food products		15828	19625	20128	22412		2827	3074	3436	3667		...	...	...	...
313	Beverages		3194	3469	3519	3914		890	839	890	923		...	...	...	...
314	Tobacco		255	210	190	179		212	199	197	190		...	...	...	...
321	Textiles		14863	24192	22569	25345		4992	5879	5910	6154		...	...	...	...
322	Wearing apparel, except footwear	a/	9717	12029	11865	13072	a/	2892	3319	3461	3776		...	...	...	...
323	Leather and fur products		4518	6393	6227	6859		1654	2112	2288	2456		...	...	...	...
324	Footwear, except rubber or plastic	a/	...	...	...	...	a/	...	...	...	...		...	...	...	...
331	Wood products, except furniture		3501	5017	5397	6374		638	768	833	916		...	...	...	...
332	Furniture and fixtures, excl. metal		2046	3025	3074	3603		434	649	713	838		...	...	...	...
341	Paper and products		5570	7473	7461	7892		1140	1304	1301	1348		...	...	...	...
342	Printing and publishing		4084	5139	4826	5029		594	635	669	690		...	...	...	...
351	Industrial chemicals	b/	18803	25004	24993	27503	b/	4610	4800	5061	5315		...	...	...	...
352	Other chemicals	b/	...	...	...	...	b/	...	...	...	...		...	...	...	...
353	Petroleum refineries	c/	1323	2019	1990	2160	c/	597	680	744	768		...	...	...	...
354	Misc. petroleum and coal products	c/	...	...	...	...	c/	...	...	...	...		...	...	...	...
355	Rubber products		2016	3168	3034	3353		622	808	796	821		...	...	...	...
356	Plastic products		8382	12269	12041	13504		1409	1752	1833	2014		...	...	...	...
361	Pottery, china and earthenware		1394	1499	1560	1685		548	531	523	552		...	...	...	...
362	Glass and products		1952	2746	2783	3113		552	662	677	731		...	...	...	...
369	Other non-metallic mineral products		12899	15715	15768	17138		2863	2960	2981	2981		...	...	...	...
371	Iron and steel		4119	7141	6649	6999		2559	2773	2875	2961		...	...	...	...
372	Non-ferrous metals		3367	5300	5163	5863		1066	1273	1307	1368		...	...	...	...
381	Fabricated metal products		9746	14131	13802	15573		1712	2131	2232	2483		...	...	...	...
382	Non-electrical machinery		19675	31493	30241	34520		4888	5637	5750	6134		...	...	...	...
383	Electrical machinery		16256	25306	24234	26614		5386	7275	8069	9091		...	...	...	...
384	Transport equipment		8281	11824	11315	12586		3118	3413	3524	3746		...	...	...	...
385	Professional and scientific equipment		2515	3916	3723	4084		720	843	887	988		...	...	...	...
390	Other manufacturing industries		6882	8896	8947	9908		1915	2357	2396	2558		...	...	...	...
3	Total manufacturing		181186	256999	251499	279282		48838	56673	59353	63469		...	...	...	...

a/ 322 includes 324.
b/ 351 includes 352.
c/ 353 includes 354.

China

ISIC Revision 2		Output					Value added					Gross fixed capital formation		
			(billions of Chinese Yuan)					(billions of Chinese Yuan)					(billions of Chinese Yuan)	
ISIC	Industry	Note	2003	2004	2005	2006	Note	2003	2004	2005	2006	Note	2005	2006
311/2	Food products		844.2	1124.4	1439.4	1768.8		213.4	...	391.4	495.9		...	...
313	Beverages		223.3	244.1	308.9	389.9		79.6	...	116.5	143.9		...	...
314	Tobacco		223.6	259.6	284.1	321.4		157.3	...	206.0	238.0		...	...
321	Textiles		772.5	1035.6	1267.2	1531.6		190.7	...	324.0	396.3		...	...
322	Wearing apparel, except footwear	a/	342.6	399.6	497.5	615.9		91.7a/	...	142.0a/	183.4a/		...	...
323	Leather and fur products		227.4	276.6	346.3	415.0		59.1	...	94.4	117.3		...	...
324	Footwear, except rubber or plastic	a/	...	...	...	...		...a/	...	...a/	...a/		...	...
331	Wood products, except furniture		99.3	138.6	182.8	242.9		26.6	...	51.1	68.6		...	...
332	Furniture and fixtures, excl. metal		72.0	115.5	142.7	188.3		18.3	...	38.5	50.1		...	...
341	Paper and products		252.6	337.2	416.1	503.5		68.1	...	114.6	138.6		...	...
342	Printing and publishing		102.7	119.9	144.3	170.7		33.4	...	46.3	55.8		...	...
351	Industrial chemicals	b/	1358.3	1814.7	2321.9	2867.3		378.5b/	...	640.7b/	781.1b/		...	...
352	Other chemicals	b/	...	...	...	...		...b/	...	...b/	...b/		...	...
353	Petroleum refineries	c/	623.5	892.7	1200.0	1514.9		128.7c/	...	198.2c/	231.4c/		...	...
354	Misc. petroleum and coal products	c/	...	...	...	...		...c/	...	...c/	...c/		...	...
355	Rubber products		131.3	181.8	219.7	273.2		37.0	...	59.5	71.5		...	...
356	Plastic products		306.4	419.0	506.8	638.1		76.3	...	127.2	166.9		...	...
361	Pottery, china and earthenware		46.3	52.2	56.1	71.5		14.9	...	19.0	24.3		...	...
362	Glass and products		82.4	123.4	150.8	190.4		24.8	...	45.3	61.0		...	...
369	Other non-metallic mineral products		436.7	570.3	712.5	910.2		135.2	...	216.4	280.3		...	...
371	Iron and steel		1000.7	1694.9	2147.1	2540.4		282.4	...	577.7	700.4		...	...
372	Non-ferrous metals		356.4	598.7	793.8	1293.6		90.2	...	193.0	319.8		...	...
381	Fabricated metal products		385.7	515.8	655.7	852.9		97.1	...	169.3	222.6		...	...
382	Non-electrical machinery		954.3	1359.0	1669.6	2168.8		259.9	...	464.9	609.6		...	...
383	Electrical machinery		2375.6	3349.4	4089.6	5124.3		550.6	...	929.6	1170.2		...	...
384	Transport equipment		1121.4	1379.6	1571.5	2038.3		289.7	...	383.1	493.3		...	...
385	Professional and scientific equipment		163.7	219.3	278.1	353.9		44.5	...	73.3	96.8		...	...
390	Other manufacturing industries		232.2	306.4	381.1	471.2		60.8	...	101.0	126.5		...	...
3	Total manufacturing		12735.2	17528.4	21783.6	27457.2		3408.9	...	5723.2	7243.7		...	...

a/ 322 includes 324.
b/ 351 includes 352.
c/ 353 includes 354.

China (Hong Kong SAR)

Supplier of information:
Census and Statistics Department, Hong Kong SAR.

Basic source of data:
Annual sample survey.

Major deviations from ISIC (Revision 2):
Data collected under the national classification system, Hong Kong Standard Industrial Classification (HSIC), have been reclassified by the national authorities to correspond with the ISIC (Revision 2). Due to the reduction of the sample size of the Annual Survey of Industrial Production (ASIP) in 2004, figures at 4-digit level are no longer available.

Reference period:
Calendar year.

Scope:
All privately owned establishments.

Method of data collection:
The inquiry is carried out through questionnaires, by telephone or follow-up site visits as required.

Type of enumeration:
Establishments with 100 or more persons engaged are fully enumerated, establishments with less than 50 persons engaged are enumerated on a sample basis.

Adjusted for non-response:
Yes.

Concepts and definitions of variables:
Output is gross output.
Value added includes net change between the beginning and the end of the year in the value of stocks of materials and supplies, rental payments and other operating expenses.

Related national publications:
Report on the Annual Survey of Industrial Production, 2006, published by the Census and Statistics Department, Hong Kong SAR.

China (Hong Kong SAR)

ISIC Revision 2		Number of establishments					Number of persons engaged					Wages and salaries paid to employees				
			(number)					(thousands)					(millions of Hong Kong Dollars)			
ISIC	Industry	Note	2003	2004	2005	2006	Note	2003	2004	2005	2006	Note	2003	2004	2005	2006
311/2	Food products		536	519	631	793		19.7	19.4	22.2	21.0		2531	2502	2450	2928
3111	Slaughtering, preparing and preserving meat		121	...	...	...		2.1	...	...	...		289	...	...	...
3112	Dairy products		13	...	...	...		1.5	...	...	...		305	...	...	...
3113	Canning, preserving of fruits and vegetables		6	...	...	...		0.3	...	...	...		49	...	...	...
3114	Canning, preserving and processing of fish		26	...	...	...		0.7	...	...	...		90	...	...	...
3115	Vegetable and animal oils and fats		1	...	...	...		-	...	...	...		...	...	...	...
3116	Grain mill products		13	...	...	...		0.4	...	...	...		70	...	...	...
3117	Bakery products		187	...	...	...		7.4	...	...	...		878	...	...	...
3118	Sugar factories and refineries		3	...	...	...		0.1	...	...	...		...	...	...	...
3119	Cocoa, chocolate and sugar confectionery		6	...	...	...		-	...	...	...		1	...	...	...
3121	Other food products		159	...	...	...		7.1	...	...	...		844	...	...	...
3122	Prepared animal feeds		1	...	...	...		-	...	...	...		...	...	...	...
313	Beverages		18	17	17	18		2.8	3.1	3.1	2.7		...	...	...	...
3131	Distilling, rectifying and blending spirits		3	...	...	...		-	...	...	...		...	...	...	...
3132	Wine industries		...	...	...	...		...	...	...	...		...	...	...	...
3133	Malt liquors and malt		3	...	...	...		0.3	...	...	...		...	...	...	...
3134	Soft drinks and carbonated waters		12	...	...	...		2.5	...	...	...		469	...	...	...
314	Tobacco		3	3	3	3		0.5	0.5	0.5	0.5		...	...	...	...
321	Textiles		1611	1580	1494	1163		23.5	22.4	22.7	17.5		3167	3243	2710	2510
3211	Spinning, weaving and finishing textiles		758	...	...	...		12.3	...	...	...		1589a/	...	...	...
3212	Made-up textile goods excl. wearing apparel		235	...	...	...		0.7	...	...	...		59	...	...	...
3213	Knitting mills		591	...	...	...		10.4	...	...	...		1475	...	...	...
3214	Carpets and rugs		-	...	...	...		-	...	...	...		-	...	...	...
3215	Cordage, rope and twine		8	...	...	...		-	...	...	...		4	...	...	...
3219	Other textiles		19	...	...	...		0.1	...	...	...		5	...	...	...
322	Wearing apparel, except footwear		1204	1330	1174	1080		23.8	24.1	19.9	16.7		2227a/	2163	2085	2102
323	Leather and fur products		28	34	30	33		0.1	0.1	0.1	0.1		10a/	16	...	...
3231	Tanneries and leather finishing		9	...	...	...		0.1	...	...	...		10	...	...	...
3232	Fur dressing and dyeing industries		...	...	...	...		...	...	...	...		...	...	...	...
3233	Leather prods. excl. footwear and wearing		19	...	...	...		-	...	...	...		...	...	...	...
324	Footwear, except rubber or plastic		20	18	16	16		0.1	0.1	0.1	0.1		10	7	7	5
331	Wood products, except furniture		143	122	116	127		0.4	0.3	0.2	0.2		25	25	...	...
3311	Sawmills, planing and other wood mills		8	...	...	...		0.1	...	...	...		6	...	...	...
3312	Wooden and cane containers		70	...	...	...		0.2	...	...	...		8	...	...	...
3319	Other wood and cork products		66	...	...	...		0.2	...	...	...		11a/	...	...	...
332	Furniture and fixtures, excl. metal		130	111	112	110		0.4	0.3	0.3	0.2		24	23	...	21
341	Paper and products		461	448	407	388		2.5	2.4	2.2	1.3		289	223	225	89
3411	Pulp, paper and paperboard articles		4	...	...	...		0.3	...	...	...		...	...	...	...
3412	Containers of paper and paperboard		313	...	...	...		1.3	...	...	...		126	...	...	...
3419	Other pulp, paper and paperboard articles		144	...	...	...		0.8	...	...	...		...	...	...	...
342	Printing and publishing		3872	3866	3814	3777		35.3	34.6	35.5	39.0		6593	6594	7026	7617
351	Industrial chemicals		108	343b/	300b/	279b/		1.3	5.6b/	5.8b/	5.4b/	b/	1086	993	851	1000
3511	Basic chemicals excl. fertilizers		41	...	...	...		0.7	...	...	...		193	...	...	...
3512	Fertilizers and pesticides		2	...	...	...		-	...	...	...		...	...	...	...
3513	Synthetic resins and plastic materials		65	...	...	...		0.6	...	...	...		156	...	...	...
352	Other chemicals		270	...b/	...b/	...b/		5.1	...b/	...b/	...b/	b/	...	...	...	...
3521	Paints, varnishes and lacquers		4	...	...	...		0.1	...	...	...		...	...	...	...
3522	Drugs and medicines		155	...	...	...		3.5	...	...	...		504	...	...	...
3523	Soap, cleaning preps., perfumes, cosmetics		48	...	...	...		0.6	...	...	...		67	...	...	...
3529	Other chemical products		64	...	...	...		1.0	...	...	...		160	...	...	...
353	Petroleum refineries	c/	3	3	3	2	c/	0.1	0.2	0.2	0.1		...	...	...	...

354	Misc. petroleum and coal products	c/	...	...	...	...	c/	...	...	...	...	...	...	...	...
355	Rubber products		61	56	58	31		0.5	0.4	0.4	0.4	...	...	...	...
3551	Tyres and tubes		7	...	...	...		0.1	...	...	...	25	...	...	...
3559	Other rubber products		54	...	...	...		0.3	...	...	...	29a/	...	...	...
356	Plastic products		612	648	600	476		3.3	3.5	4.7	2.5	393	356	581	312
361	Pottery, china and earthenware		8	191d/	190d/	86d/		0.1	2.2d/	2.7d/	1.4d/	3	421d/	338d/	294d/
362	Glass and products		27	...d/	...d/	...d/		0.2	...d/	...d/	...d/	28	...d/	...d/	...d/
369	Other non-metallic mineral products		144	...d/	...d/	...d/		2.1	...d/	...d/	...d/	370a/	...d/	...d/	...d/
3691	Structural clay products		-	...	...	...		-	...	...	...	-	...	...	...
3692	Cement, lime and plaster		17	...	...	...		1.4	...	...	...	289	...	...	...
3699	Other non-metallic mineral products		127	...	...	...		0.8	...	...	...	81	...	...	...
371	Iron and steel		18	28e/	33e/	40e/		0.4	1.2e/	1.4e/	1.5e/	...	237e/	210e/	284e/
372	Non-ferrous metals		20	...e/	...e/	...e/		0.8	...e/	...e/	...e/	100a/	...e/	...e/	...e/
381	Fabricated metal products		1454	1284	1267	1229		6.0	6.0	6.3	6.3	659	604	805	549
3811	Cutlery, hand tools and general hardware		59	...	...	...		0.2	...	...	...	15	...	...	...
3812	Furniture and fixtures primarily of metal		45	...	...	...		0.3	...	...	...	31	...	...	...
3813	Structural metal products		262	...	...	...		0.9	...	...	...	106	...	...	...
3819	Other fabricated metal products		1089	...	...	...		4.7	...	...	...	482a/	...	...	...
382	Non-electrical machinery		1815	1663	1040	1356		7.1	9.0	4.5	6.9	960a/	1164	669	1044
3821	Engines and turbines		41	...	...	...		0.2	...	...	...	23	...	...	...
3822	Agricultural machinery and equipment		4	...	...	...		0.1	...	...	...	...	...	...	...
3823	Metal and wood working machinery		52	...	...	...		0.1	...	...	...	16	...	...	...
3824	Other special industrial machinery		668	...	...	...		3.0	...	...	...	493	...	...	...
3825	Office, computing and accounting machinery		338	...	...	...		1.9	...	...	...	232	...	...	...
3829	Other non-electrical machinery and equipment		713	...	...	...		1.8	...	...	...	195	...	...	...
383	Electrical machinery		409	340	841	242		15.4	12.2	17.6	11.5	2292a/	1940	2677	1642
3831	Electrical industrial machinery		103	...	...	...		2.0	...	...	...	258	...	...	...
3832	Radio, television and communication equipment		202	...	...	...		9.9	...	...	...	1604a/	...	...	...
3833	Electrical appliances and housewares		21	...	...	...		0.4	...	...	...	29	...	...	...
3839	Other electrical apparatus and supplies		84	...	...	...		3.1	...	...	...	392a/	...	...	...
384	Transport equipment		515	412	425	411		9.5	9.0	7.5	8.7	1918	1900	1856	2070
3841	Shipbuilding and repairing		279	...	...	...		2.6	...	...	...	437	...	...	...
3842	Railroad equipment		4	...	...	...		0.1	...	...	...	...	...	...	...
3843	Motor vehicles		216	...	...	...		1.8	...	...	...	245	...	...	...
3844	Motorcycles and bicycles		1	...	...	...		-	...	...	...	...	...	...	...
3845	Aircraft		5	...	...	...		4.9	...	...	...	1211	...	...	...
3849	Other transport equipment		10	...	...	...		0.1	...	...	...	6	...	...	...
385	Professional and scientific equipment		185	177	171	137		2.5	2.2	1.2	0.9	327	294	218	129
3851	Prof. and scientific equipment n.e.c.		35	...	...	...		0.3	...	...	...	...	...	...	...
3852	Photographic and optical goods		22	...	...	...		0.5	...	...	...	63	...	...	...
3853	Watches and clocks		128	...	...	...		1.6	...	...	...	209a/	...	...	...
390	Other manufacturing industries		1482	1489	1307	1367		8.9	8.6	5.0	5.5	1060	915	650	737
3901	Jewellery and related articles		446	...	...	...		3.5	...	...	...	520	...	...	...
3902	Musical instruments		2	...	...	...		-	...	...	...	...	...	...	...
3903	Sporting and athletic goods		11	...	...	...		0.1	...	...	...	10	...	...	...
3909	Manufacturing industries, n.e.c.		1024	...	...	...		5.3	...	...	...	527a/	...	...	...
3	Total manufacturing		15156	14681	14050	13165		172.4	167.4	164.2	150.4	25093	24464	24209	24149

a/ Data are incomplete due to confidentiality rules.
b/ 351 includes 352.
c/ 353 includes 354.
d/ 361 includes 362 and 369.
e/ 371 includes 372.

China (Hong Kong SAR)

ISIC Revision 2		Output in producers' prices					Value added in producers' prices					Gross fixed capital formation		
			(millions of Hong Kong Dollars)					(millions of Hong Kong Dollars)					(millions of Hong Kong Dollars)	
ISIC	Industry	Note	2003	2004	2005	2006	Note	2003	2004	2005	2006	Note	2005	2006
311/2	Food products		13552	13602	13465	15692		5136	5031	4859	5548		137	395
3111	Slaughtering, preparing and preserving meat		2049	...	...	...		389	...	...	...		...	...
3112	Dairy products		1321	...	...	...		772	...	...	...		...	...
3113	Canning, preserving of fruits and vegetables		250	...	...	...		62	...	...	...		...	...
3114	Canning, preserving and processing of fish		579	...	...	...		274	...	...	...		...	...
3115	Vegetable and animal oils and fats		...	...	...	...		...	...	...	...		...	...
3116	Grain mill products		648	...	...	...		179	...	...	...		...	...
3117	Bakery products		3564	...	...	...		1375	...	...	...		...	...
3118	Sugar factories and refineries		...	...	...	...		...	...	...	...		...	...
3119	Cocoa, chocolate and sugar confectionery		3	...	...	...		-	...	...	...		...	...
3121	Other food products		5109	...	...	...		2077	...	...	...		...	...
3122	Prepared animal feeds		...	...	...	...		...	...	...	...		...	...
313	Beverages		...	...	...	...		...	...	...	...		...	...
3131	Distilling, rectifying and blending spirits		...	...	...	...		...	...	...	...		...	...
3132	Wine industries		...	...	...	...		...	...	...	...		...	...
3133	Malt liquors and malt		...	...	...	...		...	...	...	...		...	...
3134	Soft drinks and carbonated waters		2121	...	...	...		865	...	...	...		...	...
314	Tobacco		...	...	...	...		...	...	...	...		...	...
321	Textiles		21754	20429	21331	18884		6038	6067	4991	5580		1393	1038
3211	Spinning, weaving and finishing textiles		8100a/	...	...	...		2429a/	...	...	...		...	...
3212	Made-up textile goods excl. wearing apparel		306	...	...	...		121	...	...	...		...	...
3213	Knitting mills		13115	...	...	...		3373	...	...	...		...	...
3214	Carpets and rugs		-	...	...	...		-	...	...	...		...	...
3215	Cordage, rope and twine		18	...	...	...		9	...	...	...		...	...
3219	Other textiles		16	...	...	...		6	...	...	...		...	...
322	Wearing apparel, except footwear		23395a/	23091	17394	13800		4625a/	4454	4676	3324		131	115
323	Leather and fur products		175a/	156	...	...		19a/	29	...	...		...	...
3231	Tanneries and leather finishing		175	...	...	...		19	...	...	...		...	...
3232	Fur dressing and dyeing industries		...	...	...	...		...	...	...	...		...	...
3233	Leather prods. excl. footwear and wearing		...	...	...	...		...	...	...	...		...	...
324	Footwear, except rubber or plastic		74	64	49	35		17	13	11	8		10	7
331	Wood products, except furniture		139	153	...	...		43	47	...	...		...	...
3311	Sawmills, planing and other wood mills		32	...	...	...		8	...	...	...		...	...
3312	Wooden and cane containers		40	...	...	...		16	...	...	...		...	...
3319	Other wood and cork products		65a/	...	...	...		17a/	...	...	...		...	...
332	Furniture and fixtures, excl. metal		92	89	...	66		42	39	...	37		...	...
341	Paper and products		1546	1578	1528	498		456	348	288	124		14	17
3411	Pulp, paper and paperboard articles		...	...	...	...		...	...	...	...		...	...
3412	Containers of paper and paperboard		537	...	...	...		198	...	...	...		...	...
3419	Other pulp, paper and paperboard articles		...	...	...	...		...	...	...	...		...	...
342	Printing and publishing		28842	28773	29307	30106		11384	11270	12063	11954		-1164	343
351	Industrial chemicals	b/	7184	6530	7370	8276	b/	1955	1679	2069	2016	b/	72	197
3511	Basic chemicals excl. fertilizers		1096	...	...	...		598	...	...	...		...	...
3512	Fertilizers and pesticides		...	...	...	...		...	...	...	...		...	...
3513	Synthetic resins and plastic materials		2986	...	...	...		172	...	...	...		...	...
352	Other chemicals	b/	...	...	...	...	b/	...	...	...	...	b/	...	...
3521	Paints, varnishes and lacquers		...	...	...	...		...	...	...	...		...	...
3522	Drugs and medicines		2000	...	...	...		835	...	...	...		...	...
3523	Soap, cleaning preps., perfumes, cosmetics		250	...	...	...		91	...	...	...		...	...
3529	Other chemical products		819	...	...	...		248	...	...	...		...	...
353	Petroleum refineries		...	...	...	...		...	...	...	...		...	...

354	Misc. petroleum and coal products	...	...	...	...	...	...	...	...	...	...
355	Rubber products	...	...	...	...	...	...	...	...	...	...
3551	Tyres and tubes	111	...	...	...	55	...	...	...	...	...
3559	Other rubber products	132a/	...	...	...	58a/	...	...	...	...	...
356	Plastic products	2054	2093	1931	2132	645	633	878	503	52	49
361	Pottery, china and earthenware	12	4130c/	5065c/	3259c/	5	623c/	594c/	1015c/	227c/	18c/
362	Glass and products	159	...c/	...c/	...c/	54	...c/	...c/	...c/	...c/	...c/
369	Other non-metallic mineral products	3996a/	...c/	...c/	...c/	680a/	...c/	...c/	...c/	...c/	...c/
3691	Structural clay products	-	...	...	...	-	...	...	...	...	...
3692	Cement, lime and plaster	3538	...	...	...	563	...	...	...	...	...
3699	Other non-metallic mineral products	458	...	...	...	117	...	...	...	...	...
371	Iron and steel	...	12517d/	18039d/	28956d/	...	464d/	521d/	773d/	33d/	25d/
372	Non-ferrous metals	9529a/	...d/	...d/	...d/	438a/	...d/	...d/	...d/	...d/	...d/
381	Fabricated metal products	2444	2511	2864	2722	920	971	1345	899	6	4
3811	Cutlery, hand tools and general hardware	54	...	...	...	20	...	...	...	...	...
3812	Furniture and fixtures primarily of metal	96	...	...	...	22	...	...	...	...	...
3813	Structural metal products	360	...	...	...	143	...	...	...	...	...
3819	Other fabricated metal products	1850a/	...	...	...	707a/	...	...	...	...	...
382	Non-electrical machinery	4355a/	6154	3573	5407	2028a/	3014	1941	2712	61	211
3821	Engines and turbines	79	...	...	...	36	...	...	...	...	...
3822	Agricultural machinery and equipment	...	...	...	...	...	...	...	...	...	...
3823	Metal and wood working machinery	54	...	...	...	20	...	...	...	...	...
3824	Other special industrial machinery	2540	...	...	...	1238	...	...	...	...	...
3825	Office, computing and accounting machinery	963	...	...	...	406	...	...	...	...	...
3829	Other non-electrical machinery and equipment	719	...	...	...	328	...	...	...	...	...
383	Electrical machinery	13447a/	12605	16789	14070	4741a/	4190	5697	4803	1277	685
3831	Electrical industrial machinery	996	...	...	...	382	...	...	...	...	...
3832	Radio, television and communication equipment	10105a/	...	...	...	3583a/	...	...	...	...	...
3833	Electrical appliances and housewares	125	...	...	...	20	...	...	...	...	...
3839	Other electrical apparatus and supplies	2132a/	...	...	...	704a/	...	...	...	...	...
384	Transport equipment	8168	7930	7957	11056	2918	3001	2836	4459	310	592
3841	Shipbuilding and repairing	1221	...	...	...	560	...	...	...	...	...
3842	Railroad equipment	...	...	...	...	...	...	...	...	...	...
3843	Motor vehicles	961	...	...	...	373	...	...	...	...	...
3844	Motorcycles and bicycles	...	...	...	...	...	...	...	...	...	...
3845	Aircraft	5907	...	...	...	1955	...	...	...	...	...
3849	Other transport equipment	24	...	...	...	8	...	...	...	...	...
385	Professional and scientific equipment	2055	2239	2283	2111	658	787	553	446	15	29
3851	Prof. and scientific equipment n.e.c.	...	...	...	...	...	...	...	...	...	...
3852	Photographic and optical goods	256	...	...	...	89	...	...	...	...	...
3853	Watches and clocks	1439a/	...	...	...	492a/	...	...	...	...	...
390	Other manufacturing industries	7397	7776	9138	8789	2000	2073	2037	1746	379	207
3901	Jewellery and related articles	4760	...	...	...	887	...	...	...	...	...
3902	Musical instruments	...	...	...	...	...	...	...	...	...	...
3903	Sporting and athletic goods	129	...	...	...	22	...	...	...	...	...
3909	Manufacturing industries, n.e.c.	2489a/	...	...	...	1085a/	...	...	...	...	...
3	Total manufacturing	156434	157627	163213	171305	46745	46705	47322	47961	3049	4091

a/ Data are incomplete due to confidentiality rules.
b/ 351 includes 352.
c/ 361 includes 362 and 369.
d/ 371 includes 372.

China (Hong Kong SAR)

ISIC Revision 3			Index numbers of industrial production											
			(2000=100)											
ISIC	Industry	Note	1995	1996	1997	1998	1999	2000	2001	2002	2003	2004	2005	2006
15	Food and beverages	a/	117	116	115	105	103	100	98	106	94	99	101	110
16	Tobacco products	a/	...	...	...	...	...	...	...	...	...	...	...	...
17	Textiles		119	111	114	102	96	100	100	93	83	79	83	81
18	Wearing apparel, fur		112	107	103	97	97	100	100	93	95	95	84	84
19	Leather, leather products and footwear		...	...	...	...	...	...	...	...	...	...	...	...
20	Wood products (excl. furniture)		...	...	...	...	...	...	...	...	...	...	...	...
21	Paper and paper products	b/	119	115	118	109	98	100	99	99	98	96	96	99
22	Printing and publishing	b/	...	...	...	...	...	...	...	...	...	...	...	...
23	Coke,refined petroleum products,nuclear fuel	c/	156	156	158	137	117	100	92	76	77	76	77	83
24	Chemicals and chemical products	c/	...	...	...	...	...	...	...	...	...	...	...	...
25	Rubber and plastics products	c/	...	...	...	...	...	...	...	...	...	...	...	...
26	Non-metallic mineral products	c/	...	...	...	...	...	...	...	...	...	...	...	...
27	Basic metals	d/	181	165	156	140	113	100	85	65	60	65	71	72
28	Fabricated metal products	d/	...	...	...	...	...	...	...	...	...	...	...	...
29	Machinery and equipment n.e.c.	e/	117	111	109	101	99	100	92	72	56	63	70	67
30	Office, accounting and computing machinery	e/	...	...	...	...	...	...	...	...	...	...	...	...
31	Electrical machinery and apparatus	e/	...	...	...	...	...	...	...	...	...	...	...	...
32	Radio,television and communication equipment	e/	...	...	...	...	...	...	...	...	...	...	...	...
33	Medical, precision and optical instruments	e/	...	...	...	...	...	...	...	...	...	...	...	...
34	Motor vehicles, trailers, semi-trailers		...	...	...	...	...	...	...	...	...	...	...	...
35	Other transport equipment		...	...	...	...	...	...	...	...	...	...	...	...
36	Furniture; manufacturing n.e.c.		118	121	123	109	96	100	95	99	92	96	103	107
37	Recycling		...	...	...	...	...	...	...	...	...	...	...	...
D	Total manufacturing		123	119	118	107	101	100	96	86	78	81	83	84

a/ 15 includes 16.
b/ 21 includes 22.
c/ 23 includes 24, 25 and 26.
d/ 27 includes 28.
e/ 29 includes 30, 31, 32 and 33.

China (Macao SAR)

Supplier of information:
Statistics and Census Service, Macao SAR.

Basic source of data:
Annual sample survey.

Major deviations from ISIC (Revision 3):
None reported.

Reference period:
Calendar year.

Scope:
All establishments.

Method of data collection:
The inquiry is carried out through field interviews by enumerators, mail returns and through respondents' personal delivery of questionnaires.

Type of enumeration:
Method of systematic stratified sampling.

Adjusted for non-response:
Yes.

Concepts and definitions of variables:
No deviations from the standard UN concepts and definitions are reported.

Related national publications:
Brief report on Industrial Survey, published by the Statistics and Census Service, Macao SAR.

China (Macao SAR)

ISIC Revision 3		Number of establishments					Number of persons engaged					Wages and salaries paid to employees				
			(number)					(number)					(thousands of Macao Patacas)			
ISIC	Industry	Note	2003	2004	2005	2006	Note	2003	2004	2005	2006	Note	2003	2004	2005	2006
15	Food and beverages		138	171	179	179		1227	1283	1341	1869		60466	64574	75771	115812
16	Tobacco products		3	...b/	...b/	...b/		...a/	...b/	...b/	...b/		...a/	...b/	...b/	...b/
17	Textiles		81	85	71	69		4678	4474	4085	3263		257922	241568	221022	211295
18	Wearing apparel, fur		394	469	454	434		27316	25774	23993	23007		1245529	1269886	1125725	1169559
19	Leather, leather products and footwear		16	13	9	13		1087	724	238	639		46372	33171	10545	20639
20	Wood products (excl. furniture)		10	...b/	...b/	...b/		...	...b/	...b/	...b/		...	...b/	...b/	...b/
21	Paper and paper products		19	...b/	...b/	...b/		116	...b/	...b/	...b/		4916	...b/	...b/	...b/
22	Printing and publishing		123	133	139	131		1168	1179	1180	1030		84823	99270	97376	95722
23	Coke,refined petroleum products,nuclear fuel		-	-	-	-		-	-	-	-		-	-	-	-
24	Chemicals and chemical products		16	...b/	...b/	...b/		304	...b/	...b/	...b/		37608	...b/	...b/	...b/
25	Rubber and plastics products		15	...b/	...b/	...b/		113	...b/	...b/	...b/		4636	...b/	...b/	...b/
26	Non-metallic mineral products		20	19	21	18		288	248	324	507		28345	24882	44144	84592
27	Basic metals		-	-	-	-		-	-	-	-		-	-	-	-
28	Fabricated metal products		140	...b/	...b/	...b/		344	...b/	...b/	...b/		8757	...b/	...b/	...b/
29	Machinery and equipment n.e.c.		53	...b/	...b/	...b/		124	...b/	...b/	...b/		3960	...b/	...b/	...b/
30	Office, accounting and computing machinery		3	3	2	2		268	306	304	...a/		29622	35449	34863	...a/
31	Electrical machinery and apparatus		9	8	8	8		377	229	199	...a/		22544	19051	16956	...a/
32	Radio,television and communication equipment		...	...	...	...		...	...	...	...		...	...	...	...
33	Medical, precision and optical instruments		15c/	...b/	...b/	...b/		441c/	...b/	...b/	...b/		33823c/	...b/	...b/	...b/
34	Motor vehicles, trailers, semi-trailers		-	-	-	-		-	-	-	-		-	-	-	-
35	Other transport equipment		...c/	...b/	...b/	...b/		...c/	...b/	...b/	...b/		...c/	...b/	...b/	...b/
36	Furniture; manufacturing n.e.c.		92	369b/	355b/	334b/		446	2359b/	3024b/	2680b/		21327	162374b/	228039b/	265566b/
37	Recycling		...	...	...	...		...	...	...	...		...	...	...	...
D	Total manufacturing		1148	1270	1238	1188		38395	36576	34688	33430		1896162	1950224	1854441	1963185

a/ Data suppressed due to confidentiality rules.
b/ 36 includes 16, 20, 21, 24, 25, 28, 29, 33 and 35.
c/ 33 includes 35.

China (Macao SAR)

ISIC Revision 3		Output in producers' prices					Value added in producers' prices					Gross fixed capital formation	
			(thousands of Macao Patacas)					(thousands of Macao Patacas)				(thousands of Macao Patacas)	
ISIC	Industry	Note	2003	2004	2005	2006	Note	2003	2004	2005	2006	Note	2005	2006
15	Food and beverages		214919	246819	237095	348845		100034	112978	124439	151489		33171	20507
16	Tobacco products		...a/	...b/	...b/	...b/		...a/	...b/	...b/	...b/		...b/	...b/
17	Textiles		2613902	2760363	1967031	2010695		447686	447900	399393	506481		110391	54614
18	Wearing apparel, fur		8586425	8756970	7683613	7843966		1941682	1927777	1746630	1687005		25879	43808
19	Leather, leather products and footwear		486591	417407	53965	86614		66992	61546	10041	25460		-18	4830
20	Wood products (excl. furniture)		...	...b/	...b/	...b/		...	...b/	...b/	...b/		...b/	...b/
21	Paper and paper products		22356	...b/	...b/	...b/		6231	...b/	...b/	...b/		...b/	...b/
22	Printing and publishing		278475	304072	210689	330523		110582	125826	77131	150006		15617	10816
23	Coke,refined petroleum products,nuclear fuel		-	-	-	-		-	-	-	-		-	-
24	Chemicals and chemical products		172180	...b/	...b/	...b/		73387	...b/	...b/	...b/		...b/	...b/
25	Rubber and plastics products		25306	...b/	...b/	...b/		6917	...b/	...b/	...b/		...b/	...b/
26	Non-metallic mineral products		281328	258110	680769	1260439		61677	59135	171799	404701		59576	73889
27	Basic metals		-	-	-	-		-	-	-	-		-	-
28	Fabricated metal products		45979	...b/	...b/	...b/		19488	...b/	...b/	...b/		...b/	...b/
29	Machinery and equipment n.e.c.		14512	...b/	...b/	...b/		8511	...b/	...b/	...b/		...b/	...b/
30	Office, accounting and computing machinery		232966	418595	546901	...a/		56111	90861	78354	...a/		-1508	...a/
31	Electrical machinery and apparatus		129770	79994	83414	...a/		39921	37134	30422	...a/		636	...a/
32	Radio,television and communication equipment		...	...	...	...		...	...	...	...		...	...
33	Medical, precision and optical instruments		39649c/	...b/	...b/	...b/		18994c/	...b/	...b/	...b/		...b/	...b/
34	Motor vehicles, trailers, semi-trailers		-	-	-	-		-	-	-	-		-	-
35	Other transport equipment		...c/	...b/	...b/	...b/		...c/	...b/	...b/	...b/		...b/	...b/
36	Furniture; manufacturing n.e.c.		100053	755465b/	1043288b/	1175451b/		36440	281546b/	425239b/	430262b/		51485b/	44347b/
37	Recycling		...	...	...	...		...	...	...	...		...	...
D	Total manufacturing		13392951	13997794	12506765	13645673		3034849	3144702	3063448	3474508		295409	209696

a/ Data suppressed due to confidentiality rules.
b/ 36 includes 16, 20, 21, 24, 25, 28, 29, 33 and 35.
c/ 33 includes 35.

China (Macao SAR)

ISIC Revision 3			Index numbers of industrial production (2000=100)											
ISIC	Industry	Note	1995	1996	1997	1998	1999	2000	2001	2002	2003	2004	2005	2006
15	Food and beverages		...	...	...	...	...	...	...	...	...	...	...	...
16	Tobacco products		...	87	113	100	63	100	105	107	135	166	179	178
17	Textiles		...	84	91	92	90	100	111	137	156	144	128	142
18	Wearing apparel, fur		...	88	88	89	92	100	104	121	142	137	99	91
19	Leather, leather products and footwear		...	...	...	...	...	...	...	...	...	...	...	...
20	Wood products (excl. furniture)		...	...	...	...	...	...	...	...	...	...	...	...
21	Paper and paper products		...	...	...	...	...	...	...	...	...	...	...	...
22	Printing and publishing		...	...	...	...	...	...	...	...	...	...	...	...
23	Coke,refined petroleum products,nuclear fuel		...	...	...	...	...	...	...	...	...	...	...	...
24	Chemicals and chemical products		...	...	...	...	...	...	...	...	...	...	...	...
25	Rubber and plastics products		...	...	...	...	...	...	...	...	...	...	...	...
26	Non-metallic mineral products		...	238	249	164	167	100	100	70	153	163	381	532
27	Basic metals		...	...	...	...	...	...	...	...	...	...	...	...
28	Fabricated metal products		...	...	...	...	...	...	...	...	...	...	...	...
29	Machinery and equipment n.e.c.		...	...	...	...	...	...	...	...	...	...	...	...
30	Office, accounting and computing machinery		...	...	...	...	...	...	...	...	...	...	...	...
31	Electrical machinery and apparatus		...	...	...	...	...	...	...	...	...	...	...	...
32	Radio,television and communication equipment		...	...	...	...	...	...	...	...	...	...	...	...
33	Medical, precision and optical instruments		...	...	...	...	...	...	...	...	...	...	...	...
34	Motor vehicles, trailers, semi-trailers		...	...	...	...	...	...	...	...	...	...	...	...
35	Other transport equipment		...	...	...	...	...	...	...	...	...	...	...	...
36	Furniture; manufacturing n.e.c.		...	...	...	...	...	...	...	...	...	...	...	...
37	Recycling		...	...	...	...	...	...	...	...	...	...	...	...
D	Total manufacturing		...	89	88	86	87	100	106	123	144	135	106	105

Cook Islands

Supplier of information:
Statistics Office, Ministry of Finance and Economic Management, Rarotonga.

Basic source of data:
National accounts; census of population and dwellings.

Major deviations from ISIC (Revision 3):
None reported.

Reference period:
Calendar year.

Scope:
All establishments.

Method of data collection:
The inquiry is conducted by mail and personal visits.

Type of enumeration:
Not reported.

Adjusted for non-response:
No.

Concepts and definitions of variables:
No deviations from the standard UN concepts and definitions are reported.

Related national publications:
None reported.

Cook Islands

ISIC Revision 3	Number of establishments					Number of employees					Wages and salaries paid to employees				
		(number)					(number)					(thousands of New Zealand Dollars)			
ISIC Industry	Note	2003	2004	2005	2006	Note	2003	2004	2005	2006	Note	2003	2004	2005	2006
D Total manufacturing		...	...	...	...		...	...	...	...		4013	4501	4585	4268

ISIC Revision 3	Output					Value added					Gross fixed capital formation		
		(thousands of New Zealand Dollars)					(thousands of New Zealand Dollars)					(thousands of New Zealand Dollars)	
ISIC Industry	Note	2003	2004	2005	2006	Note	2003	2004	2005	2006	Note	2005	2006
D Total manufacturing		18169	20380	20762	19324		8446	9360	9588	9131		...	...

ISIC Revision 3	Index numbers of industrial production												
		(2000 = 100)											
ISIC Industry	Note	1995	1996	1997	1998	1999	2000	2001	2002	2003	2004	2005	2006
D Total manufacturing		...	...	...	...	...	...	...	...	...	...	...	...

Croatia

Supplier of information:
Central Bureau of Statistics of the Republic of Croatia, Zagreb.

Basic source of data:
Survey; administrative source.

Major deviations from ISIC (Revision 3):
None reported.

Reference period:
Calendar year.

Scope:
All establishments.

Method of data collection:
Mail questionnaires.

Type of enumeration:
Complete enumeration.

Adjusted for non-response:
No.

Concepts and definitions of variables:
Number of employees is as of 31 March of the reference year.
Wages and salaries was computed by UNIDO from the reported monthly wages and salaries per employee.

Related national publications:
Persons in Paid Employment by Sex and Activities; Average Monthly Gross Earnings of Persons in Paid Employment; Statistical Report; Gross Fixed Capital Formation, all published by the Central Bureau of Statistics of the Republic of Croatia, Zagreb.

Croatia

ISIC	Industry	Note	Number of establishments (number) 2003	2004	2005	2006	Note	Number of employees (number) 2003	2004	2005	2006	Note	Wages and salaries paid to employees (millions of Croatian Kunas) 2003	2004	2005	2006
151	Processed meat,fish,fruit,vegetables,fats		712	701	696	813		14393	14145	13302	13634	a/	3025.3	3129.3	3169.3	3372.0
1511	Processing/preserving of meat		443	436	431	491		7092	7017	6343	6635		...	...	...	...
1512	Processing/preserving of fish		55	55	55	68		1399	1627	1457	1533		...	...	...	...
1513	Processing/preserving of fruit & vegetables		157	155	155	182		4764	4382	4372	4409		...	...	...	...
1514	Vegetable and animal oils and fats		57	55	55	72		1138	1119	1130	1057		...	...	...	...
1520	Dairy products		137	137	137	189		4623	4577	4375	4287	a/	...	...	...	...
153	Grain mill products; starches; animal feeds		276	270	261	284		4290	3821	4091	3967	a/	...	...	...	...
1531	Grain mill products		162	160	153	167		2915	2325	2451	2350		...	...	...	...
1532	Starches and starch products		2	2	2	5		2	3	2	66		...	...	...	...
1533	Prepared animal feeds		112	108	106	112		1373	1493	1638	1551		...	...	...	...
154	Other food products		1032	1020	1014	1266		14478	14409	14059	14872	a/	...	...	...	...
1541	Bakery products		689	679	675	892		7919	8071	7943	8419		...	...	...	...
1542	Sugar		15	15	15	18		1160	1129	1090	1254		...	...	...	...
1543	Cocoa, chocolate and sugar confectionery		23	23	23	31		3072	2857	2887	2950		...	...	...	...
1544	Macaroni, noodles & similar products		89	88	87	85		232	237	205	200		...	...	...	...
1549	Other food products n.e.c.		216	215	214	240		2095	2115	1934	2049		...	...	...	...
155	Beverages		406	402	401	488		6758	6765	6464	6644	a/	...	...	...	...
1551	Distilling, rectifying & blending of spirits		61	61	61	72		946	900	834	863		...	...	...	...
1552	Wines		154	151	150	180		1777	1695	1775	1827		...	...	...	...
1553	Malt liquors and malt		50	50	50	53		2045	1934	1815	1693		...	...	...	...
1554	Soft drinks; mineral waters		141	140	140	183		1990	2236	2040	2261		...	...	...	...
1600	Tobacco products		15	14	14	15		1126	1332	1265	1079		108.2	124.7	137.3	125.4
171	Spinning, weaving and finishing of textiles		148	146	145	152		4210	3501	3235	2814	b/	364.1	353.3	345.5	368.0
1711	Textile fibre preparation; textile weaving		116	115	114	114		4138	3198	2859	2440		...	...	...	...
1712	Finishing of textiles		32	31	31	38		72	303	376	374		...	...	...	...
172	Other textiles		311	310	309	345		2471	2521	2393	2587	b/	...	...	...	...
1721	Made-up textile articles, except apparel		195	194	193	224		1412	1547	1451	1676		...	...	...	...
1722	Carpets and rugs		12	12	12	12		137	25	20	20		...	...	...	...
1723	Cordage, rope, twine and netting		14	14	14	16		182	153	146	88		...	...	...	...
1729	Other textiles n.e.c.		90	90	90	93		740	796	776	803		...	...	...	...
1730	Knitted and crocheted fabrics and articles		203	201	201	210		2425	2351	2304	2584	b/	...	...	...	...
1810	Wearing apparel, except fur apparel		1303	1293	1287	1390		26373	25538	24101	22379	c/	921.3	920.1	905.7	872.1
1820	Dressing & dyeing of fur; processing of fur		8	8	8	9		102	81	81	87	c/	...	...	...	...
191	Tanning, dressing and processing of leather		193	190	188	193		1778	1420	1524	1945	d/	277.7	264.1	266.0	293.2
1911	Tanning and dressing of leather		41	40	39	40		1310	862	1052	1403		...	...	...	...
1912	Luggage, handbags, etc.; saddlery & harness		152	150	149	153		468	558	472	542		...	...	...	...
1920	Footwear		263	255	254	265		6766	6122	5820	5587	d/	...	...	...	...
2010	Sawmilling and planing of wood		744	738	737	794		5459	5547	4986	4776	e/	459.7	489.5	497.8	544.2
202	Products of wood, cork, straw, etc.		962	951	949	1076		6413	6539	6712	7171	e/	...	...	...	...
2021	Veneer sheets, plywood, particle board, etc.		35	33	33	42		1710	1800	1481	1324		...	...	...	...
2022	Builders' carpentry and joinery		540	535	533	610		2983	3126	3763	4239		...	...	...	...
2023	Wooden containers		99	97	97	108		274	321	319	394		...	...	...	...
2029	Other wood products; articles of cork/straw		288	286	286	316		1446	1292	1149	1214		...	...	...	...
210	Paper and paper products		313	313	311	337		5555	4942	4699	4681		299.8	275.9	277.1	295.2
2101	Pulp, paper and paperboard		33	33	33	34		1713	1474	1434	1448		...	...	...	...
2102	Corrugated paper and paperboard		160	160	159	164		3054	2725	2585	2441		...	...	...	...
2109	Other articles of paper and paperboard		120	120	119	137		788	743	680	792		...	...	...	...
221	Publishing		1441	1436	1434	1694		6269	6729	7114	7310	f/	994.8	1087.1	1156.8	1254.0
2211	Publishing of books and other publications		691	689	689	778		2007	2101	2236	2307		...	...	...	...
2212	Publishing of newspapers, journals, etc.		542	540	538	657		3695	3987	4201	4290		...	...	...	...
2213	Publishing of recorded media		118	117	117	139		181	216	220	234		...	...	...	...
2219	Other publishing		90	90	90	120		386	425	457	479		...	...	...	...

222	Printing and related service activities	1676	1671	1669	1800	5690	5770	5602	5841	f/	...	...	...	...
2221	Printing	1087	1083	1081	1182	5353	5405	5261	5467		...	...	...	...
2222	Service activities related to printing	589	588	588	618	337	365	341	374		...	...	...	...
2230	Reproduction of recorded media	51	50	50	64	57	60	71	70	f/	...	...	...	...
2310	Coke oven products	...	...	...	...	...	...	...	...	g/	364.9	371.5	425.7	443.3
2320	Refined petroleum products	24	24	24	30	4265	3961	4039	3821	g/	...	...	...	...
2330	Processing of nuclear fuel	...	...	...	...	...	...	...	...	g/	...	...	...	...
241	Basic chemicals	84	84	83	103	4354	4138	4165	4256	h/	1195.6	1096.8	1078.9	1213.3
2411	Basic chemicals, except fertilizers	55	55	55	61	466	492	518	533		...	...	...	...
2412	Fertilizers and nitrogen compounds	5	5	5	12	2771	2683	2646	2652		...	...	...	...
2413	Plastics in primary forms; synthetic rubber	24	24	23	30	1117	963	1001	1071		...	...	...	...
242	Other chemicals	441	439	438	478	9123	7950	7486	7635	h/	...	...	...	...
2421	Pesticides and other agro-chemical products	8	8	8	7	564	504	379	358		...	...	...	...
2422	Paints, varnishes, printing ink and mastics	91	91	91	105	802	811	829	842		...	...	...	...
2423	Pharmaceuticals, medicinal chemicals, etc.	37	37	37	40	4856	4023	3730	3882		...	...	...	...
2424	Soap, cleaning & cosmetic preparations	188	187	187	201	1490	1371	1378	1457		...	...	...	...
2429	Other chemical products n.e.c.	117	116	115	125	1411	1241	1170	1096		...	...	...	...
2430	Man-made fibres	1	...	1	1	...	...	...	...	h/	...	...	...	...
251	Rubber products	154	153	153	169	607	616	658	730	i/	344.8	366.1	391.7	433.4
2511	Rubber tyres and tubes	33	33	33	36	129	120	124	194		...	...	...	...
2519	Other rubber products	121	120	120	133	478	496	534	536		...	...	...	...
2520	Plastic products	957	953	951	1096	6390	6296	6313	6457	i/	...	...	...	...
2610	Glass and glass products	95	95	94	115	1837	1979	1892	1950	j/	939.3	1023.6	1050.7	1130.7
269	Non-metallic mineral products n.e.c.	814	811	809	964	12618	12759	12544	12659	j/	...	...	...	...
2691	Pottery, china and earthenware	103	103	103	112	952	940	907	852		...	...	...	...
2692	Refractory ceramic products	10	9	9	9	28	27	32	33		...	...	...	...
2693	Struct.non-refractory clay; ceramic products	112	112	112	117	4149	3770	3818	3824		...	...	...	...
2694	Cement, lime and plaster	25	25	25	30	2333	2320	2254	2031		...	...	...	...
2695	Articles of concrete, cement and plaster	316	315	314	361	3564	3892	3610	3931		...	...	...	...
2696	Cutting, shaping & finishing of stone	214	214	214	288	1176	1351	1483	1584		...	...	...	...
2699	Other non-metallic mineral products n.e.c.	34	33	32	47	416	459	440	404		...	...	...	...
2710	Basic iron and steel	40	40	40	50	2315	2289	2251	2034	k/	358.2	356.3	375.2	422.1
2720	Basic precious and non-ferrous metals	61	61	61	74	2092	2032	1926	1859	k/	...	...	...	...
273	Casting of metals	95	92	92	102	3173	2860	3001	3221	k/	...	...	...	...
2731	Casting of iron and steel	47	45	45	50	2297	2211	2180	2302		...	...	...	...
2732	Casting of non-ferrous metals	48	47	47	52	876	649	821	919		...	...	...	...
281	Struct.metal products;tanks;steam generators	983	977	976	1218	9444	9859	10106	11468	m/	1024.3	1104.4	1156.5	1375.0
2811	Structural metal products	873	867	866	1095	8007	8336	8516	9837		...	...	...	...
2812	Tanks, reservoirs and containers of metal	57	57	57	68	658	659	656	712		...	...	...	...
2813	Steam generators	53	53	53	55	779	864	934	919		...	...	...	...
289	Other metal products; metal working services	1976	1965	1962	2108	10071	10293	10204	11021	m/	...	...	...	...
2891	Metal forging/pressing/stamping/roll-forming	165	164	164	170	584	726	697	797		...	...	...	...
2892	Treatment & coating of metals	516	514	513	602	3723	3506	3598	3962		...	...	...	...
2893	Cutlery, hand tools and general hardware	303	300	300	320	1858	1901	1712	1788		...	...	...	...
2899	Other fabricated metal products n.e.c.	992	987	985	1016	3906	4160	4197	4474		...	...	...	...
291	General purpose machinery	473	469	467	569	5740	6176	6426	6879	n/	660.6	731.6	811.1	946.3
2911	Engines & turbines (not for transport equipment)	47	47	47	53	1991	2257	2257	2363		...	...	...	...
2912	Pumps, compressors, taps and valves	92	90	90	98	876	875	841	798		...	...	...	...
2913	Bearings, gears, gearing & driving elements	27	27	27	37	289	385	597	679		...	...	...	...
2914	Ovens, furnaces and furnace burners	17	17	17	18	33	36	44	50		...	...	...	...
2915	Lifting and handling equipment	70	69	69	94	832	853	784	805		...	...	...	...
2919	Other general purpose machinery	220	219	217	269	1719	1770	1903	2184		...	...	...	...
292	Special purpose machinery	382	381	380	294	4952	4800	4848	4949	n/	...	...	...	...
2921	Agricultural and forestry machinery	76	76	75	80	1106	1206	1246	1242		...	...	...	...
2922	Machine tools	118	117	117	142	1504	1392	1341	1293		...	...	...	...
2923	Machinery for metallurgy	2	2	2	1	...	...	1	1		...	...	...	...
2924	Machinery for mining & construction	26	26	26	30	147	147	97	94		...	...	...	...
2925	Food/beverage/tobacco processing machinery	46	46	46	53	673	489	567	691		...	...	...	...
2926	Machinery for textile, apparel and leather	23	23	23	27	219	204	174	162		...	...	...	...
2927	Weapons and ammunition	16	16	16	16	163	158	123	91		...	...	...	...
2929	Other special purpose machinery	75	75	75	87	1139	1204	1299	1375		...	...	...	...

continued

Croatia

ISIC Revision 3		Number of establishments					Number of employees					Wages and salaries paid to employees				
			(number)					(number)					(millions of Croatian Kunas)			
ISIC	Industry	Note	2003	2004	2005	2006	Note	2003	2004	2005	2006	Note	2003	2004	2005	2006
2930	Domestic appliances n.e.c.		79	78	78	82		1019	1068	1332	1428	n/	...	...	...	...
3000	Office, accounting and computing machinery		622	620	620	649		1780	1951	1945	2045		167.8	192.3	199.5	244.5
3110	Electric motors, generators and transformers		233	232	228	234		2839	2668	2658	2724	p/	871.4	980.7	1028.9	1182.9
3120	Electricity distribution & control apparatus		213	211	210	214		3163	3666	3507	3489	p/	...	...	...	...
3130	Insulated wire and cable		19	19	18	21		819	1277	1070	1027	p/	...	...	...	...
3140	Accumulators, primary cells and batteries		28	27	27	27		288	315	247	186	p/	...	...	...	...
3150	Lighting equipment and electric lamps		75	75	75	81		919	933	860	713	p/	...	...	...	...
3190	Other electrical equipment n.e.c.		241	241	240	253		2553	2681	2934	3262	p/	...	...	...	...
3210	Electronic valves, tubes, etc.		161	161	161	163		953	1544	1703	2048	q/	320.2	374.7	396.4	463.9
3220	TV/radio transmitters; line comm. apparatus		130	130	129	135		1851	1807	1824	1951	q/	...	...	...	...
3230	TV and radio receivers and associated goods		80	79	79	91		195	135	223	178	q/	...	...	...	...
331	Medical, measuring, testing appliances, etc.		365	363	362	399		1074	1154	1240	1246	r/	102.2	116.6	127.0	141.4
3311	Medical, surgical and orthopaedic equipment		148	148	148	171		512	531	595	631		...	...	...	...
3312	Measuring/testing/navigating appliances,etc.		148	146	145	149		329	356	369	335		...	...	...	...
3313	Industrial process control equipment		69	69	69	79		233	267	276	280		...	...	...	...
3320	Optical instruments & photographic equipment		161	158	157	177		487	507	522	550	r/	...	...	...	...
3330	Watches and clocks		16	16	14	14		26	27	24	24	r/	...	...	...	...
3410	Motor vehicles		21	21	21	27		603	613	539	550	s/	183.4	192.4	206.5	238.0
3420	Automobile bodies, trailers & semi-trailers		19	19	19	29		94	216	204	271	s/	...	...	...	...
3430	Parts/accessories for automobiles		105	103	103	105		2375	2146	2257	2359	s/	...	...	...	...
351	Building and repairing of ships and boats		447	446	446	622		15440	14840	15464	15391	t/	1358.0	1433.1	1538.3	1624.3
3511	Building and repairing of ships		333	332	332	453		15182	14415	15030	14869		...	...	...	...
3512	Building/repairing of pleasure/sport. boats		114	114	114	169		258	425	434	522		...	...	...	...
3520	Railway/tramway locomotives & rolling stock		21	21	21	20		3293	3984	3890	3663	t/	...	...	...	...
3530	Aircraft and spacecraft		4	4	4	10		30	41	53	68	t/	...	...	...	...
359	Transport equipment n.e.c.		25	25	25	29		89	94	93	105	t/	...	...	...	...
3591	Motorcycles		2	2	2	4		5	4	4	3		...	...	...	...
3592	Bicycles and invalid carriages		22	22	22	23		78	85	85	98		...	...	...	...
3599	Other transport equipment n.e.c.		1	1	1	2		6	5	4	4		...	...	...	...
3610	Furniture		708	705	702	895		10486	10304	10277	10655	u/	494.3	507.1	501.4	547.7
369	Manufacturing n.e.c.		464	459	458	504		1296	1229	1006	973	u/	...	...	...	...
3691	Jewellery and related articles		84	84	84	97		203	164	185	203		...	...	...	...
3692	Musical instruments		17	17	17	17		9	14	30	22		...	...	...	...
3693	Sports goods		31	31	31	33		67	82	44	81		...	...	...	...
3694	Games and toys		55	54	54	62		159	178	114	110		...	...	...	...
3699	Other manufacturing n.e.c.		277	273	272	295		858	791	633	557		...	...	...	...
3710	Recycling of metal waste and scrap		201	201	200	253		839	915	903	904	v/	83.0	91.6	96.7	123.6
3720	Recycling of non-metal waste and scrap		83	80	79	113		416	459	493	741	v/	...	...	...	...
D	Total manufacturing		21295	21144	21072	24044		249144	246752	243325	247805		15077.2	15657.9	16278.4	17850.9

a/ 151 includes 1520, 153, 154 and 155.
b/ 171 includes 172 and 1730.
c/ 1810 includes 1820.
d/ 191 includes 1920.
e/ 2010 includes 202.
f/ 221 includes 222 and 2230.
g/ 2310 includes 2320 and 2330.
h/ 241 includes 242 and 2430.
i/ 251 includes 2520.
j/ 2610 includes 269.
k/ 2710 includes 2720 and 273.
m/ 281 includes 289.
n/ 291 includes 292 and 2930.
p/ 3110 includes 3120, 3130, 3140, 3150 and 3190.
q/ 3210 includes 3220 and 3230.
r/ 331 includes 3320 and 3330.
s/ 3410 includes 3420 and 3430.
t/ 351 includes 3520, 3530 and 359.
u/ 3610 includes 369.
v/ 3710 includes 3720.

Croatia

ISIC Revision 3		Output					Value added					Gross fixed capital formation		
			(millions of Croatian Kunas)					(millions of Croatian Kunas)					(millions of Croatian Kunas)	
ISIC	Industry	Note	2003	2004	2005	2006	Note	2003	2004	2005	2006	Note	2005	2006
151	Processed meat,fish,fruit,vegetables,fats		...	...	...	...		...	...	...	...		294.7	278.8
1511	Processing/preserving of meat		...	...	...	...		...	...	...	...		...	...
1512	Processing/preserving of fish		...	...	...	...		...	...	...	...		...	...
1513	Processing/preserving of fruit & vegetables		...	...	...	...		...	...	...	...		...	...
1514	Vegetable and animal oils and fats		...	...	...	...		...	...	...	...		...	...
1520	Dairy products		...	...	...	...		...	...	...	...		179.4	235.2
153	Grain mill products; starches; animal feeds		...	...	...	...		...	...	...	...		173.4	167.1
1531	Grain mill products		...	...	...	...		...	...	...	...		...	...
1532	Starches and starch products		...	...	...	...		...	...	...	...		...	...
1533	Prepared animal feeds		...	...	...	...		...	...	...	...		...	...
154	Other food products		...	...	...	...		...	...	...	...		378.3	662.0
1541	Bakery products		...	...	...	...		...	...	...	...		...	...
1542	Sugar		...	...	...	...		...	...	...	...		...	...
1543	Cocoa, chocolate and sugar confectionery		...	...	...	...		...	...	...	...		...	...
1544	Macaroni, noodles & similar products		...	...	...	...		...	...	...	...		...	...
1549	Other food products n.e.c.		...	...	...	...		...	...	...	...		...	...
155	Beverages		...	...	...	...		...	...	...	...		477.8	595.8
1551	Distilling, rectifying & blending of spirits		...	...	...	...		...	...	...	...		...	...
1552	Wines		...	...	...	...		...	...	...	...		...	...
1553	Malt liquors and malt		...	...	...	...		...	...	...	...		...	...
1554	Soft drinks; mineral waters		...	...	...	...		...	...	...	...		...	...
1600	Tobacco products		...	...	...	...		...	...	...	...		559.1	3.9
171	Spinning, weaving and finishing of textiles		...	...	...	...		...	...	...	...		22.4	43.7
1711	Textile fibre preparation; textile weaving		...	...	...	...		...	...	...	...		...	...
1712	Finishing of textiles		...	...	...	...		...	...	...	...		...	...
172	Other textiles		...	...	...	...		...	...	...	...		43.3	40.6
1721	Made-up textile articles, except apparel		...	...	...	...		...	...	...	...		...	...
1722	Carpets and rugs		...	...	...	...		...	...	...	...		...	...
1723	Cordage, rope, twine and netting		...	...	...	...		...	...	...	...		...	...
1729	Other textiles n.e.c.		...	...	...	...		...	...	...	...		...	...
1730	Knitted and crocheted fabrics and articles		...	...	...	...		...	...	...	...		76.7	75.8
1810	Wearing apparel, except fur apparel		...	...	...	...		...	...	...	...		107.8	260.9
1820	Dressing & dyeing of fur; processing of fur		...	...	...	...		...	...	...	...		0.1	-
191	Tanning, dressing and processing of leather		...	...	...	...		...	...	...	...		102.1	70.6
1911	Tanning and dressing of leather		...	...	...	...		...	...	...	...		...	...
1912	Luggage, handbags, etc.; saddlery & harness		...	...	...	...		...	...	...	...		...	...
1920	Footwear		...	...	...	...		...	...	...	...		14.2	23.4
2010	Sawmilling and planing of wood		...	...	...	...		...	...	...	...		71.8	83.0
202	Products of wood, cork, straw, etc.		...	...	...	...		...	...	...	...		56.0	103.8
2021	Veneer sheets, plywood, particle board, etc.		...	...	...	...		...	...	...	...		...	...
2022	Builders' carpentry and joinery		...	...	...	...		...	...	...	...		...	...
2023	Wooden containers		...	...	...	...		...	...	...	...		...	...
2029	Other wood products; articles of cork/straw		...	...	...	...		...	...	...	...		...	...
210	Paper and paper products		...	...	...	...		...	...	...	...		139.0	165.4
2101	Pulp, paper and paperboard		...	...	...	...		...	...	...	...		...	...
2102	Corrugated paper and paperboard		...	...	...	...		...	...	...	...		...	...
2109	Other articles of paper and paperboard		...	...	...	...		...	...	...	...		...	...
221	Publishing		...	...	...	...		...	...	...	...		139.8	57.8
2211	Publishing of books and other publications		...	...	...	...		...	...	...	...		31.3	18.1
2212	Publishing of newspapers, journals, etc.		...	...	...	...		...	...	...	...		...	...
2213	Publishing of recorded media		...	...	...	...		...	...	...	...		3.0	1.3
2219	Other publishing		...	...	...	...		...	...	...	...		14.4	0.4

continued

Croatia

ISIC Revision 3		Output					Value added					Gross fixed capital formation		
			(millions of Croatian Kunas)					(millions of Croatian Kunas)					(millions of Croatian Kunas)	
ISIC	Industry	Note	2003	2004	2005	2006	Note	2003	2004	2005	2006	Note	2005	2006
222	Printing and related service activities		...	...	...	...		...	...	...	...		230.2	245.5
2221	Printing		...	...	...	...		...	...	...	...		...	...
2222	Service activities related to printing		...	...	...	...		...	...	...	...		...	...
2230	Reproduction of recorded media		...	...	...	...		...	...	...	...		2.0	3.3
2310	Coke oven products		...	...	...	...		...	...	...	...		...	...
2320	Refined petroleum products		...	...	...	...		...	...	...	...		1681.3	1936.5
2330	Processing of nuclear fuel		...	...	...	...		...	...	...	...		...	...
241	Basic chemicals		...	...	...	...		...	...	...	...		173.0	124.6
2411	Basic chemicals, except fertilizers		...	...	...	...		...	...	...	...		...	...
2412	Fertilizers and nitrogen compounds		...	...	...	...		...	...	...	...		...	...
2413	Plastics in primary forms; synthetic rubber		...	...	...	...		...	...	...	...		...	...
242	Other chemicals		...	...	...	...		...	...	...	...		353.8	335.1
2421	Pesticides and other agro-chemical products		...	...	...	...		...	...	...	...		...	...
2422	Paints, varnishes, printing ink and mastics		...	...	...	...		...	...	...	...		...	...
2423	Pharmaceuticals, medicinal chemicals, etc.		...	...	...	...		...	...	...	...		...	...
2424	Soap, cleaning & cosmetic preparations		...	...	...	...		...	...	...	...		...	...
2429	Other chemical products n.e.c.		...	...	...	...		...	...	...	...		...	...
2430	Man-made fibres		...	...	...	...		...	...	...	...		...	...
251	Rubber products		...	...	...	...		...	...	...	...		39.8	22.7
2511	Rubber tyres and tubes		...	...	...	...		...	...	...	...		4.8	1.5
2519	Other rubber products		...	...	...	...		...	...	...	...		35.1	21.2
2520	Plastic products		...	...	...	...		...	...	...	...		191.6	166.7
2610	Glass and glass products		...	...	...	...		...	...	...	...		74.0	82.8
269	Non-metallic mineral products n.e.c.		...	...	...	...		...	...	...	...		647.2	624.9
2691	Pottery, china and earthenware		...	...	...	...		...	...	...	...		...	...
2692	Refractory ceramic products		...	...	...	...		...	...	...	...		...	...
2693	Struct.non-refractory clay; ceramic products		...	...	...	...		...	...	...	...		...	...
2694	Cement, lime and plaster		...	...	...	...		...	...	...	...		...	...
2695	Articles of concrete, cement and plaster		...	...	...	...		...	...	...	...		...	...
2696	Cutting, shaping & finishing of stone		...	...	...	...		...	...	...	...		...	...
2699	Other non-metallic mineral products n.e.c.		...	...	...	...		...	...	...	...		...	...
2710	Basic iron and steel		...	...	...	...		...	...	...	...		11.2	42.0
2720	Basic precious and non-ferrous metals		...	...	...	...		...	...	...	...		35.7	4.8
273	Casting of metals		...	...	...	...		...	...	...	...		54.6	42.6
2731	Casting of iron and steel		...	...	...	...		...	...	...	...		...	...
2732	Casting of non-ferrous metals		...	...	...	...		...	...	...	...		...	...
281	Struct.metal products;tanks;steam generators		...	...	...	...		...	...	...	...		167.5	281.3
2811	Structural metal products		...	...	...	...		...	...	...	...		...	...
2812	Tanks, reservoirs and containers of metal		...	...	...	...		...	...	...	...		...	...
2813	Steam generators		...	...	...	...		...	...	...	...		...	...
289	Other metal products; metal working services		...	...	...	...		...	...	...	...		271.8	327.9
2891	Metal forging/pressing/stamping/roll-forming		...	...	...	...		...	...	...	...		46.9	18.7
2892	Treatment & coating of metals		...	...	...	...		...	...	...	...		...	...
2893	Cutlery, hand tools and general hardware		...	...	...	...		...	...	...	...		...	...
2899	Other fabricated metal products n.e.c.		...	...	...	...		...	...	...	...		...	...
291	General purpose machinery		...	...	...	...		...	...	...	...		89.2	149.6
2911	Engines & turbines (not for transport equipment)		...	...	...	...		...	...	...	...		34.9	46.3
2912	Pumps, compressors, taps and valves		...	...	...	...		...	...	...	...		...	...
2913	Bearings, gears, gearing & driving elements		...	...	...	...		...	...	...	...		21.8	17.7
2914	Ovens, furnaces and furnace burners		...	...	...	...		...	...	...	...		...	...
2915	Lifting and handling equipment		...	...	...	...		...	...	...	...		13.6	26.3
2919	Other general purpose machinery		...	...	...	...		...	...	...	...		...	...

292	Special purpose machinery	...	...	...	...	...	...	...	...	104.0	94.0
2921	Agricultural and forestry machinery	...	...	...	...	...	...	...	...	...	...
2922	Machine tools	...	...	...	...	...	...	...	...	...	...
2923	Machinery for metallurgy	...	...	...	...	...	...	...	...	...	...
2924	Machinery for mining & construction	...	...	...	...	...	...	...	...	...	...
2925	Food/beverage/tobacco processing machinery	...	...	...	...	...	...	...	...	...	...
2926	Machinery for textile, apparel and leather	...	...	...	...	...	...	...	...	...	...
2927	Weapons and ammunition	...	...	...	...	...	...	...	...	...	...
2929	Other special purpose machinery	...	...	...	...	...	...	...	...	...	...
2930	Domestic appliances n.e.c.	...	...	...	...	...	...	...	...	35.3	13.1
3000	Office, accounting and computing machinery	...	...	...	...	...	...	...	...	59.1	54.6
3110	Electric motors, generators and transformers	...	...	...	...	...	...	...	...	71.4	84.5
3120	Electricity distribution & control apparatus	...	...	...	...	...	...	...	...	80.7	67.4
3130	Insulated wire and cable	...	...	...	...	...	...	...	...	9.9	93.6
3140	Accumulators, primary cells and batteries	...	...	...	...	...	...	...	...	14.3	2.6
3150	Lighting equipment and electric lamps	...	...	...	...	...	...	...	...	7.4	14.5
3190	Other electrical equipment n.e.c.	...	...	...	...	...	...	...	...	91.3	84.8
3210	Electronic valves, tubes, etc.	...	...	...	...	...	...	...	...	8.2	4.4
3220	TV/radio transmitters; line comm. apparatus	...	...	...	...	...	...	...	...	123.0	71.4
3230	TV and radio receivers and associated goods	...	...	...	...	...	...	...	...	7.9	7.9
331	Medical, measuring, testing appliances, etc.	...	...	...	...	...	...	...	...	25.3	20.0
3311	Medical, surgical and orthopaedic equipment	...	...	...	...	...	...	...	...	...	...
3312	Measuring/testing/navigating appliances,etc.	...	...	...	...	...	...	...	...	...	...
3313	Industrial process control equipment	...	...	...	...	...	...	...	...	...	...
3320	Optical instruments & photographic equipment	...	...	...	...	...	...	...	...	4.1	19.7
3330	Watches and clocks	...	...	...	...	...	...	...	...	-	...
3410	Motor vehicles	...	...	...	...	...	...	...	...	5.2	0.3
3420	Automobile bodies, trailers & semi-trailers	...	...	...	...	...	...	...	...	3.3	8.1
3430	Parts/accessories for automobiles	...	...	...	...	...	...	...	...	80.4	91.5
351	Building and repairing of ships and boats	...	...	...	...	...	...	...	...	163.3	216.1
3511	Building and repairing of ships	...	...	...	...	...	...	...	...	157.1	194.7
3512	Building/repairing of pleasure/sport. boats	...	...	...	...	...	...	...	...	6.2	21.4
3520	Railway/tramway locomotives & rolling stock	...	...	...	...	...	...	...	...	33.2	23.7
3530	Aircraft and spacecraft	...	...	...	...	...	...	...	...	0.8	...
359	Transport equipment n.e.c.	...	...	...	...	...	...	...	...	-	...
3591	Motorcycles	...	...	...	...	...	...	...	...	...	...
3592	Bicycles and invalid carriages	...	...	...	...	...	...	...	...	...	...
3599	Other transport equipment n.e.c.	...	...	...	...	...	...	...	...	...	...
3610	Furniture	...	...	...	...	...	...	...	...	175.4	416.2
369	Manufacturing n.e.c.	...	...	...	...	...	...	...	...	13.1	39.3
3691	Jewellery and related articles	...	...	...	...	...	...	...	...	...	...
3692	Musical instruments	...	...	...	...	...	...	...	...	...	...
3693	Sports goods	...	...	...	...	...	...	...	...	...	...
3694	Games and toys	...	...	...	...	...	...	...	...	...	...
3699	Other manufacturing n.e.c.	...	...	...	...	...	...	...	...	...	...
3710	Recycling of metal waste and scrap	...	...	...	...	...	...	...	...	36.3	73.6
3720	Recycling of non-metal waste and scrap	...	...	...	...	...	...	...	...	44.9	111.3
D	Total manufacturing	...	...	...	...	...	...	...	...	8056.3	8870.3

Croatia

ISIC Revision 3			Index numbers of industrial production (2000=100)											
ISIC	Industry	Note	1995	1996	1997	1998	1999	2000	2001	2002	2003	2004	2005	2006
15	Food and beverages		109	110	103	107	100	100	106	113	119	122	130	137
16	Tobacco products		90	101	92	91	100	100	112	109	114	119	114	105
17	Textiles		116	95	108	111	98	100	109	111	107	101	97	94
18	Wearing apparel, fur		126	114	113	113	102	100	101	87	83	62	58	50
19	Leather, leather products and footwear		152	133	124	114	104	100	109	92	85	83	76	98
20	Wood products (excl. furniture)		85	91	104	104	89	100	96	97	95	105	110	118
21	Paper and paper products		81	73	79	81	98	100	123	129	126	128	135	154
22	Printing and publishing		58	58	89	101	96	100	113	136	165	179	207	222
23	Coke,refined petroleum products,nuclear fuel		110	106	89	88	95	100	95	96	101	100	94	82
24	Chemicals and chemical products		99	97	97	90	91	100	93	100	90	99	97	91
25	Rubber and plastics products		98	92	105	113	110	100	110	119	126	128	146	143
26	Non-metallic mineral products		81	97	86	98	96	100	107	122	132	134	142	156
27	Basic metals		83	75	95	111	96	100	104	94	99	124	130	134
28	Fabricated metal products		76	75	89	99	99	100	107	114	137	147	161	172
29	Machinery and equipment n.e.c.		91	86	89	99	95	100	118	139	133	151	178	226
30	Office, accounting and computing machinery		200	182	176	116	84	100	106	103	71	56	73	53
31	Electrical machinery and apparatus		91	92	93	108	112	100	119	122	146	143	165	153
32	Radio,television and communication equipment		86	98	104	75	76	100	63	64	69	60	72	101
33	Medical, precision and optical instruments		138	97	100	116	108	100	118	100	105	112	135	128
34	Motor vehicles, trailers, semi-trailers		70	54	102	85	80	100	135	137	151	184	199	239
35	Other transport equipment		62	75	81	98	110	100	136	136	124	145	150	146
36	Furniture; manufacturing n.e.c.		78	77	103	98	100	100	109	111	120	126	121	128
37	Recycling		85	91	104	88	95	100	94	103	122	178	204	244
D	Total manufacturing		92	93	97	100	97	100	106	111	117	122	130	139

Cyprus

Supplier of information:
Statistical Service, Ministry of Finance, Nicosia.

Basic source of data:
Annual sample survey.

Major deviations from ISIC (Revision 3):
None reported.

Reference period:
Calendar year.

Scope:
All privately owned establishments.

Method of data collection:
Data are collected through personal interviews.

Type of enumeration:
Sample survey.

Adjusted for non-response:
Yes.

Concepts and definitions of variables:
Output is gross output, i.e.,including revenue from non-industrial activities.

Related national publications:
Industrial Statistics (annual), published by the Statistical Service, Ministry of Finance, Nicosia.

Cyprus

ISIC Revision 3		Number of establishments					Number of employees					Wages and salaries paid to employees				
			(number)					(number)					(thousands of Euros)			
ISIC	Industry	Note	2003	2004	2005	2006	Note	2003	2004	2005	2006	Note	2003	2004	2005	2006
151	Processed meat,fish,fruit,vegetables,fats		183	182	146	147		2091	2023	2062	1972		28588	30444	31683	31201
1511	Processing/preserving of meat	a/	85	85	74	74	a/	1276	1216	1249	1235	a/	16662	17706	18509	18456
1512	Processing/preserving of fish	a/	...	...	...	...	a/	...	...	...	...	a/	...	...	...	...
1513	Processing/preserving of fruit & vegetables		60	59	41	41		646	613	609	552		8984	9481	9835	9500
1514	Vegetable and animal oils and fats		38	38	31	32		169	194	204	185		2942	3257	3339	3245
1520	Dairy products		118	118	144	146		1421	1383	1404	1527		23584	25067	27797	29844
153	Grain mill products; starches; animal feeds		72	70	50	49		573	557	497	515		9100	8868	8777	8845
1531	Grain mill products		16	15	13	13		190	189	173	192		3455	3632	3496	3767
1532	Starches and starch products		1	1	-	-		...	...	-	-		...	...	-	-
1533	Prepared animal feeds		55	54	37	36		383	368	324	323		5645	5235	5281	5078
154	Other food products		695	693	547	551b/		5542	5904	6029	6117b/		62714	68060	75857	79628b/
1541	Bakery products		548	548	425	432		4212	4573	4697	4908		44015	48791	54330	58412
1542	Sugar		-	-	-	-		-	-	-	-		-	-	-	-
1543	Cocoa, chocolate and sugar confectionery		44	44	52	51		167	140	206	195		1821	1621	3843	3882
1544	Macaroni, noodles & similar products		53	53	30	29		339	353	321	326		4497	4726	4553	4846
1549	Other food products n.e.c.		50	48	40	39		824	838	805	688		12381	12922	13131	12488
155	Beverages		63	63	73	73		2250	2259	2250	2047		43996	45097	46985	48049
1551	Distilling, rectifying & blending of spirits	c/	47	47	57	57	c/	1301	1287	1279	1150	c/	25620	25843	26502	25938
1552	Wines	c/	...	...	...	...	c/	...	...	...	...	c/	...	...	...	...
1553	Malt liquors and malt	c/	...	...	...	...	c/	...	...	...	...	c/	...	...	...	...
1554	Soft drinks; mineral waters		16	16	16	16		949	972	971	897		18376	19254	20483	22111
1600	Tobacco products		3	3	3	...b/		297	318	276	...b/		6670	6975	8071	...b/
171	Spinning, weaving and finishing of textiles		20	20	27	26		86	102	44	46		1047	1152	583	647
1711	Textile fibre preparation; textile weaving		2	2	27d/	26d/		3	3	44d/	46d/		26	26	583d/	647d/
1712	Finishing of textiles		18	18	...d/	...d/		83	99	...d/	...d/		1022	1126	...d/	...d/
172	Other textiles		101	100	86	85		379	387	435	402		3656	4055	5037	5227
1721	Made-up textile articles, except apparel		79	78	70	69		311	339	383	365		3064	3595	4569	4812
1722	Carpets and rugs		-	-	-	-		-	-	-	-		-	-	-	-
1723	Cordage, rope, twine and netting		-	-	-	-		-	-	-	-		-	-	-	-
1729	Other textiles n.e.c.		22	22	16	16		68	48	52	37		593	460	468	415
1730	Knitted and crocheted fabrics and articles		25	24	17	16		239	178	92	62		2464	1931	1039	641
1810	Wearing apparel, except fur apparel		630	630	426	418		1787	1469	1170	1100		15883	13334	14041	13312
1820	Dressing & dyeing of fur; processing of fur		-	-	-	-		-	-	-	-		-	-	-	-
191	Tanning, dressing and processing of leather		27	27	20	20		57	48	37	36		578	448	419	448
1911	Tanning and dressing of leather		2	2	20e/	20e/		3	2	37e/	36e/		31	24	419e/	448e/
1912	Luggage, handbags, etc.; saddlery & harness		25	25	...e/	...e/		54	46	...e/	...e/		547	424	...e/	...e/
1920	Footwear		80	80	46	44		345	279	236	204		4178	3159	2978	2556
2010	Sawmilling and planing of wood		10	10	5	3		60	61	23	18		571	564	227	171
202	Products of wood, cork, straw, etc.		1027	1030	943	946		2586	2554	2454	2611		32481	35520	43351	45010
2021	Veneer sheets, plywood, particle board, etc.		3	3	2	2		122	120	112	114		3146	3540	3144	3250
2022	Builders' carpentry and joinery		976	983	903	909		2399	2374	2298	2449		28612	31302	39136	40819
2023	Wooden containers		44	40	3	35f/		17	13	12	48f/		173	114	150	941f/
2029	Other wood products; articles of cork/straw		4	4	35	...f/		48	47	32	...f/		550	564	921	...f/
210	Paper and paper products		46	46	37	38		801	802	797	779		12140	12635	12242	12340
2101	Pulp, paper and paperboard		-	-	-	-		-	-	-	-		-	-	-	-
2102	Corrugated paper and paperboard		17	17	10	10		214	228	223	218		3969	4143	4265	4149
2109	Other articles of paper and paperboard		29	29	27	28		587	574	574	561		8171	8492	7977	8191
221	Publishing		92	90	60	62		676	739	814	843		14694	15541	17359	17990
2211	Publishing of books and other publications		35	35	10	9		...	...	18	23		...	...	444	511
2212	Publishing of newspapers, journals, etc.		52	50	42	45		...	...	777	799		...	...	16599	17154
2213	Publishing of recorded media		-	-	-	-		-	-	-	-		-	-	-	-
2219	Other publishing		5	5	8	8		...	...	19	21		...	...	316	325

222	Printing and related service activities		310	311	286	287		1525	1459	1453	1447		22273	22384	22882	24206
2221	Printing		290	291	283	284		1525	1459	1450	1441		22273	22384	22853	24139
2222	Service activities related to printing		20	20	3	3		...	...	3	6		...	...	29	67
2230	Reproduction of recorded media		-	-	-	-		-	-	-	-		-	-	-	-
2310	Coke oven products		-	-	-	-		-	-	-	-		-	-	-	-
2320	Refined petroleum products		4	4	4g/	4g/		140	74	59g/	59g/		6301	3084	1225g/	1179g/
2330	Processing of nuclear fuel		-	-	-	-		-	-	-	-		-	-	-	-
241	Basic chemicals		1	1	...g/	...g/		38	43	...g/	...g/		834	849	...g/	...g/
2411	Basic chemicals, except fertilizers		1	1	...	...		38	43	...	...		834	849	...	...
2412	Fertilizers and nitrogen compounds		-	-	-	-		-	-	-	-		-	-	-	-
2413	Plastics in primary forms; synthetic rubber		-	-	-	-		-	-	-	-		-	-	-	-
242	Other chemicals		70	70	61	62		1680	1715	1705	1816		27232	30201	29919	31727
2421	Pesticides and other agro-chemical products		6	6	3	3		49	78	118	103		994	1657	2272	2219
2422	Paints, varnishes, printing ink and mastics		16	16	17	17		301	313	300	305		4548	4818	5068	5191
2423	Pharmaceuticals, medicinal chemicals, etc.		14	14	10	11		875	901	984	1110		14398	16724	18005	20008
2424	Soap, cleaning & cosmetic preparations		28	28	26	25		427	395	268	262		6935	6628	4029	3699
2429	Other chemical products n.e.c.		6	6	5	6		28	28	35	36		355	374	545	610
2430	Man-made fibres		-	-	-	-		-	-	-	-		-	-	-	-
251	Rubber products		9	9	9	9		23	23	23	21		267	280	325	280
2511	Rubber tyres and tubes		5	5	3	3		15	15	14	14		159	169	181	184
2519	Other rubber products		4	4	6	6		8	8	9	7		108	111	144	96
2520	Plastic products		61	61	61	62		1174	1193	1212	1165		18024	18824	20847	20331
2610	Glass and glass products		67	67	65	65		211	209	204	226		2616	2599	2882	3335
269	Non-metallic mineral products n.e.c.		306	306	264	265		2660	2677	2937	3061		51420	55890	63569	67821
2691	Pottery, china and earthenware		53	53	36	37		30	26	31	32		244	196	701	695
2692	Refractory ceramic products		74	74	34h/	34h/		323	306	198h/	194h/		4895	4852	3873h/	3979h/
2693	Struct.non-refractory clay; ceramic products		2	2	...h/	...h/		...	...	...h/	...h/		...	...	...h/	...h/
2694	Cement, lime and plaster		4	4	3	3		371	363	359	367		13691	14060	14538	15219
2695	Articles of concrete, cement and plaster		126	126	112	112		1300	1375	1625	1719		22431	26384	31616	34256
2696	Cutting, shaping & finishing of stone		40	40	76	76		554	542	669	690		8487	8974	11495	12228
2699	Other non-metallic mineral products n.e.c.		7	7	3	3		82	65	55	59		1673	1423	1345	1444
2710	Basic iron and steel	i/	3	3	3	4	i/	332	419	367	364	i/	6752	8112	6419	7109
2720	Basic precious and non-ferrous metals	i/	...	...	...	...	i/	...	...	...	...	i/	...	...	...	...
273	Casting of metals		2	2	-	-		...	...	-	-		...	...	-	-
2731	Casting of iron and steel		1	1	-	-		...	...	-	-		...	...	-	-
2732	Casting of non-ferrous metals		1	1	-	-		...	...	-	-		...	...	-	-
281	Struct.metal products;tanks;steam generators		810	812	722	745		1669	1783	2394	2452		23191	25122	39677	42348
2811	Structural metal products		778	780	706	729		1501	1658	2266	2321		20214	22825	37333	39698
2812	Tanks, reservoirs and containers of metal	j/	32	32	16	16	j/	168	125	128	131	j/	2976	2296	2344	2650
2813	Steam generators	j/	...	...	...	...	j/	...	...	...	...	j/	...	...	...	...
289	Other metal products; metal working services		340	340	319	320		859	956	869	869		11800	13701	15405	15743
2891	Metal forging/pressing/stamping/roll-forming		3	3	-	-		...	...	-	-		...	...	-	-
2892	Treatment & coating of metals		146	146	138	136		187	168	212	208		2108	2016	4037	4174
2893	Cutlery, hand tools and general hardware		32	32	37	37		98	104	108	101		1199	1415	1845	1897
2899	Other fabricated metal products n.e.c.		159	159	144	147		574	684	549	560		8492	10270	9522	9672
291	General purpose machinery		99	98	73	74		647	647	511	506		9794	10098	8193	8543
2911	Engines & turbines (not for transport equipment)		1	1	-	-		...	...	-	-		...	...	-	-
2912	Pumps, compressors, taps and valves		40	40	23k/	23k/		121	104	69k/	77k/		1895	1688	1464k/	1468k/
2913	Bearings, gears, gearing & driving elements		-	-	...k/	...k/		-	-	...k/	...k/		-	-	...k/	...k/
2914	Ovens, furnaces and furnace burners		-	-	-	-		-	-	-	-		-	-	-	-
2915	Lifting and handling equipment		8	8	12	11		56	79	78	69		957	1235	1135	1107
2919	Other general purpose machinery		50	49	38	40		470	464	364	360		6942	7174	5594	5968
292	Special purpose machinery		124	124	101	101		241	239	170	165		3120	3393	3149	3255
2921	Agricultural and forestry machinery		58	58	61	60		137	129	74	62		1789	1907	1423	1560
2922	Machine tools		46m/	46m/	5	5		73m/	78m/	-	-		960m/	1076m/	60	65
2923	Machinery for metallurgy		...m/	...m/	13n/	14n/		...m/	...m/	55n/	59n/		...m/	...m/	936n/	904n/
2924	Machinery for mining & construction		...m/	...m/	...n/	...n/		...m/	...m/	...n/	...n/		...m/	...m/	...n/	...n/
2925	Food/beverage/tobacco processing machinery		...m/	...m/	...n/	...n/		...m/	...m/	...n/	...n/		...m/	...m/	...n/	...n/
2926	Machinery for textile, apparel and leather		...m/	...m/	...n/	...n/		...m/	...m/	...n/	...n/		...m/	...m/	...n/	...n/
2927	Weapons and ammunition		20	20	17	17		31	32	30	34		371	410	540	540
2929	Other special purpose machinery		...m/	...m/	5	5		...m/	...m/	11	10		...m/	...m/	190	186

continued

Cyprus

ISIC Revision 3		Number of establishments					Number of employees					Wages and salaries paid to employees				
			(number)					(number)					(thousands of Euros)			
ISIC	Industry	Note	2003	2004	2005	2006	Note	2003	2004	2005	2006	Note	2003	2004	2005	2006
2930	Domestic appliances n.e.c.		51	52	48p/	46		235	273	253p/	236		3041	3583	3930p/	3732
3000	Office, accounting and computing machinery		2	1	...p/	-		...	...	...p/	-		...	...	...p/	-
3110	Electric motors, generators and transformers		22	22	25	25		49	51	38	34		593	651	607	588
3120	Electricity distribution & control apparatus		19	19	18	19		170	175	159	162		2454	2527	2720	2917
3130	Insulated wire and cable		1	1	35q/	37q/	q/	240	233	188	180	q/	3147	2852	2867	2779
3140	Accumulators, primary cells and batteries		1	1	...q/	...q/	q/	...	...	...	...	q/	...	...	...	...
3150	Lighting equipment and electric lamps		58r/	58r/	...q/	...q/	q/	...	...	...	...	q/	...	...	...	...
3190	Other electrical equipment n.e.c.		...r/	...r/	...q/	...q/	q/	...	...	...	...	q/	...	...	...	...
3210	Electronic valves, tubes, etc.		-	1	5t/	4t/		-	24s/	32t/	46t/		-	287s/	391t/	642t/
3220	TV/radio transmitters; line comm. apparatus		5	5	-	-		4	...s/	-	-		32	...s/	-	-
3230	TV and radio receivers and associated goods		-	-	...t/	...t/		-	-	...t/	...t/		-	-	...t/	...t/
331	Medical, measuring, testing appliances, etc.		65	66	65	68		150	161	99	109		1770	1924	1856	2081
3311	Medical, surgical and orthopaedic equipment		63	64	62	65		150u/	161u/	95	104		1770u/	1924u/	1779	1992
3312	Measuring/testing/navigating appliances,etc.		1	1	3v/	3v/		...u/	...u/	4v/	5v/		...u/	...u/	77v/	89v/
3313	Industrial process control equipment		1	1	...v/	...v/		...u/	...u/	...v/	...v/		...u/	...u/	...v/	...v/
3320	Optical instruments & photographic equipment		7	7	5	5		73	75	63	68		851	945	771	883
3330	Watches and clocks		-	-	-	-		-	-	-	-		-	-	-	-
3410	Motor vehicles		-	-	-	-		-	-	-	-		-	-	-	-
3420	Automobile bodies, trailers & semi-trailers		28	27	32	32		155	136	108	104		1914	1948	2028	2066
3430	Parts/accessories for automobiles		16	16	8	8		182	143	128	128		2303	1915	1782	1750
351	Building and repairing of ships and boats		33	32	40	39		141	141	125	129		1999	2132	2083	2073
3511	Building and repairing of ships		8	8	7	7		64	54	53	54		1006	1061	965	1025
3512	Building/repairing of pleasure/sport. boats		25	24	33	32		77	87	72	75		993	1071	1117	1048
3520	Railway/tramway locomotives & rolling stock		-	-	-	-		-	-	-	-		-	-	-	-
3530	Aircraft and spacecraft		-	-	-	-		-	-	-	-		-	-	-	-
359	Transport equipment n.e.c.		-	-	-	-		-	-	-	-		-	-	-	-
3591	Motorcycles		-	-	-	-		-	-	-	-		-	-	-	-
3592	Bicycles and invalid carriages		-	-	-	-		-	-	-	-		-	-	-	-
3599	Other transport equipment n.e.c.		-	-	-	-		-	-	-	-		-	-	-	-
3610	Furniture		622	624	457	452		1884	1788	1531	1566		23944	24238	23425	24447
369	Manufacturing n.e.c.		277	277	210	210		743	738	588	590		8343	8787	8200	8206
3691	Jewellery and related articles		224	223	147	147		520	509	370	357		5989	6151	5409	5313
3692	Musical instruments		53w/	54w/	9x/	10x/		223w/	229w/	2x/	3x/		2354w/	2636w/	92x/	89x/
3693	Sports goods		...w/	...w/	-	-		...w/	...w/	-	-		...w/	...w/	-	-
3694	Games and toys		...w/	...w/	...x/	...x/		...w/	...w/	...x/	...x/		...w/	...w/	...x/	...x/
3699	Other manufacturing n.e.c.		...w/	...w/	54	53		...w/	...w/	216	230		...w/	...w/	2698	2804
3710	Recycling of metal waste and scrap		5	5	8	8		86	91	91	95		1042	1167	1398	1393
3720	Recycling of non-metal waste and scrap		4	6	11	11		34	54	93	85		331	545	1121	1076
D	Total manufacturing		6614	6614	5565	5586		34535	34583	34020	33962		497733	520888	564114	576419

a/ 1511 includes 1512.
b/ 154 includes 1600.
c/ 1551 includes 1552 and 1553.
d/ 1711 includes 1712.
e/ 1911 includes 1912.
f/ 2023 includes 2029.
g/ 2320 includes 241.
h/ 2692 includes 2693.
i/ 2710 includes 2720.
j/ 2812 includes 2813.
k/ 2912 includes 2913.
m/ 2922 includes 2923, 2924, 2925, 2926 and 2929.
n/ 2923 includes 2924, 2925 and 2926.
p/ 2930 includes 3000.
q/ 3130 includes 3140, 3150 and 3190.
r/ 3150 includes 3190.
s/ 3210 includes 3220.
t/ 3210 includes 3230.
u/ 3311 includes 3312 and 3313.
v/ 3312 includes 3313.
w/ 3692 includes 3693, 3694 and 3699.
x/ 3692 includes 3694.

Cyprus

ISIC Revision 3		Output in producers' prices					Value added in producers' prices					Gross fixed capital formation		
			(thousands of Euros)					(thousands of Euros)					(thousands of Euros)	
ISIC	Industry	Note	2003	2004	2005	2006	Note	2003	2004	2005	2006	Note	2005	2006
151	Processed meat,fish,fruit,vegetables,fats		307880	325012	351497	368607		59423	64818	62494	68204		12557	22208
1511	Processing/preserving of meat	a/	221633	231475	262291	276628	a/	36207	36952	35296	41405	a/	9809	19096
1512	Processing/preserving of fish	a/	...	...	...	...	a/	...	...	...	...	a/	...	...
1513	Processing/preserving of fruit & vegetables		49203	51783	52885	57134		16363	18528	19739	20129		812	484
1514	Vegetable and animal oils and fats		37044	41755	36321	34845		6853	9338	7458	6670		1936	2628
1520	Dairy products		144274	145564	163933	168654		42606	44924	51808	52920		9363	8290
153	Grain mill products; starches; animal feeds		92958	109754	103652	98226		19596	21123	19634	18084		2840	7364
1531	Grain mill products		26904	30912	29140	32240		7458	8487	7677	7101		629	2570
1532	Starches and starch products		...	...	-	-		...	...	-	-		-	-
1533	Prepared animal feeds		66055	78842	74512	65986		12138	12637	11957	10983		2211	4794
154	Other food products		240060	253345	260811	307805b/		113436	119865	125488	155842b/		25556	36865b/
1541	Bakery products		164890	178834	187333	205366		77746	86216	90465	99254		21492	31017
1542	Sugar		-	-	-	-		-	-	-	-		-	-
1543	Cocoa, chocolate and sugar confectionery		7489	7178	8560	8418		3622	3448	4651	5246		516	1252
1544	Macaroni, noodles & similar products		18309	17342	15572	16777		8640	7215	6674	7814		2809	557
1549	Other food products n.e.c.		49372	49990	49346	77244		23427	22986	23698	43528		738	4039
155	Beverages		230786	236481	233981	219208		88902	104013	102443	97341		7675	8029
1551	Distilling, rectifying & blending of spirits	c/	115932	116404	113538	110746	c/	50168	61710	60925	56326	c/	4588	4333
1552	Wines	c/	...	...	...	...	c/	...	...	...	...	c/	...	...
1553	Malt liquors and malt	c/	...	...	...	...	c/	...	...	...	...	c/	...	...
1554	Soft drinks; mineral waters		114854	120077	120443	108462		38734	42303	41517	41015		3087	3696
1600	Tobacco products		124945	145751	138848	...b/		93616	108592	108134	...b/		299	...b/
171	Spinning, weaving and finishing of textiles		3614	3754	2057	3046		1611	1615	839	1316		130	142
1711	Textile fibre preparation; textile weaving		179	186	2057d/	3046d/		48	31	839d/	1316d/		130d/	142d/
1712	Finishing of textiles		3434	3568	...d/	...d/		1563	1584	...d/	...d/		...d/	...d/
172	Other textiles		17351	18967	20462	20843		6552	7521	9447	9920		533	449
1721	Made-up textile articles, except apparel		15507	17887	18923	19510		5620	6843	8519	9209		516	440
1722	Carpets and rugs		-	-	-	-		-	-	-	-		-	-
1723	Cordage, rope, twine and netting		-	-	-	-		-	-	-	-		-	-
1729	Other textiles n.e.c.		1844	1080	1539	1333		933	678	928	711		17	9
1730	Knitted and crocheted fabrics and articles		10248	7332	3310	2464		4299	3494	1715	1138		7	-21
1810	Wearing apparel, except fur apparel		71783	57554	55596	51456		30777	24638	21703	20505		3120	1237
1820	Dressing & dyeing of fur; processing of fur		-	-	-	-		-	-	-	-		-	-
191	Tanning, dressing and processing of leather		1517	1358	2021	2035		776	673	883	1075		106	-
1911	Tanning and dressing of leather		196	103	2021e/	2035e/		36	19	883e/	1075e/		106e/	-e/
1912	Luggage, handbags, etc.; saddlery & harness		1321	1256	...e/	...e/		740	654	...e/	...e/		...e/	...e/
1920	Footwear		14286	10079	10183	8782		6395	4618	5114	4531		128	183
2010	Sawmilling and planing of wood		2349	2542	1179	849		877	877	379	391		-	85
202	Products of wood, cork, straw, etc.		157284	177994	182443	187828		66138	72158	73203	77451		11198	12825
2021	Veneer sheets, plywood, particle board, etc.		19767	23322	21276	19468		6064	6511	6928	5461		1143	-834
2022	Builders' carpentry and joinery		133905	151546	158227	165273		58342	64141	64848	70710		9944	13632
2023	Wooden containers		858	323	875	3087f/		318	123	285	1280f/		111	27f/
2029	Other wood products; articles of cork/straw		2754	2802	2066	...f/		1415	1382	1141	...f/		-	...f/
210	Paper and paper products		64556	62680	57816	59164		24373	25506	22730	21901		4142	3634
2101	Pulp, paper and paperboard		-	-	-	-		-	-	-	-		-	-
2102	Corrugated paper and paperboard		19116	19394	19107	19557		7019	7620	6869	6631		453	745
2109	Other articles of paper and paperboard		45440	43286	38708	39607		17354	17886	15861	15270		3689	2889
221	Publishing		50836	57529	59476	66171		22979	26369	28267	30346		682	3706
2211	Publishing of books and other publications		...	...	1545	1994		...	...	873	1167		-	41
2212	Publishing of newspapers, journals, etc.		...	...	53992	60368		...	...	26301	28099		579	3583
2213	Publishing of recorded media		-	-	-	-		-	-	-	-		-	-
2219	Other publishing		...	...	3940	3809		...	...	1094	1080		103	82

continued

Cyprus

ISIC Revision 3		Output in producers' prices (thousands of Euros)					Value added in producers' prices (thousands of Euros)					Gross fixed capital formation (thousands of Euros)	
ISIC	Industry	Note	2003	2004	2005	2006	Note	2003	2004	2005	2006	Note	2005	2006
222	Printing and related service activities		82724	88051	90474	101711		40525	41018	41760	44128		5818	16174
2221	Printing		82724	88051	90276	101421		40525	41018	41686	44014		5464	16174
2222	Service activities related to printing		...	...	198	290		...	...	73	114		354	-
2230	Reproduction of recorded media		-	-	-	-		-	-	-	-		-	-
2310	Coke oven products		-	-	-	-		-	-	-	-		-	-
2320	Refined petroleum products		205777	65439	7280g/	8179g/		17831	7549	3041g/	3140g/		772g/	718g/
2330	Processing of nuclear fuel		-	-	-	-		-	-	-	-		-	-
241	Basic chemicals		3169	3580	...g/	...g/		1512	1975	...g/	...g/		...g/	...g/
2411	Basic chemicals, except fertilizers		3169	3580	...	...		1512	1975	...	...		...	...
2412	Fertilizers and nitrogen compounds		-	-	-	-		-	-	-	-		-	-
2413	Plastics in primary forms; synthetic rubber		-	-	-	-		-	-	-	-		-	-
242	Other chemicals		147652	163633	158129	172270		56362	64452	64993	69945		9956	5861
2421	Pesticides and other agro-chemical products		5362	6870	7381	7854		2016	3272	3511	4396		1285	337
2422	Paints, varnishes, printing ink and mastics		27098	29453	27661	28223		9307	11212	10216	10899		989	70
2423	Pharmaceuticals, medicinal chemicals, etc.		78283	92241	101018	111616		30869	35100	42765	44473		5483	5169
2424	Soap, cleaning & cosmetic preparations		34386	32316	19034	20003		13221	13746	7219	7740		2124	282
2429	Other chemical products n.e.c.		2524	2753	3036	4574		948	1123	1283	2437		75	3
2430	Man-made fibres		-	-	-	-		-	-	-	-		-	-
251	Rubber products		1199	1198	1128	1374		400	386	454	591		9	7
2511	Rubber tyres and tubes		851	873	714	988		241	258	255	389		9	7
2519	Other rubber products		349	325	413	386		159	128	200	202		-	-
2520	Plastic products		69991	74640	82061	88403		32474	34439	34980	35908		5755	5632
2610	Glass and glass products		12999	13141	13862	15048		5254	5517	5937	6539		769	630
269	Non-metallic mineral products n.e.c.		338855	410668	475133	501756		124398	151768	166081	180885		34015	45483
2691	Pottery, china and earthenware		1338	1112	1145	1319		851	663	784	938		-	34
2692	Refractory ceramic products		32236	41746	38584h/	38823h/		15813	22408	20339h/	22012h/		5155h/	7463h/
2693	Struct.non-refractory clay; ceramic products		...	...	...h/	...h/		...	...	...h/	...h/		...h/	...h/
2694	Cement, lime and plaster		79612	92230	102972	111028		34088	41386	40656	49616		4511	7070
2695	Articles of concrete, cement and plaster		173452	216220	258886	272816		53192	64337	75556	78114		20013	28001
2696	Cutting, shaping & finishing of stone		35435	39100	55017	57761		15188	18147	23639	24657		3931	2712
2699	Other non-metallic mineral products n.e.c.		16782	20259	18530	20009		5266	4827	5107	5548		405	203
2710	Basic iron and steel	i/	46250	54650	54183	71074	i/	17453	21182	21653	26237	i/	1639	2927
2720	Basic precious and non-ferrous metals	i/	...	...	...	...	i/	...	...	...	...	i/	...	...
273	Casting of metals		...	...	-	-		...	...	-	-		-	-
2731	Casting of iron and steel		...	...	-	-		...	...	-	-		-	-
2732	Casting of non-ferrous metals		...	...	-	-		...	...	-	-		-	-
281	Struct.metal products;tanks;steam generators		135496	154499	207412	229795		49761	58205	74331	82355		8495	9568
2811	Structural metal products		126575	147688	200212	220756		45232	54463	70709	77836		8097	9259
2812	Tanks, reservoirs and containers of metal	j/	8921	6810	7200	9039	j/	4530	3742	3622	4519	j/	398	309
2813	Steam generators	j/	...	...	...	...	j/	...	...	...	...	j/	...	...
289	Other metal products; metal working services		53942	70078	60085	62683		26365	31568	28223	29443		3687	2505
2891	Metal forging/pressing/stamping/roll-forming		...	...	-	-		...	...	-	-		-	-
2892	Treatment & coating of metals		11636	16343	12756	12671		6927	7873	6727	6787		350	214
2893	Cutlery, hand tools and general hardware		4900	5778	6426	6668		2821	3340	3853	4145		185	236
2899	Other fabricated metal products n.e.c.		37406	47957	40902	43344		16618	20355	17643	18511		3152	2055
291	General purpose machinery		39139	40279	35741	34591		15999	16285	14884	15032		1189	-6599
2911	Engines & turbines (not for transport equipment)		...	...	-	-		...	...	-	-		-	-
2912	Pumps, compressors, taps and valves		7060	6635	5239k/	3684k/		3207	2537	2442k/	1302k/		555k/	-7977
2913	Bearings, gears, gearing & driving elements		-	-	...k/	...k/		-	-	...k/	...k/		...k/	...
2914	Ovens, furnaces and furnace burners		-	-	-	-		-	-	-	-		-	-
2915	Lifting and handling equipment		4189	6349	7940	6766		1545	2218	2993	2747		62	488
2919	Other general purpose machinery		27890	27295	22562	24141		11248	11530	9449	10983		572	890

292	Special purpose machinery		14475	15078	12668	14110		6388	6775	5162	5972		1041	1698
2921	Agricultural and forestry machinery		8181	7576	4418	5259		3976	3870	2262	2874		251	1027
2922	Machine tools		3034m/	3540m/	219	203		1779m/	2114m/	104	96		12	17
2923	Machinery for metallurgy		...m/	...m/	3007n/	3272n/		...m/	...m/	1603n/	1680n/		331n/	315n/
2924	Machinery for mining & construction		...m/	...m/	...n/	...n/		...m/	...m/	...n/	...n/		...n/	...n/
2925	Food/beverage/tobacco processing machinery		...m/	...m/	...n/	...n/		...m/	...m/	...n/	...n/		...n/	...n/
2926	Machinery for textile, apparel and leather		...m/	...m/	...n/	...n/		...m/	...m/	...n/	...n/		...n/	...n/
2927	Weapons and ammunition		3260	3962	4463	4820		634	791	916	1011		412	330
2929	Other special purpose machinery		...m/	...m/	560	556		...m/	...m/	277	311		34	9
2930	Domestic appliances n.e.c.		16022	18385	22427p/	22468		5379	6841	8049p/	8070		993p/	701
3000	Office, accounting and computing machinery		...	...	...p/	-		...	...	...p/	-		...p/	-
3110	Electric motors, generators and transformers		1647	1733	1594	2049		888	1100	665	1080		19	32
3120	Electricity distribution & control apparatus		10559	11632	11456	15111		4630	4365	4588	5452		108	157
3130	Insulated wire and cable	q/	11748	11034	12623	14773	q/	4649	4555	4576	5064	q/	605	885
3140	Accumulators, primary cells and batteries	q/	...	...	...	...	q/	...	...	...	...	q/	...	...
3150	Lighting equipment and electric lamps	q/	...	...	...	...	q/	...	...	...	...	q/	...	...
3190	Other electrical equipment n.e.c.	q/	...	...	...	...	q/	...	...	...	...	q/	...	...
3210	Electronic valves, tubes, etc.		-	6561r/	13122s/	34900s/		-	629r/	1345s/	3949s/		1627s/	427s/
3220	TV/radio transmitters; line comm. apparatus		103	...r/	-	-		68	...r/	-	-		-	-
3230	TV and radio receivers and associated goods		-	-	...s/	...s/		-	-	...s/	...s/		...s/	...s/
331	Medical, measuring, testing appliances, etc.		5343	6160	4777	5722		3246	3732	3197	3653		306	183
3311	Medical, surgical and orthopaedic equipment		5343t/	6160t/	4454	5413		3246t/	3732t/	3019	3499		301	159
3312	Measuring/testing/navigating appliances,etc.		...t/	...t/	323u/	309u/		...t/	...t/	178u/	154u/		5u/	24u/
3313	Industrial process control equipment		...t/	...t/	...u/	...u/		...t/	...t/	...u/	...u/		...u/	...u/
3320	Optical instruments & photographic equipment		4642	3853	3110	3269		2054	1903	1517	1633		313	335
3330	Watches and clocks		-	-	-	-		-	-	-	-		-	-
3410	Motor vehicles		-	-	-	-		-	-	-	-		-	-
3420	Automobile bodies, trailers & semi-trailers		12627	8037	7709	8548		3253	3253	3140	3438		85	58
3430	Parts/accessories for automobiles		9052	7673	6728	7077		4092	3159	3011	3060		123	161
351	Building and repairing of ships and boats		8048	7390	7395	8560		4265	3998	3720	4107		154	637
3511	Building and repairing of ships		3672	2600	2419	2987		2185	1738	1488	1812		36	133
3512	Building/repairing of pleasure/sport. boats		4376	4789	4975	5573		2079	2260	2231	2295		118	504
3520	Railway/tramway locomotives & rolling stock		-	-	-	-		-	-	-	-		-	-
3530	Aircraft and spacecraft		-	-	-	-		-	-	-	-		-	-
359	Transport equipment n.e.c.		-	-	-	-		-	-	-	-		-	-
3591	Motorcycles		-	-	-	-		-	-	-	-		-	-
3592	Bicycles and invalid carriages		-	-	-	-		-	-	-	-		-	-
3599	Other transport equipment n.e.c.		-	-	-	-		-	-	-	-		-	-
3610	Furniture		92697	95788	86568	91186		43055	46746	40877	42664		3928	5828
369	Manufacturing n.e.c.		39918	41579	31823	32327		16450	17428	13952	14537		1680	1322
3691	Jewellery and related articles		29590	30488	20679	20812		11900	12586	9271	9384		712	654
3692	Musical instruments		10328v/	11091v/	260w/	207w/		4550v/	4842v/	123w/	125w/		-w/	176w/
3693	Sports goods		...v/	...v/	-	-		...v/	...v/	-	-		-	-
3694	Games and toys		...v/	...v/	...w/	...w/		...v/	...v/	...w/	...w/		...w/	...w/
3699	Other manufacturing n.e.c.		...v/	...v/	10884	11308		...v/	...v/	4559	5028		967	492
3710	Recycling of metal waste and scrap		9290	13999	18825	29540		2370	3580	5555	8076		755	1874
3720	Recycling of non-metal waste and scrap		1085	2006	4321	5049		583	1061	1900	2142		514	825
D	Total manufacturing		2909176	3006455	3077900	3146711		1072062	1174272	1191871	1168065		162691	203025

a/ 1511 includes 1512.
b/ 154 includes 1600.
c/ 1551 includes 1552 and 1553.
d/ 1711 includes 1712.
e/ 1911 includes 1912.
f/ 2023 includes 2029.
g/ 2320 includes 241.
h/ 2692 includes 2693.
i/ 2710 includes 2720.
j/ 2812 includes 2813.
k/ 2912 includes 2913.
m/ 2922 includes 2923, 2924, 2925, 2926 and 2929.
n/ 2923 includes 2924, 2925 and 2926.
p/ 2930 includes 3000.
q/ 3130 includes 3140, 3150 and 3190.
r/ 3210 includes 3220.
s/ 3210 includes 3230.
t/ 3311 includes 3312 and 3313.
u/ 3312 includes 3313.
v/ 3692 includes 3693, 3694 and 3699.
w/ 3692 includes 3694.

Cyprus

ISIC Revision 3			Index numbers of industrial production											
			(2000=100)											
ISIC	Industry	Note	1995	1996	1997	1998	1999	2000	2001	2002	2003	2004	2005	2006
15	Food and beverages		105	99	95	93	96	100	102	101	103	100	101	96
16	Tobacco products		51	55	73	88	96	100	75	51	54	59	55	13
17	Textiles		141	114	105	111	107	100	100	83	63	43	32	30
18	Wearing apparel, fur		135	117	113	113	108	100	95	76	57	53	51	42
19	Leather, leather products and footwear		181	139	138	140	115	100	93	84	47	37	21	16
20	Wood products (excl. furniture)		88	90	89	88	94	100	102	104	102	126	126	122
21	Paper and paper products		122	121	116	107	99	100	111	115	119	116	116	116
22	Printing and publishing		101	98	90	89	87	100	105	99	98	100	96	102
23	Coke,refined petroleum products,nuclear fuel		70	64	89	92	100	100	98	92	82	26	3	3
24	Chemicals and chemical products		101	103	100	100	97	100	112	113	108	118	118	126
25	Rubber and plastics products		107	103	107	102	102	100	94	100	96	94	91	92
26	Non-metallic mineral products		101	98	88	94	94	100	102	114	120	128	133	137
27	Basic metals		...	...	...	...	...	...	...	...	...	...	...	...
28	Fabricated metal products	a/	84	85	86	87	92	100	102	112	104	112	111	120
29	Machinery and equipment n.e.c.	a/	...	...	...	...	...	...	...	...	...	...	...	...
30	Office, accounting and computing machinery	a/	...	...	...	...	...	...	...	...	...	...	...	...
31	Electrical machinery and apparatus	b/	112	110	108	103	91	100	95	92	77	65	69	98
32	Radio,television and communication equipment	b/	...	...	...	...	...	...	...	...	...	...	...	...
33	Medical, precision and optical instruments		45	41	47	65	106	100	110	115	103	126	130	120
34	Motor vehicles, trailers, semi-trailers	c/	104	81	75	104	102	100	111	140	134	121	118	141
35	Other transport equipment	c/	...	...	...	...	...	...	...	...	...	...	...	...
36	Furniture; manufacturing n.e.c.		106	100	105	103	99	100	95	94	84	81	80	81
37	Recycling		...	...	...	...	...	...	...	...	...	...	...	...
D	Total manufacturing		100	95	94	95	96	100	98	96	93	94	94	93

a/ 28 includes 29 and 30.
b/ 31 includes 32.
c/ 34 includes 35.

Denmark

Supplier of information:
Danmarks Statistik, Copenhagen.
Industrial statistics for the OECD countries are compiled by the OECD secretariat, which supplies them to UNIDO.

Basic source of data:
Surveys based partly on the establishment as a local unit (employment, wages and salaries, gross fixed capital formation) and partly on kind-of-activity units (output, value added).

Major deviations from ISIC (Revision 3):
The data presented in ISIC (Revision 3) were originally classified according to NACE (Revision 1).

Reference period:
Calendar year.

Scope:
The figures for number of establishments, employment and wages and salaries were derived from the register-based statistics of establishments and employment. All establishments with any number of employees in manufacturing are covered.

Method of data collection:
Not reported.

Type of enumeration:
Not reported.

Adjusted for non-response:
Not reported

Concepts and definitions of variables:
Number of employees refers to all full-time and part-time employees and all self-employed at end November.
Wages and salaries includes all outlays which were reported to the tax authorities by establishments operating during the year. This means that outlays of even those establishments, which were not active at the end of November, are included in the figures.

Related national publications:
None reported.

Denmark

ISIC Revision 3		Number of enterprises					Number of employees					Wages and salaries paid to employees				
			(number)					(number)					(millions of Danish Kroner)			
ISIC	Industry	Note	2002	2003	2004	2005	Note	2002	2003	2004	2005	Note	2002	2003	2004	2005
151	Processed meat,fish,fruit,vegetables,fats		351	338	342	345		...	...	29860	27105		...	...	9083	8349
1511	Processing/preserving of meat		161	162	158	159		23929	23004	20886	18905		6119	6833	6764	6147
1512	Processing/preserving of fish		126	119	119	125		6467	6320	5819	5334		1393	1384	1384	1285
1513	Processing/preserving of fruit & vegetables		50	39	46	41		2477	2369	2431	2176		633	661	671	648
1514	Vegetable and animal oils and fats		14	18	19	20		...	...	724	690		...	...	265	269
1520	Dairy products		84	61	66	71		...	...	...	...		...	...	...	...
153	Grain mill products; starches; animal feeds		74	76	75	80		5145	...	...	...		1465	...	...	...
1531	Grain mill products		16	16	15	15		1093	911	896	855		336	265	290	279
1532	Starches and starch products		5	7	7	8		170	194	184	185		39	48	51	48
1533	Prepared animal feeds		53	53	53	57		3882	...	...	...		1091	...	...	...
154	Other food products		1302	1240	1248	1216		29008	27654	27166	27215		5772	5896	5932	6009
1541	Bakery products		1171	1105	1101	1065		18303	17473	17155	...		2701	2723	2676	...
1542	Sugar		2	2	2	2		...	...	...	...		...	...	...	...
1543	Cocoa, chocolate and sugar confectionery		54	51	59	61		3210	2988	2852	2945		781	790	767	779
1544	Macaroni, noodles & similar products		5	3	2	1		...	...	...	...		...	...	...	...
1549	Other food products n.e.c.		70	79	84	87		...	...	...	...		...	...	...	...
155	Beverages		34	38	42	66		5434	5519	5257	5083		1702	1797	1760	1718
1551	Distilling, rectifying & blending of spirits		5	5	4	6		...	...	...	...		...	...	...	...
1552	Wines		1	3	4	7		...	...	...	...		...	...	...	...
1553	Malt liquors and malt		14	18	23	41		...	...	...	...		...	...	...	...
1554	Soft drinks; mineral waters		14	12	11	12		1090	...	209	193		353	...	63	57
1600	Tobacco products		6	6	6	7		1385	...	...	...		452	...	...	...
171	Spinning, weaving and finishing of textiles		95	90	94	101		1277	997	836	772		317	256	244	203
1711	Textile fibre preparation; textile weaving		42	36	38	37		...	...	...	...		...	...	...	...
1712	Finishing of textiles		53	54	56	64		603	587	465	396		143	142	129	94
172	Other textiles		385	362	347	342		5132	4715	4576	4554		1261	1179	1234	1217
1721	Made-up textile articles, except apparel		267	251	240	239		2958	2807	2650	2643		655	655	654	639
1722	Carpets and rugs		18	15	15	16		857	821	809	889		246	239	250	279
1723	Cordage, rope, twine and netting		49	45	41	41		506	310	...	235		127	72	...	59
1729	Other textiles n.e.c.		51	51	51	46		811	777	...	...		233	213	...	...
1730	Knitted and crocheted fabrics and articles		76	70	62	57		1174	1121	860	742		313	305	276	209
1810	Wearing apparel, except fur apparel		434	451	425	402		3141	2874	2495	2017		768	733	668	521
1820	Dressing & dyeing of fur; processing of fur		56	53	49	47		229	103	97	93		33	14	13	14
191	Tanning, dressing and processing of leather		20	20	21	19		...	...	...	...		...	...	...	...
1911	Tanning and dressing of leather		3	3	3	3		...	...	...	...		...	...	...	...
1912	Luggage, handbags, etc.; saddlery & harness		17	17	18	16		48	...	33	27		10	...	5	4
1920	Footwear		51	48	45	40		...	339	...	...		...	89	...	...
2010	Sawmilling and planing of wood		134	113	114	117		1371	1250	1045	1086		309	293	263	253
202	Products of wood, cork, straw, etc.		555	549	550	551		13124	12695	13212	13641		3188	3273	3402	3563
2021	Veneer sheets, plywood, particle board, etc.		48	46	44	43		1122	1177	1321	1264		273	287	329	318
2022	Builders' carpentry and joinery		259	264	269	278		10232	9890	10309	10860		2520	2602	2706	2888
2023	Wooden containers		73	73	77	73		805	757	793	785		176	174	173	190
2029	Other wood products; articles of cork/straw		175	166	160	157		965	871	789	732		218	210	194	166
210	Paper and paper products		196	187	180	174		8449	8201	7825	7616		2601	2532	2566	2498
2101	Pulp, paper and paperboard		22	20	20	15		1039	980	905	664		343	307	299	227
2102	Corrugated paper and paperboard		64	66	66	59		4548	4347	4153	4160		1409	1374	1401	1406
2109	Other articles of paper and paperboard		110	101	94	100		...	...	...	...		...	...	...	...
221	Publishing		1218	1216	1201	1228		31810	31436	24485	23494		5853	5798	5371	5853
2211	Publishing of books and other publications		491	497	488	491		4075	3613	3539	3832		1116	1078	1102	1294
2212	Publishing of newspapers, journals, etc.		324	314	307	324		26381	26562	19852	18365		4414	4403	3979	4214
2213	Publishing of recorded media		99	115	128	142		190	221	225	281		45	59	61	88
2219	Other publishing		304	290	278	271		1164	1040	869	1016		278	258	230	257

222	Printing and related service activities	1473	1352	1252	1192	14025	12590	10728	10096	3995	3845	3242	3008
2221	Printing	1036	954	863	814	11282	10199	8662	8167	3271	3192	2666	2487
2222	Service activities related to printing	437	398	389	378	2743	2391	2066	1929	724	652	575	519
2230	Reproduction of recorded media	47	53	44	40	784	1209	1160	1045	194	323	317	354
2310	Coke oven products	-	-	-	-	-	-	-	-	-	-	-	-
2320	Refined petroleum products	8	7	6	6	...	...	...	...	...	...	...	...
2330	Processing of nuclear fuel	-	-	-	-	-	-	-	-	-	-	-	-
241	Basic chemicals	65	66	64	66	4191	4198	5920	3945	1586	1677	1636	1685
2411	Basic chemicals, except fertilizers	33	35	34	36	...	...	...	...	...	...	...	...
2412	Fertilizers and nitrogen compounds	10	7	6	8	...	...	15	16	...	...	4	6
2413	Plastics in primary forms; synthetic rubber	22	24	24	22	324	318	356	324	95	99	109	93
242	Other chemicals	300	292	298	292	...	...	...	...	...	...	...	...
2421	Pesticides and other agro-chemical products	10	9	8	10	...	...	...	...	...	...	...	...
2422	Paints, varnishes, printing ink and mastics	53	49	53	49	2043	1982	1951	1820	682	693	715	680
2423	Pharmaceuticals, medicinal chemicals, etc.	82	82	79	85	16401	16969	17013	17604	6202	6914	7163	7789
2424	Soap, cleaning & cosmetic preparations	88	91	90	84	2102	2238	1985	1726	628	690	615	526
2429	Other chemical products n.e.c.	67	61	68	64	2701	2588	1094	1148	953	938	424	422
2430	Man-made fibres	3	3	4	3	...	...	...	...	...	...	...	...
251	Rubber products	90	90	84	83	1602	1570	1651	1488	438	433	467	446
2511	Rubber tyres and tubes	38	38	40	34	152	143	145	141	36	37	37	35
2519	Other rubber products	52	52	44	49	1450	1427	1506	1347	401	396	430	411
2520	Plastic products	647	613	606	574	21646	20815	19841	18521	5708	5867	5836	5528
2610	Glass and glass products	159	155	150	153	2614	2592	2525	2305	695	712	712	638
269	Non-metallic mineral products n.e.c.	542	522	504	484	14800	14409	14622	14118	4439	4388	4491	4578
2691	Pottery, china and earthenware	130	126	121	110	...	...	...	...	...	...	...	...
2692	Refractory ceramic products	2	2	2	4	...	...	...	...	...	...	...	...
2693	Struct.non-refractory clay; ceramic products	29	26	27	29	...	...	...	...	...	...	...	...
2694	Cement, lime and plaster	4	4	5	5	...	...	...	...	...	...	...	...
2695	Articles of concrete, cement and plaster	226	213	202	192	8223	8065	7712	7566	2361	2416	2367	2444
2696	Cutting, shaping & finishing of stone	114	113	107	107	531	451	467	482	133	114	116	118
2699	Other non-metallic mineral products n.e.c.	37	38	40	37	3613	3769	4432	3945	1241	1215	1373	1379
2710	Basic iron and steel	92	82	79	85	3019	2299	2187	2012	866	722	659	607
2720	Basic precious and non-ferrous metals	38	39	37	37	1613	1591	1919	1881	453	470	580	578
273	Casting of metals	55	61	57	53	2195	1731	1600	1134	560	485	452	313
2731	Casting of iron and steel	22	27	26	22	...	1035	1151	...	...	290	327	...
2732	Casting of non-ferrous metals	33	34	31	31	774	696	449	...	214	195	125	...
281	Struct.metal products;tanks;steam generators	585	604	606	583	...	...	14574	...	...	...	4438	...
2811	Structural metal products	510	524	535	513	12962	12011	11807	11997	3538	3551	3525	3506
2812	Tanks, reservoirs and containers of metal	67	69	62	63	1799	1833	...	1702	502	517	...	499
2813	Steam generators	8	11	9	7	...	...	...	...	...	...	...	...
289	Other metal products; metal working services	3343	3384	3472	3623	...	...	27986	...	...	...	7576	...
2891	Metal forging/pressing/stamping/roll-forming	63	63	50	51	105	...	66	64	22	...	12	13
2892	Treatment & coating of metals	2240	2314	2430	2617	11369	10835	10851	11689	2788	2747	2775	2994
2893	Cutlery, hand tools and general hardware	288	272	268	255	...	3514	2896	...	...	982	812	...
2899	Other fabricated metal products n.e.c.	752	735	724	700	13523	13579	14173	13750	3508	3576	3976	3989
291	General purpose machinery	932	904	896	888	40478	39521	39596	38980	11815	12157	12687	12976
2911	Engines & turbines (not for transport equipment)	87	84	88	85	...	...	...	...	...	...	...	...
2912	Pumps, compressors, taps and valves	155	144	140	146	...	...	16845	16597	...	...	5125	5288
2913	Bearings, gears, gearing & driving elements	38	37	35	38	789	753	...	...	208	210	...	...
2914	Ovens, furnaces and furnace burners	48	47	44	43	421	415	400	390	110	118	110	116
2915	Lifting and handling equipment	211	206	205	198	7959	7262	7783	7657	2307	2202	2449	2455
2919	Other general purpose machinery	393	386	384	378	11857	12525	10760	10282	3529	3975	3589	3576
292	Special purpose machinery	1370	1360	1337	1327	...	20027	19520	...	...	6120	6146	...
2921	Agricultural and forestry machinery	458	458	454	458	5355	...	...	4861	1487	...	...	1409
2922	Machine tools	159	154	156	157	1966	1939	...	2094	562	573	...	668
2923	Machinery for metallurgy	36	40	42	41	180	160	...	111	39	39	...	28
2924	Machinery for mining & construction	62	61	60	68	2080	1784	1469	1680	643	571	483	572
2925	Food/beverage/tobacco processing machinery	175	168	154	161	5415	4305	3838	3823	1692	1405	1292	1288
2926	Machinery for textile, apparel and leather	21	14	15	15	810	774	...	759	230	229	...	249
2927	Weapons and ammunition	11	12	10	10	...	...	...	...	...	...	...	...
2929	Other special purpose machinery	448	453	446	417	6194	5965	...	5381	1820	1815	...	1672

continued

Denmark

ISIC Revision 3		Number of enterprises					Number of employees					Wages and salaries paid to employees				
			(number)					(number)					(millions of Danish Kroner)			
ISIC	Industry	Note	2002	2003	2004	2005	Note	2002	2003	2004	2005	Note	2002	2003	2004	2005
2930	Domestic appliances n.e.c.		63	68	61	64		...	3553	2738	...		...	1060	826	...
3000	Office, accounting and computing machinery		101	97	92	90		1566	1290	1181	1078		503	423	396	393
3110	Electric motors, generators and transformers		97	100	103	116		12128	10363	9677	10931		3501	2722	3149	3756
3120	Electricity distribution & control apparatus		144	127	131	119		3837	3653	3864	4072		1047	1056	1163	1203
3130	Insulated wire and cable		21	26	26	28		...	...	1006	1007		...	...	314	321
3140	Accumulators, primary cells and batteries		7	7	8	6		...	...	295	14		...	...	66	3
3150	Lighting equipment and electric lamps		130	114	115	112		2403	2294	2206	2153		569	572	611	588
3190	Other electrical equipment n.e.c.		519	511	500	487		3789	3630	3693	3580		1017	1003	1043	993
3210	Electronic valves, tubes, etc.		88	84	73	75		2097	1947	1636	1496		551	517	437	417
3220	TV/radio transmitters; line comm. apparatus		36	45	43	45		...	2569	1498	1215		...	831	523	481
3230	TV and radio receivers and associated goods		85	94	92	94		...	4100	3880	4098		...	1048	1119	1068
331	Medical, measuring, testing appliances, etc.		642	598	640	638		14058	13887	13121	14939		4381	4582	4290	5092
3311	Medical, surgical and orthopaedic equipment		397	347	382	379		7397	7338	7435	8935		2173	2257	2329	2898
3312	Measuring/testing/navigating appliances,etc.		174	176	183	177		6221	6094	5250	5482		2082	2185	1835	2043
3313	Industrial process control equipment		71	75	75	82		440	455	436	522		126	140	126	151
3320	Optical instruments & photographic equipment		44	44	49	45		1580	1306	1256	1161		542	463	443	419
3330	Watches and clocks		6	6	7	7		18	23	19	16		5	4	4	5
3410	Motor vehicles		-	3	3	4		-	...	...	...		-	...	...	...
3420	Automobile bodies, trailers & semi-trailers		108	95	87	86		3129	...	2382	...		898	...	709	...
3430	Parts/accessories for automobiles		50	53	48	46		3391	...	...	3895		919	...	...	1129
351	Building and repairing of ships and boats		298	277	268	278		5857	4980	4874	5288		1783	1644	1534	1706
3511	Building and repairing of ships		90	80	64	65		...	3374	...	...		...	1227	...	...
3512	Building/repairing of pleasure/sport. boats		208	197	204	213		...	1606	...	...		...	418	...	...
3520	Railway/tramway locomotives & rolling stock		1	1	3	3		...	...	...	...		...	...	...	...
3530	Aircraft and spacecraft		30	35	37	36		...	494	1304	2074		...	166	527	940
359	Transport equipment n.e.c.		51	55	55	55		1022	...	...	...		276	...	...	...
3591	Motorcycles		2	2	2	2		...	...	...	...		...	...	...	...
3592	Bicycles and invalid carriages		33	36	39	40		...	...	...	...		...	...	...	...
3599	Other transport equipment n.e.c.		16	17	14	13		367	...	...	...		103	...	...	...
3610	Furniture		1105	1021	1017	990		21420	20193	19121	18712		5183	5097	5031	5006
369	Manufacturing n.e.c.		760	731	756	752		7617	...	...	6423		2000	...	...	1840
3691	Jewellery and related articles		236	228	243	247		957	898	...	...		233	231	...	...
3692	Musical instruments		58	64	57	54		229	223	208	196		51	53	52	51
3693	Sports goods		37	34	33	34		406	381	339	361		107	116	103	102
3694	Games and toys		66	58	65	65		...	...	...	...		...	...	...	...
3699	Other manufacturing n.e.c.		363	347	358	352		...	1960	1893	1838		...	440	403	406
3710	Recycling of metal waste and scrap		17	17	19	27		...	...	...	...		...	...	...	...
3720	Recycling of non-metal waste and scrap		12	16	15	16		...	...	...	...		...	...	...	...
D	Total manufacturing		19235	18730	18611	18571		449008	429443	408374	400953		120933	121183	120820	122385

Denmark

ISIC Revision 3		Output					Value added in factor values					Gross fixed capital formation		
			(millions of Danish Kroner)					(millions of Danish Kroner)					(millions of Danish Kroner)	
ISIC	Industry	Note	2002	2003	2004	2005	Note	2002	2003	2004	2005	Note	2004	2005
151	Processed meat,fish,fruit,vegetables,fats		...	...	55544	56493		...	...	13732	12603		3026	2511
1511	Processing/preserving of meat		39732	38602	39330	39105		9566	9963	10030	9099		2139	1496
1512	Processing/preserving of fish		11091	9867	8581	9588		2286	2124	2101	1896		452	465
1513	Processing/preserving of fruit & vegetables		4191	4149	4516	4361		1079	1069	1127	1066		314	357
1514	Vegetable and animal oils and fats		...	...	3118	3439		...	...	473	542		121	194
1520	Dairy products		...	...	...	...		...	...	...	...		...	...
153	Grain mill products; starches; animal feeds		13321	...	...	...		2748	...	...	...		...	...
1531	Grain mill products		2452	2190	2414	2335		515	476	490	481		125	167
1532	Starches and starch products		796	670	699	645		267	168	197	168		89	55
1533	Prepared animal feeds		10074	...	...	...		1965	...	...	...		...	...
154	Other food products		26072	25145	24613	26491		9643	9508	9444	9449		1563	1278
1541	Bakery products		9620	9181	9229	...		4024	3915	3955	...		443	...
1542	Sugar		...	...	...	...		...	...	...	...		...	...
1543	Cocoa, chocolate and sugar confectionery		3506	3379	3280	3474		1242	1163	1168	1168		144	154
1544	Macaroni, noodles & similar products		...	...	...	...		...	...	...	...		...	...
1549	Other food products n.e.c.		...	...	...	...		...	...	...	...		...	...
155	Beverages		11475	15193	10911	10575		3495	4100	3557	3194		826	578
1551	Distilling, rectifying & blending of spirits		...	...	...	...		...	...	...	...		...	...
1552	Wines		...	...	...	...		...	...	...	...		...	...
1553	Malt liquors and malt		...	...	...	...		...	...	...	...		...	...
1554	Soft drinks; mineral waters		2882	...	589	583		704	...	158	151		19	36
1600	Tobacco products		12188	...	...	...		1910	...	...	...		...	...
171	Spinning, weaving and finishing of textiles		1019	953	875	811		412	395	365	305		45	42
1711	Textile fibre preparation; textile weaving		...	...	...	...		...	...	...	...		...	...
1712	Finishing of textiles		386	479	406	301		190	211	177	124		22	16
172	Other textiles		5204	5001	4910	5301		1971	1853	1905	1921		250	232
1721	Made-up textile articles, except apparel		2384	2440	2379	2489		945	959	935	963		116	98
1722	Carpets and rugs		1233	1177	1064	1303		415	360	382	436		25	57
1723	Cordage, rope, twine and netting		473	300	...	230		166	104	...	66		...	5
1729	Other textiles n.e.c.		1115	1084	...	...		445	431	...	...		...	...
1730	Knitted and crocheted fabrics and articles		1668	1548	1217	1011		481	418	390	294		56	31
1810	Wearing apparel, except fur apparel		4456	4040	3501	3446		1212	1089	992	818		69	77
1820	Dressing & dyeing of fur; processing of fur		184	99	95	105		56	34	25	29		1	3
191	Tanning, dressing and processing of leather		...	...	...	...		...	...	...	...		...	...
1911	Tanning and dressing of leather		...	...	...	...		...	...	...	...		...	...
1912	Luggage, handbags, etc.; saddlery & harness		45	...	33	27		13	...	10	7		1	1
1920	Footwear		...	550	...	...		...	136	...	...		...	...
2010	Sawmilling and planing of wood		1360	1256	1186	1185		455	437	412	398		110	61
202	Products of wood, cork, straw, etc.		11630	12030	12715	13886		4503	4585	4919	5376		711	682
2021	Veneer sheets, plywood, particle board, etc.		1158	1135	1385	1484		432	405	499	493		77	54
2022	Builders' carpentry and joinery		9055	9543	9925	10990		3515	3651	3903	4362		498	560
2023	Wooden containers		661	662	689	805		263	253	242	278		71	28
2029	Other wood products; articles of cork/straw		756	690	716	607		293	276	276	244		66	39
210	Paper and paper products		11340	10746	10415	10475		4087	4062	3791	3557		627	568
2101	Pulp, paper and paperboard		2054	1928	1956	1375		623	554	522	382		92	43
2102	Corrugated paper and paperboard		5734	5413	5053	5596		2153	2161	1972	1918		339	336
2109	Other articles of paper and paperboard		...	...	...	...		...	...	...	...		...	...
221	Publishing		19744	19818	18641	19997		7745	7871	7786	9047		794	531
2211	Publishing of books and other publications		5262	4947	4478	5278		2066	2051	2060	2835		169	157
2212	Publishing of newspapers, journals, etc.		12960	13392	12885	13543		5163	5311	5257	5714		529	338
2213	Publishing of recorded media		454	477	399	383		82	99	91	118		20	12
2219	Other publishing		1069	1002	879	794		433	410	378	379		75	24

continued

Denmark

ISIC Revision 3		Output					Value added in factor values					Gross fixed capital formation		
		Note	(millions of Danish Kroner)				Note	(millions of Danish Kroner)				Note	(millions of Danish Kroner)	
ISIC	Industry		2002	2003	2004	2005		2002	2003	2004	2005		2004	2005
222	Printing and related service activities		12786	11974	11246	10898		5871	5477	5026	4645		1083	708
2221	Printing		10650	10332	9724	9423		4827	4557	4166	3878		905	609
2222	Service activities related to printing		2136	1641	1521	1475		1044	919	859	768		177	98
2230	Reproduction of recorded media		770	1193	1146	1142		296	546	561	598		60	29
2310	Coke oven products		-	-	-	-		-	-	-	-		-	-
2320	Refined petroleum products		...	...	...	...		...	...	...	...		...	...
2330	Processing of nuclear fuel		-	-	-	-		-	-	-	-		-	-
241	Basic chemicals		8349	8574	8241	7841		3139	3221	3711	3753		265	502
2411	Basic chemicals, except fertilizers		...	...	...	...		...	...	...	...		...	...
2412	Fertilizers and nitrogen compounds		...	...	112	151		...	...	20	19		4	10
2413	Plastics in primary forms; synthetic rubber		473	480	552	561		130	132	163	148		28	26
242	Other chemicals		...	...	...	...		...	...	...	...		...	...
2421	Pesticides and other agro-chemical products		...	...	...	...		...	...	...	...		...	...
2422	Paints, varnishes, printing ink and mastics		3249	3226	3219	3108		892	814	826	841		177	207
2423	Pharmaceuticals, medicinal chemicals, etc.		35099	35736	38396	43498		14543	16341	16567	17848		4168	3058
2424	Soap, cleaning & cosmetic preparations		3200	3600	2461	2714		1045	1168	1048	947		113	114
2429	Other chemical products n.e.c.		3248	3605	1997	2099		1187	1241	805	703		235	104
2430	Man-made fibres		...	...	...	...		...	...	...	...		...	...
251	Rubber products		1509	1461	1566	1632		595	555	641	546		54	62
2511	Rubber tyres and tubes		250	215	225	208		70	63	74	71		10	9
2519	Other rubber products		1259	1245	1341	1425		525	492	567	476		43	53
2520	Plastic products		22336	21823	22045	22499		9589	9291	9371	9093		1733	1458
2610	Glass and glass products		2651	2621	2683	2598		1037	1070	1059	1038		282	194
269	Non-metallic mineral products n.e.c.		16823	16033	16232	18175		7108	6880	6894	7535		1383	997
2691	Pottery, china and earthenware		...	...	...	...		...	...	...	...		...	...
2692	Refractory ceramic products		...	...	...	...		...	...	...	...		...	...
2693	Struct.non-refractory clay; ceramic products		...	...	...	...		...	...	...	...		...	...
2694	Cement, lime and plaster		...	...	...	...		...	...	...	...		...	...
2695	Articles of concrete, cement and plaster		8215	8487	8158	9400		3486	3612	3499	3962		599	501
2696	Cutting, shaping & finishing of stone		467	449	426	472		214	189	200	190		45	25
2699	Other non-metallic mineral products n.e.c.		4502	4212	4763	5215		1915	1734	1870	2043		170	206
2710	Basic iron and steel		3369	3913	4959	4412		1146	915	1211	1031		192	158
2720	Basic precious and non-ferrous metals		2872	2814	3024	3244		721	735	926	839		71	101
273	Casting of metals		1647	1492	1445	953		763	670	668	358		99	77
2731	Casting of iron and steel		...	861	1016	...		...	395	486	...		71	...
2732	Casting of non-ferrous metals		634	631	428	...		291	276	183	...		28	...
281	Struct.metal products;tanks;steam generators		...	...	13839	...		...	...	5836	...		531	...
2811	Structural metal products		12190	10438	10634	11895		4811	4601	4616	4663		411	411
2812	Tanks, reservoirs and containers of metal		1500	1547	...	1675		643	671	...	635		...	75
2813	Steam generators		...	...	...	...		...	...	...	...		...	...
289	Other metal products; metal working services		...	...	25095	...		...	...	11901	...		1703	...
2891	Metal forging/pressing/stamping/roll-forming		94	...	76	80		39	...	27	28		3	4
2892	Treatment & coating of metals		8394	8166	8586	10334		4208	4155	4385	4739		763	666
2893	Cutlery, hand tools and general hardware		...	2928	2499	...		...	1403	1263	...		132	...
2899	Other fabricated metal products n.e.c.		11202	11969	13934	15062		5128	5311	6226	6023		806	734
291	General purpose machinery		39692	41630	43058	45298		16584	16716	17512	17569		1777	1569
2911	Engines & turbines (not for transport equipment)		...	...	...	...		...	...	...	...		...	...
2912	Pumps, compressors, taps and valves		...	...	18270	18706		...	...	7313	7262		1207	899
2913	Bearings, gears, gearing & driving elements		654	690	...	...		305	328	...	...		...	...
2914	Ovens, furnaces and furnace burners		435	483	395	527		180	192	156	186		10	29
2915	Lifting and handling equipment		7071	6608	7093	7921		3003	2748	3153	3134		127	159
2919	Other general purpose machinery		12887	14388	12817	12857		4784	5413	4876	4538		323	302

292	Special purpose machinery		...	20129	19554	...		...	7677	7982	...		682	...
2921	Agricultural and forestry machinery		6166	...	...	5717		2015	...	...	2014		...	154
2922	Machine tools		1759	1708	...	2379		776	751	...	991		...	146
2923	Machinery for metallurgy		134	134	...	116		62	62	...	42		...	4
2924	Machinery for mining & construction		2040	1806	1779	2260		772	696	701	923		31	262
2925	Food/beverage/tobacco processing machinery		5488	4514	3908	4318		2049	1824	1630	1654		87	122
2926	Machinery for textile, apparel and leather		690	690	...	844		323	286	...	350		...	19
2927	Weapons and ammunition		...	...	...	...		...	...	...	...		...	...
2929	Other special purpose machinery		5723	5789	...	5520		2196	2293	...	2215		...	154
2930	Domestic appliances n.e.c.		...	6299	3671	...		...	1674	1160	...		171	...
3000	Office, accounting and computing machinery		2049	2044	1692	1890		802	729	671	684		21	25
3110	Electric motors, generators and transformers		20201	18387	19474	25796		5130	3713	3152	3221		639	698
3120	Electricity distribution & control apparatus		3722	3646	5145	5215		1618	1578	2142	2025		92	110
3130	Insulated wire and cable		...	...	1513	1664		...	...	513	546		39	50
3140	Accumulators, primary cells and batteries		...	...	201	22		...	...	68	4		29	4
3150	Lighting equipment and electric lamps		2211	2081	2144	2013		738	720	783	687		49	106
3190	Other electrical equipment n.e.c.		3801	3773	4124	4104		1314	1394	1471	1427		120	99
3210	Electronic valves, tubes, etc.		1717	2004	1434	1478		817	827	536	617		37	52
3220	TV/radio transmitters; line comm. apparatus		...	5071	1837	1672		...	1274	764	794		75	25
3230	TV and radio receivers and associated goods		...	5059	4670	5315		...	1691	1551	1726		191	138
331	Medical, measuring, testing appliances, etc.		14912	16836	15802	19260		7221	8230	7769	9269		759	837
3311	Medical, surgical and orthopaedic equipment		8324	9782	9851	12009		3939	4622	4676	5792		478	480
3312	Measuring/testing/navigating appliances,etc.		6198	6650	5574	6748		3114	3418	2918	3257		264	346
3313	Industrial process control equipment		391	404	377	502		168	189	174	219		17	11
3320	Optical instruments & photographic equipment		1465	1339	1506	1659		452	458	654	724		35	30
3330	Watches and clocks		17	18	17	19		8	7	7	7		1	-
3410	Motor vehicles		-	...	...	...		-	...	...	...		...	...
3420	Automobile bodies, trailers & semi-trailers		4275	...	3574	...		1236	...	1001	...		84	...
3430	Parts/accessories for automobiles		3192	...	...	4001		1222	...	...	1636		...	165
351	Building and repairing of ships and boats		8849	7353	7849	7457		2289	2125	1426	1113		272	437
3511	Building and repairing of ships		...	5988	...	...		...	1597	...	...		...	...
3512	Building/repairing of pleasure/sport. boats		...	1367	...	...		...	528	...	...		...	...
3520	Railway/tramway locomotives & rolling stock		...	...	...	...		...	...	...	...		...	...
3530	Aircraft and spacecraft		...	554	1531	2994		...	218	671	1237		98	176
359	Transport equipment n.e.c.		974	...	...	...		384	...	...	...		...	...
3591	Motorcycles		...	...	...	...		...	...	...	...		...	...
3592	Bicycles and invalid carriages		...	...	...	...		...	...	...	...		...	...
3599	Other transport equipment n.e.c.		316	...	...	...		112	...	...	...		...	...
3610	Furniture		20963	20246	20623	21145		8017	7812	8079	7945		759	678
369	Manufacturing n.e.c.		7967	...	...	8459		3275	...	...	2391		...	437
3691	Jewellery and related articles		883	858	...	...		366	386	...	...		...	...
3692	Musical instruments		111	136	127	130		77	78	78	65		16	1
3693	Sports goods		453	424	424	469		178	193	148	133		39	11
3694	Games and toys		...	...	...	...		...	...	...	...		...	...
3699	Other manufacturing n.e.c.		...	1623	1492	1871		...	710	656	656		107	51
3710	Recycling of metal waste and scrap		...	...	...	...		...	...	...	...		...	...
3720	Recycling of non-metal waste and scrap		...	...	...	...		...	...	...	...		...	...
D	Total manufacturing		553071	547508	531539	578851		189443	189082	189888	191639		29707	25326

Denmark

ISIC Revision 3			Index numbers of industrial production											
			(2000=100)											
ISIC	Industry	Note	1995	1996	1997	1998	1999	2000	2001	2002	2003	2004	2005	2006
15	Food and beverages		96	95	100	95	98	100	100	108	115	112	111	113
16	Tobacco products		107	102	103	108	97	100	92	94	95	83	78	80
17	Textiles		90	97	91	97	98	100	94	90	88	82	80	81
18	Wearing apparel, fur		112	113	116	111	100	100	90	84	74	61	60	63
19	Leather, leather products and footwear		89	82	96	99	90	100	73	67	67	14	11	12
20	Wood products (excl. furniture)		85	81	91	96	92	100	94	95	92	101	107	117
21	Paper and paper products		105	99	103	101	98	100	98	97	91	90	89	90
22	Printing and publishing		83	92	95	94	94	100	98	94	88	94	95	92
23	Coke,refined petroleum products,nuclear fuel		100	113	98	82	87	100	94	80	78	99	117	134
24	Chemicals and chemical products		65	70	74	77	91	100	110	114	109	98	109	106
25	Rubber and plastics products		85	85	92	96	97	100	102	100	101	101	109	109
26	Non-metallic mineral products		88	88	94	99	101	100	99	89	94	94	99	106
27	Basic metals		83	79	86	89	81	100	91	69	73	68	66	66
28	Fabricated metal products		87	89	90	96	90	100	101	109	111	109	101	110
29	Machinery and equipment n.e.c.		95	93	99	105	95	100	103	103	99	105	100	110
30	Office, accounting and computing machinery		70	87	53	39	63	100	133	104	146	182	202	258
31	Electrical machinery and apparatus		67	71	79	81	99	100	115	116	113	125	157	156
32	Radio,television and communication equipment		63	81	81	86	103	100	103	120	113	75	69	73
33	Medical, precision and optical instruments		64	67	76	83	85	100	103	95	95	105	100	118
34	Motor vehicles, trailers, semi-trailers		82	82	97	105	96	100	105	96	101	95	96	101
35	Other transport equipment		165	153	149	142	115	100	110	114	94	98	127	125
36	Furniture; manufacturing n.e.c.		89	86	90	102	97	100	101	105	100	105	104	111
37	Recycling		...	...	...	...	...	...	...	...	...	...	...	...
D	Total manufacturing		87	88	92	95	95	100	102	103	102	102	104	108

Eritrea

Supplier of information:
Ministry of Trade and Industry, Asmara.

Basic source of data:
Census of the manufacturing industry.

Major deviations from ISIC (Revision 3):
None reported.

Reference period:
Calendar year.

Scope:
Establishments with 10 or more employees.

Method of data collection:
Direct interview in the field.

Type of enumeration:
Complete enumeration.

Adjusted for non-response:
No.

Concepts and definitions of variables:
Number of employees includes temporary and contract workers.
Wages and salaries excludes remuneration for time not worked but includes employers' contributions paid to social security, pension and insurance schemes as well as the benefits received by employees under these schemes and severance and termination pay.
Output includes revenue from non-industrial activities.
Value added includes net receipts of non-industrial services.

Related national publications:
Report on Census of Manufacturing Establishments, published by the Ministry of Trade and Industry, Asmara.

Eritrea

ISIC Revision 3		Number of establishments					Number of employees					Wages and salaries paid to employees				
			(number)					(number)					(thousands of Eritrean Nakfa)			
ISIC	Industry	Note	2003	2004	2005	2006	Note	2003	2004	2005	2006	Note	2003	2004	2005	2006
151	Processed meat,fish,fruit,vegetables,fats		3	3	3	3		693	743	589	569		7537	7751	5829	5538
1511	Processing/preserving of meat		1	1	1	1		610	578	522	507		6632	6890	4789	4508
1512	Processing/preserving of fish		1	1	1	1		61	55	48	48		594	415	689	753
1513	Processing/preserving of fruit & vegetables		-	-	-	-		-	-	-	-		-	-	-	-
1514	Vegetable and animal oils and fats		1	1	1	1		22	110	19	14		312	446	351	277
1520	Dairy products		5	5	5	5		198	205	225	220		2403	2918	3357	3652
153	Grain mill products; starches; animal feeds		5	6	5	5		514	543	534	522		5533	6889	7836	8606
1531	Grain mill products		3	3	2	2		407	420	427	432		4694	5704	6663	7542
1532	Starches and starch products		-	-	-	-		-	-	-	-		-	-	-	-
1533	Prepared animal feeds		2	3	3	3		107	123	107	90		839	1185	1173	1064
154	Other food products		53	52	75	72		1067	1136	1572	1331		8706	11302	13900	13652
1541	Bakery products		50	47	70	67		916	890	1349	1117		7593	8803	11178	11160
1542	Sugar		-	-	-	-		-	-	-	-		-	-	-	-
1543	Cocoa, chocolate and sugar confectionery		1	1	1	1		49	52	46	41		366	562	521	472
1544	Macaroni, noodles & similar products		2	3	3	3		102	99	84	77		747	1053	1197	1011
1549	Other food products n.e.c.		-	1	1	1		-	95	93	96		-	884	1004	1010
155	Beverages		13	22	22	22		1083	1321	1425	1420		17147	25645	23838	26854
1551	Distilling, rectifying & blending of spirits		-	-	-	-		-	-	-	-		-	-	-	-
1552	Wines		3	5	5	4		141	198	182	185		1344	2003	2201	2250
1553	Malt liquors and malt		1	2	2	3		396	442	511	513		6387	10084	10641	12603
1554	Soft drinks; mineral waters		9	15	15	15		546	681	732	722		9415	13558	10996	12000
1600	Tobacco products		1	1	1	1		49	44	49	45		2065	2065	3356	3661
171	Spinning, weaving and finishing of textiles		3	3	4	5		1964	1926	1501	1897		20062	17698	15921	24053
1711	Textile fibre preparation; textile weaving		-	-	-	-		-	-	-	-		-	-	-	-
1712	Finishing of textiles		3	3	4	5		1964	1926	1501	1897		20062	17698	15921	24053
172	Other textiles		2	1	-	-		241	223	-	-		2047	1785	-	-
1721	Made-up textile articles, except apparel		-	-	-	-		-	-	-	-		-	-	-	-
1722	Carpets and rugs		1	1	-	-		233	223	-	-		2000	1785	-	-
1723	Cordage, rope, twine and netting		-	-	-	-		-	-	-	-		-	-	-	-
1729	Other textiles n.e.c.		1	-	-	-		8	-	-	-		47	-	-	-
1730	Knitted and crocheted fabrics and articles		4	4	4	4		185	202	304	214		1734	2096	3114	2800
1810	Wearing apparel, except fur apparel		5	5	5	4		534	640	565	218		4287	5017	4880	1996
1820	Dressing & dyeing of fur; processing of fur		-	-	-	-		-	-	-	-		-	-	-	-
191	Tanning, dressing and processing of leather		6	6	6	6		311	323	311	324		3699	3975	4434	4911
1911	Tanning and dressing of leather		5	5	5	5		273	279	278	301		3458	3739	4185	4680
1912	Luggage, handbags, etc.; saddlery & harness		1	1	1	1		38	44	33	23		242	236	249	231
1920	Footwear		16	15	15	15		663	611	646	787		6404	6112	6373	9135
2010	Sawmilling and planing of wood		-	-	-	-		-	-	-	-		-	-	-	-
202	Products of wood, cork, straw, etc.		-	-	-	-		-	-	-	-		-	-	-	-
2021	Veneer sheets, plywood, particle board, etc.		-	-	-	-		-	-	-	-		-	-	-	-
2022	Builders' carpentry and joinery		-	-	-	-		-	-	-	-		-	-	-	-
2023	Wooden containers		-	-	-	-		-	-	-	-		-	-	-	-
2029	Other wood products; articles of cork/straw		-	-	-	-		-	-	-	-		-	-	-	-
210	Paper and paper products		3	4	4	4		92	114	113	113		1033	1289	1429	1352
2101	Pulp, paper and paperboard		2	3	3	3		37	70	68	78		304	470	483	617
2102	Corrugated paper and paperboard		1	1	1	1		55	44	45	35		728	819	946	734
2109	Other articles of paper and paperboard		-	-	-	-		-	-	-	-		-	-	-	-
221	Publishing		-	-	-	-		-	-	-	-		-	-	-	-
2211	Publishing of books and other publications		-	-	-	-		-	-	-	-		-	-	-	-
2212	Publishing of newspapers, journals, etc.		-	-	-	-		-	-	-	-		-	-	-	-
2213	Publishing of recorded media		-	-	-	-		-	-	-	-		-	-	-	-
2219	Other publishing		-	-	-	-		-	-	-	-		-	-	-	-

222	Printing and related service activities	7	8	8	8	425	442	447	451	5294	7608	6406	8944
2221	Printing	7	8	8	8	425	442	447	451	5294	7608	6406	8944
2222	Service activities related to printing	-	-	-	-	-	-	-	-	-	-	-	-
2230	Reproduction of recorded media	-	-	-	-	-	-	-	-	-	-	-	-
2310	Coke oven products	-	-	-	-	-	-	-	-	-	-	-	-
2320	Refined petroleum products	-	-	-	-	-	-	-	-	-	-	-	-
2330	Processing of nuclear fuel	-	-	-	-	-	-	-	-	-	-	-	-
241	Basic chemicals	2	2	2	2	24	25	26	26	427	462	464	517
2411	Basic chemicals, except fertilizers	2	2	2	2	24	25	26	26	427	462	464	517
2412	Fertilizers and nitrogen compounds	-	-	-	-	-	-	-	-	-	-	-	-
2413	Plastics in primary forms; synthetic rubber	-	-	-	-	-	-	-	-	-	-	-	-
242	Other chemicals	12	15	18	18	518	560	625	689	6888	8823	9374	11462
2421	Pesticides and other agro-chemical products	-	-	-	-	-	-	-	-	-	-	-	-
2422	Paints, varnishes, printing ink and mastics	2	3	3	3	35	58	79	95	357	773	1360	1625
2423	Pharmaceuticals, medicinal chemicals, etc.	-	-	1	2	-	-	52	152	-	-	1189	2575
2424	Soap, cleaning & cosmetic preparations	6	9	8	7	234	287	272	228	3153	5338	3831	4054
2429	Other chemical products n.e.c.	4	3	6	6	249	215	222	214	3379	2712	2994	3208
2430	Man-made fibres	-	-	-	-	-	-	-	-	-	-	-	-
251	Rubber products	2	2	2	1	27	27	27	23	326	387	443	431
2511	Rubber tyres and tubes	2	2	2	1	27	27	27	23	326	387	443	431
2519	Other rubber products	-	-	-	-	-	-	-	-	-	-	-	-
2520	Plastic products	11	12	12	11	551	555	502	564	4088	5302	5466	5268
2610	Glass and glass products	3	4	5	4	89	92	97	69	956	1116	1575	931
269	Non-metallic mineral products n.e.c.	43	47	46	43	1863	2141	1941	1737	20055	26085	30836	26056
2691	Pottery, china and earthenware	-	-	-	-	-	-	-	-	-	-	-	-
2692	Refractory ceramic products	3	3	3	3	344	385	281	271	3563	4493	5171	4607
2693	Struct.non-refractory clay; ceramic products	32	37	35	32	1123	1390	1255	1048	10166	14557	16025	13114
2694	Cement, lime and plaster	3	2	2	2	248	225	222	244	4138	4536	5884	5093
2695	Articles of concrete, cement and plaster	-	-	-	-	-	-	-	-	-	-	-	-
2696	Cutting, shaping & finishing of stone	5	5	6	6	148	141	183	174	2187	2499	3756	3242
2699	Other non-metallic mineral products n.e.c.	-	-	-	-	-	-	-	-	-	-	-	-
2710	Basic iron and steel	2	2	1	2	33	42	35	34	438	603	600	648
2720	Basic precious and non-ferrous metals	-	-	-	-	-	-	-	-	-	-	-	-
273	Casting of metals	-	-	-	-	-	-	-	-	-	-	-	-
2731	Casting of iron and steel	-	-	-	-	-	-	-	-	-	-	-	-
2732	Casting of non-ferrous metals	-	-	-	-	-	-	-	-	-	-	-	-
281	Struct.metal products;tanks;steam generators	5	5	5	5	183	153	150	104	1943	2349	2497	2032
2811	Structural metal products	5	5	5	5	183	153	150	104	1943	2349	2497	2032
2812	Tanks, reservoirs and containers of metal	-	-	-	-	-	-	-	-	-	-	-	-
2813	Steam generators	-	-	-	-	-	-	-	-	-	-	-	-
289	Other metal products; metal working services	9	9	9	8	446	403	305	307	5041	5126	3846	3958
2891	Metal forging/pressing/stamping/roll-forming	-	-	-	-	-	-	-	-	-	-	-	-
2892	Treatment & coating of metals	-	-	-	-	-	-	-	-	-	-	-	-
2893	Cutlery, hand tools and general hardware	1	1	1	1	41	43	53	56	553	526	616	618
2899	Other fabricated metal products n.e.c.	8	8	8	7	405	360	252	251	4488	4600	3230	3340
291	General purpose machinery	2	3	2	1	74	97	79	79	595	1637	1127	1074
2911	Engines & turbines (not for transport equipment)	-	-	-	-	-	-	-	-	-	-	-	-
2912	Pumps, compressors, taps and valves	-	-	-	-	-	-	-	-	-	-	-	-
2913	Bearings, gears, gearing & driving elements	1	1	-	-	5	3	-	-	66	36	-	-
2914	Ovens, furnaces and furnace burners	1	2	2	1	69	94	79	79	529	1601	1127	1074
2915	Lifting and handling equipment	-	-	-	-	-	-	-	-	-	-	-	-
2919	Other general purpose machinery	-	-	-	-	-	-	-	-	-	-	-	-
292	Special purpose machinery	-	-	-	-	-	-	-	-	-	-	-	-
2921	Agricultural and forestry machinery	-	-	-	-	-	-	-	-	-	-	-	-
2922	Machine tools	-	-	-	-	-	-	-	-	-	-	-	-
2923	Machinery for metallurgy	-	-	-	-	-	-	-	-	-	-	-	-
2924	Machinery for mining & construction	-	-	-	-	-	-	-	-	-	-	-	-
2925	Food/beverage/tobacco processing machinery	-	-	-	-	-	-	-	-	-	-	-	-
2926	Machinery for textile, apparel and leather	-	-	-	-	-	-	-	-	-	-	-	-
2927	Weapons and ammunition	-	-	-	-	-	-	-	-	-	-	-	-
2929	Other special purpose machinery	-	-	-	-	-	-	-	-	-	-	-	-

continued

Eritrea

ISIC Revision 3		Number of establishments					Number of employees					Wages and salaries paid to employees				
			(number)					(number)					(thousands of Eritrean Nakfa)			
ISIC	Industry	Note	2003	2004	2005	2006	Note	2003	2004	2005	2006	Note	2003	2004	2005	2006
2930	Domestic appliances n.e.c.		-	-	-	-		-	-	-	-		-	-	-	-
3000	Office, accounting and computing machinery		-	-	-	-		-	-	-	-		-	-	-	-
3110	Electric motors, generators and transformers		-	-	-	-		-	-	-	-		-	-	-	-
3120	Electricity distribution & control apparatus		-	-	-	-		-	-	-	-		-	-	-	-
3130	Insulated wire and cable		-	-	-	-		-	-	-	-		-	-	-	-
3140	Accumulators, primary cells and batteries		2	2	-	-		17	20	-	-		122	219	-	-
3150	Lighting equipment and electric lamps		-	-	-	-		-	-	-	-		-	-	-	-
3190	Other electrical equipment n.e.c.		-	-	-	-		-	-	-	-		-	-	-	-
3210	Electronic valves, tubes, etc.		-	-	-	-		-	-	-	-		-	-	-	-
3220	TV/radio transmitters; line comm. apparatus		-	-	-	-		-	-	-	-		-	-	-	-
3230	TV and radio receivers and associated goods		-	-	-	-		-	-	-	-		-	-	-	-
331	Medical, measuring, testing appliances, etc.		3	3	-	-		100	105	-	-		1192	1507	-	-
3311	Medical, surgical and orthopaedic equipment		2	2	-	-		40	50	-	-		289	289	-	-
3312	Measuring/testing/navigating appliances,etc.		1	1	-	-		60	55	-	-		902	1218	-	-
3313	Industrial process control equipment		-	-	-	-		-	-	-	-		-	-	-	-
3320	Optical instruments & photographic equipment		-	-	-	-		-	-	-	-		-	-	-	-
3330	Watches and clocks		-	-	-	-		-	-	-	-		-	-	-	-
3410	Motor vehicles		1	1	1	1		41	54	51	43		520	512	567	602
3420	Automobile bodies, trailers & semi-trailers		1	1	1	1		83	106	90	72		1526	2008	2111	1747
3430	Parts/accessories for automobiles		3	4	3	4		106	108	31	75		1413	1793	190	2339
351	Building and repairing of ships and boats		-	-	-	-		-	-	-	-		-	-	-	-
3511	Building and repairing of ships		-	-	-	-		-	-	-	-		-	-	-	-
3512	Building/repairing of pleasure/sport. boats		-	-	-	-		-	-	-	-		-	-	-	-
3520	Railway/tramway locomotives & rolling stock		-	-	-	-		-	-	-	-		-	-	-	-
3530	Aircraft and spacecraft		-	-	-	-		-	-	-	-		-	-	-	-
359	Transport equipment n.e.c.		-	-	-	-		-	-	-	-		-	-	-	-
3591	Motorcycles		-	-	-	-		-	-	-	-		-	-	-	-
3592	Bicycles and invalid carriages		-	-	-	-		-	-	-	-		-	-	-	-
3599	Other transport equipment n.e.c.		-	-	-	-		-	-	-	-		-	-	-	-
3610	Furniture		25	29	29	27		1354	1524	1561	1751		20749	27817	28418	32941
369	Manufacturing n.e.c.		-	-	-	-		-	-	-	-		-	-	-	-
3691	Jewellery and related articles		-	-	-	-		-	-	-	-		-	-	-	-
3692	Musical instruments		-	-	-	-		-	-	-	-		-	-	-	-
3693	Sports goods		-	-	-	-		-	-	-	-		-	-	-	-
3694	Games and toys		-	-	-	-		-	-	-	-		-	-	-	-
3699	Other manufacturing n.e.c.		-	-	-	-		-	-	-	-		-	-	-	-
3710	Recycling of metal waste and scrap		-	-	-	-		-	-	-	-		-	-	-	-
3720	Recycling of non-metal waste and scrap		-	-	-	-		-	-	-	-		-	-	-	-
D	Total manufacturing	a/	252	276	293	282	a/	13528	14485	13801	13684	a/	154230	187896	188186	205160

a/ Sum of available data.

ISIC Revision 3		Output in producers' prices					Value added in producers' prices					Gross fixed capital formation		
			(millions of Eritrean Nakfa)					(millions of Eritrean Nakfa)					(millions of Eritrean Nakfa)	
ISIC	Industry	Note	2003	2004	2005	2006	Note	2003	2004	2005	2006	Note	2005	2006
151	Processed meat,fish,fruit,vegetables,fats		51.0	74.7	23.9	15.6		4.7	23.5	5.4	1.8		58.2	25.5
1511	Processing/preserving of meat		41.1	54.6	10.7	11.2		2.4	20.5	-0.7	1.9		57.0	19.1
1512	Processing/preserving of fish		8.1	8.8	5.6	4.4		1.4	-1.3	-0.8	0.2		1.2	6.4
1513	Processing/preserving of fruit & vegetables		-	-	-	-		-	-	-	-		-	-
1514	Vegetable and animal oils and fats		1.8	11.3	7.6	...		0.9	4.3	6.9	-0.4		-	-0.1
1520	Dairy products		78.1	82.8	70.2	70.1		8.9	11.3	5.4	13.5		0.4	2.8
153	Grain mill products; starches; animal feeds		171.2	185.7	212.3	153.7		-140.6	-153.7	-276.8	-253.5		136.3	42.5
1531	Grain mill products		128.4	134.5	152.6	114.5		-145.5	-164.2	-291.7	-266.4		135.4	42.5
1532	Starches and starch products		-	-	-	-		-	-	-	-		-	-
1533	Prepared animal feeds		42.8	51.2	59.7	39.2		4.9	10.5	14.9	12.9		0.9	0.1
154	Other food products		161.3	188.7	238.2	218.8		38.3	54.1	73.5	54.9		7.3	3.2
1541	Bakery products		118.4	99.2	129.0	123.9		27.4	27.2	34.0	28.2		6.8	2.4
1542	Sugar		-	-	-	-		-	-	-	-		-	-
1543	Cocoa, chocolate and sugar confectionery		15.2	13.9	11.6	9.1		5.7	5.3	4.9	0.3		-	-
1544	Macaroni, noodles & similar products		27.7	57.9	74.5	58.7		5.2	17.2	27.7	22.5		0.2	0.8
1549	Other food products n.e.c.		-	17.7	23.1	27.0		-	4.3	6.9	3.8		0.3	-
155	Beverages		591.8	877.5	671.3	631.4		365.3	427.3	428.4	392.1		19.4	17.2
1551	Distilling, rectifying & blending of spirits		-	-	-	-		-	-	-	-		-	-
1552	Wines		24.0	33.5	34.2	22.2		14.8	14.6	19.4	10.9		0.7	-
1553	Malt liquors and malt		328.5	566.3	520.5	474.2		253.5	303.8	351.8	321.2		0.9	11.2
1554	Soft drinks; mineral waters		239.4	277.7	116.7	135.0		97.0	108.9	57.2	60.1		17.9	5.9
1600	Tobacco products		163.5	185.7	221.3	89.7		120.5	104.2	160.9	54.5		-	0.8
171	Spinning, weaving and finishing of textiles		65.6	71.7	79.0	133.1		32.0	34.8	36.0	59.0		91.8	52.7
1711	Textile fibre preparation; textile weaving		-	-	-	-		-	-	-	-		-	-
1712	Finishing of textiles		65.6	71.7	79.0	133.1		32.0	34.8	36.0	59.0		91.8	52.7
172	Other textiles		4.7	3.3	-	-		2.0	1.1	-	-		-	-
1721	Made-up textile articles, except apparel		-	-	-	-		-	-	-	-		-	-
1722	Carpets and rugs		4.5	3.3	-	-		1.9	1.1	-	-		-	-
1723	Cordage, rope, twine and netting		-	-	-	-		-	-	-	-		-	-
1729	Other textiles n.e.c.		0.1	-	-	-		0.1	-	-	-		-	-
1730	Knitted and crocheted fabrics and articles		8.7	14.8	23.3	15.7		6.1	7.6	16.6	9.5		6.4	0.3
1810	Wearing apparel, except fur apparel		13.9	26.0	22.6	15.7		7.3	13.1	9.2	5.2		0.5	0.1
1820	Dressing & dyeing of fur; processing of fur		-	-	-	-		-	-	-	-		-	-
191	Tanning, dressing and processing of leather		33.4	41.9	48.9	47.6		8.4	12.8	12.3	9.4		0.7	12.1
1911	Tanning and dressing of leather		32.6	40.7	47.7	46.8		8.0	12.3	12.0	9.0		0.7	12.1
1912	Luggage, handbags, etc.; saddlery & harness		0.8	1.2	1.2	0.9		0.4	0.4	0.3	0.4		-	-
1920	Footwear		49.2	56.4	76.9	91.8		19.1	24.7	34.8	41.2		5.0	3.4
2010	Sawmilling and planing of wood		-	-	-	-		-	-	-	-		-	-
202	Products of wood, cork, straw, etc.		-	-	-	-		-	-	-	-		-	-
2021	Veneer sheets, plywood, particle board, etc.		-	-	-	-		-	-	-	-		-	-
2022	Builders' carpentry and joinery		-	-	-	-		-	-	-	-		-	-
2023	Wooden containers		-	-	-	-		-	-	-	-		-	-
2029	Other wood products; articles of cork/straw		-	-	-	-		-	-	-	-		-	-
210	Paper and paper products		11.8	13.0	12.1	9.1		4.9	5.8	6.0	5.0		0.1	0.3
2101	Pulp, paper and paperboard		1.9	2.5	2.6	3.5		0.9	0.8	1.0	1.9		0.1	0.3
2102	Corrugated paper and paperboard		9.9	10.5	9.5	5.6		4.1	5.0	5.0	3.2		-	-
2109	Other articles of paper and paperboard		-	-	-	-		-	-	-	-		-	-
221	Publishing		-	-	-	-		-	-	-	-		-	-
2211	Publishing of books and other publications		-	-	-	-		-	-	-	-		-	-
2212	Publishing of newspapers, journals, etc.		-	-	-	-		-	-	-	-		-	-
2213	Publishing of recorded media		-	-	-	-		-	-	-	-		-	-
2219	Other publishing		-	-	-	-		-	-	-	-		-	-

continued

ISIC	Industry	Note	Output in producers' prices (millions of Eritrean Nakfa) 2003	2004	2005	2006	Note	Value added in producers' prices (millions of Eritrean Nakfa) 2003	2004	2005	2006	Note	Gross fixed capital formation (millions of Eritrean Nakfa) 2005	2006
222	Printing and related service activities		45.4	63.7	86.9	80.6		25.1	34.4	41.6	35.7		47.8	1.6
2221	Printing		45.4	63.7	86.9	80.6		25.1	34.4	41.6	35.7		47.8	1.6
2222	Service activities related to printing		-	-	-	-		-	-	-	-		-	-
2230	Reproduction of recorded media		-	-	-	-		-	-	-	-		-	-
2310	Coke oven products		-	-	-	-		-	-	-	-		-	-
2320	Refined petroleum products		-	-	-	-		-	-	-	-		-	-
2330	Processing of nuclear fuel		-	-	-	-		-	-	-	-		-	-
241	Basic chemicals		3.6	4.3	8.4	3.7		2.3	2.9	6.9	2.7		-	-
2411	Basic chemicals, except fertilizers		3.6	4.3	8.4	3.7		2.3	2.9	6.9	2.7		-	-
2412	Fertilizers and nitrogen compounds		-	-	-	-		-	-	-	-		-	-
2413	Plastics in primary forms; synthetic rubber		-	-	-	-		-	-	-	-		-	-
242	Other chemicals		148.0	172.3	205.9	191.1		59.3	64.3	63.3	73.5		12.2	26.4
2421	Pesticides and other agro-chemical products		-	-	-	-		-	-	-	-		-	-
2422	Paints, varnishes, printing ink and mastics		7.3	13.5	36.9	38.4		2.0	5.1	18.8	23.6		2.8	3.4
2423	Pharmaceuticals, medicinal chemicals, etc.		-	-	9.7	27.8		-	-	3.9	4.2		1.7	6.0
2424	Soap, cleaning & cosmetic preparations		124.2	143.6	141.0	104.7		52.6	52.5	31.0	36.1		7.7	16.6
2429	Other chemical products n.e.c.		16.4	15.2	18.3	20.2		4.7	6.7	9.6	9.6		0.1	0.3
2430	Man-made fibres		-	-	-	-		-	-	-	-		-	-
251	Rubber products		6.0	20.3	19.4	20.5		1.9	5.0	8.2	5.2		0.6	0.8
2511	Rubber tyres and tubes		6.0	20.3	19.4	20.5		1.9	5.0	8.2	5.2		0.6	0.8
2519	Other rubber products		-	-	-	-		-	-	-	-		-	-
2520	Plastic products		49.4	65.8	63.4	50.7		18.7	23.2	22.6	19.9		1.5	5.4
2610	Glass and glass products		6.1	12.5	15.0	10.9		1.9	2.3	4.1	2.4		1.5	0.3
269	Non-metallic mineral products n.e.c.		172.5	213.6	251.0	207.0		61.2	81.0	97.6	67.3		33.3	20.3
2691	Pottery, china and earthenware		-	-	-	-		-	-	-	-		-	-
2692	Refractory ceramic products		19.6	23.0	25.5	34.8		8.8	10.0	8.3	15.4		4.0	3.9
2693	Struct.non-refractory clay; ceramic products		77.4	96.7	113.2	93.1		34.9	33.0	46.8	34.9		19.3	12.7
2694	Cement, lime and plaster		57.7	66.7	72.5	60.0		9.9	23.7	19.4	8.9		0.1	0.3
2695	Articles of concrete, cement and plaster		-	-	-	-		-	-	-	-		-	-
2696	Cutting, shaping & finishing of stone		17.8	27.2	39.8	19.1		7.6	14.3	23.1	8.1		9.9	3.3
2699	Other non-metallic mineral products n.e.c.		-	-	-	-		-	-	-	-		-	-
2710	Basic iron and steel		29.8	49.7	31.6	3.4		10.8	16.1	10.4	0.9		0.5	-
2720	Basic precious and non-ferrous metals		-	-	-	-		-	-	-	-		-	-
273	Casting of metals		-	-	-	-		-	-	-	-		-	-
2731	Casting of iron and steel		-	-	-	-		-	-	-	-		-	-
2732	Casting of non-ferrous metals		-	-	-	-		-	-	-	-		-	-
281	Struct.metal products;tanks;steam generators		20.7	24.9	27.3	19.5		7.7	10.8	10.8	9.9		0.5	0.5
2811	Structural metal products		20.7	24.9	27.3	19.5		7.7	10.8	10.8	9.9		0.5	0.5
2812	Tanks, reservoirs and containers of metal		-	-	-	-		-	-	-	-		-	-
2813	Steam generators		-	-	-	-		-	-	-	-		-	-
289	Other metal products; metal working services		27.0	32.3	19.7	15.3		11.2	17.3	6.0	0.3		5.5	5.5
2891	Metal forging/pressing/stamping/roll-forming		-	-	-	-		-	-	-	-		-	-
2892	Treatment & coating of metals		-	-	-	-		-	-	-	-		-	-
2893	Cutlery, hand tools and general hardware		5.2	2.1	3.8	1.0		2.2	1.2	0.8	0.6		-	-
2899	Other fabricated metal products n.e.c.		21.8	30.2	15.8	14.3		9.0	16.1	5.3	-0.3		5.5	5.5
291	General purpose machinery		24.1	30.5	24.7	31.1		7.9	9.7	11.1	22.8		0.1	-
2911	Engines & turbines (not for transport equipment)		-	-	-	-		-	-	-	-		-	-
2912	Pumps, compressors, taps and valves		-	-	-	-		-	-	-	-		-	-
2913	Bearings, gears, gearing & driving elements		0.3	0.2	-	-		0.3	0.1	-	-		-	-
2914	Ovens, furnaces and furnace burners		23.8	30.3	24.7	31.1		7.6	9.6	11.1	22.8		0.1	-
2915	Lifting and handling equipment		-	-	-	-		-	-	-	-		-	-
2919	Other general purpose machinery		-	-	-	-		-	-	-	-		-	-

292	Special purpose machinery		-	-	-	-		-	-	-	-		-	-
2921	Agricultural and forestry machinery		-	-	-	-		-	-	-	-		-	-
2922	Machine tools		-	-	-	-		-	-	-	-		-	-
2923	Machinery for metallurgy		-	-	-	-		-	-	-	-		-	-
2924	Machinery for mining & construction		-	-	-	-		-	-	-	-		-	-
2925	Food/beverage/tobacco processing machinery		-	-	-	-		-	-	-	-		-	-
2926	Machinery for textile, apparel and leather		-	-	-	-		-	-	-	-		-	-
2927	Weapons and ammunition		-	-	-	-		-	-	-	-		-	-
2929	Other special purpose machinery		-	-	-	-		-	-	-	-		-	-
2930	Domestic appliances n.e.c.		-	-	-	-		-	-	-	-		-	-
3000	Office, accounting and computing machinery		-	-	-	-		-	-	-	-		-	-
3110	Electric motors, generators and transformers		-	-	-	-		-	-	-	-		-	-
3120	Electricity distribution & control apparatus		-	-	-	-		-	-	-	-		-	-
3130	Insulated wire and cable		-	-	-	-		-	-	-	-		-	-
3140	Accumulators, primary cells and batteries		0.7	0.8	-	-		0.2	0.2	-	-		-	-
3150	Lighting equipment and electric lamps		-	-	-	-		-	-	-	-		-	-
3190	Other electrical equipment n.e.c.		-	-	-	-		-	-	-	-		-	-
3210	Electronic valves, tubes, etc.		-	-	-	-		-	-	-	-		-	-
3220	TV/radio transmitters; line comm. apparatus		-	-	-	-		-	-	-	-		-	-
3230	TV and radio receivers and associated goods		-	-	-	-		-	-	-	-		-	-
331	Medical, measuring, testing appliances, etc.		10.8	13.3	-	-		7.6	7.7	-	-		-	-
3311	Medical, surgical and orthopaedic equipment		2.0	2.0	-	-		0.5	0.8	-	-		-	-
3312	Measuring/testing/navigating appliances,etc.		8.7	11.3	-	-		7.1	6.9	-	-		-	-
3313	Industrial process control equipment		-	-	-	-		-	-	-	-		-	-
3320	Optical instruments & photographic equipment		-	-	-	-		-	-	-	-		-	-
3330	Watches and clocks		-	-	-	-		-	-	-	-		-	-
3410	Motor vehicles		2.8	3.6	3.7	3.4		1.0	1.9	0.7	1.6		-	-
3420	Automobile bodies, trailers & semi-trailers		13.4	18.6	17.6	5.9		2.2	0.4	5.0	1.4		5.1	-5.3
3430	Parts/accessories for automobiles		9.2	7.6	5.8	14.5		6.5	3.7	4.2	6.1		0.2	0.4
351	Building and repairing of ships and boats		-	-	-	-		-	-	-	-		-	-
3511	Building and repairing of ships		-	-	-	-		-	-	-	-		-	-
3512	Building/repairing of pleasure/sport. boats		-	-	-	-		-	-	-	-		-	-
3520	Railway/tramway locomotives & rolling stock		-	-	-	-		-	-	-	-		-	-
3530	Aircraft and spacecraft		-	-	-	-		-	-	-	-		-	-
359	Transport equipment n.e.c.		-	-	-	-		-	-	-	-		-	-
3591	Motorcycles		-	-	-	-		-	-	-	-		-	-
3592	Bicycles and invalid carriages		-	-	-	-		-	-	-	-		-	-
3599	Other transport equipment n.e.c.		-	-	-	-		-	-	-	-		-	-
3610	Furniture		220.6	210.5	259.4	240.2		98.7	94.6	120.6	113.4		33.1	14.9
369	Manufacturing n.e.c.		-	-	-	-		-	-	-	-		-	-
3691	Jewellery and related articles		-	-	-	-		-	-	-	-		-	-
3692	Musical instruments		-	-	-	-		-	-	-	-		-	-
3693	Sports goods		-	-	-	-		-	-	-	-		-	-
3694	Games and toys		-	-	-	-		-	-	-	-		-	-
3699	Other manufacturing n.e.c.		-	-	-	-		-	-	-	-		-	-
3710	Recycling of metal waste and scrap		-	-	-	-		-	-	-	-		-	-
3720	Recycling of non-metal waste and scrap		-	-	-	-		-	-	-	-		-	-
D	Total manufacturing	a/	2194.5	2766.6	2739.7	2390.1	a/	801.0	942.1	924.6	755.9	a/	467.7	231.6

a/ Sum of available data.

Estonia

Supplier of information:
Statistics Estonia, Tallinn.

Basic source of data:
Annual survey.

Major deviations from ISIC (Revision 3):
None reported.

Reference period:
Calendar year.

Scope:
All enterprises.

Method of data collection:
Questionnaires.

Type of enumeration:
Sample survey.

Adjusted for non-response:
Yes.

Concepts and definitions of variables:
Number of employees includes home workers, paid working proprietors, seasonal workers, apprentices on the pay-roll, persons on strike or on short-term leave.
Wages and salaries paid to employees includes employers' contributions paid to social security, pension and insurance schemes as well as the benefits received by employees under these schemes and severance and termination pay.
Value added is valued at basic prices.
Gross fixed capital formation includes data on enterprises and self-employed entrepreneurs.

Related national publications:
Statistical Yearbook of Estonia; Financial Statistics of Enterprises, both published by Statistics Estonia, Tallinn.

Estonia

ISIC Revision 3		Number of enterprises					Number of employees					Wages and salaries paid to employees				
			(number)					(thousands)					(millions of Estonian Krooni)			
ISIC	Industry	Note	2003	2004	2005	2006	Note	2003	2004	2005	2006	Note	2003	2004	2005	2006
151	Processed meat,fish,fruit,vegetables,fats		155	159	150	136		7.2	6.7	6.1	...		462.2	469.6	475.5	...
1511	Processing/preserving of meat		58	62	59	54		2.7	2.6	2.8	2.9		189.9	206.2	230.1	274.4
1512	Processing/preserving of fish		78	75	65	54		3.9	3.4	2.6	2.4		224.9	208.2	183.3	180.2
1513	Processing/preserving of fruit & vegetables		14	17	20	21		...	...	...	0.7		...	...	...	68.1
1514	Vegetable and animal oils and fats		5	5	6	7		...	...	...	...		...	...	...	...
1520	Dairy products		28	31	30	31		2.6	2.7	2.6	2.6		221.2	241.2	268.5	289.1
153	Grain mill products; starches; animal feeds		34	33	31	30		0.5	0.3	0.4	...		31.4	30.4	36.6	...
1531	Grain mill products		19	16	14	12		...	...	...	...		...	...	...	...
1532	Starches and starch products		1	2	1	1		...	...	...	...		...	...	...	...
1533	Prepared animal feeds		14	15	16	17		0.3	0.2	0.3	0.3		19.2	20.8	26.5	28.9
154	Other food products		193	170	173	153		6.1	5.8	6.2	6.0		364.1	388.0	442.6	494.1
1541	Bakery products		150	143	143	126		4.9	4.7	4.9	4.8		257.9	281.7	311.4	356.4
1542	Sugar		-	-	-	-		-	-	-	-		-	-	-	-
1543	Cocoa, chocolate and sugar confectionery		6	6	7	8		...	...	...	...		...	...	...	...
1544	Macaroni, noodles & similar products		-	-	-	-		-	-	-	-		-	-	-	-
1549	Other food products n.e.c.		37	21	23	19		...	...	...	...		...	...	...	...
155	Beverages		42	44	41	37		2.2	2.1	2.1	2.1		219.4	229.3	262.5	295.7
1551	Distilling, rectifying & blending of spirits		11	11	12	10		...	...	...	...		...	...	...	...
1552	Wines		7	6	6	6		...	...	...	...		...	...	...	...
1553	Malt liquors and malt		10	9	8	7		0.9	0.9	...	...		93.1	109.2	...	...
1554	Soft drinks; mineral waters		14	18	15	14		0.6	0.5	0.6	0.5		66.7	53.6	70.5	61.0
1600	Tobacco products		-	-	-	-		-	-	-	-		-	-	-	-
171	Spinning, weaving and finishing of textiles		17	22	18	23		6.5	5.8	5.0	4.1		361.8	350.0	319.9	276.3
1711	Textile fibre preparation; textile weaving		14	17	15	17		...	...	...	3.9		...	...	...	259.8
1712	Finishing of textiles		3	5	3	6		...	...	...	0.2		...	...	...	16.5
172	Other textiles		98	107	123	136		3.8	4.3	4.2	4.1		240.1	283.8	302.0	344.0
1721	Made-up textile articles, except apparel		77	79	88	98		3.2	3.4	3.3	3.2		191.5	223.2	231.7	259.8
1722	Carpets and rugs		8	11	13	14		0.4	0.6	...	0.5		29.8	38.4	...	52.2
1723	Cordage, rope, twine and netting		4	3	5	5		...	...	...	...		...	...	...	...
1729	Other textiles n.e.c.		9	14	17	19		...	...	0.2	...		...	...	16.6	...
1730	Knitted and crocheted fabrics and articles		55	61	62	67		0.9	0.9	0.9	...		48.4	52.0	51.6	...
1810	Wearing apparel, except fur apparel		393	388	383	378		12.9	12.2	...	...		670.7	682.1	...	...
1820	Dressing & dyeing of fur; processing of fur		12	10	10	8		...	...	...	...		...	...	...	...
191	Tanning, dressing and processing of leather		44	50	48	47		0.7	0.7	0.7	0.7		33.1	40.7	39.5	41.2
1911	Tanning and dressing of leather		3	6	7	10		...	0.1	0.1	0.2		...	6.6	6.7	7.5
1912	Luggage, handbags, etc.; saddlery & harness		41	44	41	37		...	0.6	0.6	0.5		...	34.1	32.8	33.7
1920	Footwear		22	22	23	18		...	1.4	1.2	1.0		...	84.7	80.4	77.4
2010	Sawmilling and planing of wood		544	573	498	484		7.9	7.9	7.4	6.7		453.1	535.8	579.3	604.3
202	Products of wood, cork, straw, etc.		483	498	544	607		10.0	10.7	11.2	12.5		685.9	802.5	952.2	1225.0
2021	Veneer sheets, plywood, particle board, etc.		15	15	18	18		2.0	2.1	2.2	2.2		136.9	165.3	204.5	223.3
2022	Builders' carpentry and joinery		300	319	343	381		5.8	6.0	6.6	8.0		401.1	460.4	566.3	801.3
2023	Wooden containers		56	53	69	69		1.0	1.2	1.2	1.2		71.8	87.5	91.6	107.7
2029	Other wood products; articles of cork/straw		112	111	114	139		1.2	1.4	1.2	1.1		76.1	89.3	89.8	92.7
210	Paper and paper products		47	46	52	56		1.7	1.7	1.8	1.9		149.1	155.4	184.2	221.3
2101	Pulp, paper and paperboard		5	4	3	4		...	...	...	0.7		...	...	...	93.3
2102	Corrugated paper and paperboard		20	17	20	31		...	...	0.4	0.5		...	...	46.6	53.8
2109	Other articles of paper and paperboard		22	25	29	21		0.6	0.7	...	0.7		49.4	55.9	...	74.2
221	Publishing		234	262	270	289		3.2	3.2	3.3	3.4		368.2	402.5	442.1	514.2
2211	Publishing of books and other publications		105	113	121	131		0.9	0.9	0.9	0.9		87.3	94.6	104.1	108.8
2212	Publishing of newspapers, journals, etc.		81	81	83	92		2.1	2.1	2.1	2.2		262.6	291.7	316.7	375.1
2213	Publishing of recorded media		8	10	11	11		...	...	...	...		...	0.4	0.7	0.8
2219	Other publishing		40	58	55	55		0.2	0.2	0.3	0.3		18.3	15.8	20.6	29.5

222	Printing and related service activities	168	195	210	241	2.3	2.6	2.8	2.9	243.4	266.4	302.5	362.7
2221	Printing	163	163	174	188	2.1	2.4	2.6	...	223.2	243.6	288.0	...
2222	Service activities related to printing	5	32	36	53	0.2	0.2	0.2	...	20.2	22.8	14.5	...
2230	Reproduction of recorded media	8	12	14	12	...	0.1	0.1	...	1.9	4.1	6.4	3.1
2310	Coke oven products	-	-	-	-	-	-	-	-	-	-	-	-
2320	Refined petroleum products	5	5	7	4	1.0	1.0	1.0	1.1	54.6	64.6	71.6	97.2
2330	Processing of nuclear fuel	-	-	-	-	-	-	-	-	-	-	-	-
241	Basic chemicals	29	32	29	28	1.0	1.1	1.2	1.1	74.7	93.9	113.4	123.4
2411	Basic chemicals, except fertilizers	22	22	18	16	0.5	0.4	0.5	...	38.7	39.1	46.5	...
2412	Fertilizers and nitrogen compounds	5	7	8	9	...	...	...	0.5	...	...	...	56.9
2413	Plastics in primary forms; synthetic rubber	2	3	3	3	...	...	...	...	...	...	...	...
242	Other chemicals	70	66	68	78	1.8	1.7	1.7	1.8	166.6	183.3	209.6	255.2
2421	Pesticides and other agro-chemical products	3	2	3	5	...	...	...	...	0.2	...	0.1	...
2422	Paints, varnishes, printing ink and mastics	12	12	14	18	0.5	0.6	0.6	0.7	70.4	83.2	93.6	118.9
2423	Pharmaceuticals, medicinal chemicals, etc.	15	15	14	14	0.3	...	0.2	...	29.7	...	35.4	...
2424	Soap, cleaning & cosmetic preparations	23	22	19	17	0.2	0.2	0.2	0.2	16.0	17.5	15.7	19.2
2429	Other chemical products n.e.c.	17	15	18	24	0.8	0.7	0.7	0.7	50.3	49.3	64.8	73.6
2430	Man-made fibres	-	-	-	-	-	-	-	-	-	-	-	-
251	Rubber products	18	17	15	14	0.4	0.4	0.5	0.5	28.3	32.3	38.7	46.8
2511	Rubber tyres and tubes	7	6	6	6	0.1	0.1	0.1	0.1	8.5	8.9	10.4	14.7
2519	Other rubber products	11	11	9	8	0.3	0.3	0.4	0.4	19.8	23.4	28.3	32.1
2520	Plastic products	111	133	138	176	3.3	3.8	4.0	4.7	286.8	336.7	380.3	505.8
2610	Glass and glass products	39	43	50	57	1.0	1.1	1.2	1.3	115.1	128.9	155.3	193.7
269	Non-metallic mineral products n.e.c.	115	119	120	132	3.6	3.7	4.0	4.4	331.8	397.9	490.2	666.3
2691	Pottery, china and earthenware	12	14	14	15	0.2	0.2	...	0.2	10.5	9.5	...	15.9
2692	Refractory ceramic products	2	1	2	2	...	...	...	...	...	...	...	...
2693	Struct.non-refractory clay; ceramic products	6	7	6	9	0.4	0.4	0.4	...	42.4	46.6	56.1	...
2694	Cement, lime and plaster	2	3	3	4	...	...	...	...	...	...	...	...
2695	Articles of concrete, cement and plaster	42	41	46	55	2.3	2.4	2.6	3.0	214.5	268.0	342.5	471.9
2696	Cutting, shaping & finishing of stone	46	48	45	40	0.3	0.3	0.4	0.4	21.7	25.9	30.0	41.1
2699	Other non-metallic mineral products n.e.c.	5	5	4	7	...	...	...	0.1	5.0	5.5	6.0	7.1
2710	Basic iron and steel	1	1	1	3	...	...	...	...	...	...	...	...
2720	Basic precious and non-ferrous metals	2	1	1	2	...	...	...	...	...	...	...	...
273	Casting of metals	8	9	9	10	0.2	...	...	0.3	10.9	...	...	23.0
2731	Casting of iron and steel	3	4	3	3	...	...	...	...	...	...	...	...
2732	Casting of non-ferrous metals	5	5	6	7	...	...	...	...	...	...	...	...
281	Struct.metal products;tanks;steam generators	280	305	323	354	4.9	5.1	5.0	...	377.8	433.4	460.9	...
2811	Structural metal products	224	255	290	314	4.2	4.6	4.5	4.7	321.9	396.1	422.1	546.6
2812	Tanks, reservoirs and containers of metal	54	48	31	38	...	...	...	0.4	...	...	...	48.5
2813	Steam generators	2	2	2	2	...	...	...	...	...	...	...	...
289	Other metal products; metal working services	373	386	409	472	5.3	6.1	6.7	...	403.2	491.7	612.7	...
2891	Metal forging/pressing/stamping/roll-forming	26	34	33	29	...	...	...	...	...	...	...	...
2892	Treatment & coating of metals	146	159	185	230	...	...	...	3.6	...	...	...	385.2
2893	Cutlery, hand tools and general hardware	30	28	29	27	0.8	0.8	0.7	0.5	59.8	61.9	60.7	39.9
2899	Other fabricated metal products n.e.c.	171	165	162	186	2.4	2.4	2.4	2.8	175.3	181.9	218.4	302.2
291	General purpose machinery	110	132	158	162	2.8	2.9	2.8	3.0	227.6	256.4	308.8	365.9
2911	Engines & turbines (not for transport equipment)	5	3	2	4	...	...	...	...	...	...	...	...
2912	Pumps, compressors, taps and valves	21	23	27	29	...	0.5	0.5	0.5	...	45.8	51.2	67.6
2913	Bearings, gears, gearing & driving elements	-	-	1	2	-	-	...	...	-	-	...	...
2914	Ovens, furnaces and furnace burners	4	2	2	2	0.2	...	...	...	16.8	...	...	...
2915	Lifting and handling equipment	21	18	20	24	0.5	...	...	...	45.3	...	...	...
2919	Other general purpose machinery	59	86	106	101	1.7	1.8	1.8	1.7	131.4	144.9	181.0	196.7
292	Special purpose machinery	92	91	91	93	2.2	2.3	2.3	...	175.6	200.4	242.4	...
2921	Agricultural and forestry machinery	41	39	39	32	0.8	0.8	0.8	0.8	54.8	56.1	64.7	83.1
2922	Machine tools	13	15	10	12	0.2	0.2	0.2	0.3	19.6	27.6	33.6	41.2
2923	Machinery for metallurgy	-	-	1	-	-	-	...	-	-	-	...	-
2924	Machinery for mining & construction	3	4	6	5	...	...	...	0.4	...	...	...	41.2
2925	Food/beverage/tobacco processing machinery	13	13	6	8	...	0.3	0.2	0.3	...	28.5	30.4	41.1
2926	Machinery for textile, apparel and leather	3	...	2	...	...	...	...	...	0.8	...	...	...
2927	Weapons and ammunition	1	1	1	2	...	...	...	...	...	...	...	...
2929	Other special purpose machinery	18	19	26	34	0.5	0.4	0.7	0.8	46.9	47.3	71.8	106.8

continued

Estonia

ISIC Revision 3		Number of enterprises					Number of employees					Wages and salaries paid to employees				
			(number)					(thousands)					(millions of Estonian Krooni)			
ISIC	Industry	Note	2003	2004	2005	2006	Note	2003	2004	2005	2006	Note	2003	2004	2005	2006
2930	Domestic appliances n.e.c.		4	2	5	2		...	...	...	...		0.6	...	...	...
3000	Office, accounting and computing machinery		21	20	20	16		0.3	0.3	0.4	0.3		28.0	37.7	48.5	38.1
3110	Electric motors, generators and transformers		22	22	25	27		1.3	1.5	1.8	2.2		154.2	187.1	238.5	327.0
3120	Electricity distribution & control apparatus		15	18	23	21		0.6	0.7	0.8	0.7		62.9	75.1	97.5	86.4
3130	Insulated wire and cable		6	5	6	11		0.5	0.5	0.6	1.3		36.3	39.5	54.9	105.0
3140	Accumulators, primary cells and batteries		3	3	2	3		...	...	...	...		...	...	...	...
3150	Lighting equipment and electric lamps		14	15	13	12		0.2	0.3	0.3	...		14.0	18.3	20.3	...
3190	Other electrical equipment n.e.c.		24	32	34	34		...	...	...	1.7		...	...	...	181.4
3210	Electronic valves, tubes, etc.		43	39	31	40		1.1	1.0	1.1	1.2		71.5	82.0	93.9	115.5
3220	TV/radio transmitters; line comm. apparatus		12	18	15	18		...	...	...	...		...	...	...	...
3230	TV and radio receivers and associated goods		31	33	24	28		...	...	...	...		...	...	...	...
331	Medical, measuring, testing appliances, etc.		114	117	126	127		2.4	1.7	1.8	1.9		201.8	172.6	208.4	241.8
3311	Medical, surgical and orthopaedic equipment		48	50	54	60		0.8	0.8	0.9	0.9		73.7	81.7	102.3	115.5
3312	Measuring/testing/navigating appliances,etc.		54	52	50	43		0.6	0.6	0.6	0.7		42.2	42.9	51.5	61.4
3313	Industrial process control equipment		12	15	22	24		1.0	0.3	0.3	0.3		85.9	48.0	54.6	64.9
3320	Optical instruments & photographic equipment		8	9	9	7		...	...	...	...		1.9	2.4	...	...
3330	Watches and clocks		-	-	1	1		-	-	...	...		-	-	...	...
3410	Motor vehicles		5	5	4	6		0.1	0.1	0.1	0.1		9.0	8.7	16.7	20.2
3420	Automobile bodies, trailers & semi-trailers		15	19	18	26		0.5	0.6	0.6	0.8		36.9	57.2	64.9	93.4
3430	Parts/accessories for automobiles		13	14	12	12		1.3	1.3	1.3	1.3		128.3	141.5	147.9	168.6
351	Building and repairing of ships and boats		74	87	95	110		2.1	2.2	2.4	...		181.7	206.1	267.6	...
3511	Building and repairing of ships		58	69	64	75		1.8	1.9	2.1	2.0		162.6	183.0	239.4	287.5
3512	Building/repairing of pleasure/sport. boats		16	18	31	35		0.3	0.3	0.3	...		19.1	23.1	28.2	...
3520	Railway/tramway locomotives & rolling stock		6	5	5	6		...	...	...	...		...	...	...	...
3530	Aircraft and spacecraft		6	5	4	5		...	...	...	...		...	...	...	...
359	Transport equipment n.e.c.		-	-	-	-		-	-	-	-		-	-	-	-
3591	Motorcycles		-	-	-	-		-	-	-	-		-	-	-	-
3592	Bicycles and invalid carriages		-	-	-	-		-	-	-	-		-	-	-	-
3599	Other transport equipment n.e.c.		-	-	-	-		-	-	-	-		-	-	-	-
3610	Furniture		379	387	438	513		12.1	11.2	10.6	10.2		786.8	810.1	835.1	937.6
369	Manufacturing n.e.c.		86	94	106	103		1.4	1.6	1.6	1.5		92.3	106.4	121.1	126.8
3691	Jewellery and related articles		24	26	29	27		...	0.2	...	...		...	16.1	...	...
3692	Musical instruments		4	5	6	8		...	...	...	...		...	...	...	...
3693	Sports goods		13	12	16	16		0.3	...	0.5	0.5		17.3	...	26.9	36.1
3694	Games and toys		3	7	6	7		...	...	...	...		...	...	...	0.5
3699	Other manufacturing n.e.c.		42	44	49	45		0.7	0.8	0.8	0.7		42.8	50.3	60.0	56.6
3710	Recycling of metal waste and scrap		10	10	15	14		0.2	0.2	0.3	0.2		16.5	35.3	40.2	36.2
3720	Recycling of non-metal waste and scrap		11	12	12	18		0.1	0.1	0.2	0.3		6.0	7.7	20.4	35.9
D	Total manufacturing		4752	4994	5142	5498		127.1	129.0	129.7	131.2		9158.1	10198.3	11475.1	13548.5

Estonia

ISIC Revision 3		Output					Value added					Gross fixed capital formation		
			(millions of Estonian Krooni)					(millions of Estonian Krooni)					(millions of Estonian Krooni)	
ISIC	Industry	Note	2003	2004	2005	2006	Note	2003	2004	2005	2006	Note	2005	2006a/
151	Processed meat,fish,fruit,vegetables,fats		4159.8	4364.5	4859.7	...		891.9	857.6	978.6	...	b/	1168.5	1387.7
1511	Processing/preserving of meat		2053.4	2261.0	2646.2	2939.4		451.7	452.8	515.9	605.3		...	...
1512	Processing/preserving of fish		1447.9	1381.1	1395.4	1529.7		330.6	287.8	323.2	307.8		...	...
1513	Processing/preserving of fruit & vegetables		...	...	...	649.4		...	...	...	166.7		...	...
1514	Vegetable and animal oils and fats		...	...	...	...		...	...	...	...		...	...
1520	Dairy products		2912.4	3875.6	3908.4	4049.6		488.8	380.6	472.2	663.2	b/	...	...
153	Grain mill products; starches; animal feeds		492.6	561.3	559.7	...		89.8	89.0	115.9	...	b/	...	...
1531	Grain mill products		...	...	...	...		...	...	...	...		...	...
1532	Starches and starch products		...	...	...	...		...	...	...	...		...	...
1533	Prepared animal feeds		312.7	359.6	382.9	369.4		53.5	50.7	88.8	87.8		...	...
154	Other food products		1981.8	2107.7	2380.7	2632.4		721.0	736.0	766.7	852.9	b/	...	...
1541	Bakery products		1256.6	1340.3	1451.6	1610.5		492.2	517.3	554.2	625.5		...	...
1542	Sugar		-	-	-	-		-	-	-	-		...	...
1543	Cocoa, chocolate and sugar confectionery		...	...	...	...		...	...	...	...		...	...
1544	Macaroni, noodles & similar products		-	-	-	-		-	-	-	-		...	...
1549	Other food products n.e.c.		...	...	...	...		...	...	...	...		...	...
155	Beverages		2133.8	2277.3	2599.7	3074.4		661.4	695.1	815.6	971.9	b/	...	...
1551	Distilling, rectifying & blending of spirits		...	...	...	...		...	...	...	...		...	...
1552	Wines		...	...	...	...		...	...	...	...		...	...
1553	Malt liquors and malt		935.3	1066.3	...	...		364.4	402.0	...	...		...	...
1554	Soft drinks; mineral waters		668.2	606.4	735.3	585.5		180.8	129.3	175.5	185.9		...	...
1600	Tobacco products		-	-	-	-		-	-	-	-		-	-
171	Spinning, weaving and finishing of textiles		2083.9	1951.4	1656.4	1334.9		682.2	681.8	550.0	451.4	c/	357.9	214.6
1711	Textile fibre preparation; textile weaving		...	...	...	1235.4		...	...	...	413.2		...	...
1712	Finishing of textiles		...	...	...	99.5		...	...	...	38.2		...	...
172	Other textiles		2043.3	2226.0	2162.1	2648.3		600.1	641.9	606.0	733.8	c/	...	...
1721	Made-up textile articles, except apparel		1672.8	1838.1	1792.1	2207.2		499.1	522.8	462.2	577.5		...	...
1722	Carpets and rugs		212.8	217.1	...	286.9		61.5	71.5	...	85.4		...	...
1723	Cordage, rope, twine and netting		...	...	...	...		...	...	...	...		...	...
1729	Other textiles n.e.c.		...	...	86.0	...		...	...	38.5	...		...	...
1730	Knitted and crocheted fabrics and articles		224.3	220.2	201.6	...		90.1	94.6	84.8	...	c/	...	...
1810	Wearing apparel, except fur apparel		2433.2	2410.9	...	...		1051.1	1110.3	...	...	d/	89.4	9.7
1820	Dressing & dyeing of fur; processing of fur		...	...	...	...		...	...	...	...	d/	...	...
191	Tanning, dressing and processing of leather		141.4	173.4	158.6	168.6		57.5	73.3	66.5	65.0	e/	-92.6	8.1
1911	Tanning and dressing of leather		...	37.7	51.2	59.0		...	9.8	10.9	11.1		...	...
1912	Luggage, handbags, etc.; saddlery & harness		...	135.7	107.4	109.6		...	63.5	55.6	53.9		...	...
1920	Footwear		...	288.5	256.8	261.9		...	128.8	116.8	121.2	e/	...	...
2010	Sawmilling and planing of wood		5806.0	7123.6	7882.8	7949.5		1264.4	1484.7	1429.3	1668.6	f/	1242.5	1834.3
202	Products of wood, cork, straw, etc.		5014.1	5730.9	6786.3	8572.7		1583.4	1739.9	2050.2	2635.2	f/	...	...
2021	Veneer sheets, plywood, particle board, etc.		1165.0	1312.8	1572.5	1707.6		465.1	414.7	457.9	495.7		...	...
2022	Builders' carpentry and joinery		2849.5	3282.6	3965.3	5519.4		809.1	960.0	1180.2	1678.0		...	...
2023	Wooden containers		617.9	705.7	785.9	892.3		184.2	230.3	228.1	297.8		...	...
2029	Other wood products; articles of cork/straw		381.7	429.8	462.6	453.4		125.0	134.9	184.0	163.7		...	...
210	Paper and paper products		1475.5	1412.8	1644.2	2189.9		403.1	373.8	373.1	535.3		273.0	235.4
2101	Pulp, paper and paperboard		...	...	...	1018.7		...	...	...	248.9		...	...
2102	Corrugated paper and paperboard		...	...	437.9	527.4		...	...	121.5	149.3		...	...
2109	Other articles of paper and paperboard		459.8	455.8	...	643.8		83.9	105.1	...	137.1		...	...
221	Publishing		1587.9	1725.6	1900.6	2160.7		653.7	715.6	788.1	891.1	g/	358.1	495.2
2211	Publishing of books and other publications		360.2	392.8	420.3	453.5		170.1	172.8	175.1	203.2		...	...
2212	Publishing of newspapers, journals, etc.		1150.8	1234.8	1337.7	1526.3		451.0	509.5	570.4	634.2		...	...
2213	Publishing of recorded media		1.8	7.8	10.7	12.0		0.5	2.7	1.8	3.8		...	...
2219	Other publishing		75.1	90.2	131.9	168.9		32.1	30.6	40.8	49.9		...	...

continued

Estonia

ISIC Revision 3		Output					Value added					Gross fixed capital formation		
			(millions of Estonian Krooni)					(millions of Estonian Krooni)					(millions of Estonian Krooni)	
ISIC	Industry	Note	2003	2004	2005	2006	Note	2003	2004	2005	2006	Note	2005	2006a/
222	Printing and related service activities		1489.8	1626.4	1976.7	2362.1		547.2	571.8	721.9	874.9	g/	...	...
2221	Printing		1372.3	1502.6	1903.1	...		505.7	521.0	686.4	...		...	...
2222	Service activities related to printing		117.5	123.8	73.6	...		41.5	50.8	35.5	...		...	...
2230	Reproduction of recorded media		39.0	47.8	44.2	25.6		12.6	19.3	9.6	3.3	g/	...	...
2310	Coke oven products		-	-	-	-		-	-	-	-	h/	176.9	433.6
2320	Refined petroleum products		533.2	678.9	953.3	1384.4		126.0	215.0	345.8	569.7	h/	...	...
2330	Processing of nuclear fuel		-	-	-	-		-	-	-	-	h/	...	...
241	Basic chemicals		922.9	1411.3	1679.4	1853.7		220.3	308.5	450.3	397.7	i/	227.6	233.2
2411	Basic chemicals, except fertilizers		471.7	583.3	655.5	...		106.7	143.1	168.0	...		...	...
2412	Fertilizers and nitrogen compounds		...	...	...	871.4		...	...	...	184.6		...	...
2413	Plastics in primary forms; synthetic rubber		...	...	...	...		...	...	...	...		...	...
242	Other chemicals		1970.0	2335.6	3049.2	3533.1		602.8	623.7	778.6	863.4	i/	...	...
2421	Pesticides and other agro-chemical products		0.5	...	0.9	...		0.2	...	0.1	...		...	...
2422	Paints, varnishes, printing ink and mastics		1197.2	1504.1	2022.7	2479.8		329.9	357.4	458.3	526.8		...	...
2423	Pharmaceuticals, medicinal chemicals, etc.		177.3	...	272.9	...		100.2	...	74.8	...		...	...
2424	Soap, cleaning & cosmetic preparations		90.4	100.4	97.4	120.8		30.4	46.0	40.4	43.0		...	...
2429	Other chemical products n.e.c.		504.6	470.5	655.3	614.6		142.1	134.6	205.0	197.9		...	...
2430	Man-made fibres		-	-	-	-		-	-	-	-	i/	...	...
251	Rubber products		160.3	197.4	223.1	261.7		59.6	69.0	81.3	96.4	j/	352.3	321.4
2511	Rubber tyres and tubes		80.5	89.2	94.1	106.2		22.9	25.0	31.3	37.8		...	...
2519	Other rubber products		79.8	108.2	129.0	155.5		36.7	44.0	50.0	58.6		...	...
2520	Plastic products		2662.0	2825.2	3259.7	4447.7		695.9	741.6	808.9	1117.6	j/	...	...
2610	Glass and glass products		1118.5	1241.5	1405.4	1728.0		376.5	413.5	460.1	533.1	k/	612.3	1329.3
269	Non-metallic mineral products n.e.c.		2090.5	2570.2	3390.9	4604.1		975.5	1243.9	1586.1	2178.7	k/	...	...
2691	Pottery, china and earthenware		32.7	29.6	...	35.7		19.5	16.1	...	12.1		...	...
2692	Refractory ceramic products		...	...	...	...		...	...	...	...		...	...
2693	Struct.non-refractory clay; ceramic products		351.4	387.5	485.0	...		192.6	226.5	231.0	...		...	...
2694	Cement, lime and plaster		...	...	...	...		...	...	...	...		...	...
2695	Articles of concrete, cement and plaster		1173.3	1511.6	2097.6	2851.2		527.2	686.4	980.9	1384.3		...	...
2696	Cutting, shaping & finishing of stone		79.5	113.6	139.7	198.8		43.9	67.9	72.8	97.4		...	...
2699	Other non-metallic mineral products n.e.c.		39.9	45.1	54.1	78.1		12.9	14.7	14.3	17.1		...	...
2710	Basic iron and steel		...	...	...	...		...	...	...	...	m/	10.1	3.4
2720	Basic precious and non-ferrous metals		...	...	...	...		...	...	...	...	m/	...	...
273	Casting of metals		55.8	...	...	118.4		20.5	...	...	43.9	m/	...	...
2731	Casting of iron and steel		...	...	...	...		...	...	...	...		...	...
2732	Casting of non-ferrous metals		...	...	...	...		...	...	...	...		...	...
281	Struct.metal products;tanks;steam generators		2647.6	2974.5	3534.4	...		705.4	731.2	914.2	...	n/	592.8	1067.1
2811	Structural metal products		2286.5	2766.7	3334.6	4061.8		615.4	677.3	855.0	1178.1		...	...
2812	Tanks, reservoirs and containers of metal		...	...	...	311.6		...	...	...	94.3		...	...
2813	Steam generators		...	...	...	...		...	...	...	...		...	...
289	Other metal products; metal working services		2920.9	3646.6	5138.8	...		997.5	1155.5	1336.1	...	n/	...	...
2891	Metal forging/pressing/stamping/roll-forming		...	...	...	...		...	...	...	...		...	...
2892	Treatment & coating of metals		...	...	...	3528.6		...	...	...	911.1		...	...
2893	Cutlery, hand tools and general hardware		220.7	218.8	205.7	143.8		109.7	112.4	110.3	82.5		...	...
2899	Other fabricated metal products n.e.c.		980.0	966.3	1505.4	1883.0		332.3	345.9	474.5	717.3		...	...
291	General purpose machinery		1128.1	1296.4	1633.2	1986.1		430.0	453.7	626.0	674.9	p/	288.4	225.0
2911	Engines & turbines (not for transport equipment)		...	...	...	...		...	...	...	...		...	...
2912	Pumps, compressors, taps and valves		...	198.3	229.8	279.4		...	89.0	99.0	116.8		...	...
2913	Bearings, gears, gearing & driving elements		-	-	...	...		-	-	...	...		...	...
2914	Ovens, furnaces and furnace burners		75.4	...	...	...		30.1	...	...	...		...	...
2915	Lifting and handling equipment		244.7	...	...	...		95.9	...	...	...		...	...
2919	Other general purpose machinery		665.7	729.2	886.6	1062.3		238.3	236.4	306.3	359.8		...	...

292	Special purpose machinery	1014.9	1240.1	1446.3	...	376.5	408.9	510.2	...	p/	...	...
2921	Agricultural and forestry machinery	319.2	389.8	516.1	593.2	111.7	121.1	151.1	162.3		...	...
2922	Machine tools	232.9	238.4	234.8	274.2	61.1	62.5	80.2	75.9		...	...
2923	Machinery for metallurgy	-	-	...	-	-	-	...	-		...	...
2924	Machinery for mining & construction	...	...	...	197.2	...	...	...	72.0		...	...
2925	Food/beverage/tobacco processing machinery	...	147.0	150.1	176.0	...	58.4	68.2	82.2		...	...
2926	Machinery for textile, apparel and leather	1.7	...	...	...	1.8	...	...	...		...	...
2927	Weapons and ammunition	...	...	...	...	...	...	...	...		...	...
2929	Other special purpose machinery	226.7	277.3	368.0	520.8	80.3	91.5	145.9	199.2		...	...
2930	Domestic appliances n.e.c.	2.7	...	...	...	0.8	...	...	...	p/	...	...
3000	Office, accounting and computing machinery	369.5	455.2	521.9	605.1	52.5	71.3	90.9	82.1		2.3	3.8
3110	Electric motors, generators and transformers	788.0	1119.2	1640.6	2634.1	346.5	387.7	555.4	730.3	q/	319.6	343.4
3120	Electricity distribution & control apparatus	488.5	612.0	855.0	829.7	154.8	183.1	239.1	202.0	q/	...	...
3130	Insulated wire and cable	294.9	541.9	960.8	1032.2	90.4	106.2	147.6	206.1	q/	...	...
3140	Accumulators, primary cells and batteries	...	...	...	...	...	...	...	...	q/	...	...
3150	Lighting equipment and electric lamps	46.1	94.6	123.8	...	24.6	35.6	44.0	...	q/	...	...
3190	Other electrical equipment n.e.c.	...	...	...	571.8	...	...	...	308.4	q/	...	...
3210	Electronic valves, tubes, etc.	708.1	859.4	797.8	1043.9	150.6	204.1	224.5	255.1	r/	281.0	108.4
3220	TV/radio transmitters; line comm. apparatus	...	...	...	...	...	...	...	...	r/	...	...
3230	TV and radio receivers and associated goods	...	...	...	...	...	...	...	...	r/	...	...
331	Medical, measuring, testing appliances, etc.	1162.9	1306.3	1592.0	1541.0	372.8	401.9	457.5	441.2	s/	87.1	81.8
3311	Medical, surgical and orthopaedic equipment	346.6	429.1	509.2	602.7	127.7	171.7	204.0	239.8		...	...
3312	Measuring/testing/navigating appliances,etc.	187.6	190.2	332.9	403.5	78.5	83.6	94.9	112.3		...	...
3313	Industrial process control equipment	628.7	687.0	749.9	534.8	166.6	146.6	158.6	89.1		...	...
3320	Optical instruments & photographic equipment	6.8	10.8	...	...	0.9	3.4	...	...	s/	...	...
3330	Watches and clocks	-	-	...	...	-	-	...	...	s/	...	...
3410	Motor vehicles	40.7	43.5	81.6	106.7	12.6	16.5	34.5	40.2	t/	147.8	64.3
3420	Automobile bodies, trailers & semi-trailers	262.8	381.0	472.7	613.1	73.6	101.8	140.9	174.4	t/	...	...
3430	Parts/accessories for automobiles	1233.9	1294.3	1264.7	1380.1	383.5	410.0	405.7	431.1	t/	...	...
351	Building and repairing of ships and boats	1162.9	1403.6	1790.2	...	372.3	326.4	443.1	...	u/	134.6	449.7
3511	Building and repairing of ships	1015.9	1238.7	1587.3	1842.7	316.5	269.2	373.9	387.5		...	...
3512	Building/repairing of pleasure/sport. boats	147.0	164.9	202.9	...	55.8	57.2	69.2	...		...	...
3520	Railway/tramway locomotives & rolling stock	...	...	...	...	...	...	...	...	u/	...	...
3530	Aircraft and spacecraft	...	...	...	...	...	...	...	...	u/	...	...
359	Transport equipment n.e.c.	-	-	-	-	-	-	-	-	u/	...	...
3591	Motorcycles	-	-	-	-	-	-	-	-		...	...
3592	Bicycles and invalid carriages	-	-	-	-	-	-	-	-		...	...
3599	Other transport equipment n.e.c.	-	-	-	-	-	-	-	-		...	...
3610	Furniture	4575.1	4863.3	5151.3	5697.2	1373.9	1340.7	1487.4	1690.1	v/	295.4	447.9
369	Manufacturing n.e.c.	495.9	563.9	709.0	755.7	189.9	234.1	300.1	313.0	v/	...	...
3691	Jewellery and related articles	...	82.0	...	...	...	37.5	...	...		...	...
3692	Musical instruments	...	...	...	...	...	...	...	...		...	...
3693	Sports goods	68.5	...	138.5	215.3	31.3	...	94.0	120.4		...	...
3694	Games and toys	...	...	...	2.5	...	...	...	1.2		...	...
3699	Other manufacturing n.e.c.	294.0	320.9	420.7	383.1	96.8	112.0	134.0	124.0		...	...
3710	Recycling of metal waste and scrap	276.6	543.3	639.7	1004.7	78.1	110.4	62.6	31.6	w/	101.7	122.5
3720	Recycling of non-metal waste and scrap	24.9	33.3	146.8	147.3	10.7	16.5	59.4	94.4	w/	...	...
D	Total manufacturing	65861.1	76434.3	87605.2	102971.5	20033.7	21847.4	24908.9	29878.9		7026.6	9419.8

a/ Preliminary data.
b/ 151 includes 1520, 153, 154 and 155.
c/ 171 includes 172 and 1730.
d/ 1810 includes 1820.
e/ 191 includes 1920.
f/ 2010 includes 202.
g/ 221 includes 222 and 2230.
h/ 2310 includes 2320 and 2330.
i/ 241 includes 242 and 2430.
j/ 251 includes 2520.
k/ 2610 includes 269.
m/ 2710 includes 2720 and 273.
n/ 281 includes 289.
p/ 291 includes 292 and 2930.
q/ 3110 includes 3120, 3130, 3140, 3150 and 3190.
r/ 3210 includes 3220 and 3230.
s/ 331 includes 3320 and 3330.
t/ 3410 includes 3420 and 3430.
u/ 351 includes 3520, 3530 and 359.
v/ 3610 includes 369.
w/ 3710 includes 3720.

Estonia

ISIC Revision 3		Index numbers of industrial production												
			(2000=100)											
ISIC	Industry	Note	1995	1996	1997	1998	1999	2000	2001	2002	2003	2004	2005	2006
15	Food and beverages		112	104	122	116	93	100	110	112	115	121	127	135
16	Tobacco products		...	...	...	...	...	...	...	...	...	...	...	...
17	Textiles		49	66	80	82	82	100	116	130	142	143	131	134
18	Wearing apparel, fur		84	83	81	86	88	100	110	112	112	108	102	108
19	Leather, leather products and footwear		68	64	73	85	88	100	88	87	91	54	49	48
20	Wood products (excl. furniture)		29	41	56	68	84	100	116	128	140	162	181	192
21	Paper and paper products		34	39	54	65	69	100	109	129	128	134	147	184
22	Printing and publishing		77	65	72	80	94	100	113	128	151	173	191	213
23	Coke,refined petroleum products,nuclear fuel		...	...	...	...	...	...	...	...	...	...	...	...
24	Chemicals and chemical products		128	125	126	105	99	100	103	112	128	161	189	202
25	Rubber and plastics products		39	49	73	84	78	100	133	149	194	201	222	295
26	Non-metallic mineral products		72	70	93	105	87	100	107	118	135	154	189	222
27	Basic metals		55	42	61	92	90	100	153	199	343	268	243	248
28	Fabricated metal products		46	53	67	83	79	100	122	127	162	178	224	267
29	Machinery and equipment n.e.c.		69	66	67	70	67	100	135	162	168	177	199	230
30	Office, accounting and computing machinery		67	82	118	127	112	100	113	141	204	281	384	494
31	Electrical machinery and apparatus		54	55	58	72	84	100	122	144	174	253	353	438
32	Radio,television and communication equipment		29	32	36	53	64	100	53	59	70	102	141	154
33	Medical, precision and optical instruments		27	25	35	60	75	100	80	90	112	144	167	156
34	Motor vehicles, trailers, semi-trailers		80	74	94	83	90	100	127	141	141	151	162	172
35	Other transport equipment		68	72	79	87	91	100	120	157	180	260	253	249
36	Furniture; manufacturing n.e.c.		55	63	79	84	86	100	118	127	132	140	148	154
37	Recycling		...	...	...	...	...	...	...	...	...	...	...	...
D	Total manufacturing		69	70	83	88	86	100	110	120	133	149	166	185

Ethiopia

Supplier of information:
Central Statistical Authority, Addis Ababa.

Basic source of data:
Annual survey of the manufacturing industry.

Major deviations from ISIC (Revision 3):
None reported.

Reference period:
Fiscal year ending 8 July of the year indicated.

Scope:
Establishments with 10 or more persons engaged.

Method of data collection:
Individual sites are visited by enumerators.

Type of enumeration:
Not reported.

Adjusted for non-response:
Yes.

Concepts and definitions of variables:
Output and value added include subsidies.

Related national publications:
Statistical Abstract (annual); Results of Annual Survey of Manufacturing Industries, both published by the Central Statistical Authority, Addis Ababa.

Ethiopia

ISIC Revision 3		Number of establishments					Number of employees					Wages and salaries paid to employees				
			(number)					(number)					(thousands of Ethiopian Birr)			
ISIC	Industry	Note	2003	2004	2005	2006	Note	2003	2004	2005	2006	Note	2003	2004	2005	2006
151	Processed meat,fish,fruit,vegetables,fats		36	36	33	41		3681	2737	2390	3223		23867	19201	16885	26457
1511	Processing/preserving of meat	a/	9	8	7	8	a/	2208	1481	1230	1508	a/	15212	10270	8776	13716
1512	Processing/preserving of fish	a/	...	...	...	...	a/	...	...	...	...	a/	...	...	...	...
1513	Processing/preserving of fruit & vegetables	a/	...	...	...	...	a/	...	...	...	...	a/	...	...	...	...
1514	Vegetable and animal oils and fats		27	28	26	33		1473	1256	1160	1715		8655	8931	8109	12741
1520	Dairy products		3	3	3	3		627	757	646	689		4397	5174	4313	5153
153	Grain mill products; starches; animal feeds		66	79	79	95		4020	4825	4441	4135		24725	24297	26479	24420
1531	Grain mill products		63	75	74	90		3849	4587	4264	3963		23903	23591	25743	23706
1532	Starches and starch products		-	-	-	-		-	-	-	-		-	-	-	-
1533	Prepared animal feeds		3	4	5	5		171	238	177	172		822	706	736	714
154	Other food products		152	171	220	196		13214	13354	15074	17457		117495	127799	138214	170899
1541	Bakery products		127	141	192	160		4170	4190	6006	5748		18010	16548	22270	27846
1542	Sugar	b/	10	12	10	14	b/	7521	6937	6794	8810	b/	89724	94777	99736	122252
1543	Cocoa, chocolate and sugar confectionery	b/	...	...	...	...	b/	...	...	...	...	b/	...	...	...	...
1544	Macaroni, noodles & similar products		5	6	7	6		566	1041	1043	1058		4873	10989	9996	11403
1549	Other food products n.e.c.		10	12	11	16		957	1186	1231	1841		4888	5485	6212	9398
155	Beverages		31	33	35	38		9028	9686	9142	10156		118831	127015	137818	163816
1551	Distilling, rectifying & blending of spirits		12	9	14	11		921	1180	993	1065		9249	10433	9638	10910
1552	Wines		2	1	2	2		492	462	345	543		4284	5430	3800	9166
1553	Malt liquors and malt		7	8	7	8		3345	3659	3612	3916		47543	52438	64511	72488
1554	Soft drinks; mineral waters		10	15	12	17		4270	4385	4192	4632		57755	58714	59869	71252
1600	Tobacco products		1	1	1	1		792	785	697	755		13692	12979	13943	23009
171	Spinning, weaving and finishing of textiles		29	28	28	32		19173	20453	18122	20727		103994	133682	104486	125171
1711	Textile fibre preparation; textile weaving		29	28	28	32		19173	20453	18122	20727		103994	133682	104486	125171
1712	Finishing of textiles		-	-	-	-		-	-	-	-		-	-	-	-
172	Other textiles		2	2	2	2		2618	2266	2405	1222		11117	13088	12088	6516
1721	Made-up textile articles, except apparel		-	-	-	-		-	-	-	-		-	-	-	-
1722	Carpets and rugs		-	-	-	-		-	-	-	-		-	-	-	-
1723	Cordage, rope, twine and netting		2	2	2	2		2618	2266	2405	1222		11117	13088	12088	6516
1729	Other textiles n.e.c.		-	-	-	-		-	-	-	-		-	-	-	-
1730	Knitted and crocheted fabrics and articles		7	8	10	8		147	181	174	151		275	457	541	537
1810	Wearing apparel, except fur apparel		32	37	29	31		4278	3806	2606	4099		21529	20914	12984	25458
1820	Dressing & dyeing of fur; processing of fur		-	-	-	-		-	-	-	-		-	-	-	-
191	Tanning, dressing and processing of leather		15	17	18	18		3502	3725	3780	4050		36400	29702	40524	46804
1911	Tanning and dressing of leather		15	17	18	18		3502	3725	3780	4050		36400	29702	40524	46804
1912	Luggage, handbags, etc.; saddlery & harness		-	-	-	-		-	-	-	-		-	-	-	-
1920	Footwear		41	48	44	45		3730	3940	4133	3864		21503	24522	28163	27082
2010	Sawmilling and planing of wood	c/	...	...	...	...	c/	...	...	...	...	c/	...	...	...	...
202	Products of wood, cork, straw, etc.	c/	17	20	18	29	c/	1669	1616	1563	1759	c/	10699	11319	10620	12320
2021	Veneer sheets, plywood, particle board, etc.		...	...	...	...		...	...	...	...		...	...	...	...
2022	Builders' carpentry and joinery		...	...	...	...		...	...	...	...		...	...	...	...
2023	Wooden containers		-	-	-	-		-	-	-	-		-	-	-	-
2029	Other wood products; articles of cork/straw		...	...	...	...		...	...	...	...		...	...	...	...
210	Paper and paper products		7	7	9	13		1554	1737	1832	2085		13305	13250	19085	24498
2101	Pulp, paper and paperboard		7	7	9	13		1554	1737	1832	2085		13305	13250	19085	24498
2102	Corrugated paper and paperboard		-	-	-	-		-	-	-	-		-	-	-	-
2109	Other articles of paper and paperboard		-	-	-	-		-	-	-	-		-	-	-	-
221	Publishing		-	-	-	-		-	-	-	-		-	-	-	-
2211	Publishing of books and other publications		-	-	-	-		-	-	-	-		-	-	-	-
2212	Publishing of newspapers, journals, etc.		-	-	-	-		-	-	-	-		-	-	-	-
2213	Publishing of recorded media		-	-	-	-		-	-	-	-		-	-	-	-
2219	Other publishing		-	-	-	-		-	-	-	-		-	-	-	-

222	Printing and related service activities		66	91	73	74		4851	5203	5675	5974		41035	47641	56222	60674
2221	Printing	d/	...	...	...	...	d/	...	...	...	...	d/	...	...	...	...
2222	Service activities related to printing	d/	66	91	73	74	d/	4851	5203	5675	5974	d/	41035	47641	56222	60674
2230	Reproduction of recorded media		-	-	-	-		-	-	-	-		-	-	-	-
2310	Coke oven products		-	-	-	-		-	-	-	-		-	-	-	-
2320	Refined petroleum products		-	-	-	-		-	-	-	-		-	-	-	-
2330	Processing of nuclear fuel		-	-	-	-		-	-	-	-		-	-	-	-
241	Basic chemicals		6	7	6	7		1334	1059	1181	1180		10609	12138	11374	10086
2411	Basic chemicals, except fertilizers		6	7	6	7		1334	1059	1181	1180		10609	12138	11374	10086
2412	Fertilizers and nitrogen compounds		-	-	-	-		-	-	-	-		-	-	-	-
2413	Plastics in primary forms; synthetic rubber		-	-	-	-		-	-	-	-		-	-	-	-
242	Other chemicals		40	39	46	46		3760	4012	4794	4488		33556	34521	45396	45839
2421	Pesticides and other agro-chemical products		-	-	-	-		-	-	-	-		-	-	-	-
2422	Paints, varnishes, printing ink and mastics		8	8	8	9		611	607	640	700		7279	6972	7794	9229
2423	Pharmaceuticals, medicinal chemicals, etc.		7	7	6	4		1227	1269	1384	1091		13724	14399	21440	17907
2424	Soap, cleaning & cosmetic preparations		19	18	26	27		1437	1548	2300	2298		9763	10340	13937	16522
2429	Other chemical products n.e.c.		6	6	6	6		485	588	470	399		2790	2810	2225	2181
2430	Man-made fibres		-	-	-	-		-	-	-	-		-	-	-	-
251	Rubber products		5	4	4	4		1016	976	1053	1005		14650	16911	19575	17249
2511	Rubber tyres and tubes		5	4	4	4		1016	976	1053	1005		14650	16911	19575	17249
2519	Other rubber products		-	-	-	-		-	-	-	-		-	-	-	-
2520	Plastic products		36	38	43	59		3408	3434	4620	5894		20609	21473	27982	37307
2610	Glass and glass products		2	2	2	2		353	477	352	444		1916	3811	4055	5942
269	Non-metallic mineral products n.e.c.		113	121	142	150		7482	8661	8695	9649		69266	70454	72639	92206
2691	Pottery, china and earthenware		-	-	-	-		-	-	-	-		-	-	-	-
2692	Refractory ceramic products		-	-	-	-		-	-	-	-		-	-	-	-
2693	Struct.non-refractory clay; ceramic products		6	4	5	6		387	520	495	427		3112	3419	3568	3939
2694	Cement, lime and plaster		9	8	12	9		2729	2393	2256	3114		37617	35042	34317	50881
2695	Articles of concrete, cement and plaster		80	89	96	98		2432	3393	3458	3051		11342	15153	16071	16341
2696	Cutting, shaping & finishing of stone		-	-	-	-		-	-	-	-		-	-	-	-
2699	Other non-metallic mineral products n.e.c.		18	20	29	37		1934	2355	2486	3057		17195	16840	18683	21045
2710	Basic iron and steel		10	13	13	18		1466	1699	1762	2122		19691	21362	28000	30880
2720	Basic precious and non-ferrous metals		-	-	-	-		-	-	-	-		-	-	-	-
273	Casting of metals		-	-	-	-		-	-	-	-		-	-	-	-
2731	Casting of iron and steel		-	-	-	-		-	-	-	-		-	-	-	-
2732	Casting of non-ferrous metals		-	-	-	-		-	-	-	-		-	-	-	-
281	Struct.metal products;tanks;steam generators		42	46	48	70		1261	1387	1428	3157		8720	9562	11676	15521
2811	Structural metal products	e/	42	46	48	70	e/	1261	1387	1428	3157	e/	8720	9562	11676	15521
2812	Tanks, reservoirs and containers of metal	e/	...	...	...	...	e/	...	...	...	...	e/	...	...	...	...
2813	Steam generators		-	-	-	-		-	-	-	-		-	-	-	-
289	Other metal products; metal working services		31	32	28	36		2151	2066	2400	2639		17780	20373	22325	26366
2891	Metal forging/pressing/stamping/roll-forming		-	-	-	-		-	-	-	-		-	-	-	-
2892	Treatment & coating of metals		-	-	-	-		-	-	-	-		-	-	-	-
2893	Cutlery, hand tools and general hardware		11	9	10	10		629	509	813	883		4061	4639	6305	6949
2899	Other fabricated metal products n.e.c.		20	23	18	26		1522	1557	1587	1756		13719	15734	16020	19417
291	General purpose machinery		5	5	3	6		120	137	111	218		592	739	858	1844
2911	Engines & turbines (not for transport equipment)		-	-	-	-		-	-	-	-		-	-	-	-
2912	Pumps, compressors, taps and valves		-	-	-	-		-	-	-	-		-	-	-	-
2913	Bearings, gears, gearing & driving elements		-	-	-	-		-	-	-	-		-	-	-	-
2914	Ovens, furnaces and furnace burners		5	5	3	5		120	137	111	156		592	739	858	902
2915	Lifting and handling equipment		-	-	-	-		-	-	-	-		-	-	-	-
2919	Other general purpose machinery		-	-	-	1		-	-	-	62		-	-	-	942
292	Special purpose machinery		4	5	4	5		74	69	60	80		443	390	389	488
2921	Agricultural and forestry machinery		-	-	-	-		-	-	-	-		-	-	-	-
2922	Machine tools		-	-	-	-		-	-	-	-		-	-	-	-
2923	Machinery for metallurgy		-	-	-	-		-	-	-	-		-	-	-	-
2924	Machinery for mining & construction		-	-	-	-		-	-	-	-		-	-	-	-
2925	Food/beverage/tobacco processing machinery		4	5	4	5		74	69	60	80		443	390	389	488
2926	Machinery for textile, apparel and leather		-	-	-	-		-	-	-	-		-	-	-	-
2927	Weapons and ammunition		-	-	-	-		-	-	-	-		-	-	-	-
2929	Other special purpose machinery		-	-	-	-		-	-	-	-		-	-	-	-

continued

Ethiopia

ISIC Revision 3		Number of establishments					Number of employees					Wages and salaries paid to employees				
			(number)					(number)					(thousands of Ethiopian Birr)			
ISIC	Industry	Note	2003	2004	2005	2006	Note	2003	2004	2005	2006	Note	2003	2004	2005	2006
2930	Domestic appliances n.e.c.		-	-	-	-		-	-	-	-		-	-	-	-
3000	Office, accounting and computing machinery		-	-	-	-		-	-	-	-		-	-	-	-
3110	Electric motors, generators and transformers		-	-	-	-		-	-	-	-		-	-	-	-
3120	Electricity distribution & control apparatus		-	-	-	-		-	-	-	-		-	-	-	-
3130	Insulated wire and cable		-	-	-	-		-	-	-	-		-	-	-	-
3140	Accumulators, primary cells and batteries		1	1	1	2		50	50	50	102		95	95	95	8328
3150	Lighting equipment and electric lamps		-	-	-	-		-	-	-	-		-	-	-	-
3190	Other electrical equipment n.e.c.		-	-	-	-		-	-	-	-		-	-	-	-
3210	Electronic valves, tubes, etc.		-	-	-	-		-	-	-	-		-	-	-	-
3220	TV/radio transmitters; line comm. apparatus		-	-	-	-		-	-	-	-		-	-	-	-
3230	TV and radio receivers and associated goods		-	-	-	-		-	-	-	-		-	-	-	-
331	Medical, measuring, testing appliances, etc.		-	-	-	-		-	-	-	-		-	-	-	-
3311	Medical, surgical and orthopaedic equipment		-	-	-	-		-	-	-	-		-	-	-	-
3312	Measuring/testing/navigating appliances,etc.		-	-	-	-		-	-	-	-		-	-	-	-
3313	Industrial process control equipment		-	-	-	-		-	-	-	-		-	-	-	-
3320	Optical instruments & photographic equipment		-	-	-	-		-	-	-	-		-	-	-	-
3330	Watches and clocks		-	-	-	-		-	-	-	-		-	-	-	-
3410	Motor vehicles		-	-	-	-		-	-	-	-		-	-	-	-
3420	Automobile bodies, trailers & semi-trailers		7	6	7	8		946	1029	1148	1408		14673	18786	16942	23947
3430	Parts/accessories for automobiles		1	2	2	3		73	101	84	48		669	893	915	230
351	Building and repairing of ships and boats		-	-	-	-		-	-	-	-		-	-	-	-
3511	Building and repairing of ships		-	-	-	-		-	-	-	-		-	-	-	-
3512	Building/repairing of pleasure/sport. boats		-	-	-	-		-	-	-	-		-	-	-	-
3520	Railway/tramway locomotives & rolling stock		-	-	-	-		-	-	-	-		-	-	-	-
3530	Aircraft and spacecraft		-	-	-	-		-	-	-	-		-	-	-	-
359	Transport equipment n.e.c.		-	-	-	-		-	-	-	-		-	-	-	-
3591	Motorcycles		-	-	-	-		-	-	-	-		-	-	-	-
3592	Bicycles and invalid carriages		-	-	-	-		-	-	-	-		-	-	-	-
3599	Other transport equipment n.e.c.		-	-	-	-		-	-	-	-		-	-	-	-
3610	Furniture		158	172	256	202		5026	5153	8732	5688		26251	28762	50939	35214
369	Manufacturing n.e.c.		-	-	-	-		-	-	-	-		-	-	-	-
3691	Jewellery and related articles		-	-	-	-		-	-	-	-		-	-	-	-
3692	Musical instruments		-	-	-	-		-	-	-	-		-	-	-	-
3693	Sports goods		-	-	-	-		-	-	-	-		-	-	-	-
3694	Games and toys		-	-	-	-		-	-	-	-		-	-	-	-
3699	Other manufacturing n.e.c.		-	-	-	-		-	-	-	-		-	-	-	-
3710	Recycling of metal waste and scrap		-	-	-	-		-	-	-	-		-	-	-	-
3720	Recycling of non-metal waste and scrap		-	-	-	-		-	-	-	-		-	-	-	-
D	Total manufacturing	f/	966	1074	1207	1244	f/	101404	105381	109150	118468	f/	802384	871310	935525	1094261

a/ 1511 includes 1512 and 1513.
b/ 1542 includes 1543.
c/ 202 includes 2010.
d/ 2222 includes 2221.
e/ 2811 includes 2812.
f/ Sum of available data.

Ethiopia

ISIC Revision 3		Output in producers' prices					Value added in producers' prices					Gross fixed capital formation		
			(millions of Ethiopian Birr)					(millions of Ethiopian Birr)					(millions of Ethiopian Birr)	
ISIC	Industry	Note	2003	2004	2005	2006	Note	2003	2004	2005	2006	Note	2005	2006
151	Processed meat,fish,fruit,vegetables,fats		241.1	172.2	167.3	238.1		107.7	71.8	39.5	79.3		8.4	6.1
1511	Processing/preserving of meat	a/	125.4	61.9	57.5	61.7	a/	62.4	36.2	21.9	20.1	a/	5.1	3.2
1512	Processing/preserving of fish	a/	...	...	...	...	a/	...	...	...	...	a/	...	...
1513	Processing/preserving of fruit & vegetables	a/	...	...	...	...	a/	...	...	...	...	a/	...	...
1514	Vegetable and animal oils and fats		115.7	110.3	109.8	176.4		45.3	35.6	17.6	59.3		3.3	2.9
1520	Dairy products		50.5	60.2	68.0	99.0		23.2	28.2	24.0	43.6		2.9	8.9
153	Grain mill products; starches; animal feeds		472.0	530.7	464.1	536.9		122.4	127.9	88.8	108.4		45.6	42.0
1531	Grain mill products		466.3	517.2	448.2	522.0		120.0	123.8	85.2	103.4		45.3	41.4
1532	Starches and starch products		-	-	-	-		-	-	-	-		-	-
1533	Prepared animal feeds		5.7	13.4	15.8	14.9		2.4	4.1	3.6	4.9		0.3	0.6
154	Other food products		1550.2	1771.3	1848.5	2539.2		1093.7	1129.5	922.3	1071.3		111.2	202.9
1541	Bakery products		207.6	207.4	284.7	379.1		75.3	63.0	78.5	79.1		18.5	16.7
1542	Sugar	b/	1166.5	1274.0	1231.5	1483.0	b/	952.4	950.0	743.6	883.1	b/	86.6	92.9
1543	Cocoa, chocolate and sugar confectionery	b/	...	...	...	...	b/	...	...	...	...	b/	...	...
1544	Macaroni, noodles & similar products		106.6	183.1	192.8	191.5		34.3	64.8	54.3	51.1		2.6	68.2
1549	Other food products n.e.c.		69.6	106.8	139.4	485.6		31.7	51.7	45.8	58.0		3.5	25.1
155	Beverages		1263.5	1461.7	1870.6	1990.6		880.7	1015.4	1003.2	1099.1		208.6	223.7
1551	Distilling, rectifying & blending of spirits		76.3	91.9	131.1	137.1		61.4	74.8	95.3	92.7		5.9	16.9
1552	Wines		39.7	49.3	58.8	72.2		28.7	35.3	27.5	48.5		1.1	9.1
1553	Malt liquors and malt		671.6	773.6	927.3	1117.0		485.4	555.0	500.3	635.0		177.2	169.0
1554	Soft drinks; mineral waters		475.9	546.9	753.4	664.3		305.2	350.3	380.1	323.0		24.4	28.7
1600	Tobacco products		256.8	364.0	324.6	415.2		160.6	248.9	205.7	261.4		4.5	5.4
171	Spinning, weaving and finishing of textiles		700.2	900.7	837.6	893.6		226.4	271.7	244.5	222.9		86.9	54.1
1711	Textile fibre preparation; textile weaving		700.2	900.7	837.6	893.6		226.4	271.7	244.5	222.9		86.9	54.1
1712	Finishing of textiles		-	-	-	-		-	-	-	-		-	-
172	Other textiles		48.4	52.9	54.3	20.1		23.2	31.0	20.1	3.8		1.1	-
1721	Made-up textile articles, except apparel		-	-	-	-		-	-	-	-		-	-
1722	Carpets and rugs		-	-	-	-		-	-	-	-		-	-
1723	Cordage, rope, twine and netting		48.4	52.9	54.3	20.1		23.2	31.0	20.1	3.8		1.1	-
1729	Other textiles n.e.c.		-	-	-	-		-	-	-	-		-	-
1730	Knitted and crocheted fabrics and articles		3.3	2.8	5.4	4.8		1.5	1.6	2.5	2.3		1.8	-
1810	Wearing apparel, except fur apparel		73.1	86.5	62.6	80.5		43.3	47.0	24.8	30.7		10.3	8.8
1820	Dressing & dyeing of fur; processing of fur		-	-	-	-		-	-	-	-		-	-
191	Tanning, dressing and processing of leather		602.5	589.4	741.5	727.0		114.6	149.2	94.4	140.4		47.6	42.8
1911	Tanning and dressing of leather		602.5	589.4	741.5	727.0		114.6	149.2	94.4	140.4		47.6	42.8
1912	Luggage, handbags, etc.; saddlery & harness		-	-	-	-		-	-	-	-		-	-
1920	Footwear		188.0	223.7	243.2	295.8		75.3	87.4	87.2	102.5		39.3	32.1
2010	Sawmilling and planing of wood	c/	...	...	...	...	c/	...	...	...	...	c/	...	...
202	Products of wood, cork, straw, etc.	c/	61.2	58.4	58.0	71.8	c/	40.7	36.8	30.8	36.1	c/	1.2	2.8
2021	Veneer sheets, plywood, particle board, etc.		...	...	...	...		...	...	...	...		...	...
2022	Builders' carpentry and joinery		...	...	...	...		...	...	...	...		...	...
2023	Wooden containers		-	-	-	-		-	-	-	-		-	-
2029	Other wood products; articles of cork/straw		...	...	...	...		...	...	...	...		...	...
210	Paper and paper products		136.1	218.1	227.8	270.4		49.4	81.5	72.0	112.5		21.1	9.6
2101	Pulp, paper and paperboard		136.1	218.1	227.8	270.4		49.3	81.5	72.0	112.5		21.1	9.6
2102	Corrugated paper and paperboard		-	-	-	-		-	-	-	-		-	-
2109	Other articles of paper and paperboard		-	-	-	-		-	-	-	-		-	-
221	Publishing		-	-	-	-		-	-	-	-		-	-
2211	Publishing of books and other publications		-	-	-	-		-	-	-	-		-	-
2212	Publishing of newspapers, journals, etc.		-	-	-	-		-	-	-	-		-	-
2213	Publishing of recorded media		-	-	-	-		-	-	-	-		-	-
2219	Other publishing		-	-	-	-		-	-	-	-		-	-

continued

ISIC Revision 3		Output in producers' prices (millions of Ethiopian Birr)					Value added in producers' prices (millions of Ethiopian Birr)					Gross fixed capital formation (millions of Ethiopian Birr)	
ISIC	Industry	Note	2003	2004	2005	2006	Note	2003	2004	2005	2006	Note	2005	2006
222	Printing and related service activities		297.6	394.9	552.4	525.5		162.0	212.9	261.6	201.0		35.6	40.9
2221	Printing	d/	...	...	...	...	d/	...	...	...	...	d/	...	...
2222	Service activities related to printing	d/	297.6	394.9	552.4	525.5	d/	162.0	212.9	261.6	201.0	d/	35.6	40.9
2230	Reproduction of recorded media		-	-	-	-		-	-	-	-		-	-
2310	Coke oven products		-	-	-	-		-	-	-	-		-	-
2320	Refined petroleum products		-	-	-	-		-	-	-	-		-	-
2330	Processing of nuclear fuel		-	-	-	-		-	-	-	-		-	-
241	Basic chemicals		51.5	59.3	52.6	46.6		31.0	30.9	18.0	1.7		5.9	2.1
2411	Basic chemicals, except fertilizers		51.5	59.3	52.6	46.6		31.0	30.9	18.0	1.7		5.9	2.1
2412	Fertilizers and nitrogen compounds		-	-	-	-		-	-	-	-		-	-
2413	Plastics in primary forms; synthetic rubber		-	-	-	-		-	-	-	-		-	-
242	Other chemicals		521.9	667.1	736.2	883.3		205.0	278.7	225.8	252.4		28.2	26.1
2421	Pesticides and other agro-chemical products		-	-	-	-		-	-	-	-		-	-
2422	Paints, varnishes, printing ink and mastics		165.5	197.6	204.5	254.2		69.2	72.7	66.2	76.7		9.7	3.3
2423	Pharmaceuticals, medicinal chemicals, etc.		145.9	201.2	170.0	216.4		66.0	110.0	55.9	64.3		6.6	8.2
2424	Soap, cleaning & cosmetic preparations		189.7	243.2	335.5	383.7		62.5	87.8	98.5	106.9		10.6	14.6
2429	Other chemical products n.e.c.		20.8	25.1	26.3	29.0		7.4	8.2	5.2	4.5		1.4	-
2430	Man-made fibres		-	-	-	-		-	-	-	-		-	-
251	Rubber products		187.5	193.1	213.1	228.8		101.0	112.0	70.6	130.4		15.9	5.0
2511	Rubber tyres and tubes		187.5	193.1	213.1	228.8		101.0	112.0	70.6	130.4		15.9	5.0
2519	Other rubber products		-	-	-	-		-	-	-	-		-	-
2520	Plastic products		300.6	364.2	475.0	754.3		135.2	156.1	161.1	291.2		74.9	67.6
2610	Glass and glass products		7.2	30.3	37.6	68.9		5.1	20.3	17.8	35.6		0.2	4.1
269	Non-metallic mineral products n.e.c.		1015.7	1149.3	1126.2	1606.9		514.7	597.9	397.4	748.5		55.5	69.3
2691	Pottery, china and earthenware		-	-	-	-		-	-	-	-		-	-
2692	Refractory ceramic products		-	-	-	-		-	-	-	-		-	-
2693	Struct.non-refractory clay; ceramic products		15.4	16.5	20.2	16.5		8.7	12.1	9.6	1.3		-	-
2694	Cement, lime and plaster		841.3	942.3	893.2	1350.9		428.0	497.4	316.2	645.2		34.4	42.8
2695	Articles of concrete, cement and plaster		68.4	105.2	116.3	118.3		26.3	47.4	39.3	50.4		13.5	15.8
2696	Cutting, shaping & finishing of stone		-	-	-	-		-	-	-	-		-	-
2699	Other non-metallic mineral products n.e.c.		90.5	85.3	96.5	121.2		51.7	40.9	32.4	51.5		7.6	10.7
2710	Basic iron and steel		382.7	761.8	1085.3	1374.1		177.0	221.2	361.2	306.2		28.9	55.0
2720	Basic precious and non-ferrous metals		-	-	-	-		-	-	-	-		-	-
273	Casting of metals		-	-	-	-		-	-	-	-		-	-
2731	Casting of iron and steel		-	-	-	-		-	-	-	-		-	-
2732	Casting of non-ferrous metals		-	-	-	-		-	-	-	-		-	-
281	Struct.metal products;tanks;steam generators		82.6	111.4	178.8	225.6		32.5	46.7	49.0	70.5		6.1	18.7
2811	Structural metal products	e/	82.6	111.4	178.8	225.6	e/	32.5	46.7	49.0	70.5	e/	6.1	18.7
2812	Tanks, reservoirs and containers of metal	e/	...	...	...	...	e/	...	...	...	...	e/	...	...
2813	Steam generators		-	-	-	-		-	-	-	-		-	-
289	Other metal products; metal working services		135.5	188.2	295.2	302.2		56.9	84.8	104.2	105.9		12.3	13.1
2891	Metal forging/pressing/stamping/roll-forming		-	-	-	-		-	-	-	-		-	-
2892	Treatment & coating of metals		-	-	-	-		-	-	-	-		-	-
2893	Cutlery, hand tools and general hardware		33.9	51.7	134.8	134.7		13.2	20.7	42.5	37.6		10.7	5.7
2899	Other fabricated metal products n.e.c.		101.6	136.4	160.3	167.4		43.7	64.1	61.7	68.3		1.6	7.4
291	General purpose machinery		6.7	11.9	11.3	121.9		3.3	4.4	3.4	25.2		0.9	1.8
2911	Engines & turbines (not for transport equipment)		-	-	-	-		-	-	-	-		-	-
2912	Pumps, compressors, taps and valves		-	-	-	-		-	-	-	-		-	-
2913	Bearings, gears, gearing & driving elements		-	-	-	-		-	-	-	-		-	-
2914	Ovens, furnaces and furnace burners		6.7	11.9	11.3	11.4		3.3	4.4	3.4	4.2		0.9	1.7
2915	Lifting and handling equipment		-	-	-	-		-	-	-	-		-	-
2919	Other general purpose machinery		-	-	-	110.5		-	-	-	21.0		-	0.1

292	Special purpose machinery		1.0	1.6	1.3	3.1		0.4	0.7	0.7	1.8		0.1	-
2921	Agricultural and forestry machinery		-	-	-	-		-	-	-	-		-	-
2922	Machine tools		-	-	-	-		-	-	-	-		-	-
2923	Machinery for metallurgy		-	-	-	-		-	-	-	-		-	-
2924	Machinery for mining & construction		-	-	-	-		-	-	-	-		-	-
2925	Food/beverage/tobacco processing machinery		1.0	1.6	1.3	3.1		0.4	0.7	0.7	1.8		0.1	-
2926	Machinery for textile, apparel and leather		-	-	-	-		-	-	-	-		-	-
2927	Weapons and ammunition		-	-	-	-		-	-	-	-		-	-
2929	Other special purpose machinery		-	-	-	-		-	-	-	-		-	-
2930	Domestic appliances n.e.c.		-	-	-	-		-	-	-	-		-	-
3000	Office, accounting and computing machinery		-	-	-	-		-	-	-	-		-	-
3110	Electric motors, generators and transformers		-	-	-	-		-	-	-	-		-	-
3120	Electricity distribution & control apparatus		-	-	-	-		-	-	-	-		-	-
3130	Insulated wire and cable		-	-	-	-		-	-	-	-		-	-
3140	Accumulators, primary cells and batteries		1.1	1.1	1.1	11.5		0.1	0.1	-0.4	1.8		-	-
3150	Lighting equipment and electric lamps		-	-	-	-		-	-	-	-		-	-
3190	Other electrical equipment n.e.c.		-	-	-	-		-	-	-	-		-	-
3210	Electronic valves, tubes, etc.		-	-	-	-		-	-	-	-		-	-
3220	TV/radio transmitters; line comm. apparatus		-	-	-	-		-	-	-	-		-	-
3230	TV and radio receivers and associated goods		-	-	-	-		-	-	-	-		-	-
331	Medical, measuring, testing appliances, etc.		-	-	-	-		-	-	-	-		-	-
3311	Medical, surgical and orthopaedic equipment		-	-	-	-		-	-	-	-		-	-
3312	Measuring/testing/navigating appliances,etc.		-	-	-	-		-	-	-	-		-	-
3313	Industrial process control equipment		-	-	-	-		-	-	-	-		-	-
3320	Optical instruments & photographic equipment		-	-	-	-		-	-	-	-		-	-
3330	Watches and clocks		-	-	-	-		-	-	-	-		-	-
3410	Motor vehicles		-	-	-	-		-	-	-	-		-	-
3420	Automobile bodies, trailers & semi-trailers		187.7	270.6	237.8	420.3		57.8	103.6	43.9	110.0		15.2	17.8
3430	Parts/accessories for automobiles		2.3	4.7	5.4	2.5		1.5	2.8	3.8	1.2		0.1	-
351	Building and repairing of ships and boats		-	-	-	-		-	-	-	-		-	-
3511	Building and repairing of ships		-	-	-	-		-	-	-	-		-	-
3512	Building/repairing of pleasure/sport. boats		-	-	-	-		-	-	-	-		-	-
3520	Railway/tramway locomotives & rolling stock		-	-	-	-		-	-	-	-		-	-
3530	Aircraft and spacecraft		-	-	-	-		-	-	-	-		-	-
359	Transport equipment n.e.c.		-	-	-	-		-	-	-	-		-	-
3591	Motorcycles		-	-	-	-		-	-	-	-		-	-
3592	Bicycles and invalid carriages		-	-	-	-		-	-	-	-		-	-
3599	Other transport equipment n.e.c.		-	-	-	-		-	-	-	-		-	-
3610	Furniture		195.7	169.7	333.7	288.6		86.0	88.8	138.5	118.8		24.6	38.3
369	Manufacturing n.e.c.		-	-	-	-		-	-	-	-		-	-
3691	Jewellery and related articles		-	-	-	-		-	-	-	-		-	-
3692	Musical instruments		-	-	-	-		-	-	-	-		-	-
3693	Sports goods		-	-	-	-		-	-	-	-		-	-
3694	Games and toys		-	-	-	-		-	-	-	-		-	-
3699	Other manufacturing n.e.c.		-	-	-	-		-	-	-	-		-	-
3710	Recycling of metal waste and scrap		-	-	-	-		-	-	-	-		-	-
3720	Recycling of non-metal waste and scrap		-	-	-	-		-	-	-	-		-	-
D	Total manufacturing	f/	9024.2	10871.8	12316.4	15047.1	f/	4532.1	5289.9	4716.5	5716.4	f/	894.8	999.1

a/ 1511 includes 1512 and 1513.
b/ 1542 includes 1543.
c/ 202 includes 2010.
d/ 2222 includes 2221.
e/ 2811 includes 2812.
f/ Sum of available data.

Ethiopia

ISIC Revision 3			Index numbers of industrial production											
			(2000=100)											
ISIC	Industry	Note	1995	1996	1997	1998	1999	2000	2001	2002	2003	2004	2005	2006
15	Food and beverages		...	...	...	...	...	...	...	...	...	...	...	...
16	Tobacco products		...	...	...	...	...	...	...	...	...	...	...	...
17	Textiles		...	...	...	...	...	...	...	...	...	...	...	...
18	Wearing apparel, fur		...	...	...	...	...	...	...	...	...	...	...	...
19	Leather, leather products and footwear		...	...	...	...	...	...	...	...	...	...	...	...
20	Wood products (excl. furniture)		...	...	...	...	...	...	...	...	...	...	...	...
21	Paper and paper products		...	...	...	...	...	...	...	...	...	...	...	...
22	Printing and publishing		...	...	...	...	...	...	...	...	...	...	...	...
23	Coke,refined petroleum products,nuclear fuel		...	...	...	...	...	...	...	...	...	...	...	...
24	Chemicals and chemical products		...	...	...	...	...	...	...	...	...	...	...	...
25	Rubber and plastics products		...	...	...	...	...	...	...	...	...	...	...	...
26	Non-metallic mineral products		...	...	...	...	...	...	...	...	...	...	...	...
27	Basic metals		...	...	...	...	...	...	...	...	...	...	...	...
28	Fabricated metal products		...	...	...	...	...	...	...	...	...	...	...	...
29	Machinery and equipment n.e.c.		...	...	...	...	...	...	...	...	...	...	...	...
30	Office, accounting and computing machinery		...	...	...	...	...	...	...	...	...	...	...	...
31	Electrical machinery and apparatus		...	...	...	...	...	...	...	...	...	...	...	...
32	Radio,television and communication equipment		...	...	...	...	...	...	...	...	...	...	...	...
33	Medical, precision and optical instruments		...	...	...	...	...	...	...	...	...	...	...	...
34	Motor vehicles, trailers, semi-trailers		...	...	...	...	...	...	...	...	...	...	...	...
35	Other transport equipment		...	...	...	...	...	...	...	...	...	...	...	...
36	Furniture; manufacturing n.e.c.		...	...	...	...	...	...	...	...	...	...	...	...
37	Recycling		...	...	...	...	...	...	...	...	...	...	...	...
D	Total manufacturing		81	84	86	86	93	100	104	105	106	113	122	131

Fiji

Supplier of information:
Bureau of Statistics, Suva.

Basic source of data:
Annual census.

Major deviations from ISIC (Revision 3):
Data are collected under the National Classification of Industrial Activities (NSIC), and correspond approximately with ISIC (Revision 3).

Reference period:
Calendar year.

Scope:
All establishments.

Method of data collection:
Mail questionnaires and direct interview in the field.

Type of enumeration:
Complete enumeration.

Adjusted for non-response:
Yes.

Concepts and definitions of variables:
Wages and salaries is compensation of employees.

Related national publications:
Census of Industries (annual), published by the Bureau of Statistics, Suva.

ISIC Revision 3		Number of establishments					Number of employees					Wages and salaries paid to employees				
			(number)					(number)					(thousands of Fiji Dollars)			
ISIC	Industry	Note	2002	2003	2004	2005	Note	2002	2003	2004	2005	Note	2002	2003	2004	2005
151	Processed meat,fish,fruit,vegetables,fats		34	34	36	...		2070	2094	1918	...		13598	14673	16053	...
1511	Processing/preserving of meat		7	7	8	...		270	278	226	...		2483	2577	2323	...
1512	Processing/preserving of fish		12	12	12	...		1421	1427	1322	...		8407	9039	10424	...
1513	Processing/preserving of fruit & vegetables		12	12	13	...		283	287	291	...		1804	2053	2217	...
1514	Vegetable and animal oils and fats		3	3	3	...		96	102	79	...		903	1004	1089	...
1520	Dairy products		5	5	5	...		313	320	415	...		2581	2739	3139	...
153	Grain mill products; starches; animal feeds		...	...	...	...		...	...	...	...		...	...	...	...
1531	Grain mill products		...a/	...a/	...a/	...		...a/	...a/	...a/	...		...a/	...a/	...a/	...
1532	Starches and starch products		9a/	9a/	10a/	...		408a/	465a/	451a/	...		2875a/	3320a/	3555a/	...
1533	Prepared animal feeds		4	4	4	...		170	181	231	...		1283	1585	886	...
154	Other food products		86	97	91	...		3734	4624	4813	...		45418	46565	44115	...
1541	Bakery products		59	65	62	...		673	722	623	...		4430	5467	4620	...
1542	Sugar		5	5	5	...		2528	3340	3741	...		36981	37284	36087	...
1543	Cocoa, chocolate and sugar confectionery		13	16	14	...		389	413	350	...		3308	2949	2748	...
1544	Macaroni, noodles & similar products		5	5	5	...		20	23	18	...		206	275	278	...
1549	Other food products n.e.c.		4	6	5	...		124	126	81	...		494	590	381	...
155	Beverages		...	...	...	...		...	...	...	...		...	...	...	...
1551	Distilling, rectifying & blending of spirits		...	...	...	...		...	...	...	...		...	...	...	...
1552	Wines		...	...	...	...		...	...	...	...		...	...	...	...
1553	Malt liquors and malt		4	5	7	...		579	585	389	...		10928	11033	8949	...
1554	Soft drinks; mineral waters		8	8	9	...		470	475	409	...		5694	6138	6599	...
1600	Tobacco products		1	1	1	...		...	...	...	...		...	...	...	...
171	Spinning, weaving and finishing of textiles		...	...	...	...		...	...	...	...		...	...	...	...
1711	Textile fibre preparation; textile weaving		...	...	...	...		...	...	...	...		...	...	...	...
1712	Finishing of textiles		...	...	...	...		...	...	...	...		...	...	...	...
172	Other textiles		...	...	...	...		...	...	...	...		...	...	...	...
1721	Made-up textile articles, except apparel		...	...	...	...		...	...	...	...		...	...	...	...
1722	Carpets and rugs		...	...	...	...		...	...	...	...		...	...	...	...
1723	Cordage, rope, twine and netting		...	...	...	...		...	...	...	...		...	...	...	...
1729	Other textiles n.e.c.		...	...	...	...		...	...	...	...		...	...	...	...
1730	Knitted and crocheted fabrics and articles		...	...	...	...		...	...	...	...		...	...	...	...
1810	Wearing apparel, except fur apparel		153	159	158	...		7958	8678	9604	...		57995	59668	64528	...
1820	Dressing & dyeing of fur; processing of fur		...	...	...	...		...	...	...	...		...	...	...	...
191	Tanning, dressing and processing of leather		...	...	...	...		...	...	...	...		...	...	...	...
1911	Tanning and dressing of leather		...	...	...	...		...	...	...	...		...	...	...	...
1912	Luggage, handbags, etc.; saddlery & harness		...	...	...	...		...	...	...	...		...	...	...	...
1920	Footwear		11	8	9	...		711	803	871	...		4110	4983	7488	...
2010	Sawmilling and planing of wood		13	14	11	...		600	611	711	...		6428	7726	10607	...
202	Products of wood, cork, straw, etc.		...	...	...	...		...	...	...	...		...	...	...	...
2021	Veneer sheets, plywood, particle board, etc.		7	5	7	...		345	364	303	...		1974	1960	3946	...
2022	Builders' carpentry and joinery		...	...	...	...		...	...	...	...		...	...	...	...
2023	Wooden containers		...	...	...	...		...	...	...	...		...	...	...	...
2029	Other wood products; articles of cork/straw		...	...	...	...		...	...	...	...		...	...	...	...
210	Paper and paper products		11	12	14	...		578	584	586	...		7040	6636	5414	...
2101	Pulp, paper and paperboard		...	...	...	...		...	...	...	...		...	...	...	...
2102	Corrugated paper and paperboard		...	...	...	...		...	...	...	...		...	...	...	...
2109	Other articles of paper and paperboard		...	...	...	...		...	...	...	...		...	...	...	...
221	Publishing		10	10	10	...		440	447	329	...		5122	5052	3254	...
2211	Publishing of books and other publications		...	...	...	...		...	...	...	...		...	...	...	...
2212	Publishing of newspapers, journals, etc.		...	...	...	...		...	...	...	...		...	...	...	...
2213	Publishing of recorded media		...	...	...	...		...	...	...	...		...	...	...	...
2219	Other publishing		...	...	...	...		...	...	...	...		...	...	...	...

222	Printing and related service activities	32	34	32	...	414	425	441	...	4255	4994	5745	...
2221	Printing	...	...	...	...	...	...	...	...	...	...	...	...
2222	Service activities related to printing	...	...	...	...	...	...	...	...	...	...	...	...
2230	Reproduction of recorded media	...	...	...	...	...	...	...	...	...	...	...	...
2310	Coke oven products	...	...	...	...	...	...	...	...	...	...	...	...
2320	Refined petroleum products	...	...	...	...	...	...	...	...	...	...	...	...
2330	Processing of nuclear fuel	...	...	...	...	...	...	...	...	...	...	...	...
241	Basic chemicals	...	...	...	...	...	...	...	...	...	...	...	...
2411	Basic chemicals, except fertilizers	...	...	...	...	...	...	...	...	...	...	...	...
2412	Fertilizers and nitrogen compounds	3	3	3	...	55	57	57	...	1115	1104	1120	...
2413	Plastics in primary forms; synthetic rubber	...	...	...	...	...	...	...	...	...	...	...	...
242	Other chemicals	...	...	...	...	...	...	...	...	...	...	...	...
2421	Pesticides and other agro-chemical products	...	...	...	...	...	...	...	...	...	...	...	...
2422	Paints, varnishes, printing ink and mastics	6	5	7	...	207	210	209	...	3000	2800	2391	...
2423	Pharmaceuticals, medicinal chemicals, etc.	...	...	...	...	...	...	...	...	...	...	...	...
2424	Soap, cleaning & cosmetic preparations	8	8	8	...	280	282	201	...	3097	2999	2326	...
2429	Other chemical products n.e.c.	7	6	7	...	123	123	106	...	...	...	...	...
2430	Man-made fibres	...	...	...	...	...	...	...	...	...	...	...	...
251	Rubber products	...	...	...	...	...	...	...	...	...	...	...	...
2511	Rubber tyres and tubes	12	12	10	...	182	185	72	...	1150	1165	632	...
2519	Other rubber products	...	...	...	...	...	...	...	...	...	...	...	...
2520	Plastic products	14	16	14	...	238	259	298	...	1517	2004	2333	...
2610	Glass and glass products	4	3	5	...	126	124	103	...	2155	2234	2613	...
269	Non-metallic mineral products n.e.c.	...	...	...	...	...	...	...	...	...	...	...	...
2691	Pottery, china and earthenware	...	...	...	...	...	...	...	...	...	...	...	...
2692	Refractory ceramic products	...	...	...	...	...	...	...	...	...	...	...	...
2693	Struct.non-refractory clay; ceramic products	...	...	...	...	...	...	...	...	...	...	...	...
2694	Cement, lime and plaster	...	...	...	...	...	...	...	...	...	...	...	...
2695	Articles of concrete, cement and plaster	17	17	16	...	309	370	372	...	2383	2646	2011	...
2696	Cutting, shaping & finishing of stone	...	...	...	...	...	...	...	...	...	...	...	...
2699	Other non-metallic mineral products n.e.c.	...	...	...	...	...	...	...	...	...	...	...	...
2710	Basic iron and steel	...	5	3	...	95	112	129	...	1020	1079	965	...
2720	Basic precious and non-ferrous metals	...	...	...	...	...	...	...	...	...	...	...	...
273	Casting of metals	...	...	...	...	...	...	...	...	...	...	...	...
2731	Casting of iron and steel	...	...	...	...	...	...	...	...	...	...	...	...
2732	Casting of non-ferrous metals	...	...	...	...	...	...	...	...	...	...	...	...
281	Struct.metal products;tanks;steam generators	...	...	...	...	...	...	...	...	...	...	...	...
2811	Structural metal products	19	26	24	...	290	469	452	...	2192	2538	3297	...
2812	Tanks, reservoirs and containers of metal	...	...	...	...	...	...	...	...	...	...	...	...
2813	Steam generators	...	...	...	...	...	...	...	...	...	...	...	...
289	Other metal products; metal working services	...	...	...	...	...	...	...	...	...	...	...	...
2891	Metal forging/pressing/stamping/roll-forming	6	6	5	...	341	349	328	...	2858	2754	1139	...
2892	Treatment & coating of metals	13	9	7	...	192	155	104	...	1329	1389	1334	...
2893	Cutlery, hand tools and general hardware	...	...	...	...	...	...	...	...	...	...	...	...
2899	Other fabricated metal products n.e.c.	10	7	9	...	198	127	114	...	1307	1283	1544	...
291	General purpose machinery	...	...	...	...	...	...	...	...	...	...	...	...
2911	Engines & turbines (not for transport equipment)	4	2	6	...	16	17	28	...	183	185	240	...
2912	Pumps, compressors, taps and valves	...	...	...	...	...	...	...	...	...	...	...	...
2913	Bearings, gears, gearing & driving elements	...	...	...	...	...	...	...	...	...	...	...	...
2914	Ovens, furnaces and furnace burners	...	...	...	...	...	...	...	...	...	...	...	...
2915	Lifting and handling equipment	4	4	3	...	13	15	18	...	343	347	142	...
2919	Other general purpose machinery	4	4	3	...	10	12	10	...	37	40	58	...
292	Special purpose machinery	...	...	...	...	...	...	...	...	...	...	...	...
2921	Agricultural and forestry machinery	...	...	...	...	...	...	...	...	...	...	...	...
2922	Machine tools	...	...	...	...	...	...	...	...	...	...	...	...
2923	Machinery for metallurgy	...	...	...	...	...	...	...	...	...	...	...	...
2924	Machinery for mining & construction	...	...	...	...	...	...	...	...	...	...	...	...
2925	Food/beverage/tobacco processing machinery	...	...	...	...	...	...	...	...	...	...	...	...
2926	Machinery for textile, apparel and leather	...	...	...	...	...	...	...	...	...	...	...	...
2927	Weapons and ammunition	...	...	...	...	...	...	...	...	...	...	...	...
2929	Other special purpose machinery	...	...	...	...	...	...	...	...	...	...	...	...

continued

Fiji

ISIC Revision 3		Number of establishments					Number of employees					Wages and salaries paid to employees				
			(number)					(number)					(thousands of Fiji Dollars)			
ISIC	Industry	Note	2002	2003	2004	2005	Note	2002	2003	2004	2005	Note	2002	2003	2004	2005
2930	Domestic appliances n.e.c.		...	...	...	...		...	...	...	...		...	...	...	...
3000	Office, accounting and computing machinery		...	...	...	...		...	...	...	...		...	...	...	...
3110	Electric motors, generators and transformers		7	6	7	...		64	62	62	...		369	398	96	...
3120	Electricity distribution & control apparatus		...	...	...	...		...	...	...	...		...	...	...	...
3130	Insulated wire and cable		...	...	...	...		...	...	...	...		...	...	...	...
3140	Accumulators, primary cells and batteries		...	8	6	...		142	150	144	...		1299	1462	664	...
3150	Lighting equipment and electric lamps		...	...	...	...		...	...	...	...		...	...	...	...
3190	Other electrical equipment n.e.c.		...	...	...	...		...	...	...	...		...	...	...	...
3210	Electronic valves, tubes, etc.		...	...	...	...		...	...	...	...		...	...	...	...
3220	TV/radio transmitters; line comm. apparatus		...	...	...	...		...	...	...	...		...	...	...	...
3230	TV and radio receivers and associated goods		...	...	...	...		...	...	...	...		...	...	...	...
331	Medical, measuring, testing appliances, etc.		...	...	...	...		...	...	...	...		...	...	...	...
3311	Medical, surgical and orthopaedic equipment		...	...	...	...		...	...	...	...		...	...	...	...
3312	Measuring/testing/navigating appliances,etc.		...	...	...	...		...	...	...	...		...	...	...	...
3313	Industrial process control equipment		...	...	...	...		...	...	...	...		...	...	...	...
3320	Optical instruments & photographic equipment		...	...	...	...		...	...	...	...		...	...	...	...
3330	Watches and clocks		...	...	...	...		...	...	...	...		...	...	...	...
3410	Motor vehicles		...	...	...	...		...	...	...	...		...	...	...	...
3420	Automobile bodies, trailers & semi-trailers		5	6	9	...		60	66	104	...		317	370	1210	...
3430	Parts/accessories for automobiles		...	...	...	...		...	...	...	...		...	...	...	...
351	Building and repairing of ships and boats		...	...	...	...		...	...	...	...		...	...	...	...
3511	Building and repairing of ships		10	9	8	...		265	238	182	...		2189	2361	2790	...
3512	Building/repairing of pleasure/sport. boats		...	...	...	...		...	...	...	...		...	...	...	...
3520	Railway/tramway locomotives & rolling stock		...	...	...	...		...	...	...	...		...	...	...	...
3530	Aircraft and spacecraft		...	...	...	...		...	...	...	...		...	...	...	...
359	Transport equipment n.e.c.		...	...	...	...		...	...	...	...		...	...	...	...
3591	Motorcycles		...	...	...	...		...	...	...	...		...	...	...	...
3592	Bicycles and invalid carriages		...	...	...	...		...	...	...	...		...	...	...	...
3599	Other transport equipment n.e.c.		...	...	...	...		...	...	...	...		...	...	...	...
3610	Furniture		4	2	4	...		1037	1316	1146	...		7371	9967	10807	...
369	Manufacturing n.e.c.		...	...	...	...		...	...	...	...		...	...	...	...
3691	Jewellery and related articles		16	18	14	...		97	108	101	...		539	569	747	...
3692	Musical instruments		...	...	...	...		...	...	...	...		...	...	...	...
3693	Sports goods		...	...	...	...		...	...	...	...		...	...	...	...
3694	Games and toys		...	...	...	...		...	...	...	...		...	...	...	...
3699	Other manufacturing n.e.c.		17	22	16	...		110	116	108	...		733	789	524	...
3710	Recycling of metal waste and scrap		...	...	...	...		...	...	...	...		...	...	...	...
3720	Recycling of non-metal waste and scrap		...	...	...	...		...	...	...	...		...	...	...	...
D	Total manufacturing		593	617	602	...		23240	25578	25919	...		205802	217557	223258	...

a/ 1532 includes 1531.

Fiji

ISIC Revision 3		Output in producers' prices (thousands of Fiji Dollars)					Value added in producers' prices (thousands of Fiji Dollars)					Gross fixed capital formation (thousands of Fiji Dollars)		
ISIC	Industry	Note	2002	2003	2004	2005	Note	2002	2003	2004	2005	Note	2003	2004
151	Processed meat,fish,fruit,vegetables,fats		120147	126036	178944	...		11927	24276	30139	...		3827	...
1511	Processing/preserving of meat		35588	37029	34471	...		4919	5711	5203	...		239	81
1512	Processing/preserving of fish		43220	44988	84152	...		1039	11098	18637	...		2388	2303
1513	Processing/preserving of fruit & vegetables		17962	20786	22431	...		4590	5663	4715	...		1154	965
1514	Vegetable and animal oils and fats		23377	23233	37890	...		1379	1803	1584	...		47	...
1520	Dairy products		47693	49992	68825	...		4271	5076	8064	...		780	1441
153	Grain mill products; starches; animal feeds		...	...	...	...		...	...	...	...		...	...
1531	Grain mill products		...a/	...a/	...a/	...		...a/	...a/	...a/	...		...a/	...a/
1532	Starches and starch products		68296a/	73282a/	80906a/	...		8471a/	8145a/	11263a/	...		2364a/	2784a/
1533	Prepared animal feeds		15033	16511	15926	...		3666	4183	2712	...		489	10022
154	Other food products		355674	318465	341817	...		86922	95811	58048	...		27577	12606
1541	Bakery products		35199	38674	40614	...		7297	8758	8131	...		-82	196
1542	Sugar		275264	230418	248517	...		75308	79330	39653	...		27292	12392
1543	Cocoa, chocolate and sugar confectionery		32649	34499	37851	...		1589	4167	8155	...		59	-108
1544	Macaroni, noodles & similar products		3161	3943	3547	...		770	999	623	...		43	62
1549	Other food products n.e.c.		9401	10931	11289	...		1959	2558	1485	...		265	63
155	Beverages		...	...	...	...		...	...	...	...		...	...
1551	Distilling, rectifying & blending of spirits		...	...	...	...		...	...	...	...		...	...
1552	Wines		...	...	...	...		...	...	...	...		...	...
1553	Malt liquors and malt		111719	114592	126781	...		51023	51709	42625	...		372	1661
1554	Soft drinks; mineral waters		67279	79090	97268	...		21159	22414	36672	...		4954	5989
1600	Tobacco products		...	...	...	...		...	...	...	...		...	...
171	Spinning, weaving and finishing of textiles		...	...	...	...		...	...	...	...		...	...
1711	Textile fibre preparation; textile weaving		...	...	...	...		...	...	...	...		...	...
1712	Finishing of textiles		...	...	...	...		...	...	...	...		...	...
172	Other textiles		...	...	...	...		...	...	...	...		...	...
1721	Made-up textile articles, except apparel		...	...	...	...		...	...	...	...		...	...
1722	Carpets and rugs		...	...	...	...		...	...	...	...		...	...
1723	Cordage, rope, twine and netting		...	...	...	...		...	...	...	...		...	...
1729	Other textiles n.e.c.		...	...	...	...		...	...	...	...		...	...
1730	Knitted and crocheted fabrics and articles		...	...	...	...		...	...	...	...		...	...
1810	Wearing apparel, except fur apparel		263796	264776	294394	...		77598	83201	92641	...		4279	3944
1820	Dressing & dyeing of fur; processing of fur		...	...	...	...		...	...	...	...		...	...
191	Tanning, dressing and processing of leather		...	...	...	...		...	...	...	...		...	...
1911	Tanning and dressing of leather		...	...	...	...		...	...	...	...		...	...
1912	Luggage, handbags, etc.; saddlery & harness		...	...	...	...		...	...	...	...		...	...
1920	Footwear		23177	24673	19394	...		6037	6863	8835	...		157	45
2010	Sawmilling and planing of wood		52534	62192	74356	...		12996	15597	16594	...		2490	2922
202	Products of wood, cork, straw, etc.		...	...	...	...		...	...	...	...		...	...
2021	Veneer sheets, plywood, particle board, etc.		11655	8262	19029	...		3443	2936	9120	...		775	14
2022	Builders' carpentry and joinery		...	...	...	...		...	...	...	...		...	...
2023	Wooden containers		...	...	...	...		...	...	...	...		...	...
2029	Other wood products; articles of cork/straw		...	...	...	...		...	...	...	...		...	...
210	Paper and paper products		67723	68137	62517	...		18440	20126	16881	...		949	1373
2101	Pulp, paper and paperboard		...	...	...	...		...	...	...	...		...	...
2102	Corrugated paper and paperboard		...	...	...	...		...	...	...	...		...	...
2109	Other articles of paper and paperboard		...	...	...	...		...	...	...	...		...	...
221	Publishing		21223	23513	25961	...		11907	14043	10983	...		1068	223
2211	Publishing of books and other publications		...	...	...	...		...	...	...	...		...	...
2212	Publishing of newspapers, journals, etc.		...	...	...	...		...	...	...	...		...	...
2213	Publishing of recorded media		...	...	...	...		...	...	...	...		...	...
2219	Other publishing		...	...	...	...		...	...	...	...		...	...

continued

Fiji

ISIC Revision 3		Output in producers' prices (thousands of Fiji Dollars)					Value added in producers' prices (thousands of Fiji Dollars)					Gross fixed capital formation (thousands of Fiji Dollars)		
ISIC	Industry	Note	2002	2003	2004	2005	Note	2002	2003	2004	2005	Note	2003	2004
222	Printing and related service activities		20956	23983	30872	...		7311	9877	10429	...		4014	2469
2221	Printing		...	...	...	...		...	...	...	...		...	...
2222	Service activities related to printing		...	...	...	...		...	...	...	...		...	...
2230	Reproduction of recorded media		...	...	...	...		...	...	...	...		...	...
2310	Coke oven products		...	...	...	...		...	...	...	...		...	...
2320	Refined petroleum products		...	...	...	...		...	...	...	...		...	...
2330	Processing of nuclear fuel		...	...	...	...		...	...	...	...		...	...
241	Basic chemicals		...	...	...	...		...	...	...	...		...	...
2411	Basic chemicals, except fertilizers		...	...	...	...		...	...	...	...		...	...
2412	Fertilizers and nitrogen compounds		17922	16377	18276	...		2378	2475	-18	...		570	75
2413	Plastics in primary forms; synthetic rubber		...	...	...	...		...	...	...	...		...	...
242	Other chemicals		...	...	...	...		...	...	...	...		...	...
2421	Pesticides and other agro-chemical products		...	...	...	...		...	...	...	...		...	...
2422	Paints, varnishes, printing ink and mastics		24565	24865	29615	...		7722	7621	7487	...		400	133
2423	Pharmaceuticals, medicinal chemicals, etc.		...	...	...	...		...	...	...	...		...	...
2424	Soap, cleaning & cosmetic preparations		24746	25711	36253	...		5377	6215	10139	...		389	283
2429	Other chemical products n.e.c.		15117	13413	10384	...		6610	5954	6051	...		1089	439
2430	Man-made fibres		...	...	...	...		...	...	...	...		...	...
251	Rubber products		...	...	...	...		...	...	...	...		...	...
2511	Rubber tyres and tubes		7698	8765	8060	...		565	1708	2053	...		173	...
2519	Other rubber products		...	...	...	...		...	...	...	...		...	...
2520	Plastic products		...	...	...	...		7292	8124	10205	...		3345	4385
2610	Glass and glass products		17399	19700	18771	...		4864	6008	3838	...		132	-214
269	Non-metallic mineral products n.e.c.		...	...	...	...		...	...	...	...		...	...
2691	Pottery, china and earthenware		...	...	...	...		...	...	...	...		...	...
2692	Refractory ceramic products		...	...	...	...		...	...	...	...		...	...
2693	Struct.non-refractory clay; ceramic products		...	...	...	...		...	...	...	...		...	...
2694	Cement, lime and plaster		...	...	...	...		...	...	...	...		...	...
2695	Articles of concrete, cement and plaster		...	...	...	...		6997	7886	8543	...		...	...
2696	Cutting, shaping & finishing of stone		...	...	...	...		...	...	...	...		...	...
2699	Other non-metallic mineral products n.e.c.		...	...	...	...		...	...	...	...		...	...
2710	Basic iron and steel		16054	17446	39201	...		4258	3236	4923	...		602	1173
2720	Basic precious and non-ferrous metals		...	...	...	...		...	...	...	...		...	...
273	Casting of metals		...	...	...	...		...	...	...	...		...	...
2731	Casting of iron and steel		...	...	...	...		...	...	...	...		...	...
2732	Casting of non-ferrous metals		...	...	...	...		...	...	...	...		...	...
281	Struct.metal products;tanks;steam generators		...	...	...	...		...	...	...	...		...	...
2811	Structural metal products		19439	20781	23307	...		5477	4679	5637	...		468	173
2812	Tanks, reservoirs and containers of metal		...	...	...	...		...	...	...	...		...	...
2813	Steam generators		...	...	...	...		...	...	...	...		...	...
289	Other metal products; metal working services		...	...	...	...		...	...	...	...		...	...
2891	Metal forging/pressing/stamping/roll-forming		46882	47442	37331	...		6456	5956	5715	...		918	8
2892	Treatment & coating of metals		5503	6429	6266	...		2585	3427	3564	...		-111	31
2893	Cutlery, hand tools and general hardware		...	...	...	...		...	...	...	...		...	...
2899	Other fabricated metal products n.e.c.		17520	20088	21777	...		5421	6687	6123	...		279	33
291	General purpose machinery		...	...	...	...		...	...	...	...		...	...
2911	Engines & turbines (not for transport equipment)		1103	1344	2087	...		234	451	495	...		...	47
2912	Pumps, compressors, taps and valves		...	...	...	...		...	...	...	...		...	...
2913	Bearings, gears, gearing & driving elements		...	...	...	...		...	...	...	...		...	...
2914	Ovens, furnaces and furnace burners		...	...	...	...		...	...	...	...		...	...
2915	Lifting and handling equipment		976	1615	460	...		299	533	130	...		...	...
2919	Other general purpose machinery		...	...	...	...		55	96	82	...		...	...

292	Special purpose machinery	...	...	...	...	...	...	...	...	...	...
2921	Agricultural and forestry machinery	...	...	...	...	...	...	...	...	...	...
2922	Machine tools	...	...	...	...	...	...	...	...	...	...
2923	Machinery for metallurgy	...	...	...	...	...	...	...	...	...	...
2924	Machinery for mining & construction	...	...	...	...	...	...	...	...	...	...
2925	Food/beverage/tobacco processing machinery	...	...	...	...	...	...	...	...	...	...
2926	Machinery for textile, apparel and leather	...	...	...	...	...	...	...	...	...	...
2927	Weapons and ammunition	...	...	...	...	...	...	...	...	...	...
2929	Other special purpose machinery	...	...	...	...	...	...	...	...	...	...
2930	Domestic appliances n.e.c.	...	...	...	...	...	...	...	...	...	...
3000	Office, accounting and computing machinery	...	...	...	...	...	...	...	...	...	...
3110	Electric motors, generators and transformers	2003	2517	2686	...	612	968	2239	...	123	30
3120	Electricity distribution & control apparatus	...	...	...	...	...	...	...	...	...	...
3130	Insulated wire and cable	...	...	...	...	...	...	...	...	...	...
3140	Accumulators, primary cells and batteries	10329	10442	4356	...	2696	3170	1295	...	114	63
3150	Lighting equipment and electric lamps	...	...	...	...	...	...	...	...	...	...
3190	Other electrical equipment n.e.c.	...	...	...	...	...	...	...	...	...	...
3210	Electronic valves, tubes, etc.	...	...	...	...	...	...	...	...	...	...
3220	TV/radio transmitters; line comm. apparatus	...	...	...	...	...	...	...	...	...	...
3230	TV and radio receivers and associated goods	...	...	...	...	...	...	...	...	...	...
331	Medical, measuring, testing appliances, etc.	...	...	...	...	...	...	...	...	...	...
3311	Medical, surgical and orthopaedic equipment	...	...	...	...	...	...	...	...	...	...
3312	Measuring/testing/navigating appliances,etc.	...	...	...	...	...	...	...	...	...	...
3313	Industrial process control equipment	...	...	...	...	...	...	...	...	...	...
3320	Optical instruments & photographic equipment	...	...	...	...	...	...	...	...	...	...
3330	Watches and clocks	...	...	...	...	...	...	...	...	...	...
3410	Motor vehicles	...	...	...	...	...	...	...	...	...	...
3420	Automobile bodies, trailers & semi-trailers	4335	5129	6480	...	1223	1474	1954	...	112	8
3430	Parts/accessories for automobiles	...	...	...	...	...	...	...	...	...	...
351	Building and repairing of ships and boats	...	...	...	...	...	...	...	...	...	...
3511	Building and repairing of ships	7595	9901	9007	...	2856	4303	3076	...	16	31
3512	Building/repairing of pleasure/sport. boats	...	...	...	...	...	...	...	...	...	...
3520	Railway/tramway locomotives & rolling stock	...	...	...	...	...	...	...	...	...	...
3530	Aircraft and spacecraft	...	...	...	...	...	...	...	...	...	...
359	Transport equipment n.e.c.	...	...	...	...	...	...	...	...	...	...
3591	Motorcycles	...	...	...	...	...	...	...	...	...	...
3592	Bicycles and invalid carriages	...	...	...	...	...	...	...	...	...	...
3599	Other transport equipment n.e.c.	...	...	...	...	...	...	...	...	...	...
3610	Furniture	39850	72268	80221	...	14050	21468	22382	...	808	354
369	Manufacturing n.e.c.	...	...	...	...	...	...	...	...	...	...
3691	Jewellery and related articles	12692	14622	18054	...	1112	1955	1918	...	1079	3122
3692	Musical instruments	...	...	...	...	...	...	...	...	...	...
3693	Sports goods	...	...	...	...	...	...	...	...	...	...
3694	Games and toys	...	...	...	...	...	...	...	...	...	...
3699	Other manufacturing n.e.c.	4742	5922	5931	...	1265	1868	3193	...	-181	-301
3710	Recycling of metal waste and scrap	...	...	...	...	...	...	...	...	...	...
3720	Recycling of non-metal waste and scrap	...	...	...	...	...	...	...	...	...	...
D	Total manufacturing	1543371	1598282	1731361	...	415575	470518	466031	...	64746	58715

a/ 1532 includes 1531.

ISIC Revision 3			Index numbers of industrial production											
			(2000=100)											
ISIC	Industry	Note	1995	1996	1997	1998	1999	2000	2001	2002	2003	2004	2005	2006
15	Food and beverages	a/	113	112	97	101	120	100	110	119	126	136	152	165
16	Tobacco products	a/	...	...	...	...	...	...	...	...	...	...	...	...
17	Textiles	b/	44	58	74	97	106	100	131	115	103	128	58	42
18	Wearing apparel, fur	b/	...	...	...	...	...	...	...	...	...	...	...	...
19	Leather, leather products and footwear		...	...	...	...	...	...	...	...	...	...	...	...
20	Wood products (excl. furniture)		...	...	...	...	...	...	...	...	...	...	...	...
21	Paper and paper products	c/	85	85	89	94	98	100	86	94	85	80	79	96
22	Printing and publishing	c/	...	...	...	...	...	...	...	...	...	...	...	...
23	Coke,refined petroleum products,nuclear fuel		...	...	...	...	...	...	...	...	...	...	...	...
24	Chemicals and chemical products		...	...	...	...	...	...	...	...	...	...	...	...
25	Rubber and plastics products		...	...	...	...	...	...	...	...	...	...	...	...
26	Non-metallic mineral products		...	...	...	...	...	...	...	...	...	...	...	...
27	Basic metals		...	...	...	...	...	...	...	...	...	...	...	...
28	Fabricated metal products		...	...	...	...	...	...	...	...	...	...	...	...
29	Machinery and equipment n.e.c.		...	...	...	...	...	...	...	...	...	...	...	...
30	Office, accounting and computing machinery		...	...	...	...	...	...	...	...	...	...	...	...
31	Electrical machinery and apparatus		...	...	...	...	...	...	...	...	...	...	...	...
32	Radio,television and communication equipment		...	...	...	...	...	...	...	...	...	...	...	...
33	Medical, precision and optical instruments		...	...	...	...	...	...	...	...	...	...	...	...
34	Motor vehicles, trailers, semi-trailers		...	...	...	...	...	...	...	...	...	...	...	...
35	Other transport equipment		...	...	...	...	...	...	...	...	...	...	...	...
36	Furniture; manufacturing n.e.c.		...	...	...	...	...	...	...	...	...	...	...	...
37	Recycling		...	...	...	...	...	...	...	...	...	...	...	...
D	Total manufacturing		132	96	103	106	111	100	107	107	105	118	99	100

a/ 15 includes 16.
b/ 17 includes 18.
c/ 21 includes 22.

Finland

Supplier of information:
Statistics Finland, Helsinki.
Industrial statistics for the OECD countries are compiled by the OECD secretariat, which supplies them to UNIDO.

Basic source of data:
Annual survey; administrative data; business registers.

Major deviations from ISIC (Revision 3):
Data have been converted from NACE (Revision 1) to ISIC (Revision 3).

Reference period:
Calendar year.

Scope:
All enterprises.

Method of data collection:
Mail questionnaires.

Type of enumeration:
All enterprises with 20 or more employees are surveyed; administrative financial data is used for all other enterprises. The Business Register provides information on the principal activity and employment in enterprises not surveyed.

Adjusted for non-response:
Yes.

Concepts and definitions of variables:
Number of employees is based on the average number of employees throughout the year. Data are not converted to full-time equivalent.
Wages and salaries includes social insurance contributions payable by employees and deducted by employers.
Output is gross output. It excludes income from sales of capital assets produced on own accounts.
Gross fixed capital formation is expenditure on the purchase of fixed assets plus own-account construction of assets. Fixed assets include investments in equipment goods, buildings, other construction and other fixed assets. They are investments with a productive life of at least one year, and include assets made by a unit's labour force for its own use; additions, alterations, improvements and repairs to existing assets; new assets (whether or not in use) and used assets.

Related national publications:
Statistics on the Structure of Industry and Construction; Preliminary Data on Finnish Industries, both published by Statistics Finland, Helsinki.

Finland

ISIC	Industry	Number of enterprises Note	2002	2003	2004	2005	Number of employees Note	2002	2003	2004	2005	Wages and salaries paid to employees Note	2002	2003	2004	2005
ISIC Revision 3			(number)					(number)					(millions of Euros)			
151	Processed meat,fish,fruit,vegetables,fats		610	596	605	604		13890	14370	...	...		381.6	390.2	...	...
1511	Processing/preserving of meat		236	231	234	238		10611	10868	9896	10246		291.1	292.5	290.7	300.0
1512	Processing/preserving of fish		154	160	156	160		596	647	...	...		12.6	14.7	13.9	15.0
1513	Processing/preserving of fruit & vegetables		200	187	199	188		1987	2043	1977	1975		53.0	54.8	55.1	55.0
1514	Vegetable and animal oils and fats		20	18	16	18		696	812	...	...		24.9	28.2	...	...
1520	Dairy products		54	53	56	55		5320	5357	5255	5210		151.6	161.9	166.1	172.0
153	Grain mill products; starches; animal feeds		158	152	156	156		1507	1509	1516	1606		45.0	47.7	50.4	56.0
1531	Grain mill products		74	69	70	69		372	382	420	569		10.7	11.0	13.9	20.0
1532	Starches and starch products		7	8	7	6		163	155	103	60		5.3	5.0	3.1	2.0
1533	Prepared animal feeds		77	75	79	81		972	972	993	976		28.9	31.8	33.3	33.0
154	Other food products		1024	1012	975	954		14463	14334	13717	...		359.6	368.4	376.7	370.0
1541	Bakery products		871	857	828	817		10532	10498	9866	9675		248.9	254.8	257.9	256.0
1542	Sugar		4	5	5	5		389	458	509	512		13.9	16.5	18.4	18.0
1543	Cocoa, chocolate and sugar confectionery		36	37	35	32		...	2141	2042	1969		...	58.5	57.9	60.0
1544	Macaroni, noodles & similar products		1	1	1	1		...	...	...	...		...	...	...	...
1549	Other food products n.e.c.		112	112	106	99		...	...	...	...		...	...	...	...
155	Beverages		90	93	96	92		3887	3853	3757	3524		130.5	127.7	134.2	135.0
1551	Distilling, rectifying & blending of spirits		7	7	6	6		549	572	594	591		20.6	20.0	24.9	24.0
1552	Wines		39	36	40	38		245	259	251	259		7.2	7.9	7.5	8.0
1553	Malt liquors and malt		27	27	26	24		3050	2956	2838	2587		101.7	98.4	100.1	101.0
1554	Soft drinks; mineral waters		17	23	24	24		43	66	74	87		0.9	1.3	1.7	2.0
1600	Tobacco products		5	4	2	1		395	379	...	...		13.8	13.9	...	...
171	Spinning, weaving and finishing of textiles		185	189	192	185		834	801	775	854		19.9	19.6	18.6	22.0
1711	Textile fibre preparation; textile weaving		54	53	54	51		330	292	283	258		8.2	7.2	7.0	7.0
1712	Finishing of textiles		131	136	138	134		504	509	492	596		11.7	12.4	11.6	15.0
172	Other textiles		705	654	661	653		3721	3543	3684	3463		100.5	98.2	105.7	103.0
1721	Made-up textile articles, except apparel		308	292	289	296		1151	1138	1214	1002		24.4	25.3	28.4	24.0
1722	Carpets and rugs		162	139	140	136		137	123	128	138		2.9	2.4	2.7	3.0
1723	Cordage, rope, twine and netting		23	20	18	18		122	135	137	126		2.3	2.7	2.8	3.0
1729	Other textiles n.e.c.		212	203	214	203		2311	2147	2205	2196		71.0	67.7	71.9	74.0
1730	Knitted and crocheted fabrics and articles		151	137	127	117		1018	716	672	642		22.4	14.9	13.9	14.0
1810	Wearing apparel, except fur apparel		1168	1154	1110	1079		5415	4906	4536	4045		115.0	106.8	102.3	95.0
1820	Dressing & dyeing of fur; processing of fur		99	98	87	85		246	243	182	185		4.9	5.1	4.2	4.0
191	Tanning, dressing and processing of leather		226	208	191	182		476	462	406	374		9.4	9.2	8.5	8.0
1911	Tanning and dressing of leather		16	15	11	12		212	187	161	145		4.4	3.8	3.5	3.0
1912	Luggage, handbags, etc.; saddlery & harness		210	193	180	170		264	275	245	229		5.0	5.4	5.0	5.0
1920	Footwear		90	87	82	77		1875	1830	1661	1534		38.7	37.1	35.5	35.0
2010	Sawmilling and planing of wood		1171	1136	1110	1087		10033	8715	8580	8320		271.5	242.3	249.4	240.0
202	Products of wood, cork, straw, etc.		1668	1641	1608	1569		17510	18453	18613	18380		420.7	462.6	487.5	493.0
2021	Veneer sheets, plywood, particle board, etc.		51	47	42	39		5843	6966	6719	6191		148.8	186.9	190.0	181.0
2022	Builders' carpentry and joinery		989	991	963	938		10051	9881	10317	10615		236.5	239.1	260.3	274.0
2023	Wooden containers		201	199	192	178		971	954	972	1014		21.7	22.1	22.6	25.0
2029	Other wood products; articles of cork/straw		427	404	411	414		645	652	605	560		13.7	14.5	14.6	14.0
210	Paper and paper products		201	204	206	204		39436	38290	37144	33909		1507.6	1525.1	1536.0	1352.0
2101	Pulp, paper and paperboard		54	62	63	60		35485	34484	33417	30307		1386.7	1403.8	1409.5	1232.0
2102	Corrugated paper and paperboard		66	65	68	70		2755	2637	2562	2449		87.9	88.0	87.5	85.0
2109	Other articles of paper and paperboard		81	77	75	74		1196	1169	1165	1152		33.0	33.4	39.0	35.0
221	Publishing		1388	1374	1395	1436		17065	17142	16885	16029		541.9	551.7	567.8	561.0
2211	Publishing of books and other publications		369	348	351	349		2162	2227	2284	2332		68.6	71.5	76.3	77.0
2212	Publishing of newspapers, journals, etc.		558	558	551	545		14049	14018	13728	12776		448.7	453.3	464.5	455.0
2213	Publishing of recorded media		329	344	366	398		332	332	314	323		9.3	10.5	10.5	12.0
2219	Other publishing		132	124	127	144		522	565	559	598		15.3	16.4	16.5	18.0

222	Printing and related service activities	1276	1237	1208	1172	12390	11951	11462	11490	353.0	342.5	345.5	366.0
2221	Printing	925	906	895	873	11272	10920	10497	10516	320.4	311.4	315.6	334.0
2222	Service activities related to printing	351	331	313	299	1118	1031	965	974	32.7	31.1	30.0	31.0
2230	Reproduction of recorded media	91	91	94	93	151	154	135	149	4.5	4.8	4.1	5.0
2310	Coke oven products	3	2	1	1	...	...	...	...	...	...	...	...
2320	Refined petroleum products	12	9	10	7	...	...	...	2704	...	...	...	130.0
2330	Processing of nuclear fuel	1	1	1	1	...	...	...	...	...	...	...	...
241	Basic chemicals	104	107	113	117	9033	8835	8855	8716	343.5	348.0	378.2	378.0
2411	Basic chemicals, except fertilizers	54	57	60	56	5720	5733	5703	5261	210.0	216.6	242.2	228.0
2412	Fertilizers and nitrogen compounds	11	11	10	11	781	811	782	756	29.0	32.1	32.6	33.0
2413	Plastics in primary forms; synthetic rubber	39	39	43	50	2532	2291	2370	2699	104.6	99.3	103.5	117.0
242	Other chemicals	204	218	212	215	...	...	...	...	...	...	...	...
2421	Pesticides and other agro-chemical products	1	1	1	1	...	...	...	...	...	...	...	...
2422	Paints, varnishes, printing ink and mastics	41	43	38	40	1888	1697	1745	1915	60.5	55.5	59.9	69.0
2423	Pharmaceuticals, medicinal chemicals, etc.	36	40	35	40	5796	5410	4188	4020	170.6	178.2	142.0	140.0
2424	Soap, cleaning & cosmetic preparations	68	69	73	71	...	...	...	986	...	...	...	31.0
2429	Other chemical products n.e.c.	58	65	65	63	1099	1851	1738	...	36.7	62.3	60.3	64.0
2430	Man-made fibres	3	2	2	1	...	...	...	...	...	...	...	...
251	Rubber products	76	78	68	68	2751	2755	2707	2924	83.8	91.5	92.0	102.0
2511	Rubber tyres and tubes	19	20	18	18	1448	1474	1554	1629	49.4	55.9	58.9	64.0
2519	Other rubber products	57	58	50	50	1303	1281	1153	1295	34.4	35.5	33.1	38.0
2520	Plastic products	634	608	614	603	15013	13141	13327	12575	406.8	376.2	379.1	390.0
2610	Glass and glass products	151	156	156	163	4594	4614	4505	4463	137.2	143.0	143.1	151.0
269	Non-metallic mineral products n.e.c.	774	770	744	731	11258	11146	11260	11562	310.5	321.0	330.5	363.0
2691	Pottery, china and earthenware	170	164	149	152	...	...	...	...	...	...	...	...
2692	Refractory ceramic products	6	6	5	5	47	47	45	41	1.4	1.5	1.4	1.0
2693	Struct.non-refractory clay; ceramic products	14	13	13	11	...	...	428	...	...	...	12.6	11.0
2694	Cement, lime and plaster	2	3	4	3	...	...	842	827	...	...	27.6	28.0
2695	Articles of concrete, cement and plaster	286	295	282	274	6249	6120	6221	6302	168.1	171.5	178.3	193.0
2696	Cutting, shaping & finishing of stone	265	260	259	254	1407	1357	1325	1462	35.2	35.4	35.1	41.0
2699	Other non-metallic mineral products n.e.c.	31	29	32	32	1482	1507	1649	1626	47.4	49.4	53.6	59.0
2710	Basic iron and steel	71	71	76	75	10967	10416	11156	12235	377.4	378.0	447.0	485.0
2720	Basic precious and non-ferrous metals	20	19	18	20	3386	3249	3030	3007	116.1	113.5	115.3	116.0
273	Casting of metals	61	64	61	59	2532	2617	2942	3037	68.5	69.8	85.0	96.0
2731	Casting of iron and steel	27	27	27	27	1710	1799	2041	2134	47.5	48.4	61.2	70.0
2732	Casting of non-ferrous metals	34	37	34	32	822	818	901	903	21.0	21.3	23.7	26.0
281	Struct.metal products;tanks;steam generators	1474	1475	1498	1517	17417	17656	16161	16841	486.3	496.3	473.9	515.0
2811	Structural metal products	1356	1342	1364	1391	13592	11165	10337	11151	367.9	303.7	284.8	320.0
2812	Tanks, reservoirs and containers of metal	95	91	95	85	1673	1593	1637	1550	45.2	45.6	47.0	47.0
2813	Steam generators	23	42	39	41	2152	4898	4187	4140	73.2	147.0	142.1	148.0
289	Other metal products; metal working services	2993	3024	3061	3100	22490	22694	23108	23891	573.6	595.5	627.1	672.0
2891	Metal forging/pressing/stamping/roll-forming	101	103	98	96	500	387	359	363	12.7	9.7	9.1	9.0
2892	Treatment & coating of metals	1594	1638	1702	1756	13578	13917	14573	15702	342.4	360.5	389.6	438.0
2893	Cutlery, hand tools and general hardware	351	352	344	334	3208	3185	3106	3126	85.0	87.9	88.4	91.0
2899	Other fabricated metal products n.e.c.	947	931	917	914	5204	5205	5070	4700	133.5	137.4	140.0	134.0
291	General purpose machinery	1648	1614	1600	1564	25160	24952	24913	23306	806.0	826.4	876.4	836.0
2911	Engines & turbines (not for transport equipment)	108	107	103	103	3151	3668	4208	2542	124.4	154.8	189.1	124.0
2912	Pumps, compressors, taps and valves	143	136	128	125	4654	4399	3964	3898	134.1	130.9	121.2	121.0
2913	Bearings, gears, gearing & driving elements	45	45	43	42	1718	1677	1673	1758	50.9	51.2	53.5	59.0
2914	Ovens, furnaces and furnace burners	22	20	21	24	207	200	205	229	6.2	6.1	6.8	8.0
2915	Lifting and handling equipment	351	351	358	355	8123	8170	7910	7765	278.0	277.6	291.0	296.0
2919	Other general purpose machinery	979	955	947	915	7307	6838	6953	7113	212.5	205.8	214.9	228.0
292	Special purpose machinery	1863	1861	1848	1839	31321	30569	28802	32133	1005.2	997.9	981.4	1138.0
2921	Agricultural and forestry machinery	722	719	716	714	4116	4552	4467	4512	119.6	133.1	138.2	147.0
2922	Machine tools	164	167	157	161	3192	2936	2849	2925	93.6	86.7	85.7	93.0
2923	Machinery for metallurgy	16	17	17	17	76	154	79	73	1.7	4.4	3.1	3.0
2924	Machinery for mining & construction	185	187	189	181	3934	4001	3728	3942	130.8	133.4	132.6	145.0
2925	Food/beverage/tobacco processing machinery	128	132	135	130	2203	1910	2032	1833	64.9	55.2	61.2	57.0
2926	Machinery for textile, apparel and leather	23	21	24	24	41	43	69	72	0.9	1.1	1.9	2.0
2927	Weapons and ammunition	44	40	42	41	1245	1273	1258	1185	38.9	41.6	43.7	44.0
2929	Other special purpose machinery	581	578	568	571	16514	15700	14320	17591	554.8	542.5	514.9	648.0

continued

Finland

ISIC	Industry	Number of enterprises (number) Note	2002	2003	2004	2005	Number of employees (number) Note	2002	2003	2004	2005	Wages and salaries paid to employees (millions of Euros) Note	2002	2003	2004	2005
2930	Domestic appliances n.e.c.		40	38	39	40		1267	1235	1254	1220		31.8	31.7	33.8	34.0
3000	Office, accounting and computing machinery		56	51	52	49		389	343	352	221		10.8	9.8	10.5	8.0
3110	Electric motors, generators and transformers		87	89	88	85		11936	11149	9089	9133		392.6	370.2	325.1	336.0
3120	Electricity distribution & control apparatus		107	113	118	111		2850	3123	3364	3328		73.2	87.0	96.6	99.0
3130	Insulated wire and cable		36	34	37	37		2012	1809	1666	1706		61.1	55.0	53.3	55.0
3140	Accumulators, primary cells and batteries		5	5	5	5		14	11	12	14		0.4	0.3	0.3	...
3150	Lighting equipment and electric lamps		82	80	77	76		1307	1158	1081	1056		35.1	31.8	31.7	32.0
3190	Other electrical equipment n.e.c.		178	178	177	183		2482	2650	2362	2282		70.5	76.0	76.7	72.0
3210	Electronic valves, tubes, etc.		210	208	205	200		4385	4021	3872	3901		114.0	110.1	110.0	113.0
3220	TV/radio transmitters; line comm. apparatus		63	61	54	54		30441	30283	30869	31808		1163.3	1296.0	1421.1	1559.0
3230	TV and radio receivers and associated goods		53	52	52	55		1223	1126	1107	824		33.9	30.7	31.7	28.0
331	Medical, measuring, testing appliances, etc.		828	817	804	817		11792	11493	11158	11121		394.0	386.6	385.6	413.0
3311	Medical, surgical and orthopaedic equipment		533	525	516	519		5156	4663	4354	4321		167.7	146.7	147.4	154.0
3312	Measuring/testing/navigating appliances,etc.		227	222	222	231		3733	4103	4154	4220		118.2	132.3	136.3	153.0
3313	Industrial process control equipment		68	70	66	67		2903	2727	2650	2580		108.1	107.6	101.9	107.0
3320	Optical instruments & photographic equipment		41	43	37	36		251	221	...	...		6.5	6.3	...	...
3330	Watches and clocks		3	4	2	2		4	5	...	...		0.1	0.1	...	...
3410	Motor vehicles		29	30	28	31		2951	2867	2106	2189		84.8	73.3	69.9	72.0
3420	Automobile bodies, trailers & semi-trailers		182	183	179	170		3668	3746	3767	3852		100.8	104.5	109.6	113.0
3430	Parts/accessories for automobiles		72	68	71	75		775	778	734	764		20.5	21.4	21.5	24.0
351	Building and repairing of ships and boats		566	574	577	568		11407	10557	9306	8736		321.9	300.6	249.8	258.0
3511	Building and repairing of ships		151	143	146	134		9366	8441	7108	6303		266.8	243.2	189.7	192.0
3512	Building/repairing of pleasure/sport. boats		415	431	431	434		2041	2116	2198	2432		55.1	57.4	60.1	66.0
3520	Railway/tramway locomotives & rolling stock		8	10	10	11		642	592	566	578		15.2	15.9	16.3	18.0
3530	Aircraft and spacecraft		9	13	12	13		674	634	661	680		23.3	20.6	21.7	23.0
359	Transport equipment n.e.c.		27	23	22	24		203	386	338	553		5.2	9.6	9.6	16.0
3591	Motorcycles		1	1	2	2		...	...	...	...		...	...	...	...
3592	Bicycles and invalid carriages		11	10	10	10		...	...	...	...		...	...	...	...
3599	Other transport equipment n.e.c.		15	12	10	12		71	91	63	...		1.8	1.7	1.7	8.0
3610	Furniture		1610	1582	1577	1575		11295	10938	10646	10040		262.1	261.0	263.1	269.0
369	Manufacturing n.e.c.		984	982	1023	1011		3365	2933	2798	2654		83.9	76.4	76.1	74.0
3691	Jewellery and related articles		287	281	301	300		696	664	654	629		18.4	18.3	18.4	19.0
3692	Musical instruments		67	76	84	81		70	62	76	67		1.5	1.5	2.0	2.0
3693	Sports goods		155	152	157	157		1124	913	952	973		28.6	25.2	26.5	27.0
3694	Games and toys		65	57	55	61		210	115	95	97		4.6	2.8	2.3	3.0
3699	Other manufacturing n.e.c.		410	416	426	412		1265	1179	1021	888		30.8	28.6	26.9	23.0
3710	Recycling of metal waste and scrap		47	44	50	55		239	248	249	779		5.9	6.6	6.9	24.0
3720	Recycling of non-metal waste and scrap		24	23	26	25		129	126	126	148		3.4	3.1	3.5	5.0
D	Total manufacturing		25799	25504	25366	25190		424848	416025	403158	400482		12982.5	13142.3	13419.4	13757.0

ISIC Revision 3		Output					Value added in factor values					Gross fixed capital formation		
			(millions of Euros)					(millions of Euros)					(millions of Euros)	
ISIC	Industry	Note	2002	2003	2004	2005	Note	2002	2003	2004	2005	Note	2004	2005
151	Processed meat,fish,fruit,vegetables,fats		2611.4	2744.8	...	...		702.7	701.3	...	...		...	...
1511	Processing/preserving of meat		1932.2	2030.1	2092.1	2050.0		512.3	512.2	510.0	480.0		56.9	114.0
1512	Processing/preserving of fish		92.0	105.1	97.5	91.0		26.0	26.7	25.2	28.0		...	...
1513	Processing/preserving of fruit & vegetables		378.6	379.7	395.7	365.0		109.0	117.8	112.9	126.0		18.1	23.0
1514	Vegetable and animal oils and fats		208.6	229.9	...	...		55.4	44.6	...	...		...	...
1520	Dairy products		1766.3	1767.8	1778.2	1805.0		282.3	284.0	303.8	318.0		86.2	57.0
153	Grain mill products; starches; animal feeds		701.3	695.9	703.2	621.0		109.2	115.3	119.1	126.0		19.2	40.0
1531	Grain mill products		130.6	131.8	141.6	145.0		25.5	26.9	30.3	39.0		4.2	22.0
1532	Starches and starch products		99.9	80.6	63.5	19.0		15.4	9.3	8.4	7.0		1.9	1.0
1533	Prepared animal feeds		470.8	483.5	498.1	457.0		68.4	79.0	80.4	80.0		13.1	17.0
154	Other food products		1890.3	1944.6	1918.1	1892.0		685.4	713.0	723.7	694.0		103.8	...
1541	Bakery products		921.7	952.8	961.9	969.0		413.2	426.1	428.8	430.0		36.4	59.0
1542	Sugar		285.7	311.2	268.8	253.0		47.6	55.9	58.8	53.0		19.0	2.0
1543	Cocoa, chocolate and sugar confectionery		...	324.8	323.9	323.0		...	120.8	117.9	104.0		21.2	8.0
1544	Macaroni, noodles & similar products		...	...	...	...		...	...	...	...		...	...
1549	Other food products n.e.c.		...	...	...	...		...	...	...	...		...	...
155	Beverages		964.3	979.3	978.2	956.0		335.0	332.8	334.9	312.0		36.6	42.0
1551	Distilling, rectifying & blending of spirits		166.7	182.2	193.8	198.0		54.6	56.0	57.9	55.0		8.6	9.0
1552	Wines		35.2	42.3	40.8	41.0		12.5	12.5	16.3	18.0		2.7	2.0
1553	Malt liquors and malt		756.9	745.6	729.3	697.0		266.4	262.1	257.6	236.0		24.4	30.0
1554	Soft drinks; mineral waters		5.5	9.1	14.3	20.0		1.5	2.2	3.2	4.0		0.9	1.0
1600	Tobacco products		96.9	91.3	...	...		18.4	18.5	...	...		...	...
171	Spinning, weaving and finishing of textiles		105.7	106.9	92.6	92.0		34.8	34.9	30.1	34.0		2.2	3.0
1711	Textile fibre preparation; textile weaving		42.7	38.1	37.7	36.0		12.8	12.4	12.0	11.0		0.5	1.0
1712	Finishing of textiles		63.0	68.8	54.9	56.0		22.0	22.5	18.1	23.0		1.7	2.0
172	Other textiles		502.0	475.9	521.9	505.0		213.8	196.8	203.9	208.0		28.5	24.0
1721	Made-up textile articles, except apparel		128.6	133.8	163.5	131.0		47.5	48.5	54.2	47.0		5.2	4.0
1722	Carpets and rugs		27.1	19.8	22.1	28.0		7.5	6.3	7.7	9.0		0.9	3.0
1723	Cordage, rope, twine and netting		11.7	12.7	12.5	12.0		4.5	5.3	4.8	4.0		1.2	-
1729	Other textiles n.e.c.		334.7	309.5	323.7	334.0		154.4	136.7	137.4	148.0		21.2	18.0
1730	Knitted and crocheted fabrics and articles		86.7	60.1	53.5	52.0		36.1	24.3	23.4	22.0		0.9	1.0
1810	Wearing apparel, except fur apparel		527.3	463.1	432.5	398.0		199.6	184.0	180.2	165.0		7.5	6.0
1820	Dressing & dyeing of fur; processing of fur		21.0	20.6	17.6	17.0		7.5	9.0	7.4	8.0		0.8	1.0
191	Tanning, dressing and processing of leather		58.9	55.8	48.6	48.0		17.9	16.8	15.3	17.0		1.1	1.0
1911	Tanning and dressing of leather		26.3	24.5	19.1	19.0		6.4	6.0	4.8	5.0		0.2	1.0
1912	Luggage, handbags, etc.; saddlery & harness		32.6	31.3	29.5	28.0		11.5	10.8	10.5	12.0		0.9	1.0
1920	Footwear		167.4	153.7	158.6	149.0		70.0	62.4	64.7	59.0		5.1	3.0
2010	Sawmilling and planing of wood		3027.0	2782.2	2739.2	2728.0		506.5	478.3	451.7	432.0		128.0	93.0
202	Products of wood, cork, straw, etc.		2275.9	2825.7	2940.1	3000.0		744.0	813.7	866.9	865.0		96.2	129.0
2021	Veneer sheets, plywood, particle board, etc.		752.8	1192.5	1167.0	1125.0		253.9	303.2	293.6	282.0		25.7	33.0
2022	Builders' carpentry and joinery		1351.0	1459.7	1593.6	1684.0		416.8	440.6	499.1	505.0		60.8	87.0
2023	Wooden containers		113.0	113.9	121.3	134.0		45.4	43.3	47.6	52.0		5.4	5.0
2029	Other wood products; articles of cork/straw		59.1	59.6	58.2	58.0		27.9	26.6	26.6	26.0		4.3	4.0
210	Paper and paper products		13860.9	13675.4	13678.9	12292.0		4367.7	3581.3	3795.1	3038.0		571.6	649.0
2101	Pulp, paper and paperboard		13268.4	13091.8	13065.2	11694.0		4157.7	3374.5	3575.7	2834.0		546.7	630.0
2102	Corrugated paper and paperboard		410.8	402.5	409.7	392.0		147.7	146.9	151.1	140.0		14.8	10.0
2109	Other articles of paper and paperboard		181.7	181.1	204.0	206.0		62.2	59.9	68.2	64.0		10.0	9.0
221	Publishing		2557.4	2652.2	2577.5	2594.0		998.9	1002.7	1095.3	1017.0		70.9	67.0
2211	Publishing of books and other publications		361.4	365.8	361.8	362.0		123.7	123.9	136.2	133.0		5.2	5.0
2212	Publishing of newspapers, journals, etc.		2077.1	2146.2	2086.7	2086.0		826.9	823.2	904.2	823.0		60.9	53.0
2213	Publishing of recorded media		57.9	71.3	65.9	75.0		22.0	25.6	25.9	30.0		2.2	3.0
2219	Other publishing		61.0	69.0	63.1	70.0		26.1	30.0	28.9	31.0		2.6	6.0

continued

Finland

ISIC Revision 3		Output					Value added in factor values					Gross fixed capital formation		
			(millions of Euros)					(millions of Euros)					(millions of Euros)	
ISIC	Industry	Note	2002	2003	2004	2005	Note	2002	2003	2004	2005	Note	2004	2005
222	Printing and related service activities		1554.3	1475.2	1473.8	1651.0		652.6	605.2	603.1	672.0		104.2	111.0
2221	Printing		1453.0	1377.5	1378.6	1555.0		594.2	551.1	549.9	620.0		99.6	103.0
2222	Service activities related to printing		101.2	97.7	95.2	96.0		58.5	54.2	53.3	53.0		4.7	8.0
2230	Reproduction of recorded media		22.9	22.8	22.4	24.0		7.3	7.1	7.8	9.0		0.8	2.0
2310	Coke oven products		...	...	...	...		...	...	...	...		...	...
2320	Refined petroleum products		...	...	...	5509.0		...	...	...	777.0		...	232.0
2330	Processing of nuclear fuel		...	...	...	...		...	...	...	...		...	...
241	Basic chemicals		3396.3	3408.8	4094.3	4090.0		948.3	967.3	1164.4	1042.0		256.5	203.0
2411	Basic chemicals, except fertilizers		1773.6	1783.1	2142.8	1759.0		579.0	628.1	753.9	620.0		185.8	162.0
2412	Fertilizers and nitrogen compounds		320.3	294.3	289.8	371.0		75.4	68.9	70.5	82.0		28.9	7.0
2413	Plastics in primary forms; synthetic rubber		1302.4	1331.5	1661.7	1959.0		294.0	270.5	339.9	340.0		41.9	34.0
242	Other chemicals		...	...	...	...		...	...	...	...		...	...
2421	Pesticides and other agro-chemical products		...	...	...	...		...	...	...	...		...	...
2422	Paints, varnishes, printing ink and mastics		434.2	393.7	432.3	471.0		135.8	117.2	133.9	150.0		10.9	12.0
2423	Pharmaceuticals, medicinal chemicals, etc.		900.4	882.0	824.7	861.0		374.8	391.7	408.7	468.0		33.5	24.0
2424	Soap, cleaning & cosmetic preparations		...	...	...	166.0		...	...	...	61.0		...	7.0
2429	Other chemical products n.e.c.		235.5	373.6	365.1	357.0		73.3	123.2	135.6	145.0		25.0	...
2430	Man-made fibres		...	...	...	...		...	...	...	...		...	...
251	Rubber products		423.3	471.5	535.4	576.0		206.7	230.6	268.3	256.0		42.5	36.0
2511	Rubber tyres and tubes		275.5	320.5	392.3	410.0		143.5	168.0	211.8	189.0		36.0	32.0
2519	Other rubber products		147.9	151.0	143.1	166.0		63.3	62.5	56.5	67.0		6.5	4.0
2520	Plastic products		2010.9	1898.5	1971.5	2086.0		799.0	746.8	757.1	739.0		115.9	115.0
2610	Glass and glass products		602.9	610.2	599.2	730.0		262.9	257.6	263.3	362.0		40.3	26.0
269	Non-metallic mineral products n.e.c.		1854.5	1890.0	2047.6	2204.0		695.7	712.0	738.7	825.0		101.8	126.0
2691	Pottery, china and earthenware		...	...	...	...		...	...	...	...		...	...
2692	Refractory ceramic products		10.3	11.6	12.3	13.0		4.3	5.0	5.2	6.0		0.8	-
2693	Struct.non-refractory clay; ceramic products		...	...	52.9	46.0		...	...	20.9	19.0		2.5	...
2694	Cement, lime and plaster		...	...	245.0	247.0		...	...	99.5	103.0		11.1	12.0
2695	Articles of concrete, cement and plaster		1032.0	1043.9	1134.9	1211.0		353.5	352.7	369.5	413.0		51.3	78.0
2696	Cutting, shaping & finishing of stone		154.3	136.0	138.7	169.0		64.2	67.7	68.7	82.0		8.6	11.0
2699	Other non-metallic mineral products n.e.c.		288.9	285.8	311.9	346.0		121.5	119.2	132.2	132.0		24.8	17.0
2710	Basic iron and steel		2986.3	3577.0	5124.0	5593.0		771.1	900.0	1348.0	1385.0		535.0	164.0
2720	Basic precious and non-ferrous metals		1737.9	1591.4	2043.9	2077.0		274.1	265.6	279.0	361.0		36.3	44.0
273	Casting of metals		269.1	268.9	346.9	379.0		114.7	115.1	136.3	154.0		12.6	26.0
2731	Casting of iron and steel		181.1	178.5	238.6	266.0		78.6	77.7	92.7	109.0		8.2	20.0
2732	Casting of non-ferrous metals		88.0	90.4	108.4	114.0		36.1	37.5	43.6	45.0		4.3	6.0
281	Struct.metal products;tanks;steam generators		2521.0	2556.4	2317.6	2522.0		820.6	828.1	724.3	911.0		72.5	86.0
2811	Structural metal products		1764.2	1479.5	1321.6	1620.0		658.9	537.0	523.9	586.0		58.0	70.0
2812	Tanks, reservoirs and containers of metal		199.9	198.7	213.4	225.0		79.4	76.7	77.6	80.0		7.1	7.0
2813	Steam generators		556.9	878.2	782.6	677.0		82.3	214.4	122.8	246.0		7.4	9.0
289	Other metal products; metal working services		2377.6	2409.7	2660.9	2954.0		1109.3	1118.1	1209.8	1301.0		179.5	199.0
2891	Metal forging/pressing/stamping/roll-forming		53.8	39.5	40.5	47.0		22.7	16.1	16.9	19.0		1.4	3.0
2892	Treatment & coating of metals		1342.1	1359.8	1574.3	1845.0		624.0	648.3	716.5	819.0		126.2	143.0
2893	Cutlery, hand tools and general hardware		346.7	352.6	361.3	372.0		203.1	204.7	204.3	202.0		14.5	15.0
2899	Other fabricated metal products n.e.c.		635.0	657.8	684.8	689.0		259.5	249.0	272.1	261.0		37.4	39.0
291	General purpose machinery		4836.5	4729.9	4922.6	5579.0		1329.0	1343.3	1552.4	1597.0		88.8	102.0
2911	Engines & turbines (not for transport equipment)		1313.7	1250.6	1188.3	1340.0		127.7	220.2	223.1	214.0		8.2	11.0
2912	Pumps, compressors, taps and valves		585.7	580.2	558.3	578.0		240.1	232.0	221.0	224.0		23.3	20.0
2913	Bearings, gears, gearing & driving elements		241.1	207.1	251.6	280.0		96.0	88.9	100.7	101.0		11.4	11.0
2914	Ovens, furnaces and furnace burners		33.0	35.5	37.4	41.0		9.1	11.9	12.5	14.0		0.5	1.0
2915	Lifting and handling equipment		1609.9	1630.5	1800.9	2195.0		469.8	413.0	600.7	618.0		17.1	32.0
2919	Other general purpose machinery		1053.0	1025.9	1086.0	1144.0		386.1	377.4	394.5	426.0		28.2	28.0

292	Special purpose machinery		5212.5	5280.6	5602.4	6563.0		1693.6	1602.8	1679.4	1956.0		132.8	127.0
2921	Agricultural and forestry machinery		918.6	1004.9	1126.8	1289.0		243.7	254.1	310.9	352.0		14.2	22.0
2922	Machine tools		398.9	399.4	426.2	504.0		126.4	144.8	138.3	153.0		20.2	17.0
2923	Machinery for metallurgy		9.4	17.0	15.4	13.0		3.5	5.6	8.1	...		0.3	-
2924	Machinery for mining & construction		849.2	807.7	992.1	1174.0		283.4	241.4	261.4	310.0		14.3	18.0
2925	Food/beverage/tobacco processing machinery		200.8	173.8	199.8	186.0		104.6	84.9	94.3	90.0		3.4	5.0
2926	Machinery for textile, apparel and leather		4.0	4.2	5.6	6.0		2.1	2.1	3.1	3.0		0.2	-
2927	Weapons and ammunition		202.4	214.6	271.0	270.0		72.4	76.1	90.8	82.0		6.6	3.0
2929	Other special purpose machinery		2629.2	2659.0	2565.5	3121.0		857.6	793.7	772.6	966.0		73.6	62.0
2930	Domestic appliances n.e.c.		164.8	161.5	175.2	171.0		59.0	59.2	66.5	64.0		5.9	4.0
3000	Office, accounting and computing machinery		73.2	70.7	70.4	50.0		13.9	16.5	16.5	11.0		1.3	1.0
3110	Electric motors, generators and transformers		1915.4	1900.2	1882.1	2050.0		650.1	644.6	615.7	661.0		34.6	37.0
3120	Electricity distribution & control apparatus		340.7	403.1	464.7	501.0		130.1	148.0	164.2	169.0		10.1	7.0
3130	Insulated wire and cable		377.6	331.8	361.8	428.0		88.2	85.2	85.4	95.0		6.3	5.0
3140	Accumulators, primary cells and batteries		1.2	1.1	1.3	1.0		0.4	0.2	0.4	...		-	-
3150	Lighting equipment and electric lamps		158.6	172.2	174.0	176.0		57.5	65.8	68.0	72.0		2.6	6.0
3190	Other electrical equipment n.e.c.		367.1	390.8	375.1	377.0		131.4	145.9	139.3	143.0		7.9	11.0
3210	Electronic valves, tubes, etc.		509.1	491.5	534.5	528.0		186.1	165.3	178.6	156.0		24.1	21.0
3220	TV/radio transmitters; line comm. apparatus		15325.1	13830.0	14186.9	17190.0		5605.9	5995.0	5047.4	5118.0		234.8	347.0
3230	TV and radio receivers and associated goods		166.2	135.2	142.6	120.0		38.4	41.6	47.9	40.0		1.7	3.0
331	Medical, measuring, testing appliances, etc.		1975.5	1911.1	1950.0	2021.0		768.1	742.8	734.0	816.0		34.0	42.0
3311	Medical, surgical and orthopaedic equipment		836.5	734.0	740.4	803.0		370.4	300.5	313.6	346.0		14.1	21.0
3312	Measuring/testing/navigating appliances,etc.		636.1	699.4	706.3	756.0		228.3	267.4	247.3	284.0		17.8	18.0
3313	Industrial process control equipment		502.9	477.7	503.3	462.0		169.4	174.9	173.1	185.0		2.1	3.0
3320	Optical instruments & photographic equipment		22.3	25.2	...	...		8.9	11.2	...	...		...	...
3330	Watches and clocks		0.4	0.4	...	...		0.1	0.2	...	...		...	...
3410	Motor vehicles		389.5	347.1	340.3	426.0		149.8	111.9	94.1	123.0		23.5	18.0
3420	Automobile bodies, trailers & semi-trailers		475.8	505.6	545.8	575.0		163.9	173.6	181.2	189.0		9.4	11.0
3430	Parts/accessories for automobiles		95.6	101.0	108.1	132.0		37.8	41.9	42.4	50.0		3.3	4.0
351	Building and repairing of ships and boats		2107.4	1926.0	1231.7	1571.0		609.7	590.3	398.7	424.0		28.7	44.0
3511	Building and repairing of ships		1822.2	1643.3	929.9	1231.0		506.2	484.6	289.0	310.0		17.2	24.0
3512	Building/repairing of pleasure/sport. boats		285.2	282.7	301.8	340.0		103.6	105.7	109.7	114.0		11.5	20.0
3520	Railway/tramway locomotives & rolling stock		51.0	49.7	56.7	81.0		18.9	17.9	20.0	28.0		1.0	1.0
3530	Aircraft and spacecraft		58.6	55.4	58.7	64.0		37.7	33.9	36.3	41.0		1.6	3.0
359	Transport equipment n.e.c.		24.1	47.9	44.1	86.0		9.5	17.2	14.1	25.0		1.9	2.0
3591	Motorcycles		...	...	...	...		...	...	...	...		...	...
3592	Bicycles and invalid carriages		...	...	...	...		...	...	...	...		...	...
3599	Other transport equipment n.e.c.		6.1	5.5	6.3	47.0		3.0	2.6	3.1	15.0		0.2	...
3610	Furniture		1164.0	1135.0	1209.1	1296.0		432.3	426.9	449.3	443.0		40.8	46.0
369	Manufacturing n.e.c.		418.6	361.8	366.6	371.0		171.6	144.5	150.6	148.0		10.4	12.0
3691	Jewellery and related articles		98.2	93.6	91.5	91.0		41.8	33.6	35.1	35.0		1.4	3.0
3692	Musical instruments		7.0	6.7	8.7	8.0		3.3	3.6	4.3	4.0		0.3	-
3693	Sports goods		138.2	108.3	126.4	140.0		54.1	47.0	55.3	56.0		3.1	4.0
3694	Games and toys		22.4	10.2	9.0	9.0		9.6	4.0	3.6	4.0		0.4	-
3699	Other manufacturing n.e.c.		152.8	143.0	131.0	123.0		62.8	56.3	52.3	49.0		5.2	5.0
3710	Recycling of metal waste and scrap		65.8	102.1	86.7	450.0		16.4	15.7	21.3	65.0		5.2	10.0
3720	Recycling of non-metal waste and scrap		22.6	23.4	28.1	58.0		10.3	8.9	11.2	18.0		1.5	3.0
D	Total manufacturing		92993.0	91957.6	96238.0	103112.0		29654.7	29227.4	29798.7	30078.0		3728.0	3646.0

Finland

ISIC Revision 3			Index numbers of industrial production											
			(2000=100)											
ISIC	Industry	Note	1995	1996	1997	1998	1999	2000	2001	2002	2003	2004	2005	2006
15	Food and beverages		92	94	97	98	101	100	104	107	109	110	108	108
16	Tobacco products		...	...	...	...	...	...	...	...	...	...	...	...
17	Textiles		89	93	95	96	100	100	102	102	99	101	104	107
18	Wearing apparel, fur		115	113	112	106	106	100	104	98	83	75	73	70
19	Leather, leather products and footwear		112	108	109	113	102	100	97	99	90	88	82	86
20	Wood products (excl. furniture)		71	74	83	89	94	100	99	102	106	110	111	117
21	Paper and paper products		82	78	90	93	96	100	93	97	100	106	94	108
22	Printing and publishing		87	88	92	95	96	100	101	103	103	102	102	103
23	Coke,refined petroleum products,nuclear fuel		91	97	91	107	102	100	93	103	104	111	104	115
24	Chemicals and chemical products		80	82	87	89	92	100	102	100	101	102	100	111
25	Rubber and plastics products		72	73	78	86	89	100	98	94	93	99	104	105
26	Non-metallic mineral products		73	78	87	92	96	100	99	98	101	108	117	123
27	Basic metals		77	82	87	91	95	100	100	101	103	108	100	104
28	Fabricated metal products		71	75	84	89	86	100	105	101	105	106	109	118
29	Machinery and equipment n.e.c.		86	89	95	96	95	100	108	100	102	107	112	123
30	Office, accounting and computing machinery	a/	23	26	32	52	68	100	95	106	106	125	129	143
31	Electrical machinery and apparatus	a/	...	...	...	...	...	...	...	...	...	...	...	...
32	Radio,television and communication equipment	a/	...	...	...	...	...	...	...	...	...	...	...	...
33	Medical, precision and optical instruments	a/	...	...	...	...	...	...	...	...	...	...	...	...
34	Motor vehicles, trailers, semi-trailers		68	73	84	90	92	100	101	106	104	105	117	129
35	Other transport equipment		108	100	99	100	98	100	102	99	93	81	94	120
36	Furniture; manufacturing n.e.c.		73	74	79	88	93	100	101	90	89	94	81	88
37	Recycling		...	...	...	...	...	...	...	...	...	...	...	...
D	Total manufacturing		68	69	76	84	89	100	100	102	102	108	109	119

a/ 30 includes 31, 32 and 33.

France

Supplier of information:
Institut National de la Statistique et des Études Économiques, Paris.
Industrial statistics for the OECD countries are compiled by the OECD secretariat, which supplies them to UNIDO.

Basic source of data:
Annual survey.

Major deviations from ISIC (Revision 3):
Data were originally classified according to NAF-93 (Nomenclature d'Activités Française), which is fully compatible with NACE (Revision 1) and with ISIC (Revision 3).

Reference period:
Calendar year.

Scope:
All enterprises.

Method of data collection:
Mail questionnaires.

Type of enumeration:
The surveys are exhaustive for enterprises with 20 or more persons engaged; sample surveys are used for smaller enterprises.

Adjusted for non-response:
Yes.

Concepts and definitions of variables:
Number of employees refers to all persons receiving compensation from the enterprise, regardless of their status. It is the annual average over the twelve months of the year. Part-time employees are counted in proportion to the time they work.
Wages and salaries corresponds to the remuneration paid by the employers during the year to compensate for the work of the employees (excluding interim employed persons and workers on hire).
Output corresponds to the total value of goods and services sold, stocked or immobilized, that have been produced during the year. It excludes resale of goods. Immobilized production corresponds to the costs of work done by the enterprise on its own account. Stock production and immobilized production are estimated at production cost, excluding deductible VAT and subsidies.
Value added is defined as gross value added.
Gross fixed capital formation is the sum of the value of acquisitions (either new or used) and production of fixed capital. It includes fixed assets in progress but excludes intangible and financial assets and equipment financed by leasing. Its valuation is at acquisition costs.

Related national publications:
None reported.

France

ISIC Revision 3		Number of enterprises					Number of employees					Wages and salaries paid to employees				
			(number)					(thousands)					(millions of Euros)			
ISIC	Industry	Note	2002	2003	2004	2005	Note	2002	2003	2004	2005	Note	2002	2003	2004	2005
151	Processed meat,fish,fruit,vegetables,fats		13482	14083	13691	13293		210.1	208.4	...	...		4265.7	4288.7	...	...
1511	Processing/preserving of meat		11648	12099	11668	11216		164.8	164.3	162.3	154.2		3214.8	3279.3	3335.7	3294.0
1512	Processing/preserving of fish		482	505	509	492		15.2	15.5	15.4	15.4		313.6	333.1	329.3	339.0
1513	Processing/preserving of fruit & vegetables		1163	1284	1312	1372		26.6	26.3	26.3	26.1		586.8	610.3	624.9	633.0
1514	Vegetable and animal oils and fats		189	195	202	213		3.6	2.3	...	...		150.5	66.0	...	...
1520	Dairy products		1486	1519	1471	1462		64.9	63.3	63.0	60.2		1564.3	1611.1	1631.8	1622.0
153	Grain mill products; starches; animal feeds		1193	1204	1182	1148		33.7	36.1	36.1	35.7		949.9	1089.3	1121.0	1143.0
1531	Grain mill products		641	648	635	614		9.7	9.7	9.7	9.7		254.9	263.8	278.3	287.0
1532	Starches and starch products		12	11	9	12		4.7	4.7	4.8	4.7		158.1	166.0	167.4	182.0
1533	Prepared animal feeds		540	545	538	522		19.3	21.7	21.7	21.3		537.0	659.4	675.3	675.0
154	Other food products		46683	48186	48289	48672		256.2	256.9	261.1	252.6		4876.2	4957.4	5166.2	5189.0
1541	Bakery products		44290	45694	45774	46157		195.1	197.1	201.5	195.4		3157.2	3279.6	3438.5	3457.0
1542	Sugar		55	55	55	52		8.7	8.7	8.8	7.5		263.1	246.6	289.0	268.0
1543	Cocoa, chocolate and sugar confectionery		745	780	797	823		23.7	21.9	21.6	20.9		672.8	588.7	593.7	592.0
1544	Macaroni, noodles & similar products		291	309	305	301		4.2	4.5	4.0	4.0		91.9	129.6	106.9	123.0
1549	Other food products n.e.c.		1302	1348	1358	1339		24.4	24.6	25.1	24.8		691.3	713.1	738.0	750.0
155	Beverages		3488	3562	3510	3410		46.9	47.0	46.1	44.6		1521.8	1565.5	1625.3	1598.0
1551	Distilling, rectifying & blending of spirits		1170	1187	1150	1124		10.6	10.6	10.3	10.1		345.2	347.9	367.5	411.0
1552	Wines		1977	2016	1994	1882		14.2	13.9	14.0	13.9		426.2	437.9	445.7	474.0
1553	Malt liquors and malt		143	155	161	191		6.1	5.8	5.7	5.5		229.9	203.9	260.0	212.0
1554	Soft drinks; mineral waters		198	204	205	213		16.0	16.7	16.1	15.0		520.5	575.8	552.1	501.0
1600	Tobacco products		18	10	10	10		4.2	4.1	...	...		143.9	151.3	...	...
171	Spinning, weaving and finishing of textiles		1603	1627	1530	1419		46.4	41.7	37.1	32.8		1017.9	922.9	852.9	804.0
1711	Textile fibre preparation; textile weaving		997	1002	933	863		32.8	29.2	26.2	22.5		714.7	648.2	602.6	562.0
1712	Finishing of textiles		606	625	597	556		13.6	12.5	10.9	10.2		303.2	274.7	250.3	242.0
172	Other textiles		2940	3138	3126	3114		45.6	44.3	42.1	39.4		976.1	957.5	952.9	942.0
1721	Made-up textile articles, except apparel		1561	1700	1732	1763		18.5	18.5	17.7	16.3		365.1	373.1	367.2	362.0
1722	Carpets and rugs		74	74	75	73		3.2	3.1	2.8	2.9		75.6	71.2	72.4	78.0
1723	Cordage, rope, twine and netting		98	102	92	92		1.5	1.2	1.2	1.1		31.2	24.3	24.9	24.0
1729	Other textiles n.e.c.		1207	1262	1227	1186		22.4	21.4	20.4	19.1		504.3	488.9	488.4	478.0
1730	Knitted and crocheted fabrics and articles		792	816	739	653		19.2	17.6	13.4	11.7		397.8	379.3	288.1	265.0
1810	Wearing apparel, except fur apparel		11869	12976	12593	12077		89.2	...	76.8	69.0		1852.0	...	1727.6	1675.0
1820	Dressing & dyeing of fur; processing of fur		263	265	247	224		0.7	...	0.7	0.6		16.7	...	16.1	15.0
191	Tanning, dressing and processing of leather		1774	1878	1798	1734		20.7	20.1	19.3	19.1		412.9	416.1	415.7	433.0
1911	Tanning and dressing of leather		168	173	160	150		3.1	2.7	2.5	2.3		64.3	54.8	56.8	57.0
1912	Luggage, handbags, etc.; saddlery & harness		1606	1705	1638	1584		17.6	17.4	16.9	16.8		348.6	361.3	358.9	375.0
1920	Footwear		531	539	507	484		21.9	18.6	16.0	14.1		419.5	359.7	328.6	290.0
2010	Sawmilling and planing of wood		3624	3785	3661	3610		28.6	27.2	26.6	24.2		576.3	564.0	581.2	548.0
202	Products of wood, cork, straw, etc.		7008	7415	7411	7319		63.2	61.4	60.0	60.5		1309.4	1303.6	1311.5	1383.0
2021	Veneer sheets, plywood, particle board, etc.		169	165	156	154		9.6	9.2	8.6	8.4		219.8	218.8	215.0	215.0
2022	Builders' carpentry and joinery		3101	3351	3451	3481		26.9	25.9	26.0	27.5		550.7	542.7	564.5	627.0
2023	Wooden containers		1105	1144	1127	1131		17.7	17.6	17.0	17.0		359.0	363.7	363.5	372.0
2029	Other wood products; articles of cork/straw		2633	2755	2677	2553		9.0	8.6	8.3	7.6		179.9	178.4	168.5	170.0
210	Paper and paper products		1618	1633	1612	1561		90.6	88.2	84.4	81.8		2520.8	2511.7	2493.9	2475.0
2101	Pulp, paper and paperboard		213	211	206	203		27.3	27.1	24.8	24.4		857.4	879.1	845.3	837.0
2102	Corrugated paper and paperboard		758	771	773	738		38.5	37.4	36.1	35.2		977.8	963.5	971.4	968.0
2109	Other articles of paper and paperboard		647	651	633	620		24.8	23.7	23.4	22.2		685.6	669.1	677.2	670.0
221	Publishing		12446	13419	13896	13876		89.5	87.4	88.0	85.5		3367.2	3387.6	3487.4	3481.0
2211	Publishing of books and other publications		3349	3504	3539	3469		17.7	17.1	16.7	16.6		610.1	602.4	606.8	614.0
2212	Publishing of newspapers, journals, etc.		5627	6030	6179	6065		63.9	...	63.5	61.8		2486.2	...	2572.5	2588.0
2213	Publishing of recorded media		2465	2746	3010	3173		5.3	...	5.0	4.5		203.0	...	231.4	206.0
2219	Other publishing		1005	1139	1168	1169		2.5	2.5	2.7	2.5		68.0	71.9	76.7	74.0

222	Printing and related service activities	16766	17986	17852	17648	115.8	109.8	104.1	100.3	2999.3	2884.8	2800.3	2774.0
2221	Printing	7976	8240	8005	7677	88.4	83.4	79.5	76.8	2309.5	2217.4	2163.2	2141.0
2222	Service activities related to printing	8790	9746	9847	9971	27.4	26.4	24.5	23.5	689.8	667.4	637.1	632.0
2230	Reproduction of recorded media	467	534	544	560	3.4	2.7	2.7	2.6	81.7	66.8	67.8	67.0
2310	Coke oven products	3	3	4	5	...	0.3	...	...	...	9.7	...	...
2320	Refined petroleum products	94	93	90	85	17.8	17.6	21.2	16.9	1099.9	961.6	954.7	940.0
2330	Processing of nuclear fuel	17	16	18	19	...	11.2	...	...	...	455.6	...	...
241	Basic chemicals	904	901	884	854	74.0	70.2	108.2	68.1	2626.8	2613.9	2448.2	2712.0
2411	Basic chemicals, except fertilizers	490	485	483	466	53.8	51.3	47.7	49.1	1915.4	1961.3	1788.7	1998.0
2412	Fertilizers and nitrogen compounds	189	195	187	176	6.0	5.8	5.6	5.6	191.9	187.6	192.6	188.0
2413	Plastics in primary forms; synthetic rubber	225	221	214	212	14.1	13.1	54.9	13.4	519.6	465.1	466.9	525.0
242	Other chemicals	2972	3024	3015	2973	219.5	216.5	213.1	208.0	8028.4	8180.7	8249.6	8394.0
2421	Pesticides and other agro-chemical products	130	133	132	120	6.8	6.1	6.2	6.1	324.5	286.0	289.9	302.0
2422	Paints, varnishes, printing ink and mastics	382	392	380	383	19.9	19.2	19.6	18.1	632.4	636.6	638.3	622.0
2423	Pharmaceuticals, medicinal chemicals, etc.	586	580	583	565	105.6	101.9	99.2	103.6	4040.7	4093.9	4130.0	4431.0
2424	Soap, cleaning & cosmetic preparations	1210	1247	1249	1255	55.8	56.6	56.9	54.4	1959.0	1982.5	2017.4	2058.0
2429	Other chemical products n.e.c.	664	672	671	650	31.3	32.7	31.2	25.9	1071.8	1181.7	1174.0	980.0
2430	Man-made fibres	22	23	20	21	2.3	2.4	2.2	2.2	60.1	60.6	58.5	60.0
251	Rubber products	581	586	569	541	70.8	70.5	69.2	68.2	1916.7	1941.0	1954.5	1933.0
2511	Rubber tyres and tubes	...	149	131	122	...	...	38.0	37.5	...	...	1143.1	1119.0
2519	Other rubber products	434	437	438	419	32.5	...	31.3	30.7	809.7	...	811.4	814.0
2520	Plastic products	4632	4757	4685	4590	173.7	173.3	171.3	168.2	4145.3	4221.3	4315.6	4404.0
2610	Glass and glass products	1291	1371	1371	1358	51.1	49.9	49.5	47.9	1395.2	1409.9	1410.7	1428.0
269	Non-metallic mineral products n.e.c.	7439	7831	7830	7846	94.4	93.0	91.6	91.1	2439.9	2452.3	2542.4	2595.0
2691	Pottery, china and earthenware	1834	1976	1990	2057	12.9	12.3	11.7	...	272.3	267.4	265.6	...
2692	Refractory ceramic products	65	63	62	61	4.6	4.4	4.0	3.9	135.4	138.2	132.0	130.0
2693	Struct.non-refractory clay; ceramic products	231	246	252	247	8.9	8.9	8.6	8.5	217.1	216.8	223.4	239.0
2694	Cement, lime and plaster	73	71	71	70	6.6	6.5	6.3	6.3	259.3	251.7	265.8	259.0
2695	Articles of concrete, cement and plaster	1686	1750	1715	1666	38.3	38.0	38.7	39.5	977.4	991.3	1061.3	1099.0
2696	Cutting, shaping & finishing of stone	3117	3291	3310	3321	13.6	13.6	13.2	12.9	276.9	282.8	285.9	292.0
2699	Other non-metallic mineral products n.e.c.	433	434	430	424	9.5	9.3	9.1	9.0	301.6	304.2	308.4	311.0
2710	Basic iron and steel	346	351	348	336	61.6	60.6	56.6	54.1	1855.1	1842.3	1816.6	1786.0
2720	Basic precious and non-ferrous metals	282	287	269	266	23.0	22.1	20.9	20.2	722.1	703.1	694.3	699.0
273	Casting of metals	487	500	484	471	36.9	35.1	32.5	31.4	864.8	817.6	790.3	780.0
2731	Casting of iron and steel	133	138	131	124	17.6	16.3	14.8	14.3	422.3	376.6	359.9	357.0
2732	Casting of non-ferrous metals	354	362	353	347	19.3	18.8	17.7	17.1	442.5	440.9	430.4	423.0
281	Struct.metal products;tanks;steam generators	10736	11361	11459	11561	149.6	146.1	142.0	141.2	3712.2	3682.8	3627.4	3739.0
2811	Structural metal products	4338	4581	4762	4912	56.9	56.9	57.6	57.5	1288.6	1331.8	1384.8	1436.0
2812	Tanks, reservoirs and containers of metal	282	288	263	244	11.9	11.3	11.0	11.0	303.5	302.8	294.4	309.0
2813	Steam generators	6116	6492	6434	6405	80.9	77.9	73.5	72.6	2120.1	2048.2	1948.2	1993.0
289	Other metal products; metal working services	18762	19415	19084	18696	306.1	296.1	295.0	289.2	7421.3	7356.4	7582.8	7745.0
2891	Metal forging/pressing/stamping/roll-forming	1778	1840	1774	1740	55.2	53.9	55.3	54.3	1293.9	1283.6	1363.0	1411.0
2892	Treatment & coating of metals	12614	13084	12877	12640	149.4	143.8	143.9	141.6	3640.1	3597.5	3718.9	3804.0
2893	Cutlery, hand tools and general hardware	2084	2137	2099	2004	39.3	38.0	35.2	34.2	958.1	952.7	918.8	919.0
2899	Other fabricated metal products n.e.c.	2286	2354	2334	2312	62.1	60.4	60.6	59.0	1529.2	1522.6	1582.1	1611.0
291	General purpose machinery	6972	7274	7227	7197	181.5	177.6	174.9	177.7	5190.0	5189.6	5283.5	5511.0
2911	Engines & turbines (not for transport equipment)	229	249	249	237	9.4	8.3	7.8	8.6	367.5	309.1	273.7	341.0
2912	Pumps, compressors, taps and valves	1033	1060	1055	1041	43.2	41.1	40.3	41.1	1191.3	1144.2	1175.4	1265.0
2913	Bearings, gears, gearing & driving elements	179	180	171	163	19.2	18.8	18.4	18.6	542.8	552.5	559.5	563.0
2914	Ovens, furnaces and furnace burners	134	128	123	125	4.3	4.0	3.6	3.8	144.9	140.0	136.9	149.0
2915	Lifting and handling equipment	1479	1546	1556	1572	45.5	44.7	44.4	44.6	1265.5	1291.9	1328.5	1355.0
2919	Other general purpose machinery	3918	4111	4073	4059	59.9	60.8	60.4	61.1	1678.1	1751.9	1809.6	1839.0
292	Special purpose machinery	8767	8979	8884	8718	118.6	116.0	116.5	111.8	3376.7	3392.5	3595.9	3557.0
2921	Agricultural and forestry machinery	4375	4465	4391	4290	27.1	26.8	26.7	25.7	627.3	620.9	648.2	641.0
2922	Machine tools	925	941	936	892	16.1	15.0	14.4	13.7	464.7	444.2	443.3	438.0
2923	Machinery for metallurgy	...	72	76	81	...	2.1	2.1	2.0	...	69.7	70.9	68.0
2924	Machinery for mining & construction	465	474	472	479	...	12.2	10.7	11.3	...	372.6	336.9	355.0
2925	Food/beverage/tobacco processing machinery	918	948	957	940	15.4	15.3	14.8	14.4	399.0	416.4	409.8	413.0
2926	Machinery for textile, apparel and leather	243	248	242	232	5.4	5.2	5.0	4.4	162.5	163.7	162.1	153.0
2927	Weapons and ammunition	172	182	177	180	8.0	7.3	12.2	11.4	317.7	323.5	537.1	548.0
2929	Other special purpose machinery	1598	1649	1633	1624	31.7	32.1	30.6	28.9	955.7	981.4	987.6	941.0

continued

France

ISIC Revision 3		Number of enterprises					Number of employees					Wages and salaries paid to employees				
			(number)					(thousands)					(millions of Euros)			
ISIC	Industry	Note	2002	2003	2004	2005	Note	2002	2003	2004	2005	Note	2002	2003	2004	2005
2930	Domestic appliances n.e.c.		251	256	244	234		20.9	19.9	19.4	18.0		498.8	502.3	503.7	511.0
3000	Office, accounting and computing machinery		544	552	532	503		33.3	29.1	8.6	9.0		1733.6	1350.9	259.2	301.0
3110	Electric motors, generators and transformers		1234	1276	1268	1234		29.4	28.6	27.0	26.4		792.2	793.2	757.5	783.0
3120	Electricity distribution & control apparatus		940	959	925	896		70.2	67.2	66.0	66.6		2068.9	2215.5	2148.8	2112.0
3130	Insulated wire and cable		226	230	230	219		16.2	14.7	13.5	14.1		466.8	438.4	414.2	446.0
3140	Accumulators, primary cells and batteries		36	37	34	36		5.7	5.6	5.5	5.9		157.1	162.3	161.5	166.0
3150	Lighting equipment and electric lamps		819	869	869	858		11.3	10.9	10.9	10.8		278.1	271.0	286.4	304.0
3190	Other electrical equipment n.e.c.		926	952	940	925		36.9	35.8	37.4	32.7		1016.4	1060.8	1153.8	1057.0
3210	Electronic valves, tubes, etc.		1112	1112	1067	1050		65.8	61.7	60.3	57.3		1942.8	1917.8	1908.3	1885.0
3220	TV/radio transmitters; line comm. apparatus		1123	1136	1074	1019		69.7	60.6	53.7	43.9		2989.2	2705.2	2352.5	1909.0
3230	TV and radio receivers and associated goods		427	435	427	420		20.3	18.2	14.7	13.7		665.0	603.6	517.3	503.0
331	Medical, measuring, testing appliances, etc.		10835	11189	11105	11059		119.9	112.8	111.3	121.3		3897.0	3771.4	3748.3	4320.0
3311	Medical, surgical and orthopaedic equipment		7727	8005	8008	8037		43.3	43.9	44.7	44.5		1207.0	1271.0	1308.0	1350.0
3312	Measuring/testing/navigating appliances,etc.		1532	1552	1505	1474		54.6	49.7	47.6	59.0		2035.0	1928.0	1866.0	2426.0
3313	Industrial process control equipment		1576	1632	1592	1548		22.0	19.2	19.0	17.9		655.0	573.0	574.0	545.0
3320	Optical instruments & photographic equipment		852	912	887	870		15.4	14.7	14.1	14.0		411.5	406.8	411.7	439.0
3330	Watches and clocks		317	326	319	302		4.1	3.7	3.6	3.8		96.8	91.1	89.7	99.0
3410	Motor vehicles		223	230	226	224		166.8	172.1	168.2	167.5		5568.3	5933.2	6107.7	6223.0
3420	Automobile bodies, trailers & semi-trailers		1275	1311	1319	1289		29.4	28.8	28.3	28.2		660.2	661.0	668.0	686.0
3430	Parts/accessories for automobiles		652	657	634	619		86.9	86.5	82.7	79.5		2484.5	2389.5	2480.4	2507.0
351	Building and repairing of ships and boats		2210	2369	2482	2542		22.6	35.2	34.5	33.5		534.7	825.1	864.5	880.0
3511	Building and repairing of ships		694	759	770	762		11.6	23.9	22.7	21.6		306.9	584.4	614.3	609.0
3512	Building/repairing of pleasure/sport. boats		1516	1610	1712	1780		11.0	11.3	11.7	11.9		227.8	240.7	250.1	271.0
3520	Railway/tramway locomotives & rolling stock		62	60	61	59		14.6	14.8	14.3	14.0		480.0	503.0	517.0	507.0
3530	Aircraft and spacecraft		392	393	397	391		82.2	81.8	91.1	90.2		3123.6	3257.8	3946.4	4062.0
359	Transport equipment n.e.c.		246	253	246	232		7.3	7.0	7.2	6.2		176.0	164.5	192.8	161.0
3591	Motorcycles		78	84	81	83		...	3.1	3.0	2.7		...	81.6	81.0	79.0
3592	Bicycles and invalid carriages		129	129	126	120		3.3	...	3.6	2.9		69.4	...	95.8	67.0
3599	Other transport equipment n.e.c.		39	40	39	29		...	0.7	0.7	0.6		...	16.0	16.0	15.0
3610	Furniture		18625	19600	19538	19399		104.1	99.6	96.1	90.8		2226.1	2197.6	2205.8	2176.0
369	Manufacturing n.e.c.		8672	9330	9420	9576		47.8	45.4	44.3	42.5		1113.6	1106.3	1099.9	1128.0
3691	Jewellery and related articles		2982	3131	3100	3088		11.5	10.7	10.3	10.1		283.8	268.9	265.8	276.0
3692	Musical instruments		903	938	945	984		2.6	2.4	2.4	2.3		56.3	59.1	59.0	60.0
3693	Sports goods		563	595	592	600		7.9	7.5	7.8	7.4		204.3	206.0	215.2	230.0
3694	Games and toys		625	665	687	669		5.6	5.5	5.0	4.7		120.5	123.2	113.2	112.0
3699	Other manufacturing n.e.c.		3599	4001	4096	4235		20.1	19.3	18.9	17.9		448.7	449.1	446.7	451.0
3710	Recycling of metal waste and scrap		2457	2584	2594	2636		12.9	12.9	13.3	13.4		289.2	301.8	327.4	349.0
3720	Recycling of non-metal waste and scrap		1535	1643	1656	1610		13.2	14.0	14.1	14.1		279.7	301.9	314.4	324.0
D	Total manufacturing		248349	260018	258404	256013		3950.3	3855.4	3804.1	3662.0		108519.0	108409.0	108635.0	109848.0

France

ISIC Revision 3		Output					Value added in factor values					Gross fixed capital formation		
			(millions of Euros)					(millions of Euros)					(millions of Euros)	
ISIC	Industry	Note	2002	2003	2004	2005	Note	2002	2003	2004	2005	Note	2004	2005
151	Processed meat,fish,fruit,vegetables,fats		41789.1	40510.7	...	...		7909.3	7852.1	...	...		...	...
1511	Processing/preserving of meat		29806.9	29636.9	30632.8	30653.0		5765.9	5735.2	5808.3	5629.0		776.2	738.0
1512	Processing/preserving of fish		2851.1	3018.4	2908.7	2866.0		564.6	642.6	621.1	624.0		89.6	79.0
1513	Processing/preserving of fruit & vegetables		6271.2	6377.7	6471.7	6168.0		1230.0	1264.0	1288.2	1289.0		302.8	257.0
1514	Vegetable and animal oils and fats		2859.9	1477.7	...	...		348.8	210.3	...	...		...	...
1520	Dairy products		23293.8	23364.5	23285.6	22477.0		3116.8	3157.3	3233.3	3073.0		593.6	580.0
153	Grain mill products; starches; animal feeds		12068.0	13189.7	13646.1	13298.0		2076.2	2390.9	2453.8	2491.0		465.8	458.0
1531	Grain mill products		2834.2	2831.6	2952.9	2886.0		552.3	577.0	553.3	597.0		109.6	106.0
1532	Starches and starch products		1817.7	1815.4	1865.0	1896.0		441.8	456.2	495.1	485.0		92.9	108.0
1533	Prepared animal feeds		7416.2	8542.7	8828.2	8516.0		1082.1	1357.7	1405.5	1410.0		263.3	244.0
154	Other food products		33670.3	32666.5	33897.3	34168.0		10811.2	10542.6	11231.9	10936.0		1813.0	2085.0
1541	Bakery products		15469.6	15771.2	16532.8	16445.0		6470.1	6610.2	6985.0	6899.0		1224.9	1320.0
1542	Sugar		3486.2	2879.7	3444.4	3522.0		864.4	664.9	863.8	725.0		113.8	322.0
1543	Cocoa, chocolate and sugar confectionery		6699.4	5958.1	5737.3	5615.0		1650.5	1323.9	1347.6	1304.0		158.4	147.0
1544	Macaroni, noodles & similar products		877.5	1110.1	1061.4	1218.0		172.2	223.3	227.8	260.0		32.3	43.0
1549	Other food products n.e.c.		7137.6	6947.5	7121.4	7368.0		1653.9	1720.3	1807.8	1748.0		283.5	253.0
155	Beverages		18749.0	19191.5	19813.5	19204.0		4872.4	4880.7	5099.7	4748.0		935.6	835.0
1551	Distilling, rectifying & blending of spirits		4175.6	3987.3	4136.0	4440.0		1294.3	1155.1	1154.2	1247.0		148.7	165.0
1552	Wines		6102.1	6129.1	6171.2	6503.0		1390.3	1377.5	1439.1	1514.0		269.6	274.0
1553	Malt liquors and malt		2834.8	2537.1	3233.4	2537.0		759.3	682.6	962.7	682.0		215.8	147.0
1554	Soft drinks; mineral waters		5636.5	6538.0	6272.9	5724.0		1428.4	1665.5	1543.6	1306.0		301.5	250.0
1600	Tobacco products		9796.8	9948.1	...	...		649.0	627.5	...	...		...	...
171	Spinning, weaving and finishing of textiles		7000.9	6258.1	5837.2	4990.0		1621.8	1430.1	1286.1	1170.0		167.5	133.0
1711	Textile fibre preparation; textile weaving		5467.3	4902.3	4640.7	3868.0		1149.1	1007.2	918.9	831.0		127.4	89.0
1712	Finishing of textiles		1533.6	1355.8	1196.5	1122.0		472.7	422.9	367.2	339.0		40.1	44.0
172	Other textiles		5519.1	5397.5	5350.2	5188.0		1706.1	1662.5	1641.8	1575.0		161.7	176.0
1721	Made-up textile articles, except apparel		1915.7	1994.9	1946.1	1807.0		599.0	628.5	619.7	588.0		46.9	47.0
1722	Carpets and rugs		547.3	462.3	471.1	490.0		135.2	120.2	116.4	106.0		28.5	24.0
1723	Cordage, rope, twine and netting		183.7	136.2	137.9	120.0		57.8	43.6	43.5	41.0		4.2	4.0
1729	Other textiles n.e.c.		2872.6	2804.1	2795.2	2771.0		914.2	870.2	862.2	839.0		82.2	100.0
1730	Knitted and crocheted fabrics and articles		2133.5	2079.8	1502.2	1400.0		662.7	664.0	495.1	452.0		35.2	31.0
1810	Wearing apparel, except fur apparel		12015.0	...	11035.6	10395.0		3249.0	...	3090.7	3100.0		182.8	147.0
1820	Dressing & dyeing of fur; processing of fur		100.4	...	83.6	80.0		32.7	...	26.3	26.0		3.0	3.0
191	Tanning, dressing and processing of leather		2123.9	2052.2	2056.8	2149.0		873.7	855.8	857.4	893.0		43.8	68.0
1911	Tanning and dressing of leather		419.3	334.0	320.3	323.0		105.8	91.7	93.4	89.0		9.1	7.0
1912	Luggage, handbags, etc.; saddlery & harness		1704.6	1718.2	1736.5	1826.0		767.9	764.1	764.0	804.0		34.7	61.0
1920	Footwear		1999.0	1690.0	1527.1	1342.0		675.3	540.4	503.6	451.0		34.1	36.0
2010	Sawmilling and planing of wood		3236.2	3050.1	3254.1	3101.0		1079.6	986.8	1039.5	967.0		189.3	155.0
202	Products of wood, cork, straw, etc.		8757.9	8663.7	8765.0	8651.0		2520.9	2406.5	2463.2	2611.0		422.7	344.0
2021	Veneer sheets, plywood, particle board, etc.		1834.6	1819.4	1782.2	1839.0		400.6	352.6	370.9	378.0		182.8	66.0
2022	Builders' carpentry and joinery		3875.6	3861.7	4038.2	3884.0		1111.2	1087.6	1142.6	1274.0		141.3	185.0
2023	Wooden containers		2078.7	2031.9	2070.1	2098.0		684.0	658.7	662.0	669.0		71.5	68.0
2029	Other wood products; articles of cork/straw		969.0	950.7	874.5	831.0		325.1	307.6	287.7	289.0		27.1	25.0
210	Paper and paper products		18680.9	18006.6	17765.6	17282.0		5211.4	4901.4	4588.1	4267.0		800.0	939.0
2101	Pulp, paper and paperboard		7553.0	7238.0	6868.8	6984.0		1967.7	1726.8	1502.7	1392.0		342.9	421.0
2102	Corrugated paper and paperboard		6178.5	6053.5	5931.5	5751.0		1882.9	1875.2	1802.1	1670.0		254.7	361.0
2109	Other articles of paper and paperboard		4949.4	4715.1	4965.2	4547.0		1360.8	1299.4	1283.2	1205.0		202.3	157.0
221	Publishing		18899.7	19309.2	19884.8	19557.0		5890.2	6122.8	6314.7	6315.0		282.3	324.0
2211	Publishing of books and other publications		4218.8	4246.3	4256.5	4279.0		1241.1	1259.8	1242.8	1325.0		37.9	43.0
2212	Publishing of newspapers, journals, etc.		12317.0	...	13222.0	13176.0		4010.3	...	4367.9	4410.0		183.2	241.0
2213	Publishing of recorded media		1977.3	...	1979.8	1704.0		506.6	...	567.2	440.0		49.2	26.0
2219	Other publishing		386.7	386.8	426.6	399.0		132.1	138.9	136.8	141.0		11.9	14.0

continued

France

ISIC Revision 3		Output					Value added in factor values					Gross fixed capital formation		
			(millions of Euros)					(millions of Euros)					(millions of Euros)	
ISIC	Industry	Note	2002	2003	2004	2005	Note	2002	2003	2004	2005	Note	2004	2005
222	Printing and related service activities		13558.8	12874.9	12777.2	12680.0		5007.4	4767.8	4705.1	4555.0		513.5	611.0
2221	Printing		11015.1	10374.4	10341.9	10284.0		3848.0	3643.2	3609.5	3477.0		425.7	514.0
2222	Service activities related to printing		2543.7	2500.5	2435.3	2397.0		1159.4	1124.6	1095.7	1079.0		87.9	97.0
2230	Reproduction of recorded media		461.7	388.7	413.0	357.0		153.0	110.2	111.9	96.0		31.4	20.0
2310	Coke oven products		...	7.4	...	...		...	-11.8	...	...		...	...
2320	Refined petroleum products		49518.8	47713.4	54469.2	64552.0		2270.4	2090.4	3619.7	4904.0		787.7	974.0
2330	Processing of nuclear fuel		...	3574.9	...	...		...	1288.0	...	...		...	...
241	Basic chemicals		27915.9	27554.5	28915.6	32154.0		5434.8	5176.9	5258.1	5709.0		1509.5	2009.0
2411	Basic chemicals, except fertilizers		20060.0	19580.5	20812.3	22938.0		4229.0	4111.1	4035.3	4258.0		1165.3	1221.0
2412	Fertilizers and nitrogen compounds		1881.5	2051.9	2256.3	2286.0		218.4	228.7	294.6	316.0		64.7	124.0
2413	Plastics in primary forms; synthetic rubber		5974.5	5922.1	5847.0	6930.0		987.4	837.1	928.2	1135.0		279.5	665.0
242	Other chemicals		71634.9	73731.1	76061.4	70403.0		18886.0	20089.9	19806.7	20280.0		2103.4	1999.0
2421	Pesticides and other agro-chemical products		3410.7	3009.2	2918.8	2806.0		536.4	592.6	628.6	663.0		97.9	80.0
2422	Paints, varnishes, printing ink and mastics		3927.3	3995.0	4111.9	4102.0		1168.0	1168.2	1237.8	1186.0		136.8	110.0
2423	Pharmaceuticals, medicinal chemicals, etc.		38926.3	40168.0	42072.0	38578.0		10692.0	11498.9	10849.2	11737.0		1091.6	977.0
2424	Soap, cleaning & cosmetic preparations		18201.4	18911.9	19159.4	17875.0		4326.6	4545.3	4730.3	4685.0		478.9	517.0
2429	Other chemical products n.e.c.		7169.2	7647.0	7799.3	7042.0		2163.0	2284.9	2360.8	2009.0		298.2	315.0
2430	Man-made fibres		557.6	549.1	562.7	586.0		106.3	87.9	69.1	91.0		9.0	9.0
251	Rubber products		9645.2	9965.5	10465.7	10691.0		3409.6	3467.1	3582.3	3489.0		438.9	410.0
2511	Rubber tyres and tubes		...	...	6667.8	6951.0		...	...	2155.8	2125.0		332.1	306.0
2519	Other rubber products		3687.8	...	3797.8	3740.0		1378.4	...	1426.5	1365.0		106.8	104.0
2520	Plastic products		24979.0	25671.1	27036.7	27655.0		7705.1	7755.8	7943.7	7958.0		1231.6	1229.0
2610	Glass and glass products		7131.8	7084.4	7032.1	7206.0		2748.3	2649.6	2607.8	2549.0		346.0	346.0
269	Non-metallic mineral products n.e.c.		16222.2	16502.7	17915.5	18831.0		5219.0	5246.6	5819.5	5959.0		847.3	966.0
2691	Pottery, china and earthenware		899.8	932.5	917.8	...		403.8	405.4	397.5	...		27.9	...
2692	Refractory ceramic products		675.6	644.2	650.6	672.0		250.2	238.8	248.4	268.0		21.6	19.0
2693	Struct.non-refractory clay; ceramic products		1195.3	1193.5	1331.2	1438.0		579.6	571.2	657.1	690.0		83.3	126.0
2694	Cement, lime and plaster		2746.2	2828.9	3095.4	3199.0		1170.6	1202.9	1317.3	1261.0		169.2	217.0
2695	Articles of concrete, cement and plaster		7587.3	7714.0	8630.9	9182.0		2188.3	2168.5	2439.9	2565.0		376.0	406.0
2696	Cutting, shaping & finishing of stone		1166.5	1162.7	1181.3	1186.0		518.5	517.7	528.4	533.0		48.3	48.0
2699	Other non-metallic mineral products n.e.c.		1951.5	2026.9	2108.2	2195.0		108.0	142.1	230.9	207.0		121.1	112.0
2710	Basic iron and steel		16475.0	16448.7	18746.5	20013.0		3494.8	3647.6	4289.2	4456.0		590.6	823.0
2720	Basic precious and non-ferrous metals		8370.4	7425.6	8260.9	8533.0		1442.5	1267.1	1451.3	1569.0		241.1	220.0
273	Casting of metals		3900.5	3772.1	3857.8	3871.0		1359.6	1284.9	1295.3	1261.0		174.3	176.0
2731	Casting of iron and steel		1628.5	1520.2	1620.8	1733.0		582.3	527.4	545.3	564.0		59.1	79.0
2732	Casting of non-ferrous metals		2272.0	2251.9	2237.0	2139.0		777.2	757.4	750.0	698.0		115.2	97.0
281	Struct.metal products;tanks;steam generators		18041.7	17501.0	17778.3	18776.0		6584.4	6166.8	6246.2	6609.0		414.2	468.0
2811	Structural metal products		7514.5	7570.8	8054.2	8459.0		2471.7	2482.1	2566.9	2691.0		193.8	216.0
2812	Tanks, reservoirs and containers of metal		1686.8	1748.5	1719.5	1836.0		545.4	570.9	581.9	636.0		52.1	62.0
2813	Steam generators		8840.4	8181.7	8004.6	8482.0		3567.3	3113.8	3097.4	3283.0		168.3	191.0
289	Other metal products; metal working services		33993.2	33414.2	35516.6	37203.0		13010.5	12637.8	13375.6	13752.0		1452.4	1656.0
2891	Metal forging/pressing/stamping/roll-forming		7337.5	7291.8	8161.9	8895.0		2224.1	2171.9	2420.1	2527.0		375.3	395.0
2892	Treatment & coating of metals		13773.0	13575.7	14176.6	15037.0		6133.7	5966.2	6217.8	6451.0		585.0	760.0
2893	Cutlery, hand tools and general hardware		4004.9	3898.4	3822.7	3822.0		1678.8	1612.5	1618.1	1606.0		152.7	155.0
2899	Other fabricated metal products n.e.c.		8877.8	8648.3	9355.4	9450.0		2973.9	2887.2	3119.6	3169.0		339.4	346.0
291	General purpose machinery		28487.3	28264.2	29675.1	30852.0		9234.0	9386.9	9830.4	10343.0		593.6	663.0
2911	Engines & turbines (not for transport equipment)		2956.5	2669.9	2563.3	2535.0		703.8	623.6	622.4	611.0		39.3	48.0
2912	Pumps, compressors, taps and valves		6645.1	6409.8	6923.4	7407.0		2130.9	2101.3	2246.7	2454.0		188.6	202.0
2913	Bearings, gears, gearing & driving elements		2496.8	2510.4	2822.1	2844.0		995.1	978.0	1010.7	1056.0		97.4	99.0
2914	Ovens, furnaces and furnace burners		845.7	867.2	849.3	925.0		197.9	223.8	222.0	260.0		9.9	8.0
2915	Lifting and handling equipment		6651.0	6815.5	7288.5	7889.0		2346.8	2433.3	2553.3	2716.0		91.3	120.0
2919	Other general purpose machinery		8892.0	8991.3	9228.4	9252.0		2859.4	3027.0	3175.4	3247.0		167.2	185.0

292	Special purpose machinery	18736.6	18338.0	19340.5	19761.0	5845.5	5852.2	6075.8	6024.0	413.0	463.0
2921	Agricultural and forestry machinery	3795.7	3836.6	4238.0	4312.0	1217.5	1131.8	1243.5	1209.0	100.0	119.0
2922	Machine tools	2250.7	2096.0	2046.0	2161.0	761.4	723.9	733.4	724.0	44.8	48.0
2923	Machinery for metallurgy	...	393.3	529.0	461.0	...	108.2	112.7	117.0	13.8	13.0
2924	Machinery for mining & construction	...	2273.0	2188.8	2552.0	...	723.8	644.2	720.0	59.3	78.0
2925	Food/beverage/tobacco processing machinery	1915.3	1985.5	1931.2	1971.0	719.6	736.7	726.6	749.0	38.5	40.0
2926	Machinery for textile, apparel and leather	1012.7	1021.6	958.6	926.0	306.0	291.8	281.3	275.0	25.8	25.0
2927	Weapons and ammunition	2096.2	1989.4	2691.7	2761.0	485.3	559.7	829.4	810.0	25.4	52.0
2929	Other special purpose machinery	4844.2	4742.4	4757.1	4617.0	1559.2	1576.3	1504.7	1420.0	105.4	88.0
2930	Domestic appliances n.e.c.	3560.2	3333.1	3375.4	3231.0	1098.5	1018.8	1031.6	955.0	124.7	120.0
3000	Office, accounting and computing machinery	11278.3	10696.5	2470.9	2122.0	2685.4	2631.7	487.6	506.0	35.5	87.0
3110	Electric motors, generators and transformers	4131.1	4056.0	4033.2	4353.0	1434.8	1390.8	1348.7	1424.0	77.8	92.0
3120	Electricity distribution & control apparatus	11088.6	11618.1	11805.8	13382.0	3666.3	3658.7	3813.6	3883.0	370.0	404.0
3130	Insulated wire and cable	2453.6	2202.0	2432.0	2977.0	659.2	608.3	639.2	721.0	70.2	47.0
3140	Accumulators, primary cells and batteries	913.0	901.5	861.9	889.0	279.7	260.0	260.1	250.0	38.8	27.0
3150	Lighting equipment and electric lamps	1333.3	1323.7	1397.1	1455.0	492.9	490.1	525.4	529.0	43.6	46.0
3190	Other electrical equipment n.e.c.	6168.1	6296.7	7004.4	5813.0	1708.4	1856.0	2117.9	1844.0	242.4	184.0
3210	Electronic valves, tubes, etc.	10939.0	9855.0	10429.4	10103.0	3228.5	3258.3	3649.6	3456.0	845.8	540.0
3220	TV/radio transmitters; line comm. apparatus	15954.0	14015.7	14097.7	12128.0	3702.9	3253.1	3466.3	2931.0	264.6	145.0
3230	TV and radio receivers and associated goods	5228.6	4303.5	3293.4	3285.0	983.7	938.8	783.9	824.0	72.0	104.0
331	Medical, measuring, testing appliances, etc.	20494.0	19291.8	18454.5	20268.0	6872.2	6689.8	6954.4	7797.0	426.1	564.0
3311	Medical, surgical and orthopaedic equipment	5949.0	6157.0	6234.0	6317.0	2310.0	2493.0	2674.0	2684.0	204.0	256.0
3312	Measuring/testing/navigating appliances,etc.	11694.0	10692.0	9766.0	11643.0	3565.0	3310.0	3374.0	4200.0	186.0	273.0
3313	Industrial process control equipment	2851.0	2443.0	2455.0	2308.0	997.0	887.0	906.0	913.0	36.0	35.0
3320	Optical instruments & photographic equipment	1881.8	1796.0	1904.4	2064.0	703.7	713.0	774.1	831.0	69.0	70.0
3330	Watches and clocks	389.1	339.4	340.9	378.0	171.3	149.5	148.8	168.0	13.2	17.0
3410	Motor vehicles	162783.0	166666.0	85047.6	85026.0	12580.9	12057.4	13214.5	12683.0	4128.6	3151.0
3420	Automobile bodies, trailers & semi-trailers	3856.4	3709.6	3978.3	4117.0	1112.6	1107.5	1121.4	1185.0	86.0	89.0
3430	Parts/accessories for automobiles	21510.0	20520.6	18671.1	18187.0	4777.6	4792.9	4947.6	4614.0	646.2	978.0
351	Building and repairing of ships and boats	4092.2	5623.6	5477.3	5512.0	960.4	1497.9	1563.0	1757.0	265.4	230.0
3511	Building and repairing of ships	2726.4	4213.7	3948.1	3862.0	477.4	1022.0	1037.9	1193.0	192.7	110.0
3512	Building/repairing of pleasure/sport. boats	1365.8	1409.9	1529.2	1649.0	483.0	475.9	525.1	564.0	72.7	120.0
3520	Railway/tramway locomotives & rolling stock	2811.6	3066.2	2930.7	3038.0	788.2	720.3	803.3	857.0	58.5	40.0
3530	Aircraft and spacecraft	37624.7	35076.7	39255.6	45099.0	6379.4	6623.9	4633.3	7052.0	936.8	1056.0
359	Transport equipment n.e.c.	1058.0	1091.3	1694.6	1003.0	273.0	273.1	339.8	240.0	36.0	29.0
3591	Motorcycles	...	524.0	555.1	521.0	...	106.8	115.6	106.0	19.8	20.0
3592	Bicycles and invalid carriages	454.8	...	1036.2	387.0	133.2	...	194.5	108.0	14.6	7.0
3599	Other transport equipment n.e.c.	...	91.0	103.0	95.0	...	25.0	30.0	27.0	2.0	2.0
3610	Furniture	12534.2	12313.7	12610.5	12489.0	3825.0	3737.5	3739.8	3622.0	371.9	319.0
369	Manufacturing n.e.c.	6356.9	6163.6	5983.5	5998.0	2042.4	2047.6	2048.5	2069.0	207.8	204.0
3691	Jewellery and related articles	1596.3	1384.7	1352.6	1444.0	510.6	455.2	466.5	503.0	30.2	35.0
3692	Musical instruments	190.6	188.2	194.7	197.0	110.4	112.5	115.4	115.0	8.1	8.0
3693	Sports goods	1191.8	1216.4	1358.0	1332.0	361.5	379.8	409.5	398.0	51.0	46.0
3694	Games and toys	732.2	732.6	696.0	640.0	203.4	215.6	197.3	188.0	24.6	22.0
3699	Other manufacturing n.e.c.	2646.0	2641.7	2382.2	2386.0	856.5	884.5	859.8	866.0	93.9	93.0
3710	Recycling of metal waste and scrap	2671.0	2825.9	3952.5	2593.0	661.8	706.2	949.1	959.0	176.6	212.0
3720	Recycling of non-metal waste and scrap	1591.7	1716.2	1923.4	1957.0	548.2	572.0	630.0	633.0	172.6	158.0
D	Total manufacturing	926079.0	916222.0	856497.0	871342.0	207984.0	206130.0	209892.0	214014.0	29010.6	29970.0

France

ISIC Revision 3			Index numbers of industrial production											
			(2000=100)											
ISIC	Industry	Note	1995	1996	1997	1998	1999	2000	2001	2002	2003	2004	2005	2006
15	Food and beverages		95	97	99	100	102	100	101	103	102	104	104	105
16	Tobacco products		121	123	116	114	110	100	99	102	99	73	70	66
17	Textiles		115	110	111	112	105	100	96	89	83	77	71	65
18	Wearing apparel, fur		215	178	160	147	123	100	89	68	55	47	35	31
19	Leather, leather products and footwear		142	126	123	121	107	100	96	86	77	72	66	61
20	Wood products (excl. furniture)		90	88	94	93	92	100	99	97	96	100	100	104
21	Paper and paper products		91	89	95	94	97	100	97	98	98	101	101	100
22	Printing and publishing		88	86	88	91	97	100	99	96	95	96	95	94
23	Coke,refined petroleum products,nuclear fuel		94	99	104	107	97	100	102	95	100	100	99	96
24	Chemicals and chemical products		82	85	89	93	95	100	103	104	107	111	114	117
25	Rubber and plastics products		80	80	85	90	94	100	101	101	102	106	107	106
26	Non-metallic mineral products		93	91	93	96	96	100	99	97	96	99	99	102
27	Basic metals		90	87	93	96	93	100	98	96	93	95	91	93
28	Fabricated metal products		83	82	87	91	93	100	101	101	98	100	102	105
29	Machinery and equipment n.e.c.		89	90	92	97	95	100	100	103	102	105	108	113
30	Office, accounting and computing machinery		73	81	81	82	92	100	92	75	75	71	43	38
31	Electrical machinery and apparatus		79	79	84	89	93	100	102	95	91	90	91	97
32	Radio,television and communication equipment		57	58	66	70	81	100	94	87	90	100	97	95
33	Medical, precision and optical instruments		94	88	93	97	98	100	103	106	109	107	111	120
34	Motor vehicles, trailers, semi-trailers		66	68	74	85	93	100	107	109	107	113	112	103
35	Other transport equipment		65	66	81	89	99	100	109	102	106	109	121	128
36	Furniture; manufacturing n.e.c.		86	85	86	94	97	100	101	93	89	92	91	86
37	Recycling		...	...	...	...	...	...	...	...	...	...	...	...
D	Total manufacturing		86	85	90	94	96	100	101	100	99	101	102	103

Georgia

Supplier of information:
State Department for Statistics of Georgia, Tbilisi.

Basic source of data:
Survey.

Major deviations from ISIC (Revision 3):
None reported.

Reference period:
Calendar year.

Scope:
Not reported.

Method of data collection:
Not reported.

Type of enumeration:
Not reported.

Adjusted for non-response:
Not reported.

Concepts and definitions of variables:
No deviations from the standard UN concepts and definitions are reported.

Related national publications:
None reported.

Georgia

ISIC Revision 3		Number of establishments					Number of persons engaged					Wages and salaries paid to employees				
			(number)					(number)					(thousands of Georgian Lari)			
ISIC	Industry	Note	2003	2004	2005	2006	Note	2003	2004	2005	2006	Note	2003	2004	2005	2006
151	Processed meat,fish,fruit,vegetables,fats		63	76	108	95		959	1220	2358	2294		496	1133	2789	5236
1511	Processing/preserving of meat		33	41	47	44		359	550	758	919		171	754	1618	3226
1512	Processing/preserving of fish		2	5	6	6		...	58	83	77		6	11	105	94
1513	Processing/preserving of fruit & vegetables		19	18	38	37		548	549	1423	1227		312	352	1040	1825
1514	Vegetable and animal oils and fats		9	12	17	8		37	63	94	71		7	17	26	91
1520	Dairy products		36	43	47	51		877	1078	1159	1277		1083	1740	3211	4161
153	Grain mill products; starches; animal feeds		73	72	123	105		1225	1338	1810	2175		1185	2079	2968	4568
1531	Grain mill products		...	...	122	104		...	...	1794	2159		...	...	2945	4542
1532	Starches and starch products		...	...	-	-		...	...	-	-		...	...	-	-
1533	Prepared animal feeds		...	...	...	1		...	...	...	...		...	...	...	...
154	Other food products		1039	1338	1406	1025		7556	8301	8928	7167		5750	7351	8715	9151
1541	Bakery products		947	1241	1275	933		5324	6166	6404	5568		3664	5201	5608	5928
1542	Sugar		4	5	5	5		501	540	626	611		1121	1208	1743	2356
1543	Cocoa, chocolate and sugar confectionery		7	9	13	9		27	33	68	23		9	8	31	37
1544	Macaroni, noodles & similar products		9	10	18	17		54	63	89	98		50	51	101	119
1549	Other food products n.e.c.		72	73	95	59		1650	1499	1741	867		906	883	1233	712
155	Beverages		340	342	461	420		6953	8076	9156	9457		12233	19194	27342	35596
1551	Distilling, rectifying & blending of spirits		27	27	40	37		651	746	1055	1382		627	1143	2649	4501
1552	Wines		113	110	143	149		3162	3330	4106	4020		5296	7251	8053	9329
1553	Malt liquors and malt		14	17	27	13		1093	1584	1517	1581		1518	5211	7900	9226
1554	Soft drinks; mineral waters		186	188	251	221		2047	2416	2478	2474		4792	5589	8740	12539
1600	Tobacco products		12	12	16	13		528	469	424	426		690	3649	2546	3256
171	Spinning, weaving and finishing of textiles		5	16	8	8		184	280	198	136		336	275	266	447
1711	Textile fibre preparation; textile weaving		5	16	7	8		184	280	197	136		336	275	266	447
1712	Finishing of textiles		-	-	...	-		-	-	...	-		-	-	...	-
172	Other textiles		4	5	6	17		42	49	43	76		13	18	51	56
1721	Made-up textile articles, except apparel		...	...	5	13		...	...	17	62		...	...	38	27
1722	Carpets and rugs		-	-	-	-		-	-	-	-		-	-	-	-
1723	Cordage, rope, twine and netting		-	-	-	-		-	-	-	-		-	-	-	-
1729	Other textiles n.e.c.		...	...	...	...		...	...	...	...		...	...	...	...
1730	Knitted and crocheted fabrics and articles		3	2	...	...		12	11	...	...		2	34	...	...
1810	Wearing apparel, except fur apparel		36	42	75	69		1509	1785	1971	2051		1523	2503	3942	4320
1820	Dressing & dyeing of fur; processing of fur		...	...	...	...		...	...	...	...		...	...	...	...
191	Tanning, dressing and processing of leather		13	16	17	18		128	103	136	92		69	94	177	105
1911	Tanning and dressing of leather		10	13	14	16		91	86	91	83		52	61	82	87
1912	Luggage, handbags, etc.; saddlery & harness		3	3	3	2		37	17	45	...		17	34	95	19
1920	Footwear		26	31	64	64		133	231	350	376		64	158	244	327
2010	Sawmilling and planing of wood		184	171	385	264		1670	1619	2652	2042		1147	1242	2130	2035
202	Products of wood, cork, straw, etc.		57	59	155	135		325	533	892	706		155	346	777	817
2021	Veneer sheets, plywood, particle board, etc.		...	...	10	7		...	...	215	86		...	...	217	122
2022	Builders' carpentry and joinery		48	51	121	94		281	387	598	453		137	231	514	525
2023	Wooden containers		7	4	8	22		30	19	33	67		11	8	14	58
2029	Other wood products; articles of cork/straw		...	...	16	12		...	...	46	100		...	...	32	112
210	Paper and paper products		25	21	35	39		288	290	386	402		284	325	560	910
2101	Pulp, paper and paperboard		-	-	...	-		-	-	14	-		-	-	...	-
2102	Corrugated paper and paperboard		13	10	8	12		198	180	190	...		224	249	367	807
2109	Other articles of paper and paperboard		12	11	24	27		90	110	182	...		60	76	182	104
221	Publishing		129	130	166	173		1777	1844	2153	1611		2272	2892	3122	3742
2211	Publishing of books and other publications		24	26	42	40		502	503	635	277		528	944	802	684
2212	Publishing of newspapers, journals, etc.		101	101	120	127		1238	1320	1495	1275		1708	1916	2256	2913
2213	Publishing of recorded media		-	-	-	-		-	-	-	-		-	-	-	-
2219	Other publishing		...	...	...	5		...	...	...	59		...	...	...	145

222	Printing and related service activities	130	129	211	189	1467	1319	1704	1497	1207	1416	2321	2930
2221	Printing	115	115	198	185	1167	967	1241	1489	950	1058	1851	2553
2222	Service activities related to printing	15	14	13	4	300	352	463	8	257	359	470	369
2230	Reproduction of recorded media	-	-	-	2	-	-	-	...	-	-	-	...
2310	Coke oven products	-	-	-	-	-	-	-	-	-	-	-	-
2320	Refined petroleum products	8	9	5	2	131	199	44	...	226	298	33	...
2330	Processing of nuclear fuel	...	...	...	...	...	...	...	...	...	...	...	...
241	Basic chemicals	25	21	27	22	3558	3642	6512	3339	9838	9790	...	15275
2411	Basic chemicals, except fertilizers	23	19	23	...	346	328	360	...	656	749	1156	...
2412	Fertilizers and nitrogen compounds	2	2	3	...	3212	3314	6151	...	...	...	10920	...
2413	Plastics in primary forms; synthetic rubber	-	-	...	...	-	-	...	...	-	-	...	...
242	Other chemicals	55	57	76	82	804	909	1034	1084	685	1050	2560	3191
2421	Pesticides and other agro-chemical products	1	1	1	1	9	13	13	...	...	...	...	...
2422	Paints, varnishes, printing ink and mastics	11	8	8	5	142	119	97	89	114	116	99	119
2423	Pharmaceuticals, medicinal chemicals, etc.	40	42	57	62	639	705	810	854	555	703	1887	2736
2424	Soap, cleaning & cosmetic preparations	...	...	6	9	...	...	63	101	...	...	101	201
2429	Other chemical products n.e.c.	3	3	4	5	...	...	51	37	8	196	446	136
2430	Man-made fibres	1	...	...	...	...	...	...	...	...	...	...	...
251	Rubber products	7	6	5	3	62	61	53	...	39	39	55	...
2511	Rubber tyres and tubes	...	...	...	...	...	...	...	...	...	...	...	...
2519	Other rubber products	...	...	...	...	...	...	...	...	...	...	...	...
2520	Plastic products	44	62	116	126	582	842	1184	1667	515	1591	3053	7211
2610	Glass and glass products	3	3	6	5	281	283	310	320	923	920	1318	1729
269	Non-metallic mineral products n.e.c.	...	...	...	433	...	...	4666	6372	...	...	...	17002
2691	Pottery, china and earthenware	7	10	12	13	81	107	106	85	65	118	104	87
2692	Refractory ceramic products	...	...	...	...	...	...	...	...	...	...	...	...
2693	Struct.non-refractory clay; ceramic products	9	11	16	15	204	244	309	336	155	459	698	616
2694	Cement, lime and plaster	27	31	41	42	1584	1685	1991	3351	3606	4410	6107	9495
2695	Articles of concrete, cement and plaster	67	79	136	143	1064	1247	1628	1888	2675	2556	3337	5993
2696	Cutting, shaping & finishing of stone	55	59	103	217	382	393	574	673	196	261	379	698
2699	Other non-metallic mineral products n.e.c.	3	2	3	3	83	53	55	...	93	84	41	274
2710	Basic iron and steel	6	6	6	7	5133	2949	2467	2610	6428	8096	7463	7851
2720	Basic precious and non-ferrous metals	...	...	...	1	...	...	...	...	...	...	...	...
273	Casting of metals	9	10	11	8	669	837	747	731	1163	1475	...	7851
2731	Casting of iron and steel	...	...	...	...	...	...	...	...	...	...	...	...
2732	Casting of non-ferrous metals	...	...	...	...	...	...	...	...	...	...	...	...
281	Struct.metal products;tanks;steam generators	31	31	45	46	394	366	540	506	557	930	1313	1358
2811	Structural metal products	30	30	44	45	372	341	516	491	534	911	1293	1300
2812	Tanks, reservoirs and containers of metal	...	...	...	1	...	...	...	...	...	...	...	...
2813	Steam generators	-	-	-	-	-	-	-	-	-	-	-	-
289	Other metal products; metal working services	30	35	68	71	724	1881	715	1086	954	2170	1303	2500
2891	Metal forging/pressing/stamping/roll-forming	...	4	3	1	...	18	7	...	...	27	...	...
2892	Treatment & coating of metals	...	4	18	15	...	1483	213	93	...	1717	228	88
2893	Cutlery, hand tools and general hardware	...	...	...	4	...	...	...	25	...	...	...	76
2899	Other fabricated metal products n.e.c.	25	27	46	51	311	380	490	967	316	427	1073	2336
291	General purpose machinery	17	23	32	33	506	700	637	592	818	1905	3900	4377
2911	Engines & turbines (not for transport equipment)	8	7	6	...	310	366	272	...	651	1517	3309	...
2912	Pumps, compressors, taps and valves	...	...	...	...	...	...	...	...	...	...	...	...
2913	Bearings, gears, gearing & driving elements	-	-	-	-	-	-	-	-	-	-	-	-
2914	Ovens, furnaces and furnace burners	-	-	-	-	-	-	-	-	-	-	-	-
2915	Lifting and handling equipment	4	10	11	...	154	301	254	...	130	361	476	...
2919	Other general purpose machinery	5	5	10	...	42	26	47	...	38	26	64	...
292	Special purpose machinery	...	15	27	18	...	362	...	284	...	253	800	1148
2921	Agricultural and forestry machinery	6	5	8	3	162	138	58	...	35	39	26	...
2922	Machine tools	5	5	6	2	181	148	149	...	188	132	208	...
2923	Machinery for metallurgy	-	-	-	-	-	-	-	-	-	-	-	-
2924	Machinery for mining & construction	...	...	...	...	...	...	...	...	...	...	...	...
2925	Food/beverage/tobacco processing machinery	5	4	7	...	53	56	105	...	37	41	219	...
2926	Machinery for textile, apparel and leather	-	-	-	-	-	-	-	-	-	-	-	-
2927	Weapons and ammunition	-	-	-	-	-	-	-	-	-	-	-	-
2929	Other special purpose machinery	6	...	5	...	78	...	250	...	87	...	82	...

continued

Georgia

ISIC Revision 3		Number of establishments					Number of persons engaged					Wages and salaries paid to employees				
			(number)					(number)					(thousands of Georgian Lari)			
ISIC	Industry	Note	2003	2004	2005	2006	Note	2003	2004	2005	2006	Note	2003	2004	2005	2006
2930	Domestic appliances n.e.c.		7	9	13	26		16	25	84	41		2	5	12	10
3000	Office, accounting and computing machinery		...	...	...	...		...	...	...	...		...	...	...	...
3110	Electric motors, generators and transformers		9	9	15	15		410	322	544	431		690	689	1002	1900
3120	Electricity distribution & control apparatus		6	2	4	2		85	...	84	...		58	49	92	...
3130	Insulated wire and cable		2	2	2	1		...	...	54	...		29	40	46	...
3140	Accumulators, primary cells and batteries		3	4	4	3		...	64	26	...		13	26	26	...
3150	Lighting equipment and electric lamps		...	...	...	4		...	...	...	69		...	...	...	473
3190	Other electrical equipment n.e.c.		6	9	8	6		127	141	147	16		108	113	252	12
3210	Electronic valves, tubes, etc.		2	2	2	...		114	64	91	...		40	57	64	...
3220	TV/radio transmitters; line comm. apparatus		...	...	...	3		...	...	...	...		...	...	...	...
3230	TV and radio receivers and associated goods		4	...	...	2		60	...	...	...		21	...	...	...
331	Medical, measuring, testing appliances, etc.		14	15	15	15		292	369	445	287		203	258	714	468
3311	Medical, surgical and orthopaedic equipment		5	6	7	6		132	145	164	163		127	131	223	232
3312	Measuring/testing/navigating appliances,etc.		8	8	7	7		155	222	271	118		75	127	449	222
3313	Industrial process control equipment		...	...	...	2		...	...	...	...		...	...	...	...
3320	Optical instruments & photographic equipment		...	...	...	...		...	...	...	...		...	...	...	...
3330	Watches and clocks		...	...	...	...		...	...	...	...		...	...	...	...
3410	Motor vehicles		...	...	-	1		...	...	...	...		...	...	...	...
3420	Automobile bodies, trailers & semi-trailers		...	...	...	1		...	...	...	...		...	...	...	...
3430	Parts/accessories for automobiles		11	8	6	5		62	64	64	51		32	48	79	98
351	Building and repairing of ships and boats		11	7	6	4		468	370	495	442		1312	563	965	1575
3511	Building and repairing of ships		...	...	...	...		...	...	...	...		...	...	...	...
3512	Building/repairing of pleasure/sport. boats		...	...	...	...		...	...	...	...		...	...	...	...
3520	Railway/tramway locomotives & rolling stock		9	7	12	9		3643	2224	2088	2167		9599	5400	5723	8813
3530	Aircraft and spacecraft		...	...	...	1		...	...	...	...		...	...	...	...
359	Transport equipment n.e.c.		-	-	-	-		-	-	-	-		-	-	-	-
3591	Motorcycles		-	-	-	-		-	-	-	-		-	-	-	-
3592	Bicycles and invalid carriages		-	-	-	-		-	-	-	-		-	-	-	-
3599	Other transport equipment n.e.c.		-	-	-	-		-	-	-	-		-	-	-	-
3610	Furniture		64	63	133	153		564	547	873	922		365	384	709	1516
369	Manufacturing n.e.c.		18	17	30	20		274	282	251	206		382	345	412	647
3691	Jewellery and related articles		7	6	11	6		227	231	179	159		362	323	358	647
3692	Musical instruments		-	-	-	-		-	-	-	-		-	-	-	-
3693	Sports goods		-	-	-	-		-	-	-	-		-	-	-	-
3694	Games and toys		-	-	...	1		-	-	...	...		-	-	...	...
3699	Other manufacturing n.e.c.		11	11	18	13		47	51	70	43		20	22	52	48
3710	Recycling of metal waste and scrap		...	...	5	3		...	...	47	...		...	...	36	...
3720	Recycling of non-metal waste and scrap		...	...	...	17		...	...	...	18		...	...	...	2
D	Total manufacturing		2775	3137	4306	3835		51619	52649	61692	57530		81567	101683	130992	170754

Georgia

ISIC Revision 3		Output					Value added					Gross fixed capital formation		
		Note	(thousands of Georgian Lari)				Note	(thousands of Georgian Lari)				Note	(thousands of Georgian Lari)	
ISIC	Industry		2003	2004	2005	2006		2003	2004	2005	2006		2005	2006
151	Processed meat,fish,fruit,vegetables,fats		17608	26832	75872	94164		2158	4147	8761	10751		19876	40586
1511	Processing/preserving of meat		4036	8111	13149	30704		867	2202	4799	10801		8812	12746
1512	Processing/preserving of fish		22	329	1171	1417		5	41	250	-175		576	3923
1513	Processing/preserving of fruit & vegetables		13495	18265	61384	61782		1263	1855	3694	...		10201	23655
1514	Vegetable and animal oils and fats		55	127	168	261		24	48	18	153		287	263
1520	Dairy products		15561	22120	28232	34771		4495	6368	8151	9042		17760	16795
153	Grain mill products; starches; animal feeds		35312	81690	92213	163497		4336	6217	6515	22256		16774	21847
1531	Grain mill products		...	...	91589	162789		...	...	...	22243		16675	21531
1532	Starches and starch products		...	...	-	-		...	...	-	-		-	-
1533	Prepared animal feeds		...	...	...	...		...	...	...	...		...	...
154	Other food products		138394	156949	162804	166761		29240	34718	20869	28844		32102	21806
1541	Bakery products		47919	77476	62042	61075		11256	16804	13860	12843		17624	14810
1542	Sugar		77158	67345	88583	96532		13961	15464	5377	14025		1816	2334
1543	Cocoa, chocolate and sugar confectionery		46	61	149	256		21	23	...	57		460	78
1544	Macaroni, noodles & similar products		550	867	835	928		95	155	293	281		414	411
1549	Other food products n.e.c.		12722	11199	11195	7971		3907	2272	1191	1638		11787	4174
155	Beverages		232518	291600	440452	402333		61460	80954	108754	100370		158699	186056
1551	Distilling, rectifying & blending of spirits		13215	24957	47380	47377		7547	13849	15271	9392		12553	14511
1552	Wines		98875	109738	173246	105372		19779	21442	36733	18901		60588	57313
1553	Malt liquors and malt		19482	37828	47669	81637		3034	13062	8875	27198		27715	43082
1554	Soft drinks; mineral waters		100946	119077	172158	167947		31100	32601	47876	44880		57843	71150
1600	Tobacco products		17955	34012	38060	63080		1026	31562	3573	10988		11332	9136
171	Spinning, weaving and finishing of textiles		574	360	563	810		285	147	163	-33		2832	2667
1711	Textile fibre preparation; textile weaving		574	360	556	810		285	147	162	-33		2830	2667
1712	Finishing of textiles		-	-	...	-		-	-	...	-		...	-
172	Other textiles		1231	1527	1201	1548		206	304	185	659		391	117
1721	Made-up textile articles, except apparel		...	...	711	1455		...	...	77	618		79	97
1722	Carpets and rugs		-	-	-	-		-	-	-	-		-	-
1723	Cordage, rope, twine and netting		-	-	-	-		-	-	-	-		-	-
1729	Other textiles n.e.c.		...	...	485	...		...	...	...	...		...	...
1730	Knitted and crocheted fabrics and articles		...	...	...	...		3	...	...	...		...	...
1810	Wearing apparel, except fur apparel		4821	6294	13395	15981		1302	2871	4847	6953		7095	5375
1820	Dressing & dyeing of fur; processing of fur		...	...	...	...		...	...	...	...		...	...
191	Tanning, dressing and processing of leather		618	507	578	848		102	-19	170	320		1051	449
1911	Tanning and dressing of leather		551	411	440	668		-62	-45	150	250		475	434
1912	Luggage, handbags, etc.; saddlery & harness		67	69	138	...		42	27	20	...		576	...
1920	Footwear		1074	2322	3161	4458		122	403	526	568		887	934
2010	Sawmilling and planing of wood		10221	9931	20353	18752		3464	3774	5714	6807		12571	12897
202	Products of wood, cork, straw, etc.		1216	2629	6765	6551		...	1053	1598	2216		4659	6344
2021	Veneer sheets, plywood, particle board, etc.		...	...	1185	623		...	...	250	143		1571	1230
2022	Builders' carpentry and joinery		864	1602	4700	3861		255	724	1222	1213		2700	4301
2023	Wooden containers		341	225	357	1041		105	69	39	482		9	77
2029	Other wood products; articles of cork/straw		...	...	523	1027		...	...	88	378		379	736
210	Paper and paper products		3886	5708	8023	8680		704	1010	1657	2034		2195	3508
2101	Pulp, paper and paperboard		-	-	...	-		-	-	...	-		...	-
2102	Corrugated paper and paperboard		1978	3027	4247	5033		352	512	853	1155		1264	2262
2109	Other articles of paper and paperboard		1909	2682	3676	3647		352	498	778	879		923	1246
221	Publishing		14574	18396	22125	31191		3446	7919	9145	13244		5547	6550
2211	Publishing of books and other publications		2671	4077	4940	8769		1199	2360	2048	3978		1817	1506
2212	Publishing of newspapers, journals, etc.		11528	13763	16166	19813		2022	5207	6444	8106		2973	3962
2213	Publishing of recorded media		-	-	-	-		...	...	...	...		...	-
2219	Other publishing		...	...	...	2609		...	...	...	1160		...	1082

continued

Georgia

ISIC Revision 3		Output					Value added					Gross fixed capital formation		
			(thousands of Georgian Lari)					(thousands of Georgian Lari)					(thousands of Georgian Lari)	
ISIC	Industry	Note	2003	2004	2005	2006	Note	2003	2004	2005	2006	Note	2005	2006
222	Printing and related service activities		19578	23702	30028	36632		4715	7497	9407	13911		10449	9453
2221	Printing		19533	23419	29789	36579		4711	7447	9339	13898		10288	9449
2222	Service activities related to printing		45	283	239	53		4	50	67	13		161	4
2230	Reproduction of recorded media		-	-	-	...		-	-	-	...		-	...
2310	Coke oven products		-	-	-	-		-	-	-	-		-	-
2320	Refined petroleum products		5996	18324	1190	...		1317	3425	112	41		1121	...
2330	Processing of nuclear fuel		...	...	...	...		...	...	...	...		...	...
241	Basic chemicals		44981	89551	108238	163934		12466	25581	41723	62423		131336	120514
2411	Basic chemicals, except fertilizers		...	4387	7333	...		3539	3083	5274	...		8275	...
2412	Fertilizers and nitrogen compounds		...	85164	100901	...		6712	22498	36448	...		123051	...
2413	Plastics in primary forms; synthetic rubber		-	-	...	...		-	-	...	...		...	...
242	Other chemicals		7856	14171	19123	27449		2186	4497	6707	11310		16292	15223
2421	Pesticides and other agro-chemical products		...	...	...	...		...	...	...	...		...	...
2422	Paints, varnishes, printing ink and mastics		683	762	485	480		154	239	54	-27		1786	1843
2423	Pharmaceuticals, medicinal chemicals, etc.		7011	10710	14356	22092		1937	3392	4884	10316		13024	10757
2424	Soap, cleaning & cosmetic preparations		...	...	1160	2241		...	...	275	905		513	921
2429	Other chemical products n.e.c.		...	...	3012	2628		44	696	1460	114		954	1692
2430	Man-made fibres		...	...	...	...		22	...	...	...		...	...
251	Rubber products		663	687	916	1157		120	107	189	172		538	...
2511	Rubber tyres and tubes		...	...	...	...		...	...	...	...		...	...
2519	Other rubber products		...	...	...	...		...	...	...	...		...	...
2520	Plastic products		16210	26810	20424	51621		1589	5370	6578	14656		17693	10259
2610	Glass and glass products		20727	21062	24498	22775		11008	7709	9702	7609		23945	24713
269	Non-metallic mineral products n.e.c.		...	...	...	188362		...	...	...	47129		...	41832
2691	Pottery, china and earthenware		...	...	...	272		...	...	...	129		...	643
2692	Refractory ceramic products		...	...	...	...		...	...	...	...		...	...
2693	Struct.non-refractory clay; ceramic products		1671	2622	3975	4313		712	1063	1647	1356		6317	2432
2694	Cement, lime and plaster		39100	44946	68533	116283		9328	9240	12014	25695		6815	13124
2695	Articles of concrete, cement and plaster		16019	20266	29776	62743		4793	6383	9328	19204		18731	21946
2696	Cutting, shaping & finishing of stone		1747	2388	3784	4433		649	698	881	542		2045	2825
2699	Other non-metallic mineral products n.e.c.		262	203	199	...		163	104	61	...		1397	...
2710	Basic iron and steel		60863	93689	148875	151109		12769	4200	22119	22251		43072	3036
2720	Basic precious and non-ferrous metals		...	...	...	...		...	...	...	...		...	...
273	Casting of metals		5604	7092	7487	8640		1961	2262	3494	3830		14519	11039
2731	Casting of iron and steel		...	...	...	...		...	...	...	...		...	...
2732	Casting of non-ferrous metals		...	...	...	...		...	...	...	...		...	...
281	Struct.metal products;tanks;steam generators		4283	4672	8059	8841		1122	1694	2691	2524		2604	5777
2811	Structural metal products		4248	4654	7986	8610		1088	1677	2682	2343		2400	5745
2812	Tanks, reservoirs and containers of metal		...	...	...	...		...	...	...	...		...	...
2813	Steam generators		-	-	-	-		-	-	-	-		-	-
289	Other metal products; metal working services		4826	5663	7024	22461		1766	2501	2508	5070		4958	5394
2891	Metal forging/pressing/stamping/roll-forming		...	278	86	...		...	46	21	...		529	-
2892	Treatment & coating of metals		...	1795	807	323		...	1487	272	164		1605	1350
2893	Cutlery, hand tools and general hardware		...	...	...	283		...	...	...	109		...	6
2899	Other fabricated metal products n.e.c.		1926	3590	6128	21850		652	968	2218	4795		2822	4038
291	General purpose machinery		3314	7031	13199	15142		1806	4271	9706	9339		3827	1459
2911	Engines & turbines (not for transport equipment)		2762	5620	11431	...		1897	3828	8985	...		730	...
2912	Pumps, compressors, taps and valves		...	...	...	...		...	...	...	...		...	...
2913	Bearings, gears, gearing & driving elements		-	-	-	-		-	-	-	-		-	-
2914	Ovens, furnaces and furnace burners		-	-	-	-		-	-	-	-		-	-
2915	Lifting and handling equipment		325	1320	1188	...		50	416	448	...		2805	...
2919	Other general purpose machinery		228	87	451	...		-141	24	188	...		118	...

292	Special purpose machinery	...	778	2873	12390	...	446	1719	2412	8119	6512
2921	Agricultural and forestry machinery	139	62	51	28	32	23	29	13	558	...
2922	Machine tools	400	401	416	...	125	222	223	133	2133	...
2923	Machinery for metallurgy	-	-	-	-	-	-	-	-	-	-
2924	Machinery for mining & construction	...	...	...	...	...	...	...	...	...	...
2925	Food/beverage/tobacco processing machinery	464	90	749	...	50	46	300	...	1542	...
2926	Machinery for textile, apparel and leather	-	-	-	-	-	-	-	-	-	-
2927	Weapons and ammunition	-	-	-	-	-	-	-	-	-	-
2929	Other special purpose machinery	674	...	596	...	114	...	253	...	2874	...
2930	Domestic appliances n.e.c.	31	43	209	214	8	16	31	65	8	241
3000	Office, accounting and computing machinery	...	...	...	...	...	...	...	...	...	...
3110	Electric motors, generators and transformers	2780	1768	3488	5919	1123	685	1526	2958	5600	6843
3120	Electricity distribution & control apparatus	454	...	432	85	-160	...	116	...	673	...
3130	Insulated wire and cable	...	...	1491	...	78	149	234	...	379	...
3140	Accumulators, primary cells and batteries	...	395	296	117	...	63	57	...	150	...
3150	Lighting equipment and electric lamps	...	...	...	3487	...	17	...	1540	...	182
3190	Other electrical equipment n.e.c.	1887	1833	5489	79	534	665	1127	38	1263	11
3210	Electronic valves, tubes, etc.	...	73	87	...	-18	56	48	...	4747	...
3220	TV/radio transmitters; line comm. apparatus	...	...	...	500	...	...	...	...	...	...
3230	TV and radio receivers and associated goods	70	...	...	...	-3	62	...	...	...	...
331	Medical, measuring, testing appliances, etc.	1098	2470	4424	2686	542	949	2051	1260	2202	1893
3311	Medical, surgical and orthopaedic equipment	644	1401	1044	1629	298	547	508	662	1249	1456
3312	Measuring/testing/navigating appliances,etc.	406	1012	3299	856	228	368	1488	498	744	434
3313	Industrial process control equipment	...	...	...	...	...	...	...	...	...	...
3320	Optical instruments & photographic equipment	...	...	...	...	...	...	...	...	...	...
3330	Watches and clocks	...	...	...	...	...	...	...	...	...	...
3410	Motor vehicles	...	...	...	...	...	...	...	...	...	...
3420	Automobile bodies, trailers & semi-trailers	...	...	...	...	...	...	...	...	...	...
3430	Parts/accessories for automobiles	250	481	663	848	78	120	145	240	299	403
351	Building and repairing of ships and boats	4745	...	1192	2760	3859	785	83	1057	11903	9153
3511	Building and repairing of ships	...	...	...	...	...	...	...	...	...	...
3512	Building/repairing of pleasure/sport. boats	...	...	...	...	...	...	...	...	...	...
3520	Railway/tramway locomotives & rolling stock	42276	24760	17669	33404	22225	10541	5138	9425	55638	54508
3530	Aircraft and spacecraft	...	...	...	...	...	...	...	...	...	...
359	Transport equipment n.e.c.	-	-	-	-	-	-	-	-	-	-
3591	Motorcycles	-	-	-	-	-	-	-	-	-	-
3592	Bicycles and invalid carriages	-	-	-	-	-	-	-	-	-	-
3599	Other transport equipment n.e.c.	-	-	-	-	-	-	-	-	-	-
3610	Furniture	3167	2971	7274	14043	811	934	2412	3755	5559	3556
369	Manufacturing n.e.c.	1263	1244	1865	2640	312	196	415	1051	957	1275
3691	Jewellery and related articles	822	591	967	1930	245	79	250	893	691	1233
3692	Musical instruments	-	-	-	-	-	-	-	-	-	-
3693	Sports goods	-	-	-	-	-	-	-	-	-	-
3694	Games and toys	-	-	...	...	-	-	...	...	-	-
3699	Other manufacturing n.e.c.	441	653	891	680	67	117	163	133	266	34
3710	Recycling of metal waste and scrap	...	...	72	71	...	...	41	...	477	...
3720	Recycling of non-metal waste and scrap	...	...	74	52	...	...	...	11	...	33
D	Total manufacturing	949217	1148168	1552683	1918934	285345	309469	378439	499363	744071	720850

Georgia

ISIC Revision 3			Index numbers of industrial production											
			(2000=100)											
ISIC	Industry	Note	1995	1996	1997	1998	1999	2000	2001	2002	2003	2004	2005	2006
15	Food and beverages		...	...	...	...	...	...	...	...	...	...	...	...
16	Tobacco products		...	...	...	...	...	...	...	...	...	...	...	...
17	Textiles		...	...	...	...	...	...	...	...	...	...	...	...
18	Wearing apparel, fur		...	...	...	...	...	...	...	...	...	...	...	...
19	Leather, leather products and footwear		...	...	...	...	...	...	...	...	...	...	...	...
20	Wood products (excl. furniture)		...	...	...	...	...	...	...	...	...	...	...	...
21	Paper and paper products		...	...	...	...	...	...	...	...	...	...	...	...
22	Printing and publishing		...	...	...	...	...	...	...	...	...	...	...	...
23	Coke,refined petroleum products,nuclear fuel		...	...	...	...	...	...	...	...	...	...	...	...
24	Chemicals and chemical products		...	...	...	...	...	...	...	...	...	...	...	...
25	Rubber and plastics products		...	...	...	...	...	...	...	...	...	...	...	...
26	Non-metallic mineral products		...	...	...	...	...	...	...	...	...	...	...	...
27	Basic metals		...	...	...	...	...	...	...	...	...	...	...	...
28	Fabricated metal products		...	...	...	...	...	...	...	...	...	...	...	...
29	Machinery and equipment n.e.c.		...	...	...	...	...	...	...	...	...	...	...	...
30	Office, accounting and computing machinery		...	...	...	...	...	...	...	...	...	...	...	...
31	Electrical machinery and apparatus		...	...	...	...	...	...	...	...	...	...	...	...
32	Radio,television and communication equipment		...	...	...	...	...	...	...	...	...	...	...	...
33	Medical, precision and optical instruments		...	...	...	...	...	...	...	...	...	...	...	...
34	Motor vehicles, trailers, semi-trailers		...	...	...	...	...	...	...	...	...	...	...	...
35	Other transport equipment		...	...	...	...	...	...	...	...	...	...	...	...
36	Furniture; manufacturing n.e.c.		...	...	...	...	...	...	...	...	...	...	...	...
37	Recycling		...	...	...	...	...	...	...	...	...	...	...	...
D	Total manufacturing		...	...	...	...	...	100	98	132	163	178	250	349

Germany

Supplier of information:
Federal Statistical Office, Wiesbaden.
Industrial statistics for the OECD countries are compiled by the OECD secretariat, which supplies them to UNIDO.

Basic source of data:
Annual survey.

Major deviations from ISIC (Revision 3):
Originally, data have been compiled according to the national classification of economic activities, 1993 edition (Klassifikation der Wirtschaftszweige, Ausgabe 1993 - WZ93).

Reference period:
Calendar year.

Scope:
All enterprises.

Method of data collection:
Not reported.

Type of enumeration:
Enterprises with 20 or more persons engaged were completely enumerated; those with less than 20 persons engaged were sampled.

Adjusted for non-response:
Not reported.

Concepts and definitions of variables:
Number of employees refers to annual averages of all employees at the end of the month provided they are working for at least one third of the usual working time. Part-time and temporary employees are covered as well as apprentices.
Wages and salaries includes all payments for interim employed persons and excludes contributions to company old-age pensions institutions.
Output relates to turnover from own production based on invoice values. It includes proceeds from goods sold as purchased and from the sale of waste, power and similar items. The value of shipments also includes excise duties, costs for freight packing, postage and other charges, but excludes value added or turnover taxes.

Related national publications:
Fachserie 4, Reihe 4.3 Kostenstruktur der Unternehmen des Verarbeitenden Gewerbes sowie des Bergbaus und der Gewinnung von Steinen und Erden, published by the Federal Statistical Office, Wiesbaden.

Germany

ISIC Revision 3		Number of enterprises					Number of employees					Wages and salaries paid to employees				
			(number)					(thousands)					(millions of Euros)			
ISIC	Industry	Note	2002	2003	2004	2005	Note	2002	2003	2004	2005	Note	2002	2003	2004	2005
151	Processed meat,fish,fruit,vegetables,fats		13921	14861	13620	13535		234.1	250.2	249.4	250.5		4902	5122	5178	4960
1511	Processing/preserving of meat		13058	14015	12825	12615		181.5	201.7	202.3	200.8		3398	3673	3781	3454
1512	Processing/preserving of fish		178	163	196	190		10.6	9.7	9.7	9.4		278	251	251	243
1513	Processing/preserving of fruit & vegetables		629	619	525	646		32.8	31.1	29.9	30.4		852	850	823	833
1514	Vegetable and animal oils and fats		56	64	74	84		9.1	7.7	7.5	9.9		374	348	323	429
1520	Dairy products		342	360	295	453		39.2	44.7	41.7	38.8		1307	1542	1487	1349
153	Grain mill products; starches; animal feeds		1020	1034	1033	952		29.1	29.8	29.2	28.9		975	958	944	922
1531	Grain mill products		596	610	633	512		11.6	12.6	12.1	11.6		345	339	341	320
1532	Starches and starch products		18	27	25	24		2.7	2.7	2.8	2.8		111	111	116	122
1533	Prepared animal feeds		405	397	375	416		14.8	14.5	14.4	14.5		519	508	488	480
154	Other food products		16918	17030	15540	15721		403.5	411.3	414.4	417.6		7757	7806	7923	7727
1541	Bakery products		16004	16061	14628	14773		311.1	317.1	322.8	330.2		4796	4746	4863	4719
1542	Sugar		15	11	11	11		7.0	7.3	6.6	6.2		289	280	284	282
1543	Cocoa, chocolate and sugar confectionery		244	288	249	256		34.0	35.0	33.8	32.4		943	927	926	929
1544	Macaroni, noodles & similar products		116	159	133	145		3.1	3.5	3.8	4.0		84	85	89	93
1549	Other food products n.e.c.		539	511	518	536		48.3	48.5	47.4	44.7		1645	1767	1761	1705
155	Beverages		2086	2103	2094	2047		81.0	76.0	78.1	75.5		2728	2770	2755	2666
1551	Distilling, rectifying & blending of spirits		...	...	...	...		...	...	...	...		...	...	...	...
1552	Wines		...	...	...	...		...	...	...	...		...	...	...	...
1553	Malt liquors and malt		793	740	837	759		40.2	38.0	39.9	37.7		1528	1499	1484	1420
1554	Soft drinks; mineral waters		227	323	264	253		31.0	28.3	28.2	27.2		937	990	1012	968
1600	Tobacco products		35	26	32	33		12.4	11.9	11.6	11.6		629	599	603	630
171	Spinning, weaving and finishing of textiles		1039	1371	1244	1118		49.6	45.4	41.4	37.4		1327	1246	1131	1055
1711	Textile fibre preparation; textile weaving		473	412	392	360		35.3	30.3	27.6	25.2		968	879	799	763
1712	Finishing of textiles		566	959	852	758		14.3	15.1	13.8	12.2		359	368	333	292
172	Other textiles		2520	1949	2085	2260		56.9	52.5	50.7	50.8		1503	1401	1375	1407
1721	Made-up textile articles, except apparel		1471	963	1011	1175		22.1	19.8	17.7	19.0		512	437	402	425
1722	Carpets and rugs		82	72	107	104		7.0	5.6	5.6	5.1		204	167	173	157
1723	Cordage, rope, twine and netting		76	106	88	77		1.1	1.3	1.2	1.2		23	28	25	27
1729	Other textiles n.e.c.		891	808	879	905		26.6	25.7	26.2	25.5		764	769	775	798
1730	Knitted and crocheted fabrics and articles		399	450	364	390		14.6	15.5	12.8	12.8		350	366	323	321
1810	Wearing apparel, except fur apparel		2501	2540	2693	2316		61.2	55.5	55.2	49.8		1556	1415	1421	1341
1820	Dressing & dyeing of fur; processing of fur		453	406	365	354		2.0	1.0	0.9	1.4		31	22	13	19
191	Tanning, dressing and processing of leather		695	776	817	699		10.2	10.4	9.4	8.4		224	218	215	188
1911	Tanning and dressing of leather		76	89	77	87		3.3	3.1	2.9	2.9		93	88	82	80
1912	Luggage, handbags, etc.; saddlery & harness		619	687	740	612		6.9	7.3	6.6	5.5		131	129	133	108
1920	Footwear		471	426	482	431		14.4	12.3	12.3	10.7		357	302	314	270
2010	Sawmilling and planing of wood		2130	2281	2448	2481		25.3	24.1	25.5	29.0		598	584	632	705
202	Products of wood, cork, straw, etc.		11800	11040	13633	11548		126.3	117.9	123.6	110.0		3282	2966	3277	2789
2021	Veneer sheets, plywood, particle board, etc.		200	238	227	197		20.2	18.3	17.9	17.4		674	608	615	586
2022	Builders' carpentry and joinery		8457	7960	9939	8070		77.8	75.2	80.5	66.3		1924	1766	2080	1635
2023	Wooden containers		764	623	710	668		10.5	8.0	9.3	11.0		279	205	234	263
2029	Other wood products; articles of cork/straw		2379	2219	2757	2613		17.7	16.4	15.9	15.2		405	388	348	304
210	Paper and paper products		1911	1673	1571	1625		151.4	149.7	147.6	143.9		5231	5185	5210	5147
2101	Pulp, paper and paperboard		234	245	265	299		46.1	46.3	46.1	45.0		1762	1812	1840	1850
2102	Corrugated paper and paperboard		757	783	752	734		55.3	56.0	55.6	55.0		1722	1751	1789	1778
2109	Other articles of paper and paperboard		920	645	553	592		49.9	47.4	45.9	43.9		1747	1622	1581	1519
221	Publishing		5358	5574	4821	5818		180.2	187.6	187.0	190.1		6013	6009	5775	5648
2211	Publishing of books and other publications		2359	2023	1784	2025		33.1	28.8	30.3	31.0		1160	1043	1109	1124
2212	Publishing of newspapers, journals, etc.		1928	2177	1835	2441		142.3	151.9	149.4	151.2		4727	4777	4458	4318
2213	Publishing of recorded media		173	548	416	600		0.7	2.0	1.6	2.6		25	81	65	84
2219	Other publishing		899	826	786	752		4.1	4.8	5.7	5.3		101	109	144	122

222	Printing and related service activities	12934	12574	11294	12228	186.4	165.5	161.6	160.3	5729	4905	5050	5163
2221	Printing	8604	9084	8297	8931	150.2	130.1	128.4	128.0	4658	3952	4143	4258
2222	Service activities related to printing	4330	3490	2997	3296	36.3	35.4	33.2	32.4	1071	953	907	905
2230	Reproduction of recorded media	367	268	229	390	8.4	8.4	7.6	7.4	251	255	243	202
2310	Coke oven products	...	...	...	...	...	...	...	...	...	...	...	...
2320	Refined petroleum products	...	...	...	...	...	...	...	...	...	...	...	...
2330	Processing of nuclear fuel	...	...	...	...	...	...	...	...	...	...	...	...
241	Basic chemicals	632	700	664	771	199.4	191.9	168.9	167.4	9597	9825	8900	9037
2411	Basic chemicals, except fertilizers	...	...	...	...	...	...	...	...	...	...	...	...
2412	Fertilizers and nitrogen compounds	65	37	55	77	10.6	10.4	10.3	10.2	389	393	412	435
2413	Plastics in primary forms; synthetic rubber	...	...	...	...	...	...	...	...	...	...	...	...
242	Other chemicals	2093	2457	2590	2668	267.7	278.3	274.7	268.8	11065	12003	12110	12140
2421	Pesticides and other agro-chemical products	42	44	47	52	5.2	7.2	4.1	6.8	271	378	206	411
2422	Paints, varnishes, printing ink and mastics	430	399	480	359	47.6	45.8	46.7	44.5	1857	1868	1921	1843
2423	Pharmaceuticals, medicinal chemicals, etc.	425	637	686	715	113.5	121.8	122.6	124.3	5025	5670	5916	6145
2424	Soap, cleaning & cosmetic preparations	630	651	653	683	51.2	53.1	52.4	47.0	1917	2067	2055	1886
2429	Other chemical products n.e.c.	566	726	724	859	50.0	50.5	48.9	46.2	1996	2020	2013	1857
2430	Man-made fibres	39	52	45	46	16.8	15.7	14.7	13.7	636	604	592	559
251	Rubber products	578	688	867	767	76.7	78.1	76.4	75.4	2631	2612	2701	2755
2511	Rubber tyres and tubes	96	176	235	168	24.5	25.6	25.3	25.0	927	953	1031	1053
2519	Other rubber products	483	512	631	598	52.2	52.5	51.1	50.4	1704	1659	1670	1702
2520	Plastic products	5785	5575	6048	6386	304.4	298.9	306.2	301.6	9262	9092	9413	9374
2610	Glass and glass products	1368	1305	1201	1155	70.1	64.4	62.2	59.1	2208	2079	2013	1973
269	Non-metallic mineral products n.e.c.	8096	8587	8058	8694	187.4	183.3	179.5	177.3	5982	5850	5734	5687
2691	Pottery, china and earthenware	777	869	878	694	26.4	26.9	25.9	25.0	725	768	733	735
2692	Refractory ceramic products	92	95	126	92	7.9	7.7	7.6	7.0	287	269	277	257
2693	Struct.non-refractory clay; ceramic products	288	301	276	334	16.2	16.0	14.8	15.0	501	536	496	493
2694	Cement, lime and plaster	95	75	77	61	12.3	12.6	11.9	11.4	535	534	499	486
2695	Articles of concrete, cement and plaster	2379	2490	2274	2184	79.7	76.1	74.8	69.5	2543	2460	2404	2286
2696	Cutting, shaping & finishing of stone	4101	4301	4084	4974	22.5	21.4	21.3	26.0	562	433	468	525
2699	Other non-metallic mineral products n.e.c.	364	456	343	354	22.3	22.6	23.3	23.4	831	850	857	906
2710	Basic iron and steel	825	921	1313	1134	130.3	127.2	128.2	126.9	4940	4911	5061	5173
2720	Basic precious and non-ferrous metals	539	620	628	679	65.4	62.0	62.5	62.8	2606	2577	2626	2718
273	Casting of metals	701	689	719	737	70.8	68.7	69.7	69.3	2379	2398	2478	2518
2731	Casting of iron and steel	205	244	248	246	40.8	38.0	37.6	38.0	1421	1363	1380	1427
2732	Casting of non-ferrous metals	497	446	471	489	30.0	30.7	32.1	31.3	958	1035	1098	1091
281	Struct.metal products;tanks;steam generators	14345	13020	11852	13079	237.1	224.4	211.1	221.6	6927	6607	6208	6674
2811	Structural metal products	13486	12253	11069	12202	184.2	172.6	159.3	173.4	5022	4653	4213	4818
2812	Tanks, reservoirs and containers of metal	404	433	451	567	26.9	27.8	28.2	27.0	931	980	1033	978
2813	Steam generators	455	334	332	310	26.0	24.0	23.5	21.3	975	973	962	877
289	Other metal products; metal working services	23770	26848	26604	27340	504.9	535.6	537.6	543.6	15762	16323	16500	16800
2891	Metal forging/pressing/stamping/roll-forming	1350	1401	1208	1513	85.9	86.3	90.6	94.5	2899	2914	3110	3250
2892	Treatment & coating of metals	11658	16675	16889	17305	130.7	169.9	169.4	180.6	3613	4191	4332	4674
2893	Cutlery, hand tools and general hardware	4223	4223	4004	3887	133.1	135.3	131.6	127.8	4517	4655	4461	4296
2899	Other fabricated metal products n.e.c.	6539	4549	4503	4635	155.2	144.0	145.9	140.8	4732	4564	4597	4579
291	General purpose machinery	7347	7124	8479	7856	507.6	503.6	512.7	506.5	19683	20112	20791	20994
2911	Engines & turbines (not for transport equipment)	113	151	100	113	23.1	22.9	22.0	21.2	996	1088	1054	1071
2912	Pumps, compressors, taps and valves	1173	1281	1459	1317	122.8	124.5	128.2	126.5	4766	4967	5247	5285
2913	Bearings, gears, gearing & driving elements	782	653	1158	723	86.6	86.1	91.9	86.6	3262	3394	3632	3566
2914	Ovens, furnaces and furnace burners	209	210	200	224	13.0	12.4	11.3	11.5	534	518	489	492
2915	Lifting and handling equipment	1575	1310	1565	1639	83.7	79.6	79.0	78.9	3247	3140	3192	3219
2919	Other general purpose machinery	3496	3519	3996	3839	178.3	178.2	180.3	181.8	6879	7005	7176	7361
292	Special purpose machinery	9785	11662	12112	11428	480.7	491.8	476.1	472.1	18340	19067	18458	18595
2921	Agricultural and forestry machinery	2324	2589	2875	2479	32.9	35.6	35.4	35.3	1031	1121	1130	1186
2922	Machine tools	1636	2161	3085	3019	129.3	131.3	135.1	135.2	4976	5101	5255	5296
2923	Machinery for metallurgy	243	276	323	256	11.6	12.7	12.5	11.1	480	542	533	515
2924	Machinery for mining & construction	524	567	464	478	38.8	38.5	37.7	39.2	1502	1531	1548	1646
2925	Food/beverage/tobacco processing machinery	784	541	653	653	25.1	24.0	22.9	24.3	912	929	872	957
2926	Machinery for textile, apparel and leather	413	404	388	359	34.0	36.8	32.7	30.3	1311	1438	1266	1212
2927	Weapons and ammunition	169	169	178	147	10.9	12.0	11.8	12.1	502	540	526	556
2929	Other special purpose machinery	3692	4954	4145	4037	198.2	200.8	188.1	184.6	7625	7866	7327	7226

continued

Germany

ISIC Revision 3		Number of enterprises					Number of employees					Wages and salaries paid to employees				
			(number)					(thousands)					(millions of Euros)			
ISIC	Industry	Note	2002	2003	2004	2005	Note	2002	2003	2004	2005	Note	2002	2003	2004	2005
2930	Domestic appliances n.e.c.		302	372	448	413		65.9	65.1	62.1	60.2		2554	2650	2528	2469
3000	Office, accounting and computing machinery		853	1056	1087	1207		41.7	43.1	41.2	41.7		2048	2123	1972	2079
3110	Electric motors, generators and transformers		1221	1104	1160	1144		68.2	65.8	67.2	65.2		2217	2271	2311	2331
3120	Electricity distribution & control apparatus		2268	1900	1973	2066		293.6	275.8	276.9	269.7		13061	12498	13027	13009
3130	Insulated wire and cable		380	416	371	382		23.8	21.2	22.1	21.0		852	719	757	734
3140	Accumulators, primary cells and batteries		43	67	74	64		7.3	7.3	6.9	6.2		269	285	281	261
3150	Lighting equipment and electric lamps		992	879	878	885		38.1	35.8	35.1	34.6		1231	1247	1263	1237
3190	Other electrical equipment n.e.c.		1454	1541	1423	1470		83.9	84.1	87.9	90.6		3030	3100	3501	3638
3210	Electronic valves, tubes, etc.		1173	1164	1257	1392		71.1	72.5	71.5	72.6		2912	3210	2988	3129
3220	TV/radio transmitters; line comm. apparatus		729	937	680	922		50.8	51.1	46.9	40.6		2463	2447	2283	1956
3230	TV and radio receivers and associated goods		479	435	536	384		32.6	26.8	27.3	25.2		1213	1051	1046	1006
331	Medical, measuring, testing appliances, etc.		14287	14517	14469	15560		262.2	275.4	280.1	283.3		8538	9034	9166	9428
3311	Medical, surgical and orthopaedic equipment		11044	11381	10839	12024		140.3	153.6	154.4	158.4		3800	4219	4147	4297
3312	Measuring/testing/navigating appliances,etc.		2705	2624	3211	3008		107.7	106.3	112.2	110.7		4164	4152	4406	4488
3313	Industrial process control equipment		538	512	419	528		14.2	15.5	13.5	14.2		573	664	613	643
3320	Optical instruments & photographic equipment		917	863	898	1129		31.3	31.1	29.2	31.6		1103	1134	1131	1170
3330	Watches and clocks		267	168	188	187		5.1	4.7	4.9	4.4		150	141	159	137
3410	Motor vehicles		189	227	238	276		529.6	525.8	526.8	516.5		25546	26284	27085	27384
3420	Automobile bodies, trailers & semi-trailers		1021	1069	1249	1183		40.4	39.6	41.1	39.5		1234	1196	1246	1202
3430	Parts/accessories for automobiles		1349	988	1058	1027		302.5	300.6	304.2	309.0		12046	12418	13025	13420
351	Building and repairing of ships and boats		571	595	560	605		27.7	26.1	25.5	24.6		974	942	899	952
3511	Building and repairing of ships		170	178	173	202		23.1	21.8	20.4	20.5		850	813	756	820
3512	Building/repairing of pleasure/sport. boats		402	417	388	403		4.6	4.3	5.1	4.1		124	129	143	131
3520	Railway/tramway locomotives & rolling stock		115	108	121	131		22.7	23.2	28.6	28.5		896	978	1168	1161
3530	Aircraft and spacecraft		216	209	190	199		75.3	75.0	74.8	73.0		3751	3951	4114	4332
359	Transport equipment n.e.c.		453	309	346	293		11.6	10.2	10.1	8.9		357	295	297	271
3591	Motorcycles		97	55	48	58		1.3	1.3	1.5	1.4		40	43	45	43
3592	Bicycles and invalid carriages		168	156	146	129		6.5	6.0	5.3	4.6		199	165	156	137
3599	Other transport equipment n.e.c.		188	98	153	106		3.8	2.9	3.2	2.9		117	87	97	91
3610	Furniture		7871	8446	7918	9009		171.1	160.9	156.5	155.3		4970	4684	4527	4506
369	Manufacturing n.e.c.		5559	6012	5606	5486		73.1	71.1	62.4	60.7		1859	1796	1606	1558
3691	Jewellery and related articles		2290	2789	2470	2433		11.8	12.8	9.7	10.0		264	276	207	183
3692	Musical instruments		887	1058	998	960		7.6	7.3	6.6	6.8		191	193	175	171
3693	Sports goods		270	185	229	317		6.6	4.4	4.0	3.9		184	108	95	99
3694	Games and toys		583	516	485	546		15.4	14.4	13.2	12.6		400	377	343	329
3699	Other manufacturing n.e.c.		1529	1464	1424	1230		31.7	32.2	28.9	27.4		820	841	786	777
3710	Recycling of metal waste and scrap		287	303	440	398		5.0	5.7	6.1	5.8		153	176	179	162
3720	Recycling of non-metal waste and scrap		830	656	686	887		10.0	9.0	10.3	13.9		297	242	264	353
D	Total manufacturing		196704	201393	199783	203907		7173.6	7122.0	7067.1	7004.2		251825	253803	255468	256604

Germany

ISIC Revision 3		Output					Value added in factor values					Gross fixed capital formation		
			(millions of Euros)					(millions of Euros)					(millions of Euros)	
ISIC	Industry	Note	2002	2003	2004	2005	Note	2002	2003	2004	2005	Note	2004	2005
151	Processed meat,fish,fruit,vegetables,fats		40830	43167	57564	46705		8886	9197	9944	8883		951	908
1511	Processing/preserving of meat		25285	27862	42855	31098		5940	6387	7256	5927		593	573
1512	Processing/preserving of fish		1885	1769	1892	2017		410	397	420	449		46	50
1513	Processing/preserving of fruit & vegetables		7650	7822	7415	7792		1558	1576	1489	1608		252	216
1514	Vegetable and animal oils and fats		6010	5715	5401	5798		977	837	779	899		60	69
1520	Dairy products		19225	20573	20953	20712		2629	2979	3092	2718		496	448
153	Grain mill products; starches; animal feeds		9431	9842	10049	9361		2037	2113	2067	2035		341	303
1531	Grain mill products		3278	3513	3675	3041		674	678	700	752		164	134
1532	Starches and starch products		988	1070	1164	1275		336	324	313	295		63	65
1533	Prepared animal feeds		5165	5259	5210	5046		1027	1110	1054	989		114	104
154	Other food products		40356	39792	40450	40903		13794	13821	14460	13932		1381	1483
1541	Bakery products		16320	16678	17242	17285		7887	7920	8283	8001		600	626
1542	Sugar		2997	2747	2878	2969		870	737	847	800		153	151
1543	Cocoa, chocolate and sugar confectionery		6920	6946	7280	7435		1701	1787	1864	1810		196	216
1544	Macaroni, noodles & similar products		521	637	643	676		158	191	174	186		49	32
1549	Other food products n.e.c.		13598	12785	12407	12539		3179	3187	3293	3135		384	458
155	Beverages		19828	20144	19320	18978		5435	5692	5341	5419		1501	1432
1551	Distilling, rectifying & blending of spirits		...	...	...	...		...	...	...	...		32	274
1552	Wines		...	...	...	...		...	...	...	...		21	...
1553	Malt liquors and malt		9724	9339	9276	8935		3087	3201	3097	3123		766	699
1554	Soft drinks; mineral waters		6027	6613	5952	6022		1749	1826	1614	1655		683	...
1600	Tobacco products		15032	14306	13549	14585		1799	1510	1573	1564		176	134
171	Spinning, weaving and finishing of textiles		5807	5653	5275	4852		1934	1766	1671	1538		172	151
1711	Textile fibre preparation; textile weaving		4447	4009	4021	3698		1388	1219	1162	1110		117	108
1712	Finishing of textiles		1360	1644	1254	1154		546	547	509	428		55	42
172	Other textiles		6851	6466	6450	6769		2351	2244	2270	2355		238	237
1721	Made-up textile articles, except apparel		2298	2042	1859	2017		734	746	677	746		53	40
1722	Carpets and rugs		954	840	848	842		279	228	221	217		16	12
1723	Cordage, rope, twine and netting		112	134	117	124		40	48	43	44		5	6
1729	Other textiles n.e.c.		3488	3450	3625	3786		1298	1222	1329	1348		165	180
1730	Knitted and crocheted fabrics and articles		1534	1668	1575	1520		569	622	579	533		42	42
1810	Wearing apparel, except fur apparel		9769	8976	9464	9066		2499	2464	2459	2331		114	97
1820	Dressing & dyeing of fur; processing of fur		162	125	66	88		65	44	29	42		2	2
191	Tanning, dressing and processing of leather		1284	1271	1156	1064		375	367	351	329		16	16
1911	Tanning and dressing of leather		630	606	500	527		149	151	138	120		8	8
1912	Luggage, handbags, etc.; saddlery & harness		654	665	655	537		226	217	213	209		8	8
1920	Footwear		2384	1875	2007	1862		674	540	566	509		28	28
2010	Sawmilling and planing of wood		4114	4095	4643	5609		1091	1057	1268	1449		179	274
202	Products of wood, cork, straw, etc.		15558	14690	15339	14878		5119	5028	5161	4700		372	415
2021	Veneer sheets, plywood, particle board, etc.		4351	4082	4471	4770		1224	985	1031	1147		123	172
2022	Builders' carpentry and joinery		8114	7885	8478	7398		2745	3011	3211	2587		189	179
2023	Wooden containers		1356	876	1026	1299		465	330	381	454		31	31
2029	Other wood products; articles of cork/straw		1738	1848	1364	1412		685	702	537	512		28	33
210	Paper and paper products		30480	29599	30211	30988		9717	9362	9425	9401		2193	1568
2101	Pulp, paper and paperboard		13711	13324	13751	14659		4136	3729	3766	3856		1279	653
2102	Corrugated paper and paperboard		8690	8691	8826	8974		2964	2882	3001	3013		464	502
2109	Other articles of paper and paperboard		8079	7585	7635	7355		2617	2750	2658	2533		449	412
221	Publishing		26705	26479	26593	26874		9382	9702	9632	9978		376	389
2211	Publishing of books and other publications		6369	6138	6332	6532		2037	2132	2020	2424		49	59
2212	Publishing of newspapers, journals, etc.		19757	19232	19022	19129		7147	7193	7253	7203		315	315
2213	Publishing of recorded media		148	595	534	693		38	203	128	154		6	5
2219	Other publishing		430	515	706	520		160	174	231	198		6	9

continued

Germany

ISIC Revision 3		Output					Value added in factor values					Gross fixed capital formation		
			(millions of Euros)					(millions of Euros)					(millions of Euros)	
ISIC	Industry	Note	2002	2003	2004	2005	Note	2002	2003	2004	2005	Note	2004	2005
222	Printing and related service activities		20871	18538	19799	20882		9101	7867	8429	8657		1037	1084
2221	Printing		17954	15702	17071	18113		7458	6384	6989	7123		920	959
2222	Service activities related to printing		2918	2836	2728	2769		1643	1483	1440	1534		117	126
2230	Reproduction of recorded media		1324	1349	1312	1416		555	559	501	496		80	64
2310	Coke oven products		...	...	...	...		...	...	...	...		...	-
2320	Refined petroleum products		...	...	...	...		...	...	...	...		575	661
2330	Processing of nuclear fuel		...	...	...	...		...	...	...	...		...	54
241	Basic chemicals		58372	56604	60092	61997		19379	17907	18447	18841		2373	2807
2411	Basic chemicals, except fertilizers		...	...	...	...		...	...	...	...		974	1385
2412	Fertilizers and nitrogen compounds		2164	2172	2259	2437		672	704	794	876		121	107
2413	Plastics in primary forms; synthetic rubber		...	...	...	...		...	...	...	...		1279	1315
242	Other chemicals		58614	63702	64069	67711		20277	22110	22825	24411		2825	2610
2421	Pesticides and other agro-chemical products		1656	2430	1127	3009		503	818	355	824		31	72
2422	Paints, varnishes, printing ink and mastics		8981	9378	9664	9666		3193	3343	3475	3341		258	225
2423	Pharmaceuticals, medicinal chemicals, etc.		24777	27948	29114	32319		9398	10776	11668	13375		1513	1471
2424	Soap, cleaning & cosmetic preparations		11857	12809	12835	10819		3311	3663	3614	3150		490	355
2429	Other chemical products n.e.c.		11342	11137	11329	11897		3872	3511	3714	3722		533	487
2430	Man-made fibres		3697	3726	3718	3638		982	1079	1070	981		96	82
251	Rubber products		11009	11015	11762	12073		4571	4333	4621	4568		437	448
2511	Rubber tyres and tubes		4313	4289	5019	5127		1871	1612	1863	1839		188	198
2519	Other rubber products		6696	6726	6744	6946		2700	2721	2759	2730		250	251
2520	Plastic products		41287	41356	44175	45586		15213	15357	16016	16036		2030	1756
2610	Glass and glass products		9371	8683	8726	8736		3774	3451	3382	3290		440	530
269	Non-metallic mineral products n.e.c.		26256	25375	26556	26602		9793	9512	9853	9527		1188	1247
2691	Pottery, china and earthenware		2040	2240	2273	2267		1038	1179	1170	1111		120	121
2692	Refractory ceramic products		1307	1246	1350	1264		465	436	480	422		50	76
2693	Struct.non-refractory clay; ceramic products		1906	2069	1922	1893		861	871	802	757		122	141
2694	Cement, lime and plaster		2532	2433	2566	2698		1004	720	877	948		165	212
2695	Articles of concrete, cement and plaster		12635	11440	12407	11838		4090	3940	4184	3743		459	489
2696	Cutting, shaping & finishing of stone		1902	1714	1833	1855		918	776	784	961		62	53
2699	Other non-metallic mineral products n.e.c.		3936	4232	4204	4787		1418	1590	1555	1585		210	156
2710	Basic iron and steel		30497	31470	39362	44726		8000	8640	10191	11718		1115	1162
2720	Basic precious and non-ferrous metals		19866	18567	20810	23076		4578	4248	4629	4484		556	563
273	Casting of metals		8655	8766	9629	10644		3637	3771	3941	4267		508	388
2731	Casting of iron and steel		4869	4667	5079	5757		2195	1995	2023	2176		206	200
2732	Casting of non-ferrous metals		3787	4099	4551	4887		1442	1776	1918	2091		302	188
281	Struct.metal products;tanks;steam generators		28103	26906	27020	28411		10685	10121	10013	10360		524	499
2811	Structural metal products		20599	19288	18837	20660		7867	7173	6949	7644		385	352
2812	Tanks, reservoirs and containers of metal		3485	3916	4422	4260		1370	1546	1637	1468		106	113
2813	Steam generators		4019	3702	3761	3490		1449	1402	1428	1248		33	33
289	Other metal products; metal working services		56983	60759	65359	69169		25491	26963	27649	28506		2919	2949
2891	Metal forging/pressing/stamping/roll-forming		10819	11538	13541	15087		4525	4652	5182	5405		594	565
2892	Treatment & coating of metals		11847	14745	15758	17351		6029	7236	7299	7880		942	965
2893	Cutlery, hand tools and general hardware		15128	15657	15945	15890		7160	7393	7316	7201		716	739
2899	Other fabricated metal products n.e.c.		19190	18819	20115	20841		7777	7681	7852	8020		668	680
291	General purpose machinery		72646	75834	82501	88572		29301	29769	32820	33573		2376	2453
2911	Engines & turbines (not for transport equipment)		4851	4945	4923	5140		1530	1463	1683	1587		111	139
2912	Pumps, compressors, taps and valves		16928	18160	20354	22110		7142	7959	8877	8953		695	678
2913	Bearings, gears, gearing & driving elements		11151	11712	13441	14365		5140	5103	5834	5998		590	609
2914	Ovens, furnaces and furnace burners		1986	1832	1858	1981		825	699	686	719		29	32
2915	Lifting and handling equipment		11256	10959	11702	12964		4838	4417	4628	4840		232	274
2919	Other general purpose machinery		26474	28226	30221	32012		9826	10130	11111	11475		719	721

292	Special purpose machinery		72967	74626	76876	80582		27561	27770	27524	28534		1684	1670
2921	Agricultural and forestry machinery		6748	6971	7187	7829		1932	2067	2027	2215		158	137
2922	Machine tools		17863	18247	19790	21408		7194	7280	7666	8082		479	483
2923	Machinery for metallurgy		1667	1933	2043	2157		495	738	771	747		22	25
2924	Machinery for mining & construction		7059	7191	8146	9772		2301	2263	2507	2739		145	162
2925	Food/beverage/tobacco processing machinery		3406	3590	3618	3753		1335	1394	1345	1472		63	63
2926	Machinery for textile, apparel and leather		5004	5828	5047	4883		1970	2059	1759	1718		104	101
2927	Weapons and ammunition		1778	2001	2016	2142		673	782	820	894		56	49
2929	Other special purpose machinery		29442	28865	29030	28639		11662	11186	10628	10668		657	649
2930	Domestic appliances n.e.c.		11045	10620	9890	10117		4390	4035	3598	3624		416	432
3000	Office, accounting and computing machinery		13458	13247	13252	13427		3429	3680	4061	3786		173	143
3110	Electric motors, generators and transformers		10466	10679	11305	11646		3334	3443	3662	3746		311	280
3120	Electricity distribution & control apparatus		45949	45504	49998	49456		16290	16656	18304	16895		1254	1335
3130	Insulated wire and cable		3975	3669	4191	4395		1097	1012	1054	1153		80	92
3140	Accumulators, primary cells and batteries		1132	1219	1392	1424		369	466	432	386		45	27
3150	Lighting equipment and electric lamps		4297	4336	4556	4682		1973	2009	2055	2015		190	237
3190	Other electrical equipment n.e.c.		12928	13187	14985	15888		4935	4857	5206	5558		546	508
3210	Electronic valves, tubes, etc.		13215	15622	17035	16626		3930	5113	6262	5463		1816	1805
3220	TV/radio transmitters; line comm. apparatus		10054	10600	10491	11418		2690	3118	3206	3013		233	188
3230	TV and radio receivers and associated goods		6091	5497	5443	5240		1928	1646	1644	1774		166	161
331	Medical, measuring, testing appliances, etc.		30094	31978	32931	34744		13782	14829	15227	16296		863	883
3311	Medical, surgical and orthopaedic equipment		13257	14956	15112	15767		6661	7525	7509	7890		433	426
3312	Measuring/testing/navigating appliances,etc.		14588	14600	15560	15988		6216	6359	6812	6967		411	430
3313	Industrial process control equipment		2249	2422	2259	2990		906	944	906	1439		19	27
3320	Optical instruments & photographic equipment		3974	4086	4130	4429		1802	1826	1834	1950		141	216
3330	Watches and clocks		628	551	601	569		272	219	227	224		18	15
3410	Motor vehicles		171942	172589	180749	190237		35622	41513	39510	39179		9043	6984
3420	Automobile bodies, trailers & semi-trailers		6391	6722	7956	8108		1706	1842	2071	2019		142	124
3430	Parts/accessories for automobiles		53248	56844	60883	63573		17688	18301	19822	19755		3047	2693
351	Building and repairing of ships and boats		5568	6100	5577	5712		1165	1382	1258	1341		109	112
3511	Building and repairing of ships		4605	4900	4516	4710		920	1080	970	1070		66	65
3512	Building/repairing of pleasure/sport. boats		963	1200	1061	1001		245	302	288	271		42	47
3520	Railway/tramway locomotives & rolling stock		4437	5440	4942	6248		1344	1654	1426	1818		79	90
3530	Aircraft and spacecraft		16398	15711	16359	19022		6503	5711	5543	7184		784	871
359	Transport equipment n.e.c.		1730	1439	1372	1241		538	481	523	464		36	31
3591	Motorcycles		160	157	174	174		58	64	71	64		8	6
3592	Bicycles and invalid carriages		1217	948	824	682		313	278	294	247		14	15
3599	Other transport equipment n.e.c.		354	334	375	385		166	139	158	153		14	10
3610	Furniture		21107	20126	20683	21945		7021	6734	6832	7041		400	435
369	Manufacturing n.e.c.		7300	7151	6787	6596		3132	3081	2874	2830		281	292
3691	Jewellery and related articles		1176	1096	1065	876		489	452	434	347		22	27
3692	Musical instruments		613	594	531	521		308	339	282	289		11	9
3693	Sports goods		731	496	440	440		294	188	167	177		10	11
3694	Games and toys		1760	1761	1620	1743		741	702	640	672		140	132
3699	Other manufacturing n.e.c.		3021	3204	3131	3017		1300	1401	1353	1345		99	113
3710	Recycling of metal waste and scrap		1514	1796	2260	1941		383	389	411	363		71	77
3720	Recycling of non-metal waste and scrap		1806	1425	1512	2133		536	541	582	667		115	115
D	Total manufacturing		1294022	1329436	1409866	1451465		401497	411789	426680	429471		49735	47098

Germany

ISIC Revision 3			Index numbers of industrial production											
			(2000=100)											
ISIC	Industry	Note	1995	1996	1997	1998	1999	2000	2001	2002	2003	2004	2005	2006
15	Food and beverages		92	94	96	95	98	100	99	101	101	102	107	109
16	Tobacco products		84	87	88	92	98	100	99	88	73	66	59	56
17	Textiles		113	107	106	106	99	100	97	92	88	86	83	83
18	Wearing apparel, fur		154	142	133	126	110	100	93	80	71	67	62	53
19	Leather, leather products and footwear		120	109	107	103	103	100	95	92	80	77	70	67
20	Wood products (excl. furniture)		98	94	96	98	100	100	94	90	89	91	92	98
21	Paper and paper products		97	96	98	98	98	100	98	99	102	104	107	111
22	Printing and publishing		84	86	88	92	96	100	97	94	90	92	93	93
23	Coke,refined petroleum products,nuclear fuel		94	94	90	97	98	100	97	96	95	105	109	109
24	Chemicals and chemical products		86	89	94	94	97	100	98	102	102	104	110	115
25	Rubber and plastics products		87	86	91	94	96	100	99	101	102	105	106	110
26	Non-metallic mineral products		104	99	98	99	99	100	94	90	88	88	85	90
27	Basic metals		91	87	95	96	92	100	101	102	100	104	105	112
28	Fabricated metal products		88	86	89	93	94	100	102	101	101	103	105	112
29	Machinery and equipment n.e.c.		88	88	92	96	93	100	102	100	98	101	106	115
30	Office, accounting and computing machinery		48	53	61	74	78	100	94	85	80	88	117	142
31	Electrical machinery and apparatus		82	82	87	92	93	100	103	100	102	107	110	119
32	Radio,television and communication equipment		59	59	64	68	75	100	101	92	101	119	141	187
33	Medical, precision and optical instruments		76	78	80	85	87	100	103	101	104	109	111	123
34	Motor vehicles, trailers, semi-trailers		68	70	76	87	90	100	104	105	108	112	117	120
35	Other transport equipment		100	93	89	91	95	100	108	114	121	119	123	136
36	Furniture; manufacturing n.e.c.		106	103	100	103	100	100	97	86	83	82	83	86
37	Recycling		50	50	65	68	75	100	101	109	112	134	148	174
D	Total manufacturing		86	86	89	93	94	100	100	99	100	103	107	113

Greece

Supplier of information:
National Statistical Service of Greece, Athens.
Industrial statistics for the OECD countries are compiled by the OECD secretariat, which supplies them to UNIDO.

Basic source of data:
Annual industrial survey.

Major deviations from ISIC (Revision 3):
Data were originally classified according to the Greek classification system based on NACE (Revision 1).

Reference period:
Calendar year.

Scope:
Enterprises with 10 or more employees.

Method of data collection:
Not reported.

Type of enumeration:
Not reported

Adjusted for non-response:
Not reported.

Concepts and definitions of variables:
No deviations from the standard UN concepts and definitions are reported.

Related national publications:
None reported.

Greece

ISIC Revision 3		Number of enterprises					Number of employees					Wages and salaries paid to employees				
			(number)					(number)					(millions of Euros)			
ISIC	Industry	Note	2002	2003	2004	2005	Note	2002	2003	2004	2005	Note	2002	2003	2004	2005
151	Processed meat,fish,fruit,vegetables,fats		...	...	2750	...		...	...	18644	...		...	...	288	...
1511	Processing/preserving of meat		...	...	390	...		...	...	5814	...		...	...	91	...
1512	Processing/preserving of fish		...	...	63	...		...	...	1113	...		...	...	14	...
1513	Processing/preserving of fruit & vegetables		...	...	508	...		...	...	8069	...		...	...	119	...
1514	Vegetable and animal oils and fats		...	...	1789	...		...	...	3648	...		...	...	64	...
1520	Dairy products		...	...	752	...		...	...	8781	...		...	...	165	...
153	Grain mill products; starches; animal feeds		...	...	450	...		...	...	3664	...		...	...	65	...
1531	Grain mill products		...	...	280	...		...	...	2207	...		...	...	38	...
1532	Starches and starch products		...	...	11	...		...	...	112	...		...	...	4	...
1533	Prepared animal feeds		...	...	159	...		...	...	1345	...		...	...	24	...
154	Other food products		...	...	9780	...		...	...	25331	...		...	...	389	...
1541	Bakery products		...	...	8775	...		...	...	17779	...		...	...	246	...
1542	Sugar		...	...	4	...		...	...	1641	...		...	...	41	...
1543	Cocoa, chocolate and sugar confectionery		...	...	391	...		...	...	2736	...		...	...	47	...
1544	Macaroni, noodles & similar products		...	...	179	...		...	...	966	...		...	...	18	...
1549	Other food products n.e.c.		...	...	431	...		...	...	2209	...		...	...	37	...
155	Beverages		...	...	758	...		...	...	9374	...		...	...	237	...
1551	Distilling, rectifying & blending of spirits		...	...	245	...		...	...	868	...		...	...	15	...
1552	Wines		...	...	417	...		...	...	2478	...		...	...	45	...
1553	Malt liquors and malt		...	...	14	...		...	...	1770	...		...	...	60	...
1554	Soft drinks; mineral waters		...	...	82	...		...	...	4258	...		...	...	116	...
1600	Tobacco products		...	...	5	...		...	...	2075	...		...	...	67	...
171	Spinning, weaving and finishing of textiles		...	...	880	...		...	...	8109	...		...	...	134	...
1711	Textile fibre preparation; textile weaving		...	...	441	...		...	...	5575	...		...	...	93	...
1712	Finishing of textiles		...	...	439	...		...	...	2534	...		...	...	41	...
172	Other textiles		...	...	2016	...		...	...	5788	...		...	...	77	...
1721	Made-up textile articles, except apparel		...	...	1313	...		...	...	2973	...		...	...	38	...
1722	Carpets and rugs		...	...	72	...		...	...	861	...		...	...	12	...
1723	Cordage, rope, twine and netting		...	...	55	...		...	...	341	...		...	...	4	...
1729	Other textiles n.e.c.		...	...	576	...		...	...	1613	...		...	...	22	...
1730	Knitted and crocheted fabrics and articles		...	...	681	...		...	...	3259	...		...	...	46	...
1810	Wearing apparel, except fur apparel		...	...	10367	...		...	...	20779	...		...	...	248	...
1820	Dressing & dyeing of fur; processing of fur		...	...	2152	...		...	...	2759	...		...	...	32	...
191	Tanning, dressing and processing of leather		...	...	414	...		...	...	860	...		...	...	12	...
1911	Tanning and dressing of leather		...	...	128	...		...	...	318	...		...	...	5	...
1912	Luggage, handbags, etc.; saddlery & harness		...	...	286	...		...	...	542	...		...	...	7	...
1920	Footwear		...	...	919	...		...	...	3470	...		...	...	47	...
2010	Sawmilling and planing of wood		...	...	324	...		...	...	650	...		...	...	9	...
202	Products of wood, cork, straw, etc.		...	...	5451	...		...	...	7199	...		...	...	90	...
2021	Veneer sheets, plywood, particle board, etc.		...	...	49	...		...	...	2205	...		...	...	39	...
2022	Builders' carpentry and joinery		...	...	4352	...		...	...	3811	...		...	...	40	...
2023	Wooden containers		...	...	203	...		...	...	307	...		...	...	3	...
2029	Other wood products; articles of cork/straw		...	...	847	...		...	...	876	...		...	...	8	...
210	Paper and paper products		...	...	409	...		...	...	6893	...		...	...	131	...
2101	Pulp, paper and paperboard		...	...	83	...		...	...	1276	...		...	...	28	...
2102	Corrugated paper and paperboard		...	...	157	...		...	...	3054	...		...	...	53	...
2109	Other articles of paper and paperboard		...	...	169	...		...	...	2563	...		...	...	51	...
221	Publishing		...	...	2910	...		...	...	11405	...		...	...	236	...
2211	Publishing of books and other publications		...	...	1376	...		...	...	1877	...		...	...	29	...
2212	Publishing of newspapers, journals, etc.		...	...	1167	...		...	...	9105	...		...	...	201	...
2213	Publishing of recorded media		...	...	78	...		...	...	128	...		...	...	2	...
2219	Other publishing		...	...	289	...		...	...	295	...		...	...	4	...

222	Printing and related service activities	...	...	4426	...	...	...	7946	...	...	...	142	...
2221	Printing	...	...	2793	...	...	...	5833	...	...	...	110	...
2222	Service activities related to printing	...	...	1633	...	...	...	2113	...	...	...	32	...
2230	Reproduction of recorded media	...	...	77	...	...	...	97	...	...	...	2	...
2310	Coke oven products	...	...	79	...	...	...	61	...	...	...	1	...
2320	Refined petroleum products	...	...	73	...	...	...	3260	...	...	...	178	...
2330	Processing of nuclear fuel	...	...	4	...	...	...	3	...	...	...	-	...
241	Basic chemicals	...	...	66	...	...	...	2884	...	...	...	82	...
2411	Basic chemicals, except fertilizers	...	...	...	...	...	...	...	...	...	...	...	...
2412	Fertilizers and nitrogen compounds	...	...	6	...	...	...	1184	...	...	...	39	...
2413	Plastics in primary forms; synthetic rubber	...	...	...	...	...	...	...	...	...	...	...	...
242	Other chemicals	...	...	274	...	...	...	13137	...	...	...	278	...
2421	Pesticides and other agro-chemical products	...	...	11	...	...	...	548	...	...	...	11	...
2422	Paints, varnishes, printing ink and mastics	...	...	71	...	...	...	2171	...	...	...	40	...
2423	Pharmaceuticals, medicinal chemicals, etc.	...	...	53	...	...	...	5023	...	...	...	118	...
2424	Soap, cleaning & cosmetic preparations	...	...	92	...	...	...	4366	...	...	...	91	...
2429	Other chemical products n.e.c.	...	...	47	...	...	...	1029	...	...	...	18	...
2430	Man-made fibres	...	...	3	...	...	...	58	...	...	...	1	...
251	Rubber products	...	...	62	...	...	...	738	...	...	...	15	...
2511	Rubber tyres and tubes	...	...	...	...	...	...	...	...	...	...	...	...
2519	Other rubber products	...	...	...	...	...	...	...	...	...	...	...	...
2520	Plastic products	...	...	500	...	...	...	10076	...	...	...	159	...
2610	Glass and glass products	...	...	273	...	...	...	1205	...	...	...	24	...
269	Non-metallic mineral products n.e.c.	...	...	3706	...	...	...	18504	...	...	...	404	...
2691	Pottery, china and earthenware	...	...	...	...	...	...	...	...	...	...	...	...
2692	Refractory ceramic products	...	...	...	...	...	...	...	...	...	...	...	...
2693	Struct.non-refractory clay; ceramic products	...	...	164	...	...	...	2205	...	...	...	36	...
2694	Cement, lime and plaster	...	...	159	...	...	...	3604	...	...	...	135	...
2695	Articles of concrete, cement and plaster	...	...	1359	...	...	...	6673	...	...	...	127	...
2696	Cutting, shaping & finishing of stone	...	...	1163	...	...	...	3309	...	...	...	51	...
2699	Other non-metallic mineral products n.e.c.	...	...	92	...	...	...	590	...	...	...	12	...
2710	Basic iron and steel	...	...	975	...	...	...	5996	...	...	...	140	...
2720	Basic precious and non-ferrous metals	...	...	374	...	...	...	6476	...	...	...	149	...
273	Casting of metals	...	...	430	...	...	...	488	...	...	...	7	...
2731	Casting of iron and steel	...	...	272	...	...	...	259	...	...	...	4	...
2732	Casting of non-ferrous metals	...	...	158	...	...	...	229	...	...	...	3	...
281	Struct.metal products;tanks;steam generators	...	...	8142	...	...	...	13442	...	...	...	195	...
2811	Structural metal products	...	...	7813	...	...	...	11786	...	...	...	169	...
2812	Tanks, reservoirs and containers of metal	...	...	288	...	...	...	1557	...	...	...	25	...
2813	Steam generators	...	...	41	...	...	...	99	...	...	...	1	...
289	Other metal products; metal working services	...	...	5010	...	...	...	10770	...	...	...	169	...
2891	Metal forging/pressing/stamping/roll-forming	...	...	985	...	...	...	951	...	...	...	13	...
2892	Treatment & coating of metals	...	...	1701	...	...	...	2365	...	...	...	33	...
2893	Cutlery, hand tools and general hardware	...	...	543	...	...	...	2117	...	...	...	38	...
2899	Other fabricated metal products n.e.c.	...	...	1781	...	...	...	5337	...	...	...	87	...
291	General purpose machinery	...	...	2334	...	...	...	5980	...	...	...	97	...
2911	Engines & turbines (not for transport equipment)	...	...	88	...	...	...	475	...	...	...	10	...
2912	Pumps, compressors, taps and valves	...	...	239	...	...	...	790	...	...	...	12	...
2913	Bearings, gears, gearing & driving elements	...	...	38	...	...	...	185	...	...	...	3	...
2914	Ovens, furnaces and furnace burners	...	...	167	...	...	...	201	...	...	...	3	...
2915	Lifting and handling equipment	...	...	790	...	...	...	1813	...	...	...	28	...
2919	Other general purpose machinery	...	...	1012	...	...	...	2516	...	...	...	41	...
292	Special purpose machinery	...	...	3306	...	...	...	6952	...	...	...	132	...
2921	Agricultural and forestry machinery	...	...	1168	...	...	...	1457	...	...	...	20	...
2922	Machine tools	...	...	1208	...	...	...	1474	...	...	...	23	...
2923	Machinery for metallurgy	...	...	132	...	...	...	157	...	...	...	2	...
2924	Machinery for mining & construction	...	...	136	...	...	...	478	...	...	...	7	...
2925	Food/beverage/tobacco processing machinery	...	...	113	...	...	...	392	...	...	...	6	...
2926	Machinery for textile, apparel and leather	...	...	92	...	...	...	290	...	...	...	5	...
2927	Weapons and ammunition	...	...	96	...	...	...	2240	...	...	...	63	...
2929	Other special purpose machinery	...	...	361	...	...	...	464	...	...	...	6	...

continued

Greece

ISIC Revision 3		Number of enterprises					Number of employees					Wages and salaries paid to employees				
			(number)					(number)					(millions of Euros)			
ISIC	Industry	Note	2002	2003	2004	2005	Note	2002	2003	2004	2005	Note	2002	2003	2004	2005
2930	Domestic appliances n.e.c.		...	...	394	...		...	...	2931	...		...	...	53	...
3000	Office, accounting and computing machinery		...	...	700	...		...	...	43	...		...	...	1	...
3110	Electric motors, generators and transformers		...	...	329	...		...	...	1236	...		...	...	25	...
3120	Electricity distribution & control apparatus		...	...	243	...		...	...	1408	...		...	...	22	...
3130	Insulated wire and cable		...	...	18	...		...	...	1654	...		...	...	34	...
3140	Accumulators, primary cells and batteries		...	...	19	...		...	...	475	...		...	...	7	...
3150	Lighting equipment and electric lamps		...	...	675	...		...	...	1504	...		...	...	21	...
3190	Other electrical equipment n.e.c.		...	...	365	...		...	...	420	...		...	...	6	...
3210	Electronic valves, tubes, etc.		...	...	163	...		...	...	308	...		...	...	4	...
3220	TV/radio transmitters; line comm. apparatus		...	...	236	...		...	...	4389	...		...	...	105	...
3230	TV and radio receivers and associated goods		...	...	319	...		...	...	308	...		...	...	4	...
331	Medical, measuring, testing appliances, etc.		...	...	432	...		...	...	1408	...		...	...	21	...
3311	Medical, surgical and orthopaedic equipment		...	...	245	...		...	...	541	...		...	...	7	...
3312	Measuring/testing/navigating appliances,etc.		...	...	140	...		...	...	799	...		...	...	13	...
3313	Industrial process control equipment		...	...	47	...		...	...	68	...		...	...	1	...
3320	Optical instruments & photographic equipment		...	...	102	...		...	...	375	...		...	...	5	...
3330	Watches and clocks		...	...	57	...		...	...	82	...		...	...	1	...
3410	Motor vehicles		...	...	53	...		...	...	1360	...		...	...	30	...
3420	Automobile bodies, trailers & semi-trailers		...	...	186	...		...	...	807	...		...	...	11	...
3430	Parts/accessories for automobiles		...	...	202	...		...	...	638	...		...	...	8	...
351	Building and repairing of ships and boats		...	...	814	...		...	...	6239	...		...	...	120	...
3511	Building and repairing of ships		...	...	576	...		...	...	5786	...		...	...	114	...
3512	Building/repairing of pleasure/sport. boats		...	...	238	...		...	...	453	...		...	...	5	...
3520	Railway/tramway locomotives & rolling stock		...	...	6	...		...	...	2174	...		...	...	50	...
3530	Aircraft and spacecraft		...	...	12	...		...	...	4005	...		...	...	137	...
359	Transport equipment n.e.c.		...	...	31	...		...	...	284	...		...	...	4	...
3591	Motorcycles		...	...	12	...		...	...	17	...		...	...	-	...
3592	Bicycles and invalid carriages		...	...	11	...		...	...	214	...		...	...	3	...
3599	Other transport equipment n.e.c.		...	...	8	...		...	...	53	...		...	...	1	...
3610	Furniture		...	...	6944	...		...	...	11630	...		...	...	146	...
369	Manufacturing n.e.c.		...	...	...	...		...	...	...	...		...	...	...	...
3691	Jewellery and related articles		...	...	2124	...		...	...	2724	...		...	...	36	...
3692	Musical instruments		...	...	92	...		...	...	89	...		...	...	1	...
3693	Sports goods		...	...	72	...		...	...	300	...		...	...	3	...
3694	Games and toys		...	...	154	...		...	...	212	...		...	...	3	...
3699	Other manufacturing n.e.c.		...	...	...	...		...	...	...	...		...	...	...	...
3710	Recycling of metal waste and scrap		...	...	...	...		...	...	...	...		...	...	...	...
3720	Recycling of non-metal waste and scrap		...	...	-	...		...	...	-	...		...	...	-	...
D	Total manufacturing		...	...	87643	...		...	...	296301	...		...	...	5328	...

ISIC Revision 3		Output					Value added in factor values					Gross fixed capital formation		
			(millions of Euros)					(millions of Euros)					(millions of Euros)	
ISIC	Industry	Note	2002	2003	2004	2005	Note	2002	2003	2004	2005	Note	2004	2005
151	Processed meat,fish,fruit,vegetables,fats		...	...	2547	...		...	...	691	...		156	...
1511	Processing/preserving of meat		...	...	721	...		...	...	184	...		41	...
1512	Processing/preserving of fish		...	...	96	...		...	...	32	...		4	...
1513	Processing/preserving of fruit & vegetables		...	...	927	...		...	...	262	...		78	...
1514	Vegetable and animal oils and fats		...	...	803	...		...	...	212	...		34	...
1520	Dairy products		...	...	1644	...		...	...	429	...		103	...
153	Grain mill products; starches; animal feeds		...	...	669	...		...	...	157	...		24	...
1531	Grain mill products		...	...	364	...		...	...	91	...		14	...
1532	Starches and starch products		...	...	33	...		...	...	12	...		3	...
1533	Prepared animal feeds		...	...	273	...		...	...	54	...		7	...
154	Other food products		...	...	2958	...		...	...	1038	...		188	...
1541	Bakery products		...	...	1968	...		...	...	696	...		136	...
1542	Sugar		...	...	201	...		...	...	71	...		6	...
1543	Cocoa, chocolate and sugar confectionery		...	...	327	...		...	...	101	...		25	...
1544	Macaroni, noodles & similar products		...	...	134	...		...	...	44	...		8	...
1549	Other food products n.e.c.		...	...	327	...		...	...	126	...		14	...
155	Beverages		...	...	1738	...		...	...	683	...		108	...
1551	Distilling, rectifying & blending of spirits		...	...	124	...		...	...	48	...		6	...
1552	Wines		...	...	337	...		...	...	104	...		22	...
1553	Malt liquors and malt		...	...	354	...		...	...	186	...		27	...
1554	Soft drinks; mineral waters		...	...	922	...		...	...	344	...		54	...
1600	Tobacco products		...	...	444	...		...	...	194	...		14	...
171	Spinning, weaving and finishing of textiles		...	...	708	...		...	...	232	...		40	...
1711	Textile fibre preparation; textile weaving		...	...	513	...		...	...	146	...		23	...
1712	Finishing of textiles		...	...	195	...		...	...	86	...		16	...
172	Other textiles		...	...	482	...		...	...	183	...		29	...
1721	Made-up textile articles, except apparel		...	...	270	...		...	...	93	...		16	...
1722	Carpets and rugs		...	...	54	...		...	...	24	...		1	...
1723	Cordage, rope, twine and netting		...	...	31	...		...	...	15	...		2	...
1729	Other textiles n.e.c.		...	...	127	...		...	...	52	...		9	...
1730	Knitted and crocheted fabrics and articles		...	...	312	...		...	...	103	...		13	...
1810	Wearing apparel, except fur apparel		...	...	1555	...		...	...	524	...		62	...
1820	Dressing & dyeing of fur; processing of fur		...	...	221	...		...	...	70	...		7	...
191	Tanning, dressing and processing of leather		...	...	72	...		...	...	25	...		1	...
1911	Tanning and dressing of leather		...	...	33	...		...	...	9	...		-	...
1912	Luggage, handbags, etc.; saddlery & harness		...	...	39	...		...	...	16	...		1	...
1920	Footwear		...	...	253	...		...	...	105	...		11	...
2010	Sawmilling and planing of wood		...	...	51	...		...	...	18	...		2	...
202	Products of wood, cork, straw, etc.		...	...	674	...		...	...	236	...		38	...
2021	Veneer sheets, plywood, particle board, etc.		...	...	283	...		...	...	83	...		21	...
2022	Builders' carpentry and joinery		...	...	306	...		...	...	120	...		13	...
2023	Wooden containers		...	...	26	...		...	...	9	...		1	...
2029	Other wood products; articles of cork/straw		...	...	58	...		...	...	25	...		3	...
210	Paper and paper products		...	...	879	...		...	...	283	...		86	...
2101	Pulp, paper and paperboard		...	...	186	...		...	...	56	...		31	...
2102	Corrugated paper and paperboard		...	...	337	...		...	...	113	...		29	...
2109	Other articles of paper and paperboard		...	...	356	...		...	...	113	...		26	...
221	Publishing		...	...	1500	...		...	...	646	...		63	...
2211	Publishing of books and other publications		...	...	409	...		...	...	187	...		20	...
2212	Publishing of newspapers, journals, etc.		...	...	988	...		...	...	412	...		37	...
2213	Publishing of recorded media		...	...	28	...		...	...	13	...		3	...
2219	Other publishing		...	...	74	...		...	...	34	...		3	...

continued

Greece

ISIC Revision 3		Output					Value added in factor values					Gross fixed capital formation		
		Note	(millions of Euros)				Note	(millions of Euros)				Note	(millions of Euros)	
ISIC	Industry		2002	2003	2004	2005		2002	2003	2004	2005		2004	2005
222	Printing and related service activities		...	...	1485	...		...	...	675	...		68	...
2221	Printing		...	...	1052	...		...	...	467	...		48	...
2222	Service activities related to printing		...	...	433	...		...	...	209	...		20	...
2230	Reproduction of recorded media		...	...	20	...		...	...	10	...		1	...
2310	Coke oven products		...	...	17	...		...	...	6	...		-	...
2320	Refined petroleum products		...	...	5074	...		...	...	730	...		41	...
2330	Processing of nuclear fuel		...	...	1	...		...	...	-	...		-	...
241	Basic chemicals		...	...	751	...		...	...	168	...		35	...
2411	Basic chemicals, except fertilizers		...	...	...	...		...	...	...	...		...	...
2412	Fertilizers and nitrogen compounds		...	...	208	...		...	...	46	...		5	...
2413	Plastics in primary forms; synthetic rubber		...	...	...	...		...	...	...	...		...	...
242	Other chemicals		...	...	1876	...		...	...	676	...		122	...
2421	Pesticides and other agro-chemical products		...	...	121	...		...	...	40	...		2	...
2422	Paints, varnishes, printing ink and mastics		...	...	327	...		...	...	125	...		23	...
2423	Pharmaceuticals, medicinal chemicals, etc.		...	...	690	...		...	...	236	...		51	...
2424	Soap, cleaning & cosmetic preparations		...	...	615	...		...	...	226	...		34	...
2429	Other chemical products n.e.c.		...	...	124	...		...	...	49	...		11	...
2430	Man-made fibres		...	...	5	...		...	...	2	...		1	...
251	Rubber products		...	...	105	...		...	...	42	...		4	...
2511	Rubber tyres and tubes		...	...	...	...		...	...	...	...		...	...
2519	Other rubber products		...	...	...	...		...	...	...	...		...	...
2520	Plastic products		...	...	1086	...		...	...	406	...		79	...
2610	Glass and glass products		...	...	127	...		...	...	58	...		9	...
269	Non-metallic mineral products n.e.c.		...	...	2701	...		...	...	1076	...		145	...
2691	Pottery, china and earthenware		...	...	...	...		...	...	...	...		...	...
2692	Refractory ceramic products		...	...	...	...		...	...	...	...		...	...
2693	Struct.non-refractory clay; ceramic products		...	...	180	...		...	...	79	...		15	...
2694	Cement, lime and plaster		...	...	945	...		...	...	504	...		58	...
2695	Articles of concrete, cement and plaster		...	...	1005	...		...	...	274	...		40	...
2696	Cutting, shaping & finishing of stone		...	...	312	...		...	...	121	...		15	...
2699	Other non-metallic mineral products n.e.c.		...	...	80	...		...	...	30	...		8	...
2710	Basic iron and steel		...	...	2245	...		...	...	404	...		151	...
2720	Basic precious and non-ferrous metals		...	...	1835	...		...	...	443	...		78	...
273	Casting of metals		...	...	56	...		...	...	22	...		1	...
2731	Casting of iron and steel		...	...	33	...		...	...	12	...		1	...
2732	Casting of non-ferrous metals		...	...	23	...		...	...	10	...		-	...
281	Struct.metal products;tanks;steam generators		...	...	2212	...		...	...	791	...		68	...
2811	Structural metal products		...	...	2040	...		...	...	720	...		62	...
2812	Tanks, reservoirs and containers of metal		...	...	159	...		...	...	66	...		6	...
2813	Steam generators		...	...	13	...		...	...	5	...		1	...
289	Other metal products; metal working services		...	...	1600	...		...	...	589	...		77	...
2891	Metal forging/pressing/stamping/roll-forming		...	...	198	...		...	...	71	...		4	...
2892	Treatment & coating of metals		...	...	386	...		...	...	147	...		8	...
2893	Cutlery, hand tools and general hardware		...	...	240	...		...	...	102	...		19	...
2899	Other fabricated metal products n.e.c.		...	...	777	...		...	...	268	...		46	...
291	General purpose machinery		...	...	484	...		...	...	228	...		30	...
2911	Engines & turbines (not for transport equipment)		...	...	22	...		...	...	15	...		-	...
2912	Pumps, compressors, taps and valves		...	...	59	...		...	...	27	...		4	...
2913	Bearings, gears, gearing & driving elements		...	...	12	...		...	...	6	...		-	...
2914	Ovens, furnaces and furnace burners		...	...	19	...		...	...	9	...		1	...
2915	Lifting and handling equipment		...	...	154	...		...	...	73	...		13	...
2919	Other general purpose machinery		...	...	218	...		...	...	99	...		12	...

292	Special purpose machinery	...	...	561	...	...	...	229	...	25	...
2921	Agricultural and forestry machinery	...	...	140	...	...	...	59	...	6	...
2922	Machine tools	...	...	137	...	...	...	63	...	6	...
2923	Machinery for metallurgy	...	...	15	...	...	...	7	...	1	...
2924	Machinery for mining & construction	...	...	38	...	...	...	16	...	1	...
2925	Food/beverage/tobacco processing machinery	...	...	25	...	...	...	12	...	2	...
2926	Machinery for textile, apparel and leather	...	...	27	...	...	...	11	...	1	...
2927	Weapons and ammunition	...	...	140	...	...	...	44	...	8	...
2929	Other special purpose machinery	...	...	38	...	...	...	18	...	1	...
2930	Domestic appliances n.e.c.	...	...	331	...	...	...	129	...	8	...
3000	Office, accounting and computing machinery	...	...	12	...	...	...	6	...	3	...
3110	Electric motors, generators and transformers	...	...	160	...	...	...	59	...	2	...
3120	Electricity distribution & control apparatus	...	...	119	...	...	...	45	...	3	...
3130	Insulated wire and cable	...	...	392	...	...	...	68	...	15	...
3140	Accumulators, primary cells and batteries	...	...	64	...	...	...	23	...	9	...
3150	Lighting equipment and electric lamps	...	...	166	...	...	...	63	...	9	...
3190	Other electrical equipment n.e.c.	...	...	55	...	...	...	21	...	1	...
3210	Electronic valves, tubes, etc.	...	...	21	...	...	...	11	...	5	...
3220	TV/radio transmitters; line comm. apparatus	...	...	484	...	...	...	238	...	15	...
3230	TV and radio receivers and associated goods	...	...	25	...	...	...	12	...	10	...
331	Medical, measuring, testing appliances, etc.	...	...	177	...	...	...	85	...	4	...
3311	Medical, surgical and orthopaedic equipment	...	...	62	...	...	...	37	...	2	...
3312	Measuring/testing/navigating appliances,etc.	...	...	104	...	...	...	42	...	3	...
3313	Industrial process control equipment	...	...	10	...	...	...	7	...	-	...
3320	Optical instruments & photographic equipment	...	...	35	...	...	...	22	...	2	...
3330	Watches and clocks	...	...	13	...	...	...	8	...	-	...
3410	Motor vehicles	...	...	229	...	...	...	68	...	3	...
3420	Automobile bodies, trailers & semi-trailers	...	...	105	...	...	...	41	...	5	...
3430	Parts/accessories for automobiles	...	...	60	...	...	...	30	...	2	...
351	Building and repairing of ships and boats	...	...	673	...	...	...	219	...	45	...
3511	Building and repairing of ships	...	...	616	...	...	...	197	...	39	...
3512	Building/repairing of pleasure/sport. boats	...	...	57	...	...	...	22	...	6	...
3520	Railway/tramway locomotives & rolling stock	...	...	110	...	...	...	85	...	-	...
3530	Aircraft and spacecraft	...	...	360	...	...	...	187	...	2	...
359	Transport equipment n.e.c.	...	...	31	...	...	...	10	...	2	...
3591	Motorcycles	...	...	3	...	...	...	1	...	-	...
3592	Bicycles and invalid carriages	...	...	24	...	...	...	8	...	2	...
3599	Other transport equipment n.e.c.	...	...	5	...	...	...	2	...	-	...
3610	Furniture	...	...	897	...	...	...	390	...	29	...
369	Manufacturing n.e.c.	...	...	...	...	...	...	...	...	...	...
3691	Jewellery and related articles	...	...	207	...	...	...	92	...	15	...
3692	Musical instruments	...	...	7	...	...	...	3	...	-	...
3693	Sports goods	...	...	17	...	...	...	6	...	2	...
3694	Games and toys	...	...	15	...	...	...	7	...	-	...
3699	Other manufacturing n.e.c.	...	...	...	...	...	...	...	...	...	...
3710	Recycling of metal waste and scrap	...	...	...	...	...	...	...	...	...	...
3720	Recycling of non-metal waste and scrap	...	...	-	...	...	...	-	...	-	...
D	Total manufacturing	...	...	43880	...	...	...	14171	...	2074	...

Greece

ISIC Revision 3			Index numbers of industrial production											
			(2000=100)											
ISIC	Industry	Note	1995	1996	1997	1998	1999	2000	2001	2002	2003	2004	2005	2006
15	Food and beverages		86	84	88	101	98	100	101	101	99	107	106	109
16	Tobacco products		119	117	113	89	101	100	102	103	106	116	109	100
17	Textiles		100	99	105	104	88	100	93	90	87	78	64	56
18	Wearing apparel, fur		120	110	105	107	106	100	93	88	87	83	71	61
19	Leather, leather products and footwear		...	...	...	...	...	...	...	...	...	...	...	...
20	Wood products (excl. furniture)		106	105	88	72	72	100	89	88	84	84	79	77
21	Paper and paper products		97	90	74	116	120	100	91	88	87	89	93	94
22	Printing and publishing		95	104	111	120	99	100	99	100	103	107	122	128
23	Coke,refined petroleum products,nuclear fuel		...	...	...	...	...	...	...	...	...	...	...	...
24	Chemicals and chemical products		...	...	...	...	...	...	...	...	...	...	...	...
25	Rubber and plastics products		...	...	...	...	...	...	...	...	...	...	...	...
26	Non-metallic mineral products		...	...	...	...	...	...	...	...	...	...	...	...
27	Basic metals		...	...	...	...	...	...	...	...	...	...	...	...
28	Fabricated metal products		77	80	80	84	99	100	91	92	98	108	112	117
29	Machinery and equipment n.e.c.	a/	85	88	91	93	86	100	83	90	88	87	99	110
30	Office, accounting and computing machinery	a/	...	...	...	...	...	...	...	...	...	...	...	...
31	Electrical machinery and apparatus	b/	62	53	56	85	82	100	83	64	65	70	60	49
32	Radio,television and communication equipment	b/	...	...	...	...	...	...	...	...	...	...	...	...
33	Medical, precision and optical instruments		95	104	113	96	96	100	137	112	146	109	116	151
34	Motor vehicles, trailers, semi-trailers	c/	116	109	99	104	103	100	98	91	91	86	79	83
35	Other transport equipment	c/	...	...	...	...	...	...	...	...	...	...	...	...
36	Furniture; manufacturing n.e.c.		...	...	...	...	...	...	...	...	...	...	...	...
37	Recycling		...	...	...	...	...	...	...	...	...	...	...	...
D	Total manufacturing		87	87	89	96	95	100	98	97	97	98	97	98

a/ 29 includes 30.
b/ 31 includes 32.
c/ 34 includes 35.

Guatemala

Supplier of information:
Instituto Nacional de Estadística, Ministerio de Economía, Guatemala.

Basic source of data:
Not reported.

Major deviations from ISIC (Revision 3):
None reported.

Reference period:
Not reported.

Scope:
Not reported.

Method of data collection:
Not reported.

Type of enumeration:
Not reported.

Adjusted for non-response:
Not reported.

Concepts and definitions of variables:
No deviations from the standard UN concepts and definitions are reported.

Related national publications:
None reported.

Guatemala

ISIC Revision 3		Number of establishments					Number of persons engaged					Wages and salaries				
			(number)					(number)					(Guatemalan Quetzales)			
ISIC	Industry	Note	2003	2004	2005	2006	Note	2003	2004	2005	2006a/	Note	2003	2004	2005	2006
15	Food and beverages	b/	36	36	33	29	b/	304308	317809	330745	342607		...	...	...	...
16	Tobacco products	b/	...	...	...	...	b/	...	...	...	...		...	...	...	...
17	Textiles	c/	25	24	17	17	c/	316958	355151	334643	344940		...	...	...	...
18	Wearing apparel, fur	c/	...	...	...	...	c/	...	...	...	...		...	...	...	...
19	Leather, leather products and footwear	c/	...	...	...	...	c/	...	...	...	...		...	...	...	...
20	Wood products (excl. furniture)	d/	31	29	26	22	d/	38247	38448	38263	40672		...	...	...	...
21	Paper and paper products	d/	...	...	...	...	d/	...	...	...	...		...	...	...	...
22	Printing and publishing	d/	...	...	...	...	d/	...	...	...	...		...	...	...	...
23	Coke,refined petroleum products,nuclear fuel	e/	16	18	14	17	e/	19156	20840	21623	22383		...	...	...	...
24	Chemicals and chemical products	e/	...	...	...	...	e/	...	...	...	...		...	...	...	...
25	Rubber and plastics products	f/	20	22	17	17	f/	55376	56006	56412	56852		...	...	...	...
26	Non-metallic mineral products	f/	...	...	...	...	f/	...	...	...	...		...	...	...	...
27	Basic metals	g/	33	36	30	24	g/	38315	39940	40460	42823		...	...	...	...
28	Fabricated metal products	g/	...	...	...	...	g/	...	...	...	...		...	...	...	...
29	Machinery and equipment n.e.c.	g/	...	...	...	...	g/	...	...	...	...		...	...	...	...
30	Office, accounting and computing machinery		...	...	...	...		...	...	...	...		...	...	...	...
31	Electrical machinery and apparatus		...	...	...	...		...	...	...	...		...	...	...	...
32	Radio,television and communication equipment		...	...	...	...		...	...	...	...		...	...	...	...
33	Medical, precision and optical instruments		...	...	...	...		...	...	...	...		...	...	...	...
34	Motor vehicles, trailers, semi-trailers		...	...	...	...		...	...	...	...		...	...	...	...
35	Other transport equipment		...	...	...	...		...	...	...	...		...	...	...	...
36	Furniture; manufacturing n.e.c.	h/	15	11	11	6	h/	47875	47113	48977	48155		...	...	...	...
37	Recycling	h/	...	...	...	...	h/	...	...	...	...		...	...	...	...
D	Total manufacturing		176	176	148	132		820235	875307	871123	898432		...	...	...	...

a/ Preliminarey figures.
b/ 15 includes 16.
c/ 17 includes 18 and 19.
d/ 20 includes 21 and 22.
e/ 23 includes 24.
f/ 25 includes 26.
g/ 27 includes 28 and 29.
h/ 36 includes 37.

Guatemala

ISIC Revision 3			Index numbers of industrial production											
			(2000=100)											
ISIC	Industry	Note	1995	1996	1997	1998	1999	2000	2001	2002	2003	2004	2005	2006
15	Food and beverages		...	...	...	...	...	...	...	...	...	...	...	...
16	Tobacco products		...	...	...	...	...	...	...	...	...	...	...	...
17	Textiles		...	...	...	...	...	...	...	...	...	...	...	...
18	Wearing apparel, fur		...	...	...	...	...	...	...	...	...	...	...	...
19	Leather, leather products and footwear		...	...	...	...	...	...	...	...	...	...	...	...
20	Wood products (excl. furniture)		...	...	...	...	...	...	...	...	...	...	...	...
21	Paper and paper products		...	...	...	...	...	...	...	...	...	...	...	...
22	Printing and publishing		...	...	...	...	...	...	...	...	...	...	...	...
23	Coke,refined petroleum products,nuclear fuel		...	...	...	...	...	...	...	...	...	...	...	...
24	Chemicals and chemical products		...	...	...	...	...	...	...	...	...	...	...	...
25	Rubber and plastics products		...	...	...	...	...	...	...	...	...	...	...	...
26	Non-metallic mineral products		...	...	...	...	...	...	...	...	...	...	...	...
27	Basic metals		...	...	...	...	...	...	...	...	...	...	...	...
28	Fabricated metal products		...	...	...	...	...	...	...	...	...	...	...	...
29	Machinery and equipment n.e.c.		...	...	...	...	...	...	...	...	...	...	...	...
30	Office, accounting and computing machinery		...	...	...	...	...	...	...	...	...	...	...	...
31	Electrical machinery and apparatus		...	...	...	...	...	...	...	...	...	...	...	...
32	Radio,television and communication equipment		...	...	...	...	...	...	...	...	...	...	...	...
33	Medical, precision and optical instruments		...	...	...	...	...	...	...	...	...	...	...	...
34	Motor vehicles, trailers, semi-trailers		...	...	...	...	...	...	...	...	...	...	...	...
35	Other transport equipment		...	...	...	...	...	...	...	...	...	...	...	...
36	Furniture; manufacturing n.e.c.		...	...	...	...	...	...	...	...	...	...	...	...
37	Recycling		...	...	...	...	...	...	...	...	...	...	...	...
D	Total manufacturing		88	90	92	96	98	100	101	102	103	105	108	...

Hungary

Supplier of information:
Hungarian Central Statistical Office, Budapest.
Industrial statistics for the OECD countries are compiled by the OECD secretariat, which supplies them to UNIDO.

Basic source of data:
Annual structural business statistics; labour statistics.

Major deviations from ISIC (Revision 3):
Data collected under the national classification system have been reclassified by the national authorities to correspond approximately with ISIC (Revision 3).

Reference period:
Calendar year.

Scope:
Enterprises with 5 or more employees.

Method of data collection:
Questionnaires are distributed by mail.

Type of enumeration:
Not reported.

Adjusted for non-response:
Not reported.

Concepts and definitions of variables:
Wages and salaries refers to full time employees.
Output is the production value based on sales including changes in stocks and the resale of goods and services.
Value added is the gross value added derived from operating activities.

Related national publications:
Statistical Yearbook of Hungary; Yearbook of Industrial and Construction Statistics, both published by the Hungarian Central Statistical Office, Budapest.

Hungary

ISIC Revision 3		Number of enterprises					Number of employees					Wages and salaries paid to employees				
			(number)					(number)					(millions of Hungarian Forints)			
ISIC	Industry	Note	2002	2003	2004	2005	Note	2002	2003	2004	2005	Note	2002	2003	2004	2005
151	Processed meat,fish,fruit,vegetables,fats		...	1390	1321	1258		...	52987	49601	43747		...	77456	75724	72654
1511	Processing/preserving of meat		676	699	663	619		37734	37533	35636	31341		48640	51130	50684	47774
1512	Processing/preserving of fish		...	14	15	11		...	172	167	46		...	127	151	74
1513	Processing/preserving of fruit & vegetables		516	576	554	544		13673	13271	11768	10640		17201	17855	16559	16247
1514	Vegetable and animal oils and fats		93	101	89	84		2075	2011	2030	1720		8771	8344	8330	8558
1520	Dairy products		121	103	96	90		9442	9908	9483	8518		14966	17195	17818	17562
153	Grain mill products; starches; animal feeds		440	437	395	394		12403	11908	10679	9564		20093	21203	20460	20960
1531	Grain mill products		219	206	181	178		6322	5872	5125	4336		8382	8547	7952	7640
1532	Starches and starch products		3	3	3	4		357	332	278	237		1142	1192	1107	1067
1533	Prepared animal feeds		218	228	211	212		5724	5704	5276	4991		10569	11464	11400	12229
154	Other food products		3064	3019	2898	2814		42356	44393	41547	41881		48567	50546	52899	54745
1541	Bakery products		2204	2141	2042	1984		27683	28555	28697	29343		25146	26478	27582	30857
1542	Sugar		7	7	5	6		1589	1417	1252	1399		4106	3804	4228	3944
1543	Cocoa, chocolate and sugar confectionery		304	280	271	249		5603	5784	5529	4891		8795	10398	11652	9996
1544	Macaroni, noodles & similar products		284	299	279	278		1757	2961	1919	1931		1628	2206	1460	1612
1549	Other food products n.e.c.		265	292	301	297		5724	5676	4150	4317		8868	7659	7927	8334
155	Beverages		2164	2298	2257	2210		15640	15686	15326	14133		29689	32337	32691	33264
1551	Distilling, rectifying & blending of spirits		417	469	472	471		2029	2070	1941	1848		3426	3804	3800	4018
1552	Wines		554	619	613	616		5168	5110	4860	4705		6220	6619	6493	6722
1553	Malt liquors and malt		122	115	103	98		3378	3239	2899	2445		8989	9561	8934	8979
1554	Soft drinks; mineral waters		1071	1095	1069	1025		5065	5267	5626	5135		11055	12351	13464	13544
1600	Tobacco products		...	7	6	6		...	2069	1715	1544		...	9409	11602	9153
171	Spinning, weaving and finishing of textiles		502	...	293	269		9642	...	7066	5474		10666	...	9110	7789
1711	Textile fibre preparation; textile weaving		293	...	134	115		8600	...	6325	4822		9427	...	8254	7094
1712	Finishing of textiles		209	182	159	154		1042	795	741	652		1239	862	856	695
172	Other textiles		1473	1375	1266	1179		16182	14541	17863	13737		14820	13543	16257	14858
1721	Made-up textile articles, except apparel		506	509	463	435		9877	10137	11005	8448		7920	8648	8280	8161
1722	Carpets and rugs		78	54	54	53		886	633	1291	562		729	609	1007	620
1723	Cordage, rope, twine and netting		64	58	58	53		778	530	490	383		826	533	478	372
1729	Other textiles n.e.c.		825	754	691	638		4641	3241	5077	4344		5345	3728	6493	5705
1730	Knitted and crocheted fabrics and articles		921	808	708	637		6196	5475	4988	6275		4981	4261	3901	5507
1810	Wearing apparel, except fur apparel		6126	5764	5224	4756		66025	58425	51225	40511		52916	47528	44342	37952
1820	Dressing & dyeing of fur; processing of fur		220	199	175	160		255	300	268	91		170	228	176	174
191	Tanning, dressing and processing of leather		487	429	378	360		4026	3994	3998	4263		3887	3931	4303	5705
1911	Tanning and dressing of leather		33	32	23	17		378	312	272	108		389	330	252	198
1912	Luggage, handbags, etc.; saddlery & harness		454	397	355	343		3648	3682	3726	4155		3499	3601	4052	5507
1920	Footwear		906	642	502	433		18152	14885	11373	8736		15379	14000	10444	8731
2010	Sawmilling and planing of wood		1314	1155	1023	931		6514	7367	7257	5728		5005	6366	6191	4911
202	Products of wood, cork, straw, etc.		5359	4852	4377	4161		20568	21184	21065	19548		18586	19935	20938	22076
2021	Veneer sheets, plywood, particle board, etc.		53	56	47	45		2407	2364	2056	1686		3596	3931	3750	3795
2022	Builders' carpentry and joinery		3441	3232	2973	2816		10822	11243	11437	11206		9548	10322	10922	12303
2023	Wooden containers		328	354	350	349		2926	2957	2555	2532		2405	2359	2139	2406
2029	Other wood products; articles of cork/straw		1537	1210	1007	951		4413	4620	5017	4124		3037	3322	4127	3572
210	Paper and paper products		592	582	545	513		11620	15604	18714	18246		21162	26934	30023	31155
2101	Pulp, paper and paperboard		56	51	50	46		1558	1674	1443	1357		2818	3170	3146	3299
2102	Corrugated paper and paperboard		314	328	303	287		6003	9120	11964	11534		11395	15217	18094	18207
2109	Other articles of paper and paperboard		222	203	192	180		4059	4810	5307	5355		6924	8547	8758	9674
221	Publishing		3175	3340	3267	3188		10829	10953	10765	10069		21502	24398	26324	27186
2211	Publishing of books and other publications		1341	1422	1411	1380		3916	4083	3715	3379		8528	9232	9236	9128
2212	Publishing of newspapers, journals, etc.		1145	1268	1231	1187		5784	5783	5982	5823		11516	13239	15326	16471
2213	Publishing of recorded media		190	199	194	208		386	396	367	305		777	1167	755	843
2219	Other publishing		499	451	431	413		743	691	701	562		705	761	1007	719

222	Printing and related service activities	4322	4487	4540	4340	23683	25437	21936	19727	27357	30079	29696	30510
2221	Printing	1826	1938	1884	1832	16341	18224	16105	14811	21089	23790	23681	24185
2222	Service activities related to printing	2496	2549	2656	2508	7342	7213	5831	4916	6268	6315	5990	6325
2230	Reproduction of recorded media	280	255	229	205	576	569	424	450	777	812	554	843
2310	Coke oven products	5	3	3	3	971	931	908	883	1919	2004	2542	2753
2320	Refined petroleum products	9	5	5	6	8794	7297	6144	5824	40550	38525	41348	53876
2330	Processing of nuclear fuel	-	-	-	-	-	-	-	-	-	-	-	-
241	Basic chemicals	258	250	244	220	11602	11322	10536	9558	27819	28989	30577	30709
2411	Basic chemicals, except fertilizers	165	160	163	147	4216	4148	3805	3189	9548	10221	9588	9848
2412	Fertilizers and nitrogen compounds	16	18	20	18	1356	1233	1186	1182	2964	2638	2894	3150
2413	Plastics in primary forms; synthetic rubber	77	72	...	...	6030	5941	...	...	15258	16105	...	...
242	Other chemicals	550	528	491	471	21605	22014	22152	21721	60837	69441	76656	83345
2421	Pesticides and other agro-chemical products	41	43	43	44	872	821	774	775	1822	1826	1963	2084
2422	Paints, varnishes, printing ink and mastics	71	75	65	65	1905	1907	1595	1623	4106	4185	4102	4515
2423	Pharmaceuticals, medicinal chemicals, etc.	103	102	95	92	14149	14565	14968	15240	45700	54148	59870	66428
2424	Soap, cleaning & cosmetic preparations	164	165	159	154	3158	3276	3390	3137	6779	6721	8078	8434
2429	Other chemical products n.e.c.	171	143	129	116	1521	1445	1425	946	2430	2562	2642	1885
2430	Man-made fibres	9	10	8	7	1055	958	839	75	1871	1699	1611	99
251	Rubber products	277	268	260	242	9930	8210	9555	9305	18562	18590	20636	21952
2511	Rubber tyres and tubes	43	47	47	47	3450	3262	3293	3480	9816	10297	10570	12006
2519	Other rubber products	234	221	213	195	6480	4948	6262	5825	8771	8268	10066	9947
2520	Plastic products	2260	2215	2192	2098	29329	30999	31360	30911	41959	46869	51313	55042
2610	Glass and glass products	519	503	491	436	6282	6426	5952	4820	8649	8927	9135	8533
269	Non-metallic mineral products n.e.c.	2086	2182	2143	2061	24815	24214	23783	23445	40039	42278	44695	48915
2691	Pottery, china and earthenware	571	554	541	499	6412	5982	5510	5193	9645	9435	9060	9972
2692	Refractory ceramic products	41	50	47	45	1027	1107	1108	980	2260	2511	2642	2654
2693	Struct.non-refractory clay; ceramic products	136	93	75	66	4625	4498	4342	3875	6973	7583	8154	7640
2694	Cement, lime and plaster	315	173	122	111	1885	1689	1625	1450	4738	5072	5109	5804
2695	Articles of concrete, cement and plaster	580	680	676	652	7558	8139	7973	7947	12002	13594	14772	15999
2696	Cutting, shaping & finishing of stone	348	539	589	590	1519	1241	1382	1453	948	913	931	1116
2699	Other non-metallic mineral products n.e.c.	95	93	93	98	1789	1558	1843	2547	3450	3196	4052	5755
2710	Basic iron and steel	116	114	96	91	9741	9924	8664	9251	19072	22116	23253	26517
2720	Basic precious and non-ferrous metals	66	62	56	55	5640	5557	5330	5419	14796	16866	17717	19422
273	Casting of metals	232	247	232	215	5300	5637	4976	4994	7483	8293	8028	8955
2731	Casting of iron and steel	73	61	54	51	2439	2256	2000	1867	3158	2866	2466	2778
2732	Casting of non-ferrous metals	159	186	178	164	2861	3381	2976	3127	4325	5402	5537	6201
281	Struct.metal products;tanks;steam generators	4277	3935	3790	3625	29712	30403	30964	29000	36589	40706	42782	44302
2811	Structural metal products	3899	3537	3368	3229	24647	25272	25646	24938	29665	32717	34603	37059
2812	Tanks, reservoirs and containers of metal	325	336	358	336	3838	3745	4047	3074	5005	5554	5914	5135
2813	Steam generators	53	62	64	60	1227	1386	1271	988	1919	2435	2265	2108
289	Other metal products; metal working services	6567	6047	6371	6110	35472	36395	36508	35155	43052	46159	51943	55365
2891	Metal forging/pressing/stamping/roll-forming	272	244	230	224	1816	1543	1748	1674	2770	2384	2995	2877
2892	Treatment & coating of metals	4341	4084	4440	4249	16202	17570	19237	19348	17517	19732	25594	29468
2893	Cutlery, hand tools and general hardware	913	755	780	770	5662	5744	6026	5235	7483	8471	9639	9178
2899	Other fabricated metal products n.e.c.	1041	964	921	867	11792	11538	9497	8898	15282	15572	13715	13841
291	General purpose machinery	5296	4482	4587	4359	29719	30493	30554	29202	49199	55365	61606	62385
2911	Engines & turbines (not for transport equipment)	98	71	67	69	1761	1617	1585	1581	4349	4591	5134	5333
2912	Pumps, compressors, taps and valves	185	213	232	219	6506	7221	7835	6677	13144	15953	18447	15677
2913	Bearings, gears, gearing & driving elements	70	78	75	74	2707	2678	2339	2228	3912	4007	4228	4366
2914	Ovens, furnaces and furnace burners	44	42	42	49	276	283	302	417	292	304	377	645
2915	Lifting and handling equipment	767	749	819	830	4440	4709	5127	5447	6608	7279	8355	10170
2919	Other general purpose machinery	4132	3329	3352	3118	14029	13985	13366	12852	20919	23257	25040	26169
292	Special purpose machinery	1853	2089	2200	2169	26465	25063	24496	24532	40841	41391	45324	50677
2921	Agricultural and forestry machinery	385	528	535	528	8194	6602	5624	5571	11103	9029	8280	9277
2922	Machine tools	317	366	365	354	3789	4105	4175	3582	5928	7025	7927	8483
2923	Machinery for metallurgy	12	14	18	17	578	549	526	493	1093	1091	1107	1215
2924	Machinery for mining & construction	109	108	126	115	4257	3108	3476	3503	7216	5605	8028	9277
2925	Food/beverage/tobacco processing machinery	258	283	291	302	2863	3008	3030	3647	4155	4641	5184	5854
2926	Machinery for textile, apparel and leather	78	88	97	85	832	727	711	616	1069	964	1057	992
2927	Weapons and ammunition	32	37	36	38	1023	1025	932	602	1458	1649	1585	1265
2929	Other special purpose machinery	662	665	732	730	4929	5939	6022	6518	8844	11413	12155	14288

continued

Hungary

ISIC Revision 3		Number of enterprises					Number of employees					Wages and salaries paid to employees				
			(number)					(number)					(millions of Hungarian Forints)			
ISIC	Industry	Note	2002	2003	2004	2005	Note	2002	2003	2004	2005	Note	2002	2003	2004	2005
2930	Domestic appliances n.e.c.		110	106	109	102		9594	9632	9965	10219		13606	14761	16358	17934
3000	Office, accounting and computing machinery		405	353	322	306		14273	12820	8235	8190		23202	25007	16433	18480
3110	Electric motors, generators and transformers		491	486	486	441		8123	7943	8065	7216		12439	12960	14093	13916
3120	Electricity distribution & control apparatus		259	287	299	281		8151	8226	8963	7441		13071	14811	16886	14114
3130	Insulated wire and cable		45	47	49	44		4004	4144	4049	3686		5078	5757	5889	6176
3140	Accumulators, primary cells and batteries		30	33	29	27		1609	1837	2198	2189		2721	2739	3498	4490
3150	Lighting equipment and electric lamps		178	164	171	175		19682	19975	20672	19321		35399	39742	44795	44500
3190	Other electrical equipment n.e.c.		689	641	645	628		30863	25637	25801	27051		47984	42507	46230	53653
3210	Electronic valves, tubes, etc.		406	405	433	432		17033	16308	19825	21670		30151	31931	42153	44897
3220	TV/radio transmitters; line comm. apparatus		848	786	871	853		5876	4672	4939	5253		14335	11971	13640	16644
3230	TV and radio receivers and associated goods		330	391	465	462		16268	22483	28875	25790		25729	40833	53855	54447
331	Medical, measuring, testing appliances, etc.		3710	3334	3509	3458		15580	15680	15980	15328		22449	25032	27129	28724
3311	Medical, surgical and orthopaedic equipment		1796	1821	1897	1878		7682	8043	8092	7839		9208	10119	10343	11385
3312	Measuring/testing/navigating appliances,etc.		1401	945	916	865		6012	5656	5588	5208		9864	11007	11602	11485
3313	Industrial process control equipment		513	568	696	715		1886	1981	2300	2281		3377	3906	5184	5854
3320	Optical instruments & photographic equipment		194	215	214	214		2112	2091	2138	1991		2843	3043	3297	3671
3330	Watches and clocks		15	14	15	14		24	29	30	-		24	25	25	25
3410	Motor vehicles		61	55	50	43		9895	9959	10323	9567		29544	32032	33546	35298
3420	Automobile bodies, trailers & semi-trailers		65	74	79	88		1487	1547	1942	2583		2357	2841	3926	7144
3430	Parts/accessories for automobiles		270	281	285	277		25283	27898	28592	30645		45482	54655	59945	70694
351	Building and repairing of ships and boats		137	152	162	164		438	443	403	424		437	482	478	521
3511	Building and repairing of ships		55	64	69	63		215	198	175	150		219	203	201	198
3512	Building/repairing of pleasure/sport. boats		82	88	93	101		223	245	228	274		243	279	277	322
3520	Railway/tramway locomotives & rolling stock		76	82	88	83		6605	6841	6406	6301		10447	13898	14345	14635
3530	Aircraft and spacecraft		95	85	105	106		1261	1125	1022	984		3571	3525	3448	3994
359	Transport equipment n.e.c.		148	91	75	63		1105	1142	991	741		1166	1268	906	819
3591	Motorcycles		7	6	6	4		32	66	67	41		49	76	50	74
3592	Bicycles and invalid carriages		40	42	40	37		602	668	762	700		462	583	705	670
3599	Other transport equipment n.e.c.		101	43	29	22		471	408	162	-		656	609	151	74
3610	Furniture		3688	4149	4083	3851		21982	22335	21568	20035		20579	21253	22171	22523
369	Manufacturing n.e.c.		3027	2650	2517	2456		9805	9855	8534	8728		8795	9181	8858	9674
3691	Jewellery and related articles		556	552	551	528		1009	997	990	945		826	837	931	967
3692	Musical instruments		202	190	191	191		269	229	204	89		267	228	226	248
3693	Sports goods		123	131	129	126		812	824	739	698		802	888	805	943
3694	Games and toys		272	268	243	231		2592	2929	1899	1538		2211	2562	1862	1662
3699	Other manufacturing n.e.c.		1874	1509	1403	1380		5123	4876	4702	5458		4689	4667	5033	5854
3710	Recycling of metal waste and scrap		336	230	177	177		1303	957	908	998		1725	1065	1334	1513
3720	Recycling of non-metal waste and scrap		235	153	135	139		534	619	748	869		559	659	755	893
D	Total manufacturing		73005	69711	68042	64956		819205	815057	799186	753557		1220257	1310860	1396612	1467935

ISIC Revision 3		Output					Value added in factor values					Gross fixed capital formation		
			(millions of Hungarian Forints)					(millions of Hungarian Forints)					(millions of Hungarian Forints)	
ISIC	Industry	Note	2002	2003	2004	2005	Note	2002	2003	2004	2005	Note	2004	2005
151	Processed meat,fish,fruit,vegetables,fats		...	860989	846131	826031		...	166502	145082	151311		45878	42565
1511	Processing/preserving of meat		532758	528747	555967	553226		93757	89883	75397	93316		34125	27534
1512	Processing/preserving of fish		...	1167	1107	372		...	254	176	99		50	-
1513	Processing/preserving of fruit & vegetables		197233	213675	170625	153816		46332	51028	42304	32122		9311	12452
1514	Vegetable and animal oils and fats		114044	117401	118431	118618		30345	25337	27204	25772		2391	2580
1520	Dairy products		228672	239823	233289	218954		38266	48365	47866	39242		12583	10195
153	Grain mill products; starches; animal feeds		260524	290167	276952	246165		63412	69746	59241	61789		19051	19174
1531	Grain mill products		82096	91988	87502	70297		18343	20163	16735	16148		8330	7665
1532	Starches and starch products		30807	30485	30602	32718		13338	11083	11803	15007		1132	2828
1533	Prepared animal feeds		147597	167668	158873	143150		31730	38500	30703	30634		9588	8707
154	Other food products		388879	390651	444885	430094		114117	117071	126560	130301		30250	25103
1541	Bakery products		142155	146161	153664	155403		50705	52499	55869	63054		13967	10939
1542	Sugar		55832	44333	72075	70868		15744	11996	15553	16123		2743	2282
1543	Cocoa, chocolate and sugar confectionery		84112	108955	110051	99245		20093	28329	27657	24731		5360	4515
1544	Macaroni, noodles & similar products		21210	22192	23430	24259		4981	5301	5008	5556		2995	3200
1549	Other food products n.e.c.		85594	69010	85640	80343		22595	18920	22524	20861		5209	4142
155	Beverages		346385	382713	379805	374183		88607	100459	88911	88852		28991	31130
1551	Distilling, rectifying & blending of spirits		59670	66017	66136	68288		11370	14862	12684	15652		3725	4266
1552	Wines		63023	75325	71320	63054		18076	17119	15653	13519		8280	11857
1553	Malt liquors and malt		127359	136143	120696	118766		36031	40326	30627	29667		8179	4862
1554	Soft drinks; mineral waters		96333	105227	121652	124075		23130	28177	29948	30014		8808	10145
1600	Tobacco products		...	281899	235529	219003		...	35380	17717	21779		3246	3622
171	Spinning, weaving and finishing of textiles		61687	...	52647	44525		19242	...	15704	15578		3901	2580
1711	Textile fibre preparation; textile weaving		51580	...	46154	39117		17323	...	13866	14089		3574	2009
1712	Finishing of textiles		10107	7228	6493	5407		1919	1826	1837	1488		327	571
172	Other textiles		65526	65130	68200	59929		21891	19579	23203	26591		4530	3026
1721	Made-up textile articles, except apparel		27843	30003	30149	29146		9548	10018	9588	14040		1585	1687
1722	Carpets and rugs		2478	2612	3121	2530		1142	1040	1585	1488		403	124
1723	Cordage, rope, twine and netting		3766	2156	2064	1687		1020	558	705	595		277	74
1729	Other textiles n.e.c.		31439	30358	32867	26566		10156	7964	11325	10468		2265	1141
1730	Knitted and crocheted fabrics and articles		20919	18185	14269	15950		6803	6822	6468	9748		1158	744
1810	Wearing apparel, except fur apparel		212831	218139	200321	174156		82630	79459	74944	64171		5134	3274
1820	Dressing & dyeing of fur; processing of fur		1142	1192	1057	1017		243	355	377	273		201	74
191	Tanning, dressing and processing of leather		15331	15293	17264	30287		5491	6112	6065	7317		3850	1687
1911	Tanning and dressing of leather		3620	3018	2038	1091		583	558	478	174		101	25
1912	Luggage, handbags, etc.; saddlery & harness		11711	12275	15225	29195		4908	5554	5587	7144		3750	1662
1920	Footwear		58188	46210	35459	31998		25073	20112	16106	15081		1510	918
2010	Sawmilling and planing of wood		35861	43090	41901	37133		7969	12377	11778	9649		4933	2555
202	Products of wood, cork, straw, etc.		138632	151335	155803	160240		36055	41315	44317	46261		11878	14561
2021	Veneer sheets, plywood, particle board, etc.		38193	38398	37850	42417		8333	8167	6946	8111		2668	2654
2022	Builders' carpentry and joinery		69316	81234	83752	83320		18854	23308	24562	25847		6065	8756
2023	Wooden containers		15476	15445	17616	18579		3693	4286	5813	5432		1309	2009
2029	Other wood products; articles of cork/straw		15646	16257	16584	15925		5175	5554	6996	6871		1837	1141
210	Paper and paper products		217715	235233	237643	240162		61566	67184	63217	69107		22926	16867
2101	Pulp, paper and paperboard		51313	56126	52043	55092		11516	10170	6870	8806		2139	5407
2102	Corrugated paper and paperboard		107971	122777	123615	117303		28620	35177	35912	36091		7650	6598
2109	Other articles of paper and paperboard		58431	56329	61984	67767		21453	21837	20460	24234		13137	4862
221	Publishing		179862	195313	201429	201615		49515	57394	59945	61169		11627	10914
2211	Publishing of books and other publications		59913	63202	63041	60896		19096	21000	21970	21853		1585	1736
2212	Publishing of newspapers, journals, etc.		106853	119100	125931	128192		27260	32210	34201	36339		9563	8880
2213	Publishing of recorded media		7313	6873	5537	7417		1871	2333	1409	1612		176	74
2219	Other publishing		5758	6138	6946	5110		1288	1851	2340	1364		302	223

continued

Hungary

ISIC Revision 3		Output					Value added in factor values					Gross fixed capital formation		
			(millions of Hungarian Forints)					(millions of Hungarian Forints)					(millions of Hungarian Forints)	
ISIC	Industry	Note	2002	2003	2004	2005	Note	2002	2003	2004	2005	Note	2004	2005
222	Printing and related service activities		175756	193918	191010	197076		60302	67311	64576	68933		17717	17512
2221	Printing		131076	147987	149838	155974		45336	51941	50735	54621		12935	14536
2222	Service activities related to printing		44680	45905	41146	41102		14966	15395	13866	14312		4782	2977
2230	Reproduction of recorded media		5078	6898	5235	5854		1968	2232	1812	1488		377	223
2310	Coke oven products		25899	31576	52018	65609		-1361	1775	7298	7020		352	347
2320	Refined petroleum products		909732	963883	1082214	1394860		184964	175251	213584	286622		54157	53256
2330	Processing of nuclear fuel		-	-	-	-		-	-	-	-		-	-
241	Basic chemicals		370827	382079	446093	559328		91085	90771	98449	106934		82242	66825
2411	Basic chemicals, except fertilizers		93539	96274	92611	93341		34354	35659	33446	26913		13841	10468
2412	Fertilizers and nitrogen compounds		26361	26148	34201	39614		4713	4768	9840	9004		2038	5234
2413	Plastics in primary forms; synthetic rubber		250903	259656	...	...		52017	50344	...	...		...	...
242	Other chemicals		456542	544040	586670	630345		195970	253468	261223	294287		80783	85503
2421	Pesticides and other agro-chemical products		11419	11768	11979	12502		3814	4058	4127	5110		554	1265
2422	Paints, varnishes, printing ink and mastics		32605	32895	32816	34628		10107	9587	8682	10617		1510	1662
2423	Pharmaceuticals, medicinal chemicals, etc.		310500	389890	422462	458992		156416	212280	214138	237930		74668	78830
2424	Soap, cleaning & cosmetic preparations		84914	93129	104036	110854		19898	22141	28941	35744		3297	3249
2429	Other chemical products n.e.c.		17104	16358	15376	13370		5734	5402	5335	4887		755	496
2430	Man-made fibres		12634	10525	9286	1265		2284	1699	1233	124		805	50
251	Rubber products		119147	119658	136702	145159		36371	35811	41247	45914		9236	19894
2511	Rubber tyres and tubes		61080	63354	74542	82080		18489	18134	21794	27856		4027	14759
2519	Other rubber products		58091	56304	62160	63079		17882	17652	19478	18058		5209	5135
2520	Plastic products		384943	408379	425557	464250		111591	125719	123943	133972		40819	43260
2610	Glass and glass products		59816	62822	59216	63997		21477	20898	18371	22176		18698	29195
269	Non-metallic mineral products n.e.c.		317862	343452	362567	412433		117762	130487	129102	144812		46708	84139
2691	Pottery, china and earthenware		33990	33148	28287	42665		18926	18489	15200	21977		4731	42466
2692	Refractory ceramic products		12391	14025	13892	14809		4033	4996	5235	5457		654	645
2693	Struct.non-refractory clay; ceramic products		48640	53412	55466	52686		23616	26554	25594	22473		10998	7169
2694	Cement, lime and plaster		59525	62517	61380	64890		25025	28203	27456	29171		7978	6102
2695	Articles of concrete, cement and plaster		114749	134317	146038	157809		34986	41239	41876	47626		15175	14461
2696	Cutting, shaping & finishing of stone		8382	6645	6770	7690		2235	2029	2064	2232		856	645
2699	Other non-metallic mineral products n.e.c.		40210	39413	50760	71910		8941	8953	11677	15900		6292	12651
2710	Basic iron and steel		222525	256105	324037	342408		17566	43724	73887	61144		9689	16694
2720	Basic precious and non-ferrous metals		186373	196961	227375	234556		29617	40757	42254	50106		11199	16719
273	Casting of metals		44048	49989	52194	58317		14335	17069	17792	18777		3876	3349
2731	Casting of iron and steel		14092	11717	10746	14784		4883	4210	3574	4787		528	298
2732	Casting of non-ferrous metals		29957	38297	41474	43558		9427	12859	14244	13990		3322	3076
281	Struct.metal products;tanks;steam generators		232729	264272	295826	321101		73908	85140	91327	97831		20007	18132
2811	Structural metal products		188463	209794	241141	269705		59355	67133	72151	81162		14722	14759
2812	Tanks, reservoirs and containers of metal		34184	37815	39385	36711		10933	12605	12835	11658		1913	1538
2813	Steam generators		10083	16663	15301	14685		3620	5402	6342	5011		3372	1836
289	Other metal products; metal working services		273206	305688	361459	385916		92737	101093	118305	121197		39360	31577
2891	Metal forging/pressing/stamping/roll-forming		21477	24880	38001	53182		5369	4540	6845	7938		6946	3572
2892	Treatment & coating of metals		105687	125314	156759	175595		37294	44586	58108	63203		18220	19075
2893	Cutlery, hand tools and general hardware		41546	46539	55944	49684		17250	18210	22398	19075		6342	3671
2899	Other fabricated metal products n.e.c.		104496	108955	110756	107455		32824	33757	30954	30981		7852	5259
291	General purpose machinery		317303	353851	376358	382047		100074	111517	116418	122338		36843	35000
2911	Engines & turbines (not for transport equipment)		19704	21025	23455	25673		9670	10322	9286	10418		1434	1439
2912	Pumps, compressors, taps and valves		107290	124959	140300	117749		27211	30536	34578	34529		21945	12725
2913	Bearings, gears, gearing & driving elements		32945	35786	29042	28997		6657	8344	8028	7342		1686	2629
2914	Ovens, furnaces and furnace burners		1749	1877	2240	3076		656	634	830	1017		126	198
2915	Lifting and handling equipment		32921	39539	47060	55861		12269	13848	15376	18232		3196	3622
2919	Other general purpose machinery		122694	130640	134261	150715		43611	47833	48319	50776		8456	14362

292	Special purpose machinery	225149	232291	261399	308698	72329	75629	81915	97384	17692	17413
2921	Agricultural and forestry machinery	84768	66525	64953	78681	21648	16435	14244	18256	2617	4068
2922	Machine tools	24855	29166	42128	52959	9888	11844	13564	16421	7172	5507
2923	Machinery for metallurgy	3134	2942	3498	4068	1288	1319	1611	1811	25	50
2924	Machinery for mining & construction	37513	30587	42656	51619	11127	9409	12432	16198	1334	1513
2925	Food/beverage/tobacco processing machinery	22376	26960	32590	38175	7556	9206	11123	13097	2693	1687
2926	Machinery for textile, apparel and leather	3839	3677	4228	3547	1676	1572	1560	1414	75	174
2927	Weapons and ammunition	6244	7127	6619	5953	2211	2384	2089	2208	403	99
2929	Other special purpose machinery	42420	65307	64727	73671	16910	23434	25267	27955	3347	4316
2930	Domestic appliances n.e.c.	128330	146466	159905	185517	29908	36673	37850	43607	17918	12303
3000	Office, accounting and computing machinery	417159	497450	494663	623945	32046	140125	100337	113532	6820	6276
3110	Electric motors, generators and transformers	60205	71977	83048	91084	16108	21659	22826	23441	6417	7938
3120	Electricity distribution & control apparatus	113923	128560	154242	103486	30321	39945	45399	31825	6292	5085
3130	Insulated wire and cable	51143	52702	57303	70769	12367	12427	10620	12551	4605	2853
3140	Accumulators, primary cells and batteries	45482	91709	81110	117253	11978	27822	13086	13593	10192	5656
3150	Lighting equipment and electric lamps	354840	374977	461922	508602	138316	157244	230672	292327	5738	6598
3190	Other electrical equipment n.e.c.	662814	318496	323333	418039	69535	93789	95606	112491	31231	22672
3210	Electronic valves, tubes, etc.	252798	424737	499067	601174	48956	65916	142112	171700	76228	56208
3220	TV/radio transmitters; line comm. apparatus	129035	104923	132977	185715	36589	28355	33622	40730	21920	8731
3230	TV and radio receivers and associated goods	950427	1703718	2008046	2094510	89894	171853	160685	187600	40719	30733
331	Medical, measuring, testing appliances, etc.	117786	132719	142364	149152	48810	56354	63242	64394	10066	7466
3311	Medical, surgical and orthopaedic equipment	44437	49101	50231	54348	18562	22547	24008	24185	3070	2778
3312	Measuring/testing/navigating appliances,etc.	49928	54528	57982	59532	20822	22648	24663	25227	2491	2828
3313	Industrial process control equipment	23421	29090	34150	35273	9427	11159	14571	14982	4505	1860
3320	Optical instruments & photographic equipment	13557	15775	15930	17463	5880	7304	7499	7863	1057	2481
3330	Watches and clocks	219	203	226	223	49	51	75	74	-	-
3410	Motor vehicles	1155071	1344744	1355365	1499338	178355	210276	229615	218160	115311	106612
3420	Automobile bodies, trailers & semi-trailers	26774	31703	43814	57101	6657	8623	10595	14412	2491	1662
3430	Parts/accessories for automobiles	417305	519541	601090	788824	118150	147531	162849	206774	44619	52091
351	Building and repairing of ships and boats	2405	2638	1988	2654	705	888	629	1042	126	124
3511	Building and repairing of ships	899	989	755	843	389	380	277	322	25	25
3512	Building/repairing of pleasure/sport. boats	1506	1623	1233	1811	340	482	352	719	101	74
3520	Railway/tramway locomotives & rolling stock	54228	78394	81563	73770	20481	24880	25418	25847	2970	2481
3530	Aircraft and spacecraft	10909	12351	13514	14809	5151	6290	7927	8210	579	620
359	Transport equipment n.e.c.	6973	6670	8405	11286	1749	2359	1812	1811	252	248
3591	Motorcycles	462	431	579	372	73	178	126	99	25	25
3592	Bicycles and invalid carriages	3693	3830	7172	10418	899	1141	1384	1588	226	198
3599	Other transport equipment n.e.c.	2843	2435	679	471	802	1040	302	124	25	25
3610	Furniture	124662	128129	132977	135262	33747	36699	38177	40407	10016	8136
369	Manufacturing n.e.c.	46915	46590	47891	59929	16302	18819	17641	24061	2995	1910
3691	Jewellery and related articles	4009	4261	4656	4118	1506	1674	1636	1588	201	422
3692	Musical instruments	1045	964	1132	1265	389	406	428	521	75	25
3693	Sports goods	7823	6518	9160	15726	2089	2359	2693	7466	403	248
3694	Games and toys	7021	8927	8179	12849	3644	4743	3548	3870	1384	571
3699	Other manufacturing n.e.c.	27017	25920	24763	25971	8674	9638	9337	10617	931	645
3710	Recycling of metal waste and scrap	14019	11743	14747	14312	1895	2815	3423	6400	1007	1786
3720	Recycling of non-metal waste and scrap	4640	4844	7172	8583	826	1268	1963	2902	1585	1339
D	Total manufacturing	12796379	14472724	15620461	17117336	2993340	3568155	3774044	4165032	1123310	1080134

Hungary

ISIC Revision 3			Index numbers of industrial production											
			(2000=100)											
ISIC	Industry	Note	1995	1996	1997	1998	1999	2000	2001	2002	2003	2004	2005	2006
15	Food and beverages		99	98	91	91	93	100	99	101	101	99	95	96
16	Tobacco products		87	98	95	100	108	100	114	101	90	45	24	26
17	Textiles		76	71	73	73	80	100	86	83	73	76	70	67
18	Wearing apparel, fur		69	70	68	87	96	100	115	109	105	97	83	81
19	Leather, leather products and footwear		90	85	95	100	101	100	100	95	73	60	63	86
20	Wood products (excl. furniture)		81	82	86	90	86	100	105	111	115	121	116	113
21	Paper and paper products		66	63	82	91	89	100	102	108	111	108	110	117
22	Printing and publishing		66	60	67	68	77	100	112	101	103	102	110	110
23	Coke,refined petroleum products,nuclear fuel		102	100	97	110	102	100	99	100	93	104	116	115
24	Chemicals and chemical products		108	102	109	101	90	100	96	98	105	110	117	122
25	Rubber and plastics products		57	59	67	80	87	100	116	128	132	138	143	160
26	Non-metallic mineral products		79	80	84	94	91	100	104	107	109	105	118	126
27	Basic metals		76	83	93	90	86	100	97	101	109	117	111	128
28	Fabricated metal products		78	67	68	76	79	100	110	99	115	125	125	134
29	Machinery and equipment n.e.c.		83	78	77	85	90	100	110	145	150	155	164	196
30	Office, accounting and computing machinery		1	5	21	41	80	100	78	67	74	73	91	103
31	Electrical machinery and apparatus		31	35	39	49	61	100	159	168	124	142	152	156
32	Radio,television and communication equipment		9	13	26	35	56	100	94	109	177	238	285	333
33	Medical, precision and optical instruments		82	86	91	89	91	100	109	100	109	123	115	155
34	Motor vehicles, trailers, semi-trailers		23	29	48	71	86	100	104	105	119	128	146	185
35	Other transport equipment		52	50	61	101	97	100	109	122	149	171	169	178
36	Furniture; manufacturing n.e.c.		79	69	69	81	82	100	116	142	108	116	126	140
37	Recycling		14	38	35	84	90	100	112	83	61	104	93	105
D	Total manufacturing		54	55	64	74	83	100	104	108	116	125	135	150

Indonesia

Supplier of information:
Badan Pusat Statistik (BPS), Statistics Indonesia, Jakarta.

Basic source of data:
Annual industrial survey.

Major deviations from ISIC (Revision 3):
Data presented in accordance with ISIC (Revision 3) were originally classified according to the national classification system.

Reference period:
Calendar year.

Scope:
Large establishments (with 100 or more persons engaged) and medium scale establishments (with 20 to 99 persons engaged).

Method of data collection:
For provinces where establishments are concentrated, the inquiry is carried out by field enumerators through direct interviews; elsewhere it is carried out by mail.

Type of enumeration:
Establishments are completely enumerated.

Adjusted for non-response:
Not reported.

Concepts and definitions of variables:
Wages and salaries is compensation of employees.
Output is gross output.
Value added is total value added.
Gross fixed capital formation represents the value of acquisitions of new and used fixed assets; sales are not taken into account.

Related national publications:
Industrial Statistics (Survey of Manufacturing Industries) Volumes I and II (annual), published by the BPS, Jakarta.

Indonesia

ISIC Revision 3		Number of establishments					Number of employees					Wages and salaries paid to employees				
			(number)					(thousands)					(billions of Indonesian Rupiahs)			
ISIC	Industry	Note	2002	2003	2004	2005	Note	2002	2003	2004	2005	Note	2002	2003	2004	2005
151	Processed meat,fish,fruit,vegetables,fats		859	869	952	1090		179.4	231.4	290.5	229.9		1192.7	1871.8	2380.8	3205.5
1511	Processing/preserving of meat		33	29	30	37		5.0	8.1	5.8	7.1		64.8	105.9	68.0	85.8
1512	Processing/preserving of fish		506	502	553	584		71.0	74.8	81.7	97.2		445.7	534.5	638.7	948.8
1513	Processing/preserving of fruit & vegetables		34	46	48	76		3.7	4.3	3.7	18.2		28.8	22.6	33.6	309.9
1514	Vegetable and animal oils and fats		278	285	314	388		98.3	142.8	197.4	104.6		640.7	1197.4	1624.6	1740.3
1520	Dairy products		...	26	29	43		...	6.4	7.5	10.6		...	239.2	170.0	270.2
153	Grain mill products; starches; animal feeds		744	689	683	742		77.0	71.7	69.6	74.7		675.2	602.0	697.9	922.6
1531	Grain mill products		434	398	397	432		40.5	40.7	37.4	40.3		166.4	168.5	184.7	206.1
1532	Starches and starch products		216	212	208	223		18.8	17.4	18.6	21.1		168.6	186.6	221.1	416.2
1533	Prepared animal feeds		90	74	74	86		14.0	11.3	11.4	13.3		269.4	191.8	221.5	300.2
154	Other food products		2394	2335	2448	2559		278.2	272.4	272.0	289.1		2026.6	2176.1	2666.2	2765.8
1541	Bakery products		486	488	520	553		43.6	46.1	47.2	52.3		375.7	336.7	461.8	500.1
1542	Sugar		90	99	93	115		64.4	58.0	58.7	69.4		570.5	660.2	716.9	898.7
1543	Cocoa, chocolate and sugar confectionery		98	95	92	98		17.7	17.3	16.8	18.0		131.1	202.2	187.9	211.5
1544	Macaroni, noodles & similar products		302	294	306	305		28.9	28.0	27.8	33.2		223.3	215.1	252.7	260.6
1549	Other food products n.e.c.		1413	1355	1433	1488		123.2	122.8	121.4	116.3		723.4	760.9	1045.4	894.8
155	Beverages		237	223	251	288		23.5	23.9	27.4	32.4		190.9	240.5	252.2	434.6
1551	Distilling, rectifying & blending of spirits		6	4	4	9		0.4	0.2	0.2	0.7		2.6	2.0	2.0	5.8
1552	Wines		3	...	...	12		0.2	...	...	0.9		1.1	...	...	10.7
1553	Malt liquors and malt		-	...	...	4		-	...	...	1.1		-	...	...	78.4
1554	Soft drinks; mineral waters		222	212	240	263		22.5	23.2	26.6	29.6		184.7	234.0	245.1	339.7
1600	Tobacco products		809	781	798	858		264.7	264.2	254.8	272.3		2637.5	2482.8	2310.9	2253.1
171	Spinning, weaving and finishing of textiles		1142	1102	1056	1172		435.2	400.8	385.7	424.0		3524.2	3663.0	3827.1	3891.5
1711	Textile fibre preparation; textile weaving		741	637	554	693		355.5	300.5	250.5	279.4		2901.2	2660.9	2407.8	2933.9
1712	Finishing of textiles		400	465	502	479		79.7	100.3	135.1	144.5		623.0	1002.0	1419.3	957.7
172	Other textiles		337	327	385	414		46.3	50.1	56.3	56.8		342.9	352.5	452.5	491.6
1721	Made-up textile articles, except apparel		202	179	208	204		25.9	25.5	28.1	28.8		168.2	173.9	229.8	273.7
1722	Carpets and rugs		13	17	21	28		2.0	5.9	6.9	8.0		32.7	27.8	34.2	44.0
1723	Cordage, rope, twine and netting		26	18	26	33		6.6	5.6	5.9	3.8		52.4	45.2	61.9	44.4
1729	Other textiles n.e.c.		92	111	128	147		11.6	13.1	15.0	15.6		89.3	105.4	124.1	127.2
1730	Knitted and crocheted fabrics and articles		265	289	298	262		83.5	85.8	90.7	82.6		659.7	818.2	870.6	979.6
1810	Wearing apparel, except fur apparel		2006	1865	1885	1921		469.4	446.0	438.0	451.9		4119.3	4154.3	4412.0	4437.5
1820	Dressing & dyeing of fur; processing of fur		-	-	3	1		-	-	0.1	-		-	-	1.2	0.4
191	Tanning, dressing and processing of leather		159	144	148	164		25.5	20.2	22.1	22.7		180.9	198.8	212.0	211.2
1911	Tanning and dressing of leather		58	63	58	56		6.9	7.3	6.7	6.4		67.6	91.7	82.7	69.5
1912	Luggage, handbags, etc.; saddlery & harness		101	81	90	105		18.6	12.8	15.3	16.0		113.3	107.1	129.3	139.2
1920	Footwear		347	340	319	327		234.8	217.2	196.7	186.0		2346.5	1480.4	2551.9	2385.5
2010	Sawmilling and planing of wood		744	523	449	462		76.1	48.8	44.2	51.5		442.5	272.8	247.5	306.3
202	Products of wood, cork, straw, etc.		786	823	848	863		299.8	270.8	270.0	260.7		3142.0	2904.0	2961.8	3345.8
2021	Veneer sheets, plywood, particle board, etc.		188	195	222	217		208.9	183.1	181.1	174.2		2369.5	2138.6	2108.6	2463.6
2022	Builders' carpentry and joinery		369	371	365	362		68.5	62.6	64.6	60.2		629.7	571.8	680.6	697.6
2023	Wooden containers		12	30	37	42		0.8	0.9	1.1	1.3		3.5	6.2	6.1	9.1
2029	Other wood products; articles of cork/straw		214	224	223	242		20.0	22.4	21.7	25.0		120.6	167.8	135.3	175.4
210	Paper and paper products		314	341	376	413		94.9	102.1	103.4	119.5		1026.9	1958.2	1785.4	2754.7
2101	Pulp, paper and paperboard		110	123	142	155		61.7	68.3	71.9	85.1		741.6	1419.0	1310.8	2225.5
2102	Corrugated paper and paperboard		140	175	189	203		26.5	29.0	26.5	27.2		224.5	494.0	429.1	429.8
2109	Other articles of paper and paperboard		64	42	45	55		6.8	4.7	5.1	7.2		60.8	45.1	45.4	99.3
221	Publishing		324	277	426	441		35.0	34.3	41.8	42.9		569.0	859.6	621.1	919.2
2211	Publishing of books and other publications		309	210	131	193		32.9	26.8	16.8	23.2		539.9	675.8	317.0	518.5
2212	Publishing of newspapers, journals, etc.		11	27	39	57		1.4	4.2	6.3	7.1		14.2	142.3	82.3	247.6
2213	Publishing of recorded media		-	3	-	-		-	0.1	-	-		-	5.7	-	-
2219	Other publishing		3	34	250	190		0.5	2.9	18.2	12.5		8.7	34.6	212.4	147.6

222	Printing and related service activities	221	222	64	99	17.8	15.6	6.4	6.3	271.2	169.0	90.6	101.5
2221	Printing	179	186	44	90	16.2	14.3	5.8	6.0	257.8	156.6	85.4	99.0
2222	Service activities related to printing	42	36	20	9	1.6	1.4	0.6	0.3	13.4	12.3	5.2	2.5
2230	Reproduction of recorded media	-	-	1	5	-	-	-	0.1	-	-	0.2	1.1
2310	Coke oven products	6	...	6	6	0.7	...	0.7	0.7	0.4	...	3.3	8.5
2320	Refined petroleum products	14	27	21	46	0.7	2.2	1.6	4.5	5.1	36.3	43.2	107.4
2330	Processing of nuclear fuel	...	...	...	...	...	...	...	...	...	...	...	...
241	Basic chemicals	313	287	294	348	42.4	44.3	42.9	58.0	1230.7	1217.9	1248.9	2672.0
2411	Basic chemicals, except fertilizers	226	198	210	233	29.8	31.5	30.5	36.8	599.9	513.2	754.5	1181.0
2412	Fertilizers and nitrogen compounds	38	51	49	68	6.6	7.3	7.0	14.9	491.1	589.7	250.1	1340.1
2413	Plastics in primary forms; synthetic rubber	48	37	34	45	6.0	5.4	5.4	6.2	139.5	113.6	244.1	150.3
242	Other chemicals	582	585	597	650	124.2	128.6	128.1	141.7	1935.5	2560.9	3064.4	2913.9
2421	Pesticides and other agro-chemical products	32	34	36	41	18.9	19.9	9.0	20.8	66.0	453.8	267.1	247.7
2422	Paints, varnishes, printing ink and mastics	111	115	108	119	11.7	11.0	10.9	12.1	166.0	201.9	182.5	182.9
2423	Pharmaceuticals, medicinal chemicals, etc.	211	197	207	205	46.9	45.0	59.8	52.9	1085.7	983.8	1653.4	1626.5
2424	Soap, cleaning & cosmetic preparations	119	121	118	135	28.9	33.5	29.0	33.1	300.9	541.4	361.5	444.1
2429	Other chemical products n.e.c.	108	115	121	150	16.4	16.5	15.7	22.7	271.6	244.8	402.4	412.7
2430	Man-made fibres	9	13	12	13	6.3	16.1	6.5	8.9	47.0	661.7	454.6	119.5
251	Rubber products	428	417	427	461	151.8	149.0	146.7	151.3	1781.9	8640.5	1826.5	1831.7
2511	Rubber tyres and tubes	298	282	288	326	112.1	113.6	110.1	117.9	1231.6	8265.0	1380.3	1387.5
2519	Other rubber products	126	132	135	135	39.0	34.7	35.8	33.4	540.3	364.5	433.9	444.2
2520	Plastic products	976	950	999	1016	192.3	183.5	181.0	183.1	1860.8	1912.9	2120.6	2598.5
2610	Glass and glass products	...	37	47	71	...	20.4	22.0	29.6	...	411.0	260.0	473.3
269	Non-metallic mineral products n.e.c.	...	1350	1338	1451	...	120.3	123.3	135.5	...	1492.1	1212.3	2339.7
2691	Pottery, china and earthenware	...	61	65	72	...	29.1	30.6	32.2	...	264.7	293.6	407.0
2692	Refractory ceramic products	...	5	5	14	...	0.4	0.4	1.2	...	4.6	3.1	14.3
2693	Struct.non-refractory clay; ceramic products	...	696	648	709	...	36.5	33.9	38.2	...	132.7	140.1	243.5
2694	Cement, lime and plaster	...	354a/	368a/	387a/	...	34.8a/	37.5a/	43.7a/	...	931.5a/	608.9a/	1485.2a/
2695	Articles of concrete, cement and plaster	...	...a/	...a/	...a/	...	...a/	...a/	...a/	...	...a/	...a/	...a/
2696	Cutting, shaping & finishing of stone	...	...b/	...b/	...b/	...	...b/	...b/	...b/	...	...b/	...b/	...b/
2699	Other non-metallic mineral products n.e.c.	...	234b/	252b/	269b/	...	19.5b/	20.9b/	20.2b/	...	158.7b/	166.7b/	189.8b/
2710	Basic iron and steel	117	103	112	110	38.4	36.4	33.6	36.1	1008.7	1327.8	1434.6	1520.1
2720	Basic precious and non-ferrous metals	44	57	64	71	9.3	13.5	14.1	14.7	189.2	371.5	279.5	499.5
273	Casting of metals	33	21	20	30	5.8	2.9	5.9	5.6	40.5	44.5	250.7	98.9
2731	Casting of iron and steel	25	15	12	20	4.9	2.4	4.7	4.7	28.3	42.4	218.4	78.0
2732	Casting of non-ferrous metals	7	5	5	10	0.2	0.4	0.3	0.9	1.3	0.5	1.1	20.9
281	Struct.metal products;tanks;steam generators	178	164	165	186	19.8	19.7	19.8	23.8	355.6	300.1	332.6	405.9
2811	Structural metal products	149	130	133	145	14.1	14.0	13.5	16.4	268.1	226.3	230.7	245.4
2812	Tanks, reservoirs and containers of metal	29	34	32	41	5.7	5.7	6.4	7.4	87.5	73.8	101.9	160.6
2813	Steam generators	-	-	-	-	-	-	-	-	-	-	-	-
289	Other metal products; metal working services	696	651	664	673	92.9	79.1	100.0	99.5	971.1	1008.7	1121.1	1189.9
2891	Metal forging/pressing/stamping/roll-forming	17	16	14	21	2.4	2.2	1.5	2.3	33.0	40.2	24.3	47.9
2892	Treatment & coating of metals	53	61	56	66	4.8	3.5	3.0	4.2	45.7	44.1	44.9	102.6
2893	Cutlery, hand tools and general hardware	199	175	163	170	30.1	23.9	26.2	27.3	293.9	296.0	258.5	265.1
2899	Other fabricated metal products n.e.c.	420	393	427	414	54.9	49.0	69.1	65.4	592.3	623.8	790.8	770.9
291	General purpose machinery	192	156	153	204	28.5	16.0	16.1	27.8	484.6	274.7	293.2	420.9
2911	Engines & turbines (not for transport equipment)	35	27	39	47	4.8	2.1	3.0	7.3	116.7	29.1	59.6	96.0
2912	Pumps, compressors, taps and valves	42	34	25	35	6.7	4.7	3.2	5.3	168.8	106.2	58.1	55.3
2913	Bearings, gears, gearing & driving elements	43	34	31	38	5.8	3.9	4.2	5.9	44.0	47.4	49.9	78.2
2914	Ovens, furnaces and furnace burners	7	6	3	11	2.4	0.3	0.2	2.0	18.4	1.3	2.1	19.0
2915	Lifting and handling equipment	8	6	7	14	2.6	1.2	1.3	1.9	47.6	46.6	65.4	81.2
2919	Other general purpose machinery	55	46	46	59	6.1	3.6	4.0	5.4	87.9	42.7	57.6	91.1
292	Special purpose machinery	76	81	94	118	9.5	10.0	10.5	15.9	118.2	141.8	189.4	340.5
2921	Agricultural and forestry machinery	24	21	22	32	2.2	1.7	2.0	3.4	23.3	28.0	31.9	62.0
2922	Machine tools	17	18	20	23	1.0	1.4	3.7	4.1	14.6	32.8	75.1	100.3
2923	Machinery for metallurgy	-	-	-	-	-	-	-	-	-	-	-	-
2924	Machinery for mining & construction	5	3	9	9	0.3	0.3	0.8	1.0	11.5	3.7	17.7	17.5
2925	Food/beverage/tobacco processing machinery	4	...	...	9	0.5	...	...	0.7	7.0	...	...	8.1
2926	Machinery for textile, apparel and leather	14	18	18	16	3.7	4.2	1.9	1.6	42.4	42.2	22.0	15.9
2927	Weapons and ammunition	-	3	3	4	-	0.1	0.1	3.1	-	0.3	1.0	96.7
2929	Other special purpose machinery	10	14	20	20	1.1	1.1	1.9	1.5	9.8	17.1	37.1	18.0

continued

Indonesia

ISIC Revision 3		Number of establishments					Number of employees					Wages and salaries paid to employees				
			(number)					(thousands)					(billions of Indonesian Rupiahs)			
ISIC	Industry	Note	2002	2003	2004	2005	Note	2002	2003	2004	2005	Note	2002	2003	2004	2005
2930	Domestic appliances n.e.c.		142	86	86	88		64.1	33.1	36.1	35.1		1163.4	431.3	370.9	482.9
3000	Office, accounting and computing machinery		6	5	4	7		1.0	1.0	0.6	3.7		5.5	5.6	3.8	29.4
3110	Electric motors, generators and transformers		28	30	27	33		5.4	6.9	6.4	12.2		106.5	147.3	112.2	230.6
3120	Electricity distribution & control apparatus		45	46	50	55		5.9	6.9	8.4	8.0		94.9	119.5	123.8	121.8
3130	Insulated wire and cable		61	63	68	73		21.3	22.1	22.9	22.5		379.6	358.7	380.4	358.7
3140	Accumulators, primary cells and batteries		27	25	32	37		7.6	8.4	10.9	12.9		202.3	178.4	254.5	221.3
3150	Lighting equipment and electric lamps		22	19	18	27		6.1	3.5	4.2	9.5		83.8	55.9	41.9	101.7
3190	Other electrical equipment n.e.c.		26	25	12	27		12.4	12.7	8.9	16.1		220.9	262.5	121.3	485.4
3210	Electronic valves, tubes, etc.		102	141	156	131		45.1	74.4	86.9	92.8		744.1	1185.9	1298.5	1930.8
3220	TV/radio transmitters; line comm. apparatus		12	15	13	11		7.2	6.0	6.2	6.1		95.6	81.3	50.1	91.1
3230	TV and radio receivers and associated goods		43	43	44	49		30.6	38.9	37.9	40.9		424.8	728.8	396.0	829.1
331	Medical, measuring, testing appliances, etc.		14	11	11	26		2.2	4.1	2.7	5.8		25.4	71.2	29.2	111.5
3311	Medical, surgical and orthopaedic equipment		8	4	4	16		1.7	2.0	2.2	4.4		15.5	35.1	22.6	74.8
3312	Measuring/testing/navigating appliances,etc.		5	4	4	7		0.4	0.3	0.3	0.5		5.4	5.7	4.9	4.9
3313	Industrial process control equipment		-	-	-	-		-	-	-	-		-	-	-	-
3320	Optical instruments & photographic equipment		2	4	1	9		0.9	2.9	0.9	10.6		7.9	21.9	8.3	219.6
3330	Watches and clocks		12	11	10	12		1.3	1.1	0.6	1.1		9.4	7.6	5.9	9.6
3410	Motor vehicles		13	12	13	16		10.8	12.5	19.0	20.4		404.4	653.9	663.6	1413.5
3420	Automobile bodies, trailers & semi-trailers		76	78	69	76		11.2	11.6	10.1	11.2		67.8	76.9	72.7	120.6
3430	Parts/accessories for automobiles		167	157	167	170		37.0	39.4	42.6	40.8		619.4	836.0	890.0	785.7
351	Building and repairing of ships and boats		123	114	101	116		15.1	16.0	13.5	13.4		135.6	189.0	155.0	301.7
3511	Building and repairing of ships		123	114	100	116		15.1	16.0	13.0	13.4		135.6	189.0	148.4	301.7
3512	Building/repairing of pleasure/sport. boats		-	-	-	-		-	-	-	-		-	-	-	-
3520	Railway/tramway locomotives & rolling stock		-	-	3	4		-	-	0.1	0.9		-	-	0.3	26.5
3530	Aircraft and spacecraft		-	-	-	1		-	-	-	9.8		-	-	-	111.7
359	Transport equipment n.e.c.		162	171	169	176		34.0	39.6	33.3	34.8		320.3	706.9	457.7	636.8
3591	Motorcycles		95	108	113	123		25.6	32.4	27.5	29.0		240.4	630.9	415.8	564.6
3592	Bicycles and invalid carriages		66	62	55	51		7.2	6.1	5.8	5.7		63.1	54.0	41.5	71.3
3599	Other transport equipment n.e.c.		-	-	-	-		-	-	-	-		-	-	-	-
3610	Furniture		1343	1318	1307	1340		168.1	168.0	166.1	167.2		1184.6	1330.2	1347.3	1430.1
369	Manufacturing n.e.c.		479	473	475	525		99.4	92.2	90.0	93.6		897.8	855.2	859.4	818.1
3691	Jewellery and related articles		84	85	97	107		10.9	8.9	10.4	12.5		59.6	52.9	93.8	120.3
3692	Musical instruments		13	16	17	20		7.1	7.7	8.8	10.2		97.8	92.5	93.4	75.0
3693	Sports goods		36	39	45	49		3.5	3.3	3.8	4.2		15.9	21.9	26.4	28.6
3694	Games and toys		83	84	77	93		30.7	30.2	24.4	19.8		306.7	341.1	337.7	194.5
3699	Other manufacturing n.e.c.		260	247	236	252		47.1	41.7	42.1	46.8		417.2	340.8	305.0	398.8
3710	Recycling of metal waste and scrap		...	...	...	3		...	...	...	0.1		...	...	...	0.1
3720	Recycling of non-metal waste and scrap		29	55	55	52		1.6	2.4	2.4	2.6		10.9	17.2	16.4	22.6
D	Total manufacturing		21146	20324	20685	20729		4364.9	4273.9	4325.0	4226.6		46405.1	60550.3	53068.1	58121.3

a/ 2694 includes 2695.
b/ 2699 includes 2696.

Indonesia

ISIC Revision 3		Output in producers' prices					Value added in factor values					Gross fixed capital formation		
			(billions of Indonesian Rupiahs)					(billions of Indonesian Rupiahs)					(billions of Indonesian Rupiahs)	
ISIC	Industry	Note	2002	2003	2004	2005	Note	2002	2003	2004	2005	Note	2004	2005
151	Processed meat,fish,fruit,vegetables,fats		57985	67774	75457	118937		14465	15669	21058	33663		26371	36974
1511	Processing/preserving of meat		710	1011	1291	947		291	373	335	486		131	239
1512	Processing/preserving of fish		9209	11156	13221	22760		2046	2272	2990	5290		4390	2700
1513	Processing/preserving of fruit & vegetables		169	246	286	1539		83	127	119	575		107	581
1514	Vegetable and animal oils and fats		47454	54199	60189	92852		11951	12763	17491	27059		21735	33290
1520	Dairy products		...	5751	7583	9234		...	2168	2255	2512		985	1183
153	Grain mill products; starches; animal feeds		18747	18946	27445	32177		5226	3733	4272	4661		6938	103069
1531	Grain mill products		2916	2583	2754	3638		633	530	464	722		572	732
1532	Starches and starch products		4490	4573	4991	11256		1226	838	873	1255		2610	2836
1533	Prepared animal feeds		10960	11095	13665	17282		3245	2254	2693	2683		3753	99500
154	Other food products		28865	30894	32206	37459		10811	12477	12387	15046		83056	85075
1541	Bakery products		5352	3712	3255	5099		1485	1289	973	1299		815	936
1542	Sugar		8074	9412	8716	10148		4121	4647	4649	5158		3133	2717
1543	Cocoa, chocolate and sugar confectionery		2345	2735	3332	2199		738	790	624	762		1185	1224
1544	Macaroni, noodles & similar products		4020	4057	3442	4710		1018	1267	887	829		736	792
1549	Other food products n.e.c.		9035	10969	13450	15303		3437	4480	5250	6997		77184	79405
155	Beverages		3427	3674	4102	6246		1743	2002	2053	3018		6204	6994
1551	Distilling, rectifying & blending of spirits		21	6	6	13		14	3	4	9		1	10
1552	Wines		6	...	...	141		4	...	...	55		...	19
1553	Malt liquors and malt		-	...	...	281		-	...	...	32		...	424
1554	Soft drinks; mineral waters		3389	3645	4063	5810		1719	1992	2032	2921		6197	6541
1600	Tobacco products		52972	54230	50293	59377		23544	39320	37154	40051		8463	9681
171	Spinning, weaving and finishing of textiles		58847	61514	61346	76864		19580	19378	20301	20283		31107	29701
1711	Textile fibre preparation; textile weaving		50307	49275	41087	62500		17039	15158	13858	16234		18402	23772
1712	Finishing of textiles		8540	12239	20259	14365		2542	4220	6443	4049		12705	5929
172	Other textiles		2401	3801	5304	5826		736	1455	1784	1754		1433	11982
1721	Made-up textile articles, except apparel		1309	2794	3658	4341		413	1094	1205	1262		440	11455
1722	Carpets and rugs		401	238	254	390		81	58	47	70		126	183
1723	Cordage, rope, twine and netting		261	230	296	302		115	94	110	83		404	163
1729	Other textiles n.e.c.		429	538	1081	791		125	209	419	336		457	181
1730	Knitted and crocheted fabrics and articles		6069	7541	17414	10246		1657	2442	3930	4175		1908	206509
1810	Wearing apparel, except fur apparel		27848	31493	29864	36805		12011	12587	12069	11805		7299	6831
1820	Dressing & dyeing of fur; processing of fur		-	-	4	1		-	-	2	1		6	-
191	Tanning, dressing and processing of leather		4585	2610	2595	6852		1022	930	1162	1403		392	359
1911	Tanning and dressing of leather		2237	1891	1986	6001		396	651	923	1121		282	245
1912	Luggage, handbags, etc.; saddlery & harness		2348	719	609	831		625	279	240	274		111	113
1920	Footwear		18864	17786	16448	16020		6215	7107	5772	6283		3267	3252
2010	Sawmilling and planing of wood		5357	6676	4138	5200		2989	1833	961	1225		928	1047
202	Products of wood, cork, straw, etc.		34337	36178	35448	39555		14918	14993	14858	14776		12452	10197
2021	Veneer sheets, plywood, particle board, etc.		25264	27491	25149	30013		11302	11760	10827	11841		9596	6706
2022	Builders' carpentry and joinery		6892	6678	7524	7898		2635	2288	2661	2117		2260	3087
2023	Wooden containers		23	45	56	106		8	18	17	44		15	65
2029	Other wood products; articles of cork/straw		1954	1693	1654	1538		880	839	598	773		561	339
210	Paper and paper products		48089	37773	41979	68226		14451	15215	15763	24128		17037	49301
2101	Pulp, paper and paperboard		37559	27572	34626	59974		11927	12591	13547	21582		15636	38536
2102	Corrugated paper and paperboard		9569	9550	6548	6758		2156	2413	1982	2143		1237	10533
2109	Other articles of paper and paperboard		961	649	805	1495		368	210	234	403		165	233
221	Publishing		3875	5878	10626	12763		2348	2874	4540	4607		2020	3388
2211	Publishing of books and other publications		3509	3926	4884	8477		2083	1846	1917	2426		749	1921
2212	Publishing of newspapers, journals, etc.		111	1591	2862	3117		42	929	1517	1774		720	984
2213	Publishing of recorded media		-	35	-	-		-	16	-	-		-	-
2219	Other publishing		226	318	2849	1151		215	80	1089	400		518	484

continued

Indonesia

ISIC Revision 3		Output in producers' prices					Value added in factor values					Gross fixed capital formation		
			(billions of Indonesian Rupiahs)					(billions of Indonesian Rupiahs)					(billions of Indonesian Rupiahs)	
ISIC	Industry	Note	2002	2003	2004	2005	Note	2002	2003	2004	2005	Note	2004	2005
222	Printing and related service activities		2018	1449	1074	1388		569	504	350	401		109	66
2221	Printing		1960	1414	1060	1383		533	480	342	397		50	60
2222	Service activities related to printing		58	34	14	5		36	24	8	4		60	5
2230	Reproduction of recorded media		-	-	-	5		-	-	-	2		1	-
2310	Coke oven products		27	...	57	96		20	...	31	31		22	22
2320	Refined petroleum products		73	678	1066	1927		34	233	225	662		553	839
2330	Processing of nuclear fuel		...	...	...	...		...	...	...	...		...	...
241	Basic chemicals		38110	28604	38913	64100		9731	13134	12987	23625		11127	354254
2411	Basic chemicals, except fertilizers		25184	17823	23414	36864		5830	8800	7501	9282		5653	13637
2412	Fertilizers and nitrogen compounds		5257	4430	5806	15981		2432	2871	1333	9806		4194	339050
2413	Plastics in primary forms; synthetic rubber		7665	6346	9206	11251		1467	1461	4082	4535		1272	1561
242	Other chemicals		31485	37281	36922	42704		15000	16576	15104	19378		6690	12904
2421	Pesticides and other agro-chemical products		810	1413	3022	2184		328	551	1041	1100		275	303
2422	Paints, varnishes, printing ink and mastics		3850	3673	2716	4739		1211	1212	771	1430		351	428
2423	Pharmaceuticals, medicinal chemicals, etc.		16583	18372	17499	20137		8470	9296	8096	11545		3864	5818
2424	Soap, cleaning & cosmetic preparations		5230	6594	6965	7386		2976	2699	2601	3172		1043	1080
2429	Other chemical products n.e.c.		4704	6026	4531	8257		1923	1937	1470	2132		944	5275
2430	Man-made fibres		5504	9775	1851	3262		750	3557	596	393		469	3108
251	Rubber products		25006	26067	37491	65518		5879	6067	9784	11720		90641	8539
2511	Rubber tyres and tubes		22451	23675	32868	61612		4962	5087	8281	10460		89403	7276
2519	Other rubber products		2429	2296	4468	3906		888	962	1484	1260		1167	1263
2520	Plastic products		15759	17907	28670	32003		5074	6896	11894	10603		6774	7077
2610	Glass and glass products		...	3681	7240	9191		...	1907	2132	4406		2346	3434
269	Non-metallic mineral products n.e.c.		...	14092	20526	28093		...	7045	9757	14809		12755	20327
2691	Pottery, china and earthenware		...	2872	2768	3979		...	1405	1254	1460		2072	2823
2692	Refractory ceramic products		...	19	47	130		...	5	13	47		7	33
2693	Struct.non-refractory clay; ceramic products		...	476	595	1286		...	252	315	517		555	1076
2694	Cement, lime and plaster		...	9042a/	15476a/	20525a/		...	4552a/	7407a/	11824a/		9130a/	15353a/
2695	Articles of concrete, cement and plaster		...	...a/	...a/	...a/		...	...a/	...a/	...a/		...a/	...a/
2696	Cutting, shaping & finishing of stone		...	...b/	...b/	...b/		...	...b/	...b/	...b/		...b/	...b/
2699	Other non-metallic mineral products n.e.c.		...	1683b/	1640b/	2174b/		...	831b/	768b/	961b/		992b/	1042b/
2710	Basic iron and steel		32671	39311	43676	62129		8948	8051	7454	7676		7599	4306
2720	Basic precious and non-ferrous metals		8181	8061	8829	14031		1896	2743	3016	4461		2347	3164
273	Casting of metals		1255	605	6647	3761		479	259	1161	1906		419	600
2731	Casting of iron and steel		1177	548	5446	3539		436	242	863	1881		382	400
2732	Casting of non-ferrous metals		3	34	9	222		2	7	2	25		8	200
281	Struct.metal products;tanks;steam generators		4008	3064	7498	6325		1366	1536	3129	3288		769	1331
2811	Structural metal products		3373	2396	6760	4453		1074	1202	2733	2549		562	790
2812	Tanks, reservoirs and containers of metal		635	668	738	1872		291	334	396	740		207	541
2813	Steam generators		-	-	-	-		-	-	-	-		-	-
289	Other metal products; metal working services		97272	12289	14640	17867		4087	4684	4445	5668		3933	4740
2891	Metal forging/pressing/stamping/roll-forming		658	1044	932	2191		166	118	93	232		172	257
2892	Treatment & coating of metals		536	351	601	1136		169	232	200	400		1368	366
2893	Cutlery, hand tools and general hardware		2470	1439	2691	3201		934	567	1199	1285		379	1750
2899	Other fabricated metal products n.e.c.		93564	9373	10337	11327		2807	3706	2944	3746		2014	2227
291	General purpose machinery		6008	4924	3458	10228		2513	2025	1392	3286		1606	1796
2911	Engines & turbines (not for transport equipment)		779	252	843	1934		229	131	340	837		512	446
2912	Pumps, compressors, taps and valves		942	1088	484	1343		591	244	248	314		597	642
2913	Bearings, gears, gearing & driving elements		2265	2748	878	4181		1194	1263	407	1357		178	232
2914	Ovens, furnaces and furnace burners		10	1	9	267		6	1	4	139		7	78
2915	Lifting and handling equipment		568	540	908	1677		232	228	239	315		141	183
2919	Other general purpose machinery		1438	260	335	826		259	123	152	324		169	214

292	Special purpose machinery	630	1329	2025	2461	282	407	588	1452	658	1036
2921	Agricultural and forestry machinery	192	718	684	493	69	135	135	113	71	146
2922	Machine tools	71	225	383	1115	33	147	272	825	281	427
2923	Machinery for metallurgy	-	-	-	-	-	-	-	-	-	-
2924	Machinery for mining & construction	87	30	673	155	83	12	57	74	44	56
2925	Food/beverage/tobacco processing machinery	38	...	...	63	11	...	...	43	...	16
2926	Machinery for textile, apparel and leather	87	78	118	92	17	33	34	38	199	204
2927	Weapons and ammunition	-	1	6	343	-	1	3	236	1	116
2929	Other special purpose machinery	50	69	139	147	18	35	74	74	59	66
2930	Domestic appliances n.e.c.	5546	4663	5033	4143	1557	904	1917	2267	14407	14201
3000	Office, accounting and computing machinery	22	23	16	1762	15	16	11	645	-	163
3110	Electric motors, generators and transformers	1139	1879	2818	4045	638	782	746	1564	515	549
3120	Electricity distribution & control apparatus	879	850	2066	1552	293	442	744	755	251	273
3130	Insulated wire and cable	3833	3024	4767	4825	1001	1014	1149	1200	1162	1389
3140	Accumulators, primary cells and batteries	2908	3770	11431	8962	1049	1005	2434	3010	277	704
3150	Lighting equipment and electric lamps	1187	344	904	2592	449	126	482	863	152	308
3190	Other electrical equipment n.e.c.	2748	4068	7181	3559	683	783	1253	1968	29	900
3210	Electronic valves, tubes, etc.	16733	22531	29892	16836	9607	8960	10533	8662	2324	4367
3220	TV/radio transmitters; line comm. apparatus	234	1274	1510	2109	202	514	1074	790	184	218
3230	TV and radio receivers and associated goods	14299	15587	44247	9251	4415	6225	6215	6054	1457	980
331	Medical, measuring, testing appliances, etc.	74	246	555	1120	47	93	245	295	7	138
3311	Medical, surgical and orthopaedic equipment	40	187	501	313	24	48	209	160	4	63
3312	Measuring/testing/navigating appliances,etc.	29	33	40	95	22	29	30	41	2	7
3313	Industrial process control equipment	-	-	-	-	-	-	-	-	-	-
3320	Optical instruments & photographic equipment	41	205	29	1228	20	45	12	384	-	1053
3330	Watches and clocks	75	32	33	34	34	16	16	16	20	27
3410	Motor vehicles	41178	15914	35664	43077	20351	13393	22433	37236	3012	7217
3420	Automobile bodies, trailers & semi-trailers	821	1016	726	959	307	438	371	549	391	529
3430	Parts/accessories for automobiles	8532	10439	12658	19214	-314	4552	5758	5196	3617	3759
351	Building and repairing of ships and boats	1946	2846	2168	4299	1039	1656	889	2522	615	1957
3511	Building and repairing of ships	1946	2846	2087	4299	1039	1656	880	2522	614	1957
3512	Building/repairing of pleasure/sport. boats	-	-	-	-	-	-	-	-	-	-
3520	Railway/tramway locomotives & rolling stock	-	-	4	128	-	-	2	33	1	5
3530	Aircraft and spacecraft	-	-	-	1250	-	-	-	249	-	755
359	Transport equipment n.e.c.	23369	33345	27813	30544	9622	15891	12723	11298	2416	3011
3591	Motorcycles	19899	28823	27205	30163	8588	14506	12532	11103	2345	2946
3592	Bicycles and invalid carriages	242	440	607	376	145	222	190	194	71	63
3599	Other transport equipment n.e.c.	-	-	-	-	-	-	-	-	-	-
3610	Furniture	9729	10378	9906	9613	3736	4263	3784	3703	5047	7811
369	Manufacturing n.e.c.	7024	4594	8041	10357	2178	1816	3139	3946	996	1011
3691	Jewellery and related articles	3104	1075	1110	1671	737	370	435	521	194	207
3692	Musical instruments	423	683	2134	3477	92	217	834	1404	287	245
3693	Sports goods	144	146	326	190	72	77	90	84	41	68
3694	Games and toys	1101	1112	2593	2974	389	448	886	1165	61	82
3699	Other manufacturing n.e.c.	2248	1564	1870	2036	885	699	890	770	413	406
3710	Recycling of metal waste and scrap	...	...	...	2	...	...	...	1	...	-
3720	Recycling of non-metal waste and scrap	122	223	199	256	30	53	36	54	71	91
D	Total manufacturing	882476	838804	985946	1088682	286787	326784	358910	396438	437159	1044537

a/ 2694 includes 2695.
b/ 2699 includes 2696.

Indonesia

ISIC Revision 3			Index numbers of industrial production											
			(2000=100)											
ISIC	Industry	Note	1995	1996	1997	1998	1999	2000	2001	2002	2003	2004	2005	2006
15	Food and beverages		117	122	118	109	102	100	98	94	107	112	135	151
16	Tobacco products		...	...	...	...	...	...	...	...	...	...	...	...
17	Textiles		107	107	104	90	98	100	91	87	78	73	63	67
18	Wearing apparel, fur		107	107	104	90	98	100	91	94	118	157	145	242
19	Leather, leather products and footwear		146	144	124	103	99	100	101	102	91	84	63	61
20	Wood products (excl. furniture)		145	143	141	114	106	100	91	95	101	101	103	61
21	Paper and paper products		61	71	85	88	101	100	75	67	63	62	63	52
22	Printing and publishing		251	222	178	175	116	100	117	117	168	180	176	211
23	Coke,refined petroleum products,nuclear fuel		94	100	107	98	103	100	96	86	94	114	192	209
24	Chemicals and chemical products		...	...	...	...	...	...	...	...	...	...	...	...
25	Rubber and plastics products		...	...	...	...	...	...	...	...	...	...	...	...
26	Non-metallic mineral products		145	121	127	99	106	100	111	131	108	114	110	123
27	Basic metals		91	91	95	74	82	100	102	90	71	75	73	89
28	Fabricated metal products		62	67	64	41	55	100	111	96	98	111	109	120
29	Machinery and equipment n.e.c.		727	668	429	132	129	100	131	324	480	619	421	408
30	Office, accounting and computing machinery		...	...	...	...	...	...	...	...	...	...	...	...
31	Electrical machinery and apparatus		101	93	114	80	89	100	107	91	60	56	56	55
32	Radio,television and communication equipment		...	...	...	...	...	...	...	...	...	...	...	...
33	Medical, precision and optical instruments		...	...	...	...	...	...	...	...	...	...	...	...
34	Motor vehicles, trailers, semi-trailers		158	151	201	53	51	100	132	117	136	164	223	119
35	Other transport equipment		...	...	...	...	...	...	...	...	...	...	...	...
36	Furniture; manufacturing n.e.c.		567	641	615	384	216	100	147	90	109	128	145	142
37	Recycling		...	...	...	...	...	...	...	...	...	...	...	...
D	Total manufacturing		109	110	116	95	97	100	99	92	114	117	119	116

Iran (Islamic Republic of)

Supplier of information:
Statistical Centre of Iran, Teheran.

Basic source of data:
Census; sample survey.

Major deviations from ISIC (Revision 3):
None reported.

Reference period:
Fiscal year.

Scope:
All establishments.

Method of data collection:
Direct interview in the field.

Type of enumeration:
Sample survey is conducted for establishments with less than 10 persons engaged; establishments with 10 or more persons engaged are completely enumerated.

Adjusted for non-response:
Yes.

Concepts and definitions of variables:
Wages and salaries includes employers' contributions paid to social security, pension and insurance schemes as well as the benefits received by employees under these schemes and severance and termination pay.

Related national publications:
Survey results of manufacturing establishments with 10 to 49 workers; Survey results of manufacturing establishments with 50 workers and more, both published by the Statistical Centre of Iran, Teheran.

ISIC Revision 3		Number of establishments					Number of employees					Wages and salaries paid to employees				
			(number)					(thousands)					(billions of Iranian Rials)			
ISIC	Industry	Note	2002	2003	2004	2005	Note	2002	2003	2004	2005	Note	2002	2003	2004	2005
151	Processed meat,fish,fruit,vegetables,fats		685	743	735	751		43.1	45.3	46.7	48.1		850.0	1057.8	1225.5	1523.7
1511	Processing/preserving of meat		296	334	325	332		13.6	15.6	16.0	17.4		240.4	308.8	369.7	482.2
1512	Processing/preserving of fish		46	49	54	56		3.9	4.0	4.1	4.3		77.8	92.2	106.6	123.4
1513	Processing/preserving of fruit & vegetables		302	319	311	316		14.2	14.2	15.3	15.2		252.0	309.4	363.9	422.4
1514	Vegetable and animal oils and fats		41	41	45	47		11.4	11.6	11.3	11.2		279.8	347.4	385.2	495.6
1520	Dairy products		178	198	217	218		12.6	14.5	17.6	18.9		333.4	395.1	564.7	695.7
153	Grain mill products; starches; animal feeds		404	427	421	427		13.2	14.3	14.2	14.1		251.9	319.0	371.7	440.6
1531	Grain mill products		296	312	311	310		9.5	9.9	10.1	9.8		171.5	209.1	255.5	290.0
1532	Starches and starch products		24	23	26	28		1.4	1.3	1.2	1.3		31.1	38.2	36.4	40.6
1533	Prepared animal feeds		84	92	84	89		2.3	3.1	2.9	3.1		49.3	71.7	79.8	110.0
154	Other food products		1184	1234	1199	1180		66.5	69.8	67.8	68.6		1437.0	1659.9	1988.0	2288.6
1541	Bakery products		505	515	497	470		18.8	19.2	19.9	17.8		401.8	432.6	556.2	474.6
1542	Sugar		71	68	60	77		26.2	25.7	24.0	25.1		696.0	764.6	895.8	1052.6
1543	Cocoa, chocolate and sugar confectionery		68	71	72	72		3.9	3.8	4.5	6.3		62.7	63.2	91.9	248.9
1544	Macaroni, noodles & similar products		165	164	153	144		3.3	3.7	3.7	3.5		47.0	61.4	80.5	93.2
1549	Other food products n.e.c.		375	416	417	417		14.4	17.5	15.6	16.0		229.5	338.1	363.6	419.3
155	Beverages		84	98	101	105		13.8	14.9	13.7	13.8		381.2	496.4	597.0	590.4
1551	Distilling, rectifying & blending of spirits		16	15	13	10		0.6	0.7	0.6	0.4		7.9	14.0	17.9	17.6
1552	Wines		-	-	-	-		-	-	-	-		-	-	-	-
1553	Malt liquors and malt		4	3	4	4		0.7	0.6	0.6	0.7		25.9	26.6	36.0	40.9
1554	Soft drinks; mineral waters		64	80	84	91		12.4	13.6	12.5	12.8		347.4	455.8	543.0	531.9
1600	Tobacco products		2	2	2	2		7.3	10.5	10.6	5.5		282.3	491.5	305.2	196.4
171	Spinning, weaving and finishing of textiles		785	798	772	758		91.8	82.0	77.6	71.2		1963.2	2028.7	2074.7	2265.2
1711	Textile fibre preparation; textile weaving		670	688	670	656		88.2	78.0	73.6	67.1		1904.8	1953.7	1974.6	2145.7
1712	Finishing of textiles		115	110	102	102		3.6	4.0	4.0	4.1		58.4	75.0	100.1	119.5
172	Other textiles		881	854	803	803		30.7	32.7	31.0	30.1		467.8	586.6	699.5	827.1
1721	Made-up textile articles, except apparel		88	89	82	83		5.1	6.5	5.7	5.4		80.1	137.5	157.7	170.0
1722	Carpets and rugs		754	732	693	696		24.3	25.1	24.3	23.8		367.1	429.5	520.2	632.1
1723	Cordage, rope, twine and netting		9	7	7	6		0.5	0.4	0.4	0.4		7.7	8.3	8.6	11.4
1729	Other textiles n.e.c.		30	26	21	18		0.8	0.6	0.6	0.5		13.0	11.2	13.1	13.7
1730	Knitted and crocheted fabrics and articles		95	86	87	65		2.2	1.7	2.1	1.8		33.4	31.4	42.7	45.7
1810	Wearing apparel, except fur apparel		368	294	231	205		8.3	8.1	6.8	6.3		119.4	145.1	149.5	154.2
1820	Dressing & dyeing of fur; processing of fur		2	1	2	1		-	-	0.1	-		0.4	0.3	1.4	0.3
191	Tanning, dressing and processing of leather		120	106	103	103		3.2	2.6	2.9	2.7		51.2	46.2	61.4	64.8
1911	Tanning and dressing of leather		100	94	94	89		2.7	2.4	2.7	2.4		43.7	40.9	56.2	59.6
1912	Luggage, handbags, etc.; saddlery & harness		20	12	9	14		0.5	0.3	0.2	0.2		7.5	5.3	5.2	5.2
1920	Footwear		255	205	171	135		10.0	6.6	4.9	4.8		176.7	122.5	103.9	115.7
2010	Sawmilling and planing of wood		19	20	16	17		2.8	2.6	2.4	2.3		56.9	90.2	90.1	86.5
202	Products of wood, cork, straw, etc.		209	183	153	134		7.0	6.3	5.5	5.0		141.3	162.3	174.8	185.3
2021	Veneer sheets, plywood, particle board, etc.		60	70	62	55		3.9	4.0	3.6	3.6		94.5	125.9	138.1	151.9
2022	Builders' carpentry and joinery		85	59	48	39		1.6	1.4	1.2	0.8		23.7	22.1	23.9	20.5
2023	Wooden containers		36	32	27	23		0.5	0.5	0.4	0.3		6.8	8.2	6.9	7.1
2029	Other wood products; articles of cork/straw		28	22	16	17		1.0	0.4	0.3	0.3		16.4	6.1	5.9	5.8
210	Paper and paper products		282	285	296	295		18.0	17.6	17.9	16.7		516.7	552.9	578.8	722.6
2101	Pulp, paper and paperboard		50	52	53	56		7.8	6.9	6.4	6.0		308.0	295.7	266.7	370.3
2102	Corrugated paper and paperboard		149	156	161	157		6.0	6.9	7.2	6.5		130.2	174.2	204.7	194.0
2109	Other articles of paper and paperboard		83	77	82	82		4.2	3.9	4.2	4.3		78.5	83.0	107.4	158.4
221	Publishing		146	121	99	99		9.8	10.0	7.5	7.5		248.9	311.1	293.7	341.6
2211	Publishing of books and other publications		71	46	42	40		3.7	3.7	2.7	2.7		99.8	113.5	84.3	109.8
2212	Publishing of newspapers, journals, etc.		67	70	53	55		5.7	6.2	4.7	4.7		140.1	195.9	206.9	229.2
2213	Publishing of recorded media		1	-	-	-		0.1	-	-	-		2.7	-	-	-
2219	Other publishing		7	5	4	4		0.3	0.1	0.1	0.1		6.3	1.7	2.5	2.7

222	Printing and related service activities	281	253	233	214	6.1	5.9	5.5	5.1	102.9	129.0	132.8	150.2
2221	Printing	214	196	184	172	5.0	4.8	4.7	4.5	86.1	106.6	114.3	131.8
2222	Service activities related to printing	67	57	49	42	1.1	1.2	0.9	0.7	16.8	22.4	18.5	18.4
2230	Reproduction of recorded media	-	-	-	1	-	-	-	0.1	-	-	-	1.7
2310	Coke oven products	1	1	3	3	0.2	0.2	0.2	0.2	4.9	5.4	5.1	5.3
2320	Refined petroleum products	85	95	115	112	17.4	16.3	16.3	14.8	1028.0	1127.9	1512.5	1570.1
2330	Processing of nuclear fuel	-	-	-	-	-	-	-	-	-	-	-	-
241	Basic chemicals	229	254	299	333	23.9	23.2	22.7	23.4	1110.6	1296.8	1391.4	1457.0
2411	Basic chemicals, except fertilizers	129	138	168	182	6.2	6.2	7.1	7.8	208.0	232.2	342.5	377.2
2412	Fertilizers and nitrogen compounds	33	44	47	62	7.3	6.6	5.7	5.5	362.7	378.5	429.5	362.6
2413	Plastics in primary forms; synthetic rubber	67	72	84	89	10.4	10.3	9.9	10.1	539.9	686.2	619.4	717.1
242	Other chemicals	550	554	557	558	42.7	46.0	45.2	47.1	1037.8	1449.7	1756.0	2061.7
2421	Pesticides and other agro-chemical products	18	19	20	24	1.6	1.7	1.2	2.2	31.7	42.5	37.5	81.9
2422	Paints, varnishes, printing ink and mastics	155	145	148	148	6.6	6.9	6.8	6.7	136.8	180.1	203.9	223.2
2423	Pharmaceuticals, medicinal chemicals, etc.	133	137	146	145	17.2	18.1	18.4	18.7	489.2	688.2	840.7	973.2
2424	Soap, cleaning & cosmetic preparations	150	152	146	146	12.2	12.1	11.9	12.9	284.7	322.5	460.8	509.1
2429	Other chemical products n.e.c.	94	101	97	95	5.1	7.4	6.9	6.6	95.4	216.5	213.2	274.4
2430	Man-made fibres	20	19	23	24	3.7	3.1	2.8	2.7	220.2	181.7	129.4	165.0
251	Rubber products	134	146	134	133	17.7	18.8	17.9	16.9	537.0	657.5	826.4	794.6
2511	Rubber tyres and tubes	28	27	29	30	11.0	12.3	11.9	11.6	412.3	510.5	660.6	633.6
2519	Other rubber products	106	119	105	103	6.7	6.5	6.0	5.3	124.7	146.9	165.8	161.0
2520	Plastic products	696	742	735	752	24.3	28.3	28.2	29.1	463.3	603.3	775.3	867.6
2610	Glass and glass products	187	175	155	146	14.6	14.4	14.5	14.0	340.2	372.4	478.8	516.4
269	Non-metallic mineral products n.e.c.	3325	3444	3453	3392	127.9	134.6	134.4	130.8	2934.3	3731.3	4602.4	5032.3
2691	Pottery, china and earthenware	75	73	77	69	13.0	11.9	12.2	11.5	253.4	296.6	356.9	384.6
2692	Refractory ceramic products	29	30	28	32	2.7	3.2	2.7	3.1	93.6	111.6	101.1	144.9
2693	Struct.non-refractory clay; ceramic products	1528	1579	1596	1554	54.7	59.6	59.0	57.4	1010.7	1281.8	1621.6	1728.0
2694	Cement, lime and plaster	116	120	130	134	21.1	20.7	21.4	20.0	835.3	1100.8	1437.3	1497.6
2695	Articles of concrete, cement and plaster	363	379	351	350	14.3	15.2	14.5	14.0	360.3	431.2	481.8	554.8
2696	Cutting, shaping & finishing of stone	868	872	847	828	12.7	12.8	12.5	11.9	202.8	244.7	272.4	305.7
2699	Other non-metallic mineral products n.e.c.	346	391	424	425	9.4	11.3	12.1	13.0	178.1	264.6	331.2	416.8
2710	Basic iron and steel	165	175	184	198	44.6	42.7	43.4	42.8	1854.0	2328.1	2574.5	2850.2
2720	Basic precious and non-ferrous metals	145	148	161	160	16.1	16.1	16.5	17.4	661.5	788.4	1191.2	1368.5
273	Casting of metals	236	244	228	214	13.8	15.0	14.9	13.8	339.6	431.7	485.4	557.6
2731	Casting of iron and steel	177	188	177	169	11.7	13.0	12.4	11.7	303.8	387.6	410.9	444.6
2732	Casting of non-ferrous metals	59	56	51	45	2.1	2.0	2.5	2.1	35.8	44.1	74.5	113.0
281	Struct.metal products;tanks;steam generators	317	346	350	350	22.7	25.7	26.5	26.2	610.3	854.7	996.6	970.3
2811	Structural metal products	189	202	213	220	10.8	12.9	14.7	14.3	245.5	311.4	486.6	495.0
2812	Tanks, reservoirs and containers of metal	126	143	135	128	11.8	12.8	11.7	11.8	362.9	542.6	506.1	471.1
2813	Steam generators	2	1	2	2	0.1	-	0.1	0.1	1.9	0.7	4.0	4.1
289	Other metal products; metal working services	1003	993	915	912	40.5	41.7	41.1	42.4	839.8	1007.9	1233.3	1452.2
2891	Metal forging/pressing/stamping/roll-forming	60	60	51	47	1.3	1.4	1.7	1.5	23.9	26.7	43.9	44.7
2892	Treatment & coating of metals	305	295	277	275	8.4	8.6	9.0	9.6	182.0	195.5	267.9	293.4
2893	Cutlery, hand tools and general hardware	85	81	80	78	4.6	4.2	4.5	4.6	76.0	94.5	104.6	126.3
2899	Other fabricated metal products n.e.c.	553	557	507	512	26.1	27.4	25.8	26.7	558.0	691.2	816.9	987.8
291	General purpose machinery	449	475	443	442	35.5	34.5	34.3	34.8	844.8	915.9	1260.6	1360.0
2911	Engines & turbines (not for transport equipment)	20	22	18	17	6.0	3.6	4.1	4.0	182.8	151.8	265.7	273.0
2912	Pumps, compressors, taps and valves	145	154	143	141	8.8	9.2	8.2	7.9	187.9	226.3	231.7	251.1
2913	Bearings, gears, gearing & driving elements	37	37	35	38	1.9	2.0	1.6	1.7	48.1	54.7	65.3	74.3
2914	Ovens, furnaces and furnace burners	32	37	33	33	2.3	2.5	2.3	2.2	47.6	55.9	55.7	69.7
2915	Lifting and handling equipment	70	81	70	68	4.9	5.4	5.5	5.3	132.9	143.9	188.6	216.6
2919	Other general purpose machinery	145	144	144	145	11.7	11.7	12.6	13.6	245.5	283.4	453.7	475.2
292	Special purpose machinery	500	519	488	461	25.9	27.6	26.3	27.2	669.2	847.9	975.1	1245.7
2921	Agricultural and forestry machinery	97	104	94	95	6.9	6.9	6.3	7.3	208.6	259.6	316.1	451.2
2922	Machine tools	116	110	98	87	6.9	7.0	6.2	5.0	205.6	243.6	177.7	205.0
2923	Machinery for metallurgy	11	10	8	8	0.3	0.3	0.3	0.3	4.6	5.3	8.0	10.0
2924	Machinery for mining & construction	67	69	63	61	4.0	4.3	4.6	5.3	102.0	130.6	228.4	274.5
2925	Food/beverage/tobacco processing machinery	91	90	92	87	2.8	3.1	3.3	3.4	49.1	63.8	80.7	101.9
2926	Machinery for textile, apparel and leather	23	31	31	27	1.4	1.5	1.5	1.5	30.0	44.6	47.3	64.6
2927	Weapons and ammunition	-	-	-	-	-	-	-	-	-	-	-	-
2929	Other special purpose machinery	95	105	102	96	3.7	4.6	4.2	4.5	69.4	100.4	116.8	138.4

continued

Iran (Islamic Republic of)

ISIC Revision 3		Number of establishments					Number of employees					Wages and salaries paid to employees			
			(number)					(thousands)					(billions of Iranian Rials)		
ISIC	Industry	Note	2002	2003	2004	2005	Note	2002	2003	2004	2005	Note	2002	2003	2004	2005
2930	Domestic appliances n.e.c.		239	247	254	241		24.7	23.2	23.0	21.3		578.1	700.0	807.5	793.2
3000	Office, accounting and computing machinery		50	49	39	36		2.5	2.7	2.9	2.9		45.3	54.5	94.7	113.9
3110	Electric motors, generators and transformers		97	99	89	89		9.7	9.3	8.5	8.5		284.9	352.2	365.8	373.2
3120	Electricity distribution & control apparatus		145	157	156	160		10.9	11.3	11.9	11.9		213.2	292.3	384.5	420.6
3130	Insulated wire and cable		99	116	109	110		10.1	10.2	9.9	9.6		244.9	320.2	369.4	415.0
3140	Accumulators, primary cells and batteries		9	10	12	10		2.2	2.2	3.6	3.9		47.6	73.7	145.1	216.6
3150	Lighting equipment and electric lamps		71	76	70	67		4.9	4.8	4.9	4.6		96.2	109.5	119.4	140.6
3190	Other electrical equipment n.e.c.		62	63	53	51		5.2	6.5	7.3	7.5		117.0	150.7	252.8	282.0
3210	Electronic valves, tubes, etc.		30	38	31	33		1.4	1.6	1.2	1.1		29.0	41.0	34.6	37.8
3220	TV/radio transmitters; line comm. apparatus		20	17	16	15		3.8	4.8	4.6	4.2		89.1	168.9	181.2	221.8
3230	TV and radio receivers and associated goods		27	27	30	28		5.9	4.0	4.0	3.6		186.5	145.6	184.0	155.1
331	Medical, measuring, testing appliances, etc.		147	160	152	144		10.5	11.8	12.0	11.0		195.8	295.5	353.7	317.9
3311	Medical, surgical and orthopaedic equipment		110	122	116	108		6.5	7.0	7.1	6.7		118.3	149.1	175.6	181.4
3312	Measuring/testing/navigating appliances,etc.		32	35	34	34		3.9	4.7	4.8	4.3		75.8	145.1	176.7	134.3
3313	Industrial process control equipment		5	3	2	2		0.1	0.1	0.1	0.1		1.7	1.3	1.4	2.2
3320	Optical instruments & photographic equipment		10	12	13	13		0.5	0.6	0.6	0.6		11.8	14.8	19.3	20.8
3330	Watches and clocks		10	10	11	10		0.5	0.5	0.6	0.5		6.9	8.2	15.6	15.5
3410	Motor vehicles		18	18	21	21		41.3	43.6	44.1	47.9		1900.1	2780.2	3418.8	4134.8
3420	Automobile bodies, trailers & semi-trailers		55	48	48	51		2.8	3.9	4.8	4.6		51.4	94.7	164.3	182.0
3430	Parts/accessories for automobiles		512	609	631	611		41.6	53.2	58.2	57.4		977.5	1506.9	2023.4	2228.8
351	Building and repairing of ships and boats		16	19	16	18		6.4	7.1	7.1	7.3		228.7	314.2	283.4	349.1
3511	Building and repairing of ships		4	4	4	5		5.9	6.5	6.5	6.7		218.9	300.9	269.3	332.0
3512	Building/repairing of pleasure/sport. boats		12	15	12	13		0.5	0.6	0.5	0.6		9.8	13.3	14.1	17.1
3520	Railway/tramway locomotives & rolling stock		18	20	18	20		3.8	3.5	3.3	3.7		102.3	121.2	143.1	132.0
3530	Aircraft and spacecraft		4	4	3	2		3.2	3.2	3.2	3.2		132.2	148.6	168.8	191.6
359	Transport equipment n.e.c.		123	128	162	136		8.4	10.9	10.6	9.5		157.9	272.1	303.6	285.8
3591	Motorcycles		84	91	130	113		6.9	9.5	9.5	8.5		133.6	239.1	269.9	253.5
3592	Bicycles and invalid carriages		30	28	22	15		1.1	1.1	0.8	0.6		20.5	25.3	23.3	19.8
3599	Other transport equipment n.e.c.		9	9	10	8		0.3	0.3	0.3	0.3		3.9	7.8	10.4	12.5
3610	Furniture		371	328	314	309		12.0	12.1	11.7	12.3		180.6	258.4	332.0	450.6
369	Manufacturing n.e.c.		142	144	139	130		5.1	5.0	5.0	5.0		102.5	102.2	117.5	136.0
3691	Jewellery and related articles		17	18	17	14		0.4	0.5	0.5	0.4		5.8	9.6	11.9	8.5
3692	Musical instruments		4	3	2	2		0.1	0.1	-	-		1.1	1.2	1.0	1.0
3693	Sports goods		8	7	8	6		0.3	0.2	0.3	0.2		4.0	4.7	6.0	4.4
3694	Games and toys		13	13	10	6		0.3	0.3	0.3	0.1		4.1	4.2	5.1	2.6
3699	Other manufacturing n.e.c.		100	103	102	102		4.1	3.9	3.9	4.3		87.5	82.5	93.5	119.5
3710	Recycling of metal waste and scrap		-	3	2	-		-	0.1	-	-		-	0.8	0.7	-
3720	Recycling of non-metal waste and scrap		8	9	10	10		0.1	0.1	0.1	0.2		1.1	1.6	2.7	3.8
D	Total manufacturing		16305	16649	16283	16018		1035.4	1069.7	1063.1	1049.1		26890.9	33554.5	39935.2	44589.2

ISIC Revision 3		Output in producers' prices (billions of Iranian Rials)					Value added in producers' prices (billions of Iranian Rials)					Gross fixed capital formation (billions of Iranian Rials)	
ISIC	Industry	Note	2002	2003	2004	2005	Note	2002	2003	2004	2005	Note	2004	2005
151	Processed meat,fish,fruit,vegetables,fats		14908.4	17563.1	20449.4	23639.2		4223.3	4599.2	4693.2	5985.6		1106.8	976.7
1511	Processing/preserving of meat		3626.5	4328.1	4838.1	6250.2		815.7	1098.3	1073.4	1449.1		161.3	100.1
1512	Processing/preserving of fish		823.4	957.2	1112.5	1077.7		431.7	413.2	404.7	354.6		30.4	36.6
1513	Processing/preserving of fruit & vegetables		4102.1	4053.7	4550.6	5468.1		1380.4	1086.7	1322.5	1649.1		341.8	244.3
1514	Vegetable and animal oils and fats		6356.3	8224.1	9948.2	10843.2		1595.6	2000.9	1892.6	2532.8		573.3	595.7
1520	Dairy products		5811.9	7728.9	10638.8	13375.0		1346.6	1691.9	2258.0	3462.7		625.7	468.5
153	Grain mill products; starches; animal feeds		2295.1	3094.6	3926.9	4938.2		973.8	1237.5	1438.4	1768.6		308.8	485.6
1531	Grain mill products		920.6	1231.5	1380.3	1522.0		600.6	801.3	802.8	876.3		252.7	421.8
1532	Starches and starch products		381.9	363.0	410.9	425.9		177.6	120.8	144.4	126.8		14.9	25.2
1533	Prepared animal feeds		992.6	1500.1	2135.8	2990.2		195.5	315.4	491.3	765.5		41.2	38.6
154	Other food products		11162.7	13314.1	14316.1	17312.8		3880.0	4307.9	4858.0	6178.2		1092.6	737.7
1541	Bakery products		2112.5	2402.6	2989.8	2928.7		853.4	1023.5	1183.6	1232.3		212.8	155.0
1542	Sugar		5751.7	6304.3	6570.0	7775.9		1999.6	1921.6	2069.4	2813.9		576.5	345.3
1543	Cocoa, chocolate and sugar confectionery		622.2	568.3	803.7	1784.5		213.8	143.4	276.5	606.3		36.2	47.9
1544	Macaroni, noodles & similar products		418.6	814.7	913.8	832.8		141.2	303.6	317.9	267.4		16.8	-11.5
1549	Other food products n.e.c.		2257.6	3224.2	3038.8	3990.7		672.0	915.9	1010.4	1258.2		250.3	201.1
155	Beverages		2766.2	3199.4	3799.9	4756.1		1348.5	1438.3	1626.3	1935.6		306.7	258.8
1551	Distilling, rectifying & blending of spirits		121.0	160.4	155.6	155.6		45.1	61.9	63.4	43.2		2.3	0.4
1552	Wines		-	-	-	-		-	-	-	-		-	-
1553	Malt liquors and malt		137.9	170.1	239.3	372.9		80.9	68.4	139.7	195.7		9.3	29.5
1554	Soft drinks; mineral waters		2507.3	2868.9	3405.0	4227.6		1222.5	1308.1	1423.1	1696.7		295.2	228.9
1600	Tobacco products		844.1	1248.6	1688.0	1671.9		548.5	572.3	938.0	866.9		142.1	-2.6
171	Spinning, weaving and finishing of textiles		8697.7	10455.4	12687.2	13414.3		3394.8	3688.1	4330.1	4796.4		612.1	842.7
1711	Textile fibre preparation; textile weaving		8339.3	10064.1	12261.0	12936.8		3255.7	3520.4	4142.4	4564.3		582.4	765.9
1712	Finishing of textiles		358.4	391.3	426.2	477.5		139.2	167.7	187.7	232.2		29.7	76.8
172	Other textiles		4112.5	5319.1	6317.5	7148.5		1360.6	1790.8	1860.3	2302.8		440.8	639.4
1721	Made-up textile articles, except apparel		693.8	1138.5	1357.6	1472.0		232.8	459.8	411.0	493.0		67.2	168.4
1722	Carpets and rugs		3263.4	4056.2	4827.9	5522.6		1078.0	1295.4	1409.0	1752.7		370.7	469.7
1723	Cordage, rope, twine and netting		48.6	52.0	61.7	75.8		15.6	10.2	15.3	26.2		0.4	0.1
1729	Other textiles n.e.c.		106.5	72.4	70.3	78.2		34.2	25.5	25.0	30.9		2.5	1.2
1730	Knitted and crocheted fabrics and articles		210.7	286.7	404.0	286.2		81.6	114.1	152.4	93.6		17.8	32.8
1810	Wearing apparel, except fur apparel		699.2	699.2	747.6	984.6		286.7	306.6	320.0	429.7		12.1	30.9
1820	Dressing & dyeing of fur; processing of fur		9.6	1.1	14.5	1.4		1.6	0.3	4.7	0.5		0.2	-
191	Tanning, dressing and processing of leather		728.9	971.0	932.7	985.6		251.1	214.9	313.6	339.1		9.6	11.7
1911	Tanning and dressing of leather		667.9	899.6	908.2	962.5		233.5	196.8	303.8	328.7		9.3	11.4
1912	Luggage, handbags, etc.; saddlery & harness		61.0	71.4	24.6	23.1		17.5	18.1	9.7	10.4		0.3	0.3
1920	Footwear		859.7	852.6	668.2	795.9		328.2	335.4	241.2	267.2		31.5	39.3
2010	Sawmilling and planing of wood		156.1	196.3	161.8	181.7		93.4	132.8	104.7	108.1		-15.8	14.3
202	Products of wood, cork, straw, etc.		836.5	954.3	1069.7	1225.0		389.8	421.9	469.3	527.3		29.6	50.0
2021	Veneer sheets, plywood, particle board, etc.		578.9	773.6	837.1	1043.4		276.1	347.7	386.9	450.4		27.7	45.6
2022	Builders' carpentry and joinery		151.3	100.5	145.3	85.0		63.7	44.1	48.7	39.7		1.0	2.6
2023	Wooden containers		38.7	49.8	54.8	63.3		15.4	16.6	19.4	24.5		0.3	0.6
2029	Other wood products; articles of cork/straw		67.6	30.4	32.5	33.3		34.5	13.5	14.2	12.6		0.6	1.1
210	Paper and paper products		3003.9	4255.7	5377.3	6181.2		1084.1	1482.7	1862.8	2195.5		307.9	357.8
2101	Pulp, paper and paperboard		1215.2	1445.3	1723.2	2085.8		564.8	659.1	701.5	925.2		94.7	184.3
2102	Corrugated paper and paperboard		1228.8	1827.8	2292.2	2383.7		314.6	495.8	671.2	666.4		165.8	121.1
2109	Other articles of paper and paperboard		559.9	982.6	1361.9	1711.7		204.8	327.8	490.1	603.9		47.5	52.4
221	Publishing		2506.2	1294.5	872.5	1238.2		989.8	646.4	399.2	646.8		-24.9	6.7
2211	Publishing of books and other publications		652.2	513.2	260.9	514.6		300.2	276.9	161.5	267.1		2.2	10.6
2212	Publishing of newspapers, journals, etc.		1787.5	766.6	597.5	716.2		653.8	362.0	229.6	374.0		-27.3	-4.4
2213	Publishing of recorded media		39.5	-	-	-		23.8	-	-	-		-	-
2219	Other publishing		27.0	14.7	14.1	7.4		12.0	7.5	8.1	5.7		0.2	0.5

continued

Iran (Islamic Republic of)

ISIC Revision 3		Output in producers' prices					Value added in producers' prices					Gross fixed capital formation		
			(billions of Iranian Rials)					(billions of Iranian Rials)					(billions of Iranian Rials)	
ISIC	Industry	Note	2002	2003	2004	2005	Note	2002	2003	2004	2005	Note	2004	2005
222	Printing and related service activities		741.8	797.8	1113.0	1155.6		327.6	318.0	378.7	431.9		87.5	31.8
2221	Printing		659.5	695.6	1016.1	1094.2		290.2	271.3	332.0	402.0		82.1	30.0
2222	Service activities related to printing		82.3	102.2	96.9	61.4		37.4	46.7	46.8	29.9		5.4	1.8
2230	Reproduction of recorded media		-	-	-	46.2		-	-	-	12.9		-	-
2310	Coke oven products		7.2	7.3	28.7	48.7		5.8	5.8	5.5	21.9		1.7	7.1
2320	Refined petroleum products		21373.8	30910.1	38477.3	40863.2		10147.1	15277.4	19098.7	19810.6		451.5	236.5
2330	Processing of nuclear fuel		-	-	-	-		-	-	-	-		-	-
241	Basic chemicals		19809.0	23126.1	37175.6	38770.8		13836.2	12443.3	20482.9	19190.8		1174.5	1017.4
2411	Basic chemicals, except fertilizers		2343.9	2797.9	5195.4	6873.7		1136.6	1217.8	2251.6	2893.4		396.4	246.4
2412	Fertilizers and nitrogen compounds		2319.7	2575.1	3413.2	3835.0		1653.6	1649.3	2019.4	2451.6		-41.6	95.0
2413	Plastics in primary forms; synthetic rubber		15145.3	17753.1	28567.0	28062.2		11046.1	9576.2	16211.9	13845.9		819.7	675.9
242	Other chemicals		10969.8	15643.6	17603.9	20746.5		4249.9	6036.5	6468.6	7643.5		688.1	702.5
2421	Pesticides and other agro-chemical products		331.2	519.5	442.3	740.3		136.5	181.7	210.8	229.7		12.8	66.4
2422	Paints, varnishes, printing ink and mastics		1625.7	2269.4	2485.7	2586.8		592.8	723.0	736.3	888.1		99.3	113.9
2423	Pharmaceuticals, medicinal chemicals, etc.		4793.1	7160.5	7818.1	9190.9		2019.3	2975.3	3351.4	3783.8		319.4	305.3
2424	Soap, cleaning & cosmetic preparations		3257.1	4095.0	5042.8	6474.5		1128.1	1475.8	1475.9	2116.3		185.0	172.6
2429	Other chemical products n.e.c.		962.6	1599.1	1815.0	1754.0		373.3	680.7	694.2	625.7		71.5	44.3
2430	Man-made fibres		1324.3	1774.5	2130.1	2431.4		709.7	483.8	497.8	567.6		249.1	56.2
251	Rubber products		4160.1	4620.7	6334.6	7025.8		1918.6	1678.2	2104.9	3109.2		249.0	247.5
2511	Rubber tyres and tubes		3486.6	3783.7	4628.9	5419.8		1610.2	1336.2	1554.0	2295.7		169.5	145.5
2519	Other rubber products		673.5	837.0	1705.7	1605.9		308.4	342.0	550.9	813.5		79.6	102.1
2520	Plastic products		4142.4	5834.6	7855.7	10361.2		1439.1	1888.7	2473.0	3106.7		532.3	550.5
2610	Glass and glass products		2119.8	2679.8	3445.1	3235.1		1066.9	1337.3	1399.7	1375.3		389.7	279.1
269	Non-metallic mineral products n.e.c.		18396.5	23513.9	28785.8	33322.7		10302.2	13630.6	16826.1	19341.4		2759.6	2371.6
2691	Pottery, china and earthenware		939.9	1052.6	1355.8	1450.3		603.3	675.3	812.7	859.9		-16.1	96.7
2692	Refractory ceramic products		568.7	714.1	690.4	935.2		254.3	260.9	290.5	418.3		30.1	30.6
2693	Struct.non-refractory clay; ceramic products		4584.7	6083.3	6937.9	7869.5		2799.7	3717.2	4303.2	4603.5		1303.6	909.1
2694	Cement, lime and plaster		5699.5	7750.3	10318.2	12591.1		3725.4	5463.8	7382.8	8944.1		773.3	843.5
2695	Articles of concrete, cement and plaster		2475.1	3195.3	3841.0	4018.0		1084.0	1539.9	1768.6	1758.5		236.4	188.8
2696	Cutting, shaping & finishing of stone		2160.1	2109.4	2290.5	2455.1		1001.5	883.5	869.2	981.1		179.3	106.2
2699	Other non-metallic mineral products n.e.c.		1968.6	2608.9	3351.9	4003.6		834.1	1090.1	1399.1	1775.9		252.9	196.7
2710	Basic iron and steel		23104.1	32573.8	52627.9	57933.0		8771.1	14334.6	25064.6	27178.3		2413.5	2372.4
2720	Basic precious and non-ferrous metals		6991.8	8647.2	13710.6	19571.5		2922.2	3289.5	5447.1	6859.1		672.2	4829.3
273	Casting of metals		1863.1	2211.7	3167.5	3197.5		969.1	1076.0	1218.2	1336.3		162.4	142.5
2731	Casting of iron and steel		1634.7	1894.9	2574.1	2608.0		888.5	961.7	1020.3	1157.4		136.0	119.8
2732	Casting of non-ferrous metals		228.4	316.8	593.4	589.6		80.6	114.3	197.9	178.8		26.4	22.8
281	Struct.metal products;tanks;steam generators		4375.2	5696.5	6828.3	7472.7		2353.6	2779.3	2710.4	2742.6		243.4	241.0
2811	Structural metal products		2039.6	2873.8	4076.8	4257.2		778.1	980.9	1287.0	1341.5		121.5	102.8
2812	Tanks, reservoirs and containers of metal		2324.6	2816.6	2731.5	3192.2		1572.1	1797.0	1415.9	1389.9		120.5	138.1
2813	Steam generators		11.0	6.1	20.0	23.3		3.4	1.4	7.5	11.2		1.3	0.1
289	Other metal products; metal working services		5947.0	7443.0	10150.8	13162.9		2246.7	2619.4	3175.1	4624.9		401.7	668.0
2891	Metal forging/pressing/stamping/roll-forming		279.7	333.9	731.1	1083.8		65.4	84.6	149.2	318.8		15.5	21.9
2892	Treatment & coating of metals		1195.4	1331.6	1990.6	2189.8		509.8	529.2	731.9	974.4		58.6	88.1
2893	Cutlery, hand tools and general hardware		394.1	482.9	660.7	841.2		186.4	223.0	255.1	338.5		18.3	16.8
2899	Other fabricated metal products n.e.c.		4077.9	5294.5	6768.4	9048.2		1485.0	1782.5	2039.0	2993.2		309.2	541.1
291	General purpose machinery		5193.9	5926.9	8256.8	9908.8		2372.0	2469.6	3365.8	3556.8		476.5	339.8
2911	Engines & turbines (not for transport equipment)		1023.9	665.3	1963.6	2577.7		509.8	347.0	897.5	671.0		304.5	66.6
2912	Pumps, compressors, taps and valves		1053.8	1260.8	1325.3	1705.1		469.3	570.5	559.8	630.4		54.2	162.9
2913	Bearings, gears, gearing & driving elements		195.0	189.7	218.1	226.0		85.3	99.9	118.3	135.8		3.9	6.3
2914	Ovens, furnaces and furnace burners		317.1	395.4	421.7	428.5		126.6	177.0	156.2	147.7		24.4	11.1
2915	Lifting and handling equipment		724.7	835.4	1108.8	1195.9		317.2	340.8	389.4	538.3		25.1	16.8
2919	Other general purpose machinery		1879.4	2580.4	3219.2	3775.7		863.8	934.5	1244.6	1433.6		64.4	76.1

292	Special purpose machinery	3942.2	5916.2	7216.2	9328.3	1675.1	2360.8	2565.9	3768.9	233.8	150.0
2921	Agricultural and forestry machinery	1532.8	1801.5	2410.4	3599.9	441.3	762.6	891.4	1405.7	50.0	28.3
2922	Machine tools	820.2	1296.4	1077.3	937.3	462.2	639.4	443.1	446.3	27.9	33.3
2923	Machinery for metallurgy	28.8	22.1	36.7	45.6	13.5	9.8	18.4	26.8	1.1	0.5
2924	Machinery for mining & construction	694.0	1733.2	2369.6	3148.5	384.9	469.5	627.0	1175.6	110.3	47.2
2925	Food/beverage/tobacco processing machinery	279.3	344.9	391.8	638.2	121.6	148.6	168.4	288.3	12.2	14.4
2926	Machinery for textile, apparel and leather	195.1	198.9	290.8	244.0	79.4	80.8	161.4	115.4	6.4	0.8
2927	Weapons and ammunition	-	-	-	-	-	-	-	-	-	-
2929	Other special purpose machinery	392.1	519.2	639.5	714.6	172.2	250.1	256.2	310.8	25.9	25.5
2930	Domestic appliances n.e.c.	4783.3	5549.3	6114.8	6598.8	1651.6	1833.4	2162.1	2103.1	233.5	278.8
3000	Office, accounting and computing machinery	454.0	463.1	718.2	731.4	184.8	151.2	314.5	374.0	30.4	19.6
3110	Electric motors, generators and transformers	2315.5	2347.5	2941.3	3824.8	714.7	910.6	999.8	1538.7	194.8	99.0
3120	Electricity distribution & control apparatus	1305.8	2018.1	2549.1	2850.8	647.9	872.5	1122.0	1380.8	116.1	140.1
3130	Insulated wire and cable	3953.8	4581.0	6294.1	6916.2	1584.6	1314.6	1435.2	2218.4	317.6	221.4
3140	Accumulators, primary cells and batteries	602.1	560.2	832.2	1258.2	255.7	251.7	336.3	518.8	16.6	66.5
3150	Lighting equipment and electric lamps	678.8	648.3	802.6	815.8	293.0	292.2	367.2	368.9	18.7	15.1
3190	Other electrical equipment n.e.c.	690.7	2437.1	3368.0	3584.3	265.2	614.0	1058.5	1233.3	160.4	160.6
3210	Electronic valves, tubes, etc.	196.5	569.4	266.9	283.9	66.0	128.8	113.3	102.0	8.6	12.7
3220	TV/radio transmitters; line comm. apparatus	1333.2	1698.0	2176.7	1671.4	511.6	587.9	1198.6	747.5	79.1	65.9
3230	TV and radio receivers and associated goods	2237.3	1980.4	1907.9	1975.3	620.3	511.4	557.0	633.0	25.5	73.7
331	Medical, measuring, testing appliances, etc.	1231.6	1694.5	1925.5	1942.2	505.7	737.8	933.7	938.2	119.5	221.9
3311	Medical, surgical and orthopaedic equipment	658.4	847.3	883.9	882.5	287.5	396.2	458.6	423.8	81.2	195.2
3312	Measuring/testing/navigating appliances,etc.	568.1	841.4	1029.6	1050.6	215.9	339.2	471.5	510.6	38.2	26.6
3313	Industrial process control equipment	5.1	5.8	12.0	9.0	2.3	2.4	3.5	3.8	0.1	0.1
3320	Optical instruments & photographic equipment	46.5	62.1	189.6	223.7	22.0	29.1	94.9	112.4	16.3	16.2
3330	Watches and clocks	41.9	49.7	158.0	74.5	16.9	27.1	62.8	35.4	6.1	2.2
3410	Motor vehicles	41404.9	71787.2	93514.4	109800.0	10973.8	19245.8	18956.4	25545.2	3481.0	3683.1
3420	Automobile bodies, trailers & semi-trailers	285.3	876.4	1081.0	1591.6	115.9	258.1	310.5	432.7	32.2	119.9
3430	Parts/accessories for automobiles	10333.0	13405.8	18330.3	23605.4	3248.0	4249.5	5838.9	7317.2	964.5	550.5
351	Building and repairing of ships and boats	1530.4	4535.2	5964.8	4830.0	676.7	3031.0	3160.9	2228.9	412.6	190.2
3511	Building and repairing of ships	1463.4	4431.8	5873.6	4737.2	639.6	2978.6	3109.5	2190.1	412.2	186.9
3512	Building/repairing of pleasure/sport. boats	67.0	103.4	91.2	92.8	37.0	52.4	51.4	38.8	0.4	3.3
3520	Railway/tramway locomotives & rolling stock	322.8	292.1	428.8	695.5	104.1	151.7	276.6	325.2	30.9	20.9
3530	Aircraft and spacecraft	246.7	280.9	319.2	357.7	170.7	184.6	260.9	301.1	21.4	-
359	Transport equipment n.e.c.	2603.2	3275.3	5176.4	5274.5	852.0	1031.6	1375.4	1555.1	73.5	49.7
3591	Motorcycles	2430.5	3132.4	4984.2	5109.6	786.4	974.0	1311.9	1478.2	71.1	48.2
3592	Bicycles and invalid carriages	141.6	109.5	140.3	98.9	52.8	43.8	46.2	46.9	0.9	1.3
3599	Other transport equipment n.e.c.	31.1	33.4	51.9	65.9	12.9	13.7	17.3	30.0	1.5	0.3
3610	Furniture	1043.3	1641.7	2026.9	2740.0	466.6	730.9	867.4	1275.4	45.2	109.5
369	Manufacturing n.e.c.	547.4	674.1	742.6	829.8	224.5	258.9	302.0	324.2	33.3	57.1
3691	Jewellery and related articles	55.2	66.6	86.6	52.3	17.8	25.4	32.6	21.5	5.0	0.5
3692	Musical instruments	6.2	7.1	9.4	5.9	3.3	3.7	2.6	2.7	-	-
3693	Sports goods	32.6	27.7	25.4	23.3	11.6	10.8	11.7	12.0	0.2	33.2
3694	Games and toys	17.0	32.8	29.3	16.0	8.2	12.2	10.1	5.2	3.4	-
3699	Other manufacturing n.e.c.	436.4	540.0	591.9	732.4	183.6	206.8	245.1	282.8	24.6	23.4
3710	Recycling of metal waste and scrap	-	4.7	3.6	-	-	2.4	2.3	-	0.6	-
3720	Recycling of non-metal waste and scrap	6.5	17.8	30.2	19.1	2.1	4.0	7.8	8.1	0.6	0.3
D	Total manufacturing	272265.6	370207.9	486843.0	559212.7	110069.7	142420.9	181268.2	208200.9	22629.1	25368.5

Iran (Islamic Republic of)

ISIC Revision 3			Index numbers of industrial production											
			(2000=100)											
ISIC	Industry	Note	1995	1996	1997	1998	1999	2000	2001	2002	2003	2004	2005	2006
15	Food and beverages		71	78	84	88	95	100	94	114	129	133	...	...
16	Tobacco products		...	...	...	...	...	...	...	...	...	...	...	...
17	Textiles		97	106	107	105	104	100	98	107	105	104	...	...
18	Wearing apparel, fur		...	...	...	...	...	...	...	...	...	...	...	...
19	Leather, leather products and footwear		...	...	...	...	...	...	...	...	...	...	...	...
20	Wood products (excl. furniture)		...	...	...	...	...	...	...	...	...	...	...	...
21	Paper and paper products		...	...	...	...	...	...	...	...	...	...	...	...
22	Printing and publishing		...	...	...	...	...	...	...	...	...	...	...	...
23	Coke,refined petroleum products,nuclear fuel		...	...	...	...	...	...	...	...	...	...	...	...
24	Chemicals and chemical products		78	86	91	90	97	100	106	114	128	141	...	...
25	Rubber and plastics products		...	...	...	...	...	...	...	...	...	...	...	...
26	Non-metallic mineral products		72	77	84	82	93	100	110	123	136	140	...	...
27	Basic metals		...	...	...	...	...	...	...	...	...	...	...	...
28	Fabricated metal products		71	83	89	88	96	100	111	137	146	161	...	...
29	Machinery and equipment n.e.c.	a/	58	72	93	91	98	100	104	128	143	175	...	...
30	Office, accounting and computing machinery	a/	...	...	...	...	...	...	...	...	...	...	...	...
31	Electrical machinery and apparatus	b/	46	53	74	77	90	100	106	197	269	292	...	...
32	Radio,television and communication equipment	b/	...	...	...	...	...	...	...	...	...	...	...	...
33	Medical, precision and optical instruments		...	...	...	...	...	...	...	...	...	...	...	...
34	Motor vehicles, trailers, semi-trailers	c/	48	46	67	77	89	100	124	224	379	479	...	...
35	Other transport equipment	c/	...	...	...	...	...	...	...	...	...	...	...	...
36	Furniture; manufacturing n.e.c.		...	...	...	...	...	...	...	...	...	...	...	...
37	Recycling		...	...	...	...	...	...	...	...	...	...	...	...
D	Total manufacturing		71	75	77	92	96	100	104	108	112	115	119	...

a/ 29 includes 30.
b/ 31 includes 32.
c/ 34 includes 35.

Ireland

Supplier of information:
Irish Central Statistics Office, Dublin.
Industrial statistics for the OECD countries are compiled by the OECD secretariat, which supplies them to UNIDO.

Basic source of data:
Annual census.

Major deviations from ISIC (Revision 3):
All data have been converted from NACE (Revision 1) to ISIC (Revision 3).

Reference period:
Calendar year.

Scope:
Enterprises with three or more persons engaged.

Method of data collection:
Not reported.

Type of enumeration:
Sample survey.

Adjusted for non-response:
Not reported.

Concepts and definitions of variables:
Number of employees refers to the number of persons who are paid a fixed wage or salary. Persons at work or temporarily absent because of illness, holidays, strikes, etc., are included, as are part-time workers. The numbers given for each year refer to a week in September.
Wages and salaries represents the gross amount paid to employees before deduction of income tax, employees' contributions to social security, etc.
Output represents the net selling value of all goods manufactured during the year, whether sold or not, and the value of work done. In general, for enterprises working on commission on materials supplied to them by other firms, only the payments received by them for the work done are included. Operating subsidies related to the production or sales of the output are included in the value of output; excise duty and VAT are excluded.
Valuation of value added is exclusive of deductible VAT.
Gross fixed capital formation is the difference between acquisitions and sales of capital assets. Capital assets (land, buildings, plant and equipment) are defined as goods with an expected useful life of more than one year intended for use by the enterprise itself. Acquisitions include purchases from other enterprises and production by the enterprise itself of capital goods for its own use. Major alterations, improvements and repairs that extend the useful life of an asset or increase its productivity are included. The value of work put in place during the year is included whether or not completed. Acquisitions are valued at total cost, including installation charges and fees or duties but excluding deductible VAT and financial costs. Sales are valued at the actual price received excluding VAT.

Related national publications:
Census of Industrial Production (annual), published by the Irish Central Statistics Office, Dublin.

Ireland

ISIC Revision 3		Number of enterprises					Number of employees					Wages and salaries paid to employees				
			(number)					(number)					(millions of Euros)			
ISIC	Industry	Note	2002	2003	2004	2005	Note	2002	2003	2004	2005	Note	2002	2003	2004	2005
151	Processed meat,fish,fruit,vegetables,fats		...	268	243	232		...	19315	18364	17794		...	459	456	455
1511	Processing/preserving of meat		159	147	134	129		14174	14684	14010	13997		323	364	364	368
1512	Processing/preserving of fish		87	86	77	70		3135	2688	2528	1969		52	53	47	39
1513	Processing/preserving of fruit & vegetables		...	30	27	29		...	1880	1765	1776		...	41	43	46
1514	Vegetable and animal oils and fats		...	5	5	4		...	63	61	52		...	2	2	2
1520	Dairy products		60	54	44	42		10013	9669	7187	6323		318	327	255	234
153	Grain mill products; starches; animal feeds		70	72	68	62		2479	2186	2072	2210		70	65	64	72
1531	Grain mill products		...	...	...	...		...	...	...	...		...	...	...	...
1532	Starches and starch products		...	...	...	...		...	...	...	...		...	...	...	...
1533	Prepared animal feeds		60	61	55	49		2072	1796	1728	1831		57	51	51	57
154	Other food products		245	244	216	205		12105	12765	12341	12519		357	392	403	437
1541	Bakery products		...	...	...	...		...	...	...	...		...	...	...	...
1542	Sugar		...	...	...	...		...	...	...	...		...	...	...	...
1543	Cocoa, chocolate and sugar confectionery		25	24	...	20		2815	2710	...	2841		84	84	...	92
1544	Macaroni, noodles & similar products		...	...	...	...		...	...	...	...		...	...	...	...
1549	Other food products n.e.c.		...	...	...	...		...	...	...	...		...	...	...	...
155	Beverages		35	33	...	...		5869	5216	...	...		254	250	...	...
1551	Distilling, rectifying & blending of spirits		...	8	...	...		...	1128	...	...		...	49	...	...
1552	Wines		...	...	...	...		...	...	...	...		...	...	...	...
1553	Malt liquors and malt		...	...	...	...		...	...	...	...		...	...	...	...
1554	Soft drinks; mineral waters		...	...	14	12		...	...	1467	1254		...	...	55	44
1600	Tobacco products		...	6	...	...		...	794	...	...		...	33	...	...
171	Spinning, weaving and finishing of textiles		...	22	...	...		...	968	...	...		...	28	...	...
1711	Textile fibre preparation; textile weaving		...	...	...	...		...	...	...	...		...	...	...	...
1712	Finishing of textiles		...	...	...	5		...	...	...	53		...	...	...	1
172	Other textiles		...	112	...	...		...	2110	...	...		...	52	...	...
1721	Made-up textile articles, except apparel		...	68	...	...		...	995	...	...		...	22	...	...
1722	Carpets and rugs		11	10	7	6		537	471	271	296		14	13	7	9
1723	Cordage, rope, twine and netting		...	8	9	9		...	140	155	139		...	3	4	4
1729	Other textiles n.e.c.		...	26	21	23		...	504	414	407		...	13	11	11
1730	Knitted and crocheted fabrics and articles		43	39	...	21		2611	1219	...	557		27	21	...	5
1810	Wearing apparel, except fur apparel		...	...	83	68		...	...	2366	2068		...	...	53	51
1820	Dressing & dyeing of fur; processing of fur		...	...	5	4		...	...	49	37		...	...	1	1
191	Tanning, dressing and processing of leather		...	...	...	...		...	...	...	...		...	...	...	...
1911	Tanning and dressing of leather		...	...	...	-		...	...	...	-		...	...	...	-
1912	Luggage, handbags, etc.; saddlery & harness		...	18	12	...		...	307	257	...		...	6	5	...
1920	Footwear		...	...	...	...		...	...	...	...		...	...	...	...
2010	Sawmilling and planing of wood		45	38	35	35		1316	1555	1253	1279		34	41	35	38
202	Products of wood, cork, straw, etc.		267	269	256	242		4878	5019	4999	5244		109	120	129	141
2021	Veneer sheets, plywood, particle board, etc.		11	11	11	11		733	703	698	691		24	25	27	27
2022	Builders' carpentry and joinery		181	175	167	155		3169	3220	3219	3511		67	73	78	90
2023	Wooden containers		30	32	29	28		365	401	378	362		7	8	8	9
2029	Other wood products; articles of cork/straw		45	51	49	48		611	695	704	680		12	14	16	16
210	Paper and paper products		115	113	100	96		4873	4792	3932	3413		151	156	140	124
2101	Pulp, paper and paperboard		13	12	8	6		230	243	149	88		8	8	4	2
2102	Corrugated paper and paperboard		51	52	49	47		2507	2508	2012	2037		79	83	75	74
2109	Other articles of paper and paperboard		51	...	...	...		2137	...	...	...		65	...	...	...
221	Publishing		130	134	133	136		4409	4719	4612	4005		139	167	164	159
2211	Publishing of books and other publications		35	34	32	28		613	889	765	431		17	27	28	14
2212	Publishing of newspapers, journals, etc.		...	85	85	91		...	3681	3615	3370		...	137	130	138
2213	Publishing of recorded media		...	...	...	...		...	...	...	...		...	...	...	...
2219	Other publishing		...	...	...	...		...	...	...	...		...	...	...	...

222	Printing and related service activities	380	391	357	326	7936	7456	6450	6664	223	213	187	237
2221	Printing	328	334	310	284	7118	6676	5890	6139	200	190	170	221
2222	Service activities related to printing	52	57	47	42	818	780	560	525	23	23	17	17
2230	Reproduction of recorded media	32	31	28	24	5912	5177	5104	4587	216	207	223	210
2310	Coke oven products	-	-	-	-	-	-	-	-	-	-	-	-
2320	Refined petroleum products	...	...	...	...	...	...	...	...	...	...	...	...
2330	Processing of nuclear fuel	-	-	-	-	-	-	-	-	-	-	-	-
241	Basic chemicals	65	65	56	55	8018	7861	7649	8087	347	345	336	452
2411	Basic chemicals, except fertilizers	...	...	...	...	...	...	...	...	...	...	...	...
2412	Fertilizers and nitrogen compounds	15	16	12	10	908	516	410	390	35	18	15	15
2413	Plastics in primary forms; synthetic rubber	13	14	13	12	700	603	628	703	24	23	27	28
242	Other chemicals	...	...	...	...	...	...	...	...	...	...	...	...
2421	Pesticides and other agro-chemical products	...	6	5	5	...	175	187	192	...	4	5	5
2422	Paints, varnishes, printing ink and mastics	...	17	18	15	...	538	539	518	...	17	17	18
2423	Pharmaceuticals, medicinal chemicals, etc.	58	54	...	53	9824	9190	...	11185	331	345	...	468
2424	Soap, cleaning & cosmetic preparations	28	...	...	23	3024	...	...	2299	94	...	...	91
2429	Other chemical products n.e.c.	...	36	34	...	...	2329	2463	...	...	74	87	...
2430	Man-made fibres	...	...	...	...	...	...	...	...	...	...	...	...
251	Rubber products	33	33	27	24	1091	986	921	750	26	28	27	22
2511	Rubber tyres and tubes	7	...	...	...	64	...	...	...	1	...	...	...
2519	Other rubber products	26	27	...	...	1027	890	...	...	25	25	...	...
2520	Plastic products	243	242	249	240	8258	8670	8763	8968	197	230	244	262
2610	Glass and glass products	55	54	53	48	3974	3288	3288	3132	97	95	88	96
269	Non-metallic mineral products n.e.c.	233	253	244	244	6970	7222	7405	7562	205	214	239	268
2691	Pottery, china and earthenware	...	...	...	...	...	...	...	...	...	...	...	...
2692	Refractory ceramic products	...	...	...	...	...	...	...	...	...	...	...	...
2693	Struct.non-refractory clay; ceramic products	...	...	21	19	...	...	275	232	...	...	7	6
2694	Cement, lime and plaster	...	...	...	5	...	...	...	603	...	...	...	27
2695	Articles of concrete, cement and plaster	...	120	...	125	...	4355	...	5099	...	132	...	184
2696	Cutting, shaping & finishing of stone	57	68	62	64	860	820	802	840	21	21	21	24
2699	Other non-metallic mineral products n.e.c.	9	10	13	13	234	238	268	220	7	7	10	9
2710	Basic iron and steel	...	63	59	62	...	964	1029	1334	...	25	26	40
2720	Basic precious and non-ferrous metals	17	18	17	16	952	1032	972	960	35	39	40	42
273	Casting of metals	...	12	9	8	...	102	64	47	...	2	2	1
2731	Casting of iron and steel	...	...	...	...	...	...	...	...	...	...	...	...
2732	Casting of non-ferrous metals	...	...	...	...	...	...	...	...	...	...	...	...
281	Struct.metal products;tanks;steam generators	328	330	318	305	6780	6480	6887	6983	168	176	197	211
2811	Structural metal products	291	292	280	265	5537	5289	5586	5685	135	142	154	168
2812	Tanks, reservoirs and containers of metal	...	...	...	...	...	...	...	...	...	...	...	...
2813	Steam generators	...	...	...	...	...	...	...	...	...	...	...	...
289	Other metal products; metal working services	270	266	265	256	6478	6166	6022	5784	164	165	164	169
2891	Metal forging/pressing/stamping/roll-forming	13	12	13	13	411	377	339	310	12	12	8	8
2892	Treatment & coating of metals	86	94	98	94	1533	1627	1737	1599	37	45	47	46
2893	Cutlery, hand tools and general hardware	53	52	50	47	1408	1406	1298	1210	36	38	34	35
2899	Other fabricated metal products n.e.c.	118	108	104	102	3126	2756	2648	2665	79	71	75	81
291	General purpose machinery	170	161	160	144	7164	6467	6694	6923	213	200	206	230
2911	Engines & turbines (not for transport equipment)	...	...	...	...	...	...	...	...	...	...	...	...
2912	Pumps, compressors, taps and valves	...	...	...	...	...	...	...	...	...	...	...	...
2913	Bearings, gears, gearing & driving elements	12	11	10	9	283	274	292	355	8	8	8	10
2914	Ovens, furnaces and furnace burners	...	...	3	3	...	...	112	117	...	...	3	3
2915	Lifting and handling equipment	...	...	36	31	...	...	1813	1606	...	...	56	54
2919	Other general purpose machinery	79	73	79	72	2571	2006	2330	2709	71	57	70	88
292	Special purpose machinery	...	143	127	118	...	3200	2735	2350	...	86	77	68
2921	Agricultural and forestry machinery	...	30	27	25	...	673	606	603	...	17	16	16
2922	Machine tools	30	29	27	27	625	619	613	540	15	16	16	15
2923	Machinery for metallurgy	...	...	-	-	...	...	-	-	...	...	-	-
2924	Machinery for mining & construction	...	13	...	...	...	557	...	...	...	17	...	...
2925	Food/beverage/tobacco processing machinery	26	26	21	21	532	513	371	364	13	14	10	11
2926	Machinery for textile, apparel and leather	...	...	...	...	...	...	...	...	...	...	...	...
2927	Weapons and ammunition	-	-	-	-	-	-	-	-	-	-	-	-
2929	Other special purpose machinery	...	...	...	34	...	...	...	437	...	...	...	13

continued

Ireland

ISIC Revision 3		Number of enterprises					Number of employees					Wages and salaries paid to employees				
			(number)					(number)					(millions of Euros)			
ISIC	Industry	Note	2002	2003	2004	2005	Note	2002	2003	2004	2005	Note	2002	2003	2004	2005
2930	Domestic appliances n.e.c.		...	13	14	11		...	2361	2230	2002		...	59	64	59
3000	Office, accounting and computing machinery		70	62	50	45		14121	13092	14115	12721		464	419	506	465
3110	Electric motors, generators and transformers		33	...	...	...		4011	...	...	...		115	...	...	...
3120	Electricity distribution & control apparatus		64	...	...	50		3474	...	...	2205		82	...	...	72
3130	Insulated wire and cable		25	22	...	...		1701	1459	...	...		41	39	...	...
3140	Accumulators, primary cells and batteries		7	7	6	5		175	158	128	111		4	4	3	3
3150	Lighting equipment and electric lamps		26	25	...	18		318	343	...	230		8	10	...	8
3190	Other electrical equipment n.e.c.		32	33	32	29		2953	2984	2710	2794		65	75	68	72
3210	Electronic valves, tubes, etc.		...	34	...	...		...	6561	...	...		...	224	...	...
3220	TV/radio transmitters; line comm. apparatus		...	13	8	8		...	2034	398	543		...	70	13	15
3230	TV and radio receivers and associated goods		...	8	...	...		...	844	...	...		...	21	...	...
331	Medical, measuring, testing appliances, etc.		119	114	...	...		17284	17195	...	...		485	520	...	...
3311	Medical, surgical and orthopaedic equipment		64	63	59	62		15093	15133	16883	18747		417	451	482	572
3312	Measuring/testing/navigating appliances,etc.		39	37	38	38		1867	1804	2164	2216		56	59	70	73
3313	Industrial process control equipment		16	14	...	...		324	258	...	...		12	10	...	...
3320	Optical instruments & photographic equipment		...	...	...	11		...	...	...	3080		...	...	...	100
3330	Watches and clocks		...	...	...	...		...	...	...	...		...	...	...	...
3410	Motor vehicles		9	10	10	9		236	241	283	290		6	6	7	8
3420	Automobile bodies, trailers & semi-trailers		39	33	28	27		740	615	396	404		18	16	11	11
3430	Parts/accessories for automobiles		27	29	23	20		2574	2567	2496	2618		64	75	66	73
351	Building and repairing of ships and boats		26	27	22	22		448	486	406	280		11	10	11	8
3511	Building and repairing of ships		17	16	14	12		391	402	343	219		10	9	10	6
3512	Building/repairing of pleasure/sport. boats		9	11	8	10		57	84	63	61		1	2	1	1
3520	Railway/tramway locomotives & rolling stock		...	-	...	...		...	-	...	...		...	-	...	...
3530	Aircraft and spacecraft		...	13	...	...		...	3770	...	...		...	142	...	...
359	Transport equipment n.e.c.		...	8	...	...		...	187	...	...		...	4	...	...
3591	Motorcycles		-	...	...	...		-	...	...	...		-	...	...	...
3592	Bicycles and invalid carriages		...	...	...	...		...	...	...	...		...	...	...	...
3599	Other transport equipment n.e.c.		...	...	...	...		...	...	...	...		...	...	...	...
3610	Furniture		455	475	428	...		6562	6346	5898	...		139	145	147	...
369	Manufacturing n.e.c.		...	...	...	...		...	...	...	...		...	...	...	...
3691	Jewellery and related articles		...	...	...	...		...	...	...	...		...	...	...	...
3692	Musical instruments		...	6	4	5		...	43	24	26		...	1	1	1
3693	Sports goods		8	8	9	7		466	327	229	113		11	8	5	2
3694	Games and toys		...	...	...	...		...	...	...	...		...	...	...	...
3699	Other manufacturing n.e.c.		50	50	50	44		1898	1443	1409	1219		45	30	32	32
3710	Recycling of metal waste and scrap		...	9	...	...		...	167	...	...		...	5	...	...
3720	Recycling of non-metal waste and scrap		15	18	...	...		187	201	...	...		5	5	...	...
D	Total manufacturing		4932	4880	4519	4256		239850	228024	219030	215175		6886	6967	6982	7366

Ireland

ISIC Revision 3		Output					Value added in factor values					Gross fixed capital formation		
			(millions of Euros)					(millions of Euros)					(millions of Euros)	
ISIC	Industry	Note	2002	2003	2004	2005	Note	2002	2003	2004	2005	Note	2004	2005
151	Processed meat,fish,fruit,vegetables,fats		...	4299	4326	4179		...	806	811	848		115	104
1511	Processing/preserving of meat		3412	3696	3757	3611		592	652	633	665		97	80
1512	Processing/preserving of fish		468	399	341	324		105	76	89	76		11	9
1513	Processing/preserving of fruit & vegetables		...	190	212	229		...	75	85	102		7	15
1514	Vegetable and animal oils and fats		...	14	17	15		...	4	5	5		1	1
1520	Dairy products		3465	3764	3151	2882		585	787	723	546		61	88
153	Grain mill products; starches; animal feeds		826	812	809	750		186	164	151	155		26	29
1531	Grain mill products		...	...	...	...		...	...	...	...		...	...
1532	Starches and starch products		...	...	...	...		...	...	...	...		...	...
1533	Prepared animal feeds		719	699	694	627		142	138	132	120		23	18
154	Other food products		6323	7517	8346	8492		2673	3874	3927	3165		134	151
1541	Bakery products		...	...	...	...		...	...	...	...		...	...
1542	Sugar		...	...	...	...		...	...	...	...		...	...
1543	Cocoa, chocolate and sugar confectionery		418	402	...	431		185	176	...	181		...	14
1544	Macaroni, noodles & similar products		...	...	...	...		...	...	...	...		...	...
1549	Other food products n.e.c.		...	...	...	...		...	...	...	...		...	...
155	Beverages		2922	3084	...	...		1372	1519	...	...		...	...
1551	Distilling, rectifying & blending of spirits		...	636	...	...		...	202	...	...		...	...
1552	Wines		...	...	...	...		...	...	...	...		...	...
1553	Malt liquors and malt		...	...	...	...		...	...	...	...		...	...
1554	Soft drinks; mineral waters		...	...	301	244		...	...	133	87		11	13
1600	Tobacco products		...	1632	...	...		...	275	...	...		...	...
171	Spinning, weaving and finishing of textiles		...	125	...	...		...	38	...	...		...	...
1711	Textile fibre preparation; textile weaving		...	...	...	...		...	...	...	...		...	...
1712	Finishing of textiles		...	...	...	3		...	...	...	1		...	-
172	Other textiles		...	190	...	...		...	64	...	...		...	...
1721	Made-up textile articles, except apparel		...	83	...	...		...	26	...	...		...	...
1722	Carpets and rugs		48	41	32	32		18	15	12	11		1	6
1723	Cordage, rope, twine and netting		...	15	17	14		...	6	8	6		-	-
1729	Other textiles n.e.c.		...	51	40	41		...	17	15	19		2	1
1730	Knitted and crocheted fabrics and articles		91	63	...	19		39	25	...	7		...	-
1810	Wearing apparel, except fur apparel		...	...	225	217		...	...	100	110		5	4
1820	Dressing & dyeing of fur; processing of fur		...	...	3	3		...	...	1	1		-	-
191	Tanning, dressing and processing of leather		...	...	...	...		...	...	...	...		...	...
1911	Tanning and dressing of leather		...	...	...	-		...	...	...	-		...	-
1912	Luggage, handbags, etc.; saddlery & harness		...	23	19	...		...	12	6	...		-	...
1920	Footwear		...	...	...	...		...	...	...	...		...	...
2010	Sawmilling and planing of wood		305	352	337	352		111	120	121	106		11	17
202	Products of wood, cork, straw, etc.		632	676	731	786		197	203	267	278		28	26
2021	Veneer sheets, plywood, particle board, etc.		174	186	214	224		39	42	67	65		5	6
2022	Builders' carpentry and joinery		363	377	386	436		125	122	155	168		17	17
2023	Wooden containers		39	44	47	51		13	13	15	17		2	1
2029	Other wood products; articles of cork/straw		56	70	84	74		20	25	30	28		5	3
210	Paper and paper products		805	817	764	555		334	345	311	217		23	16
2101	Pulp, paper and paperboard		37	34	26	11		14	13	11	4		1	1
2102	Corrugated paper and paperboard		368	390	339	316		145	153	126	135		10	8
2109	Other articles of paper and paperboard		400	...	...	...		175	...	...	...		...	...
221	Publishing		597	661	720	591		329	392	457	321		28	20
2211	Publishing of books and other publications		71	89	103	56		35	48	57	29		13	1
2212	Publishing of newspapers, journals, etc.		...	557	595	481		...	337	387	274		15	18
2213	Publishing of recorded media		...	...	...	...		...	...	...	...		...	...
2219	Other publishing		...	...	...	...		...	...	...	...		...	...

continued

Ireland

ISIC Revision 3		Output					Value added in factor values					Gross fixed capital formation		
			(millions of Euros)					(millions of Euros)					(millions of Euros)	
ISIC	Industry	Note	2002	2003	2004	2005	Note	2002	2003	2004	2005	Note	2004	2005
222	Printing and related service activities		771	736	660	872		363	337	316	468		43	39
2221	Printing		714	668	608	828		332	301	286	444		41	37
2222	Service activities related to printing		56	68	53	44		31	37	31	24		2	1
2230	Reproduction of recorded media		8557	9345	12122	12097		2581	3141	3508	3428		36	41
2310	Coke oven products		-	-	-	-		-	-	-	-		-	-
2320	Refined petroleum products		...	...	...	...		...	...	...	...		...	...
2330	Processing of nuclear fuel		-	-	-	-		-	-	-	-		-	-
241	Basic chemicals		23063	21490	20531	22051		12576	12238	9479	8949		406	353
2411	Basic chemicals, except fertilizers		...	...	...	...		...	...	...	...		...	...
2412	Fertilizers and nitrogen compounds		360	300	282	284		64	57	34	33		8	4
2413	Plastics in primary forms; synthetic rubber		211	208	191	218		79	83	71	69		5	5
242	Other chemicals		...	...	...	...		...	...	...	...		...	...
2421	Pesticides and other agro-chemical products		...	29	30	31		...	2	11	8		2	2
2422	Paints, varnishes, printing ink and mastics		...	112	117	108		...	39	44	30		4	3
2423	Pharmaceuticals, medicinal chemicals, etc.		5885	5750	...	6080		3069	3110	...	2390		...	388
2424	Soap, cleaning & cosmetic preparations		874	...	...	690		259	...	...	328		...	32
2429	Other chemical products n.e.c.		...	691	690	...		...	308	300	...		23	...
2430	Man-made fibres		...	...	...	...		...	...	...	...		...	...
251	Rubber products		98	115	108	93		39	50	49	45		4	2
2511	Rubber tyres and tubes		5	...	...	...		2	...	...	...		...	...
2519	Other rubber products		92	101	...	...		37	43	...	...		...	...
2520	Plastic products		1022	1122	1200	1337		391	408	495	490		59	69
2610	Glass and glass products		397	385	345	372		202	171	157	153		18	20
269	Non-metallic mineral products n.e.c.		1244	1427	1573	1905		495	609	609	764		159	138
2691	Pottery, china and earthenware		...	...	...	...		...	...	...	...		...	...
2692	Refractory ceramic products		...	...	...	...		...	...	...	...		...	...
2693	Struct.non-refractory clay; ceramic products		...	...	35	25		...	...	17	13		2	2
2694	Cement, lime and plaster		...	...	...	429		...	...	...	184		...	24
2695	Articles of concrete, cement and plaster		...	799	...	1111		...	316	...	444		...	90
2696	Cutting, shaping & finishing of stone		92	98	94	114		35	30	34	49		5	4
2699	Other non-metallic mineral products n.e.c.		89	94	110	136		20	22	39	38		2	8
2710	Basic iron and steel		...	109	133	199		...	40	55	81		5	7
2720	Basic precious and non-ferrous metals		228	254	266	318		51	67	76	75		12	55
273	Casting of metals		...	7	7	6		...	4	4	3		-	-
2731	Casting of iron and steel		...	...	...	...		...	...	...	...		...	...
2732	Casting of non-ferrous metals		...	...	...	...		...	...	...	...		...	...
281	Struct.metal products;tanks;steam generators		744	797	916	946		251	261	330	323		23	27
2811	Structural metal products		622	667	762	793		198	205	258	251		20	24
2812	Tanks, reservoirs and containers of metal		...	...	...	...		...	...	...	...		...	...
2813	Steam generators		...	...	...	...		...	...	...	...		...	...
289	Other metal products; metal working services		684	664	663	646		289	289	302	258		22	18
2891	Metal forging/pressing/stamping/roll-forming		35	43	43	41		16	12	12	7		2	1
2892	Treatment & coating of metals		109	153	173	152		56	79	56	75		5	4
2893	Cutlery, hand tools and general hardware		137	141	129	119		65	63	69	42		4	4
2899	Other fabricated metal products n.e.c.		403	328	318	334		153	136	166	134		11	8
291	General purpose machinery		1128	1056	1227	1399		401	370	443	545		27	33
2911	Engines & turbines (not for transport equipment)		...	...	...	...		...	...	...	...		...	...
2912	Pumps, compressors, taps and valves		...	...	...	...		...	...	...	...		...	...
2913	Bearings, gears, gearing & driving elements		40	40	43	54		18	18	21	25		1	1
2914	Ovens, furnaces and furnace burners		...	...	9	8		...	...	5	4		-	-
2915	Lifting and handling equipment		...	...	304	316		...	...	130	122		8	10
2919	Other general purpose machinery		495	409	545	684		128	95	137	251		7	10

292	Special purpose machinery	...	337	293	287	...	140	118	114	11	10
2921	Agricultural and forestry machinery	...	89	80	86	...	28	23	30	3	2
2922	Machine tools	66	71	62	62	27	28	27	28	3	2
2923	Machinery for metallurgy	...	...	-	-	...	...	-	-	-	-
2924	Machinery for mining & construction	...	61	...	...	...	24	...	...	...	...
2925	Food/beverage/tobacco processing machinery	52	52	41	44	24	23	15	19	1	1
2926	Machinery for textile, apparel and leather	...	...	...	...	...	...	...	...	...	...
2927	Weapons and ammunition	-	-	-	-	-	-	-	-	-	-
2929	Other special purpose machinery	...	...	...	39	...	...	...	16	...	2
2930	Domestic appliances n.e.c.	...	438	259	251	...	196	121	96	18	19
3000	Office, accounting and computing machinery	15699	15031	15719	17568	1435	1179	1514	1988	125	154
3110	Electric motors, generators and transformers	1815	...	...	...	474	...	...	...	...	...
3120	Electricity distribution & control apparatus	487	...	...	297	198	...	...	92	...	11
3130	Insulated wire and cable	349	284	...	...	115	86	...	...	...	...
3140	Accumulators, primary cells and batteries	19	21	16	16	6	3	7	8	-	-
3150	Lighting equipment and electric lamps	26	40	...	33	9	16	...	14	...	1
3190	Other electrical equipment n.e.c.	384	562	601	781	114	205	215	160	11	6
3210	Electronic valves, tubes, etc.	...	2497	...	...	...	1291	...	...	...	...
3220	TV/radio transmitters; line comm. apparatus	...	699	80	266	...	132	28	57	2	1
3230	TV and radio receivers and associated goods	...	189	...	...	...	51	...	...	...	...
331	Medical, measuring, testing appliances, etc.	4498	4788	...	...	1890	2232	...	...	...	...
3311	Medical, surgical and orthopaedic equipment	4058	4359	3798	4585	1751	2108	1585	1983	192	340
3312	Measuring/testing/navigating appliances,etc.	395	395	452	483	132	118	154	192	13	10
3313	Industrial process control equipment	45	34	...	...	8	6	...	...	...	...
3320	Optical instruments & photographic equipment	...	...	...	828	...	...	...	551	...	74
3330	Watches and clocks	...	...	...	...	...	...	...	...	...	...
3410	Motor vehicles	49	71	54	112	16	24	18	44	4	6
3420	Automobile bodies, trailers & semi-trailers	87	81	55	65	23	21	19	20	1	2
3430	Parts/accessories for automobiles	380	430	442	489	124	152	161	157	23	17
351	Building and repairing of ships and boats	38	38	31	29	12	15	14	13	1	1
3511	Building and repairing of ships	33	29	28	24	10	10	12	12	-	1
3512	Building/repairing of pleasure/sport. boats	5	9	3	5	3	5	1	2	-	-
3520	Railway/tramway locomotives & rolling stock	...	-	...	...	...	-	...	...	...	...
3530	Aircraft and spacecraft	...	376	...	...	...	195	...	...	...	...
359	Transport equipment n.e.c.	...	32	...	...	...	12	...	...	...	...
3591	Motorcycles	-	...	...	...	-	...	...	...	...	...
3592	Bicycles and invalid carriages	...	...	...	...	...	...	...	...	...	...
3599	Other transport equipment n.e.c.	...	...	...	...	...	...	...	...	...	...
3610	Furniture	597	627	631	...	231	244	258	...	26	...
369	Manufacturing n.e.c.	...	...	...	...	...	...	...	...	...	...
3691	Jewellery and related articles	...	...	...	...	...	...	...	...	...	...
3692	Musical instruments	...	5	2	3	...	3	1	2	-	-
3693	Sports goods	58	32	18	10	32	17	8	4	-	-
3694	Games and toys	...	...	...	...	...	...	...	...	...	...
3699	Other manufacturing n.e.c.	353	185	190	174	194	63	76	69	4	3
3710	Recycling of metal waste and scrap	...	58	...	...	...	15	...	...	...	...
3720	Recycling of non-metal waste and scrap	50	49	...	...	17	18	...	...	...	...
D	Total manufacturing	99488	99835	102008	106746	35989	38608	35651	34121	3261	3841

Ireland

ISIC Revision 3			Index numbers of industrial production											
			(2000=100)											
ISIC	Industry	Note	1995	1996	1997	1998	1999	2000	2001	2002	2003	2004	2005	2006
15	Food and beverages		83	84	86	91	95	100	107	111	116	124	126	128
16	Tobacco products		...	...	...	...	...	...	...	...	...	...	...	...
17	Textiles		120	119	122	125	108	100	112	86	70	65	55	53
18	Wearing apparel, fur		164	170	163	166	150	100	98	55	60	65	57	36
19	Leather, leather products and footwear		127	119	121	122	106	100	85	84	56	36	19	17
20	Wood products (excl. furniture)		61	68	86	94	103	100	92	104	108	124	134	150
21	Paper and paper products		94	94	98	102	98	100	101	96	90	94	86	87
22	Printing and publishing		55	60	75	96	106	100	99	109	123	152	167	189
23	Coke,refined petroleum products,nuclear fuel		...	...	...	...	...	...	...	...	...	...	...	...
24	Chemicals and chemical products		30	36	49	70	88	100	123	153	159	144	145	151
25	Rubber and plastics products		101	99	96	96	97	100	100	90	96	95	89	91
26	Non-metallic mineral products		74	78	88	89	91	100	102	100	106	108	115	118
27	Basic metals		106	105	101	96	97	100	90	88	84	80	91	95
28	Fabricated metal products		76	79	82	88	92	100	92	91	92	100	95	95
29	Machinery and equipment n.e.c.		96	95	95	103	97	100	94	95	98	88	83	92
30	Office, accounting and computing machinery		46	49	56	61	73	100	92	76	93	106	114	122
31	Electrical machinery and apparatus		35	39	50	66	71	100	119	127	129	144	154	176
32	Radio,television and communication equipment		50	53	62	78	81	100	98	89	77	78	81	93
33	Medical, precision and optical instruments		36	44	54	62	73	100	135	136	165	170	191	190
34	Motor vehicles, trailers, semi-trailers	a/	50	59	67	76	80	100	104	91	89	93	92	92
35	Other transport equipment	a/	...	...	...	...	...	...	...	...	...	...	...	...
36	Furniture; manufacturing n.e.c.		...	...	...	...	...	...	...	...	...	...	...	...
37	Recycling		...	...	...	...	...	...	...	...	...	...	...	...
D	Total manufacturing		48	52	62	75	86	100	110	119	124	124	128	135

a/ 34 includes 35.

Israel

Supplier of information:
Central Bureau of Statistics, Jerusalem.

Basic source of data:
Annual manufacturing survey; administrative data.

Major deviations from ISIC (Revision 3):
None reported.

Reference period:
Calendar year.

Scope:
Prior to 2004, establishments with five or more persons engaged. From 2004 onwards, establishments with one or more persons engaged excluding the diamond industry.

Method of data collection:
Collection of balance sheets and profit-and-loss statements from income tax authorities.

Type of enumeration:
Sample survey.

Adjusted for non-response:
Yes.

Concepts and definitions of variables:
Wages and salaries includes employers' contributions paid to social security, pension and insurance schemes, as well as the benefits received by employees under these schemes, and severance and termination pay.
Output is at basic prices and includes revenue from non-industrial activities.
Value added is at basic prices.

Related national publications:
Manufacturing Survey, published by the Central Bureau of Statistics, Jerusalem.

Israel

ISIC Revision 3		Number of establishments a/					Number of employees a/					Wages and salaries paid to employees a/				
			(number)					(thousands)					(millions of Israeli New Sheqalim)			
ISIC	Industry	Note	2002	2003	2004	2005	Note	2002	2003	2004b/	2005b/	Note	2002	2003	2004	2005
151	Processed meat,fish,fruit,vegetables,fats		143	140	293	271		11.8	11.7	11.8	12.4		1217	1201	1229	1278
1511	Processing/preserving of meat		...	...	...	...		...	...	...	...		...	...	...	...
1512	Processing/preserving of fish		...	...	...	...		...	...	...	...		...	...	...	...
1513	Processing/preserving of fruit & vegetables		...	...	...	...		...	...	...	...		...	...	...	...
1514	Vegetable and animal oils and fats		...	...	...	...		...	...	...	...		...	...	...	...
1520	Dairy products		92	102	77	159		7.2	7.9	7.6	7.9		958	1040	937	1030
153	Grain mill products; starches; animal feeds		98	97	77	77		2.2	2.1	1.8	1.7		266	243	235	226
1531	Grain mill products		...	...	...	...		...	...	...	...		...	...	...	...
1532	Starches and starch products		...	...	...	...		...	...	...	...		...	...	...	...
1533	Prepared animal feeds		...	...	...	...		...	...	...	...		...	...	...	...
154	Other food products		672	732	1828	2075		26.6	25.8	23.7	24.9		2161	2164	2093	2178
1541	Bakery products		...	...	...	...		...	...	...	...		...	...	...	...
1542	Sugar		...	...	...	...		...	...	...	...		...	...	...	...
1543	Cocoa, chocolate and sugar confectionery		...	...	...	...		...	...	...	...		...	...	...	...
1544	Macaroni, noodles & similar products		...	...	...	...		...	...	...	...		...	...	...	...
1549	Other food products n.e.c.		...	...	...	...		...	...	...	...		...	...	...	...
155	Beverages	c/	54	78	261	267	c/	6.4	6.3	6.9	6.4	c/	843	838	866	801
1551	Distilling, rectifying & blending of spirits		...	...	...	...		...	...	...	...		...	...	...	...
1552	Wines		...	...	...	...		...	...	...	...		...	...	...	...
1553	Malt liquors and malt		...	...	...	...		...	...	...	...		...	...	...	...
1554	Soft drinks; mineral waters		...	...	...	...		...	...	...	...		...	...	...	...
1600	Tobacco products	c/	...	...	...	...	c/	...	...	...	...	c/	...	...	...	...
171	Spinning, weaving and finishing of textiles	d/	106	87	135	128	d/	4.8	4.2	4.7	4.4	d/	509	433	565	540
1711	Textile fibre preparation; textile weaving		...	...	...	...		...	...	...	...		...	...	...	...
1712	Finishing of textiles		...	...	...	...		...	...	...	...		...	...	...	...
172	Other textiles	e/	125	125	375	297	e/	3.5	3.3	3.0	2.7	e/	286	274	253	289
1721	Made-up textile articles, except apparel		...	...	...	...		...	...	...	...		...	...	...	...
1722	Carpets and rugs	d/	...	...	...	...	d/	...	...	...	...	d/	...	...	...	...
1723	Cordage, rope, twine and netting		...	...	...	...		...	...	...	...		...	...	...	...
1729	Other textiles n.e.c.		...	...	...	...		...	...	...	...		...	...	...	...
1730	Knitted and crocheted fabrics and articles		118	93	110	101		8.7	7.6	5.4	4.4		679	615	482	462
1810	Wearing apparel, except fur apparel		463	379	1006	850		8.9	7.8	7.4	6.3		593	564	430	377
1820	Dressing & dyeing of fur; processing of fur	f/	...	...	...	...	f/	...	...	...	...	f/	...	...	...	...
191	Tanning, dressing and processing of leather	f/	82	79	259	302	f/	1.8	1.9	1.7	1.5	f/	139	144	130	125
1911	Tanning and dressing of leather		...	...	...	...		...	...	...	...		...	...	...	...
1912	Luggage, handbags, etc.; saddlery & harness		...	...	...	...		...	...	...	...		...	...	...	...
1920	Footwear		38	38	174	209		1.2	1.2	1.3	1.2		99	97	106	104
2010	Sawmilling and planing of wood	g/	20	20	36	40	g/	0.6	0.5	0.8	0.7	g/	52	59	87	85
202	Products of wood, cork, straw, etc.	h/	158	150	773	643	h/	3.4	3.6	4.0	3.3	h/	319	347	301	268
2021	Veneer sheets, plywood, particle board, etc.	g/	...	...	...	...	g/	...	...	...	...	g/	...	...	...	...
2022	Builders' carpentry and joinery		...	...	...	...		...	...	...	...		...	...	...	...
2023	Wooden containers		...	...	...	...		...	...	...	...		...	...	...	...
2029	Other wood products; articles of cork/straw		...	...	...	...		...	...	...	...		...	...	...	...
210	Paper and paper products		192	200	301	274		8.3	8.3	8.5	9.9		937	917	901	995
2101	Pulp, paper and paperboard		...	...	...	...		...	...	...	...		...	...	...	...
2102	Corrugated paper and paperboard		...	...	...	...		...	...	...	...		...	...	...	...
2109	Other articles of paper and paperboard		...	...	...	...		...	...	...	...		...	...	...	...
221	Publishing		274	299	848	871		12.5	12.2	13.2	13.5		1278	1267	1213	1294
2211	Publishing of books and other publications		...	...	...	...		...	...	...	...		...	...	...	...
2212	Publishing of newspapers, journals, etc.		...	...	...	...		...	...	...	...		...	...	...	...
2213	Publishing of recorded media		...	...	...	...		...	...	...	...		...	...	...	...
2219	Other publishing		...	...	...	...		...	...	...	...		...	...	...	...

222	Printing and related service activities	i/	483	455	1691	1319	i/	9.7	8.8	10.3	10.7	i/	943	864	995	1130
2221	Printing		...	...	...	...		...	...	...	...		...	...	...	...
2222	Service activities related to printing		...	...	...	...		...	...	...	...		...	...	...	...
2230	Reproduction of recorded media	i/	...	...	...	...	i/	...	...	...	...	i/	...	...	...	...
2310	Coke oven products	j/	...	...	...	...	j/	...	...	...	...	j/	...	...	...	...
2320	Refined petroleum products	j/	...	...	...	...	j/	...	...	...	...	j/	...	...	...	...
2330	Processing of nuclear fuel	j/	...	...	...	...	j/	...	...	...	...	j/	...	...	...	...
241	Basic chemicals		...	...	...	...		...	...	...	...		...	...	...	...
2411	Basic chemicals, except fertilizers	k/	52	47	92	111	k/	4.1	4.0	4.7	5.0	k/	944	965	1158	1269
2412	Fertilizers and nitrogen compounds	k/	...	...	...	...	k/	...	...	...	...	k/	...	...	...	...
2413	Plastics in primary forms; synthetic rubber	j/	21	22	29	30	j/	3.8	3.9	3.4	3.6	j/	771	801	788	879
242	Other chemicals		286	262	296	253		15.6	16.5	14.4	14.6		2491	2673	2540	2721
2421	Pesticides and other agro-chemical products		...	...	...	...		...	...	...	...		...	...	...	...
2422	Paints, varnishes, printing ink and mastics		...	...	...	...		...	...	...	...		...	...	...	...
2423	Pharmaceuticals, medicinal chemicals, etc.		...	...	...	...		...	...	...	...		...	...	...	...
2424	Soap, cleaning & cosmetic preparations		...	...	...	...		...	...	...	...		...	...	...	...
2429	Other chemical products n.e.c.		...	...	...	...		...	...	...	...		...	...	...	...
2430	Man-made fibres	j/	...	...	...	...	j/	...	...	...	...	j/	...	...	...	...
251	Rubber products		28	34	66	65		1.7	1.9	1.7	1.9		187	225	203	226
2511	Rubber tyres and tubes		...	...	...	...		...	...	...	...		...	...	...	...
2519	Other rubber products		...	...	...	...		...	...	...	...		...	...	...	...
2520	Plastic products		443	401	544	554		18.7	17.8	16.0	17.8		1851	1937	1948	2106
2610	Glass and glass products	m/	...	...	...	...	m/	...	...	...	...	m/	...	...	...	...
269	Non-metallic mineral products n.e.c.		...	...	...	...		...	...	...	...		...	...	...	...
2691	Pottery, china and earthenware	m/	69	64	153	153	m/	2.5	2.5	2.2	2.2	m/	278	276	232	248
2692	Refractory ceramic products		...	...	...	...		...	...	...	...		...	...	...	...
2693	Struct.non-refractory clay; ceramic products	m/	...	...	...	...	m/	...	...	...	...	m/	...	...	...	...
2694	Cement, lime and plaster	n/	123	115	143	196	n/	5.6	5.1	5.1	5.5	n/	785	801	686	727
2695	Articles of concrete, cement and plaster	n/	...	...	...	...	n/	...	...	...	...	n/	...	...	...	...
2696	Cutting, shaping & finishing of stone	p/	175	164	487	510	p/	2.1	2.1	2.5	3.0	p/	166	161	239	289
2699	Other non-metallic mineral products n.e.c.	p/	...	...	...	...	p/	...	...	...	...	p/	...	...	...	...
2710	Basic iron and steel		39	50	53	74		2.3	2.2	1.9	2.1		302	296	287	306
2720	Basic precious and non-ferrous metals		34	30	121	84		2.0	2.0	1.8	1.5		205	226	200	190
273	Casting of metals		12	10	115	123		1.3	1.2	1.7	1.9		151	144	209	253
2731	Casting of iron and steel		...	...	...	...		...	...	...	...		...	...	...	...
2732	Casting of non-ferrous metals		...	...	...	...		...	...	...	...		...	...	...	...
281	Struct.metal products;tanks;steam generators		623	482	973	900		13.7	13.4	11.5	10.0		1186	1251	1005	890
2811	Structural metal products		...	...	...	...		...	...	...	...		...	...	...	...
2812	Tanks, reservoirs and containers of metal		...	...	...	...		...	...	...	...		...	...	...	...
2813	Steam generators		...	...	...	...		...	...	...	...		...	...	...	...
289	Other metal products; metal working services		1017	1078	3676	3413		29.7	30.2	28.2	30.3		3260	3431	2954	3087
2891	Metal forging/pressing/stamping/roll-forming		...	...	...	...		...	...	...	...		...	...	...	...
2892	Treatment & coating of metals		...	...	...	...		...	...	...	...		...	...	...	...
2893	Cutlery, hand tools and general hardware		...	...	...	...		...	...	...	...		...	...	...	...
2899	Other fabricated metal products n.e.c.		...	...	...	...		...	...	...	...		...	...	...	...
291	General purpose machinery		268	245	370	257		9.8	9.0	8.1	8.0		1484	1458	1294	1382
2911	Engines & turbines (not for transport equipment)		...	...	...	...		...	...	...	...		...	...	...	...
2912	Pumps, compressors, taps and valves		...	...	...	...		...	...	...	...		...	...	...	...
2913	Bearings, gears, gearing & driving elements		...	...	...	...		...	...	...	...		...	...	...	...
2914	Ovens, furnaces and furnace burners		...	...	...	...		...	...	...	...		...	...	...	...
2915	Lifting and handling equipment		...	...	...	...		...	...	...	...		...	...	...	...
2919	Other general purpose machinery		...	...	...	...		...	...	...	...		...	...	...	...
292	Special purpose machinery		26	29	242	90		2.5	2.6	3.7	3.3		431	500	600	578
2921	Agricultural and forestry machinery		...	...	...	...		...	...	...	...		...	...	...	...
2922	Machine tools		...	...	...	...		...	...	...	...		...	...	...	...
2923	Machinery for metallurgy		...	...	...	...		...	...	...	...		...	...	...	...
2924	Machinery for mining & construction		...	...	...	...		...	...	...	...		...	...	...	...
2925	Food/beverage/tobacco processing machinery		...	...	...	...		...	...	...	...		...	...	...	...
2926	Machinery for textile, apparel and leather		...	...	...	...		...	...	...	...		...	...	...	...
2927	Weapons and ammunition		...	...	...	...		...	...	...	...		...	...	...	...
2929	Other special purpose machinery		...	...	...	...		...	...	...	...		...	...	...	...

continued

Israel

ISIC Revision 3		Number of establishments a/					Number of employees a/					Wages and salaries paid to employees a/				
			(number)					(thousands)					(millions of Israeli New Sheqalim)			
ISIC	Industry	Note	2002	2003	2004	2005	Note	2002	2003	2004b/	2005b/	Note	2002	2003	2004	2005
2930	Domestic appliances n.e.c.	q/	82	87	99	79	q/	3.8	3.7	3.1	3.1	q/	504	478	400	386
3000	Office, accounting and computing machinery	q/	...	...	...	...	q/	...	...	...	...	q/	...	...	...	...
3110	Electric motors, generators and transformers		87	63	187	182		2.5	2.5	1.7	1.7		323	318	218	229
3120	Electricity distribution & control apparatus	r/	128	107	161	225	r/	3.4	3.5	3.1	3.7	r/	419	449	390	450
3130	Insulated wire and cable	s/	28	27	39	29	s/	1.8	1.7	1.8	1.7	s/	253	248	298	248
3140	Accumulators, primary cells and batteries	s/	...	...	...	...	s/	...	...	...	...	s/	...	...	...	...
3150	Lighting equipment and electric lamps	r/	...	...	...	...	r/	...	...	...	...	r/	...	...	...	...
3190	Other electrical equipment n.e.c.	r/	...	...	...	...	r/	...	...	...	...	r/	...	...	...	...
3210	Electronic valves, tubes, etc.		145	128	328	168		14.3	14.5	15.7	16.9		1979	2092	2338	2588
3220	TV/radio transmitters; line comm. apparatus		63	68	132	134		10.5	9.5	11.4	11.8		2668	2301	2864	2887
3230	TV and radio receivers and associated goods		36	32	50	76		3.6	3.4	2.2	2.8		862	807	521	743
331	Medical, measuring, testing appliances, etc.	t/	260	213	257	229	t/	28.2	27.2	25.6	26.1	t/	6764	6604	6350	6964
3311	Medical, surgical and orthopaedic equipment		...	...	...	...		...	...	...	...		...	...	...	...
3312	Measuring/testing/navigating appliances,etc.		...	...	...	...		...	...	...	...		...	...	...	...
3313	Industrial process control equipment		...	...	...	...		...	...	...	...		...	...	...	...
3320	Optical instruments & photographic equipment		63	69	36	49		4.1	4.8	2.7	2.6		860	908	668	688
3330	Watches and clocks	t/	...	...	...	...	t/	...	...	...	...	t/	...	...	...	...
3410	Motor vehicles	u/	...	...	...	...	u/	...	...	...	...	u/	...	...	...	...
3420	Automobile bodies, trailers & semi-trailers	u/	100	82	94	73	u/	2.7	2.8	2.5	2.7	u/	314	328	328	346
3430	Parts/accessories for automobiles	u/	...	...	...	...	u/	...	...	...	...	u/	...	...	...	...
351	Building and repairing of ships and boats	v/	...	...	...	...	v/	...	...	...	...	v/	...	...	...	...
3511	Building and repairing of ships		...	...	...	...		...	...	...	...		...	...	...	...
3512	Building/repairing of pleasure/sport. boats		...	...	...	...		...	...	...	...		...	...	...	...
3520	Railway/tramway locomotives & rolling stock	v/	59	38	29	28	v/	12.0	11.9	12.1	12.5	v/	2903	3025	2820	2414
3530	Aircraft and spacecraft	v/	...	...	...	...	v/	...	...	...	...	v/	...	...	...	...
359	Transport equipment n.e.c.	v/	...	...	...	...	v/	...	...	...	...	v/	...	...	...	...
3591	Motorcycles		...	...	...	...		...	...	...	...		...	...	...	...
3592	Bicycles and invalid carriages		...	...	...	...		...	...	...	...		...	...	...	...
3599	Other transport equipment n.e.c.		...	...	...	...		...	...	...	...		...	...	...	...
3610	Furniture		332	383	3733	3811		11.0	10.0	14.0	12.6		1022	895	1153	987
369	Manufacturing n.e.c.		250	274	1018	969		5.4	5.8	6.9	6.6		455	447	481	537
3691	Jewellery and related articles		...	...	...	...		...	...	...	...		...	...	...	...
3692	Musical instruments		...	...	...	...		...	...	...	...		...	...	...	...
3693	Sports goods		...	...	...	...		...	...	...	...		...	...	...	...
3694	Games and toys		...	...	...	...		...	...	...	...		...	...	...	...
3699	Other manufacturing n.e.c.		...	...	...	...		...	...	...	...		...	...	...	...
3710	Recycling of metal waste and scrap		...	...	...	...		...	...	...	...		...	...	...	...
3720	Recycling of non-metal waste and scrap		...	...	...	...		...	...	...	...		...	...	...	...
D	Total manufacturing		7999	7719	21767	20748		339.0	331.8	323.6	329.2		45887	45835	44668	46519

a/ Methodological break between 2003 and 2004.
b/ Number of persons engaged.
c/ 155 includes 1600.
d/ 171 includes 1722.
e/ 172 excludes 1722.
f/ 191 includes 1820.
g/ 2010 includes 2021.
h/ 202 excludes 2021.
i/ 222 includes 2230.
j/ 2413 includes 2310, 2320, 2330 and 2430.
k/ 2411 includes 2412.
m/ 2691 includes 2610 and 2693.
n/ 2694 includes 2695.
p/ 2696 includes 2699.
q/ 2930 includes 3000.
r/ 3120 includes 3150 and 3190.
s/ 3130 includes 3140.
t/ 331 includes 3330.
u/ 3420 includes 3410 and 3430.
v/ 3520 includes 351, 3530 and 359.

ISIC Revision 3		Output a/					Value added a/					Gross fixed capital formation a/		
			(millions of Israeli New Sheqalim)					(millions of Israeli New Sheqalim)					(millions of Israeli New Sheqalim)	
ISIC	Industry	Note	2002	2003	2004	2005	Note	2002	2003	2004	2005	Note	2004	2005
151	Processed meat,fish,fruit,vegetables,fats		8353	8581	10429	10633		1717	1954	1723	1748		280	...
1511	Processing/preserving of meat		...	...	...	...		...	...	...	...		...	...
1512	Processing/preserving of fish		...	...	...	...		...	...	...	...		...	...
1513	Processing/preserving of fruit & vegetables		...	...	...	...		...	...	...	...		...	...
1514	Vegetable and animal oils and fats		...	...	...	...		...	...	...	...		...	...
1520	Dairy products		5425	5970	5495	6394		1641	1716	1493	1724		351	...
153	Grain mill products; starches; animal feeds		3521	3436	3687	3800		585	599	506	502		117	...
1531	Grain mill products		...	...	...	...		...	...	...	...		...	...
1532	Starches and starch products		...	...	...	...		...	...	...	...		...	...
1533	Prepared animal feeds		...	...	...	...		...	...	...	...		...	...
154	Other food products		8477	8417	9271	9163		3419	3296	3207	3158		490	...
1541	Bakery products		...	...	...	...		...	...	...	...		...	...
1542	Sugar		...	...	...	...		...	...	...	...		...	...
1543	Cocoa, chocolate and sugar confectionery		...	...	...	...		...	...	...	...		...	...
1544	Macaroni, noodles & similar products		...	...	...	...		...	...	...	...		...	...
1549	Other food products n.e.c.		...	...	...	...		...	...	...	...		...	...
155	Beverages	b/	4471	4901	4501	4254	b/	1365	1473	1246	1451		282b/	...
1551	Distilling, rectifying & blending of spirits		...	...	...	...		...	...	...	...		...	...
1552	Wines		...	...	...	...		...	...	...	...		...	...
1553	Malt liquors and malt		...	...	...	...		...	...	...	...		...	...
1554	Soft drinks; mineral waters		...	...	...	...		...	...	...	...		...	...
1600	Tobacco products	b/	...	...	...	...	b/	...	...	...	...		...b/	...
171	Spinning, weaving and finishing of textiles	c/	2657	2608	2947	3069	c/	967	844	881	802		108c/	...
1711	Textile fibre preparation; textile weaving		...	...	...	...		...	...	...	...		...	...
1712	Finishing of textiles		...	...	...	...		...	...	...	...		...	...
172	Other textiles	d/	1270	1247	1414	1953	d/	391	396	366	578	d/	51	...
1721	Made-up textile articles, except apparel		...	...	...	...		...	...	...	...		...	...
1722	Carpets and rugs	c/	...	...	...	...	c/	...	...	...	...		...c/	...
1723	Cordage, rope, twine and netting		...	...	...	...		...	...	...	...		...	...
1729	Other textiles n.e.c.		...	...	...	...		...	...	...	...		...	...
1730	Knitted and crocheted fabrics and articles		2776	2253	1909	1846		970	756	558	590		60	...
1810	Wearing apparel, except fur apparel		2506	2738	1911	1581		833	1059	704	550		46	...
1820	Dressing & dyeing of fur; processing of fur	e/	...	...	...	...	e/	...	...	...	...		...e/	...
191	Tanning, dressing and processing of leather	e/	687	688	471	515	e/	227	238	167	175		8e/	...
1911	Tanning and dressing of leather		...	...	...	...		...	...	...	...		...	...
1912	Luggage, handbags, etc.; saddlery & harness		...	...	...	...		...	...	...	...		...	...
1920	Footwear		464	452	387	421		156	151	143	150		5	...
2010	Sawmilling and planing of wood	f/	376	508	699	679	f/	82	99	134	141		11f/	...
202	Products of wood, cork, straw, etc.	g/	1414	1488	1179	1113	g/	448	519	387	321	g/	23	...
2021	Veneer sheets, plywood, particle board, etc.	f/	...	...	...	...	f/	...	...	...	...		...f/	...
2022	Builders' carpentry and joinery		...	...	...	...		...	...	...	...		...	...
2023	Wooden containers		...	...	...	...		...	...	...	...		...	...
2029	Other wood products; articles of cork/straw		...	...	...	...		...	...	...	...		...	...
210	Paper and paper products		4507	4686	4641	5221		1532	1518	1350	1482		201	...
2101	Pulp, paper and paperboard		...	...	...	...		...	...	...	...		...	...
2102	Corrugated paper and paperboard		...	...	...	...		...	...	...	...		...	...
2109	Other articles of paper and paperboard		...	...	...	...		...	...	...	...		...	...
221	Publishing		4508	4540	3654	3919		1829	1829	1631	1797		142	...
2211	Publishing of books and other publications		...	...	...	...		...	...	...	...		...	...
2212	Publishing of newspapers, journals, etc.		...	...	...	...		...	...	...	...		...	...
2213	Publishing of recorded media		...	...	...	...		...	...	...	...		...	...
2219	Other publishing		...	...	...	...		...	...	...	...		...	...

continued

Israel

ISIC Revision 3		Output a/					Value added a/					Gross fixed capital formation a/		
			(millions of Israeli New Sheqalim)					(millions of Israeli New Sheqalim)					(millions of Israeli New Sheqalim)	
ISIC	Industry	Note	2002	2003	2004	2005	Note	2002	2003	2004	2005	Note	2004	2005
222	Printing and related service activities	h/	3540	3074	3335	3608	h/	1666	1465	1417	1569		319h/	...
2221	Printing		...	...	...	...		...	...	...	...		...	...
2222	Service activities related to printing		...	...	...	...		...	...	...	...		...	...
2230	Reproduction of recorded media	h/	...	...	...	...	h/	...	...	...	...		...h/	...
2310	Coke oven products	i/	...	...	...	...	i/	...	...	...	...		...i/	...
2320	Refined petroleum products	i/	...	...	...	...	i/	...	...	...	...		...i/	...
2330	Processing of nuclear fuel	i/	...	...	...	...	i/	...	...	...	...		...i/	...
241	Basic chemicals		...	...	...	...		...	...	...	...		...	...
2411	Basic chemicals, except fertilizers	j/	5285	5410	6646	7934	j/	1469	1539	1844	2618		315j/	...
2412	Fertilizers and nitrogen compounds	j/	...	...	...	...	j/	...	...	...	...		...j/	...
2413	Plastics in primary forms; synthetic rubber	i/	14798	17896	23007	32372	i/	1341	1920	2915	4301		280i/	...
242	Other chemicals		16046	17248	19358	21470		6381	6521	7369	8460		1085	...
2421	Pesticides and other agro-chemical products		...	...	...	...		...	...	...	...		...	...
2422	Paints, varnishes, printing ink and mastics		...	...	...	...		...	...	...	...		...	...
2423	Pharmaceuticals, medicinal chemicals, etc.		...	...	...	...		...	...	...	...		...	...
2424	Soap, cleaning & cosmetic preparations		...	...	...	...		...	...	...	...		...	...
2429	Other chemical products n.e.c.		...	...	...	...		...	...	...	...		...	...
2430	Man-made fibres	i/	...	...	...	...	i/	...	...	...	...		...i/	...
251	Rubber products		615	832	989	995		210	300	349	327		26	...
2511	Rubber tyres and tubes		...	...	...	...		...	...	...	...		...	...
2519	Other rubber products		...	...	...	...		...	...	...	...		...	...
2520	Plastic products		9538	10009	10600	12756		3521	3494	3302	3829		1043	...
2610	Glass and glass products	k/	...	...	...	...	k/	...	...	...	...		...k/	...
269	Non-metallic mineral products n.e.c.		...	...	...	...		...	...	...	...		...	...
2691	Pottery, china and earthenware	k/	1216	1165	934	1023	k/	456	425	351	376		32k/	...
2692	Refractory ceramic products		...	...	...	...		...	...	...	...		...	...
2693	Struct.non-refractory clay; ceramic products	k/	...	...	...	...	k/	...	...	...	...		...k/	...
2694	Cement, lime and plaster	m/	4434	4241	3910	4681	m/	1343	1318	1175	1227		100m/	...
2695	Articles of concrete, cement and plaster	m/	...	...	...	...	m/	...	...	...	...		...m/	...
2696	Cutting, shaping & finishing of stone	n/	711	645	1205	1394	n/	267	229	400	432		72n/	...
2699	Other non-metallic mineral products n.e.c.	n/	...	...	...	...	n/	...	...	...	...		...n/	...
2710	Basic iron and steel		2054	1939	2870	3342		510	520	611	457		118	...
2720	Basic precious and non-ferrous metals		1270	1429	1528	1553		239	310	282	283		52	...
273	Casting of metals		413	348	818	995		234	189	253	359		42	...
2731	Casting of iron and steel		...	...	...	...		...	...	...	...		...	...
2732	Casting of non-ferrous metals		...	...	...	...		...	...	...	...		...	...
281	Struct.metal products;tanks;steam generators		4622	4647	4229	4545		1596	1706	1274	1367		63	...
2811	Structural metal products		...	...	...	...		...	...	...	...		...	...
2812	Tanks, reservoirs and containers of metal		...	...	...	...		...	...	...	...		...	...
2813	Steam generators		...	...	...	...		...	...	...	...		...	...
289	Other metal products; metal working services		12508	13306	12635	14235		6109	6335	5795	6299		638	...
2891	Metal forging/pressing/stamping/roll-forming		...	...	...	...		...	...	...	...		...	...
2892	Treatment & coating of metals		...	...	...	...		...	...	...	...		...	...
2893	Cutlery, hand tools and general hardware		...	...	...	...		...	...	...	...		...	...
2899	Other fabricated metal products n.e.c.		...	...	...	...		...	...	...	...		...	...
291	General purpose machinery		4517	4263	4235	4699		1637	1705	1470	1650		90	...
2911	Engines & turbines (not for transport equipment)		...	...	...	...		...	...	...	...		...	...
2912	Pumps, compressors, taps and valves		...	...	...	...		...	...	...	...		...	...
2913	Bearings, gears, gearing & driving elements		...	...	...	...		...	...	...	...		...	...
2914	Ovens, furnaces and furnace burners		...	...	...	...		...	...	...	...		...	...
2915	Lifting and handling equipment		...	...	...	...		...	...	...	...		...	...
2919	Other general purpose machinery		...	...	...	...		...	...	...	...		...	...

292	Special purpose machinery		1544	1907	2759	3154		320	580	832	859		134	...
2921	Agricultural and forestry machinery		...	...	...	...		...	...	...	...		...	...
2922	Machine tools		...	...	...	...		...	...	...	...		...	...
2923	Machinery for metallurgy		...	...	...	...		...	...	...	...		...	...
2924	Machinery for mining & construction		...	...	...	...		...	...	...	...		...	...
2925	Food/beverage/tobacco processing machinery		...	...	...	...		...	...	...	...		...	...
2926	Machinery for textile, apparel and leather		...	...	...	...		...	...	...	...		...	...
2927	Weapons and ammunition		...	...	...	...		...	...	...	...		...	...
2929	Other special purpose machinery		...	...	...	...		...	...	...	...		...	...
2930	Domestic appliances n.e.c.	p/	2018	1944	2037	2216	p/	543	518	545	563		33p/	...
3000	Office, accounting and computing machinery	p/	...	...	...	...	p/	...	...	...	...		...p/	...
3110	Electric motors, generators and transformers		1199	1851	854	874		448	716	311	351		13	...
3120	Electricity distribution & control apparatus	q/	1518	1701	1520	1681	q/	569	667	470	532		35q/	...
3130	Insulated wire and cable	r/	1183	1252	1566	1699	r/	321	402	468	439		22r/	...
3140	Accumulators, primary cells and batteries	r/	...	...	...	...	r/	...	...	...	...		...r/	...
3150	Lighting equipment and electric lamps	q/	...	...	...	...	q/	...	...	...	...		...q/	...
3190	Other electrical equipment n.e.c.	q/	...	...	...	...	q/	...	...	...	...		...q/	...
3210	Electronic valves, tubes, etc.		9376	8673	8834	9480		4193	4792	4078	4453		1632	...
3220	TV/radio transmitters; line comm. apparatus		9223	8570	11509	12694		3104	3055	4191	4932		471	...
3230	TV and radio receivers and associated goods		3039	2584	1564	2111		1186	861	623	756		44	...
331	Medical, measuring, testing appliances, etc.	s/	22637	22013	23297	25081	s/	9020	8922	9222	9234		789s/	...
3311	Medical, surgical and orthopaedic equipment		...	...	...	...		...	...	...	...		...	...
3312	Measuring/testing/navigating appliances,etc.		...	...	...	...		...	...	...	...		...	...
3313	Industrial process control equipment		...	...	...	...		...	...	...	...		...	...
3320	Optical instruments & photographic equipment		2579	2663	2149	2239		1128	1119	730	950		210	...
3330	Watches and clocks	s/	...	...	...	...	s/	...	...	...	...		...s/	...
3410	Motor vehicles	t/	...	...	...	...	t/	...	...	...	...		...t/	...
3420	Automobile bodies, trailers & semi-trailers	t/	1197	1319	1269	1510	t/	499	484	464	517		45t/	...
3430	Parts/accessories for automobiles	t/	...	...	...	...	t/	...	...	...	...		...t/	...
351	Building and repairing of ships and boats	u/	...	...	...	...	u/	...	...	...	...		...u/	...
3511	Building and repairing of ships		...	...	...	...		...	...	...	...		...	...
3512	Building/repairing of pleasure/sport. boats		...	...	...	...		...	...	...	...		...	...
3520	Railway/tramway locomotives & rolling stock	u/	8014	7712	7862	7865	u/	3614	3762	4281	3364		406u/	...
3530	Aircraft and spacecraft	u/	...	...	...	...	u/	...	...	...	...		...u/	...
359	Transport equipment n.e.c.	u/	...	...	...	...	u/	...	...	...	...		...u/	...
3591	Motorcycles		...	...	...	...		...	...	...	...		...	...
3592	Bicycles and invalid carriages		...	...	...	...		...	...	...	...		...	...
3599	Other transport equipment n.e.c.		...	...	...	...		...	...	...	...		...	...
3610	Furniture		5273	4602	5447	4710		1875	1649	1646	1600		205	...
369	Manufacturing n.e.c.		3145	3141	2472	2947		840	762	672	881		54	...
3691	Jewellery and related articles		...	...	...	...		...	...	...	...		...	...
3692	Musical instruments		...	...	...	...		...	...	...	...		...	...
3693	Sports goods		...	...	...	...		...	...	...	...		...	...
3694	Games and toys		...	...	...	...		...	...	...	...		...	...
3699	Other manufacturing n.e.c.		...	...	...	...		...	...	...	...		...	...
3710	Recycling of metal waste and scrap		...	...	...	...		...	...	...	...		...	...
3720	Recycling of non-metal waste and scrap		...	...	...	...		...	...	...	...		...	...
D	Total manufacturing		208451	212552	225663	253170		72622	74721	73792	80776		10783	...

a/ Methodological break between 2003 and 2004.
b/ 155 includes 1600.
c/ 171 includes 1722.
d/ 172 excludes 1722.
e/ 191 includes 1820.
f/ 2010 includes 2021.
g/ 202 excludes 2021.
h/ 222 includes 2230.
i/ 2413 includes 2310, 2320, 2330 and 2430.
j/ 2411 includes 2412.

k/ 2691 includes 2610 and 2693.
m/ 2694 includes 2695.
n/ 2696 includes 2699.
p/ 2930 includes 3000.
q/ 3120 includes 3150 and 3190.
r/ 3130 includes 3140.
s/ 331 includes 3330.
t/ 3420 includes 3410 and 3430.
u/ 3520 includes 351, 3530 and 359.

Israel

ISIC Revision 3			Index numbers of industrial production											
			(2000=100)											
ISIC	Industry	Note	1995	1996	1997	1998	1999	2000	2001	2002	2003	2004	2005	2006
15	Food and beverages	a/	95	95	98	99	100	100	99	97	95	97	97	99
16	Tobacco products	a/	...	...	...	...	...	...	...	...	...	...	...	...
17	Textiles		103	98	98	101	106	100	91	87	84	85	85	88
18	Wearing apparel, fur		...	...	...	...	...	...	...	...	...	...	...	...
19	Leather, leather products and footwear		...	...	...	...	...	...	...	...	...	...	...	...
20	Wood products (excl. furniture)		...	...	...	...	...	...	...	...	...	...	...	...
21	Paper and paper products		101	102	101	103	100	100	96	96	93	93	97	99
22	Printing and publishing		95	98	98	101	100	100	97	93	90	95	97	101
23	Coke,refined petroleum products,nuclear fuel	b/	80	88	89	100	97	100	106	123	129	146	152	188
24	Chemicals and chemical products	b/	...	...	...	...	...	...	...	...	...	...	...	...
25	Rubber and plastics products		86	91	90	92	97	100	103	112	119	125	138	144
26	Non-metallic mineral products		136	150	136	119	109	100	93	88	83	76	80	83
27	Basic metals		97	103	105	99	98	100	93	84	75	81	83	83
28	Fabricated metal products		87	91	96	95	92	100	96	94	93	99	104	116
29	Machinery and equipment n.e.c.		91	94	86	86	89	100	93	86	83	77	76	82
30	Office, accounting and computing machinery		...	...	...	...	...	...	...	...	...	...	...	...
31	Electrical machinery and apparatus		...	...	...	...	...	...	...	...	...	...	...	...
32	Radio,television and communication equipment		...	...	...	...	...	...	...	...	...	...	...	...
33	Medical, precision and optical instruments		...	...	...	...	...	...	...	...	...	...	...	...
34	Motor vehicles, trailers, semi-trailers		...	...	...	...	...	...	...	...	...	...	...	...
35	Other transport equipment		...	...	...	...	...	...	...	...	...	...	...	...
36	Furniture; manufacturing n.e.c.		...	...	...	...	...	...	...	...	...	...	...	...
37	Recycling		...	...	...	...	...	...	...	...	...	...	...	...
D	Total manufacturing		81	85	87	89	91	100	95	93	93	99	103	113

a/ 15 includes 16.
b/ 23 includes 24.

Italy

Supplier of information:
Istituto Nazionale di Statistica (National Institute of Statistics), Rome.
Industrial statistics for the OECD countries are compiled by the OECD secretariat, which supplies them to UNIDO.

Basic source of data:
Annual surveys; adminstrative data.

Major deviations from ISIC (Revision 3):
Data have been converted from national NACE-related classification system to ISIC (Revision 3).

Reference period:
Calendar year.

Scope:
All enterprises.

Method of data collection:
Not reported.

Type of enumeration:
Enterprises with over 100 employees are completely enumerated, enterprises below that threshold are sampled.

Adjusted for non-response:
Not reported.

Concepts and definitions of variables:
Output is gross output. It is net of indirect taxes and subsidies, and is calculated on a shipment basis. The valuation is at selling prices, excluding VAT.
Value added is in the national accounting concept. The valuation excludes all indirect taxes and subsidies.
Gross fixed capital formation (value of sales not deducted) is defined as the value of purchases of fixed assets, including own-account construction. Fixed assets covered are those with a productive life of at least one year. Assets made by a unit's labour force for its own use; additions, alterations, improvements and repairs to existing assets; new assets (not yet in use, or previously used outside the country) and used assets are all included. The valuation is at full cost incurred, including installation expenses.

Related national publications:
None reported.

Italy

ISIC Revision 3		Number of enterprises					Number of employees					Wages and salaries paid to employees				
			(number)					(thousands)					(millions of Euros)			
ISIC	Industry	Note	2002	2003	2004	2005	Note	2002	2003	2004	2005	Note	2002	2003	2004	2005
151	Processed meat,fish,fruit,vegetables,fats		10357	10359	...	...		93.2	...	...	...		1912.0	...	...	...
1511	Processing/preserving of meat		3706	3769	3794	3854		51.9	54.0	52.6	53.4		1075.5	1116.0	1168.4	1168.0
1512	Processing/preserving of fish		455	451	...	...		5.6	...	...	...		112.7	...	...	...
1513	Processing/preserving of fruit & vegetables		1960	2010	2017	2024		27.7	27.8	30.3	29.4		538.5	531.8	576.3	560.0
1514	Vegetable and animal oils and fats		4236	4129	4057	4031		7.9	8.0	7.6	7.4		185.3	172.9	176.5	159.0
1520	Dairy products		3727	4378	4307	4339		45.1	48.4	45.0	40.4		1076.9	1160.7	1060.4	981.0
153	Grain mill products; starches; animal feeds		2392	2275	2211	2171		16.5	16.5	16.4	16.5		385.6	425.1	448.4	458.0
1531	Grain mill products		1761	1645	1581	1546		7.5	7.0	7.0	7.1		155.0	152.2	170.2	175.0
1532	Starches and starch products		36	34	32	32		1.1	0.7	1.3	1.3		28.6	20.2	44.5	47.0
1533	Prepared animal feeds		595	596	598	593		8.0	8.8	8.1	8.1		201.9	252.8	233.7	237.0
154	Other food products		50410	50113	50437	51224		131.4	143.3	154.8	163.9		2522.2	2658.4	2985.1	3157.0
1541	Bakery products		39738	40535	40527	40687		80.3	92.8	91.5	100.4		1408.2	1512.7	1398.2	1527.0
1542	Sugar		31	34	31	32		3.5	3.0	3.0	3.2		63.1	96.0	90.6	107.0
1543	Cocoa, chocolate and sugar confectionery		495	517	523	518		13.5	13.6	18.4	18.4		327.5	336.4	498.9	498.0
1544	Macaroni, noodles & similar products		5579	5641	5709	5893		14.2	13.7	20.6	19.7		282.9	265.9	462.7	464.0
1549	Other food products n.e.c.		4567	3386	3647	4094		19.9	20.2	21.3	22.1		440.5	447.4	534.7	561.0
155	Beverages		2914	2841	2806	2822		32.6	33.3	33.3	33.0		798.7	886.1	888.9	932.0
1551	Distilling, rectifying & blending of spirits		658	656	675	661		4.3	4.3	4.7	5.0		106.2	112.7	127.7	148.0
1552	Wines		1922	1814	...	...		14.0	...	...	...		317.1	...	...	...
1553	Malt liquors and malt		24	55	...	...		2.9	...	...	...		88.5	...	...	...
1554	Soft drinks; mineral waters		310	316	297	311		11.5	12.7	11.9	12.0		287.0	366.9	339.0	363.0
1600	Tobacco products		68	2	...	...		8.2	...	...	...		136.3	...	...	...
171	Spinning, weaving and finishing of textiles		9423	9341	8748	8279		141.6	138.6	126.2	118.8		2774.2	2852.4	2646.8	2521.0
1711	Textile fibre preparation; textile weaving		7770	7255	6727	6279		105.5	100.3	89.7	84.9		2030.9	2026.9	1862.5	1764.0
1712	Finishing of textiles		1653	2086	2021	2000		36.1	38.3	36.5	33.8		743.3	825.5	784.3	756.0
172	Other textiles		9645	9198	8984	8957		51.4	49.4	48.2	46.7		904.8	879.4	875.4	873.0
1721	Made-up textile articles, except apparel		5348	5045	4947	4982		18.9	17.9	17.8	17.5		308.9	295.7	294.1	297.0
1722	Carpets and rugs		204	203	193	194		1.7	1.7	1.7	1.8		30.8	34.6	34.8	33.0
1723	Cordage, rope, twine and netting		233	230	217	208		1.4	1.4	1.4	1.3		21.1	21.7	22.9	20.0
1729	Other textiles n.e.c.		3860	3720	3627	3573		29.4	28.3	27.4	26.2		543.9	527.4	523.7	523.0
1730	Knitted and crocheted fabrics and articles		8462	8619	7848	7197		54.6	54.9	51.4	45.6		836.3	854.6	822.7	767.0
1810	Wearing apparel, except fur apparel		43234	38509	36950	35704		224.1	220.2	205.7	194.9		3208.5	3161.1	3233.6	3057.0
1820	Dressing & dyeing of fur; processing of fur		2110	1939	1810	1728		2.8	2.8	2.6	1.2		40.9	39.8	42.3	22.0
191	Tanning, dressing and processing of leather		9779	9349	8888	8567		53.1	53.5	50.9	48.8		920.6	941.9	971.4	946.0
1911	Tanning and dressing of leather		2531	2492	2397	2308		27.0	27.3	25.7	24.5		505.6	515.2	546.2	498.0
1912	Luggage, handbags, etc.; saddlery & harness		7248	6857	6491	6259		26.1	26.2	25.2	24.3		415.0	426.7	425.2	448.0
1920	Footwear		12959	12203	11582	11022		111.0	107.8	97.1	89.3		1687.3	1628.0	1593.7	1502.0
2010	Sawmilling and planing of wood		5632	5085	5009	4893		15.1	15.3	14.8	14.5		239.1	255.3	260.5	258.0
202	Products of wood, cork, straw, etc.		42703	40938	39284	37865		98.4	95.2	97.1	96.5		1524.8	1521.1	1640.9	1703.0
2021	Veneer sheets, plywood, particle board, etc.		471	434	412	404		10.5	10.5	10.4	10.7		206.1	202.1	218.4	237.0
2022	Builders' carpentry and joinery		29577	28529	27291	26204		52.1	51.7	54.7	53.4		759.4	790.0	856.0	897.0
2023	Wooden containers		1775	1733	1722	1699		9.3	9.6	9.5	9.8		139.7	150.2	167.2	152.0
2029	Other wood products; articles of cork/straw		10880	10242	9859	9558		26.4	23.4	22.5	22.6		419.6	378.8	399.3	417.0
210	Paper and paper products		4597	4490	4362	4311		75.0	75.7	75.8	73.4		1725.9	1777.5	1832.2	1792.0
2101	Pulp, paper and paperboard		371	363	346	335		18.0	18.7	17.3	16.8		500.1	503.8	478.3	474.0
2102	Corrugated paper and paperboard		1697	1661	1636	1616		28.4	26.9	27.8	27.2		603.1	594.5	643.7	621.0
2109	Other articles of paper and paperboard		2529	2466	2380	2360		28.6	30.1	30.7	29.4		622.7	679.3	710.2	697.0
221	Publishing		6828	6933	7009	7208		35.7	36.0	35.1	35.2		1341.9	1395.4	1477.8	1454.0
2211	Publishing of books and other publications		3228	3264	3253	3322		13.2	13.4	10.6	10.9		411.6	432.8	320.5	307.0
2212	Publishing of newspapers, journals, etc.		2400	2445	2489	2545		21.0	20.5	21.9	22.2		895.1	909.5	1095.4	1087.0
2213	Publishing of recorded media		634	682	709	752		0.6	0.7	0.9	0.6		11.4	17.4	22.9	19.0
2219	Other publishing		566	542	558	589		0.9	1.4	1.6	1.5		23.9	35.8	39.0	41.0

222	Printing and related service activities	20262	19603	19355	19272	93.7	94.9	92.4	91.2	1864.9	2041.8	1981.0	2049.0
2221	Printing	12996	13045	12922	12888	69.7	71.3	69.2	68.4	1420.2	1587.9	1515.4	1569.0
2222	Service activities related to printing	7266	6558	6433	6384	24.0	23.6	23.2	22.8	444.7	453.9	465.6	480.0
2230	Reproduction of recorded media	413	392	412	421	1.7	1.7	1.2	1.1	44.8	40.6	29.7	26.0
2310	Coke oven products	6	5	...	7	...	0.3	...	0.3	...	7.4	...	8.0
2320	Refined petroleum products	440	426	402	385	16.9	17.4	16.7	16.5	667.7	615.5	633.0	653.0
2330	Processing of nuclear fuel	1	-	...	-	...	-	...	-	...	-	...	-
241	Basic chemicals	1217	1145	1097	1096	50.0	48.0	46.6	44.6	1421.6	1443.0	1484.2	1464.0
2411	Basic chemicals, except fertilizers	495	488	489	496	25.7	22.9	22.6	21.4	742.8	698.9	721.5	702.0
2412	Fertilizers and nitrogen compounds	191	190	189	185	...	2.3	2.4	2.5	...	62.7	76.7	71.0
2413	Plastics in primary forms; synthetic rubber	531	467	419	415	...	22.8	21.6	20.7	...	681.4	686.1	691.0
242	Other chemicals	4965	4779	4688	4659	142.1	140.9	139.1	140.6	4670.0	4809.9	4793.5	5000.0
2421	Pesticides and other agro-chemical products	44	40	39	39	2.1	2.2	2.2	2.2	64.6	73.1	76.2	78.0
2422	Paints, varnishes, printing ink and mastics	1032	1028	1012	1012	18.1	20.0	20.5	20.8	483.3	571.5	596.2	619.0
2423	Pharmaceuticals, medicinal chemicals, etc.	704	663	668	646	71.2	71.3	70.2	67.3	2668.1	2750.1	2744.4	2688.0
2424	Soap, cleaning & cosmetic preparations	1581	1544	1511	1521	25.5	24.6	24.9	27.7	721.9	731.8	727.2	884.0
2429	Other chemical products n.e.c.	1604	1504	1458	1441	25.2	22.8	21.3	22.6	732.1	683.4	649.5	732.0
2430	Man-made fibres	49	51	54	57	7.0	5.9	5.7	5.1	176.6	154.7	141.8	127.0
251	Rubber products	1663	1621	1595	1584	44.7	44.8	43.2	43.5	1033.4	1033.6	1056.7	1141.0
2511	Rubber tyres and tubes	241	219	203	196	15.0	14.7	14.1	13.9	418.4	404.8	421.8	437.0
2519	Other rubber products	1422	1402	1392	1388	29.7	30.1	29.1	29.6	615.0	628.8	635.0	703.0
2520	Plastic products	11335	11187	11051	10964	142.4	147.9	146.9	142.5	2915.0	3090.8	3129.6	3185.0
2610	Glass and glass products	5468	5379	5310	5217	38.5	39.8	38.1	38.2	824.2	844.4	888.1	906.0
269	Non-metallic mineral products n.e.c.	21789	21493	21190	21020	172.2	172.5	172.4	172.5	3572.4	3723.9	3887.9	4022.0
2691	Pottery, china and earthenware	4148	4068	3944	3816	18.8	17.0	17.5	16.7	341.1	286.9	321.5	321.0
2692	Refractory ceramic products	137	128	131	138	2.7	2.6	2.5	2.7	63.9	65.2	65.8	79.0
2693	Struct.non-refractory clay; ceramic products	1049	1036	1015	1020	44.7	43.8	42.4	41.4	1123.8	1155.6	1173.4	1182.0
2694	Cement, lime and plaster	315	319	297	289	11.4	11.5	11.4	11.6	314.6	320.5	337.2	349.0
2695	Articles of concrete, cement and plaster	4715	4724	4678	4650	51.0	54.3	54.3	55.3	972.3	1131.5	1166.6	1223.0
2696	Cutting, shaping & finishing of stone	10362	10231	10146	10136	34.6	34.4	34.7	35.2	577.6	576.9	600.2	638.0
2699	Other non-metallic mineral products n.e.c.	1063	987	979	971	9.0	8.8	9.7	9.5	179.0	187.4	223.2	231.0
2710	Basic iron and steel	1957	1534	1543	1563	73.9	77.0	73.2	71.9	1799.3	1948.9	1955.3	1988.0
2720	Basic precious and non-ferrous metals	830	687	736	731	23.5	22.4	22.7	22.6	585.4	570.6	613.4	614.0
273	Casting of metals	1549	1512	1478	1436	32.9	33.2	33.7	33.3	751.4	766.2	821.0	823.0
2731	Casting of iron and steel	326	310	299	282	13.9	13.7	12.9	12.4	347.2	331.0	324.8	322.0
2732	Casting of non-ferrous metals	1223	1202	1179	1154	19.0	19.5	20.9	20.8	404.2	435.2	496.2	501.0
281	Struct.metal products;tanks;steam generators	35044	34857	35017	35563	155.7	167.4	165.9	168.4	2854.2	3225.9	3478.9	3303.0
2811	Structural metal products	33969	33842	33998	34526	133.8	145.3	142.9	145.2	2380.2	2717.8	2893.6	2712.0
2812	Tanks, reservoirs and containers of metal	1002	950	952	969	20.1	20.5	21.3	21.4	426.7	460.1	530.9	536.0
2813	Steam generators	73	65	67	68	1.7	1.6	1.8	1.8	47.3	48.0	54.4	55.0
289	Other metal products; metal working services	62033	62959	62047	61375	383.3	394.2	388.1	389.3	7329.2	7992.7	8268.4	8546.0
2891	Metal forging/pressing/stamping/roll-forming	2575	2565	2547	2566	48.2	47.6	47.4	48.0	1063.4	1071.8	1145.3	1176.0
2892	Treatment & coating of metals	32604	33438	33177	33151	183.6	195.4	198.0	196.7	3337.0	3853.9	4098.5	4191.0
2893	Cutlery, hand tools and general hardware	3231	3019	2817	2720	38.4	35.8	32.8	32.1	794.9	782.5	750.6	758.0
2899	Other fabricated metal products n.e.c.	23623	23937	23506	22938	113.0	115.4	110.0	112.6	2133.9	2284.5	2274.0	2422.0
291	General purpose machinery	25855	24111	23929	23941	265.8	262.7	253.9	253.4	6301.9	6538.4	6585.8	6936.0
2911	Engines & turbines (not for transport equipment)	633	616	627	648	14.9	14.0	13.8	13.8	440.9	417.3	436.8	471.0
2912	Pumps, compressors, taps and valves	1989	1969	1938	1953	47.7	49.2	49.4	49.7	1106.5	1202.9	1291.3	1328.0
2913	Bearings, gears, gearing & driving elements	514	534	525	535	27.2	28.3	26.9	27.3	658.1	716.2	712.2	768.0
2914	Ovens, furnaces and furnace burners	1267	1208	1165	1105	7.6	8.6	8.2	7.8	163.7	203.8	205.5	212.0
2915	Lifting and handling equipment	4597	4533	4548	4701	42.7	43.6	43.1	41.6	957.0	1050.3	1104.5	1104.0
2919	Other general purpose machinery	16855	15251	15126	14999	125.8	119.1	112.5	113.0	2975.7	2948.0	2835.5	3053.0
292	Special purpose machinery	16482	16475	16426	16554	205.7	204.4	198.2	192.6	4960.3	5117.1	5245.4	5311.0
2921	Agricultural and forestry machinery	4183	4280	4177	4160	27.4	28.5	29.0	29.1	583.5	617.1	656.0	666.0
2922	Machine tools	3684	3019	2954	3057	50.6	46.2	44.3	43.8	1206.8	1151.9	1207.0	1266.0
2923	Machinery for metallurgy	491	547	544	522	7.6	8.0	8.1	8.3	198.5	222.6	231.0	237.0
2924	Machinery for mining & construction	697	814	801	817	12.0	13.8	15.7	15.8	290.4	345.2	421.1	424.0
2925	Food/beverage/tobacco processing machinery	1785	1922	1974	2013	21.0	21.2	21.6	21.2	534.9	521.0	583.6	605.0
2926	Machinery for textile, apparel and leather	2410	2401	2301	2167	27.3	26.6	22.9	20.6	620.0	647.0	541.0	521.0
2927	Weapons and ammunition	147	176	151	138	6.2	6.4	6.5	6.2	179.0	198.0	203.9	198.0
2929	Other special purpose machinery	3085	3316	3524	3680	53.5	53.6	50.2	47.8	1347.2	1414.3	1401.9	1395.0

continued

Italy

ISIC Revision 3		Number of enterprises					Number of employees					Wages and salaries paid to employees			
			(number)					(thousands)					(millions of Euros)		
ISIC	Industry	Note	2002	2003	2004	2005	Note	2002	2003	2004	2005	Note	2002	2003	2004	2005
2930	Domestic appliances n.e.c.		848	871	847	821		58.5	57.5	58.1	56.7		1280.3	1283.8	1349.2	1363.0
3000	Office, accounting and computing machinery		1863	1925	1884	1880		14.4	13.6	12.8	12.2		347.3	326.7	333.3	311.0
3110	Electric motors, generators and transformers		2233	2147	2131	2149		29.9	27.7	27.1	25.7		681.5	622.9	588.1	589.0
3120	Electricity distribution & control apparatus		2159	2116	2180	2244		37.0	36.3	35.2	34.3		886.8	882.5	924.7	909.0
3130	Insulated wire and cable		499	480	459	442		12.9	12.9	12.8	12.5		283.5	298.5	305.7	324.0
3140	Accumulators, primary cells and batteries		130	124	121	111		3.9	3.6	3.4	2.8		97.0	85.7	83.1	74.0
3150	Lighting equipment and electric lamps		2127	2126	2083	2046		16.1	17.0	16.5	16.4		329.5	346.0	353.2	369.0
3190	Other electrical equipment n.e.c.		11947	10958	10709	10790		79.9	80.4	74.0	73.8		1644.1	1649.4	1618.8	1681.0
3210	Electronic valves, tubes, etc.		1072	1038	1030	992		31.8	31.9	30.6	30.6		775.0	805.6	814.8	800.0
3220	TV/radio transmitters; line comm. apparatus		7762	7110	6465	6010		50.2	45.1	41.4	39.4		1357.2	1331.2	1245.7	1173.0
3230	TV and radio receivers and associated goods		400	402	403	381		6.8	6.5	6.1	5.6		135.5	122.9	127.4	125.0
331	Medical, measuring, testing appliances, etc.		19964	19558	18915	18811		69.4	68.2	71.1	73.3		1690.3	1706.2	1872.3	2012.0
3311	Medical, surgical and orthopaedic equipment		16593	16154	15531	15350		26.8	26.3	28.7	31.0		544.0	571.0	622.0	728.0
3312	Measuring/testing/navigating appliances,etc.		2228	2129	2135	2142		29.4	28.7	29.3	29.0		797.0	787.0	866.0	881.0
3313	Industrial process control equipment		1143	1275	1249	1319		13.3	13.1	13.1	13.3		350.0	348.0	384.0	403.0
3320	Optical instruments & photographic equipment		2629	2498	2478	2408		24.0	23.7	22.9	22.6		521.2	450.3	465.5	516.0
3330	Watches and clocks		131	123	118	118		1.1	0.8	0.8	0.8		23.8	17.0	17.8	18.0
3410	Motor vehicles		63	47	70	98		65.3	59.4	66.5	67.5		1542.1	1445.5	1674.8	1722.0
3420	Automobile bodies, trailers & semi-trailers		384	426	483	541		15.1	15.7	15.3	14.7		319.1	336.5	345.7	352.0
3430	Parts/accessories for automobiles		1498	1443	1421	1426		86.9	86.0	82.3	81.1		2005.5	2008.7	2039.3	2096.0
351	Building and repairing of ships and boats		3228	3419	3628	3861		27.2	29.9	31.3	33.4		576.2	668.1	718.3	778.0
3511	Building and repairing of ships		1316	1389	1431	1449		19.2	20.3	20.4	20.9		437.8	476.7	506.0	534.0
3512	Building/repairing of pleasure/sport. boats		1912	2030	2197	2412		8.0	9.5	10.9	12.5		138.5	191.4	212.3	244.0
3520	Railway/tramway locomotives & rolling stock		96	105	121	140		10.1	10.6	10.8	11.2		273.3	273.2	297.6	315.0
3530	Aircraft and spacecraft		126	130	137	163		28.4	25.5	27.2	28.3		831.8	776.3	882.0	961.0
359	Transport equipment n.e.c.		1112	931	872	841		20.7	20.3	19.5	18.7		433.7	453.6	459.4	447.0
3591	Motorcycles		339	330	340	324		15.0	14.9	14.2	14.1		330.0	356.8	359.9	361.0
3592	Bicycles and invalid carriages		713	538	481	470		5.4	5.3	5.0	4.2		99.7	92.4	93.6	80.0
3599	Other transport equipment n.e.c.		60	63	51	47		0.2	0.2	0.3	0.3		4.0	4.0	6.0	6.0
3610	Furniture		32163	31312	30985	30712		160.8	167.6	162.0	155.9		2792.6	2940.6	2959.8	2840.0
369	Manufacturing n.e.c.		18073	17914	17606	17391		66.5	67.0	65.4	63.0		1097.8	1158.0	1164.9	1155.0
3691	Jewellery and related articles		10439	10043	9762	9455		33.2	32.8	30.9	29.5		518.8	524.7	502.6	502.0
3692	Musical instruments		706	734	733	740		1.7	1.9	1.8	1.7		28.9	32.7	35.8	32.0
3693	Sports goods		641	645	630	651		4.4	4.1	4.9	4.5		88.8	80.0	107.2	87.0
3694	Games and toys		788	783	785	767		4.5	4.8	4.6	4.0		76.5	90.2	86.9	75.0
3699	Other manufacturing n.e.c.		5499	5709	5696	5778		22.6	23.5	23.2	23.3		384.8	430.4	432.4	458.0
3710	Recycling of metal waste and scrap		1292	1249	1299	1364		3.8	4.2	4.5	4.9		66.7	70.9	81.0	95.0
3720	Recycling of non-metal waste and scrap		991	982	1008	1096		6.2	6.4	6.9	7.8		112.3	121.7	150.6	177.0
D	Total manufacturing		549388	534222	524359	519323		3967.1	3981.4	3895.5	3836.6		83923.3	86580.7	88757.4	89779.0

Italy

ISIC Revision 3		Output					Value added in factor values					Gross fixed capital formation		
			(millions of Euros)					(millions of Euros)					(millions of Euros)	
ISIC	Industry	Note	2002	2003	2004	2005	Note	2002	2003	2004	2005	Note	2004	2005
151	Processed meat,fish,fruit,vegetables,fats		29727.0	...	...	...		4810.1	...	...	...		...	...
1511	Processing/preserving of meat		16001.3	17229.7	17533.0	18424.0		2660.0	2763.6	2655.0	2672.0		637.2	592.0
1512	Processing/preserving of fish		1742.7	...	...	...		268.2	...	...	...		...	...
1513	Processing/preserving of fruit & vegetables		7119.3	7352.0	7152.8	6613.0		1286.9	1340.1	1425.6	1334.0		410.3	587.0
1514	Vegetable and animal oils and fats		4863.7	4544.4	7555.2	5696.0		595.0	546.8	797.6	563.0		236.3	139.0
1520	Dairy products		14792.9	16649.8	14891.7	15629.0		2804.5	3123.6	2779.0	2727.0		604.2	490.0
153	Grain mill products; starches; animal feeds		9325.5	9329.0	9833.2	9211.0		1207.6	1222.0	1324.9	1299.0		509.3	267.0
1531	Grain mill products		4084.0	3680.8	4270.6	3563.0		497.4	474.3	578.5	569.0		243.8	149.0
1532	Starches and starch products		557.1	373.6	653.8	676.0		173.9	100.2	181.9	170.0		25.2	24.0
1533	Prepared animal feeds		4684.4	5274.6	4908.8	4972.0		536.4	647.5	564.5	561.0		240.2	94.0
154	Other food products		23503.9	23846.1	27215.4	29086.0		7545.3	7352.3	8104.1	8385.0		1256.2	1128.0
1541	Bakery products		10760.2	10504.7	9766.3	10412.0		3996.3	3937.8	3587.6	3921.0		500.2	409.0
1542	Sugar		728.2	1019.2	1024.5	1435.0		137.7	156.5	169.3	164.0		49.6	54.0
1543	Cocoa, chocolate and sugar confectionery		3626.2	3684.3	5455.9	5620.0		977.0	940.3	1402.4	1378.0		187.9	190.0
1544	Macaroni, noodles & similar products		2969.7	3045.4	4626.9	4732.0		826.3	737.8	1169.4	1207.0		247.1	230.0
1549	Other food products n.e.c.		5419.6	5592.4	6341.8	6887.0		1608.0	1579.9	1775.4	1716.0		271.5	245.0
155	Beverages		13376.6	14090.6	13920.6	13673.0		2408.4	2539.7	2486.0	2512.0		534.1	571.0
1551	Distilling, rectifying & blending of spirits		1709.5	1470.5	2099.5	2405.0		361.5	325.3	431.4	454.0		43.5	47.0
1552	Wines		6774.4	...	...	...		1076.6	...	...	...		...	...
1553	Malt liquors and malt		1253.1	...	...	...		271.2	...	...	...		...	...
1554	Soft drinks; mineral waters		3639.7	4899.4	4245.6	4328.0		699.2	1009.6	806.3	836.0		201.5	154.0
1600	Tobacco products		8929.8	...	...	...		352.0	...	...	...		...	...
171	Spinning, weaving and finishing of textiles		20897.0	20242.1	21410.9	18572.0		6133.6	5941.1	5504.2	5169.0		646.4	584.0
1711	Textile fibre preparation; textile weaving		16993.3	15876.9	16640.4	14979.0		4560.6	4204.7	3855.1	3741.0		432.1	474.0
1712	Finishing of textiles		3903.7	4365.2	4770.5	3594.0		1573.0	1736.4	1649.1	1428.0		214.3	110.0
172	Other textiles		8510.9	8016.6	7142.2	7744.0		2303.0	2116.0	2087.3	2118.0		365.9	315.0
1721	Made-up textile articles, except apparel		2929.5	2634.2	2394.9	2754.0		793.6	716.1	697.2	733.0		110.0	78.0
1722	Carpets and rugs		290.0	294.2	345.2	261.0		72.8	67.4	76.8	60.0		5.3	57.0
1723	Cordage, rope, twine and netting		220.3	202.5	177.8	181.0		56.1	55.3	56.7	53.0		19.9	14.0
1729	Other textiles n.e.c.		5071.1	4885.8	4224.3	4548.0		1380.5	1277.2	1256.5	1273.0		230.7	166.0
1730	Knitted and crocheted fabrics and articles		8302.1	7509.4	7210.1	6742.0		2048.5	1925.2	1886.1	1771.0		210.8	133.0
1810	Wearing apparel, except fur apparel		30268.2	26298.9	29784.4	25896.0		7775.8	6876.4	7343.2	6688.0		779.2	588.0
1820	Dressing & dyeing of fur; processing of fur		539.1	335.8	460.1	228.0		138.0	101.3	121.4	62.0		7.6	3.0
191	Tanning, dressing and processing of leather		11166.2	11386.4	11298.1	10849.0		2221.6	2192.0	2251.7	2205.0		401.3	274.0
1911	Tanning and dressing of leather		7528.9	7161.7	7040.7	6239.0		1303.0	1191.9	1271.9	1115.0		321.6	191.0
1912	Luggage, handbags, etc.; saddlery & harness		3637.3	4224.7	4257.4	4611.0		918.6	1000.1	979.8	1090.0		79.7	83.0
1920	Footwear		14260.3	13193.5	12402.4	12950.0		3735.6	3327.8	3341.7	3137.0		313.9	268.0
2010	Sawmilling and planing of wood		2374.6	2612.5	2873.2	2570.0		695.8	747.7	734.3	752.0		139.1	277.0
202	Products of wood, cork, straw, etc.		13888.7	13731.9	15378.3	14651.0		4208.8	4088.6	4328.9	4443.0		565.5	872.0
2021	Veneer sheets, plywood, particle board, etc.		2273.1	2073.4	2530.9	2621.0		501.4	420.3	550.3	595.0		124.8	272.0
2022	Builders' carpentry and joinery		6360.3	6648.7	7516.0	7226.0		2241.2	2247.5	2330.3	2415.0		281.4	396.0
2023	Wooden containers		1562.4	1619.8	1575.5	1684.0		368.8	411.3	403.2	428.0		59.0	50.0
2029	Other wood products; articles of cork/straw		3692.9	3390.0	3755.9	3120.0		1097.4	1009.5	1045.1	1006.0		100.3	155.0
210	Paper and paper products		18789.1	17926.3	17697.5	17935.0		4719.8	4451.8	4576.3	4331.0		699.1	694.0
2101	Pulp, paper and paperboard		5788.4	5275.4	4997.9	5297.0		1484.7	1208.9	1174.8	1114.0		215.8	227.0
2102	Corrugated paper and paperboard		5837.7	5472.1	5897.8	5466.0		1536.1	1424.3	1476.8	1395.0		239.0	231.0
2109	Other articles of paper and paperboard		7163.1	7178.8	6801.7	7172.0		1698.9	1818.5	1924.7	1822.0		244.2	236.0
221	Publishing		11499.4	11549.4	13085.8	12821.0		3679.9	3537.7	4097.3	3827.0		240.3	212.0
2211	Publishing of books and other publications		4411.8	4651.1	4259.0	4049.0		1497.5	1381.3	1457.6	1454.0		24.3	31.0
2212	Publishing of newspapers, journals, etc.		6511.1	6258.1	8189.2	7937.0		2031.2	2001.5	2480.7	2154.0		188.0	167.0
2213	Publishing of recorded media		236.9	285.2	227.8	288.0		60.0	52.6	58.8	64.0		20.1	4.0
2219	Other publishing		339.7	355.0	409.8	547.0		91.2	102.3	100.2	155.0		8.0	10.0

continued

Italy

ISIC Revision 3		Output					Value added in factor values					Gross fixed capital formation		
			(millions of Euros)					(millions of Euros)					(millions of Euros)	
ISIC	Industry	Note	2002	2003	2004	2005	Note	2002	2003	2004	2005	Note	2004	2005
222	Printing and related service activities		13315.5	13928.2	14085.3	13419.0		4858.6	4838.6	4818.3	4670.0		554.7	686.0
2221	Printing		9701.5	11391.8	11023.2	10518.0		3516.0	3748.1	3714.3	3557.0		417.1	521.0
2222	Service activities related to printing		3613.9	2536.4	3062.1	2901.0		1342.5	1090.6	1104.0	1113.0		137.6	165.0
2230	Reproduction of recorded media		620.0	440.9	299.5	354.0		164.4	127.2	77.2	110.0		21.8	46.0
2310	Coke oven products		...	110.9	...	144.0		...	24.5	...	38.0		...	7.0
2320	Refined petroleum products		37306.7	27975.5	31508.9	34971.0		2125.2	2083.5	2474.7	2960.0		770.9	947.0
2330	Processing of nuclear fuel		...	-	...	-		...	-	...	-		...	-
241	Basic chemicals		19135.0	18387.3	21944.5	23232.0		3386.9	2996.1	3159.3	3446.0		586.2	894.0
2411	Basic chemicals, except fertilizers		7606.2	6575.5	8064.2	8843.0		1722.6	1421.7	1490.4	1456.0		318.2	480.0
2412	Fertilizers and nitrogen compounds		...	919.0	1343.4	1180.0		...	171.2	247.6	219.0		20.0	73.0
2413	Plastics in primary forms; synthetic rubber		...	10892.8	12536.8	13209.0		...	1403.3	1421.4	1770.0		247.8	341.0
242	Other chemicals		46909.0	44547.5	42569.2	44715.0		12205.3	12382.1	11662.3	12017.0		1529.5	1409.0
2421	Pesticides and other agro-chemical products		661.7	796.7	937.5	861.0		140.5	165.5	188.3	184.0		17.9	27.0
2422	Paints, varnishes, printing ink and mastics		4750.5	5386.7	5966.8	5908.0		1221.2	1475.6	1439.7	1481.0		193.9	272.0
2423	Pharmaceuticals, medicinal chemicals, etc.		23386.8	21484.7	20358.8	19718.0		6770.7	6870.1	6463.9	6206.0		874.5	687.0
2424	Soap, cleaning & cosmetic preparations		8822.1	9454.6	8661.8	10505.0		2057.1	2152.6	1948.0	2351.0		198.7	140.0
2429	Other chemical products n.e.c.		9287.9	7424.8	6644.3	7722.0		2015.8	1718.3	1622.4	1795.0		244.5	283.0
2430	Man-made fibres		1836.0	1470.5	1470.7	1478.0		331.3	261.2	223.7	204.0		26.4	29.0
251	Rubber products		7011.3	7111.1	7548.1	7979.0		2174.1	2132.5	2233.7	2286.0		302.2	377.0
2511	Rubber tyres and tubes		2938.3	2881.6	2781.1	3289.0		832.6	769.8	828.9	792.0		148.6	141.0
2519	Other rubber products		4073.0	4229.5	4766.9	4690.0		1341.5	1362.6	1404.7	1494.0		153.6	236.0
2520	Plastic products		25893.8	27327.3	27415.2	28762.0		7556.6	7506.7	7288.0	7402.0		1124.9	1074.0
2610	Glass and glass products		6200.9	6475.9	6569.1	6175.0		2145.8	2131.4	2156.4	2039.0		570.4	385.0
269	Non-metallic mineral products n.e.c.		31232.6	31791.7	32481.8	34388.0		10179.5	10409.4	10452.6	10198.0		1837.4	1906.0
2691	Pottery, china and earthenware		1821.8	1544.4	1437.2	1631.0		812.6	648.6	635.2	626.0		94.3	127.0
2692	Refractory ceramic products		507.7	468.5	442.0	519.0		171.9	149.1	149.0	164.0		10.6	21.0
2693	Struct.non-refractory clay; ceramic products		7480.1	7599.0	7935.9	7800.0		2683.3	2770.6	2864.3	2741.0		455.5	485.0
2694	Cement, lime and plaster		3609.1	3696.9	3849.7	3852.0		1563.9	1574.4	1533.2	1274.0		277.3	292.0
2695	Articles of concrete, cement and plaster		10983.4	12163.2	12013.8	12753.0		2923.0	3245.8	3064.7	3164.0		691.1	573.0
2696	Cutting, shaping & finishing of stone		5156.7	4756.4	4807.8	5689.0		1542.2	1552.4	1657.3	1670.0		244.9	330.0
2699	Other non-metallic mineral products n.e.c.		1673.7	1563.3	1995.4	2144.0		482.6	468.5	548.9	560.0		63.7	77.0
2710	Basic iron and steel		22686.0	24670.9	30824.4	32075.0		4024.5	4427.8	5982.3	5868.0		968.2	1087.0
2720	Basic precious and non-ferrous metals		8221.4	8260.9	8935.1	10204.0		1335.5	1323.9	1452.9	1363.0		379.9	339.0
273	Casting of metals		6172.5	5911.9	6621.0	6552.0		1668.6	1594.4	1768.7	1738.0		252.1	379.0
2731	Casting of iron and steel		2167.7	2218.3	2235.0	2514.0		709.2	693.2	668.4	703.0		86.6	185.0
2732	Casting of non-ferrous metals		4004.8	3693.6	4386.0	4037.0		959.4	901.2	1100.2	1035.0		165.6	195.0
281	Struct.metal products;tanks;steam generators		21423.6	23735.7	27055.8	25624.0		6938.9	7373.3	7774.7	7637.0		995.1	771.0
2811	Structural metal products		17628.9	19884.7	22777.7	20897.0		5865.3	6265.5	6670.1	6401.0		845.8	547.0
2812	Tanks, reservoirs and containers of metal		3423.4	3523.1	3851.8	4197.0		976.9	1017.4	1016.9	1128.0		143.3	219.0
2813	Steam generators		371.3	327.9	426.3	530.0		96.7	90.4	87.7	108.0		6.0	5.0
289	Other metal products; metal working services		50793.4	52268.2	58244.2	61193.0		18535.4	19401.2	19193.9	20384.0		3335.6	2459.0
2891	Metal forging/pressing/stamping/roll-forming		10190.2	8884.8	10809.7	12361.0		2696.1	2450.0	2522.2	2995.0		465.3	443.0
2892	Treatment & coating of metals		19344.9	21295.0	24494.0	24236.0		8248.0	9287.8	9308.7	9404.0		1596.0	1085.0
2893	Cutlery, hand tools and general hardware		4684.0	4421.4	4387.1	4506.0		1938.4	1797.5	1721.9	1786.0		248.7	221.0
2899	Other fabricated metal products n.e.c.		16574.3	17667.0	18553.4	20089.0		5652.9	5865.9	5641.1	6200.0		1025.6	711.0
291	General purpose machinery		48913.3	48058.2	50017.0	52150.0		15179.1	14726.5	15189.6	15906.0		1675.3	1480.0
2911	Engines & turbines (not for transport equipment)		4748.8	4149.4	4354.0	4568.0		1291.4	1108.2	1243.0	1307.0		102.3	94.0
2912	Pumps, compressors, taps and valves		9448.2	9632.3	10269.9	10623.0		2965.2	2889.5	2951.9	3163.0		409.4	474.0
2913	Bearings, gears, gearing & driving elements		3894.1	4415.0	4841.5	4974.0		1432.4	1433.2	1607.3	1662.0		199.6	261.0
2914	Ovens, furnaces and furnace burners		1373.7	1644.7	1694.6	1639.0		362.3	500.0	485.6	463.0		38.1	28.0
2915	Lifting and handling equipment		7276.0	7610.3	7198.7	8822.0		2084.2	2165.4	2285.2	2536.0		268.4	204.0
2919	Other general purpose machinery		22172.5	20606.5	21658.2	21524.0		7043.6	6630.3	6616.6	6776.0		657.5	418.0

292	Special purpose machinery	36424.8	36349.1	37269.9	38210.0	10652.8	10529.7	10786.3	10894.0	1028.7	1083.0
2921	Agricultural and forestry machinery	5963.7	6052.0	6578.8	6406.0	1406.7	1463.6	1468.8	1589.0	224.3	129.0
2922	Machine tools	7927.2	7198.9	7829.6	7880.0	2647.5	2220.8	2484.3	2545.0	172.7	160.0
2923	Machinery for metallurgy	1383.1	1518.0	1579.8	1936.0	380.3	445.8	468.9	540.0	47.5	51.0
2924	Machinery for mining & construction	3324.0	3158.5	3837.1	4339.0	700.9	716.0	888.2	987.0	136.0	261.0
2925	Food/beverage/tobacco processing machinery	3842.8	3738.1	4043.3	4007.0	1204.7	1215.1	1224.0	1161.0	71.9	117.0
2926	Machinery for textile, apparel and leather	4690.3	4506.0	3394.0	3424.0	1344.7	1263.5	1021.3	1035.0	78.9	93.0
2927	Weapons and ammunition	1178.6	1324.4	1260.6	1278.0	374.3	375.7	410.4	360.0	39.3	31.0
2929	Other special purpose machinery	8115.1	8853.1	8746.7	8941.0	2593.6	2829.2	2820.4	2677.0	258.1	240.0
2930	Domestic appliances n.e.c.	11099.3	10743.7	11820.2	11801.0	2768.6	2583.6	2658.0	2663.0	310.1	306.0
3000	Office, accounting and computing machinery	3811.1	3127.0	3864.6	3110.0	481.9	631.6	666.1	579.0	46.1	67.0
3110	Electric motors, generators and transformers	5682.6	4749.6	4958.9	4873.0	1280.3	1339.1	1310.3	1384.0	210.0	153.0
3120	Electricity distribution & control apparatus	5662.8	5991.9	6520.9	5920.0	1942.9	2049.0	2173.5	2062.0	292.8	204.0
3130	Insulated wire and cable	3097.0	2998.9	3577.4	4022.0	589.9	566.5	549.7	602.0	120.5	91.0
3140	Accumulators, primary cells and batteries	707.9	599.0	612.0	651.0	165.2	147.9	139.3	128.0	8.1	6.0
3150	Lighting equipment and electric lamps	2909.4	2825.5	2981.9	2877.0	926.4	889.7	890.5	877.0	109.5	133.0
3190	Other electrical equipment n.e.c.	11368.0	10402.6	12318.7	11779.0	3679.7	3482.2	3671.2	3787.0	473.8	257.0
3210	Electronic valves, tubes, etc.	5199.8	4959.5	4717.2	4479.0	1865.6	1947.0	1759.1	1793.0	739.9	514.0
3220	TV/radio transmitters; line comm. apparatus	8256.2	8584.1	8250.9	7415.0	2324.2	2721.4	2440.2	2153.0	205.4	217.0
3230	TV and radio receivers and associated goods	1082.1	918.7	1221.4	811.0	225.6	218.7	202.3	210.0	24.4	16.0
331	Medical, measuring, testing appliances, etc.	11353.1	10711.9	11581.3	12962.0	4223.1	3889.0	4367.9	4796.0	330.4	314.0
3311	Medical, surgical and orthopaedic equipment	4333.0	4075.0	4419.0	5556.0	1802.0	1573.0	1797.0	2116.0	153.0	177.0
3312	Measuring/testing/navigating appliances,etc.	4940.0	4384.0	4952.0	5110.0	1706.0	1563.0	1800.0	1826.0	154.0	102.0
3313	Industrial process control equipment	2080.0	2253.0	2210.0	2297.0	716.0	754.0	771.0	854.0	24.0	35.0
3320	Optical instruments & photographic equipment	3938.4	3006.6	3062.5	3380.0	1378.3	1089.7	1164.9	1270.0	112.1	140.0
3330	Watches and clocks	208.3	184.8	178.8	172.0	57.8	41.6	37.6	40.0	2.2	1.0
3410	Motor vehicles	23458.5	23075.7	24699.5	24858.0	1356.6	1998.3	2330.6	2810.0	1335.1	1495.0
3420	Automobile bodies, trailers & semi-trailers	2313.8	2363.7	2518.2	2642.0	618.5	616.4	591.4	628.0	85.3	47.0
3430	Parts/accessories for automobiles	15571.9	15809.7	15343.1	16258.0	4203.3	4292.3	4225.6	4051.0	736.0	788.0
351	Building and repairing of ships and boats	4726.5	5454.1	6086.9	7243.0	1237.6	1427.2	1689.8	1920.0	169.8	178.0
3511	Building and repairing of ships	3630.0	3675.6	3946.9	4356.0	952.0	977.6	1017.5	1141.0	88.5	94.0
3512	Building/repairing of pleasure/sport. boats	1096.5	1778.6	2140.0	2887.0	285.6	449.6	672.4	779.0	81.4	84.0
3520	Railway/tramway locomotives & rolling stock	1766.7	1376.3	2457.8	2498.0	446.9	489.4	674.1	494.0	26.9	36.0
3530	Aircraft and spacecraft	6115.4	4349.3	5637.3	6051.0	2012.8	1486.4	1785.0	1887.0	198.5	226.0
359	Transport equipment n.e.c.	4116.1	4281.8	4340.7	3992.0	961.7	926.0	943.4	927.0	262.6	116.0
3591	Motorcycles	3145.9	3391.8	3384.4	3292.0	690.9	709.6	685.0	736.0	242.1	94.0
3592	Bicycles and invalid carriages	943.6	857.0	913.9	658.0	261.8	207.2	245.3	180.0	18.7	22.0
3599	Other transport equipment n.e.c.	27.0	33.0	42.0	42.0	9.0	9.0	13.0	12.0	2.0	1.0
3610	Furniture	25310.2	22812.0	25412.9	24386.0	6677.4	6308.4	6326.7	6590.0	788.0	683.0
369	Manufacturing n.e.c.	11239.4	10843.0	10637.6	11031.0	2713.2	2922.6	2838.4	2794.0	423.9	328.0
3691	Jewellery and related articles	6293.2	5099.1	4966.7	5170.0	1199.9	1246.7	1130.4	1166.0	118.7	120.0
3692	Musical instruments	220.7	252.0	270.3	224.0	83.1	84.9	85.9	81.0	5.6	8.0
3693	Sports goods	826.9	715.4	934.0	832.0	240.7	209.5	264.4	251.0	34.2	17.0
3694	Games and toys	714.2	948.3	870.8	813.0	200.9	230.9	247.0	195.0	92.0	50.0
3699	Other manufacturing n.e.c.	3184.4	3828.2	3595.8	3992.0	988.6	1150.6	1110.7	1102.0	173.4	134.0
3710	Recycling of metal waste and scrap	1174.7	1196.9	1750.3	1968.0	204.7	223.4	305.5	303.0	75.0	82.0
3720	Recycling of non-metal waste and scrap	1408.4	1347.9	1950.9	2216.0	400.7	346.9	429.7	476.0	115.7	110.0
D	Total manufacturing	795929.0	777939.0	829690.0	830676.0	203014.0	201629.0	207570.0	208907.0	31768.3	29890.0

Italy

ISIC Revision 3			Index numbers of industrial production (2000=100)											
ISIC	Industry	Note	1995	1996	1997	1998	1999	2000	2001	2002	2003	2004	2005	2006
15	Food and beverages		90	90	92	94	98	100	104	105	107	108	109	110
16	Tobacco products		115	118	118	116	103	100	104	86	92	51	44	43
17	Textiles		98	94	101	99	97	100	99	93	89	86	82	80
18	Wearing apparel, fur		110	112	111	113	103	100	104	95	92	92	81	83
19	Leather, leather products and footwear		112	112	113	105	101	100	95	87	84	75	68	67
20	Wood products (excl. furniture)		86	81	80	86	90	100	100	102	103	107	106	106
21	Paper and paper products		87	85	90	92	97	100	100	104	104	109	110	110
22	Printing and publishing		90	85	91	97	101	100	97	96	99	107	104	101
23	Coke,refined petroleum products,nuclear fuel		98	98	103	107	102	100	102	101	104	105	109	105
24	Chemicals and chemical products		93	94	98	98	98	100	97	101	98	101	99	103
25	Rubber and plastics products		88	84	92	94	95	100	98	95	95	95	90	93
26	Non-metallic mineral products		89	87	89	91	95	100	102	102	101	100	99	98
27	Basic metals		99	99	101	101	93	100	96	95	96	101	101	108
28	Fabricated metal products		94	91	93	99	98	100	103	99	102	104	103	106
29	Machinery and equipment n.e.c.		92	95	95	96	95	100	101	102	98	99	98	102
30	Office, accounting and computing machinery		146	144	117	124	92	100	94	62	45	48	25	12
31	Electrical machinery and apparatus		102	91	96	99	98	100	95	84	80	78	75	82
32	Radio,television and communication equipment		111	113	113	107	104	100	90	78	78	78	72	78
33	Medical, precision and optical instruments		87	88	89	89	90	100	99	110	93	92	90	94
34	Motor vehicles, trailers, semi-trailers		86	84	95	93	94	100	91	86	82	82	76	81
35	Other transport equipment		85	90	99	100	96	100	90	87	81	82	77	81
36	Furniture; manufacturing n.e.c.		85	82	83	90	98	100	102	98	92	93	90	89
37	Recycling		...	...	...	...	...	100	103	106	108	105	100	108
D	Total manufacturing		94	93	96	97	97	100	99	97	96	96	94	96

Jamaica

Supplier of information:
Statisitical Institute of Jamaica, Kingston.

Basic source of data:
Quarterly survey on registered establishments.

Major deviations from ISIC (Revision 2):
None reported.

Reference period:
Calendar year.

Scope:
Establishments with 10 or more persons engaged.

Method of data collection:
Direct interview in the field.

Type of enumeration:
Sample survey.

Adjusted for non-response:
Yes.

Concepts and definitions of variables:
Number of employees is estimated number of employees in large establishments.
Wages and salaries includes direct wages and salaries and remuneration for time not worked. Figures were computed by UNIDO from reported weekly wages and salaries per employee.

Related national publications:
None reported.

Jamaica

ISIC Revision 2		Establishments					Number of employees					Wages and salaries paid to employees				
			(number)					(number)					(thousands of Jamaican Dollars)			
ISIC	Industry	Note	2003	2004	2005	2006	Note	2003	2004	2005	2006	Note	2003	2004	2005	2006
311/2	Food products		...	...	...	...		6607	6828	6599	6351		1966904	2141698	2395516	2370879
3111	Slaughtering, preparing and preserving meat		...	...	...	...		...	...	...	...		...	...	...	...
3112	Dairy products		...	...	...	...		...	...	...	...		...	...	...	...
3113	Canning, preserving of fruits and vegetables		...	...	...	...		...	...	...	...		...	...	...	...
3114	Canning, preserving and processing of fish		...	...	...	...		...	...	...	...		...	...	...	...
3115	Vegetable and animal oils and fats		...	...	...	...		...	...	...	...		...	...	...	...
3116	Grain mill products		...	...	...	...		...	...	...	...		...	...	...	...
3117	Bakery products		...	...	...	...		...	...	...	...		...	...	...	...
3118	Sugar factories and refineries		...	...	...	...		6607	6828	6599	6351		1966904	2141698	2395516	2370879
3119	Cocoa, chocolate and sugar confectionery		...	...	...	...		...	...	...	...		...	...	...	...
3121	Other food products		...	...	...	...		...	...	...	...		...	...	...	...
3122	Prepared animal feeds		...	...	...	...		...	...	...	...		...	...	...	...
313	Beverages		...	...	...	...		2640	2555	2660	2715		1657656	1982271	2401927	2714327
3131	Distilling, rectifying and blending spirits		...	...	...	...		...	...	...	...		...	...	...	...
3132	Wine industries		...	...	...	...		...	...	...	...		...	...	...	...
3133	Malt liquors and malt		...	...	...	...		...	...	...	...		...	...	...	...
3134	Soft drinks and carbonated waters		...	...	...	...		...	...	...	...		...	...	...	...
314	Tobacco		...	...	...	...		129	146	...	...		149615	203147	...	...
321	Textiles		...	...	...	...		159	159	164	178		43366	47715	53846	62879
3211	Spinning, weaving and finishing textiles		...	...	...	...		...	...	...	...		...	...	...	...
3212	Made-up textile goods excl. wearing apparel		...	...	...	...		...	...	...	...		...	...	...	...
3213	Knitting mills		...	...	...	...		...	...	...	...		...	...	...	...
3214	Carpets and rugs		...	...	...	...		...	...	...	...		...	...	...	...
3215	Cordage, rope and twine		...	...	...	...		...	...	...	...		...	...	...	...
3219	Other textiles		...	...	...	...		...	...	...	...		...	...	...	...
322	Wearing apparel, except footwear		...	...	...	...		6301	6233	6413	6467		1205104	1188209	1512647	1575154
323	Leather and fur products		...	...	...	...		165	148	138	154		32501	33231	31696	41217
3231	Tanneries and leather finishing		...	...	...	...		...	...	...	...		...	...	...	...
3232	Fur dressing and dyeing industries		...	...	...	...		...	...	...	...		...	...	...	...
3233	Leather prods. excl. footwear and wearing		...	...	...	...		...	...	...	...		...	...	...	...
324	Footwear, except rubber or plastic		...	...	...	...		...	...	...	...		...	...	...	...
331	Wood products, except furniture		...	...	...	...		553	567	599	656		125923	170034	183586	214906
3311	Sawmills, planing and other wood mills		...	...	...	...		...	...	...	...		...	...	...	...
3312	Wooden and cane containers		...	...	...	...		...	...	...	...		...	...	...	...
3319	Other wood and cork products		...	...	...	...		...	...	...	...		...	...	...	...
332	Furniture and fixtures, excl. metal		...	...	...	...		1613	1657	1644	1643		528419	533700	597561	549439
341	Paper and products		...	...	...	...		1282	1210	1318	1396		550937	634108	722301	757135
3411	Pulp, paper and paperboard articles		...	...	...	...		...	...	...	...		...	...	...	...
3412	Containers of paper and paperboard		...	...	...	...		...	...	...	...		...	...	...	...
3419	Other pulp, paper and paperboard articles		...	...	...	...		...	...	...	...		...	...	...	...
342	Printing and publishing		...	...	...	...		2433	2420	2424	2558		1015797	1166663	1188128	1599783
351	Industrial chemicals		...	...	...	...		677	741	733	731		381717	456296	446148	525060
3511	Basic chemicals excl. fertilizers		...	...	...	...		...	...	...	...		...	...	...	...
3512	Fertilizers and pesticides		...	...	...	...		...	...	...	...		...	...	...	...
3513	Synthetic resins and plastic materials		...	...	...	...		...	...	...	...		...	...	...	...
352	Other chemicals		...	...	...	...		1786	1760	1769	1875		918783	979539	987031	1089270
3521	Paints, varnishes and lacquers		...	...	...	...		...	...	...	...		...	...	...	...
3522	Drugs and medicines		...	...	...	...		...	...	...	...		...	...	...	...
3523	Soap, cleaning preps., perfumes, cosmetics		...	...	...	...		...	...	...	...		...	...	...	...
3529	Other chemical products		...	...	...	...		...	...	...	...		...	...	...	...
353	Petroleum refineries		...	...	...	...		257	253	256	277		392073	393970	370912	496866

354	Misc. petroleum and coal products	...	...	...	...	...	...	...	...	...	...	...	...
355	Rubber products	...	...	...	...	124	131	129	115	23097	30736	31177	34170
3551	Tyres and tubes	...	...	...	...	...	...	...	...	...	...	...	...
3559	Other rubber products	...	...	...	...	...	...	...	...	...	...	...	...
356	Plastic products	...	...	...	...	958	924	938	936	291224	323603	361138	358567
361	Pottery, china and earthenware	...	...	...	...	...	...	...	...	...	...	...	...
362	Glass and products	...	...	...	...	...	...	...	...	...	...	...	...
369	Other non-metallic mineral products	...	...	...	...	1359	1286	1350	1441	694101	693329	...	...
3691	Structural clay products	...	...	...	...	...	...	...	...	...	...	...	...
3692	Cement, lime and plaster	...	...	...	...	...	...	...	...	...	...	...	...
3699	Other non-metallic mineral products	...	...	...	...	...	...	...	...	...	...	...	...
371	Iron and steel	...	...	...	...	...	...	...	...	...	...	...	...
372	Non-ferrous metals	...	...	...	...	...	...	...	...	...	...	...	...
381	Fabricated metal products	...	...	...	...	2348	2216	2273	2253	1016693	1118327	1330651	1371077
3811	Cutlery, hand tools and general hardware	...	...	...	...	...	...	...	...	...	...	...	...
3812	Furniture and fixtures primarily of metal	...	...	...	...	...	...	...	...	...	...	...	...
3813	Structural metal products	...	...	...	...	...	...	...	...	...	...	...	...
3819	Other fabricated metal products	...	...	...	...	...	...	...	...	...	...	...	...
382	Non-electrical machinery	...	...	...	...	...	...	...	...	...	...	...	...
3821	Engines and turbines	...	...	...	...	...	...	...	...	...	...	...	...
3822	Agricultural machinery and equipment	...	...	...	...	...	...	...	...	...	...	...	...
3823	Metal and wood working machinery	...	...	...	...	...	...	...	...	...	...	...	...
3824	Other special industrial machinery	...	...	...	...	...	...	...	...	...	...	...	...
3825	Office, computing and accounting machinery	...	...	...	...	...	...	...	...	...	...	...	...
3829	Other non-electrical machinery and equipment	...	...	...	...	...	...	...	...	...	...	...	...
383	Electrical machinery	...	...	...	...	...	...	...	...	...	...	...	...
3831	Electrical industrial machinery	...	...	...	...	...	...	...	...	...	...	...	...
3832	Radio, television and communication equipment	...	...	...	...	...	...	...	...	...	...	...	...
3833	Electrical appliances and housewares	...	...	...	...	...	...	...	...	...	...	...	...
3839	Other electrical apparatus and supplies	...	...	...	...	...	...	...	...	...	...	...	...
384	Transport equipment	...	...	...	...	...	...	...	...	...	...	...	...
3841	Shipbuilding and repairing	...	...	...	...	...	...	...	...	...	...	...	...
3842	Railroad equipment	...	...	...	...	...	...	...	...	...	...	...	...
3843	Motor vehicles	...	...	...	...	...	...	...	...	...	...	...	...
3844	Motorcycles and bicycles	...	...	...	...	...	...	...	...	...	...	...	...
3845	Aircraft	...	...	...	...	...	...	...	...	...	...	...	...
3849	Other transport equipment	...	...	...	...	...	...	...	...	...	...	...	...
385	Professional and scientific equipment	...	...	...	...	...	...	...	...	...	...	...	...
3851	Prof. and scientific equipment n.e.c.	...	...	...	...	...	...	...	...	...	...	...	...
3852	Photographic and optical goods	...	...	...	...	...	...	...	...	...	...	...	...
3853	Watches and clocks	...	...	...	...	...	...	...	...	...	...	...	...
390	Other manufacturing industries	...	...	...	...	...	...	...	...	...	...	...	...
3901	Jewellery and related articles	...	...	...	...	...	...	...	...	...	...	...	...
3902	Musical instruments	...	...	...	...	...	...	...	...	...	...	...	...
3903	Sporting and athletic goods	...	...	...	...	...	...	...	...	...	...	...	...
3909	Manufacturing industries, n.e.c.	...	...	...	...	...	...	...	...	...	...	...	...
3	Total manufacturing	...	...	...	...	39818	40178	40747	41257	15077640	16588690	18213583	19574301

Japan

Supplier of information:
Ministry of Economy, Trade and Industry (METI), Tokyo.
Industrial statistics for the OECD countries are compiled by the OECD secretariat, which supplies them to UNIDO.

Basic source of data:
Manufacturing census; survey.

Major deviations from ISIC (Revision 3):
All data have been converted from the Japanese Standard Industrial Classification to ISIC (Revision 3).

Reference period:
Calendar year.

Scope:
Census covers all establishments only in years where the last digit is 0, 3, 5 or 8. In all other years, the survey is limited to those establishments with four or more persons engaged. Data on investment cover establishments with 30 or more persons engaged.

Method of data collection:
Questionnaires are distributed and collected by enumerators.

Type of enumeration:
Not reported.

Adjusted for non-response:
No.

Concepts and definitions of variables:
Number of employees includes all employees with contracts of more than one month, temporary employees provided by employment agencies and employees working for 18 days or more in two consecutive months.
Wages and salaries relates to total cash payments, including basic wages, bonuses and other premiums, allowances and employees' retirement and termination allowances.
Output represents the value of shipments of finished goods, adjusted for changes in stocks of finished goods and work in progress. The value of goods shipped in the same condition as received is excluded.
Value added is output less the value of raw materials, fuels and electricity consumed, the cost of contract and commission work done by others, value of excise taxes and depreciation.
Gross fixed capital formation is defined as the value of purchases of fixed assets, including own account construction, less the value of sales. Fixed assets covered are those with a productive life of more than one year and include repairs to existing assets, new assets whether not yet in use or previously used abroad and used assets. Valuation is at full cost incurred, including delivery price, cost of installation and fees and taxes. For own-produced assets, the cost of work put in progress covers labour costs, materials and supplies and includes an allocation for overheads. The amount realized is taken for sales of used assets.

Related national publications:
Census of Manufactures published by Ministry of Economy, Trade and Industry (METI), Tokyo.

Japan

ISIC Revision 3		Number of establishments					Number of employees					Wages and salaries paid to employees				
			(number)					(thousands)					(billions of Japanese Yen)			
ISIC	Industry	Note	2002	2003	2004	2005	Note	2002	2003	2004	2005	Note	2002	2003	2004	2005
151	Processed meat,fish,fruit,vegetables,fats		12075	...	...	...		310	304	294	290		538	525	506	504
1511	Processing/preserving of meat		1173	...	...	...		59	61	59	58		145	147	144	141
1512	Processing/preserving of fish		8453	...	...	...		185	178	173	171		266	251	242	242
1513	Processing/preserving of fruit & vegetables		2344	...	...	...		58	58	55	54		94	93	88	89
1514	Vegetable and animal oils and fats		105	...	...	...		6	7	6	6		33	34	32	32
1520	Dairy products		711	...	...	...		39	38	37	37		144	138	136	135
153	Grain mill products; starches; animal feeds		1573	...	...	...		30	29	29	28		77	71	71	68
1531	Grain mill products		778	...	...	...		15	14	14	14		35	34	34	32
1532	Starches and starch products		105	...	...	...		3	3	3	3		14	12	12	12
1533	Prepared animal feeds		690	...	...	...		12	12	12	11		28	25	26	24
154	Other food products		23602	...	...	...		741	734	720	713		1520	1502	1473	1464
1541	Bakery products		5903	...	...	...		218	212	208	207		477	465	456	455
1542	Sugar		114	...	...	...		5	5	4	4		23	22	20	19
1543	Cocoa, chocolate and sugar confectionery		1056	...	...	...		41	41	41	41		111	109	111	111
1544	Macaroni, noodles & similar products		3486	...	...	...		57	56	53	52		94	89	85	81
1549	Other food products n.e.c.		13043	...	...	...		420	420	414	409		815	816	802	799
155	Beverages		2636	...	...	...		68	66	65	64		224	214	211	209
1551	Distilling, rectifying & blending of spirits		358	...	...	...		11	11	12	12		42	40	40	44
1552	Wines		1473	...	...	...		26	25	24	22		52	48	45	41
1553	Malt liquors and malt		55	...	...	...		5	4	4	4		34	29	26	25
1554	Soft drinks; mineral waters		750	...	...	...		25	26	26	26		96	97	99	99
1600	Tobacco products		31	...	...	...		5	5	5	3		38	34	34	24
171	Spinning, weaving and finishing of textiles		6452	...	...	...		102	98	90	86		205	191	177	169
1711	Textile fibre preparation; textile weaving		4287	...	...	...		59	57	51	48		101	95	88	83
1712	Finishing of textiles		2165	...	...	...		43	41	38	37		103	95	89	86
172	Other textiles		6808	...	...	...		95	91	88	87		140	131	135	136
1721	Made-up textile articles, except apparel		4226	...	...	...		53	51	48	47		54	48	49	46
1722	Carpets and rugs		299	...	...	...		6	6	5	5		14	14	13	13
1723	Cordage, rope, twine and netting		515	...	...	...		7	7	7	7		9	8	10	9
1729	Other textiles n.e.c.		1768	...	...	...		29	28	28	28		63	61	64	67
1730	Knitted and crocheted fabrics and articles		4852	...	...	...		80	74	67	62		99	88	82	76
1810	Wearing apparel, except fur apparel		9277	...	...	...		166	152	138	128		186	167	155	144
1820	Dressing & dyeing of fur; processing of fur		43	...	...	...		-	-	-	-		1	1	1	1
191	Tanning, dressing and processing of leather		1765	...	...	...		19	19	17	18		26	26	23	28
1911	Tanning and dressing of leather		384	...	...	...		6	6	5	6		16	17	14	19
1912	Luggage, handbags, etc.; saddlery & harness		1381	...	...	...		13	13	12	12		9	9	9	9
1920	Footwear		1783	...	...	...		26	24	22	21		39	34	32	33
2010	Sawmilling and planing of wood		5793	...	...	...		59	56	53	51		44	44	45	41
202	Products of wood, cork, straw, etc.		9645	...	...	...		110	108	101	100		157	149	143	142
2021	Veneer sheets, plywood, particle board, etc.		1032	...	...	...		24	24	23	23		59	58	59	59
2022	Builders' carpentry and joinery		4910	...	...	...		54	53	49	49		79	74	68	69
2023	Wooden containers		893	...	...	...		10	9	9	8		6	6	6	5
2029	Other wood products; articles of cork/straw		2810	...	...	...		23	22	20	20		12	11	11	9
210	Paper and paper products		8423	...	...	...		213	207	201	198		656	626	618	603
2101	Pulp, paper and paperboard		893	...	...	...		56	54	51	49		281	267	255	246
2102	Corrugated paper and paperboard		5009	...	...	...		100	98	96	94		231	221	221	217
2109	Other articles of paper and paperboard		2521	...	...	...		57	55	55	54		144	138	142	140
221	Publishing		...	...	...	...		...	...	...	...		...	...	...	...
2211	Publishing of books and other publications		...	...	...	...		...	...	...	...		...	...	...	...
2212	Publishing of newspapers, journals, etc.		...	...	...	...		...	...	...	...		...	...	...	...
2213	Publishing of recorded media		...	...	...	...		...	...	...	...		...	...	...	...
2219	Other publishing		...	...	...	...		...	...	...	...		...	...	...	...

222	Printing and related service activities	19493	...	...	...	357	349	334	328	894	853	828	839
2221	Printing	14842	...	...	...	286	280	268	265	758	724	695	712
2222	Service activities related to printing	4651	...	...	...	71	69	66	63	136	128	133	126
2230	Reproduction of recorded media	98	...	...	...	6	6	6	6	24	26	25	24
2310	Coke oven products	810	...	...	...	8	8	8	8	11	11	12	12
2320	Refined petroleum products	224	...	...	...	15	15	15	15	106	107	105	107
2330	Processing of nuclear fuel	6	...	...	...	4	4	4	4	28	29	29	31
241	Basic chemicals	1605	...	...	...	111	110	106	106	642	630	613	618
2411	Basic chemicals, except fertilizers	1235	...	...	...	72	71	72	73	399	390	399	414
2412	Fertilizers and nitrogen compounds	160	...	...	...	4	6	5	4	14	23	19	15
2413	Plastics in primary forms; synthetic rubber	210	...	...	...	34	33	29	28	230	216	195	190
242	Other chemicals	3424	...	...	...	211	204	203	203	1060	1011	1008	1013
2421	Pesticides and other agro-chemical products	72	...	...	...	4	4	4	4	22	23	20	22
2422	Paints, varnishes, printing ink and mastics	1029	...	...	...	42	41	41	44	192	181	184	203
2423	Pharmaceuticals, medicinal chemicals, etc.	961	...	...	...	92	88	87	86	517	487	485	474
2424	Soap, cleaning & cosmetic preparations	822	...	...	...	44	44	43	43	173	174	167	168
2429	Other chemical products n.e.c.	540	...	...	...	29	27	28	26	155	146	153	146
2430	Man-made fibres	64	...	...	...	14	11	10	9	75	59	52	44
251	Rubber products	2927	...	...	...	105	105	105	108	384	376	377	396
2511	Rubber tyres and tubes	114	...	...	...	20	20	20	22	109	106	106	115
2519	Other rubber products	2813	...	...	...	85	85	85	87	276	270	271	281
2520	Plastic products	16784	...	...	...	391	398	397	394	1022	1036	1058	1049
2610	Glass and glass products	1122	...	...	...	51	50	50	49	221	211	217	210
269	Non-metallic mineral products n.e.c.	14092	...	...	...	251	241	226	220	532	498	475	471
2691	Pottery, china and earthenware	2277	...	...	...	40	40	36	35	119	121	113	110
2692	Refractory ceramic products	610	...	...	...	17	16	15	15	57	51	48	48
2693	Struct.non-refractory clay; ceramic products	507	...	...	...	7	7	7	6	14	13	12	12
2694	Cement, lime and plaster	207	...	...	...	8	8	7	8	39	37	35	35
2695	Articles of concrete, cement and plaster	6673	...	...	...	121	114	106	102	194	172	158	152
2696	Cutting, shaping & finishing of stone	2351	...	...	...	25	24	22	21	19	17	16	16
2699	Other non-metallic mineral products n.e.c.	1467	...	...	...	32	32	32	33	90	88	93	99
2710	Basic iron and steel	2614	...	...	...	141	136	134	136	729	700	725	767
2720	Basic precious and non-ferrous metals	1149	...	...	...	54	53	52	54	249	241	247	256
273	Casting of metals	1690	...	...	...	46	46	47	48	156	155	164	166
2731	Casting of iron and steel	991	...	...	...	34	34	34	35	126	127	131	136
2732	Casting of non-ferrous metals	699	...	...	...	12	12	13	12	30	28	34	30
281	Struct.metal products;tanks;steam generators	16924	...	...	...	280	275	263	260	659	640	613	580
2811	Structural metal products	10414	...	...	...	190	180	171	170	468	420	402	396
2812	Tanks, reservoirs and containers of metal	6387	...	...	...	76	75	74	76	92	85	87	88
2813	Steam generators	123	...	...	...	15	20	19	14	100	135	123	96
289	Other metal products; metal working services	22344	...	...	...	425	427	422	433	1061	1065	1076	1132
2891	Metal forging/pressing/stamping/roll-forming	5514	...	...	...	118	117	116	123	314	313	317	350
2892	Treatment & coating of metals	6380	...	...	...	103	104	105	107	199	201	210	222
2893	Cutlery, hand tools and general hardware	2798	...	...	...	56	54	53	55	162	158	152	160
2899	Other fabricated metal products n.e.c.	7652	...	...	...	149	152	148	149	387	392	397	400
291	General purpose machinery	12462	...	...	...	375	364	362	376	1459	1380	1402	1483
2911	Engines & turbines (not for transport equipment)	762	...	...	...	38	33	31	40	218	162	153	209
2912	Pumps, compressors, taps and valves	2284	...	...	...	78	79	79	81	294	298	307	322
2913	Bearings, gears, gearing & driving elements	1239	...	...	...	61	61	61	63	273	283	287	299
2914	Ovens, furnaces and furnace burners	144	...	...	...	3	3	3	3	9	9	10	10
2915	Lifting and handling equipment	1817	...	...	...	50	47	46	47	176	169	166	173
2919	Other general purpose machinery	6216	...	...	...	147	141	142	142	490	458	479	469
292	Special purpose machinery	20408	...	...	...	458	453	471	482	1507	1455	1585	1634
2921	Agricultural and forestry machinery	869	...	...	...	30	30	29	29	115	115	112	113
2922	Machine tools	6667	...	...	...	126	128	133	140	369	374	407	439
2923	Machinery for metallurgy	127	...	...	...	3	3	3	3	13	13	12	13
2924	Machinery for mining & construction	1175	...	...	...	35	35	39	39	135	137	149	157
2925	Food/beverage/tobacco processing machinery	1725	...	...	...	38	35	34	35	115	104	107	108
2926	Machinery for textile, apparel and leather	769	...	...	...	21	19	18	18	75	63	66	64
2927	Weapons and ammunition	38	...	...	...	6	2	6	6	36	11	36	36
2929	Other special purpose machinery	9038	...	...	...	199	201	208	211	649	638	696	704

continued

Japan

ISIC Revision 3		Number of establishments					Number of employees					Wages and salaries paid to employees				
			(number)					(thousands)					(billions of Japanese Yen)			
ISIC	Industry	Note	2002	2003	2004	2005	Note	2002	2003	2004	2005	Note	2002	2003	2004	2005
2930	Domestic appliances n.e.c.		2255	...	...	...		105	93	86	84		394	360	334	325
3000	Office, accounting and computing machinery		2033	...	...	...		140	133	126	118		672	626	601	566
3110	Electric motors, generators and transformers		1905	...	...	...		70	68	65	69		249	238	233	258
3120	Electricity distribution & control apparatus		3954	...	...	...		125	119	115	114		472	431	420	414
3130	Insulated wire and cable		488	...	...	...		34	29	27	25		161	131	124	120
3140	Accumulators, primary cells and batteries		191	...	...	...		21	20	17	16		102	102	90	86
3150	Lighting equipment and electric lamps		956	...	...	...		37	37	38	37		136	143	144	149
3190	Other electrical equipment n.e.c.		2622	...	...	...		122	114	112	116		430	406	415	442
3210	Electronic valves, tubes, etc.		2411	...	...	...		267	261	255	248		1271	1250	1254	1236
3220	TV/radio transmitters; line comm. apparatus		592	...	...	...		69	68	64	62		371	349	346	332
3230	TV and radio receivers and associated goods		5101	...	...	...		283	282	281	268		1160	1157	1190	1155
331	Medical, measuring, testing appliances, etc.		4586	...	...	...		160	149	155	156		647	574	612	613
3311	Medical, surgical and orthopaedic equipment		1490	...	...	...		49	48	49	50		184	174	176	174
3312	Measuring/testing/navigating appliances,etc.		2844	...	...	...		99	93	98	97		401	371	407	408
3313	Industrial process control equipment		252	...	...	...		12	8	8	8		63	30	29	31
3320	Optical instruments & photographic equipment		1482	...	...	...		47	44	42	41		156	143	143	138
3330	Watches and clocks		199	...	...	...		11	10	10	10		43	44	38	41
3410	Motor vehicles		55	...	...	...		152	154	152	157		1152	1158	1158	1162
3420	Automobile bodies, trailers & semi-trailers		221	...	...	...		39	39	34	36		253	249	204	228
3430	Parts/accessories for automobiles		8873	...	...	...		490	497	512	534		2311	2349	2442	2564
351	Building and repairing of ships and boats		1094	...	...	...		41	38	39	38		170	153	166	155
3511	Building and repairing of ships		1094	...	...	...		41	38	...	38		170	153	...	155
3512	Building/repairing of pleasure/sport. boats		-	...	...	...		-	-	...	...		-	-	...	...
3520	Railway/tramway locomotives & rolling stock		350	...	...	...		15	15	15	14		66	65	66	62
3530	Aircraft and spacecraft		260	...	...	...		25	32	29	30		136	184	156	177
359	Transport equipment n.e.c.		540	...	...	...		12	11	13	12		37	29	37	36
3591	Motorcycles		-	...	...	...		-	-	...	...		-	-	...	...
3592	Bicycles and invalid carriages		309	...	...	...		7	7	7	6		19	17	20	19
3599	Other transport equipment n.e.c.		231	...	...	...		5	5	6	5		17	11	18	17
3610	Furniture		6706	...	...	...		104	101	96	95		212	201	198	194
369	Manufacturing n.e.c.		9610	...	...	...		147	141	131	134		307	281	265	284
3691	Jewellery and related articles		652	...	...	...		10	9	9	8		16	16	15	15
3692	Musical instruments		325	...	...	...		12	11	10	10		56	46	47	46
3693	Sports goods		757	...	...	...		16	15	14	14		38	32	31	30
3694	Games and toys		950	...	...	...		14	13	10	11		24	20	11	18
3699	Other manufacturing n.e.c.		6926	...	...	...		95	93	89	92		173	167	161	175
3710	Recycling of metal waste and scrap		596a/	...	...	...	a/	10	10	12	12	a/	13	15	21	24
3720	Recycling of non-metal waste and scrap		...a/	...	...	...	a/	...	...	...	...	a/	...	...	...	...
D	Total manufacturing		290789	...	...	...		7893	7723	7565	7549		25832	25059	25113	25367

a/ 3710 includes 3720.

ISIC Revision 3		Output					Value added					Gross fixed capital formation		
			(billions of Japanese Yen)					(billions of Japanese Yen)					(billions of Japanese Yen)	
ISIC	Industry	Note	2002	2003	2004	2005	Note	2002	2003	2004	2005	Note	2004	2005
151	Processed meat,fish,fruit,vegetables,fats		7010	6835	6769	6701		2216	2152	2118	2048		112	152
1511	Processing/preserving of meat		1868	1876	1939	1915		453	458	472	434		31	36
1512	Processing/preserving of fish		3611	3389	3280	3301		1219	1162	1129	1101		44	62
1513	Processing/preserving of fruit & vegetables		857	845	823	820		355	348	340	338		15	25
1514	Vegetable and animal oils and fats		674	724	726	665		188	184	177	175		24	30
1520	Dairy products		2269	2157	2209	2208		723	655	679	658		65	71
153	Grain mill products; starches; animal feeds		2410	2390	2524	2412		509	468	505	453		40	65
1531	Grain mill products		1302	1294	1354	1250		245	223	239	203		15	22
1532	Starches and starch products		236	225	236	249		70	63	66	75		7	10
1533	Prepared animal feeds		873	870	934	913		194	182	199	175		17	33
154	Other food products		12815	12889	12850	12920		5757	5824	5698	5665		370	426
1541	Bakery products		2916	2922	2910	2901		1545	1553	1540	1525		90	95
1542	Sugar		297	300	291	288		87	86	76	70		17	18
1543	Cocoa, chocolate and sugar confectionery		1104	1104	1135	1180		560	555	565	585		34	48
1544	Macaroni, noodles & similar products		992	965	938	920		410	411	390	372		20	26
1549	Other food products n.e.c.		7506	7597	7576	7631		3154	3217	3127	3113		208	239
155	Beverages		6226	6046	6128	5764		2288	2203	2168	2052		140	212
1551	Distilling, rectifying & blending of spirits		1328	1319	1417	1535		531	481	536	573		41	58
1552	Wines		687	645	596	545		314	303	278	245		11	17
1553	Malt liquors and malt		2146	1906	1863	1711		537	463	404	408		33	34
1554	Soft drinks; mineral waters		2065	2176	2251	1973		907	957	950	825		55	104
1600	Tobacco products		2925	2795	2986	2375		673	502	590	491		35	60
171	Spinning, weaving and finishing of textiles		1575	1502	1390	1291		714	696	636	576		29	36
1711	Textile fibre preparation; textile weaving		961	915	839	765		402	392	352	310		15	19
1712	Finishing of textiles		613	586	551	526		312	304	284	267		15	17
172	Other textiles		1582	1509	1501	1515		664	633	611	621		24	38
1721	Made-up textile articles, except apparel		742	687	665	652		312	294	274	273		5	11
1722	Carpets and rugs		186	175	177	175		54	48	47	49		2	5
1723	Cordage, rope, twine and netting		90	84	87	92		41	38	40	43		1	2
1729	Other textiles n.e.c.		564	562	571	595		257	253	250	255		14	21
1730	Knitted and crocheted fabrics and articles		858	806	734	676		373	356	323	292		10	12
1810	Wearing apparel, except fur apparel		1190	1095	1007	936		622	573	523	482		9	10
1820	Dressing & dyeing of fur; processing of fur		9	7	6	6		5	4	4	3		-	-
191	Tanning, dressing and processing of leather		336	334	315	341		138	135	131	133		5	6
1911	Tanning and dressing of leather		144	153	149	179		50	52	52	59		3	5
1912	Luggage, handbags, etc.; saddlery & harness		191	181	166	162		87	83	79	74		2	1
1920	Footwear		377	332	316	299		153	134	127	118		2	3
2010	Sawmilling and planing of wood		1073	1044	1017	958		400	388	376	337		13	19
202	Products of wood, cork, straw, etc.		2046	2012	2000	1962		832	800	790	764		35	47
2021	Veneer sheets, plywood, particle board, etc.		600	607	652	645		216	211	234	225		22	20
2022	Builders' carpentry and joinery		1073	1056	1024	1004		437	422	399	390		11	22
2023	Wooden containers		115	108	101	97		56	51	49	46		1	2
2029	Other wood products; articles of cork/straw		257	240	223	215		123	115	108	104		2	3
210	Paper and paper products		7123	7070	7182	7065		2645	2651	2711	2575		309	323
2101	Pulp, paper and paperboard		3420	3452	3460	3416		1197	1221	1243	1168		197	199
2102	Corrugated paper and paperboard		2316	2262	2314	2281		876	855	869	848		61	69
2109	Other articles of paper and paperboard		1387	1356	1407	1368		571	575	598	559		51	55
221	Publishing		...	...	...	...		...	...	...	...		...	...
2211	Publishing of books and other publications		...	...	...	...		...	...	...	...		...	...
2212	Publishing of newspapers, journals, etc.		...	...	...	...		...	...	...	...		...	...
2213	Publishing of recorded media		...	...	...	...		...	...	...	...		...	...
2219	Other publishing		...	...	...	...		...	...	...	...		...	...

continued

Japan

ISIC Revision 3		Output					Value added					Gross fixed capital formation		
		Note	(billions of Japanese Yen)				Note	(billions of Japanese Yen)				Note	(billions of Japanese Yen)	
ISIC	Industry		2002	2003	2004	2005		2002	2003	2004	2005		2004	2005
222	Printing and related service activities		7411	7228	7036	6945		3463	3368	3294	3225		190	271
2221	Printing		6492	6348	6171	6105		2871	2810	2747	2701		165	216
2222	Service activities related to printing		919	880	865	841		592	558	546	524		26	56
2230	Reproduction of recorded media		177	358	379	399		112	203	204	222		7	11
2310	Coke oven products		592	578	599	668		170	162	156	133		13	18
2320	Refined petroleum products		8974	9329	9871	12758		748	510	552	664		182	115
2330	Processing of nuclear fuel		83	80	153	80		8	8	68	13		39	26
241	Basic chemicals		9183	9620	10147	11291		3565	3594	3647	3735		488	634
2411	Basic chemicals, except fertilizers		5927	6221	6739	7785		2358	2410	2395	2543		319	426
2412	Fertilizers and nitrogen compounds		226	270	283	269		69	83	108	88		11	9
2413	Plastics in primary forms; synthetic rubber		3030	3129	3125	3238		1138	1101	1144	1105		158	199
242	Other chemicals		12921	13131	13469	13213		7235	7412	7605	7210		503	507
2421	Pesticides and other agro-chemical products		288	282	263	279		95	92	99	97		10	9
2422	Paints, varnishes, printing ink and mastics		2101	2052	2133	2267		783	765	776	806		60	91
2423	Pharmaceuticals, medicinal chemicals, etc.		6814	7043	7216	7001		4365	4544	4662	4373		264	234
2424	Soap, cleaning & cosmetic preparations		2429	2463	2503	2501		1424	1452	1490	1475		76	78
2429	Other chemical products n.e.c.		1288	1291	1355	1165		568	559	578	458		93	95
2430	Man-made fibres		574	506	465	454		193	183	155	157		33	27
251	Rubber products		2757	2784	2882	3005		1305	1281	1332	1322		152	160
2511	Rubber tyres and tubes		943	938	1028	1066		493	470	513	485		81	77
2519	Other rubber products		1814	1846	1854	1939		811	810	820	836		72	83
2520	Plastic products		9565	10011	10574	10800		3889	4102	4344	4349		411	520
2610	Glass and glass products		1686	1699	1908	1828		829	883	991	933		166	143
269	Non-metallic mineral products n.e.c.		5965	5688	5509	5619		2942	2840	2727	2680		165	252
2691	Pottery, china and earthenware		558	611	589	617		307	339	327	349		30	45
2692	Refractory ceramic products		354	315	314	335		159	146	144	143		11	12
2693	Struct.non-refractory clay; ceramic products		118	112	100	95		69	66	56	50		2	4
2694	Cement, lime and plaster		544	525	510	537		242	243	224	223		29	50
2695	Articles of concrete, cement and plaster		3167	2932	2769	2750		1473	1369	1289	1226		54	83
2696	Cutting, shaping & finishing of stone		464	417	380	369		292	268	243	224		8	12
2699	Other non-metallic mineral products n.e.c.		761	777	847	915		398	411	444	464		33	47
2710	Basic iron and steel		9478	10237	12148	14611		3142	3564	4117	5284		526	536
2720	Basic precious and non-ferrous metals		3423	3466	3873	4225		803	836	1040	1103		135	188
273	Casting of metals		1001	1044	1175	1266		456	469	512	544		40	49
2731	Casting of iron and steel		766	809	894	1003		348	365	394	437		30	37
2732	Casting of non-ferrous metals		236	234	281	263		107	104	118	107		10	12
281	Struct.metal products;tanks;steam generators		7293	6883	7073	6890		3200	3030	2961	2742		119	125
2811	Structural metal products		5159	4734	4693	4879		2128	1956	1847	1836		80	72
2812	Tanks, reservoirs and containers of metal		1175	1122	1177	1268		581	562	580	603		12	30
2813	Steam generators		959	1027	1204	743		490	512	534	303		27	24
289	Other metal products; metal working services		8379	8506	8795	9518		3889	3956	4153	4336		315	414
2891	Metal forging/pressing/stamping/roll-forming		2667	2729	2844	3199		1122	1143	1185	1268		117	151
2892	Treatment & coating of metals		1439	1502	1606	1705		832	865	924	949		51	84
2893	Cutlery, hand tools and general hardware		991	975	987	1085		491	486	565	622		32	43
2899	Other fabricated metal products n.e.c.		3281	3300	3358	3529		1444	1462	1479	1497		115	136
291	General purpose machinery		10934	10820	11166	12592		4374	4413	4494	4983		272	388
2911	Engines & turbines (not for transport equipment)		1623	1358	1283	1894		555	509	474	671		35	54
2912	Pumps, compressors, taps and valves		2203	2365	2554	2801		924	1019	1066	1091		57	84
2913	Bearings, gears, gearing & driving elements		1544	1643	1763	1898		679	707	756	795		86	126
2914	Ovens, furnaces and furnace burners		105	94	130	155		23	24	35	58		-	2
2915	Lifting and handling equipment		1601	1549	1604	1883		601	579	602	752		24	31
2919	Other general purpose machinery		3858	3811	3833	3961		1590	1575	1562	1616		70	92

292	Special purpose machinery		11986	12633	15250	16592		4813	5076	5853	6461		388	491
2921	Agricultural and forestry machinery		956	919	955	1026		379	329	325	329		20	23
2922	Machine tools		2607	2926	3489	4018		1114	1253	1459	1717		86	114
2923	Machinery for metallurgy		99	112	129	148		36	47	47	62		1	3
2924	Machinery for mining & construction		1373	1623	1996	2230		443	569	642	695		51	58
2925	Food/beverage/tobacco processing machinery		826	835	928	968		370	370	403	433		12	16
2926	Machinery for textile, apparel and leather		431	415	425	408		182	174	184	165		10	8
2927	Weapons and ammunition		458	111	359	400		181	39	114	154		9	18
2929	Other special purpose machinery		5236	5692	6969	7395		2108	2294	2680	2907		198	250
2930	Domestic appliances n.e.c.		3741	3585	3417	3427		1463	1445	1359	1377		76	76
3000	Office, accounting and computing machinery		7979	7195	7205	6769		1696	1558	1651	1672		216	282
3110	Electric motors, generators and transformers		1609	1613	1759	1836		573	601	664	679		40	80
3120	Electricity distribution & control apparatus		3203	3138	3034	3132		1216	1209	1061	1126		67	79
3130	Insulated wire and cable		1376	1262	1314	1414		318	339	345	350		37	40
3140	Accumulators, primary cells and batteries		929	897	829	830		298	287	257	235		41	54
3150	Lighting equipment and electric lamps		1070	1154	1191	1264		446	459	482	498		51	53
3190	Other electrical equipment n.e.c.		3100	3114	3498	3856		1059	1039	1213	1273		228	290
3210	Electronic valves, tubes, etc.		9878	10709	11184	10827		3434	4005	4521	4144		1057	1107
3220	TV/radio transmitters; line comm. apparatus		4112	4760	4519	4372		1059	1208	1144	1200		68	60
3230	TV and radio receivers and associated goods		11331	12719	13467	13124		3426	3881	4019	4019		822	926
331	Medical, measuring, testing appliances, etc.		4419	4169	4691	4823		1897	1913	2099	2179		124	128
3311	Medical, surgical and orthopaedic equipment		1577	1523	1529	1638		765	768	782	807		49	39
3312	Measuring/testing/navigating appliances,etc.		2581	2480	2981	3001		1013	1065	1231	1287		73	87
3313	Industrial process control equipment		261	165	181	184		119	80	86	86		3	3
3320	Optical instruments & photographic equipment		960	1011	1038	967		368	377	389	364		53	69
3330	Watches and clocks		307	314	329	334		65	70	62	74		13	10
3410	Motor vehicles		21542	22106	22391	24025		5860	5672	5486	6223		466	644
3420	Automobile bodies, trailers & semi-trailers		2817	2982	2131	2522		529	536	368	398		42	74
3430	Parts/accessories for automobiles		18804	19962	21290	22408		6016	6314	6513	6770		954	1263
351	Building and repairing of ships and boats		1886	1715	1903	1864		711	633	659	559		54	65
3511	Building and repairing of ships		1886	1715	1903	1864		711	633	659	559		...	65
3512	Building/repairing of pleasure/sport. boats		...	...	...	...		...	...	...	...		...	...
3520	Railway/tramway locomotives & rolling stock		474	433	498	498		192	188	206	157		9	10
3530	Aircraft and spacecraft		1116	1274	1045	1078		418	421	436	422		33	35
359	Transport equipment n.e.c.		405	373	427	359		158	130	159	128		11	10
3591	Motorcycles		...	...	...	...		...	...	...	...		...	...
3592	Bicycles and invalid carriages		226	181	205	180		100	69	83	70		6	6
3599	Other transport equipment n.e.c.		179	192	222	179		57	62	77	58		5	5
3610	Furniture		1812	1825	1764	1759		792	796	761	755		23	36
369	Manufacturing n.e.c.		3890	3503	2923	3317		1442	1300	1238	1274		53	74
3691	Jewellery and related articles		232	224	211	214		101	87	80	83		1	1
3692	Musical instruments		268	173	161	164		79	56	54	55		5	6
3693	Sports goods		318	280	271	271		154	143	141	137		5	7
3694	Games and toys		866	660	163	356		187	109	78	89		5	5
3699	Other manufacturing n.e.c.		2206	2166	2117	2312		922	906	886	910		37	55
3710	Recycling of metal waste and scrap	a/	339	443	659	760	a/	150	183	207	268	a/	12	24
3720	Recycling of non-metal waste and scrap	a/	...	...	...	...	a/	...	...	...	...	a/	...	...
D	Total manufacturing		269304	273677	283913	295747		97429	98629	101489	103508		9894	11852

a/ 3710 includes 3720.

Japan

ISIC Revision 3			Index numbers of industrial production											
			(2000=100)											
ISIC	Industry	Note	1995	1996	1997	1998	1999	2000	2001	2002	2003	2004	2005	2006
15	Food and beverages		101	102	101	99	100	100	99	98	98	98	98	97
16	Tobacco products		...	...	...	...	...	...	...	...	...	...	...	...
17	Textiles		130	127	127	112	105	100	93	85	79	76	72	70
18	Wearing apparel, fur		148	141	133	119	112	100	87	77	70	62	56	53
19	Leather, leather products and footwear		142	139	130	116	105	100	96	83	78	76	71	66
20	Wood products (excl. furniture)		140	138	129	110	104	100	90	82	80	79	77	76
21	Paper and paper products		95	96	99	96	98	100	97	97	97	98	99	99
22	Printing and publishing		104	106	107	104	103	100	98	97	96	94	95	100
23	Coke,refined petroleum products,nuclear fuel		97	97	100	100	100	100	101	100	102	100	102	100
24	Chemicals and chemical products		95	96	99	94	99	100	99	99	100	102	101	104
25	Rubber and plastics products		101	104	106	100	99	100	95	94	96	97	98	100
26	Non-metallic mineral products		115	115	116	103	99	100	93	88	86	86	86	87
27	Basic metals		100	99	104	92	91	100	97	98	102	105	105	108
28	Fabricated metal products		112	113	111	100	100	100	93	87	85	85	84	83
29	Machinery and equipment n.e.c.		100	105	109	96	90	100	89	82	88	101	107	114
30	Office, accounting and computing machinery		...	...	...	...	...	...	...	...	...	...	...	...
31	Electrical machinery and apparatus		72	79	83	79	85	100	85	87	96	107	109	124
32	Radio,television and communication equipment		67	69	76	73	81	100	81	86	100	110	111	131
33	Medical, precision and optical instruments		94	100	104	102	95	100	84	74	81	97	100	108
34	Motor vehicles, trailers, semi-trailers		94	96	105	96	96	100	100	106	110	114	118	127
35	Other transport equipment		97	103	108	96	102	100	103	110	89	115	136	119
36	Furniture; manufacturing n.e.c.		103	102	112	104	101	100	88	81	77	76	78	89
37	Recycling		...	...	...	...	...	...	...	...	...	...	...	...
D	Total manufacturing		96	98	101	94	95	100	93	92	95	100	101	105

Jordan

Supplier of information:
Department of Statistics, Amman.

Basic source of data:
Annual industrial survey.

Major deviations from ISIC (Revision 3):
None reported.

Reference period:
Fiscal year.

Scope:
All establishments.

Method of data collection:
Direct interview in the field.

Type of enumeration:
Sample survey.

Adjusted for non-response:
Yes.

Concepts and definitions of variables:
Output refers to gross output.
Value added refers to total value added.

Related national publications:
Industry Survey (annual); Statistical Yearbook, both published by the Department of Statistics, Amman.

Jordan

ISIC Revision 3		Number of establishments					Number of employees					Wages and salaries paid to employees				
			(number)					(number)					(thousands of Jordanian Dinars)			
ISIC	Industry	Note	2003	2004	2005	2006	Note	2003	2004	2005	2006	Note	2003	2004	2005	2006
151	Processed meat,fish,fruit,vegetables,fats		126	136	154	163		4207	4296	4658	4690		10310	11096	12482	14099
1511	Processing/preserving of meat		15	25	25	26		1915	2163	2382	2411		4780	5550	6239	7731
1512	Processing/preserving of fish		-	-	-	-		-	-	-	-		-	-	-	-
1513	Processing/preserving of fruit & vegetables		10	17	24	25		859	911	996	1096		1755	1948	2253	1716
1514	Vegetable and animal oils and fats		101	94	105	112		1433	1222	1280	1183		3775	3598	3990	4652
1520	Dairy products		603	642	621	627		4226	4388	5658	5700		6412	6972	7534	7141
153	Grain mill products; starches; animal feeds		186	203	210	213		1328	1534	2022	2072		3157	3744	4578	6293
1531	Grain mill products		118	31	38	46		967	876	1233	1252		2285	2313	2905	4293
1532	Starches and starch products		-	-	-	-		-	-	-	-		-	-	-	-
1533	Prepared animal feeds		68	172	172	167		361	658	789	820		872	1431	1673	2000
154	Other food products		2413	2808	2823	2586		13655	14781	15184	14897		18723	20862	22108	26012
1541	Bakery products		1791	2066	2077	1983		9682	10820	11171	10814		12787	15217	16157	17625
1542	Sugar		-	-	-	-		-	-	-	-		-	-	-	-
1543	Cocoa, chocolate and sugar confectionery		65	67	70	64		961	1002	1076	1083		1474	1745	1963	2447
1544	Macaroni, noodles & similar products		-	-	-	-		-	-	-	-		-	-	-	-
1549	Other food products n.e.c.		557	675	676	539		3012	2959	2937	3000		4462	3900	3988	5940
155	Beverages		37	62	63	67		3106	3648	3729	3763		9491	11009	13488	13121
1551	Distilling, rectifying & blending of spirits		9	10	8	7		404	441	457	412		1337	1522	1653	2460
1552	Wines		-	-	-	-		-	-	-	-		-	-	-	-
1553	Malt liquors and malt		-	-	-	-		-	-	-	-		-	-	-	-
1554	Soft drinks; mineral waters		28	52	55	60		2702	3207	3272	3351		8154	9487	11835	10661
1600	Tobacco products		6	10	9	10		1162	1238	1146	1414		4986	5017	4765	5753
171	Spinning, weaving and finishing of textiles		18	22	23	24		642	613	650	411		1976	1798	1950	1880
1711	Textile fibre preparation; textile weaving		18	22	23	24		642	613	650	411		1976	1798	1950	1880
1712	Finishing of textiles		-	-	-	-		-	-	-	-		-	-	-	-
172	Other textiles		448	540	548	532		1625	1743	2227	2497		2633	2393	2889	4755
1721	Made-up textile articles, except apparel		381	431	433	405		778	876	1216	1393		623	510	854	1729
1722	Carpets and rugs		29	21	27	27		654	553	739	820		1806	1579	1758	2395
1723	Cordage, rope, twine and netting		-	-	-	-		-	-	-	-		-	-	-	-
1729	Other textiles n.e.c.		38	88	88	100		193	314	272	284		204	304	277	631
1730	Knitted and crocheted fabrics and articles		83	103	100	100		762	898	679	815		1122	921	589	1487
1810	Wearing apparel, except fur apparel		1927	2025	2061	2114		17207	18002	18427	19850		23788	24855	29716	34289
1820	Dressing & dyeing of fur; processing of fur		-	-	-	-		-	-	-	-		-	-	-	-
191	Tanning, dressing and processing of leather		75	94	73	70		386	392	435	445		822	954	1027	1046
1911	Tanning and dressing of leather		24	24	23	20		194	219	184	223		652	732	653	797
1912	Luggage, handbags, etc.; saddlery & harness		51	70	50	50		192	173	251	222		170	222	374	249
1920	Footwear		175	226	226	200		1258	1523	1406	1230		1932	1656	1523	1090
2010	Sawmilling and planing of wood		158	31	34	40		435	413	614	511		345	1032	1098	885
202	Products of wood, cork, straw, etc.		1161	1203	1535	1186		2714	2920	3349	3360		1884	2452	3605	2471
2021	Veneer sheets, plywood, particle board, etc.		-	-	-	-		-	-	-	-		-	-	-	-
2022	Builders' carpentry and joinery		1000	1020	1350	1055		2228	2454	2932	3000		1533	1893	2599	2062
2023	Wooden containers		29	56	58	32		178	210	180	140		138	209	169	215
2029	Other wood products; articles of cork/straw		132	127	127	99		308	256	237	220		213	350	837	194
210	Paper and paper products		93	117	117	113		2979	3296	3509	3571		8025	9139	9863	10118
2101	Pulp, paper and paperboard		14	22	20	19		777	680	640	633		2197	2010	2026	1849
2102	Corrugated paper and paperboard		54	56	57	53		960	1043	1117	1166		2896	3438	3375	4955
2109	Other articles of paper and paperboard		25	39	40	41		1242	1573	1752	1772		2932	3691	4462	3314
221	Publishing		52	51	51	66		2037	2674	2570	2522		8755	13000	13754	14808
2211	Publishing of books and other publications		-	-	-	-		-	-	-	-		-	-	-	-
2212	Publishing of newspapers, journals, etc.		52	51	51	66		2037	2674	2570	2522		8755	13000	13754	14808
2213	Publishing of recorded media		-	-	-	-		-	-	-	-		-	-	-	-
2219	Other publishing		-	-	-	-		-	-	-	-		-	-	-	-

222	Printing and related service activities	375	414	420	458	2582	2900	3337	3047	4997	5867	8277	7804
2221	Printing	337	340	345	415	2327	2595	2894	2841	4746	5488	7284	7581
2222	Service activities related to printing	38	74	75	43	255	305	443	206	251	379	993	223
2230	Reproduction of recorded media	-	-	-	-	-	-	-	-	-	-	-	-
2310	Coke oven products	-	-	-	-	-	-	-	-	-	-	-	-
2320	Refined petroleum products	1	1	1	1	3493	3571	3431	3577	20069	20409	20541	21891
2330	Processing of nuclear fuel	-	-	-	-	-	-	-	-	-	-	-	-
241	Basic chemicals	48	67	74	62	2965	3301	3284	3146	17040	17527	19665	20384
2411	Basic chemicals, except fertilizers	13	13	17	21	1096	1096	1102	1086	6524	6602	6639	6699
2412	Fertilizers and nitrogen compounds	13	13	13	15	1416	1577	1542	1543	9457	9445	11271	11689
2413	Plastics in primary forms; synthetic rubber	22	41	44	26	453	628	640	517	1059	1480	1755	1996
242	Other chemicals	200	206	206	225	8645	9925	10996	10903	32515	41442	50543	53413
2421	Pesticides and other agro-chemical products	4	8	7	5	109	246	220	157	248	754	578	548
2422	Paints, varnishes, printing ink and mastics	51	48	50	68	1472	1575	1578	1793	3882	4338	4474	5932
2423	Pharmaceuticals, medicinal chemicals, etc.	25	23	24	29	4137	4791	5603	5360	20107	27405	35578	37169
2424	Soap, cleaning & cosmetic preparations	105	113	112	111	2635	3048	3334	3386	7432	8159	9004	8930
2429	Other chemical products n.e.c.	15	14	13	12	292	265	261	207	846	786	909	834
2430	Man-made fibres	-	-	-	-	-	-	-	-	-	-	-	-
251	Rubber products	37	32	31	26	268	236	201	209	498	473	617	465
2511	Rubber tyres and tubes	16	14	13	8	156	133	122	110	322	293	468	294
2519	Other rubber products	21	18	18	18	112	103	79	99	176	180	149	171
2520	Plastic products	186	199	199	257	4377	4245	4218	4360	9233	9157	9664	10911
2610	Glass and glass products	36	34	34	27	359	380	488	583	795	735	1078	1454
269	Non-metallic mineral products n.e.c.	2277	2372	2459	2434	13660	15551	16152	16929	28322	34313	37156	43044
2691	Pottery, china and earthenware	15	17	15	26	358	307	314	311	804	697	668	451
2692	Refractory ceramic products	-	-	-	-	-	-	-	-	-	-	-	-
2693	Struct.non-refractory clay; ceramic products	14	18	20	23	985	1159	853	934	2077	2235	2029	2095
2694	Cement, lime and plaster	4	6	11	26	1857	2034	1901	1904	10118	11747	12062	12963
2695	Articles of concrete, cement and plaster	1563	1578	1631	1515	6427	7124	7574	7479	9364	11686	12936	15459
2696	Cutting, shaping & finishing of stone	668	733	762	834	3795	4580	5097	5878	5372	6948	8063	10829
2699	Other non-metallic mineral products n.e.c.	13	20	20	10	238	347	413	423	587	1000	1398	1247
2710	Basic iron and steel	32	33	36	32	1871	2157	2389	2051	6705	7557	9265	8411
2720	Basic precious and non-ferrous metals	6	6	6	5	910	917	977	1047	2123	2223	2376	2947
273	Casting of metals	18	80	82	80	646	581	598	600	2003	1360	1593	770
2731	Casting of iron and steel	18	80	82	80	646	581	598	600	2003	1360	1593	770
2732	Casting of non-ferrous metals	-	-	-	-	-	-	-	-	-	-	-	-
281	Struct.metal products;tanks;steam generators	3085	3106	3148	3336	8057	7713	7978	8468	6506	7241	8407	10498
2811	Structural metal products	2941	2970	3015	3229	7551	7439	7672	8187	6235	7016	8227	10206
2812	Tanks, reservoirs and containers of metal	144	136	133	107	506	274	306	281	271	225	180	292
2813	Steam generators	-	-	-	-	-	-	-	-	-	-	-	-
289	Other metal products; metal working services	1095	940	980	986	4642	4330	5068	5126	6784	7594	8431	8488
2891	Metal forging/pressing/stamping/roll-forming	-	-	-	-	-	-	-	-	-	-	-	-
2892	Treatment & coating of metals	83	394	415	614	474	1187	1516	1576	571	1315	1723	2038
2893	Cutlery, hand tools and general hardware	117	121	133	131	476	487	658	700	723	869	947	635
2899	Other fabricated metal products n.e.c.	895	425	432	241	3692	2656	2894	2850	5490	5410	5761	5815
291	General purpose machinery	51	63	65	53	1527	1692	1810	1738	4386	4968	5629	5901
2911	Engines & turbines (not for transport equipment)	-	-	-	-	-	-	-	-	-	-	-	-
2912	Pumps, compressors, taps and valves	-	-	-	-	-	-	-	-	-	-	-	-
2913	Bearings, gears, gearing & driving elements	-	-	-	-	-	-	-	-	-	-	-	-
2914	Ovens, furnaces and furnace burners	-	-	-	-	-	-	-	-	-	-	-	-
2915	Lifting and handling equipment	16	23	24	26	228	338	380	382	608	836	1078	1531
2919	Other general purpose machinery	35	40	41	27	1299	1354	1430	1356	3778	4132	4551	4370
292	Special purpose machinery	197	218	228	168	977	995	1057	1031	1618	1768	1745	2295
2921	Agricultural and forestry machinery	70	67	69	67	266	219	195	241	330	341	243	326
2922	Machine tools	8	7	7	7	101	138	124	120	246	360	198	124
2923	Machinery for metallurgy	-	-	-	-	-	-	-	-	-	-	-	-
2924	Machinery for mining & construction	99	107	111	72	382	331	485	400	553	462	841	519
2925	Food/beverage/tobacco processing machinery	11	16	18	12	134	171	148	140	171	240	151	54
2926	Machinery for textile, apparel and leather	-	-	-	-	-	-	-	-	-	-	-	-
2927	Weapons and ammunition	-	-	-	-	-	-	-	-	-	-	-	-
2929	Other special purpose machinery	9	21	23	10	94	136	105	130	318	365	312	1272

continued

Jordan

ISIC Revision 3		Number of establishments					Number of employees					Wages and salaries paid to employees				
			(number)					(number)					(thousands of Jordanian Dinars)			
ISIC	Industry	Note	2003	2004	2005	2006	Note	2003	2004	2005	2006	Note	2003	2004	2005	2006
2930	Domestic appliances n.e.c.		39	34	37	59		1167	1295	1289	1135		2838	3022	3084	3319
3000	Office, accounting and computing machinery		-	-	-	-		-	-	-	-		-	-	-	-
3110	Electric motors, generators and transformers		5	6	7	7		99	108	144	123		270	275	432	468
3120	Electricity distribution & control apparatus		14	15	16	35		176	250	345	537		447	654	921	1220
3130	Insulated wire and cable		4	5	6	7		853	1466	1757	2378		2384	3893	4736	5379
3140	Accumulators, primary cells and batteries		-	-	-	-		-	-	-	-		-	-	-	-
3150	Lighting equipment and electric lamps		26	31	36	40		599	471	532	598		1310	1194	1299	1795
3190	Other electrical equipment n.e.c.		-	-	-	-		-	-	-	-		-	-	-	-
3210	Electronic valves, tubes, etc.		-	-	-	-		-	-	-	-		-	-	-	-
3220	TV/radio transmitters; line comm. apparatus		-	-	-	-		-	-	-	-		-	-	-	-
3230	TV and radio receivers and associated goods		-	-	-	-		-	-	-	-		-	-	-	-
331	Medical, measuring, testing appliances, etc.		164	183	184	208		994	985	1225	1006		2074	2027	2724	2378
3311	Medical, surgical and orthopaedic equipment		164	183	184	208		994	985	1225	1006		2074	2027	2724	2378
3312	Measuring/testing/navigating appliances,etc.		-	-	-	-		-	-	-	-		-	-	-	-
3313	Industrial process control equipment		-	-	-	-		-	-	-	-		-	-	-	-
3320	Optical instruments & photographic equipment		-	-	-	-		-	-	-	-		-	-	-	-
3330	Watches and clocks		-	-	-	-		-	-	-	-		-	-	-	-
3410	Motor vehicles		-	-	-	-		-	-	-	-		-	-	-	-
3420	Automobile bodies, trailers & semi-trailers		136	159	166	181		924	1065	1140	1165		2262	2494	2662	3327
3430	Parts/accessories for automobiles		19	22	25	36		562	660	688	687		1106	1391	1525	1694
351	Building and repairing of ships and boats		3	6	6	8		10	44	91	183		24	129	350	1864
3511	Building and repairing of ships		-	-	-	-		-	-	-	-		-	-	-	-
3512	Building/repairing of pleasure/sport. boats		3	6	6	8		10	44	91	183		24	129	350	1864
3520	Railway/tramway locomotives & rolling stock		-	-	-	-		-	-	-	-		-	-	-	-
3530	Aircraft and spacecraft		-	-	-	-		-	-	-	-		-	-	-	-
359	Transport equipment n.e.c.		-	-	-	-		-	-	-	-		-	-	-	-
3591	Motorcycles		-	-	-	-		-	-	-	-		-	-	-	-
3592	Bicycles and invalid carriages		-	-	-	-		-	-	-	-		-	-	-	-
3599	Other transport equipment n.e.c.		-	-	-	-		-	-	-	-		-	-	-	-
3610	Furniture		3075	3108	3113	3109		8372	8949	10277	10786		9062	10525	13783	17111
369	Manufacturing n.e.c.		276	267	274	200		1522	1117	1916	1415		1967	1745	1944	2118
3691	Jewellery and related articles		221	213	218	125		1138	776	1629	1015		1045	890	1045	1092
3692	Musical instruments		-	-	-	-		-	-	-	-		-	-	-	-
3693	Sports goods		-	-	-	-		-	-	-	-		-	-	-	-
3694	Games and toys		-	-	-	-		-	-	-	-		-	-	-	-
3699	Other manufacturing n.e.c.		55	54	56	75		384	341	287	400		922	855	899	1026
3710	Recycling of metal waste and scrap		-	-	-	-		-	-	-	-		-	-	-	-
3720	Recycling of non-metal waste and scrap		-	-	-	-		-	-	-	-		-	-	-	-
D	Total manufacturing	a/	18966	19934	20487	20151	a/	127986	137604	147651	150576	a/	271699	306883	349416	384597

a/ Sum of available data.

ISIC Revision 3		Output in producers' prices					Value added in producers' prices					Gross fixed capital formation		
			(millions of Jordanian Dinars)					(millions of Jordanian Dinars)					(millions of Jordanian Dinars)	
ISIC	Industry	Note	2003	2004	2005	2006	Note	2003	2004	2005	2006	Note	2005	2006
151	Processed meat,fish,fruit,vegetables,fats		194.7	258.7	302.1	358.3		48.9	60.8	73.0	89.3		14.8	14.4
1511	Processing/preserving of meat		89.8	100.0	117.2	133.9		22.4	22.8	28.6	33.5		10.9	11.1
1512	Processing/preserving of fish		-	-	-	-		-	-	-	-		-	-
1513	Processing/preserving of fruit & vegetables		16.2	18.8	22.2	30.3		4.7	5.5	6.3	9.1		0.5	2.3
1514	Vegetable and animal oils and fats		88.7	139.9	162.7	194.1		21.8	32.5	38.1	46.7		3.4	1.0
1520	Dairy products		75.8	88.6	94.2	98.9		16.7	20.1	20.2	20.5		3.9	2.7
153	Grain mill products; starches; animal feeds		123.9	149.7	134.9	127.4		17.3	21.8	20.9	16.5		3.0	5.0
1531	Grain mill products		86.5	90.6	82.6	85.8		9.8	10.2	10.5	10.1		1.8	4.2
1532	Starches and starch products		-	-	-	-		-	-	-	-		-	-
1533	Prepared animal feeds		37.3	59.1	52.3	41.6		7.5	11.6	10.5	6.4		1.2	0.8
154	Other food products		176.0	196.0	214.6	250.1		54.1	61.9	66.7	72.0		10.6	12.0
1541	Bakery products		110.9	120.1	125.8	143.8		34.2	38.3	38.4	41.7		7.4	2.9
1542	Sugar		-	-	-	-		-	-	-	-		-	-
1543	Cocoa, chocolate and sugar confectionery		18.0	19.2	26.4	27.6		4.9	5.3	7.1	6.6		0.1	-
1544	Macaroni, noodles & similar products		-	-	-	-		-	-	-	-		-	-
1549	Other food products n.e.c.		47.1	56.7	62.5	78.7		15.0	18.3	21.2	23.7		3.0	9.1
155	Beverages		104.2	126.7	140.0	156.6		51.9	64.4	70.4	76.3		7.4	9.2
1551	Distilling, rectifying & blending of spirits		25.1	31.7	35.5	35.9		16.7	22.0	24.4	24.9		0.6	2.2
1552	Wines		-	-	-	-		-	-	-	-		-	-
1553	Malt liquors and malt		-	-	-	-		-	-	-	-		-	-
1554	Soft drinks; mineral waters		79.1	95.0	104.5	120.7		35.3	42.5	46.0	51.4		6.8	7.0
1600	Tobacco products		216.2	241.5	244.1	282.4		133.2	151.6	155.4	180.9		6.6	9.7
171	Spinning, weaving and finishing of textiles		27.0	22.3	22.9	15.9		12.5	10.4	9.6	6.8		0.3	0.6
1711	Textile fibre preparation; textile weaving		27.0	22.3	22.9	15.9		12.5	10.4	9.6	6.8		0.3	0.6
1712	Finishing of textiles		-	-	-	-		-	-	-	-		-	-
172	Other textiles		21.1	24.4	29.4	45.8		9.5	10.6	13.2	18.7		0.1	11.7
1721	Made-up textile articles, except apparel		4.1	5.1	8.2	8.9		2.1	2.4	4.1	4.0		-	11.7
1722	Carpets and rugs		15.6	17.3	19.3	33.8		6.7	7.3	8.0	13.0		0.1	-
1723	Cordage, rope, twine and netting		-	-	-	-		-	-	-	-		-	-
1729	Other textiles n.e.c.		1.4	2.1	1.9	3.1		0.7	1.0	1.0	1.7		-	-
1730	Knitted and crocheted fabrics and articles		5.0	4.9	3.8	6.2		2.3	2.2	1.5	2.7		0.1	0.1
1810	Wearing apparel, except fur apparel		171.4	280.9	310.6	325.7		101.3	163.7	168.4	175.2		4.1	4.3
1820	Dressing & dyeing of fur; processing of fur		-	-	-	-		-	-	-	-		-	-
191	Tanning, dressing and processing of leather		4.4	6.6	4.9	4.8		1.3	2.3	1.4	1.2		0.1	0.1
1911	Tanning and dressing of leather		3.7	5.0	3.7	3.6		0.9	1.3	0.7	0.7		0.1	0.1
1912	Luggage, handbags, etc.; saddlery & harness		0.7	1.6	1.2	1.2		0.4	1.0	0.7	0.5		-	-
1920	Footwear		13.4	14.7	13.9	19.6		5.0	4.4	4.3	7.3		-	-
2010	Sawmilling and planing of wood		4.6	5.5	7.8	8.5		1.5	1.5	1.6	1.5		-	-
202	Products of wood, cork, straw, etc.		18.8	21.7	23.3	27.3		7.2	8.3	9.1	11.4		0.1	0.1
2021	Veneer sheets, plywood, particle board, etc.		-	-	-	-		-	-	-	-		-	-
2022	Builders' carpentry and joinery		16.6	18.3	19.6	21.8		6.1	6.6	7.3	8.5		0.1	0.1
2023	Wooden containers		0.9	1.2	1.2	1.4		0.4	0.5	0.5	0.6		-	-
2029	Other wood products; articles of cork/straw		1.4	2.1	2.6	4.2		0.7	1.2	1.3	2.2		-	-
210	Paper and paper products		106.9	123.4	134.8	140.2		35.6	44.3	46.6	46.1		8.4	5.3
2101	Pulp, paper and paperboard		20.3	22.0	24.7	29.3		5.6	6.5	7.3	8.8		1.2	0.7
2102	Corrugated paper and paperboard		40.6	50.7	56.7	61.8		15.0	20.1	21.9	22.5		6.2	4.1
2109	Other articles of paper and paperboard		45.9	50.6	53.5	49.1		15.1	17.8	17.4	14.9		0.9	0.5
221	Publishing		50.3	60.5	63.6	87.6		28.6	32.3	34.1	49.9		8.8	11.8
2211	Publishing of books and other publications		-	-	-	-		-	-	-	-		-	-
2212	Publishing of newspapers, journals, etc.		50.3	60.5	63.6	87.6		28.6	32.3	34.1	49.9		8.8	11.8
2213	Publishing of recorded media		-	-	-	-		-	-	-	-		-	-
2219	Other publishing		-	-	-	-		-	-	-	-		-	-

continued

Jordan

ISIC Revision 3		Output in producers' prices					Value added in producers' prices					Gross fixed capital formation		
			(millions of Jordanian Dinars)					(millions of Jordanian Dinars)					(millions of Jordanian Dinars)	
ISIC	Industry	Note	2003	2004	2005	2006	Note	2003	2004	2005	2006	Note	2005	2006
222	Printing and related service activities		38.6	47.0	52.4	56.4		15.3	18.0	20.4	20.6		1.5	8.7
2221	Printing		36.8	44.5	49.4	53.8		14.2	16.5	18.5	18.9		1.5	8.6
2222	Service activities related to printing		1.7	2.5	3.0	2.6		1.1	1.5	1.8	1.7		-	0.2
2230	Reproduction of recorded media		-	-	-	-		-	-	-	-		-	-
2310	Coke oven products		-	-	-	-		-	-	-	-		-	-
2320	Refined petroleum products		598.0	903.2	1223.4	1629.9		67.3	76.6	79.1	84.4		6.1	6.0
2330	Processing of nuclear fuel		-	-	-	-		-	-	-	-		-	-
241	Basic chemicals		335.4	296.1	319.0	337.7		71.8	92.0	100.0	102.0		7.9	7.9
2411	Basic chemicals, except fertilizers		97.1	104.1	112.6	110.2		52.2	55.1	59.4	58.3		3.7	5.0
2412	Fertilizers and nitrogen compounds		229.0	177.0	187.1	202.4		16.4	31.6	34.2	36.3		3.7	1.8
2413	Plastics in primary forms; synthetic rubber		9.3	15.0	19.3	25.0		3.1	5.3	6.3	7.4		0.4	1.2
242	Other chemicals		327.7	404.7	472.7	507.2		124.9	154.0	173.4	184.1		24.6	26.3
2421	Pesticides and other agro-chemical products		7.9	14.6	12.6	14.9		1.8	3.4	3.3	3.7		1.7	-
2422	Paints, varnishes, printing ink and mastics		58.8	77.0	87.6	98.8		16.0	21.2	23.0	24.0		2.9	1.3
2423	Pharmaceuticals, medicinal chemicals, etc.		168.0	203.9	257.0	268.5		75.7	92.3	112.9	119.2		14.1	22.7
2424	Soap, cleaning & cosmetic preparations		84.8	97.5	101.0	111.5		29.1	33.5	29.9	33.3		5.6	1.6
2429	Other chemical products n.e.c.		8.3	11.7	14.5	13.5		2.3	3.5	4.3	3.9		0.3	0.6
2430	Man-made fibres		-	-	-	-		-	-	-	-		-	-
251	Rubber products		3.8	3.8	3.5	4.1		1.6	1.7	1.5	1.1		0.1	0.5
2511	Rubber tyres and tubes		2.3	2.1	2.5	3.0		0.9	0.9	1.1	0.7		0.1	-
2519	Other rubber products		1.5	1.7	1.0	1.1		0.7	0.9	0.4	0.5		-	0.4
2520	Plastic products		106.4	127.7	149.1	156.4		37.9	45.8	49.5	49.5		10.7	5.9
2610	Glass and glass products		4.4	7.0	8.7	11.5		1.9	3.1	3.8	4.8		0.1	1.1
269	Non-metallic mineral products n.e.c.		333.9	413.3	509.0	619.1		165.9	203.7	247.6	299.8		29.0	74.2
2691	Pottery, china and earthenware		5.8	3.9	5.2	4.3		3.0	1.9	2.6	2.3		0.1	0.2
2692	Refractory ceramic products		-	-	-	-		-	-	-	-		-	-
2693	Struct.non-refractory clay; ceramic products		15.0	19.7	21.2	17.3		6.9	9.6	10.6	9.0		0.7	1.0
2694	Cement, lime and plaster		174.7	208.1	253.2	302.5		108.8	131.1	158.5	191.2		-3.0	17.0
2695	Articles of concrete, cement and plaster		88.3	125.9	161.0	207.1		27.0	40.2	50.1	64.9		25.5	51.9
2696	Cutting, shaping & finishing of stone		44.7	48.9	61.4	81.0		18.0	18.2	23.3	30.2		5.3	3.2
2699	Other non-metallic mineral products n.e.c.		5.4	6.9	7.1	7.0		2.2	2.7	2.4	2.3		0.4	0.8
2710	Basic iron and steel		145.0	230.5	292.6	257.7		51.7	81.1	97.1	84.4		3.4	12.0
2720	Basic precious and non-ferrous metals		33.3	40.3	47.0	66.4		14.1	17.3	20.6	28.1		1.9	4.7
273	Casting of metals		7.5	5.7	7.2	14.5		2.9	2.3	3.1	7.0		6.9	0.6
2731	Casting of iron and steel		7.5	5.7	7.2	14.5		2.9	2.3	3.1	7.0		6.9	0.6
2732	Casting of non-ferrous metals		-	-	-	-		-	-	-	-		-	-
281	Struct.metal products;tanks;steam generators		65.1	76.3	87.8	115.0		22.6	26.6	30.0	37.2		0.3	1.3
2811	Structural metal products		62.0	74.5	85.8	111.4		21.6	26.0	29.2	36.3		0.3	1.3
2812	Tanks, reservoirs and containers of metal		3.2	1.8	2.1	3.7		1.0	0.6	0.8	0.9		-	-
2813	Steam generators		-	-	-	-		-	-	-	-		-	-
289	Other metal products; metal working services		73.7	115.5	128.2	158.7		27.9	47.0	51.1	62.8		7.7	8.5
2891	Metal forging/pressing/stamping/roll-forming		-	-	-	-		-	-	-	-		-	-
2892	Treatment & coating of metals		2.6	5.5	7.7	9.7		1.7	3.4	4.1	4.8		-	-
2893	Cutlery, hand tools and general hardware		5.2	6.3	8.3	11.2		1.8	2.2	3.4	4.8		0.1	0.3
2899	Other fabricated metal products n.e.c.		65.9	103.7	112.2	137.7		24.4	41.5	43.6	53.2		7.6	8.1
291	General purpose machinery		31.7	45.7	56.1	57.7		10.7	15.8	18.1	18.1		1.9	1.7
2911	Engines & turbines (not for transport equipment)		-	-	-	-		-	-	-	-		-	-
2912	Pumps, compressors, taps and valves		-	-	-	-		-	-	-	-		-	-
2913	Bearings, gears, gearing & driving elements		-	-	-	-		-	-	-	-		-	-
2914	Ovens, furnaces and furnace burners		-	-	-	-		-	-	-	-		-	-
2915	Lifting and handling equipment		6.5	12.2	12.8	14.9		1.5	3.2	2.4	1.9		0.5	0.2
2919	Other general purpose machinery		25.2	33.5	43.2	42.8		9.2	12.6	15.7	16.1		1.4	1.5

292	Special purpose machinery		17.8	19.5	23.3	28.2		6.6	7.1	8.4	9.4		0.4	0.3
2921	Agricultural and forestry machinery		8.7	9.6	11.0	13.9		2.3	2.5	3.0	3.4		0.4	-
2922	Machine tools		2.9	2.6	2.8	3.0		1.3	1.2	1.0	1.1		-	-
2923	Machinery for metallurgy		-	-	-	-		-	-	-	-		-	-
2924	Machinery for mining & construction		3.0	3.3	5.2	6.2		1.5	1.6	2.5	3.0		-	0.3
2925	Food/beverage/tobacco processing machinery		1.5	2.1	2.1	2.5		0.6	0.9	0.9	1.1		-	-
2926	Machinery for textile, apparel and leather		-	-	-	-		-	-	-	-		-	-
2927	Weapons and ammunition		-	-	-	-		-	-	-	-		-	-
2929	Other special purpose machinery		1.7	1.9	2.1	2.6		0.8	1.0	1.1	0.8		-	-
2930	Domestic appliances n.e.c.		22.7	25.2	31.6	39.4		7.9	8.9	11.4	15.0		0.7	0.7
3000	Office, accounting and computing machinery		-	-	-	-		-	-	-	-		-	-
3110	Electric motors, generators and transformers		4.5	6.0	7.3	10.3		1.2	1.6	1.6	1.4		0.3	0.2
3120	Electricity distribution & control apparatus		4.6	7.9	9.8	10.8		1.7	3.0	3.8	4.0		0.1	0.1
3130	Insulated wire and cable		68.8	113.9	160.3	210.9		15.9	26.6	38.0	45.5		24.1	15.7
3140	Accumulators, primary cells and batteries		-	-	-	-		-	-	-	-		-	-
3150	Lighting equipment and electric lamps		10.3	11.2	15.7	19.0		5.0	5.4	7.6	9.1		0.1	0.3
3190	Other electrical equipment n.e.c.		-	-	-	-		-	-	-	-		-	-
3210	Electronic valves, tubes, etc.		-	-	-	-		-	-	-	-		-	-
3220	TV/radio transmitters; line comm. apparatus		-	-	-	-		-	-	-	-		-	-
3230	TV and radio receivers and associated goods		-	-	-	-		-	-	-	-		-	-
331	Medical, measuring, testing appliances, etc.		12.3	12.5	17.2	16.5		5.3	5.3	7.2	6.6		0.3	2.1
3311	Medical, surgical and orthopaedic equipment		12.3	12.5	17.2	16.5		5.3	5.3	7.2	6.6		0.3	2.1
3312	Measuring/testing/navigating appliances,etc.		-	-	-	-		-	-	-	-		-	-
3313	Industrial process control equipment		-	-	-	-		-	-	-	-		-	-
3320	Optical instruments & photographic equipment		-	-	-	-		-	-	-	-		-	-
3330	Watches and clocks		-	-	-	-		-	-	-	-		-	-
3410	Motor vehicles		-	-	-	-		-	-	-	-		-	-
3420	Automobile bodies, trailers & semi-trailers		22.9	28.2	31.4	32.5		8.3	10.3	11.1	11.0		0.6	0.1
3430	Parts/accessories for automobiles		8.8	10.3	11.4	11.8		2.9	3.5	4.1	4.1		3.3	0.3
351	Building and repairing of ships and boats		0.2	0.9	5.1	5.8		0.1	0.4	3.3	2.5		0.7	0.4
3511	Building and repairing of ships		-	-	-	-		-	-	-	-		-	-
3512	Building/repairing of pleasure/sport. boats		0.2	0.9	5.1	5.8		0.1	0.4	3.3	2.5		0.7	0.4
3520	Railway/tramway locomotives & rolling stock		-	-	-	-		-	-	-	-		-	-
3530	Aircraft and spacecraft		-	-	-	-		-	-	-	-		-	-
359	Transport equipment n.e.c.		-	-	-	-		-	-	-	-		-	-
3591	Motorcycles		-	-	-	-		-	-	-	-		-	-
3592	Bicycles and invalid carriages		-	-	-	-		-	-	-	-		-	-
3599	Other transport equipment n.e.c.		-	-	-	-		-	-	-	-		-	-
3610	Furniture		67.6	77.5	92.4	110.7		28.0	33.2	40.2	46.5		2.7	3.3
369	Manufacturing n.e.c.		20.2	23.3	26.5	29.3		6.8	8.1	8.4	9.8		0.1	0.3
3691	Jewellery and related articles		8.6	10.4	11.2	13.1		3.9	4.6	4.7	5.7		0.2	-
3692	Musical instruments		-	-	-	-		-	-	-	-		-	-
3693	Sports goods		-	-	-	-		-	-	-	-		-	-
3694	Games and toys		-	-	-	-		-	-	-	-		-	-
3699	Other manufacturing n.e.c.		11.7	12.9	15.3	16.2		2.8	3.6	3.7	4.1		-0.1	0.3
3710	Recycling of metal waste and scrap		-	-	-	-		-	-	-	-		-	-
3720	Recycling of non-metal waste and scrap		-	-	-	-		-	-	-	-		-	-
D	Total manufacturing	a/	3679.0	4679.1	5533.5	6472.8	a/	1233.1	1559.0	1736.5	1924.9	a/	203.7	270.0

a/ Sum of available data.

Jordan

ISIC Revision 3			Index numbers of industrial production											
			(2000=100)											
ISIC	Industry	Note	1995	1996	1997	1998	1999	2000	2001	2002	2003	2004	2005	2006
15	Food and beverages		111	91	81	96	102	100	101	112	91	106	125	131
16	Tobacco products		49	51	47	66	75	100	128	159	173	194	226	254
17	Textiles		116	155	153	146	115	100	69	84	93	91	72	83
18	Wearing apparel, fur		155	137	100	105	114	100	81	77	66	85	93	98
19	Leather, leather products and footwear		147	127	148	161	88	100	80	76	74	84	35	41
20	Wood products (excl. furniture)		110	102	79	107	143	100	324	189	64	100	45	43
21	Paper and paper products		124	122	135	117	102	100	101	104	94	118	133	141
22	Printing and publishing		75	96	97	131	125	100	98	83	73	84	97	100
23	Coke,refined petroleum products,nuclear fuel		85	87	91	90	91	100	101	102	103	111	118	113
24	Chemicals and chemical products		113	89	131	115	96	100	111	107	101	117	125	135
25	Rubber and plastics products		138	138	124	139	128	100	149	171	133	137	167	153
26	Non-metallic mineral products		116	117	121	113	101	100	114	121	120	136	154	163
27	Basic metals		141	154	110	91	106	100	125	119	130	143	166	139
28	Fabricated metal products		...	...	...	...	90	100	141	127	123	148	164	185
29	Machinery and equipment n.e.c.		127	144	167	163	113	100	91	71	86	104	114	203
30	Office, accounting and computing machinery		...	...	...	...	...	...	...	...	...	...	...	...
31	Electrical machinery and apparatus		94	76	93	93	97	100	109	116	118	167	205	220
32	Radio,television and communication equipment		49	67	35	75	88	100	90	92	156	229	282	515
33	Medical, precision and optical instruments		...	...	...	...	114	100	92	130	105	79	66	47
34	Motor vehicles, trailers, semi-trailers		200	44	151	68	98	100	83	130	133	135	144	122
35	Other transport equipment		...	...	...	...	...	...	...	...	...	...	...	...
36	Furniture; manufacturing n.e.c.		78	92	66	99	109	100	107	100	105	119	144	151
37	Recycling		...	...	...	...	...	...	...	...	...	...	...	...
D	Total manufacturing		91	87	92	95	93	100	114	120	109	124	138	147

Kazakhstan

Supplier of information:
Agency on Statistics of the Republic of Kazakhstan, Almaty.

Basic source of data:
Statistical reports.

Major deviations from ISIC (Revision 3):
None reported.

Reference period:
Calendar year.

Scope:
Not reported.

Method of data collection:
Not reported.

Type of enumeration:
Not reported.

Adjusted for non-response:
Not reported

Concepts and definitions of variables:
Figures for wages and salaries were computed by UNIDO from reported monthly wages and salaries per employee.

Related national publications:
None reported.

Kazakhstan

ISIC	Industry (ISIC Revision 3)	Note	Number of establishments (number) 2003	2004	2005	2006	Note	Number of employees (thousands) 2003	2004	2005	2006	Note	Wages and salaries paid to employees (millions of Kazakhstan Tenge) 2003	2004	2005	2006
151	Processed meat,fish,fruit,vegetables,fats		1389	1335	1379	1275		69.3a/	...	...	...		14403.3a/	...	...	...
1511	Processing/preserving of meat		1032	1001	1041	973		...	...	...	...		...	...	...	...
1512	Processing/preserving of fish		56	67	71	69		...	...	...	...		...	...	...	...
1513	Processing/preserving of fruit & vegetables		50	50	53	53		...	...	...	...		...	...	...	...
1514	Vegetable and animal oils and fats		251	217	214	180		...	...	...	...		...	...	...	...
1520	Dairy products		430	394	372	342		...a/	...	...	...		...a/	...	...	...
153	Grain mill products; starches; animal feeds		1308	1230	1114	997		...a/	...	...	...		...a/	...	...	...
1531	Grain mill products		1138	1039	991	889		...	...	...	...		...	...	...	...
1532	Starches and starch products		1	2	4	5		...	...	...	...		...	...	...	...
1533	Prepared animal feeds		169	189	119	103		...	...	...	...		...	...	...	...
154	Other food products		1344	1230	1165	1088		...a/	...	...	...		...a/	...	...	...
1541	Bakery products		1100	1003	960	897		...	...	...	...		...	...	...	...
1542	Sugar		9	10	12	13		...	...	...	...		...	...	...	...
1543	Cocoa, chocolate and sugar confectionery		20	19	19	20		...	...	...	...		...	...	...	...
1544	Macaroni, noodles & similar products		200	182	157	139		...	...	...	...		...	...	...	...
1549	Other food products n.e.c.		15	16	17	19		...	...	...	...		...	...	...	...
155	Beverages		302	294	278	268		...a/	...	...	...		...a/	...	...	...
1551	Distilling, rectifying & blending of spirits		55	51	49	45		...	...	...	...		...	...	...	...
1552	Wines		37	41	38	33		...	...	...	...		...	...	...	...
1553	Malt liquors and malt		73	72	70	71		...	...	...	...		...	...	...	...
1554	Soft drinks; mineral waters		137	130	121	119		...	...	...	...		...	...	...	...
1600	Tobacco products		9	8	6	6		2.0	...	...	...		2475.5	...	...	...
171	Spinning, weaving and finishing of textiles		45	38	42	42		16.4b/	...	...	...		2261.6b/	...	...	...
1711	Textile fibre preparation; textile weaving		45	38	42	42		...	...	...	...		...	...	...	...
1712	Finishing of textiles		-	-	-	-			...	...	...			...	...	...
172	Other textiles		...	193	194	191		...b/	...	...	...		...b/	...	...	...
1721	Made-up textile articles, except apparel		161	159	155	152		...	...	...	...		...	...	...	...
1722	Carpets and rugs		1	1	1	2		...	...	...	...		...	...	...	...
1723	Cordage, rope, twine and netting		...	1	2	2		...	...	...	...		...	...	...	...
1729	Other textiles n.e.c.		30	32	36	35		...	...	...	...		...	...	...	...
1730	Knitted and crocheted fabrics and articles		31	31	26	25		...b/	...	...	...		...b/	...	...	...
1810	Wearing apparel, except fur apparel		387	398	394	369		6.9c/	...	...	...		848.9c/	...	...	...
1820	Dressing & dyeing of fur; processing of fur		25	24	15	13		...c/	...	...	...		...c/	...	...	...
191	Tanning, dressing and processing of leather		15	12	15	13		1.6d/	...	...	...		240.9d/	...	...	...
1911	Tanning and dressing of leather		10	9	11	11		...	...	...	...		...	...	...	...
1912	Luggage, handbags, etc.; saddlery & harness		5	3	4	2		...	...	...	...		...	...	...	...
1920	Footwear		33	31	29	30		...d/	...	...	...		...d/	...	...	...
2010	Sawmilling and planing of wood		150	140	128	116		2.3e/	...	...	...		397.3e/	...	...	...
202	Products of wood, cork, straw, etc.		315	304	295	309		...e/	...	...	...		...e/	...	...	...
2021	Veneer sheets, plywood, particle board, etc.		4	5	4	8		...	...	...	...		...	...	...	...
2022	Builders' carpentry and joinery		222	229	224	224		...	...	...	...		...	...	...	...
2023	Wooden containers		13	4	9	15		...	...	...	...		...	...	...	...
2029	Other wood products; articles of cork/straw		76	66	58	62		...	...	...	...		...	...	...	...
210	Paper and paper products		19	30	44	46		2.1	...	...	...		751.9	...	...	...
2101	Pulp, paper and paperboard		3	1	2	4		...	...	...	...		...	...	...	...
2102	Corrugated paper and paperboard		8	15	22	23		...	...	...	...		...	...	...	...
2109	Other articles of paper and paperboard		8	14	20	19		...	...	...	...		...	...	...	...
221	Publishing		592	666	761	802		6.8f/	...	...	...		2509.2f/	...	...	...
2211	Publishing of books and other publications		71	75	76	79		...	...	...	...		...	...	...	...
2212	Publishing of newspapers, journals, etc.		457	492	559	606		...	...	...	...		...	...	...	...
2213	Publishing of recorded media		-	-	1	1			...	...	...			...	...	...
2219	Other publishing		64	99	125	116		...	...	...	...		...	...	...	...

222	Printing and related service activities		483	482	504	526	...f/	...	...	...	...f/	...	...	...
2221	Printing		450	450	474	504	...	...	...	...	...	...	...	...
2222	Service activities related to printing		33	24	21	22	...	...	...	...	...	...	...	...
2230	Reproduction of recorded media		8	8	9	9	...f/	...	...	...	...f/	...	...	...
2310	Coke oven products		...	...	1	1	12.2g/	...	...	...	7431.8g/	...	...	...
2320	Refined petroleum products		10	11	13	16	...g/	...	...	...	...g/	...	...	...
2330	Processing of nuclear fuel		-	-	-	-	...g/	...	...	...	...g/	...	...	...
241	Basic chemicals		108	94	96	92	17.1h/	...	...	...	4623.0h/	...	...	...
2411	Basic chemicals, except fertilizers		93	80	77	72	...	...	...	...	...	...	...	...
2412	Fertilizers and nitrogen compounds		5	5	7	5	...	...	...	...	...	...	...	...
2413	Plastics in primary forms; synthetic rubber		10	9	12	15	...	...	...	...	...	...	...	...
242	Other chemicals		172	177	184	190	...h/	...	...	...	...h/	...	...	...
2421	Pesticides and other agro-chemical products		8	6	8	9	...	...	...	...	...	...	...	...
2422	Paints, varnishes, printing ink and mastics		42	40	38	45	...	...	...	...	...	...	...	...
2423	Pharmaceuticals, medicinal chemicals, etc.		74	77	87	88	...	...	...	...	...	...	...	...
2424	Soap, cleaning & cosmetic preparations		22	21	19	17	...	...	...	...	...	...	...	...
2429	Other chemical products n.e.c.		26	33	32	31	...	...	...	...	...	...	...	...
2430	Man-made fibres		1	3	2	1	...h/	...	...	...	...h/	...	...	...
251	Rubber products		32	24	25	24	5.0i/	...	...	...	955.3i/	...	...	...
2511	Rubber tyres and tubes		1	...	...	...	...	...	...	...	...	...	...	...
2519	Other rubber products		31	24	25	24	...	...	...	...	...	...	...	...
2520	Plastic products		262	369	467	565	...i/	...	...	...	...i/	...	...	...
2610	Glass and glass products		30	37	40	42	21.5j/	...	...	...	6034.4j/	...	...	...
269	Non-metallic mineral products n.e.c.		494	559	652	778	...j/	...	...	...	...j/	...	...	...
2691	Pottery, china and earthenware		14	12	13	16	...	...	...	...	...	...	...	...
2692	Refractory ceramic products		8	6	6	7	...	...	...	...	...	...	...	...
2693	Struct.non-refractory clay; ceramic products		61	69	87	100	...	...	...	...	...	...	...	...
2694	Cement, lime and plaster		27	22	19	20	...	...	...	...	...	...	...	...
2695	Articles of concrete, cement and plaster		316	379	461	561	...	...	...	...	...	...	...	...
2696	Cutting, shaping & finishing of stone		46	45	41	46	...	...	...	...	...	...	...	...
2699	Other non-metallic mineral products n.e.c.		22	26	25	28	...	...	...	...	...	...	...	...
2710	Basic iron and steel		21	23	26	29	132.8k/	...	...	...	46960.2k/	...	...	...
2720	Basic precious and non-ferrous metals		52	50	48	53	...k/	...	...	...	...k/	...	...	...
273	Casting of metals		13	14	18	16	...k/	...	...	...	...k/	...	...	...
2731	Casting of iron and steel		12	12	15	14	...	...	...	...	...	...	...	...
2732	Casting of non-ferrous metals		1	2	3	2	...	...	...	...	...	...	...	...
281	Struct.metal products;tanks;steam generators		337	355	405	426	11.9m/	...	...	...	2488.9m/	...	...	...
2811	Structural metal products		293	301	353	365	...	...	...	...	...	...	...	...
2812	Tanks, reservoirs and containers of metal		12	16	14	18	...	...	...	...	...	...	...	...
2813	Steam generators		32	38	38	43	...	...	...	...	...	...	...	...
289	Other metal products; metal working services		190	227	256	265	...m/	...	...	...	...m/	...	...	...
2891	Metal forging/pressing/stamping/roll-forming		4	4	7	5	...	...	...	...	...	...	...	...
2892	Treatment & coating of metals		13	19	20	19	...	...	...	...	...	...	...	...
2893	Cutlery, hand tools and general hardware		23	28	32	32	...	...	...	...	...	...	...	...
2899	Other fabricated metal products n.e.c.		150	176	197	209	...	...	...	...	...	...	...	...
291	General purpose machinery		56	56	47	55	33.1n/	...	...	...	8588.3n/	...	...	...
2911	Engines & turbines (not for transport equipment)		6	4	2	3	...	...	...	...	...	...	...	...
2912	Pumps, compressors, taps and valves		17	19	10	19	...	...	...	...	...	...	...	...
2913	Bearings, gears, gearing & driving elements		5	4	7	6	...	...	...	...	...	...	...	...
2914	Ovens, furnaces and furnace burners		3	3	5	2	...	...	...	...	...	...	...	...
2915	Lifting and handling equipment		9	9	7	6	...	...	...	...	...	...	...	...
2919	Other general purpose machinery		16	17	16	19	...	...	...	...	...	...	...	...
292	Special purpose machinery		98	106	106	94	...n/	...	...	...	...n/	...	...	...
2921	Agricultural and forestry machinery		35	39	37	35	...	...	...	...	...	...	...	...
2922	Machine tools	p/	14	12	15	15	...	...	...	...	...	...	...	...
2923	Machinery for metallurgy		3	7	3	4	...	...	...	...	...	...	...	...
2924	Machinery for mining & construction		24	27	30	34	...	...	...	...	...	...	...	...
2925	Food/beverage/tobacco processing machinery		8	7	5	7	...	...	...	...	...	...	...	...
2926	Machinery for textile, apparel and leather		1	2	3	3	...	...	...	...	...	...	...	...
2927	Weapons and ammunition		-	-	-	-	...	...	...	...	...	...	...	...
2929	Other special purpose machinery		13	12	13	16	...	...	...	...	...	...	...	...

continued

Kazakhstan

ISIC Revision 3		Number of establishments					Number of employees					Wages and salaries paid to employees			
			(number)					(thousands)					(millions of Kazakhstan Tenge)		
ISIC	Industry	Note	2003	2004	2005	2006	Note	2003	2004	2005	2006	Note	2003	2004	2005	2006
2930	Domestic appliances n.e.c.		4	6	9	10		...n/	...	...	...		...n/	...	...	...
3000	Office, accounting and computing machinery		15	22	28	30		0.1	...	...	...		31.8	...	...	...
3110	Electric motors, generators and transformers		4	4	4	3		7.1q/	...	...	...		1791.2q/	...	...	...
3120	Electricity distribution & control apparatus		10	16	17	19		...q/	...	...	...		...q/	...	...	...
3130	Insulated wire and cable		14	16	16	13		...q/	...	...	...		...q/	...	...	...
3140	Accumulators, primary cells and batteries		9	6	6	3		...q/	...	...	...		...q/	...	...	...
3150	Lighting equipment and electric lamps		1	2	3	3		...q/	...	...	...		...q/	...	...	...
3190	Other electrical equipment n.e.c.		6	8	9	11		...q/	...	...	...		...q/	...	...	...
3210	Electronic valves, tubes, etc.		1	1	1	2		0.6r/	...	...	...		410.1r/	...	...	...
3220	TV/radio transmitters; line comm. apparatus		5	6	6	6		...r/	...	...	...		...r/	...	...	...
3230	TV and radio receivers and associated goods		6	4	5	5		...r/	...	...	...		...r/	...	...	...
331	Medical, measuring, testing appliances, etc.		50	55	57	55		3.1s/	...	...	...		716.2s/	...	...	...
3311	Medical, surgical and orthopaedic equipment		32	38	40	39		...	...	...	...		...	...	...	...
3312	Measuring/testing/navigating appliances,etc.		14	15	15	15		...	...	...	...		...	...	...	...
3313	Industrial process control equipment		4	2	2	1		...	...	...	...		...	...	...	...
3320	Optical instruments & photographic equipment		3	3	2	2		...s/	...	...	...		...s/	...	...	...
3330	Watches and clocks		-	2	-	-		...s/	...	...	...		...s/	...	...	...
3410	Motor vehicles		4	3	5	5		1.5t/	...	...	...		355.9t/	...	...	...
3420	Automobile bodies, trailers & semi-trailers		4	5	5	6		...t/	...	...	...		...t/	...	...	...
3430	Parts/accessories for automobiles		6	8	8	5		...t/	...	...	...		...t/	...	...	...
351	Building and repairing of ships and boats		3	5	7	11		30.0u/	...	...	...		8329.0u/	...	...	...
3511	Building and repairing of ships		3	5	7	11		...	...	...	...		...	...	...	...
3512	Building/repairing of pleasure/sport. boats		-	-	-	-		...	...	...	...		...	...	...	...
3520	Railway/tramway locomotives & rolling stock		10	9	8	10		...u/	...	...	...		...u/	...	...	...
3530	Aircraft and spacecraft		...	1	-	-		...u/	...	...	...		...u/	...	...	...
359	Transport equipment n.e.c.		...	2	2	2		...u/	...	...	...		...u/	...	...	...
3591	Motorcycles		-	-	-	-		...	...	...	...		...	...	...	...
3592	Bicycles and invalid carriages		-	-	-	-		...	...	...	...		...	...	...	...
3599	Other transport equipment n.e.c.		...	2	2	2		...	...	...	...		...	...	...	...
3610	Furniture		297	351	400	414		3.4v/	...	...	...		526.9v/	...	...	...
369	Manufacturing n.e.c.		46	49	48	58		...v/	...	...	...		...v/	...	...	...
3691	Jewellery and related articles		16	15	16	17		...	...	...	...		...	...	...	...
3692	Musical instruments		3	5	2	3		...	...	...	...		...	...	...	...
3693	Sports goods		1	3	3	3		...	...	...	...		...	...	...	...
3694	Games and toys		3	4	3	5		...	...	...	...		...	...	...	...
3699	Other manufacturing n.e.c.		23	22	24	30		...	...	...	...		...	...	...	...
3710	Recycling of metal waste and scrap		54	52	53	54		3.5w/	...	...	...		964.7w/	...	...	...
3720	Recycling of non-metal waste and scrap		8	7	6	4		...w/	...	...	...		...w/	...	...	...
D	Total manufacturing		10911	11076	11274	11248		390.3	...	...	...		116261.0	...	...	...

a/ 151 includes 1520, 153, 154 and 155.
b/ 171 includes 172 and 1730.
c/ 1810 includes 1820.
d/ 191 includes 1920.
e/ 2010 includes 202.
f/ 221 includes 222 and 2230.
g/ 2310 includes 2320 and 2330.
h/ 241 includes 242 and 2430.
i/ 251 includes 2520.
j/ 2610 includes 269.
k/ 2710 includes 2720 and 273.
m/ 281 includes 289.
n/ 291 includes 292 and 2930.
p/ 2922 includes repair.
q/ 3110 includes 3120, 3130, 3140, 3150 and 3190.
r/ 3210 includes 3220 and 3230.
s/ 331 includes 3320 and 3330.
t/ 3410 includes 3420 and 3430.
u/ 351 includes 3520, 3530 and 359.
v/ 3610 includes 369.
w/ 3710 includes 3720.

Kazakhstan

ISIC Revision 3		Output					Value added					Gross fixed capital formation		
			(millions of Kazakhstan Tenge)					(millions of Kazakhstan Tenge)					(millions of Kazakhstan Tenge)	
ISIC	Industry	Note	2003	2004	2005	2006	Note	2003	2004	2005	2006	Note	2005	2006
151	Processed meat,fish,fruit,vegetables,fats		40059	53094	66226	78255		...	...	...	...		...	...
1511	Processing/preserving of meat		14180	19786	24288	28801		...	...	...	...		...	...
1512	Processing/preserving of fish		2509	3075	5683	4782		...	...	...	...		...	...
1513	Processing/preserving of fruit & vegetables		5855	8928	11833	14924		...	...	...	...		...	...
1514	Vegetable and animal oils and fats		17515	21305	24422	29748		...	...	...	...		...	...
1520	Dairy products		17124	21970	29340	36656		...	...	...	...		...	...
153	Grain mill products; starches; animal feeds		31321	45352	48617	54113		...	...	...	...		...	...
1531	Grain mill products		27653	41024	44190	48800		...	...	...	...		...	...
1532	Starches and starch products		157	457	550	632		...	...	...	...		...	...
1533	Prepared animal feeds		3668	3871	3877	4681		...	...	...	...		...	...
154	Other food products		44426	52278	60951	67800		...	...	...	...		...	...
1541	Bakery products		10019	13246	14550	15845		...	...	...	...		...	...
1542	Sugar		19635	21169	24430	27182		...	...	...	...		...	...
1543	Cocoa, chocolate and sugar confectionery		10570	12433	16260	18655		...	...	...	...		...	...
1544	Macaroni, noodles & similar products		3401	4361	4450	5217		...	...	...	...		...	...
1549	Other food products n.e.c.		801	1069	1261	901		...	...	...	...		...	...
155	Beverages		40800	49545	68998	80159		...	...	...	...		...	...
1551	Distilling, rectifying & blending of spirits		6437	8462	15811	14949		...	...	...	...		...	...
1552	Wines		5132	3848	5852	4224		...	...	...	...		...	...
1553	Malt liquors and malt		14808	19451	23824	30370		...	...	...	...		...	...
1554	Soft drinks; mineral waters		14423	17784	23511	30616		...	...	...	...		...	...
1600	Tobacco products		34465	39935	45693	51811		...	...	...	...		...	...
171	Spinning, weaving and finishing of textiles		24144	23647	22242	20712		...	...	...	...		...	...
1711	Textile fibre preparation; textile weaving		24144	23647	22242	20712		...	...	...	...		...	...
1712	Finishing of textiles		-	-	-	-		...	...	...	...		...	...
172	Other textiles		2266	2701	3566	4115		...	...	...	...		...	...
1721	Made-up textile articles, except apparel		1406	1715	2261	2726		...	...	...	...		...	...
1722	Carpets and rugs		184	190	209	236		...	...	...	...		...	...
1723	Cordage, rope, twine and netting		10	2	1	3		...	...	...	...		...	...
1729	Other textiles n.e.c.		666	794	1095	1150		...	...	...	...		...	...
1730	Knitted and crocheted fabrics and articles		257	368	437	478		...	...	...	...		...	...
1810	Wearing apparel, except fur apparel		4398	4277	5621	6094		...	...	...	...		...	...
1820	Dressing & dyeing of fur; processing of fur		289	380	289	271		...	...	...	...		...	...
191	Tanning, dressing and processing of leather		1189	2033	605	618		...	...	...	...		...	...
1911	Tanning and dressing of leather		1159	1340	594	610		...	...	...	...		...	...
1912	Luggage, handbags, etc.; saddlery & harness		30	20	11	9		...	...	...	...		...	...
1920	Footwear		899	1092	1181	1517		...	...	...	...		...	...
2010	Sawmilling and planing of wood		844	1205	1682	1610		...	...	...	...		...	...
202	Products of wood, cork, straw, etc.		2257	2652	3118	4007		...	...	...	...		...	...
2021	Veneer sheets, plywood, particle board, etc.		130	141	163	194		...	...	...	...		...	...
2022	Builders' carpentry and joinery		1658	2109	2437	3116		...	...	...	...		...	...
2023	Wooden containers		30	52	99	153		...	...	...	...		...	...
2029	Other wood products; articles of cork/straw		439	350	416	544		...	...	...	...		...	...
210	Paper and paper products		3649	4722	6613	8688		...	...	...	...		...	...
2101	Pulp, paper and paperboard		602	1541	1789	2233		...	...	...	...		...	...
2102	Corrugated paper and paperboard		2176	2200	3630	4908		...	...	...	...		...	...
2109	Other articles of paper and paperboard		871	981	1194	1555		...	...	...	...		...	...
221	Publishing		7829	10359	12860	17049		...	...	...	...		...	...
2211	Publishing of books and other publications		1394	1713	1925	2182		...	...	...	...		...	...
2212	Publishing of newspapers, journals, etc.		5933	7889	9776	12813		...	...	...	...		...	...
2213	Publishing of recorded media		-	-	35	81		...	...	...	...		...	...
2219	Other publishing		502	757	1124	1973		...	...	...	...		...	...

continued

ISIC Revision 3		Output					Value added					Gross fixed capital formation		
			(millions of Kazakhstan Tenge)					(millions of Kazakhstan Tenge)					(millions of Kazakhstan Tenge)	
ISIC	Industry	Note	2003	2004	2005	2006	Note	2003	2004	2005	2006	Note	2005	2006
222	Printing and related service activities		12495	15394	19000	22886		...	...	...	...		...	...
2221	Printing		12167	14497	18361	22174		...	...	...	...		...	...
2222	Service activities related to printing		328	515	639	712		...	...	...	...		...	...
2230	Reproduction of recorded media		162	382	472	512		...	...	...	...		...	...
2310	Coke oven products		17	120	20	1260		...	...	...	...		...	...
2320	Refined petroleum products		120427	127894	154632	154114		...	...	...	...		...	...
2330	Processing of nuclear fuel		-	-	-	-		...	...	...	...		...	...
241	Basic chemicals		26924	29585	37223	34411		...	...	...	...		...	...
2411	Basic chemicals, except fertilizers		22367	24067	31653	28997		...	...	...	...		...	...
2412	Fertilizers and nitrogen compounds		3990	5197	4984	4348		...	...	...	...		...	...
2413	Plastics in primary forms; synthetic rubber		567	321	586	1066		...	...	...	...		...	...
242	Other chemicals		12262	13574	16675	19631		...	...	...	...		...	...
2421	Pesticides and other agro-chemical products		2328	1839	995	1512		...	...	...	...		...	...
2422	Paints, varnishes, printing ink and mastics		1607	1863	2578	2962		...	...	...	...		...	...
2423	Pharmaceuticals, medicinal chemicals, etc.		4168	5051	6875	8765		...	...	...	...		...	...
2424	Soap, cleaning & cosmetic preparations		2372	2047	1831	1781		...	...	...	...		...	...
2429	Other chemical products n.e.c.		1787	2774	4396	4611		...	...	...	...		...	...
2430	Man-made fibres		8	11	14	22		...	...	...	...		...	...
251	Rubber products		2033	2485	3455	3965		...	...	...	...		...	...
2511	Rubber tyres and tubes		...	...	...	...		...	...	...	...		...	...
2519	Other rubber products		2033	2485	3455	3965		...	...	...	...		...	...
2520	Plastic products		11268	17355	23820	34117		...	...	...	...		...	...
2610	Glass and glass products		2605	4175	4950	5712		...	...	...	...		...	...
269	Non-metallic mineral products n.e.c.		41957	66977	103389	144391		...	...	...	...		...	...
2691	Pottery, china and earthenware		382	701	603	664		...	...	...	...		...	...
2692	Refractory ceramic products		308	644	535	564		...	...	...	...		...	...
2693	Struct.non-refractory clay; ceramic products		1583	2295	2770	4126		...	...	...	...		...	...
2694	Cement, lime and plaster		9761	14017	19992	25038		...	...	...	...		...	...
2695	Articles of concrete, cement and plaster		27732	47342	75958	110499		...	...	...	...		...	...
2696	Cutting, shaping & finishing of stone		708	638	953	1005		...	...	...	...		...	...
2699	Other non-metallic mineral products n.e.c.		1483	1340	2578	2495		...	...	...	...		...	...
2710	Basic iron and steel		221165	276916	273242	276966		...	...	...	...		...	...
2720	Basic precious and non-ferrous metals		228898	307361	396852	708060		...	...	...	...		...	...
273	Casting of metals		5538	12643	10358	15122		...	...	...	...		...	...
2731	Casting of iron and steel		5504	12575	10313	14976		...	...	...	...		...	...
2732	Casting of non-ferrous metals		34	68	45	146		...	...	...	...		...	...
281	Struct.metal products;tanks;steam generators		14646	20992	33597	65560		...	...	...	...		...	...
2811	Structural metal products		12903	18707	29712	61272		...	...	...	...		...	...
2812	Tanks, reservoirs and containers of metal		815	1255	2277	1917		...	...	...	...		...	...
2813	Steam generators		928	1030	1608	2371		...	...	...	...		...	...
289	Other metal products; metal working services		7660	9640	15404	21780		...	...	...	...		...	...
2891	Metal forging/pressing/stamping/roll-forming		189	256	319	294		...	...	...	...		...	...
2892	Treatment & coating of metals		406	1051	1494	3663		...	...	...	...		...	...
2893	Cutlery, hand tools and general hardware		175	202	158	174		...	...	...	...		...	...
2899	Other fabricated metal products n.e.c.		6890	8131	13433	17649		...	...	...	...		...	...
291	General purpose machinery		8135	12187	14757	17495		...	...	...	...		...	...
2911	Engines & turbines (not for transport equipment)		81	397	68	116		...	...	...	...		...	...
2912	Pumps, compressors, taps and valves		1959	2653	1453	3532		...	...	...	...		...	...
2913	Bearings, gears, gearing & driving elements		5003	7621	11097	11395		...	...	...	...		...	...
2914	Ovens, furnaces and furnace burners		60	23	30	29		...	...	...	...		...	...
2915	Lifting and handling equipment		520	802	1152	1475		...	...	...	...		...	...
2919	Other general purpose machinery		512	691	957	948		...	...	...	...		...	...

292	Special purpose machinery		8848	13449	13065	12536		...	...	...	...		...	...
2921	Agricultural and forestry machinery		1435	1739	1653	1617		...	...	...	...		...	...
2922	Machine tools	a/	135	208	240	467		...	...	...	...		...	...
2923	Machinery for metallurgy		784	1046	1584	1320		...	...	...	...		...	...
2924	Machinery for mining & construction		2730	4562	6418	7926		...	...	...	...		...	...
2925	Food/beverage/tobacco processing machinery		46	43	45	292		...	...	...	...		...	...
2926	Machinery for textile, apparel and leather		29	37	381	914		...	...	...	...		...	...
2927	Weapons and ammunition		-	-	-	-		...	...	...	...		...	...
2929	Other special purpose machinery		3689	5814	4170	4091		...	...	...	...		...	...
2930	Domestic appliances n.e.c.		589	853	1410	1938		...	...	...	...		...	...
3000	Office, accounting and computing machinery		1350	2209	3587	4151		...	...	...	...		...	...
3110	Electric motors, generators and transformers		709	760	1248	2647		...	...	...	...		...	...
3120	Electricity distribution & control apparatus		2193	2572	3022	4417		...	...	...	...		...	...
3130	Insulated wire and cable		2154	2779	4003	6194		...	...	...	...		...	...
3140	Accumulators, primary cells and batteries		2048	2728	4337	4151		...	...	...	...		...	...
3150	Lighting equipment and electric lamps		83	160	95	233		...	...	...	...		...	...
3190	Other electrical equipment n.e.c.		1382	2544	3359	4983		...	...	...	...		...	...
3210	Electronic valves, tubes, etc.		3	2	377	416		...	...	...	...		...	...
3220	TV/radio transmitters; line comm. apparatus		253	424	876	2686		...	...	...	...		...	...
3230	TV and radio receivers and associated goods		9137	8758	7014	8910		...	...	...	...		...	...
331	Medical, measuring, testing appliances, etc.		2303	2700	3621	3920		...	...	...	...		...	...
3311	Medical, surgical and orthopaedic equipment		1410	1743	2238	2490		...	...	...	...		...	...
3312	Measuring/testing/navigating appliances,etc.		891	952	1353	1330		...	...	...	...		...	...
3313	Industrial process control equipment		2	5	30	100		...	...	...	...		...	...
3320	Optical instruments & photographic equipment		14	15	25	16		...	...	...	...		...	...
3330	Watches and clocks		-	20	-	-		...	...	...	...		...	...
3410	Motor vehicles		3208	3541	5280	16300		...	...	...	...		...	...
3420	Automobile bodies, trailers & semi-trailers		338	187	354	157		...	...	...	...		...	...
3430	Parts/accessories for automobiles		212	309	291	293		...	...	...	...		...	...
351	Building and repairing of ships and boats		337	486	742	1120		...	...	...	...		...	...
3511	Building and repairing of ships		337	486	742	1120		...	...	...	...		...	...
3512	Building/repairing of pleasure/sport. boats		-	-	-	-		...	...	...	...		...	...
3520	Railway/tramway locomotives & rolling stock		3421	1879	3675	5265		...	...	...	...		...	...
3530	Aircraft and spacecraft		22	277	-	-		...	...	...	...		...	...
359	Transport equipment n.e.c.		239	28	33	29		...	...	...	...		...	...
3591	Motorcycles		-	-	-	-		...	...	...	...		...	...
3592	Bicycles and invalid carriages		-	2	-	-		...	...	...	...		...	...
3599	Other transport equipment n.e.c.		239	26	33	29		...	...	...	...		...	...
3610	Furniture		5820	7652	9275	12543		...	...	...	...		...	...
369	Manufacturing n.e.c.		2012	2367	3867	3680		...	...	...	...		...	...
3691	Jewellery and related articles		1855	2143	3487	3213		...	...	...	...		...	...
3692	Musical instruments		2	-	1	4		...	...	...	...		...	...
3693	Sports goods		23	84	184	88		...	...	...	...		...	...
3694	Games and toys		28	38	60	206		...	...	...	...		...	...
3699	Other manufacturing n.e.c.		104	102	135	169		...	...	...	...		...	...
3710	Recycling of metal waste and scrap		3917	10525	10544	22507		...	...	...	...		...	...
3720	Recycling of non-metal waste and scrap		24	28	70	94		...	...	...	...		...	...
D	Total manufacturing		1096721	1536622	1851566	2406501		...	...	...	...		...	...

a/ 2922 includes repair.

Kazakhstan

ISIC Revision 3			Index numbers of industrial production											
			(2000=100)											
ISIC	Industry	Note	1995	1996	1997	1998	1999	2000	2001	2002	2003	2004	2005	2006
15	Food and beverages	a/	...	...	...	...	...	100	108	118	130	142	165	177
16	Tobacco products	a/	...	...	...	...	...	...	...	...	...	...	...	...
17	Textiles	b/	...	...	...	...	...	100	126	146	139	143	163	168
18	Wearing apparel, fur	b/	...	...	...	...	...	...	...	...	...	...	...	...
19	Leather, leather products and footwear		...	...	...	...	...	...	...	...	...	...	...	...
20	Wood products (excl. furniture)		...	...	...	...	...	100	120	150	179	164	188	172
21	Paper and paper products	c/	...	...	...	...	...	100	140	175	184	216	284	329
22	Printing and publishing	c/	...	...	...	...	...	...	...	...	...	...	...	...
23	Coke,refined petroleum products,nuclear fuel		...	...	...	...	...	100	119	130	147	153	178	186
24	Chemicals and chemical products		...	...	...	...	...	100	161	183	215	240	229	238
25	Rubber and plastics products		...	...	...	...	...	...	...	...	...	...	...	...
26	Non-metallic mineral products		...	...	...	...	...	100	146	172	221	286	387	463
27	Basic metals	d/	...	...	...	...	...	100	107	114	115	120	113	121
28	Fabricated metal products	d/	...	...	...	...	...	...	...	...	...	...	...	...
29	Machinery and equipment n.e.c.	e/	...	...	...	...	...	100	141	155	188	248	309	369
30	Office, accounting and computing machinery	e/	...	...	...	...	...	...	...	...	...	...	...	...
31	Electrical machinery and apparatus	e/	...	...	...	...	...	...	...	...	...	...	...	...
32	Radio,television and communication equipment	e/	...	...	...	...	...	...	...	...	...	...	...	...
33	Medical, precision and optical instruments	e/	...	...	...	...	...	...	...	...	...	...	...	...
34	Motor vehicles, trailers, semi-trailers	e/	...	...	...	...	...	...	...	...	...	...	...	...
35	Other transport equipment	e/	...	...	...	...	...	...	...	...	...	...	...	...
36	Furniture; manufacturing n.e.c.		...	...	...	...	...	...	...	...	...	...	...	...
37	Recycling		...	...	...	...	...	...	...	...	...	...	...	...
D	Total manufacturing		...	...	...	...	...	100	115	124	134	147	158	170

a/ 15 includes 16.
b/ 17 includes 18.
c/ 21 includes 22.
d/ 27 includes 28.
e/ 29 includes 30, 31, 32, 33, 34 and 35.

Kenya

Supplier of information:
Kenya National Bureau of Statistics, Nairobi.

Basic source of data:
Annual enumeration of employed and self-employed persons survey; monthly survey of industrial production.

Major deviations from ISIC (Revision 3):
The data for number of establishments, number of employees and wages and salaries were originally classified according to the ISIC (Revision 2).
Total Manufacturing includes output and value added from the export processing zones and micro small enterprises.

Reference period:
Calendar year.

Scope:
All establishments with 4 or more persons engaged.

Method of data collection:
The survey is conducted by mail, followed by interviews of field enumerators.

Type of enumeration:
Complete enumeration for number of establishments, number of employees and wages and salaries; sample survey for output and value added.

Adjusted for non-response:
Yes.

Concepts and definitions of variables:
Output and value added are valued at basic prices.

Related national publications:
Statistical Abstract (annual); Economic Survey Report, both published by the Kenya National Bureau of Statistics, Nairobi.

Kenya

ISIC Revision 3		Number of establishments					Number of employees					Wages and salaries paid to employees				
			(number)					(number)					(millions of Kenyan Shillings)			
ISIC	Industry	Note	2003	2004	2005	2006	Note	2003	2004	2005	2006	Note	2003	2004	2005	2006
15	Food and beverages		...	...	...	...		...	...	...	...		...	...	...	...
16	Tobacco products		...	...	...	...		...	...	...	...		...	...	...	...
17	Textiles		...	...	...	...		...	...	...	...		...	...	...	...
18	Wearing apparel, fur		...	...	...	...		...	...	...	...		...	...	...	...
19	Leather, leather products and footwear		...	...	...	...		...	...	...	...		...	...	...	...
20	Wood products (excl. furniture)		...	...	...	...		...	...	...	...		...	...	...	...
21	Paper and paper products		...	...	...	...		...	...	...	...		...	...	...	...
22	Printing and publishing		...	...	...	...		...	...	...	...		...	...	...	...
23	Coke,refined petroleum products,nuclear fuel		...	...	...	...		...	...	...	...		...	...	...	...
24	Chemicals and chemical products		...	...	...	...		...	...	...	...		...	...	...	...
25	Rubber and plastics products		...	...	...	...		...	...	...	...		...	...	...	...
26	Non-metallic mineral products		...	...	...	...		...	...	...	...		...	...	...	...
27	Basic metals		...	...	...	...		...	...	...	...		...	...	...	...
28	Fabricated metal products		...	...	...	...		...	...	...	...		...	...	...	...
29	Machinery and equipment n.e.c.		...	...	...	...		...	...	...	...		...	...	...	...
30	Office, accounting and computing machinery		...	...	...	...		...	...	...	...		...	...	...	...
31	Electrical machinery and apparatus		...	...	...	...		...	...	...	...		...	...	...	...
32	Radio,television and communication equipment		...	...	...	...		...	...	...	...		...	...	...	...
33	Medical, precision and optical instruments		...	...	...	...		...	...	...	...		...	...	...	...
34	Motor vehicles, trailers, semi-trailers		...	...	...	...		...	...	...	...		...	...	...	...
35	Other transport equipment		...	...	...	...		...	...	...	...		...	...	...	...
36	Furniture; manufacturing n.e.c.		...	...	...	...		...	...	...	...		...	...	...	...
37	Recycling		...	...	...	...		...	...	...	...		...	...	...	...
D	Total manufacturing		4774	5244	4875	4915		239755	237926	247516	253751		33296	38931	46509	57988

Kenya

ISIC Revision 3		Output					Value added					Gross fixed capital formation		
			(millions of Kenyan Shillings)					(millions of Kenyan Shillings)					(millions of Kenyan Shillings)	
ISIC	Industry	Note	2003	2004	2005	2006	Note	2003	2004	2005	2006	Note	2005	2006
151	Processed meat,fish,fruit,vegetables,fats		40664	44587	45677	51554		8539	9363	9592	10826		...	...
1511	Processing/preserving of meat		...	...	...	...		...	...	...	...		...	...
1512	Processing/preserving of fish		...	...	...	...		...	...	...	...		...	...
1513	Processing/preserving of fruit & vegetables		...	...	...	...		...	...	...	...		...	...
1514	Vegetable and animal oils and fats		...	...	...	...		...	...	...	...		...	...
1520	Dairy products		4172	4640	5533	6350		1085	1206	1439	1651		...	...
153	Grain mill products; starches; animal feeds		36600	48139	54385	58424		7686	10109	11421	12269		...	...
1531	Grain mill products		...	...	...	...		...	...	...	...		...	...
1532	Starches and starch products		...	...	...	...		...	...	...	...		...	...
1533	Prepared animal feeds		...	...	...	...		...	...	...	...		...	...
154	Other food products		40948	41528	47895	51809		7669	7607	8749	9399		...	...
1541	Bakery products		16529	11885	13421	14233		3471	2496	2818	2989		...	...
1542	Sugar		10579	13500	15819	15712		2222	2835	3322	3300		...	...
1543	Cocoa, chocolate and sugar confectionery		...	...	...	...		...	...	...	...		...	...
1544	Macaroni, noodles & similar products		...	...	...	...		...	...	...	...		...	...
1549	Other food products n.e.c.		13840	16143	18655	21864		1976	2276	2609	3110		...	...
155	Beverages		18436	21236	26566	30737		7559	8707	10892	12602		...	...
1551	Distilling, rectifying & blending of spirits		...	...	...	...		...	...	...	...		...	...
1552	Wines		...	...	...	...		...	...	...	...		...	...
1553	Malt liquors and malt		...	...	...	...		...	...	...	...		...	...
1554	Soft drinks; mineral waters		...	...	...	...		...	...	...	...		...	...
1600	Tobacco products		2990	3297	5188	6675		1076	1187	1868	2403		...	...
171	Spinning, weaving and finishing of textiles	a/	11116	10317	10784	11451	a/	2891	2683	2804	2977		...	...
1711	Textile fibre preparation; textile weaving		...	...	...	...		...	...	...	...		...	...
1712	Finishing of textiles		...	...	...	...		...	...	...	...		...	...
172	Other textiles	a/	...	...	...	...	a/	...	...	...	...		...	...
1721	Made-up textile articles, except apparel		...	...	...	...		...	...	...	...		...	...
1722	Carpets and rugs		...	...	...	...		...	...	...	...		...	...
1723	Cordage, rope, twine and netting		...	...	...	...		...	...	...	...		...	...
1729	Other textiles n.e.c.		...	...	...	...		...	...	...	...		...	...
1730	Knitted and crocheted fabrics and articles	a/	...	...	...	...	a/	...	...	...	...		...	...
1810	Wearing apparel, except fur apparel	b/	5937	6166	9306	13421	b/	1544	1603	2419	3490		...	...
1820	Dressing & dyeing of fur; processing of fur	b/	...	...	...	...	b/	...	...	...	...		...	...
191	Tanning, dressing and processing of leather		2296	2514	3617	4445		597	654	940	1156		...	...
1911	Tanning and dressing of leather		...	...	...	...		...	...	...	...		...	...
1912	Luggage, handbags, etc.; saddlery & harness		...	...	...	...		...	...	...	...		...	...
1920	Footwear		9970	6636	8339	8855		2592	1590	1374	2140		...	...
2010	Sawmilling and planing of wood	c/	2719	2587	2186	2268	c/	1522	1449	1224	1270		...	...
202	Products of wood, cork, straw, etc.	c/	...	...	...	...	c/	...	...	...	...		...	...
2021	Veneer sheets, plywood, particle board, etc.		...	...	...	...		...	...	...	...		...	...
2022	Builders' carpentry and joinery		...	...	...	...		...	...	...	...		...	...
2023	Wooden containers		...	...	...	...		...	...	...	...		...	...
2029	Other wood products; articles of cork/straw		...	...	...	...		...	...	...	...		...	...
210	Paper and paper products		19677	19415	26258	26630		5116	5048	6827	6924		...	...
2101	Pulp, paper and paperboard		...	...	...	...		...	...	...	...		...	...
2102	Corrugated paper and paperboard		...	...	...	...		...	...	...	...		...	...
2109	Other articles of paper and paperboard		...	...	...	...		...	...	...	...		...	...
221	Publishing	d/	13218	12727	14835	13565	d/	4097	3945	4599	4205		...	...
2211	Publishing of books and other publications		...	...	...	...		...	...	...	...		...	...
2212	Publishing of newspapers, journals, etc.		...	...	...	...		...	...	...	...		...	...
2213	Publishing of recorded media		...	...	...	...		...	...	...	...		...	...
2219	Other publishing		...	...	...	...		...	...	...	...		...	...

continued

Kenya

ISIC Revision 3		Output					Value added					Gross fixed capital formation		
			(millions of Kenyan Shillings)					(millions of Kenyan Shillings)					(millions of Kenyan Shillings)	
ISIC	Industry	Note	2003	2004	2005	2006	Note	2003	2004	2005	2006	Note	2005	2006
222	Printing and related service activities	d/	...	...	...	...	d/	...	...	...	...		...	...
2221	Printing		...	...	...	...		...	...	...	...		...	...
2222	Service activities related to printing		...	...	...	...		...	...	...	...		...	...
2230	Reproduction of recorded media	d/	...	...	...	...	d/	...	...	...	...		...	...
2310	Coke oven products	e/	33196	50668	70460	79793	e/	3146	8554	17684	19308		...	...
2320	Refined petroleum products	e/	...	...	...	...	e/	...	...	...	...		...	...
2330	Processing of nuclear fuel	e/	...	...	...	...	e/	...	...	...	...		...	...
241	Basic chemicals		6849	7996	7519	7257		2466	2878	2707	2612		...	...
2411	Basic chemicals, except fertilizers		...	...	...	...		...	...	...	...		...	...
2412	Fertilizers and nitrogen compounds		...	...	...	...		...	...	...	...		...	...
2413	Plastics in primary forms; synthetic rubber		...	...	...	...		...	...	...	...		...	...
242	Other chemicals		13310	15502	14975	16885		4792	5581	5391	6079		...	...
2421	Pesticides and other agro-chemical products		...	...	...	...		...	...	...	...		...	...
2422	Paints, varnishes, printing ink and mastics		...	...	...	...		...	...	...	...		...	...
2423	Pharmaceuticals, medicinal chemicals, etc.		...	...	...	...		...	...	...	...		...	...
2424	Soap, cleaning & cosmetic preparations		...	...	...	...		...	...	...	...		...	...
2429	Other chemical products n.e.c.		...	...	...	...		...	...	...	...		...	...
2430	Man-made fibres		...	...	...	...		...	...	...	...		...	...
251	Rubber products		8311	8904	10044	9491		1550	1963	2162	2760		...	...
2511	Rubber tyres and tubes		...	...	...	...		...	...	...	...		...	...
2519	Other rubber products		...	...	...	...		...	...	...	...		...	...
2520	Plastic products		4313	4677	6325	8690		2237	2111	2749	2694		...	...
2610	Glass and glass products	f/	20125	22382	25664	26619	f/	13282	14772	16938	17568		...	...
269	Non-metallic mineral products n.e.c.	f/	...	...	...	...	f/	...	...	...	...		...	...
2691	Pottery, china and earthenware		...	...	...	...		...	...	...	...		...	...
2692	Refractory ceramic products		...	...	...	...		...	...	...	...		...	...
2693	Struct.non-refractory clay; ceramic products		...	...	...	...		...	...	...	...		...	...
2694	Cement, lime and plaster		...	...	...	...		...	...	...	...		...	...
2695	Articles of concrete, cement and plaster		...	...	...	...		...	...	...	...		...	...
2696	Cutting, shaping & finishing of stone		...	...	...	...		...	...	...	...		...	...
2699	Other non-metallic mineral products n.e.c.		...	...	...	...		...	...	...	...		...	...
2710	Basic iron and steel	g/	13233	14247	15397	18626	g/	5425	5841	6313	7637		...	...
2720	Basic precious and non-ferrous metals	g/	...	...	...	...	g/	...	...	...	...		...	...
273	Casting of metals	g/	...	...	...	...	g/	...	...	...	...		...	...
2731	Casting of iron and steel		...	...	...	...		...	...	...	...		...	...
2732	Casting of non-ferrous metals		...	...	...	...		...	...	...	...		...	...
281	Struct.metal products;tanks;steam generators	g/	...	...	...	...	g/	...	...	...	...		...	...
2811	Structural metal products		...	...	...	...		...	...	...	...		...	...
2812	Tanks, reservoirs and containers of metal		...	...	...	...		...	...	...	...		...	...
2813	Steam generators		...	...	...	...		...	...	...	...		...	...
289	Other metal products; metal working services	g/	...	...	...	...	g/	...	...	...	...		...	...
2891	Metal forging/pressing/stamping/roll-forming		...	...	...	...		...	...	...	...		...	...
2892	Treatment & coating of metals		...	...	...	...		...	...	...	...		...	...
2893	Cutlery, hand tools and general hardware		...	...	...	...		...	...	...	...		...	...
2899	Other fabricated metal products n.e.c.		...	...	...	...		...	...	...	...		...	...
291	General purpose machinery	h/	1804	2317	2621	2608	h/	649	834	943	938		...	...
2911	Engines & turbines (not for transport equipment)		...	...	...	...		...	...	...	...		...	...
2912	Pumps, compressors, taps and valves		...	...	...	...		...	...	...	...		...	...
2913	Bearings, gears, gearing & driving elements		...	...	...	...		...	...	...	...		...	...
2914	Ovens, furnaces and furnace burners		...	...	...	...		...	...	...	...		...	...
2915	Lifting and handling equipment		...	...	...	...		...	...	...	...		...	...
2919	Other general purpose machinery		...	...	...	...		...	...	...	...		...	...

292	Special purpose machinery	h/	...	...	...	...	h/	...	...	...	...		...	...
2921	Agricultural and forestry machinery		...	...	...	...		...	...	...	...		...	...
2922	Machine tools		...	...	...	...		...	...	...	...		...	...
2923	Machinery for metallurgy		...	...	...	...		...	...	...	...		...	...
2924	Machinery for mining & construction		...	...	...	...		...	...	...	...		...	...
2925	Food/beverage/tobacco processing machinery		...	...	...	...		...	...	...	...		...	...
2926	Machinery for textile, apparel and leather		...	...	...	...		...	...	...	...		...	...
2927	Weapons and ammunition		...	...	...	...		...	...	...	...		...	...
2929	Other special purpose machinery		...	...	...	...		...	...	...	...		...	...
2930	Domestic appliances n.e.c.	h/	...	...	...	...	h/	...	...	...	...		...	...
3000	Office, accounting and computing machinery	h/	...	...	...	...	h/	...	...	...	...		...	...
3110	Electric motors, generators and transformers	i/	6055	7602	8391	8136	i/	2180	2736	3020	2928		...	...
3120	Electricity distribution & control apparatus	i/	...	...	...	...	i/	...	...	...	...		...	...
3130	Insulated wire and cable	i/	...	...	...	...	i/	...	...	...	...		...	...
3140	Accumulators, primary cells and batteries	i/	...	...	...	...	i/	...	...	...	...		...	...
3150	Lighting equipment and electric lamps	i/	...	...	...	...	i/	...	...	...	...		...	...
3190	Other electrical equipment n.e.c.	i/	...	...	...	...	i/	...	...	...	...		...	...
3210	Electronic valves, tubes, etc.	i/	...	...	...	...	i/	...	...	...	...		...	...
3220	TV/radio transmitters; line comm. apparatus	i/	...	...	...	...	i/	...	...	...	...		...	...
3230	TV and radio receivers and associated goods	i/	...	...	...	...	i/	...	...	...	...		...	...
331	Medical, measuring, testing appliances, etc.		...	...	...	...		...	...	...	...		...	...
3311	Medical, surgical and orthopaedic equipment		...	...	...	...		...	...	...	...		...	...
3312	Measuring/testing/navigating appliances,etc.		...	...	...	...		...	...	...	...		...	...
3313	Industrial process control equipment		...	...	...	...		...	...	...	...		...	...
3320	Optical instruments & photographic equipment		...	...	...	...		...	...	...	...		...	...
3330	Watches and clocks		...	...	...	...		...	...	...	...		...	...
3410	Motor vehicles	j/	11957	16739	11423	16711	j/	2236	2913	2236	2940		...	...
3420	Automobile bodies, trailers & semi-trailers	j/	...	...	...	...	j/	...	...	...	...		...	...
3430	Parts/accessories for automobiles	j/	...	...	...	...	j/	...	...	...	...		...	...
351	Building and repairing of ships and boats	j/	...	...	...	...	j/	...	...	...	...		...	...
3511	Building and repairing of ships		...	...	...	...		...	...	...	...		...	...
3512	Building/repairing of pleasure/sport. boats		...	...	...	...		...	...	...	...		...	...
3520	Railway/tramway locomotives & rolling stock	j/	...	...	...	...	j/	...	...	...	...		...	...
3530	Aircraft and spacecraft	j/	...	...	...	...	j/	...	...	...	...		...	...
359	Transport equipment n.e.c.	j/	...	...	...	...	j/	...	...	...	...		...	...
3591	Motorcycles		...	...	...	...		...	...	...	...		...	...
3592	Bicycles and invalid carriages		...	...	...	...		...	...	...	...		...	...
3599	Other transport equipment n.e.c.		...	...	...	...		...	...	...	...		...	...
3610	Furniture	k/	4273	4449	4823	6126	k/	1752	1824	1978	2512		...	...
369	Manufacturing n.e.c.	k/	...	...	...	...	k/	...	...	...	...		...	...
3691	Jewellery and related articles		...	...	...	...		...	...	...	...		...	...
3692	Musical instruments		...	...	...	...		...	...	...	...		...	...
3693	Sports goods		...	...	...	...		...	...	...	...		...	...
3694	Games and toys		...	...	...	...		...	...	...	...		...	...
3699	Other manufacturing n.e.c.		...	...	...	...		...	...	...	...		...	...
3710	Recycling of metal waste and scrap		...	...	...	...		...	...	...	...		...	...
3720	Recycling of non-metal waste and scrap		...	...	...	...		...	...	...	...		...	...
D	Total manufacturing		384256	444648	507807	563645		109885	127443	150896	165803		...	...

a/ 171 includes 172 and 1730.
b/ 1810 includes 1820.
c/ 2010 includes 202.
d/ 221 includes 222 and 2230.
e/ 2310 includes 2320 and 2330.
f/ 2610 includes 269.
g/ 2710 includes 2720, 273, 281 and 289.
h/ 291 includes 292, 2930 and 3000.
i/ 3110 includes 3120, 3130, 3140, 3150, 3190, 3210, 3220 and 3230.
j/ 3410 includes 3420, 3430, 351, 3520, 3530 and 359.
k/ 3610 includes 369.

Kenya

ISIC Revision 3		Index numbers of industrial production												
			(2000=100)											
ISIC	Industry	Note	1995	1996	1997	1998	1999	2000	2001	2002	2003	2004	2005	2006
15	Food and beverages		97	97	98	100	103	100	101	106	106	117	118	120
16	Tobacco products		133	140	148	126	120	100	97	77	79	89	122	171
17	Textiles		118	109	104	103	103	100	99	104	92	77	84	89
18	Wearing apparel, fur		92	91	85	89	93	100	103	107	113	112	161	227
19	Leather, leather products and footwear		120	126	113	106	89	100	109	149	147	138	214	228
20	Wood products (excl. furniture)		98	100	100	98	110	100	95	79	68	54	52	53
21	Paper and paper products		59	74	76	86	92	100	102	105	140	130	165	160
22	Printing and publishing		106	110	110	110	110	100	100	103	101	100	99	68
23	Coke,refined petroleum products,nuclear fuel		75	81	90	90	94	100	112	104	131	149	144	156
24	Chemicals and chemical products		...	...	...	...	...	...	...	...	...	...	...	...
25	Rubber and plastics products		...	...	...	...	...	...	...	...	...	...	...	...
26	Non-metallic mineral products		...	...	...	...	...	...	...	...	...	...	...	...
27	Basic metals		...	...	...	...	...	...	...	...	...	...	...	...
28	Fabricated metal products		87	103	125	106	113	100	100	101	100	104	108	118
29	Machinery and equipment n.e.c.		91	132	103	101	99	100	103	100	101	103	102	105
30	Office, accounting and computing machinery		...	...	...	...	...	...	...	...	...	...	...	...
31	Electrical machinery and apparatus		134	141	113	118	100	100	106	109	115	137	142	130
32	Radio,television and communication equipment		...	...	...	...	...	...	...	...	...	...	...	...
33	Medical, precision and optical instruments		...	...	...	...	...	...	...	...	...	...	...	...
34	Motor vehicles, trailers, semi-trailers		...	...	...	...	...	...	...	...	...	...	...	...
35	Other transport equipment		219	296	246	179	149	100	88	199	200	459	404	531
36	Furniture; manufacturing n.e.c.		...	...	...	...	...	...	...	...	...	...	...	...
37	Recycling		...	...	...	...	...	...	...	...	...	...	...	...
D	Total manufacturing		94	98	104	114	101	100	101	102	103	110	119	126

Kyrgyzstan

Supplier of information:
National Statistical Committee of the Kyrgyz Republic, Bishkek City.

Basic source of data:
Annual industrial survey.

Major deviations from ISIC (Revision 3):
Data collected under the national classification system have been reclassified by the national authorities to correspond with ISIC (Revision 3).

Reference period:
Calendar year.

Scope:
All establishments.

Method of data collection:
Not reported.

Type of enumeration:
Not reported.

Adjusted for non-response:
No.

Concepts and definitions of variables:
No deviations from the standard UN concepts and definitions are reported.

Related national publications:
None reported.

Kyrgyzstan

ISIC Revision 3		Number of establishments					Number of employees					Wages and salaries paid to employees				
			(number)					(number)					(millions of Kyrgyzstan Soms)			
ISIC	Industry	Note	2003	2004	2005	2006	Note	2003	2004	2005	2006	Note	2003	2004	2005	2006
151	Processed meat,fish,fruit,vegetables,fats		114	103	104	101		1182	1369	1349	1639		13.5	24.2	36.1	55.2
1511	Processing/preserving of meat		57	45	41	40		377	552	502	505		6.7	14.8	15.6	20.6
1512	Processing/preserving of fish		6	5	6	6		37	26	33	39		0.3	0.2	0.3	0.4
1513	Processing/preserving of fruit & vegetables		40	35	37	39		726	675	502	590		6.2	8.6	7.8	10.1
1514	Vegetable and animal oils and fats		11	18	20	16		42	116	312	505		0.3	0.7	12.5	23.9
1520	Dairy products		52	45	43	38		1954	1930	1848	1788		56.3	77.7	90.7	103.3
153	Grain mill products; starches; animal feeds		169	135	122	107		2616	2118	1579	1539		41.3	34.5	29.1	27.9
1531	Grain mill products		134	109	96	85		2219	1784	1320	1395		30.4	26.3	22.1	24.5
1532	Starches and starch products		3	2	2	2		243	190	165	95		8.4	7.0	5.7	2.9
1533	Prepared animal feeds		32	24	24	20		154	144	94	49		2.5	1.2	1.2	0.5
154	Other food products		153	136	125	119		3708	3697	3882	4329		109.4	133.8	131.8	162.4
1541	Bakery products		113	102	92	86		1371	1400	1482	1737		17.9	19.4	23.5	28.5
1542	Sugar		4	5	5	7		1559	1570	1738	1962		74.7	99.1	97.7	118.6
1543	Cocoa, chocolate and sugar confectionery		10	9	11	10		167	92	163	153		1.5	0.9	2.1	5.6
1544	Macaroni, noodles & similar products		12	8	7	7		58	33	60	86		0.5	0.1	0.7	0.9
1549	Other food products n.e.c.		14	12	10	9		553	602	439	391		14.9	14.2	7.8	8.8
155	Beverages		123	115	106	101		4792	4690	4670	4514		147.4	156.7	167.3	161.4
1551	Distilling, rectifying & blending of spirits		39	35	30	32		2078	1826	1814	1637		79.4	72.7	67.8	54.5
1552	Wines		32	29	26	20		595	534	507	474		12.4	12.3	15.8	17.0
1553	Malt liquors and malt		13	13	13	11		489	478	461	445		17.2	21.6	27.4	19.5
1554	Soft drinks; mineral waters		39	38	37	38		1630	1852	1888	1958		38.4	50.1	56.3	70.4
1600	Tobacco products		28	23	20	17		1025	976	725	758		73.1	78.3	82.7	91.4
171	Spinning, weaving and finishing of textiles		37	46	51	51		4416	4115	4093	3873		82.6	81.6	105.8	108.2
1711	Textile fibre preparation; textile weaving		32	40	45	46		3558	3083	3140	3159		62.8	54.4	77.5	82.6
1712	Finishing of textiles		5	6	6	5		858	1032	953	714		19.9	27.2	28.3	25.6
172	Other textiles		28	28	30	29		642	513	444	411		9.9	5.6	6.6	6.0
1721	Made-up textile articles, except apparel		6	7	4	4		129	43	24	25		0.7	0.3	0.2	0.3
1722	Carpets and rugs		5	7	9	9		102	134	150	142		1.6	1.6	1.8	1.5
1723	Cordage, rope, twine and netting		-	-	-	-		-	-	-	-		-	-	-	-
1729	Other textiles n.e.c.		17	14	17	16		411	336	270	244		7.6	3.6	4.5	4.3
1730	Knitted and crocheted fabrics and articles		3	5	5	4		941	762	731	728		12.7	12.4	23.5	26.5
1810	Wearing apparel, except fur apparel		101	101	95	87		2250	1726	1677	1612		24.3	19.5	19.6	20.1
1820	Dressing & dyeing of fur; processing of fur		7	5	4	1		121	91	78	37		1.0	0.9	0.8	0.5
191	Tanning, dressing and processing of leather		12	8	7	7		294	214	212	157		5.9	5.4	5.7	5.3
1911	Tanning and dressing of leather		8	7	6	5		192	139	129	102		3.1	2.8	2.9	3.6
1912	Luggage, handbags, etc.; saddlery & harness		4	1	1	2		102	75	83	55		2.8	2.6	2.9	1.7
1920	Footwear		10	8	9	9		113	103	70	124		1.6	1.6	1.0	6.8
2010	Sawmilling and planing of wood		52	51	51	46		396	370	451	473		3.0	2.7	4.2	5.1
202	Products of wood, cork, straw, etc.		...	...	...	...		...	...	...	...		...	...	...	...
2021	Veneer sheets, plywood, particle board, etc.		...	...	...	...		...	...	...	...		...	...	...	...
2022	Builders' carpentry and joinery		27	25	24	25		299	248	235	270		3.9	4.5	4.9	4.9
2023	Wooden containers		3	1	...	...		50	...	...	...		1.0	...	...	...
2029	Other wood products; articles of cork/straw		8	11	13	14		34	59	367	291		0.3	0.7	8.9	6.1
210	Paper and paper products		19	15	10	10		532	519	583	439		24.1	20.5	20.4	17.2
2101	Pulp, paper and paperboard		1	2	2	3		11	16	19	45		0.1	0.2	0.2	0.4
2102	Corrugated paper and paperboard		8	7	5	5		198	247	310	384		5.8	7.2	11.6	16.7
2109	Other articles of paper and paperboard		10	6	3	2		323	256	254	10		18.3	13.1	8.6	0.1
221	Publishing		88	118	119	138		1117	1430	1350	1337		34.2	43.9	50.0	47.6
2211	Publishing of books and other publications		7	21	18	27		97	180	173	148		2.0	4.2	3.1	3.5
2212	Publishing of newspapers, journals, etc.		75	92	96	105		997	1236	1158	1164		31.9	39.4	46.3	43.5
2213	Publishing of recorded media		-	-	-	-		-	-	-	-		-	-	-	-
2219	Other publishing		6	5	5	6		23	14	19	25		0.2	0.2	0.6	0.6

222	Printing and related service activities	98	101	101	97	2002	1811	1778	1713	75.7	72.2	67.9	75.8
2221	Printing	89	99	97	95	1947	1781	1748	1686	74.5	71.1	66.8	74.7
2222	Service activities related to printing	9	2	4	2	55	30	30	27	1.3	1.1	1.1	1.0
2230	Reproduction of recorded media	...	...	...	...	...	...	...	...	...	...	...	...
2310	Coke oven products	...	...	...	...	...	...	...	...	...	...	...	...
2320	Refined petroleum products	4	4	3	3	370	238	255	262	18.0	30.8	92.1	109.7
2330	Processing of nuclear fuel	1	2	1	1	644	834	786	783	31.1	45.3	41.9	45.8
241	Basic chemicals	14	20	21	20	1713	1470	1679	1725	45.9	45.8	73.6	86.0
2411	Basic chemicals, except fertilizers	14	20	21	20	1713	1470	1679	1725	45.9	45.8	73.6	86.0
2412	Fertilizers and nitrogen compounds	-	-	-	-	-	-	-	-	-	-	-	-
2413	Plastics in primary forms; synthetic rubber	-	-	-	-	-	-	-	-	-	-	-	-
242	Other chemicals	43	50	53	57	646	575	773	662	10.2	11.7	10.1	12.8
2421	Pesticides and other agro-chemical products	-	-	-	-	-	-	-	-	-	-	-	-
2422	Paints, varnishes, printing ink and mastics	6	8	7	9	70	83	252	177	0.9	1.3	1.4	1.8
2423	Pharmaceuticals, medicinal chemicals, etc.	26	31	32	35	492	403	383	385	8.1	8.9	6.5	8.6
2424	Soap, cleaning & cosmetic preparations	8	8	12	11	67	74	112	78	0.7	0.8	1.5	1.7
2429	Other chemical products n.e.c.	3	3	2	2	17	15	26	22	0.5	0.6	0.8	0.8
2430	Man-made fibres	-	-	-	-	-	-	-	-	-	-	-	-
251	Rubber products	3	4	5	6	57	50	55	53	0.8	0.8	0.7	1.0
2511	Rubber tyres and tubes	-	-	-	-	-	-	-	-	-	-	-	-
2519	Other rubber products	3	4	5	6	57	50	55	53	0.8	0.8	0.7	1.0
2520	Plastic products	41	46	61	76	940	1199	1410	1433	22.5	26.6	27.2	38.4
2610	Glass and glass products	9	8	7	6	1325	1481	1611	1572	55.7	84.0	108.9	119.1
269	Non-metallic mineral products n.e.c.	...	...	...	...	...	...	...	...	...	...	...	...
2691	Pottery, china and earthenware	...	...	...	...	...	...	...	...	...	...	...	...
2692	Refractory ceramic products	17	14	20	18	1596	1773	2212	2169	31.8	52.0	81.4	88.0
2693	Struct.non-refractory clay; ceramic products	5	7	4	4	52	80	46	79	0.3	0.8	1.0	1.7
2694	Cement, lime and plaster	7	7	5	5	1490	1656	1715	2039	109.4	133.4	170.7	212.4
2695	Articles of concrete, cement and plaster	74	79	81	80	2575	2844	2883	2239	67.1	77.9	89.4	91.3
2696	Cutting, shaping & finishing of stone	11	11	13	14	257	276	341	372	5.0	6.2	4.6	6.0
2699	Other non-metallic mineral products n.e.c.	8	12	16	16	150	142	267	268	2.7	2.6	5.2	5.1
2710	Basic iron and steel	-	-	-	-	-	-	-	-	-	-	-	-
2720	Basic precious and non-ferrous metals	6	7	10	9	3724	3006	4080	4901	562.4	1298.9	1499.9	2021.3
273	Casting of metals	5	4	5	9	145	101	126	113	2.4	1.3	2.4	2.4
2731	Casting of iron and steel	5	4	5	9	145	101	126	113	2.4	1.3	2.4	2.4
2732	Casting of non-ferrous metals	-	-	-	-	-	-	-	-	-	-	-	-
281	Struct.metal products;tanks;steam generators	45	29	35	34	943	1143	1304	898	21.1	25.4	34.6	29.2
2811	Structural metal products	41	27	31	31	867	1076	1221	826	19.2	23.0	31.9	25.9
2812	Tanks, reservoirs and containers of metal	-	-	-	-	-	-	-	-	-	-	-	-
2813	Steam generators	4	2	4	3	76	67	83	72	1.9	2.4	2.7	3.3
289	Other metal products; metal working services	48	41	41	41	1145	1559	1460	1252	22.7	45.6	45.5	42.9
2891	Metal forging/pressing/stamping/roll-forming	2	3	4	3	29	46	65	65	1.0	2.3	3.7	3.9
2892	Treatment & coating of metals	4	2	1	1	89	16	11	12	2.5	0.8	0.6	0.7
2893	Cutlery, hand tools and general hardware	7	9	8	10	444	464	401	393	10.1	12.4	13.1	12.4
2899	Other fabricated metal products n.e.c.	35	27	28	27	583	1033	983	782	9.0	30.1	28.0	25.9
291	General purpose machinery	32	...	...	18	542	...	...	292	7.0	...	...	5.9
2911	Engines & turbines (not for transport equipment)	-	-	-	-	-	-	-	-	-	-	-	-
2912	Pumps, compressors, taps and valves	11	9	7	5	300	247	219	137	3.6	2.9	1.9	1.9
2913	Bearings, gears, gearing & driving elements	4	...	1	1	138	...	4	10	2.3	...	-	0.2
2914	Ovens, furnaces and furnace burners	3	3	4	2	10	16	4	3	0.2	0.1	0.1	0.1
2915	Lifting and handling equipment	2	1	...	1	13	9	...	5	0.1	0.3	...	0.1
2919	Other general purpose machinery	12	13	11	9	81	197	168	137	0.7	4.1	3.7	3.7
292	Special purpose machinery	...	...	...	...	...	...	...	...	...	...	...	...
2921	Agricultural and forestry machinery	92	75	64	50	294	819	220	526	10.5	11.0	5.2	10.7
2922	Machine tools	9	4	7	7	781	28	36	31	21.3	0.5	0.8	0.9
2923	Machinery for metallurgy	...	...	...	...	...	...	...	...	...	...	...	...
2924	Machinery for mining & construction	4	3	4	5	365	361	645	643	17.5	23.5	47.4	48.6
2925	Food/beverage/tobacco processing machinery	7	7	5	6	288	255	200	133	7.0	5.7	4.1	4.7
2926	Machinery for textile, apparel and leather	-	-	-	-	-	-	-	-	-	-	-	-
2927	Weapons and ammunition	1	4	4	4	668	1690	1702	1486	17.2	69.7	96.0	103.4
2929	Other special purpose machinery	7	6	4	3	460	561	531	416	22.2	29.8	25.9	21.1

continued

ISIC Revision 3		Number of establishments					Number of employees					Wages and salaries paid to employees				
			(number)					(number)					(millions of Kyrgyzstan Soms)			
ISIC	Industry	Note	2003	2004	2005	2006	Note	2003	2004	2005	2006	Note	2003	2004	2005	2006
2930	Domestic appliances n.e.c.		10	9	12	12		495	485	541	523		6.2	7.4	10.1	10.1
3000	Office, accounting and computing machinery		27	22	14	15		315	108	84	173		7.6	2.4	2.0	4.2
3110	Electric motors, generators and transformers		9	10	7	8		533	404	330	286		21.8	16.2	12.9	10.1
3120	Electricity distribution & control apparatus		5	6	4	5		383	358	410	467		6.3	7.7	10.1	13.5
3130	Insulated wire and cable		1	1	1	1		260	266	163	78		7.2	7.7	4.9	2.2
3140	Accumulators, primary cells and batteries		3	3	2	4		92	92	86	65		2.2	1.9	1.5	1.2
3150	Lighting equipment and electric lamps		2	3	2	2		3990	4196	4053	3756		152.3	177.3	165.7	173.7
3190	Other electrical equipment n.e.c.		6	8	6	6		75	68	66	39		1.3	1.5	1.4	1.0
3210	Electronic valves, tubes, etc.		6	7	6	5		451	451	394	243		13.1	15.2	15.4	14.1
3220	TV/radio transmitters; line comm. apparatus		8	6	7	6		91	56	43	31		1.5	1.1	0.9	0.6
3230	TV and radio receivers and associated goods		7	5	5	4		222	100	75	68		2.5	1.9	1.4	1.3
331	Medical, measuring, testing appliances, etc.		18	13	12	12		1367	410	309	207		63.4	11.8	11.7	11.2
3311	Medical, surgical and orthopaedic equipment		1	2	2	2		135	137	143	150		5.9	5.6	7.6	9.5
3312	Measuring/testing/navigating appliances,etc.		9	6	5	3		79	241	118	8		1.4	5.5	2.9	0.1
3313	Industrial process control equipment		8	5	5	7		1153	32	48	49		56.1	0.8	1.3	1.6
3320	Optical instruments & photographic equipment		2	2	2	2		39	1	42	30		0.4	-	1.4	1.4
3330	Watches and clocks		-	-	-	-		-	-	-	-		-	-	-	-
3410	Motor vehicles		1	1	1	1		67	60	41	27		1.6	1.5	1.1	0.7
3420	Automobile bodies, trailers & semi-trailers		3	2	...	...		21	5	...	...		0.5	-	...	...
3430	Parts/accessories for automobiles		1	2	2	2		767	638	656	596		23.3	25.0	30.7	20.8
351	Building and repairing of ships and boats		...	-	-	-		...	-	-	-		...	-	-	-
3511	Building and repairing of ships		...	-	-	-		...	-	-	-		...	-	-	-
3512	Building/repairing of pleasure/sport. boats		-	-	-	-		-	-	-	-		-	-	-	-
3520	Railway/tramway locomotives & rolling stock		1	1	1	1		8	17	12	9		0.2	0.5	0.4	0.4
3530	Aircraft and spacecraft		2	1	1	3		77	33	9	40		4.0	0.5	0.2	1.2
359	Transport equipment n.e.c.		...	...	...	2		...	...	...	...		...	...	...	...
3591	Motorcycles		...	...	...	1		...	...	...	...		...	...	...	...
3592	Bicycles and invalid carriages		1	1	1	1		7	8	7	...		1.3	0.8	0.1	...
3599	Other transport equipment n.e.c.		...	...	...	...		...	...	...	...		...	...	...	...
3610	Furniture		38	36	36	35		1026	1128	1091	1010		16.2	22.1	20.2	23.2
369	Manufacturing n.e.c.		18	15	11	13		426	518	506	582		5.5	6.6	5.0	5.0
3691	Jewellery and related articles		13	8	6	7		228	254	305	384		3.2	2.5	2.7	2.9
3692	Musical instruments		...	...	...	1		...	...	...	10		...	...	...	-
3693	Sports goods		-	-	-	-		-	-	-	-		-	-	-	-
3694	Games and toys		-	-	-	-		-	-	-	-		-	-	-	-
3699	Other manufacturing n.e.c.		5	7	5	5		198	193	201	188		2.2	2.4	2.4	2.1
3710	Recycling of metal waste and scrap		8	5	2	3		40	23	16	29		0.5	0.2	0.1	0.1
3720	Recycling of non-metal waste and scrap		-	-	-	-		-	-	-	-		-	-	-	-
D	Total manufacturing		1802	1709	1666	1635		60406	58776	59788	58638		2172.2	3122.9	3628.7	4335.8

ISIC Revision 3		Output in producers' prices					Value added					Gross fixed capital formation		
			(millions of Kyrgyzstan Soms)					(millions of Kyrgyzstan Soms)					(millions of Kyrgyzstan Soms)	
ISIC	Industry	Note	2003	2004	2005	2006	Note	2003	2004	2005	2006	Note	2005	2006
151	Processed meat,fish,fruit,vegetables,fats		395.6	505.2	548.7	1121.4		195.4	219.7	117.2	...		...	...
1511	Processing/preserving of meat		179.5	196.1	244.4	249.0		61.6	66.9	51.9	...		...	...
1512	Processing/preserving of fish		10.0	14.2	14.8	16.0		0.4	0.1	1.6	...		...	...
1513	Processing/preserving of fruit & vegetables		184.1	253.9	56.8	106.2		13.2	85.3	-2.0	...		...	...
1514	Vegetable and animal oils and fats		22.0	41.1	232.7	750.1		...	...	65.6	...		...	...
1520	Dairy products		891.8	950.9	1293.5	1387.8		170.6	170.5	291.6	...		...	...
153	Grain mill products; starches; animal feeds		615.0	694.6	976.7	1040.2		...	...	...	...		...	...
1531	Grain mill products		508.2	595.1	917.6	999.6		162.9	...	...	...		...	...
1532	Starches and starch products		30.0	30.0	0.3	0.1		...	...	...	...		...	...
1533	Prepared animal feeds		76.8	69.5	58.8	40.5		12.2	20.3	-6.2	...		...	...
154	Other food products		2424.3	2742.2	2210.4	2703.1		492.7	543.0	554.9	...		...	...
1541	Bakery products		1281.3	1415.7	1552.8	1689.3		213.0	298.0	336.4	...		...	...
1542	Sugar		764.9	936.6	394.0	766.5		143.0	113.5	158.9	...		...	...
1543	Cocoa, chocolate and sugar confectionery		10.5	12.7	17.3	16.7		3.1	4.0	1.3	...		...	...
1544	Macaroni, noodles & similar products		37.1	33.3	44.9	65.0		4.7	0.4	-0.9	...		...	...
1549	Other food products n.e.c.		330.5	343.9	201.4	165.5		128.8	127.1	59.3	...		...	...
155	Beverages		1533.4	1698.4	1804.0	1666.8		417.8	435.2	573.9	...		...	...
1551	Distilling, rectifying & blending of spirits		946.4	804.3	796.9	648.9		193.0	109.9	136.3	...		...	...
1552	Wines		95.8	121.8	135.2	180.9		25.0	32.4	40.9	...		...	...
1553	Malt liquors and malt		99.3	167.0	181.9	166.0		41.3	82.8	95.9	...		...	...
1554	Soft drinks; mineral waters		391.9	605.3	690.1	671.0		158.6	210.1	300.9	...		...	...
1600	Tobacco products		1091.0	1125.1	1083.9	1113.7		279.8	368.0	336.9	...		...	...
171	Spinning, weaving and finishing of textiles		837.0	893.4	881.6	987.4		96.4	235.5	288.3	...		...	...
1711	Textile fibre preparation; textile weaving		774.0	785.7	757.8	913.1		88.8	205.9	256.0	...		...	...
1712	Finishing of textiles		63.0	107.6	123.8	74.3		7.6	29.6	32.3	...		...	...
172	Other textiles		169.1	179.1	187.9	205.5		19.9	95.5	83.5	...		...	...
1721	Made-up textile articles, except apparel		12.4	8.9	13.0	15.8		2.3	...	...	...		...	...
1722	Carpets and rugs		53.1	77.6	80.6	85.3		14.1	28.3	23.2	...		...	...
1723	Cordage, rope, twine and netting		-	-	-	-		-	-	-	...		...	...
1729	Other textiles n.e.c.		103.6	92.7	94.3	104.4		3.6	...	...	...		...	...
1730	Knitted and crocheted fabrics and articles		77.9	19.7	127.6	127.7		...	...	...	...		...	...
1810	Wearing apparel, except fur apparel		236.9	1179.1	1212.6	3471.9		48.9	...	317.3	...		...	...
1820	Dressing & dyeing of fur; processing of fur		5.5	...	31.2	17.2		...	...	2.7	...		...	...
191	Tanning, dressing and processing of leather		98.1	66.8	61.7	67.1		19.9	6.9	9.4	...		...	...
1911	Tanning and dressing of leather		88.0	55.9	52.3	53.8		16.5	3.6	10.6	...		...	...
1912	Luggage, handbags, etc.; saddlery & harness		10.1	10.9	9.4	13.4		3.4	3.3	-1.2	...		...	...
1920	Footwear		16.1	25.2	13.5	33.8		1.4	4.8	4.4	...		...	...
2010	Sawmilling and planing of wood		21.4	21.4	24.8	34.0		8.2	6.5	24.9	...		...	...
202	Products of wood, cork, straw, etc.		...	...	...	64.5		...	...	...	...		...	...
2021	Veneer sheets, plywood, particle board, etc.		...	...	...	...		...	...	...	...		...	...
2022	Builders' carpentry and joinery		27.4	28.1	24.8	35.7		4.8	5.3	1.0	...		...	...
2023	Wooden containers		12.8	...	...	0.1		1.4	-	8.0	...		...	...
2029	Other wood products; articles of cork/straw		7.2	5.9	19.8	28.7		0.7	-0.1	1.9	...		...	...
210	Paper and paper products		123.9	178.8	176.7	171.9		...	...	...	...		...	...
2101	Pulp, paper and paperboard		0.7	0.6	3.0	4.0		...	...	51.9	...		...	...
2102	Corrugated paper and paperboard		80.8	141.6	150.1	163.9		...	...	...	...		...	...
2109	Other articles of paper and paperboard		42.4	36.7	23.6	3.9		...	...	...	...		...	...
221	Publishing		126.9	175.2	197.8	172.8		...	...	...	...		...	...
2211	Publishing of books and other publications		5.0	33.5	19.5	28.0		...	...	...	...		...	...
2212	Publishing of newspapers, journals, etc.		119.8	140.6	176.2	143.7		...	...	...	...		...	...
2213	Publishing of recorded media		-	-	-	-		-	-	-	...		...	...
2219	Other publishing		2.0	1.1	2.1	1.1		...	...	...	...		...	...

continued

ISIC Revision 3		Output in producers' prices					Value added					Gross fixed capital formation		
			(millions of Kyrgyzstan Soms)					(millions of Kyrgyzstan Soms)					(millions of Kyrgyzstan Soms)	
ISIC	Industry	Note	2003	2004	2005	2006	Note	2003	2004	2005	2006	Note	2005	2006
222	Printing and related service activities		414.6	366.0	325.2	384.4		...	...	...	...		...	...
2221	Printing		406.4	15.7	18.5	19.5		...	...	...	...		...	...
2222	Service activities related to printing		8.2	350.4	306.7	364.8		...	...	...	...		...	...
2230	Reproduction of recorded media		...	...	...	...		...	...	...	...		...	...
2310	Coke oven products		...	...	...	...		...	...	...	...		...	...
2320	Refined petroleum products		398.6	388.3	429.7	475.3		72.2	-27.3	140.9	...		...	...
2330	Processing of nuclear fuel		87.1	143.0	124.8	103.1		43.0	...	...	...		...	...
241	Basic chemicals		142.1	395.6	573.3	534.2		13.5	89.6	146.7	...		...	...
2411	Basic chemicals, except fertilizers		142.1	395.6	573.3	534.2		13.5	89.6	146.7	...		...	...
2412	Fertilizers and nitrogen compounds		-	-	-	-		-	-	-	...		...	...
2413	Plastics in primary forms; synthetic rubber		-	-	-	-		-	-	-	...		...	...
242	Other chemicals		123.2	187.8	211.2	240.9		...	...	35.9	...		...	...
2421	Pesticides and other agro-chemical products		-	-	-	-		-	-	-	...		...	...
2422	Paints, varnishes, printing ink and mastics		53.8	78.4	88.1	101.2		3.7	-1.8	6.4	...		...	...
2423	Pharmaceuticals, medicinal chemicals, etc.		41.1	65.8	62.5	84.2		13.5	21.3	14.8	...		...	...
2424	Soap, cleaning & cosmetic preparations		25.0	38.4	52.7	47.6		4.5	8.2	14.7	...		...	...
2429	Other chemical products n.e.c.		3.3	5.2	7.9	8.0		...	...	...	...		...	...
2430	Man-made fibres		-	-	-	-		-	-	-	...		...	...
251	Rubber products		5.7	5.7	7.5	15.1		1.6	1.8	16.9	...		...	...
2511	Rubber tyres and tubes		-	-	-	-		-	-	-	...		...	...
2519	Other rubber products		5.7	5.7	7.5	15.1		1.6	1.8	16.9	...		...	...
2520	Plastic products		481.4	948.8	1107.4	1199.8		98.4	187.9	172.4	...		...	...
2610	Glass and glass products		734.7	1323.6	1223.5	1386.8		360.7	751.3	416.7	...		...	...
269	Non-metallic mineral products n.e.c.		...	...	5889.6	7684.0		...	...	...	...		...	...
2691	Pottery, china and earthenware		...	...	2944.8	3842.0		...	...	...	...		...	...
2692	Refractory ceramic products		137.5	215.8	296.5	350.9		...	...	...	...		...	...
2693	Struct.non-refractory clay; ceramic products		4.7	9.6	10.1	17.4		...	...	...	...		...	...
2694	Cement, lime and plaster		1191.2	1504.5	1816.1	2495.5		357.3	438.4	541.3	...		...	...
2695	Articles of concrete, cement and plaster		410.6	536.1	770.0	791.4		...	...	...	...		...	...
2696	Cutting, shaping & finishing of stone		31.2	24.7	34.3	67.1		8.2	10.7	3.9	...		...	...
2699	Other non-metallic mineral products n.e.c.		224.7	13.7	17.8	119.8		80.7	3.6	6.0	...		...	...
2710	Basic iron and steel		-	-	-	-		-	-	-	...		...	...
2720	Basic precious and non-ferrous metals		22140.5	23508.4	18636.0	16157.4		6780.9	8036.2	6498.9	...		...	...
273	Casting of metals		232.8	10.7	10.9	14.6		35.3	0.7	96.5	...		...	...
2731	Casting of iron and steel		232.8	10.7	10.9	14.6		35.3	0.7	96.5	...		...	...
2732	Casting of non-ferrous metals		-	-	-	-		-	-	-	...		...	...
281	Struct.metal products;tanks;steam generators		97.8	137.5	186.7	188.8		...	...	...	...		...	...
2811	Structural metal products		87.4	124.4	165.5	162.9		...	...	...	...		...	...
2812	Tanks, reservoirs and containers of metal		-	-	-	-		-	-	-	...		...	...
2813	Steam generators		10.5	13.1	21.2	25.9		...	...	...	...		...	...
289	Other metal products; metal working services		176.1	295.9	299.9	326.1		...	...	...	...		...	...
2891	Metal forging/pressing/stamping/roll-forming		25.8	85.9	89.7	88.0		...	...	...	...		...	...
2892	Treatment & coating of metals		43.7	10.7	2.1	4.2		...	...	...	...		...	...
2893	Cutlery, hand tools and general hardware		50.4	46.9	71.0	76.6		...	...	...	...		...	...
2899	Other fabricated metal products n.e.c.		56.1	152.4	137.1	157.4		...	...	...	...		...	...
291	General purpose machinery		54.9	83.5	...	115.7		...	...	...	...		...	...
2911	Engines & turbines (not for transport equipment)		-	-	-	-		-	-	-	...		...	...
2912	Pumps, compressors, taps and valves		16.3	19.1	11.9	7.7		...	...	...	...		...	...
2913	Bearings, gears, gearing & driving elements		7.0	24.8	22.9	26.7		...	...	...	...		...	...
2914	Ovens, furnaces and furnace burners		1.2	0.7	0.3	-		...	...	...	...		...	...
2915	Lifting and handling equipment		0.2	0.6	...	0.1		...	...	...	...		...	...
2919	Other general purpose machinery		30.3	38.3	42.9	81.1		...	...	...	...		...	...

292	Special purpose machinery	296.3	...	...	...	...	...	...	...	...	...
2921	Agricultural and forestry machinery	47.6	39.9	37.9	26.0	16.4	9.4	12.8	...	...	...
2922	Machine tools	71.9	1.6	3.3	3.3	46.0	0.3	1.7	...	...	...
2923	Machinery for metallurgy	-	...	...	...	...	...	...	...	...	...
2924	Machinery for mining & construction	68.9	97.0	185.6	165.4	...	...	...	...	...	...
2925	Food/beverage/tobacco processing machinery	32.0	14.8	17.9	12.9	...	...	...	...	...	...
2926	Machinery for textile, apparel and leather	-	-	-	-	-	-	-	...	...	...
2927	Weapons and ammunition	28.8	590.5	745.5	783.7	...	316.2	60.6	...	...	...
2929	Other special purpose machinery	47.1	116.8	42.9	45.3	...	89.0	86.0	...	...	...
2930	Domestic appliances n.e.c.	27.4	24.5	40.2	36.2	7.8	11.2	13.2	...	...	...
3000	Office, accounting and computing machinery	20.3	24.0	17.0	14.1	6.4	0.7	3.3	...	...	...
3110	Electric motors, generators and transformers	73.6	56.0	63.2	41.4	...	...	...	...	...	...
3120	Electricity distribution & control apparatus	46.6	58.8	84.5	135.5	...	...	...	...	...	...
3130	Insulated wire and cable	58.6	74.6	20.7	1.0	...	...	...	...	...	...
3140	Accumulators, primary cells and batteries	21.0	21.2	11.8	5.3	...	...	...	...	...	...
3150	Lighting equipment and electric lamps	862.1	1049.6	743.2	737.3	...	...	...	...	...	...
3190	Other electrical equipment n.e.c.	3.5	3.5	5.1	3.7	...	...	...	...	...	...
3210	Electronic valves, tubes, etc.	66.8	86.6	77.1	82.9	...	...	...	...	...	...
3220	TV/radio transmitters; line comm. apparatus	11.2	74.1	65.5	60.4	...	30.1	22.3	...	...	...
3230	TV and radio receivers and associated goods	3.7	9.3	9.1	20.4	...	...	...	...	...	...
331	Medical, measuring, testing appliances, etc.	418.9	37.1	26.7	26.3	...	...	...	...	...	...
3311	Medical, surgical and orthopaedic equipment	16.4	15.6	20.1	22.3	12.2	11.8	10.2	...	...	...
3312	Measuring/testing/navigating appliances,etc.	32.5	20.8	4.1	1.3	...	...	...	...	...	...
3313	Industrial process control equipment	370.1	0.7	2.5	2.7	...	...	...	...	...	...
3320	Optical instruments & photographic equipment	3.5	0.2	7.5	10.0	...	...	...	...	...	...
3330	Watches and clocks	-	-	-	-	-	-	-	...	...	...
3410	Motor vehicles	3.6	2.7	1.3	1.3	...	...	...	...	...	...
3420	Automobile bodies, trailers & semi-trailers	0.6	0.9	...	...	...	...	53.6	...	...	...
3430	Parts/accessories for automobiles	148.9	195.6	229.1	141.5	...	...	...	...	...	...
351	Building and repairing of ships and boats	17.9	...	-	-	...	-	-	...	...	...
3511	Building and repairing of ships	17.9	...	-	-	...	-	-	...	...	...
3512	Building/repairing of pleasure/sport. boats	-	-	-	-	-	-	-	...	...	...
3520	Railway/tramway locomotives & rolling stock	2.0	2.4	1.9	2.4	...	...	...	...	...	...
3530	Aircraft and spacecraft	15.9	17.7	3.8	34.0	...	...	...	...	...	...
359	Transport equipment n.e.c.	...	...	...	...	...	...	...	...	...	...
3591	Motorcycles	...	...	...	...	...	-	...	...	...	...
3592	Bicycles and invalid carriages	5.8	1.6	1.3	...	...	...	...	...	...	...
3599	Other transport equipment n.e.c.	...	...	0.1	0.2	...	...	...	...	...	...
3610	Furniture	227.8	245.8	213.7	300.1	10.4	54.4	35.6	...	...	...
369	Manufacturing n.e.c.	...	...	51.7	37.9	...	...	...	...	...	...
3691	Jewellery and related articles	14.0	53.7	48.4	34.2	...	...	...	...	...	...
3692	Musical instruments	...	...	...	-	...	...	...	...	...	...
3693	Sports goods	-	-	-	-	-	-	-	...	...	...
3694	Games and toys	-	-	-	-	-	-	-	...	...	...
3699	Other manufacturing n.e.c.	3.5	3.6	3.3	3.6	...	...	...	...	...	...
3710	Recycling of metal waste and scrap	6.3	14.6	9.9	5.3	...	...	...	...	...	...
3720	Recycling of non-metal waste and scrap	-	-	-	-	-	-	-	...	...	...
D	Total manufacturing	38160.5	43506.7	42698.5	45946.8	10905.2	13901.5	12985.2	...	...	...

Kyrgyzstan

ISIC Revision 3			Index numbers of industrial production											
			(2000=100)											
ISIC	Industry	Note	1995	1996	1997	1998	1999	2000	2001	2002	2003	2004	2005	2006
15	Food and beverages	a/	...	...	...	...	...	100	94	102	110	115	114	124
16	Tobacco products	a/	...	...	...	...	...	...	...	...	...	...	...	...
17	Textiles	b/	...	...	...	...	...	100	116	135	132	184	209	248
18	Wearing apparel, fur	b/	...	...	...	...	...	...	...	...	...	...	...	...
19	Leather, leather products and footwear		...	...	...	...	...	...	...	...	...	...	...	...
20	Wood products (excl. furniture)		...	...	...	...	...	100	223	267	247	248	254	373
21	Paper and paper products		...	...	...	...	...	...	...	...	...	...	...	...
22	Printing and publishing		...	...	...	...	...	...	...	...	...	...	...	...
23	Coke,refined petroleum products,nuclear fuel		...	...	...	...	...	...	...	...	...	...	...	...
24	Chemicals and chemical products		...	...	...	...	...	100	107	179	191	273	237	212
25	Rubber and plastics products		...	...	...	...	...	...	...	...	...	...	...	...
26	Non-metallic mineral products		...	...	...	...	...	100	99	96	119	149	126	128
27	Basic metals	c/	...	...	...	...	...	100	114	79	99	94	72	46
28	Fabricated metal products	c/	...	...	...	...	...	...	...	...	...	...	...	...
29	Machinery and equipment n.e.c.		...	...	...	...	...	100	114	107	107	114	107	112
30	Office, accounting and computing machinery	d/	...	...	...	...	...	100	116	125	152	144	104	101
31	Electrical machinery and apparatus	d/	...	...	...	...	...	...	...	...	...	...	...	...
32	Radio,television and communication equipment	d/	...	...	...	...	...	...	...	...	...	...	...	...
33	Medical, precision and optical instruments	d/	...	...	...	...	...	...	...	...	...	...	...	...
34	Motor vehicles, trailers, semi-trailers	e/	...	...	...	...	...	100	192	225	165	188	193	105
35	Other transport equipment	e/	...	...	...	...	...	...	...	...	...	...	...	...
36	Furniture; manufacturing n.e.c.		...	...	...	...	...	...	...	...	...	...	...	...
37	Recycling		...	...	...	...	...	...	...	...	...	...	...	...
D	Total manufacturing		...	...	...	...	...	100	109	97	131	146	129	107

a/ 15 includes 16.
b/ 17 includes 18.
c/ 27 includes 28.
d/ 30 includes 31, 32 and 33.
e/ 34 includes 35.

Latvia

Supplier of information:
Central Statistical Bureau of Latvia, Riga.

Basic source of data:
Survey.

Major deviations from ISIC (Revision 3):
Data collected under the national classification system have been reclassified by the national authorities to correspond with ISIC (Revision 3).

Reference period:
Calendar year.

Scope:
All registered enterprises.

Method of data collection:
Mail questionnaires.

Type of enumeration:
Sample survey.

Adjusted for non-response:
Yes.

Concepts and definitions of variables:
<u>Wages and salaries</u> excludes payments in kind and housing and family allowances paid directly by the employer.

Related national publications:
None reported.

Latvia

ISIC Revision 3		Number of enterprises					Number of employees					Wages and salaries paid to employees				
			(number)					(number)					(thousands of Latvian Lats)			
ISIC	Industry	Note	2003	2004	2005	2006	Note	2003	2004	2005	2006	Note	2003	2004	2005	2006
151	Processed meat,fish,fruit,vegetables,fats		312	278	279	271		14136	13909	14743	14694		20464	21030	25699	31666
1511	Processing/preserving of meat		154	124	132	124		5982	5935	5902	6147		9124	9853	12016	15622
1512	Processing/preserving of fish		119	119	116	110		7242	7194	7842	7505		9232	9684	11655	13361
1513	Processing/preserving of fruit & vegetables		35	32	28	31		847	753	863	842	a/	2108	1493	2028	2684
1514	Vegetable and animal oils and fats		4	3	3	6		65	27	136	200	a/	...	...	...	...
1520	Dairy products		51	42	48	53		4166	4211	4118	4241		9291	10452	11572	15330
153	Grain mill products; starches; animal feeds		48	43	47	37		1372	1341	1373	1217		4195	4079	4737	4832
1531	Grain mill products		34	30	33	24		835	803	814	680	b/	3074	2883	3270	3322
1532	Starches and starch products		1	1	1	1		68	67	63	47	b/	...	...	...	...
1533	Prepared animal feeds		13	12	13	12		469	471	496	490		1121	1196	1467	1510
154	Other food products		386	367	344	324		11738	12193	11340	10912		20442	22587	24310	27883
1541	Bakery products		305	278	270	254		8864	9227	8444	8136		12129	13777	14394	17551
1542	Sugar		2	2	2	2		798	730	651	673	c/	5274	5139	5640	6302
1543	Cocoa, chocolate and sugar confectionery		19	17	17	19		734	716	764	778	c/	...	...	...	...
1544	Macaroni, noodles & similar products		19	25	12	9		270	439	379	380		214	411	397	500
1549	Other food products n.e.c.		41	45	43	40		1072	1081	1102	945		2825	3260	3880	3531
155	Beverages		63	60	60	56		3681	3814	3829	4043		12128	13339	14265	18592
1551	Distilling, rectifying & blending of spirits		15	14	14	14		1180	1166	1235	1312		4283	4379	5115	6613
1552	Wines		-	-	-	-		-	-	-	-		-	-	-	-
1553	Malt liquors and malt		22	18	20	19		1832	1839	1761	1627		6189	6353	5972	7005
1554	Soft drinks; mineral waters		26	28	26	23		669	809	833	1104		1656	2607	3179	4974
1600	Tobacco products		2	2	3	3		347	329	328	317		...	...	...	...
171	Spinning, weaving and finishing of textiles		56	45	43	56		2907	1555	1648	1601		7124	3126	3466	4398
1711	Textile fibre preparation; textile weaving		35	26	28	36		2896	1541	1634	1585		7118	3116	3450	4372
1712	Finishing of textiles		21	19	15	20		11	14	14	16		7	11	17	27
172	Other textiles		167	188	166	162		2672	2848	2703	2361		3766	4351	4247	5024
1721	Made-up textile articles, except apparel		126	116	110	106	d/	1948	1920	1739	1599	d/	2921	3158	2834	3394
1722	Carpets and rugs		1	3	4	2	d/	...	...	...	...	d/	...	...	...	...
1723	Cordage, rope, twine and netting		12	12	15	14		266	477	507	449		310	596	708	881
1729	Other textiles n.e.c.		28	57	37	40		458	451	457	313		534	597	704	749
1730	Knitted and crocheted fabrics and articles		379	277	215	212		4573	4324	3897	3243		8583	8720	9298	8806
1810	Wearing apparel, except fur apparel		1041	913	855	886		13672	13828	13227	12619		19172	20413	21883	25946
1820	Dressing & dyeing of fur; processing of fur		30	24	41	37		45	65	64	59		32	45	59	66
191	Tanning, dressing and processing of leather		37	44	42	43		333	326	301	291		353	380	405	464
1911	Tanning and dressing of leather		2	6	4	4		83	76	72	54	e/	353	380	405	464
1912	Luggage, handbags, etc.; saddlery & harness		35	38	38	39		250	250	229	237	e/	...	...	...	...
1920	Footwear		27	29	41	31		333	378	325	251		365	493	463	418
2010	Sawmilling and planing of wood		1026	1044	1105	1012		22009	20966	21746	19123		30675	33614	36022	42668
202	Products of wood, cork, straw, etc.		594	598	642	704		10854	11635	11579	12727		27008	30187	31692	42064
2021	Veneer sheets, plywood, particle board, etc.		18	16	22	23		5126	5319	4783	4818		19110	21275	20878	25086
2022	Builders' carpentry and joinery		326	325	379	437		3362	3614	3963	4785		4418	5218	6491	11295
2023	Wooden containers		67	104	112	94		965	1103	1144	1498		1361	1167	1331	2146
2029	Other wood products; articles of cork/straw		183	153	129	150		1401	1599	1689	1626		2119	2528	2993	3536
210	Paper and paper products		64	67	67	64		1659	1663	1595	1612		3634	3989	4760	5847
2101	Pulp, paper and paperboard		1	1	2	2		148	152	160	184	f/	...	...	...	...
2102	Corrugated paper and paperboard		33	39	37	35		873	1002	921	874	f/	2519	2919	3444	4020
2109	Other articles of paper and paperboard		30	27	28	27		638	509	514	554		1115	1071	1316	1827
221	Publishing		352	361	343	377		5919	6479	6042	4646		15572	18634	21131	20822
2211	Publishing of books and other publications		117	113	125	134		826	942	1067	885		1906	2049	2879	3101
2212	Publishing of newspapers, journals, etc.		171	201	170	174		4888	5348	4766	3584		13402	16346	17877	17249
2213	Publishing of recorded media		43	18	18	28		70	80	79	65		...g/	...g/	...g/	102
2219	Other publishing		21	29	30	41		135	109	130	112		264g/	238g/	375g/	371

222	Printing and related service activities	324	376	389	433	3716	4639	4339	4713		7711	9737	10165	14107
2221	Printing	255	307	319	327	3428	4411	4040	4426		7266	9476	9748	13589
2222	Service activities related to printing	69	69	70	106	288	228	299	287		445	261	417	518
2230	Reproduction of recorded media	14	16	13	20	24	57	59	58		31	73	84	173
2310	Coke oven products	-	-	-	-	-	-	-	-		-	-	-	-
2320	Refined petroleum products	1	2	3	4	47	39	42	42		...	72	...	...
2330	Processing of nuclear fuel	-	-	-	-	-	-	-	-		-	-	-	-
241	Basic chemicals	36	38	32	28	437	475	475	348		635	772	825	621
2411	Basic chemicals, except fertilizers	29	31	25	23	312	350	341	279		343	423	461	621h/
2412	Fertilizers and nitrogen compounds	5	4	5	4	115	120	122	66		292i/	349i/	365i/	...h/
2413	Plastics in primary forms; synthetic rubber	2	3	2	1	10	5	12	3		...i/	...i/	...i/	...h/
242	Other chemicals	86	86	105	96	3654	3586	3714	3823		9889	11162	12883	17639
2421	Pesticides and other agro-chemical products	2	2	3	4	9	6	13	15	j/	...	...	...	...
2422	Paints, varnishes, printing ink and mastics	17	19	19	13	686	560	474	466	j/	1525	1614	1246	1385
2423	Pharmaceuticals, medicinal chemicals, etc.	24	25	26	25	1850	1813	1839	1953		5697	6295	7779	11253
2424	Soap, cleaning & cosmetic preparations	22	26	33	31	841	979	1120	1102		2280	2818	3197	3973
2429	Other chemical products n.e.c.	21	14	24	23	268	228	268	287		387	435	661	1028
2430	Man-made fibres	2	1	1	1	359	151	143	141		...	...	...	...
251	Rubber products	16	18	15	16	287	298	265	292		714	806	749	1088
2511	Rubber tyres and tubes	5	5	4	5	78	85	59	58		212	242	251	328
2519	Other rubber products	11	13	11	11	209	213	206	234		502	564	498	760
2520	Plastic products	133	169	171	207	3127	3561	3818	4277		5203	7302	9078	12533
2610	Glass and glass products	26	29	28	37	1148	2066	2164	1918		1993	5791	7115	7496
269	Non-metallic mineral products n.e.c.	285	255	287	338	2992	3259	3840	4070		6194	7948	10361	16651
2691	Pottery, china and earthenware	90	40	38	49	311	292	272	281	k/	241	285	277	343
2692	Refractory ceramic products	2	3	3	3	2	5	17	19	k/	...	...	...	...
2693	Struct.non-refractory clay; ceramic products	6	6	6	8	510	546	461	499		1395	1684	1388	1872
2694	Cement, lime and plaster	1	1	3	4	168	160	231	224	m/	...	...	...	...
2695	Articles of concrete, cement and plaster	91	113	125	150	1722	1962	2425	2591	m/	4283	5579	8126	13610
2696	Cutting, shaping & finishing of stone	92	90	110	116	249	253	388	399		155	189	338	499
2699	Other non-metallic mineral products n.e.c.	3	2	2	8	30	41	46	57		120	211	232	328
2710	Basic iron and steel	9	9	9	11	3066	3083	3026	3139	n/	10894	12316	12961	19450
2720	Basic precious and non-ferrous metals	8	9	7	8	398	412	431	401	n/	...	...	...	...
273	Casting of metals	2	3	2	3	30	50	37	55	n/	...	...	...	...
2731	Casting of iron and steel	-	1	1	1	-	18	35	43		-	...	...	...
2732	Casting of non-ferrous metals	2	2	1	2	30	32	2	12		...	...	...	...
281	Struct.metal products;tanks;steam generators	182	218	227	285	3176	3459	3695	4582		5794	6862	8904	14200
2811	Structural metal products	162	192	201	257	2743	3002	3251	4173		4960	5904	7798	13108
2812	Tanks, reservoirs and containers of metal	15	22	23	26	337	380	373	376	p/	834	959	1106	1092
2813	Steam generators	5	4	3	2	96	77	71	33	p/	...	...	...	...
289	Other metal products; metal working services	308	320	346	379	4811	4925	5178	5111		8796	10059	11904	13799
2891	Metal forging/pressing/stamping/roll-forming	17	16	16	21	450	260	269	228		721	477	589	715
2892	Treatment & coating of metals	89	99	123	149	527	689	937	1209		1150	1413	2170	3323
2893	Cutlery, hand tools and general hardware	49	42	36	33	848	861	785	754		1400	1475	1448	1781
2899	Other fabricated metal products n.e.c.	153	163	171	176	2986	3115	3187	2920		5525	6693	7696	7981
291	General purpose machinery	111	113	109	128	2605	2634	2614	2722		4829	6446	7416	9268
2911	Engines & turbines (not for transport equipment)	9	6	7	7	270	273	265	207		753	1105	1147	964
2912	Pumps, compressors, taps and valves	17	17	19	21	371	364	323	366		657	877	1137	1367
2913	Bearings, gears, gearing & driving elements	3	1	2	2	825	684	643	634	q/	1628	1910	1993	2422
2914	Ovens, furnaces and furnace burners	5	3	2	2	20	109	105	119	q/	...	...	...	...
2915	Lifting and handling equipment	25	30	23	27	427	562	546	374		711	1423	1685	1281
2919	Other general purpose machinery	52	56	56	69	692	642	732	1022		1080	1131	1454	3234
292	Special purpose machinery	134	154	162	159	4382	4671	4663	4498		8450	9466	10872	13206
2921	Agricultural and forestry machinery	52	56	59	64	936	1033	1231	1348		1403	1785	2658	4287
2922	Machine tools	40	47	49	41	2665	2691	2512	2325		4949	5235	5294	6097
2923	Machinery for metallurgy	-	-	-	-	-	-	-	-		-	-	-	-
2924	Machinery for mining & construction	5	6	9	10	17	22	55	29	r/	...	...	...	...
2925	Food/beverage/tobacco processing machinery	14	14	15	18	149	111	105	158	r/	188	167	270	422
2926	Machinery for textile, apparel and leather	3	3	2	1	17	16	15	7		...	...	...	...
2927	Weapons and ammunition	1	1	1	1	15	16	13	43		...	...	...	...
2929	Other special purpose machinery	19	27	27	24	583	782	732	588		1873	2232	2612	2278

continued

Latvia

ISIC Revision 3		Number of enterprises					Number of employees					Wages and salaries paid to employees				
			(number)					(number)					(thousands of Latvian Lats)			
ISIC	Industry	Note	2003	2004	2005	2006	Note	2003	2004	2005	2006	Note	2003	2004	2005	2006
2930	Domestic appliances n.e.c.		6	10	8	5		59	77	48	14		75	91	74	83
3000	Office, accounting and computing machinery		27	26	24	25		153	246	177	173		467	668	707	866
3110	Electric motors, generators and transformers		41	31	31	32		518	540	605	610		1669	1880	2463	2924
3120	Electricity distribution & control apparatus		13	13	14	14		955	985	1047	1088		2672	3212	4014	4967
3130	Insulated wire and cable		3	3	6	7		305	435	512	610		...	...	...	...
3140	Accumulators, primary cells and batteries		1	3	4	4		...	36	45	14		...	...	...	...
3150	Lighting equipment and electric lamps		7	7	7	11		452	401	345	263	s/	...	...	...	...
3190	Other electrical equipment n.e.c.		15	13	14	15		872	892	851	991	s/	3443	2946	3609	5153
3210	Electronic valves, tubes, etc.		11	12	8	7		339	311	334	287		478	568	573	654
3220	TV/radio transmitters; line comm. apparatus		19	13	19	17		631	624	384	405		1439	1839	1739	2581
3230	TV and radio receivers and associated goods		13	13	18	16		316	386	355	328		477	857	740	828
331	Medical, measuring, testing appliances, etc.		108	145	151	165		1501	1640	1518	1561		3105	3516	3694	4652
3311	Medical, surgical and orthopaedic equipment		65	101	103	107		591	758	647	689		861	1049	1115	1441
3312	Measuring/testing/navigating appliances,etc.		36	36	36	41		889	851	825	745		2244t/	2467t/	2579t/	2891
3313	Industrial process control equipment		7	8	12	17		21	31	46	127		...t/	...t/	...t/	320
3320	Optical instruments & photographic equipment		6	4	8	10		90	102	209	214		268	379	886	1218
3330	Watches and clocks		1	...	...	-		...	...	...	-		...	...	...	-
3410	Motor vehicles		1	1	2	2		172	...	20	176		...	...	...	...
3420	Automobile bodies, trailers & semi-trailers		7	7	8	7		416	591	572	539		541	1006	1209	1678
3430	Parts/accessories for automobiles		11	14	15	12		168	235	361	506		433	733	1219	2417
351	Building and repairing of ships and boats		92	98	111	124		2688	2677	2714	2620		6471	6594	7410	8508
3511	Building and repairing of ships		73	75	92	98		2581	2528	2589	2425		6348	6315	7206	7837
3512	Building/repairing of pleasure/sport. boats		19	23	19	26		107	149	125	195		123	279	203	671
3520	Railway/tramway locomotives & rolling stock		18	12	16	16		3395	3431	3079	2765		6340	7193	8140	8940
3530	Aircraft and spacecraft		3	4	5	7		25	42	46	42		47	62	...	...
359	Transport equipment n.e.c.		1	1	1	1		20	15	10	6		...	...	...	...
3591	Motorcycles		-	-	-	-		-	-	-	-		-	-	-	-
3592	Bicycles and invalid carriages		1	1	1	1		20	15	10	6		...	...	...	...
3599	Other transport equipment n.e.c.		-	-	-	-		-	-	-	-		-	-	-	-
3610	Furniture		434	513	568	664		9421	10993	11058	11673		15226	19231	22250	29202
369	Manufacturing n.e.c.		463	310	293	311		2163	2304	2508	2202		3156	3825	4320	5075
3691	Jewellery and related articles		157	132	115	124		148	182	192	153		146	238	248	283
3692	Musical instruments		9	11	10	12		25	35	29	24		37	55	65	69
3693	Sports goods		13	20	19	16		43	67	65	49		25	70	62	58
3694	Games and toys		39	43	41	34		874	954	815	682		1256	1511	1580	1753
3699	Other manufacturing n.e.c.		245	104	108	125		1073	1066	1407	1294		1693	1950	2365	2912
3710	Recycling of metal waste and scrap		35	30	43	41		348	410	537	583		438	574	1018	1358
3720	Recycling of non-metal waste and scrap		9	10	12	17		34	63	90	126		61	100	219	456
D	Total manufacturing		7657	7491	7633	8011		159716	164665	164786	161943		304226	342662	385331	481963

a/ 1513 includes 1514.
b/ 1531 includes 1532.
c/ 1542 includes 1543.
d/ 1721 includes 1722.
e/ 1911 includes 1912.
f/ 2102 includes 2101.
g/ 2219 includes 2213.
h/ 2411 includes 2412 and 2413.
i/ 2412 includes 2413.
j/ 2422 includes 2421.
k/ 2691 includes 2692.
m/ 2695 includes 2694.
n/ 2710 includes 2720 and 273.
p/ 2812 includes 2813.
q/ 2913 includes 2914.
r/ 2925 includes 2924.
s/ 3190 includes 3150.
t/ 3312 includes 3313.

ISIC Revision 3		Output in factor values					Value added in factor values					Gross fixed capital formation		
			(thousands of Latvian Lats)					(thousands of Latvian Lats)					(thousands of Latvian Lats)	
ISIC	Industry	Note	2003	2004	2005	2006	Note	2003	2004	2005	2006	Note	2005	2006
151	Processed meat,fish,fruit,vegetables,fats		211538	227834	288056	344876		40678	39736	63041	79053		48007	43505
1511	Processing/preserving of meat		116212	134992	160703	207908		21450	19078	30653	45114		30512	16736
1512	Processing/preserving of fish		72263	77519	101207	104182		14259	17810	23433	23543		9281	8817
1513	Processing/preserving of fruit & vegetables	a/	23062	15323	26145	32787	a/	4969	2847	8954	10396	a/	8214	17952
1514	Vegetable and animal oils and fats	a/	...	...	...	...	a/	...	...	...	...	a/	...	...
1520	Dairy products		113733	137318	167680	200418		26241	28234	36661	37974		21280	22583
153	Grain mill products; starches; animal feeds		46184	52792	62419	61743		10277	11111	13778	5714		6204	8297
1531	Grain mill products	b/	28427	31867	38697	39296	b/	6337	7382	9030	11427	b/	3164	4070
1532	Starches and starch products	b/	...	...	...	...	b/	...	...	...	...	b/	...	...
1533	Prepared animal feeds		17758	20925	23722	22447		3940	3729	4748	5714		3041	4227
154	Other food products		149847	171908	181296	204687		48638	52811	54164	76895		22328	23861
1541	Bakery products		74667	88726	94218	109291		24033	27178	31576	41392		16381	16957
1542	Sugar	c/	43317	50300	51467	56538	c/	13841	15233	11845	20287	c/	1972	2695
1543	Cocoa, chocolate and sugar confectionery	c/	...	...	...	...	c/	...	...	...	...	c/	...	...
1544	Macaroni, noodles & similar products		3180	4117	4684	5978		953	1211	1094	1792		528	1864
1549	Other food products n.e.c.		28684	28766	30927	32880		9812	9189	9649	13424		3447	2345
155	Beverages		129812	162954	194084	230640		59297	43529	35131	51369		26959	22901
1551	Distilling, rectifying & blending of spirits		65731	81613	102755	119164		37685	22131	7949	14413		9669	2578
1552	Wines		-	-	-	-		-	-	-	-		-	-
1553	Malt liquors and malt		46919	51204	57164	69501		16129	12460	18079	26884		14960	11056
1554	Soft drinks; mineral waters		17162	30138	34166	41976		5484	8937	9103	10073		2330	9267
1600	Tobacco products		...	...	...	...		...	...	...	...		...	...
171	Spinning, weaving and finishing of textiles		41815	20301	28839	29591		14267	5617	8095	7101		2069	2588
1711	Textile fibre preparation; textile weaving		41639	20157	28612	29367		14232	5587	8028	7041		2067	2575
1712	Finishing of textiles		176	144	228	224		35	30	67	61		2	13
172	Other textiles		25679	27715	24439	34222		8565	7101	9568	11867		4998	3325
1721	Made-up textile articles, except apparel	d/	19855	19092	14203	22321	d/	6400	5112	6024	8055	d/	3162	2104
1722	Carpets and rugs	d/	...	...	...	...	d/	...	...	...	...	d/	...	...
1723	Cordage, rope, twine and netting		2400	5266	5986	7134		709	770	1885	1935		632	763
1729	Other textiles n.e.c.		3421	3357	4250	4767		1456	1219	1658	1877		1204	458
1730	Knitted and crocheted fabrics and articles		40366	42372	49244	51492		17153	18851	22230	16593		5694	7427
1810	Wearing apparel, except fur apparel		73539	82019	88910	109385		37276	37457	40699	50465		5431	5273
1820	Dressing & dyeing of fur; processing of fur		151	446	318	465		71	134	108	166		25	17
191	Tanning, dressing and processing of leather		2048	2424	2898	3513		688	719	816	929		186	114
1911	Tanning and dressing of leather	e/	2048	2424	2898	3513	e/	688	719	816	929	e/	186	114
1912	Luggage, handbags, etc.; saddlery & harness	e/	...	...	...	...	e/	...	...	...	...	e/	...	...
1920	Footwear		1368	1705	1674	2083		635	864	746	873		158	265
2010	Sawmilling and planing of wood		393753	450555	524285	546743		108916	111116	146138	144131		62018	61116
202	Products of wood, cork, straw, etc.		188858	243192	265769	373911		56686	70163	76996	87426		52584	94728
2021	Veneer sheets, plywood, particle board, etc.		110236	139266	144228	185603		33844	44556	47562	42590		17481	38861
2022	Builders' carpentry and joinery		39372	56818	70482	115719		12183	13698	16308	29453		30408	47492
2023	Wooden containers		25268	28024	30026	48463		6643	5409	6962	10175		1823	4593
2029	Other wood products; articles of cork/straw		13983	19085	21034	24127		4015	6500	6165	5208		2872	3782
210	Paper and paper products		39423	37008	45409	53797		11166	10400	10743	15630		8315	7995
2101	Pulp, paper and paperboard	f/	...	...	...	...	f/	...	...	...	...	f/	...	...
2102	Corrugated paper and paperboard	f/	25960	27437	32394	36337	f/	7611	7668	6857	8858	f/	4006	4097
2109	Other articles of paper and paperboard		13462	9571	13015	17460		3555	2732	3887	6772		4309	3898
221	Publishing		73480	77857	94054	99317		33486	37356	46073	46460		5157	3217
2211	Publishing of books and other publications		13845	13600	19272	20304		5971	5937	8025	8890		1000	748
2212	Publishing of newspapers, journals, etc.		55377	61947	71761	72316		26070	30539	37014	34779		4092	2285
2213	Publishing of recorded media		...g/	...g/	...g/	3767		...g/	...g/	...g/	1715		13	55
2219	Other publishing		4258g/	2310g/	3021g/	2930		1444g/	880g/	1034g/	1076		51	129

continued

Latvia

ISIC Revision 3		Output in factor values					Value added in factor values					Gross fixed capital formation		
			(thousands of Latvian Lats)					(thousands of Latvian Lats)					(thousands of Latvian Lats)	
ISIC	Industry	Note	2003	2004	2005	2006	Note	2003	2004	2005	2006	Note	2005	2006
222	Printing and related service activities		64076	81506	91580	138909		28368	25507	29285	36899		19281	27707
2221	Printing		61593	78661	86149	129605		27375	24769	27969	34630		18827	26746
2222	Service activities related to printing		2484	2845	5431	9304		993	738	1316	2270		454	961
2230	Reproduction of recorded media		623	1195	558	3257		78	213	208	1770		32	536
2310	Coke oven products		-	-	-	-		-	-	-	-		-	-
2320	Refined petroleum products		...	...	...	...		...	...	...	...		33	316
2330	Processing of nuclear fuel		-	-	-	-		-	-	-	-		-	-
241	Basic chemicals		5901	6462	7496	7198		1821	1959	2236	1720		1031	708
2411	Basic chemicals, except fertilizers		3322	3860	4225	7198h/		1226	1381	1675	1720h/		783	708h/
2412	Fertilizers and nitrogen compounds		2579i/	2602i/	3271i/	...h/		593i/	573i/	561i/	...h/		248i/	...h/
2413	Plastics in primary forms; synthetic rubber		...i/	...i/	...i/	...h/		...i/	...i/	...i/	...h/		...i/	...h/
242	Other chemicals		56067	65435	83369	105327		26152	29753	39860	48626		9119	21006
2421	Pesticides and other agro-chemical products	j/	...	...	...	...	j/	...	...	...	...	j/	...	...
2422	Paints, varnishes, printing ink and mastics	j/	15402	15003	14100	15813	j/	6120	3892	3082	4125	j/	673	460
2423	Pharmaceuticals, medicinal chemicals, etc.		25723	34499	46515	60585		13037	18991	27008	31814		5514	7507
2424	Soap, cleaning & cosmetic preparations		11664	13130	17089	19486		5591	5719	7511	9226		1695	1783
2429	Other chemical products n.e.c.		3278	2803	5665	9444		1403	1151	2260	3461		1237	11257
2430	Man-made fibres		...	...	...	...		...	...	...	...		...	...
251	Rubber products		6889	8760	7583	9911		2377	1840	1821	3032		561	538
2511	Rubber tyres and tubes		2174	2575	2372	2385		1147	644	506	810		61	56
2519	Other rubber products		4715	6185	5211	7526		1230	1197	1315	2221		501	483
2520	Plastic products		63108	78669	99449	137752		17748	21069	28200	30295		12886	18177
2610	Glass and glass products		10819	39066	48864	53664		2349	13394	12899	14654		8809	27923
269	Non-metallic mineral products n.e.c.		63708	82704	122472	198112		26627	30871	41428	65739		28195	49722
2691	Pottery, china and earthenware	k/	985	1197	1571	1783	k/	295	474	813	995	k/	938	341
2692	Refractory ceramic products	k/	...	...	...	...	k/	...	...	...	...	k/	...	...
2693	Struct.non-refractory clay; ceramic products		5013	6511	5311	7803		2301	2893	1821	4648		3210	4673
2694	Cement, lime and plaster	m/	...	...	...	...	m/	...	...	...	...	m/	...	...
2695	Articles of concrete, cement and plaster	m/	53157	68626	106279	174175	m/	22658	25902	36426	56541	m/	22980	43222
2696	Cutting, shaping & finishing of stone		1582	1726	3620	...		470	567	1042	1582		954	1034
2699	Other non-metallic mineral products n.e.c.		2972	4645	5691	...		905	1036	1327	1972		113	452
2710	Basic iron and steel	n/	152102	221473	218405	264107	n/	47043	73032	44125	69437	n/	17936	11478
2720	Basic precious and non-ferrous metals	n/	...	...	...	...	n/	...	...	...	...	n/	...	...
273	Casting of metals	n/	...	...	...	...	n/	...	...	...	...	n/	...	...
2731	Casting of iron and steel		-	...	...	...		-	...	...	...		...	...
2732	Casting of non-ferrous metals		...	...	...	...		...	...	...	...		...	...
281	Struct.metal products;tanks;steam generators		42157	60853	83860	127374		14774	17097	25086	37738		6917	14028
2811	Structural metal products		37725	54631	77143	120857		13136	15150	22823	35524		6234	12834
2812	Tanks, reservoirs and containers of metal	p/	4432	6223	6717	6517	p/	1638	1947	2263	2213	p/	683	1193
2813	Steam generators	p/	...	...	...	...	p/	...	...	...	...	p/	...	...
289	Other metal products; metal working services		54193	63412	85719	102445		19181	22975	30003	33403		11054	10833
2891	Metal forging/pressing/stamping/roll-forming		4236	2346	3542	3895		1897	911	1687	976		745	481
2892	Treatment & coating of metals		5264	8851	15268	24367		2647	3422	6723	10534		2656	4545
2893	Cutlery, hand tools and general hardware		6061	9158	10453	10059		2530	3046	3017	3743		1392	782
2899	Other fabricated metal products n.e.c.		38633	43057	56456	64125		12107	15596	18577	18150		6262	5025
291	General purpose machinery		32312	40286	45954	61077		12339	13833	17594	20614		6211	5945
2911	Engines & turbines (not for transport equipment)		6964	7744	7574	5117		1669	2524	2463	1444		126	761
2912	Pumps, compressors, taps and valves		3774	5060	6124	8493		1590	2210	2355	2445		1963	281
2913	Bearings, gears, gearing & driving elements	q/	8065	8889	10107	11797	q/	3356	2471	3735	1444	q/	1670	1015
2914	Ovens, furnaces and furnace burners	q/	...	...	...	...	q/	...	...	...	...	q/	...	...
2915	Lifting and handling equipment		5988	8952	8342	10839		3052	3347	3227	2445		706	1549
2919	Other general purpose machinery		7522	9641	13808	24830		2672	3281	5815	9314		1746	2340

292	Special purpose machinery		37339	42906	51418	59930		17853	18277	20371	24582		6653	5066
2921	Agricultural and forestry machinery		6470	9242	13560	18928		1964	2904	5786	8785		2531	1101
2922	Machine tools		23159	24456	24921	28565		11221	10894	9481	11211		2401	1980
2923	Machinery for metallurgy		-	-	-	-		-	-	-	-		-	-
2924	Machinery for mining & construction	r/	...	...	...	...		56	88	209	256		117	144
2925	Food/beverage/tobacco processing machinery	r/	1497	1617	2353	3652		742	470	590	824		103	249
2926	Machinery for textile, apparel and leather		...	...	...	...		...	...	...	...		...	...
2927	Weapons and ammunition		...	...	...	...		...	...	...	...		...	...
2929	Other special purpose machinery		5965	7311	10411	8648		3784	3793	4242	3456		1347	1731
2930	Domestic appliances n.e.c.		458	1136	667	245		175	103	121	120		30	34
3000	Office, accounting and computing machinery		6527	6800	9294	18898		1301	1987	3568	5110		709	207
3110	Electric motors, generators and transformers		15683	19596	22615	20093		5347	5340	6721	6728		1071	452
3120	Electricity distribution & control apparatus		16172	20984	24238	33189		6650	7469	8719	11849		2656	1990
3130	Insulated wire and cable		...	...	...	...		...	...	...	...		...	...
3140	Accumulators, primary cells and batteries		...	...	...	...		...	...	...	...		...	...
3150	Lighting equipment and electric lamps	s/	...	...	...	...	s/	...	...	...	...	s/	...	...
3190	Other electrical equipment n.e.c.	s/	25338	21489	24780	29921	s/	9039	6438	8254	10528	s/	1746	4648
3210	Electronic valves, tubes, etc.		2424	3162	3336	2666		982	1281	1157	1485		343	419
3220	TV/radio transmitters; line comm. apparatus		10909	18578	15120	20080		5044	9662	8478	9411		6301	1135
3230	TV and radio receivers and associated goods		3194	3661	3458	3841		994	1830	1886	1902		339	202
331	Medical, measuring, testing appliances, etc.		20720	19495	24275	29819		7160	6879	10396	13181		3527	3876
3311	Medical, surgical and orthopaedic equipment		4127	5724	5846	10110		2468	1938	2837	4572		1216	1466
3312	Measuring/testing/navigating appliances,etc.		16593t/	13771t/	18429t/	16862		4691t/	4942t/	7559t/	7671		2311t/	2093
3313	Industrial process control equipment		...t/	...t/	...t/	2847		...t/	...t/	...t/	938		...t/	317
3320	Optical instruments & photographic equipment		1413	1925	3642	5111		820	900	2675	2143		289	1044
3330	Watches and clocks		...	...	...	-		...	...	...	-		...	-
3410	Motor vehicles		...	...	...	...		933	...	...	...		...	...
3420	Automobile bodies, trailers & semi-trailers		6346	9940	10542	23943		1470	2112	1963	4086		1094	441
3430	Parts/accessories for automobiles		3369	6414	11792	19525		1245	1806	4066	4287		6264	4207
351	Building and repairing of ships and boats		40459	49655	60971	68365		11232	11856	16193	19415		5056	4087
3511	Building and repairing of ships		39304	47836	59332	65481		10973	11485	15832	18199		4846	3508
3512	Building/repairing of pleasure/sport. boats		1155	1819	1639	2885		259	371	360	1217		209	579
3520	Railway/tramway locomotives & rolling stock		28248	34265	39296	45376		11385	13484	12924	14542		4906	2741
3530	Aircraft and spacecraft		90	105	...	...		54	-34	...	...		...	...
359	Transport equipment n.e.c.		29	...	...	...		7	...	...	...		...	...
3591	Motorcycles		-	-	-	-		-	-	-	-		-	-
3592	Bicycles and invalid carriages		29	...	...	...		7	...	...	...		...	...
3599	Other transport equipment n.e.c.		-	-	-	-		-	-	-	-		-	-
3610	Furniture		88983	119152	138543	186597		33399	45992	49497	64679		24394	25590
369	Manufacturing n.e.c.		13487	18069	21325	28984		7102	8815	9449	12353		2788	1851
3691	Jewellery and related articles		764	1445	1645	1482		219	368	585	387		92	57
3692	Musical instruments		107	155	220	393		63	112	128	176		114	32
3693	Sports goods		276	857	910	660		91	351	164	160		63	120
3694	Games and toys		4938	5479	5047	6862		3159	2998	2897	3778		134	82
3699	Other manufacturing n.e.c.		7402	10133	13502	19588		3571	4985	5675	7852		2385	1561
3710	Recycling of metal waste and scrap		11933	36912	47568	62055		1428	4072	2451	6392		2292	2615
3720	Recycling of non-metal waste and scrap		151	479	1748	3494		53	51	776	1209		1932	3822
D	Total manufacturing		2460840	2952992	3478303	4267682		822162	880110	1030800	1239907		467932	563392

a/ 1513 includes 1514.
b/ 1531 includes 1532.
c/ 1542 includes 1543.
d/ 1721 includes 1722.
e/ 1911 includes 1912.
f/ 2102 includes 2101.
g/ 2219 includes 2213.
h/ 2411 includes 2412 and 2413.
i/ 2412 includes 2413.
j/ 2422 includes 2421.

k/ 2691 includes 2692.
m/ 2695 includes 2694.
n/ 2710 includes 2720 and 273.
p/ 2812 includes 2813.
q/ 2913 includes 2914.
r/ 2925 includes 2924.
s/ 3190 includes 3150.
t/ 3312 includes 3313.

Latvia

ISIC Revision 3			Index numbers of industrial production											
			(2000=100)											
ISIC	Industry	Note	1995	1996	1997	1998	1999	2000	2001	2002	2003	2004	2005	2006
15	Food and beverages		101	112	128	124	102	100	105	111	118	126	132	138
16	Tobacco products		...	...	...	...	...	...	...	...	...	...	...	...
17	Textiles		84	129	142	139	92	100	105	109	104	97	116	143
18	Wearing apparel, fur		51	48	59	67	89	100	103	99	97	102	99	90
19	Leather, leather products and footwear		585	601	441	350	156	100	94	55	63	79	82	70
20	Wood products (excl. furniture)		54	67	96	110	90	100	108	114	132	140	144	142
21	Paper and paper products		39	62	106	103	90	100	114	128	123	119	129	138
22	Printing and publishing		77	84	94	126	103	100	97	91	100	103	111	127
23	Coke,refined petroleum products,nuclear fuel		...	...	...	...	...	...	...	...	...	...	...	...
24	Chemicals and chemical products		251	243	282	237	126	100	110	127	111	134	152	191
25	Rubber and plastics products		88	94	120	165	90	100	120	137	156	179	215	235
26	Non-metallic mineral products		97	101	95	142	103	100	111	128	135	152	189	198
27	Basic metals		31	31	43	73	100	100	117	115	140	152	144	148
28	Fabricated metal products		59	87	149	156	90	100	109	106	122	128	144	163
29	Machinery and equipment n.e.c.		146	139	137	86	82	100	128	141	173	187	195	192
30	Office, accounting and computing machinery		...	...	...	...	...	...	...	...	...	...	...	...
31	Electrical machinery and apparatus		76	69	96	95	84	100	117	145	168	185	207	225
32	Radio,television and communication equipment		223	257	286	216	80	100	127	156	282	334	298	363
33	Medical, precision and optical instruments		...	...	...	...	...	...	...	...	...	...	...	...
34	Motor vehicles, trailers, semi-trailers		...	...	...	...	...	...	...	...	...	...	...	...
35	Other transport equipment		103	86	69	69	71	100	75	77	70	71	78	70
36	Furniture; manufacturing n.e.c.		115	106	114	134	88	100	122	132	141	155	163	174
37	Recycling		149	124	160	179	84	100	62	51	61	68	60	50
D	Total manufacturing		92	99	116	120	96	100	108	114	123	131	139	146

Lesotho

Supplier of information:
Bureau of Statistics, Maseru.

Basic source of data:
Quarterly sample survey.

Major deviations from ISIC (Revision 3):
None reported.

Reference period:
Calendar year.

Scope:
Establishments with 20 or more persons engaged.

Method of data collection:
Data were collected directly in the field and by e-mail.

Type of enumeration:
Sample survey.

Adjusted for non-response:
Yes.

Concepts and definitions of variables:
No deviations from the standard UN concepts and definitions are reported.

Related national publications:
Performance of Manufacturing Sector, published by the Bureau of Statistics, Maseru.

Lesotho

ISIC Revision 3		Number of establishments					Number of employees					Wages and salaries paid to employees				
			(number)					(number)					(thousands of Lesotho Maloti)			
ISIC	Industry	Note	2003	2004	2005	2006	Note	2003	2004	2005	2006	Note	2003	2004	2005	2006
151	Processed meat,fish,fruit,vegetables,fats		...	...	...	...		...	...	...	...		...	...	...	...
1511	Processing/preserving of meat		...	...	...	...		164	...	...	...		760	...	...	...
1512	Processing/preserving of fish		...	...	...	...		...	...	...	...		...	...	...	...
1513	Processing/preserving of fruit & vegetables		...	...	...	...		...	...	...	...		...	...	...	...
1514	Vegetable and animal oils and fats		...	...	...	...		...	...	...	...		...	...	...	...
1520	Dairy products		1	1	1	1		100	119	120	118		608	720	799	814
153	Grain mill products; starches; animal feeds		...	...	...	...		...	...	...	...		...	...	...	...
1531	Grain mill products		2	2	2	2		2114	1804	1074	1736		20249	21114	20662	22289
1532	Starches and starch products		...	...	...	...		...	...	...	...		...	...	...	...
1533	Prepared animal feeds		...	...	...	...		...	...	...	...		...	...	...	...
154	Other food products		...	...	...	...		...	...	...	...		...	...	...	...
1541	Bakery products		2	2	2	2		1096	1138	1160	1288		6291	6446	6974	7994
1542	Sugar		...	...	...	...		...	...	...	...		...	...	...	...
1543	Cocoa, chocolate and sugar confectionery		...	...	...	...		...	...	...	...		...	...	...	...
1544	Macaroni, noodles & similar products		...	...	...	...		...	...	...	...		...	...	...	...
1549	Other food products n.e.c.		...	...	...	...		...	...	...	...		...	...	...	...
155	Beverages		...	...	...	...		...	...	...	...		...	...	...	...
1551	Distilling, rectifying & blending of spirits		...	...	...	...		...	...	...	...		...	...	...	...
1552	Wines		...	...	...	...		...	...	...	...		...	...	...	...
1553	Malt liquors and malt		1	1	1	1		1327	1313	1245	1155		19066	14244	21294	25982
1554	Soft drinks; mineral waters		...	...	...	...		...	...	...	...		...	...	...	...
1600	Tobacco products		...	...	...	...		...	...	...	...		...	...	...	...
171	Spinning, weaving and finishing of textiles		...	...	...	...		...	...	...	...		...	...	...	...
1711	Textile fibre preparation; textile weaving		2	2	1	1		...	...	...	...		...	...	...	...
1712	Finishing of textiles		...	...	...	...		...	...	...	...		...	...	...	...
172	Other textiles		...	...	...	...		...	...	...	...		...	...	...	...
1721	Made-up textile articles, except apparel		2	2	2	2		6300	18405	13176	21508		13267	52839	36878	62133
1722	Carpets and rugs		...	...	...	...		...	...	...	...		...	...	...	...
1723	Cordage, rope, twine and netting		...	...	...	...		...	...	...	...		...	...	...	...
1729	Other textiles n.e.c.		2	2	2	3		2309	12481	11465	16175		5312	30830	35376	37969
1730	Knitted and crocheted fabrics and articles		...	...	...	...		...	...	...	...		...	...	...	...
1810	Wearing apparel, except fur apparel		11	20	17	16		64140	89443	65423	67280		156479	222574	178564	168984
1820	Dressing & dyeing of fur; processing of fur		...	...	...	...		...	...	...	...		...	...	...	...
191	Tanning, dressing and processing of leather		...	...	...	...		...	...	...	...		...	...	...	...
1911	Tanning and dressing of leather		...	...	...	...		...	...	...	...		...	...	...	...
1912	Luggage, handbags, etc.; saddlery & harness		...	...	...	...		...	...	...	...		...	...	...	...
1920	Footwear		3	3	3	3		9638	8591	1942	2159		27526	22843	5074	6193
2010	Sawmilling and planing of wood		...	...	...	...		...	...	...	...		...	...	...	...
202	Products of wood, cork, straw, etc.		...	...	...	...		...	...	...	...		...	...	...	...
2021	Veneer sheets, plywood, particle board, etc.		...	...	...	...		...	...	...	...		...	...	...	...
2022	Builders' carpentry and joinery		...	...	...	...		...	...	...	...		...	...	...	...
2023	Wooden containers		...	...	...	...		...	...	...	...		...	...	...	...
2029	Other wood products; articles of cork/straw		...	...	...	...		...	...	...	...		...	...	...	...
210	Paper and paper products		...	...	...	...		...	...	...	...		...	...	...	...
2101	Pulp, paper and paperboard		...	...	...	...		...	...	...	...		...	...	...	...
2102	Corrugated paper and paperboard		...	...	...	...		...	...	...	...		...	...	...	...
2109	Other articles of paper and paperboard		...	...	...	...		...	...	...	...		...	...	...	...
221	Publishing		...	...	...	...		...	...	...	...		...	...	...	...
2211	Publishing of books and other publications		...	...	...	...		...	...	...	...		...	...	...	...
2212	Publishing of newspapers, journals, etc.		...	...	...	...		...	...	...	...		...	...	...	...
2213	Publishing of recorded media		...	...	...	...		...	...	...	...		...	...	...	...
2219	Other publishing		...	...	...	...		...	...	...	...		...	...	...	...

222	Printing and related service activities	...	...	...	...	...	...	...	...	...	...	...	...
2221	Printing	4	4	4	4	479	943	543	569	1920	4459	2193	2550
2222	Service activities related to printing	...	...	...	...	...	...	...	...	...	...	...	...
2230	Reproduction of recorded media	...	...	...	...	...	...	...	...	...	...	...	...
2310	Coke oven products	...	...	...	...	...	...	...	...	...	...	...	...
2320	Refined petroleum products	1	1	1	1	142	156	178	162	246	325	465	406
2330	Processing of nuclear fuel	...	...	...	...	...	...	...	...	...	...	...	...
241	Basic chemicals	...	...	...	...	...	...	...	...	...	...	...	...
2411	Basic chemicals, except fertilizers	...	...	...	...	...	...	...	...	...	...	...	...
2412	Fertilizers and nitrogen compounds	...	...	...	...	...	...	...	...	...	...	...	...
2413	Plastics in primary forms; synthetic rubber	...	...	...	...	...	...	...	...	...	...	...	...
242	Other chemicals	...	...	...	...	...	...	...	...	...	...	...	...
2421	Pesticides and other agro-chemical products	...	...	...	...	...	...	...	...	...	...	...	...
2422	Paints, varnishes, printing ink and mastics	...	...	...	...	...	...	...	...	...	...	...	...
2423	Pharmaceuticals, medicinal chemicals, etc.	1	1	1	1	439	422	1283	1250	4610	3692	5751	5796
2424	Soap, cleaning & cosmetic preparations	...	...	...	...	...	...	...	...	...	...	...	...
2429	Other chemical products n.e.c.	...	...	...	...	...	...	...	...	...	...	...	...
2430	Man-made fibres	...	...	...	...	...	...	...	...	...	...	...	...
251	Rubber products	...	...	...	...	...	...	...	...	...	...	...	...
2511	Rubber tyres and tubes	...	...	...	...	...	...	...	...	...	...	...	...
2519	Other rubber products	...	...	...	...	...	...	...	...	...	...	...	...
2520	Plastic products	...	...	...	...	...	...	...	...	...	...	...	...
2610	Glass and glass products	...	...	...	...	...	...	...	...	...	...	...	...
269	Non-metallic mineral products n.e.c.	...	...	...	...	...	...	...	...	...	...	...	...
2691	Pottery, china and earthenware	...	...	...	...	...	...	...	...	...	...	...	...
2692	Refractory ceramic products	1	2	2	1	24	94	79	73	52	186	159	420
2693	Struct.non-refractory clay; ceramic products	1	1	1	1	591	570	382	1320	...	...	...	...
2694	Cement, lime and plaster	...	...	...	...	...	...	...	...	...	...	...	...
2695	Articles of concrete, cement and plaster	4	3	1	2	...	...	...	...	5215	5367	5100	1950
2696	Cutting, shaping & finishing of stone	...	...	...	...	...	...	...	...	...	...	...	...
2699	Other non-metallic mineral products n.e.c.	...	...	...	...	...	...	...	...	...	...	...	...
2710	Basic iron and steel	1	1	1	1	443	681	978	1063	2217	3282	5214	5891
2720	Basic precious and non-ferrous metals	...	...	...	...	...	...	...	...	...	...	...	...
273	Casting of metals	...	...	...	...	...	...	...	...	...	...	...	...
2731	Casting of iron and steel	...	...	...	...	...	...	...	...	...	...	...	...
2732	Casting of non-ferrous metals	...	...	...	...	...	...	...	...	...	...	...	...
281	Struct.metal products;tanks;steam generators	...	...	...	...	...	...	...	...	...	...	...	...
2811	Structural metal products	...	...	...	...	...	...	...	...	...	...	...	...
2812	Tanks, reservoirs and containers of metal	...	...	...	...	...	...	...	...	...	...	...	...
2813	Steam generators	...	...	...	...	...	...	...	...	...	...	...	...
289	Other metal products; metal working services	...	...	...	...	...	...	...	...	...	...	...	...
2891	Metal forging/pressing/stamping/roll-forming	...	...	...	...	...	...	...	...	...	...	...	...
2892	Treatment & coating of metals	...	...	...	...	...	...	...	...	...	...	...	...
2893	Cutlery, hand tools and general hardware	...	...	...	...	...	...	...	...	...	...	...	...
2899	Other fabricated metal products n.e.c.	1	1	1	1	338	321	331	75	1037	1171	1338	409
291	General purpose machinery	...	...	...	...	...	...	...	...	...	...	...	...
2911	Engines & turbines (not for transport equipment)	...	...	...	...	...	...	...	...	...	...	...	...
2912	Pumps, compressors, taps and valves	...	...	...	...	...	...	...	...	...	...	...	...
2913	Bearings, gears, gearing & driving elements	...	...	...	...	...	...	...	...	...	...	...	...
2914	Ovens, furnaces and furnace burners	...	...	...	...	...	...	...	...	...	...	...	...
2915	Lifting and handling equipment	...	...	...	...	...	...	...	...	...	...	...	...
2919	Other general purpose machinery	...	...	...	...	...	...	...	...	...	...	...	...
292	Special purpose machinery	...	...	...	...	...	...	...	...	...	...	...	...
2921	Agricultural and forestry machinery	...	...	...	...	...	...	...	...	...	...	...	...
2922	Machine tools	...	...	...	...	...	...	...	...	...	...	...	...
2923	Machinery for metallurgy	...	...	...	...	...	...	...	...	...	...	...	...
2924	Machinery for mining & construction	...	...	...	...	...	...	...	...	...	...	...	...
2925	Food/beverage/tobacco processing machinery	...	...	...	...	...	...	...	...	...	...	...	...
2926	Machinery for textile, apparel and leather	...	...	...	...	...	...	...	...	...	...	...	...
2927	Weapons and ammunition	...	...	...	...	...	...	...	...	...	...	...	...
2929	Other special purpose machinery	...	...	...	...	...	...	...	...	...	...	...	...

continued

Lesotho

ISIC Revision 3		Number of establishments					Number of employees					Wages and salaries paid to employees				
			(number)					(number)					(thousands of Lesotho Maloti)			
ISIC	Industry	Note	2003	2004	2005	2006	Note	2003	2004	2005	2006	Note	2003	2004	2005	2006
2930	Domestic appliances n.e.c.		...	...	...	...		...	...	...	...		...	...	...	...
3000	Office, accounting and computing machinery		...	...	...	...		...	...	...	...		...	...	...	...
3110	Electric motors, generators and transformers		...	...	...	...		...	...	...	...		...	...	...	...
3120	Electricity distribution & control apparatus		...	...	...	...		...	...	...	...		...	...	...	...
3130	Insulated wire and cable		...	...	...	...		...	...	...	...		...	...	...	...
3140	Accumulators, primary cells and batteries		...	...	...	...		...	...	...	...		...	...	...	...
3150	Lighting equipment and electric lamps		...	...	...	...		...	...	...	...		...	...	...	...
3190	Other electrical equipment n.e.c.		...	...	...	...		...	...	...	...		...	...	...	...
3210	Electronic valves, tubes, etc.		...	...	...	...		...	...	...	...		...	...	...	...
3220	TV/radio transmitters; line comm. apparatus		...	...	...	...		...	...	...	...		...	...	...	...
3230	TV and radio receivers and associated goods		1	1	1	1		1140	1432	1387	1372		2641	3681	4106	3902
331	Medical, measuring, testing appliances, etc.		...	...	...	...		...	...	...	...		...	...	...	...
3311	Medical, surgical and orthopaedic equipment		...	...	...	...		...	...	...	...		...	...	...	...
3312	Measuring/testing/navigating appliances,etc.		...	...	...	...		...	...	...	...		...	...	...	...
3313	Industrial process control equipment		...	...	...	...		...	...	...	...		...	...	...	...
3320	Optical instruments & photographic equipment		...	...	...	...		...	...	...	...		...	...	...	...
3330	Watches and clocks		...	...	...	...		...	...	...	...		...	...	...	...
3410	Motor vehicles		...	...	...	...		...	...	...	...		...	...	...	...
3420	Automobile bodies, trailers & semi-trailers		...	...	...	...		...	...	...	...		...	...	...	...
3430	Parts/accessories for automobiles		...	...	...	...		...	...	...	...		...	...	...	...
351	Building and repairing of ships and boats		...	...	...	...		...	...	...	...		...	...	...	...
3511	Building and repairing of ships		...	...	...	...		...	...	...	...		...	...	...	...
3512	Building/repairing of pleasure/sport. boats		...	...	...	...		...	...	...	...		...	...	...	...
3520	Railway/tramway locomotives & rolling stock		...	...	...	...		...	...	...	...		...	...	...	...
3530	Aircraft and spacecraft		...	...	...	...		...	...	...	...		...	...	...	...
359	Transport equipment n.e.c.		...	...	...	...		...	...	...	...		...	...	...	...
3591	Motorcycles		...	...	...	...		...	...	...	...		...	...	...	...
3592	Bicycles and invalid carriages		...	...	...	...		...	...	...	...		...	...	...	...
3599	Other transport equipment n.e.c.		...	...	...	...		...	...	...	...		...	...	...	...
3610	Furniture		2	2	1	1		815	759	698	742		1819	1647	1996	2084
369	Manufacturing n.e.c.		...	...	...	...		...	...	...	...		...	...	...	...
3691	Jewellery and related articles		...	...	...	...		...	...	...	...		...	...	...	...
3692	Musical instruments		...	...	...	...		...	...	...	...		...	...	...	...
3693	Sports goods		...	...	...	...		...	...	...	...		...	...	...	...
3694	Games and toys		...	...	...	...		...	...	...	...		...	...	...	...
3699	Other manufacturing n.e.c.		...	...	...	...		...	...	...	...		...	...	...	...
3710	Recycling of metal waste and scrap		...	...	...	...		...	...	...	...		...	...	...	...
3720	Recycling of non-metal waste and scrap		...	...	...	...		...	...	...	...		...	...	...	...
D	Total manufacturing		43	52	45	45		91599	138672	101464	118045		260890	395451	331943	355766

Lithuania

Supplier of information:
Statistics Lithuania, Vilnius.

Basic source of data:
Annual survey; administrative data.

Major deviations from ISIC (Revision 3):
None reported.

Reference period:
Calendar year.

Scope:
All registered enterprises.

Method of data collection:
The survey was based on information obtained through mail questionnaires, online survey and administrative data.

Type of enumeration:
Complete enumeration.

Adjusted for non-response:
Yes.

Concepts and definitions of variables:
Output includes revenue from non-industrial activities.
Value added includes cost of non-industrial activities.

Related national publications:
None reported.

Lithuania

ISIC Revision 3		Number of enterprises					Number of employees					Wages and salaries paid to employees				
			(number)					(number)					(millions of Lithuanian Litas)			
ISIC	Industry	Note	2003	2004	2005	2006	Note	2003	2004	2005	2006	Note	2003	2004	2005	2006
151	Processed meat,fish,fruit,vegetables,fats		452	396	358	316		15127	15468	16439	16567		114.3	132.5	153.2	191.5
1511	Processing/preserving of meat		312	275	239	216		9715	9777	10667	10706		60.6	69.5	85.8	111.6
1512	Processing/preserving of fish		89	73	70	56		4484	4772	4763	4835		44.0	52.6	55.1	66.7
1513	Processing/preserving of fruit & vegetables		41	38	39	36		822	830	917	876		8.0	9.0	10.9	10.9
1514	Vegetable and animal oils and fats		10	10	10	8		106	89	92	150		1.7	1.4	1.4	2.4
1520	Dairy products		39	33	36	33		10466	10931	9576	9140		131.9	244.5	147.9	160.8
153	Grain mill products; starches; animal feeds		107	92	81	77		3034	2928	3329	2915		41.5	46.3	54.7	61.7
1531	Grain mill products		81	69	61	53		1236	1205	1711	1290		12.4	13.6	20.3	20.8
1532	Starches and starch products		2	2	2	2		80	78	77	63		0.8	0.8	0.8	0.8
1533	Prepared animal feeds		24	21	18	22		1718	1645	1541	1562		28.3	31.9	33.6	40.2
154	Other food products		643	580	521	490		18786	18021	17238	17332		176.6	183.3	184.4	217.3
1541	Bakery products		550	493	439	409		13932	13451	12525	12731		100.8	108.4	109.3	128.1
1542	Sugar		3	3	4	3		1151	1066	920	767		19.5	19.2	17.9	17.1
1543	Cocoa, chocolate and sugar confectionery		25	27	23	23		2276	2171	2291	2374		41.7	42.3	41.7	53.9
1544	Macaroni, noodles & similar products		25	20	19	20		627	514	537	517		3.6	3.6	4.1	5.2
1549	Other food products n.e.c.		40	37	36	35		800	819	965	943		11.0	9.9	11.4	13.0
155	Beverages		133	129	115	112		5951	5478	4943	4733		104.3	100.6	98.2	110.5
1551	Distilling, rectifying & blending of spirits		4	4	4	4		1152	1002	706	678		22.7	21.2	16.1	18.3
1552	Wines		4	4	4	4		1036	909	814	752		18.1	15.8	15.1	14.7
1553	Malt liquors and malt		77	76	71	68		2495	2446	2388	2358		55.7	54.9	57.6	65.9
1554	Soft drinks; mineral waters		48	45	36	36		1268	1121	1035	945		7.8	8.7	9.4	11.6
1600	Tobacco products		1	1	1	1		483	488	531	556		23.0	22.7	25.8	28.1
171	Spinning, weaving and finishing of textiles		83	74	75	73		10951	10387	10250	9296		125.9	124.7	123.3	134.0
1711	Textile fibre preparation; textile weaving		65	57	58	54		10571	9760	9896	8897		122.0	116.8	118.7	127.5
1712	Finishing of textiles		18	17	17	19		380	627	354	399		4.0	7.8	4.6	6.5
172	Other textiles		112	118	117	120		3551	3510	3797	4545		39.3	43.5	45.4	59.7
1721	Made-up textile articles, except apparel		75	77	76	82		2686	2642	2794	3384		31.0	32.7	32.5	41.6
1722	Carpets and rugs		2	2	3	3		72	62	74	71		0.9	0.7	1.0	1.1
1723	Cordage, rope, twine and netting		9	9	10	10		366	323	384	543		3.4	4.4	4.6	7.6
1729	Other textiles n.e.c.		26	30	28	25		427	483	545	547		3.9	5.7	7.3	9.4
1730	Knitted and crocheted fabrics and articles		177	166	156	139		4799	4736	3676	3517		39.5	45.3	35.9	37.6
1810	Wearing apparel, except fur apparel		933	835	805	758		47838	37877	34190	29993		317.1	320.1	315.2	319.3
1820	Dressing & dyeing of fur; processing of fur		26	21	20	18		562	567	536	523		4.3	4.7	5.0	5.4
191	Tanning, dressing and processing of leather		55	54	60	51		1207	1002	1050	866		9.3	9.1	11.4	8.4
1911	Tanning and dressing of leather		15	14	13	10		633	447	401	293		6.6	5.8	6.3	4.5
1912	Luggage, handbags, etc.; saddlery & harness		40	40	47	41		574	555	649	573		2.7	3.3	5.1	3.9
1920	Footwear		47	44	34	32		1372	1305	954	809		11.6	12.9	11.1	10.0
2010	Sawmilling and planing of wood		882	845	836	784		13469	13864	13428	13995		86.9	103.7	114.5	144.4
202	Products of wood, cork, straw, etc.		767	729	702	713		14891	15177	15054	15486		131.6	145.0	162.3	212.2
2021	Veneer sheets, plywood, particle board, etc.		43	40	50	44		3582	3410	3853	3422		49.9	49.9	62.1	67.9
2022	Builders' carpentry and joinery		401	392	377	388		6041	6594	6158	7127		47.1	54.5	57.2	91.8
2023	Wooden containers		117	106	104	105		2768	2463	2678	2556		17.4	18.4	21.0	26.6
2029	Other wood products; articles of cork/straw		206	191	171	176		2500	2710	2365	2381		17.3	22.2	22.0	25.9
210	Paper and paper products		104	103	93	87		2175	2062	1965	2243		30.4	32.3	34.6	42.6
2101	Pulp, paper and paperboard		12	8	7	8		576	413	363	412		10.1	7.6	8.0	9.7
2102	Corrugated paper and paperboard		25	27	25	29		865	801	759	1123		12.5	14.9	14.4	22.7
2109	Other articles of paper and paperboard		67	68	61	50		734	848	843	708		7.9	9.9	12.2	10.2
221	Publishing		566	552	578	588		6476	6500	6564	6358		97.2	99.4	117.2	111.1
2211	Publishing of books and other publications		209	199	217	219		1291	1288	1443	1479		17.9	18.0	23.4	26.7
2212	Publishing of newspapers, journals, etc.		267	256	256	260		4745	4762	4628	4361		76.1	77.9	89.4	78.7
2213	Publishing of recorded media		16	18	16	19		131	98	124	130		0.9	0.7	0.8	1.1
2219	Other publishing		74	79	89	90		309	352	369	388		2.3	2.8	3.7	4.5

222	Printing and related service activities	295	284	279	294	3628	3840	3828	4733	43.1	47.7	51.4	77.4
2221	Printing	217	214	208	226	3126	3326	3267	4177	36.8	41.7	43.9	68.4
2222	Service activities related to printing	78	70	71	68	502	514	561	556	6.3	6.0	7.4	9.0
2230	Reproduction of recorded media	27	21	18	18	70	78	86	53	0.4	0.5	0.8	0.8
2310	Coke oven products	-	-	-	-	-	-	-	-	-	-	-	-
2320	Refined petroleum products	4	3	3	3	3585	3531	3454	3466	133.7	135.2	145.4	144.2
2330	Processing of nuclear fuel	-	-	-	-	-	-	-	-	-	-	-	-
241	Basic chemicals	28	29	29	29	3044	3142	3420	3772	70.6	79.1	105.5	135.2
2411	Basic chemicals, except fertilizers	20	20	18	16	430	438	441	481	8.9	11.0	12.8	14.8
2412	Fertilizers and nitrogen compounds	4	6	5	7	2471	2554	2634	2774	60.6	66.8	81.9	103.2
2413	Plastics in primary forms; synthetic rubber	4	3	6	6	143	150	345	517	1.1	1.3	10.8	17.2
242	Other chemicals	97	89	85	89	2082	1909	1832	1838	27.7	30.7	30.9	35.6
2421	Pesticides and other agro-chemical products	1	1	-	-	...	...	-	-	...	...	-	-
2422	Paints, varnishes, printing ink and mastics	29	27	26	32	251	263	356	405	2.7	3.2	4.6	6.2
2423	Pharmaceuticals, medicinal chemicals, etc.	19	17	18	17	1084	944	841	800	18.0	19.6	18.3	20.1
2424	Soap, cleaning & cosmetic preparations	28	26	23	22	518	510	500	497	5.3	5.7	6.1	6.8
2429	Other chemical products n.e.c.	20	18	18	18	229	192	135	136	1.8	2.1	1.8	2.5
2430	Man-made fibres	1	1	1	1	704	176	405	424	6.5	4.6	5.8	8.1
251	Rubber products	29	29	32	30	256	259	255	330	2.1	2.5	3.0	4.6
2511	Rubber tyres and tubes	9	9	14	11	84	94	105	102	0.8	1.0	1.3	1.7
2519	Other rubber products	20	20	18	19	172	165	150	228	1.3	1.4	1.6	2.9
2520	Plastic products	345	340	340	360	7363	8187	8369	9098	81.2	106.0	119.7	154.2
2610	Glass and glass products	59	56	62	63	1612	1671	2168	2307	21.4	23.8	33.0	43.9
269	Non-metallic mineral products n.e.c.	504	492	483	479	8204	8328	8491	8951	101.0	112.1	130.5	172.9
2691	Pottery, china and earthenware	84	76	75	66	1048	990	924	727	6.8	6.7	6.6	6.3
2692	Refractory ceramic products	8	8	8	7	356	378	218	227	4.8	5.3	2.8	4.5
2693	Struct.non-refractory clay; ceramic products	15	17	16	15	1192	1136	979	987	14.6	14.6	14.4	16.5
2694	Cement, lime and plaster	3	3	4	3	742	744	769	797	14.2	14.5	16.8	20.8
2695	Articles of concrete, cement and plaster	135	121	121	122	3519	3612	4058	4514	47.3	56.1	71.7	100.9
2696	Cutting, shaping & finishing of stone	245	251	242	246	1009	1095	1080	1161	4.2	5.2	5.9	8.0
2699	Other non-metallic mineral products n.e.c.	14	16	17	20	338	373	463	538	9.0	9.7	12.3	15.9
2710	Basic iron and steel	13	8	10	15	244	112	77	122	4.5	1.3	1.1	1.7
2720	Basic precious and non-ferrous metals	4	2	5	5	21	19	79	74	0.1	0.1	0.6	0.7
273	Casting of metals	17	15	15	15	835	799	832	724	11.1	11.5	11.9	13.2
2731	Casting of iron and steel	9	7	7	7	720	688	716	591	10.2	10.6	10.7	11.7
2732	Casting of non-ferrous metals	8	8	8	8	115	111	116	133	0.9	0.9	1.2	1.4
281	Struct.metal products;tanks;steam generators	248	244	263	288	5734	6487	7130	8141	54.6	81.4	97.6	149.8
2811	Structural metal products	218	214	231	253	4222	4832	4931	5427	36.8	55.3	62.6	88.2
2812	Tanks, reservoirs and containers of metal	28	28	31	34	1448	1385	1947	2485	16.4	18.0	27.5	53.3
2813	Steam generators	2	2	1	1	64	270	252	229	1.3	8.1	7.5	8.2
289	Other metal products; metal working services	417	422	428	452	7419	8720	9073	9371	72.9	98.1	123.8	142.4
2891	Metal forging/pressing/stamping/roll-forming	37	38	47	50	902	1107	1077	907	13.3	18.3	17.3	18.2
2892	Treatment & coating of metals	82	88	98	111	828	1080	1299	1707	7.4	11.0	16.1	26.1
2893	Cutlery, hand tools and general hardware	72	62	57	53	1033	936	632	789	8.5	7.9	8.7	11.5
2899	Other fabricated metal products n.e.c.	226	234	226	238	4656	5597	6065	5968	43.7	60.8	81.7	86.6
291	General purpose machinery	146	144	149	151	5304	5014	4755	5399	68.8	71.1	71.8	103.3
2911	Engines & turbines (not for transport equipment)	15	14	12	11	1151	1045	824	767	14.9	15.8	14.6	15.5
2912	Pumps, compressors, taps and valves	18	16	17	17	597	360	322	401	7.5	4.8	4.5	5.4
2913	Bearings, gears, gearing & driving elements	8	10	13	12	140	130	166	175	0.9	1.1	1.6	2.2
2914	Ovens, furnaces and furnace burners	9	9	6	6	104	125	61	366	1.5	2.0	0.4	6.3
2915	Lifting and handling equipment	25	23	24	26	863	761	820	782	12.3	12.5	14.4	17.7
2919	Other general purpose machinery	71	72	77	79	2449	2593	2562	2908	31.6	34.9	36.3	56.1
292	Special purpose machinery	145	141	139	140	3306	3126	2821	3148	40.7	43.4	43.5	58.6
2921	Agricultural and forestry machinery	44	46	45	47	1039	1013	804	888	8.9	9.4	8.9	12.0
2922	Machine tools	28	29	32	32	300	288	315	353	1.7	2.0	2.4	3.5
2923	Machinery for metallurgy	-	-	-	-	-	-	-	-	-	-	-	-
2924	Machinery for mining & construction	4	4	3	4	233	181	28	75	3.5	4.0	0.3	1.3
2925	Food/beverage/tobacco processing machinery	11	11	10	12	189	190	171	298	3.8	4.0	3.5	6.1
2926	Machinery for textile, apparel and leather	4	3	5	3	47	40	60	53	0.6	0.6	1.0	0.8
2927	Weapons and ammunition	4	5	5	4	92	94	103	96	1.5	1.6	1.6	1.7
2929	Other special purpose machinery	50	43	39	38	1406	1320	1340	1385	20.7	21.7	25.8	33.2

continued

ISIC Revision 3		Number of enterprises					Number of employees					Wages and salaries paid to employees				
			(number)					(number)					(millions of Lithuanian Litas)			
ISIC	Industry	Note	2003	2004	2005	2006	Note	2003	2004	2005	2006	Note	2003	2004	2005	2006
2930	Domestic appliances n.e.c.		37	34	28	28		2455	2399	2265	2194		32.6	35.0	33.5	38.2
3000	Office, accounting and computing machinery		46	43	42	39		414	483	313	402		3.8	5.0	3.5	5.8
3110	Electric motors, generators and transformers		66	58	56	52		490	494	501	486		4.5	5.6	5.1	7.4
3120	Electricity distribution & control apparatus		45	39	40	48		1647	1530	1433	1777		21.0	20.6	20.6	28.0
3130	Insulated wire and cable		9	8	12	7		879	1010	909	688		9.3	11.6	11.8	12.0
3140	Accumulators, primary cells and batteries		5	3	2	2		76	65	58	57		1.5	1.6	1.5	1.9
3150	Lighting equipment and electric lamps		10	10	11	11		120	161	230	273		1.4	2.7	3.6	4.3
3190	Other electrical equipment n.e.c.		34	31	27	29		3505	3593	3303	3101		44.3	46.7	45.3	49.6
3210	Electronic valves, tubes, etc.		15	13	12	12		4373	4948	6208	3442		75.9	90.8	99.9	73.3
3220	TV/radio transmitters; line comm. apparatus		21	21	18	16		342	372	295	338		4.4	5.4	5.6	8.8
3230	TV and radio receivers and associated goods		36	39	34	37		3449	3884	1900	1956		40.9	48.3	27.1	33.7
331	Medical, measuring, testing appliances, etc.		205	222	242	279		3370	3467	3492	3581		45.1	49.3	57.5	65.3
3311	Medical, surgical and orthopaedic equipment		137	149	172	197		1545	1755	1848	2170		18.6	20.8	26.5	33.4
3312	Measuring/testing/navigating appliances,etc.		59	61	58	64		1749	1583	1424	1155		25.0	26.2	27.4	26.4
3313	Industrial process control equipment		9	12	12	18		76	129	220	256		1.5	2.3	3.6	5.5
3320	Optical instruments & photographic equipment		16	10	7	9		185	162	169	209		5.6	5.5	6.3	7.9
3330	Watches and clocks		1	-	2	2		...	-	1	1		...	-	-	-
3410	Motor vehicles		3	4	4	4		66	147	159	121		0.6	1.2	1.9	1.6
3420	Automobile bodies, trailers & semi-trailers		12	10	11	13		298	360	461	722		3.4	4.9	6.5	16.5
3430	Parts/accessories for automobiles		14	15	14	16		379	202	263	330		0.7	1.3	2.2	4.0
351	Building and repairing of ships and boats		86	85	100	107		5131	4546	4655	5071		88.1	84.9	96.0	125.9
3511	Building and repairing of ships		77	77	85	97		5023	4414	4430	4832		87.0	83.0	93.1	121.5
3512	Building/repairing of pleasure/sport. boats		9	8	15	10		108	132	225	239		1.1	1.8	2.9	4.3
3520	Railway/tramway locomotives & rolling stock		5	6	6	5		650	768	752	709		3.1	14.6	16.2	18.4
3530	Aircraft and spacecraft		15	13	17	19		344	375	416	447		4.7	4.7	6.9	7.8
359	Transport equipment n.e.c.		7	6	9	12		1059	911	965	943		18.3	15.1	17.8	17.6
3591	Motorcycles		-	-	-	-		-	-	-	-		-	-	-	-
3592	Bicycles and invalid carriages		4	3	4	6		1038	884	932	914		18.1	15.0	17.5	17.4
3599	Other transport equipment n.e.c.		3	3	5	6		21	27	33	29		0.1	0.2	0.3	0.2
3610	Furniture		545	571	644	701		18437	20089	22575	24442		190.5	227.8	267.6	353.6
369	Manufacturing n.e.c.		238	228	236	227		2481	2477	2406	2573		20.7	24.1	28.0	36.1
3691	Jewellery and related articles		89	87	98	95		844	873	877	832		5.3	7.2	8.7	10.2
3692	Musical instruments		8	8	7	7		35	26	26	28		0.2	0.2	0.2	0.3
3693	Sports goods		14	14	15	15		109	98	104	118		0.7	0.7	0.8	1.1
3694	Games and toys		20	19	20	19		234	234	196	214		1.6	1.7	1.9	2.0
3699	Other manufacturing n.e.c.		107	100	96	91		1259	1246	1203	1381		12.9	14.2	16.3	22.6
3710	Recycling of metal waste and scrap		30	30	34	41		1096	1118	1139	1189		9.5	13.4	16.8	23.7
3720	Recycling of non-metal waste and scrap		23	23	20	28		517	533	362	482		3.5	4.4	3.9	6.3
D	Total manufacturing		9030	8614	8557	8568		266312	259793	255825	256359		2858.8	3243.9	3401.5	4048.2

ISIC Revision 3		Output in factor values					Value added in factor values					Gross fixed capital formation	
		(millions of Lithuanian Litas)					(millions of Lithuanian Litas)					(millions of Lithuanian Litas)	
ISIC Industry	Note	2003	2004	2005	2006	Note	2003	2004	2005	2006	Note	2005	2006
151 Processed meat,fish,fruit,vegetables,fats		1337.7	1669.9	2132.9	2351.2		193.0	272.4	327.0	348.1		97.4	93.0
1511 Processing/preserving of meat		771.3	992.8	1305.4	1510.5		98.4	138.8	165.6	202.3		67.0	64.7
1512 Processing/preserving of fish		437.2	548.4	672.9	681.8		70.4	107.3	121.7	115.0		23.6	18.9
1513 Processing/preserving of fruit & vegetables		97.3	95.9	125.9	129.3		18.3	20.8	32.3	25.0		6.0	4.9
1514 Vegetable and animal oils and fats		31.9	32.8	28.7	29.6		5.9	5.4	7.4	5.8		0.8	4.5
1520 Dairy products		1298.1	1575.3	1782.2	2082.6		287.1	326.7	349.8	468.4		92.5	129.6
153 Grain mill products; starches; animal feeds		782.0	834.7	901.9	1066.3		145.7	152.0	140.3	182.4		96.1	136.7
1531 Grain mill products		147.2	199.3	217.8	213.6		22.6	37.5	48.2	49.5		61.2	87.2
1532 Starches and starch products		6.1	5.5	4.0	4.1		1.5	1.3	1.0	1.2		2.3	7.3
1533 Prepared animal feeds		628.7	629.9	680.2	848.5		121.6	113.2	91.1	131.7		32.7	42.1
154 Other food products		1248.5	1257.6	1290.0	1405.9		372.4	376.4	402.1	423.4		87.4	107.0
1541 Bakery products		526.1	544.6	518.3	606.4		174.6	189.8	179.2	202.7		49.6	47.7
1542 Sugar		257.6	277.7	278.8	234.5		62.7	69.9	83.0	58.3		8.4	24.8
1543 Cocoa, chocolate and sugar confectionery		339.4	304.1	324.7	383.8		97.9	91.6	92.6	115.6		9.4	16.0
1544 Macaroni, noodles & similar products		32.6	35.3	40.0	45.6		12.7	4.5	20.9	16.7		11.8	5.0
1549 Other food products n.e.c.		92.8	95.9	128.2	135.6		24.5	20.6	26.3	30.1		8.1	13.4
155 Beverages		984.6	1027.4	1130.3	1312.5		332.6	367.2	375.7	408.0		60.7	81.7
1551 Distilling, rectifying & blending of spirits		139.1	135.7	158.6	224.2		51.9	42.7	52.6	55.8		15.6	18.7
1552 Wines		182.7	202.2	190.6	205.4		52.8	80.2	57.4	54.5		9.2	3.6
1553 Malt liquors and malt		572.2	591.8	678.2	754.6		207.5	223.5	246.7	268.4		26.5	48.7
1554 Soft drinks; mineral waters		90.6	97.7	103.0	128.3		20.5	20.8	18.9	29.3		9.4	10.8
1600 Tobacco products		234.2	270.9	450.6	487.4		82.2	92.3	148.3	107.7		45.1	64.6
171 Spinning, weaving and finishing of textiles		664.8	646.8	677.5	629.1		192.9	211.3	209.0	213.0		71.4	40.1
1711 Textile fibre preparation; textile weaving		644.4	590.4	640.1	585.8		186.0	200.4	200.0	201.6		67.9	36.8
1712 Finishing of textiles		20.4	56.3	37.4	43.3		6.9	10.9	9.0	11.5		3.5	3.3
172 Other textiles		287.4	365.0	367.5	431.6		83.3	103.0	110.8	123.8		39.8	37.3
1721 Made-up textile articles, except apparel		222.5	241.6	209.8	258.1		68.1	76.2	66.2	76.7		9.8	26.7
1722 Carpets and rugs		3.5	3.0	4.8	4.4		1.5	1.5	2.4	2.7		0.5	1.6
1723 Cordage, rope, twine and netting		33.0	55.6	56.3	66.2		2.7	9.5	16.6	20.0		18.1	6.3
1729 Other textiles n.e.c.		28.4	64.9	96.5	102.9		11.0	15.8	25.7	24.4		11.3	2.7
1730 Knitted and crocheted fabrics and articles		174.2	209.1	180.1	169.7		71.3	77.2	62.9	64.5		11.9	9.4
1810 Wearing apparel, except fur apparel		1177.6	1187.5	1184.3	1194.5		553.7	548.7	543.7	520.8		49.0	44.3
1820 Dressing & dyeing of fur; processing of fur		21.9	21.9	28.2	36.0		5.3	7.6	9.8	11.3		3.3	2.8
191 Tanning, dressing and processing of leather		78.5	88.3	87.5	61.2		19.5	-5.5	15.1	24.7		4.6	17.5
1911 Tanning and dressing of leather		68.4	62.7	47.4	44.6		14.6	-11.1	3.7	16.3		3.6	17.1
1912 Luggage, handbags, etc.; saddlery & harness		10.0	25.6	40.1	16.6		4.9	5.6	11.4	8.4		0.9	0.3
1920 Footwear		46.6	44.5	46.3	43.4		17.3	17.1	16.2	18.1		1.6	4.3
2010 Sawmilling and planing of wood		852.5	973.0	1117.0	1187.2		200.7	218.5	257.1	283.5		89.0	110.9
202 Products of wood, cork, straw, etc.		908.5	1036.6	1226.0	1432.2		257.4	298.3	345.5	436.9		137.7	305.1
2021 Veneer sheets, plywood, particle board, etc.		350.0	385.7	478.2	494.5		93.3	119.7	139.7	150.2		74.4	210.4
2022 Builders' carpentry and joinery		311.5	374.5	411.6	569.6		93.6	103.8	111.1	177.8		46.2	68.5
2023 Wooden containers		131.6	146.7	183.1	199.6		37.7	35.7	52.1	59.6		7.9	15.4
2029 Other wood products; articles of cork/straw		115.6	129.8	153.1	168.6		32.9	39.2	42.6	49.2		9.2	10.8
210 Paper and paper products		329.9	320.1	343.0	421.0		78.4	80.3	83.6	99.8		29.7	33.0
2101 Pulp, paper and paperboard		89.9	81.7	87.0	100.9		21.8	26.3	21.7	24.3		8.2	7.6
2102 Corrugated paper and paperboard		159.5	150.3	152.7	234.8		37.1	32.0	35.8	49.0		9.9	10.7
2109 Other articles of paper and paperboard		80.5	88.1	103.3	85.3		19.5	22.0	26.1	26.5		11.6	14.7
221 Publishing		513.2	554.1	648.5	678.1		194.1	210.3	236.4	200.3		60.0	94.6
2211 Publishing of books and other publications		114.2	125.5	161.2	194.0		44.0	50.0	62.7	58.6		14.9	32.6
2212 Publishing of newspapers, journals, etc.		351.8	380.3	442.0	424.3		137.2	146.0	157.8	126.2		39.5	59.3
2213 Publishing of recorded media		18.3	15.8	14.7	26.5		4.2	3.9	6.3	5.6		1.2	0.7
2219 Other publishing		29.0	32.5	30.6	33.3		8.7	10.4	9.5	9.9		4.5	2.0

continued

Lithuania

ISIC Revision 3		Output in factor values					Value added in factor values					Gross fixed capital formation		
			(millions of Lithuanian Litas)					(millions of Lithuanian Litas)					(millions of Lithuanian Litas)	
ISIC	Industry	Note	2003	2004	2005	2006	Note	2003	2004	2005	2006	Note	2005	2006
222	Printing and related service activities		345.7	361.9	398.1	580.6		119.1	115.5	141.3	193.0		30.0	70.3
2221	Printing		296.8	310.9	339.7	512.9		101.8	98.9	120.3	171.1		28.4	62.6
2222	Service activities related to printing		48.9	51.0	58.4	67.7		17.3	16.6	21.0	21.8		1.6	7.7
2230	Reproduction of recorded media		3.3	3.3	4.5	7.7		1.5	1.9	2.8	3.0		0.7	1.2
2310	Coke oven products		-	-	-	-		-	-	-	-		-	-
2320	Refined petroleum products		5330.5	7695.2	11417.1	11661.4		520.6	1214.4	1557.7	477.9		160.7	335.1
2330	Processing of nuclear fuel		-	-	-	-		-	-	-	-		-	-
241	Basic chemicals		1166.3	1391.1	1811.5	2534.4		184.5	248.9	446.7	414.4		524.7	242.7
2411	Basic chemicals, except fertilizers		51.0	57.0	64.2	78.9		21.6	25.7	29.8	37.6		5.1	10.4
2412	Fertilizers and nitrogen compounds		1107.0	1324.3	1684.4	1687.4		159.7	219.3	395.5	340.1		76.8	90.5
2413	Plastics in primary forms; synthetic rubber		8.3	9.8	63.0	768.1		3.1	4.0	21.3	36.7		442.9	141.8
242	Other chemicals		187.4	241.6	246.6	288.2		41.7	59.1	68.3	82.3		28.7	31.4
2421	Pesticides and other agro-chemical products		...	...	-	-		...	...	-	-		-	-
2422	Paints, varnishes, printing ink and mastics		32.9	45.8	62.6	73.3		8.9	9.0	14.5	18.0		3.1	3.6
2423	Pharmaceuticals, medicinal chemicals, etc.		92.7	123.9	110.7	116.5		21.6	36.1	40.7	44.7		22.0	9.4
2424	Soap, cleaning & cosmetic preparations		34.9	37.8	35.3	41.9		8.3	9.9	9.3	12.5		1.3	2.4
2429	Other chemical products n.e.c.		27.0	34.1	37.9	56.5		2.9	4.2	3.8	7.1		2.3	16.0
2430	Man-made fibres		20.4	8.3	64.6	81.2		4.0	0.4	5.5	18.8		0.1	0.2
251	Rubber products		13.4	14.0	18.4	30.8		4.6	5.0	5.8	9.6		2.5	1.8
2511	Rubber tyres and tubes		7.0	7.2	10.3	10.5		2.5	2.6	2.7	3.3		0.2	0.2
2519	Other rubber products		6.4	6.8	8.2	20.3		2.1	2.5	3.1	6.3		2.3	1.5
2520	Plastic products		1238.6	1389.3	1649.4	2021.6		251.2	269.6	331.4	522.1		153.1	134.1
2610	Glass and glass products		160.5	168.9	277.7	365.5		45.1	50.8	75.7	92.1		39.6	36.6
269	Non-metallic mineral products n.e.c.		663.7	756.3	959.1	1396.1		226.8	271.5	309.9	529.5		155.1	177.8
2691	Pottery, china and earthenware		21.7	19.9	19.5	15.8		11.6	11.5	10.1	8.9		2.7	0.8
2692	Refractory ceramic products		31.3	35.8	20.0	32.0		11.6	14.2	6.5	7.2		14.8	9.1
2693	Struct.non-refractory clay; ceramic products		58.9	64.1	61.9	67.9		22.7	30.1	30.1	35.3		3.0	3.6
2694	Cement, lime and plaster		108.7	126.1	148.1	242.5		33.2	31.8	31.6	84.4		20.6	14.3
2695	Articles of concrete, cement and plaster		328.8	378.3	547.7	798.0		99.6	130.1	176.2	300.4		58.8	126.7
2696	Cutting, shaping & finishing of stone		22.8	30.9	34.1	39.3		8.2	10.4	11.8	16.3		4.3	5.1
2699	Other non-metallic mineral products n.e.c.		91.5	101.0	127.8	200.6		40.0	43.5	43.7	76.9		51.0	18.4
2710	Basic iron and steel		61.4	12.4	9.6	12.5		9.0	3.2	1.8	2.9		0.1	3.4
2720	Basic precious and non-ferrous metals		0.7	0.4	18.8	16.8		0.2	0.2	2.7	3.9		1.1	1.5
273	Casting of metals		39.4	43.4	41.6	53.4		15.0	16.9	15.5	21.7		1.4	2.6
2731	Casting of iron and steel		34.2	39.4	36.6	46.6		12.6	14.5	13.7	18.5		1.1	2.3
2732	Casting of non-ferrous metals		5.2	4.0	5.0	6.8		2.4	2.4	1.8	3.2		0.2	0.3
281	Struct.metal products;tanks;steam generators		408.7	537.9	721.5	1052.7		116.5	160.9	212.0	322.2		51.8	69.5
2811	Structural metal products		313.4	416.6	544.1	745.4		83.3	115.9	146.5	208.6		38.4	54.3
2812	Tanks, reservoirs and containers of metal		92.9	108.2	162.2	295.4		31.0	33.2	54.8	103.3		13.2	15.2
2813	Steam generators		2.4	13.1	15.3	11.9		2.1	11.7	10.8	10.2		0.1	-
289	Other metal products; metal working services		400.9	620.1	815.1	1033.2		138.3	177.1	231.7	252.1		76.0	87.0
2891	Metal forging/pressing/stamping/roll-forming		66.5	81.9	72.0	205.2		24.2	26.0	23.4	18.7		7.9	5.9
2892	Treatment & coating of metals		48.5	92.3	120.0	172.1		13.3	17.1	29.2	45.8		12.4	10.6
2893	Cutlery, hand tools and general hardware		37.1	36.4	39.5	52.0		14.3	12.8	17.6	20.5		1.7	2.3
2899	Other fabricated metal products n.e.c.		248.7	409.5	583.6	603.9		86.5	121.3	161.5	167.1		54.0	68.2
291	General purpose machinery		298.6	323.7	373.8	579.9		107.6	121.4	139.2	214.1		31.7	38.8
2911	Engines & turbines (not for transport equipment)		63.7	57.4	42.3	46.7		22.2	19.3	12.2	22.5		2.4	1.9
2912	Pumps, compressors, taps and valves		23.9	20.5	22.5	31.3		2.8	8.3	8.4	10.8		1.7	1.4
2913	Bearings, gears, gearing & driving elements		4.8	5.3	7.2	7.6		1.7	2.1	3.2	3.6		0.9	1.3
2914	Ovens, furnaces and furnace burners		8.6	10.6	3.2	35.5		3.1	4.5	0.6	12.3		0.1	0.9
2915	Lifting and handling equipment		52.7	45.6	58.3	102.4		20.7	20.8	25.1	33.9		6.2	4.4
2919	Other general purpose machinery		144.8	184.3	240.2	356.3		57.1	66.5	89.7	130.9		20.4	28.9

292	Special purpose machinery	179.7	184.6	184.6	242.9	69.3	68.6	69.9	117.4	5.9	16.4
2921	Agricultural and forestry machinery	40.1	47.4	47.4	66.7	14.3	16.6	18.0	24.4	2.9	3.0
2922	Machine tools	7.9	8.9	13.6	19.2	3.4	3.3	5.6	7.5	0.6	0.9
2923	Machinery for metallurgy	-	-	-	-	-	-	-	-	-	-
2924	Machinery for mining & construction	16.0	12.0	2.0	7.8	4.4	5.7	0.8	3.4	0.1	0.3
2925	Food/beverage/tobacco processing machinery	17.4	27.4	13.2	43.3	7.0	5.3	3.0	28.3	0.2	9.9
2926	Machinery for textile, apparel and leather	3.4	1.4	3.3	3.4	1.4	0.6	2.1	1.3	0.3	0.3
2927	Weapons and ammunition	13.1	8.2	7.8	6.6	4.9	2.8	2.5	1.3	0.1	0.1
2929	Other special purpose machinery	81.8	79.3	97.3	95.9	33.9	34.4	37.7	51.1	1.9	1.9
2930	Domestic appliances n.e.c.	304.7	331.1	321.4	322.6	75.1	89.4	90.1	65.4	10.7	45.3
3000	Office, accounting and computing machinery	32.3	29.2	38.7	57.5	12.3	13.2	9.5	13.6	2.4	2.7
3110	Electric motors, generators and transformers	23.2	31.3	29.9	36.2	5.6	9.3	9.6	11.3	1.7	1.3
3120	Electricity distribution & control apparatus	132.9	126.1	134.1	167.1	34.3	37.3	41.0	52.3	4.6	4.7
3130	Insulated wire and cable	89.0	134.7	145.8	209.1	25.6	30.4	29.5	42.1	1.2	1.0
3140	Accumulators, primary cells and batteries	9.5	6.3	7.8	10.6	3.6	2.9	2.1	4.2	-	0.1
3150	Lighting equipment and electric lamps	9.9	26.5	70.7	67.5	2.3	7.2	9.3	13.9	1.1	1.9
3190	Other electrical equipment n.e.c.	502.3	540.3	394.0	453.4	123.3	160.2	74.5	170.1	3.3	2.9
3210	Electronic valves, tubes, etc.	508.1	562.8	454.2	255.9	183.9	192.6	107.7	50.6	13.8	6.3
3220	TV/radio transmitters; line comm. apparatus	52.3	50.6	59.0	70.5	8.9	6.2	15.1	25.3	10.9	5.6
3230	TV and radio receivers and associated goods	425.8	549.2	381.6	471.3	83.7	128.7	46.6	52.8	14.7	6.6
331	Medical, measuring, testing appliances, etc.	256.6	310.4	310.0	371.0	102.0	111.6	140.7	149.0	26.6	42.4
3311	Medical, surgical and orthopaedic equipment	113.9	122.3	144.8	181.3	45.5	50.5	70.8	72.1	16.9	35.8
3312	Measuring/testing/navigating appliances,etc.	136.8	173.4	149.9	132.7	53.1	57.8	65.3	58.5	9.1	4.0
3313	Industrial process control equipment	5.9	14.7	15.4	57.0	3.4	3.3	4.6	18.4	0.6	2.6
3320	Optical instruments & photographic equipment	23.9	23.6	29.5	41.8	10.1	10.3	14.5	17.1	0.6	1.4
3330	Watches and clocks	-	-	0.1	0.2	-	-	0.1	-	-	-
3410	Motor vehicles	3.1	26.7	28.3	21.6	0.7	5.6	6.3	2.7	2.5	0.2
3420	Automobile bodies, trailers & semi-trailers	75.7	116.2	162.0	306.8	13.0	25.1	24.9	53.9	6.7	21.2
3430	Parts/accessories for automobiles	3.5	6.5	12.6	21.6	1.2	2.2	3.9	5.9	15.6	6.8
351	Building and repairing of ships and boats	312.6	392.5	458.6	574.1	134.7	141.5	176.8	223.2	23.3	56.0
3511	Building and repairing of ships	304.0	375.2	421.3	524.6	132.7	136.8	160.3	205.6	21.8	48.8
3512	Building/repairing of pleasure/sport. boats	8.5	17.4	37.3	49.5	2.0	4.7	16.5	17.5	1.5	7.2
3520	Railway/tramway locomotives & rolling stock	27.1	101.5	140.1	158.4	6.0	25.6	26.9	36.5	12.9	2.6
3530	Aircraft and spacecraft	25.9	24.6	49.9	46.1	11.5	10.9	17.4	14.3	1.0	3.7
359	Transport equipment n.e.c.	152.6	147.3	191.4	153.9	23.4	34.1	27.2	35.4	7.2	4.1
3591	Motorcycles	-	-	-	-	-	-	-	-	-	-
3592	Bicycles and invalid carriages	151.7	146.2	190.1	152.0	23.1	33.8	26.8	34.5	7.2	4.1
3599	Other transport equipment n.e.c.	1.0	1.1	1.3	1.9	0.3	0.3	0.4	0.9	-	-
3610	Furniture	1208.8	1394.6	1622.2	2089.4	375.6	437.8	467.2	585.5	133.1	194.6
369	Manufacturing n.e.c.	93.6	116.4	150.0	188.3	39.7	46.3	62.6	75.6	8.6	11.8
3691	Jewellery and related articles	27.8	38.6	54.0	75.4	10.4	13.7	19.7	23.2	3.9	2.1
3692	Musical instruments	1.0	0.9	2.0	0.9	0.5	0.4	1.2	0.3	0.4	0.1
3693	Sports goods	3.3	3.5	4.0	6.0	0.9	1.4	1.4	2.1	0.1	0.5
3694	Games and toys	8.4	9.3	7.5	9.4	3.4	2.7	2.5	3.8	0.3	0.2
3699	Other manufacturing n.e.c.	53.1	64.1	82.5	96.5	24.5	28.1	37.8	46.1	4.0	8.9
3710	Recycling of metal waste and scrap	180.5	201.3	281.3	415.0	23.5	47.1	24.4	48.4	11.8	14.2
3720	Recycling of non-metal waste and scrap	31.7	39.4	29.4	45.1	10.5	11.7	11.7	13.2	6.5	8.0
D	Total manufacturing	25944.8	31124.5	38108.6	43503.9	6252.1	7726.7	8690.7	8973.8	2561.0	3007.6

Lithuania

ISIC Revision 3			Index numbers of industrial production											
			(2000=100)											
ISIC	Industry	Note	1995	1996	1997	1998	1999	2000	2001	2002	2003	2004	2005	2006
15	Food and beverages		99	98	101	103	93	100	102	101	111	115	124	139
16	Tobacco products		50	63	76	104	110	100	108	96	80	88	147	222
17	Textiles		100	102	100	99	92	100	114	115	104	112	109	120
18	Wearing apparel, fur		61	75	83	82	94	100	108	106	119	107	99	101
19	Leather, leather products and footwear		98	94	99	85	82	100	84	72	59	35	38	40
20	Wood products (excl. furniture)		49	55	62	64	75	100	114	141	175	187	206	219
21	Paper and paper products		116	109	114	100	81	100	124	132	146	158	176	202
22	Printing and publishing		62	66	92	99	109	100	104	91	120	128	125	136
23	Coke,refined petroleum products,nuclear fuel		105	119	147	166	109	100	149	140	149	185	193	176
24	Chemicals and chemical products		67	75	78	88	93	100	89	111	113	113	129	172
25	Rubber and plastics products		50	60	65	80	82	100	130	151	235	264	326	384
26	Non-metallic mineral products		117	115	108	112	104	100	103	106	141	161	216	289
27	Basic metals		39	29	27	31	67	100	104	83	61	47	59	50
28	Fabricated metal products		133	145	154	149	88	100	123	132	207	269	333	426
29	Machinery and equipment n.e.c.		142	111	107	99	107	100	122	159	163	183	204	220
30	Office, accounting and computing machinery		157	154	138	85	92	100	111	88	96	107	96	133
31	Electrical machinery and apparatus		29	36	53	85	92	100	104	117	184	222	206	189
32	Radio,television and communication equipment		51	58	60	65	77	100	112	141	191	218	228	204
33	Medical, precision and optical instruments		199	99	101	118	110	100	109	105	124	150	158	189
34	Motor vehicles, trailers, semi-trailers		151	123	148	121	61	100	202	332	414	787	1037	2057
35	Other transport equipment		60	77	72	89	83	100	113	109	114	133	190	219
36	Furniture; manufacturing n.e.c.		70	64	68	77	80	100	119	151	187	250	283	359
37	Recycling		34	26	31	22	25	100	110	100	130	184	167	153
D	Total manufacturing		89	90	95	103	92	100	116	119	136	152	165	179

Luxembourg

Supplier of information:
Service central de la statistique et des études économiques (STATEC), Luxembourg. Industrial statistics for the OECD countries are compiled by the OECD secretariat, which supplies them to UNIDO.

Basic source of data:
Annual sample survey, administrative sources and annual accounts of large establishments.

Major deviations from ISIC (Revision 3):
Data, originally compiled according to NACE (Revision 1) have been regrouped to correspond to ISIC (Revision 3).

Reference period:
Calendar year.

Scope:
All enterprises included in the business register.

Method of data collection:
Establishments with more than 50 employees are completely enumerated, while for the other establishments a sample survey is carried out.

Type of enumeration:
Not reported.

Adjusted for non-response:
Yes.

Concepts and definitions of variables:
Output corresponds to the turnover adjusted for changes in the value of stocks of finished goods and work in progress, less the acquisition of goods and services shipped in the same condition as received, plus the immobilised production and other operating incomes (excluding subsidies). Excluded are value added tax (VAT) invoiced to the client by the producer, and VAT deductible on purchase of raw materials and intermediate products. The valuation is at market prices.
Value added relates to the gross value of operating activities, taking into account subsidies and indirect taxes. It is calculated as output less acquisition of goods and services, other taxes on products related to turnover but not deductible and taxes related to production. It excludes receipts and costs belonging to the business accounts under items "financial receipts/charges" and "exceptional receipts/charges".

Related national publications:
Annuaire statistique, published by the Service central de la statistique et des études économiques (STATEC), Luxembourg.

Luxembourg

ISIC Revision 3		Number of enterprises					Number of employees					Wages and salaries paid to employees				
			(number)					(number)					(millions of Euros)			
ISIC	Industry	Note	2002	2003	2004	2005	Note	2002	2003	2004	2005	Note	2002	2003	2004	2005
15	Food and beverages		209	200	194	190	a/	4321	4977	5205	5143	a/	118	126	130	148
16	Tobacco products		1	1	1	1	a/	...	...	...	...	a/	...	...	...	...
17	Textiles		27	23	22	21		1287	906b/	892b/	1075b/		51	58b/	59b/	63b/
18	Wearing apparel, fur		16	19	18	17		25	...b/	...b/	...b/		1	...b/	...b/	...b/
19	Leather, leather products and footwear		-	-	-	-		-	-	-	-		-	-	-	-
20	Wood products (excl. furniture)		19	20	22	21		513	568	591	591		18	18	17	19
21	Paper and paper products		2	2	2	2		245	3032c/	3334c/	3061c/		10	121c/	125c/	123c/
22	Printing and publishing		181	182	182	186		2596	...c/	...c/	...c/		104	...c/	...c/	...c/
23	Coke,refined petroleum products,nuclear fuel		-	-	-	-		-	-	-	-		-	-	-	-
24	Chemicals and chemical products		16	14	15	15		1475	1446	1312	1290		59	48	50	50
25	Rubber and plastics products		25	20	23	25		3971	5855	6186	6158		186	274	280	290
26	Non-metallic mineral products		44	41	42	41		2785	3245	3060	2988		102	123	120	119
27	Basic metals		16	9	10	9		5962	6928	6631	6188		254	315	331	338
28	Fabricated metal products		204	211	203	207		4593	4183	4387	4157		163	133	143	142
29	Machinery and equipment n.e.c.		49	38	39	41		2548	2305	2301	2379		104	93	95	105
30	Office, accounting and computing machinery		1	1	1	1		...	...	...	...		...	...	...	...
31	Electrical machinery and apparatus		21	19	18	17		466	...	...	...		18	...	...	...
32	Radio,television and communication equipment		3	2	4	3		...	...	...	...		...	...	...	...
33	Medical, precision and optical instruments		56	53	54	55		1933	1860	1944	2051		55	53	51	64
34	Motor vehicles, trailers, semi-trailers		10	10	10	9	d/	273	365	410	447	d/	8	10	12	12
35	Other transport equipment		2	2	2	3	d/	...	...	...	...	d/	...	...	...	...
36	Furniture; manufacturing n.e.c.		66	70	67	69		694	261	273	254		18	7	7	8
37	Recycling		16	17	18	17		228	265	278	279		8	8	9	9
D	Total manufacturing		984	954	947	950		33955	36722	37381	36642		1275	1403	1447	1509

a/ 15 includes 16.
b/ 17 includes 18.
c/ 21 includes 22.
d/ 34 includes 35.

Luxembourg

ISIC Revision 3		Output					Value added in factor values					Gross fixed capital formation	
		Note	(millions of Euros)				Note	(millions of Euros)				Note	(millions of Euros)	
ISIC	Industry		2002	2003	2004	2005		2002	2003	2004	2005		2004	2005
15	Food and beverages	a/	685	724	779	846	a/	229	232	247	270		46a/	40a/
16	Tobacco products	a/	...	...	...	...	a/	...	...	...	...		...a/	...a/
17	Textiles		527	471b/	513b/	541b/		169	210b/	194b/	189b/		178b/	6b/
18	Wearing apparel, fur		2	...b/	...b/	...b/		1	...b/	...b/	...b/		...b/	...b/
19	Leather, leather products and footwear		-	-	-	-		-	-	-	-		-	-
20	Wood products (excl. furniture)		136	144	186	168		37	37	52	48		4	14
21	Paper and paper products		149	549c/	650c/	660c/		26	217c/	227c/	212c/		17c/	9c/
22	Printing and publishing		301	...c/	...c/	...c/		153	...c/	...c/	...c/		...c/	...c/
23	Coke,refined petroleum products,nuclear fuel		-	-	-	-		-	-	-	-		-	-
24	Chemicals and chemical products		518	369	350	277		112	98	94	74		23	8
25	Rubber and plastics products		987	1250	1310	1358		378	483	456	427		41	39
26	Non-metallic mineral products		597	651	666	666		241	230	261	261		42	20
27	Basic metals		1551	2159	2663	2616		417	459	502	561		183	192
28	Fabricated metal products		907	633	742	694		253	203	256	242		26	26
29	Machinery and equipment n.e.c.		546	529	533	509		163	143	150	162		18	26
30	Office, accounting and computing machinery		...	...	...	...		...	...	...	...		...	...
31	Electrical machinery and apparatus		50	...	...	...		18	...	...	...		...	...
32	Radio,television and communication equipment		...	...	...	...		...	...	...	...		...	...
33	Medical, precision and optical instruments		163	167	178	320		71	81	84	134		7	4
34	Motor vehicles, trailers, semi-trailers	d/	26	42	55	66	d/	10	18	22	26		1d/	2d/
35	Other transport equipment	d/	...	...	...	...	d/	...	...	...	...		...d/	...d/
36	Furniture; manufacturing n.e.c.		56	26	26	28		14	12	12	13		1	-
37	Recycling		33	37	42	53		14	12	11	18		5	2
D	Total manufacturing		7238	7808	8753	8869		2309	2459	2596	2662		594	392

a/ 15 includes 16.
b/ 17 includes 18.
c/ 21 includes 22.
d/ 34 includes 35.

Luxembourg

ISIC Revision 3			Index numbers of industrial production (2000=100)											
ISIC	Industry	Note	1995	1996	1997	1998	1999	2000	2001	2002	2003	2004	2005	2006
15	Food and beverages		94	93	93	95	99	100	113	116	114	117	126	117
16	Tobacco products		...	...	...	...	...	...	...	...	...	...	...	...
17	Textiles	a/	102	83	95	100	93	100	102	104	108	109	113	116
18	Wearing apparel, fur	a/	...	...	...	...	...	...	...	...	...	...	...	...
19	Leather, leather products and footwear	a/	...	...	...	...	...	...	...	...	...	...	...	...
20	Wood products (excl. furniture)		20	37	50	74	92	100	97	121	134	151	151	149
21	Paper and paper products	b/	75	77	80	83	92	100	115	117	131	148	150	144
22	Printing and publishing	b/	...	...	...	...	...	...	...	...	...	...	...	...
23	Coke,refined petroleum products,nuclear fuel		...	...	...	...	...	...	...	...	...	...	...	...
24	Chemicals and chemical products		60	67	74	110	94	100	109	115	119	118	115	104
25	Rubber and plastics products		90	91	94	95	93	100	107	117	127	135	143	149
26	Non-metallic mineral products		76	78	84	84	94	100	101	100	100	97	94	95
27	Basic metals		83	78	85	75	95	100	99	96	98	102	92	107
28	Fabricated metal products		80	77	83	97	97	100	95	92	94	95	98	104
29	Machinery and equipment n.e.c.		84	104	90	104	108	100	92	93	97	90	113	110
30	Office, accounting and computing machinery	c/	80	80	92	96	90	100	107	109	105	118	130	136
31	Electrical machinery and apparatus	c/	...	...	...	...	...	...	...	...	...	...	...	...
32	Radio,television and communication equipment	c/	...	...	...	...	...	...	...	...	...	...	...	...
33	Medical, precision and optical instruments	c/	...	...	...	...	...	...	...	...	...	...	...	...
34	Motor vehicles, trailers, semi-trailers	d/	85	78	95	101	101	100	96	111	120	130	132	130
35	Other transport equipment	d/	...	...	...	...	...	...	...	...	...	...	...	...
36	Furniture; manufacturing n.e.c.	d/	...	...	...	...	...	...	...	...	...	...	...	...
37	Recycling		...	...	...	...	...	...	...	...	...	...	...	...
D	Total manufacturing		81	81	86	94	95	100	103	104	109	114	116	118

a/ 17 includes 18 and 19.
b/ 21 includes 22.
c/ 30 includes 31, 32 and 33.
d/ 34 includes 35 and 36.

Madagascar

Supplier of information:
Institut National de la Statistique, Ministère de l'Economie, des Finances et du Budget, Antananarivo.

Basic source of data:
Enterprise survey.

Major deviations from ISIC (Revision 3):
None reported.

Reference period:
Calendar year.

Scope:
All enterprises.

Method of data collection:
Data were collected by direct interview in the field and by mail questionnaire.

Type of enumeration:
Sample survey. Value added is estimated based on the index of industrial production (2001=100).

Adjusted for non-response:
Yes.

Concepts and definitions of variables:
Wages and salaries is compensation of employees.

Related national publications:
None reported.

Madagascar

ISIC Revision 3		Establishments					Number of employees					Wages and salaries paid to employees				
			(number)					(number)					(millions of Madagascar Ariary)			
ISIC	Industry	Note	2003	2004	2005	2006	Note	2003	2004	2005	2006	Note	2003	2004	2005	2006
151	Processed meat,fish,fruit,vegetables,fats		...	...	...	...		5498	2039	2711	2829		736	751	998	1139
1511	Processing/preserving of meat		...	...	...	...		...	...	...	...		...	...	...	...
1512	Processing/preserving of fish		...	...	...	...		...	...	...	...		...	...	...	...
1513	Processing/preserving of fruit & vegetables		...	...	...	...		...	...	...	...		...	...	...	...
1514	Vegetable and animal oils and fats		...	...	...	...		...	...	...	...		...	...	...	...
1520	Dairy products		...	...	...	...		15191	5633	7489	7816		579	592	787	899
153	Grain mill products; starches; animal feeds		...	...	...	...		22437	16077	21374	22308		3079	3144	4180	4773
1531	Grain mill products		...	...	...	...		...	...	...	...		...	...	...	...
1532	Starches and starch products		...	...	...	...		...	...	...	...		...	...	...	...
1533	Prepared animal feeds		...	...	...	...		...	...	...	...		...	...	...	...
154	Other food products		...	...	...	...		10764	3991	5306	5538		1157	1181	1570	1793
1541	Bakery products		...	...	...	...		...	...	...	...		...	...	...	...
1542	Sugar		...	...	...	...		...	...	...	...		...	...	...	...
1543	Cocoa, chocolate and sugar confectionery		...	...	...	...		...	...	...	...		...	...	...	...
1544	Macaroni, noodles & similar products		...	...	...	...		...	...	...	...		...	...	...	...
1549	Other food products n.e.c.		...	...	...	...		...	...	...	...		...	...	...	...
155	Beverages		...	...	...	...		11780	8440	11221	11711		7058	7206	9580	10938
1551	Distilling, rectifying & blending of spirits		...	...	...	...		...	...	...	...		...	...	...	...
1552	Wines		...	...	...	...		...	...	...	...		...	...	...	...
1553	Malt liquors and malt		...	...	...	...		...	...	...	...		...	...	...	...
1554	Soft drinks; mineral waters		...	...	...	...		...	...	...	...		...	...	...	...
1600	Tobacco products		...	...	...	...		2334	1672	2223	2320		457	473	629	718
171	Spinning, weaving and finishing of textiles		...	...	...	...		6756	3093	4112	4292		597	614	816	932
1711	Textile fibre preparation; textile weaving		...	...	...	...		...	...	...	...		...	...	...	...
1712	Finishing of textiles		...	...	...	...		...	...	...	...		...	...	...	...
172	Other textiles		...	...	...	...		75186	34418	45759	47758		6930	7128	9477	10820
1721	Made-up textile articles, except apparel		...	...	...	...		...	...	...	...		...	...	...	...
1722	Carpets and rugs		...	...	...	...		...	...	...	...		...	...	...	...
1723	Cordage, rope, twine and netting		...	...	...	...		...	...	...	...		...	...	...	...
1729	Other textiles n.e.c.		...	...	...	...		...	...	...	...		...	...	...	...
1730	Knitted and crocheted fabrics and articles		...	...	...	...		142486	102094	135734	141663		24693	25400	33769	38556
1810	Wearing apparel, except fur apparel		...	...	...	...		192897	138215	183757	191784		43554	44800	59562	68005
1820	Dressing & dyeing of fur; processing of fur		...	...	...	...		...	...	...	...		...	...	...	...
191	Tanning, dressing and processing of leather		...	...	...	...		15140	10848	14422	15052		888	891	1185	1353
1911	Tanning and dressing of leather		...	...	...	...		...	...	...	...		...	...	...	...
1912	Luggage, handbags, etc.; saddlery & harness		...	...	...	...		...	...	...	...		...	...	...	...
1920	Footwear		...	...	...	...		4514	3234	4300	4488		1162	1166	1550	1770
2010	Sawmilling and planing of wood		...	...	...	...		11039	7910	10516	10975		666	718	955	1090
202	Products of wood, cork, straw, etc.		...	...	...	...		32439	23243	30902	32252		3418	3685	4899	5593
2021	Veneer sheets, plywood, particle board, etc.		...	...	...	...		...	...	...	...		...	...	...	...
2022	Builders' carpentry and joinery		...	...	...	...		...	...	...	...		...	...	...	...
2023	Wooden containers		...	...	...	...		...	...	...	...		...	...	...	...
2029	Other wood products; articles of cork/straw		...	...	...	...		...	...	...	...		...	...	...	...
210	Paper and paper products		...	...	...	...		...	...	...	...		...	...	...	...
2101	Pulp, paper and paperboard		...	...	...	...		...	...	...	...		...	...	...	...
2102	Corrugated paper and paperboard		...	...	...	...		...	...	...	...		...	...	...	...
2109	Other articles of paper and paperboard		...	...	...	...		...	...	...	...		...	...	...	...
221	Publishing		...	...	...	...		1384	992	1319	1377		346	365	365	417
2211	Publishing of books and other publications		...	...	...	...		...	...	...	...		...	...	...	...
2212	Publishing of newspapers, journals, etc.		...	...	...	...		...	...	...	...		...	...	...	...
2213	Publishing of recorded media		...	...	...	...		...	...	...	...		...	...	...	...
2219	Other publishing		...	...	...	...		...	...	...	...		...	...	...	...

222	Printing and related service activities	...	...	...	...	9489	6799	9039	9434	4798	5056	6722	7675
2221	Printing	...	...	...	...	...	...	...	...	...	...	...	...
2222	Service activities related to printing	...	...	...	...	...	...	...	...	...	...	...	...
2230	Reproduction of recorded media	...	...	...	...	...	...	...	...	...	...	...	...
2310	Coke oven products	...	...	...	...	...	...	...	...	...	...	...	...
2320	Refined petroleum products	...	...	...	...	...	...	...	...	...	...	...	...
2330	Processing of nuclear fuel	...	...	...	...	...	...	...	...	...	...	...	...
241	Basic chemicals	...	...	...	...	3537	2534	3369	3516	2704	2748	3653	4171
2411	Basic chemicals, except fertilizers	...	...	...	...	...	...	...	...	...	...	...	...
2412	Fertilizers and nitrogen compounds	...	...	...	...	...	...	...	...	...	...	...	...
2413	Plastics in primary forms; synthetic rubber	...	...	...	...	...	...	...	...	...	...	...	...
242	Other chemicals	...	...	...	...	443	317	421	439	84	85	113	129
2421	Pesticides and other agro-chemical products	...	...	...	...	...	...	...	...	...	...	...	...
2422	Paints, varnishes, printing ink and mastics	...	...	...	...	...	...	...	...	...	...	...	...
2423	Pharmaceuticals, medicinal chemicals, etc.	...	...	...	...	...	...	...	...	...	...	...	...
2424	Soap, cleaning & cosmetic preparations	...	...	...	...	...	...	...	...	...	...	...	...
2429	Other chemical products n.e.c.	...	...	...	...	...	...	...	...	...	...	...	...
2430	Man-made fibres	...	...	...	...	...	...	...	...	...	...	...	...
251	Rubber products	...	...	...	...	2005	1437	1910	1993	368	377	501	572
2511	Rubber tyres and tubes	...	...	...	...	...	...	...	...	...	...	...	...
2519	Other rubber products	...	...	...	...	...	...	...	...	...	...	...	...
2520	Plastic products	...	...	...	...	79577	57018	75805	79116	17769	18200	24197	27627
2610	Glass and glass products	...	...	...	...	...	...	...	...	...	...	...	...
269	Non-metallic mineral products n.e.c.	...	...	...	...	19562	14017	18636	19450	9489	10600	14093	16091
2691	Pottery, china and earthenware	...	...	...	...	...	...	...	...	...	...	...	...
2692	Refractory ceramic products	...	...	...	...	...	...	...	...	...	...	...	...
2693	Struct.non-refractory clay; ceramic products	...	...	...	...	...	...	...	...	...	...	...	...
2694	Cement, lime and plaster	...	...	...	...	...	...	...	...	...	...	...	...
2695	Articles of concrete, cement and plaster	...	...	...	...	...	...	...	...	...	...	...	...
2696	Cutting, shaping & finishing of stone	...	...	...	...	...	...	...	...	...	...	...	...
2699	Other non-metallic mineral products n.e.c.	...	...	...	...	...	...	...	...	...	...	...	...
2710	Basic iron and steel	...	...	...	...	2100	1505	2001	2088	22	23	31	35
2720	Basic precious and non-ferrous metals	...	...	...	...	200	144	191	199	37	38	51	58
273	Casting of metals	...	...	...	...	...	...	...	...	...	...	...	...
2731	Casting of iron and steel	...	...	...	...	...	...	...	...	...	...	...	...
2732	Casting of non-ferrous metals	...	...	...	...	...	...	...	...	...	...	...	...
281	Struct.metal products;tanks;steam generators	...	...	...	...	9060	6492	8631	9008	2235	2115	2812	3211
2811	Structural metal products	...	...	...	...	...	...	...	...	...	...	...	...
2812	Tanks, reservoirs and containers of metal	...	...	...	...	...	...	...	...	...	...	...	...
2813	Steam generators	...	...	...	...	...	...	...	...	...	...	...	...
289	Other metal products; metal working services	...	...	...	...	16302	11681	15530	16208	1934	1829	2432	2777
2891	Metal forging/pressing/stamping/roll-forming	...	...	...	...	...	...	...	...	...	...	...	...
2892	Treatment & coating of metals	...	...	...	...	...	...	...	...	...	...	...	...
2893	Cutlery, hand tools and general hardware	...	...	...	...	...	...	...	...	...	...	...	...
2899	Other fabricated metal products n.e.c.	...	...	...	...	...	...	...	...	...	...	...	...
291	General purpose machinery	...	...	...	...	111	79	105	110	50	55	73	83
2911	Engines & turbines (not for transport equipment)	...	...	...	...	...	...	...	...	...	...	...	...
2912	Pumps, compressors, taps and valves	...	...	...	...	...	...	...	...	...	...	...	...
2913	Bearings, gears, gearing & driving elements	...	...	...	...	...	...	...	...	...	...	...	...
2914	Ovens, furnaces and furnace burners	...	...	...	...	...	...	...	...	...	...	...	...
2915	Lifting and handling equipment	...	...	...	...	...	...	...	...	...	...	...	...
2919	Other general purpose machinery	...	...	...	...	...	...	...	...	...	...	...	...
292	Special purpose machinery	...	...	...	...	1068	766	1018	1062	232	257	342	390
2921	Agricultural and forestry machinery	...	...	...	...	...	...	...	...	...	...	...	...
2922	Machine tools	...	...	...	...	...	...	...	...	...	...	...	...
2923	Machinery for metallurgy	...	...	...	...	...	...	...	...	...	...	...	...
2924	Machinery for mining & construction	...	...	...	...	...	...	...	...	...	...	...	...
2925	Food/beverage/tobacco processing machinery	...	...	...	...	...	...	...	...	...	...	...	...
2926	Machinery for textile, apparel and leather	...	...	...	...	...	...	...	...	...	...	...	...
2927	Weapons and ammunition	...	...	...	...	...	...	...	...	...	...	...	...
2929	Other special purpose machinery	...	...	...	...	...	...	...	...	...	...	...	...

continued

Madagascar

ISIC Revision 3		Establishments					Number of employees					Wages and salaries paid to employees				
			(number)					(number)					(millions of Madagascar Ariary)			
ISIC	Industry	Note	2003	2004	2005	2006	Note	2003	2004	2005	2006	Note	2003	2004	2005	2006
2930	Domestic appliances n.e.c.		...	...	...	...		...	...	...	...		...	...	...	...
3000	Office, accounting and computing machinery		...	...	...	...		...	...	...	...		...	...	...	...
3110	Electric motors, generators and transformers		...	...	...	...		...	...	...	...		...	...	...	...
3120	Electricity distribution & control apparatus		...	...	...	...		...	...	...	...		...	...	...	...
3130	Insulated wire and cable		...	...	...	...		...	...	...	...		...	...	...	...
3140	Accumulators, primary cells and batteries		...	...	...	...		1467	1051	1397	1458		1077	1076	1431	1634
3150	Lighting equipment and electric lamps		...	...	...	...		...	...	...	...		...	...	...	...
3190	Other electrical equipment n.e.c.		...	...	...	...		...	...	...	...		...	...	...	...
3210	Electronic valves, tubes, etc.		...	...	...	...		...	...	...	...		...	...	...	...
3220	TV/radio transmitters; line comm. apparatus		...	...	...	...		...	...	...	...		...	...	...	...
3230	TV and radio receivers and associated goods		...	...	...	...		...	...	...	...		...	...	...	...
331	Medical, measuring, testing appliances, etc.		...	...	...	...		...	...	...	...		...	...	...	...
3311	Medical, surgical and orthopaedic equipment		...	...	...	...		...	...	...	...		...	...	...	...
3312	Measuring/testing/navigating appliances,etc.		...	...	...	...		...	...	...	...		...	...	...	...
3313	Industrial process control equipment		...	...	...	...		...	...	...	...		...	...	...	...
3320	Optical instruments & photographic equipment		...	...	...	...		...	...	...	...		...	...	...	...
3330	Watches and clocks		...	...	...	...		...	...	...	...		...	...	...	...
3410	Motor vehicles		...	...	...	...		...	...	...	...		...	...	...	...
3420	Automobile bodies, trailers & semi-trailers		...	...	...	...		...	...	...	...		...	...	...	...
3430	Parts/accessories for automobiles		...	...	...	...		...	...	...	...		...	...	...	...
351	Building and repairing of ships and boats		...	...	...	...		979	701	932	973		440	455	605	691
3511	Building and repairing of ships		...	...	...	...		...	...	...	...		...	...	...	...
3512	Building/repairing of pleasure/sport. boats		...	...	...	...		...	...	...	...		...	...	...	...
3520	Railway/tramway locomotives & rolling stock		...	...	...	...		...	...	...	...		...	...	...	...
3530	Aircraft and spacecraft		...	...	...	...		...	...	...	...		...	...	...	...
359	Transport equipment n.e.c.		...	...	...	...		...	...	...	...		...	...	...	...
3591	Motorcycles		...	...	...	...		...	...	...	...		...	...	...	...
3592	Bicycles and invalid carriages		...	...	...	...		...	...	...	...		...	...	...	...
3599	Other transport equipment n.e.c.		...	...	...	...		...	...	...	...		...	...	...	...
3610	Furniture		...	...	...	...		37198	26653	35435	36983		7189	7983	10613	12117
369	Manufacturing n.e.c.		...	...	...	...		2948	2112	2808	2931		2349	2608	3467	3958
3691	Jewellery and related articles		...	...	...	...		...	...	...	...		...	...	...	...
3692	Musical instruments		...	...	...	...		...	...	...	...		...	...	...	...
3693	Sports goods		...	...	...	...		...	...	...	...		...	...	...	...
3694	Games and toys		...	...	...	...		...	...	...	...		...	...	...	...
3699	Other manufacturing n.e.c.		...	...	...	...		...	...	...	...		...	...	...	...
3710	Recycling of metal waste and scrap		...	...	...	...		...	...	...	...		...	...	...	...
3720	Recycling of non-metal waste and scrap		...	...	...	...		...	...	...	...		...	...	...	...
D	Total manufacturing		...	...	...	...		736938	495955	659371	687131		146109	151893	201940	230015

Madagascar

ISIC Revision 3		Output in producers' prices					Value added in producers' prices					Gross fixed capital formation		
			(millions of Madagascar Ariary)					(millions of Madagascar Ariary)					(millions of Madagascar Ariary)	
ISIC	Industry	Note	2003	2004	2005	2006	Note	2003	2004	2005	2006	Note	2005	2006
151	Processed meat,fish,fruit,vegetables,fats		6428	6564	6660	7238		2142	2187	2187	2279		1218	1366
1511	Processing/preserving of meat		...	...	...	...		...	...	...	...		...	...
1512	Processing/preserving of fish		...	...	...	...		...	...	...	...		...	...
1513	Processing/preserving of fruit & vegetables		...	...	...	...		...	...	...	...		...	...
1514	Vegetable and animal oils and fats		...	...	...	...		...	...	...	...		...	...
1520	Dairy products		17530	17900	18163	19740		4925	5029	5029	5240		9184	10306
153	Grain mill products; starches; animal feeds		28890	29500	29933	32532		...	...	...	...		32992	37022
1531	Grain mill products		...	...	...	...		...	...	...	...		...	...
1532	Starches and starch products		...	...	...	...		...	...	...	...		...	...
1533	Prepared animal feeds		...	...	...	...		...	...	...	...		...	...
154	Other food products		53864	55000	55806	60651		43385	44300	44300	46161		23004	25815
1541	Bakery products		...	...	...	...		...	...	...	...		...	...
1542	Sugar		...	...	...	...		...	...	...	...		...	...
1543	Cocoa, chocolate and sugar confectionery		...	...	...	...		...	...	...	...		...	...
1544	Macaroni, noodles & similar products		...	...	...	...		...	...	...	...		...	...
1549	Other food products n.e.c.		...	...	...	...		...	...	...	...		...	...
155	Beverages		450566	460000	485965	521197		195898	200000	201000	211251		231166	259405
1551	Distilling, rectifying & blending of spirits		...	...	...	...		...	...	...	...		...	...
1552	Wines		...	...	...	...		...	...	...	...		...	...
1553	Malt liquors and malt		...	...	...	...		...	...	...	...		...	...
1554	Soft drinks; mineral waters		...	...	...	...		...	...	...	...		...	...
1600	Tobacco products		3666	3800	3839	4030		2785	2887	2800	2853		563	632
171	Spinning, weaving and finishing of textiles		2771	2850	2578	2831		...	...	...	...		1214	1363
1711	Textile fibre preparation; textile weaving		...	...	...	...		...	...	...	...		...	...
1712	Finishing of textiles		...	...	...	...		...	...	...	...		...	...
172	Other textiles		29749	30600	27680	30399		12541	12900	13674	14631		22668	25437
1721	Made-up textile articles, except apparel		...	...	...	...		...	...	...	...		...	...
1722	Carpets and rugs		...	...	...	...		...	...	...	...		...	...
1723	Cordage, rope, twine and netting		...	...	...	...		...	...	...	...		...	...
1729	Other textiles n.e.c.		...	...	...	...		...	...	...	...		...	...
1730	Knitted and crocheted fabrics and articles		53081	54600	49389	54241		35193	36200	38372	41058		10710	12018
1810	Wearing apparel, except fur apparel		236241	243000	219810	241404		103051	106000	112360	120225		217700	244294
1820	Dressing & dyeing of fur; processing of fur		...	...	...	...		...	...	...	...		...	...
191	Tanning, dressing and processing of leather		4910	4926	4708	5092		2995	3004	3184	...		3867	4339
1911	Tanning and dressing of leather		...	...	...	...		...	...	...	...		...	...
1912	Luggage, handbags, etc.; saddlery & harness		...	...	...	...		...	...	...	...		...	...
1920	Footwear		7885	7911	7562	8179		4308	4322	4257	4436		4508	5058
2010	Sawmilling and planing of wood		4272	4606	4528	4908		1930	2081	2143	2231		7238	8122
202	Products of wood, cork, straw, etc.		13634	14700	14451	15665		9646	10400	10712	11151		75409	84622
2021	Veneer sheets, plywood, particle board, etc.		...	...	...	...		...	...	...	...		...	...
2022	Builders' carpentry and joinery		...	...	...	...		...	...	...	...		...	...
2023	Wooden containers		...	...	...	...		...	...	...	...		...	...
2029	Other wood products; articles of cork/straw		...	...	...	...		...	...	...	...		...	...
210	Paper and paper products		...	...	...	...		...	...	...	...		...	...
2101	Pulp, paper and paperboard		...	...	...	...		...	...	...	...		...	...
2102	Corrugated paper and paperboard		...	...	...	...		...	...	...	...		...	...
2109	Other articles of paper and paperboard		...	...	...	...		...	...	...	...		...	...
221	Publishing		1369	1443	1533	1642		400	421	447	514		639	717
2211	Publishing of books and other publications		...	...	...	...		...	...	...	...		...	...
2212	Publishing of newspapers, journals, etc.		...	...	...	...		...	...	...	...		...	...
2213	Publishing of recorded media		...	...	...	...		...	...	...	...		...	...
2219	Other publishing		...	...	...	...		...	...	...	...		...	...

continued

ISIC Revision 3		Output in producers' prices					Value added in producers' prices					Gross fixed capital formation		
			(millions of Madagascar Ariary)					(millions of Madagascar Ariary)					(millions of Madagascar Ariary)	
ISIC	Industry	Note	2003	2004	2005	2006	Note	2003	2004	2005	2006	Note	2005	2006
222	Printing and related service activities		22776	24000	25499	27319		7626	8036	8538	9819		9516	10678
2221	Printing		...	...	...	...		...	...	...	...		...	...
2222	Service activities related to printing		...	...	...	...		...	...	...	...		...	...
2230	Reproduction of recorded media		...	...	...	...		...	...	...	...		...	...
2310	Coke oven products		...	...	...	...		...	...	...	...		...	...
2320	Refined petroleum products		...	...	...	...		...	...	...	...		...	...
2330	Processing of nuclear fuel		...	...	...	...		...	...	...	...		...	...
241	Basic chemicals		18600	18900	18512	18966		10333	10500	10285	11828		49375	55407
2411	Basic chemicals, except fertilizers		...	...	...	...		...	...	...	...		...	...
2412	Fertilizers and nitrogen compounds		...	...	...	...		...	...	...	...		...	...
2413	Plastics in primary forms; synthetic rubber		...	...	...	...		...	...	...	...		...	...
242	Other chemicals		230	234	229	235		160	162	158	182		7	8
2421	Pesticides and other agro-chemical products		...	...	...	...		...	...	...	...		...	...
2422	Paints, varnishes, printing ink and mastics		...	...	...	...		...	...	...	...		...	...
2423	Pharmaceuticals, medicinal chemicals, etc.		...	...	...	...		...	...	...	...		...	...
2424	Soap, cleaning & cosmetic preparations		...	...	...	...		...	...	...	...		...	...
2429	Other chemical products n.e.c.		...	...	...	...		...	...	...	...		...	...
2430	Man-made fibres		...	...	...	...		...	...	...	...		...	...
251	Rubber products		2255	2309	2607	2981		...	...	...	...		2655	2979
2511	Rubber tyres and tubes		...	...	...	...		...	...	...	...		...	...
2519	Other rubber products		...	...	...	...		...	...	...	...		...	...
2520	Plastic products		126922	130000	146774	167819		37198	38100	43016	49468		44550	49992
2610	Glass and glass products		...	...	...	...		...	...	...	...		...	...
269	Non-metallic mineral products n.e.c.		8021	8960	9731	11193		...	...	...	...		46794	52511
2691	Pottery, china and earthenware		...	...	...	...		...	...	...	...		...	...
2692	Refractory ceramic products		...	...	...	...		...	...	...	...		...	...
2693	Struct.non-refractory clay; ceramic products		...	...	...	...		...	...	...	...		...	...
2694	Cement, lime and plaster		...	...	...	...		...	...	...	...		...	...
2695	Articles of concrete, cement and plaster		...	...	...	...		...	...	...	...		...	...
2696	Cutting, shaping & finishing of stone		...	...	...	...		...	...	...	...		...	...
2699	Other non-metallic mineral products n.e.c.		...	...	...	...		...	...	...	...		...	...
2710	Basic iron and steel		453	468	474	508		...	134	143	146		164	184
2720	Basic precious and non-ferrous metals		766	791	801	859		...	113	121	139		122	137
273	Casting of metals		...	...	...	...		...	...	...	...		...	...
2731	Casting of iron and steel		...	...	...	...		...	...	...	...		...	...
2732	Casting of non-ferrous metals		...	...	...	...		...	...	...	...		...	...
281	Struct.metal products;tanks;steam generators		44922	42500	42366	44171		...	...	...	...		20311	22792
2811	Structural metal products		...	...	...	...		...	...	...	...		...	...
2812	Tanks, reservoirs and containers of metal		...	...	...	...		...	...	...	...		...	...
2813	Steam generators		...	...	...	...		...	...	...	...		...	...
289	Other metal products; metal working services		23782	22500	22429	23384		11521	10900	11630	11909		4648	5216
2891	Metal forging/pressing/stamping/roll-forming		...	...	...	...		...	...	...	...		...	...
2892	Treatment & coating of metals		...	...	...	...		...	...	...	...		...	...
2893	Cutlery, hand tools and general hardware		...	...	...	...		...	...	...	...		...	...
2899	Other fabricated metal products n.e.c.		...	...	...	...		...	...	...	...		...	...
291	General purpose machinery		319	354	363	393		...	...	...	...		155	174
2911	Engines & turbines (not for transport equipment)		...	...	...	...		...	...	...	...		...	...
2912	Pumps, compressors, taps and valves		...	...	...	...		...	...	...	...		...	...
2913	Bearings, gears, gearing & driving elements		...	...	...	...		...	...	...	...		...	...
2914	Ovens, furnaces and furnace burners		...	...	...	...		...	...	...	...		...	...
2915	Lifting and handling equipment		...	...	...	...		...	...	...	...		...	...
2919	Other general purpose machinery		...	...	...	...		...	...	...	...		...	...

292	Special purpose machinery	1941	2151	2205	2390	1630	1807	1928	2217	412	462
2921	Agricultural and forestry machinery	...	...	...	...	...	...	...	...	...	...
2922	Machine tools	...	...	...	...	...	...	...	...	...	...
2923	Machinery for metallurgy	...	...	...	...	...	...	...	...	...	...
2924	Machinery for mining & construction	...	...	...	...	...	...	...	...	...	...
2925	Food/beverage/tobacco processing machinery	...	...	...	...	...	...	...	...	...	...
2926	Machinery for textile, apparel and leather	...	...	...	...	...	...	...	...	...	...
2927	Weapons and ammunition	...	...	...	...	...	...	...	...	...	...
2929	Other special purpose machinery	...	...	...	...	...	...	...	...	...	...
2930	Domestic appliances n.e.c.	...	...	...	...	...	...	...	...	...	...
3000	Office, accounting and computing machinery	...	...	...	...	...	...	...	...	...	...
3110	Electric motors, generators and transformers	...	...	...	...	...	...	...	...	...	...
3120	Electricity distribution & control apparatus	...	...	...	...	...	...	...	...	...	...
3130	Insulated wire and cable	...	...	...	...	...	...	...	...	...	...
3140	Accumulators, primary cells and batteries	11404	11400	10845	11678	4080	4079	4283	4925	110	123
3150	Lighting equipment and electric lamps	...	...	...	...	...	...	...	...	...	...
3190	Other electrical equipment n.e.c.	...	...	...	...	...	...	...	...	...	...
3210	Electronic valves, tubes, etc.	...	...	...	...	...	...	...	...	...	...
3220	TV/radio transmitters; line comm. apparatus	...	...	...	...	...	...	...	...	...	...
3230	TV and radio receivers and associated goods	...	...	...	...	...	...	...	...	...	...
331	Medical, measuring, testing appliances, etc.	...	...	...	...	...	...	...	...	...	...
3311	Medical, surgical and orthopaedic equipment	...	...	...	...	...	...	...	...	...	...
3312	Measuring/testing/navigating appliances,etc.	...	...	...	...	...	...	...	...	...	...
3313	Industrial process control equipment	...	...	...	...	...	...	...	...	...	...
3320	Optical instruments & photographic equipment	...	...	...	...	...	...	...	...	...	...
3330	Watches and clocks	...	...	...	...	...	...	...	...	...	...
3410	Motor vehicles	...	...	...	...	...	...	...	...	...	...
3420	Automobile bodies, trailers & semi-trailers	...	...	...	...	...	...	...	...	...	...
3430	Parts/accessories for automobiles	...	...	...	...	...	...	...	...	...	...
351	Building and repairing of ships and boats	1980	2045	2055	2179	635	655	688	791	1751	1964
3511	Building and repairing of ships	...	...	...	...	...	...	...	...	...	...
3512	Building/repairing of pleasure/sport. boats	...	...	...	...	...	...	...	...	...	...
3520	Railway/tramway locomotives & rolling stock	...	...	...	...	...	...	...	...	...	...
3530	Aircraft and spacecraft	...	...	...	...	...	...	...	...	...	...
359	Transport equipment n.e.c.	...	...	...	...	...	...	...	...	...	...
3591	Motorcycles	...	...	...	...	...	...	...	...	...	...
3592	Bicycles and invalid carriages	...	...	...	...	...	...	...	...	...	...
3599	Other transport equipment n.e.c.	...	...	...	...	...	...	...	...	...	...
3610	Furniture	24494	27200	28033	29847	11991	13316	13715	14277	41537	46611
369	Manufacturing n.e.c.	32508	36100	37205	39612	12877	14300	14729	15333	7752	8699
3691	Jewellery and related articles	...	...	...	...	...	...	...	...	...	...
3692	Musical instruments	...	...	...	...	...	...	...	...	...	...
3693	Sports goods	...	...	...	...	...	...	...	...	...	...
3694	Games and toys	...	...	...	...	...	...	...	...	...	...
3699	Other manufacturing n.e.c.	...	...	...	...	...	...	...	...	...	...
3710	Recycling of metal waste and scrap	...	...	...	...	...	...	...	...	...	...
3720	Recycling of non-metal waste and scrap	...	...	...	...	...	...	...	...	...	...
D	Total manufacturing	1236351	1269994	1282853	1393283	599019	613649	637333	583065	871936	978455

Madagascar

ISIC Revision 3			Index numbers of industrial production											
			(2000=100)											
ISIC	Industry	Note	1995	1996	1997	1998	1999	2000	2001	2002	2003	2004	2005	2006
15	Food and beverages		72	72	68	75	95	100	109	95	117	119	140	158
16	Tobacco products		58	75	69	82	93	100	107	99	107	111	116	122
17	Textiles	a/	126	117	133	129	116	100	130	72	94	96	122	134
18	Wearing apparel, fur	a/	...	...	...	...	...	...	...	...	...	...	...	...
19	Leather, leather products and footwear		33	38	24	22	82	100	102	71	89	89	106	115
20	Wood products (excl. furniture)		23	17	18	40	49	100	91	70	81	87	100	109
21	Paper and paper products		120	93	105	107	65	100	80	64	69	63	63	62
22	Printing and publishing		169	86	84	136	95	100	101	99	115	121	159	170
23	Coke,refined petroleum products,nuclear fuel		60	65	91	86	85	100	107	56	118	124	100	100
24	Chemicals and chemical products		65	33	115	101	104	100	133	118	123	125	138	141
25	Rubber and plastics products		...	...	...	...	...	...	...	...	...	...	...	...
26	Non-metallic mineral products		81	79	75	90	94	100	105	84	120	134	168	194
27	Basic metals		...	...	...	...	...	...	...	...	...	...	...	...
28	Fabricated metal products		82	118	125	134	138	100	137	122	143	135	219	168
29	Machinery and equipment n.e.c.		...	...	...	...	...	...	...	...	...	...	...	...
30	Office, accounting and computing machinery		...	...	...	...	...	...	...	...	...	...	...	...
31	Electrical machinery and apparatus		75	76	84	85	85	100	99	70	85	85	102	110
32	Radio,television and communication equipment		...	...	...	...	...	...	...	...	...	...	...	...
33	Medical, precision and optical instruments		...	...	...	...	...	...	...	...	...	...	...	...
34	Motor vehicles, trailers, semi-trailers		...	...	...	...	...	...	...	...	...	...	...	...
35	Other transport equipment		118	132	112	124	131	100	88	76	86	89	106	112
36	Furniture; manufacturing n.e.c.		...	...	...	...	...	...	...	...	...	...	...	...
37	Recycling		...	...	...	...	...	...	...	...	...	...	...	...
D	Total manufacturing		67	67	82	84	88	100	109	84	112	117	130	149

a/ 17 includes 18.

Malaysia

Supplier of information:
Department of Statistics, Putrajaya.

Basic source of data:
Census (every 5 years); annual survey.

Major deviations from ISIC (Revision 3):
The data presented in ISIC (Revision 3) were originally classified according to the Malaysia Standard Industrial Classification 2000, which conforms closely with ISIC (Revision 3).

Reference period:
Calendar year; however, data given for a financial year are accepted and incorporated into the calendar year which adheres to the major part of the financial year.

Scope:
All establishments.

Method of data collection:
The annual survey is conducted by mail, e-mail and through field contacts.

Type of enumeration:
For 2005, complete enumeration.
For 2002 to 2004 , establishments with 30 or more employees are completely enumerated. For establishments with less than 30 employees data refer to overall estimates of the manufacturing sector based on a stratified sampling technique.

Adjusted for non-response:
Yes.

Concepts and definitions of variables:
Wages and salaries is compensation of employees.
Output is at basic prices.
Value added is at basic prices.

Related national publications:
Census of Manufacturing Industries, 2006; Annual Survey of Manufacturing Industries, both published by the Department of Statistics, Putrajaya.

Malaysia

ISIC Revision 3		Number of establishments					Number of employees					Wages and salaries paid to employees				
			(number)					(thousands)					(millions of Malaysian Ringgits)			
ISIC	Industry	Note	2002	2003	2004	2005	Note	2002	2003	2004	2005	Note	2002	2003	2004	2005
151	Processed meat,fish,fruit,vegetables,fats		700	686	662	888		53.4	57.9	58.6	63.8		936	1033	1059	1196
1511	Processing/preserving of meat		61	54	50	80		5.2	6.0	7.3	7.2		93	100	137	131
1512	Processing/preserving of fish		146	131	141	252		8.2	8.8	10.1	11.0		104	105	131	138
1513	Processing/preserving of fruit & vegetables		38	54	44	58		1.6	1.9	1.8	2.0		22	35	28	36
1514	Vegetable and animal oils and fats		455	447	427	498		38.3	41.2	39.5	43.6		717	793	763	891
1520	Dairy products		48	41	43	56		4.9	4.1	4.1	7.0		174	156	146	313
153	Grain mill products; starches; animal feeds		412	387	374	382		11.6	11.4	10.8	11.3		279	277	297	277
1531	Grain mill products		311	278	279	278		6.9	6.2	6.3	6.3		164	144	178	149
1532	Starches and starch products		30	25	25	27		1.0	0.9	0.7	0.7		16	16	10	11
1533	Prepared animal feeds		71	84	70	77		3.8	4.3	3.8	4.3		99	117	109	117
154	Other food products		1817	1752	1688	2853		51.0	50.2	51.4	61.7		864	897	933	1096
1541	Bakery products		849	762	771	1204		20.0	18.9	20.8	23.8		262	259	298	330
1542	Sugar		8	8	7	13		2.1	1.9	1.9	2.0		71	72	69	75
1543	Cocoa, chocolate and sugar confectionery		38	66	57	64		4.3	6.4	5.2	5.6		95	130	112	128
1544	Macaroni, noodles & similar products		264	258	226	325		4.3	4.3	4.4	6.1		54	71	75	98
1549	Other food products n.e.c.		658	658	627	1247		20.3	18.6	19.1	24.3		382	365	379	465
155	Beverages		123	122	117	193		5.8	5.8	6.1	7.2		169	203	229	188
1551	Distilling, rectifying & blending of spirits	a/	28	26	26	32	a/	1.0	1.0	1.1	1.4	a/	69	71	76	63
1552	Wines		-	-	-	3		-	-	-	-		-	-	-	2
1553	Malt liquors and malt	a/	...	...	...	...	a/	...	...	...	...	a/	...	...	...	...
1554	Soft drinks; mineral waters		95	96	91	158		4.8	4.8	5.0	5.8		100	132	153	123
1600	Tobacco products		216	231	214	170		9.9	9.0	9.5	6.6		172	132	154	187
171	Spinning, weaving and finishing of textiles		142	117	124	235		27.4	21.4	19.7	21.0		445	396	393	405
1711	Textile fibre preparation; textile weaving		57	49	47	72		21.5	14.6	13.5	14.5		319	265	258	269
1712	Finishing of textiles		85	68	77	163		5.9	6.8	6.2	6.5		126	131	135	136
172	Other textiles		259	243	235	422		6.1	6.6	7.0	7.6		102	115	121	136
1721	Made-up textile articles, except apparel		188	170	170	271		2.7	3.0	3.4	3.1		37	46	51	42
1722	Carpets and rugs		14	14	14	18		1.3	1.3	1.5	1.5		28	26	28	32
1723	Cordage, rope, twine and netting		9	8	8	13		0.8	0.7	0.7	0.8		11	12	12	18
1729	Other textiles n.e.c.		48	51	43	120		1.3	1.6	1.4	2.2		26	31	30	44
1730	Knitted and crocheted fabrics and articles		89	91	87	104		10.9	11.0	10.5	10.6		176	181	173	161
1810	Wearing apparel, except fur apparel		2671	2318	2516	5556b/		78.4	71.7	78.5	65.1b/		1105	969	1132	921b/
1820	Dressing & dyeing of fur; processing of fur		-	-	-	...b/		-	-	-	...b/		-	-	-	...b/
191	Tanning, dressing and processing of leather		59	51	48	80		2.3	2.2	2.0	2.5		34	32	32	38
1911	Tanning and dressing of leather		11	7	8	8		0.4	0.4	0.4	0.3		6	6	6	5
1912	Luggage, handbags, etc.; saddlery & harness		48	44	40	72		1.9	1.9	1.6	2.2		28	26	26	33
1920	Footwear		204	176	266	299		5.0	4.2	5.9	5.7		76	72	114	97
2010	Sawmilling and planing of wood		469	428	434	605		32.7	29.7	31.6	38.2		432	422	459	585
202	Products of wood, cork, straw, etc.		777	761	720	931		78.1	83.5	84.2	92.6		941	1037	1107	1196
2021	Veneer sheets, plywood, particle board, etc.		136	126	129	180		56.8	59.6	62.5	71.3		636	670	772	874
2022	Builders' carpentry and joinery		351	341	339	356		15.2	17.3	16.2	15.1		214	268	247	224
2023	Wooden containers		70	81	49	109		1.0	1.6	0.9	1.5		14	21	12	23
2029	Other wood products; articles of cork/straw		220	213	203	286		5.1	5.0	4.7	4.8		77	78	76	75
210	Paper and paper products		390	397	412	537		33.5	31.2	34.7	37.0		715	680	750	786
2101	Pulp, paper and paperboard		77	93	86	115		8.1	7.2	7.7	7.7		184	174	187	183
2102	Corrugated paper and paperboard		186	182	187	220		19.2	17.6	19.4	19.5		400	362	398	404
2109	Other articles of paper and paperboard		127	122	139	202		6.2	6.3	7.6	9.8		131	144	165	199
221	Publishing		162	160	197	255		15.8	15.3	17.0	18.1		544	538	599	663
2211	Publishing of books and other publications		70	76	67	152		3.5	3.9	3.8	5.8		89	103	102	149
2212	Publishing of newspapers, journals, etc.		43	39	42	51		5.6	5.8	6.1	7.2		228	230	248	344
2213	Publishing of recorded media		5	45c/	88c/	9		0.3	5.6c/	7.1c/	0.3		5	205c/	249c/	5
2219	Other publishing		44	...c/	...c/	43		6.5	...c/	...c/	4.8		222	...c/	...c/	165

222	Printing and related service activities	646	635	611	1234	20.4	19.4	20.1	30.3	449	433	457	669
2221	Printing	268	276	309	790	7.5	8.8	9.1	17.6	148	177	181	378
2222	Service activities related to printing	378	359	302	444	12.8	10.6	11.0	12.6	301	256	276	291
2230	Reproduction of recorded media	5	3	3	8	0.2	0.2	0.2	0.5	4	4	3	10
2310	Coke oven products	-	-	-	...d/	-	-	-	...d/	-	-	-	...d/
2320	Refined petroleum products	41	50	39	32d/	5.6	4.6	4.4	4.8d/	341	329	317	311d/
2330	Processing of nuclear fuel	-	-	-	-	-	-	-	-	-	-	-	-
241	Basic chemicals	213	216	209	291	21.7	22.4	22.7	27.0	1038	1133	1188	1464
2411	Basic chemicals, except fertilizers	110	108	105	135	11.8	12.0	12.9	15.3	596	627	697	953
2412	Fertilizers and nitrogen compounds	22	23	24	39	1.7	1.9	1.9	2.2	81	96	101	119
2413	Plastics in primary forms; synthetic rubber	81	85	80	117	8.3	8.5	7.9	9.4	361	410	390	392
242	Other chemicals	470	472	506	598	26.5	27.7	29.6	33.4	775	838	938	1022
2421	Pesticides and other agro-chemical products	29	24	28	28	2.0	1.9	1.6	2.1	47	47	39	54
2422	Paints, varnishes, printing ink and mastics	109	122	113	149	6.0	6.7	7.1	8.8	206	236	247	294
2423	Pharmaceuticals, medicinal chemicals, etc.	114	108	119	159	6.4	7.2	8.0	8.9	138	145	174	198
2424	Soap, cleaning & cosmetic preparations	130	127	126	144	5.6	5.5	5.6	6.4	139	154	160	183
2429	Other chemical products n.e.c.	88e/	91e/	120	118	6.4e/	6.3e/	7.4	7.3	245e/	256e/	318	293
2430	Man-made fibres	...e/	...e/	3	4	...e/	...e/	0.2	0.2	...e/	...e/	12	10
251	Rubber products	455	430	438	466	67.1	69.6	72.7	82.1	1134	1211	1323	1520
2511	Rubber tyres and tubes	82	73	75	71	8.5	8.6	8.6	9.0	191	226	214	250
2519	Other rubber products	373	357	363	395	58.6	61.0	64.1	73.1	943	985	1109	1270
2520	Plastic products	1116	1131	996	1349	99.8	102.6	101.6	119.5	1886	2005	1999	2243
2610	Glass and glass products	112	110	96	236	11.8	10.1	8.6	9.1	335	309	281	290
269	Non-metallic mineral products n.e.c.	729	720	758	1024	45.8	45.9	47.4	56.1	991	1060	1144	1353
2691	Pottery, china and earthenware	77	73	76	91	7.6	7.1	7.7	9.2	121	124	139	170
2692	Refractory ceramic products	65	81	109	110	9.0	10.0	11.8	11.2	173	192	252	230
2693	Struct.non-refractory clay; ceramic products	107	85	72	99	5.6	4.8	4.8	8.0	97	93	91	155
2694	Cement, lime and plaster	50	47	46	67	4.7	4.4	4.7	5.6	173	189	193	265
2695	Articles of concrete, cement and plaster	288	285	338	467	13.4	14.0	13.8	15.6	296	328	343	370
2696	Cutting, shaping & finishing of stone	62	69	54	84	1.2	1.2	1.0	1.6	17	15	15	30
2699	Other non-metallic mineral products n.e.c.	80	80	63	106	4.3	4.4	3.6	4.9	114	119	111	133
2710	Basic iron and steel	188	209	234	489	20.2	21.3	21.8	24.7	584	630	713	707
2720	Basic precious and non-ferrous metals	85	94	80	117	11.0	11.3	10.8	11.2	307	340	330	350
273	Casting of metals	274	270	258	325	9.9	9.3	10.1	11.7	229	221	255	285
2731	Casting of iron and steel	251	246	236	293	8.3	7.6	8.3	9.7	193	184	208	234
2732	Casting of non-ferrous metals	23	24	22	32	1.6	1.7	1.8	2.0	36	37	47	51
281	Struct.metal products;tanks;steam generators	1224	1204	1130	1724	21.5	21.2	21.5	26.0	419	421	449	519
2811	Structural metal products	1173	1149	1075	1659	18.5	18.2	18.0	21.9	345	354	360	418
2812	Tanks, reservoirs and containers of metal	51	55	55	61	3.0	2.9	3.4	3.9	74	67	89	96
2813	Steam generators	-	-	-	4	-	-	-	0.2	-	-	-	5
289	Other metal products; metal working services	1068	1027	1055	1301	45.3	47.4	50.5	55.5	991	1039	1182	1241
2891	Metal forging/pressing/stamping/roll-forming	268	233	265	297	5.1	5.4	7.1	10.2	96	104	144	200
2892	Treatment & coating of metals	57	56	51	101	2.4	3.1	3.3	5.2	49	60	69	98
2893	Cutlery, hand tools and general hardware	141	132	131	165	2.0	2.1	2.4	2.0	39	39	51	33
2899	Other fabricated metal products n.e.c.	602	606	608	738	35.8	36.8	37.7	38.1	807	836	918	910
291	General purpose machinery	327	324	392	432	24.7	22.3	24.8	27.6	718	673	750	839
2911	Engines & turbines (not for transport equipment)	15	8	8	19	0.6	0.7	0.8	0.6	16	17	15	12
2912	Pumps, compressors, taps and valves	45	46	37	42	6.2	5.6	5.0	5.9	186	200	186	192
2913	Bearings, gears, gearing & driving elements	34	27	103	41	1.5	1.6	3.7	1.7	45	57	115	58
2914	Ovens, furnaces and furnace burners	11	8	5	7	0.3	0.3	0.2	0.3	6	6	4	10
2915	Lifting and handling equipment	41	38	35	41	1.9	1.8	1.6	3.1	47	46	50	80
2919	Other general purpose machinery	181	197	204	282	14.1	12.2	13.5	16.0	418	347	380	487
292	Special purpose machinery	693	712	591	680	16.7	16.8	16.6	19.1	446	440	474	532
2921	Agricultural and forestry machinery	50	56	47	96	1.3	1.3	1.3	1.5	34	34	35	39
2922	Machine tools	486	501	401	377	11.8	11.3	11.6	11.5	311	292	322	327
2923	Machinery for metallurgy	4	5	5	11	0.1	0.1	0.1	0.1	3	3	3	4
2924	Machinery for mining & construction	25	40	41	49	0.9	1.1	1.0	1.7	31	37	39	50
2925	Food/beverage/tobacco processing machinery	27	21	24	30	0.6	0.5	0.6	0.8	17	12	14	21
2926	Machinery for textile, apparel and leather	52	16	8	10f/	0.2	0.1	0.1	0.6f/	4	2	1	19f/
2927	Weapons and ammunition	6	4	3	...f/	-	-	0.5	...f/	1	1	14	...f/
2929	Other special purpose machinery	43	69	62	107	1.6	2.3	1.5	2.8	45	59	46	72

continued

Malaysia

ISIC Revision 3		Number of establishments					Number of employees					Wages and salaries paid to employees				
			(number)					(thousands)					(millions of Malaysian Ringgits)			
ISIC	Industry	Note	2002	2003	2004	2005	Note	2002	2003	2004	2005	Note	2002	2003	2004	2005
2930	Domestic appliances n.e.c.		71	68	96	52		6.7	8.2	11.7	7.2		181	200	300	189
3000	Office, accounting and computing machinery		66	57	61	67		59.6	57.3	64.3	81.5		1402	1399	1686	2215
3110	Electric motors, generators and transformers		69	71	82	61		16.4	16.7	14.7	14.0		227	272	256	264
3120	Electricity distribution & control apparatus		116	129	105	138		10.8	10.8	10.1	10.3		278	286	265	239
3130	Insulated wire and cable		130	125	119	123		23.1	23.7	22.9	20.5		519	534	561	457
3140	Accumulators, primary cells and batteries		21	17	21	21		3.0	3.1	4.8	3.8		66	65	121	100
3150	Lighting equipment and electric lamps		40	46	35	48		7.2	7.4	6.9	6.8		175	183	177	195
3190	Other electrical equipment n.e.c.		53	63	93	83		5.9	6.7	8.8	10.3		112	135	172	182
3210	Electronic valves, tubes, etc.		248	275	227	271		170.9	183.0	179.6	193.1		4201	4533	4678	5091
3220	TV/radio transmitters; line comm. apparatus		30	31	30	32		12.7	15.6	19.3	21.3		268	371	424	555
3230	TV and radio receivers and associated goods		150	132	120	123		95.6	98.4	86.3	76.4		1973	2070	2179	2105
331	Medical, measuring, testing appliances, etc.		27	26	27	90		12.4	13.7	12.8	12.3		298	317	323	327
3311	Medical, surgical and orthopaedic equipment		6	7	7	60		6.4	7.5	6.8	7.1		164	185	185	218
3312	Measuring/testing/navigating appliances,etc.		21g/	19g/	20g/	25		6.0g/	6.1g/	6.0g/	4.7		134g/	132g/	138g/	97
3313	Industrial process control equipment		...g/	...g/	...g/	5		...g/	...g/	...g/	0.4		...g/	...g/	...g/	12
3320	Optical instruments & photographic equipment		14	15	15	17		5.7	5.8	5.7	8.6		157	141	145	179
3330	Watches and clocks		12	10	10	10		5.2	5.3	6.5	4.2		116	114	144	119
3410	Motor vehicles		29	15	31	17		21.4	19.2	23.4	23.4		595	526	767	692
3420	Automobile bodies, trailers & semi-trailers		102	117	101	100		2.9	3.1	3.3	2.9		62	61	77	66
3430	Parts/accessories for automobiles		165	200	170	187		22.8	25.8	24.3	25.5		506	556	521	575
351	Building and repairing of ships and boats		128	117	149	179		16.2	17.0	18.1	10.2		551	572	480	302
3511	Building and repairing of ships		112	100	131	147		15.3	16.0	16.9	8.7		529	548	450	263
3512	Building/repairing of pleasure/sport. boats		16	17	18	32		0.9	1.0	1.2	1.5		22	24	30	39
3520	Railway/tramway locomotives & rolling stock		-	-	-	-		-	-	-	-		-	-	-	-
3530	Aircraft and spacecraft		5	6	6	6		2.6	2.4	2.6	3.8		103	105	121	170
359	Transport equipment n.e.c.		72	63	69	86		6.6	6.9	8.8	10.2		146	158	195	224
3591	Motorcycles		37	36	35	47		4.1	4.3	4.7	6.2		88	100	108	139
3592	Bicycles and invalid carriages		28	22	28	31		2.0	1.9	3.2	3.3		47	44	69	70
3599	Other transport equipment n.e.c.		7	5	6	8		0.5	0.7	0.9	0.7		11	14	18	15
3610	Furniture		1351	1385	1409	1793		72.0	70.1	77.2	87.0		1002	1030	1148	1338
369	Manufacturing n.e.c.		611	592	630	815		22.3	22.8	22.6	25.0		420	432	444	506
3691	Jewellery and related articles		171	171	193	242		3.0	2.7	3.1	4.1		66	62	73	98
3692	Musical instruments		23h/	20h/	23h/	5		1.9h/	1.7h/	2.0h/	0.4		29h/	29h/	27h/	6
3693	Sports goods		...h/	...h/	...h/	28		...h/	...h/	...h/	2.1		...h/	...h/	...h/	34
3694	Games and toys		21	17	21	26		5.9	6.4	6.3	5.6		106	110	116	113
3699	Other manufacturing n.e.c.		396	384	393	514		11.4	12.0	11.3	12.9		219	231	228	255
3710	Recycling of metal waste and scrap		4	13i/	3	12		0.2	0.3i/	0.1	0.5		5	6i/	2	10
3720	Recycling of non-metal waste and scrap		7	...i/	18	50		0.2	...i/	0.4	1.2		3	...i/	8	22
D	Total manufacturing		19705	19141	19163	28257		1477.2	1490.5	1530.5	1654.7		31177	32292	34707	37731

a/ 1551 includes 1553.
b/ 1810 includes 1820.
c/ 2213 includes 2219.
d/ 2320 includes 2310.
e/ 2429 includes 2430.
f/ 2926 includes 2927.
g/ 3312 includes 3313.
h/ 3692 includes 3693.
i/ 3710 includes 3720.

ISIC Revision 3		Output in producers' prices					Value added in producers' prices					Gross fixed capital formation		
		(millions of Malaysian Ringgits)					(millions of Malaysian Ringgits)					(millions of Malaysian Ringgits)	
ISIC	Industry	Note	2002	2003	2004	2005	Note	2002	2003	2004	2005	Note	2004	2005
151	Processed meat,fish,fruit,vegetables,fats		39685	50869	52295	53112		4501	5090	5478	4741		568	1169
1511	Processing/preserving of meat		1252	1382	1741	1379		237	254	242	214		41	29
1512	Processing/preserving of fish		1305	1447	1846	2035		292	321	381	384		49	70
1513	Processing/preserving of fruit & vegetables		182	271	226	329		47	68	61	73		8	12
1514	Vegetable and animal oils and fats		36946	47769	48482	49369		3925	4447	4794	4070		470	1058
1520	Dairy products		2300	2185	2282	4273		571	563	610	822		46	419
153	Grain mill products; starches; animal feeds		5846	5842	7036	6133		946	865	860	750		227	141
1531	Grain mill products		2853	2475	3311	2991		563	450	499	385		196	108
1532	Starches and starch products		130	91	80	90		36	22	20	15		6	3
1533	Prepared animal feeds		2863	3276	3645	3052		347	393	341	350		25	30
154	Other food products		8400	8942	9892	11433		2537	2731	2845	2685		586	585
1541	Bakery products		1607	1718	2066	2314		552	589	687	636		155	151
1542	Sugar		1636	1692	1729	1886		322	442	468	339		36	29
1543	Cocoa, chocolate and sugar confectionery		1369	1828	2047	2376		319	408	379	412		88	125
1544	Macaroni, noodles & similar products		465	574	621	894		156	168	167	209		15	24
1549	Other food products n.e.c.		3323	3130	3429	3963		1188	1124	1144	1089		292	256
155	Beverages		2057	2133	2303	3656		619	631	641	1515		40	62
1551	Distilling, rectifying & blending of spirits	a/	599	627	601	1646	a/	305	321	285	1182	a/	-	45
1552	Wines		-	-	-	14		-	-	-	3		-	-
1553	Malt liquors and malt	a/	...	...	...	...	a/	...	...	...	...	a/	...	...
1554	Soft drinks; mineral waters		1458	1506	1702	1996		314	310	356	330		40	17
1600	Tobacco products		1775	1518	1589	1935		360	410	383	416		98	38
171	Spinning, weaving and finishing of textiles		4629	4191	4482	5164		1080	965	1077	838		134	149
1711	Textile fibre preparation; textile weaving		3522	3085	3347	4027		791	587	676	515		36	73
1712	Finishing of textiles		1107	1106	1135	1137		289	378	401	323		98	76
172	Other textiles		643	642	708	750		243	252	268	230		20	15
1721	Made-up textile articles, except apparel		189	220	277	219		68	86	105	67		4	2
1722	Carpets and rugs		190	158	170	211		61	55	56	58		2	4
1723	Cordage, rope, twine and netting		76	83	85	100		29	30	29	31		-	2
1729	Other textiles n.e.c.		188	181	176	220		85	81	78	74		14	7
1730	Knitted and crocheted fabrics and articles		1262	1227	1291	1209		394	416	408	272		63	35
1810	Wearing apparel, except fur apparel		5104	5050	5804	5110b/		1752	1632	1860	1396b/		77	176b/
1820	Dressing & dyeing of fur; processing of fur		-	-	-	...b/		-	-	-	...b/		-	...b/
191	Tanning, dressing and processing of leather		188	175	211	256		58	57	62	65		8	6
1911	Tanning and dressing of leather		61	57	55	58		12	15	14	9		1	1
1912	Luggage, handbags, etc.; saddlery & harness		127	118	156	198		46	42	48	56		7	5
1920	Footwear		317	349	599	512		123	130	226	158		27	10
2010	Sawmilling and planing of wood		3230	3183	3588	5002		914	874	965	1034		57	106
202	Products of wood, cork, straw, etc.		8460	9725	11267	12357		2776	3165	3717	2987		470	786
2021	Veneer sheets, plywood, particle board, etc.		6378	7174	8719	10129		2072	2276	2909	2406		370	723
2022	Builders' carpentry and joinery		1569	1985	2001	1713		516	682	608	413		86	40
2023	Wooden containers		85	136	77	114		26	42	25	35		-	3
2029	Other wood products; articles of cork/straw		428	430	470	401		162	165	175	133		14	20
210	Paper and paper products		6753	6267	7610	7974		2223	1931	2234	1804		352	297
2101	Pulp, paper and paperboard		1822	1875	2420	2325		684	590	744	558		65	98
2102	Corrugated paper and paperboard		3819	3004	3520	3709		1168	889	983	764		175	133
2109	Other articles of paper and paperboard		1112	1388	1670	1940		371	452	507	482		112	66
221	Publishing		2860	2975	3421	3813		1274	1469	1589	1349		223	164
2211	Publishing of books and other publications		500	620	675	891		232	271	295	276		39	37
2212	Publishing of newspapers, journals, etc.		1099	1170	1252	1925		348	508	521	761		90	103
2213	Publishing of recorded media		36	1185c/	1494c/	54		12	690c/	773c/	11		94c/	1
2219	Other publishing		1225	...c/	...c/	943		682	...c/	...c/	301		...c/	23

continued

Malaysia

ISIC Revision 3		Output in producers' prices					Value added in producers' prices					Gross fixed capital formation		
		Note	(millions of Malaysian Ringgits)				Note	(millions of Malaysian Ringgits)				Note	(millions of Malaysian Ringgits)	
ISIC	Industry		2002	2003	2004	2005		2002	2003	2004	2005		2004	2005
222	Printing and related service activities		2105	2127	2348	3749		890	890	950	1247		180	245
2221	Printing		729	915	951	2275		284	354	370	713		71	124
2222	Service activities related to printing		1376	1212	1397	1474		606	536	580	534		109	121
2230	Reproduction of recorded media		25	30	33	63		10	11	10	20		4	9
2310	Coke oven products		-	-	-	...d/		-	-	-	...d/		-	...d/
2320	Refined petroleum products		44941	47746	62205	78820d/		10000	12646	16183	16058d/		396	754d/
2330	Processing of nuclear fuel		-	-	-	-		-	-	-	-		-	-
241	Basic chemicals		22289	29631	42669	43900		7517	9436	12735	11959		5994	883
2411	Basic chemicals, except fertilizers		12028	16535	24303	26838		4925	6194	8369	9372		1147	1189
2412	Fertilizers and nitrogen compounds		1235	1742	2048	3319		438	621	656	1121		361	67
2413	Plastics in primary forms; synthetic rubber		9026	11354	16318	13743		2154	2621	3710	1466		4486	-373
242	Other chemicals		8260	9788	12952	12988		2600	3129	3700	3079		297	394
2421	Pesticides and other agro-chemical products		573	679	727	713		142	165	132	146		6	17
2422	Paints, varnishes, printing ink and mastics		2045	2367	2462	2935		609	718	691	615		67	75
2423	Pharmaceuticals, medicinal chemicals, etc.		861	927	1157	1215		399	447	528	454		85	95
2424	Soap, cleaning & cosmetic preparations		1461	1727	2107	2378		447	592	616	503		33	3
2429	Other chemical products n.e.c.		3320e/	4088e/	6499	5747		1003e/	1207e/	1733	1361		106	204
2430	Man-made fibres		...e/	...e/	277	268		...e/	...e/	34	20		5	4
251	Rubber products		10908	13060	15242	18930		2961	3228	3462	3517		558	945
2511	Rubber tyres and tubes		1475	1724	1776	2235		495	600	512	501		92	213
2519	Other rubber products		9433	11336	13466	16695		2466	2628	2950	3016		466	732
2520	Plastic products		16048	17261	16644	19221		5838	5984	5251	4886		900	1200
2610	Glass and glass products		3448	2960	3056	2733		1667	1273	1397	820		129	365
269	Non-metallic mineral products n.e.c.		9250	9945	11792	12223		3772	4157	4339	3410		618	879
2691	Pottery, china and earthenware		496	497	558	802		245	245	272	296		27	96
2692	Refractory ceramic products		1163	1300	1667	1560		518	619	785	615		157	276
2693	Struct.non-refractory clay; ceramic products		502	477	508	920		229	227	235	346		227	172
2694	Cement, lime and plaster		3142	3267	3395	3786		1442	1591	1359	1034		72	200
2695	Articles of concrete, cement and plaster		3017	3408	4735	3898		933	1060	1318	752		107	99
2696	Cutting, shaping & finishing of stone		102	77	79	129		42	31	33	48		9	5
2699	Other non-metallic mineral products n.e.c.		828	919	850	1128		363	384	337	319		19	31
2710	Basic iron and steel		9829	12729	17462	18754		2179	3003	3459	1987		188	735
2720	Basic precious and non-ferrous metals		4663	6048	8540	8038		906	1156	1277	911		180	171
273	Casting of metals		2432	2383	2663	3464		637	591	688	585		104	131
2731	Casting of iron and steel		2020	1873	2194	2599		533	485	574	456		93	116
2732	Casting of non-ferrous metals		412	510	469	865		104	106	114	129		11	15
281	Struct.metal products;tanks;steam generators		2690	2765	3204	3729		896	907	1030	974		88	104
2811	Structural metal products		2163	2114	2172	2684		736	724	726	711		83	81
2812	Tanks, reservoirs and containers of metal		527	651	1032	1012		160	183	304	247		5	18
2813	Steam generators		-	-	-	33		-	-	-	16		-	5
289	Other metal products; metal working services		9239	10934	12833	13570		2624	2966	3686	2815		440	533
2891	Metal forging/pressing/stamping/roll-forming		801	1066	1406	1754		220	244	347	389		40	69
2892	Treatment & coating of metals		473	461	512	894		164	183	194	214		43	50
2893	Cutlery, hand tools and general hardware		255	327	376	221		102	133	156	64		17	5
2899	Other fabricated metal products n.e.c.		7710	9080	10539	10701		2138	2406	2989	2148		340	409
291	General purpose machinery		7484	6244	7107	9902		2082	2069	2362	2044		185	365
2911	Engines & turbines (not for transport equipment)		77	84	50	53		30	34	26	20		-	6
2912	Pumps, compressors, taps and valves		2043	1789	1786	2062		644	548	539	370		17	68
2913	Bearings, gears, gearing & driving elements		375	470	874	489		157	198	386	195		117	69
2914	Ovens, furnaces and furnace burners		36	38	47	84		11	12	11	19		1	1
2915	Lifting and handling equipment		294	287	352	1119		105	107	119	160		5	26
2919	Other general purpose machinery		4659	3576	3998	6095		1135	1170	1281	1280		45	195

292	Special purpose machinery		2697	2778	3345	3940		1010	1006	1219	1086		109	219
2921	Agricultural and forestry machinery		195	260	315	333		83	102	116	103		6	2
2922	Machine tools		1768	1696	2216	2214		647	623	820	644		93	156
2923	Machinery for metallurgy		24	25	29	39		5	4	4	7		-	-
2924	Machinery for mining & construction		306	344	367	689		132	116	118	128		1	49
2925	Food/beverage/tobacco processing machinery		91	73	73	116		40	31	30	35		1	-2
2926	Machinery for textile, apparel and leather		63	25	5	104f/		17	7	2	37f/		-	1f/
2927	Weapons and ammunition		2	4	70	...f/		1	1	29	...f/		3	...f/
2929	Other special purpose machinery		248	351	270	445		85	122	100	132		5	13
2930	Domestic appliances n.e.c.		2650	2287	4018	3909		415	479	974	593		174	84
3000	Office, accounting and computing machinery		43487	58704	60720	64596		6074	7478	9956	8573		1259	3232
3110	Electric motors, generators and transformers		1980	1809	1879	2291		539	492	468	425		5	75
3120	Electricity distribution & control apparatus		2335	2725	2520	1983		666	794	764	461		48	57
3130	Insulated wire and cable		5158	4735	5936	6072		1350	1210	1436	1007		136	151
3140	Accumulators, primary cells and batteries		523	572	966	877		177	189	280	233		30	90
3150	Lighting equipment and electric lamps		1564	1862	2075	2161		499	611	759	431		121	165
3190	Other electrical equipment n.e.c.		672	888	1309	1362		273	377	469	403		43	42
3210	Electronic valves, tubes, etc.		65386	73819	82135	84896		14832	17338	16819	13618		4234	4024
3220	TV/radio transmitters; line comm. apparatus		5806	9999	12968	16741		1454	1861	2235	1981		175	258
3230	TV and radio receivers and associated goods		35273	37773	39984	41839		5247	5314	6674	4145		733	578
331	Medical, measuring, testing appliances, etc.		2442	2186	2671	3065		717	728	847	805		108	142
3311	Medical, surgical and orthopaedic equipment		860	942	956	1129		421	466	473	436		81	113
3312	Measuring/testing/navigating appliances,etc.		1582g/	1244g/	1715g/	1747		296g/	262g/	374g/	293		27g/	17
3313	Industrial process control equipment		...g/	...g/	...g/	189		...g/	...g/	...g/	76		...g/	12
3320	Optical instruments & photographic equipment		1689	1696	1870	2697		291	294	343	403		-5	70
3330	Watches and clocks		552	487	1064	445		231	206	241	162		36	18
3410	Motor vehicles		16348	13973	21431	17359		4128	3975	4027	2234		1136	639
3420	Automobile bodies, trailers & semi-trailers		508	526	670	713		146	130	174	229		20	39
3430	Parts/accessories for automobiles		5009	5352	4344	5243		1825	1686	1464	1272		239	223
351	Building and repairing of ships and boats		2856	3049	2964	3022		1183	1265	411	585		79	125
3511	Building and repairing of ships		2740	2923	2793	2811		1135	1216	348	516		67	107
3512	Building/repairing of pleasure/sport. boats		116	126	171	211		48	49	63	69		12	18
3520	Railway/tramway locomotives & rolling stock		-	-	-	-		-	-	-	-		-	-
3530	Aircraft and spacecraft		416	461	697	1550		159	179	284	250		23	33
359	Transport equipment n.e.c.		1792	1944	2841	2763		510	515	693	597		50	76
3591	Motorcycles		1080	1119	1477	1661		290	302	359	394		26	54
3592	Bicycles and invalid carriages		635	706	1208	979		192	165	275	169		21	9
3599	Other transport equipment n.e.c.		77	119	156	123		28	48	59	34		3	13
3610	Furniture		7391	7402	8945	10186		2242	2223	2536	2400		391	461
369	Manufacturing n.e.c.		2805	2794	2877	4170		865	897	984	858		97	144
3691	Jewellery and related articles		673	594	606	1713		120	113	189	207		12	28
3692	Musical instruments		194h/	179h/	182h/	33		65h/	57h/	49h/	8		-3h/	-
3693	Sports goods		...h/	...h/	...h/	242		...h/	...h/	...h/	54		...h/	9
3694	Games and toys		470	498	509	465		214	218	223	130		19	35
3699	Other manufacturing n.e.c.		1468	1523	1580	1717		466	509	523	459		69	72
3710	Recycling of metal waste and scrap		62	112i/	79	242		10	17i/	11	22		-1	-2
3720	Recycling of non-metal waste and scrap		21	...i/	86	357		7	...i/	19	43		9	10
D	Total manufacturing		456542	516857	601799	655520		109800	121891	137873	118210		22510	22827

a/ 1551 includes 1553.
b/ 1810 includes 1820.
c/ 2213 includes 2219.
d/ 2320 includes 2310.
e/ 2429 includes 2430.
f/ 2926 includes 2927.
g/ 3312 includes 3313.
h/ 3692 includes 3693.
i/ 3710 includes 3720.

Malaysia

ISIC Revision 3			Index numbers of industrial production											
			(2000=100)											
ISIC	Industry	Note	1995	1996	1997	1998	1999	2000	2001	2002	2003	2004	2005	2006
15	Food and beverages		68	74	79	76	88	100	107	114	127	132	142	149
16	Tobacco products		58	62	74	67	57	100	94	85	88	91	89	84
17	Textiles		95	96	103	94	98	100	95	92	87	82	79	79
18	Wearing apparel, fur		80	78	79	80	83	100	87	78	80	66	77	94
19	Leather, leather products and footwear		126	126	94	61	54	100	140	145	103	154	176	118
20	Wood products (excl. furniture)		107	119	117	104	96	100	101	95	96	108	110	114
21	Paper and paper products		79	75	84	77	87	100	102	115	124	127	137	155
22	Printing and publishing		...	...	...	...	...	...	...	...	...	...	...	...
23	Coke,refined petroleum products,nuclear fuel		77	87	94	84	83	100	122	116	117	119	131	149
24	Chemicals and chemical products		65	80	92	88	93	100	101	102	117	131	139	147
25	Rubber and plastics products		47	52	65	68	85	100	88	92	115	131	146	157
26	Non-metallic mineral products		80	100	110	81	83	100	110	115	126	120	123	127
27	Basic metals		71	83	93	66	95	100	99	102	113	118	112	115
28	Fabricated metal products		66	82	91	76	75	100	104	105	112	145	138	175
29	Machinery and equipment n.e.c.		104	100	102	66	69	100	104	110	116	112	97	83
30	Office, accounting and computing machinery		67	65	71	68	77	100	87	67	60	55	59	67
31	Electrical machinery and apparatus		43	55	64	61	71	100	83	89	98	118	126	135
32	Radio,television and communication equipment		49	54	63	61	71	100	82	90	99	120	124	136
33	Medical, precision and optical instruments		89	86	88	88	87	100	79	86	93	108	104	116
34	Motor vehicles, trailers, semi-trailers		82	100	114	55	84	100	119	126	119	130	141	138
35	Other transport equipment		...	...	...	...	...	...	...	...	...	...	...	...
36	Furniture; manufacturing n.e.c.		...	...	...	...	...	...	...	...	...	...	...	...
37	Recycling		...	...	...	...	...	...	...	...	...	...	...	...
D	Total manufacturing		63	70	79	71	80	100	93	98	108	121	128	137

Morocco

Supplier of information:
Ministère du Commerce, de l 'Industrie et des Nouvelles Technologies (MCINT), Rabat.

Basic source of data:
Annual industrial survey.

Major deviations from ISIC (Revision 3):
Data collected under the national classification system have been reclassified by UNIDO to correspond with ISIC (Revision 3).

Reference period:
Fiscal year.

Scope:
Enterprises with 10 or more employees or a turnover of more than 100,000 dirhams per year.

Method of data collection:
Direct interview in the field.

Type of enumeration:
Complete enumeration.

Adjusted for non-response:
Yes.

Concepts and definitions of variables:
Wages and salaries is compensation of employees.

Related national publications:
None reported.

Morocco

ISIC Revision 3		Number of enterprises					Number of employees					Wages and salaries paid to employees				
			(number)					(number)					(millions of Moroccan Dirhams)			
ISIC	Industry	Note	2003	2004	2005	2006	Note	2003	2004	2005	2006	Note	2003	2004	2005	2006
151	Processed meat,fish,fruit,vegetables,fats		501	504	530	527		49182	40584	29330	39617		1394	1461	1542	...
1511	Processing/preserving of meat		39	41	48	48		1210	1534	1952	2257		40	46	73	...
1512	Processing/preserving of fish		203	197	192	182		34966	27510	17297	25060		822	892	896	...
1513	Processing/preserving of fruit & vegetables		102	100	114	112		8000	6417	5141	6503		202	192	208	...
1514	Vegetable and animal oils and fats		157	166	176	185		5006	5123	4940	5797		330	331	365	...
1520	Dairy products		59	65	77	73		8580	11162	9661	11029		684	748	816	...
153	Grain mill products; starches; animal feeds		200	202	207	205		9248	8975	8941	9015		442	451	480	...
1531	Grain mill products		165	166	170	170		7271	6816	6662	6788		312	308	322	...
1532	Starches and starch products		5	4	5	6		142	123	145	154		21	19	21	...
1533	Prepared animal feeds		30	32	32	29		1835	2036	2134	2073		108	124	137	...
154	Other food products		1111	1146	1209	1192		20581	20228	18554	19854		1346	1380	1389	...
1541	Bakery products		992	1034	1105	1089		9912	10285	10631	11654		279	309	335	...
1542	Sugar		14	14	13	11		5627	5244	3204	2935		703	704	659	...
1543	Cocoa, chocolate and sugar confectionery		19	17	19	15		1157	1169	1170	1108		70	73	73	...
1544	Macaroni, noodles & similar products		22	18	16	15		722	704	620	690		34	28	26	...
1549	Other food products n.e.c.		64	63	56	62		3163	2826	2929	3467		260	266	296	...
155	Beverages		31	33	32	29		5653	5625	4333	5883		660	641	656	...
1551	Distilling, rectifying & blending of spirits		4	4	4	4		134	152	81	136		6	5	6	...
1552	Wines		10	8	8	7		744	744	421	1316		79	70	77	...
1553	Malt liquors and malt		3	3	3	3		886	993	908	843		142	117	119	...
1554	Soft drinks; mineral waters		14	18	17	15		3889	3736	2923	3588		433	449	455	...
1600	Tobacco products		4	3	3	3		2314	1590	1590	1590		444	391	328	...
171	Spinning, weaving and finishing of textiles		272	262	259	324		21689	22226	21418	21900		963	958	968	...
1711	Textile fibre preparation; textile weaving		190	179	176	162		17931	17269	15275	14630		824	779	754	...
1712	Finishing of textiles		82	83	83	82		3758	4957	6143	7270		139	179	214	...
172	Other textiles		230	230	226	218		8131	7866	9742	10374		274	284	310	...
1721	Made-up textile articles, except apparel		63	67	70	69		2975	3157	4649	4998		116	110	141	...
1722	Carpets and rugs		25	20	20	19		2189	1440	1796	1912		72	68	73	...
1723	Cordage, rope, twine and netting		5	4	5	6		303	420	588	657		10	9	20	...
1729	Other textiles n.e.c.		137	139	131	124		2664	2849	2709	2807		76	97	75	...
1730	Knitted and crocheted fabrics and articles		128	108	107	93		9423	8467	8511	8416		272	244	249	...
1810	Wearing apparel, except fur apparel		1093	1030	977	891		166757	159065	149932	149599		4488	4561	4460	...
1820	Dressing & dyeing of fur; processing of fur		-	-	-	-		-	-	-	-		-	-	-	...
191	Tanning, dressing and processing of leather		99	95	102	102		3441	3178	3183	3212		130	115	124	...
1911	Tanning and dressing of leather		57	53	59	58		1813	1718	1689	1662		84	73	77	...
1912	Luggage, handbags, etc.; saddlery & harness		42	42	43	44		1628	1460	1494	1550		46	42	47	...
1920	Footwear		243	239	239	233		12946	13207	13170	14147		406	433	447	...
2010	Sawmilling and planing of wood		70	67	72	69		1295	1390	1400	1359		40	44	47	...
202	Products of wood, cork, straw, etc.		406	430	436	445		8274	7668	7092	8110		288	304	326	...
2021	Veneer sheets, plywood, particle board, etc.		4	4	3	3		1222	1080	1011	1076		87	92	78	...
2022	Builders' carpentry and joinery		350	372	376	383		4218	4389	4565	4883		111	114	151	...
2023	Wooden containers		23	23	24	22		1855	1199	552	1065		53	55	55	...
2029	Other wood products; articles of cork/straw		29	31	33	37		979	1000	964	1086		38	44	43	...
210	Paper and paper products		98	88	85	79		6946	6468	5129	4951		460	441	399	...
2101	Pulp, paper and paperboard		18	13	13	10		1588	1252	1132	1094		116	118	95	...
2102	Corrugated paper and paperboard		57	51	47	45		4619	4496	3235	3150		307	293	271	...
2109	Other articles of paper and paperboard		23	24	25	24		739	720	762	707		36	30	33	...
221	Publishing		45	38	41	24		2278	1996	2028	1729		129	121	129	...
2211	Publishing of books and other publications		10	10	6	7		610	578	491	468		26	26	24	...
2212	Publishing of newspapers, journals, etc.		12	11	10	9		1375	1183	1201	1222		87	80	81	...
2213	Publishing of recorded media		1	1	1	1		6	6	6	6		-	-	-	...
2219	Other publishing		22	16	24	7		287	229	330	39		16	15	24	...

222	Printing and related service activities	409	423	436	443	6453	6378	6536	7169	368	366	402	...
2221	Printing	407	421	435	422	6444	6373	6534	6752	368	366	402	...
2222	Service activities related to printing	2	2	1	21	9	5	2	417	-	-	-	...
2230	Reproduction of recorded media	-	-	-	-	-	-	-	-	-	-	-	...
2310	Coke oven products	1	1	1	1	64	63	63	77	7	7	8	...
2320	Refined petroleum products	11	10	25	24	2247	2112	2597	2863	350	380	462	...
2330	Processing of nuclear fuel	-	-	-	-	-	-	-	-	-	-	-	...
241	Basic chemicals	47	47	48	44	9569	10796	8594	8290	1654	1779	1730	...
2411	Basic chemicals, except fertilizers	27	27	27	24	7927	7607	3976	3535	1451	1618	228	...
2412	Fertilizers and nitrogen compounds	4	5	7	7	230	2198	3646	3639	62	60	1386	...
2413	Plastics in primary forms; synthetic rubber	16	15	14	13	1412	991	972	1116	142	101	117	...
242	Other chemicals	174	179	193	187	14932	16615	17787	19563	1961	1905	2256	...
2421	Pesticides and other agro-chemical products	3	3	5	5	212	194	232	215	59	44	53	...
2422	Paints, varnishes, printing ink and mastics	35	41	42	43	2222	2467	2640	2545	259	298	319	...
2423	Pharmaceuticals, medicinal chemicals, etc.	35	35	41	40	5422	5426	6386	6309	908	939	1167	...
2424	Soap, cleaning & cosmetic preparations	48	55	60	57	5163	7269	7486	8282	570	486	577	...
2429	Other chemical products n.e.c.	53	45	45	42	1913	1259	1043	2212	166	138	140	...
2430	Man-made fibres	2	2	2	2	418	425	955	630	11	16	22	...
251	Rubber products	25	27	26	26	1201	1093	1185	1082	128	99	93	...
2511	Rubber tyres and tubes	5	5	4	3	602	410	291	337	91	47	46	...
2519	Other rubber products	20	22	22	23	599	683	894	745	37	51	46	...
2520	Plastic products	260	245	252	239	10708	10747	10931	10413	525	533	577	...
2610	Glass and glass products	44	44	43	40	1994	1865	1585	1909	112	115	116	...
269	Non-metallic mineral products n.e.c.	641	660	721	708	29417	27829	30464	44698	1464	1470	1582	...
2691	Pottery, china and earthenware	17	16	15	14	1665	1566	1281	1408	82	86	87	...
2692	Refractory ceramic products	23	23	28	29	4541	4030	5617	8599	234	234	301	...
2693	Struct.non-refractory clay; ceramic products	86	82	90	82	4758	4258	4510	13836	145	155	159	...
2694	Cement, lime and plaster	23	23	26	24	2753	2770	2616	2770	478	462	390	...
2695	Articles of concrete, cement and plaster	334	358	384	376	12603	11985	11424	12197	442	431	550	...
2696	Cutting, shaping & finishing of stone	134	137	158	162	2312	2440	2481	2762	56	61	66	...
2699	Other non-metallic mineral products n.e.c.	24	21	20	21	785	780	2535	3126	27	39	29	...
2710	Basic iron and steel	64	68	67	66	2713	2723	2624	2811	234	233	260	...
2720	Basic precious and non-ferrous metals	27	35	35	34	1460	2926	1135	1252	99	99	102	...
273	Casting of metals	20	21	22	21	610	456	455	648	27	15	17	...
2731	Casting of iron and steel	17	16	17	16	570	374	388	575	26	13	15	...
2732	Casting of non-ferrous metals	3	5	5	5	40	82	67	73	1	2	3	...
281	Struct.metal products;tanks;steam generators	305	324	367	358	10636	11741	11109	14360	525	551	670	...
2811	Structural metal products	274	290	334	326	7856	8886	9062	11399	409	437	537	...
2812	Tanks, reservoirs and containers of metal	27	29	27	26	2626	2731	1974	2872	114	111	130	...
2813	Steam generators	4	5	6	6	154	124	73	89	3	2	3	...
289	Other metal products; metal working services	456	451	467	446	11366	11333	10523	10512	615	637	608	...
2891	Metal forging/pressing/stamping/roll-forming	17	13	9	11	1150	974	868	931	104	94	98	...
2892	Treatment & coating of metals	283	274	288	279	4005	4368	4059	3826	194	195	217	...
2893	Cutlery, hand tools and general hardware	38	38	35	25	1406	1173	1511	1402	51	48	61	...
2899	Other fabricated metal products n.e.c.	118	126	135	131	4805	4818	4085	4353	265	300	232	...
291	General purpose machinery	127	112	116	111	3577	3080	3343	3999	189	181	200	...
2911	Engines & turbines (not for transport equipment)	20	17	16	17	240	195	122	139	14	12	3	...
2912	Pumps, compressors, taps and valves	28	23	23	20	1206	1018	1043	1389	70	62	72	...
2913	Bearings, gears, gearing & driving elements	28	22	21	21	391	252	293	333	14	8	13	...
2914	Ovens, furnaces and furnace burners	1	1	1	1	10	10	12	15	-	-	-	...
2915	Lifting and handling equipment	8	9	11	9	297	337	352	321	33	38	37	...
2919	Other general purpose machinery	42	40	44	43	1433	1268	1521	1802	58	61	75	...
292	Special purpose machinery	44	51	52	53	677	749	776	756	37	39	44	...
2921	Agricultural and forestry machinery	11	12	15	15	363	361	361	325	24	22	27	...
2922	Machine tools	14	19	19	19	91	182	214	218	3	7	8	...
2923	Machinery for metallurgy	1	1	1	1	31	31	24	15	2	2	2	...
2924	Machinery for mining & construction	4	5	3	4	49	47	31	41	2	2	1	...
2925	Food/beverage/tobacco processing machinery	-	-	-	-	-	-	-	-	-	-	-	...
2926	Machinery for textile, apparel and leather	3	3	3	3	35	29	34	32	2	2	2	...
2927	Weapons and ammunition	-	-	-	-	-	-	-	-	-	-	-	...
2929	Other special purpose machinery	11	11	11	12	108	99	112	125	4	4	5	...

continued

Morocco

ISIC Revision 3		Number of enterprises					Number of employees					Wages and salaries paid to employees				
			(number)					(number)					(millions of Moroccan Dirhams)			
ISIC	Industry	Note	2003	2004	2005	2006	Note	2003	2004	2005	2006	Note	2003	2004	2005	2006
2930	Domestic appliances n.e.c.		26	24	23	25		1649	1308	981	1161		132	88	87	...
3000	Office, accounting and computing machinery		3	3	8	7		13	91	162	159		-	16	19	...
3110	Electric motors, generators and transformers		30	28	32	31		1160	802	801	845		52	51	51	...
3120	Electricity distribution & control apparatus		35	35	39	35		3721	3093	4876	4711		336	347	392	...
3130	Insulated wire and cable		9	9	11	11		685	622	1272	1464		46	47	135	...
3140	Accumulators, primary cells and batteries		6	5	5	4		1243	1255	713	477		136	143	52	...
3150	Lighting equipment and electric lamps		35	37	41	36		1544	1407	1482	1475		77	69	77	...
3190	Other electrical equipment n.e.c.		36	33	38	40		15970	15199	17227	20164		598	692	848	...
3210	Electronic valves, tubes, etc.		11	10	9	6		5897	5692	5220	5232		434	457	457	...
3220	TV/radio transmitters; line comm. apparatus		1	1	2	1		15	16	42	34		1	1	4	...
3230	TV and radio receivers and associated goods		3	4	2	2		85	100	41	45		4	4	2	...
331	Medical, measuring, testing appliances, etc.		21	21	23	24		522	701	878	1543		33	34	49	...
3311	Medical, surgical and orthopaedic equipment		12	13	15	15		193	223	307	288		8	9	10	...
3312	Measuring/testing/navigating appliances,etc.		9	8	8	9		329	478	571	1255		24	25	39	...
3313	Industrial process control equipment		-	-	-	-		-	-	-	-		-	-	-	...
3320	Optical instruments & photographic equipment		5	5	5	5		82	71	70	87		3	2	2	...
3330	Watches and clocks		-	-	-	-		-	-	-	-		-	-	-	...
3410	Motor vehicles		9	10	8	5		2454	2628	1914	1703		318	317	263	...
3420	Automobile bodies, trailers & semi-trailers		35	36	43	43		1352	1146	1347	1760		57	51	57	...
3430	Parts/accessories for automobiles		41	41	39	35		2255	2052	2107	1844		130	134	120	...
351	Building and repairing of ships and boats		47	43	39	40		1538	1302	904	1140		92	86	80	...
3511	Building and repairing of ships		42	40	38	37		1246	1012	884	872		78	71	79	...
3512	Building/repairing of pleasure/sport. boats		5	3	1	3		292	290	20	268		13	14	1	...
3520	Railway/tramway locomotives & rolling stock		1	1	-	-		195	146	-	-		15	15	-	...
3530	Aircraft and spacecraft		-	-	3	2		-	-	380	470		-	-	14	...
359	Transport equipment n.e.c.		15	16	13	12		449	723	463	452		33	45	40	...
3591	Motorcycles		7	9	7	7		284	569	317	319		28	41	35	...
3592	Bicycles and invalid carriages		4	3	3	2		105	95	93	69		3	3	3	...
3599	Other transport equipment n.e.c.		4	4	3	3		60	59	53	64		2	2	2	...
3610	Furniture		136	165	182	158		4810	4712	4976	5536		286	320	370	...
369	Manufacturing n.e.c.		60	59	61	56		2150	2101	2220	2324		109	102	117	...
3691	Jewellery and related articles		11	12	12	11		587	766	824	911		23	30	37	...
3692	Musical instruments		-	-	-	-		-	-	-	-		-	-	-	...
3693	Sports goods		1	1	2	2		3	6	13	21		-	-	-	...
3694	Games and toys		2	2	3	3		29	45	124	140		1	2	4	...
3699	Other manufacturing n.e.c.		46	44	44	40		1531	1284	1259	1252		85	70	75	...
3710	Recycling of metal waste and scrap		-	-	-	-		-	-	-	-		-	-	-	...
3720	Recycling of non-metal waste and scrap		2	3	2	2		61	70	67	50		1	2	1	...
D	Total manufacturing		7814	7829	8103	7887		492630	475863	452819	494499		23618	24024	25056	...

ISIC Revision 3		Output in factor values					Value added in factor values					Gross fixed capital formation		
		Note	(millions of Moroccan Dirhams)				Note	(millions of Moroccan Dirhams)				Note	(millions of Moroccan Dirhams)	
ISIC	Industry		2003	2004	2005	2006		2003	2004	2005	2006		2005	2006
151	Processed meat,fish,fruit,vegetables,fats		17191	17666	17898	18850		3394	3347	3276	3626		604	641
1511	Processing/preserving of meat		533	745	816	910		91	116	112	164		100	76
1512	Processing/preserving of fish		7164	6882	6897	7568		1739	1626	1636	1846		171	193
1513	Processing/preserving of fruit & vegetables		2566	2342	2359	2253		466	488	534	510		121	127
1514	Vegetable and animal oils and fats		6929	7697	7826	8119		1097	1116	994	1106		213	245
1520	Dairy products		7273	7733	8744	9051		1970	1949	2007	2285		604	572
153	Grain mill products; starches; animal feeds		14315	13670	15740	15801		1380	1577	1743	1399		390	534
1531	Grain mill products		11435	10767	11731	11862		957	1183	1323	1007		300	491
1532	Starches and starch products		157	119	160	168		53	43	49	52		13	11
1533	Prepared animal feeds		2723	2783	3849	3771		371	352	370	340		77	32
154	Other food products		10696	9658	9503	10103		2899	3146	3074	3251		790	527
1541	Bakery products		1617	1737	1781	1839		556	607	627	650		52	89
1542	Sugar		6068	5287	4881	4890		1500	1731	1480	1435		528	201
1543	Cocoa, chocolate and sugar confectionery		503	533	405	508		121	135	124	161		18	22
1544	Macaroni, noodles & similar products		539	473	512	531		75	67	82	81		8	30
1549	Other food products n.e.c.		1968	1627	1924	2335		648	607	760	924		184	185
155	Beverages		5155	4912	5191	5305		2781	2663	2894	2922		348	345
1551	Distilling, rectifying & blending of spirits		72	83	89	84		22	24	18	18		3	4
1552	Wines		836	655	809	620		344	291	317	393		16	30
1553	Malt liquors and malt		1424	1531	1522	1578		1102	1164	1158	1202		108	77
1554	Soft drinks; mineral waters		2823	2643	2771	3023		1313	1183	1402	1309		220	234
1600	Tobacco products		4920	5385	4911	4911		4834	5276	11583	11583		187	187
171	Spinning, weaving and finishing of textiles		6477	6222	6191	5902		1908	1869	1832	1781		592	606
1711	Textile fibre preparation; textile weaving		5754	5344	5219	4861		1646	1544	1466	1375		486	502
1712	Finishing of textiles		723	878	972	1041		262	324	366	406		106	104
172	Other textiles		1343	1478	1650	2073		502	494	555	599		179	227
1721	Made-up textile articles, except apparel		623	700	902	999		188	209	268	291		73	132
1722	Carpets and rugs		320	297	276	317		127	114	118	118		14	46
1723	Cordage, rope, twine and netting		60	65	120	340		36	11	34	45		67	13
1729	Other textiles n.e.c.		340	415	351	417		152	159	134	145		25	36
1730	Knitted and crocheted fabrics and articles		1483	1155	1080	1066		459	369	343	334		61	74
1810	Wearing apparel, except fur apparel		14908	14712	14335	14772		6628	6496	6178	5962		625	480
1820	Dressing & dyeing of fur; processing of fur		-	-	-	-		-	-	-	-		-	-
191	Tanning, dressing and processing of leather		709	506	546	561		217	163	193	179		4	7
1911	Tanning and dressing of leather		554	372	397	387		155	105	129	111		3	6
1912	Luggage, handbags, etc.; saddlery & harness		156	134	148	174		62	58	64	68		1	1
1920	Footwear		1533	1535	1599	1673		600	656	639	698		91	78
2010	Sawmilling and planing of wood		887	826	900	380		116	130	128	77		9	11
202	Products of wood, cork, straw, etc.		1891	1977	2215	2569		528	542	559	630		74	96
2021	Veneer sheets, plywood, particle board, etc.		694	800	739	793		177	200	165	185		40	46
2022	Builders' carpentry and joinery		562	568	819	972		174	160	207	248		18	18
2023	Wooden containers		367	306	389	532		90	87	105	121		6	7
2029	Other wood products; articles of cork/straw		269	303	268	272		88	95	83	76		10	25
210	Paper and paper products		4789	4304	3579	3712		1439	1487	1080	1128		286	303
2101	Pulp, paper and paperboard		1210	1071	1060	1238		459	514	358	406		96	95
2102	Corrugated paper and paperboard		3263	2952	2163	2160		890	900	648	643		173	176
2109	Other articles of paper and paperboard		317	280	356	314		89	73	74	79		18	32
221	Publishing		481	470	466	345		198	200	218	175		71	39
2211	Publishing of books and other publications		117	158	125	112		39	43	34	36		3	5
2212	Publishing of newspapers, journals, etc.		284	229	229	227		129	127	131	137		53	34
2213	Publishing of recorded media		1	1	1	1		-	-	-	-		-	-
2219	Other publishing		78	82	112	5		30	29	53	2		14	-

continued

Morocco

ISIC Revision 3		Output in factor values					Value added in factor values					Gross fixed capital formation		
		Note	(millions of Moroccan Dirhams)				Note	(millions of Moroccan Dirhams)				Note	(millions of Moroccan Dirhams)	
ISIC	Industry		2003	2004	2005	2006		2003	2004	2005	2006		2005	2006
222	Printing and related service activities		1934	1879	2065	2284		646	631	677	728		111	186
2221	Printing		1933	1879	2065	2168		646	631	677	679		111	178
2222	Service activities related to printing		-	-	-	116		-	-	-	49		-	8
2230	Reproduction of recorded media		-	-	-	-		-	-	-	-		-	-
2310	Coke oven products		130	150	166	96		18	25	9	28		3	6
2320	Refined petroleum products		10451	18049	26813	30206		1218	1679	2644	1898		1084	2470
2330	Processing of nuclear fuel		-	-	-	-		-	-	-	-		-	-
241	Basic chemicals		12482	12998	15963	16707		3752	4057	4375	4631		1089	1266
2411	Basic chemicals, except fertilizers		10606	11906	7934	8446		3253	3620	1698	2517		69	1170
2412	Fertilizers and nitrogen compounds		923	110	6390	6908		172	126	2368	1779		949	5
2413	Plastics in primary forms; synthetic rubber		953	982	1639	1353		327	310	309	335		71	91
242	Other chemicals		10247	10270	11333	11653		4247	3877	5199	4367		515	508
2421	Pesticides and other agro-chemical products		98	61	122	129		120	88	105	101		14	13
2422	Paints, varnishes, printing ink and mastics		1827	2276	2250	2411		861	682	524	673		107	63
2423	Pharmaceuticals, medicinal chemicals, etc.		3899	3831	4828	4728		1950	1938	2364	2366		217	322
2424	Soap, cleaning & cosmetic preparations		3395	3336	3445	3543		980	891	1928	890		131	66
2429	Other chemical products n.e.c.		1028	766	688	842		336	279	278	337		46	44
2430	Man-made fibres		32	30	32	19		17	20	24	16		5	1
251	Rubber products		533	205	251	518		195	148	132	113		10	3
2511	Rubber tyres and tubes		374	18	15	320		134	48	47	47		-	-
2519	Other rubber products		159	186	235	198		61	100	85	66		9	3
2520	Plastic products		3798	4005	4608	4929		1088	1084	1166	1234		315	266
2610	Glass and glass products		568	594	605	691		261	262	274	266		125	61
269	Non-metallic mineral products n.e.c.		12596	12408	14712	22139		5600	5039	6117	6931		1610	3814
2691	Pottery, china and earthenware		690	746	539	592		266	286	259	271		42	50
2692	Refractory ceramic products		1356	1342	2089	2883		448	337	560	760		294	113
2693	Struct.non-refractory clay; ceramic products		709	736	830	945		252	274	281	277		212	149
2694	Cement, lime and plaster		6192	5944	6059	9559		3519	2943	3361	4264		745	3128
2695	Articles of concrete, cement and plaster		2964	2979	4525	5390		914	937	1118	1168		267	314
2696	Cutting, shaping & finishing of stone		382	399	469	2529		112	135	469	126		45	50
2699	Other non-metallic mineral products n.e.c.		302	261	201	241		89	127	69	65		5	10
2710	Basic iron and steel		6409	5580	7519	9111		1449	1180	1449	1662		1720	240
2720	Basic precious and non-ferrous metals		993	1009	1282	1541		213	354	492	333		139	103
273	Casting of metals		83	83	87	114		32	20	29	70		-	20
2731	Casting of iron and steel		79	78	79	104		30	18	25	66		-	20
2732	Casting of non-ferrous metals		4	5	8	10		2	2	4	4		-	-
281	Struct.metal products;tanks;steam generators		2873	3256	4590	4838		877	948	1134	1298		87	152
2811	Structural metal products		2264	2636	3729	4117		672	711	865	1043		63	126
2812	Tanks, reservoirs and containers of metal		603	611	755	704		203	233	266	251		23	22
2813	Steam generators		6	10	105	17		2	4	4	4		2	4
289	Other metal products; metal working services		4057	4053	5123	5679		1206	1298	1353	1468		219	231
2891	Metal forging/pressing/stamping/roll-forming		433	357	465	495		175	140	142	148		4	28
2892	Treatment & coating of metals		1513	1363	2342	2771		440	406	548	625		76	49
2893	Cutlery, hand tools and general hardware		274	259	422	415		96	79	121	128		34	34
2899	Other fabricated metal products n.e.c.		1838	2075	1895	1998		495	674	541	567		105	120
291	General purpose machinery		780	676	1007	1026		315	282	350	400		65	30
2911	Engines & turbines (not for transport equipment)		62	52	11	12		19	16	6	6		-	1
2912	Pumps, compressors, taps and valves		241	199	310	329		103	86	109	92		19	8
2913	Bearings, gears, gearing & driving elements		66	27	59	65		22	13	42	59		2	7
2914	Ovens, furnaces and furnace burners		1	1	1	2		-	-	-	-		-	-
2915	Lifting and handling equipment		146	137	155	160		68	68	78	75		1	2
2919	Other general purpose machinery		264	260	471	458		103	97	114	168		44	12

292	Special purpose machinery	118	159	156	154	71	73	73	121	8	41
2921	Agricultural and forestry machinery	69	74	85	86	51	43	43	92	-	36
2922	Machine tools	10	37	32	26	4	12	14	12	1	1
2923	Machinery for metallurgy	10	8	8	8	2	6	6	5	-	-
2924	Machinery for mining & construction	9	7	4	6	3	1	1	1	-	1
2925	Food/beverage/tobacco processing machinery	-	-	-	-	-	-	-	-	-	-
2926	Machinery for textile, apparel and leather	8	9	9	10	6	3	3	3	-	-
2927	Weapons and ammunition	-	-	-	-	-	-	-	-	-	-
2929	Other special purpose machinery	11	24	19	18	5	9	7	8	6	3
2930	Domestic appliances n.e.c.	839	675	692	700	247	176	181	187	11	35
3000	Office, accounting and computing machinery	4	84	153	128	1	37	26	27	-	-
3110	Electric motors, generators and transformers	329	252	209	197	87	64	62	63	2	2
3120	Electricity distribution & control apparatus	1194	1197	1352	1425	591	557	712	765	83	57
3130	Insulated wire and cable	724	744	1909	2800	190	166	390	510	57	115
3140	Accumulators, primary cells and batteries	956	1119	298	224	279	261	106	71	5	1
3150	Lighting equipment and electric lamps	329	280	345	360	131	105	116	114	13	10
3190	Other electrical equipment n.e.c.	5297	5600	6905	8982	1202	1215	1479	1754	459	522
3210	Electronic valves, tubes, etc.	1183	1354	1261	1269	592	661	645	644	61	65
3220	TV/radio transmitters; line comm. apparatus	5	4	6	8	1	1	6	3	-	2
3230	TV and radio receivers and associated goods	19	19	8	8	4	5	3	3	1	-
331	Medical, measuring, testing appliances, etc.	241	263	438	863	84	87	114	191	16	244
3311	Medical, surgical and orthopaedic equipment	28	28	33	36	12	13	13	23	-	1
3312	Measuring/testing/navigating appliances,etc.	213	235	406	827	72	74	101	168	15	243
3313	Industrial process control equipment	-	-	-	-	-	-	-	-	-	-
3320	Optical instruments & photographic equipment	7	6	6	7	3	2	3	3	-	-
3330	Watches and clocks	-	-	-	-	-	-	-	-	-	-
3410	Motor vehicles	2296	2434	2221	1102	877	875	646	343	139	97
3420	Automobile bodies, trailers & semi-trailers	725	409	488	1508	143	87	104	246	8	32
3430	Parts/accessories for automobiles	731	724	664	634	242	236	217	211	51	32
351	Building and repairing of ships and boats	252	248	249	271	128	126	111	130	5	15
3511	Building and repairing of ships	218	206	240	228	111	99	110	121	5	8
3512	Building/repairing of pleasure/sport. boats	33	43	10	43	18	27	2	9	-	7
3520	Railway/tramway locomotives & rolling stock	36	36	-	-	23	17	-	-	-	-
3530	Aircraft and spacecraft	-	-	75	187	-	-	18	60	21	7
359	Transport equipment n.e.c.	180	197	278	322	81	90	98	112	11	6
3591	Motorcycles	157	174	258	298	73	81	92	96	11	6
3592	Bicycles and invalid carriages	15	16	13	15	6	6	5	3	-	-
3599	Other transport equipment n.e.c.	7	7	8	9	2	2	2	3	-	-
3610	Furniture	1176	1423	1791	2183	397	511	581	621	75	119
369	Manufacturing n.e.c.	748	704	751	768	205	185	209	226	35	56
3691	Jewellery and related articles	320	369	385	369	57	59	72	82	25	44
3692	Musical instruments	-	-	-	-	-	-	-	-	-	-
3693	Sports goods	1	1	2	3	-	-	1	1	-	-
3694	Games and toys	3	10	32	42	3	4	16	18	2	1
3699	Other manufacturing n.e.c.	425	323	331	354	145	121	121	125	9	11
3710	Recycling of metal waste and scrap	-	-	-	-	-	-	-	-	-	-
3720	Recycling of non-metal waste and scrap	23	27	32	34	2	3	3	3	-	-
D	Total manufacturing	179432	185411	210994	232759	56571	56809	67631	68480	13078	15542

Morocco

ISIC Revision 3			Index numbers of industrial production											
			(2000=100)											
ISIC	Industry	Note	1995	1996	1997	1998	1999	2000	2001	2002	2003	2004	2005	2006
15	Food and beverages		...	...	...	...	...	...	...	...	...	...	...	...
16	Tobacco products		100	105	104	103	99	100	105	109	111	118	124	131
17	Textiles		98	97	102	103	105	100	110	113	109	109	113	123
18	Wearing apparel, fur		62	66	70	74	82	100	96	96	96	97	103	100
19	Leather, leather products and footwear		95	105	109	101	102	100	107	106	110	106	111	109
20	Wood products (excl. furniture)		77	79	79	80	74	100	91	88	89	97	88	78
21	Paper and paper products		69	80	82	85	85	100	105	110	129	152	159	192
22	Printing and publishing		76	74	91	86	99	100	97	108	118	114	134	134
23	Coke,refined petroleum products,nuclear fuel		93	90	96	94	110	100	104	101	73	98	107	112
24	Chemicals and chemical products		85	87	94	95	99	100	103	110	112	120	126	129
25	Rubber and plastics products		67	71	72	73	84	100	93	102	96	116	116	131
26	Non-metallic mineral products		91	97	102	97	100	100	106	116	128	133	140	148
27	Basic metals		76	75	84	83	92	100	103	119	142	140	155	162
28	Fabricated metal products		76	76	78	76	92	100	109	109	107	120	128	132
29	Machinery and equipment n.e.c.		81	73	77	78	86	100	93	96	107	110	110	116
30	Office, accounting and computing machinery		608	629	744	585	588	100	100	100	100	163	163	163
31	Electrical machinery and apparatus		71	71	72	74	91	100	100	109	116	120	124	123
32	Radio,television and communication equipment		...	...	...	144	168	100	151	147	170	170	180	310
33	Medical, precision and optical instruments		54	43	55	64	77	100	82	113	101	140	144	141
34	Motor vehicles, trailers, semi-trailers		67	77	81	85	103	100	106	106	95	96	107	149
35	Other transport equipment		...	...	...	82	106	100	125	120	135	112	113	120
36	Furniture; manufacturing n.e.c.		...	...	...	...	...	...	...	...	...	...	...	...
37	Recycling		...	...	...	...	...	...	...	...	...	...	...	...
D	Total manufacturing		80	82	85	88	94	100	103	107	110	115	121	128

Netherlands

Supplier of information:
Central Bureau of Statistics, Voorburg.
Industrial statistics for the OECD countries are compiled by the OECD secretariat, which supplies them to UNIDO.

Basic source of data:
Survey on annual production statistics; survey on investment; annual census; VAT register.

Major deviations from ISIC (Revision 3):
Data presented by OECD in accordance with ISIC (Revision 3) were originally classified according to a classification system compatible with NACE (Revision 1).

Reference period:
Calendar year.

Scope:
All enterprises.

Method of data collection:
Not reported.

Type of enumeration:
Enterprises with 20 and more employees are completely enumerated, while smaller enterprises are surveyed through sampling.

Adjusted for non-response:
Yes.

Concepts and definitions of variables:
Number of employees is not converted to full time equivalent.
Wages and salaries includes gratuities, tips, severance payments, workplace and performance bonuses, ex-gratia payments, thirteenth month pay and seniority attendance.
Output is gross output. It excludes income from sales of capital assets produced on own accounts.
Value added refers to the national accounting concept.
Gross fixed capital formation is defined as the value of fixed assets purchased or constructed by the unit's own labour force for its own use, during the reference year. Major additions, alterations and improvements to fixed assets carried out by third parties are included. Transactions in fixed assets includes land, buildings, site preparation and other construction work, land which is not used for the establishment's business, transport equipment, machinery and other equipment, as well as additions, alterations and improvements which prolong the service life or increase productive capacity of capital goods. Fixed assets are valued at acquisition costs, including transportation costs and costs of installation, taxes and insurance for goods in transit.

Related national publications:
Summary of Manufacturing Industries (annual), published by Central Bureau of Statistics, Voorburg.

Netherlands

ISIC Revision 3		Number of enterprises					Number of employees					Wages and salaries paid to employees				
			(number)					(number)					(millions of Euros)			
ISIC	Industry	Note	2002	2003	2004	2005	Note	2002	2003	2004	2005	Note	2002	2003	2004	2005
151	Processed meat,fish,fruit,vegetables,fats		1105	1100	1030	1015		38538	36397	34636	33592		1144.4	1155.0	1164.0	...
1511	Processing/preserving of meat		820	815	760	735		23613	21900	19864	19075		647.4	656.8	633.0	587.0
1512	Processing/preserving of fish		135	130	125	120		3265	3109	3086	3263		79.0	...	...	77.0
1513	Processing/preserving of fruit & vegetables		135	135	125	135		9225	9192	9435	9060		305.5	312.0	339.0	325.0
1514	Vegetable and animal oils and fats		15	20	20	25		2435	2196	2251	2194		112.5	...	...	...
1520	Dairy products		245	240	255	255		11424	11208	10730	10260		413.7	425.8	416.0	457.0
153	Grain mill products; starches; animal feeds		285	285	270	280		13150	11625	11597	10605		454.5	464.2	471.0	457.0
1531	Grain mill products		65	70	70	80		1624	1375	1304	1249		47.9	...	...	...
1532	Starches and starch products		10	15	10	10		3039	2817	2547	2264		114.9	...	...	...
1533	Prepared animal feeds		210	205	185	185		8487	7433	7746	7092		291.7	282.8	301.0	292.0
154	Other food products		3065	3025	2870	2910		65691	58610	57271	56799		1473.4	1535.0	1572.0	1552.0
1541	Bakery products		2740	2725	2580	2620		45656	39333	38022	37417		743.9	763.4	790.0	760.0
1542	Sugar		5	5	5	5		...	...	...	...		62.3	...	...	...
1543	Cocoa, chocolate and sugar confectionery		150	140	135	135		6997	6321	6172	6333		246.4	252.3	234.0	245.0
1544	Macaroni, noodles & similar products		10	10	5	5		...	42	...	...		...	...	...	...
1549	Other food products n.e.c.		160	150	140	150		...	...	...	...		...	...	...	...
155	Beverages		105	115	120	130		9332	8865	8234	7720		...	378.1	356.0	338.0
1551	Distilling, rectifying & blending of spirits		30	30	30	30		...	...	...	...		...	...	...	...
1552	Wines		15	20	25	25		...	...	...	...		...	...	...	...
1553	Malt liquors and malt		35	35	45	50		...	5532	5069	...		...	...	...	...
1554	Soft drinks; mineral waters		25	20	20	20		2464	2348	2242	1956		97.4	92.5	88.0	88.0
1600	Tobacco products		20	20	20	20		5064	4768	4753	4292		...	203.8	217.0	...
171	Spinning, weaving and finishing of textiles		230	290	325	285		4553	5068	3743	3445		156.5	...	...	114.0
1711	Textile fibre preparation; textile weaving		60	80	80	70		2282	1904	1748	1713		74.6	...	...	61.0
1712	Finishing of textiles		170	210	245	215		2271	3164	1995	1732		81.8	58.6	58.0	54.0
172	Other textiles		745	945	1045	955		12162	10316	10020	8838		317.9	308.7	284.0	289.0
1721	Made-up textile articles, except apparel		555	700	780	705		5966	4763	5035	4204		118.4	105.2	89.0	104.0
1722	Carpets and rugs		70	75	75	65		3318	2920	2676	2478		110.1	109.6	99.0	105.0
1723	Cordage, rope, twine and netting		30	40	40	35		336	333	272	240		9.8	9.8	13.0	...
1729	Other textiles n.e.c.		90	125	145	150		2542	2300	2037	1916		79.6	84.1	83.0	...
1730	Knitted and crocheted fabrics and articles		70	75	80	65		977	707	450	346		28.2	...	...	9.0
1810	Wearing apparel, except fur apparel		1590	1120	1285	1510		...	...	2837	3083		106.7	...	...	...
1820	Dressing & dyeing of fur; processing of fur		10	5	10	10		...	...	7	13		-	...	...	...
191	Tanning, dressing and processing of leather		270	275	195	210		937	893	786	719		27.9	18.2	23.0	21.0
1911	Tanning and dressing of leather		60	60	40	45		370	390	337	296		12.6	9.9	11.0	10.0
1912	Luggage, handbags, etc.; saddlery & harness		210	215	155	165		567	503	449	423		15.3	8.3	12.0	11.0
1920	Footwear		165	160	105	105		1132	1093	977	783		30.9	37.3	29.0	30.0
2010	Sawmilling and planing of wood		200	200	190	190		1204	1087	1096	1055		18.7	24.0	26.0	33.0
202	Products of wood, cork, straw, etc.		2145	2140	1825	1785		17391	16806	15712	15981		492.1	470.7	479.0	479.0
2021	Veneer sheets, plywood, particle board, etc.		25	25	25	25		288	245	221	241		6.9	4.3	9.0	5.0
2022	Builders' carpentry and joinery		1315	1310	1115	1095		12885	12398	11627	11856		367.6	355.1	359.0	363.0
2023	Wooden containers		180	185	150	140		2458	2123	2031	2011		61.9	58.3	53.0	62.0
2029	Other wood products; articles of cork/straw		625	620	535	525		1760	2040	1833	1873		55.7	53.0	58.0	49.0
210	Paper and paper products		450	445	440	435		24519	23687	22733	22059		866.6	855.6	852.0	844.0
2101	Pulp, paper and paperboard		70	65	75	85		5742	5813	5948	6189		254.4	233.5	240.0	262.0
2102	Corrugated paper and paperboard		215	215	195	195		10058	9252	8734	8670		314.5	318.3	308.0	300.0
2109	Other articles of paper and paperboard		165	165	175	155		...	...	...	...		297.7	...	...	...
221	Publishing		2800	2670	2815	2780		36813	34945	33075	34420		1292.6	1303.2	1267.0	1315.0
2211	Publishing of books and other publications		1150	1115	1180	1170		7741	7965	7526	8826		297.6	298.9	300.0	319.0
2212	Publishing of newspapers, journals, etc.		1120	1025	1085	1080		27803	25702	24306	24121		951.9	967.1	930.0	955.0
2213	Publishing of recorded media		420	420	440	430		682	641	469	687		24.2	17.5	16.0	17.0
2219	Other publishing		110	105	105	100		587	637	774	787		19.0	19.7	21.0	25.0

222	Printing and related service activities	3915	3665	3635	3425	39383	36532	36198	34577	1249.4	1192.8	1212.0	1178.0
2221	Printing	2980	2775	2750	2595	32110	30642	30053	28960	1032.9	996.7	1014.0	1007.0
2222	Service activities related to printing	935	885	880	830	7273	5890	6145	5617	216.5	196.1	198.0	170.0
2230	Reproduction of recorded media	195	210	215	225	2295	1545	1455	1258	70.5	60.5	46.0	41.0
2310	Coke oven products	-	-	-	-	...	-	...	-	...	-	-	-
2320	Refined petroleum products	40	35	35	30	...	...	...	...	...	...	...	...
2330	Processing of nuclear fuel	-	-	-	-	...	...	...	...	...	...	...	...
241	Basic chemicals	290	255	290	240	28838	27221	27176	26111	1440.5	1409.4	1422.0	1476.0
2411	Basic chemicals, except fertilizers	135	120	135	120	...	...	...	...	...	...	...	...
2412	Fertilizers and nitrogen compounds	35	25	30	25	2175	1872	1953	1915	81.4	82.7	84.0	87.0
2413	Plastics in primary forms; synthetic rubber	120	105	125	100	...	...	...	...	...	...	...	...
242	Other chemicals	600	520	585	475	40703	38285	36623	36070	1497.6	...	...	1536.0
2421	Pesticides and other agro-chemical products	20	15	20	15	640	684	600	604	26.7	...	...	...
2422	Paints, varnishes, printing ink and mastics	135	120	125	105	8529	7368	6826	6699	299.6	299.1	281.0	287.0
2423	Pharmaceuticals, medicinal chemicals, etc.	145	130	155	125	16282	15322	15952	16335	583.7	614.0	627.0	696.0
2424	Soap, cleaning & cosmetic preparations	160	135	160	130	5081	5318	4936	4915	157.1	175.9	167.0	...
2429	Other chemical products n.e.c.	140	120	125	100	10171	9593	8309	7517	430.5	422.8	378.0	358.0
2430	Man-made fibres	20	20	25	20	2306	2317	2732	2720	117.9	...	...	137.0
251	Rubber products	90	95	105	100	3313	3503	3589	3362	117.8	116.2	119.0	111.0
2511	Rubber tyres and tubes	15	15	15	15	...	...	...	...	...	...	...	...
2519	Other rubber products	75	80	90	80	...	...	...	...	72.2	...	...	...
2520	Plastic products	1015	1070	1180	1080	31204	30540	29089	28673	953.7	951.2	935.0	944.0
2610	Glass and glass products	440	530	425	470	6305	6119	5972	5648	221.7	214.1	233.0	208.0
269	Non-metallic mineral products n.e.c.	1355	1490	1155	1145	24925	22556	22921	21931	813.0	799.0	804.0	784.0
2691	Pottery, china and earthenware	285	320	210	215	...	...	...	...	...	...	...	...
2692	Refractory ceramic products	10	10	5	10	...	...	...	...	...	...	...	...
2693	Struct.non-refractory clay; ceramic products	60	65	55	55	...	...	...	...	95.7	...	...	...
2694	Cement, lime and plaster	10	5	5	5	...	...	...	...	...	...	...	...
2695	Articles of concrete, cement and plaster	555	595	470	455	14611	13687	13440	12878	...	474.4	474.0	463.0
2696	Cutting, shaping & finishing of stone	360	425	335	335	2145	1764	2182	2006	55.3	66.1	61.0	66.0
2699	Other non-metallic mineral products n.e.c.	75	80	65	65	2752	2396	2513	2462	102.3	97.3	99.0	95.0
2710	Basic iron and steel	60	75	80	75	...	...	...	...	...	...	...	616.0
2720	Basic precious and non-ferrous metals	75	70	70	70	6800	6348	6274	5830	...	245.3	250.0	241.0
273	Casting of metals	120	125	120	115	...	...	...	...	137.5	...	...	119.0
2731	Casting of iron and steel	25	30	30	25	...	...	...	...	...	...	...	...
2732	Casting of non-ferrous metals	95	95	100	95	2388	2345	1726	1697	...	...	...	...
281	Struct.metal products;tanks;steam generators	2270	2335	2310	2150	44584	44330	41728	42375	1528.5	...	...	1478.0
2811	Structural metal products	2080	2165	2150	2005	38708	38040	36411	36464	1181.4	1161.4	1173.0	1246.0
2812	Tanks, reservoirs and containers of metal	175	155	145	135	5006	5518	4591	5176	312.0	309.0	304.0	198.0
2813	Steam generators	15	15	15	10	870	772	726	735	35.1	...	...	34.0
289	Other metal products; metal working services	5010	5140	5345	4975	48281	46645	46481	44132	1454.7	...	...	1502.0
2891	Metal forging/pressing/stamping/roll-forming	425	440	465	455	9097	8625	8449	8208	273.9	273.8	281.0	287.0
2892	Treatment & coating of metals	3465	3600	3765	3495	21134	20229	20769	19986	607.9	598.4	622.0	639.0
2893	Cutlery, hand tools and general hardware	360	350	350	315	5057	4924	4543	4261	160.7	...	...	153.0
2899	Other fabricated metal products n.e.c.	760	750	765	710	12993	12867	12720	11677	412.3	398.6	426.0	424.0
291	General purpose machinery	2350	2375	2365	2445	49821	47446	47761	48207	1680.8	1666.6	1729.0	1814.0
2911	Engines & turbines (not for transport equipment)	270	290	290	320	3692	3395	3348	4126	133.9	129.7	119.0	150.0
2912	Pumps, compressors, taps and valves	285	285	285	295	9206	9157	9112	9230	327.1	332.4	338.0	372.0
2913	Bearings, gears, gearing & driving elements	50	50	55	55	1644	1483	1825	1754	47.1	48.8	84.0	71.0
2914	Ovens, furnaces and furnace burners	40	40	40	40	650	733	760	723	21.8	22.4	27.0	26.0
2915	Lifting and handling equipment	410	405	415	415	12176	11955	12193	12285	401.2	417.9	438.0	454.0
2919	Other general purpose machinery	1295	1300	1275	1310	22453	20723	20523	20088	749.6	715.5	723.0	741.0
292	Special purpose machinery	1745	1705	1800	1895	...	...	...	33182	1247.8	1276.0	1308.0	1339.0
2921	Agricultural and forestry machinery	740	765	855	905	7692	7344	7798	7965	249.2	...	...	233.0
2922	Machine tools	175	110	135	165	2940	2639	2353	2219	102.2	90.7	91.0	...
2923	Machinery for metallurgy	15	15	15	15	...	...	...	...	...	...	...	...
2924	Machinery for mining & construction	100	95	90	95	1630	1298	1432	1437	...	52.0	63.0	54.0
2925	Food/beverage/tobacco processing machinery	250	245	240	245	7791	7425	7643	7882	277.3	288.8	314.0	318.0
2926	Machinery for textile, apparel and leather	60	65	60	60	1487	1531	794	875	46.5	43.3	34.0	39.0
2927	Weapons and ammunition	10	10	10	5	...	...	...	1	18.3	...	...	...
2929	Other special purpose machinery	395	400	400	405	...	...	...	...	494.6	...	...	...

continued

Netherlands

ISIC Revision 3		Number of enterprises					Number of employees					Wages and salaries paid to employees				
			(number)					(number)					(millions of Euros)			
ISIC	Industry	Note	2002	2003	2004	2005	Note	2002	2003	2004	2005	Note	2002	2003	2004	2005
2930	Domestic appliances n.e.c.		100	90	90	100		...	...	...	1987		57.7	56.9	59.0	61.0
3000	Office, accounting and computing machinery		385	285	180	200		...	...	...	...		227.2	235.8	237.0	227.0
3110	Electric motors, generators and transformers		210	235	220	250		4415	3709	3404	3437		156.7	130.9	141.0	128.0
3120	Electricity distribution & control apparatus		100	115	110	120		4687	3806	3339	3648		142.6	124.0	138.0	138.0
3130	Insulated wire and cable		50	55	50	60		3368	2861	2946	2455		125.4	116.1	111.0	109.0
3140	Accumulators, primary cells and batteries		10	10	10	15		291	174	221	192		6.0	7.7	17.0	9.0
3150	Lighting equipment and electric lamps		265	290	275	300		2649	2599	2436	2236		67.7	78.7	81.0	73.0
3190	Other electrical equipment n.e.c.		260	290	265	295		4567	4139	4438	4105		157.0	162.4	169.0	174.0
3210	Electronic valves, tubes, etc.		250	205	150	195		7058	4000	4634	3448		142.5	139.1	177.0	141.0
3220	TV/radio transmitters; line comm. apparatus		95	75	55	70		1013	818	758	842		32.2	26.5	23.0	26.0
3230	TV and radio receivers and associated goods		160	125	85	120		...	...	...	...		...	...	...	...
331	Medical, measuring, testing appliances, etc.		1880	2015	2180	1970		21962	21380	22994	23316		...	734.8	791.0	...
3311	Medical, surgical and orthopaedic equipment		1385	1485	1575	1425		10742	10131	11218	11144		...	287.1	314.0	333.0
3312	Measuring/testing/navigating appliances,etc.		390	410	465	420		9485	9611	10309	10805		359.1	383.9	418.0	427.0
3313	Industrial process control equipment		105	120	140	125		1735	1638	1467	1367		68.2	63.7	59.0	...
3320	Optical instruments & photographic equipment		115	120	130	120		1288	1347	1450	1843		38.6	45.3	42.0	...
3330	Watches and clocks		35	35	40	35		99	115	122	128		6.8	...	...	4.0
3410	Motor vehicles		150	125	95	110		10357	10514	10322	9640		400.1	407.5	402.0	424.0
3420	Automobile bodies, trailers & semi-trailers		505	460	375	410		8779	8346	8311	8062		254.4	256.6	247.0	249.0
3430	Parts/accessories for automobiles		95	95	85	95		5500	6085	4567	4577		168.7	186.0	164.0	165.0
351	Building and repairing of ships and boats		1405	1225	1595	1580		15388	13691	13140	11948		510.0	478.8	480.0	496.0
3511	Building and repairing of ships		515	460	570	560		10425	9075	8152	6995		364.1	334.5	325.0	341.0
3512	Building/repairing of pleasure/sport. boats		890	770	1025	1020		4963	4616	4988	4953		145.9	144.3	154.0	155.0
3520	Railway/tramway locomotives & rolling stock		10	10	10	15		...	...	...	...		16.6	18.3	20.0	17.0
3530	Aircraft and spacecraft		65	65	75	80		4668	7010	4853	5061		168.7	178.0	197.0	203.0
359	Transport equipment n.e.c.		140	125	160	165		...	...	...	...		98.4	96.0	95.0	95.0
3591	Motorcycles		30	25	35	35		413	435	438	375		11.0	...	...	...
3592	Bicycles and invalid carriages		80	75	95	90		...	...	...	...		66.9	...	...	...
3599	Other transport equipment n.e.c.		30	25	35	40		704	655	589	394		20.4	18.6	16.0	15.0
3610	Furniture		4960	5050	5470	5220		28358	26462	24042	23752		759.8	720.0	684.0	689.0
369	Manufacturing n.e.c.		1875	1885	2060	2020		5891	5577	5135	4947		181.7	165.2	162.0	179.0
3691	Jewellery and related articles		590	615	690	675		897	788	778	700		24.5	22.2	25.0	24.0
3692	Musical instruments		215	220	245	235		439	481	433	435		16.0	12.7	16.0	14.0
3693	Sports goods		130	130	135	135		626	577	534	539		20.2	19.2	13.0	22.0
3694	Games and toys		280	290	325	305		659	678	647	692		18.6	13.5	19.0	28.0
3699	Other manufacturing n.e.c.		660	630	665	670		3270	3053	2743	2581		102.4	97.5	89.0	90.0
3710	Recycling of metal waste and scrap		45	50	45	50		696	377	478	475		19.0	15.3	17.0	17.0
3720	Recycling of non-metal waste and scrap		180	150	170	160		2544	2824	2391	2373		69.1	78.3	87.0	83.0
D	Total manufacturing		46435	46010	46595	45600		814133	767970	743299	725287		27055.5	26743.8	26947.0	27087.0

Netherlands

ISIC Revision 3		Output					Value added in factor values					Gross fixed capital formation		
			(millions of Euros)					(millions of Euros)					(millions of Euros)	
ISIC	Industry	Note	2002	2003	2004	2005	Note	2002	2003	2004	2005	Note	2004	2005
151	Processed meat,fish,fruit,vegetables,fats		14250.4	13880.7	14540.0	...		2303.3	2315.2	2298.0	...		280.0	355.0
1511	Processing/preserving of meat		7865.2	7327.7	7635.0	7986.0		1180.0	1186.7	1225.0	1196.0		133.0	170.0
1512	Processing/preserving of fish		657.5	...	...	643.0		125.5	...	...	131.0		13.0	9.0
1513	Processing/preserving of fruit & vegetables		2759.3	2682.8	2887.0	2796.0		666.7	723.4	773.0	672.0		110.0	139.0
1514	Vegetable and animal oils and fats		2968.3	...	...	...		331.0	...	...	...		25.0	38.0
1520	Dairy products		6863.1	6821.4	6586.0	6485.0		829.1	835.3	467.0	861.0		138.0	250.0
153	Grain mill products; starches; animal feeds		6358.7	6094.5	6657.0	6127.0		981.1	1051.1	1079.0	993.0		...	196.0
1531	Grain mill products		564.6	...	...	...		104.5	...	...	...		17.0	37.0
1532	Starches and starch products		1232.0	...	...	...		288.3	...	...	...		...	62.0
1533	Prepared animal feeds		4562.1	4295.7	4931.0	4445.0		588.3	656.7	693.0	615.0		81.0	98.0
154	Other food products		10208.2	11228.7	11976.0	12133.0		3171.7	3439.5	3875.0	3814.0		449.0	462.0
1541	Bakery products		3267.7	3372.4	3548.0	3583.0		1332.7	1342.0	1418.0	1410.0		...	...
1542	Sugar		719.0	...	...	...		184.2	...	...	...		...	...
1543	Cocoa, chocolate and sugar confectionery		2586.2	2984.5	2885.0	2941.0		507.1	572.7	658.0	687.0		66.0	95.0
1544	Macaroni, noodles & similar products		...	...	...	...		...	...	...	...		...	-
1549	Other food products n.e.c.		...	...	...	...		...	...	...	...		161.0	125.0
155	Beverages		...	3897.7	3831.0	3459.0		...	1131.2	1271.0	999.0		456.0	307.0
1551	Distilling, rectifying & blending of spirits		...	...	...	...		...	...	...	...		...	...
1552	Wines		...	...	...	...		...	...	...	...		...	1.0
1553	Malt liquors and malt		...	...	...	...		...	...	...	...		...	...
1554	Soft drinks; mineral waters		1019.2	1031.7	933.0	955.0		247.1	272.7	247.0	219.0		58.0	83.0
1600	Tobacco products		...	5480.8	5348.0	...		...	1743.8	1700.0	...		...	30.0
171	Spinning, weaving and finishing of textiles		647.3	...	...	566.0		236.6	...	...	195.0		...	...
1711	Textile fibre preparation; textile weaving		381.1	...	...	306.0		121.2	...	...	94.0		...	...
1712	Finishing of textiles		266.2	250.8	253.0	260.0		115.4	108.9	76.0	100.0		5.0	7.0
172	Other textiles		1991.1	1907.3	1881.0	1830.0		579.3	547.9	515.0	543.0		49.0	41.0
1721	Made-up textile articles, except apparel		542.0	473.5	434.0	470.0		201.6	190.0	163.0	174.0		12.0	11.0
1722	Carpets and rugs		978.6	975.9	955.0	940.0		214.1	200.6	184.0	229.0		18.0	22.0
1723	Cordage, rope, twine and netting		53.1	44.9	57.0	...		17.6	17.4	20.0	...		...	1.0
1729	Other textiles n.e.c.		417.4	413.1	436.0	...		146.1	139.9	149.0	...		...	8.0
1730	Knitted and crocheted fabrics and articles		135.3	...	...	37.0		44.4	...	...	13.0		...	1.0
1810	Wearing apparel, except fur apparel		631.8	...	...	...		194.3	...	...	...		...	...
1820	Dressing & dyeing of fur; processing of fur		0.1	...	...	...		-	...	...	...		...	-
191	Tanning, dressing and processing of leather		198.9	126.3	149.0	144.0		54.9	32.6	40.0	38.0		3.0	2.0
1911	Tanning and dressing of leather		115.9	77.0	79.0	70.0		27.2	17.4	20.0	16.0		2.0	1.0
1912	Luggage, handbags, etc.; saddlery & harness		83.0	49.8	69.0	74.0		27.6	15.2	20.0	22.0		1.0	1.0
1920	Footwear		144.2	163.0	129.0	159.0		53.0	67.5	50.0	58.0		8.0	4.0
2010	Sawmilling and planing of wood		100.0	126.3	170.0	171.0		19.7	16.6	45.0	60.0		7.0	6.0
202	Products of wood, cork, straw, etc.		2412.2	2331.3	2442.0	2555.0		861.1	820.0	833.0	862.0		79.0	94.0
2021	Veneer sheets, plywood, particle board, etc.		38.8	29.8	41.0	36.0		10.5	8.9	16.0	10.0		2.0	1.0
2022	Builders' carpentry and joinery		1727.9	1713.2	1804.0	1859.0		625.0	608.4	602.0	645.0		51.0	69.0
2023	Wooden containers		379.7	343.7	330.0	379.0		107.8	102.0	93.0	103.0		11.0	...
2029	Other wood products; articles of cork/straw		265.9	244.6	267.0	281.0		117.9	100.8	122.0	103.0		15.0	...
210	Paper and paper products		5457.4	5362.8	5487.0	5521.0		1723.9	1671.4	1657.0	1597.0		326.0	356.0
2101	Pulp, paper and paperboard		1761.4	1656.3	1700.0	1915.0		534.5	475.3	488.0	487.0		123.0	170.0
2102	Corrugated paper and paperboard		1818.0	1847.2	1867.0	1841.0		581.5	607.0	573.0	554.0		91.0	93.0
2109	Other articles of paper and paperboard		1878.0	...	...	...		607.9	...	...	...		...	...
221	Publishing		6791.2	6592.2	6763.0	7294.0		2805.9	2767.1	2603.0	2722.0		90.0	85.0
2211	Publishing of books and other publications		1748.5	1674.5	1634.0	1846.0		694.7	680.3	665.0	717.0		15.0	22.0
2212	Publishing of newspapers, journals, etc.		4692.6	4690.6	4866.0	5171.0		2004.2	2008.2	1879.0	1926.0		69.0	59.0
2213	Publishing of recorded media		256.2	128.3	168.0	168.0		71.2	41.8	23.0	34.0		2.0	3.0
2219	Other publishing		93.9	98.7	96.0	110.0		35.8	36.8	35.0	44.0		3.0	2.0

continued

Netherlands

ISIC	Industry	Note	Output (millions of Euros) 2002	2003	2004	2005	Note	Value added in factor values (millions of Euros) 2002	2003	2004	2005	Note	Gross fixed capital formation (millions of Euros) 2004	2005
222	Printing and related service activities		5529.5	5157.9	5173.0	5103.0		2206.1	2080.0	2035.0	2020.0		240.0	250.0
2221	Printing		4783.3	4509.4	4511.0	4511.0		1849.4	1760.1	1727.0	1752.0		209.0	214.0
2222	Service activities related to printing		746.3	648.5	662.0	592.0		356.7	319.8	308.0	268.0		32.0	35.0
2230	Reproduction of recorded media		586.2	364.8	298.0	272.0		180.8	130.5	69.0	53.0		6.0	4.0
2310	Coke oven products		...	-	-	-		...	-	-	-		...	...
2320	Refined petroleum products		...	...	...	...		...	...	...	...		...	...
2330	Processing of nuclear fuel		...	...	...	...		...	...	...	...		...	...
241	Basic chemicals		21070.0	21945.1	28508.0	32826.0		4626.6	4733.9	5586.0	6633.0		856.0	839.0
2411	Basic chemicals, except fertilizers		...	...	...	...		...	...	...	...		...	416.0
2412	Fertilizers and nitrogen compounds		959.0	1004.4	1197.0	1407.0		206.8	257.4	367.0	364.0		42.0	66.0
2413	Plastics in primary forms; synthetic rubber		...	...	...	...		...	...	...	...		...	...
242	Other chemicals		14193.5	...	...	11217.0		3218.7	...	...	3568.0		448.0	336.0
2421	Pesticides and other agro-chemical products		225.3	...	...	...		59.0	...	...	...		8.0	5.0
2422	Paints, varnishes, printing ink and mastics		1880.6	1864.9	1764.0	1826.0		566.9	584.7	561.0	557.0		35.0	45.0
2423	Pharmaceuticals, medicinal chemicals, etc.		7655.3	7676.6	8017.0	5329.0		1308.2	1245.3	1281.0	1765.0		291.0	185.0
2424	Soap, cleaning & cosmetic preparations		1159.3	1335.9	1355.0	...		315.8	390.9	417.0	...		44.0	39.0
2429	Other chemical products n.e.c.		3273.0	2905.7	2501.0	2484.0		968.7	900.7	821.0	805.0		70.0	63.0
2430	Man-made fibres		578.5	...	...	1009.0		257.8	...	...	334.0		40.0	98.0
251	Rubber products		517.5	484.3	506.0	584.0		202.9	197.0	218.0	216.0		26.0	25.0
2511	Rubber tyres and tubes		...	...	...	...		...	...	...	...		...	...
2519	Other rubber products		346.0	...	...	...		118.1	...	...	...		...	9.0
2520	Plastic products		5446.5	5355.8	5469.0	5782.0		1829.0	1781.1	1733.0	1771.0		257.0	252.0
2610	Glass and glass products		1163.7	1044.3	1096.0	1037.0		436.1	422.8	428.0	376.0		58.0	30.0
269	Non-metallic mineral products n.e.c.		4717.0	4446.0	4428.0	4632.0		1796.0	1686.0	1665.0	1593.0		183.0	163.0
2691	Pottery, china and earthenware		...	...	...	...		...	...	...	...		...	...
2692	Refractory ceramic products		...	...	...	...		...	...	...	...		...	...
2693	Struct.non-refractory clay; ceramic products		472.1	...	...	...		224.9	...	...	...		...	...
2694	Cement, lime and plaster		...	...	...	...		...	...	...	...		...	...
2695	Articles of concrete, cement and plaster		...	2842.2	2721.0	2821.0		...	998.3	941.0	877.0		95.0	88.0
2696	Cutting, shaping & finishing of stone		254.5	265.7	275.0	274.0		107.7	106.9	116.0	116.0		8.0	6.0
2699	Other non-metallic mineral products n.e.c.		637.1	546.8	585.0	645.0		219.8	207.5	197.0	197.0		24.0	25.0
2710	Basic iron and steel		...	...	...	4365.0		...	...	...	1565.0		66.0	91.0
2720	Basic precious and non-ferrous metals		...	1802.4	2114.0	2145.0		...	452.8	496.0	452.0		64.0	56.0
273	Casting of metals		598.3	...	...	610.0		212.8	...	...	189.0		13.0	17.0
2731	Casting of iron and steel		...	...	...	...		...	...	...	...		...	...
2732	Casting of non-ferrous metals		...	...	...	...		...	...	...	...		7.0	7.0
281	Struct.metal products;tanks;steam generators		7822.7	...	...	7963.0		2465.0	...	...	2389.0		138.0	134.0
2811	Structural metal products		6030.0	5755.3	5859.0	6612.0		1938.4	1860.0	1837.0	1988.0		111.0	111.0
2812	Tanks, reservoirs and containers of metal		1355.1	1436.3	1422.0	1159.0		476.8	487.3	479.0	356.0		25.0	21.0
2813	Steam generators		437.6	...	...	193.0		49.8	...	...	45.0		2.0	3.0
289	Other metal products; metal working services		6643.7	...	...	7519.0		2563.8	...	...	2757.0		274.0	276.0
2891	Metal forging/pressing/stamping/roll-forming		1419.9	1393.0	1536.0	1625.0		456.3	454.8	520.0	508.0		75.0	61.0
2892	Treatment & coating of metals		2384.7	2392.6	2519.0	2789.0		1091.7	1053.7	1109.0	1186.0		119.0	117.0
2893	Cutlery, hand tools and general hardware		560.6	...	...	597.0		265.0	...	...	253.0		16.0	18.0
2899	Other fabricated metal products n.e.c.		2278.5	2231.4	2512.0	2508.0		750.9	746.0	832.0	811.0		64.0	80.0
291	General purpose machinery		8110.1	7715.3	8243.0	9168.0		2891.8	2825.4	2908.0	3154.0		177.0	164.0
2911	Engines & turbines (not for transport equipment)		705.4	637.6	586.0	807.0		246.6	241.9	212.0	288.0		15.0	20.0
2912	Pumps, compressors, taps and valves		1814.6	1741.6	1806.0	2026.0		609.9	594.5	596.0	697.0		36.0	35.0
2913	Bearings, gears, gearing & driving elements		203.3	221.2	375.0	360.0		75.6	88.2	145.0	119.0		8.0	6.0
2914	Ovens, furnaces and furnace burners		115.3	107.8	133.0	125.0		41.1	38.9	45.0	39.0		2.0	2.0
2915	Lifting and handling equipment		2071.1	2039.0	2263.0	2576.0		717.3	743.4	787.0	853.0		48.0	39.0
2919	Other general purpose machinery		3200.4	2968.1	3080.0	3274.0		1201.3	1118.5	1123.0	1159.0		68.0	63.0

292	Special purpose machinery	6932.3	6647.0	8051.0	7960.0	1857.2	1789.0	2337.0	2458.0	...	...
2921	Agricultural and forestry machinery	1364.8	...	...	1320.0	443.4	...	...	420.0	26.0	23.0
2922	Machine tools	440.5	405.2	458.0	...	162.2	130.8	145.0	...	4.0	7.0
2923	Machinery for metallurgy	...	...	...	...	...	...	...	...	-	...
2924	Machinery for mining & construction	...	232.2	310.0	256.0	...	81.2	102.0	92.0	3.0	5.0
2925	Food/beverage/tobacco processing machinery	1166.8	1199.9	1353.0	1387.0	444.6	440.9	486.0	490.0	27.0	27.0
2926	Machinery for textile, apparel and leather	202.4	197.7	171.0	190.0	85.0	81.2	73.0	59.0	2.0	5.0
2927	Weapons and ammunition	76.4	...	...	...	24.5	...	...	...	...	...
2929	Other special purpose machinery	3404.2	...	...	...	599.9	...	...	...	...	104.0
2930	Domestic appliances n.e.c.	315.6	327.1	330.0	329.0	110.7	111.4	119.0	115.0	...	...
3000	Office, accounting and computing machinery	1631.1	1296.8	1439.0	1246.0	302.6	292.9	306.0	346.0	...	...
3110	Electric motors, generators and transformers	853.6	644.3	649.0	586.0	240.2	222.6	240.0	228.0	14.0	12.0
3120	Electricity distribution & control apparatus	662.9	580.6	671.0	698.0	262.3	241.2	262.0	279.0	8.0	10.0
3130	Insulated wire and cable	568.6	543.5	585.0	667.0	194.7	207.6	162.0	173.0	...	10.0
3140	Accumulators, primary cells and batteries	31.9	53.9	93.0	54.0	9.5	20.3	20.0	22.0	...	-
3150	Lighting equipment and electric lamps	371.3	417.6	401.0	363.0	139.0	143.2	148.0	121.0	7.0	7.0
3190	Other electrical equipment n.e.c.	855.0	865.3	928.0	887.0	303.1	321.6	313.0	294.0	29.0	23.0
3210	Electronic valves, tubes, etc.	615.2	587.5	748.0	638.0	197.8	189.8	268.0	230.0	22.0	11.0
3220	TV/radio transmitters; line comm. apparatus	165.1	135.0	133.0	140.0	48.8	50.1	52.0	51.0	3.0	3.0
3230	TV and radio receivers and associated goods	...	...	...	...	...	...	...	...	...	...
331	Medical, measuring, testing appliances, etc.	...	3318.0	3296.0	...	...	1348.0	1381.0	...	68.0	62.0
3311	Medical, surgical and orthopaedic equipment	...	1434.3	1270.0	1419.0	...	606.9	595.0	668.0	43.0	27.0
3312	Measuring/testing/navigating appliances,etc.	1556.9	1632.6	1824.0	2110.0	522.3	637.7	708.0	868.0	23.0	32.0
3313	Industrial process control equipment	247.4	251.1	202.0	...	98.9	102.9	78.0	...	2.0	3.0
3320	Optical instruments & photographic equipment	180.1	204.5	191.0	...	75.3	84.0	84.0	...	7.0	21.0
3330	Watches and clocks	26.3	...	...	25.0	13.0	...	...	8.0	-	-
3410	Motor vehicles	4823.9	4720.5	6266.0	5890.0	1141.3	1171.2	1543.0	1476.0	80.0	90.0
3420	Automobile bodies, trailers & semi-trailers	1320.6	1338.3	1423.0	1483.0	379.7	385.6	381.0	385.0	21.0	21.0
3430	Parts/accessories for automobiles	988.0	948.5	952.0	979.0	297.3	309.5	253.0	280.0	23.0	53.0
351	Building and repairing of ships and boats	3264.9	3032.9	3310.0	3356.0	730.8	636.8	862.0	835.0	29.0	...
3511	Building and repairing of ships	2396.9	2140.1	2369.0	2477.0	488.4	389.9	608.0	604.0	16.0	...
3512	Building/repairing of pleasure/sport. boats	868.1	892.9	941.0	879.0	242.5	246.9	254.0	231.0	13.0	22.0
3520	Railway/tramway locomotives & rolling stock	89.2	115.3	150.0	126.0	21.7	27.3	38.0	42.0	...	...
3530	Aircraft and spacecraft	718.3	746.5	717.0	871.0	245.8	286.2	296.0	333.0	...	25.0
359	Transport equipment n.e.c.	696.4	675.3	684.0	695.0	186.0	169.4	184.0	188.0	13.0	10.0
3591	Motorcycles	59.8	...	...	...	16.6	...	...	...	2.0	1.0
3592	Bicycles and invalid carriages	537.6	...	...	...	135.9	...	...	...	9.0	8.0
3599	Other transport equipment n.e.c.	99.0	98.9	85.0	71.0	33.5	24.2	26.0	22.0	2.0	1.0
3610	Furniture	3578.5	3329.2	3255.0	3444.0	1313.9	1212.5	1113.0	1163.0	81.0	73.0
369	Manufacturing n.e.c.	966.9	941.0	899.0	918.0	368.2	332.4	299.0	312.0	129.0	107.0
3691	Jewellery and related articles	132.0	123.6	123.0	116.0	51.4	43.1	42.0	40.0	3.0	2.0
3692	Musical instruments	62.2	51.9	59.0	65.0	28.3	23.7	26.0	25.0	2.0	1.0
3693	Sports goods	97.1	111.4	63.0	109.0	41.3	51.9	22.0	38.0	1.0	2.0
3694	Games and toys	109.2	92.1	128.0	121.0	39.8	26.7	34.0	47.0	2.0	2.0
3699	Other manufacturing n.e.c.	566.5	561.5	526.0	507.0	207.4	187.0	175.0	163.0	121.0	100.0
3710	Recycling of metal waste and scrap	204.7	224.6	325.0	371.0	37.8	37.4	56.0	48.0	7.0	5.0
3720	Recycling of non-metal waste and scrap	664.2	721.1	834.0	744.0	196.4	202.1	219.0	203.0	53.0	98.0
D	Total manufacturing	203411.0	201049.0	216827.0	228640.0	54466.9	53994.1	56568.0	57637.0	6393.0	6559.0

Netherlands

ISIC Revision 3			Index numbers of industrial production (2000=100)											
ISIC	Industry	Note	1995	1996	1997	1998	1999	2000	2001	2002	2003	2004	2005	2006
15	Food and beverages		96	97	96	95	98	100	100	100	101	103	108	111
16	Tobacco products		98	93	94	97	95	100	100	116	107	102	103	102
17	Textiles		82	83	85	93	97	100	102	98	95	83	83	86
18	Wearing apparel, fur		127	113	107	100	89	100	90	86	83	64	69	79
19	Leather, leather products and footwear		117	103	111	109	103	100	92	86	90	96	96	91
20	Wood products (excl. furniture)		90	88	92	101	101	100	101	88	91	93	95	96
21	Paper and paper products		86	84	93	91	97	100	96	101	103	109	110	111
22	Printing and publishing		89	88	91	96	99	100	98	95	89	88	89	90
23	Coke,refined petroleum products,nuclear fuel		135	134	83	90	86	100	95	113	116	123	125	123
24	Chemicals and chemical products		85	87	88	89	96	100	112	123	124	132	133	139
25	Rubber and plastics products		85	84	90	95	98	100	99	103	99	102	107	111
26	Non-metallic mineral products		90	93	89	91	96	100	100	95	89	95	97	100
27	Basic metals		90	89	96	98	95	100	99	101	105	119	115	113
28	Fabricated metal products		89	92	90	93	93	100	101	98	95	98	104	106
29	Machinery and equipment n.e.c.		77	80	87	87	83	100	99	96	95	105	107	113
30	Office, accounting and computing machinery	a/	68	69	67	70	78	100	82	70	70	73	75	78
31	Electrical machinery and apparatus	a/	...	...	...	...	...	...	...	...	...	...	...	...
32	Radio,television and communication equipment	a/	...	...	...	...	...	...	...	...	...	...	...	...
33	Medical, precision and optical instruments	a/	...	...	...	...	...	...	...	...	...	...	...	...
34	Motor vehicles, trailers, semi-trailers		59	61	71	89	99	100	105	102	102	103	102	105
35	Other transport equipment		92	91	95	100	101	100	115	109	103	103	105	108
36	Furniture; manufacturing n.e.c.	b/	80	83	88	92	99	100	98	98	97	97	99	100
37	Recycling	b/	...	...	...	...	...	...	...	...	...	...	...	...
D	Total manufacturing		85	86	87	90	94	100	100	100	99	102	104	107

a/ 30 includes 31, 32 and 33.
b/ 36 includes 37.

Netherlands Antilles

Supplier of information:
Central Bureau of Statistics, Willemstad.

Basic source of data:
Annual survey.

Major deviations from ISIC (Revision 3):
None reported.

Reference period:
Calendar year.

Scope:
All registered enterprises.

Method of data collection:
Questionnaires; direct interview in the field.

Type of enumeration:
Sample survey. All enterprises with nine or more persons engaged are included every year. A sample is taken from smaller enterprises, which remain in the sample for four consecutive years.

Adjusted for non-response:
Yes.

Concepts and definitions of variables:
Output excludes value of goods shipped in the same condition as received less the amount paid for these goods, but includes subsidies.
Value added includes subsidies.

Related national publications:
Business Statistics; National Accounts, both published by the Central Bureau of Statistics, Willemstad.

Netherlands Antilles

ISIC Revision 3	Number of enterprises					Number of employees					Wages and salaries paid to employees				
		(number)					(number)					(millions of Netherlands Antillean Guilders)			
ISIC Industry	Note	2003	2004	2005	2006	Note	2003	2004	2005	2006	Note	2003	2004	2005	2006
D Total manufacturing		323	310	373	353		3951	3835	4150	3958		136.0	136.8	119.1	...

ISIC Revision 3	Output in producers' prices					Value added in producers' prices					Gross fixed capital formation		
		(millions of Netherlands Antillean Guilders)					(millions of Netherlands Antillean Guilders)					(millions of Netherlands Antillean Guilders)	
ISIC Industry	Note	2003	2004	2005	2006	Note	2003	2004	2005	2006	Note	2005	2006
D Total manufacturing		564.6	562.7	557.6	...		176.9	200.9	155.9	...		18.9	...

ISIC Revision 3	Index numbers of industrial production												
		(2000 = 100)											
ISIC Industry	Note	1995	1996	1997	1998	1999	2000	2001	2002	2003	2004	2005	2006
D Total manufacturing		...	...	...	...	...	...	...	...	...	...	...	...

New Zealand

Supplier of information:
Statistics New Zealand, Wellington.
Industrial statistics for the OECD countries are compiled by the OECD secretariat, which supplies them to UNIDO.

Basic source of data:
Annual business frame update survey.

Major deviations from ISIC (Revision 3):
Data collected under the national classification system have been reclassified to correspond with ISIC (Rev. 3). Some accuracy is lost in this translation as not all ISIC (Rev. 3) categories are represented.

Reference period:
Fiscal year beginning 1 April of the year indicated.

Scope:
Establishments with paid employees.

Method of data collection:
Questionnaires are distributed by mail.

Type of enumeration:
Not reported.

Adjusted for non-response:
No.

Concepts and definitions of variables:
Number of employees is converted to full-time equivalent.

Related national publications:
Business Activity Statistics; Labour Market Statistics, both published by Statistics New Zealand, Wellington.

New Zealand

ISIC Revision 3		Number of enterprises					Number of employees					Wages and salaries paid to employees				
			(number)					(number)					(millions of New Zealand Dollars)			
ISIC	Industry	Note	2004	2005	2006	2007	Note	2004	2005	2006	2007	Note	2004	2005	2006	2007
151	Processed meat,fish,fruit,vegetables,fats		552	549	546	525		44530	45110	44990	43710		2822a/	...	...	...
1511	Processing/preserving of meat		256	246	258	251		31550	31790	32160	30980		...	...	...	...
1512	Processing/preserving of fish		129	128	121	114		7500	7550	7270	7310		...	...	...	...
1513	Processing/preserving of fruit & vegetables		123	122	120	119		5240	5370	5160	5150		...	...	...	...
1514	Vegetable and animal oils and fats		44	53	47	41		250	410	400	270		...	...	...	...
1520	Dairy products		80	80	78	77		12280	12580	11930	11220		...a/	...	...	...
153	Grain mill products; starches; animal feeds		76	83	85	82		580	650	660	670		...a/	...	...	...
1531	Grain mill products		8	7	8	4		45	45	75	70		...	...	...	...
1532	Starches and starch products		...	...	...	...		...	...	...	...		...	...	...	...
1533	Prepared animal feeds		68	76	77	78		540	600	580	600		...	...	...	...
154	Other food products		673	697	715	757		15890	16430	16420	18440		...a/	...	...	...
1541	Bakery products		219	216	216	226		8270	7710	7640	9180		...	...	...	...
1542	Sugar		4	4	5	7		210	230	210	220		...	...	...	...
1543	Cocoa, chocolate and sugar confectionery		84	78	83	87		1980	1930	2010	2070		...	...	...	...
1544	Macaroni, noodles & similar products		23	21	21	23		690	720	740	760		...	...	...	...
1549	Other food products n.e.c.		343	378	390	414		4750	5850	5820	6220		...	...	...	...
155	Beverages		322	341	375	398		8090	8160	8510	8590		...a/	...	...	...
1551	Distilling, rectifying & blending of spirits		20	21	24	26		450	600	580	520		...	...	...	...
1552	Wines		210	226	256	276		4260	4320	4620	4730		...	...	...	...
1553	Malt liquors and malt		47	52	53	53		1720	1480	1510	1510		...	...	...	...
1554	Soft drinks; mineral waters		45	42	42	43		1660	1770	1800	1830		...	...	...	...
1600	Tobacco products		2	2	2	1		440	430	430	140		...	...	...	...
171	Spinning, weaving and finishing of textiles		123	115	112	103		2540	2490	2490	2940		267b/	...	...	...
1711	Textile fibre preparation; textile weaving		91	80	78	74		2250	2150	2170	2610		...	...	...	...
1712	Finishing of textiles		32	35	34	29		280	350	320	320		...	...	...	...
172	Other textiles		625	640	655	649		4910	4750	4340	3580		...b/	...	...	...
1721	Made-up textile articles, except apparel		439	459	474	476		2220	2130	1970	1930		...	...	...	...
1722	Carpets and rugs		25	31	30	30		1510	1630	1490	790		...	...	...	...
1723	Cordage, rope, twine and netting		21	21	22	21		310	290	200	200		...	...	...	...
1729	Other textiles n.e.c.		140	129	129	122		870	680	680	650		...	...	...	...
1730	Knitted and crocheted fabrics and articles		83	78	70	65		1320	1220	1020	950		...b/	...	...	...
1810	Wearing apparel, except fur apparel		1039	1037	998	957		7670	6680	6400	5830		204c/	...	...	...
1820	Dressing & dyeing of fur; processing of fur		...	...	...	...		...	...	...	...		...c/	...	...	...
191	Tanning, dressing and processing of leather		125	123	124	114		1940	2070	1720	1490		79d/	...	...	...
1911	Tanning and dressing of leather		39	41	38	35		1680	1830	1530	1320		...	...	...	...
1912	Luggage, handbags, etc.; saddlery & harness		86	82	86	79		260	230	180	170		...	...	...	...
1920	Footwear		44	41	39	36		750	780	600	550		...d/	...	...	...
2010	Sawmilling and planing of wood		592	588	537	525		10220	10320	9600	9720		719e/	...	...	...
202	Products of wood, cork, straw, etc.		1682	1760	1773	1728		10490	11260	11580	11570		...e/	...	...	...
2021	Veneer sheets, plywood, particle board, etc.		64	46	47	44		2610	2550	2860	2770		...	...	...	...
2022	Builders' carpentry and joinery		1171	1257	1280	1252		5710	6640	6710	6640		...	...	...	...
2023	Wooden containers		447	457	446	432		2170	2060	2010	2150		...	...	...	...
2029	Other wood products; articles of cork/straw		...	...	...	...		...	...	...	...		...	...	...	...
210	Paper and paper products		109	109	107	110		6490	6190	5700	5530		376	397	376	...
2101	Pulp, paper and paperboard		12	13	17	17		3180	3250	2940	2690		...	...	...	...
2102	Corrugated paper and paperboard		37	44	39	38		2190	2120	2010	2080		...	...	...	...
2109	Other articles of paper and paperboard		60	52	51	55		1130	820	750	750		...	...	...	...
221	Publishing		865	946	966	1034		19410	19450	17430	16050		881f/	...	...	...
2211	Publishing of books and other publications		275	315	329	363		1330	1270	1330	1290		...	...	...	...
2212	Publishing of newspapers, journals, etc.		518	540	542	563		17990	18040	15950	14640		...	...	...	...
2213	Publishing of recorded media		72	91	95	108		90	130	130	110		...	...	...	...
2219	Other publishing		...	...	...	...		...	...	...	...		...	...	...	...

222	Printing and related service activities	1308	1302	1291	1270	10810	11300	11280	10890	...f/	...	...	...
2221	Printing	1006	1020	1014	993	9590	10210	10260	9930	...	...	...	...
2222	Service activities related to printing	302	282	277	277	1220	1090	1020	970	...	...	...	...
2230	Reproduction of recorded media	...	...	...	...	...	...	...	...	...f/	...	...	...
2310	Coke oven products	16	19	20	23	60	130	130	120	...	...	...	...
2320	Refined petroleum products	1	1	3	9	290	310	300	320	...	...	...	...
2330	Processing of nuclear fuel	...	...	...	...	...	...	...	...	...	...	...	...
241	Basic chemicals	163	147	149	149	4130	3600	3500	3450	...	...	...	...
2411	Basic chemicals, except fertilizers	21	19	18	19	750	650	670	710	...	...	...	...
2412	Fertilizers and nitrogen compounds	70	84	83	85	1670	1740	1650	1670	...	...	...	...
2413	Plastics in primary forms; synthetic rubber	72	44	48	45	1700	1210	1170	1080	...	...	...	...
242	Other chemicals	401	394	399	399	6970	7310	7670	7430	...	...	...	...
2421	Pesticides and other agro-chemical products	13	12	12	11	150	140	150	220	...	...	...	...
2422	Paints, varnishes, printing ink and mastics	88	104	100	87	2270	2430	2650	2410	...	...	...	...
2423	Pharmaceuticals, medicinal chemicals, etc.	102	96	104	105	1790	1940	2350	2200	...	...	...	...
2424	Soap, cleaning & cosmetic preparations	126	125	121	130	2090	2050	1770	1780	...	...	...	...
2429	Other chemical products n.e.c.	72	57	62	66	680	760	760	810	...	...	...	...
2430	Man-made fibres	...	...	...	...	...	...	...	...	...	...	...	...
251	Rubber products	90	81	76	76	960	930	850	860	464g/	...	...	...
2511	Rubber tyres and tubes	14	13	12	11	110	100	70	85	...	...	...	...
2519	Other rubber products	76	68	64	65	840	830	780	770	...	...	...	...
2520	Plastic products	548	558	572	575	10300	10640	10760	10950	...g/	...	...	...
2610	Glass and glass products	147	138	142	146	1440	1690	1640	1690	65	66	66	...
269	Non-metallic mineral products n.e.c.	624	628	647	641	6610	7130	6960	6880	257	300	312	...
2691	Pottery, china and earthenware	179	166	154	141	370	380	340	290	...	...	...	...
2692	Refractory ceramic products	9	7	8	5	190	140	130	110	...	...	...	...
2693	Struct.non-refractory clay; ceramic products	9	11	11	12	55	60	160	140	...	...	...	...
2694	Cement, lime and plaster	42	41	52	45	470	430	580	550	...	...	...	...
2695	Articles of concrete, cement and plaster	254	274	280	291	4820	5210	4780	4850	...	...	...	...
2696	Cutting, shaping & finishing of stone	...	...	...	...	...	...	...	...	...	...	...	...
2699	Other non-metallic mineral products n.e.c.	131	129	142	147	720	910	970	930	...	...	...	...
2710	Basic iron and steel	223	177	183	180	2840	2780	2920	2880	302h/	...	...	...
2720	Basic precious and non-ferrous metals	27	29	28	26	2830	3260	2290	2030	...h/	...	...	...
273	Casting of metals	48	36	35	32	690	450	360	290	...h/	...	...	...
2731	Casting of iron and steel	...	...	...	...	...	...	...	...	...	...	...	...
2732	Casting of non-ferrous metals	48	36	35	32	690	450	350	290	...	...	...	...
281	Struct.metal products;tanks;steam generators	1146	1162	1156	1126	10500	11540	10950	11110	976i/	...	...	...
2811	Structural metal products	1100	1114	1112	1084	9190	10210	9900	10130	...	...	...	...
2812	Tanks, reservoirs and containers of metal	46	48	44	42	1310	1330	1040	990	...	...	...	...
2813	Steam generators	...	...	...	...	...	...	...	...	...	...	...	...
289	Other metal products; metal working services	2159	2286	2343	2353	12360	12630	13130	13170	...i/	...	...	...
2891	Metal forging/pressing/stamping/roll-forming	369	428	430	439	3660	3760	3990	4090	...	...	...	...
2892	Treatment & coating of metals	310	313	320	322	1370	1380	1480	1500	...	...	...	...
2893	Cutlery, hand tools and general hardware	109	103	106	108	1110	1050	1040	960	...	...	...	...
2899	Other fabricated metal products n.e.c.	1371	1442	1487	1484	6230	6430	6610	6620	...	...	...	...
291	General purpose machinery	252	250	253	240	1940	2190	2240	2200	788j/	...	...	...
2911	Engines & turbines (not for transport equipment)	...	...	...	...	...	...	...	...	...	...	...	...
2912	Pumps, compressors, taps and valves	48	54	52	51	310	330	340	390	...	...	...	...
2913	Bearings, gears, gearing & driving elements	...	...	...	...	...	...	...	...	...	...	...	...
2914	Ovens, furnaces and furnace burners	...	...	...	...	...	...	...	...	...	...	...	...
2915	Lifting and handling equipment	146	159	165	159	1140	1410	1350	1270	...	...	...	...
2919	Other general purpose machinery	58	37	36	30	490	450	540	540	...	...	...	...
292	Special purpose machinery	2892	2854	2901	2970	14560	14430	14800	15030	...j/	...	...	...
2921	Agricultural and forestry machinery	376	376	372	365	2690	2580	2830	2760	...	...	...	...
2922	Machine tools	263	278	273	263	1380	1470	1430	1450	...	...	...	...
2923	Machinery for metallurgy	...	...	...	...	...	...	...	...	...	...	...	...
2924	Machinery for mining & construction	24	36	43	44	200	250	300	300	...	...	...	...
2925	Food/beverage/tobacco processing machinery	30	51	51	60	120	250	270	240	...	...	...	...
2926	Machinery for textile, apparel and leather	...	...	...	...	...	...	...	...	...	...	...	...
2927	Weapons and ammunition	...	...	...	...	...	...	...	...	...	...	...	...
2929	Other special purpose machinery	2199	2113	2162	2238	10170	9900	9970	10280	...	...	...	...

continued

New Zealand

ISIC Revision 3		Number of enterprises					Number of employees					Wages and salaries paid to employees				
			(number)					(number)					(millions of New Zealand Dollars)			
ISIC	Industry	Note	2004	2005	2006	2007	Note	2004	2005	2006	2007	Note	2004	2005	2006	2007
2930	Domestic appliances n.e.c.		51	51	60	64		3940	3930	3780	3660		...j/	...	...	...
3000	Office, accounting and computing machinery		84	64	56	58		270	230	230	230		...	...	...	...
3110	Electric motors, generators and transformers		...	...	...	...		...	...	...	...		...	...	...	...
3120	Electricity distribution & control apparatus		257	238	232	239		2290	1960	1760	1810		...	...	...	...
3130	Insulated wire and cable		7	7	7	8		610	640	640	650		...	...	...	...
3140	Accumulators, primary cells and batteries		6	7	7	6		350	360	350	190		...	...	...	...
3150	Lighting equipment and electric lamps		72	70	71	67		480	530	470	450		...	...	...	...
3190	Other electrical equipment n.e.c.		...	...	...	...		...	...	...	...		...	...	...	...
3210	Electronic valves, tubes, etc.		...	...	...	...		...	...	...	...		164k/	...	...	...
3220	TV/radio transmitters; line comm. apparatus		53	55	52	52		1100	1000	940	980		...k/	...	...	...
3230	TV and radio receivers and associated goods		238	255	254	250		2560	2750	2800	2840		...k/	...	...	...
331	Medical, measuring, testing appliances, etc.		341	372	376	385		2080	2470	2780	3090		101m/	...	...	...
3311	Medical, surgical and orthopaedic equipment		227	236	243	254		1400	1590	1760	2140		...	...	...	...
3312	Measuring/testing/navigating appliances,etc.		...	...	...	...		...	...	...	...		...	...	...	...
3313	Industrial process control equipment		114	136	133	131		690	890	1030	950		...	...	...	...
3320	Optical instruments & photographic equipment		29	23	24	24		200	180	190	210		...m/	...	...	...
3330	Watches and clocks		...	...	...	...		...	...	...	...		...m/	...	...	...
3410	Motor vehicles		48	47	46	50		160	140	110	120		152n/	...	...	...
3420	Automobile bodies, trailers & semi-trailers		224	261	288	301		1800	2050	2070	1890		...n/	...	...	...
3430	Parts/accessories for automobiles		316	325	326	312		2600	2320	2010	1640		...n/	...	...	...
351	Building and repairing of ships and boats		728	729	754	748		4550	4350	4270	4350		398p/	...	...	...
3511	Building and repairing of ships		64	59	60	51		880	760	710	650		...	...	...	...
3512	Building/repairing of pleasure/sport. boats		664	670	694	697		3680	3590	3560	3710		...	...	...	...
3520	Railway/tramway locomotives & rolling stock		2	2	4	2		420	450	460	450		...p/	...	...	...
3530	Aircraft and spacecraft		159	157	169	187		1590	1680	1740	1750		...p/	...	...	...
359	Transport equipment n.e.c.		41	44	51	42		200	260	290	250		...p/	...	...	...
3591	Motorcycles		...	...	...	...		...	...	...	...		...	...	...	...
3592	Bicycles and invalid carriages		41	44	51	42		200	250	280	250		...	...	...	...
3599	Other transport equipment n.e.c.		...	...	...	...		...	...	...	...		...	...	...	...
3610	Furniture		1990	1997	1921	1850		9720	9220	8660	8340		366q/	...	...	...
369	Manufacturing n.e.c.		1099	1112	1112	1072		3420	3670	3530	3530		...q/	...	...	...
3691	Jewellery and related articles		382	394	390	379		820	790	790	770		...	...	...	...
3692	Musical instruments		...	...	...	...		...	...	...	...		...	...	...	...
3693	Sports goods		...	...	...	...		...	...	...	...		...	...	...	...
3694	Games and toys		237	233	230	227		610	720	690	670		...	...	...	...
3699	Other manufacturing n.e.c.		480	485	492	466		1990	2160	2050	2110		...	...	...	...
3710	Recycling of metal waste and scrap		1	2	2	2		45	45	35	3		...	...	...	...
3720	Recycling of non-metal waste and scrap		...	...	...	...		...	...	...	...		...	...	...	...
D	Total manufacturing		22783	23069	23192	23095		273210	277080	270670	266730		10187	10899	11130	...

a/ 151 includes 1520, 153, 154 and 155.
b/ 171 includes 172 and 1730.
c/ 1810 includes 1820.
d/ 191 includes 1920.
e/ 2010 includes 202.
f/ 221 includes 222 and 2230.
g/ 251 includes 2520.
h/ 2710 includes 2720 and 273.
i/ 281 includes 289.
j/ 291 includes 292 and 2930.
k/ 3210 includes 3220 and 3230.
m/ 331 includes 3320 and 3330.
n/ 3410 includes 3420 and 3430.
p/ 351 includes 3520, 3530 and 359.
q/ 3610 includes 369.

New Zealand

ISIC Revision 3		Output					Value added					Gross fixed capital formation		
			(millions of New Zealand Dollars)					(millions of New Zealand Dollars)					(millions of New Zealand Dollars)	
ISIC	Industry	Note	2004	2005	2006	2007	Note	2004	2005	2006	2007	Note	2005	2006
15	Food and beverages		25006	25921	27630	...		5220	5795	6519	...		1085	1020
16	Tobacco products		...	...	...	...		...	...	...	...		...	...
17	Textiles		1905a/	1950a/	1848a/	...		741a/	732a/	697a/	...		66a/	64a/
18	Wearing apparel, fur		...a/	...a/	...a/	...		...a/	...a/	...a/	...		...a/	...a/
19	Leather, leather products and footwear		...	...	...	...		...	...	...	...		...	...
20	Wood products (excl. furniture)		4117	4443	4570	...		1139	1274	1289	...		134	274
21	Paper and paper products		2508	2717	2692	...		766	800	764	...		195b/	171
22	Printing and publishing		3741	3812	3712	...		1540	1623	1657	...		...b/	202
23	Coke,refined petroleum products,nuclear fuel		...	...	...	...		...	...	...	...		...	...
24	Chemicals and chemical products		...	...	...	...		...	...	...	...		...	...
25	Rubber and plastics products		2444	2627	2593	...		986	1024	965	...		118	57
26	Non-metallic mineral products		1964	2267	2328	...		769	886	891	...		146	154
27	Basic metals		1951	2260	2425	...		509	756	781	...		108	142
28	Fabricated metal products		4891	5006	4923	...		1785	1870	1823	...		136	103
29	Machinery and equipment n.e.c.		3680	4001	4118	...		1395	1550	1593	...		146	114
30	Office, accounting and computing machinery		1955c/	2247c/	2348c/	...		692c/	797c/	830c/	...		65c/	75c/
31	Electrical machinery and apparatus		...c/	...c/	...c/	...		...c/	...c/	...c/	...		...c/	...c/
32	Radio,television and communication equipment		...c/	...c/	...c/	...		...c/	...c/	...c/	...		...c/	...c/
33	Medical, precision and optical instruments		...c/	...c/	...c/	...		...c/	...c/	...c/	...		...c/	...c/
34	Motor vehicles, trailers, semi-trailers		2089d/	2215d/	2217d/	...		936d/	946d/	929d/	...		102d/	38d/
35	Other transport equipment		...d/	...d/	...d/	...		...d/	...d/	...d/	...		...d/	...d/
36	Furniture; manufacturing n.e.c.		1695	1791	1776	...		666	716	695	...		64	40
37	Recycling		...	...	...	...		...	...	...	...		...	...
D	Total manufacturing		64388	68049	69782	...		20426	22180	22974	...		2676	2663

a/ 17 includes 18.
b/ 21 includes 22.
c/ 30 includes 31, 32 and 33.
d/ 34 includes 35.

New Zealand

ISIC Revision 3			Index numbers of industrial production (2000=100)											
ISIC	Industry	Note	1995	1996	1997	1998	1999	2000	2001	2002	2003	2004	2005	2006
15	Food and beverages	a/	94	98	98	102	98	100	102	104	122	130	131	134
16	Tobacco products	a/	...	...	...	...	...	...	...	...	...	...	...	...
17	Textiles	b/	103	99	107	99	96	100	89	84	87	84	88	77
18	Wearing apparel, fur	b/	...	...	...	...	...	...	...	...	...	...	...	...
19	Leather, leather products and footwear	b/	...	...	...	...	...	...	...	...	...	...	...	...
20	Wood products (excl. furniture)		94	92	96	91	87	100	103	99	107	106	109	105
21	Paper and paper products	c/	103	108	107	106	98	100	99	104	102	103	108	106
22	Printing and publishing	c/	...	...	...	...	...	...	...	...	...	...	...	...
23	Coke,refined petroleum products,nuclear fuel	d/	104	104	106	100	97	100	106	105	108	99	104	97
24	Chemicals and chemical products	d/	...	...	...	...	...	...	...	...	...	...	...	...
25	Rubber and plastics products	d/	...	...	...	...	...	...	...	...	...	...	...	...
26	Non-metallic mineral products		93	97	98	99	94	100	101	102	111	120	127	132
27	Basic metals	e/	87	89	90	92	90	100	103	107	114	121	121	119
28	Fabricated metal products	e/	...	...	...	...	...	...	...	...	...	...	...	...
29	Machinery and equipment n.e.c.	f/	97	100	103	100	97	100	109	111	115	121	124	122
30	Office, accounting and computing machinery	f/	...	...	...	...	...	...	...	...	...	...	...	...
31	Electrical machinery and apparatus	f/	...	...	...	...	...	...	...	...	...	...	...	...
32	Radio,television and communication equipment	f/	...	...	...	...	...	...	...	...	...	...	...	...
33	Medical, precision and optical instruments	f/	...	...	...	...	...	...	...	...	...	...	...	...
34	Motor vehicles, trailers, semi-trailers	f/	...	...	...	...	...	...	...	...	...	...	...	...
35	Other transport equipment	f/	...	...	...	...	...	...	...	...	...	...	...	...
36	Furniture; manufacturing n.e.c.		...	...	...	...	...	...	...	...	...	...	...	...
37	Recycling		...	...	...	...	...	...	...	...	...	...	...	...
D	Total manufacturing		96	98	99	99	95	100	103	103	112	115	118	116

a/ 15 includes 16.
b/ 17 includes 18 and 19.
c/ 21 includes 22.
d/ 23 includes 24 and 25.
e/ 27 includes 28.
f/ 29 includes 30, 31, 32, 33, 34 and 35.

Norway

Supplier of information:
Statistics Norway, Oslo.
Industrial statistics for the OECD countries are compiled by the OECD secretariat, which supplies them to UNIDO.

Basic source of data:
Annual industrial inquiry.

Major deviations from ISIC (Revision 3):
Data presented in ISIC (Revision 3) were originally classified according to the NACE (Revision 1).

Reference period:
Calendar year.

Scope:
All enterprises.

Method of data collection:
Not reported.

Type of enumeration:
Not reported.

Adjusted for non-response:
Not reported.

Concepts and definitions of variables:
Number of establishments refers to local kind of activity units.
Number of employees is calculated as the average number of employees throughout the year, whether full- or part-time; homeworkers are not included.
Wages and salaries comprises all payments, whether in cash or in kind, made by the employer in connection with work done, to all persons included in the count of employees (also employed outworkers). It includes taxes, social insurance and pension contributions payable by the employee, but deducted by the employer. Bonuses, production awards, holiday allowances and wages paid during periods of sickness, military leave or other absences and commission earned by salesmen and representatives are also included. Fees paid to shareholders committees are included to some extend.
Output refers to gross output and is valued in producers' prices, excluding all subsidies and including all indirect taxes exept VAT. Included are the values of all goods produced on own account, repair work for others, mounting or installation of own products and merchandise, contract work, other work, own-account investment work, own-account repair work, rental receipts and gross profit of goods sold in the same condition as purchased.
Value added is value of output, less cost of goods and services consumed. It includes subsidies, less indirect taxes (except VAT) and investment levy.
Gross fixed capital formation is defined as the acquisition of fixed durable assets, new and used, with an expected productive life of more than one year, including own-account investment work less receipts from sales of fixed durable assets.

Related national publications:
Industristatistikk (annual), published by Statistics Norway, Oslo.

Norway

ISIC Revision 3		Number of enterprises					Number of employees					Wages and salaries paid to employees				
			(number)					(number)					(millions of Norwegian Kroner)			
ISIC	Industry	Note	2001	2002	2003	2004	Note	2001	2002	2003	2004	Note	2001	2002	2003	2004
151	Processed meat,fish,fruit,vegetables,fats		698	712	679	...		27383	...	26483	25484		7125	...	7410	7683
1511	Processing/preserving of meat		184	194	194	...		13396	13810	13883	13480		3458	3715	3920	4062
1512	Processing/preserving of fish		466	464	425	...		11828	11609	10380	9587		2994	3088	2762	2726
1513	Processing/preserving of fruit & vegetables		36	43	46	...		1419	...	1352	1357		402	...	386	415
1514	Vegetable and animal oils and fats		12	11	14	...		740	763	868	1060		272	357	343	480
1520	Dairy products		24	19	19	...		5492	5561	6182	6252		1641	1882	1980	2064
153	Grain mill products; starches; animal feeds		106	103	104	...		...	...	...	2201		...	...	...	818
1531	Grain mill products		45	36	34	...		...	...	...	...		...	...	...	...
1532	Starches and starch products		1	1	1	...		...	...	...	...		...	...	...	...
1533	Prepared animal feeds		60	66	69	...		1636	1719	1830	1535		572	652	661	574
154	Other food products		449	452	448	...		13029	13162	12927	13049		3015	3255	3244	3356
1541	Bakery products		400	393	386	...		...	...	8185	8359		...	...	1795	1892
1542	Sugar		-	-	-	...		-	-	-	-		-	-	-	-
1543	Cocoa, chocolate and sugar confectionery		9	10	10	...		2347	2444	2364	2277		586	682	686	645
1544	Macaroni, noodles & similar products		2	2	2	...		...	...	...	26		...	...	...	8
1549	Other food products n.e.c.		38	47	50	...		2137	2469	...	2387		732	779	...	813
155	Beverages		29	31	26	...		...	5297	5353	5159		...	1756	1790	1809
1551	Distilling, rectifying & blending of spirits		2	2	3	...		...	...	...	...		...	...	...	...
1552	Wines		-	-	-	...		-	-	-	...		-	-	-	...
1553	Malt liquors and malt		9	11	7	...		3517	3302	3291	3105		1073	1133	1139	1127
1554	Soft drinks; mineral waters		18	18	16	...		1719	...	...	1760		533	...	...	552
1600	Tobacco products		2	2	2	...		...	...	...	438		...	...	...	172
171	Spinning, weaving and finishing of textiles		43	38	38	...		...	833	...	804		...	208	...	203
1711	Textile fibre preparation; textile weaving		17	16	16	...		...	630	...	576		...	155	...	143
1712	Finishing of textiles		26	22	22	...		147	203	213	228		33	53	53	60
172	Other textiles		205	201	182	...		2972	2704	2473	2403		711	704	635	646
1721	Made-up textile articles, except apparel		102	104	93	...		1092	1059	1003	1042		260	277	265	275
1722	Carpets and rugs		4	5	4	...		31	33	...	32		6	8	...	8
1723	Cordage, rope, twine and netting		67	59	55	...		1315	1170	1079	1000		311	302	267	275
1729	Other textiles n.e.c.		32	33	30	...		534	442	...	329		134	118	...	90
1730	Knitted and crocheted fabrics and articles		37	31	28	...		...	630	...	553		...	134	...	128
1810	Wearing apparel, except fur apparel		107	82	72	...		1086	963	910	960		219	223	214	229
1820	Dressing & dyeing of fur; processing of fur		11	12	12	...		99	112	100	113		22	26	23	23
191	Tanning, dressing and processing of leather		17	12	13	...		172	181	205	172		49	41	51	50
1911	Tanning and dressing of leather		4	3	3	...		144	136	159	143		39	33	39	39
1912	Luggage, handbags, etc.; saddlery & harness		13	9	10	...		28	45	46	29		10	8	12	12
1920	Footwear		16	13	12	...		245	181	186	173		47	41	40	40
2010	Sawmilling and planing of wood		275	273	249	...		4455	4380	4303	4249		1152	1136	1140	1168
202	Products of wood, cork, straw, etc.		637	653	622	...		9832	10154	9946	9933		2518	2714	2671	2838
2021	Veneer sheets, plywood, particle board, etc.		26	29	23	...		1477	1419	1132	1051		430	428	348	349
2022	Builders' carpentry and joinery		471	488	460	...		7482	7893	8008	8034		1893	2085	2126	2278
2023	Wooden containers		51	50	50	...		364	343	318	330		83	80	77	79
2029	Other wood products; articles of cork/straw		89	86	89	...		509	499	488	518		112	120	120	132
210	Paper and paper products		83	78	79	...		8423	8142	8008	7633		2899	2744	2756	2751
2101	Pulp, paper and paperboard		27	26	24	...		5317	5238	5050	4849		1924	1822	1764	1762
2102	Corrugated paper and paperboard		26	25	25	...		2102	2026	2047	1929		670	656	695	710
2109	Other articles of paper and paperboard		30	27	30	...		...	...	...	855		...	...	...	280
221	Publishing		731	746	658	...		22682	21677	21020	20081		6700	6709	6761	7013
2211	Publishing of books and other publications		172	166	127	...		3078	2885	2840	2938		1185	1036	1026	1161
2212	Publishing of newspapers, journals, etc.		398	411	393	...		18947	18096	17424	16339		5298	5432	5486	5585
2213	Publishing of recorded media		51	52	48	...		145	139	163	187		35	41	48	55
2219	Other publishing		110	117	90	...		512	557	593	617		182	200	200	213

222	Printing and related service activities	990	961	867	...	9490	8820	8355	8318	2944	2828	2727	2778
2221	Printing	666	656	605	...	7703	7130	6774	6671	2428	2330	2255	2297
2222	Service activities related to printing	324	305	262	...	1787	1690	1581	1647	517	498	471	480
2230	Reproduction of recorded media	38	31	28	...	174	158	129	129	52	46	39	40
2310	Coke oven products	-	...	-	...	-	...	-	...	-	...	-	...
2320	Refined petroleum products	-	...	-	...	-	...	-	...	-	...	-	...
2330	Processing of nuclear fuel	-	...	-	...	-	...	-	-	-	...	-	-
241	Basic chemicals	55	52	50	...	8995	8708	7344	7293	3654	3826	3149	3520
2411	Basic chemicals, except fertilizers	36	36	34	...	...	...	...	5008	...	...	...	2223
2412	Fertilizers and nitrogen compounds	9	8	8	...	2435	1918	737	936	515	758	335	680
2413	Plastics in primary forms; synthetic rubber	10	8	8	...	...	...	...	1349	...	...	...	618
242	Other chemicals	82	87	87	...	5867	5951	6113	5984	2318	2521	2580	2607
2421	Pesticides and other agro-chemical products	-	-	-	...	-	-	-	1	-	-	-	-
2422	Paints, varnishes, printing ink and mastics	23	25	21	...	1210	1171	1117	1092	427	490	465	475
2423	Pharmaceuticals, medicinal chemicals, etc.	14	18	18	...	2953	3073	3172	3055	1222	1316	1369	1378
2424	Soap, cleaning & cosmetic preparations	21	20	22	...	822	...	933	957	330	...	347	352
2429	Other chemical products n.e.c.	24	24	26	...	882	...	891	879	339	...	399	402
2430	Man-made fibres	-	-	-	...	-	-	-	-	-	-	-	-
251	Rubber products	40	36	36	...	753	484	633	614	199	186	209	207
2511	Rubber tyres and tubes	19	17	15	...	...	...	123	...	...	...	34	...
2519	Other rubber products	21	19	21	...	...	...	510	488	...	...	174	168
2520	Plastic products	268	263	250	...	5313	5187	5040	4774	1507	1495	1508	1502
2610	Glass and glass products	55	64	65	...	2025	2157	2027	1993	617	636	633	662
269	Non-metallic mineral products n.e.c.	342	343	332	...	7530	8420	8246	7972	2426	2763	2705	2877
2691	Pottery, china and earthenware	20	20	23	...	...	...	...	...	...	...	...	...
2692	Refractory ceramic products	3	3	2	...	...	76	...	12	...	31	...	3
2693	Struct.non-refractory clay; ceramic products	3	2	2	...	43	...	...	...	10	...	...	...
2694	Cement, lime and plaster	5	6	4	...	468	478	...	496	249	199	...	206
2695	Articles of concrete, cement and plaster	207	207	196	...	3893	3945	4077	4073	1248	1282	1308	1420
2696	Cutting, shaping & finishing of stone	87	87	87	...	487	...	...	696	130	...	...	194
2699	Other non-metallic mineral products n.e.c.	17	18	18	...	1836	2736	2488	2035	600	943	900	872
2710	Basic iron and steel	62	61	54	...	...	3765	3488	3248	...	1282	1234	1306
2720	Basic precious and non-ferrous metals	20	20	21	...	7593	7222	7878	7489	2792	3188	3224	3678
273	Casting of metals	30	28	26	...	...	1533	1447	1470	...	484	448	474
2731	Casting of iron and steel	12	12	11	...	1248	1166	1043	980	381	370	329	330
2732	Casting of non-ferrous metals	18	16	15	...	...	367	404	490	...	114	118	145
281	Struct.metal products;tanks;steam generators	409	433	428	...	9091	8470	7798	7527	2634	2500	2334	2404
2811	Structural metal products	384	406	401	...	8534	7914	7296	6967	2475	2325	2171	2215
2812	Tanks, reservoirs and containers of metal	20	22	21	...	366	...	301	381	101	...	94	130
2813	Steam generators	5	5	6	...	191	...	201	179	58	...	69	59
289	Other metal products; metal working services	751	807	800	...	9896	10803	10682	10644	2891	3305	3194	3453
2891	Metal forging/pressing/stamping/roll-forming	14	17	14	...	226	224	192	197	62	62	57	61
2892	Treatment & coating of metals	398	439	457	...	4063	4720	4773	5114	1192	1510	1433	1691
2893	Cutlery, hand tools and general hardware	90	91	79	...	1535	1667	1640	1390	482	491	504	439
2899	Other fabricated metal products n.e.c.	249	260	250	...	4072	4192	4077	3943	1155	1243	1200	1261
291	General purpose machinery	653	657	639	...	13737	14235	12859	13254	4943	5286	4839	5398
2911	Engines & turbines (not for transport equipment)	49	51	51	...	3700	3683	3769	3562	1528	1637	1612	1548
2912	Pumps, compressors, taps and valves	86	84	83	...	2671	2590	2307	2208	964	984	942	936
2913	Bearings, gears, gearing & driving elements	10	8	7	...	163	131	127	127	61	41	42	43
2914	Ovens, furnaces and furnace burners	14	14	11	...	291	318	279	268	109	125	97	90
2915	Lifting and handling equipment	127	126	115	...	2815	2758	2649	3401	999	981	941	1489
2919	Other general purpose machinery	367	374	372	...	4097	4755	3728	3688	1280	1519	1206	1293
292	Special purpose machinery	424	420	406	...	7584	6737	7308	6859	2641	2505	2723	2558
2921	Agricultural and forestry machinery	134	132	133	...	1680	839	1609	1589	522	284	523	512
2922	Machine tools	46	49	47	...	590	619	593	740	187	198	193	253
2923	Machinery for metallurgy	7	6	5	...	56	22	16	17	15	5	4	3
2924	Machinery for mining & construction	64	59	61	...	1016	1196	1180	744	357	463	443	244
2925	Food/beverage/tobacco processing machinery	74	77	64	...	986	865	587	553	296	280	172	165
2926	Machinery for textile, apparel and leather	14	12	8	...	59	47	31	39	15	14	7	11
2927	Weapons and ammunition	13	12	13	...	2073	2016	2094	1971	835	876	928	898
2929	Other special purpose machinery	72	73	75	...	1124	1133	1198	1206	414	386	452	472

continued

Norway

ISIC Revision 3		Number of enterprises					Number of employees					Wages and salaries paid to employees				
			(number)					(number)					(millions of Norwegian Kroner)			
ISIC	Industry	Note	2001	2002	2003	2004	Note	2001	2002	2003	2004	Note	2001	2002	2003	2004
2930	Domestic appliances n.e.c.		23	24	22	...		1366	1300	1140	1163		396	407	346	314
3000	Office, accounting and computing machinery		14	16	13	...		468	388	...	169		192	156	...	80
3110	Electric motors, generators and transformers		54	56	50	...		1580	1586	1260	1214		555	559	457	475
3120	Electricity distribution & control apparatus		68	65	68	...		1135	...	1175	1225		340	...	355	420
3130	Insulated wire and cable		12	13	15	...		1332	1355	1306	1333		556	565	551	588
3140	Accumulators, primary cells and batteries		1	2	3	...		...	...	...	17		...	...	...	5
3150	Lighting equipment and electric lamps		38	36	33	...		1236	1177	...	1064		371	374	...	372
3190	Other electrical equipment n.e.c.		125	123	110	...		...	1090	1128	1236		...	398	412	455
3210	Electronic valves, tubes, etc.		49	48	48	...		2786	2593	2328	1905		854	830	749	680
3220	TV/radio transmitters; line comm. apparatus		19	23	17	...		2852	2600	1790	1785		1363	1203	931	976
3230	TV and radio receivers and associated goods		13	13	16	...		594	436	...	312		215	156	...	98
331	Medical, measuring, testing appliances, etc.		254	259	292	...		14247	13652	7538	7599		5434	5687	3197	3326
3311	Medical, surgical and orthopaedic equipment		174	176	200	...		1750	1825	1916	2027		573	603	647	716
3312	Measuring/testing/navigating appliances,etc.		67	71	76	...		3260	3316	3235	3267		1396	1465	1467	1548
3313	Industrial process control equipment		13	12	16	...		9237	8511	2387	2305		3465	3619	1083	1063
3320	Optical instruments & photographic equipment		10	8	10	...		229	207	...	222		76	66	...	74
3330	Watches and clocks		-	-	1	...		-	-	...	12		-	-	...	3
3410	Motor vehicles		6	8	5	...		379	348	153	219		112	130	66	55
3420	Automobile bodies, trailers & semi-trailers		58	57	53	...		1212	1221	1251	1236		342	337	359	364
3430	Parts/accessories for automobiles		52	58	52	...		4167	4120	3784	3439		1285	1344	1285	1283
351	Building and repairing of ships and boats		592	584	570	...		30211	30170	30060	27729		10551	11094	12016	12025
3511	Building and repairing of ships		470	462	447	...		29113	29077	28913	26437		10243	10792	11685	11608
3512	Building/repairing of pleasure/sport. boats		122	122	123	...		1098	1093	1147	1292		307	302	331	417
3520	Railway/tramway locomotives & rolling stock		5	5	7	...		412	343	334	326		149	130	130	139
3530	Aircraft and spacecraft		12	14	14	...		1059	1088	1053	1048		427	439	456	480
359	Transport equipment n.e.c.		8	10	10	...		268	269	278	289		72	74	81	86
3591	Motorcycles		-	-	-	...		-	-	-	...		-	-	-	...
3592	Bicycles and invalid carriages		5	7	9	...		223	...	...	...		59	...	...	...
3599	Other transport equipment n.e.c.		3	3	1	...		45	...	...	22		13	...	...	7
3610	Furniture		490	478	450	...		9387	8574	8182	8064		2358	2268	2202	2337
369	Manufacturing n.e.c.		206	199	186	...		2707	2393	2290	2288		715	677	650	661
3691	Jewellery and related articles		68	62	62	...		739	670	671	596		179	181	167	167
3692	Musical instruments		7	7	6	...		31	28	28	28		8	7	7	8
3693	Sports goods		22	24	26	...		942	929	891	881		270	277	288	276
3694	Games and toys		9	11	9	...		49	34	34	43		14	10	8	10
3699	Other manufacturing n.e.c.		100	95	83	...		946	732	666	740		244	202	179	201
3710	Recycling of metal waste and scrap		40	39	45	...		521	595	709	701		171	218	245	256
3720	Recycling of non-metal waste and scrap		50	51	38	...		421	287	231	277		104	92	78	102
D	Total manufacturing		9888	...	9460	...		279356	...	259840	252109		87602	...	86891	90115

Norway

ISIC Revision 3		Output					Value added					Gross fixed capital formation		
		Note	(millions of Norwegian Kroner)				Note	(millions of Norwegian Kroner)				Note	(millions of Norwegian Kroner)	
ISIC	Industry		2001	2002	2003	2004		2001	2002	2003	2004		2003	2004
151	Processed meat,fish,fruit,vegetables,fats		57565	...	56444	67384		11572	...	11344	11501		1588	1599
1511	Processing/preserving of meat		27129	29449	30608	39421		5500	5567	5682	5938		663	712
1512	Processing/preserving of fish		25142	25550	20264	21513		4492	4046	4251	3963		678	685
1513	Processing/preserving of fruit & vegetables		2634	...	2672	2680		891	...	781	814		150	116
1514	Vegetable and animal oils and fats		2660	2819	2900	3770		689	683	631	785		96	85
1520	Dairy products		12420	14266	13497	13820		2636	2988	3525	3011		547	555
153	Grain mill products; starches; animal feeds		...	...	...	9906		...	...	...	1851		...	374
1531	Grain mill products		...	...	...	...		...	...	...	...		...	...
1532	Starches and starch products		...	...	...	...		...	...	...	...		...	...
1533	Prepared animal feeds		8014	9085	9363	7330		1225	1667	1814	1269		295	270
154	Other food products		12845	13979	13801	14818		5745	6070	6276	6431		991	698
1541	Bakery products		...	...	6199	6687		...	...	2820	2780		475	315
1542	Sugar		-	-	-	-		-	-	-	-		-	-
1543	Cocoa, chocolate and sugar confectionery		2868	3363	3498	3535		1590	1810	1925	1927		115	124
1544	Macaroni, noodles & similar products		...	...	...	28		...	...	...	8		...	1
1549	Other food products n.e.c.		4555	4513	...	4569		1577	1655	...	1717		...	258
155	Beverages		...	12200	13027	12991		...	7618	8340	8386		351	309
1551	Distilling, rectifying & blending of spirits		...	...	...	...		...	...	...	...		...	...
1552	Wines		-	-	-	...		-	-	-	...		-	...
1553	Malt liquors and malt		7815	8594	8926	8828		5922	6302	6414	6466		223	195
1554	Soft drinks; mineral waters		3160	...	...	3437		1324	...	...	1663		...	92
1600	Tobacco products		...	...	...	6401		...	...	...	5881		...	43
171	Spinning, weaving and finishing of textiles		...	708	...	762		...	273	...	316		...	13
1711	Textile fibre preparation; textile weaving		...	472	...	492		...	194	...	208		...	7
1712	Finishing of textiles		126	236	247	270		47	79	75	109		10	7
172	Other textiles		2753	2674	2368	2591		1113	1016	958	964		147	86
1721	Made-up textile articles, except apparel		1031	1114	1081	1172		403	426	414	429		30	23
1722	Carpets and rugs		16	21	...	22		8	9	...	12		...	1
1723	Cordage, rope, twine and netting		1243	1123	922	1074		532	446	404	412		93	54
1729	Other textiles n.e.c.		464	416	...	324		170	135	...	110		...	8
1730	Knitted and crocheted fabrics and articles		...	469	...	428		...	207	...	167		...	6
1810	Wearing apparel, except fur apparel		877	964	1042	1016		380	378	363	426		15	23
1820	Dressing & dyeing of fur; processing of fur		120	135	120	136		64	29	37	42		1	3
191	Tanning, dressing and processing of leather		300	244	241	227		76	57	60	69		6	3
1911	Tanning and dressing of leather		254	202	202	169		47	39	46	45		1	2
1912	Luggage, handbags, etc.; saddlery & harness		46	42	38	58		28	18	14	24		6	1
1920	Footwear		150	152	146	146		72	61	54	54		7	1
2010	Sawmilling and planing of wood		7903	7420	6369	8600		2179	1772	1633	1877		524	228
202	Products of wood, cork, straw, etc.		10557	11226	11547	12123		3596	3970	3836	4325		387	464
2021	Veneer sheets, plywood, particle board, etc.		1985	2018	1669	1800		533	679	540	550		50	44
2022	Builders' carpentry and joinery		7832	8436	9053	9363		2768	2991	2988	3437		291	355
2023	Wooden containers		394	376	360	394		129	119	122	126		14	39
2029	Other wood products; articles of cork/straw		346	396	465	565		167	181	186	213		32	26
210	Paper and paper products		18052	14575	15715	17992		7468	4750	4770	4731		480	794
2101	Pulp, paper and paperboard		13822	10727	11643	12705		5875	3314	3280	3278		387	680
2102	Corrugated paper and paperboard		2912	2791	2860	4175		1090	1030	1064	1053		61	77
2109	Other articles of paper and paperboard		...	...	...	1112		...	...	...	401		...	38
221	Publishing		23721	23407	23812	25157		10237	10094	10780	11129		539	477
2211	Publishing of books and other publications		5466	5042	5103	5266		2196	2091	2325	2399		66	98
2212	Publishing of newspapers, journals, etc.		17134	17076	17636	18356		7689	7601	8064	8265		459	340
2213	Publishing of recorded media		326	389	325	461		58	104	90	131		4	5
2219	Other publishing		796	901	748	1073		294	298	302	336		10	33

continued

Norway

ISIC Revision 3		Output					Value added					Gross fixed capital formation		
			(millions of Norwegian Kroner)					(millions of Norwegian Kroner)					(millions of Norwegian Kroner)	
ISIC	Industry	Note	2001	2002	2003	2004	Note	2001	2002	2003	2004	Note	2003	2004
222	Printing and related service activities		11151	10646	10148	10904		4751	4299	4230	4525		427	557
2221	Printing		9384	8965	8503	9035		3955	3615	3535	3748		391	497
2222	Service activities related to printing		1767	1681	1646	1868		797	685	695	778		36	60
2230	Reproduction of recorded media		213	200	122	145		80	74	60	62		2	4
2310	Coke oven products		-	...	-	...		-	...	-	...		-	...
2320	Refined petroleum products		-	...	-	...		-	...	-	...		-	...
2330	Processing of nuclear fuel		-	...	-	-		-	...	-	-		-	-
241	Basic chemicals		28056	25186	24396	30083		7565	6748	7475	9259		1457	1919
2411	Basic chemicals, except fertilizers		...	...	...	19039		...	...	...	7488		...	1688
2412	Fertilizers and nitrogen compounds		4603	2705	3999	5331		-123	-124	724	740		111	84
2413	Plastics in primary forms; synthetic rubber		...	...	...	5712		...	...	...	1033		...	147
242	Other chemicals		12703	12997	13029	13104		4910	5372	5312	5814		682	774
2421	Pesticides and other agro-chemical products		-	-	-	-		-	-	-	-		-	-
2422	Paints, varnishes, printing ink and mastics		2200	2196	1922	2175		617	740	646	633		42	59
2423	Pharmaceuticals, medicinal chemicals, etc.		6726	7002	7072	7092		2993	3149	3134	3687		500	593
2424	Soap, cleaning & cosmetic preparations		2105	...	2253	2109		703	...	793	797		43	25
2429	Other chemical products n.e.c.		1671	...	1783	1728		597	...	739	698		97	97
2430	Man-made fibres		-	-	-	-		-	-	-	-		-	-
251	Rubber products		617	717	618	619		267	262	280	306		17	17
2511	Rubber tyres and tubes		...	...	122	...		...	...	54	...		4	...
2519	Other rubber products		...	...	495	474		...	...	226	239		13	13
2520	Plastic products		6512	6344	6323	6864		2505	2227	2284	2297		382	258
2610	Glass and glass products		2427	2542	2344	2605		1050	1002	915	1048		121	143
269	Non-metallic mineral products n.e.c.		10973	12427	12235	13924		4323	4438	4367	4808		516	734
2691	Pottery, china and earthenware		...	...	...	...		...	...	...	...		...	...
2692	Refractory ceramic products		...	56	...	8		...	17	...	3		...	-
2693	Struct.non-refractory clay; ceramic products		62	...	...	...		39	...	...	...		...	...
2694	Cement, lime and plaster		910	941	...	993		481	394	...	372		...	83
2695	Articles of concrete, cement and plaster		6350	6454	6569	7671		2241	2152	2227	2556		322	357
2696	Cutting, shaping & finishing of stone		524	...	...	695		203	...	...	298		...	42
2699	Other non-metallic mineral products n.e.c.		2551	3848	3651	3925		1075	1379	1273	1306		153	226
2710	Basic iron and steel		...	8743	9032	13036		...	1991	2369	4070		390	328
2720	Basic precious and non-ferrous metals		34514	29404	30615	28968		8868	6387	7674	9028		2931	2956
273	Casting of metals		...	1460	1345	1556		...	652	580	581		45	68
2731	Casting of iron and steel		1036	1017	868	983		518	478	400	405		29	49
2732	Casting of non-ferrous metals		...	444	477	572		...	174	180	176		16	18
281	Struct.metal products;tanks;steam generators		8769	8567	7742	8667		3578	3452	3078	3381		170	192
2811	Structural metal products		8221	8018	7218	8043		3387	3236	2843	3116		163	184
2812	Tanks, reservoirs and containers of metal		344	...	310	405		121	...	126	172		2	5
2813	Steam generators		204	...	214	218		70	...	109	94		5	3
289	Other metal products; metal working services		9962	11142	10525	12176		4278	4818	4661	5210		331	534
2891	Metal forging/pressing/stamping/roll-forming		204	175	171	195		96	84	76	79		2	6
2892	Treatment & coating of metals		3643	4499	4070	5429		1642	2109	2006	2440		109	322
2893	Cutlery, hand tools and general hardware		1671	1781	1761	1527		741	806	770	679		46	32
2899	Other fabricated metal products n.e.c.		4444	4687	4523	5026		1798	1819	1810	2013		174	174
291	General purpose machinery		24775	25445	23650	25221		7725	8344	7906	8217		494	576
2911	Engines & turbines (not for transport equipment)		9187	9474	8093	6990		2385	2615	2593	2124		78	89
2912	Pumps, compressors, taps and valves		5961	6386	7489	7332		1840	1979	2122	1959		142	96
2913	Bearings, gears, gearing & driving elements		215	170	180	219		93	67	71	74		5	18
2914	Ovens, furnaces and furnace burners		439	458	440	378		163	196	157	124		3	3
2915	Lifting and handling equipment		4373	4091	3442	5840		1520	1450	1281	2161		106	139
2919	Other general purpose machinery		4600	4867	4005	4460		1726	2038	1681	1775		160	231

292	Special purpose machinery		10317	10044	10136	9935		3991	3701	3742	3506		266	285
2921	Agricultural and forestry machinery		1786	934	1721	2312		714	380	708	801		78	61
2922	Machine tools		584	586	531	898		287	298	271	403		23	26
2923	Machinery for metallurgy		43	20	19	12		23	9	9	5		1	-
2924	Machinery for mining & construction		1932	2573	1764	904		602	777	571	360		35	32
2925	Food/beverage/tobacco processing machinery		1054	928	542	634		383	355	218	244		18	8
2926	Machinery for textile, apparel and leather		43	35	22	49		22	19	10	26		-	1
2927	Weapons and ammunition		3058	3349	3289	2778		1236	1322	1325	1061		87	83
2929	Other special purpose machinery		1816	1620	2250	2349		724	541	627	605		24	74
2930	Domestic appliances n.e.c.		1356	1340	1329	1179		538	559	573	423		58	110
3000	Office, accounting and computing machinery		1228	856	...	391		220	115	...	121		...	5
3110	Electric motors, generators and transformers		2345	2336	1800	1999		676	786	562	545		38	34
3120	Electricity distribution & control apparatus		1215	...	1257	1569		561	...	558	734		30	28
3130	Insulated wire and cable		2789	2332	2393	3314		876	771	1013	1114		42	97
3140	Accumulators, primary cells and batteries		...	...	...	26		...	...	...	3		...	1
3150	Lighting equipment and electric lamps		1235	1279	...	1381		444	481	...	525		...	35
3190	Other electrical equipment n.e.c.		...	1490	1564	1736		...	601	653	696		33	30
3210	Electronic valves, tubes, etc.		4066	3240	3123	2911		920	839	1096	945		92	244
3220	TV/radio transmitters; line comm. apparatus		5881	5167	4620	4770		1801	1698	1464	1502		44	35
3230	TV and radio receivers and associated goods		1392	897	...	494		499	289	...	189		...	16
331	Medical, measuring, testing appliances, etc.		19812	19274	12129	12637		7674	7513	4568	4768		170	270
3311	Medical, surgical and orthopaedic equipment		2177	2316	2483	2680		798	942	1079	1152		28	71
3312	Measuring/testing/navigating appliances,etc.		5195	5240	4941	5124		1938	2005	2047	2055		103	174
3313	Industrial process control equipment		12440	11718	4704	4833		4939	4566	1442	1562		39	24
3320	Optical instruments & photographic equipment		222	188	...	227		129	94	...	105		...	6
3330	Watches and clocks		-	-	...	8		-	-	...	3		...	-
3410	Motor vehicles		806	744	182	269		283	161	97	39		4	8
3420	Automobile bodies, trailers & semi-trailers		1437	1322	1438	1763		518	414	471	498		14	17
3430	Parts/accessories for automobiles		4597	5107	5058	5143		1681	1943	1978	2015		195	207
351	Building and repairing of ships and boats		47022	49913	48429	47801		13914	14456	15721	14992		787	661
3511	Building and repairing of ships		45661	48577	46857	45661		13510	14023	15225	14356		761	614
3512	Building/repairing of pleasure/sport. boats		1361	1335	1573	2141		404	433	495	636		26	47
3520	Railway/tramway locomotives & rolling stock		896	331	381	685		233	132	172	295		38	38
3530	Aircraft and spacecraft		2218	1923	2230	2548		906	877	936	1036		372	280
359	Transport equipment n.e.c.		328	324	359	408		113	120	138	162		3	10
3591	Motorcycles		-	-	-	...		-	-	-	...		-	...
3592	Bicycles and invalid carriages		281	...	...	...		103	...	...	...		...	...
3599	Other transport equipment n.e.c.		47	...	...	42		10	...	...	13		...	1
3610	Furniture		9384	8992	8743	9768		3516	3319	3286	3733		335	331
369	Manufacturing n.e.c.		2384	2077	2119	2464		1095	990	958	1066		55	86
3691	Jewellery and related articles		580	460	472	562		285	242	246	272		7	11
3692	Musical instruments		21	20	16	27		12	10	8	14		1	-
3693	Sports goods		856	880	940	1097		409	404	388	436		31	37
3694	Games and toys		65	34	31	49		27	14	6	18		1	3
3699	Other manufacturing n.e.c.		861	683	660	728		363	320	310	326		15	35
3710	Recycling of metal waste and scrap		1375	1664	1759	2220		404	388	438	624		164	194
3720	Recycling of non-metal waste and scrap		507	590	346	526		173	165	107	163		57	52
D	Total manufacturing		463593	...	441593	481809		156087	...	151410	161608		17097	17812

Norway

ISIC Revision 3			Index numbers of industrial production											
			(2000=100)											
ISIC	Industry	Note	1995	1996	1997	1998	1999	2000	2001	2002	2003	2004	2005	2006
15	Food and beverages	a/	104	106	107	106	102	100	99	98	94	94	91	92
16	Tobacco products	a/	...	...	...	...	...	...	...	...	...	...	...	...
17	Textiles	b/	133	135	133	126	109	100	95	87	75	72	72	80
18	Wearing apparel, fur	b/	...	...	...	...	...	...	...	...	...	...	...	...
19	Leather, leather products and footwear	b/	...	...	...	...	...	...	...	...	...	...	...	...
20	Wood products (excl. furniture)		94	95	103	103	98	100	97	95	87	92	99	100
21	Paper and paper products		102	95	100	100	98	100	96	89	91	95	93	86
22	Printing and publishing		100	103	103	104	102	100	101	98	98	99	103	105
23	Coke,refined petroleum products,nuclear fuel	c/	93	95	97	100	100	100	100	100	102	105	109	110
24	Chemicals and chemical products	c/	...	...	...	...	...	...	...	...	...	...	...	...
25	Rubber and plastics products		114	114	119	111	111	100	98	94	78	80	79	80
26	Non-metallic mineral products		97	102	106	107	103	100	96	101	93	92	97	106
27	Basic metals		86	88	92	96	99	100	96	94	94	104	103	104
28	Fabricated metal products		96	103	110	117	107	100	102	103	96	96	102	114
29	Machinery and equipment n.e.c.		91	95	102	106	103	100	102	102	97	99	106	113
30	Office, accounting and computing machinery	d/	85	89	92	100	103	100	97	94	85	88	93	95
31	Electrical machinery and apparatus	d/	...	...	...	...	...	...	...	...	...	...	...	...
32	Radio,television and communication equipment	d/	...	...	...	...	...	...	...	...	...	...	...	...
33	Medical, precision and optical instruments	d/	...	...	...	...	...	...	...	...	...	...	...	...
34	Motor vehicles, trailers, semi-trailers		108	112	115	115	107	100	100	101	90	83	89	98
35	Other transport equipment		95	96	97	109	108	100	101	109	102	101	106	126
36	Furniture; manufacturing n.e.c.	e/	94	99	110	117	109	100	93	91	86	92	94	92
37	Recycling	e/	...	...	...	...	...	...	...	...	...	...	...	...
D	Total manufacturing		97	99	103	106	103	100	99	98	94	95	98	103

a/ 15 includes 16.
b/ 17 includes 18 and 19.
c/ 23 includes 24.
d/ 30 includes 31, 32 and 33.
e/ 36 includes 37.

Oman

Supplier of information:
Ministry of Commerce and Industry, Muscat.

Basic source of data:
Annual survey.

Major deviations from ISIC (Revision 3):
None reported.

Reference period:
Calendar year.

Scope:
Establishments with 10 or more employees.

Method of data collection:
Prior to 2006, the inquiries were carried out through enumerators' site visits; in 2006, the survey was conducted on-line.

Type of enumeration:
Complete enumeration.

Adjusted for non-response:
No.

Concepts and definitions of variables:
No deviations from the standard UN concepts and definitions are reported.

Related national publications:
Industrial Statistical Book; Features of the Manufacturing Sector of Large and Medium Industries; Annual Industrial Report, all published by the Industrial Information Department, Ministry of Commerce and Industry, Muscat.

Oman

ISIC Revision 3		Number of establishments					Number of employees					Wages and salaries paid to employees				
			(number)					(number)					(thousands of Omani Rials)			
ISIC	Industry	Note	2003	2004	2005	2006	Note	2003	2004	2005	2006	Note	2003	2004	2005	2006
151	Processed meat,fish,fruit,vegetables,fats		30	31	29	33		1847	2056	2214	2640		4644	5472	5995	6468
1511	Processing/preserving of meat		3	4	3	4		165	217	437	492		240	372	926	1230
1512	Processing/preserving of fish		17	18	18	18		804	895	875	769		1704	2541	2341	1349
1513	Processing/preserving of fruit & vegetables		8	8	6	9		536	613	435	827		1220	1083	905	1518
1514	Vegetable and animal oils and fats		2	1	2	2		342	331	467	552		1481	1476	1823	2371
1520	Dairy products		5	4	4	5		625	730	909	1241		1573	1805	1965	2464
153	Grain mill products; starches; animal feeds		7	6	8	7		436	425	515	512		2122	2280	2613	2827
1531	Grain mill products		3	3	4	3		273	283	287	272		1570	1741	1852	1906
1532	Starches and starch products		-	-	-	-		-	-	-	-		-	-	-	-
1533	Prepared animal feeds		4	3	4	4		163	142	228	240		552	539	761	922
154	Other food products		40	40	42	...		2452	2810	2758	...		4870	5596	6203	...
1541	Bakery products		32	32	35	32		1886	2278	2322	1922		3345	4140	4978	3988
1542	Sugar		-	-	-	-		-	-	-	-		-	-	-	-
1543	Cocoa, chocolate and sugar confectionery		1	2	1	1		80	225	96	122		165	464	239	300
1544	Macaroni, noodles & similar products		1	2	1	...		14	47	51	...		25	72	75	...
1549	Other food products n.e.c.		6	4	5	6		472	260	289	300		1334	920	910	945
155	Beverages		11	11	15	14		1521	1403	1738	1631		4117	4281	5006	5113
1551	Distilling, rectifying & blending of spirits		-	-	-	-		-	-	-	-		-	-	-	-
1552	Wines		-	-	-	-		-	-	-	-		-	-	-	-
1553	Malt liquors and malt		-	-	-	-		-	-	-	-		-	-	-	-
1554	Soft drinks; mineral waters		11	11	15	14		1521	1403	1738	1631		4117	4281	5006	5113
1600	Tobacco products		-	-	-	-		-	-	-	-		-	-	-	-
171	Spinning, weaving and finishing of textiles		2	2	2	2		287	274	272	266		903	934	980	839
1711	Textile fibre preparation; textile weaving		1	1	1	1		225	221	217	208		683	687	683	538
1712	Finishing of textiles		1	1	1	1		62	53	55	58		221	246	297	301
172	Other textiles		2	2	3	2		39	44	62	41		50	82	116	104
1721	Made-up textile articles, except apparel		2	2	2	1		39	44	45	25		50	82	78	54
1722	Carpets and rugs		-	-	1	1		-	-	17	16		-	-	38	50
1723	Cordage, rope, twine and netting		-	-	-	-		-	-	-	-		-	-	-	-
1729	Other textiles n.e.c.		-	-	-	-		-	-	-	-		-	-	-	-
1730	Knitted and crocheted fabrics and articles		-	-	-	-		-	-	-	-		-	-	-	-
1810	Wearing apparel, except fur apparel		13	9	7	5		3605	2407	1809	1599		4059	2211	2192	2031
1820	Dressing & dyeing of fur; processing of fur		-	-	-	-		-	-	-	-		-	-	-	-
191	Tanning, dressing and processing of leather		-	-	-	-		-	-	-	-		-	-	-	-
1911	Tanning and dressing of leather		-	-	-	-		-	-	-	-		-	-	-	-
1912	Luggage, handbags, etc.; saddlery & harness		-	-	-	-		-	-	-	-		-	-	-	-
1920	Footwear		4	4	3	2		161	170	147	110		333	299	293	216
2010	Sawmilling and planing of wood		-	-	-	-		-	-	-	-		-	-	-	-
202	Products of wood, cork, straw, etc.		7	14	14	14		510	896	823	822		1230	1783	1791	1648
2021	Veneer sheets, plywood, particle board, etc.		-	-	2	1		-	-	228	212		-	-	580	578
2022	Builders' carpentry and joinery		7	14	12	13		510	896	595	610		1230	1783	1211	1070
2023	Wooden containers		-	-	-	-		-	-	-	-		-	-	-	-
2029	Other wood products; articles of cork/straw		-	-	-	-		-	-	-	-		-	-	-	-
210	Paper and paper products		9	8	12	11		601	555	695	649		1640	1501	1886	1760
2101	Pulp, paper and paperboard		1	1	-	-		41	44	-	-		80	74	-	-
2102	Corrugated paper and paperboard		5	4	6	5		456	416	481	434		1107	1050	1229	1105
2109	Other articles of paper and paperboard		3	3	6	6		104	95	214	215		452	377	657	655
221	Publishing		12	10	9	7		631	591	816	527		1635	1449	2889	1720
2211	Publishing of books and other publications		8	6	5	3		365	309	287	213		856	679	700	611
2212	Publishing of newspapers, journals, etc.		3	3	3	3		256	272	519	297		766	757	2176	1086
2213	Publishing of recorded media		1	1	1	1		10	10	10	17		14	14	14	23
2219	Other publishing		-	-	-	-		-	-	-	-		-	-	-	-

222	Printing and related service activities	14	23	21	20	726	813	716	744	2752	1670	1640	1729
2221	Printing	14	22	20	20	726	804	705	744	2752	1657	1621	1729
2222	Service activities related to printing	-	1	1	-	-	9	11	-	-	13	19	-
2230	Reproduction of recorded media	1	1	1	1	36	36	36	36	47	178	52	55
2310	Coke oven products	-	-	-	-	-	-	-	-	-	-	-	-
2320	Refined petroleum products	11	13	13	11	1178	1157	1201	1261	15880	8211	14126	12538
2330	Processing of nuclear fuel	-	-	-	-	-	-	-	-	-	-	-	-
241	Basic chemicals	15	16	16	17	719	751	1168	1142	2135	2304	5973	6366
2411	Basic chemicals, except fertilizers	12	12	12	14	476	480	511	536	1503	1524	1476	1683
2412	Fertilizers and nitrogen compounds	2	3	3	2	28	57	483	468	42	79	3785	4256
2413	Plastics in primary forms; synthetic rubber	1	1	1	1	215	214	174	138	590	700	712	426
242	Other chemicals	24	25	26	26	1253	1335	1532	1628	4100	4566	5139	5460
2421	Pesticides and other agro-chemical products	-	-	-	-	-	-	-	-	-	-	-	-
2422	Paints, varnishes, printing ink and mastics	6	6	6	6	347	387	389	326	1583	1914	1873	1715
2423	Pharmaceuticals, medicinal chemicals, etc.	2	3	5	4	189	297	498	604	417	869	1371	1601
2424	Soap, cleaning & cosmetic preparations	13	13	11	10	669	566	532	498	1916	1551	1548	1571
2429	Other chemical products n.e.c.	3	3	4	6	48	85	113	200	184	231	346	572
2430	Man-made fibres	-	-	-	-	-	-	-	-	-	-	-	-
251	Rubber products	1	2	4	4	32	51	89	88	65	105	149	176
2511	Rubber tyres and tubes	-	-	2	2	-	-	26	22	-	-	44	41
2519	Other rubber products	1	2	2	2	32	51	63	66	65	105	106	135
2520	Plastic products	28	34	38	39	1332	1542	1929	2176	2645	3172	4254	4998
2610	Glass and glass products	9	9	11	10	886	902	968	1173	1979	2065	2170	2802
269	Non-metallic mineral products n.e.c.	94	96	109	105	6120	7212	7631	8002	14714	17140	19341	20769
2691	Pottery, china and earthenware	1	1	1	1	139	165	182	213	273	332	388	474
2692	Refractory ceramic products	2	2	2	2	172	221	248	260	706	861	1012	1263
2693	Struct.non-refractory clay; ceramic products	-	-	-	-	-	-	-	-	-	-	-	-
2694	Cement, lime and plaster	6	7	7	7	811	815	878	872	3833	4400	4970	5551
2695	Articles of concrete, cement and plaster	36	36	40	36	1735	1765	1740	1757	3558	3583	3271	3765
2696	Cutting, shaping & finishing of stone	10	11	14	14	1568	2292	2683	2966	2858	4216	5223	5645
2699	Other non-metallic mineral products n.e.c.	39	39	45	45	1695	1954	1900	1934	3486	3749	4476	4070
2710	Basic iron and steel	3	3	5	5	562	573	750	960	1493	1578	1946	2547
2720	Basic precious and non-ferrous metals	3	3	3	3	573	573	605	639	2375	2561	2976	3098
273	Casting of metals	3	2	2	2	69	60	50	54	152	134	149	144
2731	Casting of iron and steel	1	1	1	1	45	45	36	37	109	109	121	115
2732	Casting of non-ferrous metals	2	1	1	1	24	15	14	17	43	26	28	29
281	Struct.metal products;tanks;steam generators	31	29	30	31	2035	1882	2056	3289	4368	4461	4346	7103
2811	Structural metal products	31	28	30	31	2035	1762	2056	3289	4368	4258	4346	7103
2812	Tanks, reservoirs and containers of metal	-	1	-	-	-	120	-	-	-	202	-	-
2813	Steam generators	-	-	-	-	-	-	-	-	-	-	-	-
289	Other metal products; metal working services	18	21	21	17	1271	1354	1503	1169	1755	3398	3597	3257
2891	Metal forging/pressing/stamping/roll-forming	1	2	2	1	93	100	111	12	157	177	172	13
2892	Treatment & coating of metals	6	6	7	7	190	135	276	306	343	187	561	627
2893	Cutlery, hand tools and general hardware	1	1	-	1	34	24	-	19	20	26	-	25
2899	Other fabricated metal products n.e.c.	10	12	12	8	954	1095	1116	832	1236	3008	2864	2593
291	General purpose machinery	6	7	7	5	330	407	304	252	713	1025	893	740
2911	Engines & turbines (not for transport equipment)	1	1	1	1	163	153	45	47	311	349	109	95
2912	Pumps, compressors, taps and valves	2	2	2	2	66	109	112	133	203	391	421	485
2913	Bearings, gears, gearing & driving elements	-	-	-	-	-	-	-	-	-	-	-	-
2914	Ovens, furnaces and furnace burners	-	-	-	-	-	-	-	-	-	-	-	-
2915	Lifting and handling equipment	-	-	-	-	-	-	-	-	-	-	-	-
2919	Other general purpose machinery	3	4	4	2	101	145	147	72	199	284	363	160
292	Special purpose machinery	3	3	4	3	163	145	172	155	644	571	718	819
2921	Agricultural and forestry machinery	-	-	-	-	-	-	-	-	-	-	-	-
2922	Machine tools	1	-	1	1	35	-	25	25	100	-	66	68
2923	Machinery for metallurgy	-	-	-	-	-	-	-	-	-	-	-	-
2924	Machinery for mining & construction	1	2	2	1	45	55	63	58	338	315	353	458
2925	Food/beverage/tobacco processing machinery	-	-	-	-	-	-	-	-	-	-	-	-
2926	Machinery for textile, apparel and leather	-	-	-	-	-	-	-	-	-	-	-	-
2927	Weapons and ammunition	1	1	1	1	83	90	84	72	205	256	299	294
2929	Other special purpose machinery	-	-	-	-	-	-	-	-	-	-	-	-

continued

ISIC Revision 3		Number of establishments					Number of employees					Wages and salaries paid to employees				
			(number)					(number)					(thousands of Omani Rials)			
ISIC	Industry	Note	2003	2004	2005	2006	Note	2003	2004	2005	2006	Note	2003	2004	2005	2006
2930	Domestic appliances n.e.c.		2	2	2	1		119	127	131	21		367	329	370	28
3000	Office, accounting and computing machinery		2	-	-	-		40	-	-	-		219	-	-	-
3110	Electric motors, generators and transformers		-	-	-	-		-	-	-	-		-	-	-	-
3120	Electricity distribution & control apparatus		7	5	7	7		283	306	304	401		1423	1004	999	1246
3130	Insulated wire and cable		1	1	1	1		259	308	338	459		926	1165	1966	1788
3140	Accumulators, primary cells and batteries		2	2	2	2		322	337	349	400		683	703	779	843
3150	Lighting equipment and electric lamps		1	1	1	1		38	38	33	34		68	64	91	92
3190	Other electrical equipment n.e.c.		-	-	-	-		-	-	-	-		-	-	-	-
3210	Electronic valves, tubes, etc.		-	-	-	-		-	-	-	-		-	-	-	-
3220	TV/radio transmitters; line comm. apparatus		-	-	-	-		-	-	-	-		-	-	-	-
3230	TV and radio receivers and associated goods		-	-	-	-		-	-	-	-		-	-	-	-
331	Medical, measuring, testing appliances, etc.		-	-	-	-		-	-	-	-		-	-	-	-
3311	Medical, surgical and orthopaedic equipment		-	-	-	-		-	-	-	-		-	-	-	-
3312	Measuring/testing/navigating appliances,etc.		-	-	-	-		-	-	-	-		-	-	-	-
3313	Industrial process control equipment		-	-	-	-		-	-	-	-		-	-	-	-
3320	Optical instruments & photographic equipment		1	1	1	1		58	59	60	61		290	390	485	457
3330	Watches and clocks		-	-	-	-		-	-	-	-		-	-	-	-
3410	Motor vehicles		-	-	-	1		-	-	-	32		-	-	-	48
3420	Automobile bodies, trailers & semi-trailers		3	3	-	-		120	318	-	-		214	2021	-	-
3430	Parts/accessories for automobiles		-	1	2	2		-	47	94	79		-	89	201	148
351	Building and repairing of ships and boats		-	-	-	-		-	-	-	-		-	-	-	-
3511	Building and repairing of ships		-	-	-	-		-	-	-	-		-	-	-	-
3512	Building/repairing of pleasure/sport. boats		-	-	-	-		-	-	-	-		-	-	-	-
3520	Railway/tramway locomotives & rolling stock		-	-	-	-		-	-	-	-		-	-	-	-
3530	Aircraft and spacecraft		-	-	-	-		-	-	-	-		-	-	-	-
359	Transport equipment n.e.c.		-	-	-	-		-	-	-	-		-	-	-	-
3591	Motorcycles		-	-	-	-		-	-	-	-		-	-	-	-
3592	Bicycles and invalid carriages		-	-	-	-		-	-	-	-		-	-	-	-
3599	Other transport equipment n.e.c.		-	-	-	-		-	-	-	-		-	-	-	-
3610	Furniture		14	16	13	13		1547	1861	1560	1642		2896	3356	3027	3160
369	Manufacturing n.e.c.		6	6	7	6		263	311	381	378		778	761	945	920
3691	Jewellery and related articles		2	2	2	1		102	102	85	55		290	259	234	91
3692	Musical instruments		-	-	-	-		-	-	-	-		-	-	-	-
3693	Sports goods		-	-	-	-		-	-	-	-		-	-	-	-
3694	Games and toys		-	-	-	-		-	-	-	-		-	-	-	-
3699	Other manufacturing n.e.c.		4	4	5	5		161	209	296	323		488	502	711	829
3710	Recycling of metal waste and scrap		1	1	1	1		21	25	25	23		37	73	67	74
3720	Recycling of non-metal waste and scrap		-	-	-	-		-	-	-	-		-	-	-	-
D	Total manufacturing	a/	446	467	496	476	a/	33070	34891	36743	38680	a/	90892	90786	108326	111825

a/ Sum of available data.

ISIC Revision 3		Output					Value added					Gross fixed capital formation		
			(thousands of Omani Rials)					(thousands of Omani Rials)					(thousands of Omani Rials)	
ISIC	Industry	Note	2003	2004	2005	2006	Note	2003	2004	2005	2006	Note	2005	2006
151	Processed meat,fish,fruit,vegetables,fats		51581	57316	65777	77361		16547	15912	21211	19078		66437	61099
1511	Processing/preserving of meat		1837	2344	6427	10466		758	933	1929	4091		13446	22153
1512	Processing/preserving of fish		16313	20014	19727	14013		6430	6150	9891	3871		19139	15383
1513	Processing/preserving of fruit & vegetables		11207	7571	7503	10604		5076	3785	2823	4385		15719	13639
1514	Vegetable and animal oils and fats		22224	27386	32119	42278		4283	5044	6568	6731		18133	9924
1520	Dairy products		48079	73057	61344	59527		15690	16389	14666	11489		8045	17506
153	Grain mill products; starches; animal feeds		40099	47992	45007	49902		8480	8708	7161	9588		39272	27623
1531	Grain mill products		23870	29710	28568	31930		4820	5164	4592	6907		21090	13627
1532	Starches and starch products		-	-	-	-		-	-	-	-		-	-
1533	Prepared animal feeds		16230	18282	16439	17972		3660	3543	2569	2681		18182	13997
154	Other food products		29056	40156	47458	...		13500	17383	18940	...		21263	...
1541	Bakery products		16316	26312	32924	34218		8582	10939	13094	14839		11618	8713
1542	Sugar		-	-	-	-		-	-	-	-		-	-
1543	Cocoa, chocolate and sugar confectionery		1603	5196	2742	3515		744	1834	1295	1661		1364	1482
1544	Macaroni, noodles & similar products		189	422	399	...		56	220	148	...		150	...
1549	Other food products n.e.c.		10947	8226	11393	10763		4117	4391	4403	4070		8131	10334
155	Beverages		30513	33462	41272	39721		10617	12888	14443	15423		24869	16420
1551	Distilling, rectifying & blending of spirits		-	-	-	-		-	-	-	-		-	-
1552	Wines		-	-	-	-		-	-	-	-		-	-
1553	Malt liquors and malt		-	-	-	-		-	-	-	-		-	-
1554	Soft drinks; mineral waters		30513	33462	41272	39721		10617	12888	14443	15423		24869	16420
1600	Tobacco products		-	-	-	-		-	-	-	-		-	-
171	Spinning, weaving and finishing of textiles		3790	4963	6762	3720		1655	2649	3318	1601		5755	6293
1711	Textile fibre preparation; textile weaving		2427	3552	5143	1703		1036	2022	2639	690		4812	4591
1712	Finishing of textiles		1363	1411	1619	2017		619	627	679	911		943	1702
172	Other textiles		294	663	718	748		54	222	262	328		270	2
1721	Made-up textile articles, except apparel		294	663	539	576		54	222	161	198		264	-
1722	Carpets and rugs		-	-	179	172		-	-	102	130		5	2
1723	Cordage, rope, twine and netting		-	-	-	-		-	-	-	-		-	-
1729	Other textiles n.e.c.		-	-	-	-		-	-	-	-		-	-
1730	Knitted and crocheted fabrics and articles		-	-	-	-		-	-	-	-		-	-
1810	Wearing apparel, except fur apparel		17766	9233	7691	6779		8288	4549	3285	3074		3144	803
1820	Dressing & dyeing of fur; processing of fur		-	-	-	-		-	-	-	-		-	-
191	Tanning, dressing and processing of leather		-	-	-	-		-	-	-	-		-	-
1911	Tanning and dressing of leather		-	-	-	-		-	-	-	-		-	-
1912	Luggage, handbags, etc.; saddlery & harness		-	-	-	-		-	-	-	-		-	-
1920	Footwear		1631	1941	2164	1925		674	358	702	835		982	841
2010	Sawmilling and planing of wood		-	-	-	-		-	-	-	-		-	-
202	Products of wood, cork, straw, etc.		4856	8314	12170	16941		2231	3693	7011	10567		3097	1722
2021	Veneer sheets, plywood, particle board, etc.		-	-	2817	8211		-	-	2629	5419		641	524
2022	Builders' carpentry and joinery		4856	8314	9353	8730		2231	3693	4382	5148		2456	1198
2023	Wooden containers		-	-	-	-		-	-	-	-		-	-
2029	Other wood products; articles of cork/straw		-	-	-	-		-	-	-	-		-	-
210	Paper and paper products		11368	13362	16394	18193		4111	4621	5137	5579		11873	9277
2101	Pulp, paper and paperboard		577	1339	-	-		251	937	-	-		-	-
2102	Corrugated paper and paperboard		7696	8887	11117	12499		2487	3045	2971	3683		8152	7348
2109	Other articles of paper and paperboard		3094	3137	5277	5694		1373	639	2166	1896		3721	1929
221	Publishing		7114	7164	8140	9317		4626	4659	4758	1883		3864	3169
2211	Publishing of books and other publications		3849	3122	3475	2840		2015	1597	1598	1476		3146	1600
2212	Publishing of newspapers, journals, etc.		3167	3949	4572	6373		2579	3035	3079	368		701	1552
2213	Publishing of recorded media		98	93	93	104		32	27	81	39		17	17
2219	Other publishing		-	-	-	-		-	-	-	-		-	-

continued

ISIC Revision 3		Output					Value added					Gross fixed capital formation		
			(thousands of Omani Rials)					(thousands of Omani Rials)					(thousands of Omani Rials)	
ISIC	Industry	Note	2003	2004	2005	2006	Note	2003	2004	2005	2006	Note	2005	2006
222	Printing and related service activities		9556	9407	10035	10482		6582	5042	4643	5203		16335	12499
2221	Printing		9556	9292	9905	10482		6582	4999	4596	5203		16335	12499
2222	Service activities related to printing		-	115	130	-		-	43	47	-		-	-
2230	Reproduction of recorded media		569	691	522	575		48	190	48	533		265	152
2310	Coke oven products		-	-	-	-		-	-	-	-		-	-
2320	Refined petroleum products		961905	1030293	1416665	1711532		406431	448981	587982	674300		502159	1180974
2330	Processing of nuclear fuel		-	-	-	-		-	-	-	-		-	-
241	Basic chemicals		26384	31021	147278	143944		11808	12295	119116	105410		391528	362541
2411	Basic chemicals, except fertilizers		17172	14265	14663	20949		8614	8227	8234	8677		43125	32221
2412	Fertilizers and nitrogen compounds		199	269	119474	109754		91	126	108799	92292		331186	322805
2413	Plastics in primary forms; synthetic rubber		9013	16487	13141	13241		3103	3942	2083	4440		17216	7515
242	Other chemicals		52212	53361	61938	59904		19430	20662	20408	22531		42109	33019
2421	Pesticides and other agro-chemical products		-	-	-	-		-	-	-	-		-	-
2422	Paints, varnishes, printing ink and mastics		12940	15899	16810	17521		5963	7510	7759	8495		2741	3712
2423	Pharmaceuticals, medicinal chemicals, etc.		13059	16877	20321	18897		3806	5182	3796	5138		27550	20651
2424	Soap, cleaning & cosmetic preparations		25096	18969	21937	17192		9144	7025	7408	6461		10637	7620
2429	Other chemical products n.e.c.		1117	1616	2871	6294		516	945	1445	2437		1182	1037
2430	Man-made fibres		-	-	-	-		-	-	-	-		-	-
251	Rubber products		398	829	1132	2193		156	490	694	1496		225	314
2511	Rubber tyres and tubes		-	-	98	325		-	-	87	125		54	43
2519	Other rubber products		398	829	1034	1868		156	490	607	1371		171	271
2520	Plastic products		24034	33472	46226	59846		9411	11267	14402	14963		26274	26649
2610	Glass and glass products		17937	21100	24056	26868		8313	9352	10397	8328		24130	26566
269	Non-metallic mineral products n.e.c.		109625	137041	176689	211514		65208	89118	116193	141295		198811	171212
2691	Pottery, china and earthenware		507	1087	1390	1710		331	786	1044	1243		2665	2458
2692	Refractory ceramic products		4856	5262	7204	8318		696	3052	3755	5109		5364	9594
2693	Struct.non-refractory clay; ceramic products		-	-	-	-		-	-	-	-		-	-
2694	Cement, lime and plaster		44301	57620	78161	103240		29445	40965	59958	77014		122541	100453
2695	Articles of concrete, cement and plaster		21307	20209	20396	27573		10620	9694	8759	14124		15798	20926
2696	Cutting, shaping & finishing of stone		10397	21011	25363	29604		7715	17581	19251	22179		25639	17963
2699	Other non-metallic mineral products n.e.c.		28258	31852	44175	41070		16401	17039	23425	21626		26804	19818
2710	Basic iron and steel		47855	75069	100747	127370		7969	12394	9646	20182		25580	15186
2720	Basic precious and non-ferrous metals		14576	23910	25937	26612		6354	12476	10022	6959		60558	49798
273	Casting of metals		793	1267	720	810		482	883	357	352		400	538
2731	Casting of iron and steel		591	821	347	372		352	720	162	224		236	387
2732	Casting of non-ferrous metals		203	446	373	438		130	163	194	128		164	151
281	Struct.metal products;tanks;steam generators		18193	21157	24604	44310		10831	7760	8589	19992		11776	9774
2811	Structural metal products		18193	20841	24604	44310		10831	7790	8589	19992		11776	9774
2812	Tanks, reservoirs and containers of metal		-	316	-	-		-	-30	-	-		-	-
2813	Steam generators		-	-	-	-		-	-	-	-		-	-
289	Other metal products; metal working services		14361	20606	23838	25626		5585	13074	9248	11441		6903	7789
2891	Metal forging/pressing/stamping/roll-forming		1616	5376	5701	19		43	5286	732	14		928	-
2892	Treatment & coating of metals		1551	928	2774	6646		1038	521	1489	1450		993	1244
2893	Cutlery, hand tools and general hardware		34	139	-	75		17	99	-	10		-	698
2899	Other fabricated metal products n.e.c.		11160	14163	15363	18886		4487	7168	7027	9967		4982	5848
291	General purpose machinery		5761	10948	12266	12493		1991	4021	5560	6537		3775	3625
2911	Engines & turbines (not for transport equipment)		1623	1375	884	844		510	667	216	199		149	130
2912	Pumps, compressors, taps and valves		2002	7258	8451	10412		474	2558	4436	6087		1228	1027
2913	Bearings, gears, gearing & driving elements		-	-	-	-		-	-	-	-		-	-
2914	Ovens, furnaces and furnace burners		-	-	-	-		-	-	-	-		-	-
2915	Lifting and handling equipment		-	-	-	-		-	-	-	-		-	-
2919	Other general purpose machinery		2136	2315	2930	1238		1007	796	908	252		2398	2468

292	Special purpose machinery		2634	2363	3213	3716		2238	1985	2346	2907		3094	3861
2921	Agricultural and forestry machinery		-	-	-	-		-	-	-	-		-	-
2922	Machine tools		198	-	290	482		8	-	201	325		1231	983
2923	Machinery for metallurgy		-	-	-	-		-	-	-	-		-	-
2924	Machinery for mining & construction		1952	1395	1805	2570		1908	1286	1447	2325		253	424
2925	Food/beverage/tobacco processing machinery		-	-	-	-		-	-	-	-		-	-
2926	Machinery for textile, apparel and leather		-	-	-	-		-	-	-	-		-	-
2927	Weapons and ammunition		484	968	1117	664		321	699	699	257		1609	2454
2929	Other special purpose machinery		-	-	-	-		-	-	-	-		-	-
2930	Domestic appliances n.e.c.		2305	2372	3008	545		377	786	1302	116		510	156
3000	Office, accounting and computing machinery		592	-	-	-		168	-	-	-		-	-
3110	Electric motors, generators and transformers		-	-	-	-		-	-	-	-		-	-
3120	Electricity distribution & control apparatus		8093	11176	11914	17259		2082	2364	3129	5116		2504	5823
3130	Insulated wire and cable		22148	38885	62360	114161		3302	3739	8767	5900		25859	17173
3140	Accumulators, primary cells and batteries		5695	7828	10039	12109		2072	3195	3166	3468		2387	3340
3150	Lighting equipment and electric lamps		540	477	365	444		318	255	160	174		58	30
3190	Other electrical equipment n.e.c.		-	-	-	-		-	-	-	-		-	-
3210	Electronic valves, tubes, etc.		-	-	-	-		-	-	-	-		-	-
3220	TV/radio transmitters; line comm. apparatus		-	-	-	-		-	-	-	-		-	-
3230	TV and radio receivers and associated goods		-	-	-	-		-	-	-	-		-	-
331	Medical, measuring, testing appliances, etc.		-	-	-	-		-	-	-	-		-	-
3311	Medical, surgical and orthopaedic equipment		-	-	-	-		-	-	-	-		-	-
3312	Measuring/testing/navigating appliances,etc.		-	-	-	-		-	-	-	-		-	-
3313	Industrial process control equipment		-	-	-	-		-	-	-	-		-	-
3320	Optical instruments & photographic equipment		2537	2876	3389	3804		1097	1625	1798	1677		2961	2448
3330	Watches and clocks		-	-	-	-		-	-	-	-		-	-
3410	Motor vehicles		-	-	-	189		-	-	-	165		-	-
3420	Automobile bodies, trailers & semi-trailers		659	1615	-	-		340	1356	-	-		-	-
3430	Parts/accessories for automobiles		-	169	2686	616		-	108	2366	321		12	101
351	Building and repairing of ships and boats		-	-	-	-		-	-	-	-		-	-
3511	Building and repairing of ships		-	-	-	-		-	-	-	-		-	-
3512	Building/repairing of pleasure/sport. boats		-	-	-	-		-	-	-	-		-	-
3520	Railway/tramway locomotives & rolling stock		-	-	-	-		-	-	-	-		-	-
3530	Aircraft and spacecraft		-	-	-	-		-	-	-	-		-	-
359	Transport equipment n.e.c.		-	-	-	-		-	-	-	-		-	-
3591	Motorcycles		-	-	-	-		-	-	-	-		-	-
3592	Bicycles and invalid carriages		-	-	-	-		-	-	-	-		-	-
3599	Other transport equipment n.e.c.		-	-	-	-		-	-	-	-		-	-
3610	Furniture		20238	29404	28909	27898		11082	17109	15860	15405		5587	5656
369	Manufacturing n.e.c.		2530	3870	5889	6697		516	2322	2510	3224		7505	5240
3691	Jewellery and related articles		599	353	477	416		459	223	369	336		158	82
3692	Musical instruments		-	-	-	-		-	-	-	-		-	-
3693	Sports goods		-	-	-	-		-	-	-	-		-	-
3694	Games and toys		-	-	-	-		-	-	-	-		-	-
3699	Other manufacturing n.e.c.		1931	3517	5413	6281		57	2099	2141	2888		7347	5158
3710	Recycling of metal waste and scrap		900	1573	1603	1294		237	318	1570	244		249	3362
3720	Recycling of non-metal waste and scrap		-	-	-	-		-	-	-	-		-	-
D	Total manufacturing	a/	1619179	1870403	2520924	2985446	a/	670902	775197	1061174	1178255	a/	1550425	2113113

a/ Sum of available data.

Oman

ISIC Revision 3			Index numbers of industrial production											
			(2000=100)											
ISIC	Industry	Note	1995	1996	1997	1998	1999	2000	2001	2002	2003	2004	2005	2006
15	Food and beverages		...	...	...	...	...	...	...	...	...	...	...	...
16	Tobacco products		...	...	...	...	...	...	...	...	...	...	...	...
17	Textiles		...	...	...	...	...	...	...	...	...	...	...	...
18	Wearing apparel, fur		...	...	...	...	...	...	...	...	...	...	...	...
19	Leather, leather products and footwear		...	...	...	...	...	...	...	...	...	...	...	...
20	Wood products (excl. furniture)		...	...	...	...	...	...	...	...	...	...	...	...
21	Paper and paper products		...	...	...	...	...	...	...	...	...	...	...	...
22	Printing and publishing		...	...	...	...	...	...	...	...	...	...	...	...
23	Coke,refined petroleum products,nuclear fuel		...	...	...	...	...	...	...	...	...	...	...	...
24	Chemicals and chemical products		...	...	...	...	...	...	...	...	...	...	...	...
25	Rubber and plastics products		...	...	...	...	...	...	...	...	...	...	...	...
26	Non-metallic mineral products		...	...	...	...	...	...	...	...	...	...	...	...
27	Basic metals		...	...	...	...	...	...	...	...	...	...	...	...
28	Fabricated metal products		...	...	...	...	...	...	...	...	...	...	...	...
29	Machinery and equipment n.e.c.		...	...	...	...	...	...	...	...	...	...	...	...
30	Office, accounting and computing machinery		...	...	...	...	...	...	...	...	...	...	...	...
31	Electrical machinery and apparatus		...	...	...	...	...	...	...	...	...	...	...	...
32	Radio,television and communication equipment		...	...	...	...	...	...	...	...	...	...	...	...
33	Medical, precision and optical instruments		...	...	...	...	...	...	...	...	...	...	...	...
34	Motor vehicles, trailers, semi-trailers		...	...	...	...	...	...	...	...	...	...	...	...
35	Other transport equipment		...	...	...	...	...	...	...	...	...	...	...	...
36	Furniture; manufacturing n.e.c.		...	...	...	...	...	...	...	...	...	...	...	...
37	Recycling		...	...	...	...	...	...	...	...	...	...	...	...
D	Total manufacturing		75	70	72	71	71	100	130	146	156	162	178	...

Panama

Supplier of information:
Dirección de Estadística y Censo, Contraloría General de la República, Panamá.

Basic source of data:
Industrial survey.

Major deviations from ISIC (Revision 3):
None reported.

Reference period:
Calendar year.

Scope:
Establishments with 5 or more employees.

Method of data collection:
Individual sites are visited by enumerators.

Type of enumeration:
Sample survey.

Adjusted for non-response:
Yes.

Concepts and definitions of variables:
Wages and salaries is compensation of employees.

Related national publications:
V. Censos Nacionales Económicos Volumen III, estructura productiva y financiera de la Industria Manufacturera, año 2001; Encuesta entre empresas no financieras, published by the Dirección de Estadística y Censo, Panamá.

Panama

ISIC	Industry	Establishments: Note	Establishments: 2002	Establishments: 2003	Establishments: 2004a/	Establishments: 2005a/	Employees: Note	Employees: 2002	Employees: 2003	Employees: 2004a/	Employees: 2005a/	Wages: Note	Wages: 2002	Wages: 2003	Wages: 2004a/	Wages: 2005a/
	ISIC Revision 3		Number of establishments (number)					Number of employees (number)					Wages and salaries paid to employees (thousands of Panamanian Balboas)			
151	Processed meat,fish,fruit,vegetables,fats		...	...	57	56		...	...	7879	9216		...	...	31840	44691
1511	Processing/preserving of meat		...	...	31	31		...	...	5019	6454		...	...	22502	35435
1512	Processing/preserving of fish		...	...	17	17		...	...	2418	2350		...	...	7760	7684
1513	Processing/preserving of fruit & vegetables		...	...	9	8		...	...	442	411		...	...	1578	1572
1514	Vegetable and animal oils and fats		...	...	...b/	...b/		...	...	...b/	...b/		...	...	...b/	...b/
1520	Dairy products		...	...	22	22		...	...	2777	2917		...	...	15909	16915
153	Grain mill products; starches; animal feeds		...	...	64	62		...	...	3384	2390		...	...	12605	8724
1531	Grain mill products		...	...	49	49		...	...	1848	1858		...	...	6273	6812
1532	Starches and starch products		...	...	...	...		...	...	...	...		...	...	...	...
1533	Prepared animal feeds		...	...	15	13		...	...	1536	532		...	...	6333	1912
154	Other food products		...	...	219	181		...	...	6913	7193		...	...	30460	28626
1541	Bakery products		...	...	157	128		...	...	3584	4005		...	...	16031	13542
1542	Sugar		...	...	4	4		...	...	1525	1601		...	...	5695	5982
1543	Cocoa, chocolate and sugar confectionery		...	...	...c/	...c/		...	...	...c/	...c/		...	...	...c/	...c/
1544	Macaroni, noodles & similar products		...	...	7	7		...	...	85	74		...	...	303	316
1549	Other food products n.e.c.		...	...	51c/	42c/		...	...	1720c/	1513c/		...	...	8431c/	8787c/
155	Beverages		...	...	16	15		...	...	2060	1966		...	...	13875	16712
1551	Distilling, rectifying & blending of spirits		...	...	9d/	9d/		...	...	1272d/	1529d/		...	...	8329d/	12053d/
1552	Wines		...	...	...	...		...	...	...	...		...	...	...	...
1553	Malt liquors and malt		...	...	...d/	...d/		...	...	...d/	...d/		...	...	...d/	...d/
1554	Soft drinks; mineral waters		...	...	7	6		...	...	788	437		...	...	5546	4659
1600	Tobacco products		...	...	...	...		...	...	...	...		...	...	...	...
171	Spinning, weaving and finishing of textiles		...	...	...	...		...	...	...	...		...	...	...	...
1711	Textile fibre preparation; textile weaving		...	...	...	...		...	...	...	...		...	...	...	...
1712	Finishing of textiles		...	...	...	...		...	...	...	...		...	...	...	...
172	Other textiles		...	...	...	...		...	...	...	...		...	...	...	...
1721	Made-up textile articles, except apparel		...	...	10e/	9e/		...	...	250e/	251e/		...	...	1101e/	1009e/
1722	Carpets and rugs		...	...	...	...		...	...	...	...		...	...	...	...
1723	Cordage, rope, twine and netting		...	...	...e/	...e/		...	...	...e/	...e/		...	...	...e/	...e/
1729	Other textiles n.e.c.		...	...	...e/	...e/		...	...	...e/	...e/		...	...	...e/	...e/
1730	Knitted and crocheted fabrics and articles		...	...	...e/	...e/		...	...	...e/	...e/		...	...	...e/	...e/
1810	Wearing apparel, except fur apparel		...	...	34f/	26f/		...	...	2029f/	1567f/		...	...	14137f/	15734f/
1820	Dressing & dyeing of fur; processing of fur		...	...	...f/	...f/		...	...	...f/	...f/		...	...	...f/	...f/
191	Tanning, dressing and processing of leather		...	...	...	...		...	...	...	...		...	...	...	...
1911	Tanning and dressing of leather		...	...	4g/	4g/		...	...	97g/	127g/		...	...	567g/	250g/
1912	Luggage, handbags, etc.; saddlery & harness		...	...	...g/	...g/		...	...	...g/	...g/		...	...	...g/	...g/
1920	Footwear		...	...	9	7		...	...	113	81		...	...	403	286
2010	Sawmilling and planing of wood		...	...	7	6		...	...	105	115		...	...	412	422
202	Products of wood, cork, straw, etc.		...	...	18	18		...	...	469	592		...	...	1523	1870
2021	Veneer sheets, plywood, particle board, etc.		...	...	...h/	...h/		...	...	...h/	...h/		...	...	...h/	...h/
2022	Builders' carpentry and joinery		...	...	11h/	11h/		...	...	327h/	441h/		...	...	1017h/	1344h/
2023	Wooden containers		...	...	7i/	7i/		...	...	142i/	151i/		...	...	506i/	526i/
2029	Other wood products; articles of cork/straw		...	...	...i/	...i/		...	...	...i/	...i/		...	...	...i/	...i/
210	Paper and paper products		...	...	23	25		...	...	1637	1843		...	...	11851	13262
2101	Pulp, paper and paperboard		...	...	...j/	...j/		...	...	...j/	...j/		...	...	...j/	...j/
2102	Corrugated paper and paperboard		...	...	12j/	13j/		...	...	839j/	878j/		...	...	6735j/	7137j/
2109	Other articles of paper and paperboard		...	...	10	12		...	...	798	965		...	...	5116	6124
221	Publishing		...	...	21	21		...	...	1460	1544		...	...	12301	11563
2211	Publishing of books and other publications		...	...	...	...		...	...	...	...		...	...	...	...
2212	Publishing of newspapers, journals, etc.		...	...	7	7		...	...	1171	1175		...	...	10858	9621
2213	Publishing of recorded media		...	...	...	...		...	...	...	...		...	...	...	...
2219	Other publishing		...	...	14	14		...	...	288	369		...	...	1443	1943

222	Printing and related service activities	...	...	79	82	...	...	1451	1586	...	...	8010	9377
2221	Printing	...	...	79k/	82k/	...	...	1451k/	1586k/	...	...	8010k/	9377k/
2222	Service activities related to printing	...	...	...k/	...k/	...	...	...k/	...k/	...	...	...k/	...k/
2230	Reproduction of recorded media	...	...	...	...	...	...	...	...	...	...	...	...
2310	Coke oven products	...	...	...	...	...	...	...	...	...	...	...	...
2320	Refined petroleum products	...	...	...	...	...	...	...	...	...	...	...	...
2330	Processing of nuclear fuel	...	...	...	...	...	...	...	...	...	...	...	...
241	Basic chemicals	...	...	...	...	...	...	...	...	...	...	...	...
2411	Basic chemicals, except fertilizers	...	...	...m/	...m/	...	...	...m/	...m/	...	...	...m/	...m/
2412	Fertilizers and nitrogen compounds	...	...	3m/	3m/	...	...	160m/	185m/	...	...	1311m/	1430m/
2413	Plastics in primary forms; synthetic rubber	...	...	...	...	...	...	...	...	...	...	...	...
242	Other chemicals	...	...	41	35	...	...	1098	1034	...	...	7892	7870
2421	Pesticides and other agro-chemical products	...	...	...n/	...n/	...	...	...n/	...n/	...	...	...n/	...n/
2422	Paints, varnishes, printing ink and mastics	...	...	5n/	8n/	...	...	192n/	226n/	...	...	1694n/	2228n/
2423	Pharmaceuticals, medicinal chemicals, etc.	...	...	9	9	...	...	450	450	...	...	3928	3692
2424	Soap, cleaning & cosmetic preparations	...	...	20	12	...	...	415	330	...	...	2081	1805
2429	Other chemical products n.e.c.	...	...	7	5	...	...	42	28	...	...	189	145
2430	Man-made fibres	...	...	...	...	...	...	...	...	...	...	...	...
251	Rubber products	...	...	3	3	...	...	79	81	...	...	455	453
2511	Rubber tyres and tubes	...	...	3	3	...	...	79	81	...	...	455	453
2519	Other rubber products	...	...	...	...	...	...	...	...	...	...	...	...
2520	Plastic products	...	...	34	32	...	...	1902	1675	...	...	10557	9699
2610	Glass and glass products	...	...	6	6	...	...	389	338	...	...	1887	1749
269	Non-metallic mineral products n.e.c.	...	...	39	42	...	...	1445	1369	...	...	9231	9277
2691	Pottery, china and earthenware	...	...	5p/	5p/	...	...	71p/	68p/	...	...	198p/	201p/
2692	Refractory ceramic products	...	...	...	...	...	...	...	...	...	...	...	...
2693	Struct.non-refractory clay; ceramic products	...	...	...p/	...p/	...	...	...p/	...p/	...	...	...p/	...p/
2694	Cement, lime and plaster	...	...	3	3	...	...	394	508	...	...	3132	5037
2695	Articles of concrete, cement and plaster	...	...	31	34	...	...	980	793	...	...	5900	4039
2696	Cutting, shaping & finishing of stone	...	...	...	...	...	...	...	...	...	...	...	...
2699	Other non-metallic mineral products n.e.c.	...	...	...	...	...	...	...	...	...	...	...	...
2710	Basic iron and steel	...	...	...	...	...	...	...	...	...	...	...	...
2720	Basic precious and non-ferrous metals	...	...	6q/	4q/	...	...	490q/	383q/	...	...	2651q/	2297q/
273	Casting of metals	...	...	...	...	...	...	...	...	...	...	...	...
2731	Casting of iron and steel	...	...	...q/	...q/	...	...	...q/	...q/	...	...	...q/	...q/
2732	Casting of non-ferrous metals	...	...	...	...	...	...	...	...	...	...	...	...
281	Struct.metal products;tanks;steam generators	...	...	60	61	...	...	1202	1263	...	...	6095	6279
2811	Structural metal products	...	...	55	56	...	...	760	765	...	...	3436	3571
2812	Tanks, reservoirs and containers of metal	...	...	5	5	...	...	442	497	...	...	2659	2708
2813	Steam generators	...	...	...	...	...	...	...	...	...	...	...	...
289	Other metal products; metal working services	...	...	23	22	...	...	617	582	...	...	3787	2754
2891	Metal forging/pressing/stamping/roll-forming	...	...	...	...	...	...	...	...	...	...	...	...
2892	Treatment & coating of metals	...	...	3r/	3r/	...	...	26r/	25r/	...	...	93r/	82r/
2893	Cutlery, hand tools and general hardware	...	...	...r/	...r/	...	...	...r/	...r/	...	...	...r/	...r/
2899	Other fabricated metal products n.e.c.	...	...	20	19	...	...	591	557	...	...	3693	2672
291	General purpose machinery	...	...	...	...	...	...	...	...	...	...	...	...
2911	Engines & turbines (not for transport equipment)	...	...	...	...	...	...	...	...	...	...	...	...
2912	Pumps, compressors, taps and valves	...	...	...	...	...	...	...	...	...	...	...	...
2913	Bearings, gears, gearing & driving elements	...	...	...s/	...s/	...	...	...s/	...s/	...	...	...s/	...s/
2914	Ovens, furnaces and furnace burners	...	...	...	...	...	...	...	...	...	...	...	...
2915	Lifting and handling equipment	...	...	...	...	...	...	...	...	...	...	...	...
2919	Other general purpose machinery	...	...	...s/	...s/	...	...	...s/	...s/	...	...	...s/	...s/
292	Special purpose machinery	...	...	8	8	...	...	75	96	...	...	341	423
2921	Agricultural and forestry machinery	...	...	8s/	8s/	...	...	75s/	96s/	...	...	341s/	423s/
2922	Machine tools	...	...	...	...	...	...	...	...	...	...	...	...
2923	Machinery for metallurgy	...	...	...	...	...	...	...	...	...	...	...	...
2924	Machinery for mining & construction	...	...	...	...	...	...	...	...	...	...	...	...
2925	Food/beverage/tobacco processing machinery	...	...	...	...	...	...	...	...	...	...	...	...
2926	Machinery for textile, apparel and leather	...	...	...	...	...	...	...	...	...	...	...	...
2927	Weapons and ammunition	...	...	...	...	...	...	...	...	...	...	...	...
2929	Other special purpose machinery	...	...	...	...	...	...	...	...	...	...	...	...

continued

Panama

ISIC Revision 3		Number of establishments					Number of employees					Wages and salaries paid to employees				
			(number)					(number)					(thousands of Panamanian Balboas)			
ISIC	Industry	Note	2002	2003	2004a/	2005a/	Note	2002	2003	2004a/	2005a/	Note	2002	2003	2004a/	2005a/
2930	Domestic appliances n.e.c.		...	...	...	...		...	...	...	...		...	...	...	...
3000	Office, accounting and computing machinery		...	...	...	...		...	...	...	...		...	...	...	...
3110	Electric motors, generators and transformers		...	...	3	3		...	...	39	35		...	...	208	206
3120	Electricity distribution & control apparatus		...	...	...	...		...	...	...	...		...	...	...	...
3130	Insulated wire and cable		...	...	...	...		...	...	...	...		...	...	...	...
3140	Accumulators, primary cells and batteries		...	...	...t/	...t/		...	...	...t/	...t/		...	...	...t/	...t/
3150	Lighting equipment and electric lamps		...	...	12t/	12t/		...	...	366t/	410t/		...	...	1982t/	2215t/
3190	Other electrical equipment n.e.c.		...	...	...	...		...	...	...	...		...	...	...	...
3210	Electronic valves, tubes, etc.		...	...	...	...		...	...	...	...		...	...	...	...
3220	TV/radio transmitters; line comm. apparatus		...	...	...	...		...	...	...	...		...	...	...	...
3230	TV and radio receivers and associated goods		...	...	...b/	...b/		...	...	...b/	...b/		...	...	...b/	...b/
331	Medical, measuring, testing appliances, etc.		...	...	5	5		...	...	36	34		...	...	237	263
3311	Medical, surgical and orthopaedic equipment		...	...	5u/	5u/		...	...	36u/	34u/		...	...	237u/	263u/
3312	Measuring/testing/navigating appliances,etc.		...	...	...u/	...u/		...	...	...u/	...u/		...	...	...u/	...u/
3313	Industrial process control equipment		...	...	...	...		...	...	...	...		...	...	...	...
3320	Optical instruments & photographic equipment		...	...	...	...		...	...	...	...		...	...	...	...
3330	Watches and clocks		...	...	...	...		...	...	...	...		...	...	...	...
3410	Motor vehicles		...	...	...v/	...v/		...	...	...v/	...v/		...	...	...v/	...v/
3420	Automobile bodies, trailers & semi-trailers		...	...	6v/	7v/		...	...	97v/	138v/		...	...	423v/	669v/
3430	Parts/accessories for automobiles		...	...	...v/	...v/		...	...	...v/	...v/		...	...	...v/	...v/
351	Building and repairing of ships and boats		...	...	12	13		...	...	820	826		...	...	3346	5971
3511	Building and repairing of ships		...	...	12w/	13w/		...	...	820w/	826w/		...	...	3346w/	5971w/
3512	Building/repairing of pleasure/sport. boats		...	...	...w/	...w/		...	...	...w/	...w/		...	...	...w/	...w/
3520	Railway/tramway locomotives & rolling stock		...	...	...	...		...	...	...	...		...	...	...	...
3530	Aircraft and spacecraft		...	...	3	4		...	...	30	95		...	...	206	350
359	Transport equipment n.e.c.		...	...	...	...		...	...	...	...		...	...	...	...
3591	Motorcycles		...	...	...	...		...	...	...	...		...	...	...	...
3592	Bicycles and invalid carriages		...	...	...	...		...	...	...	...		...	...	...	...
3599	Other transport equipment n.e.c.		...	...	...	...		...	...	...	...		...	...	...	...
3610	Furniture		...	...	78	78		...	...	1585	1809		...	...	6870	6563
369	Manufacturing n.e.c.		...	...	18	18		...	...	900	1148		...	...	5822	6397
3691	Jewellery and related articles		...	...	...b/	...b/		...	...	...b/	...b/		...	...	...b/	...b/
3692	Musical instruments		...	...	...	...		...	...	...	...		...	...	...	...
3693	Sports goods		...	...	...	...		...	...	...	...		...	...	...	...
3694	Games and toys		...	...	...	...		...	...	...	...		...	...	...	...
3699	Other manufacturing n.e.c.		...	...	18b/	18b/		...	...	900b/	1148b/		...	...	5822b/	6397b/
3710	Recycling of metal waste and scrap		...	...	...	...		...	...	...	...		...	...	...	...
3720	Recycling of non-metal waste and scrap		...	...	...	...		...	...	...	...		...	...	...	...
D	Total manufacturing		...	...	943	891		...	...	41951	42889		...	...	218295	234308

a/ Provisional data.
b/ 3699 includes 1514, 3230 and 3691.
c/ 1549 includes 1543.
d/ 1551 includes 1553.
e/ 1721 includes 1723, 1729 and 1730.
f/ 1810 includes 1820.
g/ 1911 includes 1912.
h/ 2022 includes 2021.
i/ 2023 includes 2029.
j/ 2102 includes 2101.
k/ 2221 includes 2222.
m/ 2412 includes 2411.
n/ 2422 includes 2421.
p/ 2691 includes 2693.
q/ 2720 includes 2731.
r/ 2892 includes 2893.
s/ 2921 includes 2913 and 2919.
t/ 3150 includes 3140.
u/ 3311 includes 3312.
v/ 3420 includes 3410 and 3430.
w/ 3511 includes 3512.

Panama

ISIC Revision 3		Output in producers' prices					Value added					Gross fixed capital formation		
			(thousands of Panamanian Balboas)					(thousands of Panamanian Balboas)					(thousands of Panamanian Balboas)	
ISIC	Industry	Note	2002	2003	2004a/	2005a/	Note	2002	2003	2004	2005	Note	2004a/	2005a/
151	Processed meat,fish,fruit,vegetables,fats		...	...	436269	464962		...	...	...	...		176915	256090
1511	Processing/preserving of meat		...	...	290816	344687		...	...	...	...		108236	175259
1512	Processing/preserving of fish		...	...	96662	100355		...	...	...	...		47201	56126
1513	Processing/preserving of fruit & vegetables		...	...	48792	19920		...	...	...	...		21479	24705
1514	Vegetable and animal oils and fats		...	...	...b/	...b/		...	...	...	...		...b/	...b/
1520	Dairy products		...	...	162955	213586		...	...	...	...		158044	170783
153	Grain mill products; starches; animal feeds		...	...	240971	197220		...	...	...	...		120518	76994
1531	Grain mill products		...	...	156668	157884		...	...	...	...		43397	46768
1532	Starches and starch products		...	...	...	...		...	...	...	...		...	...
1533	Prepared animal feeds		...	...	84303	39336		...	...	...	...		77121	30226
154	Other food products		...	...	245365	213884		...	...	...	...		325293	325244
1541	Bakery products		...	...	81432	70071		...	...	...	...		45249	47834
1542	Sugar		...	...	65623	63510		...	...	...	...		243752	244614
1543	Cocoa, chocolate and sugar confectionery		...	...	...c/	...c/		...	...	...	...		...c/	...c/
1544	Macaroni, noodles & similar products		...	...	1845	2264		...	...	...	...		1608	1444
1549	Other food products n.e.c.		...	...	96465c/	78038c/		...	...	...	...		34685c/	31351c/
155	Beverages		...	...	203172	221565		...	...	...	...		220110	244029
1551	Distilling, rectifying & blending of spirits		...	...	113618d/	118805d/		...	...	...	...		147136d/	172674d/
1552	Wines		...	...	...	...		...	...	...	...		...	...
1553	Malt liquors and malt		...	...	...d/	...d/		...	...	...	...		...d/	...d/
1554	Soft drinks; mineral waters		...	...	89555	102760		...	...	...	...		72974	71355
1600	Tobacco products		...	...	...	...		...	...	...	...		...	...
171	Spinning, weaving and finishing of textiles		...	...	...	...		...	...	...	...		...	...
1711	Textile fibre preparation; textile weaving		...	...	...	...		...	...	...	...		...	...
1712	Finishing of textiles		...	...	...	...		...	...	...	...		...	...
172	Other textiles		...	...	...	...		...	...	...	...		...	...
1721	Made-up textile articles, except apparel		...	...	6090e/	5221e/		...	...	...	...		10696e/	9769e/
1722	Carpets and rugs		...	...	...	...		...	...	...	...		...	...
1723	Cordage, rope, twine and netting		...	...	...e/	...e/		...	...	...	...		...e/	...e/
1729	Other textiles n.e.c.		...	...	...e/	...e/		...	...	...	...		...e/	...e/
1730	Knitted and crocheted fabrics and articles		...	...	...e/	...e/		...	...	...	...		...e/	...e/
1810	Wearing apparel, except fur apparel		...	...	34228f/	31007f/		...	...	...	...		5828f/	5036f/
1820	Dressing & dyeing of fur; processing of fur		...	...	...f/	...f/		...	...	...	...		...f/	...f/
191	Tanning, dressing and processing of leather		...	...	...	...		...	...	...	...		...	...
1911	Tanning and dressing of leather		...	...	11908g/	11626g/		...	...	...	...		3823g/	3648g/
1912	Luggage, handbags, etc.; saddlery & harness		...	...	...g/	...g/		...	...	...	...		...g/	...g/
1920	Footwear		...	...	2975	2090		...	...	...	...		1264	335
2010	Sawmilling and planing of wood		...	...	6586	6064		...	...	...	...		1392	1401
202	Products of wood, cork, straw, etc.		...	...	15800	17826		...	...	...	...		2345	2455
2021	Veneer sheets, plywood, particle board, etc.		...	...	...h/	...h/		...	...	...	...		...h/	...h/
2022	Builders' carpentry and joinery		...	...	13729h/	16107h/		...	...	...	...		1764h/	1912h/
2023	Wooden containers		...	...	2070i/	1719i/		...	...	...	...		581i/	542i/
2029	Other wood products; articles of cork/straw		...	...	...i/	...i/		...	...	...	...		...i/	...i/
210	Paper and paper products		...	...	108366	118420		...	...	...	...		117885	120725
2101	Pulp, paper and paperboard		...	...	...j/	...j/		...	...	...	...		...j/	...j/
2102	Corrugated paper and paperboard		...	...	53703j/	60630j/		...	...	...	...		66869j/	69190j/
2109	Other articles of paper and paperboard		...	...	54662	57790		...	...	...	...		51016	51534
221	Publishing		...	...	68222	70512		...	...	...	...		53695	58472
2211	Publishing of books and other publications		...	...	...	...		...	...	...	...		...	...
2212	Publishing of newspapers, journals, etc.		...	...	55382	58789		...	...	...	...		47665	50350
2213	Publishing of recorded media		...	...	...	...		...	...	...	...		...	...
2219	Other publishing		...	...	12839	11722		...	...	...	...		6030	8122

continued

Panama

ISIC Revision 3		Output in producers' prices					Value added					Gross fixed capital formation		
			(thousands of Panamanian Balboas)					(thousands of Panamanian Balboas)					(thousands of Panamanian Balboas)	
ISIC	Industry	Note	2002	2003	2004a/	2005a/	Note	2002	2003	2004	2005	Note	2004a/	2005a/
222	Printing and related service activities		...	...	50086	49990		...	...	...	...		34299	35133
2221	Printing		...	...	50086k/	49990k/		...	...	...	...		34299k/	35133k/
2222	Service activities related to printing		...	...	...k/	...k/		...	...	...	...		...k/	...k/
2230	Reproduction of recorded media		...	...	...	...		...	...	...	...		...	...
2310	Coke oven products		...	...	...	...		...	...	...	...		...	...
2320	Refined petroleum products		...	...	...	...		...	...	...	...		...	...
2330	Processing of nuclear fuel		...	...	...	...		...	...	...	...		...	...
241	Basic chemicals		...	...	...	...		...	...	...	...		...	...
2411	Basic chemicals, except fertilizers		...	...	...m/	...m/		...	...	...	...		...m/	...m/
2412	Fertilizers and nitrogen compounds		...	...	16273m/	22120m/		...	...	...	...		17655m/	18042m/
2413	Plastics in primary forms; synthetic rubber		...	...	...	...		...	...	...	...		...	...
242	Other chemicals		...	...	73341	78393		...	...	...	...		40836	39653
2421	Pesticides and other agro-chemical products		...	...	...n/	...n/		...	...	...	...		...n/	...n/
2422	Paints, varnishes, printing ink and mastics		...	...	23811n/	27935n/		...	...	...	...		12015n/	11229n/
2423	Pharmaceuticals, medicinal chemicals, etc.		...	...	27109	31547		...	...	...	...		19610	19720
2424	Soap, cleaning & cosmetic preparations		...	...	20067	18567		...	...	...	...		8826	8281
2429	Other chemical products n.e.c.		...	...	2354	344		...	...	...	...		385	424
2430	Man-made fibres		...	...	...	...		...	...	...	...		...	...
251	Rubber products		...	...	1599	2306		...	...	...	...		1776	1807
2511	Rubber tyres and tubes		...	...	1599	2306		...	...	...	...		1776	1807
2519	Other rubber products		...	...	...	...		...	...	...	...		...	...
2520	Plastic products		...	...	92091	93932		...	...	...	...		82104	78732
2610	Glass and glass products		...	...	23388	24453		...	...	...	...		43722	39951
269	Non-metallic mineral products n.e.c.		...	...	180897	165550		...	...	...	...		261155	284652
2691	Pottery, china and earthenware		...	...	1734p/	1433p/		...	...	...	...		8073p/	8094p/
2692	Refractory ceramic products		...	...	...	...		...	...	...	...		...	...
2693	Struct.non-refractory clay; ceramic products		...	...	...p/	...p/		...	...	...	...		...p/	...p/
2694	Cement, lime and plaster		...	...	108336	116952		...	...	...	...		209613	238898
2695	Articles of concrete, cement and plaster		...	...	70827	47164		...	...	...	...		43469	37661
2696	Cutting, shaping & finishing of stone		...	...	...	...		...	...	...	...		...	...
2699	Other non-metallic mineral products n.e.c.		...	...	...	...		...	...	...	...		...	...
2710	Basic iron and steel		...	...	...	...		...	...	...	...		...	...
2720	Basic precious and non-ferrous metals		...	...	54509q/	41657q/		...	...	...	...		31874q/	26637q/
273	Casting of metals		...	...	...	...		...	...	...	...		...	...
2731	Casting of iron and steel		...	...	...q/	...q/		...	...	...	...		...q/	...q/
2732	Casting of non-ferrous metals		...	...	...	...		...	...	...	...		...	...
281	Struct.metal products;tanks;steam generators		...	...	36926	50527		...	...	...	...		18650	21063
2811	Structural metal products		...	...	21462	20890		...	...	...	...		4340	5177
2812	Tanks, reservoirs and containers of metal		...	...	15464	29637		...	...	...	...		14311	15886
2813	Steam generators		...	...	...	...		...	...	...	...		...	...
289	Other metal products; metal working services		...	...	14870	17083		...	...	...	...		6722	9416
2891	Metal forging/pressing/stamping/roll-forming		...	...	...	...		...	...	...	...		...	...
2892	Treatment & coating of metals		...	...	272r/	263r/		...	...	...	...		302r/	280r/
2893	Cutlery, hand tools and general hardware		...	...	...r/	...r/		...	...	...	...		...r/	...r/
2899	Other fabricated metal products n.e.c.		...	...	14598	16820		...	...	...	...		6420	9135
291	General purpose machinery		...	...	...	...		...	...	...	...		...	...
2911	Engines & turbines (not for transport equipment)		...	...	...	...		...	...	...	...		...	...
2912	Pumps, compressors, taps and valves		...	...	...	...		...	...	...	...		...	...
2913	Bearings, gears, gearing & driving elements		...	...	...s/	...s/		...	...	...	...		...s/	...s/
2914	Ovens, furnaces and furnace burners		...	...	...	...		...	...	...	...		...	...
2915	Lifting and handling equipment		...	...	...	...		...	...	...	...		...	...
2919	Other general purpose machinery		...	...	...s/	...s/		...	...	...	...		...s/	...s/

292	Special purpose machinery	...	...	1730	1931	...	...	...	...	756	847
2921	Agricultural and forestry machinery	...	...	1730s/	1931s/	...	...	...	...	756s/	847s/
2922	Machine tools	...	...	...	...	...	...	...	...	...	...
2923	Machinery for metallurgy	...	...	...	...	...	...	...	...	...	...
2924	Machinery for mining & construction	...	...	...	...	...	...	...	...	...	...
2925	Food/beverage/tobacco processing machinery	...	...	...	...	...	...	...	...	...	...
2926	Machinery for textile, apparel and leather	...	...	...	...	...	...	...	...	...	...
2927	Weapons and ammunition	...	...	...	...	...	...	...	...	...	...
2929	Other special purpose machinery	...	...	...	...	...	...	...	...	...	...
2930	Domestic appliances n.e.c.	...	...	...	...	...	...	...	...	...	...
3000	Office, accounting and computing machinery	...	...	...	...	...	...	...	...	...	...
3110	Electric motors, generators and transformers	...	...	770	885	...	...	...	...	754	765
3120	Electricity distribution & control apparatus	...	...	...	...	...	...	...	...	...	...
3130	Insulated wire and cable	...	...	...	...	...	...	...	...	...	...
3140	Accumulators, primary cells and batteries	...	...	...t/	...t/	...	...	...	...	...t/	...t/
3150	Lighting equipment and electric lamps	...	...	10211t/	8325t/	...	...	...	...	5127t/	5215t/
3190	Other electrical equipment n.e.c.	...	...	...	...	...	...	...	...	...	...
3210	Electronic valves, tubes, etc.	...	...	...	...	...	...	...	...	...	...
3220	TV/radio transmitters; line comm. apparatus	...	...	...	...	...	...	...	...	...	...
3230	TV and radio receivers and associated goods	...	...	...b/	...b/	...	...	...	...	...b/	...b/
331	Medical, measuring, testing appliances, etc.	...	...	1420	2023	...	...	...	...	208	317
3311	Medical, surgical and orthopaedic equipment	...	...	1420u/	2023u/	...	...	...	...	208u/	317u/
3312	Measuring/testing/navigating appliances,etc.	...	...	...u/	...u/	...	...	...	...	...u/	...u/
3313	Industrial process control equipment	...	...	...	...	...	...	...	...	...	...
3320	Optical instruments & photographic equipment	...	...	...	...	...	...	...	...	...	...
3330	Watches and clocks	...	...	...	...	...	...	...	...	...	...
3410	Motor vehicles	...	...	...v/	...v/	...	...	...	...	...v/	...v/
3420	Automobile bodies, trailers & semi-trailers	...	...	2221v/	4513v/	...	...	...	...	2490v/	2845v/
3430	Parts/accessories for automobiles	...	...	...v/	...v/	...	...	...	...	...v/	...v/
351	Building and repairing of ships and boats	...	...	23536	26937	...	...	...	...	8457	10028
3511	Building and repairing of ships	...	...	23536w/	26937w/	...	...	...	...	8457w/	10028w/
3512	Building/repairing of pleasure/sport. boats	...	...	...w/	...w/	...	...	...	...	...w/	...w/
3520	Railway/tramway locomotives & rolling stock	...	...	...	...	...	...	...	...	...	...
3530	Aircraft and spacecraft	...	...	825	994	...	...	...	...	673	702
359	Transport equipment n.e.c.	...	...	...	...	...	...	...	...	...	...
3591	Motorcycles	...	...	...	...	...	...	...	...	...	...
3592	Bicycles and invalid carriages	...	...	...	...	...	...	...	...	...	...
3599	Other transport equipment n.e.c.	...	...	...	...	...	...	...	...	...	...
3610	Furniture	...	...	36536	43036	...	...	...	...	19017	20446
369	Manufacturing n.e.c.	...	...	54169	70152	...	...	...	...	53917	44204
3691	Jewellery and related articles	...	...	...b/	...b/	...	...	...	...	...b/	...b/
3692	Musical instruments	...	...	...	...	...	...	...	...	...	...
3693	Sports goods	...	...	...	...	...	...	...	...	...	...
3694	Games and toys	...	...	...	...	...	...	...	...	...	...
3699	Other manufacturing n.e.c.	...	...	54169b/	70152b/	...	...	...	...	53917b/	44204b/
3710	Recycling of metal waste and scrap	...	...	...	...	...	...	...	...	...	...
3720	Recycling of non-metal waste and scrap	...	...	...	...	...	...	...	...	...	...
D	Total manufacturing	...	...	2218307	2278790	...	...	...	...	1828001	1915436

a/ Provisional data.
b/ 3699 includes 1514, 3230 and 3691.
c/ 1549 includes 1543.
d/ 1551 includes 1553.
e/ 1721 includes 1723, 1729 and 1730.
f/ 1810 includes 1820.
g/ 1911 includes 1912.
h/ 2022 includes 2021.
i/ 2023 includes 2029.
j/ 2102 includes 2101.
k/ 2221 includes 2222.
m/ 2412 includes 2411.
n/ 2422 includes 2421.
p/ 2691 includes 2693.
q/ 2720 includes 2731.
r/ 2892 includes 2893.
s/ 2921 includes 2913 and 2919.
t/ 3150 includes 3140.
u/ 3311 includes 3312.
v/ 3420 includes 3410 and 3430.
w/ 3511 includes 3512.

Panama

ISIC Revision 3			Index numbers of industrial production											
			(2000=100)											
ISIC	Industry	Note	1995	1996	1997	1998	1999	2000	2001	2002	2003	2004	2005	2006
15	Food and beverages		92	94	102	110	103	100	99	99	100	101	105	109
16	Tobacco products		...	...	...	...	...	...	...	...	...	...	...	...
17	Textiles		92	93	105	102	102	100	101	79	58	57	49	38
18	Wearing apparel, fur		194	176	157	147	113	100	85	64	47	33	30	27
19	Leather, leather products and footwear		186	153	139	130	120	100	86	98	74	68	56	66
20	Wood products (excl. furniture)		167	148	161	149	146	100	89	63	64	72	73	74
21	Paper and paper products		163	148	138	121	113	100	86	99	91	81	83	90
22	Printing and publishing		89	81	81	102	104	100	93	112	140	143	152	158
23	Coke,refined petroleum products,nuclear fuel		...	...	...	...	...	...	...	...	...	...	...	...
24	Chemicals and chemical products		124	116	116	117	105	100	85	85	82	80	79	83
25	Rubber and plastics products		110	103	115	111	103	100	92	98	102	86	96	97
26	Non-metallic mineral products		80	72	79	95	105	100	89	103	114	126	121	146
27	Basic metals		74	83	110	92	131	100	41	52	52	57	54	54
28	Fabricated metal products		71	71	81	96	95	100	97	52	50	50	54	58
29	Machinery and equipment n.e.c.		110	82	95	133	143	100	73	42	27	24	26	25
30	Office, accounting and computing machinery		...	...	...	...	...	...	...	...	...	...	...	...
31	Electrical machinery and apparatus		231	275	278	232	95	100	75	52	57	62	64	48
32	Radio,television and communication equipment		...	...	...	...	...	...	...	...	...	...	...	...
33	Medical, precision and optical instruments		...	...	...	...	...	...	...	...	...	...	...	...
34	Motor vehicles, trailers, semi-trailers		107	102	116	118	110	100	101	92	110	72	99	89
35	Other transport equipment		70	73	69	66	90	100	86	68	62	76	82	78
36	Furniture; manufacturing n.e.c.		111	105	120	134	113	100	73	75	54	48	51	51
37	Recycling		...	...	...	...	...	...	...	...	...	...	...	...
D	Total manufacturing		100	100	106	110	105	100	93	95	96	97	99	105

Peru

Supplier of information:
Instituto Nacional de Estadística e Informática (INEI), Lima.

Basic source of data:
Annual survey on registered establishments.

Major deviations from ISIC (Revision 3):
None reported.

Reference period:
Calendar year.

Scope:
Establishments with 5 or more persons engaged.

Method of data collection:
Mail questionnaire and online survey (self entry).

Type of enumeration:
Sample survey.

Adjusted for non-response:
No.

Concepts and definitions of variables:
Wages and salaries is compensation of employees.
Output is at basic prices.
Value added is at basic prices

Related national publications:
Oferta y Demanda Global 1991-2007; Encuesta Nacional de Hogares (ENAHO); both published by Instituto Nacional de Estadística e Informática (INEI), Lima.

Peru

ISIC Revision 3		Number of establishments					Number of persons engaged					Wages and salaries paid to employees				
			(number)					(thousands)					(millions of Peruvian New Soles)			
ISIC	Industry	Note	2004	2005	2006	2007	Note	2004	2005	2006	2007	Note	2004	2005	2006	2007
151	Processed meat,fish,fruit,vegetables,fats		203	214	167	...	a/	179.2	179.8	192.2	203.1	a/	1889.0	1975.1	2189.5	2308.8
1511	Processing/preserving of meat		15	17	11	...		...	...	...	...		...	...	...	...
1512	Processing/preserving of fish		144	148	119	...		...	...	...	...		...	...	...	...
1513	Processing/preserving of fruit & vegetables		33	36	22	...		...	...	...	...		...	...	...	...
1514	Vegetable and animal oils and fats		11	13	15	...		...	...	...	...		...	...	...	...
1520	Dairy products		14	9	6	...		15.9	15.9	17.5	17.6		149.5	168.5	188.5	209.4
153	Grain mill products; starches; animal feeds		47	45	32	...	a/	...	...	...	...	a/	...	...	...	...
1531	Grain mill products		34	33	26	...		...	...	...	...		...	...	...	...
1532	Starches and starch products		1	1	1	...		...	...	...	...		...	...	...	...
1533	Prepared animal feeds		12	11	5	...		...	...	...	...		...	...	...	...
154	Other food products		91	74	47	...	a/	...	...	...	...	a/	...	...	...	...
1541	Bakery products		23	18	17	...		...	...	...	...		...	...	...	...
1542	Sugar		7	6	2	...		...	...	...	...		...	...	...	...
1543	Cocoa, chocolate and sugar confectionery		13	10	8	...		...	...	...	...		...	...	...	...
1544	Macaroni, noodles & similar products		7	6	5	...		...	...	...	...		...	...	...	...
1549	Other food products n.e.c.		41	34	15	...		...	...	...	...		...	...	...	...
155	Beverages		32	31	26	...	b/	22.3	22.3	20.2	20.2	b/	584.1	631.3	608.7	644.4
1551	Distilling, rectifying & blending of spirits		2	3	1	...		...	...	...	...		...	...	...	...
1552	Wines		4	5	2	...		...	...	...	...		...	...	...	...
1553	Malt liquors and malt		7	4	7	...		...	...	...	...		...	...	...	...
1554	Soft drinks; mineral waters		19	19	16	...		...	...	...	...		...	...	...	...
1600	Tobacco products		1	1	1	...	b/	...	...	...	...	b/	...	...	...	...
171	Spinning, weaving and finishing of textiles		88	82	70	...	c/	212.2	214.4	171.1	154.5	c/	616.9	647.2	624.0	647.8
1711	Textile fibre preparation; textile weaving		78	68	61	...		...	...	...	...		...	...	...	...
1712	Finishing of textiles		10	14	9	...		...	...	...	...		...	...	...	...
172	Other textiles		27	27	20	...	c/	...	...	...	...	c/	...	...	...	...
1721	Made-up textile articles, except apparel		4	6	3	...		...	...	...	...		...	...	...	...
1722	Carpets and rugs		2	2	1	...		...	...	...	...		...	...	...	...
1723	Cordage, rope, twine and netting		5	4	6	...		...	...	...	...		...	...	...	...
1729	Other textiles n.e.c.		16	15	10	...		...	...	...	...		...	...	...	...
1730	Knitted and crocheted fabrics and articles		26	16	19	...	c/	...	...	...	...	c/	...	...	...	...
1810	Wearing apparel, except fur apparel		75	55	47	...	d/	209.2	211.6	197.8	198.6	d/	711.9	741.5	715.0	751.9
1820	Dressing & dyeing of fur; processing of fur		1	1	1	...	d/	...	...	...	...	d/	...	...	...	...
191	Tanning, dressing and processing of leather		7	3	6	...		7.8	8.2	8.5	8.6		28.8	25.8	24.8	26.0
1911	Tanning and dressing of leather		6	3	6	...		...	...	...	...		...	...	...	...
1912	Luggage, handbags, etc.; saddlery & harness		1	-	-	...		...	...	...	...		...	...	...	...
1920	Footwear		14	11	10	...		50.7	49.7	47.4	47.6		67.8	50.9	39.8	50.6
2010	Sawmilling and planing of wood		17	11	10	...		...	...	...	...		...	...	...	...
202	Products of wood, cork, straw, etc.		11	8	12	...		...	...	...	...		...	...	...	...
2021	Veneer sheets, plywood, particle board, etc.		3	3	8	...		...	...	...	...		...	...	...	...
2022	Builders' carpentry and joinery		7	4	3	...		...	...	...	...		...	...	...	...
2023	Wooden containers		-	-	1	...		...	...	...	...		...	...	...	...
2029	Other wood products; articles of cork/straw		1	1	-	...		...	...	...	...		...	...	...	...
210	Paper and paper products		22	21	24	...		7.0	7.2	7.3	7.6		125.8	127.0	122.4	141.5
2101	Pulp, paper and paperboard		3	3	4	...		...	...	...	...		...	...	...	...
2102	Corrugated paper and paperboard		9	7	9	...		...	...	...	...		...	...	...	...
2109	Other articles of paper and paperboard		10	11	11	...		...	...	...	...		...	...	...	...
221	Publishing		16	13	17	...	e/	40.3	41.0	46.8	50.9	e/	328.8	328.8	317.0	342.5
2211	Publishing of books and other publications		6	5	6	...		...	...	...	...		...	...	...	...
2212	Publishing of newspapers, journals, etc.		10	8	11	...		...	...	...	...		...	...	...	...
2213	Publishing of recorded media		-	-	-	...		...	...	...	...		...	...	...	...
2219	Other publishing		-	-	-	...		...	...	...	...		...	...	...	...

222	Printing and related service activities	45	31	31	...	e/	...	...	...	...	e/	...	...	...	...
2221	Printing	39	25	29	...		...	...	...	...		...	...	...	...
2222	Service activities related to printing	6	6	2	...		...	...	...	...		...	...	...	...
2230	Reproduction of recorded media	-	-	-	...	e/	...	...	...	...	e/	...	...	...	...
2310	Coke oven products	-	-	-	...	f/	2.5	2.5	2.5	2.6	f/	253.4	251.1	259.5	270.6
2320	Refined petroleum products	1	-	1	...	f/	...	...	...	...	f/	...	...	...	...
2330	Processing of nuclear fuel	-	-	-	...	f/	...	...	...	...	f/	...	...	...	...
241	Basic chemicals	33	20	21	...		6.1	5.8	5.2	5.3		271.3	272.0	280.9	283.5
2411	Basic chemicals, except fertilizers	25	13	18	...		...	...	...	...		...	...	...	...
2412	Fertilizers and nitrogen compounds	2	3	1	...		...	...	...	...		...	...	...	...
2413	Plastics in primary forms; synthetic rubber	6	4	2	...		...	...	...	...		...	...	...	...
242	Other chemicals	112	103	96	...		21.6	22.5	24.8	26.8		650.0	651.1	660.1	730.8
2421	Pesticides and other agro-chemical products	4	4	4	...		...	...	...	...		...	...	...	...
2422	Paints, varnishes, printing ink and mastics	25	21	19	...		...	...	...	...		...	...	...	...
2423	Pharmaceuticals, medicinal chemicals, etc.	34	27	28	...		...	...	...	...		...	...	...	...
2424	Soap, cleaning & cosmetic preparations	17	14	21	...		...	...	...	...		...	...	...	...
2429	Other chemical products n.e.c.	32	37	24	...		...	...	...	...		...	...	...	...
2430	Man-made fibres	9	4	3	...		...	...	...	...		...	...	...	...
251	Rubber products	14	13	14	...	g/	16.3	17.4	18.6	19.9	g/	345.5	349.8	356.9	379.8
2511	Rubber tyres and tubes	5	6	9	...		...	...	...	...		...	...	...	...
2519	Other rubber products	9	7	5	...		...	...	...	...		...	...	...	...
2520	Plastic products	92	86	65	...	g/	...	...	...	...	g/	...	...	...	...
2610	Glass and glass products	7	6	5	...	h/	50.7	49.4	49.4	50.4	h/	439.0	439.5	467.7	500.3
269	Non-metallic mineral products n.e.c.	37	34	24	...	h/	...	...	...	...	h/	...	...	...	...
2691	Pottery, china and earthenware	2	3	2	...		...	...	...	...		...	...	...	...
2692	Refractory ceramic products	1	2	1	...		...	...	...	...		...	...	...	...
2693	Struct.non-refractory clay; ceramic products	7	3	1	...		...	...	...	...		...	...	...	...
2694	Cement, lime and plaster	6	7	6	...		...	...	...	...		...	...	...	...
2695	Articles of concrete, cement and plaster	6	10	9	...		...	...	...	...		...	...	...	...
2696	Cutting, shaping & finishing of stone	4	4	2	...		...	...	...	...		...	...	...	...
2699	Other non-metallic mineral products n.e.c.	11	5	3	...		...	...	...	...		...	...	...	...
2710	Basic iron and steel	4	6	8	...		6.2	6.3	6.5	6.8		211.4	227.6	239.4	263.6
2720	Basic precious and non-ferrous metals	6	6	8	...		5.9	5.8	5.3	4.8		282.9	278.6	274.6	295.8
273	Casting of metals	14	14	10	...		...	...	...	...		...	...	...	...
2731	Casting of iron and steel	6	6	5	...		...	...	...	...		...	...	...	...
2732	Casting of non-ferrous metals	8	8	5	...		...	...	...	...		...	...	...	...
281	Struct.metal products;tanks;steam generators	25	26	25	...	i/	82.9	77.8	82.8	87.4	i/	283.0	284.1	355.3	413.1
2811	Structural metal products	20	21	24	...		...	...	...	...		...	...	...	...
2812	Tanks, reservoirs and containers of metal	4	3	1	...		...	...	...	...		...	...	...	...
2813	Steam generators	1	2	-	...		...	...	...	...		...	...	...	...
289	Other metal products; metal working services	46	46	29	...	i/	...	...	...	...	i/	...	...	...	...
2891	Metal forging/pressing/stamping/roll-forming	2	2	1	...		...	...	...	...		...	...	...	...
2892	Treatment & coating of metals	3	2	1	...		...	...	...	...		...	...	...	...
2893	Cutlery, hand tools and general hardware	7	6	3	...		...	...	...	...		...	...	...	...
2899	Other fabricated metal products n.e.c.	34	36	24	...		...	...	...	...		...	...	...	...
291	General purpose machinery	11	12	8	...	j/	27.5	30.2	33.1	36.2	j/	116.9	123.4	153.0	173.4
2911	Engines & turbines (not for transport equipment)	-	-	-	...		...	...	...	...		...	...	...	...
2912	Pumps, compressors, taps and valves	4	2	1	...		...	...	...	...		...	...	...	...
2913	Bearings, gears, gearing & driving elements	-	-	-	...		...	...	...	...		...	...	...	...
2914	Ovens, furnaces and furnace burners	-	-	-	...		...	...	...	...		...	...	...	...
2915	Lifting and handling equipment	2	2	3	...		...	...	...	...		...	...	...	...
2919	Other general purpose machinery	5	8	4	...		...	...	...	...		...	...	...	...
292	Special purpose machinery	7	6	7	...	j/	...	...	...	...	j/	...	...	...	...
2921	Agricultural and forestry machinery	-	-	-	...		...	...	...	...		...	...	...	...
2922	Machine tools	1	2	1	...		...	...	...	...		...	...	...	...
2923	Machinery for metallurgy	-	-	-	...		...	...	...	...		...	...	...	...
2924	Machinery for mining & construction	4	3	5	...		...	...	...	...		...	...	...	...
2925	Food/beverage/tobacco processing machinery	-	-	-	...		...	...	...	...		...	...	...	...
2926	Machinery for textile, apparel and leather	-	-	-	...		...	...	...	...		...	...	...	...
2927	Weapons and ammunition	-	-	-	...		...	...	...	...		...	...	...	...
2929	Other special purpose machinery	2	1	1	...		...	...	...	...		...	...	...	...

continued

ISIC Revision 3		Number of establishments					Number of persons engaged					Wages and salaries paid to employees				
			(number)					(thousands)					(millions of Peruvian New Soles)			
ISIC	Industry	Note	2004	2005	2006	2007	Note	2004	2005	2006	2007	Note	2004	2005	2006	2007
2930	Domestic appliances n.e.c.		2	2	5	...	j/	...	...	...	...	j/	...	...	...	...
3000	Office, accounting and computing machinery		-	-	-	...		...	...	...	...		...	...	...	...
3110	Electric motors, generators and transformers		8	3	4	...	k/	8.4	8.9	9.3	9.7	k/	241.8	236.6	352.0	430.3
3120	Electricity distribution & control apparatus		4	6	5	...	k/	...	...	...	...	k/	...	...	...	...
3130	Insulated wire and cable		2	2	3	...	k/	...	...	...	...	k/	...	...	...	...
3140	Accumulators, primary cells and batteries		5	2	5	...	k/	...	...	...	...	k/	...	...	...	...
3150	Lighting equipment and electric lamps		1	-	1	...	k/	...	...	...	...	k/	...	...	...	...
3190	Other electrical equipment n.e.c.		5	4	-	...	k/	...	...	...	...	k/	...	...	...	...
3210	Electronic valves, tubes, etc.		1	1	-	...		...	...	...	...		...	...	...	...
3220	TV/radio transmitters; line comm. apparatus		-	-	-	...		...	...	...	...		...	...	...	...
3230	TV and radio receivers and associated goods		-	-	-	...		...	...	...	...		...	...	...	...
331	Medical, measuring, testing appliances, etc.		2	2	1	...		...	...	...	...		...	...	...	...
3311	Medical, surgical and orthopaedic equipment		2	2	1	...		...	...	...	...		...	...	...	...
3312	Measuring/testing/navigating appliances,etc.		-	-	-	...		...	...	...	...		...	...	...	...
3313	Industrial process control equipment		-	-	-	...		...	...	...	...		...	...	...	...
3320	Optical instruments & photographic equipment		1	1	1	...		...	...	...	...		...	...	...	...
3330	Watches and clocks		-	-	-	...		...	...	...	...		...	...	...	...
3410	Motor vehicles		-	1	-	...	m/	8.8	8.8	8.8	8.8	m/	132.8	133.0	152.1	211.1
3420	Automobile bodies, trailers & semi-trailers		3	3	4	...	m/	...	...	...	...	m/	...	...	...	...
3430	Parts/accessories for automobiles		9	8	6	...	m/	...	...	...	...	m/	...	...	...	...
351	Building and repairing of ships and boats		3	-	3	...	m/	...	...	...	...	m/	...	...	...	...
3511	Building and repairing of ships		3	-	3	...		...	...	...	...		...	...	...	...
3512	Building/repairing of pleasure/sport. boats		-	-	-	...		...	...	...	...		...	...	...	...
3520	Railway/tramway locomotives & rolling stock		-	-	-	...	m/	...	...	...	...	m/	...	...	...	...
3530	Aircraft and spacecraft		-	1	-	...	m/	...	...	...	...	m/	...	...	...	...
359	Transport equipment n.e.c.		3	1	2	...	m/	...	...	...	...	m/	...	...	...	...
3591	Motorcycles		-	-	-	...		...	...	...	...		...	...	...	...
3592	Bicycles and invalid carriages		3	1	2	...		...	...	...	...		...	...	...	...
3599	Other transport equipment n.e.c.		-	-	-	...		...	...	...	...		...	...	...	...
3610	Furniture		12	13	10	...		160.7	162.5	159.2	161.3		353.1	358.3	381.3	393.1
369	Manufacturing n.e.c.		50	38	15	...		41.7	42.0	43.5	45.0		213.5	210.0	202.4	257.5
3691	Jewellery and related articles		2	2	2	...		...	...	...	...		...	...	...	...
3692	Musical instruments		-	-	-	...		...	...	...	...		...	...	...	...
3693	Sports goods		-	-	-	...		...	...	...	...		...	...	...	...
3694	Games and toys		-	1	-	...		...	...	...	...		...	...	...	...
3699	Other manufacturing n.e.c.		48	35	13	...		...	...	...	...		...	...	...	...
3710	Recycling of metal waste and scrap		-	-	-	...		...	...	...	...		...	...	...	...
3720	Recycling of non-metal waste and scrap		2	3	2	...		...	...	...	...		...	...	...	...
D	Total manufacturing		1268	1126	937	...		1183.8	1189.8	1157.7	1173.6		8296.7	8511.0	8965.0	9725.8

a/ 151 includes 153 and 154.
b/ 155 includes 1600.
c/ 171 includes 172 and 1730.
d/ 1810 includes 1820.
e/ 221 includes 222 and 2230.
f/ 2310 includes 2320 and 2330.
g/ 251 includes 2520.
h/ 2610 includes 269.
i/ 281 includes 289.
j/ 291 includes 292 and 2930.

k/ 3110 includes 3120, 3130, 3140, 3150 and 3190.
m/ 3410 includes 3420, 3430, 351, 3520, 3530 and 359.

ISIC Revision 3		Output in factor values					Value added in factor values					Gross fixed capital formation		
			(millions of Peruvian New Soles)					(millions of Peruvian New Soles)					(millions of Peruvian New Soles)	
ISIC	Industry	Note	2004	2005	2006	2007	Note	2004	2005	2006	2007	Note	2006	2007
151	Processed meat,fish,fruit,vegetables,fats		18663.4	19570.5	22218.6	24547.7		5866.9	6093.4	7127.5	7836.1		...	...
1511	Processing/preserving of meat		9172.7	9625.1	9950.9	10923.8		1824.0	1911.4	1979.0	2174.8		...	...
1512	Processing/preserving of fish		2414.5	2713.2	4357.3	4505.4		1036.6	1132.7	1805.6	1860.3		...	...
1513	Processing/preserving of fruit & vegetables		728.1	916.0	1157.9	1862.3		238.9	300.1	380.8	613.0		...	...
1514	Vegetable and animal oils and fats		6348.2	6316.1	6752.6	7256.2		2767.4	2749.2	2962.1	3188.1		...	...
1520	Dairy products		2346.9	2582.9	2867.8	3177.9		624.0	687.6	762.5	846.4		...	...
153	Grain mill products; starches; animal feeds		5669.2	6323.8	6008.4	7328.5		799.7	898.0	855.4	1098.3		...	...
1531	Grain mill products		4051.4	4617.3	4142.8	5116.7		594.2	678.0	607.5	808.9		...	...
1532	Starches and starch products		89.7	107.2	136.7	144.9		38.6	46.1	58.7	62.4		...	...
1533	Prepared animal feeds		1528.1	1599.3	1728.9	2066.8		166.9	173.9	189.1	227.0		...	...
154	Other food products		7216.8	7345.1	8165.2	8687.2		2461.2	2503.5	2768.8	2938.5		...	...
1541	Bakery products		2907.2	3006.1	3209.8	3304.6		1334.8	1380.7	1474.9	1535.9		...	...
1542	Sugar		1547.0	1409.1	1829.5	1726.7		390.4	356.9	464.0	437.1		...	...
1543	Cocoa, chocolate and sugar confectionery		1074.2	1271.4	1276.7	1581.9		209.3	250.2	251.7	312.1		...	...
1544	Macaroni, noodles & similar products		489.0	541.3	544.5	594.8		146.8	162.4	163.1	183.0		...	...
1549	Other food products n.e.c.		1199.4	1117.1	1304.8	1479.1		380.0	353.4	415.0	470.4		...	...
155	Beverages		4457.7	4870.3	5533.4	5977.9		1475.4	1620.1	1847.1	2002.6		...	...
1551	Distilling, rectifying & blending of spirits		252.3	226.6	215.7	229.8		83.2	78.3	72.3	76.9		...	...
1552	Wines		215.4	256.6	270.6	303.7		59.3	71.9	73.7	83.9		...	...
1553	Malt liquors and malt		2139.9	2542.2	2933.3	3225.0		766.6	908.2	1060.0	1166.6		...	...
1554	Soft drinks; mineral waters		1850.1	1844.9	2113.8	2219.5		566.3	561.7	641.2	675.1		...	...
1600	Tobacco products		179.5	120.5	-	-		43.7	31.4	-	-		...	...
171	Spinning, weaving and finishing of textiles		3938.2	3949.4	4123.7	4469.2		1050.4	1057.4	1102.8	1194.1		...	...
1711	Textile fibre preparation; textile weaving		3778.1	3790.2	3958.3	4288.8		1028.8	1036.0	1080.5	1169.8		...	...
1712	Finishing of textiles		160.1	159.2	165.4	180.5		21.6	21.4	22.3	24.3		...	...
172	Other textiles		1471.4	1548.3	1577.0	1671.3		423.5	442.8	451.3	479.2		...	...
1721	Made-up textile articles, except apparel		195.3	203.2	212.6	218.4		62.2	64.7	67.7	69.5		...	...
1722	Carpets and rugs		308.1	320.5	335.3	344.1		84.6	88.0	92.0	94.5		...	...
1723	Cordage, rope, twine and netting		267.5	262.4	264.6	293.2		102.9	100.9	101.7	112.7		...	...
1729	Other textiles n.e.c.		700.4	762.2	764.6	815.7		173.9	189.3	189.9	202.6		...	...
1730	Knitted and crocheted fabrics and articles		2675.7	2893.3	2890.6	3073.5		1028.5	1112.2	1111.2	1181.5		...	...
1810	Wearing apparel, except fur apparel		6536.4	6800.8	6747.9	7350.2		2638.7	2744.3	2724.1	2966.1		...	...
1820	Dressing & dyeing of fur; processing of fur		114.9	114.7	114.5	123.0		30.6	30.6	30.5	32.8		...	...
191	Tanning, dressing and processing of leather		279.1	236.7	225.4	237.0		60.8	55.3	49.1	51.7		...	...
1911	Tanning and dressing of leather		214.9	184.7	188.4	192.2		44.0	41.3	39.5	40.8		...	...
1912	Luggage, handbags, etc.; saddlery & harness		64.1	52.0	37.1	44.9		16.8	14.0	9.6	10.9		...	...
1920	Footwear		315.4	247.9	151.1	192.1		115.0	89.5	53.8	67.7		...	...
2010	Sawmilling and planing of wood		774.4	861.3	890.9	860.8		290.7	323.4	334.5	323.2		...	...
202	Products of wood, cork, straw, etc.		706.5	769.4	808.0	857.2		256.4	281.3	296.0	314.2		...	...
2021	Veneer sheets, plywood, particle board, etc.		79.6	98.8	109.2	122.4		37.7	46.8	51.8	58.0		...	...
2022	Builders' carpentry and joinery		385.9	402.3	420.2	455.1		127.5	132.9	138.9	150.4		...	...
2023	Wooden containers		29.9	33.3	34.6	34.8		11.1	12.3	12.8	12.9		...	...
2029	Other wood products; articles of cork/straw		211.1	235.0	243.9	244.9		80.1	89.2	92.6	93.0		...	...
210	Paper and paper products		2964.3	3498.2	3920.8	4529.6		1105.2	1320.0	1472.6	1707.1		...	...
2101	Pulp, paper and paperboard		1305.3	1374.8	1556.4	1800.0		433.7	458.4	514.4	599.0		...	...
2102	Corrugated paper and paperboard		316.4	366.1	429.2	461.1		114.0	132.0	154.7	166.2		...	...
2109	Other articles of paper and paperboard		1342.6	1757.3	1935.2	2268.5		557.5	729.6	803.5	941.9		...	...
221	Publishing		1206.3	1285.3	1396.9	1494.5		506.8	536.2	582.8	623.2		...	...
2211	Publishing of books and other publications		345.7	401.8	455.1	486.7		138.2	160.6	181.9	194.5		...	...
2212	Publishing of newspapers, journals, etc.		677.3	658.9	708.4	754.7		300.2	292.0	314.0	334.5		...	...
2213	Publishing of recorded media		6.6	6.2	6.8	6.8		3.2	3.0	3.3	3.3		...	...
2219	Other publishing		176.7	218.5	226.7	246.3		65.2	80.6	83.6	90.9		...	...

continued

ISIC Revision 3		Output in factor values					Value added in factor values					Gross fixed capital formation		
			(millions of Peruvian New Soles)					(millions of Peruvian New Soles)					(millions of Peruvian New Soles)	
ISIC	Industry	Note	2004	2005	2006	2007	Note	2004	2005	2006	2007	Note	2006	2007
222	Printing and related service activities		1821.3	2251.0	2334.7	2536.6		713.1	883.8	917.3	995.9		...	...
2221	Printing		1668.0	2061.7	2138.5	2323.3		644.7	799.2	829.7	900.7		...	...
2222	Service activities related to printing		153.3	189.2	196.2	213.2		68.5	84.5	87.7	95.3		...	...
2230	Reproduction of recorded media		...	...	...	...		...	...	...	...		...	...
2310	Coke oven products		...	...	...	...		...	...	...	...		...	...
2320	Refined petroleum products		10507.4	14942.5	16142.1	16590.0		1837.5	2467.4	2617.6	2695.9		...	...
2330	Processing of nuclear fuel		...	...	...	...		...	...	...	...		...	...
241	Basic chemicals		2317.1	2813.7	2978.9	3529.4		1064.3	1288.1	1360.3	1618.2		...	...
2411	Basic chemicals, except fertilizers		1487.0	1880.9	1912.1	2147.4		713.9	893.7	909.6	1040.0		...	...
2412	Fertilizers and nitrogen compounds		659.0	768.0	861.7	1176.3		281.4	328.0	368.0	495.3		...	...
2413	Plastics in primary forms; synthetic rubber		171.1	164.8	205.1	205.7		69.0	66.4	82.7	82.9		...	...
242	Other chemicals		6187.8	6790.3	8189.4	9421.5		2544.4	2800.7	3371.2	3855.9		...	...
2421	Pesticides and other agro-chemical products		360.4	483.3	560.4	555.5		139.8	187.4	217.3	208.8		...	...
2422	Paints, varnishes, printing ink and mastics		761.5	888.2	1094.9	1349.7		315.6	368.1	453.8	559.4		...	...
2423	Pharmaceuticals, medicinal chemicals, etc.		1193.2	1363.6	1789.8	2071.0		563.3	643.4	847.3	980.4		...	...
2424	Soap, cleaning & cosmetic preparations		1907.9	1991.5	2492.4	3022.1		638.3	669.7	835.6	1012.8		...	...
2429	Other chemical products n.e.c.		1964.7	2063.7	2252.0	2423.3		887.4	932.1	1017.2	1094.6		...	...
2430	Man-made fibres		229.1	234.8	257.8	292.8		117.6	120.5	132.4	150.3		...	...
251	Rubber products		937.9	928.1	989.5	1014.4		294.1	291.0	310.3	318.1		...	...
2511	Rubber tyres and tubes		708.3	700.1	746.8	765.7		223.4	220.8	235.5	241.4		...	...
2519	Other rubber products		229.6	228.0	242.7	248.7		70.8	70.3	74.8	76.7		...	...
2520	Plastic products		2022.6	2286.8	2423.7	2680.3		667.6	753.0	800.4	881.8		...	...
2610	Glass and glass products		1232.8	1349.0	1343.0	1704.1		445.9	492.5	490.8	616.1		...	...
269	Non-metallic mineral products n.e.c.		4478.7	4970.2	5960.0	7139.0		2133.4	2369.6	2837.6	3380.7		...	...
2691	Pottery, china and earthenware		416.8	519.3	599.3	856.9		169.0	210.6	243.0	347.2		...	...
2692	Refractory ceramic products		181.1	226.0	287.6	444.1		95.4	119.1	151.5	234.1		...	...
2693	Struct.non-refractory clay; ceramic products		1073.4	1104.3	1373.2	1648.9		468.9	482.4	599.8	720.9		...	...
2694	Cement, lime and plaster		1985.0	2224.5	2594.6	2809.9		1038.6	1163.9	1357.5	1471.1		...	...
2695	Articles of concrete, cement and plaster		677.5	734.4	916.3	1145.2		300.6	325.8	406.5	509.6		...	...
2696	Cutting, shaping & finishing of stone		61.0	70.9	85.8	108.5		23.8	27.7	33.6	42.3		...	...
2699	Other non-metallic mineral products n.e.c.		83.9	90.8	103.1	125.4		37.1	40.2	45.6	55.5		...	...
2710	Basic iron and steel		2698.8	3416.5	3990.0	4584.7		1051.7	1331.2	1556.1	1788.0		...	...
2720	Basic precious and non-ferrous metals		14049.1	16960.3	23923.8	19188.8		1892.6	2247.8	3210.4	2509.7		...	...
273	Casting of metals		898.8	1231.3	1309.7	1483.5		343.1	463.0	490.0	548.7		...	...
2731	Casting of iron and steel		282.3	349.9	367.3	385.8		128.8	164.4	168.2	176.7		...	...
2732	Casting of non-ferrous metals		616.4	881.4	942.4	1097.6		214.3	298.6	321.8	372.0		...	...
281	Struct.metal products;tanks;steam generators		1085.5	1335.6	1622.5	2253.9		469.5	571.7	698.4	975.9		...	...
2811	Structural metal products		903.2	1116.2	1367.2	1935.6		387.8	473.4	584.0	833.3		...	...
2812	Tanks, reservoirs and containers of metal		171.6	206.5	240.2	299.5		75.9	91.3	106.2	132.4		...	...
2813	Steam generators		10.8	12.9	15.1	18.8		5.8	7.0	8.2	10.2		...	...
289	Other metal products; metal working services		2254.7	2392.6	3044.3	3366.2		927.5	987.0	1237.4	1376.6		...	...
2891	Metal forging/pressing/stamping/roll-forming		58.4	66.2	80.1	93.3		29.2	33.1	40.1	46.7		...	...
2892	Treatment & coating of metals		567.3	643.1	777.8	907.6		292.0	330.1	400.2	466.8		...	...
2893	Cutlery, hand tools and general hardware		203.9	174.8	191.9	171.3		96.2	82.4	90.5	80.8		...	...
2899	Other fabricated metal products n.e.c.		1425.0	1508.5	1994.5	2194.0		510.1	541.3	706.6	782.4		...	...
291	General purpose machinery		142.4	134.8	128.9	180.4		60.9	55.9	53.8	80.2		...	...
2911	Engines & turbines (not for transport equipment)		9.2	7.8	9.0	1.3		4.4	3.5	3.9	0.7		...	...
2912	Pumps, compressors, taps and valves		82.0	87.7	80.0	83.9		31.5	32.5	29.7	33.0		...	...
2913	Bearings, gears, gearing & driving elements		7.7	8.0	8.6	10.5		3.2	3.3	3.5	4.2		...	...
2914	Ovens, furnaces and furnace burners		2.8	2.9	3.1	3.8		1.8	1.9	2.0	2.5		...	...
2915	Lifting and handling equipment		23.9	24.7	25.8	32.2		12.8	13.2	13.7	17.8		...	...
2919	Other general purpose machinery		16.7	3.5	2.4	48.7		7.3	1.5	1.0	22.1		...	...

292	Special purpose machinery	189.0	215.4	262.7	275.4	71.4	83.0	106.9	107.2	...	...
2921	Agricultural and forestry machinery	26.1	27.0	28.1	35.1	9.2	9.4	9.8	12.4	...	...
2922	Machine tools	15.7	16.0	16.7	20.8	8.4	8.4	8.8	11.0	...	...
2923	Machinery for metallurgy	0.9	0.9	1.0	1.2	0.5	0.5	0.6	0.7	...	...
2924	Machinery for mining & construction	60.6	82.9	123.9	103.0	29.0	39.8	61.2	49.9	...	...
2925	Food/beverage/tobacco processing machinery	6.2	6.4	6.9	8.4	2.6	2.7	2.9	3.5	...	...
2926	Machinery for textile, apparel and leather	5.1	5.3	5.7	6.9	2.0	2.1	2.2	2.7	...	...
2927	Weapons and ammunition	10.3	10.7	11.5	13.9	4.8	5.0	5.3	6.5	...	...
2929	Other special purpose machinery	64.0	66.1	69.0	86.0	15.0	15.2	16.1	20.5	...	...
2930	Domestic appliances n.e.c.	460.2	476.8	520.5	624.5	170.2	175.8	191.8	230.6	...	...
3000	Office, accounting and computing machinery	20.0	20.7	21.6	26.9	8.7	8.9	9.4	11.8	...	...
3110	Electric motors, generators and transformers	110.2	141.8	159.3	196.2	39.7	51.1	57.5	70.8	...	...
3120	Electricity distribution & control apparatus	175.6	90.5	119.4	137.2	87.2	44.9	59.3	68.1	...	...
3130	Insulated wire and cable	491.3	511.7	1002.9	1338.0	157.2	154.3	293.3	404.0	...	...
3140	Accumulators, primary cells and batteries	98.8	107.8	131.7	148.5	39.8	43.4	53.0	59.7	...	...
3150	Lighting equipment and electric lamps	15.8	16.1	30.0	39.6	5.5	5.6	10.5	13.9	...	...
3190	Other electrical equipment n.e.c.	49.7	51.7	101.3	133.8	18.8	19.6	38.4	50.7	...	...
3210	Electronic valves, tubes, etc.	7.0	6.9	11.8	14.7	2.1	2.1	3.5	4.4	...	...
3220	TV/radio transmitters; line comm. apparatus	15.6	15.6	26.6	33.1	3.9	3.8	6.5	8.2	...	...
3230	TV and radio receivers and associated goods	34.4	34.3	58.5	72.9	10.2	10.2	17.4	21.7	...	...
331	Medical, measuring, testing appliances, etc.	0.3	-	-	-	0.1	-	-	-	...	...
3311	Medical, surgical and orthopaedic equipment	0.1	-	-	-	-	-	-	-	...	...
3312	Measuring/testing/navigating appliances,etc.	0.1	-	-	-	-	-	-	-	...	...
3313	Industrial process control equipment	-	-	-	-	-	-	-	-	...	...
3320	Optical instruments & photographic equipment	-	-	-	-	-	-	-	-	...	...
3330	Watches and clocks	-	-	-	-	-	-	-	-	...	...
3410	Motor vehicles	27.1	31.3	41.2	49.9	6.9	7.7	9.9	11.9	...	...
3420	Automobile bodies, trailers & semi-trailers	11.8	4.3	0.7	-	2.1	0.7	0.1	-	...	...
3430	Parts/accessories for automobiles	448.9	537.0	609.4	831.2	121.6	145.3	163.4	222.1	...	...
351	Building and repairing of ships and boats	253.2	368.6	505.5	783.7	92.8	135.1	185.3	287.3	...	...
3511	Building and repairing of ships	200.0	291.4	399.8	620.7	73.7	107.4	147.3	228.7	...	...
3512	Building/repairing of pleasure/sport. boats	53.2	77.3	105.7	163.0	19.1	27.8	38.0	58.6	...	...
3520	Railway/tramway locomotives & rolling stock	1.2	1.8	2.5	3.8	0.4	0.5	0.7	1.1	...	...
3530	Aircraft and spacecraft	1.6	2.4	3.3	5.2	0.3	0.5	0.7	1.0	...	...
359	Transport equipment n.e.c.	63.2	85.6	121.3	171.9	17.1	22.8	31.8	44.9	...	...
3591	Motorcycles	20.4	33.6	55.0	80.7	5.7	9.4	15.4	22.6	...	...
3592	Bicycles and invalid carriages	21.5	22.5	23.8	30.3	7.0	7.3	7.8	9.9	...	...
3599	Other transport equipment n.e.c.	21.3	29.5	42.5	60.9	4.3	6.0	8.6	12.4	...	...
3610	Furniture	1220.6	1155.4	1312.4	1602.6	349.5	334.1	380.5	464.5	...	...
369	Manufacturing n.e.c.	1846.4	1990.0	2138.5	2820.1	770.6	831.3	908.5	1205.1	...	...
3691	Jewellery and related articles	357.3	358.4	306.8	312.7	112.8	113.1	96.8	98.7	...	...
3692	Musical instruments	11.3	12.5	13.8	18.9	2.7	3.0	3.4	4.6	...	...
3693	Sports goods	25.2	27.2	30.0	38.4	5.3	5.7	6.3	8.0	...	...
3694	Games and toys	140.6	155.7	169.3	232.2	61.9	68.6	74.6	102.3	...	...
3699	Other manufacturing n.e.c.	1312.0	1436.2	1618.6	2217.9	587.9	640.8	727.4	991.5	...	...
3710	Recycling of metal waste and scrap	...	...	...	...	...	...	...	...	...	...
3720	Recycling of non-metal waste and scrap	...	...	...	...	...	...	...	...	...	...
D	Total manufacturing	115922.1	130921.9	149459.7	158205.7	35316.7	39030.9	44182.2	48563.3	...	...

Peru

ISIC Revision 3			Index numbers of industrial production											
			(2000=100)											
ISIC	Industry	Note	1995	1996	1997	1998	1999	2000	2001	2002	2003	2004	2005	2006
15	Food and beverages		86	86	89	85	96	100	97	102	102	108	115	125
16	Tobacco products		...	...	...	...	...	...	...	...	...	...	...	...
17	Textiles		71	77	84	82	90	100	95	118	130	155	164	162
18	Wearing apparel, fur		105	103	107	97	87	100	100	106	117	124	126	123
19	Leather, leather products and footwear		124	124	116	105	88	100	74	55	44	40	32	23
20	Wood products (excl. furniture)		80	100	97	98	90	100	103	134	122	135	139	136
21	Paper and paper products		53	57	61	66	79	100	100	107	109	138	169	190
22	Printing and publishing		107	104	101	101	90	100	120	148	162	177	199	209
23	Coke,refined petroleum products,nuclear fuel		99	100	107	108	101	100	103	104	102	108	126	124
24	Chemicals and chemical products		85	89	104	95	96	100	102	106	109	116	128	146
25	Rubber and plastics products		68	80	80	88	93	100	109	117	118	121	130	138
26	Non-metallic mineral products		88	96	105	109	96	100	98	109	118	131	148	169
27	Basic metals		78	85	90	95	95	100	104	101	104	106	107	112
28	Fabricated metal products		87	87	97	96	90	100	101	104	114	114	129	153
29	Machinery and equipment n.e.c.		171	158	150	137	89	100	102	86	71	58	62	65
30	Office, accounting and computing machinery		...	...	...	...	...	...	...	...	...	...	...	...
31	Electrical machinery and apparatus		117	111	115	106	94	100	91	84	78	95	85	106
32	Radio,television and communication equipment		...	...	...	...	...	...	...	...	...	...	...	...
33	Medical, precision and optical instruments		...	...	...	...	...	...	...	...	...	...	...	...
34	Motor vehicles, trailers, semi-trailers		203	124	128	151	87	100	100	61	68	82	95	106
35	Other transport equipment		347	298	349	162	55	100	105	144	145	149	208	298
36	Furniture; manufacturing n.e.c.		113	126	136	118	101	100	99	102	104	125	129	141
37	Recycling		...	...	...	...	...	...	...	...	...	...	...	...
D	Total manufacturing		92	94	99	95	94	100	101	106	110	118	127	137

Philippines

Supplier of information:
National Statistics Office, Manila.

Basic source of data:
Annual survey.

Major deviations from ISIC (Revision 3):
Data collected under the national classification system (1994 PSIC) have been adjusted to correspond with ISIC (Revision 3); except rice and corn milling, which is part of ISIC 1531, and is included in ISIC 1549. Manufacture of furniture (ISIC 3610) includes repair of furniture.

Reference period:
Calendar year.

Scope:
Establishments with 20 or more persons engaged.

Method of data collection:
The inquiry is carried out through personal visits.

Type of enumeration:
Sample survey.

Adjusted for non-response:
Yes.

Concepts and definitions of variables:
Wages and salaries is compensation of employees. It includes overtime payment and other benefits.
Output includes value of goods shipped in the same condition as received plus the amount paid for these goods.
Value added includes value of non-industrial services done for others, and excludes cost of non-industrial services done by others.

Related national publications:
None reported.

Philippines

ISIC Revision 3		Number of establishments					Number of employees					Wages and salaries paid to employees				
			(number)					(thousands)					(millions of Philippine Pesos)			
ISIC	Industry	Note	2002	2003	2004	2005	Note	2002	2003	2004	2005	Note	2002	2003	2004	2005
151	Processed meat,fish,fruit,vegetables,fats		...	317	...	338		...	56.0	...	55.1		...	6881	...	9376
1511	Processing/preserving of meat		...	...	...	...		...	...	...	...		...	...	...	...
1512	Processing/preserving of fish		...	...	...	...		...	...	...	...		...	...	...	...
1513	Processing/preserving of fruit & vegetables		...	...	...	...		...	...	...	...		...	...	...	...
1514	Vegetable and animal oils and fats		...	...	...	...		...	...	...	...		...	...	...	...
1520	Dairy products		...	18	...	27		...	5.7	...	6.2		...	2223	...	3629
153	Grain mill products; starches; animal feeds		...	106	...	128		...	10.2	...	11.0		...	1461	...	1305
1531	Grain mill products		...	...	...	...		...	...	...	...		...	...	...	...
1532	Starches and starch products		...	...	...	...		...	...	...	...		...	...	...	...
1533	Prepared animal feeds		...	...	...	...		...	...	...	...		...	...	...	...
154	Other food products		...	...	...	...		...	...	...	...		...	...	...	...
1541	Bakery products		...	222	...	358		...	26.0	...	32.5		...	2696	...	3515
1542	Sugar		...	25	...	22		...	13.1	...	10.8		...	2202	...	2127
1543	Cocoa, chocolate and sugar confectionery		...	...a/	...	...a/		...	...a/	...	...a/		...	...a/	...	...a/
1544	Macaroni, noodles & similar products		...	...a/	...	...a/		...	...a/	...	...a/		...	...a/	...	...a/
1549	Other food products n.e.c.		...	274a/	...	294a/		...	21.6a/	...	31.3a/		...	2965a/	...	4244a/
155	Beverages		...	96	...	115		...	21.3	...	17.4		...	4609	...	4942
1551	Distilling, rectifying & blending of spirits		...	...	...	...		...	...	...	...		...	...	...	...
1552	Wines		...	...	...	...		...	...	...	...		...	...	...	...
1553	Malt liquors and malt		...	...	...	...		...	...	...	...		...	...	...	...
1554	Soft drinks; mineral waters		...	...	...	...		...	...	...	...		...	...	...	...
1600	Tobacco products		...	14	...	15		...	9.6	...	9.6		...	1376	...	2092
171	Spinning, weaving and finishing of textiles		...	96	...	105		...	14.0	...	13.3		...	1478	...	1482
1711	Textile fibre preparation; textile weaving		...	...	...	...		...	...	...	...		...	...	...	...
1712	Finishing of textiles		...	...	...	...		...	...	...	...		...	...	...	...
172	Other textiles		...	203b/	...	190b/		...	25.6b/	...	21.9b/		...	2693b/	...	2644b/
1721	Made-up textile articles, except apparel		...	...	...	...		...	...	...	...		...	...	...	...
1722	Carpets and rugs		...	...	...	...		...	...	...	...		...	...	...	...
1723	Cordage, rope, twine and netting		...	...	...	...		...	...	...	...		...	...	...	...
1729	Other textiles n.e.c.		...	...	...	...		...	...	...	...		...	...	...	...
1730	Knitted and crocheted fabrics and articles		...	...b/	...	...b/		...	...b/	...	...b/		...	...b/	...	...b/
1810	Wearing apparel, except fur apparel		...	700c/	...	791c/		...	142.8c/	...	158.6c/		...	12175c/	...	15563c/
1820	Dressing & dyeing of fur; processing of fur		...	...c/	...	...c/		...	...c/	...	...c/		...	...c/	...	...c/
191	Tanning, dressing and processing of leather		...	132d/	...	195d/		...	19.5d/	...	20.6d/		...	1463d/	...	1450d/
1911	Tanning and dressing of leather		...	...	...	...		...	...	...	...		...	...	...	...
1912	Luggage, handbags, etc.; saddlery & harness		...	...	...	...		...	...	...	...		...	...	...	...
1920	Footwear		...	...d/	...	...d/		...	...d/	...	...d/		...	...d/	...	...d/
2010	Sawmilling and planing of wood		...	170e/	...	203e/		...	20.9e/	...	20.4e/		...	1521e/	...	1825e/
202	Products of wood, cork, straw, etc.		...	...e/	...	...e/		...	...e/	...	...e/		...	...e/	...	...e/
2021	Veneer sheets, plywood, particle board, etc.		...	...	...	...		...	...	...	...		...	...	...	...
2022	Builders' carpentry and joinery		...	...	...	...		...	...	...	...		...	...	...	...
2023	Wooden containers		...	...	...	...		...	...	...	...		...	...	...	...
2029	Other wood products; articles of cork/straw		...	...	...	...		...	...	...	...		...	...	...	...
210	Paper and paper products		...	165	...	192		...	20.8	...	21.3		...	2833	...	2863
2101	Pulp, paper and paperboard		...	...	...	...		...	...	...	...		...	...	...	...
2102	Corrugated paper and paperboard		...	...	...	...		...	...	...	...		...	...	...	...
2109	Other articles of paper and paperboard		...	...	...	...		...	...	...	...		...	...	...	...
221	Publishing		...	63	...	68		...	7.3	...	5.8		...	1441	...	1277
2211	Publishing of books and other publications		...	...	...	...		...	...	...	...		...	...	...	...
2212	Publishing of newspapers, journals, etc.		...	...	...	...		...	...	...	...		...	...	...	...
2213	Publishing of recorded media		...	...	...	...		...	...	...	...		...	...	...	...
2219	Other publishing		...	...	...	...		...	...	...	...		...	...	...	...

222	Printing and related service activities	...	266f/	...	324f/	...	12.7f/	...	14.5f/	...	1305f/	...	1705f/
2221	Printing	...	...	...	...	...	...	...	...	...	...	...	...
2222	Service activities related to printing	...	...	...	...	...	...	...	...	...	...	...	...
2230	Reproduction of recorded media	...	...f/	...	...f/	...	...f/	...	...f/	...	...f/	...	...f/
2310	Coke oven products	...	3	...	4	...	0.1	...	1.5	...	33	...	1617
2320	Refined petroleum products	...	3	...	...	...	0.9	...	...	...	744	...	...
2330	Processing of nuclear fuel	...	...	...	...	...	...	...	...	...	...	...	...
241	Basic chemicals	...	133	...	149	...	10.6	...	12.1	...	1604	...	1931
2411	Basic chemicals, except fertilizers	...	...	...	...	...	...	...	...	...	...	...	...
2412	Fertilizers and nitrogen compounds	...	...	...	...	...	...	...	...	...	...	...	...
2413	Plastics in primary forms; synthetic rubber	...	...	...	...	...	...	...	...	...	...	...	...
242	Other chemicals	...	245g/	...	256g/	...	33.5g/	...	37.8g/	...	9818g/	...	13267g/
2421	Pesticides and other agro-chemical products	...	...	...	...	...	...	...	...	...	...	...	...
2422	Paints, varnishes, printing ink and mastics	...	...	...	...	...	...	...	...	...	...	...	...
2423	Pharmaceuticals, medicinal chemicals, etc.	...	...	...	...	...	...	...	...	...	...	...	...
2424	Soap, cleaning & cosmetic preparations	...	...	...	...	...	...	...	...	...	...	...	...
2429	Other chemical products n.e.c.	...	...	...	...	...	...	...	...	...	...	...	...
2430	Man-made fibres	...	...g/	...	...g/	...	...g/	...	...g/	...	...g/	...	...g/
251	Rubber products	...	104	...	81	...	10.9	...	7.7	...	1343	...	1294
2511	Rubber tyres and tubes	...	...	...	...	...	...	...	...	...	...	...	...
2519	Other rubber products	...	...	...	...	...	...	...	...	...	...	...	...
2520	Plastic products	...	331	...	331	...	39.5	...	35.4	...	4100	...	3937
2610	Glass and glass products	...	52	...	43	...	7.0	...	4.4	...	1238	...	1184
269	Non-metallic mineral products n.e.c.	...	194	...	196	...	22.6	...	22.2	...	3724	...	4161
2691	Pottery, china and earthenware	...	...	...	...	...	...	...	...	...	...	...	...
2692	Refractory ceramic products	...	...	...	...	...	...	...	...	...	...	...	...
2693	Struct.non-refractory clay; ceramic products	...	...	...	...	...	...	...	...	...	...	...	...
2694	Cement, lime and plaster	...	...	...	...	...	...	...	...	...	...	...	...
2695	Articles of concrete, cement and plaster	...	...	...	...	...	...	...	...	...	...	...	...
2696	Cutting, shaping & finishing of stone	...	...	...	...	...	...	...	...	...	...	...	...
2699	Other non-metallic mineral products n.e.c.	...	...	...	...	...	...	...	...	...	...	...	...
2710	Basic iron and steel	...	199	...	210	...	19.7	...	17.9	...	2409	...	2563
2720	Basic precious and non-ferrous metals	...	27	...	23	...	3.0	...	3.0	...	509	...	640
273	Casting of metals	...	39	...	42	...	5.1	...	4.0	...	601	...	518
2731	Casting of iron and steel	...	...	...	...	...	...	...	...	...	...	...	...
2732	Casting of non-ferrous metals	...	...	...	...	...	...	...	...	...	...	...	...
281	Struct.metal products;tanks;steam generators	...	339h/	...	383h/	...	35.3h/	...	32.5h/	...	4027h/	...	3950h/
2811	Structural metal products	...	...	...	...	...	...	...	...	...	...	...	...
2812	Tanks, reservoirs and containers of metal	...	...	...	...	...	...	...	...	...	...	...	...
2813	Steam generators	...	...	...	...	...	...	...	...	...	...	...	...
289	Other metal products; metal working services	...	...h/	...	...h/	...	...h/	...	...h/	...	...h/	...	...h/
2891	Metal forging/pressing/stamping/roll-forming	...	...	...	...	...	...	...	...	...	...	...	...
2892	Treatment & coating of metals	...	...	...	...	...	...	...	...	...	...	...	...
2893	Cutlery, hand tools and general hardware	...	...	...	...	...	...	...	...	...	...	...	...
2899	Other fabricated metal products n.e.c.	...	...	...	...	...	...	...	...	...	...	...	...
291	General purpose machinery	...	284i/	...	280i/	...	29.9i/	...	25.1i/	...	3542i/	...	4034i/
2911	Engines & turbines (not for transport equipment)	...	...	...	...	...	...	...	...	...	...	...	...
2912	Pumps, compressors, taps and valves	...	...	...	...	...	...	...	...	...	...	...	...
2913	Bearings, gears, gearing & driving elements	...	...	...	...	...	...	...	...	...	...	...	...
2914	Ovens, furnaces and furnace burners	...	...	...	...	...	...	...	...	...	...	...	...
2915	Lifting and handling equipment	...	...	...	...	...	...	...	...	...	...	...	...
2919	Other general purpose machinery	...	...	...	...	...	...	...	...	...	...	...	...
292	Special purpose machinery	...	...i/	...	...i/	...	...i/	...	...i/	...	...i/	...	...i/
2921	Agricultural and forestry machinery	...	...	...	...	...	...	...	...	...	...	...	...
2922	Machine tools	...	...	...	...	...	...	...	...	...	...	...	...
2923	Machinery for metallurgy	...	...	...	...	...	...	...	...	...	...	...	...
2924	Machinery for mining & construction	...	...	...	...	...	...	...	...	...	...	...	...
2925	Food/beverage/tobacco processing machinery	...	...	...	...	...	...	...	...	...	...	...	...
2926	Machinery for textile, apparel and leather	...	...	...	...	...	...	...	...	...	...	...	...
2927	Weapons and ammunition	...	...	...	...	...	...	...	...	...	...	...	...
2929	Other special purpose machinery	...	...	...	...	...	...	...	...	...	...	...	...

continued

Philippines

ISIC Revision 3		Number of establishments					Number of employees					Wages and salaries paid to employees				
			(number)					(thousands)					(millions of Philippine Pesos)			
ISIC	Industry	Note	2002	2003	2004	2005	Note	2002	2003	2004	2005	Note	2002	2003	2004	2005
2930	Domestic appliances n.e.c.		...	...i/	...	...i/		...	...i/	...	...i/		...	...i/	...	...i/
3000	Office, accounting and computing machinery		...	28	...	45		...	37.0	...	58.2		...	5356	...	8718
3110	Electric motors, generators and transformers		...	50j/	...	45j/		...	14.4j/	...	10.5j/		...	1694j/	...	1848j/
3120	Electricity distribution & control apparatus		...	...j/	...	...j/		...	...j/	...	...j/		...	...j/	...	...j/
3130	Insulated wire and cable		...	34	...	47		...	14.1	...	19.0		...	1687	...	2536
3140	Accumulators, primary cells and batteries		...	63k/	...	71k/		...	23.7k/	...	27.3k/		...	3192k/	...	4587k/
3150	Lighting equipment and electric lamps		...	...k/	...	...k/		...	...k/	...	...k/		...	...k/	...	...k/
3190	Other electrical equipment n.e.c.		...	...k/	...	...k/		...	...k/	...	...k/		...	...k/	...	...k/
3210	Electronic valves, tubes, etc.		...	182m/	...	181m/		...	135.2m/	...	136.1m/		...	20909m/	...	24065m/
3220	TV/radio transmitters; line comm. apparatus		...	...m/	...	...m/		...	...m/	...	...m/		...	...m/	...	...m/
3230	TV and radio receivers and associated goods		...	33	...	29		...	14.1	...	9.2		...	2313	...	1009
331	Medical, measuring, testing appliances, etc.		...	70n/	...	68n/		...	26.3n/	...	19.4n/		...	3294n/	...	3300n/
3311	Medical, surgical and orthopaedic equipment		...	...	...	...		...	...	...	...		...	...	...	...
3312	Measuring/testing/navigating appliances,etc.		...	...	...	...		...	...	...	...		...	...	...	...
3313	Industrial process control equipment		...	...	...	...		...	...	...	...		...	...	...	...
3320	Optical instruments & photographic equipment		...	...n/	...	...n/		...	...n/	...	...n/		...	...n/	...	...n/
3330	Watches and clocks		...	...n/	...	...n/		...	...n/	...	...n/		...	...n/	...	...n/
3410	Motor vehicles		...	117p/	...	126p/		...	20.2p/	...	23.4p/		...	3939p/	...	4618p/
3420	Automobile bodies, trailers & semi-trailers		...	...p/	...	...p/		...	...p/	...	...p/		...	...p/	...	...p/
3430	Parts/accessories for automobiles		...	...p/	...	...p/		...	...p/	...	...p/		...	...p/	...	...p/
351	Building and repairing of ships and boats		...	68q/	...	64q/		...	10.8q/	...	11.1q/		...	2300q/	...	3862q/
3511	Building and repairing of ships		...	...	...	...		...	...	...	...		...	...	...	...
3512	Building/repairing of pleasure/sport. boats		...	...	...	...		...	...	...	...		...	...	...	...
3520	Railway/tramway locomotives & rolling stock		...	...q/	...	...q/		...	...q/	...	...q/		...	...q/	...	...q/
3530	Aircraft and spacecraft		...	...q/	...	...q/		...	...q/	...	...q/		...	...q/	...	...q/
359	Transport equipment n.e.c.		...	...q/	...	...q/		...	...q/	...	...q/		...	...q/	...	...q/
3591	Motorcycles		...	...	...	...		...	...	...	...		...	...	...	...
3592	Bicycles and invalid carriages		...	...	...	...		...	...	...	...		...	...	...	...
3599	Other transport equipment n.e.c.		...	...	...	...		...	...	...	...		...	...	...	...
3610	Furniture		...	269	...	348		...	25.4	...	37.7		...	2233	...	3667
369	Manufacturing n.e.c.		...	153	...	147		...	15.3	...	15.5		...	1752	...	1691
3691	Jewellery and related articles		...	...	...	...		...	...	...	...		...	...	...	...
3692	Musical instruments		...	...	...	...		...	...	...	...		...	...	...	...
3693	Sports goods		...	...	...	...		...	...	...	...		...	...	...	...
3694	Games and toys		...	...	...	...		...	...	...	...		...	...	...	...
3699	Other manufacturing n.e.c.		...	...	...	...		...	...	...	...		...	...	...	...
3710	Recycling of metal waste and scrap		...	14r/	...	20r/		...	2.1r/	...	1.1r/		...	150r/	...	82r/
3720	Recycling of non-metal waste and scrap		...	...r/	...	...r/		...	...r/	...	...r/		...	...r/	...	...r/
D	Total manufacturing		...	5901	...	6554		...	983.9	...	1022.1		...	131831	...	159119

a/ 1549 includes 1543 and 1544.
b/ 172 includes 1730.
c/ 1810 includes 1820.
d/ 191 includes 1920.
e/ 2010 includes 202.
f/ 222 includes 2230.
g/ 242 includes 2430.
h/ 281 includes 289.
i/ 291 includes 292 and 2930.
j/ 3110 includes 3120.
k/ 3140 includes 3150 and 3190.
m/ 3210 includes 3220.
n/ 331 includes 3320 and 3330.
p/ 3410 includes 3420 and 3430.
q/ 351 includes 3520, 3530 and 359.
r/ 3710 includes 3720.

Philippines

ISIC Revision 3		Output in producers' prices					Value added in producers' prices					Gross fixed capital formation		
			(millions of Philippine Pesos)					(millions of Philippine Pesos)					(millions of Philippine Pesos)	
ISIC	Industry	Note	2002	2003	2004	2005	Note	2002	2003	2004	2005	Note	2004	2005
151	Processed meat,fish,fruit,vegetables,fats		...	143862	...	165404		...	33532	...	31690		...	4152
1511	Processing/preserving of meat		...	...	...	...		...	...	...	...		...	...
1512	Processing/preserving of fish		...	...	...	...		...	...	...	...		...	...
1513	Processing/preserving of fruit & vegetables		...	...	...	...		...	...	...	...		...	...
1514	Vegetable and animal oils and fats		...	...	...	...		...	...	...	...		...	...
1520	Dairy products		...	44589	...	74397		...	15912	...	13934		...	2745
153	Grain mill products; starches; animal feeds		...	61307	...	61756		...	7999	...	11730		...	2326
1531	Grain mill products		...	...	...	...		...	...	...	...		...	...
1532	Starches and starch products		...	...	...	...		...	...	...	...		...	...
1533	Prepared animal feeds		...	...	...	...		...	...	...	...		...	...
154	Other food products		...	...	...	...		...	...	...	...		...	...
1541	Bakery products		...	31588	...	42438		...	6618	...	10133		...	2989
1542	Sugar		...	16922	...	19502		...	7794	...	8382		...	1779
1543	Cocoa, chocolate and sugar confectionery		...	...a/	...	...a/		...	...a/	...	...a/		...	...a/
1544	Macaroni, noodles & similar products		...	...a/	...	...a/		...	...a/	...	...a/		...	...a/
1549	Other food products n.e.c.		...	46014a/	...	80682a/		...	11473a/	...	30554a/		...	1252a/
155	Beverages		...	84659	...	84434		...	35687	...	33939		...	2474
1551	Distilling, rectifying & blending of spirits		...	...	...	...		...	...	...	...		...	...
1552	Wines		...	...	...	...		...	...	...	...		...	...
1553	Malt liquors and malt		...	...	...	...		...	...	...	...		...	...
1554	Soft drinks; mineral waters		...	...	...	...		...	...	...	...		...	...
1600	Tobacco products		...	32639	...	61150		...	15453	...	20894		...	1789
171	Spinning, weaving and finishing of textiles		...	15602	...	14080		...	3515	...	3073		...	259
1711	Textile fibre preparation; textile weaving		...	...	...	...		...	...	...	...		...	...
1712	Finishing of textiles		...	...	...	...		...	...	...	...		...	...
172	Other textiles		...	20880b/	...	25160b/		...	5742b/	...	8237b/		...	675b/
1721	Made-up textile articles, except apparel		...	...	...	...		...	...	...	...		...	...
1722	Carpets and rugs		...	...	...	...		...	...	...	...		...	...
1723	Cordage, rope, twine and netting		...	...	...	...		...	...	...	...		...	...
1729	Other textiles n.e.c.		...	...	...	...		...	...	...	...		...	...
1730	Knitted and crocheted fabrics and articles		...	...b/	...	...b/		...	...b/	...	...b/		...	...b/
1810	Wearing apparel, except fur apparel		...	58620c/	...	66641c/		...	22867c/	...	25638c/		...	888c/
1820	Dressing & dyeing of fur; processing of fur		...	...c/	...	...c/		...	...c/	...	...c/		...	...c/
191	Tanning, dressing and processing of leather		...	12690d/	...	15260d/		...	5518d/	...	5347d/		...	746d/
1911	Tanning and dressing of leather		...	...	...	...		...	...	...	...		...	...
1912	Luggage, handbags, etc.; saddlery & harness		...	...	...	...		...	...	...	...		...	...
1920	Footwear		...	...d/	...	...d/		...	...d/	...	...d/		...	...d/
2010	Sawmilling and planing of wood		...	12614e/	...	19109e/		...	3661e/	...	3969e/		...	2119e/
202	Products of wood, cork, straw, etc.		...	...e/	...	...e/		...	...e/	...	...e/		...	...e/
2021	Veneer sheets, plywood, particle board, etc.		...	...	...	...		...	...	...	...		...	...
2022	Builders' carpentry and joinery		...	...	...	...		...	...	...	...		...	...
2023	Wooden containers		...	...	...	...		...	...	...	...		...	...
2029	Other wood products; articles of cork/straw		...	...	...	...		...	...	...	...		...	...
210	Paper and paper products		...	38985	...	50342		...	10458	...	9720		...	2975
2101	Pulp, paper and paperboard		...	...	...	...		...	...	...	...		...	...
2102	Corrugated paper and paperboard		...	...	...	...		...	...	...	...		...	...
2109	Other articles of paper and paperboard		...	...	...	...		...	...	...	...		...	...
221	Publishing		...	10284	...	9123		...	2542	...	2880		...	197
2211	Publishing of books and other publications		...	...	...	...		...	...	...	...		...	...
2212	Publishing of newspapers, journals, etc.		...	...	...	...		...	...	...	...		...	...
2213	Publishing of recorded media		...	...	...	...		...	...	...	...		...	...
2219	Other publishing		...	...	...	...		...	...	...	...		...	...

continued

Philippines

ISIC Revision 3		Output in producers' prices					Value added in producers' prices					Gross fixed capital formation		
		Note	(millions of Philippine Pesos)				Note	(millions of Philippine Pesos)				Note	(millions of Philippine Pesos)	
ISIC	Industry		2002	2003	2004	2005		2002	2003	2004	2005		2004	2005
222	Printing and related service activities		...	8226f/	...	13245f/		...	3366f/	...	3939f/		...	494f/
2221	Printing		...	...	...	...		...	...	...	...		...	...
2222	Service activities related to printing		...	...	...	...		...	...	...	...		...	...
2230	Reproduction of recorded media		...	...f/	...	...f/		...	...f/	...	...f/		...	...f/
2310	Coke oven products		...	484	...	340461		...	94	...	93623		...	6350
2320	Refined petroleum products		...	268688	...	...		...	77773	...	...		...	...
2330	Processing of nuclear fuel		...	...	...	...		...	...	...	...		...	...
241	Basic chemicals		...	39883	...	52287		...	15700	...	9076		...	3252
2411	Basic chemicals, except fertilizers		...	...	...	...		...	...	...	...		...	...
2412	Fertilizers and nitrogen compounds		...	...	...	...		...	...	...	...		...	...
2413	Plastics in primary forms; synthetic rubber		...	...	...	...		...	...	...	...		...	...
242	Other chemicals		...	132010g/	...	165176g/		...	34338g/	...	44810g/		...	3821g/
2421	Pesticides and other agro-chemical products		...	...	...	...		...	...	...	...		...	...
2422	Paints, varnishes, printing ink and mastics		...	...	...	...		...	...	...	...		...	...
2423	Pharmaceuticals, medicinal chemicals, etc.		...	...	...	...		...	...	...	...		...	...
2424	Soap, cleaning & cosmetic preparations		...	...	...	...		...	...	...	...		...	...
2429	Other chemical products n.e.c.		...	...	...	...		...	...	...	...		...	...
2430	Man-made fibres		...	...g/	...	...g/		...	...g/	...	...g/		...	...g/
251	Rubber products		...	10694	...	13605		...	3767	...	3712		...	2983
2511	Rubber tyres and tubes		...	...	...	...		...	...	...	...		...	...
2519	Other rubber products		...	...	...	...		...	...	...	...		...	...
2520	Plastic products		...	38440	...	47257		...	11421	...	13798		...	1559
2610	Glass and glass products		...	11249	...	12279		...	3869	...	4506		...	1908
269	Non-metallic mineral products n.e.c.		...	49345	...	69748		...	17926	...	22495		...	1872
2691	Pottery, china and earthenware		...	...	...	...		...	...	...	...		...	...
2692	Refractory ceramic products		...	...	...	...		...	...	...	...		...	...
2693	Struct.non-refractory clay; ceramic products		...	...	...	...		...	...	...	...		...	...
2694	Cement, lime and plaster		...	...	...	...		...	...	...	...		...	...
2695	Articles of concrete, cement and plaster		...	...	...	...		...	...	...	...		...	...
2696	Cutting, shaping & finishing of stone		...	...	...	...		...	...	...	...		...	...
2699	Other non-metallic mineral products n.e.c.		...	...	...	...		...	...	...	...		...	...
2710	Basic iron and steel		...	53505	...	77787		...	10607	...	13466		...	1372
2720	Basic precious and non-ferrous metals		...	35396	...	55667		...	3961	...	5662		...	560
273	Casting of metals		...	8763	...	9609		...	2563	...	2763		...	303
2731	Casting of iron and steel		...	...	...	...		...	...	...	...		...	...
2732	Casting of non-ferrous metals		...	...	...	...		...	...	...	...		...	...
281	Struct.metal products;tanks;steam generators		...	47959h/	...	54046h/		...	10599h/	...	12043h/		...	1868h/
2811	Structural metal products		...	...	...	...		...	...	...	...		...	...
2812	Tanks, reservoirs and containers of metal		...	...	...	...		...	...	...	...		...	...
2813	Steam generators		...	...	...	...		...	...	...	...		...	...
289	Other metal products; metal working services		...	...h/	...	...h/		...	...h/	...	...h/		...	...h/
2891	Metal forging/pressing/stamping/roll-forming		...	...	...	...		...	...	...	...		...	...
2892	Treatment & coating of metals		...	...	...	...		...	...	...	...		...	...
2893	Cutlery, hand tools and general hardware		...	...	...	...		...	...	...	...		...	...
2899	Other fabricated metal products n.e.c.		...	...	...	...		...	...	...	...		...	...
291	General purpose machinery		...	70869i/	...	74285i/		...	14017i/	...	12920i/		...	646i/
2911	Engines & turbines (not for transport equipment)		...	...	...	...		...	...	...	...		...	...
2912	Pumps, compressors, taps and valves		...	...	...	...		...	...	...	...		...	...
2913	Bearings, gears, gearing & driving elements		...	...	...	...		...	...	...	...		...	...
2914	Ovens, furnaces and furnace burners		...	...	...	...		...	...	...	...		...	...
2915	Lifting and handling equipment		...	...	...	...		...	...	...	...		...	...
2919	Other general purpose machinery		...	...	...	...		...	...	...	...		...	...

292	Special purpose machinery	...	...i/	...	...i/	...	...i/	...	...i/	...	...i/
2921	Agricultural and forestry machinery	...	...	...	...	...	...	...	...	...	...
2922	Machine tools	...	...	...	...	...	...	...	...	...	...
2923	Machinery for metallurgy	...	...	...	...	...	...	...	...	...	...
2924	Machinery for mining & construction	...	...	...	...	...	...	...	...	...	...
2925	Food/beverage/tobacco processing machinery	...	...	...	...	...	...	...	...	...	...
2926	Machinery for textile, apparel and leather	...	...	...	...	...	...	...	...	...	...
2927	Weapons and ammunition	...	...	...	...	...	...	...	...	...	...
2929	Other special purpose machinery	...	...	...	...	...	...	...	...	...	...
2930	Domestic appliances n.e.c.	...	...i/	...	...i/	...	...i/	...	...i/	...	...i/
3000	Office, accounting and computing machinery	...	163768	...	262922	...	18703	...	38008	...	4865
3110	Electric motors, generators and transformers	...	18580j/	...	31582j/	...	3392j/	...	9609j/	...	116j/
3120	Electricity distribution & control apparatus	...	...j/	...	...j/	...	...j/	...	...j/	...	...j/
3130	Insulated wire and cable	...	18395	...	36176	...	3610	...	5900	...	957
3140	Accumulators, primary cells and batteries	...	31671k/	...	53403k/	...	8252k/	...	17515k/	...	2180k/
3150	Lighting equipment and electric lamps	...	...k/	...	...k/	...	...k/	...	...k/	...	...k/
3190	Other electrical equipment n.e.c.	...	...k/	...	...k/	...	...k/	...	...k/	...	...k/
3210	Electronic valves, tubes, etc.	...	380746m/	...	456378m/	...	75567m/	...	81774m/	...	21948m/
3220	TV/radio transmitters; line comm. apparatus	...	...m/	...	...m/	...	...m/	...	...m/	...	...m/
3230	TV and radio receivers and associated goods	...	45269	...	30251	...	5539	...	5463	...	879
331	Medical, measuring, testing appliances, etc.	...	28390n/	...	45063n/	...	10078n/	...	19515n/	...	4270n/
3311	Medical, surgical and orthopaedic equipment	...	...	...	...	...	...	...	...	...	...
3312	Measuring/testing/navigating appliances,etc.	...	...	...	...	...	...	...	...	...	...
3313	Industrial process control equipment	...	...	...	...	...	...	...	...	...	...
3320	Optical instruments & photographic equipment	...	...n/	...	...n/	...	...n/	...	...n/	...	...n/
3330	Watches and clocks	...	...n/	...	...n/	...	...n/	...	...n/	...	...n/
3410	Motor vehicles	...	111065p/	...	125754p/	...	23950p/	...	21573p/	...	3474p/
3420	Automobile bodies, trailers & semi-trailers	...	...p/	...	...p/	...	...p/	...	...p/	...	...p/
3430	Parts/accessories for automobiles	...	...p/	...	...p/	...	...p/	...	...p/	...	...p/
351	Building and repairing of ships and boats	...	31699q/	...	53351q/	...	5877q/	...	9862q/	...	788q/
3511	Building and repairing of ships	...	...	...	...	...	...	...	...	...	...
3512	Building/repairing of pleasure/sport. boats	...	...	...	...	...	...	...	...	...	...
3520	Railway/tramway locomotives & rolling stock	...	...q/	...	...q/	...	...q/	...	...q/	...	...q/
3530	Aircraft and spacecraft	...	...q/	...	...q/	...	...q/	...	...q/	...	...q/
359	Transport equipment n.e.c.	...	...q/	...	...q/	...	...q/	...	...q/	...	...q/
3591	Motorcycles	...	...	...	...	...	...	...	...	...	...
3592	Bicycles and invalid carriages	...	...	...	...	...	...	...	...	...	...
3599	Other transport equipment n.e.c.	...	...	...	...	...	...	...	...	...	...
3610	Furniture	...	16018	...	31202	...	5198	...	8546	...	649
369	Manufacturing n.e.c.	...	10941	...	10111	...	3590	...	3356	...	479
3691	Jewellery and related articles	...	...	...	...	...	...	...	...	...	...
3692	Musical instruments	...	...	...	...	...	...	...	...	...	...
3693	Sports goods	...	...	...	...	...	...	...	...	...	...
3694	Games and toys	...	...	...	...	...	...	...	...	...	...
3699	Other manufacturing n.e.c.	...	...	...	...	...	...	...	...	...	...
3710	Recycling of metal waste and scrap	...	631r/	...	1063r/	...	211r/	...	784r/	...	29r/
3720	Recycling of non-metal waste and scrap	...	...r/	...	...r/	...	...r/	...	...r/	...	...r/
D	Total manufacturing	...	2263936	...	2912185	...	562741	...	684838	...	94984

a/ 1549 includes 1543 and 1544.
b/ 172 includes 1730.
c/ 1810 includes 1820.
d/ 191 includes 1920.
e/ 2010 includes 202.
f/ 222 includes 2230.
g/ 242 includes 2430.
h/ 281 includes 289.
i/ 291 includes 292 and 2930.
j/ 3110 includes 3120.

k/ 3140 includes 3150 and 3190.
m/ 3210 includes 3220.
n/ 331 includes 3320 and 3330.
p/ 3410 includes 3420 and 3430.
q/ 351 includes 3520, 3530 and 359.
r/ 3710 includes 3720.

Philippines

ISIC Revision 3			Index numbers of industrial production											
			(2000=100)											
ISIC	Industry	Note	1995	1996	1997	1998	1999	2000	2001	2002	2003	2004	2005	2006
15	Food and beverages		...	...	...	...	...	100	101	102	102	95	107	110
16	Tobacco products		...	...	...	...	...	100	90	96	46	35	30	21
17	Textiles		...	...	...	...	...	100	92	111	130	127	144	129
18	Wearing apparel, fur		...	...	...	...	...	...	...	...	...	...	...	...
19	Leather, leather products and footwear		...	...	...	...	...	100	97	93	50	6	6	6
20	Wood products (excl. furniture)		...	...	...	...	...	100	107	97	157	159	88	62
21	Paper and paper products		...	...	...	...	...	100	77	67	61	68	71	72
22	Printing and publishing		...	...	...	...	...	100	98	77	85	102	84	87
23	Coke,refined petroleum products,nuclear fuel		...	...	...	...	...	...	...	...	...	...	...	...
24	Chemicals and chemical products		...	...	...	...	...	100	88	75	67	69	74	71
25	Rubber and plastics products		...	...	...	...	...	100	79	75	85	109	116	104
26	Non-metallic mineral products		...	...	...	...	...	100	86	107	102	105	106	91
27	Basic metals		...	...	...	...	...	100	91	83	107	135	107	146
28	Fabricated metal products		...	...	...	...	...	100	114	131	123	127	133	133
29	Machinery and equipment n.e.c.		...	...	...	...	...	100	133	110	129	130	69	35
30	Office, accounting and computing machinery		...	...	...	...	...	...	...	...	...	...	...	...
31	Electrical machinery and apparatus		...	...	...	...	...	100	84	86	71	80	77	46
32	Radio,television and communication equipment		...	...	...	...	...	...	...	...	...	...	...	...
33	Medical, precision and optical instruments		...	...	...	...	...	...	...	...	...	...	...	...
34	Motor vehicles, trailers, semi-trailers		...	...	...	...	...	100	95	99	93	99	115	98
35	Other transport equipment		...	...	...	...	...	...	...	...	...	...	...	...
36	Furniture; manufacturing n.e.c.		...	...	...	...	...	100	86	83	84	109	167	170
37	Recycling		...	...	...	...	...	...	...	...	...	...	...	...
D	Total manufacturing		88	92	96	86	88	100	98	92	92	93	95	86

Poland

Supplier of information:
Central Statistical Office of Poland, Warsaw.
Industrial statistics for the OECD countries are compiled by the OECD secretariat, which supplies them to UNIDO.

Basic source of data:
Annual surveys.

Major deviations from ISIC (Revision 3):
Data presented in accordance with ISIC (Revision 3) were originally classified according to the NACE (Revision 1) at the 2-digit level.

Reference period:
Calendar year.

Scope:
All enterprises.

Method of data collection:
Not reported.

Type of enumeration:
Not reported.

Adjusted for non-response:
Not reported.

Concepts and definitions of variables:
Number of employees includes part-time employees expressed in terms of full-time equivalents.
Gross fixed capital formation includes outlays on productive and non-productive investment, outlays on capital repairs are excluded. The value of sales of fixed assets is not deducted.

Related national publications:
None reported.

Poland

ISIC Revision 3		Number of enterprises					Number of employees					Wages and salaries paid to employees				
			(number)					(thousands)					(millions of Polish Zlotys)			
ISIC	Industry	Note	2002	2003	2004	2005	Note	2002	2003	2004	2005	Note	2002	2003	2004	2005
151	Processed meat,fish,fruit,vegetables,fats		...	5545	5638	5244		...	160.8	173.0	176.8		...	3120.2	3280.6	3387.0
1511	Processing/preserving of meat		4271	3834	3882	3597		99.5	109.2	116.9	119.9		1735.8	1928.8	2010.4	2073.0
1512	Processing/preserving of fish		...	438	439	419		...	11.2	12.6	14.6		...	194.9	215.0	252.0
1513	Processing/preserving of fruit & vegetables		1158	1185	1221	1126		34.9	37.5	40.3	39.0		805.8	884.3	940.2	940.0
1514	Vegetable and animal oils and fats		...	88	96	102		...	2.9	3.2	3.3		...	112.2	115.0	122.0
1520	Dairy products		793	779	774	723		48.5	47.0	45.7	44.6		1102.5	1120.1	1153.9	1163.0
153	Grain mill products; starches; animal feeds		1922	1680	1707	1526		22.1	21.7	21.8	22.5		626.1	615.5	655.5	696.0
1531	Grain mill products		1321	1103	1130	1003		10.8	10.6	10.5	10.2		233.0	239.3	242.6	243.0
1532	Starches and starch products		11	14	15	17		1.0	1.2	1.1	1.3		21.2	28.2	29.0	36.0
1533	Prepared animal feeds		590	563	562	506		10.3	9.9	10.2	11.0		371.9	348.0	383.9	417.0
154	Other food products		9990	8958	9139	8583		140.1	139.8	145.3	142.1		2790.5	2923.1	2878.1	2821.0
1541	Bakery products		7921	7096	7245	6841		80.0	84.3	89.6	89.5		1197.3	1286.4	1315.0	1330.0
1542	Sugar		92	75	56	48		17.0	15.1	11.7	10.9		484.1	528.8	403.8	347.0
1543	Cocoa, chocolate and sugar confectionery		505	439	451	423		17.8	18.0	19.2	18.7		441.7	479.1	497.0	492.0
1544	Macaroni, noodles & similar products		675	590	609	539		5.4	5.4	6.0	5.2		88.3	90.2	96.0	84.0
1549	Other food products n.e.c.		797	758	778	732		19.8	16.9	18.7	17.7		579.0	538.5	566.8	567.0
155	Beverages		1071	1013	1018	922		33.8	34.0	31.3	28.9		1163.8	1187.9	1143.9	1128.0
1551	Distilling, rectifying & blending of spirits		187	194	203	193		6.2	6.0	5.9	5.5		229.9	237.1	244.4	230.0
1552	Wines		...	152	140	119		...	2.8	2.4	2.2		...	59.0	53.0	51.0
1553	Malt liquors and malt		...	81	86	80		...	10.2	9.2	8.8		...	513.9	483.0	472.0
1554	Soft drinks; mineral waters		...	586	589	530		...	15.1	13.7	12.3		...	378.4	364.0	375.0
1600	Tobacco products		...	16	17	20		...	6.3	6.5	6.8		...	327.3	337.2	352.0
171	Spinning, weaving and finishing of textiles		983	1013	1047	1053		29.9	28.9	29.5	25.6		...	541.2	536.9	502.0
1711	Textile fibre preparation; textile weaving		...	314	316	305		...	23.3	22.3	18.4		...	446.1	427.3	388.0
1712	Finishing of textiles		682	699	731	748		3.7	5.6	7.2	7.2		58.6	95.0	109.5	114.0
172	Other textiles		2273	2242	2228	2234		26.6	27.7	32.2	31.7		521.1	547.8	599.3	612.0
1721	Made-up textile articles, except apparel		1641	1604	1602	1594		13.8	14.3	17.3	16.8		231.1	239.8	268.4	274.0
1722	Carpets and rugs		64	65	61	58		1.8	1.8	1.8	1.5		43.6	40.0	40.3	31.0
1723	Cordage, rope, twine and netting		146	138	133	132		1.4	0.9	1.0	1.0		23.1	19.8	22.2	23.0
1729	Other textiles n.e.c.		422	435	432	450		9.6	10.7	12.1	12.5		223.0	247.7	268.4	284.0
1730	Knitted and crocheted fabrics and articles		2599	2334	2306	2184		17.7	18.7	20.9	18.7		289.7	308.4	322.3	326.0
1810	Wearing apparel, except fur apparel		21117	18604	18723	16924		145.5	137.1	143.6	138.2		1976.5	1928.3	1951.5	1844.0
1820	Dressing & dyeing of fur; processing of fur		1026	871	865	739		1.8	1.8	2.0	1.9		23.9	25.1	23.5	21.0
191	Tanning, dressing and processing of leather		1720	1723	1674	1238		7.3	7.7	8.1	7.3		119.2	128.0	125.8	119.0
1911	Tanning and dressing of leather		211	225	219	161		2.6	2.8	2.6	2.1		50.5	54.6	53.9	45.0
1912	Luggage, handbags, etc.; saddlery & harness		1509	1498	1455	1077		4.7	4.9	5.5	5.2		68.7	73.5	72.0	75.0
1920	Footwear		4341	4229	4129	2964		28.1	26.2	25.7	22.4		417.8	394.2	382.5	350.0
2010	Sawmilling and planing of wood		4547	4536	4854	4252		30.1	26.5	30.9	30.5		491.4	416.2	460.8	478.0
202	Products of wood, cork, straw, etc.		17501	16179	17190	14099		69.6	71.0	84.1	77.8		1218.9	1302.3	1431.4	1378.0
2021	Veneer sheets, plywood, particle board, etc.		214	215	233	204		12.2	12.7	13.3	13.0		310.1	327.8	354.0	358.0
2022	Builders' carpentry and joinery		9055	8309	8786	7210		33.6	34.7	40.7	38.4		561.3	604.5	656.4	628.0
2023	Wooden containers		2278	2095	2272	1872		8.4	7.7	10.0	9.4		128.1	123.6	142.1	138.0
2029	Other wood products; articles of cork/straw		5954	5560	5899	4813		15.4	16.0	20.1	16.9		219.5	246.4	278.9	253.0
210	Paper and paper products		2219	1812	2316	2175		33.3	35.4	38.8	40.2		943.1	1033.9	1187.4	1134.0
2101	Pulp, paper and paperboard		105	88	110	111		10.0	9.3	9.2	10.1		379.2	394.2	371.2	396.0
2102	Corrugated paper and paperboard		1223	1000	1280	1211		15.2	17.0	18.8	19.4		365.3	421.0	519.2	481.0
2109	Other articles of paper and paperboard		891	724	926	853		8.1	9.1	10.8	10.6		198.3	218.7	296.5	258.0
221	Publishing		5404	5111	5789	5516		29.7	31.6	32.0	32.4		1331.6	1337.9	1336.3	1460.0
2211	Publishing of books and other publications		3010	2753	3073	2861		13.9	12.9	13.1	11.6		618.3	533.2	532.8	412.0
2212	Publishing of newspapers, journals, etc.		1233	1277	1474	1472		13.6	16.6	16.5	18.0		659.6	754.5	751.9	867.0
2213	Publishing of recorded media		189	189	224	246		0.3	0.2	0.3	0.7		6.6	5.3	6.8	26.0
2219	Other publishing		972	892	1018	937		1.8	1.9	2.1	2.1		47.4	45.3	44.4	155.0

222	Printing and related service activities	11416	10426	11626	11023	34.7	39.5	41.8	42.2	878.7	990.4	992.3	1062.0
2221	Printing	8056	7431	8270	7825	31.7	35.4	37.1	37.9	820.9	901.9	905.4	976.0
2222	Service activities related to printing	3360	2995	3356	3198	3.0	4.1	4.7	4.3	57.9	88.4	87.4	87.0
2230	Reproduction of recorded media	178	186	211	221	0.7	1.1	1.3	0.9	23.5	30.4	34.9	19.0
2310	Coke oven products	8	9	10	12	6.5	6.2	6.1	6.2	226.8	233.6	253.5	277.0
2320	Refined petroleum products	69	83	90	82	11.8	10.9	9.6	8.9	629.1	595.7	710.3	572.0
2330	Processing of nuclear fuel	-	-	-	-	-	-	-	-	-	-	-	-
241	Basic chemicals	599	542	586	554	31.7	29.7	29.5	28.9	1009.1	988.6	1048.4	1081.0
2411	Basic chemicals, except fertilizers	...	335	355	322	...	...	12.7	14.0	654.5a/	...	449.5	500.0
2412	Fertilizers and nitrogen compounds	99	86	84	74	10.4	10.1	9.9	8.3	354.5	345.4	359.4	340.0
2413	Plastics in primary forms; synthetic rubber	...	121	147	158	...	...	7.0	6.6	...a/	...	239.5	240.0
242	Other chemicals	...	1669	1760	1620	...	63.7	66.0	69.7	...	2507.8	2619.7	2763.0
2421	Pesticides and other agro-chemical products	...	41	44	42	...	1.5	1.4	1.5	...	52.8	55.7	58.0
2422	Paints, varnishes, printing ink and mastics	...	321	331	297	...	6.4	6.6	6.9	...	247.3	270.3	283.0
2423	Pharmaceuticals, medicinal chemicals, etc.	216	222	230	220	23.1	24.2	24.9	24.6	1065.4	1157.1	1204.6	1209.0
2424	Soap, cleaning & cosmetic preparations	812	745	797	725	22.3	23.1	23.6	24.6	853.3	835.9	851.9	920.0
2429	Other chemical products n.e.c.	...	340	358	336	...	8.5	9.6	12.2	...	214.7	237.2	294.0
2430	Man-made fibres	...	15	16	15	...	4.0	3.4	1.2	...	96.4	80.1	36.0
251	Rubber products	834	804	769	768	21.4	22.8	26.4	28.5	632.2	685.0	769.6	851.0
2511	Rubber tyres and tubes	...	160	151	142	...	8.4	9.3	9.7	632.3b/	337.4	366.2	408.0
2519	Other rubber products	...	644	618	626	...	14.4	17.1	18.8	...b/	347.1	403.3	444.0
2520	Plastic products	8440	8516	8131	8306	77.3	84.6	94.4	102.1	1759.0	1934.9	2120.8	2252.0
2610	Glass and glass products	1673	1403	1439	1279	38.1	39.4	40.8	39.9	860.2	910.3	964.2	950.0
269	Non-metallic mineral products n.e.c.	...	9684	10000	9012	...	79.7	83.1	81.9	...	2063.0	2203.2	2236.0
2691	Pottery, china and earthenware	...	543	560	514	...	12.8	13.0	13.3	...	282.5	310.5	313.0
2692	Refractory ceramic products	81	74	75	68	3.2	2.6	2.6	2.5	85.2	73.5	75.6	73.0
2693	Struct.non-refractory clay; ceramic products	605	518	535	467	14.2	14.1	14.8	13.8	353.0	359.0	392.5	389.0
2694	Cement, lime and plaster	97	86	88	78	9.6	8.0	7.0	6.8	386.1	337.0	323.7	323.0
2695	Articles of concrete, cement and plaster	6648	5302	5402	4665	35.2	30.5	32.5	32.2	802.0	724.6	796.7	811.0
2696	Cutting, shaping & finishing of stone	3305	2906	3073	2956	7.2	6.6	7.5	7.1	112.3	117.9	112.7	111.0
2699	Other non-metallic mineral products n.e.c.	...	255	267	264	...	5.1	5.6	6.2	...	168.5	191.5	214.0
2710	Basic iron and steel	205	234	246	259	41.9	36.5	34.8	33.4	1251.3	1154.5	1207.3	1195.0
2720	Basic precious and non-ferrous metals	84	101	112	116	11.0	10.9	10.7	10.8	359.5	363.8	361.2	378.0
273	Casting of metals	399	413	413	421	18.7	18.8	19.6	21.7	409.7	436.9	468.1	548.0
2731	Casting of iron and steel	197	208	208	208	15.1	14.9	15.2	16.9	334.8	339.2	361.2	426.0
2732	Casting of non-ferrous metals	202	205	205	213	3.6	3.9	4.4	4.9	74.8	97.2	106.8	121.0
281	Struct.metal products;tanks;steam generators	5524	5977	6165	6315	70.2	74.9	83.5	89.9	1695.0	1860.2	2057.0	2268.0
2811	Structural metal products	4276	4713	4899	5104	49.6	53.9	60.9	65.8	1167.3	1299.2	1449.5	1602.0
2812	Tanks, reservoirs and containers of metal	754	805	818	817	10.2	10.5	11.8	14.1	232.2	239.3	268.0	322.0
2813	Steam generators	494	459	448	394	10.4	10.5	10.9	10.0	295.5	321.6	339.5	344.0
289	Other metal products; metal working services	23511	23748	23624	22805	93.3	103.2	116.5	125.9	2012.8	2281.2	2566.7	2772.0
2891	Metal forging/pressing/stamping/roll-forming	277	321	336	393	6.0	6.6	7.4	7.7	140.8	157.9	185.6	204.0
2892	Treatment & coating of metals	13189	13730	13817	13974	24.1	30.5	37.6	44.1	464.0	633.1	744.7	899.0
2893	Cutlery, hand tools and general hardware	1589	1531	1502	1348	14.3	14.2	14.8	15.7	333.7	327.8	364.0	374.0
2899	Other fabricated metal products n.e.c.	8456	8166	7969	7090	48.9	51.9	56.7	58.4	1074.3	1162.4	1272.5	1295.0
291	General purpose machinery	5820	5674	6138	6457	67.3	67.0	69.0	71.5	1831.9	1847.8	1938.4	2136.0
2911	Engines & turbines (not for transport equipment)	174	185	198	219	9.5	8.5	7.9	8.5	343.3	314.1	310.1	349.0
2912	Pumps, compressors, taps and valves	538	496	518	494	11.1	10.9	10.9	11.5	294.7	287.7	300.6	326.0
2913	Bearings, gears, gearing & driving elements	138	131	137	137	10.8	10.7	11.2	11.3	295.1	299.6	323.7	344.0
2914	Ovens, furnaces and furnace burners	173	160	174	176	1.6	1.6	1.9	2.3	41.7	44.0	51.6	71.0
2915	Lifting and handling equipment	1158	1081	1149	1114	10.3	9.7	10.0	10.0	243.0	237.6	254.0	268.0
2919	Other general purpose machinery	3639	3621	3962	4317	23.8	25.6	27.2	27.9	613.7	664.3	698.9	778.0
292	Special purpose machinery	7017	6641	7056	7156	93.7	87.5	91.1	91.5	2287.1	2268.4	2368.0	2472.0
2921	Agricultural and forestry machinery	2291	2036	2161	2136	15.5	14.0	15.6	14.8	332.1	310.6	338.6	342.0
2922	Machine tools	874	843	905	969	15.3	12.5	12.2	11.9	361.1	325.1	321.0	322.0
2923	Machinery for metallurgy	91	87	91	85	6.3	5.8	6.3	6.2	180.5	173.8	188.3	175.0
2924	Machinery for mining & construction	862	864	923	928	25.6	25.1	26.2	26.8	651.5	664.8	710.7	766.0
2925	Food/beverage/tobacco processing machinery	765	717	757	741	6.3	6.7	7.2	7.2	160.1	177.3	186.1	190.0
2926	Machinery for textile, apparel and leather	454	399	408	365	2.1	1.7	1.4	1.0	44.4	38.7	33.5	27.0
2927	Weapons and ammunition	62	60	67	68	8.0	6.1	5.6	6.7	167.0	133.7	125.4	155.0
2929	Other special purpose machinery	1618	1635	1744	1864	14.7	15.4	16.5	17.0	390.8	443.9	464.5	495.0

continued

Poland

ISIC Revision 3		Number of enterprises					Number of employees					Wages and salaries paid to employees				
			(number)					(thousands)					(millions of Polish Zlotys)			
ISIC	Industry	Note	2002	2003	2004	2005	Note	2002	2003	2004	2005	Note	2002	2003	2004	2005
2930	Domestic appliances n.e.c.		433	390	404	377		14.5	15.1	16.4	18.1		371.5	418.4	455.4	499.0
3000	Office, accounting and computing machinery		823	1012	858	926		3.8	3.3	4.0	5.6		130.4	117.0	134.0	160.0
3110	Electric motors, generators and transformers		1267	1149	1255	1272		9.6	12.1	12.4	13.6		221.4	348.4	366.2	387.0
3120	Electricity distribution & control apparatus		771	826	977	1136		18.3	17.9	18.6	19.9		516.1	493.6	514.2	556.0
3130	Insulated wire and cable		115	109	112	111		13.2	12.7	9.8	10.6		374.2	367.8	257.6	279.0
3140	Accumulators, primary cells and batteries		107	96	101	96		2.5	2.5	2.3	2.5		86.0	92.0	89.6	95.0
3150	Lighting equipment and electric lamps		717	658	708	700		13.8	13.0	13.5	13.8		319.8	313.7	332.3	338.0
3190	Other electrical equipment n.e.c.		1552	1459	1625	1676		22.8	25.5	29.9	32.0		529.6	642.8	706.2	771.0
3210	Electronic valves, tubes, etc.		407	332	343	330		4.2	4.3	5.9	9.9		104.2	99.9	134.0	239.0
3220	TV/radio transmitters; line comm. apparatus		1505	1184	1232	1232		8.7	7.1	8.4	9.0		464.4	260.9	286.5	299.0
3230	TV and radio receivers and associated goods		1174	935	1023	1121		12.3	12.4	13.8	11.1		410.4	479.1	470.8	400.0
331	Medical, measuring, testing appliances, etc.		9997	9066	10009	9278		35.0	34.2	36.5	36.2		979.4	928.8	981.4	1000.0
3311	Medical, surgical and orthopaedic equipment		6689	6001	6589	6068		12.7	13.1	14.5	14.8		318.2	318.5	343.6	351.0
3312	Measuring/testing/navigating appliances,etc.		1745	1633	1834	1763		13.8	13.6	14.1	13.9		393.1	390.2	404.7	412.0
3313	Industrial process control equipment		1563	1432	1586	1447		8.6	7.4	7.9	7.6		268.1	220.0	233.1	237.0
3320	Optical instruments & photographic equipment		1113	923	1018	911		1.9	1.9	2.2	2.0		47.1	44.9	50.2	47.0
3330	Watches and clocks		123	101	109	91		0.3	0.4	0.4	0.4		6.2	7.0	6.8	7.0
3410	Motor vehicles		75	73	89	71		22.6	22.5	26.6	28.3		750.3	844.7	1030.8	1087.0
3420	Automobile bodies, trailers & semi-trailers		143	145	203	183		4.5	4.7	5.8	6.5		98.0	100.8	127.2	146.0
3430	Parts/accessories for automobiles		852	792	1101	885		48.9	52.3	67.4	72.0		1214.3	1356.4	1799.9	1978.0
351	Building and repairing of ships and boats		1710	1543	2552	2124		32.7	31.3	32.3	32.8		1026.1	953.8	1075.6	1125.0
3511	Building and repairing of ships		1475	1295	2097	1732		30.7	29.1	29.4	29.2		982.9	904.1	1010.8	1044.0
3512	Building/repairing of pleasure/sport. boats		235	248	455	392		2.0	2.2	2.9	3.6		43.6	49.7	64.7	82.0
3520	Railway/tramway locomotives & rolling stock		102	98	128	122		17.6	17.0	17.2	17.4		403.5	407.0	441.4	440.0
3530	Aircraft and spacecraft		40	37	52	49		14.5	14.0	14.1	14.0		390.0	391.1	407.4	459.0
359	Transport equipment n.e.c.		132	127	185	149		3.5	3.7	3.9	3.7		60.6	65.1	74.2	70.0
3591	Motorcycles		...	12	17	13		...	...	...	...		...c/	...	...	...
3592	Bicycles and invalid carriages		...	67	100	79		...	...	...	...		51.3c/	...	...	...
3599	Other transport equipment n.e.c.		51	48	68	57		0.5	0.6	0.7	0.8		9.3	11.0	12.2	13.0
3610	Furniture		13409	13038	14136	12369		107.2	120.6	147.1	145.1		1960.3	2272.4	2633.2	2644.0
369	Manufacturing n.e.c.		10048	9516	10119	8376		26.0	26.5	33.7	28.4		417.8	439.5	482.6	432.0
3691	Jewellery and related articles		2443	2344	2539	2149		4.1	4.2	5.7	4.5		69.8	70.0	75.6	64.0
3692	Musical instruments		425	402	435	360		0.5	0.5	0.7	0.6		6.6	8.4	9.5	8.0
3693	Sports goods		338	320	345	292		1.0	1.3	1.6	1.5		19.3	23.3	26.7	27.0
3694	Games and toys		799	742	796	670		3.3	2.9	3.3	2.8		53.6	48.0	50.7	44.0
3699	Other manufacturing n.e.c.		6043	5708	6004	4905		17.1	17.5	22.4	19.0		268.5	289.9	320.0	289.0
3710	Recycling of metal waste and scrap		274	340	376	418		4.1	3.8	4.5	4.4		123.8	114.0	138.5	135.0
3720	Recycling of non-metal waste and scrap		582	678	676	741		3.0	3.3	4.0	4.6		66.3	64.7	70.2	81.0
D	Total manufacturing		210200	197397	207197	191561		2033.8	2064.5	2229.8	2245.2		48373.6	50128.6	53636.2	55314.0

a/ 2411 includes 2413.
b/ 2511 includes 2519.
c/ 3592 includes 3591.

Poland

ISIC	Industry	Note	2002	2003	2004	2005	Note	2002	2003	2004	2005	Note	2004	2005
ISIC Revision 3		Output (millions of Polish Zlotys)					Value added in factor values (millions of Polish Zlotys)					Gross fixed capital formation (millions of Polish Zlotys)		
151	Processed meat,fish,fruit,vegetables,fats		...	39865.2	43164.4	47278.0		...	7090.4	6788.4	7492.0		3219.5	2514.0
1511	Processing/preserving of meat		22726.8	24634.2	27470.4	29832.0		3808.8	4077.5	3018.0	3503.0		2011.7	1437.0
1512	Processing/preserving of fish		...	2287.4	2769.5	3533.0		...	458.4	553.6	585.0		195.1	195.0
1513	Processing/preserving of fruit & vegetables		9289.4	10634.7	10404.4	11332.0		2477.6	2224.9	2805.7	2929.0		861.9	802.0
1514	Vegetable and animal oils and fats		...	2308.9	2520.1	2581.0		...	329.5	411.0	475.0		150.7	80.0
1520	Dairy products		12761.5	13499.7	15975.5	17101.0		2560.6	2638.0	2863.2	2829.0		1024.9	859.0
153	Grain mill products; starches; animal feeds		10739.1	10632.1	12248.2	11540.0		2236.5	2084.5	2450.8	2486.0		460.8	452.0
1531	Grain mill products		3380.6	3761.2	3959.6	3483.0		709.0	794.6	918.0	760.0		196.9	146.0
1532	Starches and starch products		157.8	267.5	261.6	252.0		45.9	48.0	76.5	70.0		22.2	29.0
1533	Prepared animal feeds		7200.6	6602.9	8026.9	7805.0		1482.0	1241.6	1456.3	1655.0		241.7	276.0
154	Other food products		25211.3	25968.2	28274.4	27852.0		7675.1	7317.9	8758.5	8511.0		1497.9	1775.0
1541	Bakery products		8797.6	10322.8	9991.1	10596.0		2635.4	2620.4	2628.7	3044.0		585.8	587.0
1542	Sugar		5747.6	4250.9	5637.2	4591.0		2133.2	1326.5	2083.7	1295.0		244.9	343.0
1543	Cocoa, chocolate and sugar confectionery		3856.6	4666.7	5380.6	5745.0		1027.2	1491.5	1703.9	1884.0		319.1	479.0
1544	Macaroni, noodles & similar products		760.3	849.1	892.7	842.0		206.0	191.4	236.8	208.0		47.1	43.0
1549	Other food products n.e.c.		6048.8	5878.3	6372.8	6078.0		1673.7	1688.1	2105.9	2080.0		300.1	324.0
155	Beverages		18824.6	19756.0	20207.2	20913.0		9790.1	11228.2	11739.4	12437.0		1167.0	1027.0
1551	Distilling, rectifying & blending of spirits		5720.2	6134.8	6809.7	6373.0		4324.2	4602.4	5216.2	4811.0		88.7	74.0
1552	Wines		...	1198.0	1153.0	1092.0		...	575.0	556.0	564.0		28.0	25.0
1553	Malt liquors and malt		...	8669.0	8562.0	9447.0		...	4994.0	4814.7	5774.0		627.4	598.0
1554	Soft drinks; mineral waters		...	3754.6	3683.0	4000.0		...	1056.8	1152.1	1287.0		422.8	329.0
1600	Tobacco products		...	11769.8	12749.3	13909.0		...	9242.7	10316.6	11444.0		230.0	259.0
171	Spinning, weaving and finishing of textiles		3418.0	3568.1	3828.8	3303.0		1126.0	1044.5	1119.0	1064.0		292.0	209.0
1711	Textile fibre preparation; textile weaving		...	2921.8	3024.4	2506.0		...	847.4	879.1	800.0		208.2	159.0
1712	Finishing of textiles		474.1	646.3	804.4	798.0		174.4	197.1	239.9	264.0		83.7	50.0
172	Other textiles		3880.6	4164.7	4837.3	4726.0		1397.2	1358.6	1555.9	1459.0		359.0	338.0
1721	Made-up textile articles, except apparel		1558.0	1633.1	1998.1	1965.0		526.2	486.6	581.2	552.0		100.0	111.0
1722	Carpets and rugs		268.1	292.1	306.9	194.0		104.5	99.4	104.6	74.0		7.2	25.0
1723	Cordage, rope, twine and netting		163.9	147.4	191.5	211.0		45.5	36.5	53.9	61.0		11.3	19.0
1729	Other textiles n.e.c.		1890.9	2092.0	2340.8	2356.0		720.6	736.1	816.2	772.0		240.4	183.0
1730	Knitted and crocheted fabrics and articles		2034.4	2101.2	2387.4	2145.0		664.2	656.9	699.4	669.0		148.9	201.0
1810	Wearing apparel, except fur apparel		8316.2	8048.2	8544.8	7109.0		3413.8	3254.4	3518.2	3026.0		311.4	314.0
1820	Dressing & dyeing of fur; processing of fur		155.5	146.1	172.5	125.0		49.4	51.5	55.7	41.0		6.8	7.0
191	Tanning, dressing and processing of leather		881.0	913.4	909.0	770.0		220.6	233.2	260.3	234.0		30.8	55.0
1911	Tanning and dressing of leather		464.0	459.8	446.3	350.0		95.7	92.0	100.0	86.0		19.9	10.0
1912	Luggage, handbags, etc.; saddlery & harness		417.0	453.6	462.6	419.0		125.0	141.2	160.2	148.0		10.9	45.0
1920	Footwear		2493.8	2178.2	2347.6	2324.0		822.0	728.1	764.6	761.0		87.4	86.0
2010	Sawmilling and planing of wood		4004.4	3233.7	4129.8	4453.0		1208.9	868.9	1129.4	1164.0		342.2	522.0
202	Products of wood, cork, straw, etc.		11576.1	12933.9	15946.6	15638.0		3356.0	3796.0	4775.3	4272.0		1587.1	1016.0
2021	Veneer sheets, plywood, particle board, etc.		4298.7	4998.4	6084.5	6106.0		1247.5	1447.0	1985.5	1761.0		994.1	502.0
2022	Builders' carpentry and joinery		4390.1	4925.8	5913.8	5750.0		1285.7	1444.8	1688.5	1521.0		354.4	336.0
2023	Wooden containers		1040.3	1040.9	1378.0	1342.0		276.6	295.7	345.8	329.0		69.3	46.0
2029	Other wood products; articles of cork/straw		1846.9	1968.8	2570.3	2439.0		546.2	608.5	755.5	661.0		169.3	132.0
210	Paper and paper products		11383.2	13051.4	14552.3	14644.0		3448.1	3646.8	4310.0	4102.0		983.2	1588.0
2101	Pulp, paper and paperboard		5872.9	6341.1	6765.8	6963.0		1986.6	2055.9	2208.6	1954.0		376.6	772.0
2102	Corrugated paper and paperboard		3766.8	4547.9	5216.2	5231.0		955.1	1046.2	1338.6	1386.0		396.5	610.0
2109	Other articles of paper and paperboard		1743.2	2162.4	2570.3	2450.0		506.5	544.7	762.3	763.0		210.0	206.0
221	Publishing		8603.6	8271.2	8819.1	9232.0		3234.1	3214.8	3597.4	4077.0		170.7	238.0
2211	Publishing of books and other publications		4086.2	3515.3	3657.7	2974.0		1585.0	1352.4	1486.6	1321.0		81.9	76.0
2212	Publishing of newspapers, journals, etc.		3887.1	4292.3	4681.6	5555.0		1463.9	1725.5	1966.0	2409.0		74.2	106.0
2213	Publishing of recorded media		125.0	55.0	77.9	265.0		30.1	13.6	19.9	94.0		1.4	43.0
2219	Other publishing		505.3	408.3	402.4	437.0		155.1	123.6	124.5	253.0		12.7	13.0

continued

Poland

ISIC Revision 3		Output					Value added in factor values					Gross fixed capital formation		
			(millions of Polish Zlotys)					(millions of Polish Zlotys)					(millions of Polish Zlotys)	
ISIC	Industry	Note	2002	2003	2004	2005	Note	2002	2003	2004	2005	Note	2004	2005
222	Printing and related service activities		8520.7	8961.5	9535.3	9600.0		2626.1	2676.7	3116.2	3379.0		655.5	783.0
2221	Printing		7587.9	8146.7	8617.7	8734.0		2373.9	2436.9	2853.7	3104.0		608.4	737.0
2222	Service activities related to printing		933.1	814.8	917.1	867.0		252.3	239.8	262.1	275.0		47.1	47.0
2230	Reproduction of recorded media		200.6	308.9	346.3	253.0		82.2	118.8	148.9	80.0		41.6	36.0
2310	Coke oven products		2134.7	2726.9	7554.3	5631.0		415.8	663.9	3433.6	1386.0		147.1	179.0
2320	Refined petroleum products		32116.5	35801.3	39845.3	46213.0		15310.1	17263.6	18420.9	19535.0		1488.0	1429.0
2330	Processing of nuclear fuel		-	-	-	-		-	-	-	-		-	-
241	Basic chemicals		11716.9	14228.7	17326.3	17393.0		2973.7	3466.0	4564.8	4253.0		1456.7	1484.0
2411	Basic chemicals, except fertilizers		...	...	6770.3	7754.0		...	...	1806.6	2021.0		422.4	452.0
2412	Fertilizers and nitrogen compounds		3756.4	4708.5	5609.2	4394.0		773.8	1168.1	1552.2	1190.0		202.3	210.0
2413	Plastics in primary forms; synthetic rubber		...	...	4946.9	5244.0		...	...	1205.9	1042.0		832.0	822.0
242	Other chemicals		...	22495.6	25634.8	27172.0		...	7759.6	9136.4	9727.0		1385.7	1320.0
2421	Pesticides and other agro-chemical products		...	551.3	655.0	683.0		...	160.1	189.7	212.0		18.6	33.0
2422	Paints, varnishes, printing ink and mastics		...	2681.1	2959.6	2931.0		...	736.9	820.7	833.0		177.5	149.0
2423	Pharmaceuticals, medicinal chemicals, etc.		6401.8	7055.6	7842.2	8341.0		3242.9	3347.2	4039.3	4313.0		605.7	519.0
2424	Soap, cleaning & cosmetic preparations		10029.7	10382.6	11951.2	12106.0		2951.3	2967.1	3390.1	3561.0		470.8	397.0
2429	Other chemical products n.e.c.		...	1825.0	2226.7	3111.0		...	548.2	696.7	808.0		113.2	223.0
2430	Man-made fibres		...	1204.2	1295.1	653.0		...	246.8	260.7	129.0		29.9	5.0
251	Rubber products		4776.6	6095.2	7409.5	7924.0		1691.1	2010.6	2347.6	2426.0		885.0	1142.0
2511	Rubber tyres and tubes		...	3321.3	3877.7	4142.0		...	1095.5	1169.7	1196.0		574.5	821.0
2519	Other rubber products		...	2773.9	3531.8	3782.0		...	915.1	1178.3	1230.0		310.5	321.0
2520	Plastic products		16799.8	20294.9	23744.9	26002.0		5126.1	5768.3	6459.3	7082.0		1726.1	2028.0
2610	Glass and glass products		5485.6	6177.0	6962.7	7091.0		2125.1	2445.7	2866.8	2833.0		772.7	847.0
269	Non-metallic mineral products n.e.c.		...	18027.8	21027.0	21044.0		...	6741.1	7911.5	7906.0		1983.6	2246.0
2691	Pottery, china and earthenware		...	1424.6	1577.6	1590.0		...	663.5	724.7	722.0		234.0	505.0
2692	Refractory ceramic products		575.9	591.7	650.0	631.0		174.7	167.2	188.3	186.0		40.3	48.0
2693	Struct.non-refractory clay; ceramic products		2548.6	2891.0	3400.1	3141.0		1052.7	1318.6	1615.2	1378.0		493.4	480.0
2694	Cement, lime and plaster		3475.9	3547.4	4180.0	4148.0		1605.8	1652.9	1906.2	1862.0		395.2	225.0
2695	Articles of concrete, cement and plaster		6905.2	6690.9	7585.6	7894.0		2075.3	2066.1	2375.7	2627.0		604.8	700.0
2696	Cutting, shaping & finishing of stone		1027.2	1042.7	1194.6	1120.0		250.0	236.7	276.6	336.0		55.2	82.0
2699	Other non-metallic mineral products n.e.c.		...	1839.9	2439.9	2520.0		...	635.7	824.8	795.0		161.2	205.0
2710	Basic iron and steel		13549.6	14969.6	25826.3	20743.0		2757.3	2539.0	6631.3	4482.0		434.6	671.0
2720	Basic precious and non-ferrous metals		3498.3	4198.1	5305.9	5260.0		872.9	885.2	1061.5	1001.0		231.3	345.0
273	Casting of metals		2045.2	2576.0	3144.8	3504.0		748.7	826.2	981.9	1137.0		151.2	221.0
2731	Casting of iron and steel		1423.0	1693.0	2057.9	2408.0		553.2	588.7	680.4	849.0		63.8	104.0
2732	Casting of non-ferrous metals		622.2	882.6	1086.4	1095.0		195.2	237.6	301.9	288.0		87.4	117.0
281	Struct.metal products;tanks;steam generators		10921.9	13043.9	15516.1	16068.0		3684.6	4385.1	5286.9	5528.0		589.8	765.0
2811	Structural metal products		7533.5	9176.2	11454.6	11779.0		2459.9	2971.5	3758.6	3954.0		396.1	465.0
2812	Tanks, reservoirs and containers of metal		1840.0	2131.6	2510.1	2732.0		650.4	718.0	794.5	870.0		126.3	138.0
2813	Steam generators		1548.4	1736.1	1551.3	1556.0		574.4	695.6	733.8	704.0		67.4	162.0
289	Other metal products; metal working services		15187.8	18579.1	23175.4	24452.0		5256.1	5785.5	7534.0	7848.0		1174.3	1913.0
2891	Metal forging/pressing/stamping/roll-forming		1063.9	1312.8	1890.4	2086.0		288.1	310.2	460.8	521.0		61.6	138.0
2892	Treatment & coating of metals		3482.5	5146.7	6492.8	7741.0		1267.2	1588.7	2192.8	2484.0		311.4	390.0
2893	Cutlery, hand tools and general hardware		1908.3	1698.2	1970.5	2007.0		725.2	712.3	855.6	892.0		116.8	557.0
2899	Other fabricated metal products n.e.c.		8733.2	10421.3	12821.7	12618.0		2975.6	3174.3	4024.8	3950.0		684.5	828.0
291	General purpose machinery		9529.8	10519.9	11972.5	14084.0		3832.3	4059.1	4600.1	5123.0		563.6	695.0
2911	Engines & turbines (not for transport equipment)		1797.2	1836.4	1944.7	2580.0		817.4	814.8	799.0	1087.0		102.8	75.0
2912	Pumps, compressors, taps and valves		1589.6	1597.9	1784.0	1900.0		656.1	639.3	715.7	733.0		95.1	112.0
2913	Bearings, gears, gearing & driving elements		1357.8	1669.6	2032.1	2094.0		519.6	681.9	827.0	743.0		123.1	120.0
2914	Ovens, furnaces and furnace burners		257.7	278.5	368.5	461.0		91.4	104.7	141.2	164.0		9.1	15.0
2915	Lifting and handling equipment		1246.7	1314.2	1535.0	1802.0		489.9	431.6	502.5	596.0		44.4	57.0
2919	Other general purpose machinery		3280.7	3822.8	4308.2	5247.0		1257.9	1386.8	1615.2	1800.0		189.7	317.0

292	Special purpose machinery	10987.5	11916.8	13826.7	16278.0	4610.0	4506.5	5318.5	5949.0	665.4	804.0
2921	Agricultural and forestry machinery	2348.0	2510.9	3080.5	3387.0	793.5	778.7	922.6	975.0	116.8	145.0
2922	Machine tools	1409.1	1461.1	1574.9	1767.0	643.0	593.1	667.7	700.0	72.4	103.0
2923	Machinery for metallurgy	486.4	503.3	642.4	651.0	295.5	283.3	339.5	343.0	10.4	22.0
2924	Machinery for mining & construction	3381.4	3597.1	4294.6	5255.0	1368.2	1330.0	1637.8	2051.0	247.6	251.0
2925	Food/beverage/tobacco processing machinery	874.9	1053.7	1273.8	1309.0	332.5	381.4	457.2	469.0	49.3	64.0
2926	Machinery for textile, apparel and leather	188.6	171.1	167.5	176.0	79.8	65.6	70.6	62.0	5.4	5.0
2927	Weapons and ammunition	630.3	735.2	694.9	1262.0	322.9	246.4	292.0	342.0	58.4	52.0
2929	Other special purpose machinery	1668.7	1883.9	2098.6	2471.0	774.2	828.4	931.2	1008.0	104.6	163.0
2930	Domestic appliances n.e.c.	3084.4	4652.1	6194.9	7314.0	881.8	1270.6	1604.8	1675.0	584.0	550.0
3000	Office, accounting and computing machinery	2250.0	1117.5	1274.7	1794.0	429.3	291.7	358.5	399.0	35.8	38.0
3110	Electric motors, generators and transformers	1205.1	2110.9	2537.7	2635.0	479.1	699.5	837.5	815.0	116.3	118.0
3120	Electricity distribution & control apparatus	3145.0	2894.9	3320.4	3553.0	1123.3	1054.6	1282.4	1313.0	160.2	151.0
3130	Insulated wire and cable	4208.8	5209.1	4762.2	5111.0	1048.8	1300.5	996.8	976.0	100.0	135.0
3140	Accumulators, primary cells and batteries	851.7	993.9	1048.9	1233.0	260.8	319.4	285.2	296.0	43.0	46.0
3150	Lighting equipment and electric lamps	2641.6	2937.6	3350.7	3484.0	899.9	1099.0	1267.1	1251.0	167.5	243.0
3190	Other electrical equipment n.e.c.	3607.5	4885.3	6133.4	6473.0	1283.0	1553.9	1895.8	1961.0	318.2	293.0
3210	Electronic valves, tubes, etc.	568.2	715.8	1204.1	1286.0	226.0	198.0	274.3	375.0	43.0	222.0
3220	TV/radio transmitters; line comm. apparatus	4077.7	2526.3	3399.2	3385.0	1177.3	683.3	684.5	736.0	110.5	51.0
3230	TV and radio receivers and associated goods	7618.4	8415.1	9214.3	8802.0	1542.2	1762.0	1480.7	1277.0	506.5	276.0
331	Medical, measuring, testing appliances, etc.	4967.6	4899.8	5550.8	6186.0	2256.6	2164.2	2361.2	2617.0	217.3	294.0
3311	Medical, surgical and orthopaedic equipment	1719.3	1790.2	1991.8	2386.0	788.8	799.4	869.6	1014.0	97.8	143.0
3312	Measuring/testing/navigating appliances,etc.	1955.7	1948.1	2292.4	2459.0	904.2	867.2	938.9	1010.0	81.0	95.0
3313	Industrial process control equipment	1292.6	1161.5	1266.6	1341.0	563.6	497.6	552.7	593.0	38.5	56.0
3320	Optical instruments & photographic equipment	306.3	296.1	316.9	354.0	127.3	119.2	130.8	152.0	12.7	14.0
3330	Watches and clocks	23.9	28.2	27.6	29.0	10.8	13.6	14.0	14.0	0.5	1.0
3410	Motor vehicles	16833.4	22551.9	35622.7	36525.0	2785.4	3686.4	5238.4	5529.0	1157.1	1217.0
3420	Automobile bodies, trailers & semi-trailers	714.0	910.3	1409.2	1494.0	180.9	206.8	297.4	321.0	70.6	72.0
3430	Parts/accessories for automobiles	10779.9	14885.2	22795.2	23881.0	3055.8	3960.1	6363.8	6508.0	2301.9	2097.0
351	Building and repairing of ships and boats	5005.0	5082.4	6775.3	7263.0	1660.2	1086.7	1756.9	2147.0	244.9	296.0
3511	Building and repairing of ships	4762.4	4730.5	6277.3	6705.0	1578.8	978.5	1575.8	1966.0	207.3	243.0
3512	Building/repairing of pleasure/sport. boats	242.6	352.4	497.9	558.0	81.4	108.7	181.1	182.0	37.1	52.0
3520	Railway/tramway locomotives & rolling stock	2132.8	2681.6	2832.9	2608.0	778.4	1030.4	962.4	919.0	75.1	76.0
3530	Aircraft and spacecraft	1157.2	1167.2	1505.2	1631.0	624.9	528.8	731.5	802.0	166.1	185.0
359	Transport equipment n.e.c.	536.6	604.5	772.3	717.0	144.3	146.1	189.2	152.0	19.9	34.0
3591	Motorcycles	...	...	...	...	...	...	...	...	...	...
3592	Bicycles and invalid carriages	...	...	...	...	...	...	...	...	...	...
3599	Other transport equipment n.e.c.	56.7	72.6	79.2	103.0	17.4	18.5	26.3	25.0	5.9	8.0
3610	Furniture	14480.0	19047.6	22978.9	22922.0	4374.7	5444.9	6487.4	6428.0	1280.6	1496.0
369	Manufacturing n.e.c.	2996.1	3462.5	4413.2	3837.0	910.7	1087.6	1247.6	1138.0	207.8	193.0
3691	Jewellery and related articles	538.9	612.9	752.4	688.0	159.3	218.2	234.9	212.0	23.5	27.0
3692	Musical instruments	56.7	74.4	89.2	82.0	13.9	19.4	23.1	24.0	6.8	4.0
3693	Sports goods	118.0	136.4	177.9	194.0	42.4	52.8	68.4	74.0	9.5	8.0
3694	Games and toys	320.2	333.5	373.0	322.0	84.9	100.8	118.6	113.0	14.0	16.0
3699	Other manufacturing n.e.c.	1962.3	2305.4	3020.7	2551.0	610.2	696.5	802.6	714.0	153.9	140.0
3710	Recycling of metal waste and scrap	1102.5	1486.6	2525.0	1890.0	312.5	331.3	488.9	397.0	107.3	158.0
3720	Recycling of non-metal waste and scrap	557.8	563.1	715.2	854.0	151.2	150.0	184.7	234.0	44.8	74.0
D	Total manufacturing	453204.0	506350.0	609225.0	627685.0	149179.0	160792.0	192204.0	194304.0	34392.4	36702.0

Poland

ISIC Revision 3			Index numbers of industrial production											
			(2000=100)											
ISIC	Industry	Note	1995	1996	1997	1998	1999	2000	2001	2002	2003	2004	2005	2006
15	Food and beverages		76	85	90	97	99	100	103	107	113	119	125	135
16	Tobacco products		121	115	123	131	123	100	89	93	95	101	97	93
17	Textiles		95	99	105	102	97	100	98	99	108	118	113	122
18	Wearing apparel, fur		79	87	97	106	104	100	96	94	90	84	75	76
19	Leather, leather products and footwear		107	121	127	106	101	100	93	91	84	84	75	79
20	Wood products (excl. furniture)		56	58	68	76	88	100	96	94	101	113	123	132
21	Paper and paper products		55	63	74	81	92	100	102	115	127	139	148	156
22	Printing and publishing		46	57	68	81	98	100	102	105	109	118	117	125
23	Coke,refined petroleum products,nuclear fuel		92	92	93	81	81	100	103	87	88	94	84	93
24	Chemicals and chemical products		83	88	96	93	92	100	102	109	122	133	138	153
25	Rubber and plastics products		46	54	66	78	91	100	106	120	144	164	179	204
26	Non-metallic mineral products		60	64	74	83	93	100	97	100	109	120	124	149
27	Basic metals		94	94	106	101	91	100	84	81	84	101	94	108
28	Fabricated metal products		46	54	64	79	88	100	110	121	139	165	183	216
29	Machinery and equipment n.e.c.		84	95	102	102	98	100	99	102	119	138	163	186
30	Office, accounting and computing machinery		...	...	...	...	...	...	...	...	...	...	...	...
31	Electrical machinery and apparatus		51	61	71	79	90	100	102	103	126	138	150	170
32	Radio,television and communication equipment		43	52	69	83	88	100	107	116	113	153	165	240
33	Medical, precision and optical instruments		62	75	95	97	102	100	105	103	115	121	146	178
34	Motor vehicles, trailers, semi-trailers		35	50	63	75	88	100	86	86	113	176	181	222
35	Other transport equipment		75	71	79	86	87	100	97	81	75	94	97	105
36	Furniture; manufacturing n.e.c.		52	62	74	83	93	100	102	115	138	158	162	182
37	Recycling		...	...	...	...	...	...	...	...	...	...	...	...
D	Total manufacturing		65	73	82	88	93	100	100	102	112	129	135	153

Portugal

Supplier of information:
National Institute of Statistics, Lisbon.
Industrial statistics for the OECD countries are compiled by the OECD secretariat, which supplies them to UNIDO.

Basic source of data:
Annual survey, administrative data.

Major deviations from ISIC (Revision 3):
Data presented by OECD in accordance with ISIC (Revision 3) were originally classified according to a classification system compatible with NACE (Revision 1).

Reference period:
Calendar year.

Scope:
All enterprises.

Method of data collection:
Not reported.

Type of enumeration:
Enterprises with 100 or more employees are completely enumerated; enterprises with less than 100 employees are sampled.

Adjusted for non-response:
Not reported.

Concepts and definitions of variables:
Number of employees is calculated as the average number of employees throughout the year, whether full- or part-time; homeworkers are not included.
Wages and salaries comprises payments to all persons included in the count of employees (also employed outworkers), whether in cash or in kind or made by the employer in connection with work done. It includes taxes, social insurance and pension contributions payable by the employee, but deducted by the employer. Bonuses, production awards, holiday allowances and wages paid during periods of sickness, military leave or other absences, and commission earned by salesmen and representatives are also included. Fees paid to shareholders committee are included to some extend.
Output refers to gross output and is valued in producers' prices, excluding all subsidies, and including all indirect taxes except VAT. Included are the values of all goods produced on own account, repair work for others, mounting or installation of own products and merchandise, contract work, other work, own-account investment work, own-account repair work, rental receipts and gross profit of goods sold in the same condition as purchased.
Value added is the value of output, less cost of goods and services consumed; included are subsidies, less indirect taxes (except VAT) and investment levy.
Gross fixed capital formation is defined as the acquisition of fixed durable assets, new and used, with an expected productive life of more than one year, including own-account investment work less receipts from sales of fixed durable assets.

Related national publications:
Industrial Statistics (Volume I and Volume II), published by the National Institute of Statistics, Lisbon.

Portugal

ISIC Revision 3		Number of enterprises					Number of employees					Wages and salaries paid to employees				
			(number)					(thousands)					(millions of Euros)			
ISIC	Industry	Note	2002	2003	2004	2005	Note	2002	2003	2004	2005	Note	2002	2003	2004	2005
151	Processed meat,fish,fruit,vegetables,fats		1215	1168	1162	1505		26.7	26.8	26.3	27.4		243.6	254.9	263.0	281.0
1511	Processing/preserving of meat		441	455	490	630		15.3	15.2	14.9	15.5		128.1	136.4	138.0	147.0
1512	Processing/preserving of fish		95	94	100	150		5.6	5.4	5.6	6.1		47.4	46.8	53.0	57.0
1513	Processing/preserving of fruit & vegetables		156	153	156	221		3.9	3.9	3.8	3.9		46.6	47.8	50.0	53.0
1514	Vegetable and animal oils and fats		523	466	416	504		1.8	2.3	2.0	1.9		21.5	23.9	22.0	24.0
1520	Dairy products		312	297	314	393		7.4	7.6	7.0	6.7		87.4	93.5	92.0	91.0
153	Grain mill products; starches; animal feeds		506	506	469	436		6.5	6.5	6.4	6.2		80.2	81.0	82.0	81.0
1531	Grain mill products		...	...	...	302		...	...	...	...		...	...	...	...
1532	Starches and starch products		...	...	...	4		...	...	...	...		...	...	...	...
1533	Prepared animal feeds		117	110	114	130		4.5	4.5	4.6	4.3		54.9	55.0	56.0	56.0
154	Other food products		6022	6080	6026	7166		40.9	48.0	47.1	49.2		345.1	389.7	403.0	420.0
1541	Bakery products		5765	5814	5761	6652		34.6	41.7	40.9	42.4		249.4	292.7	303.0	314.0
1542	Sugar		5	5	...	6		0.8	0.8	...	0.7		14.0	13.5	...	15.0
1543	Cocoa, chocolate and sugar confectionery		107	106	105	142		1.2	1.1	1.1	1.2		10.9	10.8	11.0	11.0
1544	Macaroni, noodles & similar products		4	4	4	11		0.2	0.2	0.2	0.4		2.2	2.3	3.0	4.0
1549	Other food products n.e.c.		141	151	...	355		4.0	4.1	...	...		68.6	71.0	...	...
155	Beverages		511	489	525	768		12.7	12.3	12.8	12.7		171.9	172.7	187.0	189.0
1551	Distilling, rectifying & blending of spirits		...	...	131	264		...	...	0.4	...		...	...	5.0	...
1552	Wines		...	...	...	436		...	...	...	...		...	...	...	...
1553	Malt liquors and malt		...	...	...	8		...	...	...	...		...	...	...	...
1554	Soft drinks; mineral waters		46	...	43	60		3.3	...	3.1	3.1		44.4	...	42.0	43.0
1600	Tobacco products		4	4	4	4		1.4	1.3	1.3	1.3		28.4	29.9	32.0	32.0
171	Spinning, weaving and finishing of textiles		835	803	838	944		37.0	35.3	33.3	32.6		323.9	320.2	308.0	301.0
1711	Textile fibre preparation; textile weaving		462	462	466	508		26.7	25.0	23.9	...		230.3	227.5	220.0	...
1712	Finishing of textiles		373	341	372	436		10.3	10.3	9.4	10.2		93.6	92.8	88.0	93.0
172	Other textiles		2488	2340	...	4770		33.3	30.4	...	30.2		257.6	237.0	...	231.0
1721	Made-up textile articles, except apparel		1106	976	...	2057		16.9	13.3	...	13.6		142.2	107.1	...	107.0
1722	Carpets and rugs		194	...	184	181		2.2	...	2.2	2.1		16.2	...	18.0	17.0
1723	Cordage, rope, twine and netting		38	44	43	55		4.0	3.8	3.8	3.6		34.3	34.2	35.0	34.0
1729	Other textiles n.e.c.		1150	...	1158	2477		10.3	...	9.2	10.9		64.9	...	75.0	72.0
1730	Knitted and crocheted fabrics and articles		1446	1467	...	1344		22.6	19.4	...	18.2		165.6	152.5	...	141.0
1810	Wearing apparel, except fur apparel		12099	12355	11999	11930		139.1	128.3	120.1	...		872.7	857.2	831.0	...
1820	Dressing & dyeing of fur; processing of fur		42	41	43	43		0.4	0.5	0.4	...		3.6	4.0	4.0	...
191	Tanning, dressing and processing of leather		569	564	...	519		4.6	4.4	...	...		36.5	36.7	...	...
1911	Tanning and dressing of leather		135	125	...	119		2.7	2.7	...	2.3		26.1	26.5	...	24.0
1912	Luggage, handbags, etc.; saddlery & harness		434	439	...	400		1.9	1.7	...	...		10.4	10.2	...	...
1920	Footwear		2726	2866	...	3149		56.2	56.0	...	48.2		379.1	374.6	...	332.0
2010	Sawmilling and planing of wood		1030	981	992	942		9.9	9.2	8.7	8.6		69.8	68.9	66.0	67.0
202	Products of wood, cork, straw, etc.		7530	7272	7397	8708		36.0	35.2	37.7	38.0		304.1	309.2	340.0	330.0
2021	Veneer sheets, plywood, particle board, etc.		39	39	36	52		2.6	2.5	2.5	2.4		29.8	32.2	35.0	36.0
2022	Builders' carpentry and joinery		5151	5012	...	6226		16.0	16.1	...	18.5		107.2	110.4	...	122.0
2023	Wooden containers		154	158	...	182		1.0	1.0	...	1.1		7.3	7.4	...	9.0
2029	Other wood products; articles of cork/straw		2186	2063	1970	2248		16.5	15.6	15.9	15.9		159.8	159.3	169.0	164.0
210	Paper and paper products		427	417	463	536		12.8	12.3	12.8	12.5		201.5	203.6	216.0	213.0
2101	Pulp, paper and paperboard		57	54	53	57		5.3	5.0	5.0	4.7		119.2	118.8	125.0	122.0
2102	Corrugated paper and paperboard		267	257	289	327		5.8	5.6	5.4	5.5		65.0	65.8	64.0	67.0
2109	Other articles of paper and paperboard		103	106	121	152		1.7	1.8	2.4	2.4		17.3	19.1	27.0	24.0
221	Publishing		1102	1076	1255	1540		10.3	14.4	10.9	12.0		197.8	301.9	236.0	233.0
2211	Publishing of books and other publications		308	238	295	418		2.8	2.9	2.9	3.5		48.8	53.6	57.0	56.0
2212	Publishing of newspapers, journals, etc.		670	666	758	833		7.2	11.1	7.5	7.8		144.9	243.8	173.0	170.0
2213	Publishing of recorded media		67	75	85	121		0.2	0.1	0.2	0.3		2.0	1.4	3.0	3.0
2219	Other publishing		57	97	117	168		0.2	0.3	0.3	0.4		2.2	3.1	3.0	4.0

222	Printing and related service activities	2987	3237	3251	4699	22.9	24.8	24.4	24.8	258.9	281.0	308.0	276.0
2221	Printing	1561	1629	1660	1633	17.2	17.7	18.3	17.0	201.4	210.8	235.0	211.0
2222	Service activities related to printing	1426	1608	1591	3066	5.6	7.0	6.1	7.8	57.6	70.2	73.0	65.0
2230	Reproduction of recorded media	34	39	36	60	0.3	0.3	0.2	0.2	3.2	4.0	3.0	3.0
2310	Coke oven products	-	-	-	-	-	-	-	-	-	-	-	-
2320	Refined petroleum products	1	1	1	1	2.3	2.1	2.1	...	84.2	84.8	91.0	...
2330	Processing of nuclear fuel	-	-	-	-	-	-	-	-	-	-	-	-
241	Basic chemicals	176	158	180	225	5.2	5.0	4.7	...	117.7	113.5	114.0	...
2411	Basic chemicals, except fertilizers	...	80	90	116	...	2.4	2.4	2.1	...	50.0	50.0	51.0
2412	Fertilizers and nitrogen compounds	16	17	15	21	1.0	1.0	0.8	0.7	22.7	22.6	18.0	18.0
2413	Plastics in primary forms; synthetic rubber	...	61	75	88	...	1.5	1.6	...	...	41.0	47.0	...
242	Other chemicals	654	642	...	783	16.0	15.8	...	...	280.5	288.8	...	...
2421	Pesticides and other agro-chemical products	4	5	...	8	0.2	0.3	...	...	3.0	6.1	...	...
2422	Paints, varnishes, printing ink and mastics	148	147	153	166	4.5	4.6	4.6	4.7	69.6	74.3	80.0	83.0
2423	Pharmaceuticals, medicinal chemicals, etc.	104	100	105	146	6.7	6.4	6.2	6.5	142.8	141.7	134.0	144.0
2424	Soap, cleaning & cosmetic preparations	193	194	...	217	2.7	2.6	...	2.4	39.6	40.5	...	35.0
2429	Other chemical products n.e.c.	205	196	...	246	1.9	1.9	...	1.9	25.4	26.2	...	27.0
2430	Man-made fibres	17	18	18	19	0.7	0.8	0.8	0.5	12.0	13.0	13.0	9.0
251	Rubber products	129	125	127	134	5.5	5.3	5.4	5.3	68.2	69.8	75.0	68.0
2511	Rubber tyres and tubes	62	57	...	60	3.3	3.0	...	3.0	47.1	47.2	...	42.0
2519	Other rubber products	67	68	71	74	2.2	2.2	2.4	2.3	21.1	22.5	28.0	26.0
2520	Plastic products	941	893	1005	1074	19.9	19.0	19.6	20.3	227.4	231.0	242.0	248.0
2610	Glass and glass products	425	432	468	505	8.2	8.1	7.2	...	107.6	115.9	104.0	...
269	Non-metallic mineral products n.e.c.	4325	4290	4241	5578	57.1	54.4	52.4	...	594.1	590.0	590.0	...
2691	Pottery, china and earthenware	...	...	...	1209	...	...	...	...	...	...	...	...
2692	Refractory ceramic products	22	18	16	28	0.5	0.4	0.4	0.3	7.8	5.0	4.0	4.0
2693	Struct.non-refractory clay; ceramic products	285	268	266	322	9.9	9.0	8.8	8.8	111.8	101.2	105.0	113.0
2694	Cement, lime and plaster	28	26	28	33	1.9	1.8	1.7	...	46.0	47.3	47.0	...
2695	Articles of concrete, cement and plaster	790	813	840	865	10.1	10.6	10.3	9.9	123.3	132.5	135.0	130.0
2696	Cutting, shaping & finishing of stone	2009	1998	2001	3029	14.2	13.5	14.3	15.4	119.4	117.5	129.0	136.0
2699	Other non-metallic mineral products n.e.c.	64	60	64	92	1.2	1.4	1.4	...	15.8	18.8	21.0	...
2710	Basic iron and steel	113	109	...	154	2.8	3.3	...	2.9	41.6	49.8	...	48.0
2720	Basic precious and non-ferrous metals	60	60	...	95	2.3	2.5	...	2.5	30.3	33.9	...	36.0
273	Casting of metals	269	268	...	248	5.7	5.5	...	5.5	62.8	61.6	...	66.0
2731	Casting of iron and steel	48	49	47	45	3.3	3.1	3.0	3.1	39.8	37.0	34.0	41.0
2732	Casting of non-ferrous metals	221	219	...	203	2.4	2.4	...	2.3	23.1	24.6	...	25.0
281	Struct.metal products;tanks;steam generators	4975	4953	5723	6467	29.5	30.6	34.3	37.3	295.2	308.3	350.0	375.0
2811	Structural metal products	4879	4849	5612	6334	26.5	27.8	31.6	34.8	255.9	269.3	310.0	337.0
2812	Tanks, reservoirs and containers of metal	85	92	100	120	2.4	2.2	2.2	2.1	26.9	25.8	29.0	27.0
2813	Steam generators	11	12	11	13	0.6	0.6	0.5	0.5	12.4	13.2	11.0	11.0
289	Other metal products; metal working services	9080	8862	8989	12146	43.3	42.3	42.2	47.8	414.9	403.2	412.0	435.0
2891	Metal forging/pressing/stamping/roll-forming	528	504	509	1612	2.0	1.7	1.9	3.2	15.3	14.3	15.0	19.0
2892	Treatment & coating of metals	5236	5170	5193	5411	14.9	14.6	14.1	16.6	139.6	136.5	133.0	149.0
2893	Cutlery, hand tools and general hardware	1578	1546	1512	2209	11.2	10.6	10.4	11.0	101.5	94.4	99.0	96.0
2899	Other fabricated metal products n.e.c.	1738	1642	1775	2914	15.2	15.4	15.8	17.0	158.5	157.9	165.0	170.0
291	General purpose machinery	1293	1258	1357	2776	13.8	14.0	14.0	16.2	167.4	176.3	192.0	196.0
2911	Engines & turbines (not for transport equipment)	48	46	45	42	0.1	0.1	0.1	0.2	2.9	2.7	3.0	3.0
2912	Pumps, compressors, taps and valves	128	128	...	113	2.6	2.5	...	2.5	30.2	29.7	...	31.0
2913	Bearings, gears, gearing & driving elements	33	37	...	44	0.6	0.7	...	0.7	7.5	8.9	...	11.0
2914	Ovens, furnaces and furnace burners	39	39	...	51	0.3	0.3	...	0.4	3.4	3.2	...	6.0
2915	Lifting and handling equipment	190	205	182	633	3.2	3.7	3.5	4.2	48.1	57.4	57.0	63.0
2919	Other general purpose machinery	855	803	...	1893	6.9	6.6	...	8.0	75.2	75.0	...	82.0
292	Special purpose machinery	2250	2160	2439	6122	25.8	23.9	24.3	29.5	323.0	317.5	332.0	351.0
2921	Agricultural and forestry machinery	331	309	326	341	2.9	2.7	2.7	3.0	30.4	29.3	30.0	33.0
2922	Machine tools	154	139	126	171	2.3	2.2	2.2	2.5	25.9	27.7	29.0	33.0
2923	Machinery for metallurgy	31	29	33	28	0.2	0.2	0.1	0.1	2.1	1.8	1.0	1.0
2924	Machinery for mining & construction	150	165	...	604	1.8	1.9	...	2.3	18.2	19.0	...	22.0
2925	Food/beverage/tobacco processing machinery	216	199	...	1402	2.4	2.4	...	3.6	30.8	31.4	...	34.0
2926	Machinery for textile, apparel and leather	127	93	135	560	2.0	1.8	1.6	2.0	24.3	22.6	20.0	20.0
2927	Weapons and ammunition	13	17	16	19	0.4	0.4	0.4	0.4	5.9	6.1	6.0	6.0
2929	Other special purpose machinery	1228	1209	...	2997	13.9	12.4	...	15.6	185.6	179.5	...	203.0

continued

Portugal

ISIC Revision 3		Number of enterprises					Number of employees					Wages and salaries paid to employees				
			(number)					(thousands)					(millions of Euros)			
ISIC	Industry	Note	2002	2003	2004	2005	Note	2002	2003	2004	2005	Note	2002	2003	2004	2005
2930	Domestic appliances n.e.c.		92	96	95	529		4.1	4.0	3.9	3.6		45.8	47.6	50.0	39.0
3000	Office, accounting and computing machinery		41	41	46	74		0.2	0.8	0.8	0.8		2.9	13.7	13.0	12.0
3110	Electric motors, generators and transformers		203	203	...	1861		1.8	2.1	...	...		25.6	35.7	...	...
3120	Electricity distribution & control apparatus		...	...	158	1339		...	...	4.8	5.8		...	...	65.0	63.0
3130	Insulated wire and cable		28	29	27	31		2.0	2.0	1.8	2.1		33.3	32.9	31.0	35.0
3140	Accumulators, primary cells and batteries		...	...	...	6		...	...	...	...		...	...	...	...
3150	Lighting equipment and electric lamps		337	326	...	306		3.4	3.3	...	3.2		33.6	33.1	...	32.0
3190	Other electrical equipment n.e.c.		180	192	...	649		19.5	16.8	...	13.6		214.3	182.3	...	167.0
3210	Electronic valves, tubes, etc.		105	87	104	116		2.8	3.1	3.7	...		38.3	45.2	51.0	...
3220	TV/radio transmitters; line comm. apparatus		78	84	82	88		4.0	3.2	3.2	...		107.7	93.2	99.0	...
3230	TV and radio receivers and associated goods		77	75	80	83		5.5	5.8	5.6	5.0		73.1	79.3	81.0	75.0
331	Medical, measuring, testing appliances, etc.		686	717	...	1045		3.6	4.0	...	5.2		42.7	49.9	...	63.0
3311	Medical, surgical and orthopaedic equipment		521	543	...	817		2.1	2.0	...	3.1		19.4	19.7	...	28.0
3312	Measuring/testing/navigating appliances,etc.		71	71	85	92		0.5	1.0	1.0	1.0		6.4	12.6	13.0	16.0
3313	Industrial process control equipment		94	103	...	136		1.0	1.0	...	1.1		16.9	17.6	...	19.0
3320	Optical instruments & photographic equipment		21	18	22	26		1.5	1.5	1.5	1.4		19.2	20.1	21.0	19.0
3330	Watches and clocks		17	15	...	26		0.2	0.2	...	0.2		1.8	1.7	...	2.0
3410	Motor vehicles		22	24	25	41		8.3	8.0	6.7	6.7		147.1	135.8	120.0	125.0
3420	Automobile bodies, trailers & semi-trailers		187	190	207	208		3.4	3.4	3.5	3.4		33.4	34.5	40.0	42.0
3430	Parts/accessories for automobiles		199	220	231	263		12.2	11.5	12.3	13.0		143.6	146.5	171.0	178.0
351	Building and repairing of ships and boats		268	244	271	769		5.5	4.7	4.2	4.7		71.0	61.2	61.0	59.0
3511	Building and repairing of ships		209	182	191	214		5.1	4.3	3.6	3.5		68.3	57.7	56.0	52.0
3512	Building/repairing of pleasure/sport. boats		59	62	80	555		0.4	0.5	0.6	1.2		2.6	3.5	5.0	6.0
3520	Railway/tramway locomotives & rolling stock		7	7	...	9		2.6	2.5	...	1.8		47.7	45.1	...	34.0
3530	Aircraft and spacecraft		25	25	28	40		2.2	2.0	1.9	1.9		35.7	34.5	38.0	38.0
359	Transport equipment n.e.c.		60	62	...	79		1.6	1.9	...	2.1		14.4	19.8	...	22.0
3591	Motorcycles		20	19	...	24		0.6	0.6	...	0.6		5.3	6.6	...	6.0
3592	Bicycles and invalid carriages		30	34	34	41		0.9	1.2	1.3	1.3		8.5	12.6	13.0	14.0
3599	Other transport equipment n.e.c.		10	9	...	14		0.1	0.1	...	0.2		0.6	0.5	...	2.0
3610	Furniture		6933	6925	7233	7944		46.4	47.0	51.8	49.7		344.6	358.0	389.0	361.0
369	Manufacturing n.e.c.		2278	2255	2233	2616		9.7	9.2	9.1	9.6		82.7	78.9	78.0	79.0
3691	Jewellery and related articles		1150	1097	...	1082		3.6	3.6	...	3.5		33.6	31.6	...	30.0
3692	Musical instruments		22	23	...	30		-	0.1	...	0.1		0.5	0.5	...	1.0
3693	Sports goods		45	43	53	65		0.7	0.2	0.3	0.3		6.1	2.6	3.0	3.0
3694	Games and toys		53	55	63	66		0.5	0.8	0.7	0.7		3.5	5.5	5.0	6.0
3699	Other manufacturing n.e.c.		1008	1037	...	1373		4.9	4.5	...	5.0		39.0	38.7	...	41.0
3710	Recycling of metal waste and scrap		59	71	...	112		0.6	0.7	...	0.8		6.7	8.0	...	10.0
3720	Recycling of non-metal waste and scrap		120	142	...	219		0.9	1.0	...	1.1		9.3	11.0	...	12.0
D	Total manufacturing		78789	78431	80558	104262		866.5	849.5	831.6	850.6		8502.8	8672.5	8813.0	8731.0

Portugal

ISIC Revision 3		Output					Value added in factor values					Gross fixed capital formation		
			(millions of Euros)					(millions of Euros)					(millions of Euros)	
ISIC	Industry	Note	2002	2003	2004	2005	Note	2002	2003	2004	2005	Note	2004	2005
151	Processed meat,fish,fruit,vegetables,fats		3145.6	3133.5	3338.0	3312.0		530.4	577.7	587.0	594.0		200.0	147.0
1511	Processing/preserving of meat		1404.2	1424.2	1512.0	1486.0		246.4	276.2	264.0	290.0		77.0	61.0
1512	Processing/preserving of fish		625.6	627.5	687.0	629.0		99.1	106.5	118.0	122.0		38.0	32.0
1513	Processing/preserving of fruit & vegetables		463.4	503.1	555.0	547.0		112.6	117.5	136.0	118.0		61.0	32.0
1514	Vegetable and animal oils and fats		652.4	578.7	585.0	651.0		72.3	77.5	70.0	64.0		24.0	22.0
1520	Dairy products		1421.9	1459.6	1486.0	1444.0		260.2	279.7	272.0	277.0		110.0	39.0
153	Grain mill products; starches; animal feeds		1487.6	1417.7	1490.0	1332.0		219.1	214.5	217.0	218.0		40.0	33.0
1531	Grain mill products		...	...	...	...		...	...	...	...		...	...
1532	Starches and starch products		...	...	...	...		...	...	...	...		...	...
1533	Prepared animal feeds		1068.7	996.7	1032.0	939.0		148.5	141.0	142.0	142.0		21.0	18.0
154	Other food products		2096.8	2276.6	2371.0	2407.0		771.1	831.2	876.0	862.0		171.0	127.0
1541	Bakery products		1025.7	1183.1	1276.0	1283.0		432.3	484.9	532.0	534.0		112.0	90.0
1542	Sugar		287.6	279.5	...	270.0		61.5	62.8	...	43.0		...	3.0
1543	Cocoa, chocolate and sugar confectionery		51.8	54.0	56.0	57.0		17.0	18.9	21.0	20.0		4.0	5.0
1544	Macaroni, noodles & similar products		30.3	29.6	31.0	55.0		8.0	5.9	7.0	15.0		4.0	-
1549	Other food products n.e.c.		701.4	731.0	...	...		252.2	258.8	...	...		...	...
155	Beverages		1985.7	2040.1	2091.0	2037.0		483.1	508.8	504.0	531.0		183.0	123.0
1551	Distilling, rectifying & blending of spirits		...	...	51.0	...		...	...	15.0	...		4.0	...
1552	Wines		...	...	...	...		...	...	...	...		...	...
1553	Malt liquors and malt		...	...	...	...		...	...	...	...		...	...
1554	Soft drinks; mineral waters		535.4	...	518.0	517.0		116.2	...	108.0	110.0		40.0	23.0
1600	Tobacco products		403.2	407.7	418.0	431.0		173.2	180.5	176.0	188.0		20.0	5.0
171	Spinning, weaving and finishing of textiles		1874.5	1816.7	1751.0	1568.0		598.5	574.9	561.0	485.0		153.0	143.0
1711	Textile fibre preparation; textile weaving		1448.4	1409.9	1371.0	...		433.3	406.4	397.0	...		108.0	...
1712	Finishing of textiles		426.1	406.8	380.0	395.0		165.2	168.5	163.0	159.0		45.0	34.0
172	Other textiles		1469.7	1283.6	...	1236.0		436.7	426.6	...	410.0		...	72.0
1721	Made-up textile articles, except apparel		822.3	652.6	...	555.0		214.5	181.2	...	173.0		...	33.0
1722	Carpets and rugs		84.6	...	93.0	86.0		31.4	...	33.0	29.0		5.0	4.0
1723	Cordage, rope, twine and netting		179.8	188.5	192.0	199.0		59.1	62.0	61.0	58.0		14.0	9.0
1729	Other textiles n.e.c.		382.9	...	404.0	395.0		131.7	...	158.0	150.0		44.0	26.0
1730	Knitted and crocheted fabrics and articles		1019.7	965.1	...	827.0		287.6	265.4	...	231.0		...	35.0
1810	Wearing apparel, except fur apparel		3537.7	3752.2	3848.0	...		1355.8	1353.2	1361.0	...		149.0	...
1820	Dressing & dyeing of fur; processing of fur		22.4	22.2	20.0	...		7.1	6.8	7.0	...		1.0	...
191	Tanning, dressing and processing of leather		276.2	251.9	...	...		59.2	62.1	...	...		...	...
1911	Tanning and dressing of leather		232.0	211.3	...	189.0		42.2	45.8	...	43.0		...	8.0
1912	Luggage, handbags, etc.; saddlery & harness		44.2	40.7	...	...		17.1	16.2	...	...		...	...
1920	Footwear		2155.7	1980.1	...	1726.0		624.1	603.5	...	547.0		...	63.0
2010	Sawmilling and planing of wood		435.9	443.9	457.0	495.0		126.8	125.0	123.0	135.0		27.0	27.0
202	Products of wood, cork, straw, etc.		2813.5	2814.5	2845.0	2756.0		637.5	673.8	712.0	700.0		154.0	110.0
2021	Veneer sheets, plywood, particle board, etc.		380.8	363.0	414.0	427.0		86.6	80.6	103.0	104.0		29.0	10.0
2022	Builders' carpentry and joinery		614.5	641.5	...	647.0		196.2	220.7	...	223.0		...	45.0
2023	Wooden containers		56.4	49.1	...	62.0		14.3	13.7	...	17.0		...	3.0
2029	Other wood products; articles of cork/straw		1761.8	1761.0	1671.0	1619.0		340.4	358.9	358.0	357.0		71.0	52.0
210	Paper and paper products		2345.7	2266.4	2293.0	2301.0		817.9	699.4	678.0	720.0		221.0	73.0
2101	Pulp, paper and paperboard		1694.8	1589.6	1604.0	1644.0		626.2	508.9	476.0	532.0		160.0	27.0
2102	Corrugated paper and paperboard		519.7	524.1	492.0	494.0		151.8	153.1	149.0	143.0		42.0	34.0
2109	Other articles of paper and paperboard		131.2	152.8	197.0	164.0		39.9	37.3	53.0	45.0		20.0	12.0
221	Publishing		1055.7	1418.1	1298.0	1224.0		370.4	504.5	427.0	428.0		40.0	31.0
2211	Publishing of books and other publications		327.5	381.0	372.0	336.0		121.6	140.6	127.0	128.0		14.0	8.0
2212	Publishing of newspapers, journals, etc.		697.4	1006.6	885.0	824.0		239.8	357.6	290.0	283.0		22.0	21.0
2213	Publishing of recorded media		15.6	16.0	22.0	28.0		4.6	2.1	5.0	7.0		2.0	1.0
2219	Other publishing		15.2	14.5	19.0	36.0		4.3	4.3	6.0	10.0		2.0	1.0

continued

Portugal

ISIC Revision 3		Output					Value added in factor values					Gross fixed capital formation		
			(millions of Euros)					(millions of Euros)					(millions of Euros)	
ISIC	Industry	Note	2002	2003	2004	2005	Note	2002	2003	2004	2005	Note	2004	2005
222	Printing and related service activities		1238.7	1269.0	1398.0	1283.0		561.4	581.4	628.0	573.0		172.0	143.0
2221	Printing		917.9	975.9	1062.0	970.0		439.9	455.3	499.0	445.0		143.0	106.0
2222	Service activities related to printing		320.9	293.1	336.0	313.0		121.5	126.2	129.0	128.0		29.0	37.0
2230	Reproduction of recorded media		21.1	28.1	12.0	12.0		6.0	7.1	3.0	6.0		3.0	-
2310	Coke oven products		-	-	-	-		-	-	-	-		-	-
2320	Refined petroleum products		5250.7	5578.8	6299.0	...		379.3	520.3	603.0	...		105.0	...
2330	Processing of nuclear fuel		-	-	-	-		-	-	-	-		-	-
241	Basic chemicals		1428.7	1497.4	1728.0	...		287.8	299.8	357.0	...		60.0	...
2411	Basic chemicals, except fertilizers		...	605.0	615.0	599.0		...	186.0	192.0	191.0		28.0	24.0
2412	Fertilizers and nitrogen compounds		216.0	221.9	221.0	233.0		47.7	52.1	46.0	39.0		5.0	9.0
2413	Plastics in primary forms; synthetic rubber		...	670.0	892.0	...		...	62.0	120.0	...		26.0	...
242	Other chemicals		2058.6	2101.9	...	...		670.2	707.7	...	...		...	...
2421	Pesticides and other agro-chemical products		34.0	58.2	...	...		8.6	17.8	...	...		...	...
2422	Paints, varnishes, printing ink and mastics		484.9	521.9	551.0	579.0		158.7	172.0	170.0	165.0		22.0	14.0
2423	Pharmaceuticals, medicinal chemicals, etc.		1017.6	979.5	928.0	965.0		359.2	364.7	347.0	368.0		57.0	26.0
2424	Soap, cleaning & cosmetic preparations		324.4	338.4	...	233.0		88.0	94.9	...	73.0		...	47.0
2429	Other chemical products n.e.c.		197.6	204.0	...	198.0		55.7	58.4	...	59.0		...	20.0
2430	Man-made fibres		141.0	161.0	182.0	101.0		34.1	31.5	33.0	14.0		12.0	25.0
251	Rubber products		497.4	495.1	564.0	530.0		193.2	210.0	243.0	141.0		34.0	21.0
2511	Rubber tyres and tubes		394.1	387.2	...	409.0		155.9	169.7	...	95.0		...	17.0
2519	Other rubber products		103.3	107.9	140.0	121.0		37.4	40.2	50.0	46.0		8.0	5.0
2520	Plastic products		1543.7	1601.6	1738.0	1899.0		481.0	507.5	519.0	525.0		168.0	128.0
2610	Glass and glass products		665.5	703.5	708.0	...		263.5	275.9	278.0	...		95.0	...
269	Non-metallic mineral products n.e.c.		3910.5	3697.0	3817.0	...		1565.9	1427.5	1398.0	...		321.0	...
2691	Pottery, china and earthenware		...	...	...	...		...	...	...	...		...	...
2692	Refractory ceramic products		31.7	30.2	25.0	22.0		13.6	12.0	9.0	8.0		1.0	2.0
2693	Struct.non-refractory clay; ceramic products		638.0	546.7	575.0	589.0		278.8	221.7	231.0	226.0		56.0	46.0
2694	Cement, lime and plaster		808.5	697.9	720.0	...		445.8	354.3	334.0	...		84.0	...
2695	Articles of concrete, cement and plaster		1185.7	1109.0	1200.0	1234.0		285.7	276.8	270.0	288.0		73.0	90.0
2696	Cutting, shaping & finishing of stone		565.5	577.3	580.0	659.0		221.4	217.0	231.0	255.0		42.0	66.0
2699	Other non-metallic mineral products n.e.c.		122.8	145.6	178.0	...		35.8	43.2	48.0	...		17.0	...
2710	Basic iron and steel		769.8	1025.0	...	1231.0		150.3	172.8	...	168.0		...	18.0
2720	Basic precious and non-ferrous metals		291.9	302.8	...	342.0		68.2	68.5	...	66.0		...	19.0
273	Casting of metals		288.2	259.6	...	319.0		122.3	107.5	...	118.0		...	24.0
2731	Casting of iron and steel		173.5	148.2	152.0	196.0		79.6	64.9	65.0	72.0		17.0	16.0
2732	Casting of non-ferrous metals		114.7	111.4	...	123.0		42.7	42.6	...	45.0		...	8.0
281	Struct.metal products;tanks;steam generators		1687.8	1679.3	2005.0	2296.0		521.3	520.5	610.0	726.0		127.0	94.0
2811	Structural metal products		1435.7	1431.5	1750.0	2056.0		451.0	462.0	539.0	661.0		118.0	85.0
2812	Tanks, reservoirs and containers of metal		166.8	155.8	175.0	176.0		49.0	44.7	53.0	53.0		7.0	9.0
2813	Steam generators		85.3	91.9	79.0	64.0		21.3	13.8	18.0	12.0		2.0	-
289	Other metal products; metal working services		2329.2	2250.3	2399.0	2478.0		849.1	839.9	871.0	899.0		168.0	175.0
2891	Metal forging/pressing/stamping/roll-forming		112.2	94.2	105.0	136.0		35.2	29.7	36.0	40.0		8.0	10.0
2892	Treatment & coating of metals		756.2	731.7	706.0	721.0		277.7	290.4	275.0	297.0		51.0	51.0
2893	Cutlery, hand tools and general hardware		538.9	491.6	523.0	483.0		208.9	195.9	209.0	193.0		42.0	28.0
2899	Other fabricated metal products n.e.c.		921.8	932.7	1065.0	1139.0		327.3	323.9	352.0	370.0		67.0	87.0
291	General purpose machinery		939.3	1021.2	1120.0	1230.0		335.7	351.0	389.0	395.0		61.0	39.0
2911	Engines & turbines (not for transport equipment)		12.8	10.8	14.0	12.0		4.3	4.5	5.0	6.0		-	1.0
2912	Pumps, compressors, taps and valves		207.6	237.3	...	266.0		71.9	74.5	...	76.0		...	9.0
2913	Bearings, gears, gearing & driving elements		34.9	40.0	...	52.0		14.4	15.4	...	21.0		...	2.0
2914	Ovens, furnaces and furnace burners		13.1	12.8	...	22.0		5.3	4.9	...	9.0		...	1.0
2915	Lifting and handling equipment		272.9	306.3	321.0	358.0		98.9	117.6	122.0	129.0		7.0	7.0
2919	Other general purpose machinery		398.0	414.0	...	519.0		140.9	134.1	...	155.0		...	20.0

292	Special purpose machinery	1263.7	1251.3	1408.0	1512.0	577.5	540.2	599.0	630.0	116.0	110.0
2921	Agricultural and forestry machinery	137.1	128.2	141.0	156.0	54.5	49.4	53.0	56.0	8.0	8.0
2922	Machine tools	94.3	103.5	124.0	142.0	40.5	44.3	53.0	64.0	16.0	12.0
2923	Machinery for metallurgy	10.0	8.9	6.0	8.0	3.9	3.5	3.0	3.0	1.0	1.0
2924	Machinery for mining & construction	102.0	104.9	...	118.0	33.6	34.7	...	39.0	...	8.0
2925	Food/beverage/tobacco processing machinery	130.7	124.3	...	152.0	53.0	54.0	...	64.0	...	6.0
2926	Machinery for textile, apparel and leather	74.7	76.0	71.0	71.0	46.4	47.8	40.0	38.0	6.0	8.0
2927	Weapons and ammunition	34.3	36.4	44.0	41.0	6.7	3.9	7.0	11.0	1.0	-
2929	Other special purpose machinery	680.5	669.0	...	824.0	339.0	302.4	...	356.0	...	68.0
2930	Domestic appliances n.e.c.	442.3	443.0	424.0	361.0	119.3	131.1	128.0	113.0	13.0	13.0
3000	Office, accounting and computing machinery	34.0	127.0	90.0	66.0	6.6	25.3	24.0	21.0	3.0	3.0
3110	Electric motors, generators and transformers	138.2	180.7	...	...	45.1	48.9	...	...	...	...
3120	Electricity distribution & control apparatus	...	...	370.0	391.0	...	...	138.0	143.0	20.0	15.0
3130	Insulated wire and cable	344.7	347.5	396.0	486.0	64.2	70.6	65.0	80.0	21.0	8.0
3140	Accumulators, primary cells and batteries	...	...	...	...	...	...	...	...	...	...
3150	Lighting equipment and electric lamps	166.6	156.3	...	164.0	61.3	55.0	...	62.0	...	9.0
3190	Other electrical equipment n.e.c.	1164.2	1061.7	...	874.0	338.8	301.3	...	222.0	...	11.0
3210	Electronic valves, tubes, etc.	846.3	973.3	1274.0	...	114.9	128.4	162.0	...	101.0	...
3220	TV/radio transmitters; line comm. apparatus	894.1	743.1	811.0	...	228.1	195.4	225.0	...	14.0	...
3230	TV and radio receivers and associated goods	1130.0	1190.0	1220.0	1115.0	191.6	228.1	248.0	210.0	54.0	25.0
331	Medical, measuring, testing appliances, etc.	236.9	280.1	...	368.0	83.7	90.2	...	122.0	...	13.0
3311	Medical, surgical and orthopaedic equipment	88.1	87.9	...	124.0	37.0	35.0	...	55.0	...	8.0
3312	Measuring/testing/navigating appliances,etc.	35.9	62.3	69.0	123.0	16.1	23.4	27.0	28.0	8.0	3.0
3313	Industrial process control equipment	112.8	130.0	...	121.0	30.6	31.7	...	39.0	...	3.0
3320	Optical instruments & photographic equipment	121.2	127.6	123.0	116.0	46.4	46.8	43.0	45.0	10.0	5.0
3330	Watches and clocks	5.4	4.4	...	4.0	2.8	2.6	...	2.0	...	1.0
3410	Motor vehicles	2852.3	2456.6	2146.0	1978.0	448.3	339.4	306.0	302.0	103.0	9.0
3420	Automobile bodies, trailers & semi-trailers	169.1	165.4	227.0	225.0	53.7	46.1	66.0	58.0	10.0	10.0
3430	Parts/accessories for automobiles	1339.1	1413.4	1652.0	1701.0	336.6	364.3	413.0	394.0	145.0	95.0
351	Building and repairing of ships and boats	330.6	290.1	271.0	316.0	99.9	76.9	82.0	100.0	32.0	11.0
3511	Building and repairing of ships	307.2	260.9	234.0	269.0	93.5	68.6	70.0	86.0	28.0	8.0
3512	Building/repairing of pleasure/sport. boats	23.4	29.2	38.0	48.0	6.4	8.3	12.0	14.0	4.0	3.0
3520	Railway/tramway locomotives & rolling stock	223.8	212.7	...	122.0	90.2	73.3	...	40.0	...	2.0
3530	Aircraft and spacecraft	80.9	116.9	143.0	134.0	31.4	42.7	52.0	49.0	5.0	2.0
359	Transport equipment n.e.c.	81.4	158.9	...	180.0	27.0	42.0	...	49.0	...	12.0
3591	Motorcycles	22.0	30.4	...	27.0	9.1	11.3	...	10.0	...	2.0
3592	Bicycles and invalid carriages	56.3	125.9	128.0	139.0	16.3	29.2	32.0	35.0	5.0	10.0
3599	Other transport equipment n.e.c.	3.1	2.5	...	14.0	1.1	1.0	...	4.0	...	-
3610	Furniture	1891.3	2022.2	2125.0	1998.0	632.1	632.4	678.0	636.0	117.0	93.0
369	Manufacturing n.e.c.	536.0	464.5	480.0	490.0	169.8	150.7	152.0	143.0	25.0	17.0
3691	Jewellery and related articles	218.5	184.5	...	157.0	63.6	52.2	...	45.0	...	4.0
3692	Musical instruments	1.8	2.3	...	3.0	0.8	0.7	...	1.0	...	-
3693	Sports goods	80.0	19.7	29.0	27.0	16.4	4.9	6.0	5.0	1.0	1.0
3694	Games and toys	15.3	23.2	20.0	24.0	6.7	9.7	8.0	10.0	1.0	1.0
3699	Other manufacturing n.e.c.	220.3	234.7	...	280.0	82.3	83.2	...	82.0	...	11.0
3710	Recycling of metal waste and scrap	113.3	126.1	...	113.0	17.3	18.9	...	36.0	...	13.0
3720	Recycling of non-metal waste and scrap	91.3	81.6	...	81.0	24.2	26.5	...	31.0	...	7.0
D	Total manufacturing	65481.3	66221.6	69712.0	69352.0	18208.2	18344.9	19002.0	18510.0	4180.0	2901.0

Portugal

ISIC Revision 3			Index numbers of industrial production											
			(2000=100)											
ISIC	Industry	Note	1995	1996	1997	1998	1999	2000	2001	2002	2003	2004	2005	2006
15	Food and beverages		87	89	91	94	98	100	102	104	104	107	106	110
16	Tobacco products		61	58	61	77	82	100	109	118	115	120	127	127
17	Textiles		115	107	110	108	104	100	101	99	92	86	79	74
18	Wearing apparel, fur		129	127	115	113	105	100	103	94	90	82	74	72
19	Leather, leather products and footwear		144	145	145	131	118	100	98	90	78	72	64	59
20	Wood products (excl. furniture)		92	97	105	107	99	100	96	98	100	97	97	101
21	Paper and paper products		86	84	90	93	94	100	116	125	144	149	150	154
22	Printing and publishing		...	...	...	...	...	100	97	96	97	95	97	97
23	Coke,refined petroleum products,nuclear fuel		112	101	112	120	117	100	104	103	107	107	110	113
24	Chemicals and chemical products		96	98	100	100	100	100	94	100	104	102	102	103
25	Rubber and plastics products		64	71	78	82	95	100	106	115	115	118	131	131
26	Non-metallic mineral products		78	80	89	92	97	100	99	97	91	91	89	88
27	Basic metals		81	78	89	91	102	100	92	93	92	95	91	99
28	Fabricated metal products		76	83	91	97	99	100	104	111	110	110	108	114
29	Machinery and equipment n.e.c.		80	88	96	100	100	100	99	99	95	90	88	85
30	Office, accounting and computing machinery		...	...	...	...	...	100	87	71	58	63	78	90
31	Electrical machinery and apparatus		78	82	89	93	101	100	100	95	83	78	66	60
32	Radio,television and communication equipment		39	42	42	49	71	100	114	115	161	175	207	266
33	Medical, precision and optical instruments		...	...	...	...	...	100	179	181	120	113	108	112
34	Motor vehicles, trailers, semi-trailers		84	107	120	123	116	100	107	105	98	93	87	91
35	Other transport equipment		96	104	98	125	115	100	92	79	69	64	60	56
36	Furniture; manufacturing n.e.c.		87	96	97	107	103	100	107	108	108	109	97	91
37	Recycling		...	...	...	...	...	100	99	101	97	102	103	102
D	Total manufacturing		87	92	96	98	100	100	102	103	102	101	100	102

Puerto Rico

Supplier of information:
Puerto Rico Planning Board, San Juan.

Basic source of data:
Annual survey.

Major deviations from ISIC (Revision 2):
Data, except for employment data, are collected according to the national classification system (Standard Industrial Classification System), which is not strictly comparable to ISIC (Revision 2). Employment data are reported according to NAICS (North American Industrial Classification System), which is also not strictly comparable to ISIC (Revision 2).

Reference period:
Fiscal year ending 30 June of the year indicated.

Scope:
All establishments with at least one paid employee and operating during a specified week in March.

Method of data collection:
Individual sites are visited by enumerators.

Type of enumeration:
Not reported.

Adjusted for non-response:
Yes.

Concepts and definitions of variables:
No deviations from the standard UN concepts and definitions are reported.

Related national publications:
None reported.

Puerto Rico

ISIC Revision 2		Establishments					Number of persons engaged					Wages and salaries paid to employees				
		Note	(number)				Note	(number)				Note	(millions of US Dollars)			
ISIC	Industry		2003	2004	2005	2006		2003	2004	2005	2006		2003	2004	2005	2006
311/2	Food products		...	...	...	...		13440	...	...	...		366.2	254.1	257.1	257.6
3111	Slaughtering, preparing and preserving meat		...	...	...	...		...	...	...	...		49.3	28.8	32.6	33.7
3112	Dairy products		...	...	...	...		...	...	...	...		45.7	43.6	43.3	42.0
3113	Canning, preserving of fruits and vegetables		...	...	...	...		...	...	...	...		30.2	18.2	18.3	18.5
3114	Canning, preserving and processing of fish		...	...	...	...		...	...	...	...		9.7	9.0	5.4	5.2
3115	Vegetable and animal oils and fats		...	...	...	...		...	...	...	...		-	-	-	-
3116	Grain mill products		...	...	...	...		...	...	...	...		27.5	16.5	17.9	18.3
3117	Bakery products		...	...	...	...		...	...	...	...		100.9	89.8	93.1	92.2
3118	Sugar factories and refineries		...	...	...	...		...	...	...	...	a/	44.4	20.0	18.5	20.2
3119	Cocoa, chocolate and sugar confectionery		...	...	...	...		...	...	...	...	a/	...	...	...	...
3121	Other food products		...	...	...	...		...	...	...	...		58.2	27.8	28.0	27.4
3122	Prepared animal feeds		...	...	...	...		...	...	...	...		-	-	-	-
313	Beverages		...	...	...	...		3040b/	...	...	...		120.1	121.0	121.8	137.9
3131	Distilling, rectifying and blending spirits		...	...	...	...		...	...	...	...		29.4	30.3	31.0	32.1
3132	Wine industries		...	...	...	...		...	...	...	...		-	-	-	-
3133	Malt liquors and malt		...	...	...	...		...	...	...	...		10.1	11.0	10.0	11.0
3134	Soft drinks and carbonated waters		...	...	...	...		...	...	...	...		80.6	79.7	80.9	94.7
314	Tobacco		...	...	...	...		...b/	...	...	...		28.0	34.5	40.5	41.9
321	Textiles		...	...	...	...		...	...	...	...		7.1	4.1	3.8	3.6
3211	Spinning, weaving and finishing textiles		...	...	...	...		...	...	...	...		...	...	...	...
3212	Made-up textile goods excl. wearing apparel		...	...	...	...		...	...	...	...		...	...	...	...
3213	Knitting mills		...	...	...	...		...	...	...	...		...	...	...	...
3214	Carpets and rugs		...	...	...	...		...	...	...	...		...	...	...	...
3215	Cordage, rope and twine		...	...	...	...		...	...	...	...		...	...	...	...
3219	Other textiles		...	...	...	...		...	...	...	...		...	...	...	...
322	Wearing apparel, except footwear		...	...	...	...		8480	...	...	...		145.9	136.6	131.9	121.6
323	Leather and fur products		...	...	...	...		...	...	...	...	c/	20.5	24.7	26.8	24.6
3231	Tanneries and leather finishing		...	...	...	...		...	...	...	...		...	...	...	...
3232	Fur dressing and dyeing industries		...	...	...	...		...	...	...	...		...	...	...	...
3233	Leather prods. excl. footwear and wearing		...	...	...	...		...	...	...	...		...	...	...	...
324	Footwear, except rubber or plastic		...	...	...	...		...	...	...	...	c/	...	...	...	...
331	Wood products, except furniture		...	...	...	...		...	...	...	...		18.8	20.8	21.6	21.4
3311	Sawmills, planing and other wood mills		...	...	...	...		...	...	...	...		...	...	...	...
3312	Wooden and cane containers		...	...	...	...		...	...	...	...		...	...	...	...
3319	Other wood and cork products		...	...	...	...		...	...	...	...		...	...	...	...
332	Furniture and fixtures, excl. metal		...	...	...	...		3800	...	...	...		22.7	22.0	22.3	20.5
341	Paper and products		...	...	...	...		...	...	...	...		38.9	37.5	36.4	34.3
3411	Pulp, paper and paperboard articles		...	...	...	...		...	...	...	...		...	...	...	...
3412	Containers of paper and paperboard		...	...	...	...		...	...	...	...		...	...	...	...
3419	Other pulp, paper and paperboard articles		...	...	...	...		...	...	...	...		...	...	...	...
342	Printing and publishing		...	...	...	...		...	...	...	...		162.5	175.6	181.9	177.3
351	Industrial chemicals		...	...	...	...		30410d/	...	...	...		...	...	...	...
3511	Basic chemicals excl. fertilizers		...	...	...	...		...	...	...	...		...	...	...	...
3512	Fertilizers and pesticides		...	...	...	...		...	...	...	...		...	...	...	...
3513	Synthetic resins and plastic materials		...	...	...	...		...	...	...	...		...	...	...	...
352	Other chemicals		...	...	...	...		...d/	...	...	...		1332.1	1486.3	1479.7	1589.3
3521	Paints, varnishes and lacquers		...	...	...	...		...	...	...	...		16.8	17.9	17.6	29.8
3522	Drugs and medicines		...	...	...	...		...	...	...	...		1181.0	1341.1	1340.8	1437.0
3523	Soap, cleaning preps., perfumes, cosmetics		...	...	...	...		...	...	...	...		...	...	...	...
3529	Other chemical products		...	...	...	...		...	...	...	...		134.3	127.3	121.3	122.5
353	Petroleum refineries		...	...	...	...		...	...	...	...		20.6	22.4	23.4	24.9

354	Misc. petroleum and coal products		...	...	...	...	...	...	...	...		22.9	29.5	28.6	25.6
355	Rubber products		...	...	...	...	280	...	...	...	e/	92.8	95.6	94.5	92.4
3551	Tyres and tubes		...	...	...	...	...	...	...	...		...	...	...	...
3559	Other rubber products		...	...	...	...	...	...	...	...		...	...	...	...
356	Plastic products		...	...	...	...	3050	...	...	...	e/	...	...	...	...
361	Pottery, china and earthenware		...	...	...	...	...	...	...	...		...	...	...	...
362	Glass and products		...	...	...	...	...	...	...	...		23.0	24.3	24.4	22.8
369	Other non-metallic mineral products		...	...	...	...	...	...	...	...		114.7	110.1	110.8	113.3
3691	Structural clay products		...	...	...	...	...	...	...	...		...	...	...	...
3692	Cement, lime and plaster		...	...	...	...	...	...	...	...		...	...	...	...
3699	Other non-metallic mineral products		...	...	...	...	...	...	...	...		...	...	...	...
371	Iron and steel		...	...	...	...	...	...	...	...	f/	19.7	20.2	22.1	23.3
372	Non-ferrous metals		...	...	...	...	...	...	...	...	f/	...	...	...	...
381	Fabricated metal products		...	...	...	...	6260	...	...	...		94.2	101.7	98.4	95.4
3811	Cutlery, hand tools and general hardware		...	...	...	...	...	...	...	...		...	...	...	...
3812	Furniture and fixtures primarily of metal		...	...	...	...	...	...	...	...		...	...	...	...
3813	Structural metal products		...	...	...	...	...	...	...	...		...	...	...	...
3819	Other fabricated metal products		...	...	...	...	...	...	...	...		...	...	...	...
382	Non-electrical machinery		...	...	...	...	...	...	...	...		149.5	151.2	143.7	137.9
3821	Engines and turbines		...	...	...	...	...	...	...	...		...	...	...	...
3822	Agricultural machinery and equipment		...	...	...	...	...	...	...	...		...	...	...	...
3823	Metal and wood working machinery		...	...	...	...	...	...	...	...		...	...	...	...
3824	Other special industrial machinery		...	...	...	...	...	...	...	...		...	...	...	...
3825	Office, computing and accounting machinery		...	...	...	...	...	...	...	...		...	...	...	...
3829	Other non-electrical machinery and equipment		...	...	...	...	...	...	...	...		...	...	...	...
383	Electrical machinery		...	...	...	...	...	...	...	...		290.9	313.8	322.4	315.0
3831	Electrical industrial machinery		...	...	...	...	...	...	...	...		...	...	...	...
3832	Radio, television and communication equipment		...	...	...	...	...	...	...	...		...	...	...	...
3833	Electrical appliances and housewares		...	...	...	...	...	...	...	...		...	...	...	...
3839	Other electrical apparatus and supplies		...	...	...	...	...	...	...	...		...	...	...	...
384	Transport equipment		...	...	...	...	...	...	...	...		12.9	12.1	8.8	7.7
3841	Shipbuilding and repairing		...	...	...	...	...	...	...	...		...	...	...	...
3842	Railroad equipment		...	...	...	...	...	...	...	...		...	...	...	...
3843	Motor vehicles		...	...	...	...	...	...	...	...		...	...	...	...
3844	Motorcycles and bicycles		...	...	...	...	...	...	...	...		...	...	...	...
3845	Aircraft		...	...	...	...	...	...	...	...		...	...	...	...
3849	Other transport equipment		...	...	...	...	...	...	...	...		...	...	...	...
385	Professional and scientific equipment		...	...	...	...	...	...	...	...		446.9	483.2	542.4	599.6
3851	Prof. and scientific equipment n.e.c.		...	...	...	...	...	...	...	...		...	...	...	...
3852	Photographic and optical goods		...	...	...	...	...	...	...	...		...	...	...	...
3853	Watches and clocks		...	...	...	...	...	...	...	...		...	...	...	...
390	Other manufacturing industries		...	...	...	...	...	...	...	...		20.0	18.5	17.0	17.3
3901	Jewellery and related articles		...	...	...	...	...	...	...	...		...	...	...	...
3902	Musical instruments		...	...	...	...	...	...	...	...		...	...	...	...
3903	Sporting and athletic goods		...	...	...	...	...	...	...	...		...	...	...	...
3909	Manufacturing industries, n.e.c.		...	...	...	...	...	...	...	...		...	...	...	...
3	Total manufacturing		...	...	...	...	118200	...	...	...		3474.7	3706.4	3761.0	3911.5

a/ 3118 includes 3119.
b/ 313 includes 314.
c/ 323 includes 324.
d/ 351 includes 352.
e/ 355 includes 356.
f/ 371 includes 372.

Puerto Rico

ISIC Revision 2		Output					Value added					Gross fixed capital formation		
			(millions of US Dollars)					(millions of US Dollars)					(millions of US Dollars)	
ISIC	Industry	Note	2003	2004	2005	2006	Note	2003	2004	2005	2006	Note	2005	2006
311/2	Food products		1947.4	2006.8	2108.1	2107.5		468.5	450.6	473.4	456.2		...	...
3111	Slaughtering, preparing and preserving meat		223.8	224.4	261.1	277.3		54.2	49.4	56.9	57.6		...	...
3112	Dairy products		339.8	336.2	351.9	322.1		60.1	57.5	68.0	49.9		...	...
3113	Canning, preserving of fruits and vegetables		167.0	176.7	171.3	174.9		33.5	34.6	29.8	29.6		...	...
3114	Canning, preserving and processing of fish		70.0	85.0	119.7	126.6		10.7	20.0	17.9	14.9		...	...
3115	Vegetable and animal oils and fats		-	-	-	-		-	-	-	-		...	...
3116	Grain mill products		275.0	316.8	326.4	325.9		32.5	36.0	41.6	40.1		...	...
3117	Bakery products		432.1	430.1	433.6	436.6		158.5	147.9	153.7	150.2		...	...
3118	Sugar factories and refineries	a/	122.6	129.6	138.8	147.6	a/	52.6	47.1	44.1	50.6		...	...
3119	Cocoa, chocolate and sugar confectionery	a/	...	...	...	...	a/	...	...	...	...		...	...
3121	Other food products		316.9	307.2	305.5	296.5		66.7	58.3	65.4	63.3		...	...
3122	Prepared animal feeds		-	-	-	-		-	-	-	-		...	...
313	Beverages		3245.7	4307.0	4583.5	5071.6		1433.6	1751.7	1838.8	2508.2		...	...
3131	Distilling, rectifying and blending spirits		202.4	212.0	237.0	232.4		450.3	472.5	448.2	478.7		...	...
3132	Wine industries		-	-	-	-		-	-	-	-		...	...
3133	Malt liquors and malt		88.8	104.7	106.0	120.7		41.5	45.9	46.8	45.8		...	...
3134	Soft drinks and carbonated waters		2954.5	3990.4	4240.4	4718.5		941.9	1233.3	1339.8	1977.7		...	...
314	Tobacco		250.7	230.5	266.1	275.1		157.1	148.4	159.0	158.0		...	...
321	Textiles		33.0	21.8	15.7	14.5		8.3	5.3	4.5	4.5		...	...
3211	Spinning, weaving and finishing textiles		...	...	...	...		...	...	...	...		...	...
3212	Made-up textile goods excl. wearing apparel		...	...	...	...		...	...	...	...		...	...
3213	Knitting mills		...	...	...	...		...	...	...	...		...	...
3214	Carpets and rugs		...	...	...	...		...	...	...	...		...	...
3215	Cordage, rope and twine		...	...	...	...		...	...	...	...		...	...
3219	Other textiles		...	...	...	...		...	...	...	...		...	...
322	Wearing apparel, except footwear		789.5	793.9	750.0	562.3		352.6	343.9	325.3	227.7		...	...
323	Leather and fur products	b/	130.1	139.8	149.7	74.5	b/	44.4	51.5	52.5	29.1		...	...
3231	Tanneries and leather finishing		...	...	...	...		...	...	...	...		...	...
3232	Fur dressing and dyeing industries		...	...	...	...		...	...	...	...		...	...
3233	Leather prods. excl. footwear and wearing		...	...	...	...		...	...	...	...		...	...
324	Footwear, except rubber or plastic	b/	...	...	...	...	b/	...	...	...	...		...	...
331	Wood products, except furniture	c/	283.2	294.1	303.7	313.1	c/	96.3	97.3	91.1	85.5		...	...
3311	Sawmills, planing and other wood mills		...	...	...	...		...	...	...	...		...	...
3312	Wooden and cane containers		...	...	...	...		...	...	...	...		...	...
3319	Other wood and cork products		...	...	...	...		...	...	...	...		...	...
332	Furniture and fixtures, excl. metal	c/	...	...	...	...	c/	...	...	...	...		...	...
341	Paper and products		235.0	227.1	217.1	207.5		79.4	66.4	58.6	55.8		...	...
3411	Pulp, paper and paperboard articles		...	...	...	...		...	...	...	...		...	...
3412	Containers of paper and paperboard		...	...	...	...		...	...	...	...		...	...
3419	Other pulp, paper and paperboard articles		...	...	...	...		...	...	...	...		...	...
342	Printing and publishing		640.2	667.8	677.1	674.3		286.4	284.9	297.4	303.6		...	...
351	Industrial chemicals		135.0	129.5	137.0	223.7		50.6	47.3	52.5	53.7		...	...
3511	Basic chemicals excl. fertilizers		...	...	...	...		...	...	...	...		...	...
3512	Fertilizers and pesticides		...	...	...	...		...	...	...	...		...	...
3513	Synthetic resins and plastic materials		...	...	...	...		...	...	...	...		...	...
352	Other chemicals		44037.6	44959.1	44271.9	50411.9		19549.7	20452.8	21370.6	22580.5		...	...
3521	Paints, varnishes and lacquers		...	...	...	...		...	...	...	...		...	...
3522	Drugs and medicines		42785.0	43626.8	42716.5	48715.0		...	...	...	...		...	...
3523	Soap, cleaning preps., perfumes, cosmetics		...	...	...	...		...	...	...	...		...	...
3529	Other chemical products		1252.6	1332.3	1555.4	1696.9		...	...	...	...		...	...
353	Petroleum refineries		1246.3	1923.4	2384.4	3304.6	d/	32.2	133.8	117.4	119.3		...	...

354	Misc. petroleum and coal products		179.8	276.0	201.1	175.2	d/	...	...	...	...		...	...
355	Rubber products	e/	580.2	629.3	649.8	661.8	e/	197.8	208.2	216.0	221.2		...	...
3551	Tyres and tubes		...	...	...	...		...	...	...	...		...	...
3559	Other rubber products		...	...	...	...		...	...	...	...		...	...
356	Plastic products	e/	...	...	...	...	e/	...	...	...	...		...	...
361	Pottery, china and earthenware	f/	613.8	611.9	659.0	653.4	g/	238.6	234.8	251.6	283.6		...	...
362	Glass and products	f/	...	...	...	...	g/	...	...	...	...		...	...
369	Other non-metallic mineral products		140.1	155.2	166.7	182.0	g/	...	...	...	...		...	...
3691	Structural clay products		...	...	...	...		...	...	...	...		...	...
3692	Cement, lime and plaster		...	...	...	...		...	...	...	...		...	...
3699	Other non-metallic mineral products		...	...	...	...		...	...	...	...		...	...
371	Iron and steel	h/	265.0	317.3	381.1	532.4	h/	83.8	51.3	60.0	81.1		...	...
372	Non-ferrous metals	h/	...	...	...	...	h/	...	...	...	...		...	...
381	Fabricated metal products		546.9	553.5	602.7	595.0		180.5	201.0	208.7	191.7		...	...
3811	Cutlery, hand tools and general hardware		...	...	...	...		...	...	...	...		...	...
3812	Furniture and fixtures primarily of metal		...	...	...	...		...	...	...	...		...	...
3813	Structural metal products		...	...	...	...		...	...	...	...		...	...
3819	Other fabricated metal products		...	...	...	...		...	...	...	...		...	...
382	Non-electrical machinery		5857.7	3802.7	2631.1	2366.7		3506.5	3372.0	3306.8	3214.8		...	...
3821	Engines and turbines		...	...	...	...		...	...	...	...		...	...
3822	Agricultural machinery and equipment		...	...	...	...		...	...	...	...		...	...
3823	Metal and wood working machinery		...	...	...	...		...	...	...	...		...	...
3824	Other special industrial machinery		...	...	...	...		...	...	...	...		...	...
3825	Office, computing and accounting machinery		...	...	...	...		...	...	...	...		...	...
3829	Other non-electrical machinery and equipment		...	...	...	...		...	...	...	...		...	...
383	Electrical machinery		3146.1	5491.8	4024.7	4042.5		1770.7	1818.3	1904.1	1851.8		...	...
3831	Electrical industrial machinery		...	...	...	...		...	...	...	...		...	...
3832	Radio, television and communication equipment		...	...	...	...		...	...	...	...		...	...
3833	Electrical appliances and housewares		...	...	...	...		...	...	...	...		...	...
3839	Other electrical apparatus and supplies		...	...	...	...		...	...	...	...		...	...
384	Transport equipment		51.5	41.0	33.2	31.0		23.2	21.8	13.6	12.0		...	...
3841	Shipbuilding and repairing		...	...	...	...		...	...	...	...		...	...
3842	Railroad equipment		...	...	...	...		...	...	...	...		...	...
3843	Motor vehicles		...	...	...	...		...	...	...	...		...	...
3844	Motorcycles and bicycles		...	...	...	...		...	...	...	...		...	...
3845	Aircraft		...	...	...	...		...	...	...	...		...	...
3849	Other transport equipment		...	...	...	...		...	...	...	...		...	...
385	Professional and scientific equipment		6424.6	7837.5	9037.6	10516.4		2981.4	3539.6	3698.4	4156.8		...	...
3851	Prof. and scientific equipment n.e.c.		...	...	...	...		...	...	...	...		...	...
3852	Photographic and optical goods		...	...	...	...		...	...	...	...		...	...
3853	Watches and clocks		...	...	...	...		...	...	...	...		...	...
390	Other manufacturing industries		100.6	86.3	82.0	74.8		39.4	33.9	31.7	31.9		...	...
3901	Jewellery and related articles		...	...	...	...		...	...	...	...		...	...
3902	Musical instruments		...	...	...	...		...	...	...	...		...	...
3903	Sporting and athletic goods		...	...	...	...		...	...	...	...		...	...
3909	Manufacturing industries, n.e.c.		...	...	...	...		...	...	...	...		...	...
3	Total manufacturing		70880.0	75503.5	74333.5	83071.7		31530.4	33267.5	34534.0	36546.5		...	...

a/ 3118 includes 3119.
b/ 323 includes 324.
c/ 331 includes 332.
d/ 353 includes 354.
e/ 355 includes 356.
f/ 361 includes 362.
g/ 361 includes 362 and 369.
h/ 371 includes 372.

Qatar

Supplier of information:
The Planning Council, Department of Statistics, Doha.

Basic source of data:
Annual industrial survey.

Major deviations from ISIC (Revision 3):
None reported.

Reference period:
Calendar year.

Scope:
Establishments with 10 or more persons engaged.

Method of data collection:
Questionnaires are distributed by mail and collected by field enumerators.

Type of enumeration:
Not reported.

Adjusted for non-response:
Yes.

Concepts and definitions of variables:
No deviations from the standard UN concepts and definitions are reported.

Related national publications:
None reported.

Qatar

ISIC Revision 3		Number of establishments					Number of employees					Wages and salaries paid to employees				
			(number)					(number)					(thousands of Qatari Riyals)			
ISIC	Industry	Note	2003	2004	2005	2006	Note	2003	2004	2005	2006	Note	2003	2004	2005	2006
151	Processed meat,fish,fruit,vegetables,fats		2	6	6	6		224	256	264	275		5506	6143	6836	7459
1511	Processing/preserving of meat		1	1	1	1		206	206	229	246		5192	5192	5768	6230
1512	Processing/preserving of fish		-	-	-	-		-	-	-	-		-	-	-	-
1513	Processing/preserving of fruit & vegetables		1	5	5	5		18	35	35	29		314	951	1068	1229
1514	Vegetable and animal oils and fats		-	-	-	-		-	-	-	-		-	-	-	-
1520	Dairy products		4	8	8	8		381	569	771	801		6310	9789	13109	13668
153	Grain mill products; starches; animal feeds		7	9	9	9		172	209	215	243		5996	6791	7651	8423
1531	Grain mill products		7	9	9	9		172	209	215	243		5996	6791	7651	8423
1532	Starches and starch products		-	-	-	-		-	-	-	-		-	-	-	-
1533	Prepared animal feeds		-	-	-	-		-	-	-	-		-	-	-	-
154	Other food products		239	252	252	252		444	721	950	967		17036	23206	31533	32383
1541	Bakery products		210	228	228	228		418	624	681	695		14065	20671	25938	26669
1542	Sugar		-	-	-	-		-	-	-	-		-	-	-	-
1543	Cocoa, chocolate and sugar confectionery		3	7	7	7		...	10	10	10		960	317	305	317
1544	Macaroni, noodles & similar products		-	-	-	-		-	-	-	-		-	-	-	-
1549	Other food products n.e.c.		26	17	17	17		26	87	259	262		2011	2218	5290	5397
155	Beverages		5	9	9	9		288	693	461	1063		7945	14727	21727	22352
1551	Distilling, rectifying & blending of spirits		-	-	-	-		-	-	-	-		-	-	-	-
1552	Wines		-	-	-	-		-	-	-	-		-	-	-	-
1553	Malt liquors and malt		-	-	-	-		-	-	-	-		-	-	-	-
1554	Soft drinks; mineral waters		5	9	9	9		288	693	461	1063		7945	14727	21727	22352
1600	Tobacco products		...	...	...	...		...	...	...	...		...	...	...	...
171	Spinning, weaving and finishing of textiles		...	...	...	...		...	...	...	...		...	...	...	...
1711	Textile fibre preparation; textile weaving		...	...	...	...		...	...	...	...		...	...	...	...
1712	Finishing of textiles		...	...	...	...		...	...	...	...		...	...	...	...
172	Other textiles		79	53	53	53		...	181	512	526		5485	5300	10774	11056
1721	Made-up textile articles, except apparel		79	53	53	53		...	181	512	526		5485	5300	10774	11056
1722	Carpets and rugs		-	-	-	-		-	-	-	-		-	-	-	-
1723	Cordage, rope, twine and netting		-	-	-	-		-	-	-	-		-	-	-	-
1729	Other textiles n.e.c.		-	-	-	-		-	-	-	-		-	-	-	-
1730	Knitted and crocheted fabrics and articles		...	...	...	...		...	...	...	...		...	...	...	...
1810	Wearing apparel, except fur apparel	a/	1189	1146	1146	1146	a/	9287	8980	9680	9935	a/	82888	136342	133534	140552
1820	Dressing & dyeing of fur; processing of fur	a/	...	...	...	...	a/	...	...	...	...	a/	...	...	...	...
191	Tanning, dressing and processing of leather		...	1	1	1		...	...	...	...		...	30	30	45
1911	Tanning and dressing of leather		...	-	-	-		...	-	...	...		...	-	-	-
1912	Luggage, handbags, etc.; saddlery & harness		...	1	1	1		...	...	...	...		...	30	30	45
1920	Footwear		2	2	2	2		84	106	156	170		1308	2258	3310	3602
2010	Sawmilling and planing of wood		3	2	2	2		277	172	215	223		4858	1158	1447	1505
202	Products of wood, cork, straw, etc.		58	189	189	189		193	4634	5658	6174		7890	66183	86153	93568
2021	Veneer sheets, plywood, particle board, etc.		-	-	-	-		-	-	-	-		-	-	-	-
2022	Builders' carpentry and joinery		58	174	174	174		193	3970	5453	5964		7890	63145	82431	89769
2023	Wooden containers		-	-	-	-		-	-	-	-		-	-	-	-
2029	Other wood products; articles of cork/straw		-	15	15	15		-	219	205	210		-	3038	3722	3799
210	Paper and paper products		4	9	9	9		156	318	388	419		3386	5533	7289	7761
2101	Pulp, paper and paperboard		-	-	-	-		-	-	-	-		-	-	-	-
2102	Corrugated paper and paperboard		2	6	6	6		62	194	175	194		1255	2748	2470	2748
2109	Other articles of paper and paperboard		2	3	3	3		94	124	213	225		2131	2785	4819	5013
221	Publishing	b/	20	40	40	40	b/	1730	1974	2890	3037	b/	68812	84540	122129	128556
2211	Publishing of books and other publications		...	...	...	...		...	...	...	...		...	...	...	...
2212	Publishing of newspapers, journals, etc.		...	...	...	...		...	...	...	...		...	...	...	...
2213	Publishing of recorded media		...	...	...	...		...	...	...	...		...	...	...	...
2219	Other publishing		...	...	...	...		...	...	...	...		...	...	...	...

222	Printing and related service activities	b/	...	...	...	...	b/	...	...	...	...	b/	...	...	...	...
2221	Printing		...	...	...	...		...	...	...	...		...	...	...	...
2222	Service activities related to printing		...	...	...	...		...	...	...	...		...	...	...	...
2230	Reproduction of recorded media	b/	...	...	...	...	b/	...	...	...	...	b/	...	...	...	...
2310	Coke oven products		...	...	...	...		...	...	...	...		...	...	...	...
2320	Refined petroleum products		2	3	3	3		1556	1806	1826	1839		214837	241464	243087	301582
2330	Processing of nuclear fuel		...	...	...	...		...	...	...	...		...	...	...	...
241	Basic chemicals		11	32	32	32		1677	2576	3090	2895		172710	221511	290048	313127
2411	Basic chemicals, except fertilizers		1	7	7	7		124	706	947	947		2496	...	110049	110090
2412	Fertilizers and nitrogen compounds		2	1	1	1		955	1046	1423	1131		160182	119170	162342	183200
2413	Plastics in primary forms; synthetic rubber		8	24	24	24		598	817	720	817		10032	19601	17657	19837
242	Other chemicals		7	10	10	10		253	362	406	444		8800	13421	14949	14331
2421	Pesticides and other agro-chemical products		-	-	-	-		-	-	-	-		-	-	-	-
2422	Paints, varnishes, printing ink and mastics		2	3	3	3		127	159	159	173		6758	7745	7745	8519
2423	Pharmaceuticals, medicinal chemicals, etc.		-	-	-	-		-	-	-	-		-	-	-	-
2424	Soap, cleaning & cosmetic preparations		3	4	4	4		59	132	150	158		668	2875	3259	3411
2429	Other chemical products n.e.c.		2	3	3	3		67	71	97	113		1374	2801	3945	2401
2430	Man-made fibres		...	...	...	...		...	...	...	...		...	...	...	...
251	Rubber products		...	2	2	2		...	...	...	...		...	201	201	221
2511	Rubber tyres and tubes		...	...	...	...		...	...	...	...		...	...	...	...
2519	Other rubber products		...	...	...	...		...	...	...	...		...	...	...	...
2520	Plastic products		7	12	12	12		208	204	207	204		4183	4551	4567	4551
2610	Glass and glass products		2	16	16	16		...	189	229	248		103	4768	5025	5662
269	Non-metallic mineral products n.e.c.		82	125	125	125		3961	6830	8405	9056		84237	142587	168399	185239
2691	Pottery, china and earthenware		-	-	-	-		-	-	-	-		-	-	-	-
2692	Refractory ceramic products		-	-	-	-		-	-	-	-		-	-	-	-
2693	Struct.non-refractory clay; ceramic products		-	-	-	-		-	-	-	-		-	-	-	-
2694	Cement, lime and plaster		4	6	6	6		410	1451	1306	1581		8433	29218	26449	37404
2695	Articles of concrete, cement and plaster		63	82	82	82		2747	3832	3965	4284		61385	88153	91323	96488
2696	Cutting, shaping & finishing of stone		9	23	23	23		590	895	2207	2224		9941	14590	35769	35768
2699	Other non-metallic mineral products n.e.c.		6	14	14	14		214	652	927	967		4478	10626	14858	15579
2710	Basic iron and steel		2	4	4	4		1288	1454	1477	1613		113689	134017	135990	169454
2720	Basic precious and non-ferrous metals		28	8	...	...		48	...	...	...		1718	...	...	...
273	Casting of metals		2	8	8	8		30	212	140	140		1017	4481	3118	3059
2731	Casting of iron and steel		2	8	8	8		30	212	140	140		1017	4481	3118	3059
2732	Casting of non-ferrous metals		-	-	-	-		-	-	-	-		-	-	-	-
281	Struct.metal products;tanks;steam generators	c/	296	419	419	419	c/	1694	6898	5890	6898	c/	3041	110758	104182	116835
2811	Structural metal products		...	...	...	...		...	...	...	...		...	...	...	...
2812	Tanks, reservoirs and containers of metal		...	...	...	...		...	...	...	...		...	...	...	...
2813	Steam generators		...	...	...	...		...	...	...	...		...	...	...	...
289	Other metal products; metal working services	c/	...	...	...	...	c/	...	...	...	...	c/	...	...	...	...
2891	Metal forging/pressing/stamping/roll-forming		...	...	...	...		...	...	...	...		...	...	...	...
2892	Treatment & coating of metals		...	...	...	...		...	...	...	...		...	...	...	...
2893	Cutlery, hand tools and general hardware		...	...	...	...		...	...	...	...		...	...	...	...
2899	Other fabricated metal products n.e.c.		...	...	...	...		...	...	...	...		...	...	...	...
291	General purpose machinery		...	...	...	...		...	...	...	...		...	...	...	...
2911	Engines & turbines (not for transport equipment)		...	...	...	...		...	...	...	...		...	...	...	...
2912	Pumps, compressors, taps and valves		...	...	...	...		...	...	...	...		...	...	...	...
2913	Bearings, gears, gearing & driving elements		...	...	...	...		...	...	...	...		...	...	...	...
2914	Ovens, furnaces and furnace burners		...	...	...	...		...	...	...	...		...	...	...	...
2915	Lifting and handling equipment		...	...	...	...		...	...	...	...		...	...	...	...
2919	Other general purpose machinery		...	...	...	...		...	...	...	...		...	...	...	...
292	Special purpose machinery		...	...	...	...		...	...	...	...		...	...	...	...
2921	Agricultural and forestry machinery		...	...	...	...		...	...	...	...		...	...	...	...
2922	Machine tools		...	...	...	...		...	...	...	...		...	...	...	...
2923	Machinery for metallurgy		...	...	...	...		...	...	...	...		...	...	...	...
2924	Machinery for mining & construction		...	...	...	...		...	...	...	...		...	...	...	...
2925	Food/beverage/tobacco processing machinery		...	...	...	...		...	...	...	...		...	...	...	...
2926	Machinery for textile, apparel and leather		...	...	...	...		...	...	...	...		...	...	...	...
2927	Weapons and ammunition		...	...	...	...		...	...	...	...		...	...	...	...
2929	Other special purpose machinery		...	...	...	...		...	...	...	...		...	...	...	...

continued

Qatar

ISIC Revision 3		Number of establishments					Number of employees					Wages and salaries paid to employees				
			(number)					(number)					(thousands of Qatari Riyals)			
ISIC	Industry	Note	2003	2004	2005	2006	Note	2003	2004	2005	2006	Note	2003	2004	2005	2006
2930	Domestic appliances n.e.c.		3	2	2	2		48	71	56	71		1637	2938	2379	2938
3000	Office, accounting and computing machinery		...	...	...	...		...	...	...	...		...	...	...	...
3110	Electric motors, generators and transformers		...	...	...	...		...	...	...	...		...	...	...	...
3120	Electricity distribution & control apparatus		...	1	1	1		...	26	32	33		...	860	1080	1118
3130	Insulated wire and cable		...	...	...	...		...	...	...	...		...	...	...	...
3140	Accumulators, primary cells and batteries		...	...	...	...		...	...	...	...		...	...	...	...
3150	Lighting equipment and electric lamps		...	...	...	...		...	...	...	...		...	...	...	...
3190	Other electrical equipment n.e.c.		...	...	...	...		...	...	...	...		...	...	...	...
3210	Electronic valves, tubes, etc.		...	...	...	...		...	...	...	...		...	...	...	...
3220	TV/radio transmitters; line comm. apparatus		...	...	...	...		...	...	...	...		...	...	...	...
3230	TV and radio receivers and associated goods		...	...	...	...		...	...	...	...		...	...	...	...
331	Medical, measuring, testing appliances, etc.		...	...	...	...		...	...	...	...		...	...	...	...
3311	Medical, surgical and orthopaedic equipment		...	...	...	...		...	...	...	...		...	...	...	...
3312	Measuring/testing/navigating appliances,etc.		...	...	...	...		...	...	...	...		...	...	...	...
3313	Industrial process control equipment		...	...	...	...		...	...	...	...		...	...	...	...
3320	Optical instruments & photographic equipment		...	...	...	...		...	...	...	...		...	...	...	...
3330	Watches and clocks		...	...	...	...		...	...	...	...		...	...	...	...
3410	Motor vehicles		...	...	...	...		...	...	...	...		...	...	...	...
3420	Automobile bodies, trailers & semi-trailers		...	1	1	1		...	29	49	50		...	486	806	826
3430	Parts/accessories for automobiles		1	2	2	2		21	59	59	64		239	1480	1480	1627
351	Building and repairing of ships and boats		2	11	11	11		10	...	...	...		450	1421	1526	1526
3511	Building and repairing of ships		-	2	2	2		-	...	...	...		-	118	118	118
3512	Building/repairing of pleasure/sport. boats		2	9	9	9		10	10	10	10		419	1303	1408	1408
3520	Railway/tramway locomotives & rolling stock		...	...	...	...		...	...	...	...		...	...	...	...
3530	Aircraft and spacecraft		...	...	...	...		...	...	...	...		...	...	...	...
359	Transport equipment n.e.c.		...	...	...	...		...	...	...	...		...	...	...	...
3591	Motorcycles		...	...	...	...		...	...	...	...		...	...	...	...
3592	Bicycles and invalid carriages		...	...	...	...		...	...	...	...		...	...	...	...
3599	Other transport equipment n.e.c.		...	...	...	...		...	...	...	...		...	...	...	...
3610	Furniture		212	257	257	257		1430	2838	3680	3680		40120	62288	77644	78667
369	Manufacturing n.e.c.		...	31	31	31		...	96	101	101		...	3209	2808	3326
3691	Jewellery and related articles		...	31	31	31		...	96	101	101		...	3209	2808	3326
3692	Musical instruments		...	-	-	-		...	-	-	-		...	-	-	-
3693	Sports goods		...	-	-	-		...	-	-	-		...	-	-	-
3694	Games and toys		...	-	-	-		...	-	-	-		...	-	-	-
3699	Other manufacturing n.e.c.		...	-	-	-		...	-	-	-		...	-	-	-
3710	Recycling of metal waste and scrap	d/	1	14	4	4	d/	41	120	77	120	d/	715	2488	1637	2488
3720	Recycling of non-metal waste and scrap	d/	...	...	...	...	d/	...	...	...	...	d/	...	...	...	...
D	Total manufacturing		2270	2684	...	...		...	...	...	...		...	...	...	...

a/ 1810 includes 1820.
b/ 221 includes 222 and 2230.
c/ 281 includes 289.
d/ 3710 includes 3720.

Qatar

ISIC Revision 3			Output in producers' prices (millions of Qatari Riyals)					Value added in producers' prices (millions of Qatari Riyals)					Gross fixed capital formation (millions of Qatari Riyals)	
ISIC	Industry	Note	2003	2004	2005	2006	Note	2003	2004	2005	2006	Note	2005	2006
151	Processed meat,fish,fruit,vegetables,fats		53.8	62.4	69.5	76.2		12.9	20.7	23.0	25.0		...	...
1511	Processing/preserving of meat		52.2	51.9	57.6	62.2		11.9	15.6	17.3	18.8		...	...
1512	Processing/preserving of fish		-	-	-	-		-	-	-	-		...	...
1513	Processing/preserving of fruit & vegetables		1.6	10.5	11.9	14.0		1.0	5.1	5.7	6.2		...	...
1514	Vegetable and animal oils and fats		-	-	-	-		-	-	-	-		...	...
1520	Dairy products		44.7	77.5	103.8	108.2		19.0	33.9	45.5	47.4		...	...
153	Grain mill products; starches; animal feeds		25.7	32.9	42.0	45.4		...	...	...	...		...	...
1531	Grain mill products		25.7	32.9	42.0	45.4		...	...	-34.3	-38.8		...	...
1532	Starches and starch products		-	-	-	-		-	-	...	...		...	...
1533	Prepared animal feeds		-	-	-	-		-	-	...	...		...	...
154	Other food products		92.9	157.9	213.2	218.8		44.8	86.8	114.0	116.9		...	...
1541	Bakery products		78.8	138.2	170.8	175.5		38.4	76.5	93.7	96.2		...	...
1542	Sugar		-	-	-	-		-	-	-	-		...	...
1543	Cocoa, chocolate and sugar confectionery		4.2	5.4	5.2	5.5		2.4	3.7	3.6	3.7		...	...
1544	Macaroni, noodles & similar products		-	-	-	-		-	-	-	-		...	...
1549	Other food products n.e.c.		9.9	14.3	37.2	37.8		4.0	6.6	16.7	17.0		...	...
155	Beverages		54.0	99.5	146.2	150.5		19.8	36.2	53.3	54.8		...	...
1551	Distilling, rectifying & blending of spirits		-	-	-	-		-	-	-	-		...	...
1552	Wines		-	-	-	-		-	-	-	-		...	...
1553	Malt liquors and malt		-	-	-	-		-	-	-	-		...	...
1554	Soft drinks; mineral waters		54.0	99.5	146.2	150.5		19.8	36.2	53.3	54.8		...	...
1600	Tobacco products		...	...	...	...		...	...	...	...		...	...
171	Spinning, weaving and finishing of textiles		...	...	...	...		...	...	...	...		...	...
1711	Textile fibre preparation; textile weaving		...	...	...	...		...	...	...	...		...	...
1712	Finishing of textiles		...	...	...	...		...	...	...	...		...	...
172	Other textiles		27.4	...	50.2	51.5		16.4	13.7	24.9	25.5		...	...
1721	Made-up textile articles, except apparel		27.4	...	50.2	51.5		16.4	13.7	24.9	25.5		...	...
1722	Carpets and rugs		-	-	-	-		-	-	-	-		...	...
1723	Cordage, rope, twine and netting		-	-	-	-		-	-	-	-		...	...
1729	Other textiles n.e.c.		-	-	-	-		-	-	-	-		...	...
1730	Knitted and crocheted fabrics and articles		...	...	...	...		...	...	...	...		...	...
1810	Wearing apparel, except fur apparel	a/	413.3	400.4	400.8	414.2		186.9a/	...	214.4a/	221.9a/		...	...
1820	Dressing & dyeing of fur; processing of fur	a/	...	...	...	...		...a/	...	...a/	...a/		...	...
191	Tanning, dressing and processing of leather		...	...	...	...		...	0.1	0.1	0.1		...	...
1911	Tanning and dressing of leather		...	...	...	...		...	-	-	-		...	...
1912	Luggage, handbags, etc.; saddlery & harness		...	...	...	...		...	0.1	0.1	0.1		...	...
1920	Footwear		2.9	11.6	17.0	18.5		0.9	2.4	3.5	3.8		...	...
2010	Sawmilling and planing of wood		24.3	10.3	13.0	13.5		16.4	6.2	7.7	8.0		...	...
202	Products of wood, cork, straw, etc.		38.2	275.7	361.0	391.2		22.3	179.7	234.8	254.8		...	...
2021	Veneer sheets, plywood, particle board, etc.		-	-	-	-		-	-	-	-		...	...
2022	Builders' carpentry and joinery		38.2	258.3	339.0	368.9		22.3	167.7	220.5	240.2		...	...
2023	Wooden containers		-	-	-	-		-	-	-	-		...	...
2029	Other wood products; articles of cork/straw		-	17.4	22.0	22.3		-	12.0	14.3	14.6		...	...
210	Paper and paper products		21.9	141.1	235.4	245.3		7.4	40.4	65.0	68.0		...	...
2101	Pulp, paper and paperboard		-	-	-	-		-	-	-	-		...	...
2102	Corrugated paper and paperboard		7.4	10.9	10.0	10.8		3.0	5.9	5.3	5.9		...	...
2109	Other articles of paper and paperboard		14.5	130.3	225.4	234.5		4.4	34.5	59.7	62.1		...	...
221	Publishing	b/	226.4	315.1	456.0	479.7		141.1b/	...	330.5b/	347.5b/		...	...
2211	Publishing of books and other publications		...	...	...	...		...	...	...	...		...	...
2212	Publishing of newspapers, journals, etc.		...	...	...	...		...	...	...	...		...	...
2213	Publishing of recorded media		...	...	...	...		...	...	...	...		...	...
2219	Other publishing		...	...	...	...		...	...	...	...		...	...

continued

Qatar

ISIC Revision 3		Output in producers' prices (millions of Qatari Riyals)					Value added in producers' prices (millions of Qatari Riyals)					Gross fixed capital formation (millions of Qatari Riyals)		
ISIC	Industry	Note	2003	2004	2005	2006	Note	2003	2004	2005	2006	Note	2005	2006
222	Printing and related service activities	b/	...	...	...	...		...b/	...	...b/	...b/		...	...
2221	Printing		...	...	...	...		...	...	...	...		...	...
2222	Service activities related to printing		...	...	...	...		...	...	...	...		...	...
2230	Reproduction of recorded media	b/	...	...	...	...		...b/	...	...b/	...b/		...	...
2310	Coke oven products		...	...	...	...		...	...	...	...		...	...
2320	Refined petroleum products		3825.7	7508.7	7641.8	10967.1		2964.3	3332.9	4967.0	6930.3		...	...
2330	Processing of nuclear fuel		...	...	...	...		...	...	...	...		...	...
241	Basic chemicals		1457.6	2875.4	3771.1	3794.5		1165.2	3118.0	2736.7	2624.5		...	...
2411	Basic chemicals, except fertilizers		15.8	737.4	979.8	980.2		12.4	406.2	539.5	539.7		...	...
2412	Fertilizers and nitrogen compounds		1353.9	1879.5	2560.5	2554.1		1112.3	1532.5	2087.7	1961.2		...	...
2413	Plastics in primary forms; synthetic rubber		87.8	258.5	230.8	260.2		40.4	...	109.5	123.6		...	...
242	Other chemicals		76.2	112.4	127.7	137.6		27.5	69.2	76.6	82.7		...	...
2421	Pesticides and other agro-chemical products		-	-	-	-		-	-	-	-		...	...
2422	Paints, varnishes, printing ink and mastics		52.7	60.9	60.9	67.0		15.0	43.2	43.2	47.5		...	...
2423	Pharmaceuticals, medicinal chemicals, etc.		-	-	-	-		-	-	-	-		...	...
2424	Soap, cleaning & cosmetic preparations		8.1	25.1	28.5	29.9		3.2	12.2	13.9	14.5		...	...
2429	Other chemical products n.e.c.		15.4	27.1	38.5	40.7		9.2	13.8	19.5	20.7		...	...
2430	Man-made fibres		...	...	...	...		...	...	...	...		...	...
251	Rubber products		...	3.7	3.7	4.0		...	3.2	3.2	3.5		...	...
2511	Rubber tyres and tubes		...	...	...	...		...	...	...	...		...	...
2519	Other rubber products		...	...	...	...		...	...	...	...		...	...
2520	Plastic products		20.8	45.3	42.9	45.3		10.7	30.7	28.7	30.7		...	...
2610	Glass and glass products		0.4	22.6	25.1	27.5		0.2	11.6	12.8	14.0		...	...
269	Non-metallic mineral products n.e.c.		856.7	2059.5	2170.6	3206.4		347.5	1035.8	1058.6	1487.9		...	...
2691	Pottery, china and earthenware		-	-	-	-		-	-	-	-		...	...
2692	Refractory ceramic products		-	-	-	-		-	-	-	-		...	...
2693	Struct.non-refractory clay; ceramic products		-	-	-	-		-	-	-	-		...	...
2694	Cement, lime and plaster		193.3	664.8	601.8	1559.5		141.8	472.0	427.3	825.6		...	...
2695	Articles of concrete, cement and plaster		559.5	1206.1	1250.1	1319.8		169.6	498.3	516.5	545.2		...	...
2696	Cutting, shaping & finishing of stone		46.8	53.5	129.8	129.1		21.9	23.4	55.9	55.3		...	...
2699	Other non-metallic mineral products n.e.c.		57.0	135.1	188.9	198.0		14.1	42.1	58.9	61.8		...	...
2710	Basic iron and steel		1999.0	2937.4	2980.8	3613.8		1275.9	198.6	2015.4	2405.0		...	...
2720	Basic precious and non-ferrous metals		49.1	...	...	...		27.8	...	...	...		...	...
273	Casting of metals		3.6	53.9	38.0	36.6		2.5	14.2	10.4	9.6		...	...
2731	Casting of iron and steel		3.6	53.9	38.0	36.6		2.5	14.2	10.4	9.6		...	...
2732	Casting of non-ferrous metals		-	-	-	-		-	-	-	-		...	...
281	Struct.metal products;tanks;steam generators	c/	266.6	863.1	788.7	894.4	c/	156.8	548.8	497.1	565.7		...	...
2811	Structural metal products		...	...	...	...		...	...	...	...		...	...
2812	Tanks, reservoirs and containers of metal		...	...	...	...		...	...	...	...		...	...
2813	Steam generators		...	...	...	...		...	...	...	...		...	...
289	Other metal products; metal working services	c/	...	...	...	...	c/	...	...	...	...		...	...
2891	Metal forging/pressing/stamping/roll-forming		...	...	...	...		...	...	...	...		...	...
2892	Treatment & coating of metals		...	...	...	...		...	...	...	...		...	...
2893	Cutlery, hand tools and general hardware		...	...	...	...		...	...	...	...		...	...
2899	Other fabricated metal products n.e.c.		...	...	...	...		...	...	...	...		...	...
291	General purpose machinery		...	...	...	...		...	...	...	...		...	...
2911	Engines & turbines (not for transport equipment)		...	...	...	...		...	...	...	...		...	...
2912	Pumps, compressors, taps and valves		...	...	...	...		...	...	...	...		...	...
2913	Bearings, gears, gearing & driving elements		...	...	...	...		...	...	...	...		...	...
2914	Ovens, furnaces and furnace burners		...	...	...	...		...	...	...	...		...	...
2915	Lifting and handling equipment		...	...	...	...		...	...	...	...		...	...
2919	Other general purpose machinery		...	...	...	...		...	...	...	...		...	...

292	Special purpose machinery		...	...	...	...		...	...	...	...		...	...
2921	Agricultural and forestry machinery		...	...	...	...		...	...	...	...		...	...
2922	Machine tools		...	...	...	...		...	...	...	...		...	...
2923	Machinery for metallurgy		...	...	...	...		...	...	...	...		...	...
2924	Machinery for mining & construction		...	...	...	...		...	...	...	...		...	...
2925	Food/beverage/tobacco processing machinery		...	...	...	...		...	...	...	...		...	...
2926	Machinery for textile, apparel and leather		...	...	...	...		...	...	...	...		...	...
2927	Weapons and ammunition		...	...	...	...		...	...	...	...		...	...
2929	Other special purpose machinery		...	...	...	...		...	...	...	...		...	...
2930	Domestic appliances n.e.c.		5.2	10.7	8.6	10.7		1.6	10.1	8.2	10.1		...	...
3000	Office, accounting and computing machinery		...	...	...	...		...	...	...	...		...	...
3110	Electric motors, generators and transformers		...	...	...	...		...	...	...	...		...	...
3120	Electricity distribution & control apparatus		...	17.3	21.8	22.5		...	4.9	6.1	6.4		...	...
3130	Insulated wire and cable		...	...	...	...		...	...	...	...		...	...
3140	Accumulators, primary cells and batteries		...	...	...	...		...	...	...	...		...	...
3150	Lighting equipment and electric lamps		...	...	...	...		...	...	...	...		...	...
3190	Other electrical equipment n.e.c.		...	...	...	...		...	...	...	...		...	...
3210	Electronic valves, tubes, etc.		...	...	...	...		...	...	...	...		...	...
3220	TV/radio transmitters; line comm. apparatus		...	...	...	...		...	...	...	...		...	...
3230	TV and radio receivers and associated goods		...	...	...	...		...	...	...	...		...	...
331	Medical, measuring, testing appliances, etc.		...	...	...	...		...	...	...	...		...	...
3311	Medical, surgical and orthopaedic equipment		...	...	...	...		...	...	...	...		...	...
3312	Measuring/testing/navigating appliances,etc.		...	...	...	...		...	...	...	...		...	...
3313	Industrial process control equipment		...	...	...	...		...	...	...	...		...	...
3320	Optical instruments & photographic equipment		...	...	...	...		...	...	...	...		...	...
3330	Watches and clocks		...	...	...	...		...	...	...	...		...	...
3410	Motor vehicles		...	...	...	...		...	...	...	...		...	...
3420	Automobile bodies, trailers & semi-trailers		...	1.3	2.1	2.2		...	0.7	1.1	1.1		...	...
3430	Parts/accessories for automobiles		0.8	10.7	10.7	11.7		0.4	6.7	6.7	7.4		...	...
351	Building and repairing of ships and boats		1.4	5.4	5.4	5.4		0.9	3.2	3.4	3.4		...	...
3511	Building and repairing of ships		-	...	0.5	0.5		-	0.3	0.3	0.3		...	...
3512	Building/repairing of pleasure/sport. boats		1.4	5.4	4.9	4.9		0.9	2.9	3.1	3.1		...	...
3520	Railway/tramway locomotives & rolling stock		...	...	...	...		...	...	...	...		...	...
3530	Aircraft and spacecraft		...	...	...	...		...	...	...	...		...	...
359	Transport equipment n.e.c.		...	...	...	...		...	...	...	...		...	...
3591	Motorcycles		...	...	...	...		...	...	...	...		...	...
3592	Bicycles and invalid carriages		...	...	...	...		...	...	...	...		...	...
3599	Other transport equipment n.e.c.		...	...	...	...		...	...	...	...		...	...
3610	Furniture		170.7	481.3	552.7	573.6		101.6	240.0	275.9	286.2		...	...
369	Manufacturing n.e.c.		...	...	...	...		...	4.9	4.1	5.0		...	...
3691	Jewellery and related articles		...	7.6	6.7	7.9		...	4.9	4.1	5.0		...	...
3692	Musical instruments		...	-	...	...		...	-	-	-		...	...
3693	Sports goods		...	-	...	...		...	-	-	-		...	...
3694	Games and toys		...	-	...	...		...	-	-	-		...	...
3699	Other manufacturing n.e.c.		...	-	...	...		...	-	-	-		...	...
3710	Recycling of metal waste and scrap		...	17.9d/	11.7d/	17.8d/	d/	2.3	14.8	9.7	14.8		...	...
3720	Recycling of non-metal waste and scrap		...	...d/	...d/	...d/	d/	...	...	...	...		...	...
D	Total manufacturing		...	...	...	...		...	...	...	...		...	...

a/ 1810 includes 1820.
b/ 221 includes 222 and 2230.
c/ 281 includes 289.
d/ 3710 includes 3720.

Republic of Korea

Supplier of information:
National Statistical Office, Taejon.
Industrial statistics for the OECD countries are compiled by the OECD secretariat, which supplies them to UNIDO.

Basic source of data:
Annual survey and the Census of Mining and Manufacturing.

Major deviations from ISIC (Revision 3):
Data are collected under the national classification system which is compatible with ISIC (Revision 3).

Reference period:
Calendar year.

Scope:
Establishments with 5 or more employees.

Method of data collection:
The inquiry is carried out for large establishments through questionnaires, and for small establishments through personal interviews. The surveyors visit all units.

Type of enumeration:
During census years all establishments with 5 persons or more engaged are completely enumerated.

Adjusted for non-response:
Not reported.

Concepts and definitions of variables:
Number of employees is not converted to full-time equivalent.
Wages and salaries includes all money payment and payment in kind paid or supplied by the employer during the reference period to all employees counted on the payroll.
Output is gross output measured as the total value of all goods produced and services rendered to others by the establishment during the year.
Value added is gross output minus cost of production.
Gross fixed capital formation is the value of fixed assets purchased or constructed by the unit's own labour force for its own use during the reference year. The value of corresponding sales is not subtracted from it. Transactions in fixed assets include land, buildings, other construction and land improvements, transport equipment, machinery and other equipment.

Related national publications:
Report on the Industrial Census, Report on the Mining and Manufacturing Survey, both published by the National Statistical Office of the Republic of Korea, Seoul.

Republic of Korea

ISIC Revision 3		Establishments					Number of employees					Wages and salaries paid to employees				
			(number)					(thousands)					(billions of Korean Won)			
ISIC	Industry	Note	2003	2004	2005	2006	Note	2003	2004	2005	2006	Note	2003	2004	2005	2006
151	Processed meat,fish,fruit,vegetables,fats		...	...	...	...		63.0	61.0	60.9	61.7		915	912	975	1031
1511	Processing/preserving of meat		...	...	...	...		23.5	23.2	24.0	25.6		386	387	436	475
1512	Processing/preserving of fish		...	...	...	...		22.5	20.9	21.0	19.4		288	275	293	287
1513	Processing/preserving of fruit & vegetables		...	...	...	...		14.1	14.1	13.6	14.1		181	193	197	206
1514	Vegetable and animal oils and fats		...	...	...	...		2.8	2.8	2.3	2.6		60	57	48	63
1520	Dairy products		...	...	...	...		8.7	10.2	10.2	10.2		218	250	301	304
153	Grain mill products; starches; animal feeds		...	...	...	...		16.0	16.7	16.6	16.9		370	401	422	448
1531	Grain mill products		...	...	...	...		7.0	7.9	7.7	7.9		144	165	171	181
1532	Starches and starch products		...	...	...	...		1.6	1.8	1.5	1.4		38	45	44	44
1533	Prepared animal feeds		...	...	...	...		7.3	7.1	7.4	7.6		188	191	207	223
154	Other food products		...	...	...	...		74.8	73.2	72.7	72.0		1255	1292	1372	1401
1541	Bakery products		...	...	...	...		18.6	17.9	18.1	16.7		323	325	343	317
1542	Sugar		...	...	...	...		0.5	0.6	0.6	0.6		19	24	26	27
1543	Cocoa, chocolate and sugar confectionery		...	...	...	...		4.5	4.5	4.1	4.3		81	89	90	97
1544	Macaroni, noodles & similar products		...	...	...	...		8.2	8.2	7.7	7.0		174	182	187	180
1549	Other food products n.e.c.		...	...	...	...		42.9	42.0	42.1	43.5		658	671	726	781
155	Beverages		...	...	...	...		14.4	14.1	13.8	14.0		358	363	398	412
1551	Distilling, rectifying & blending of spirits		...	...	...	...		3.0	3.2	3.1	3.3		85	87	111	115
1552	Wines		...	...	...	...		1.7	1.7	1.8	1.8		31	30	34	37
1553	Malt liquors and malt		...	...	...	...		1.7	1.7	1.7	1.7		67	67	71	73
1554	Soft drinks; mineral waters		...	...	...	...		7.9	7.4	7.2	7.2		177	179	182	188
1600	Tobacco products		...	...	...	...		3.1	2.6	2.4	2.3		122	117	96	97
171	Spinning, weaving and finishing of textiles		...	...	...	...		111.6	96.7	63.0	75.6		1990	1780	1560	1505
1711	Textile fibre preparation; textile weaving		...	...	...	...		60.5	51.3	43.5	39.4		1061	945	808	778
1712	Finishing of textiles		...	...	...	...		51.1	45.4	39.3	36.3		929	835	752	727
172	Other textiles		...	...	...	...		40.5	40.5	42.2	39.0		681	746	809	770
1721	Made-up textile articles, except apparel		...	...	...	...		22.5	21.4	21.8	19.6		348	343	368	339
1722	Carpets and rugs		...	...	...	...		1.3	1.3	1.4	1.1		24	27	31	23
1723	Cordage, rope, twine and netting		...	...	...	...		3.6	3.5	3.3	3.0		61	60	61	58
1729	Other textiles n.e.c.		...	...	...	...		13.1	14.4	15.7	15.4		248	316	349	349
1730	Knitted and crocheted fabrics and articles		...	...	...	...		24.0	21.1	19.5	18.2		432	383	360	356
1810	Wearing apparel, except fur apparel		...	...	...	...		120.3	107.3	102.4	100.3		1893	1717	1680	1708
1820	Dressing & dyeing of fur; processing of fur		...	...	...	...		1.7	1.6	1.6	1.6		35	31	33	33
191	Tanning, dressing and processing of leather		...	...	...	...		13.9	12.1	11.5	10.8		272	237	228	224
1911	Tanning and dressing of leather		...	...	...	...		7.7	6.6	5.6	4.4		154	137	117	92
1912	Luggage, handbags, etc.; saddlery & harness		...	...	...	...		6.2	4.7	5.1	6.4		118	86	97	132
1920	Footwear		...	...	...	...		22.5	19.3	17.7	16.9		362	317	303	300
2010	Sawmilling and planing of wood		...	...	...	...		7.8	6.9	6.7	6.9		130	121	121	131
202	Products of wood, cork, straw, etc.		...	...	...	...		17.6	17.1	18.0	18.0		313	347	383	386
2021	Veneer sheets, plywood, particle board, etc.		...	...	...	...		6.2	5.5	5.2	5.0		124	134	132	132
2022	Builders' carpentry and joinery		...	...	...	...		5.1	4.9	5.1	5.0		87	94	108	102
2023	Wooden containers		...	...	...	...		4.4	4.8	5.7	6.0		76	92	113	119
2029	Other wood products; articles of cork/straw		...	...	...	...		1.9	1.9	2.0	2.0		26	27	31	33
210	Paper and paper products		...	...	...	...		58.4	56.8	58.3	56.9		1292	1338	1415	1404
2101	Pulp, paper and paperboard		...	...	...	...		17.8	18.0	18.4	17.8		512	557	575	556
2102	Corrugated paper and paperboard		...	...	...	...		24.1	25.4	26.0	25.8		444	490	528	540
2109	Other articles of paper and paperboard		...	...	...	...		16.5	13.4	13.9	13.4		336	291	312	307
221	Publishing		...	...	...	...		54.5	51.6	50.7	52.0		1300	1305	1320	1377
2211	Publishing of books and other publications		...	...	...	...		23.2	22.0	21.2	22.2		518	528	543	575
2212	Publishing of newspapers, journals, etc.		...	...	...	...		28.7	27.1	26.8	26.8		700	694	685	705
2213	Publishing of recorded media		...	...	...	...		0.6	0.5	0.5	0.5		12	11	12	11
2219	Other publishing		...	...	...	...		2.0	2.0	2.2	2.5		70	72	80	86

222	Printing and related service activities	...	...	...	...	39.2	40.5	41.0	40.6	769	855	880	882
2221	Printing	...	...	...	...	30.4	30.8	30.6	29.3	601	664	666	643
2222	Service activities related to printing	...	...	...	...	8.8	9.7	10.5	11.3	168	191	214	240
2230	Reproduction of recorded media	...	...	...	...	1.4	1.1	1.1	1.1	31	23	26	26
2310	Coke oven products	...	...	...	...	-	-	-	-	-	-	-	-
2320	Refined petroleum products	...	...	...	...	9.2	9.0	9.2	9.1	447	472	598	642
2330	Processing of nuclear fuel	...	...	...	...	0.6	0.6	0.6	0.6	23	24	27	32
241	Basic chemicals	...	...	...	...	46.3	46.1	45.4	47.9	1586	1730	1748	1894
2411	Basic chemicals, except fertilizers	...	...	...	...	24.3	23.7	23.8	24.7	888	984	1040	1094
2412	Fertilizers and nitrogen compounds	...	...	...	...	4.5	4.5	4.8	5.0	105	116	122	128
2413	Plastics in primary forms; synthetic rubber	...	...	...	...	17.5	17.9	16.8	18.2	594	629	586	671
242	Other chemicals	...	...	...	...	75.9	78.2	76.3	77.7	1827	2002	2030	2114
2421	Pesticides and other agro-chemical products	...	...	...	...	2.3	2.7	2.1	2.3	54	71	54	69
2422	Paints, varnishes, printing ink and mastics	...	...	...	...	12.0	11.9	12.1	12.6	303	322	334	355
2423	Pharmaceuticals, medicinal chemicals, etc.	...	...	...	...	27.0	27.3	26.6	27.0	680	735	746	766
2424	Soap, cleaning & cosmetic preparations	...	...	...	...	13.7	14.4	14.1	14.4	291	320	350	359
2429	Other chemical products n.e.c.	...	...	...	...	20.8	22.0	21.4	21.4	500	555	547	565
2430	Man-made fibres	...	...	...	...	12.3	8.7	6.5	5.8	447	275	206	190
251	Rubber products	...	...	...	...	34.7	38.6	38.9	37.2	745	896	937	1000
2511	Rubber tyres and tubes	...	...	...	...	12.3	14.0	13.3	12.5	329	401	386	449
2519	Other rubber products	...	...	...	...	22.5	24.6	25.6	24.7	416	495	551	551
2520	Plastic products	...	...	...	...	141.9	143.4	155.5	156.5	2652	2876	3265	3366
2610	Glass and glass products	...	...	...	...	21.8	22.3	23.2	23.5	523	571	635	647
269	Non-metallic mineral products n.e.c.	...	...	...	...	63.0	62.1	60.4	59.7	1371	1440	1450	1477
2691	Pottery, china and earthenware	...	...	...	...	7.1	6.8	6.7	6.4	130	124	127	130
2692	Refractory ceramic products	...	...	...	...	3.6	3.3	3.1	2.9	89	94	86	89
2693	Struct.non-refractory clay; ceramic products	...	...	...	...	4.5	4.1	3.6	3.7	73	74	68	74
2694	Cement, lime and plaster	...	...	...	...	5.9	6.1	5.5	5.3	209	237	213	205
2695	Articles of concrete, cement and plaster	...	...	...	...	28.2	29.0	28.6	28.4	586	639	663	675
2696	Cutting, shaping & finishing of stone	...	...	...	...	4.4	4.1	4.0	3.7	82	79	81	76
2699	Other non-metallic mineral products n.e.c.	...	...	...	...	9.3	2.9	3.1	9.2	202	66	73	228
2710	Basic iron and steel	...	...	...	...	65.6	70.5	71.2	73.2	1912	2539	2648	2700
2720	Basic precious and non-ferrous metals	...	...	...	...	23.5	25.5	26.3	25.8	579	672	719	741
273	Casting of metals	...	...	...	...	15.9	16.4	16.8	16.7	340	379	408	404
2731	Casting of iron and steel	...	...	...	...	11.7	11.9	12.2	12.1	258	289	304	301
2732	Casting of non-ferrous metals	...	...	...	...	4.2	4.5	4.6	4.6	82	90	103	103
281	Struct.metal products;tanks;steam generators	...	...	...	...	59.0	63.0	66.9	70.2	1315	1491	1652	1774
2811	Structural metal products	...	...	...	...	46.3	48.7	51.7	54.2	905	1019	1145	1226
2812	Tanks, reservoirs and containers of metal	...	...	...	...	6.2	8.2	8.9	9.3	128	193	216	233
2813	Steam generators	...	...	...	...	6.6	6.1	6.3	6.7	281	279	291	315
289	Other metal products; metal working services	...	...	...	...	140.0	152.7	169.9	175.8	2625	3029	3578	3862
2891	Metal forging/pressing/stamping/roll-forming	...	...	...	...	26.2	29.4	34.0	35.4	468	564	693	755
2892	Treatment & coating of metals	...	...	...	...	51.3	59.4	68.8	74.1	941	1152	1411	1585
2893	Cutlery, hand tools and general hardware	...	...	...	...	20.4	21.2	22.9	22.7	376	420	483	508
2899	Other fabricated metal products n.e.c.	...	...	...	...	42.0	42.6	44.2	43.7	840	893	990	1013
291	General purpose machinery	...	...	...	...	124.8	123.0	127.6	131.7	2805	2907	3143	3385
2911	Engines & turbines (not for transport equipment)	...	...	...	...	6.4	7.7	8.9	10.1	170	207	259	310
2912	Pumps, compressors, taps and valves	...	...	...	...	30.9	28.3	29.3	30.3	678	629	700	752
2913	Bearings, gears, gearing & driving elements	...	...	...	...	11.3	11.4	12.0	12.1	259	281	312	323
2914	Ovens, furnaces and furnace burners	...	...	...	...	2.7	3.1	2.9	3.2	63	74	71	78
2915	Lifting and handling equipment	...	...	...	...	18.2	18.9	19.2	19.6	414	474	483	506
2919	Other general purpose machinery	...	...	...	...	55.4	53.6	55.2	56.4	1221	1241	1319	1416
292	Special purpose machinery	...	...	...	...	133.2	143.1	153.4	192.2	3047	3472	3863	4997
2921	Agricultural and forestry machinery	...	...	...	...	7.0	8.4	8.7	8.7	135	192	224	220
2922	Machine tools	...	...	...	...	20.9	22.1	22.9	24.5	495	545	596	650
2923	Machinery for metallurgy	...	...	...	...	1.2	1.2	1.2	1.1	28	28	31	29
2924	Machinery for mining & construction	...	...	...	...	11.4	12.3	12.2	13.3	317	345	320	401
2925	Food/beverage/tobacco processing machinery	...	...	...	...	2.6	2.3	2.5	2.5	50	46	52	55
2926	Machinery for textile, apparel and leather	...	...	...	...	7.6	7.3	6.5	6.0	153	153	143	136
2927	Weapons and ammunition	...	...	...	...	6.1	7.1	8.2	8.0	190	234	290	292
2929	Other special purpose machinery	...	...	...	...	76.3	82.5	91.3	95.7	1679	1929	2207	2429

continued

Republic of Korea

ISIC Revision 3		Establishments					Number of employees					Wages and salaries paid to employees				
			(number)					(thousands)					(billions of Korean Won)			
ISIC	Industry	Note	2003	2004	2005	2006	Note	2003	2004	2005	2006	Note	2003	2004	2005	2006
2930	Domestic appliances n.e.c.		...	...	...	...		34.1	32.7	31.9	32.3		725	785	730	786
3000	Office, accounting and computing machinery		...	...	...	...		40.4	28.7	26.0	25.1		1102	707	646	657
3110	Electric motors, generators and transformers		...	...	...	...		43.0	39.6	37.6	35.6		884	864	852	837
3120	Electricity distribution & control apparatus		...	...	...	...		37.9	38.1	40.1	42.1		783	830	901	995
3130	Insulated wire and cable		...	...	...	...		15.8	14.4	15.5	15.7		353	316	368	400
3140	Accumulators, primary cells and batteries		...	...	...	...		6.9	6.5	5.2	4.8		174	192	138	139
3150	Lighting equipment and electric lamps		...	...	...	...		14.9	13.7	13.8	14.7		251	256	276	319
3190	Other electrical equipment n.e.c.		...	...	...	...		24.6	25.3	25.0	24.8		461	524	541	594
3210	Electronic valves, tubes, etc.		...	...	...	...		188.2	220.6	240.1	242.1		4729	6003	6982	7385
3220	TV/radio transmitters; line comm. apparatus		...	...	...	...		72.5	74.2	78.5	87.3		1601	1659	1982	2320
3230	TV and radio receivers and associated goods		...	...	...	...		40.0	51.1	54.1	55.4		827	1363	1645	1772
331	Medical, measuring, testing appliances, etc.		...	...	...	...		33.0	35.5	39.8	43.8		649	746	891	1001
3311	Medical, surgical and orthopaedic equipment		...	...	...	...		13.4	14.3	15.5	17.6		240	271	305	363
3312	Measuring/testing/navigating appliances,etc.		...	...	...	...		16.7	17.8	19.6	20.7		343	396	474	504
3313	Industrial process control equipment		...	...	...	...		2.9	3.5	4.7	5.5		65	79	112	133
3320	Optical instruments & photographic equipment		...	...	...	...		11.6	12.0	14.2	14.4		187	223	297	316
3330	Watches and clocks		...	...	...	...		2.1	1.9	1.9	1.4		38	38	39	29
3410	Motor vehicles		...	...	...	...		78.4	81.0	83.1	83.6		3365	3879	4424	4381
3420	Automobile bodies, trailers & semi-trailers		...	...	...	...		3.7	3.9	4.0	4.8		77	84	90	111
3430	Parts/accessories for automobiles		...	...	...	...		131.5	144.0	149.9	161.3		2997	3546	3862	4277
351	Building and repairing of ships and boats		...	...	...	...		85.7	89.8	91.7	103.8		3080	3545	3806	4184
3511	Building and repairing of ships		...	...	...	...		85.5	89.6	91.5	103.7		3078	3542	3803	4181
3512	Building/repairing of pleasure/sport. boats		...	...	...	...		0.1	0.2	0.2	0.2		2	3	3	3
3520	Railway/tramway locomotives & rolling stock		...	...	...	...		5.5	5.3	4.7	5.7		181	178	169	239
3530	Aircraft and spacecraft		...	...	...	...		6.7	6.9	6.9	7.4		234	256	263	303
359	Transport equipment n.e.c.		...	...	...	...		3.3	3.2	2.9	3.0		66	67	68	69
3591	Motorcycles		...	...	...	...		2.5	2.6	2.4	2.3		53	57	59	56
3592	Bicycles and invalid carriages		...	...	...	...		0.4	0.3	0.2	0.3		7	5	4	5
3599	Other transport equipment n.e.c.		...	...	...	...		0.3	0.3	0.3	0.4		6	5	5	8
3610	Furniture		...	...	...	...		41.7	40.9	42.4	44.2		728	781	825	926
369	Manufacturing n.e.c.		...	...	...	...		36.7	33.3	33.0	31.5		622	591	609	602
3691	Jewellery and related articles		...	...	...	...		4.4	4.0	3.6	3.3		68	65	58	55
3692	Musical instruments		...	...	...	...		5.2	3.8	3.1	2.5		97	73	64	53
3693	Sports goods		...	...	...	...		5.9	5.7	5.2	4.6		101	98	99	92
3694	Games and toys		...	...	...	...		3.9	3.6	3.6	2.9		61	64	63	54
3699	Other manufacturing n.e.c.		...	...	...	...		17.3	16.2	17.5	18.1		296	290	325	349
3710	Recycling of metal waste and scrap		...	...	...	...		2.0	2.0	2.7	2.7		39	41	64	64
3720	Recycling of non-metal waste and scrap		...	...	...	...		2.9	3.4	4.0	3.9		50	60	73	74
D	Total manufacturing		...	...	...	...		2624.3	2661.3	2727.3	2777.7		59185	64846	70131	74014

Republic of Korea

ISIC Revision 3		Output					Value added					Gross fixed capital formation		
			(billions of Korean Won)					(billions of Korean Won)					(billions of Korean Won)	
ISIC	Industry	Note	2003	2004	2005	2006	Note	2003	2004	2005	2006	Note	2005	2006
151	Processed meat,fish,fruit,vegetables,fats		9738	10768	11349	11867		3115	3486	3517	3628		421	542
1511	Processing/preserving of meat		4588	5446	6191	6307		1332	1620	1694	1735		201	262
1512	Processing/preserving of fish		2380	2480	2464	2471		852	867	884	859		89	127
1513	Processing/preserving of fruit & vegetables		1394	1389	1440	1591		589	595	623	638		88	108
1514	Vegetable and animal oils and fats		1376	1453	1255	1497		342	404	316	395		43	44
1520	Dairy products		4067	5072	5614	5594		1569	2210	2393	2413		201	159
153	Grain mill products; starches; animal feeds		9880	11061	10490	10432		2283	2883	2797	2763		524	483
1531	Grain mill products		4826	5213	4934	4858		949	1254	1173	1165		307	271
1532	Starches and starch products		777	928	801	840		254	299	313	318		56	62
1533	Prepared animal feeds		4278	4920	4756	4734		1081	1330	1310	1280		161	150
154	Other food products		13097	13251	13878	14057		5899	5980	6214	6154		885	899
1541	Bakery products		2523	2519	2602	2339		1328	1365	1373	1206		275	185
1542	Sugar		803	846	841	954		312	315	293	296		17	18
1543	Cocoa, chocolate and sugar confectionery		1221	1458	1423	1366		749	884	885	776		50	94
1544	Macaroni, noodles & similar products		1826	1990	1908	1614		686	723	686	616		75	49
1549	Other food products n.e.c.		6724	6438	7104	7783		2824	2694	2977	3259		467	553
155	Beverages		7076	7830	7067	7021		3884	4724	4156	4071		401	342
1551	Distilling, rectifying & blending of spirits		1612	1870	1821	1965		892	1034	994	1053		116	125
1552	Wines		449	482	480	427		283	323	322	273		37	44
1553	Malt liquors and malt		1713	1941	1517	1529		1065	1511	1126	1134		87	34
1554	Soft drinks; mineral waters		3303	3537	3248	3100		1644	1857	1713	1611		162	139
1600	Tobacco products		3800	4190	2785	2920		2486	2744	1566	1627		42	134
171	Spinning, weaving and finishing of textiles		13591	12941	11113	10736		5676	5320	3873	4224		532	516
1711	Textile fibre preparation; textile weaving		8562	8352	6906	6565		3282	3067	2586	2346		326	289
1712	Finishing of textiles		5029	4590	4206	4171		2394	2253	1982	1879		206	226
172	Other textiles		5145	6453	7385	7132		2080	2368	2759	2536		427	398
1721	Made-up textile articles, except apparel		2788	2846	3230	3033		1114	1055	1228	1048		144	110
1722	Carpets and rugs		172	180	308	208		72	64	123	78		16	14
1723	Cordage, rope, twine and netting		391	420	443	444		151	153	160	159		16	13
1729	Other textiles n.e.c.		1794	3008	3404	3447		743	1096	1247	1252		252	261
1730	Knitted and crocheted fabrics and articles		4190	3609	3428	3432		1532	1285	1286	1243		107	108
1810	Wearing apparel, except fur apparel		12064	11917	12072	12667		5576	5811	6130	6367		326	305
1820	Dressing & dyeing of fur; processing of fur		254	202	335	336		96	85	159	151		52	9
191	Tanning, dressing and processing of leather		2839	2513	2308	2194		882	836	795	757		73	74
1911	Tanning and dressing of leather		1887	1621	1417	1104		484	473	417	320		36	39
1912	Luggage, handbags, etc.; saddlery & harness		952	756	771	1090		398	315	334	437		31	34
1920	Footwear		2268	2113	1909	2012		1001	899	855	869		49	55
2010	Sawmilling and planing of wood		1089	1183	1135	1363		376	401	408	435		54	53
202	Products of wood, cork, straw, etc.		2650	3128	3301	3220		952	1137	1101	1129		219	276
2021	Veneer sheets, plywood, particle board, etc.		1331	1462	1369	1306		434	473	378	355		132	137
2022	Builders' carpentry and joinery		645	786	863	868		250	312	297	348		36	54
2023	Wooden containers		534	733	910	870		206	282	345	341		44	71
2029	Other wood products; articles of cork/straw		140	147	159	176		63	69	81	84		7	14
210	Paper and paper products		14337	14762	14746	14743		5468	5274	5313	5283		1002	1020
2101	Pulp, paper and paperboard		7739	8037	7810	7635		2973	2758	2696	2690		506	534
2102	Corrugated paper and paperboard		3965	4472	4491	4583		1423	1620	1647	1634		284	325
2109	Other articles of paper and paperboard		2633	2253	2445	2525		1073	896	969	959		212	161
221	Publishing		7569	7473	7963	8093		4714	4628	4757	4917		519	335
2211	Publishing of books and other publications		3264	3652	3974	4119		2011	2298	2483	2571		252	161
2212	Publishing of newspapers, journals, etc.		3607	3429	3539	3522		2153	2098	2022	2088		114	135
2213	Publishing of recorded media		71	69	74	84		35	39	43	47		2	6
2219	Other publishing		627	324	376	368		516	194	208	212		150	33

continued

Republic of Korea

ISIC Revision 3		Output					Value added					Gross fixed capital formation		
		Note	(billions of Korean Won)				Note	(billions of Korean Won)				Note	(billions of Korean Won)	
ISIC	Industry		2003	2004	2005	2006		2003	2004	2005	2006		2005	2006
222	Printing and related service activities		4018	4434	4601	4690		2043	2298	2389	2413		354	417
2221	Printing		3365	3621	3686	3613		1647	1816	1863	1802		264	307
2222	Service activities related to printing		652	813	915	1078		396	482	527	611		90	110
2230	Reproduction of recorded media		221	156	185	194		115	88	108	111		7	12
2310	Coke oven products		-	-	-	-		-	-	-	-		-	-
2320	Refined petroleum products		36940	47640	60504	69832		5227	7041	10985	11611		818	809
2330	Processing of nuclear fuel		122	103	119	118		72	62	75	78		19	23
241	Basic chemicals		37610	48435	50711	51840		10905	13165	13217	11324		4434	3014
2411	Basic chemicals, except fertilizers		21261	27742	31007	31486		6116	7334	8137	6611		2780	2174
2412	Fertilizers and nitrogen compounds		1201	1458	1593	1473		439	567	568	571		75	95
2413	Plastics in primary forms; synthetic rubber		15148	19236	18112	18881		4350	5263	4512	4142		1579	744
242	Other chemicals		22519	24519	24910	26819		11921	12462	12547	13741		1395	1849
2421	Pesticides and other agro-chemical products		1100	1217	1167	1142		539	604	490	555		21	31
2422	Paints, varnishes, printing ink and mastics		3453	3860	3944	4379		1283	1452	1365	1527		142	189
2423	Pharmaceuticals, medicinal chemicals, etc.		7587	7999	8735	9381		4676	4826	5515	5949		374	785
2424	Soap, cleaning & cosmetic preparations		5155	5001	5138	5548		3225	2997	2898	3307		383	226
2429	Other chemical products n.e.c.		5225	6442	5925	6369		2198	2584	2279	2404		475	618
2430	Man-made fibres		5907	4276	3899	3493		1792	1420	1288	786		139	188
251	Rubber products		6139	7538	8381	8350		2827	3636	3955	3727		644	699
2511	Rubber tyres and tubes		3212	4047	4370	4339		1608	2218	2376	2205		344	446
2519	Other rubber products		2926	3491	4011	4011		1218	1418	1579	1522		300	253
2520	Plastic products		22660	24804	29456	31471		8616	9181	10855	11480		2213	2498
2610	Glass and glass products		5001	5845	6618	7117		2612	3208	3377	3403		1538	983
269	Non-metallic mineral products n.e.c.		17486	17622	16527	16851		7687	7741	7299	7262		961	1028
2691	Pottery, china and earthenware		478	490	507	503		309	309	310	306		23	36
2692	Refractory ceramic products		755	804	773	802		327	374	340	333		48	37
2693	Struct.non-refractory clay; ceramic products		427	427	390	406		212	236	210	212		31	33
2694	Cement, lime and plaster		3394	3704	3292	3233		1961	1958	1788	1565		235	166
2695	Articles of concrete, cement and plaster		9947	9711	8993	9141		3734	3713	3455	3624		493	588
2696	Cutting, shaping & finishing of stone		579	565	583	581		274	274	281	269		20	27
2699	Other non-metallic mineral products n.e.c.		1908	1053	1055	2186		871	415	422	953		48	142
2710	Basic iron and steel		42104	58610	62776	61195		13928	20055	20189	19157		6185	6335
2720	Basic precious and non-ferrous metals		11839	15484	17856	24722		2657	3934	3932	4751		571	948
273	Casting of metals		2277	2929	3832	3975		979	1162	1345	1374		251	266
2731	Casting of iron and steel		1655	2145	2535	2317		752	898	1010	962		162	151
2732	Casting of non-ferrous metals		622	783	1297	1658		227	264	334	412		88	115
281	Struct.metal products;tanks;steam generators		10371	13481	15393	17050		3613	4933	5155	5498		905	1114
2811	Structural metal products		7787	9745	11077	12257		2736	3523	3983	4194		732	787
2812	Tanks, reservoirs and containers of metal		908	1657	1907	2243		352	563	665	775		126	171
2813	Steam generators		1676	2080	2409	2550		525	847	507	529		47	156
289	Other metal products; metal working services		15980	20540	24629	26562		7208	9081	10644	11434		2202	2724
2891	Metal forging/pressing/stamping/roll-forming		3544	4971	6344	6787		1350	1784	2238	2440		580	681
2892	Treatment & coating of metals		4014	5454	6869	7986		2288	3000	3742	4197		769	1049
2893	Cutlery, hand tools and general hardware		2379	2788	3381	3392		1064	1305	1508	1464		310	330
2899	Other fabricated metal products n.e.c.		6043	7327	8034	8397		2505	2991	3156	3333		543	665
291	General purpose machinery		24668	27791	30452	33239		9734	11100	11364	12191		1790	2199
2911	Engines & turbines (not for transport equipment)		1647	2159	3239	3779		519	692	812	1144		253	400
2912	Pumps, compressors, taps and valves		4709	4639	5205	5964		1980	1999	2076	2269		344	477
2913	Bearings, gears, gearing & driving elements		1885	2150	2486	2537		935	981	1000	1020		195	276
2914	Ovens, furnaces and furnace burners		466	705	594	674		198	261	224	269		31	68
2915	Lifting and handling equipment		3733	4287	4733	5149		1378	1561	1707	1826		234	264
2919	Other general purpose machinery		12227	13850	14195	15136		4724	5606	5546	5661		734	714

292	Special purpose machinery	22529	29129	31857	45337	9149	11425	12200	17126	2363	3223
2921	Agricultural and forestry machinery	1104	1762	2008	2099	428	669	851	799	153	164
2922	Machine tools	3846	4854	5616	6348	1463	1800	2043	2407	328	386
2923	Machinery for metallurgy	156	198	225	225	64	74	77	85	10	19
2924	Machinery for mining & construction	3907	4777	4737	5577	1314	1487	1145	1677	149	246
2925	Food/beverage/tobacco processing machinery	335	316	324	338	132	132	143	146	19	18
2926	Machinery for textile, apparel and leather	1082	1153	943	920	452	452	384	365	70	59
2927	Weapons and ammunition	1245	1598	2074	2041	541	646	778	795	182	93
2929	Other special purpose machinery	10853	14472	15930	17372	4754	6166	6778	7413	1452	1813
2930	Domestic appliances n.e.c.	8545	9182	10151	10418	2764	3155	3644	3440	359	424
3000	Office, accounting and computing machinery	20264	12123	7960	8356	5361	3956	3003	3220	385	323
3110	Electric motors, generators and transformers	7570	7967	7724	7372	2499	2620	2492	2456	378	355
3120	Electricity distribution & control apparatus	6391	7320	8073	9200	2568	2782	3107	3327	434	560
3130	Insulated wire and cable	4469	5344	5702	7335	1226	1859	1640	2281	210	340
3140	Accumulators, primary cells and batteries	1446	1666	1238	1283	571	671	465	452	57	66
3150	Lighting equipment and electric lamps	1849	1961	2124	2521	750	785	874	1045	182	230
3190	Other electrical equipment n.e.c.	4284	4876	5380	5854	1532	1688	1842	1853	213	357
3210	Electronic valves, tubes, etc.	57597	79227	81279	87764	29614	43667	42524	43156	26532	27287
3220	TV/radio transmitters; line comm. apparatus	36089	39902	45107	45230	12676	15095	16737	18229	2076	1427
3230	TV and radio receivers and associated goods	9797	16688	13663	13771	2881	4670	4973	5532	797	1175
331	Medical, measuring, testing appliances, etc.	4370	5055	6004	6800	2032	2353	2724	3030	368	476
3311	Medical, surgical and orthopaedic equipment	1515	1683	1948	2305	783	908	1016	1191	131	173
3312	Measuring/testing/navigating appliances,etc.	2280	2578	3186	3439	997	1102	1381	1439	172	225
3313	Industrial process control equipment	576	794	870	1055	252	344	327	400	66	78
3320	Optical instruments & photographic equipment	1081	1741	2529	2957	532	715	959	1002	311	354
3330	Watches and clocks	267	240	222	183	96	85	85	67	9	7
3410	Motor vehicles	47627	52750	57015	60627	18131	17924	18461	20038	3239	2365
3420	Automobile bodies, trailers & semi-trailers	860	885	887	1008	265	291	306	361	68	59
3430	Parts/accessories for automobiles	26418	34428	39880	46078	9875	11899	13275	15444	3290	3804
351	Building and repairing of ships and boats	22303	25757	30038	37140	8267	9078	9413	12194	1581	2372
3511	Building and repairing of ships	22294	25745	30024	37129	8263	9072	9406	12188	1580	2371
3512	Building/repairing of pleasure/sport. boats	9	12	14	12	4	6	8	6	1	1
3520	Railway/tramway locomotives & rolling stock	1409	1459	1701	1910	617	617	746	816	50	118
3530	Aircraft and spacecraft	1421	1460	1509	1822	560	847	707	955	67	198
359	Transport equipment n.e.c.	462	477	498	513	165	174	179	176	28	35
3591	Motorcycles	380	405	425	402	134	147	149	131	22	29
3592	Bicycles and invalid carriages	35	23	27	41	14	9	12	15	2	1
3599	Other transport equipment n.e.c.	47	49	45	70	18	17	18	29	4	4
3610	Furniture	5839	6899	7571	8571	2115	2685	2719	3009	399	445
369	Manufacturing n.e.c.	3945	3899	3926	3795	1711	1675	1663	1618	154	224
3691	Jewellery and related articles	515	582	473	373	176	198	158	135	12	10
3692	Musical instruments	463	396	319	253	249	176	140	101	10	14
3693	Sports goods	543	583	572	552	261	277	252	245	21	43
3694	Games and toys	427	441	486	340	201	194	219	151	17	28
3699	Other manufacturing n.e.c.	1996	1897	2075	2277	824	831	894	985	94	129
3710	Recycling of metal waste and scrap	693	1283	1434	1401	186	307	307	308	70	48
3720	Recycling of non-metal waste and scrap	330	461	588	600	148	203	247	245	63	40
D	Total manufacturing	677371	794853	851789	912763	255813	301863	312792	326844	73943	76699

Republic of Korea

ISIC Revision 3			Index numbers of industrial production											
			(2000=100)											
ISIC	Industry	Note	1995	1996	1997	1998	1999	2000	2001	2002	2003	2004	2005	2006
15	Food and beverages		97	101	99	10	97	100	105	108	106	108	108	110
16	Tobacco products		90	96	99	103	98	100	100	100	130	141	114	127
17	Textiles		117	111	104	95	101	100	90	85	75	69	60	60
18	Wearing apparel, fur		143	138	110	80	87	100	92	96	84	84	89	97
19	Leather, leather products and footwear		211	180	153	108	108	100	94	88	76	65	59	60
20	Wood products (excl. furniture)		121	122	122	77	97	100	107	113	114	109	104	115
21	Paper and paper products		89	94	98	87	96	100	99	105	105	109	109	112
22	Printing and publishing		...	...	...	...	...	...	...	...	...	...	...	...
23	Coke,refined petroleum products,nuclear fuel		71	83	101	90	98	100	96	88	91	94	97	98
24	Chemicals and chemical products		...	...	...	...	...	...	...	...	...	...	...	...
25	Rubber and plastics products		93	99	101	80	94	100	102	109	112	116	118	126
26	Non-metallic mineral products		105	112	114	87	94	100	102	104	110	108	101	107
27	Basic metals		82	87	92	81	92	100	101	106	112	118	118	122
28	Fabricated metal products		107	113	116	91	95	100	93	96	97	100	98	104
29	Machinery and equipment n.e.c.		92	96	94	64	80	100	95	102	109	122	126	138
30	Office, accounting and computing machinery		24	30	36	48	73	100	102	126	148	188	222	271
31	Electrical machinery and apparatus		84	88	88	66	84	100	100	112	112	119	123	123
32	Radio,television and communication equipment		...	...	...	...	...	...	...	...	...	...	...	...
33	Medical, precision and optical instruments		99	94	92	83	92	100	102	101	103	104	99	106
34	Motor vehicles, trailers, semi-trailers		77	87	87	57	88	100	99	107	114	128	138	149
35	Other transport equipment		52	61	67	100	109	100	122	119	128	145	156	169
36	Furniture; manufacturing n.e.c.		...	...	...	...	...	...	...	...	...	...	...	...
37	Recycling		...	...	...	...	...	...	...	...	...	...	...	...
D	Total manufacturing		64	70	73	68	85	100	100	108	114	127	135	146

Republic of Moldova

Supplier of information:
National Bureau of Statistics of the Republic of Moldova, Chisinau.

Basic source of data:
Not reported.

Major deviations from ISIC (Revision 3):
None reported.

Reference period:
Calendar year.

Scope:
All self-sustained establishments. Data exclude the area of the left bank of the Dniester and the town of Bender.

Method of data collection:
Not reported.

Type of enumeration:
Not reported.

Adjusted for non-response:
Not reported.

Concepts and definitions of variables:
No deviations from the standard UN concepts and definitions are reported.

Related national publications:
None reported.

ISIC Revision 3		Number of establishments					Number of employees					Wages and salaries paid to employees				
			(number)					(number)					(millions of Moldovan Lei)			
ISIC	Industry	Note	2003	2004	2005	2006	Note	2003	2004	2005	2006	Note	2003	2004	2005	2006
151	Processed meat,fish,fruit,vegetables,fats		44	46	53	51		9587	9742	9305	8873		95.5	115.1	135.5	157.9
1511	Processing/preserving of meat		12	12	14	14		2402	2366	2139	2271		28.1	30.8	36.1	46.4
1512	Processing/preserving of fish		2	2	2	2		206	220	262	160		2.6	3.4	4.0	3.4
1513	Processing/preserving of fruit & vegetables		29	30	35	34		5830	5874	5653	5185		43.3	52.9	65.7	74.9
1514	Vegetable and animal oils and fats		1	2	2	1		1149	1282	1251	1257		21.4	27.9	29.7	33.3
1520	Dairy products		20	15	15	13		3652	3938	3603	3421		46.3	60.1	69.1	73.2
153	Grain mill products; starches; animal feeds		22	19	17	17		2703	1966	1966	1804		22.4	17.3	20.7	22.8
1531	Grain mill products		18	15	13	11		...	1390	1380	1250		...	9.3	11.2	12.4
1532	Starches and starch products		-	-	-	-		-	-	-	-		-	-	-	-
1533	Prepared animal feeds		4	4	4	6		574	576	586	554		6.4	8.0	9.4	10.4
154	Other food products		66	62	69	68		11626	11041	10641	10751		154.3	167.9	202.5	232.1
1541	Bakery products		52	46	53	54		5826	5805	5948	6288		88.4	100.0	110.8	127.1
1542	Sugar		6	7	7	6		3982	3401	2889	2649		39.5	38.3	49.4	60.3
1543	Cocoa, chocolate and sugar confectionery		3	3	3	3		1422	1418	1437	1473		21.6	24.7	35.5	38.4
1544	Macaroni, noodles & similar products		2	3	3	3		40	59	51	50		0.1	0.4	0.5	0.5
1549	Other food products n.e.c.		3	3	3	2		...	...	...	...		...	...	...	...
155	Beverages		158	154	162	161		16641	19514	20205	18431		218.9	287.1	337.0	271.7
1551	Distilling, rectifying & blending of spirits		13	15	14	14		...	...	...	...		...	...	...	...
1552	Wines		130	124	130	129		12298	14207	14958	13046		139.5	176.6	207.3	141.7
1553	Malt liquors and malt		5	4	5	5		...	...	...	...		...	...	...	...
1554	Soft drinks; mineral waters		10	11	13	13		...	...	...	...		...	...	...	...
1600	Tobacco products		12	10	10	9		2248	2099	2074	1843		46.4	48.4	55.3	50.1
171	Spinning, weaving and finishing of textiles		3	2	4	5		...	...	...	...		...	...	...	...
1711	Textile fibre preparation; textile weaving		2	2	2	3		...	...	...	...		...	...	...	...
1712	Finishing of textiles		1	...	2	2		...	...	...	...		...	...	...	...
172	Other textiles		9	7	7	5		...	...	...	...		...	...	...	...
1721	Made-up textile articles, except apparel		3	1	1	1		...	...	...	...		...	...	...	...
1722	Carpets and rugs		5	5	4	2		...	...	...	...		...	...	...	...
1723	Cordage, rope, twine and netting		-	-	-	-		...	...	...	...		...	...	...	...
1729	Other textiles n.e.c.		1	1	2	2		...	...	...	...		...	...	...	...
1730	Knitted and crocheted fabrics and articles		6	5	5	4		...	...	...	...		...	...	...	...
1810	Wearing apparel, except fur apparel		33	36	42	42		...	...	...	...		...	...	...	...
1820	Dressing & dyeing of fur; processing of fur		2	1	1	1		...	...	...	...		...	...	...	...
191	Tanning, dressing and processing of leather		4	3	3	3		...	...	...	...		...	...	...	...
1911	Tanning and dressing of leather		1	1	1	1		...	...	...	...		...	...	...	...
1912	Luggage, handbags, etc.; saddlery & harness		3	2	2	2		...	...	...	...		...	...	...	...
1920	Footwear		8	9	9	9		...	...	...	...		...	...	...	...
2010	Sawmilling and planing of wood		1	3	4	3		...	...	...	...		...	...	...	...
202	Products of wood, cork, straw, etc.		...	...	...	...		...	...	...	...		...	...	...	...
2021	Veneer sheets, plywood, particle board, etc.		1	...	...	...		...	...	...	...		...	...	...	...
2022	Builders' carpentry and joinery		9	6	5	7		...	...	...	...		...	...	...	...
2023	Wooden containers		4	3	3	2		...	...	...	...		...	...	...	...
2029	Other wood products; articles of cork/straw		...	...	...	...		...	...	...	...		...	...	...	...
210	Paper and paper products		...	13	17	15		1193	1368	1691	1564		21.5	26.3	37.0	37.5
2101	Pulp, paper and paperboard		-	-	1	1		...	...	...	...		...	...	...	...
2102	Corrugated paper and paperboard		8	9	11	9		...	...	...	...		...	...	...	...
2109	Other articles of paper and paperboard		...	4	5	5		...	...	...	...		...	...	...	...
221	Publishing		...	...	...	...		...	...	...	...		...	...	...	...
2211	Publishing of books and other publications		...	...	1	1		...	...	...	...		...	...	...	...
2212	Publishing of newspapers, journals, etc.		1	1	1	1		...	...	...	...		...	...	...	...
2213	Publishing of recorded media		-	-	...	...		...	...	...	...		...	...	...	...
2219	Other publishing		...	...	...	...		...	...	...	...		...	...	...	...

222	Printing and related service activities	...	...	...	...	...	...	...	...	...	...	...	...
2221	Printing	26	21	23	22	...	...	...	...	...	...	...	...
2222	Service activities related to printing	...	...	...	...	...	...	...	...	...	...	...	...
2230	Reproduction of recorded media	...	...	...	...	...	...	...	...	...	...	...	...
2310	Coke oven products	...	...	...	...	...	...	...	...	...	...	...	...
2320	Refined petroleum products	...	...	1	1	...	...	...	...	...	...	...	...
2330	Processing of nuclear fuel	...	...	...	...	...	...	...	...	...	...	...	...
241	Basic chemicals	3	2	2	2	...	...	...	...	...	...	...	...
2411	Basic chemicals, except fertilizers	2	1	1	1	...	...	...	...	...	...	...	...
2412	Fertilizers and nitrogen compounds	-	-	-	-	...	...	...	...	...	...	...	...
2413	Plastics in primary forms; synthetic rubber	1	1	1	1	...	...	...	...	...	...	...	...
242	Other chemicals	11	11	...	...	...	...	...	...	...	...	...	...
2421	Pesticides and other agro-chemical products	-	...	1	...	...	...	...	...	...	...	...	...
2422	Paints, varnishes, printing ink and mastics	2	3	3	3	...	...	...	...	...	...	...	...
2423	Pharmaceuticals, medicinal chemicals, etc.	5	6	6	7	...	...	...	...	...	...	...	...
2424	Soap, cleaning & cosmetic preparations	2	1	2	2	...	...	...	...	...	...	...	...
2429	Other chemical products n.e.c.	2	1	...	...	...	...	...	...	...	...	...	...
2430	Man-made fibres	-	-	-	-	...	...	...	...	...	...	...	...
251	Rubber products	2	2	2	...	...	...	...	...	...	...	...	...
2511	Rubber tyres and tubes	1	1	1	...	...	...	...	...	...	...	...	...
2519	Other rubber products	1	1	1	...	...	...	...	...	...	...	...	...
2520	Plastic products	10	12	17	18	...	...	...	...	...	...	...	...
2610	Glass and glass products	4	5	5	4	...	...	...	...	...	...	...	...
269	Non-metallic mineral products n.e.c.	...	...	...	...	...	...	...	...	...	...	...	...
2691	Pottery, china and earthenware	1	1	1	1	...	...	...	...	...	...	...	...
2692	Refractory ceramic products	-	-	-	-	...	...	...	...	...	...	...	...
2693	Struct.non-refractory clay; ceramic products	8	5	5	4	...	...	...	...	...	...	...	...
2694	Cement, lime and plaster	3	3	3	3	...	...	...	...	...	...	...	...
2695	Articles of concrete, cement and plaster	13	13	15	15	...	...	...	...	...	...	...	...
2696	Cutting, shaping & finishing of stone	3	1	2	2	...	...	...	...	...	...	...	...
2699	Other non-metallic mineral products n.e.c.	...	...	...	...	...	...	...	...	...	...	...	...
2710	Basic iron and steel	...	...	...	...	...	...	...	...	...	...	...	...
2720	Basic precious and non-ferrous metals	...	...	...	...	...	...	...	...	...	...	...	...
273	Casting of metals	3	3	3	2	...	...	...	...	...	...	...	...
2731	Casting of iron and steel	2	2	2	2	...	...	...	...	...	...	...	...
2732	Casting of non-ferrous metals	1	1	1	-	...	...	...	...	...	...	...	...
281	Struct.metal products;tanks;steam generators	10	16	19	18	...	...	...	...	...	...	...	...
2811	Structural metal products	9	14	16	15	...	...	...	...	...	...	...	...
2812	Tanks, reservoirs and containers of metal	1	2	3	3	...	...	...	...	...	...	...	...
2813	Steam generators	-	-	-	-	...	...	...	...	...	...	...	...
289	Other metal products; metal working services	18	17	16	19	...	...	...	...	...	...	...	...
2891	Metal forging/pressing/stamping/roll-forming	6	1	1	1	...	...	...	...	...	...	...	...
2892	Treatment & coating of metals	1	2	2	2	...	...	...	...	...	...	...	...
2893	Cutlery, hand tools and general hardware	2	4	4	4	...	...	...	...	...	...	...	...
2899	Other fabricated metal products n.e.c.	9	10	9	12	...	...	...	...	...	...	...	...
291	General purpose machinery	...	10	...	...	...	...	...	...	...	...	...	...
2911	Engines & turbines (not for transport equipment)	2	2	1	1	...	...	...	...	...	...	...	...
2912	Pumps, compressors, taps and valves	4	5	4	4	...	...	...	...	...	...	...	...
2913	Bearings, gears, gearing & driving elements	-	...	...	...	...	...	...	...	...	...	...	...
2914	Ovens, furnaces and furnace burners	2	...	1	2	...	...	...	...	...	...	...	...
2915	Lifting and handling equipment	1	1	2	2	...	...	...	...	...	...	...	...
2919	Other general purpose machinery	...	1	1	2	...	...	...	...	...	...	...	...
292	Special purpose machinery	...	...	...	...	...	...	...	...	...	...	...	...
2921	Agricultural and forestry machinery	13	9	15	15	...	...	...	...	...	...	...	...
2922	Machine tools	7	6	5	4	...	...	...	...	...	...	...	...
2923	Machinery for metallurgy	-	-	-	...	...	...	...	...	...	...	...	...
2924	Machinery for mining & construction	...	...	...	...	...	...	...	...	...	...	...	...
2925	Food/beverage/tobacco processing machinery	4	2	3	3	...	...	...	...	...	...	...	...
2926	Machinery for textile, apparel and leather	2	2	2	1	...	...	...	...	...	...	...	...
2927	Weapons and ammunition	-	...	...	...	...	...	...	...	...	...	...	...
2929	Other special purpose machinery	2	...	...	...	...	...	...	...	...	...	...	...

continued

Republic of Moldova

ISIC Revision 3		Number of establishments					Number of employees					Wages and salaries paid to employees				
			(number)					(number)					(millions of Moldovan Lei)			
ISIC	Industry	Note	2003	2004	2005	2006	Note	2003	2004	2005	2006	Note	2003	2004	2005	2006
2930	Domestic appliances n.e.c.		5	4	3	3		...	...	...	...		...	...	...	...
3000	Office, accounting and computing machinery		1	1	1	1		446	525	512	462		3.6	5.1	5.5	7.9
3110	Electric motors, generators and transformers		3	2	2	2		...	...	...	...		...	...	...	...
3120	Electricity distribution & control apparatus		1	3	3	2		...	...	...	...		...	...	...	...
3130	Insulated wire and cable		...	1	1	2		...	...	...	...		...	...	...	...
3140	Accumulators, primary cells and batteries		...	1	2	1		...	...	...	...		...	...	...	...
3150	Lighting equipment and electric lamps		...	...	...	1		...	...	...	...		4.6	...	...	...
3190	Other electrical equipment n.e.c.		...	2	2	1		...	...	...	...		...	...	...	...
3210	Electronic valves, tubes, etc.		...	...	...	...		...	...	...	...		...	...	...	...
3220	TV/radio transmitters; line comm. apparatus		...	...	1	1		...	...	...	...		...	...	...	...
3230	TV and radio receivers and associated goods		3	1	1	1		...	...	...	...		...	...	...	...
331	Medical, measuring, testing appliances, etc.		...	6	8	6		...	...	...	...		...	...	...	...
3311	Medical, surgical and orthopaedic equipment		...	1	1	1		...	...	...	...		...	...	...	...
3312	Measuring/testing/navigating appliances,etc.		5	4	6	4		...	...	...	...		...	...	...	...
3313	Industrial process control equipment		...	1	1	1		...	...	...	...		...	...	...	...
3320	Optical instruments & photographic equipment		...	...	...	...		...	...	...	...		...	...	...	...
3330	Watches and clocks		...	...	...	...		...	...	...	...		...	...	...	...
3410	Motor vehicles		...	...	...	...		...	...	...	...		...	...	...	...
3420	Automobile bodies, trailers & semi-trailers		...	...	...	...		...	...	...	...		...	...	...	...
3430	Parts/accessories for automobiles		1	...	...	...		...	...	...	...		...	...	...	...
351	Building and repairing of ships and boats		...	...	...	...		...	...	...	...		...	...	...	...
3511	Building and repairing of ships		...	...	...	...		...	...	...	...		...	...	...	...
3512	Building/repairing of pleasure/sport. boats		...	...	...	...		...	...	...	...		...	...	...	...
3520	Railway/tramway locomotives & rolling stock		...	1	1	1		...	...	...	...		...	...	...	...
3530	Aircraft and spacecraft		...	...	...	...		...	...	...	...		...	...	...	...
359	Transport equipment n.e.c.		1	...	...	...		...	...	...	...		...	...	...	...
3591	Motorcycles		-	...	...	...		...	...	...	...		...	...	...	...
3592	Bicycles and invalid carriages		-	...	...	...		...	...	...	...		...	...	...	...
3599	Other transport equipment n.e.c.		1	...	...	...		...	...	...	...		...	...	...	...
3610	Furniture		11	12	18	18		...	...	...	...		...	...	...	...
369	Manufacturing n.e.c.		...	2	...	...		...	...	...	...		...	...	...	...
3691	Jewellery and related articles		1	1	1	1		...	...	...	...		...	...	...	...
3692	Musical instruments		-	-	-	-		...	...	...	...		...	...	...	...
3693	Sports goods		...	...	...	...		...	...	...	...		...	...	...	...
3694	Games and toys		...	...	1	1		...	...	...	...		...	...	...	...
3699	Other manufacturing n.e.c.		1	1	1	1		...	...	...	...		...	...	...	...
3710	Recycling of metal waste and scrap		3	3	3	3		...	...	...	...		...	...	...	...
3720	Recycling of non-metal waste and scrap		...	...	...	...		...	...	...	...		...	...	...	...
D	Total manufacturing		606	575	637	620		103554	107480	106059	104162		1261.0	1558.5	1809.3	1993.3

ISIC Revision 3		Output in producers' prices					Value added					Gross fixed capital formation		
			(millions of Moldovan Lei)					(millions of Moldovan Lei)					(millions of Moldovan Lei)	
ISIC	Industry	Note	2003	2004	2005	2006	Note	2003	2004	2005	2006	Note	2005	2006
151	Processed meat,fish,fruit,vegetables,fats		1872.4	1722.0	2079.3	2411.6	a/	2366.2	2368.5	2420.3	2290.2		...	...
1511	Processing/preserving of meat		595.2	615.7	652.6	749.2		...	...	...	...		...	...
1512	Processing/preserving of fish		41.0	45.5	58.5	64.1		...	...	...	...		...	...
1513	Processing/preserving of fruit & vegetables		760.0	550.2	690.2	881.8		...	...	...	...		...	...
1514	Vegetable and animal oils and fats		476.2	510.6	678.1	716.6		...	...	...	...		...	...
1520	Dairy products		541.2	639.1	721.0	813.1	a/	...	...	...	...		...	...
153	Grain mill products; starches; animal feeds		209.0	115.5	103.4	...	a/	...	...	...	...		...	...
1531	Grain mill products		188.9	95.1	...	165.0		...	...	...	...		...	...
1532	Starches and starch products		-	-	-	-		...	...	...	...		...	...
1533	Prepared animal feeds		20.0	20.4	...	38.4		...	...	...	...		...	...
154	Other food products		1338.7	1511.5	1814.6	2180.9	a/	...	...	...	...		...	...
1541	Bakery products		645.6	775.5	771.5	861.5		...	...	...	...		...	...
1542	Sugar		393.1	423.4	659.7	905.1		...	...	...	...		...	...
1543	Cocoa, chocolate and sugar confectionery		227.0	234.0	286.5	333.9		...	...	...	...		...	...
1544	Macaroni, noodles & similar products		7.1	9.8	18.6	20.0		...	...	...	...		...	...
1549	Other food products n.e.c.		65.8	68.7	78.4	60.4		...	...	...	...		...	...
155	Beverages		4308.5	4764.0	5524.4	3616.8	a/	...	...	...	...		...	...
1551	Distilling, rectifying & blending of spirits		600.4	726.6	836.4	546.2		...	...	...	...		...	...
1552	Wines		3269.9	3494.1	4032.8	2227.3		...	...	...	...		...	...
1553	Malt liquors and malt		317.7	407.1	476.7	561.0		...	...	...	...		...	...
1554	Soft drinks; mineral waters		120.5	136.2	178.5	282.3		...	...	...	...		...	...
1600	Tobacco products		424.9	424.4	429.9	347.5		65.2	80.2	79.6	73.9		...	...
171	Spinning, weaving and finishing of textiles		13.7	9.1	10.5	81.4	b/	189.4	143.0	152.8	227.5		...	...
1711	Textile fibre preparation; textile weaving		8.5	5.1	5.1	74.6		...	...	...	...		...	...
1712	Finishing of textiles		5.1	4.0	5.4	6.8		...	...	...	...		...	...
172	Other textiles		154.6	193.8	318.5	452.3	b/	...	...	...	...		...	...
1721	Made-up textile articles, except apparel		7.8	17.5	16.6	15.6		...	...	...	...		...	...
1722	Carpets and rugs		139.3	167.3	293.1	427.6		...	...	...	...		...	...
1723	Cordage, rope, twine and netting		-	-	-	-		...	...	...	...		...	...
1729	Other textiles n.e.c.		7.6	8.9	8.8	9.1		...	...	...	...		...	...
1730	Knitted and crocheted fabrics and articles		47.2	39.3	40.2	52.4	b/	...	...	...	...		...	...
1810	Wearing apparel, except fur apparel		374.6	491.2	576.3	728.5	c/	203.1	358.8	370.4	552.8		...	...
1820	Dressing & dyeing of fur; processing of fur		2.4	0.3	1.4	0.7	c/	...	...	...	...		...	...
191	Tanning, dressing and processing of leather		73.9	61.8	69.9	80.0	d/	71.7	124.6	146.8	165.9		...	...
1911	Tanning and dressing of leather		29.1	26.7	29.3	29.2		...	...	...	...		...	...
1912	Luggage, handbags, etc.; saddlery & harness		44.8	35.0	40.6	50.8		...	...	...	...		...	...
1920	Footwear		82.4	98.5	134.4	168.0	d/	...	...	...	...		...	...
2010	Sawmilling and planing of wood		17.2	30.9	29.5	47.2	e/	35.2	64.5	99.8	58.5		...	...
202	Products of wood, cork, straw, etc.		80.3	64.8	61.1	...	e/	...	...	...	...		...	...
2021	Veneer sheets, plywood, particle board, etc.		16.0	...	...	...		...	...	...	...		...	...
2022	Builders' carpentry and joinery		40.3	46.6	46.6	64.1		...	...	...	...		...	...
2023	Wooden containers		10.8	11.5	6.3	8.2		...	...	...	...		...	...
2029	Other wood products; articles of cork/straw		13.2	6.7	8.2	6.3		...	...	...	...		...	...
210	Paper and paper products		250.7	382.5	499.9	516.3		37.9	61.0	77.5	76.2		...	...
2101	Pulp, paper and paperboard		-	-	146.6	229.9		...	...	...	...		...	...
2102	Corrugated paper and paperboard		226.1	145.1	186.7	112.6		...	...	...	...		...	...
2109	Other articles of paper and paperboard		24.6	237.4	166.6	173.8		...	...	...	...		...	...
221	Publishing		225.7	185.3	222.3	185.2	f/	159.3	166.2	200.7	195.4	f/	19.0	25.3
2211	Publishing of books and other publications		137.9	102.6	126.0	101.5		...	...	...	...		...	...
2212	Publishing of newspapers, journals, etc.		71.5	80.9	91.7	82.1		...	...	...	...		...	...
2213	Publishing of recorded media		-	-	0.6	0.2		...	...	...	...		...	...
2219	Other publishing		16.3	1.8	4.0	1.4		...	...	...	...		...	...

continued

ISIC Revision 3		Output in producers' prices					Value added					Gross fixed capital formation		
			(millions of Moldovan Lei)					(millions of Moldovan Lei)					(millions of Moldovan Lei)	
ISIC	Industry	Note	2003	2004	2005	2006	Note	2003	2004	2005	2006	Note	2005	2006
222	Printing and related service activities		259.7	200.2	251.7	247.8	f/	...	...	...	...	f/	...	...
2221	Printing		224.5	192.9	244.4	241.9		...	...	...	...		...	...
2222	Service activities related to printing		35.2	7.3	7.3	5.9		...	...	...	...		...	...
2230	Reproduction of recorded media		1.3	1.4	0.5	0.8	f/	...	...	...	...	f/	...	...
2310	Coke oven products		...	...	...	...	g/	42.7	46.4	55.6	63.6		...	...
2320	Refined petroleum products		0.4	2.7	8.7	11.6	g/	...	...	...	...		...	...
2330	Processing of nuclear fuel		...	...	...	...	g/	...	...	...	...		...	...
241	Basic chemicals		15.3	20.5	24.5	28.6	g/	...	...	...	...		...	...
2411	Basic chemicals, except fertilizers		5.6	4.0	4.2	5.2		...	...	...	...		...	...
2412	Fertilizers and nitrogen compounds		-	-	-	-		...	...	...	...		...	...
2413	Plastics in primary forms; synthetic rubber		9.8	16.5	20.2	23.3		...	...	...	...		...	...
242	Other chemicals		136.3	156.2	207.2	267.7	g/	...	...	...	...		...	...
2421	Pesticides and other agro-chemical products		-	0.1	12.8	1.5		...	...	...	...		...	...
2422	Paints, varnishes, printing ink and mastics		23.5	56.3	74.4	112.2		...	...	...	...		...	...
2423	Pharmaceuticals, medicinal chemicals, etc.		61.3	61.0	60.2	93.7		...	...	...	...		...	...
2424	Soap, cleaning & cosmetic preparations		27.8	25.0	36.2	33.5		...	...	...	...		...	...
2429	Other chemical products n.e.c.		23.7	13.8	23.6	26.7		...	...	...	...		...	...
2430	Man-made fibres		-	-	-	-	g/	...	...	...	...		...	...
251	Rubber products		23.2	21.0	5.7	...	h/	62.9	85.9	124.7	185.1		...	...
2511	Rubber tyres and tubes		2.5	3.3	0.1	...		...	...	...	...		...	...
2519	Other rubber products		20.7	17.6	5.7	7.2		...	...	...	...		...	...
2520	Plastic products		226.8	325.0	494.1	832.5	h/	...	...	...	...		...	...
2610	Glass and glass products		507.2	546.8	687.7	754.3	i/	507.4	570.7	604.4	831.3		...	...
269	Non-metallic mineral products n.e.c.		737.2	962.0	1305.4	1941.1	i/	...	...	...	...		...	...
2691	Pottery, china and earthenware		0.9	0.9	3.2	4.8		...	...	...	...		...	...
2692	Refractory ceramic products		-	-	-	-		...	...	...	...		...	...
2693	Struct.non-refractory clay; ceramic products		110.7	145.9	142.6	178.5		...	...	...	...		...	...
2694	Cement, lime and plaster		137.7	401.4	588.7	956.9		...	...	...	...		...	...
2695	Articles of concrete, cement and plaster		463.4	396.8	550.4	763.5		...	...	...	...		...	...
2696	Cutting, shaping & finishing of stone		24.2	16.8	18.5	29.1		...	...	...	...		...	...
2699	Other non-metallic mineral products n.e.c.		0.3	0.2	2.1	8.3		...	...	...	...		...	...
2710	Basic iron and steel		...	...	...	...	j/	5.9	7.7	23.7	41.3		...	...
2720	Basic precious and non-ferrous metals		...	...	...	...	j/	...	...	...	...		...	...
273	Casting of metals		12.7	18.2	...	107.8	j/	...	...	...	...		...	...
2731	Casting of iron and steel		10.1	17.3	59.8	107.8		...	...	...	...		...	...
2732	Casting of non-ferrous metals		2.6	0.9	...	-		...	...	...	...		...	...
281	Struct.metal products;tanks;steam generators		148.9	214.1	311.2	368.6	k/	84.8	103.1	133.4	121.4	k/	440.4	688.6
2811	Structural metal products		125.8	192.9	278.9	323.2		...	...	...	...		...	...
2812	Tanks, reservoirs and containers of metal		23.0	21.2	32.3	45.4		...	...	...	...		...	...
2813	Steam generators		-	-	-	-		...	...	...	...		...	...
289	Other metal products; metal working services		121.9	133.9	124.2	160.7	k/	...	...	...	...	k/	...	...
2891	Metal forging/pressing/stamping/roll-forming		36.1	3.9	2.9	3.2		...	...	...	...		...	...
2892	Treatment & coating of metals		8.7	13.5	11.2	13.6		...	...	...	...		...	...
2893	Cutlery, hand tools and general hardware		4.4	17.8	17.6	30.1		...	...	...	...		...	...
2899	Other fabricated metal products n.e.c.		72.7	98.7	92.5	113.7		...	...	...	...		...	...
291	General purpose machinery		108.4	192.5	172.7	221.6	m/	188.4	161.2	160.2	174.2	m/	1010.9	1088.0
2911	Engines & turbines (not for transport equipment)		5.3	7.6	8.8	7.8		...	...	...	...		...	...
2912	Pumps, compressors, taps and valves		81.0	116.0	107.3	116.5		...	...	...	...		...	...
2913	Bearings, gears, gearing & driving elements		-	1.0	1.2	1.3		...	...	...	...		...	...
2914	Ovens, furnaces and furnace burners		5.6	33.8	11.8	24.7		...	...	...	...		...	...
2915	Lifting and handling equipment		9.5	16.6	20.5	24.5		...	...	...	...		...	...
2919	Other general purpose machinery		7.0	17.6	23.1	46.8		...	...	...	...		...	...

292	Special purpose machinery		236.5	206.1	229.8	251.9	m/	...	...	...	...	m/	...	...
2921	Agricultural and forestry machinery		146.0	142.2	146.9	159.5		...	...	...	...		...	...
2922	Machine tools		38.2	25.5	34.9	46.9		...	...	...	...		...	...
2923	Machinery for metallurgy		-	-	-	-		...	...	...	...		...	...
2924	Machinery for mining & construction		0.5	1.8	4.1	8.8		...	...	...	...		...	...
2925	Food/beverage/tobacco processing machinery		23.7	20.9	27.2	18.9		...	...	...	...		...	...
2926	Machinery for textile, apparel and leather		7.0	6.6	7.1	5.6		...	...	...	...		...	...
2927	Weapons and ammunition		-	...	...	-		...	...	...	...		...	...
2929	Other special purpose machinery		21.0	9.1	9.6	12.2		...	...	...	...		...	...
2930	Domestic appliances n.e.c.		83.6	62.0	45.7	31.2	m/	...	...	...	...	m/	...	...
3000	Office, accounting and computing machinery		38.8	26.0	35.5	34.0		8.0	4.6	6.9	15.2		257.7	244.4
3110	Electric motors, generators and transformers		18.7	41.1	48.3	65.2	n/	29.6	51.1	81.5	93.0	n/	218.9	264.7
3120	Electricity distribution & control apparatus		2.5	6.9	21.2	31.6	n/	...	...	...	...	n/	...	...
3130	Insulated wire and cable		...	5.5	9.3	15.3	n/	...	...	...	...	n/	...	...
3140	Accumulators, primary cells and batteries		...	5.8	16.4	11.4	n/	...	...	...	...	n/	...	...
3150	Lighting equipment and electric lamps		...	7.3	5.5	8.9	n/	...	...	...	...	n/	...	...
3190	Other electrical equipment n.e.c.		...	14.0	17.9	20.6	n/	...	...	...	...	n/	...	...
3210	Electronic valves, tubes, etc.		...	0.7	0.2	0.2	p/	44.9	24.0	20.2	20.9	p/	267.9	417.1
3220	TV/radio transmitters; line comm. apparatus		5.8	21.4	9.7	22.2	p/	...	...	...	...	p/	...	...
3230	TV and radio receivers and associated goods		31.3	27.1	22.8	15.2	p/	...	...	...	...	p/	...	...
331	Medical, measuring, testing appliances, etc.		115.4	134.0	111.0	213.9	q/	67.8	75.0	71.5	117.2	q/	274.7	364.4
3311	Medical, surgical and orthopaedic equipment		14.9	22.3	18.3	21.4		...	...	...	...		...	...
3312	Measuring/testing/navigating appliances,etc.		100.5	91.7	65.1	133.3		...	...	...	...		...	...
3313	Industrial process control equipment		...	20.0	27.7	59.2		...	...	...	...		...	...
3320	Optical instruments & photographic equipment		...	2.7	1.5	2.1	q/	...	...	...	...	q/	...	...
3330	Watches and clocks		...	...	...	...	q/	...	...	...	...	q/	...	...
3410	Motor vehicles		...	...	...	...	r/	3.4	4.7	5.6	12.3		...	...
3420	Automobile bodies, trailers & semi-trailers		0.1	...	2.0	2.7	r/	...	...	...	...		...	...
3430	Parts/accessories for automobiles		8.4	...	...	...	r/	...	...	...	...		...	...
351	Building and repairing of ships and boats		...	...	...	...	r/	...	...	...	...	s/	920.2	1683.3
3511	Building and repairing of ships		...	...	...	...		...	...	...	...		...	...
3512	Building/repairing of pleasure/sport. boats		...	...	...	...		...	...	...	...		...	...
3520	Railway/tramway locomotives & rolling stock		3.4	8.1	6.9	6.1	r/	...	...	...	...	s/	...	...
3530	Aircraft and spacecraft		0.4	0.3	0.3	1.1	r/	...	...	...	...	s/	...	...
359	Transport equipment n.e.c.		1.5	...	...	...	r/	...	...	...	...	s/	...	...
3591	Motorcycles		-	...	...	...		...	...	...	...		...	...
3592	Bicycles and invalid carriages		-	...	...	...		...	...	...	...		...	...
3599	Other transport equipment n.e.c.		1.5	...	-	-		...	...	...	...		...	...
3610	Furniture		183.8	241.2	363.1	434.6	t/	72.5	115.6	149.7	209.9		149.0t/	...
369	Manufacturing n.e.c.		20.1	22.5	25.9	31.1	t/	...	...	...	...		...t/	...
3691	Jewellery and related articles		12.2	13.1	15.4	18.9		...	...	...	...		...	...
3692	Musical instruments		-	-	-	-		...	...	...	...		...	...
3693	Sports goods		0.1	1.4	0.8	1.0		...	...	...	...		...	...
3694	Games and toys		3.1	5.0	6.3	9.5		...	...	...	...		...	...
3699	Other manufacturing n.e.c.		4.7	2.9	3.4	1.8		...	...	...	...		...	...
3710	Recycling of metal waste and scrap		209.1	304.0	363.9	603.6	u/	19.1	33.9	36.7	73.4		...	...
3720	Recycling of non-metal waste and scrap		-	0.4	0.2	0.3	u/	...	...	...	...		...	...
D	Total manufacturing		13311.2	14665.4	17627.1	18717.9		4265.3	4650.8	5022.0	...		3558.6	4775.7

a/ 151 includes 1520, 153, 154 and 155.
b/ 171 includes 172 and 1730.
c/ 1810 includes 1820.
d/ 191 includes 1920.
e/ 2010 includes 202.
f/ 221 includes 222 and 2230.
g/ 2310 includes 2320, 2330, 241, 242 and 2430.
h/ 251 includes 2520.
i/ 2610 includes 269.
j/ 2710 includes 2720 and 273.
k/ 281 includes 289.
m/ 291 includes 292 and 2930.
n/ 3110 includes 3120, 3130, 3140, 3150 and 3190.
p/ 3210 includes 3220 and 3230.
q/ 331 includes 3320 and 3330.
r/ 3410 includes 3420, 3430, 351, 3520, 3530 and 359.
s/ 351 includes 3520, 3530 and 359.
t/ 3610 includes 369.
u/ 3710 includes 3720.

Republic of Moldova

ISIC Revision 3			Index numbers of industrial production (2000=100)											
ISIC	Industry	Note	1995	1996	1997	1998	1999	2000	2001	2002	2003	2004	2005	2006
15	Food and beverages		...	...	136	109	88	100	118	138	164	174	182	149
16	Tobacco products		...	...	92	85	106	100	97	65	65	62	59	46
17	Textiles		...	...	81	64	75	100	128	147	163	185	182	220
18	Wearing apparel, fur		...	...	67	69	79	100	113	118	119	140	147	153
19	Leather, leather products and footwear		...	...	137	92	83	100	99	131	159	200	231	239
20	Wood products (excl. furniture)		...	...	80	65	57	100	144	147	117	108	93	97
21	Paper and paper products		...	...	116	102	60	100	140	181	330	354	421	377
22	Printing and publishing		...	...	80	84	79	100	112	120	159	160	180	163
23	Coke,refined petroleum products,nuclear fuel		...	...	...	...	...	...	...	...	...	...	...	...
24	Chemicals and chemical products		...	...	48	60	101	100	127	137	109	130	167	187
25	Rubber and plastics products		...	...	85	77	53	100	113	192	284	314	369	459
26	Non-metallic mineral products		...	...	79	72	60	100	109	138	150	171	206	231
27	Basic metals		...	...	110	102	99	100	131	102	119	132	196	239
28	Fabricated metal products		...	...	126	105	91	100	102	125	178	220	249	292
29	Machinery and equipment n.e.c.		...	...	115	105	74	100	123	136	161	178	162	164
30	Office, accounting and computing machinery		...	...	...	...	...	...	...	...	...	...	...	...
31	Electrical machinery and apparatus		...	...	122	85	104	100	95	93	127	189	106	109
32	Radio,television and communication equipment		...	...	523	213	106	100	102	180	215	222	130	124
33	Medical, precision and optical instruments		...	...	77	95	113	100	96	110	151	155	130	226
34	Motor vehicles, trailers, semi-trailers		...	...	...	...	...	...	...	...	...	...	...	...
35	Other transport equipment		...	...	...	...	...	...	...	...	...	...	...	...
36	Furniture; manufacturing n.e.c.		...	...	...	...	...	...	...	...	...	...	...	...
37	Recycling		...	...	...	...	...	...	...	...	...	...	...	...
D	Total manufacturing		...	...	116	97	85	100	115	130	154	168	179	168

Romania

Supplier of information:
National Institute of Statistics, Bucharest.

Basic source of data:
Annual sample survey; administrative source.

Major deviations from ISIC (Revision 3):
None reported.

Reference period:
Calendar year.

Scope:
All registered enterprises.

Method of data collection:
Direct interview in the field.

Type of enumeration:
Sample survey.

Adjusted for non-response:
Yes.

Concepts and definitions of variables:
Wages and salaries excludes housing and family allowances paid directly by the employer and payments in kind.
Output data refers to turnover.

Related national publications:
Annuaire Statistique de la Roumanie, published by the National Institute of Statistics, Bucharest.

Romania

ISIC Revision 3		Number of enterprises					Number of employees					Wages and salaries paid to employees				
			(number)					(thousands)					(millions of Romanian Lei)			
ISIC	Industry	Note	2003	2004	2005	2006	Note	2003	2004	2005	2006	Note	2003	2004	2005	2006
151	Processed meat,fish,fruit,vegetables,fats		1904	1825	1721	1647		42.1	42.2	43.0	45.4		335.6	394.4	460.9	580.3
1511	Processing/preserving of meat		1238	1161	1073	1004		29.6	30.1	31.1	34.0		215.6	255.6	302.6	399.5
1512	Processing/preserving of fish		53	49	42	43		1.6	1.6	1.6	1.8		11.0	13.4	15.9	19.1
1513	Processing/preserving of fruit & vegetables		289	298	315	310		5.3	4.9	5.0	4.7		42.4	49.3	56.3	68.2
1514	Vegetable and animal oils and fats		324	317	291	290		5.5	5.6	5.3	5.0		66.6	76.1	86.1	93.5
1520	Dairy products		862	834	779	764		17.2	17.7	18.0	17.6		148.7	174.0	212.6	245.3
153	Grain mill products; starches; animal feeds		1933	1936	1843	1736		16.2	17.8	17.4	16.9		119.5	150.1	168.4	197.4
1531	Grain mill products		1745	1743	1661	1571		12.9	14.6	14.3	13.8		90.4	115.3	130.9	152.8
1532	Starches and starch products		31	31	27	24		0.7	0.7	0.6	0.6		5.8	7.3	8.2	9.4
1533	Prepared animal feeds		157	162	155	141		2.7	2.6	2.5	2.4		23.3	27.5	29.3	35.2
154	Other food products		5299	5632	5770	5740		89.2	92.6	93.7	94.2		565.4	687.9	823.8	966.8
1541	Bakery products		4380	4705	4885	4882		69.8	72.1	73.7	74.2		380.4	463.9	542.3	632.6
1542	Sugar		29	26	19	20		3.3	3.3	2.7	2.6		36.7	38.6	49.1	54.5
1543	Cocoa, chocolate and sugar confectionery		229	240	245	244		7.0	7.5	7.4	7.6		77.5	93.5	112.5	141.2
1544	Macaroni, noodles & similar products		98	93	87	80		1.0	0.9	0.9	0.8		4.2	4.7	8.1	6.6
1549	Other food products n.e.c.		563	568	534	514		8.1	8.8	8.9	9.0		66.6	87.2	111.8	131.9
155	Beverages		1174	1163	1122	1033		31.6	30.0	29.6	29.7		400.5	462.1	553.6	631.6
1551	Distilling, rectifying & blending of spirits		387	353	311	278		10.3	8.8	7.3	6.9		75.7	73.2	68.4	75.3
1552	Wines		175	210	203	197		3.9	4.4	4.9	5.3		35.2	41.6	44.7	63.8
1553	Malt liquors and malt		81	74	65	52		7.4	6.9	6.6	6.4		143.7	158.8	206.5	216.1
1554	Soft drinks; mineral waters		531	526	543	506		9.9	10.0	10.7	11.2		145.9	188.5	234.0	276.4
1600	Tobacco products		39	40	34	29		4.0	3.2	3.0	2.4		91.6	86.1	95.9	114.4
171	Spinning, weaving and finishing of textiles		443	447	422	412		36.3	32.4	27.3	22.2		281.8	306.5	273.3	284.6
1711	Textile fibre preparation; textile weaving		362	350	313	295		32.7	27.6	21.8	17.5		247.6	262.3	218.9	221.3
1712	Finishing of textiles		81	97	109	117		3.6	4.7	5.6	4.6		34.2	44.2	54.4	63.3
172	Other textiles		1464	1506	1485	1472		24.7	21.5	21.7	21.7		150.8	172.0	190.0	211.8
1721	Made-up textile articles, except apparel		1061	1091	1102	1092		15.3	13.8	14.3	15.1		86.9	109.3	118.2	142.2
1722	Carpets and rugs		65	62	49	49		3.5	2.5	1.9	1.4		21.2	18.4	16.0	13.4
1723	Cordage, rope, twine and netting		30	35	31	25		0.7	0.6	0.5	0.5		5.7	6.6	6.0	6.4
1729	Other textiles n.e.c.		308	318	303	306		5.2	4.5	4.9	4.7		37.0	37.7	49.8	49.8
1730	Knitted and crocheted fabrics and articles		637	634	612	586		36.1	33.9	29.3	26.6		253.0	289.7	292.4	297.3
1810	Wearing apparel, except fur apparel		5328	5691	5864	5745		325.2	316.7	285.2	254.9		1983.2	2426.0	2452.1	2506.0
1820	Dressing & dyeing of fur; processing of fur		93	97	98	100		1.3	1.0	1.0	1.0		7.1	6.8	6.5	9.0
191	Tanning, dressing and processing of leather		476	470	468	433		10.2	10.9	10.2	9.8		64.7	83.9	96.9	105.4
1911	Tanning and dressing of leather		103	92	84	72		1.4	1.6	1.3	1.1		10.2	12.9	11.7	12.5
1912	Luggage, handbags, etc.; saddlery & harness		373	378	384	361		8.8	9.3	8.9	8.7		54.5	71.0	85.2	92.9
1920	Footwear		1499	1632	1660	1648		103.3	99.0	90.5	86.7		657.7	753.4	804.9	873.3
2010	Sawmilling and planing of wood		3773	4249	4337	4261		53.9	51.0	46.6	43.0		287.9	294.3	305.0	332.9
202	Products of wood, cork, straw, etc.		3020	3144	3194	3176		34.7	38.4	37.3	36.3		206.4	294.1	341.3	386.3
2021	Veneer sheets, plywood, particle board, etc.		240	236	256	251		8.6	10.6	9.3	8.6		58.3	95.1	99.6	113.7
2022	Builders' carpentry and joinery		1542	1700	1775	1817		16.0	17.8	18.5	18.5		91.4	128.6	167.3	189.6
2023	Wooden containers		204	206	210	212		1.3	1.4	1.5	1.6		7.4	7.7	9.4	12.1
2029	Other wood products; articles of cork/straw		1034	1002	953	896		8.8	8.6	8.0	7.6		49.3	62.7	65.0	70.9
210	Paper and paper products		690	758	773	789		17.8	17.1	16.3	16.1		177.4	197.8	198.9	234.9
2101	Pulp, paper and paperboard		54	59	47	42		7.3	6.4	5.0	4.3		82.8	86.6	76.0	76.4
2102	Corrugated paper and paperboard		324	346	366	378		6.5	6.5	7.9	7.0		62.8	70.0	87.1	96.2
2109	Other articles of paper and paperboard		312	353	360	369		4.0	4.2	3.4	4.8		31.8	41.2	35.8	62.3
221	Publishing		1754	1991	2186	2286		13.7	13.8	15.1	15.9		147.4	182.5	262.0	243.7
2211	Publishing of books and other publications		1001	1090	1120	1102		5.0	4.8	5.1	4.9		43.0	54.6	71.8	72.4
2212	Publishing of newspapers, journals, etc.		526	643	762	853		8.3	8.5	9.3	10.3		101.9	123.4	183.7	162.8
2213	Publishing of recorded media		76	100	133	151		0.1	0.2	0.2	0.2		0.7	0.8	1.8	2.0
2219	Other publishing		151	158	171	180		0.2	0.4	0.5	0.6		1.8	3.7	4.7	6.5

222	Printing and related service activities	1690	1964	2103	2153	16.7	19.0	19.9	19.8	158.5	214.7	261.2	327.3
2221	Printing	1313	1500	1588	1593	15.3	17.4	18.2	17.8	143.5	191.0	237.3	295.7
2222	Service activities related to printing	377	464	515	560	1.4	1.6	1.8	2.0	15.0	23.7	23.9	31.6
2230	Reproduction of recorded media	141	149	163	169	0.5	0.5	0.5	0.5	3.3	3.8	5.2	5.9
2310	Coke oven products	1	...	...	1	...	...	...	-	...	...	...	...
2320	Refined petroleum products	31	30	31	35	9.3	8.7	7.3	6.9	216.5	230.5	232.1	...
2330	Processing of nuclear fuel	...	...	1	1	...	...	...	-	...	...	...	...
241	Basic chemicals	340	344	345	341	33.2	29.5	26.9	24.5	497.7	498.2	522.0	557.2
2411	Basic chemicals, except fertilizers	239	242	234	229	20.1	18.4	17.0	16.1	303.8	306.8	333.5	375.2
2412	Fertilizers and nitrogen compounds	16	25	26	24	9.2	7.2	6.6	6.4	137.8	122.2	136.9	134.0
2413	Plastics in primary forms; synthetic rubber	85	77	85	88	3.9	3.9	3.3	2.0	56.1	69.2	51.6	48.0
242	Other chemicals	916	903	862	837	22.4	22.0	21.6	21.3	302.3	365.4	417.5	510.7
2421	Pesticides and other agro-chemical products	29	30	24	25	0.7	0.7	0.7	0.6	9.2	10.6	12.3	12.7
2422	Paints, varnishes, printing ink and mastics	201	197	190	193	4.4	4.4	4.7	4.7	50.5	58.4	72.2	89.2
2423	Pharmaceuticals, medicinal chemicals, etc.	150	136	135	132	9.1	8.9	8.9	9.3	151.7	188.0	213.5	278.8
2424	Soap, cleaning & cosmetic preparations	274	262	257	246	3.9	3.8	3.7	3.5	52.9	61.9	69.3	85.4
2429	Other chemical products n.e.c.	262	278	256	241	4.2	4.2	3.6	3.1	38.0	46.5	50.2	44.6
2430	Man-made fibres	24	22	19	21	5.6	4.2	3.7	2.1	47.3	41.2	44.3	31.8
251	Rubber products	457	436	412	412	14.6	14.7	14.0	12.6	176.5	192.9	206.4	224.4
2511	Rubber tyres and tubes	137	113	103	100	6.7	6.7	6.5	5.7	99.9	98.3	110.9	117.8
2519	Other rubber products	320	323	309	312	7.9	7.9	7.5	6.9	76.6	94.6	95.5	106.6
2520	Plastic products	1588	1853	2088	2302	27.1	29.3	31.5	34.0	223.9	279.7	352.8	447.1
2610	Glass and glass products	469	525	556	571	23.2	19.0	16.0	12.7	191.7	180.2	167.0	167.6
269	Non-metallic mineral products n.e.c.	1710	1948	2203	2357	50.7	51.7	49.0	47.2	575.1	660.8	746.4	855.4
2691	Pottery, china and earthenware	225	226	237	220	14.3	12.3	11.0	10.0	128.2	125.7	135.4	140.6
2692	Refractory ceramic products	43	56	50	44	4.4	3.4	2.8	1.8	41.5	38.1	28.5	24.1
2693	Struct.non-refractory clay; ceramic products	287	299	324	327	8.4	9.7	9.9	8.9	78.6	119.0	127.8	129.2
2694	Cement, lime and plaster	73	82	73	88	6.5	7.5	4.9	4.6	145.7	147.6	167.7	188.7
2695	Articles of concrete, cement and plaster	694	837	1013	1129	10.3	12.2	13.2	14.8	105.2	148.6	186.0	259.9
2696	Cutting, shaping & finishing of stone	282	346	389	434	2.6	2.8	3.1	3.2	22.7	25.7	33.9	36.8
2699	Other non-metallic mineral products n.e.c.	106	102	117	115	4.2	3.7	4.0	3.7	53.2	56.1	67.1	76.1
2710	Basic iron and steel	156	144	133	130	58.5	49.3	47.8	43.1	838.2	916.6	1027.0	1116.8
2720	Basic precious and non-ferrous metals	92	82	77	78	12.1	11.1	11.7	11.1	202.1	224.3	253.6	319.3
273	Casting of metals	248	251	240	238	9.2	8.1	7.3	6.4	85.4	84.8	89.3	89.6
2731	Casting of iron and steel	100	108	104	100	7.4	6.1	5.6	4.5	74.2	67.0	71.9	66.6
2732	Casting of non-ferrous metals	148	143	136	138	1.8	2.0	1.7	1.9	11.2	17.8	17.4	23.0
281	Struct.metal products;tanks;steam generators	2918	3387	3830	4097	51.4	55.4	58.3	60.4	445.4	618.1	717.2	916.6
2811	Structural metal products	2759	3230	3667	3947	38.6	41.9	44.7	48.0	285.5	390.2	458.2	604.9
2812	Tanks, reservoirs and containers of metal	127	124	132	124	7.2	8.5	9.0	8.2	71.6	121.7	150.0	193.6
2813	Steam generators	32	33	31	26	5.6	5.0	4.7	4.2	88.3	106.2	109.0	118.1
289	Other metal products; metal working services	1702	1940	2145	2264	38.8	39.4	40.8	41.3	382.5	480.6	565.7	655.7
2891	Metal forging/pressing/stamping/roll-forming	115	141	153	170	4.3	3.7	3.7	3.9	39.0	40.9	53.2	63.4
2892	Treatment & coating of metals	418	614	788	905	5.9	7.9	11.1	12.2	75.1	143.5	183.9	220.2
2893	Cutlery, hand tools and general hardware	230	248	251	269	10.0	9.8	9.2	8.3	100.3	117.8	126.7	136.0
2899	Other fabricated metal products n.e.c.	939	937	953	920	18.6	18.0	16.9	16.8	168.1	178.4	201.9	236.1
291	General purpose machinery	608	686	750	765	43.0	40.9	39.7	38.6	522.9	577.0	663.7	721.5
2911	Engines & turbines (not for transport equipment)	38	43	41	42	8.6	7.3	7.6	7.6	126.3	128.3	144.9	170.7
2912	Pumps, compressors, taps and valves	118	130	135	126	9.8	9.5	7.1	7.2	98.9	104.7	105.3	120.2
2913	Bearings, gears, gearing & driving elements	49	57	61	61	15.3	14.7	13.9	12.6	204.1	230.6	251.6	249.7
2914	Ovens, furnaces and furnace burners	25	24	25	22	0.4	0.3	0.3	0.4	5.4	4.4	6.7	10.8
2915	Lifting and handling equipment	198	233	266	285	5.8	5.8	7.3	7.3	56.2	66.3	107.7	114.4
2919	Other general purpose machinery	180	199	222	229	3.2	3.3	3.5	3.5	32.0	42.7	47.5	55.7
292	Special purpose machinery	684	737	743	739	86.1	72.9	62.0	52.7	983.0	982.0	882.5	920.9
2921	Agricultural and forestry machinery	87	87	92	91	11.7	9.2	8.3	7.0	116.8	108.9	111.3	108.3
2922	Machine tools	213	234	236	236	10.6	9.1	8.8	8.1	115.1	122.6	136.9	150.1
2923	Machinery for metallurgy	32	30	30	31	10.8	9.1	8.1	7.4	102.8	109.3	113.8	126.2
2924	Machinery for mining & construction	85	94	90	85	18.5	18.7	15.9	12.7	219.8	260.8	225.4	232.3
2925	Food/beverage/tobacco processing machinery	81	86	85	86	2.1	2.0	1.5	1.3	17.1	19.2	16.6	18.4
2926	Machinery for textile, apparel and leather	41	47	46	45	2.1	1.8	1.6	1.3	23.0	20.9	23.3	18.3
2927	Weapons and ammunition	23	24	23	23	18.6	13.2	11.4	9.2	237.9	202.3	160.6	158.3
2929	Other special purpose machinery	122	135	141	142	11.9	9.6	6.2	5.8	150.5	138.0	94.6	109.0

continued

Romania

ISIC Revision 3		Number of enterprises					Number of employees					Wages and salaries paid to employees				
			(number)					(thousands)					(millions of Romanian Lei)			
ISIC	Industry	Note	2003	2004	2005	2006	Note	2003	2004	2005	2006	Note	2003	2004	2005	2006
2930	Domestic appliances n.e.c.		90	83	120	85		10.7	10.8	11.4	11.8		114.4	136.8	157.5	185.5
3000	Office, accounting and computing machinery		465	480	478	515		2.7	2.7	3.7	4.2		24.6	23.8	41.3	83.3
3110	Electric motors, generators and transformers		183	196	200	213		11.9	11.7	10.6	10.2		127.4	135.1	151.3	160.5
3120	Electricity distribution & control apparatus		198	219	233	225		9.5	9.8	10.2	9.0		112.9	141.1	151.8	...
3130	Insulated wire and cable		42	47	49	53		3.7	3.8	4.3	4.9		47.9	55.8	64.2	89.3
3140	Accumulators, primary cells and batteries		24	15	16	14		0.8	0.8	0.7	0.8		11.0	14.7	...	...
3150	Lighting equipment and electric lamps		126	122	113	120		6.4	6.2	3.6	3.5		82.4	97.5	...	56.7
3190	Other electrical equipment n.e.c.		209	223	243	266		30.7	33.0	51.4	55.4		297.8	377.9	614.1	834.4
3210	Electronic valves, tubes, etc.		74	72	72	72		5.6	5.6	5.2	5.3		81.5	100.3	98.9	116.1
3220	TV/radio transmitters; line comm. apparatus		71	77	85	97		3.7	3.5	3.3	3.2		96.3	104.6	109.1	126.1
3230	TV and radio receivers and associated goods		76	72	80	78		0.7	0.7	0.6	0.6		6.8	6.5	7.4	9.6
331	Medical, measuring, testing appliances, etc.		700	801	902	989		10.3	11.1	13.7	14.2		107.4	143.3	213.4	271.3
3311	Medical, surgical and orthopaedic equipment		320	383	463	528		1.9	2.4	2.9	2.8		15.1	25.0	29.5	28.5
3312	Measuring/testing/navigating appliances,etc.		157	167	171	181		4.6	4.5	7.0	8.1		48.5	57.8	125.2	177.6
3313	Industrial process control equipment		223	251	268	280		3.9	4.1	3.7	3.4		43.8	60.5	58.7	65.2
3320	Optical instruments & photographic equipment		147	156	171	182		1.3	1.2	1.2	1.2		12.1	14.1	...	...
3330	Watches and clocks		9	9	7	6		0.2	0.2	0.1	0.1		1.0	1.1	...	...
3410	Motor vehicles		17	28	27	27		19.2	14.6	16.3	17.0		262.2	269.0	...	...
3420	Automobile bodies, trailers & semi-trailers		51	55	64	60		2.2	2.6	2.4	2.3		19.6	28.9	...	...
3430	Parts/accessories for automobiles		317	338	321	324		39.7	46.3	42.0	43.1		427.9	593.7	650.0	774.4
351	Building and repairing of ships and boats		310	405	475	521		27.9	28.3	29.3	30.7		405.8	471.3	564.2	675.9
3511	Building and repairing of ships		284	371	430	478		27.6	28.1	29.0	30.4		402.2	468.6	560.9	672.6
3512	Building/repairing of pleasure/sport. boats		26	34	45	43		0.4	0.3	0.3	0.3		3.6	2.7	3.3	3.3
3520	Railway/tramway locomotives & rolling stock		151	152	145	140		32.6	27.3	24.7	23.2		398.3	383.6	400.8	423.6
3530	Aircraft and spacecraft		26	29	24	27		7.1	6.6	6.1	6.1		129.2	129.7	143.7	174.7
359	Transport equipment n.e.c.		20	16	16	14		0.2	0.2	0.3	0.4		1.5	1.8	2.2	4.0
3591	Motorcycles		...	...	...	1		...	...	-	-		...	...	...	...
3592	Bicycles and invalid carriages		10	11	11	11		0.2	0.2	0.3	0.4		1.4	1.7	...	...
3599	Other transport equipment n.e.c.		10	5	5	2		-	-	-	-		0.1	0.1	...	...
3610	Furniture		3087	3554	3932	4132		100.0	101.0	98.1	92.6		696.4	819.9	915.1	1014.7
369	Manufacturing n.e.c.		979	1058	1150	1205		13.4	13.3	13.9	12.1		87.1	90.2	118.5	127.2
3691	Jewellery and related articles		271	284	307	322		2.7	2.7	2.7	2.5		17.5	16.2	20.0	23.2
3692	Musical instruments		31	40	44	42		1.7	1.7	1.6	1.3		12.6	13.4	14.9	14.9
3693	Sports goods		47	49	50	60		0.9	0.9	1.0	1.1		7.5	9.5	14.2	18.8
3694	Games and toys		105	108	111	121		3.1	2.7	2.9	2.1		17.4	16.5	24.1	17.8
3699	Other manufacturing n.e.c.		525	577	638	660		5.0	5.3	5.7	5.1		32.1	34.6	45.3	52.5
3710	Recycling of metal waste and scrap		921	1058	1047	1027		9.5	11.3	10.5	10.8		75.4	106.5	109.5	142.4
3720	Recycling of non-metal waste and scrap		139	204	257	324		0.6	1.4	1.9	2.3		3.5	6.9	18.2	24.3
D	Total manufacturing		52595	56919	59296	60084		1710.8	1669.1	1608.7	1540.6		15361.4	17766.5	19671.2	22307.9

ISIC Revision 3		Output in factor values					Value added in factor values					Gross fixed capital formation		
			(millions of Romanian Lei)					(millions of Romanian Lei)					(millions of Romanian Lei)	
ISIC	Industry	Note	2003	2004	2005	2006	Note	2003	2004	2005	2006	Note	2005	2006
151	Processed meat,fish,fruit,vegetables,fats		5161.9	6827.6	7759.3	8330.7		719.1	711.0	1016.2	1153.3		...	...
1511	Processing/preserving of meat		3264.3	4385.9	5296.7	5973.7		468.8	446.3	774.2	850.1		...	...
1512	Processing/preserving of fish		97.9	126.8	151.5	185.7		18.1	24.6	32.7	35.9		...	...
1513	Processing/preserving of fruit & vegetables		569.1	638.8	811.8	895.7		97.1	81.2	131.0	139.7		...	...
1514	Vegetable and animal oils and fats		1230.7	1676.1	1499.3	1275.6		135.1	158.9	78.3	127.6		...	...
1520	Dairy products		1491.2	1915.5	2272.7	2753.7		276.1	224.9	408.5	491.5		...	...
153	Grain mill products; starches; animal feeds		1877.5	2368.4	1918.7	2068.1		212.3	267.1	252.7	295.0		...	...
1531	Grain mill products		1314.8	1783.3	1380.7	1428.8		182.1	228.7	199.8	241.8		...	...
1532	Starches and starch products		69.2	86.6	83.5	102.2		4.5	10.1	16.3	19.8		...	...
1533	Prepared animal feeds		493.5	498.5	454.5	537.1		25.8	28.3	36.6	33.4		...	...
154	Other food products		5747.4	7191.3	7345.6	8819.0		979.1	1348.6	1505.3	1802.1		...	...
1541	Bakery products		3246.6	3815.9	3691.0	4061.3		601.4	836.0	900.0	996.1		...	...
1542	Sugar		458.6	591.1	684.0	1350.3		25.3	61.0	38.7	139.5		...	...
1543	Cocoa, chocolate and sugar confectionery		765.5	988.3	1121.2	1300.7		123.8	158.3	214.6	252.6		...	...
1544	Macaroni, noodles & similar products		48.2	63.4	90.0	83.1		-20.3	6.0	11.5	13.6		...	...
1549	Other food products n.e.c.		1228.4	1732.6	1759.4	2023.6		248.9	287.4	340.5	400.3		...	...
155	Beverages		5372.7	5898.9	6670.3	7797.4		1239.5	1351.3	1626.1	1903.7		...	...
1551	Distilling, rectifying & blending of spirits		1427.8	1226.1	1158.7	1095.7		205.1	166.6	98.1	73.4		...	...
1552	Wines		364.5	503.9	530.6	706.4		68.8	79.6	112.0	122.8		...	...
1553	Malt liquors and malt		1581.2	1805.5	2309.4	2784.2		509.8	532.1	717.5	927.9		...	...
1554	Soft drinks; mineral waters		1999.3	2363.3	2671.6	3211.1		455.8	573.0	698.5	779.6		...	...
1600	Tobacco products		2527.7	2809.3	2958.6	3228.9		182.1	194.4	251.6	209.3		...	...
171	Spinning, weaving and finishing of textiles		1484.7	1872.2	1611.6	1760.0		461.2	486.5	423.4	430.5		...	...
1711	Textile fibre preparation; textile weaving		1276.8	1572.0	1324.7	1479.2		358.0	367.9	301.7	323.3		...	...
1712	Finishing of textiles		207.9	300.2	286.9	280.8		103.2	118.6	121.7	107.2		...	...
172	Other textiles		693.0	739.8	839.4	988.5		254.9	283.0	288.0	336.8		...	...
1721	Made-up textile articles, except apparel		376.5	424.8	507.4	647.5		142.8	190.0	183.4	227.4		...	...
1722	Carpets and rugs		68.0	56.0	45.7	38.1		30.8	23.9	15.1	10.5		...	...
1723	Cordage, rope, twine and netting		36.5	31.5	27.9	35.7		13.0	10.8	9.9	13.9		...	...
1729	Other textiles n.e.c.		212.1	227.4	258.4	267.2		68.3	58.2	79.6	85.0		...	...
1730	Knitted and crocheted fabrics and articles		892.7	994.4	907.2	896.1		385.5	400.6	362.6	378.6		...	...
1810	Wearing apparel, except fur apparel		6192.9	7427.2	7141.7	7364.8		2879.3	3311.6	3146.7	3138.8		...	...
1820	Dressing & dyeing of fur; processing of fur		32.5	27.5	23.7	33.5		12.3	7.2	7.6	13.1		...	...
191	Tanning, dressing and processing of leather		342.0	404.1	399.2	407.0		109.8	126.4	134.1	142.3		...	...
1911	Tanning and dressing of leather		156.3	170.2	149.0	139.5		25.9	26.8	20.5	14.3		...	...
1912	Luggage, handbags, etc.; saddlery & harness		185.7	233.8	250.2	267.5		83.9	99.6	113.6	128.0		...	...
1920	Footwear		2220.5	2560.6	2548.9	2931.0		940.6	1012.2	1010.8	1106.3		...	...
2010	Sawmilling and planing of wood		2817.4	3268.2	3184.4	3415.9		618.7	623.2	624.6	651.3		...	...
202	Products of wood, cork, straw, etc.		1647.6	2607.1	2749.3	3443.0		419.8	640.4	538.4	691.1		...	...
2021	Veneer sheets, plywood, particle board, etc.		600.0	1068.0	1042.3	1389.0		148.1	250.7	183.4	254.3		...	...
2022	Builders' carpentry and joinery		641.0	1064.2	1230.4	1502.5		151.1	269.3	233.3	293.0		...	...
2023	Wooden containers		73.6	91.1	106.5	123.2		17.4	16.6	20.9	26.9		...	...
2029	Other wood products; articles of cork/straw		333.0	383.9	370.1	428.3		103.1	103.8	100.8	116.9		...	...
210	Paper and paper products		1815.8	2025.8	1819.6	2058.8		352.0	383.4	326.5	385.3		...	...
2101	Pulp, paper and paperboard		768.7	845.4	644.9	671.3		132.3	127.3	77.9	91.5		...	...
2102	Corrugated paper and paperboard		710.8	770.4	800.2	914.6		151.6	162.6	172.9	187.5		...	...
2109	Other articles of paper and paperboard		336.4	410.1	374.5	472.9		68.1	93.6	75.7	106.3		...	...
221	Publishing		1037.3	1241.3	1468.1	1715.8		260.0	369.2	472.7	487.5		...	...
2211	Publishing of books and other publications		400.0	413.8	463.3	514.8		104.9	137.4	162.0	179.8		...	...
2212	Publishing of newspapers, journals, etc.		604.4	765.7	935.6	1116.0		149.5	218.4	291.4	281.0		...	...
2213	Publishing of recorded media		14.9	28.0	41.0	41.5		2.2	3.8	6.5	9.6		...	...
2219	Other publishing		17.9	33.8	28.2	43.5		3.5	9.6	12.8	17.1		...	...

continued

Romania

ISIC	Industry	Note	Output in factor values (millions of Romanian Lei) 2003	2004	2005	2006	Note	Value added in factor values (millions of Romanian Lei) 2003	2004	2005	2006	Note	Gross fixed capital formation (millions of Romanian Lei) 2005	2006
222	Printing and related service activities		1447.3	1919.4	1988.5	2201.8		521.5	591.9	725.4	772.7		...	...
2221	Printing		1306.4	1747.0	1817.1	2003.7		455.1	517.8	626.4	679.6		...	...
2222	Service activities related to printing		140.9	172.4	171.4	198.1		66.4	74.0	99.0	93.1		...	...
2230	Reproduction of recorded media		32.0	40.9	41.6	42.6		10.2	14.7	14.9	14.3		...	...
2310	Coke oven products		...	...	...	1.3		...	...	...	...		...	...
2320	Refined petroleum products		6444.7	8434.1	12230.5	11600.3		-17.1	306.3	653.6	...		...	...
2330	Processing of nuclear fuel		...	...	...	-		...	...	...	...		...	...
241	Basic chemicals		4193.2	6619.3	5511.3	5675.6		656.5	859.2	931.9	877.4		...	...
2411	Basic chemicals, except fertilizers		2038.6	2912.7	3057.1	3475.0		410.3	637.2	623.5	662.6		...	...
2412	Fertilizers and nitrogen compounds		1179.2	1145.9	1441.4	1293.2		179.7	135.5	218.6	111.4		...	...
2413	Plastics in primary forms; synthetic rubber		975.4	2560.8	1012.8	907.4		66.5	86.4	89.8	103.4		...	...
242	Other chemicals		2567.6	3488.2	3719.7	4040.1		744.7	857.7	1040.2	1192.1		...	...
2421	Pesticides and other agro-chemical products		83.0	109.1	133.3	148.5		22.6	26.2	33.0	34.8		...	...
2422	Paints, varnishes, printing ink and mastics		632.0	715.0	787.2	961.7		138.4	149.9	164.3	204.6		...	...
2423	Pharmaceuticals, medicinal chemicals, etc.		942.7	1223.3	1371.0	1640.1		404.9	472.8	597.1	689.8		...	...
2424	Soap, cleaning & cosmetic preparations		645.8	1110.4	1096.7	934.4		119.8	144.6	185.6	195.3		...	...
2429	Other chemical products n.e.c.		264.1	330.4	331.5	355.4		58.9	64.2	60.2	67.6		...	...
2430	Man-made fibres		333.7	237.5	252.6	204.9		68.3	28.5	33.5	32.2		...	...
251	Rubber products		1771.2	1789.4	1867.9	2082.6		363.3	470.1	461.6	433.1		...	...
2511	Rubber tyres and tubes		1365.4	1297.7	1380.2	1525.1		237.6	317.6	310.6	274.9		...	...
2519	Other rubber products		405.8	491.8	487.7	557.5		125.6	152.5	151.0	158.2		...	...
2520	Plastic products		2413.9	3243.1	3875.4	5084.4		585.4	700.2	780.2	983.4		...	...
2610	Glass and glass products		769.4	863.5	801.0	938.1		267.1	288.8	210.4	199.7		...	...
269	Non-metallic mineral products n.e.c.		4066.9	5501.9	5986.4	7822.5		1388.6	1862.0	1922.9	2583.8		...	...
2691	Pottery, china and earthenware		586.3	529.8	508.3	486.6		243.1	209.3	172.1	177.2		...	...
2692	Refractory ceramic products		165.9	189.1	135.0	126.4		40.4	37.5	31.5	29.8		...	...
2693	Struct.non-refractory clay; ceramic products		375.6	581.5	610.6	747.5		155.3	208.0	223.8	229.7		...	...
2694	Cement, lime and plaster		1388.7	1850.0	2030.9	2760.1		588.0	844.6	850.4	1196.5		...	...
2695	Articles of concrete, cement and plaster		1037.0	1638.9	1847.1	2669.0		237.6	410.8	441.7	682.0		...	...
2696	Cutting, shaping & finishing of stone		127.7	169.1	196.9	227.8		39.2	40.3	75.9	71.2		...	...
2699	Other non-metallic mineral products n.e.c.		385.7	543.5	657.6	805.1		85.0	111.5	127.5	197.4		...	...
2710	Basic iron and steel		6973.4	11958.9	11962.6	12728.9		1514.4	2882.9	1794.2	2248.0		...	...
2720	Basic precious and non-ferrous metals		2041.9	2625.8	2929.4	4214.6		369.8	511.9	468.8	1045.1		...	...
273	Casting of metals		421.8	567.0	589.0	697.7		93.0	108.7	107.9	123.3		...	...
2731	Casting of iron and steel		252.4	299.2	339.6	377.8		67.2	79.1	80.0	83.1		...	...
2732	Casting of non-ferrous metals		169.5	267.8	249.4	319.9		25.9	29.6	27.9	40.2		...	...
281	Struct.metal products;tanks;steam generators		2389.7	3540.1	4209.0	5576.2		677.5	941.7	1119.7	1474.0		1556.9	...
2811	Structural metal products		1881.9	2781.4	3266.6	4497.3		477.2	645.9	765.5	1085.9		...	...
2812	Tanks, reservoirs and containers of metal		336.6	522.2	706.7	846.6		98.6	165.9	227.4	262.1		...	...
2813	Steam generators		171.2	236.5	235.7	232.3		101.7	129.9	126.8	126.0		...	...
289	Other metal products; metal working services		1957.9	2528.0	2886.2	3643.2		636.2	750.8	816.5	993.4		...	...
2891	Metal forging/pressing/stamping/roll-forming		286.9	306.3	358.3	459.0		74.7	73.2	78.9	119.5		...	...
2892	Treatment & coating of metals		231.3	397.5	557.8	844.8		127.2	193.6	257.5	325.5		...	...
2893	Cutlery, hand tools and general hardware		366.1	457.0	476.4	512.1		154.5	165.4	163.7	173.3		...	...
2899	Other fabricated metal products n.e.c.		1073.6	1367.3	1493.7	1827.3		279.9	318.5	316.4	375.1		...	...
291	General purpose machinery		1859.3	2356.4	2465.0	2849.2		610.0	728.1	874.0	875.0		3121.9	...
2911	Engines & turbines (not for transport equipment)		418.7	448.3	419.1	485.5		133.9	118.9	267.6	173.5		...	...
2912	Pumps, compressors, taps and valves		281.8	399.6	337.2	483.7		102.7	114.1	107.6	93.7		...	...
2913	Bearings, gears, gearing & driving elements		691.1	886.8	914.7	931.9		299.3	320.8	320.0	326.9		...	...
2914	Ovens, furnaces and furnace burners		30.1	25.3	48.8	65.6		9.0	6.1	10.1	15.3		...	...
2915	Lifting and handling equipment		229.5	330.4	423.1	471.4		8.7	98.9	91.5	163.8		...	...
2919	Other general purpose machinery		208.1	266.0	322.1	411.1		56.4	69.4	77.2	101.8		...	...

292	Special purpose machinery	2797.9	3372.1	2884.3	3157.8	920.5	988.5	878.7	978.3	7276.2	...
2921	Agricultural and forestry machinery	314.8	473.7	406.2	416.3	81.6	134.6	98.9	81.6	920.4	...
2922	Machine tools	384.1	410.1	484.1	541.7	140.8	140.7	178.2	202.1	1509.4	...
2923	Machinery for metallurgy	260.7	332.2	350.9	401.3	86.1	92.8	90.7	105.4	4846.4	...
2924	Machinery for mining & construction	670.5	920.7	792.4	942.5	203.3	284.7	257.4	321.9	...	...
2925	Food/beverage/tobacco processing machinery	64.8	87.1	86.7	89.9	22.3	25.8	28.0	29.1	...	...
2926	Machinery for textile, apparel and leather	76.2	70.0	68.9	53.9	27.4	18.9	24.1	17.5	...	...
2927	Weapons and ammunition	350.0	265.1	344.0	309.8	161.0	129.9	78.0	66.5	...	...
2929	Other special purpose machinery	676.8	813.2	351.1	402.4	198.1	161.2	123.4	154.2	...	...
2930	Domestic appliances n.e.c.	1198.6	1545.1	1708.2	1826.8	313.8	330.2	337.6	379.0	156.1	...
3000	Office, accounting and computing machinery	500.5	773.5	1067.5	1487.3	24.4	48.7	121.4	-162.7	2142.6	...
3110	Electric motors, generators and transformers	570.4	671.3	690.9	835.6	189.9	193.5	194.9	187.2	1268.9	...
3120	Electricity distribution & control apparatus	599.9	805.8	837.1	1020.2	196.2	240.6	245.2	...	...	...
3130	Insulated wire and cable	456.3	705.5	782.1	1457.4	100.0	117.8	131.5	282.8	...	...
3140	Accumulators, primary cells and batteries	101.2	121.7	126.1	145.6	29.7	32.0	...	...	...	...
3150	Lighting equipment and electric lamps	554.1	619.3	250.0	322.2	259.3	261.6	...	100.3	...	...
3190	Other electrical equipment n.e.c.	1386.0	1427.5	2896.9	4271.2	456.7	513.0	702.6	1078.2	...	...
3210	Electronic valves, tubes, etc.	262.4	312.3	250.8	337.1	161.4	204.2	139.8	156.4	2408.9	...
3220	TV/radio transmitters; line comm. apparatus	594.4	774.2	812.5	1011.2	193.4	211.6	229.5	238.2	...	...
3230	TV and radio receivers and associated goods	105.9	98.1	84.5	110.2	18.5	11.2	27.6	18.1	...	...
331	Medical, measuring, testing appliances, etc.	620.7	854.6	1245.4	1560.4	224.8	297.5	504.0	497.9	951.1	...
3311	Medical, surgical and orthopaedic equipment	71.8	109.6	141.6	157.5	22.1	36.0	48.3	54.4	...	...
3312	Measuring/testing/navigating appliances,etc.	326.4	425.5	814.0	1076.3	118.7	136.2	343.1	343.8	...	...
3313	Industrial process control equipment	222.5	319.5	289.8	326.6	84.0	125.3	112.6	99.7	...	...
3320	Optical instruments & photographic equipment	40.2	50.0	55.7	73.9	20.9	24.3	...	...	...	...
3330	Watches and clocks	5.2	5.1	3.3	3.4	1.0	1.9	...	...	...	...
3410	Motor vehicles	2275.2	3331.7	5224.5	6786.1	333.3	464.5	...	...	10564.4	...
3420	Automobile bodies, trailers & semi-trailers	90.6	197.5	187.7	256.1	22.6	40.6	...	...	...	...
3430	Parts/accessories for automobiles	2415.1	3448.7	4002.1	5132.8	773.4	915.3	852.1	1177.0	...	...
351	Building and repairing of ships and boats	1410.7	1826.9	2186.4	2607.1	574.0	633.6	671.2	647.2	569.7	...
3511	Building and repairing of ships	1384.5	1810.8	2170.1	2586.6	566.6	630.5	666.6	641.4	...	...
3512	Building/repairing of pleasure/sport. boats	26.2	16.1	16.3	20.5	7.5	3.2	4.6	5.8	...	...
3520	Railway/tramway locomotives & rolling stock	1474.8	1475.1	1444.5	1671.1	515.2	504.0	529.9	622.8	697.4	...
3530	Aircraft and spacecraft	390.1	448.1	494.7	697.1	180.0	183.8	230.6	290.5	480.3	...
359	Transport equipment n.e.c.	12.9	22.7	31.9	41.0	3.8	7.2	5.4	9.9	75.5	...
3591	Motorcycles	...	...	...	0.1	...	...	...	...	...	...
3592	Bicycles and invalid carriages	12.5	22.1	31.4	40.4	3.7	7.0	...	...	...	...
3599	Other transport equipment n.e.c.	0.4	0.6	0.5	0.5	0.1	0.3	...	...	...	...
3610	Furniture	3637.8	4735.8	5259.7	5879.5	1100.4	1297.1	1367.7	1479.1	1084.8	...
369	Manufacturing n.e.c.	399.5	441.0	557.7	678.9	156.6	157.9	181.6	202.9	...	...
3691	Jewellery and related articles	53.9	57.2	83.5	106.5	25.2	26.4	34.8	33.2	...	...
3692	Musical instruments	51.2	59.4	58.6	56.1	24.6	24.4	23.9	25.0	...	...
3693	Sports goods	34.2	35.6	42.4	75.6	13.4	15.1	19.6	29.8	...	...
3694	Games and toys	71.7	70.1	88.6	102.7	31.3	27.5	28.4	33.4	...	...
3699	Other manufacturing n.e.c.	188.6	218.8	284.6	338.0	62.0	64.6	74.9	81.5	...	...
3710	Recycling of metal waste and scrap	1873.2	3836.8	3343.9	5088.5	180.0	298.2	294.7	407.7	...	...
3720	Recycling of non-metal waste and scrap	40.1	111.1	125.6	239.6	9.5	30.2	34.3	51.4	...	...
D	Total manufacturing	104852.1	137904.0	149488.4	174114.3	25750.5	31653.0	33057.4	38315.0	32354.7	...

Romania

ISIC Revision 3		Note	Index numbers of industrial production											
			(2000=100)											
ISIC	Industry		1995	1996	1997	1998	1999	2000	2001	2002	2003	2004	2005	2006
15	Food and beverages		102	103	87	86	90	100	121	135	142	135	140	163
16	Tobacco products		86	91	95	104	99	100	125	113	107	117	110	100
17	Textiles		160	151	134	116	99	100	102	106	148	151	136	120
18	Wearing apparel, fur		65	82	90	67	84	100	118	123	125	119	100	91
19	Leather, leather products and footwear		90	92	90	84	88	100	106	110	114	110	98	101
20	Wood products (excl. furniture)		103	112	103	90	93	100	86	79	86	120	148	162
21	Paper and paper products		112	116	100	86	96	100	111	123	123	118	124	134
22	Printing and publishing		193	224	192	81	80	100	147	125	146	171	197	191
23	Coke,refined petroleum products,nuclear fuel		130	119	117	114	95	100	109	126	114	120	137	133
24	Chemicals and chemical products		152	134	102	79	82	100	92	94	99	134	137	156
25	Rubber and plastics products		162	163	130	108	98	100	117	127	164	179	167	170
26	Non-metallic mineral products		115	126	121	106	99	100	102	106	106	123	119	134
27	Basic metals		123	114	115	114	78	100	113	138	111	127	129	130
28	Fabricated metal products		184	114	95	94	98	100	99	99	98	97	98	114
29	Machinery and equipment n.e.c.		175	216	191	126	98	100	117	117	108	114	114	115
30	Office, accounting and computing machinery		...	...	...	...	...	...	...	...	...	...	...	...
31	Electrical machinery and apparatus		86	100	110	94	95	100	113	119	130	149	153	171
32	Radio,television and communication equipment		204	267	275	226	189	100	111	99	115	128	83	79
33	Medical, precision and optical instruments		102	131	126	88	97	100	125	127	151	136	120	113
34	Motor vehicles, trailers, semi-trailers		73	120	116	129	138	100	92	103	121	148	202	246
35	Other transport equipment		73	79	86	96	92	100	98	95	114	106	107	124
36	Furniture; manufacturing n.e.c.		81	114	111	84	91	100	109	126	133	118	138	170
37	Recycling		...	...	...	...	...	...	...	...	...	...	...	...
D	Total manufacturing		109	117	110	94	92	100	110	117	122	129	132	144

Russian Federation

Supplier of information:
Russian Federation State Committee on Statistics, Moscow.

Basic source of data:
Administrative source.

Major deviations from ISIC (Revision 3):
Data presented in accordance with ISIC (Revision 3) were originally classified according to OKVED - Russian Classification of Economic Activities harmonized with NACE (Revision 1).

Reference period:
Calendar year.

Scope:
All registered enterprises.

Method of data collection:
Mail questionnaire.

Type of enumeration:
Complete enumeration for large and medium enterprises. Sample survey for small enterprises.

Adjusted for non-response:
Yes.

Concepts and definitions of variables:
Wages and salaries was computed by UNIDO from reported monthly average of wages and salaries per employee.
Output includes value of all products and value of industrial work done or industrial services rendered.

Related national publications:
None reported.

ISIC Revision 3		Number of enterprises					Number of employees					Wages and salaries paid to employees				
			(number)					(thousands)					(millions of Russian Roubles)			
ISIC	Industry	Note	2003	2004	2005	2006	Note	2003	2004	2005	2006	Note	2003	2004	2005	2006
151	Processed meat,fish,fruit,vegetables,fats		23362	23983	24946	21452		384.5	382.1	336.4	348.4		23515.4	27087.3	27594.6	34980.7
1511	Processing/preserving of meat		2868	4178	5070	5747		213.8	215.1	218.0	226.2		12349.8	14519.3	17493.9	22623.3
1512	Processing/preserving of fish		8531	8233	8171	6513		86.5	85.9	50.6	51.0		6768.6	7622.2	4566.6	5412.7
1513	Processing/preserving of fruit & vegetables		2562	2711	2876	2515		35.2	31.9	28.2	29.8		1676.2	1731.1	2279.0	3029.5
1514	Vegetable and animal oils and fats		2545	2565	2567	1998		49.0	49.3	39.6	41.4		2721.7	3214.2	3257.4	3913.3
1520	Dairy products		5460	5623	5908	5553		225.7	215.5	212.4	207.4		12607.3	14600.1	16432.0	19084.9
153	Grain mill products; starches; animal feeds		6611	6757	7022	6309		162.4	154.1	119.1	111.5		7409.5	8535.7	8528.0	9568.5
1531	Grain mill products		4730	4789	4929	4404		...	...	...	...		...	...	...	...
1532	Starches and starch products		194	198	201	176		...	...	...	...		...	...	...	...
1533	Prepared animal feeds		1687	1729	1796	1556		...	...	...	...		...	...	...	...
154	Other food products		20819	21626	22629	20032		575.9	551.7	562.7	562.1		31272.5	36751.6	45319.9	55208.4
1541	Bakery products		13651	14218	14726	11942		...	...	...	...		...	...	...	...
1542	Sugar		335	330	337	280		...	...	...	...		...	...	...	...
1543	Cocoa, chocolate and sugar confectionery		2894	2759	2733	2161		...	...	...	...		...	...	...	...
1544	Macaroni, noodles & similar products		1306	1303	1308	1132		...	...	...	...		...	...	...	...
1549	Other food products n.e.c.		2633	2875	3108	2900		...	...	...	...		...	...	...	...
155	Beverages		7994	8232	8495	7644		218.0	219.1	201.2	192.3		17604.0	21615.4	24978.4	28611.1
1551	Distilling, rectifying & blending of spirits		2151	2143	2126	1887		...	...	...	...		...	...	...	...
1552	Wines		893	869	848	677		...	...	...	...		...	...	...	...
1553	Malt liquors and malt		1209	1215	1219	1033		...	...	...	...		...	...	...	...
1554	Soft drinks; mineral waters		3741	3965	4167	3839		...	...	...	...		...	...	...	...
1600	Tobacco products		316	324	327	274		21.2	19.1	15.2	14.1		3363.8	3628.8	3965.8	4291.0
171	Spinning, weaving and finishing of textiles		2388	2540	2693	2456		201.4	169.6	163.7	141.8		8034.7	8095.5	8502.0	8800.5
1711	Textile fibre preparation; textile weaving		2334	2373	2410	2071		...	...	...	...		...	...	...	...
1712	Finishing of textiles		54	124	191	240		...	...	...	...		...	...	...	...
172	Other textiles		2275	2914	3432	3647		107.0	100.3	59.6	56.0		3473.4	3913.1	3169.1	3625.9
1721	Made-up textile articles, except apparel		857	1362	1791	2173		75.2	68.1	21.7	21.7		2012.7	2122.8	1034.7	1206.9
1722	Carpets and rugs		129	132	146	116		...	...	...	...		...	...	...	...
1723	Cordage, rope, twine and netting		130	155	171	168		...	...	...	...		...	...	...	...
1729	Other textiles n.e.c.		1159	1265	1324	1190		...	...	...	...		...	...	...	...
1730	Knitted and crocheted fabrics and articles		3912	3854	3845	2482		30.5	25.7	25.9	23.6		1123.9	1117.6	1364.1	1549.5
1810	Wearing apparel, except fur apparel		5587	7489	8520	9336		255.6	246.3	238.9	234.0		6467.9	8777.5	10127.1	13144.6
1820	Dressing & dyeing of fur; processing of fur		2103	2070	2046	1315		16.5	14.4	7.3	7.1		529.2	507.7	360.1	434.8
191	Tanning, dressing and processing of leather		1778	1792	1814	1309		24.5	21.5	18.8	19.0		1150.9	1191.5	1260.3	1542.2
1911	Tanning and dressing of leather		665	642	638	403		12.2	11.4	10.2	10.7		675.6	740.0	789.8	972.3
1912	Luggage, handbags, etc.; saddlery & harness		1113	1150	1176	906		12.3	10.0	8.6	8.3		475.4	451.6	470.4	570.1
1920	Footwear		4153	4028	4026	2704		69.4	59.5	50.7	48.3		2488.2	2475.7	2656.4	3022.9
2010	Sawmilling and planing of wood		12591	14384	16335	15777		194.5	184.5	146.0	131.7		8156.8	9115.0	9412.1	9969.3
202	Products of wood, cork, straw, etc.		24300	24805	25539	18076		194.7	196.0	211.5	204.0		9362.8	11936.8	15883.4	18034.4
2021	Veneer sheets, plywood, particle board, etc.		334	488	576	637		113.5	115.2	95.3	97.2		6168.6	8090.4	9191.1	10592.1
2022	Builders' carpentry and joinery		14264	14773	15391	11924		44.9	47.3	94.4	88.1		2015.2	2475.3	5774.3	6490.5
2023	Wooden containers		761	804	818	805		7.8	7.3	12.6	9.9		260.8	320.3	538.4	499.0
2029	Other wood products; articles of cork/straw		8941	8716	8663	4628		28.5	26.3	9.3	8.8		890.9	1049.9	380.6	452.8
210	Paper and paper products		3044	3476	3918	3955		154.8	142.4	131.1	130.6		13982.9	14487.4	15221.0	17687.8
2101	Pulp, paper and paperboard		217	341	405	473		120.1	102.5	87.2	78.4		11666.0	11228.2	11055.1	11415.3
2102	Corrugated paper and paperboard		1315	1455	1564	1541		34.7	39.9	39.9	...		2317.3	3260.2	3789.8	...
2109	Other articles of paper and paperboard		462	687	843	960		...	...	...	...		...	...	...	...
221	Publishing		29959	33032	36351	33232		87.1	95.5	139.8	142.4		7804.2	9915.1	17042.3	20006.8
2211	Publishing of books and other publications		3427	5106	5982	6654		...	...	...	...		...	...	...	...
2212	Publishing of newspapers, journals, etc.		4176	5832	6929	7668		...	...	...	...		...	...	...	...
2213	Publishing of recorded media		127	208	286	386		...	...	...	...		...	...	...	...
2219	Other publishing		1602	2205	2402	2488		...	...	...	...		...	...	...	...

222	Printing and related service activities		12402	13446	14806	14288		130.9	130.0	121.8	127.2		8993.2	10537.8	12112.6	14774.4
2221	Printing		3646	4843	5482	5913		...	...	...	...		...	...	...	...
2222	Service activities related to printing		832	1145	1376	1559		...	...	...	...		...	...	...	...
2230	Reproduction of recorded media		715	748	802	676		3.3	2.2	0.5	0.4		125.1	106.7	54.4	34.2
2310	Coke oven products		26	28	35	35		12.4	13.0	23.1	23.0		1452.5	1875.9	3805.7	4588.5
2320	Refined petroleum products		2108	2370	2692	2558		106.8	124.9	113.0	111.0		15549.4	20840.1	27879.0	31318.7
2330	Processing of nuclear fuel	a/	...	...	...	...	a/	...	...	...	...	a/	...	...	...	...
241	Basic chemicals		2740	3178	3616	3610		382.8	336.1	338.5	327.3		30307.7	33112.9	42981.2	48761.8
2411	Basic chemicals, except fertilizers		1914	2108	2302	2162		...	...	...	...		...	...	...	...
2412	Fertilizers and nitrogen compounds		226	283	319	317		...	...	...	...		...	...	...	...
2413	Plastics in primary forms; synthetic rubber		600	725	831	851		...	...	...	...		...	...	...	...
242	Other chemicals		12022	12600	13242	11554		213.2	187.4	202.8	205.9		14460.8	15994.2	11774.7	26368.0
2421	Pesticides and other agro-chemical products		94	114	135	147		2.6	1.5	2.0	1.9		116.4	85.5	156.3	182.9
2422	Paints, varnishes, printing ink and mastics		1762	1903	2054	1987		31.4	31.7	25.7	27.3		1685.9	2138.8	2241.7	2663.3
2423	Pharmaceuticals, medicinal chemicals, etc.		4958	4953	5083	4902		84.5	81.5	86.0	90.6		5655.0	6794.2	8791.0	11116.0
2424	Soap, cleaning & cosmetic preparations		2766	2837	2935	2547		35.1	36.2	40.2	43.4		2928.9	3699.3	5605.8	6470.3
2429	Other chemical products n.e.c.		1777	1938	2074	1952		59.7	36.4	49.0	42.8		4074.7	3276.2	5773.6	5934.6
2430	Man-made fibres		182	188	190	167		27.8	26.8	21.7	17.2		1311.4	1630.1	1533.8	1488.1
251	Rubber products		1743	1905	2084	1944		118.4	116.8	118.3	108.7		7548.7	9090.2	10484.2	11844.0
2511	Rubber tyres and tubes		387	404	433	391		...	...	...	...		...	...	...	...
2519	Other rubber products		1354	1440	1518	1337		...	...	...	...		...	...	...	...
2520	Plastic products		11441	12836	14112	13771		110.8	122.6	138.5	161.8		6063.4	8020.9	10715.1	16617.8
2610	Glass and glass products		2191	2495	2772	2660		97.0	84.7	77.4	73.9		5709.2	6008.2	6611.4	7941.3
269	Non-metallic mineral products n.e.c.		23176	24113	25311	20563		601.4	579.6	571.7	569.6		38163.4	45457.1	55099.5	69157.2
2691	Pottery, china and earthenware		987	1031	1078	861		81.0	71.9	66.4	65.9		5303.3	5397.2	6248.0	7491.6
2692	Refractory ceramic products		202	275	315	343		14.6	17.4	18.7	18.3		1090.3	1580.0	1922.9	2294.4
2693	Struct.non-refractory clay; ceramic products		5696	5668	5746	3945		92.9	87.9	90.5	82.4		4778.8	5816.5	7162.8	8133.8
2694	Cement, lime and plaster		713	725	754	684		54.6	52.6	57.4	59.2		4025.6	4868.2	6545.2	8613.7
2695	Articles of concrete, cement and plaster		9969	10220	10429	7797		256.7	255.7	275.3	278.4		17054.6	21106.2	27135.0	34840.4
2696	Cutting, shaping & finishing of stone		1580	1763	1958	1802		33.4	29.6	6.0	5.4		1573.5	1514.7	532.8	571.7
2699	Other non-metallic mineral products n.e.c.		3000	3056	3148	2635		68.1	64.6	57.4	60.0		4335.1	5177.7	5551.0	7210.2
2710	Basic iron and steel		142	200	253	286		497.1	485.3	452.8	419.5		45344.0	54601.8	62614.7	69247.9
2720	Basic precious and non-ferrous metals		1000	1123	1226	1145		284.1	261.9	238.1	191.5		42089.4	44958.6	41282.3	39180.0
273	Casting of metals		846	907	988	917		31.8	34.7	57.7	57.7		1676.9	2276.0	5041.9	5949.6
2731	Casting of iron and steel		192	282	325	370		...	...	...	...		...	...	...	...
2732	Casting of non-ferrous metals		100	135	166	183		...	...	...	...		...	...	...	...
281	Struct.metal products;tanks;steam generators		14212	15328	16839	15601		236.6	232.4	198.5	217.4		15156.7	18098.8	18679.4	25356.2
2811	Structural metal products		10438	11208	11995	10728		149.0	146.1	133.8	156.5		8175.9	9776.8	12143.0	18044.8
2812	Tanks, reservoirs and containers of metal		3223	3189	3230	2370		52.3	48.4	28.4	26.1		3909.6	4153.6	2458.2	2565.9
2813	Steam generators		550	658	729	736		35.3	38.0	36.4	34.8		3070.4	4167.3	4076.7	4745.4
289	Other metal products; metal working services		8318	9635	11079	10993		188.4	191.3	272.4	285.6		10626.9	13172.4	22546.9	29016.9
2891	Metal forging/pressing/stamping/roll-forming		215	347	479	616		22.9	25.7	38.4	42.7		1580.4	2046.9	3486.9	4818.9
2892	Treatment & coating of metals		859	1646	2367	3143		4.1	11.8	56.7	71.1		251.4	772.8	4557.9	7303.7
2893	Cutlery, hand tools and general hardware		1556	1662	1755	1471		52.6	49.7	69.0	64.8		3182.6	3355.2	5088.5	5876.5
2899	Other fabricated metal products n.e.c.		5688	5965	6426	5661		108.8	104.2	108.4	106.9		5606.0	6998.1	9413.4	11017.1
291	General purpose machinery		16837	19089	21413	21354		987.4	941.6	935.7	903.5		68963.1	80790.3	102690.4	122554.2
2911	Engines & turbines (not for transport equipment)		682	915	1046	1168		...	...	...	...		...	...	...	...
2912	Pumps, compressors, taps and valves		2757	2958	3153	2990		...	...	...	...		...	...	...	...
2913	Bearings, gears, gearing & driving elements		236	277	319	246		...	...	...	...		...	...	...	...
2914	Ovens, furnaces and furnace burners		349	433	562	631		...	...	...	...		...	...	...	...
2915	Lifting and handling equipment		1609	2227	2824	3257		...	...	...	...		...	...	...	...
2919	Other general purpose machinery		11204	12153	13142	12352		...	...	...	...		...	...	...	...
292	Special purpose machinery		13683	14351	15030	13030	a/	...	...	...	...	a/	...	...	...	...
2921	Agricultural and forestry machinery		4168	4124	4125	3343		...	...	...	...		...	...	...	...
2922	Machine tools		3770	3926	4112	3377		...	...	...	...		...	...	...	...
2923	Machinery for metallurgy		344	390	396	350		...	...	...	...		...	...	...	...
2924	Machinery for mining & construction		1838	1822	1826	1517		...	...	...	...		...	...	...	...
2925	Food/beverage/tobacco processing machinery		1091	1117	1134	911		...	...	...	...		...	...	...	...
2926	Machinery for textile, apparel and leather		408	424	417	316		...	...	...	...		...	...	...	...
2927	Weapons and ammunition	a/	...	...	...	...	a/	...	...	...	...	a/	...	...	...	...
2929	Other special purpose machinery		1723	2148	2522	2617		...	...	...	...		...	...	...	...

continued

Russian Federation

ISIC Revision 3		Number of enterprises					Number of employees					Wages and salaries paid to employees				
			(number)					(thousands)					(millions of Russian Roubles)			
ISIC	Industry	Note	2003	2004	2005	2006	Note	2003	2004	2005	2006	Note	2003	2004	2005	2006
2930	Domestic appliances n.e.c.		1269	1301	1318	957		29.3	33.1	61.0	56.2		2049.8	2729.0	5464.6	6105.7
3000	Office, accounting and computing machinery		3505	3903	4251	3406		25.8	22.6	18.6	20.0		1549.8	1562.7	1705.3	2292.5
3110	Electric motors, generators and transformers	b/	1853	2875	3723	4550		103.0	94.8	99.2	98.0		7754.4	9488.8	10707.5	13288.5
3120	Electricity distribution & control apparatus	b/	...	...	...	...		54.5	63.8	88.8	86.3		3447.7	5067.7	9086.7	10992.1
3130	Insulated wire and cable		295	346	894	...		38.4	37.8	39.6	38.0		2775.6	3527.4	4310.7	5305.9
3140	Accumulators, primary cells and batteries		305	311	333	275		21.0	18.7	19.0	17.3		1327.9	1402.3	1648.0	1838.6
3150	Lighting equipment and electric lamps		307	381	439	454		30.7	29.3	28.1	25.7		1233.9	1604.5	1790.6	2051.3
3190	Other electrical equipment n.e.c.		1333	1945	2484	3002		78.5	84.9	107.8	104.0		5177.3	6959.1	10584.4	12228.3
3210	Electronic valves, tubes, etc.	a/	...	...	...	...	a/	...	...	...	...	a/	...	...	...	...
3220	TV/radio transmitters; line comm. apparatus	a/	...	...	...	...	a/	...	...	...	...	a/	...	...	...	...
3230	TV and radio receivers and associated goods	a/	...	...	...	...	a/	...	...	...	...	a/	...	...	...	...
331	Medical, measuring, testing appliances, etc.		11819	12187	12685	10350		264.1	266.0	253.0	256.0		16056.1	19818.9	25781.4	32655.6
3311	Medical, surgical and orthopaedic equipment		5310	5500	5734	4569		86.4	74.5	48.4	49.3		5183.1	5089.9	4870.2	6406.6
3312	Measuring/testing/navigating appliances,etc.		6380	6497	6676	5417		176.6	189.4	201.3	202.0		10849.6	14393.8	20421.1	25425.2
3313	Industrial process control equipment		129	190	273	361		1.1	2.1	3.3	4.5		91.3	334.3	489.4	790.6
3320	Optical instruments & photographic equipment		648	723	773	683		20.5	26.5	28.1	23.8		1150.7	2017.3	2488.5	2795.2
3330	Watches and clocks		265	307	325	284		13.9	10.3	6.3	5.1		657.3	626.7	401.8	396.1
3410	Motor vehicles	c/	3013	2879	2857	2171		423.7	383.7	300.6	276.9		31999.3	36606.9	35224.9	40052.3
3420	Automobile bodies, trailers & semi-trailers	c/	...	...	...	...		23.5	17.0	21.5	21.8		1632.4	988.7	1858.4	2470.0
3430	Parts/accessories for automobiles		717	970	1218	1414		102.6	110.7	184.8	176.3		5762.5	7825.5	15734.4	18540.1
351	Building and repairing of ships and boats	a/	...	...	...	...	a/	...	...	...	...	a/	...	...	...	...
3511	Building and repairing of ships	a/	...	...	...	...	a/	...	...	...	...	a/	...	...	...	...
3512	Building/repairing of pleasure/sport. boats	a/	...	...	...	...	a/	...	...	...	...	a/	...	...	...	...
3520	Railway/tramway locomotives & rolling stock		901	1026	1199	1217		153.1	176.7	185.6	195.0		12155.0	17434.3	22703.0	27985.0
3530	Aircraft and spacecraft	a/	...	...	...	...	a/	...	...	...	...	a/	...	...	...	...
359	Transport equipment n.e.c.	a/	...	...	...	...	a/	...	...	...	...	a/	...	...	...	...
3591	Motorcycles		15	23	30	35		...	...	...	...		...	...	...	...
3592	Bicycles and invalid carriages		30	33	41	49		...	...	...	...		...	...	...	...
3599	Other transport equipment n.e.c.		22	30	34	37		...	...	...	...		...	...	...	...
3610	Furniture		17787	18836	20455	17707		140.6	142.2	141.6	140.8		5169.9	7050.3	8850.9	11668.6
369	Manufacturing n.e.c.		6405	7220	8177	7531		65.1	63.2	91.7	92.6		4173.3	4718.7	7816.6	9983.2
3691	Jewellery and related articles		3544	3924	4345	3923		24.6	24.4	29.3	41.7		2080.0	2587.2	3856.7	6089.0
3692	Musical instruments		312	313	323	218		3.0	2.8	1.6	1.3		123.1	138.1	71.5	84.0
3693	Sports goods		761	757	809	638		8.4	8.8	2.8	3.6		255.5	332.1	236.0	299.5
3694	Games and toys		1039	1092	1164	876		9.7	10.5	19.6	16.1		439.2	538.9	1025.8	1162.6
3699	Other manufacturing n.e.c.		749	1093	1431	1694		19.5	16.7	38.4	29.8		1275.5	1122.5	2626.0	2348.1
3710	Recycling of metal waste and scrap		3473	4479	5569	6140		41.0	42.8	57.6	55.5		2782.7	3846.7	5566.2	6974.1
3720	Recycling of non-metal waste and scrap		8064	7734	7745	6486		22.1	24.8	7.0	8.2		920.9	1353.6	599.6	874.2
D	Total manufacturing		434666	452376	478533	409742		10302.9	9919.8	9511.6	9240.5		692723.1	815290.9	961169.3	1130818.2

a/ Data suppressed due to confidentiality rules.
b/ 3110 includes 3120.
c/ 3410 includes 3420.

Russian Federation

ISIC Revision 3		Output in producers' prices					Value added					Gross fixed capital formation		
			(millions of Russian Roubles)					(millions of Russian Roubles)					(millions of Russian Roubles)	
ISIC	Industry	Note	2003	2004	2005	2006	Note	2003	2004	2005	2006	Note	2005	2006
151	Processed meat,fish,fruit,vegetables,fats		326019	421668	504652	604875		72489	116342	152278	184136		...	...
1511	Processing/preserving of meat		202398	230986	278200	332452		44308	56450	71945	84047		...	...
1512	Processing/preserving of fish		44345	78088	97261	118602		12008	40278	57513	77053		...	...
1513	Processing/preserving of fruit & vegetables		30136	38168	44924	66118		5711	6581	10271	13048		...	...
1514	Vegetable and animal oils and fats		49140	74426	84267	87703		10461	13033	12549	9988		...	...
1520	Dairy products		171266	224738	240795	261800		34106	42747	49733	54394		...	...
153	Grain mill products; starches; animal feeds		117940	133404	127145	144878		24585	26412	28601	33620		...	...
1531	Grain mill products		...	...	...	...		...	...	...	...		...	...
1532	Starches and starch products		...	...	...	...		...	...	...	...		...	...
1533	Prepared animal feeds		21558	27692	30826	40776		3632	4423	5073	6874		...	...
154	Other food products		280118	333309	409274	485551		79690	100189	134699	155899		...	...
1541	Bakery products		118061	139260	158246	176557		41000	54440	68783	73376		...	...
1542	Sugar		63231	69092	81601	104149		13424	13948	20423	30191		...	...
1543	Cocoa, chocolate and sugar confectionery		...	...	...	...		...	...	...	...		...	...
1544	Macaroni, noodles & similar products		...	...	...	...		...	...	...	...		...	...
1549	Other food products n.e.c.		...	...	...	...		...	...	...	...		...	...
155	Beverages		262599	304361	379216	459523		97148	109640	131328	178690		...	...
1551	Distilling, rectifying & blending of spirits		...	...	...	...		...	...	...	...		...	...
1552	Wines		...	...	...	...		...	...	...	...		...	...
1553	Malt liquors and malt		...	...	...	...		...	...	...	...		...	...
1554	Soft drinks; mineral waters		...	...	...	...		...	...	...	...		...	...
1600	Tobacco products		87360	78034	89831	97160		32306	19704	33462	34769		...	...
171	Spinning, weaving and finishing of textiles		82056	109428	87757	98781		17304	24970	20447	27647		...	...
1711	Textile fibre preparation; textile weaving		...	...	...	...		...	...	...	...		...	...
1712	Finishing of textiles		...	...	...	...		...	...	...	...		...	...
172	Other textiles		...	...	...	...		...	...	...	...		...	...
1721	Made-up textile articles, except apparel		...	...	...	...		...	...	...	...		...	...
1722	Carpets and rugs		...	...	...	...		...	...	...	...		...	...
1723	Cordage, rope, twine and netting		...	...	...	...		...	...	...	...		...	...
1729	Other textiles n.e.c.		...	...	...	...		...	...	...	...		...	...
1730	Knitted and crocheted fabrics and articles		...	...	...	...		...	...	...	...		...	...
1810	Wearing apparel, except fur apparel		59631	81926	80942	95032		19209	28715	32001	40479		...	...
1820	Dressing & dyeing of fur; processing of fur		...	...	...	...		...	...	...	...		...	...
191	Tanning, dressing and processing of leather		24111	27709	28500	36724		6145	10190	9833	13643		...	...
1911	Tanning and dressing of leather		...	...	...	...		...	...	...	...		...	...
1912	Luggage, handbags, etc.; saddlery & harness		...	...	...	...		...	...	...	...		...	...
1920	Footwear		...	...	...	...		...	...	...	...		...	...
2010	Sawmilling and planing of wood		39875	53183	82507	97363		13967	22480	34449	39559		...	...
202	Products of wood, cork, straw, etc.		67122	90155	121042	145054		24960	33149	46731	58388		...	...
2021	Veneer sheets, plywood, particle board, etc.		...	...	...	...		...	...	...	...		...	...
2022	Builders' carpentry and joinery		...	...	...	...		...	...	...	...		...	...
2023	Wooden containers		...	...	...	...		...	...	...	...		...	...
2029	Other wood products; articles of cork/straw		...	...	...	...		...	...	...	...		...	...
210	Paper and paper products		132094	160732	181696	214369		40793	43556	55983	64646		...	...
2101	Pulp, paper and paperboard		...	...	...	...		...	...	...	...		...	...
2102	Corrugated paper and paperboard		...	...	...	...		...	...	...	...		...	...
2109	Other articles of paper and paperboard		...	...	...	...		...	...	...	...		...	...
221	Publishing		36472	68787	93584	117037		18858	33555	50682	62460		...	...
2211	Publishing of books and other publications		...	...	...	...		...	...	...	...		...	...
2212	Publishing of newspapers, journals, etc.		...	...	...	...		...	...	...	...		...	...
2213	Publishing of recorded media		...	...	...	...		...	...	...	...		...	...
2219	Other publishing		...	...	...	...		...	...	...	...		...	...

continued

Russian Federation

ISIC Revision 3		Output in producers' prices					Value added					Gross fixed capital formation		
			(millions of Russian Roubles)					(millions of Russian Roubles)					(millions of Russian Roubles)	
ISIC	Industry	Note	2003	2004	2005	2006	Note	2003	2004	2005	2006	Note	2005	2006
222	Printing and related service activities		53314	69837	82675	108933		21483	26314	31085	39755		...	...
2221	Printing		...	...	...	...		...	...	...	...		...	...
2222	Service activities related to printing		...	...	...	...		...	...	...	...		...	...
2230	Reproduction of recorded media		718	3447	4496	6533		210	1203	992	1482		...	...
2310	Coke oven products		17795	39512	31125	45248		4146	16803	9097	8170		...	...
2320	Refined petroleum products		748203	1015744	1957464	2255038		240751	372503	743486	776361		...	...
2330	Processing of nuclear fuel	a/	...	...	...	...	a/	...	...	...	...		...	...
241	Basic chemicals		492842	588358	769236	883574		165515	189924	242457	250589		...	...
2411	Basic chemicals, except fertilizers		...	...	...	...		...	...	...	...		...	...
2412	Fertilizers and nitrogen compounds		...	...	...	...		...	...	...	...		...	...
2413	Plastics in primary forms; synthetic rubber		...	...	...	...		...	...	...	...		...	...
242	Other chemicals		128231	151819	204022	238364		43211	50515	65651	78069		...	...
2421	Pesticides and other agro-chemical products		...	...	...	...		...	...	...	...		...	...
2422	Paints, varnishes, printing ink and mastics		20423	22946	38559	38673		5438	8017	12757	13679		...	...
2423	Pharmaceuticals, medicinal chemicals, etc.		44017	47945	64359	77011		18114	19943	25796	31590		...	...
2424	Soap, cleaning & cosmetic preparations		40090	50847	63628	80645		12724	14440	18953	23142		...	...
2429	Other chemical products n.e.c.		23701	30081	37475	42035		6936	8114	8145	9658		...	...
2430	Man-made fibres		16078	19356	13957	31324		1446	2740	1915	10826		...	...
251	Rubber products		122995	183514	228303	333827		29568	47180	64865	87423		...	...
2511	Rubber tyres and tubes		...	...	...	...		...	...	...	...		...	...
2519	Other rubber products		...	...	...	...		...	...	...	...		...	...
2520	Plastic products		...	2610	...	...		...	44002	...	...		...	...
2610	Glass and glass products		31442	...	50734	77713		12161	18472	18206	30677		...	...
269	Non-metallic mineral products n.e.c.		209471	286128	403875	532457		72006	100180	151721	194040		...	...
2691	Pottery, china and earthenware		...	...	...	...		...	...	...	...		...	...
2692	Refractory ceramic products		...	...	...	...		...	...	...	...		...	...
2693	Struct.non-refractory clay; ceramic products		...	...	...	...		...	...	...	...		...	...
2694	Cement, lime and plaster		37064	48306	87626	132109		11938	15648	34075	52865		...	...
2695	Articles of concrete, cement and plaster		...	...	...	...		...	...	...	...		...	...
2696	Cutting, shaping & finishing of stone		...	...	...	...		...	...	...	...		...	...
2699	Other non-metallic mineral products n.e.c.		...	...	...	...		...	...	...	...		...	...
2710	Basic iron and steel		621201	978125	1119389	1284790		183439	343967	335868	388936		...	...
2720	Basic precious and non-ferrous metals		519809	651863	801604	1130631		156900	221207	290239	464220		...	...
273	Casting of metals		10276	14139	13117	20818		2094	3906	3268	5922		...	...
2731	Casting of iron and steel		...	...	...	...		...	...	...	...		...	...
2732	Casting of non-ferrous metals		...	...	...	...		...	...	...	...		...	...
281	Struct.metal products;tanks;steam generators		78068	100601	137669	189735		26911	31518	42824	56995		...	...
2811	Structural metal products		...	...	...	...		...	...	...	...		...	...
2812	Tanks, reservoirs and containers of metal		...	...	...	...		...	...	...	...		...	...
2813	Steam generators		...	...	...	...		...	...	...	...		...	...
289	Other metal products; metal working services		65736	90528	132105	162294		20895	27774	36268	41099		...	...
2891	Metal forging/pressing/stamping/roll-forming		...	...	...	...		...	...	...	...		...	...
2892	Treatment & coating of metals		...	...	...	...		...	...	...	...		...	...
2893	Cutlery, hand tools and general hardware		...	...	...	...		...	...	...	...		...	...
2899	Other fabricated metal products n.e.c.		...	...	...	...		...	...	...	...		...	...
291	General purpose machinery		203113	235686	278950	352657		82571	97092	114646	125335		...	...
2911	Engines & turbines (not for transport equipment)		...	...	...	...		...	...	...	...		...	...
2912	Pumps, compressors, taps and valves		...	...	...	...		...	...	...	...		...	...
2913	Bearings, gears, gearing & driving elements		...	...	...	...		...	...	...	...		...	...
2914	Ovens, furnaces and furnace burners		...	...	...	...		...	...	...	...		...	...
2915	Lifting and handling equipment		...	...	...	...		...	...	...	...		...	...
2919	Other general purpose machinery		...	...	...	...		...	...	...	...		...	...

292	Special purpose machinery		137219	168094	210484	264223		51091	56732	75713	89317		...	...
2921	Agricultural and forestry machinery		...	...	...	...		...	...	...	...		...	...
2922	Machine tools		...	...	...	...		...	...	...	...		...	...
2923	Machinery for metallurgy		...	...	...	...		...	...	...	...		...	...
2924	Machinery for mining & construction		...	...	...	...		...	...	...	...		...	...
2925	Food/beverage/tobacco processing machinery		...	...	...	...		...	...	...	...		...	...
2926	Machinery for textile, apparel and leather		...	...	...	...		...	...	...	...		...	...
2927	Weapons and ammunition	a/	...	...	...	...	a/	...	...	...	...		...	...
2929	Other special purpose machinery		...	...	...	...		...	...	...	...		...	...
2930	Domestic appliances n.e.c.		21344	31990	39639	46171		8685	12356	10567	11715		...	...
3000	Office, accounting and computing machinery		6738	19585	23976	33395		2689	6983	6812	8776		...	...
3110	Electric motors, generators and transformers	b/	60258	86706	111737	137452	b/	21887	33493	43903	42980		...	...
3120	Electricity distribution & control apparatus	b/	...	...	...	...	b/	...	...	...	...		...	...
3130	Insulated wire and cable		...	48079	57118	99596		7413	11113	9359	17824		...	...
3140	Accumulators, primary cells and batteries		...	...	...	...		...	...	...	...		...	...
3150	Lighting equipment and electric lamps		...	...	...	...		...	...	...	...		...	...
3190	Other electrical equipment n.e.c.		...	66268	76254	84013		13671	23283	23934	24717		...	...
3210	Electronic valves, tubes, etc.	a/	...	...	...	...	a/	...	...	...	...		...	...
3220	TV/radio transmitters; line comm. apparatus	a/	...	...	...	...	a/	...	...	...	...		...	...
3230	TV and radio receivers and associated goods	a/	...	...	...	...	a/	...	...	...	...		...	...
331	Medical, measuring, testing appliances, etc.		...	110460	119203	149609		32624	48623	55157	66690		...	...
3311	Medical, surgical and orthopaedic equipment		...	...	...	...		...	...	...	...		...	...
3312	Measuring/testing/navigating appliances,etc.		...	...	...	...		...	...	...	...		...	...
3313	Industrial process control equipment		...	...	...	...		...	...	...	...		...	...
3320	Optical instruments & photographic equipment		...	11828	11518	13040		4888	4808	5796	5665		...	...
3330	Watches and clocks		...	...	...	...		...	...	...	...		...	...
3410	Motor vehicles	c/	319146	431359	498685	651361	c/	76845	97869	96377	122551		...	...
3420	Automobile bodies, trailers & semi-trailers	c/	...	...	...	...	c/	...	...	...	...		...	...
3430	Parts/accessories for automobiles		...	...	...	...		...	...	...	...		...	...
351	Building and repairing of ships and boats	a/	...	...	...	...	a/	...	...	...	...		...	...
3511	Building and repairing of ships	a/	...	...	...	...	a/	...	...	...	...		...	...
3512	Building/repairing of pleasure/sport. boats	a/	...	...	...	...	a/	...	...	...	...		...	...
3520	Railway/tramway locomotives & rolling stock		62835	117224	131381	145004		20748	31230	38270	42458		...	...
3530	Aircraft and spacecraft	a/	...	...	...	...	a/	...	...	...	...		...	...
359	Transport equipment n.e.c.	a/	...	...	...	...	a/	...	...	...	...		...	...
3591	Motorcycles		...	...	...	...		...	...	...	...		...	...
3592	Bicycles and invalid carriages		...	...	...	...		...	...	...	...		...	...
3599	Other transport equipment n.e.c.		...	...	...	...		...	...	...	...		...	...
3610	Furniture		52790	52050	74423	99325		18188	18723	25999	35444		...	...
369	Manufacturing n.e.c.		76640	87527	104892	122323		37242	30190	36282	42763		...	...
3691	Jewellery and related articles		50792	68698	82125	92970		24938	23417	28931	35148		...	...
3692	Musical instruments		...	...	...	...		...	...	...	...		...	...
3693	Sports goods		...	...	...	...		...	...	...	...		...	...
3694	Games and toys		...	...	...	...		...	...	...	...		...	...
3699	Other manufacturing n.e.c.		...	...	...	...		...	...	...	...		...	...
3710	Recycling of metal waste and scrap		43519	76576	114072	144843		7400	17923	23839	29628		...	...
3720	Recycling of non-metal waste and scrap		17345	5028	4853	8809		2140	2074	2317	2833		...	...
D	Total manufacturing		6300016	8225398	10610914	12976573		1976313	2687557	3521018	4185586		...	...

a/ Data suppressed due to confidentiality rules.
b/ 3110 includes 3120.
c/ 3410 includes 3420.

Russian Federation

ISIC Revision 3			Index numbers of industrial production (2000=100)											
ISIC	Industry	Note	1995	1996	1997	1998	1999	2000	2001	2002	2003	2004	2005	2006
15	Food and beverages		99	92	89	87	97	100	108	116	126	132	141	152
16	Tobacco products		34	33	52	61	81	100	106	112	110	110	117	119
17	Textiles		97	71	73	61	80	100	108	108	108	108	118	134
18	Wearing apparel, fur		88	77	79	83	81	100	108	102	105	96	93	102
19	Leather, leather products and footwear		136	99	88	69	93	100	114	127	141	140	141	172
20	Wood products (excl. furniture)		109	87	82	79	88	100	98	102	112	121	130	134
21	Paper and paper products		78	63	64	69	86	100	108	114	122	130	137	145
22	Printing and publishing		75	81	79	79	83	100	113	114	124	128	129	140
23	Coke,refined petroleum products,nuclear fuel		103	102	101	93	98	100	103	108	110	113	117	126
24	Chemicals and chemical products		79	70	73	68	87	100	100	101	106	113	118	123
25	Rubber and plastics products		73	66	68	65	79	100	102	102	107	122	142	173
26	Non-metallic mineral products		116	90	85	80	90	100	104	105	113	122	128	148
27	Basic metals		84	81	84	79	87	100	102	107	115	118	122	132
28	Fabricated metal products		112	91	91	85	86	100	121	129	137	148	189	216
29	Machinery and equipment n.e.c.		118	95	95	83	95	100	106	97	115	140	139	152
30	Office, accounting and computing machinery		181	118	139	295	107	100	114	149	193	313	401	558
31	Electrical machinery and apparatus		97	83	71	61	79	100	112	111	124	145	149	187
32	Radio,television and communication equipment		...	...	...	...	...	...	...	...	...	...	...	...
33	Medical, precision and optical instruments		42	47	46	44	60	100	106	75	164	214	365	416
34	Motor vehicles, trailers, semi-trailers		81	81	92	81	95	100	102	99	106	115	116	133
35	Other transport equipment		90	82	90	80	88	100	62	62	74	83	92	90
36	Furniture; manufacturing n.e.c.		106	88	90	79	90	100	111	114	129	145	160	181
37	Recycling		72	65	84	79	89	100	102	108	114	118	121	130
D	Total manufacturing		93	83	85	80	90	100	102	103	114	125	133	141

Saudi Arabia

Supplier of information:
Central Department of Statistics and Information, Ministry of Economy and Planning, Riyadh.

Basic source of data:
Survey.

Major deviations from ISIC (Revision 3):
None reported.

Reference period:
Calendar year.

Scope:
All privately owned establishments.

Method of data collection:
Direct interview in the field.

Type of enumeration:
Complete enumeration.

Adjusted for non-response:
No.

Concepts and definitions of variables:
No deviations from the standard UN concepts and definitions are reported.

Related national publications:
None reported.

Saudi Arabia

ISIC Revision 3		Number of establishments					Number of persons engaged					Wages and salaries paid to employees				
			(number)					(number)					(millions of Saudi Riyals)			
ISIC	Industry	Note	2003	2004	2005	2006	Note	2003	2004	2005	2006a/	Note	2003	2004	2005	2006
151	Processed meat,fish,fruit,vegetables,fats		5756	...	...	...		17671	...	...	121358b/		...	...	...	3116.6b/
1511	Processing/preserving of meat		5374	...	...	...		12396	...	...	...		...	...	...	...
1512	Processing/preserving of fish		40	...	...	...		231	...	...	...		...	...	...	...
1513	Processing/preserving of fruit & vegetables		167	...	...	...		4009	...	...	...		...	...	...	...
1514	Vegetable and animal oils and fats		175	...	...	...		1035	...	...	...		...	...	...	...
1520	Dairy products		160	...	...	...		10156	...	...	...b/		...	...	...	...b/
153	Grain mill products; starches; animal feeds		1529	...	...	...		5053	...	...	...b/		...	...	...	...b/
1531	Grain mill products		1412	...	...	...		2650	...	...	...		...	...	...	...
1532	Starches and starch products		20	...	...	...		244	...	...	...		...	...	...	...
1533	Prepared animal feeds		97	...	...	...		2159	...	...	...		...	...	...	...
154	Other food products		8775	...	...	...		40465	...	...	...b/		...	...	...	...b/
1541	Bakery products		8001	...	...	...		31078	...	...	...		...	...	...	...
1542	Sugar		35	...	...	...		515	...	...	...		...	...	...	...
1543	Cocoa, chocolate and sugar confectionery		393	...	...	...		4553	...	...	...		...	...	...	...
1544	Macaroni, noodles & similar products		32	...	...	...		680	...	...	...		...	...	...	...
1549	Other food products n.e.c.		314	...	...	...		3639	...	...	...		...	...	...	...
155	Beverages		232	...	...	...		9702	...	...	...b/		...	...	...	...b/
1551	Distilling, rectifying & blending of spirits		...	...	...	...		...	...	...	...		...	...	...	...
1552	Wines		...	...	...	...		...	...	...	...		...	...	...	...
1553	Malt liquors and malt		...	...	...	...		...	...	...	...		...	...	...	...
1554	Soft drinks; mineral waters		...	...	...	...		...	...	...	...		...	...	...	...
1600	Tobacco products		66	...	...	...		163	...	...	90		...	...	...	1.7
171	Spinning, weaving and finishing of textiles		30	...	...	...		465	...	...	6628c/		...	...	...	108.0c/
1711	Textile fibre preparation; textile weaving		30	...	...	...		465	...	...	...		...	...	...	...
1712	Finishing of textiles		-	...	...	...		-	...	...	...		...	...	...	...
172	Other textiles		809	...	...	...		6117	...	...	...c/		...	...	...	...c/
1721	Made-up textile articles, except apparel		742	...	...	...		3542	...	...	...		...	...	...	...
1722	Carpets and rugs		53	...	...	...		2535	...	...	...		...	...	...	...
1723	Cordage, rope, twine and netting		5	...	...	...		11	...	...	...		...	...	...	...
1729	Other textiles n.e.c.		9	...	...	...		29	...	...	...		...	...	...	...
1730	Knitted and crocheted fabrics and articles		3	...	...	...		57	...	...	...c/		...	...	...	...c/
1810	Wearing apparel, except fur apparel		34836	...	...	...		73589	...	...	79137d/		...	...	...	951.8d/
1820	Dressing & dyeing of fur; processing of fur		14	...	...	...		327	...	...	...d/		...	...	...	...d/
191	Tanning, dressing and processing of leather		42	...	...	...		883	...	...	1756e/		...	...	...	23.9e/
1911	Tanning and dressing of leather		21	...	...	...		460	...	...	...		...	...	...	...
1912	Luggage, handbags, etc.; saddlery & harness		21	...	...	...		423	...	...	...		...	...	...	...
1920	Footwear		132	...	...	...		958	...	...	...e/		...	...	...	...e/
2010	Sawmilling and planing of wood		86	...	...	...		350	...	...	20104f/		...	...	...	324.3f/
202	Products of wood, cork, straw, etc.		3542	...	...	...		20682	...	...	...f/		...	...	...	...f/
2021	Veneer sheets, plywood, particle board, etc.		36	...	...	...		891	...	...	...		...	...	...	...
2022	Builders' carpentry and joinery		3140	...	...	...		16698	...	...	...		...	...	...	...
2023	Wooden containers		92	...	...	...		992	...	...	...		...	...	...	...
2029	Other wood products; articles of cork/straw		274	...	...	...		2101	...	...	...		...	...	...	...
210	Paper and paper products		232	...	...	...		9878	...	...	17028		...	...	...	604.3
2101	Pulp, paper and paperboard		67	...	...	...		2215	...	...	...		...	...	...	...
2102	Corrugated paper and paperboard		80	...	...	...		4568	...	...	...		...	...	...	...
2109	Other articles of paper and paperboard		85	...	...	...		3095	...	...	...		...	...	...	...
221	Publishing		406	...	...	...		5201	...	...	24815g/		...	...	...	620.5g/
2211	Publishing of books and other publications		86	...	...	...		760	...	...	...		...	...	...	...
2212	Publishing of newspapers, journals, etc.		209	...	...	...		4042	...	...	...		...	...	...	...
2213	Publishing of recorded media		99	...	...	...		299	...	...	...		...	...	...	...
2219	Other publishing		12	...	...	...		100	...	...	...		...	...	...	...

222	Printing and related service activities	1092	...	...	...	17293	...	...	...g/	...	...	...	...g/
2221	Printing	1042	...	...	...	16962	...	...	...	...	...	...	...
2222	Service activities related to printing	50	...	...	...	331	...	...	...	...	...	...	...
2230	Reproduction of recorded media	227	...	...	...	664	...	...	...g/	...	...	...	...g/
2310	Coke oven products	-	...	...	...	-	...	...	2357h/	...	...	...	200.9h/
2320	Refined petroleum products	67	...	...	...	5058	...	...	...h/	...	...	...	...h/
2330	Processing of nuclear fuel	-	...	...	...	-	...	...	...h/	...	...	...	...h/
241	Basic chemicals	273	...	...	...	17998	...	...	40993i/	...	...	...	1985.2i/
2411	Basic chemicals, except fertilizers	139	...	...	...	11349	...	...	...	...	...	...	...
2412	Fertilizers and nitrogen compounds	21	...	...	...	3827	...	...	...	...	...	...	...
2413	Plastics in primary forms; synthetic rubber	113	...	...	...	2822	...	...	...	...	...	...	...
242	Other chemicals	432	...	...	...	12475	...	...	...i/	...	...	...	...i/
2421	Pesticides and other agro-chemical products	21	...	...	...	312	...	...	...	...	...	...	...
2422	Paints, varnishes, printing ink and mastics	176	...	...	...	4750	...	...	...	...	...	...	...
2423	Pharmaceuticals, medicinal chemicals, etc.	74	...	...	...	2183	...	...	...	...	...	...	...
2424	Soap, cleaning & cosmetic preparations	116	...	...	...	3474	...	...	...	...	...	...	...
2429	Other chemical products n.e.c.	45	...	...	...	1756	...	...	...	...	...	...	...
2430	Man-made fibres	4	...	...	...	221	...	...	...i/	...	...	...	...i/
251	Rubber products	135	...	...	...	5847	...	...	27006j/	...	...	...	578.6j/
2511	Rubber tyres and tubes	62	...	...	...	368	...	...	...	...	...	...	...
2519	Other rubber products	73	...	...	...	5479	...	...	...	...	...	...	...
2520	Plastic products	858	...	...	...	27131	...	...	...j/	...	...	...	...j/
2610	Glass and glass products	414	...	...	...	4882	...	...	65209k/	...	...	...	1371.1k/
269	Non-metallic mineral products n.e.c.	2766	...	...	...	54642	...	...	...k/	...	...	...	...k/
2691	Pottery, china and earthenware	30	...	...	...	422	...	...	...	...	...	...	...
2692	Refractory ceramic products	68	...	...	...	986	...	...	...	...	...	...	...
2693	Struct.non-refractory clay; ceramic products	265	...	...	...	5224	...	...	...	...	...	...	...
2694	Cement, lime and plaster	133	...	...	...	10494	...	...	...	...	...	...	...
2695	Articles of concrete, cement and plaster	1885	...	...	...	30038	...	...	...	...	...	...	...
2696	Cutting, shaping & finishing of stone	380	...	...	...	7246	...	...	...	...	...	...	...
2699	Other non-metallic mineral products n.e.c.	5	...	...	...	232	...	...	...	...	...	...	...
2710	Basic iron and steel	588	...	...	...	18803	...	...	16643m/	...	...	...	527.8m/
2720	Basic precious and non-ferrous metals	65	...	...	...	5233	...	...	...m/	...	...	...	...m/
273	Casting of metals	192	...	...	...	2357	...	...	...m/	...	...	...	...m/
2731	Casting of iron and steel	91	...	...	...	961	...	...	...	...	...	...	...
2732	Casting of non-ferrous metals	101	...	...	...	1396	...	...	...	...	...	...	...
281	Struct.metal products;tanks;steam generators	12040	...	...	...	62496	...	...	84429n/	...	...	...	1441.3n/
2811	Structural metal products	12011	...	...	...	61323	...	...	...	...	...	...	...
2812	Tanks, reservoirs and containers of metal	29	...	...	...	1173	...	...	...	...	...	...	...
2813	Steam generators	-	...	...	...	-	...	...	...	...	...	...	...
289	Other metal products; metal working services	2422	...	...	...	14014	...	...	...n/	...	...	...	...n/
2891	Metal forging/pressing/stamping/roll-forming	47	...	...	...	325	...	...	...	...	...	...	...
2892	Treatment & coating of metals	1281	...	...	...	7180	...	...	...	...	...	...	...
2893	Cutlery, hand tools and general hardware	736	...	...	...	1617	...	...	...	...	...	...	...
2899	Other fabricated metal products n.e.c.	358	...	...	...	4892	...	...	...	...	...	...	...
291	General purpose machinery	363	...	...	...	10643	...	...	23327p/	...	...	...	521.1p/
2911	Engines & turbines (not for transport equipment)	18	...	...	...	549	...	...	...	...	...	...	...
2912	Pumps, compressors, taps and valves	47	...	...	...	899	...	...	...	...	...	...	...
2913	Bearings, gears, gearing & driving elements	7	...	...	...	292	...	...	...	...	...	...	...
2914	Ovens, furnaces and furnace burners	-	...	...	...	-	...	...	...	...	...	...	...
2915	Lifting and handling equipment	12	...	...	...	301	...	...	...	...	...	...	...
2919	Other general purpose machinery	279	...	...	...	8602	...	...	...	...	...	...	...
292	Special purpose machinery	285	...	...	...	2968	...	...	...p/	...	...	...	...p/
2921	Agricultural and forestry machinery	123	...	...	...	697	...	...	...	...	...	...	...
2922	Machine tools	51	...	...	...	480	...	...	...	...	...	...	...
2923	Machinery for metallurgy	-	...	...	...	-	...	...	...	...	...	...	...
2924	Machinery for mining & construction	13	...	...	...	297	...	...	...	...	...	...	...
2925	Food/beverage/tobacco processing machinery	39	...	...	...	116	...	...	...	...	...	...	...
2926	Machinery for textile, apparel and leather	21	...	...	...	166	...	...	...	...	...	...	...
2927	Weapons and ammunition	3	...	...	...	4	...	...	...	...	...	...	...
2929	Other special purpose machinery	35	...	...	...	1208	...	...	...	...	...	...	...

continued

Saudi Arabia

ISIC Revision 3		Number of establishments					Number of persons engaged					Wages and salaries paid to employees				
			(number)					(number)					(millions of Saudi Riyals)			
ISIC	Industry	Note	2003	2004	2005	2006	Note	2003	2004	2005	2006a/	Note	2003	2004	2005	2006
2930	Domestic appliances n.e.c.		126	...	...	...		3861	...	...	...p/		...	...	...	...p/
3000	Office, accounting and computing machinery		28	...	...	...		355	...	...	452		...	...	...	5.5
3110	Electric motors, generators and transformers		295	...	...	...		2928	...	...	13030q/		...	...	...	355.3q/
3120	Electricity distribution & control apparatus		91	...	...	...		2058	...	...	...q/		...	...	...	...q/
3130	Insulated wire and cable		58	...	...	...		5057	...	...	...q/		...	...	...	...q/
3140	Accumulators, primary cells and batteries		4	...	...	...		284	...	...	...q/		...	...	...	...q/
3150	Lighting equipment and electric lamps		33	...	...	...		1219	...	...	...q/		...	...	...	...q/
3190	Other electrical equipment n.e.c.		56	...	...	...		831	...	...	...q/		...	...	...	...q/
3210	Electronic valves, tubes, etc.		22	...	...	...		773	...	...	931r/		...	...	...	27.1r/
3220	TV/radio transmitters; line comm. apparatus		26	...	...	...		377	...	...	...r/		...	...	...	...r/
3230	TV and radio receivers and associated goods		62	...	...	...		343	...	...	...r/		...	...	...	...r/
331	Medical, measuring, testing appliances, etc.		101	...	...	...		2311	...	...	2086s/		...	...	...	40.9s/
3311	Medical, surgical and orthopaedic equipment		84	...	...	...		1856	...	...	...		...	...	...	...
3312	Measuring/testing/navigating appliances,etc.		17	...	...	...		455	...	...	...		...	...	...	...
3313	Industrial process control equipment		-	...	...	...		-	...	...	...		...	...	...	...
3320	Optical instruments & photographic equipment		31	...	...	...		325	...	...	...s/		...	...	...	...s/
3330	Watches and clocks		-	...	...	...		-	...	...	...s/		...	...	...	...s/
3410	Motor vehicles		29	...	...	...		1746	...	...	4586t/		...	...	...	89.0t/
3420	Automobile bodies, trailers & semi-trailers		71	...	...	...		1534	...	...	...t/		...	...	...	...t/
3430	Parts/accessories for automobiles		71	...	...	...		2226	...	...	...t/		...	...	...	...t/
351	Building and repairing of ships and boats		47	...	...	...		435	...	...	1045u/		...	...	...	26.3u/
3511	Building and repairing of ships		14	...	...	...		221	...	...	...		...	...	...	...
3512	Building/repairing of pleasure/sport. boats		33	...	...	...		214	...	...	...		...	...	...	...
3520	Railway/tramway locomotives & rolling stock		3	...	...	...		133	...	...	...u/		...	...	...	...u/
3530	Aircraft and spacecraft		21	...	...	...		919	...	...	...u/		...	...	...	...u/
359	Transport equipment n.e.c.		47	...	...	...		194	...	...	...u/		...	...	...	...u/
3591	Motorcycles		-	...	...	...		-	...	...	...		...	...	...	...
3592	Bicycles and invalid carriages		41	...	...	...		122	...	...	...		...	...	...	...
3599	Other transport equipment n.e.c.		6	...	...	...		72	...	...	...		...	...	...	...
3610	Furniture		8271	...	...	...		45762	...	...	52514v/		...	...	...	748.6v/
369	Manufacturing n.e.c.		337	...	...	...		4913	...	...	...v/		...	...	...	...v/
3691	Jewellery and related articles		187	...	...	...		3867	...	...	...		...	...	...	...
3692	Musical instruments		4	...	...	...		7	...	...	...		...	...	...	...
3693	Sports goods		26	...	...	...		211	...	...	...		...	...	...	...
3694	Games and toys		27	...	...	...		247	...	...	...		...	...	...	...
3699	Other manufacturing n.e.c.		93	...	...	...		581	...	...	...		...	...	...	...
3710	Recycling of metal waste and scrap		94	...	...	...		636	...	...	3084w/		...	...	...	49.6w/
3720	Recycling of non-metal waste and scrap		48	...	...	...		2452	...	...	...w/		...	...	...	...w/
D	Total manufacturing		88845	...	...	...		546114	...	...	608608		...	...	...	13719.4

a/ Number of employees.
b/ 151 includes 1520, 153, 154 and 155.
c/ 171 includes 172 and 1730.
d/ 1810 includes 1820.
e/ 191 includes 1920.
f/ 2010 includes 202.
g/ 221 includes 222 and 2230.
h/ 2310 includes 2320 and 2330.
i/ 241 includes 242 and 2430.
j/ 251 includes 2520.
k/ 2610 includes 269.
m/ 2710 includes 2720 and 273.
n/ 281 includes 289.
p/ 291 includes 292 and 2930.
q/ 3110 includes 3120, 3130, 3140, 3150 and 3190.
r/ 3210 includes 3220 and 3230.
s/ 331 includes 3320 and 3330.
t/ 3410 includes 3420 and 3430.
u/ 351 includes 3520, 3530 and 359.
v/ 3610 includes 369.
w/ 3710 includes 3720.

Saudi Arabia

ISIC Revision 3		Output (millions of Saudi Riyals)					Value added (millions of Saudi Riyals)					Gross fixed capital formation (millions of Saudi Riyals)	
ISIC	Industry	Note	2003	2004	2005	2006	Note	2003	2004	2005	2006	Note	2005	2006
15	Food and beverages		...	...	...	46043.8		...	...	...	16653.4		...	5379.5
16	Tobacco products		...	...	...	15.7		...	...	...	3.9		...	-
17	Textiles		...	...	...	2083.2		...	...	...	1258.1		...	88.1
18	Wearing apparel, fur		...	...	...	3674.2		...	...	...	2136.1		...	71.2
19	Leather, leather products and footwear		...	...	...	5661.0		...	...	...	630.0		...	0.6
20	Wood products (excl. furniture)		...	...	...	2074.7		...	...	...	881.3		...	46.6
21	Paper and paper products		...	...	...	7842.7		...	...	...	2996.7		...	586.0
22	Printing and publishing		...	...	...	6451.9		...	...	...	2652.7		...	128.2
23	Coke,refined petroleum products,nuclear fuel		...	...	...	32072.0		...	...	...	1451.3		...	778.0
24	Chemicals and chemical products		...	...	...	49487.0		...	...	...	23244.6		...	2105.3
25	Rubber and plastics products		...	...	...	10774.3		...	...	...	4307.0		...	508.3
26	Non-metallic mineral products		...	...	...	16463.6		...	...	...	7781.1		...	3584.4
27	Basic metals		...	...	...	13186.2		...	...	...	2273.4		...	2097.4
28	Fabricated metal products		...	...	...	12077.1		...	...	...	4860.8		...	812.7
29	Machinery and equipment n.e.c.		...	...	...	6630.3		...	...	...	3615.5		...	199.5
30	Office, accounting and computing machinery		...	...	...	60.0		...	...	...	23.1		...	0.8
31	Electrical machinery and apparatus		...	...	...	11377.9		...	...	...	6683.9		...	841.8
32	Radio,television and communication equipment		...	...	...	315.6		...	...	...	209.1		...	14.2
33	Medical, precision and optical instruments		...	...	...	797.4		...	...	...	587.1		...	15.5
34	Motor vehicles, trailers, semi-trailers		...	...	...	2187.2		...	...	...	779.4		...	62.4
35	Other transport equipment		...	...	...	500.2		...	...	...	98.3		...	3.9
36	Furniture; manufacturing n.e.c.		...	...	...	4882.2		...	...	...	2093.4		...	180.1
37	Recycling		...	...	...	356.6		...	...	...	248.6		...	2.8
D	Total manufacturing		...	...	...	235014.8		...	...	...	85468.6		...	17507.3

Saudi Arabia

ISIC Revision 3			Index numbers of industrial production (2000=100)											
ISIC	Industry	Note	1995	1996	1997	1998	1999	2000	2001	2002	2003	2004	2005	2006
15	Food and beverages		...	...	...	...	...	...	...	...	...	...	...	...
16	Tobacco products		...	...	...	...	...	...	...	...	...	...	...	...
17	Textiles		...	...	...	...	...	...	...	...	...	...	...	...
18	Wearing apparel, fur		...	...	...	...	...	...	...	...	...	...	...	...
19	Leather, leather products and footwear		...	...	...	...	...	...	...	...	...	...	...	...
20	Wood products (excl. furniture)		...	...	...	...	...	...	...	...	...	...	...	...
21	Paper and paper products		...	...	...	...	...	...	...	...	...	...	...	...
22	Printing and publishing		...	...	...	...	...	...	...	...	...	...	...	...
23	Coke,refined petroleum products,nuclear fuel		...	...	...	...	...	...	...	...	...	...	...	...
24	Chemicals and chemical products		...	...	...	...	...	...	...	...	...	...	...	...
25	Rubber and plastics products		...	...	...	...	...	...	...	...	...	...	...	...
26	Non-metallic mineral products		...	...	...	...	...	...	...	...	...	...	...	...
27	Basic metals		...	...	...	...	...	...	...	...	...	...	...	...
28	Fabricated metal products		...	...	...	...	...	...	...	...	...	...	...	...
29	Machinery and equipment n.e.c.		...	...	...	...	...	...	...	...	...	...	...	...
30	Office, accounting and computing machinery		...	...	...	...	...	...	...	...	...	...	...	...
31	Electrical machinery and apparatus		...	...	...	...	...	...	...	...	...	...	...	...
32	Radio,television and communication equipment		...	...	...	...	...	...	...	...	...	...	...	...
33	Medical, precision and optical instruments		...	...	...	...	...	...	...	...	...	...	...	...
34	Motor vehicles, trailers, semi-trailers		...	...	...	...	...	...	...	...	...	...	...	...
35	Other transport equipment		...	...	...	...	...	...	...	...	...	...	...	...
36	Furniture; manufacturing n.e.c.		...	...	...	...	...	...	...	...	...	...	...	...
37	Recycling		...	...	...	...	...	...	...	...	...	...	...	...
D	Total manufacturing		75	86	89	91	95	100	104	108	116	124	132	...

Serbia

Supplier of information:
Republic Statistical Office of Serbia.

Basic source of data:
Annual Survey.

Major deviations from ISIC (Revision 3):
Data presented in ISIC (Revision 3) were originally classified according to the NACE (Revision 1).

Reference period:
Calendar year.

Scope:
All establishments (excluding data for Kosovo and Metohia).

Method of data collection:
Inquiry is carried out through questionnaires.

Type of enumeration:
Sample survey.

Adjusted for non-response:
Yes.

Concepts and definitions of variables:
Output is valued at basic prices.
Value added is valued at basic prices.

Related national publications:
System of National Accounts of the Republic of Serbia, 1997-2004, published by the Republic Statistical Office of Serbia.

Serbia

ISIC Revision 3	Number of establishments					Number of employees					Wages and salaries paid to employees				
		(number)					(number)					(millions of Serbian Dinars)			
ISIC Industry	Note	2003	2004	2005	2006	Note	2003	2004	2005	2006	Note	2003	2004	2005	2006
D Total manufacturing		...	...	...	...		...	...	...	...		...	...	...	...

ISIC Revision 3	Output					Value added					Gross fixed capital formation		
		(millions of Serbian Dinars)					(millions of Serbian Dinars)					(millions of Serbian Dinars)	
ISIC Industry	Note	2003	2004	2005	2006	Note	2003	2004	2005	2006	Note	2005	2006
D Total manufacturing		554571	730161	882162	1153977		163901	208430	252242	310680		67805	...

ISIC Revision 3	Index numbers of industrial production												
		(2000 = 100)											
ISIC Industry	Note	1995	1996	1997	1998	1999	2000	2001	2002	2003	2004	2005	2006
D Total manufacturing		...	...	...	...	...	...	...	...	...	...	...	...

Singapore

Supplier of information:
Research and Statistics Unit, Economic Development Board, Singapore.

Basic source of data:
Annual census of manufacturing activities.

Major deviations from ISIC (Revision 3):
The data presented in ISIC (Revision 3) were originally classified according to ISIC (Revision 4).

Reference period:
Financial year.

Scope:
All establishments.

Method of data collection:
The census was based on information obtained through mail questionnaires and online surveys.

Type of enumeration:
Complete enumeration.

Adjusted for non-response:
Yes.

Concepts and definitions of variables:
Number of persons engaged is as 30 June of the reference year.
Wages and salaries is compensation of employees.
Output refers to total output.

Related national publications:
Report on the Census of Industrial Production, published by the Economic Development Board, Singapore.

Singapore

ISIC	Industry	Note	Number of establishments (number) 2003	2004	2005	2006	Note	Number of employees (number) 2003	2004	2005	2006	Note	Wages and salaries paid to employees (millions of Singapore Dollars) 2003	2004	2005	2006
151	Processed meat,fish,fruit,vegetables,fats		132	135	125	117		4233	4250	4169	4189		107.3	108.7	110.5	112.0
1511	Processing/preserving of meat		55	58	58	56		1800	1862	1798	1901		43.7	40.5	42.7	43.6
1512	Processing/preserving of fish		44	46	41	36		1405	1418	1421	1293		28.8	32.8	31.6	30.9
1513	Processing/preserving of fruit & vegetables		16	16	11	10		249	224	201	220		6.6	6.4	5.7	6.1
1514	Vegetable and animal oils and fats		17	15	15	15		779	746	749	775		28.2	29.0	30.5	31.3
1520	Dairy products		...	...	...	...		...	...	...	...		...	...	...	...
153	Grain mill products; starches; animal feeds		8	8	8	9		374	373	457	539		16.6	16.5	20.3	23.9
1531	Grain mill products		...	...	...	...		...	...	...	...		...	...	...	...
1532	Starches and starch products		...	...	...	...		...	...	...	...		...	...	...	...
1533	Prepared animal feeds		...	...	...	...		...	...	...	...		...	...	...	...
154	Other food products		523a/	556b/	544b/	572b/		12715a/	14394b/	14490b/	15523b/		346.4a/	447.4b/	423.4b/	448.5b/
1541	Bakery products		227	241	229	236		4573	4537	4561	5289		101.4	100.9	98.2	106.1
1542	Sugar		...	...	...	...		...	...	...	...		...	...	...	...
1543	Cocoa, chocolate and sugar confectionery		5	5	7	12		309	325	410	444		15.1	15.8	18.0	20.4
1544	Macaroni, noodles & similar products		64	52	48	49		1109	940	981	955		23.2	20.4	20.0	23.0
1549	Other food products n.e.c.		227	...	...	...		6724	...	...	...		206.7	...	...	...
155	Beverages		18	...b/	...b/	...b/		1833	...b/	...b/	...b/		85.9	...b/	...b/	...b/
1551	Distilling, rectifying & blending of spirits		...	...	...	...		...	...	...	...		...	...	...	...
1552	Wines		...	...	...	...		...	...	...	...		...	...	...	...
1553	Malt liquors and malt		...	...	...	...		...	...	...	...		...	...	...	...
1554	Soft drinks; mineral waters		...	...	...	...		...	...	...	...		...	...	...	...
1600	Tobacco products		...a/	...b/	...b/	...b/		...a/	...b/	...b/	...b/		...a/	...b/	...b/	...b/
171	Spinning, weaving and finishing of textiles		9	10	8	5		493	606	414	262		15.2	16.2	12.1	8.4
1711	Textile fibre preparation; textile weaving		...	...	...	...		...	...	...	...		...	...	...	...
1712	Finishing of textiles		...	...	...	...		...	...	...	...		...	...	...	...
172	Other textiles		105	114	93	86		783	642	709	697		18.4	14.0	18.1	21.9
1721	Made-up textile articles, except apparel		...	...	...	...		...	...	...	...		...	...	...	...
1722	Carpets and rugs		...	...	...	...		...	...	...	...		...	...	...	...
1723	Cordage, rope, twine and netting		...	...	...	...		...	...	...	...		...	...	...	...
1729	Other textiles n.e.c.		...	...	...	...		...	...	...	...		...	...	...	...
1730	Knitted and crocheted fabrics and articles		14	14	12	9		479	594	381	359		10.3	12.3	8.0	7.6
1810	Wearing apparel, except fur apparel		582	587	502	462		8746	8503	7227	6684		159.0	154.8	143.2	130.7
1820	Dressing & dyeing of fur; processing of fur		...	...	...	...		...	...	...	...		...	...	...	...
191	Tanning, dressing and processing of leather		28	29	24	23		912	886	877	1038		28.2	28.7	28.8	31.5
1911	Tanning and dressing of leather		...	...	...	...		...	...	...	...		...	...	...	...
1912	Luggage, handbags, etc.; saddlery & harness		...	...	...	...		...	...	...	...		...	...	...	...
1920	Footwear		32	31	24	22		133	164	96	87		2.6	3.0	1.2	1.5
2010	Sawmilling and planing of wood		7	7	...	...		97	90	...	...		2.8	2.6	...	...
202	Products of wood, cork, straw, etc.		105	107	104	99		1662	1533	1760	1606		39.3	36.7	43.2	41.1
2021	Veneer sheets, plywood, particle board, etc.		...	...	...	...		...	...	...	...		...	...	...	...
2022	Builders' carpentry and joinery		29	31	29	30		771	724	709	697		19.7	19.4	18.8	18.0
2023	Wooden containers		38	36	35	35		684	588	703	671		14.5	12.2	15.7	17.4
2029	Other wood products; articles of cork/straw		38	40	40	34		207	221	348	238		5.1	5.0	8.8	5.7
210	Paper and paper products		128	129	124	121		4302	4342	4495	4423		143.3	149.6	159.3	151.7
2101	Pulp, paper and paperboard		...	...	...	...		...	...	...	...		...	...	...	...
2102	Corrugated paper and paperboard		95	99	95	91		3584	3567	3662	3609		116.0	116.4	126.5	122.0
2109	Other articles of paper and paperboard		33	30	29	30		718	775	833	814		27.3	33.2	32.9	29.7
221	Publishing		...	...	...	...		...	...	...	...		...	...	...	...
2211	Publishing of books and other publications		...	...	...	...		...	...	...	...		...	...	...	...
2212	Publishing of newspapers, journals, etc.		...	...	...	...		...	...	...	...		...	...	...	...
2213	Publishing of recorded media		...	...	...	...		...	...	...	...		...	...	...	...
2219	Other publishing		...	...	...	...		...	...	...	...		...	...	...	...

222	Printing and related service activities		910	916	835	815		17051	15633	16025	16097		650.3	587.0	638.8	660.1
2221	Printing		791	790	718	702		15109	13753	14009	14504		586.5	529.5	577.1	611.7
2222	Service activities related to printing		119	126	117	113		1942	1880	2016	1593		63.8	57.5	61.6	48.4
2230	Reproduction of recorded media		10	11	10	12		1291	1463	1513	1554		45.7	48.6	51.6	57.3
2310	Coke oven products		...	...	...	...		...	...	...	...		...	...	...	...
2320	Refined petroleum products		17	17	17	18		3122	3045	3200	3166		373.5	343.4	363.6	378.7
2330	Processing of nuclear fuel		...	...	...	...		...	...	...	...		...	...	...	...
241	Basic chemicals		63	307c/	307c/	304c/		4101	19485c/	19447c/	19702c/		270.5	1339.8c/	1304.8c/	1378.9c/
2411	Basic chemicals, except fertilizers		30	...	...	...		1814	...	...	...		101.9	...	...	...
2412	Fertilizers and nitrogen compounds		...	...	...	...		...	...	...	...		...	...	...	...
2413	Plastics in primary forms; synthetic rubber		33	...	...	...		2287	...	...	...		168.6	...	...	...
242	Other chemicals		241	...c/	...c/	...c/		15466	...c/	...c/	...c/		1000.5	...c/	...c/	...c/
2421	Pesticides and other agro-chemical products		...	...	...	...		...	...	...	...		...	...	...	...
2422	Paints, varnishes, printing ink and mastics		38	...	39	38		2030	...	2103	2141		112.5	...	109.0	112.8
2423	Pharmaceuticals, medicinal chemicals, etc.		40	...	...	...		3584	...	...	...		227.8	...	...	...
2424	Soap, cleaning & cosmetic preparations		48	...	48	51		1533	...	1349	1403		85.4	...	85.2	95.4
2429	Other chemical products n.e.c.		115	...	...	...		8319	...	...	...		574.8	...	...	...
2430	Man-made fibres		...	...c/	...c/	...c/		...	...c/	...c/	...c/		...	...c/	...c/	...c/
251	Rubber products		57	55	51	49		2513	2575	2566	2748		96.1	100.1	102.6	109.6
2511	Rubber tyres and tubes		...	...	...	...		...	...	...	...		...	...	...	...
2519	Other rubber products		...	...	...	...		...	...	...	...		...	...	...	...
2520	Plastic products		365	339	302	278		17309	17123	15655	14400		472.4	475.1	447.5	445.3
2610	Glass and glass products		37	40	41	45		1682	1573	1618	1609		55.3	57.7	54.9	50.6
269	Non-metallic mineral products n.e.c.		109	106	95	92		3482	3511	3540	3567		114.4	116.0	112.4	117.1
2691	Pottery, china and earthenware		...	...	...	...		...	...	...	...		...	...	...	...
2692	Refractory ceramic products		...	...	...	...		...	...	...	...		...	...	...	...
2693	Struct.non-refractory clay; ceramic products		7	...	...	...		112	...	...	...		4.9	...	...	...
2694	Cement, lime and plaster		...	...	...	...		...	...	...	...		...	...	...	...
2695	Articles of concrete, cement and plaster		19	...	17	15		1203	...	1301	1294		43.6	...	40.9	44.7
2696	Cutting, shaping & finishing of stone		...	...	26	22		...	...	350	274		...	...	8.6	3.7
2699	Other non-metallic mineral products n.e.c.		83	...	...	...		2167	...	...	...		66.0	...	...	...
2710	Basic iron and steel	d/	25	26	21	20	d/	1407	1385	1853	2040	d/	67.9	65.7	82.7	95.5
2720	Basic precious and non-ferrous metals	d/	...	...	...	...	d/	...	...	...	...	d/	...	...	...	...
273	Casting of metals	d/	...	...	...	...	d/	...	...	...	...	d/	...	...	...	...
2731	Casting of iron and steel		...	...	...	...		...	...	...	...		...	...	...	...
2732	Casting of non-ferrous metals		...	...	...	...		...	...	...	...		...	...	...	...
281	Struct.metal products;tanks;steam generators		485	486	443	416		10830	10425	10292	10871		257.8	252.0	247.4	272.6
2811	Structural metal products		458	460	420	395		10274	9901	9754	10187		235.5	230.5	225.4	246.6
2812	Tanks, reservoirs and containers of metal		17	15	13	10		356	317	385	511		13.1	11.5	14.5	17.0
2813	Steam generators		10	11	10	11		200	207	153	173		9.2	10.0	7.5	9.0
289	Other metal products; metal working services		737	759	730	749		27299	27139	27958	28393		872.2	870.4	914.0	969.3
2891	Metal forging/pressing/stamping/roll-forming		78	73	68	67		7411	7108	7636	7122		234.7	214.0	221.1	251.9
2892	Treatment & coating of metals		149	159	147	138		4584	4408	4734	4362		123.8	119.0	131.3	118.7
2893	Cutlery, hand tools and general hardware		25	24	23	20		574	619	641	578		19.4	19.0	20.5	19.1
2899	Other fabricated metal products n.e.c.		485	503	492	524		14730	15004	14947	16331		494.2	518.3	541.2	579.6
291	General purpose machinery		360	380	357	351		13342	13102	12865	13080		507.2	509.9	514.4	544.4
2911	Engines & turbines (not for transport equipment)		...	...	...	...		...	...	...	...		...	...	...	...
2912	Pumps, compressors, taps and valves		28	36	34	37		689	811	586	678		32.3	39.9	34.1	36.1
2913	Bearings, gears, gearing & driving elements		20	19	16	16		2546	1793	1783	1639		82.2	65.6	62.9	58.1
2914	Ovens, furnaces and furnace burners		...	...	...	...		...	...	...	...		...	...	...	...
2915	Lifting and handling equipment		115	121	112	113		4476	4263	4284	4942		182.3	188.0	196.2	232.5
2919	Other general purpose machinery		197	204	195	185		5631	6235	6212	5821		210.4	216.4	221.2	217.7
292	Special purpose machinery		1192	1230	1145	1189		27372	29063	32645	37648		1012.4	1102.2	1306.8	1520.8
2921	Agricultural and forestry machinery		...	...	...	...		...	...	...	...		...	...	...	...
2922	Machine tools		545	598	581	601		10023	10116	11314	11604		335.6	345.7	395.4	386.5
2923	Machinery for metallurgy		...	...	...	...		...	...	...	...		...	...	...	...
2924	Machinery for mining & construction		109	117	110	115		7049	7866	9039	11543		317.3	347.3	427.0	542.7
2925	Food/beverage/tobacco processing machinery		26	24	15	14		153	146	150	178		5.0	5.4	4.9	5.7
2926	Machinery for textile, apparel and leather		...	...	...	...		...	...	...	...		...	...	...	...
2927	Weapons and ammunition		...	...	...	...		...	...	...	...		...	...	...	...
2929	Other special purpose machinery		451	435	381	391		5922	6201	7581	9074		184.2	193.6	267.5	326.0

continued

Singapore

ISIC	Industry	Note	Establishments 2003	Establishments 2004	Establishments 2005	Establishments 2006	Note	Employees 2003	Employees 2004	Employees 2005	Employees 2006	Note	Wages 2003	Wages 2004	Wages 2005	Wages 2006
ISIC Revision 3			Number of establishments				Number of employees					Wages and salaries paid to employees				
			(number)					(number)					(millions of Singapore Dollars)			
2930	Domestic appliances n.e.c.		11	9	9	7		1456	1348	1366	1551		42.4	39.3	37.2	41.2
3000	Office, accounting and computing machinery		36	30	25	22		30916	28662	30588	26241		1029.2	911.8	1005.9	1028.4
3110	Electric motors, generators and transformers		68	148e/	52	50		1898	3823e/	2123	1912		65.8	131.3e/	71.4	68.8
3120	Electricity distribution & control apparatus		61	...e/	89	91		1511	...e/	2001	2018		51.6	...e/	68.8	71.4
3130	Insulated wire and cable		51	51	48	52		3876	3820	3860	4226		143.0	141.1	142.7	162.8
3140	Accumulators, primary cells and batteries		7	8	6	7		862	890	795	736		41.1	41.3	35.3	36.2
3150	Lighting equipment and electric lamps		9	9	9	9		199	213	206	205		7.7	7.7	7.7	7.7
3190	Other electrical equipment n.e.c.		15	15	16	15		521	470	499	646		20.0	19.7	23.4	26.2
3210	Electronic valves, tubes, etc.		162	154	124	127		49623	56690	55688	58021		2110.7	2418.7	2471.1	2622.4
3220	TV/radio transmitters; line comm. apparatus		14	16	14	11		4007	4229	4680	5381		183.0	261.2	331.2	237.7
3230	TV and radio receivers and associated goods		8	9	10	11		2962	2865	2737	2199		127.8	108.1	101.0	98.1
331	Medical, measuring, testing appliances, etc.		94	106	110	120		7111	8183	9035	10213		274.1	311.0	368.7	445.7
3311	Medical, surgical and orthopaedic equipment		48	58	62	70		4333	5536	6268	6625		138.3	174.6	212.5	244.3
3312	Measuring/testing/navigating appliances,etc.		31	32	30	30		801	688	730	1303		28.9	25.9	28.9	63.8
3313	Industrial process control equipment		15	16	18	20		1977	1959	2037	2285		106.8	110.5	127.3	137.7
3320	Optical instruments & photographic equipment		20	17f/	17	17f/		2383	2309f/	2398	2495f/		87.5	90.8f/	96.9f/	103.8f/
3330	Watches and clocks		5	...f/	...	...f/		912	...f/	...	...f/		25.0	...f/	...f/	...f/
3410	Motor vehicles	g/	66	66	59	56	g/	4325	4116	4444	4680	g/	176.0	175.7	189.6	204.0
3420	Automobile bodies, trailers & semi-trailers	g/	...	...	...	...	g/	...	...	...	...	g/	...	...	...	...
3430	Parts/accessories for automobiles	g/	...	...	...	...	g/	...	...	...	...	g/	...	...	...	...
351	Building and repairing of ships and boats		484	513	489	468		30816	33290	36688	41965		734.8	796.0	888.2	1040.2
3511	Building and repairing of ships		264	...	...	...		22798	...	...	...		524.6	...	...	...
3512	Building/repairing of pleasure/sport. boats		220	...	...	...		8018	...	...	...		210.2	...	...	...
3520	Railway/tramway locomotives & rolling stock		...	...	...	...		...	...	...	...		...	...	...	...
3530	Aircraft and spacecraft		54	68	63	68		12931	14584	16493	18169		753.2	910.7	1005.1	1136.1
359	Transport equipment n.e.c.		...	...	...	...		...	...	...	...		...	...	...	...
3591	Motorcycles		...	...	...	...		...	...	...	...		...	...	...	...
3592	Bicycles and invalid carriages		...	...	...	...		...	...	...	...		...	...	...	...
3599	Other transport equipment n.e.c.		...	...	...	...		...	...	...	...		...	...	...	...
3610	Furniture		682	687	589	536		6480	6745	6153	5641		153.1	152.7	138.0	126.2
369	Manufacturing n.e.c.		424	420	368	347		4564	3700	3607	3319		136.4	100.5	108.8	96.9
3691	Jewellery and related articles		135	...	115	102		977	...	848	836		22.1	...	19.8	23.7
3692	Musical instruments		...	...	...	...		...	...	...	...		...	...	...	...
3693	Sports goods		...	...	...	...		...	...	...	...		...	...	...	...
3694	Games and toys		7	...	...	...		71	...	...	...		1.5	...	...	...
3699	Other manufacturing n.e.c.		282	...	253	245		3516	...	2759	2483		112.8	...	89.0	73.2
3710	Recycling of metal waste and scrap		27	...	...	...		727	...	...	...		27.5	...	...	...
3720	Recycling of non-metal waste and scrap		...	...	...	...		...	...	...	...		...	...	...	...
D	Total manufacturing		8597	8725	8037	7892		351109	357836	369610	381909		12961.3	13476.0	14300.9	15254.9

a/ 154 includes 1600.
b/ 154 includes 155 and 1600.
c/ 241 includes 242 and 2430.
d/ 2710 includes 2720 and 273.
e/ 3110 includes 3120.
f/ 3320 includes 3330.
g/ 3410 includes 3420 and 3430.

Singapore

ISIC Revision 3		Output					Value added					Gross fixed capital formation		
			(millions of Singapore Dollars)					(millions of Singapore Dollars)					(millions of Singapore Dollars)	
ISIC	Industry	Note	2003	2004	2005	2006	Note	2003	2004	2005	2006	Note	2005	2006
151	Processed meat,fish,fruit,vegetables,fats		934.8	1001.9	1088.1	1168.9		178.6	182.9	197.3	233.4		24.9	22.5
1511	Processing/preserving of meat		250.9	253.7	277.2	314.0		71.4	68.0	68.7	77.2		6.0	8.5
1512	Processing/preserving of fish		168.2	202.0	246.8	249.1		45.7	55.1	49.0	47.7		10.1	5.2
1513	Processing/preserving of fruit & vegetables		25.7	26.7	26.5	30.3		9.1	8.9	8.7	10.2		0.5	0.9
1514	Vegetable and animal oils and fats		490.1	519.5	537.6	575.5		52.3	50.9	70.9	98.4		8.2	7.9
1520	Dairy products		...	...	...	...		...	...	...	...		...	...
153	Grain mill products; starches; animal feeds		117.8	132.9	159.0	184.7		19.0	19.4	26.7	29.3		7.5	2.5
1531	Grain mill products		...	...	...	...		...	...	...	...		...	...
1532	Starches and starch products		...	...	...	...		...	...	...	...		...	...
1533	Prepared animal feeds		...	...	...	...		...	...	...	...		...	...
154	Other food products		2340.2a/	3605.3b/	3715.3b/	3807.2b/		625.7a/	968.0b/	901.9b/	972.9b/		170.3b/	137.1b/
1541	Bakery products		407.2	438.6	497.7	507.2		151.8	157.6	164.2	172.5		20.7	25.8
1542	Sugar		...	...	...	...		...	...	...	...		...	...
1543	Cocoa, chocolate and sugar confectionery		304.8	313.2	315.3	359.4		43.5	48.4	48.9	52.8		23.1	17.2
1544	Macaroni, noodles & similar products		102.3	95.1	96.7	105.0		37.4	30.4	28.7	31.0		2.4	2.4
1549	Other food products n.e.c.		1525.8	...	...	...		393.1	...	...	...		...	...
155	Beverages		601.2	...b/	...b/	...b/		178.9	...b/	...b/	...b/		...b/	...b/
1551	Distilling, rectifying & blending of spirits		...	...	...	...		...	...	...	...		...	...
1552	Wines		...	...	...	...		...	...	...	...		...	...
1553	Malt liquors and malt		...	...	...	...		...	...	...	...		...	...
1554	Soft drinks; mineral waters		...	...	...	...		...	...	...	...		...	...
1600	Tobacco products		...a/	...b/	...b/	...b/		...a/	...b/	...b/	...b/		...b/	...b/
171	Spinning, weaving and finishing of textiles		139.4	126.4	106.5	75.7		24.7	23.3	16.8	13.7		2.0	0.9
1711	Textile fibre preparation; textile weaving		...	...	...	...		...	...	...	...		...	...
1712	Finishing of textiles		...	...	...	...		...	...	...	...		...	...
172	Other textiles		73.5	58.9	68.7	63.6		23.4	17.7	21.0	19.7		4.8	1.1
1721	Made-up textile articles, except apparel		...	...	...	...		...	...	...	...		...	...
1722	Carpets and rugs		...	...	...	...		...	...	...	...		...	...
1723	Cordage, rope, twine and netting		...	...	...	...		...	...	...	...		...	...
1729	Other textiles n.e.c.		...	...	...	...		...	...	...	...		...	...
1730	Knitted and crocheted fabrics and articles		87.4	91.5	58.6	53.1		17.5	19.2	9.6	9.9		-	-
1810	Wearing apparel, except fur apparel		791.5	816.0	650.3	554.5		194.6	212.8	202.6	182.1		8.6	11.4
1820	Dressing & dyeing of fur; processing of fur		...	...	...	...		...	...	...	...		...	...
191	Tanning, dressing and processing of leather		195.6	195.3	209.6	225.8		46.9	47.6	52.6	52.3		3.4	4.2
1911	Tanning and dressing of leather		...	...	...	...		...	...	...	...		...	...
1912	Luggage, handbags, etc.; saddlery & harness		...	...	...	...		...	...	...	...		...	...
1920	Footwear		11.9	17.3	5.9	13.1		2.9	5.1	1.3	2.2		0.6	0.1
2010	Sawmilling and planing of wood		9.9	10.7	...	...		4.8	4.1	...	...		...	...
202	Products of wood, cork, straw, etc.		246.2	266.8	264.1	273.7		54.2	55.4	59.5	56.4		3.5	12.4
2021	Veneer sheets, plywood, particle board, etc.		...	...	...	...		...	...	...	...		...	...
2022	Builders' carpentry and joinery		133.2	139.4	126.4	134.9		30.4	31.0	24.4	27.3		0.9	1.4
2023	Wooden containers		55.9	61.7	76.8	83.8		16.9	15.8	21.8	19.7		1.4	10.0
2029	Other wood products; articles of cork/straw		57.0	65.7	61.0	55.0		6.8	8.6	13.3	9.4		1.2	1.0
210	Paper and paper products		874.7	912.7	997.4	986.4		201.2	214.0	257.1	254.2		31.6	18.6
2101	Pulp, paper and paperboard		...	...	...	...		...	...	...	...		...	...
2102	Corrugated paper and paperboard		743.5	735.2	791.0	780.7		167.8	184.3	206.9	208.1		19.0	16.2
2109	Other articles of paper and paperboard		131.1	177.5	206.4	205.7		33.4	29.7	50.2	46.1		12.6	2.4
221	Publishing		...	...	...	...		...	...	...	...		...	...
2211	Publishing of books and other publications		...	...	...	...		...	...	...	...		...	...
2212	Publishing of newspapers, journals, etc.		...	...	...	...		...	...	...	...		...	...
2213	Publishing of recorded media		...	...	...	...		...	...	...	...		...	...
2219	Other publishing		...	...	...	...		...	...	...	...		...	...

continued

Singapore

ISIC Revision 3		Output					Value added					Gross fixed capital formation		
			(millions of Singapore Dollars)					(millions of Singapore Dollars)					(millions of Singapore Dollars)	
ISIC	Industry	Note	2003	2004	2005	2006	Note	2003	2004	2005	2006	Note	2005	2006
222	Printing and related service activities		2511.3	2496.7	2576.9	2690.8		1174.8	1212.0	1226.7	1235.7		130.2	123.0
2221	Printing		2365.8	2356.1	2437.1	2578.4		1091.2	1132.0	1147.6	1172.9		117.2	116.0
2222	Service activities related to printing		145.4	140.7	139.8	112.4		83.7	80.0	79.2	62.8		12.9	7.1
2230	Reproduction of recorded media		182.8	213.7	225.4	248.0		82.2	89.8	76.8	88.5		14.3	12.2
2310	Coke oven products		...	...	...	...		...	...	...	...		...	...
2320	Refined petroleum products		21969.6	28270.1	40302.6	46112.1		1522.0	2550.3	2662.9	2623.8		290.1	542.9
2330	Processing of nuclear fuel		...	...	...	...		...	...	...	...		...	...
241	Basic chemicals		4580.0	39721.6c/	43076.1c/	53744.0c/		923.4	13384.3c/	12415.2c/	15480.4c/		958.4c/	2591.8c/
2411	Basic chemicals, except fertilizers		849.9	...	...	...		332.6	...	...	...		...	...
2412	Fertilizers and nitrogen compounds		...	...	...	...		...	...	...	...		...	...
2413	Plastics in primary forms; synthetic rubber		3730.0	...	...	...		590.8	...	...	...		...	...
242	Other chemicals		23873.8	...c/	...c/	...c/		8125.0	...c/	...c/	...c/		...c/	...c/
2421	Pesticides and other agro-chemical products		...	...	...	...		...	...	...	...		...	...
2422	Paints, varnishes, printing ink and mastics		839.0	...	937.2	947.9		242.1	...	225.2	211.0		14.5	25.2
2423	Pharmaceuticals, medicinal chemicals, etc.		10216.9	...	...	...		5746.1	...	...	...		...	...
2424	Soap, cleaning & cosmetic preparations		504.6	...	572.7	598.6		149.1	...	171.8	174.3		7.2	5.5
2429	Other chemical products n.e.c.		12313.2	...	...	...		1987.6	...	...	...		...	...
2430	Man-made fibres		...	...c/	...c/	...c/		...	...c/	...c/	...c/		...c/	...c/
251	Rubber products		448.1	483.5	509.2	575.9		175.1	200.6	208.6	230.7		15.4	25.9
2511	Rubber tyres and tubes		...	...	...	...		...	...	...	...		...	...
2519	Other rubber products		...	...	...	...		...	...	...	...		...	...
2520	Plastic products		2397.0	2349.7	2324.6	2359.7		832.9	809.5	749.5	723.9		121.5	114.0
2610	Glass and glass products		442.4	473.9	410.3	364.2		196.3	223.5	175.8	148.9		157.5	46.4
269	Non-metallic mineral products n.e.c.		935.2	966.9	919.5	1093.3		202.0	174.9	179.3	220.0		14.2	102.2
2691	Pottery, china and earthenware		...	...	...	...		...	...	...	...		...	...
2692	Refractory ceramic products		...	...	...	...		...	...	...	...		...	...
2693	Struct.non-refractory clay; ceramic products		16.8	...	...	...		8.8	...	...	...		...	...
2694	Cement, lime and plaster		...	...	...	...		...	...	...	...		...	...
2695	Articles of concrete, cement and plaster		496.9	...	499.8	558.5		53.9	...	40.5	74.1		4.2	13.2
2696	Cutting, shaping & finishing of stone		...	...	27.5	13.0		...	...	8.9	3.6		0.1	0.8
2699	Other non-metallic mineral products n.e.c.		421.5	...	...	...		139.3	...	...	...		...	...
2710	Basic iron and steel	d/	508.7	762.2	1003.2	1209.6	d/	91.4	105.8	330.1	342.0	d/	19.7	118.0
2720	Basic precious and non-ferrous metals	d/	...	...	...	...	d/	...	...	...	...	d/	...	...
273	Casting of metals	d/	...	...	...	...	d/	...	...	...	...	d/	...	...
2731	Casting of iron and steel		...	...	...	...		...	...	...	...		...	...
2732	Casting of non-ferrous metals		...	...	...	...		...	...	...	...		...	...
281	Struct.metal products;tanks;steam generators		1212.2	1275.7	1152.4	1314.3		359.0	354.3	366.4	399.5		46.6	48.7
2811	Structural metal products		1116.1	1183.3	1039.1	1156.9		324.5	325.7	329.8	350.2		43.9	44.2
2812	Tanks, reservoirs and containers of metal		53.6	43.0	70.9	105.3		19.2	8.8	20.8	29.5		1.2	4.0
2813	Steam generators		42.6	49.4	42.4	52.1		15.3	19.8	15.7	19.8		1.5	0.5
289	Other metal products; metal working services		5383.9	6096.4	6348.2	7163.4		1527.9	1608.2	1702.6	1786.8		326.0	322.3
2891	Metal forging/pressing/stamping/roll-forming		1458.0	1543.0	1355.5	1551.4		409.5	372.9	374.8	421.8		104.3	61.9
2892	Treatment & coating of metals		471.6	482.8	479.3	492.6		193.6	210.7	219.4	208.2		27.1	38.6
2893	Cutlery, hand tools and general hardware		105.6	117.2	131.0	146.5		50.4	56.5	70.2	73.3		8.1	6.0
2899	Other fabricated metal products n.e.c.		3348.7	3953.4	4382.3	4972.9		874.3	968.0	1038.1	1083.5		186.6	215.8
291	General purpose machinery		2713.7	2986.2	3394.9	3593.7		1021.7	1126.3	1213.8	1196.0		107.4	91.5
2911	Engines & turbines (not for transport equipment)		...	...	...	...		...	...	...	...		...	...
2912	Pumps, compressors, taps and valves		163.7	228.5	250.7	263.6		41.5	61.2	56.3	53.1		6.8	10.8
2913	Bearings, gears, gearing & driving elements		521.6	298.0	292.9	277.5		211.0	139.9	141.2	121.2		36.6	14.7
2914	Ovens, furnaces and furnace burners		...	...	...	...		...	...	...	...		...	...
2915	Lifting and handling equipment		718.7	740.4	948.6	1138.3		237.0	266.1	331.8	353.0		12.0	11.4
2919	Other general purpose machinery		1309.8	1719.3	1902.6	1914.2		532.1	659.2	684.5	668.6		52.0	54.6

292	Special purpose machinery		5346.0	6713.4	8374.0	10732.7		1714.7	2125.9	2472.8	2866.9		305.7	405.9
2921	Agricultural and forestry machinery		...	...	...	...		...	...	...	...		...	...
2922	Machine tools		1272.8	1447.2	1703.4	1651.5		523.1	548.2	652.2	617.3		113.2	97.4
2923	Machinery for metallurgy		...	...	...	...		...	...	...	...		...	...
2924	Machinery for mining & construction		1921.4	2428.7	3773.9	5471.0		599.8	823.9	986.5	1104.0		99.1	213.9
2925	Food/beverage/tobacco processing machinery		19.6	29.2	27.6	32.6		6.3	9.4	6.4	6.1		0.5	0.5
2926	Machinery for textile, apparel and leather		...	...	...	...		...	...	...	...		...	...
2927	Weapons and ammunition		...	...	...	...		...	...	...	...		...	...
2929	Other special purpose machinery		916.0	1163.2	1413.0	1679.5		292.3	307.1	446.0	495.1		56.0	52.6
2930	Domestic appliances n.e.c.		229.4	250.2	269.2	298.0		92.2	106.4	109.3	117.1		17.3	17.2
3000	Office, accounting and computing machinery		30182.0	28496.5	30400.7	25300.3		4229.2	4488.8	5299.2	4246.3		1324.0	1090.0
3110	Electric motors, generators and transformers		711.6	1339.0e/	886.4	874.8		151.1	238.4e/	127.8	148.8		13.9	12.7
3120	Electricity distribution & control apparatus		254.6	...e/	529.2	656.3		78.5	...e/	114.7	126.1		9.5	22.1
3130	Insulated wire and cable		897.1	960.9	1069.0	1546.8		330.1	322.4	334.7	463.7		68.0	74.7
3140	Accumulators, primary cells and batteries		281.8	280.3	259.4	267.9		119.9	110.8	99.1	98.6		3.6	5.0
3150	Lighting equipment and electric lamps		33.3	33.4	38.3	37.9		9.3	10.2	9.6	9.6		0.4	0.5
3190	Other electrical equipment n.e.c.		90.8	98.4	119.2	154.4		27.6	35.7	44.0	53.8		2.0	5.0
3210	Electronic valves, tubes, etc.		30021.8	38493.5	39615.2	42383.5		7061.9	9048.1	9140.8	11087.3		4077.1	5167.4
3220	TV/radio transmitters; line comm. apparatus		1798.7	5923.3	6669.1	5490.7		159.4	805.9	1842.6	1563.5		26.4	26.7
3230	TV and radio receivers and associated goods		1507.0	1113.0	1164.1	735.0		227.7	168.1	237.8	117.1		15.4	21.4
331	Medical, measuring, testing appliances, etc.		2895.8	2934.5	3316.4	3840.5		1293.1	1150.6	1377.8	1484.3		135.2	140.9
3311	Medical, surgical and orthopaedic equipment		1914.8	1977.0	2266.0	2355.0		1032.2	883.6	1115.6	1237.5		108.0	94.1
3312	Measuring/testing/navigating appliances,etc.		194.8	117.4	145.4	419.5		43.3	45.1	52.5	27.0		2.4	23.3
3313	Industrial process control equipment		786.2	840.1	905.0	1065.9		217.6	221.9	209.8	219.7		24.8	23.6
3320	Optical instruments & photographic equipment		380.1	495.4f/	533.3f/	612.1f/		162.1	192.5f/	215.2f/	240.3f/		32.4f/	43.0f/
3330	Watches and clocks		142.9	...f/	...f/	...f/		52.9	...f/	...f/	...f/		...f/	...f/
3410	Motor vehicles	g/	1243.2	1093.3	1073.2	1141.8	g/	335.8	273.2	279.8	255.7	g/	20.5	21.8
3420	Automobile bodies, trailers & semi-trailers	g/	...	...	...	...	g/	...	...	...	...	g/	...	...
3430	Parts/accessories for automobiles	g/	...	...	...	...	g/	...	...	...	...	g/	...	...
351	Building and repairing of ships and boats		3309.3	4058.0	5041.8	6925.4		1059.0	1273.2	1479.9	1835.0		110.9	186.3
3511	Building and repairing of ships		2692.4	...	...	...		784.7	...	...	...		...	...
3512	Building/repairing of pleasure/sport. boats		616.9	...	...	...		274.3	...	...	...		...	...
3520	Railway/tramway locomotives & rolling stock		...	...	...	...		...	...	...	...		...	...
3530	Aircraft and spacecraft		3833.4	4687.9	5495.1	6491.6		1635.3	2002.1	2291.2	2554.7		203.9	296.5
359	Transport equipment n.e.c.		...	...	...	...		...	...	...	...		...	...
3591	Motorcycles		...	...	...	...		...	...	...	...		...	...
3592	Bicycles and invalid carriages		...	...	...	...		...	...	...	...		...	...
3599	Other transport equipment n.e.c.		...	...	...	...		...	...	...	...		...	...
3610	Furniture		664.9	629.3	597.5	563.5		194.7	189.0	171.3	168.5		13.4	12.7
369	Manufacturing n.e.c.		871.5	703.6	760.9	774.6		248.2	167.1	171.4	136.7		10.7	7.3
3691	Jewellery and related articles		273.6	...	386.1	434.3		27.6	...	30.5	27.0		0.8	0.6
3692	Musical instruments		...	...	...	...		...	...	...	...		...	...
3693	Sports goods		..	...	...	...		...	...	...	...		...	...
3694	Games and toys		4.2	...	...	...		-0.1	...	...	...		...	...
3699	Other manufacturing n.e.c.		593.7	...	374.9	340.2		220.6	...	140.9	109.6		9.9	6.6
3710	Recycling of metal waste and scrap		418.9	...	...	...		69.2	...	...	...		...	...
3720	Recycling of non-metal waste and scrap		...	...	...	...		...	...	...	...		...	...
D	Total manufacturing		158696.8	191636.2	217086.1	237880.1		37058.0	46317.7	49042.5	54126.7		8876.9	11945.3

a/ 154 includes 1600.
b/ 154 includes 155 and 1600.
c/ 241 includes 242 and 2430.
d/ 2710 includes 2720 and 273.
e/ 3110 includes 3120.
f/ 3320 includes 3330.
g/ 3410 includes 3420 and 3430.

Singapore

ISIC Revision 3			Index numbers of industrial production (2000=100)											
ISIC	Industry	Note	1995	1996	1997	1998	1999	2000	2001	2002	2003	2004	2005	2006
15	Food and beverages	a/	118	119	112	99	98	100	104	101	101	103	110	114
16	Tobacco products	a/	...	...	...	...	...	...	...	...	...	...	...	...
17	Textiles		115	85	91	88	85	100	85	61	64	55	42	35
18	Wearing apparel, fur		96	79	76	84	88	100	84	73	71	70	58	52
19	Leather, leather products and footwear		90	77	70	71	86	100	93	80	72	80	84	84
20	Wood products (excl. furniture)		105	109	99	100	94	100	87	73	80	95	94	107
21	Paper and paper products		127	121	112	97	101	100	93	100	100	106	112	116
22	Printing and publishing		86	86	88	80	88	100	87	80	79	80	82	86
23	Coke,refined petroleum products,nuclear fuel		111	117	121	120	110	100	101	101	107	120	131	127
24	Chemicals and chemical products		48	53	81	78	90	100	104	130	137	143	143	151
25	Rubber and plastics products		99	91	87	72	81	100	75	82	77	75	80	79
26	Non-metallic mineral products		118	131	127	111	100	100	75	76	69	79	68	65
27	Basic metals		98	98	103	85	94	100	101	103	89	105	123	145
28	Fabricated metal products		106	103	100	95	92	100	81	79	72	76	75	81
29	Machinery and equipment n.e.c.		80	85	90	82	79	100	84	85	85	102	125	160
30	Office, accounting and computing machinery		...	...	...	...	...	...	...	...	...	...	...	...
31	Electrical machinery and apparatus		105	104	106	92	92	100	88	91	89	93	101	116
32	Radio,television and communication equipment		60	64	66	64	80	100	79	82	86	99	108	113
33	Medical, precision and optical instruments		61	62	69	80	90	100	104	115	118	124	130	133
34	Motor vehicles, trailers, semi-trailers	b/	89	84	91	103	99	100	123	135	127	152	184	229
35	Other transport equipment	b/	...	...	...	...	...	...	...	...	...	...	...	...
36	Furniture; manufacturing n.e.c.		147	141	136	108	102	100	100	89	91	84	85	97
37	Recycling		...	...	...	...	...	...	...	...	...	...	...	...
D	Total manufacturing		71	73	76	76	87	100	88	96	99	113	123	138

a/ 15 includes 16.
b/ 34 includes 35.

Slovakia

Supplier of information:
Statistical Office of the Slovak Republic, Bratislava.
Industrial statistics for the OECD countries are compiled by the OECD secretariat, which supplies them to UNIDO.

Basic source of data:
Annual industrial survey.

Major deviations from ISIC (Revision 3):
Data presented in accordance with ISIC (Revision 3) were originally classified in the National Branch of Economic Activities (OKEC), which was compatible with NACE (Revision 1) .

Reference period:
Calendar year.

Scope:
All enterprises.

Method of data collection:
Questionnaires are distributed by mail.

Type of enumeration:
Not reported.

Adjusted for non-response:
Yes.

Concepts and definitions of variables:
No deviations from the standard UN concepts and definitions are reported.

Related national publications:
None reported.

Slovakia

ISIC Revision 3		Number of enterprises					Number of employees					Wages and salaries paid to employees				
			(number)					(number)					(millions of Slovak Koruny)			
ISIC	Industry	Note	2002	2003	2004	2005	Note	2002	2003	2004	2005	Note	2002	2003	2004	2005
151	Processed meat,fish,fruit,vegetables,fats		151	...	...	...		11826	...	...	...		1823	...	...	...
1511	Processing/preserving of meat		85	106	94	98		8482	8770	8589	8215		1234	1319	1449	1386
1512	Processing/preserving of fish		11	9	9	8		1056	954	990	917		158	154	180	158
1513	Processing/preserving of fruit & vegetables		42	...	...	...		1136	...	...	...		171	...	...	...
1514	Vegetable and animal oils and fats		13	7	7	9		1152	1047	979	932		260	249	260	270
1520	Dairy products		49	53	51	40		4810	4644	3990	3567		824	875	824	791
153	Grain mill products; starches; animal feeds		108	117	100	74		4728	4452	3634	3143		892	904	820	741
1531	Grain mill products		35	47	36	26		1610	1744	1324	1151		256	278	256	228
1532	Starches and starch products		3	7	10	10		417	450	460	396		124	129	144	147
1533	Prepared animal feeds		70	63	54	38		2701	2258	1850	1596		512	494	420	367
154	Other food products		289	319	325	333		17264	16437	15730	16153		2463	2527	2782	2814
1541	Bakery products		208	217	220	228		12498	11817	11135	11729		1563	1589	1621	1722
1542	Sugar		5	6	4	5		992	986	951	749		226	228	248	235
1543	Cocoa, chocolate and sugar confectionery		12	13	13	13		1109	1162	1155	1142		231	253	272	282
1544	Macaroni, noodles & similar products		15	14	21	19		175	244	371	313		13	21	32	58
1549	Other food products n.e.c.		49	69	67	68		2490	2228	2118	2220		435	427	608	517
155	Beverages		165	173	186	152		8165	7500	7368	6480		1524	1660	1605	1509
1551	Distilling, rectifying & blending of spirits		67	...	...	...		1379	...	...	...		196	...	...	...
1552	Wines		26	...	...	...		950	...	...	...		167	...	...	...
1553	Malt liquors and malt		15	16	20	13		3475	3175	2848	2409		717	846	756	691
1554	Soft drinks; mineral waters		57	54	76	40		2361	2182	2499	2136		440	465	500	459
1600	Tobacco products		...	...	...	...		...	...	...	...		...	...	...	...
171	Spinning, weaving and finishing of textiles		26	26	26	...		6901	6117	4906	...		879	867	776	...
1711	Textile fibre preparation; textile weaving		22	21	21	...		6689	5955	4770	...		854	846	756	...
1712	Finishing of textiles		4	5	5	...		212	162	136	...		26	21	20	...
172	Other textiles		70	125	77	112		3290	4089	3802	4084		424	576	572	641
1721	Made-up textile articles, except apparel		42	86	46	69		2346	2924	2625	2775		278	378	372	405
1722	Carpets and rugs		...	...	...	...		...	...	...	...		...	...	...	...
1723	Cordage, rope, twine and netting		...	...	...	...		...	...	...	...		...	...	...	...
1729	Other textiles n.e.c.		...	...	26	35		...	...	870	1010		...	...	148	178
1730	Knitted and crocheted fabrics and articles		40	50	60	...		8464	7998	7432	...		905	892	933	...
1810	Wearing apparel, except fur apparel		207	320	278	229		28492	28261	25947	24061		2989	3145	3094	2976
1820	Dressing & dyeing of fur; processing of fur		5	5	6	7		237	223	199	149		30	29	24	23
191	Tanning, dressing and processing of leather		25	...	...	...		1967	...	...	...		269	...	...	...
1911	Tanning and dressing of leather		6	10	10	11		935	1139	966	990		145	195	188	208
1912	Luggage, handbags, etc.; saddlery & harness		19	...	...	...		1032	...	...	...		124	...	...	...
1920	Footwear		68	112	76	73		14654	14047	12973	12941		1588	1697	1709	1768
2010	Sawmilling and planing of wood		190	282	240	305		5428	4974	4602	6044		627	618	604	838
202	Products of wood, cork, straw, etc.		265	344	251	337		7837	8412	7823	8350		1003	1158	1221	1386
2021	Veneer sheets, plywood, particle board, etc.		37	43	26	32		3825	3717	3149	3024		534	560	564	594
2022	Builders' carpentry and joinery		117	153	136	167		1819	2895	2979	3128		208	353	404	440
2023	Wooden containers		26	53	6	35		415	572	310	585		77	91	44	104
2029	Other wood products; articles of cork/straw		85	95	83	103		1778	1228	1385	1613		184	154	208	247
210	Paper and paper products		68	75	85	73		9273	8839	7875	7684		2054	1987	1949	2019
2101	Pulp, paper and paperboard		12	14	12	12		5121	4736	4045	3121		1281	1227	1105	938
2102	Corrugated paper and paperboard		28	20	27	24		1761	1785	1759	1806		324	324	364	401
2109	Other articles of paper and paperboard		...	...	...	...		...	...	...	...		...	...	...	...
221	Publishing		296	417	374	366		5453	5821	6308	5475		1353	1452	1593	1486
2211	Publishing of books and other publications		43	56	70	40		1985	2183	2248	1442		397	415	464	344
2212	Publishing of newspapers, journals, etc.		102	156	91	...		2677	2548	2568	...		789	797	808	...
2213	Publishing of recorded media		6	6	3	...		7	1	-	...		-	-	-	...
2219	Other publishing		145	199	210	214		784	1089	1492	1638		167	241	324	324

222	Printing and related service activities	245	201	200	216	5046	3863	4476	4345	1016	792	949	1042
2221	Printing	133	115	109	123	4110	3416	3740	3575	824	714	816	880
2222	Service activities related to printing	112	86	91	93	936	447	736	770	192	79	132	158
2230	Reproduction of recorded media	17	17	13	19	55	48	12	272	9	12	4	66
2310	Coke oven products	-	-	-	-	-	-	-	-	-	-	-	-
2320	Refined petroleum products	...	...	...	...	...	...	...	...	...	...	...	...
2330	Processing of nuclear fuel	-	-	-	...	-	-	-	...	-	-	-	...
241	Basic chemicals	44	54	46	40	7336	6298	5338	5191	1575	1423	1333	1482
2411	Basic chemicals, except fertilizers	...	...	...	...	...	...	...	...	...	...	...	...
2412	Fertilizers and nitrogen compounds	...	...	...	...	...	...	...	...	...	...	...	...
2413	Plastics in primary forms; synthetic rubber	...	...	...	...	...	...	...	...	...	...	...	...
242	Other chemicals	100	101	116	121	7246	6498	5385	5184	1605	1523	1245	1363
2421	Pesticides and other agro-chemical products	...	...	...	3	...	...	...	11	...	...	...	-
2422	Paints, varnishes, printing ink and mastics	14	...	...	11	673	...	...	461	120	...	...	112
2423	Pharmaceuticals, medicinal chemicals, etc.	...	25	27	28	...	3372	2669	2757	...	867	648	760
2424	Soap, cleaning & cosmetic preparations	41	30	49	58	1270	1059	1016	911	248	207	180	185
2429	Other chemical products n.e.c.	22	29	26	21	1741	1439	1191	1044	380	332	312	305
2430	Man-made fibres	6	7	7	7	3391	2950	2336	2034	722	685	556	486
251	Rubber products	28	40	34	36	6352	6890	6741	6430	1592	1863	1993	1945
2511	Rubber tyres and tubes	14	18	18	19	3979	4093	3879	3570	1153	1323	1373	1366
2519	Other rubber products	14	22	16	17	2373	2797	2862	2860	440	539	620	583
2520	Plastic products	258	377	350	421	9514	11856	11918	13301	1622	2211	2329	2733
2610	Glass and glass products	39	44	43	50	8100	7771	7591	7953	1426	1514	1577	1710
269	Non-metallic mineral products n.e.c.	180	223	241	287	15740	14990	14634	13784	3095	3091	3346	3420
2691	Pottery, china and earthenware	...	...	...	...	...	...	...	...	...	...	...	...
2692	Refractory ceramic products	12	14	14	13	4780	4750	4352	3850	845	867	848	818
2693	Struct.non-refractory clay; ceramic products	14	...	17	...	2178	...	2224	...	376	...	420	...
2694	Cement, lime and plaster	10	9	7	...	2551	2573	2678	...	679	747	880	...
2695	Articles of concrete, cement and plaster	89	111	123	163	3759	3171	3101	3504	730	606	728	841
2696	Cutting, shaping & finishing of stone	30	...	48	43	607	...	650	392	81	...	100	54
2699	Other non-metallic mineral products n.e.c.	10	12	11	9	964	979	959	918	218	224	228	259
2710	Basic iron and steel	34	...	...	26	25597	...	...	21847	6374	...	...	8086
2720	Basic precious and non-ferrous metals	15	15	10	12	4667	3620	2739	2567	1037	880	720	730
273	Casting of metals	19	...	...	28	1507	...	...	2884	303	...	...	618
2731	Casting of iron and steel	...	...	...	...	...	...	...	...	...	...	...	...
2732	Casting of non-ferrous metals	...	...	...	...	...	...	...	...	...	...	...	...
281	Struct.metal products;tanks;steam generators	307	293	341	...	10013	9662	11238	...	1665	1734	2265	...
2811	Structural metal products	253	239	281	305	7891	8144	9296	10021	1289	1460	1853	2154
2812	Tanks, reservoirs and containers of metal	40	42	51	43	1409	1348	1776	1737	239	236	368	371
2813	Steam generators	14	12	9	...	713	170	166	...	137	37	44	...
289	Other metal products; metal working services	607	739	762	...	20573	21057	21135	...	3300	3663	4122	...
2891	Metal forging/pressing/stamping/roll-forming	16	19	20	...	1038	1063	1204	...	205	220	276	...
2892	Treatment & coating of metals	294	360	398	451	8141	8935	8994	9441	1255	1564	1697	1976
2893	Cutlery, hand tools and general hardware	114	133	124	143	2934	2820	2659	3087	431	448	476	567
2899	Other fabricated metal products n.e.c.	183	227	220	221	8460	8239	8278	8050	1409	1431	1673	1710
291	General purpose machinery	215	335	334	326	19037	20989	22297	21709	3445	4116	4923	5292
2911	Engines & turbines (not for transport equipment)	14	12	16	15	535	486	457	446	98	91	96	100
2912	Pumps, compressors, taps and valves	32	40	34	39	3444	3721	3891	3850	593	656	736	768
2913	Bearings, gears, gearing & driving elements	16	17	17	22	9367	9594	10332	10901	1768	1951	2393	2791
2914	Ovens, furnaces and furnace burners	9	12	9	16	100	165	70	134	21	21	16	23
2915	Lifting and handling equipment	56	59	57	46	2098	2166	2112	1920	333	369	436	428
2919	Other general purpose machinery	88	195	201	188	3493	4857	5435	4458	636	1029	1245	1181
292	Special purpose machinery	267	275	254	264	20061	19142	18247	17067	3748	3767	4022	3898
2921	Agricultural and forestry machinery	64	57	40	60	2348	2007	1715	1700	401	328	344	340
2922	Machine tools	27	31	27	33	3344	3003	2809	3242	555	556	580	710
2923	Machinery for metallurgy	7	7	4	6	489	483	386	630	124	108	100	178
2924	Machinery for mining & construction	33	30	32	34	3341	2959	2950	3145	593	519	588	695
2925	Food/beverage/tobacco processing machinery	20	30	32	18	1053	1034	1042	812	184	195	200	178
2926	Machinery for textile, apparel and leather	7	9	8	9	980	1123	900	751	132	178	152	151
2927	Weapons and ammunition	8	7	5	6	787	716	442	405	132	129	92	93
2929	Other special purpose machinery	101	104	106	98	7719	7817	8003	6382	1627	1755	1965	1556

continued

Slovakia

ISIC Revision 3		Number of enterprises					Number of employees					Wages and salaries paid to employees				
			(number)					(number)					(millions of Slovak Koruny)			
ISIC	Industry	Note	2002	2003	2004	2005	Note	2002	2003	2004	2005	Note	2002	2003	2004	2005
2930	Domestic appliances n.e.c.		40	25	24	25		3127	3401	3441	3117		529	593	648	645
3000	Office, accounting and computing machinery		31	40	33	51		1177	1891	2886	3533		218	369	684	845
3110	Electric motors, generators and transformers		37	33	40	49		6595	4847	5122	6063		1131	929	1069	1390
3120	Electricity distribution & control apparatus		107	76	125	138		3318	2953	3268	3317		589	560	640	683
3130	Insulated wire and cable		26	29	28	30		10089	11140	11566	13045		1503	1730	1937	2366
3140	Accumulators, primary cells and batteries		5	5	5	5		106	60	59	54		21	12	12	12
3150	Lighting equipment and electric lamps		18	18	25	25		2567	2917	3296	4083		418	527	680	849
3190	Other electrical equipment n.e.c.		120	224	177	127		12340	17012	17601	18317		1661	2489	2986	3134
3210	Electronic valves, tubes, etc.		42	42	45	38		4742	5295	6036	5977		803	929	1177	1154
3220	TV/radio transmitters; line comm. apparatus		53	58	58	66		2747	2841	2112	2014		593	593	468	479
3230	TV and radio receivers and associated goods		25	33	28	12		1808	1633	1715	2553		273	257	316	521
331	Medical, measuring, testing appliances, etc.		199	221	189	...		6711	6756	6513	...		1349	1398	1473	...
3311	Medical, surgical and orthopaedic equipment		95	110	74	113		2764	2824	2352	2900		482	568	508	706
3312	Measuring/testing/navigating appliances,etc.		73	78	76	97		2355	2598	2535	2484		482	502	544	587
3313	Industrial process control equipment		31	33	39	...		1592	1334	1626	...		384	328	420	...
3320	Optical instruments & photographic equipment		...	...	...	...		...	...	...	...		...	...	...	...
3330	Watches and clocks		...	...	...	...		...	...	...	...		...	...	...	...
3410	Motor vehicles		...	...	...	...		...	...	...	...		...	...	...	...
3420	Automobile bodies, trailers & semi-trailers		...	...	...	...		...	...	...	...		...	...	...	...
3430	Parts/accessories for automobiles		35	39	49	54		6809	9949	10632	11028		1251	2050	2529	2717
351	Building and repairing of ships and boats		9	10	9	...		979	864	1004	...		145	133	180	...
3511	Building and repairing of ships		...	...	...	...		...	...	...	...		...	...	...	...
3512	Building/repairing of pleasure/sport. boats		...	...	...	...		...	...	...	...		...	...	...	...
3520	Railway/tramway locomotives & rolling stock		12	12	11	14		7140	6854	6328	5530		1315	1365	1637	1436
3530	Aircraft and spacecraft		7	8	8	9		568	515	437	928		98	100	96	239
359	Transport equipment n.e.c.		18	13	21	...		325	243	324	...		43	37	52	...
3591	Motorcycles		...	...	3	...		...	...	24	...		...	...	4	...
3592	Bicycles and invalid carriages		...	...	...	...		...	...	...	...		...	...	...	...
3599	Other transport equipment n.e.c.		...	...	...	...		...	...	...	...		...	...	...	...
3610	Furniture		214	242	188	285		11808	12187	12242	13509		1819	2062	2293	2629
369	Manufacturing n.e.c.		108	126	106	118		3298	3184	2760	2961		474	411	396	498
3691	Jewellery and related articles		10	23	18	19		489	484	569	535		68	62	84	81
3692	Musical instruments		...	5	3	5		...	9	12	18		...	-	-	-
3693	Sports goods		...	17	16	16		...	574	258	239		...	79	40	39
3694	Games and toys		23	25	20	25		453	645	580	819		73	100	96	185
3699	Other manufacturing n.e.c.		61	56	49	53		1853	1472	1341	1350		269	170	176	193
3710	Recycling of metal waste and scrap		30	43	26	44		371	453	511	820		102	120	144	201
3720	Recycling of non-metal waste and scrap		13	21	14	5		261	275	272	440		38	46	48	116
D	Total manufacturing		5609	6764	6389	6848		408092	410540	400279	403816		71798	77730	83718	90727

Slovakia

ISIC Revision 3		Output					Value added in factor values					Gross fixed capital formation		
			(millions of Slovak Koruny)					(millions of Slovak Koruny)					(millions of Slovak Koruny)	
ISIC	Industry	Note	2002	2003	2004	2005	Note	2002	2003	2004	2005	Note	2004	2005
151	Processed meat,fish,fruit,vegetables,fats		25176	...	...	...		2809	...	...	...		...	...
1511	Processing/preserving of meat		17244	16840	17938	18149		1166	1406	884	1312		1673	691
1512	Processing/preserving of fish		1375	1265	1289	1274		243	295	368	340		112	131
1513	Processing/preserving of fruit & vegetables		1597	...	...	...		410	...	...	...		...	...
1514	Vegetable and animal oils and fats		4961	4381	4534	4535		990	763	632	695		76	77
1520	Dairy products		16544	16359	15625	15459		1499	1303	1425	1127		1393	988
153	Grain mill products; starches; animal feeds		14512	13596	11843	10808		2651	2756	2289	1926		1341	1281
1531	Grain mill products		3279	3307	3138	2744		333	577	464	386		168	401
1532	Starches and starch products		2421	2332	2637	2825		948	904	852	826		644	320
1533	Prepared animal feeds		8813	7953	6067	5238		1370	1274	969	714		528	560
154	Other food products		21962	21948	25150	24665		5277	5721	6311	6145		1885	3466
1541	Bakery products		9205	8870	8833	8901		2638	2606	2269	2370		676	2019
1542	Sugar		3620	3846	6083	5118		803	1066	1645	1262		344	811
1543	Cocoa, chocolate and sugar confectionery		3710	3900	4647	4701		645	739	832	791		508	259
1544	Macaroni, noodles & similar products		77	104	260	475		21	37	44	127		-	23
1549	Other food products n.e.c.		5354	5232	5319	5466		1170	1274	1517	1594		352	355
155	Beverages		18085	18339	17814	17844		3501	4248	4030	4173		1253	1779
1551	Distilling, rectifying & blending of spirits		2441	...	...	...		342	...	...	...		...	...
1552	Wines		1827	...	...	...		508	...	...	...		...	...
1553	Malt liquors and malt		8009	8821	8345	7473		1934	2477	2121	1579		512	895
1554	Soft drinks; mineral waters		5811	5402	5475	5987		717	1008	981	1386		520	494
1600	Tobacco products		...	...	...	...		...	...	...	...		...	...
171	Spinning, weaving and finishing of textiles		5614	4634	4506	...		1652	1120	993	...		432	...
1711	Textile fibre preparation; textile weaving		5478	4522	4402	...		1627	1108	969	...		420	...
1712	Finishing of textiles		137	112	104	...		26	12	24	...		12	...
172	Other textiles		1990	2921	2822	3702		679	933	969	1204		124	262
1721	Made-up textile articles, except apparel		1063	1560	1413	2158		504	660	608	830		32	158
1722	Carpets and rugs		...	...	...	...		...	...	...	...		...	...
1723	Cordage, rope, twine and netting		...	...	...	...		...	...	...	...		...	...
1729	Other textiles n.e.c.		...	...	820	841		...	...	284	282		44	39
1730	Knitted and crocheted fabrics and articles		3245	3066	3594	...		1430	1419	1513	...		384	...
1810	Wearing apparel, except fur apparel		9307	9737	10322	9129		4572	4734	4486	4122		252	602
1820	Dressing & dyeing of fur; processing of fur		128	133	104	58		4	12	-4	-4		4	-
191	Tanning, dressing and processing of leather		1853	...	...	...		615	...	...	...		...	...
1911	Tanning and dressing of leather		1247	1527	1441	1390		389	290	368	401		40	66
1912	Luggage, handbags, etc.; saddlery & harness		606	...	...	...		226	...	...	...		...	...
1920	Footwear		9102	11505	12063	11858		3023	2755	2950	3211		212	313
2010	Sawmilling and planing of wood		4073	4049	4827	6377		867	859	1101	1505		316	710
202	Products of wood, cork, straw, etc.		9849	11086	12283	14729		2173	2228	2633	3458		700	1417
2021	Veneer sheets, plywood, particle board, etc.		6028	6543	7496	8442		1259	996	1241	1760		496	745
2022	Builders' carpentry and joinery		1558	2373	2549	3204		312	535	648	803		76	255
2023	Wooden containers		628	718	296	645		171	232	76	189		8	73
2029	Other wood products; articles of cork/straw		1636	1452	1941	2439		431	465	668	706		120	344
210	Paper and paper products		32763	31133	32590	34291		9589	7319	6672	7353		5227	5249
2101	Pulp, paper and paperboard		21573	20251	21100	18883		6835	4829	4010	4022		3970	1254
2102	Corrugated paper and paperboard		4560	4319	4591	4609		1029	954	1069	1108		356	529
2109	Other articles of paper and paperboard		...	...	...	...		...	...	...	...		...	...
221	Publishing		9444	11181	11726	10615		3104	3572	3822	3729		360	448
2211	Publishing of books and other publications		2771	3199	3450	2733		845	1004	1061	845		184	162
2212	Publishing of newspapers, journals, etc.		5520	5916	4943	...		1712	1855	1601	...		156	...
2213	Publishing of recorded media		13	-	4	...		4	-	-	...		-	...
2219	Other publishing		1144	2070	3334	2594		542	709	1161	1031		20	208

continued

Slovakia

ISIC Revision 3		Output					Value added in factor values					Gross fixed capital formation		
			(millions of Slovak Koruny)					(millions of Slovak Koruny)					(millions of Slovak Koruny)	
ISIC	Industry	Note	2002	2003	2004	2005	Note	2002	2003	2004	2005	Note	2004	2005
222	Printing and related service activities		9192	8032	7944	8453		2515	2186	2133	2355		864	903
2221	Printing		7945	7090	7324	7743		2113	1726	1853	2061		848	803
2222	Service activities related to printing		1251	946	620	710		401	456	280	297		16	100
2230	Reproduction of recorded media		94	349	84	2285		30	37	32	452		12	598
2310	Coke oven products		-	-	-	-		-	-	-	-		-	-
2320	Refined petroleum products		...	...	...	...		...	...	...	...		...	...
2330	Processing of nuclear fuel		-	-	-	...		-	-	-	...		-	...
241	Basic chemicals		21428	17731	18986	22866		3637	2842	3594	4447		1153	1502
2411	Basic chemicals, except fertilizers		...	...	...	...		...	...	...	...		...	...
2412	Fertilizers and nitrogen compounds		...	...	...	...		...	...	...	...		...	...
2413	Plastics in primary forms; synthetic rubber		...	...	...	...		...	...	...	...		...	...
242	Other chemicals		15908	15326	11770	12938		3719	3489	2493	2968		804	1162
2421	Pesticides and other agro-chemical products		...	...	...	12		...	...	...	4		...	-
2422	Paints, varnishes, printing ink and mastics		1430	...	...	1116		260	...	...	243		...	46
2423	Pharmaceuticals, medicinal chemicals, etc.		...	7746	6408	7257		...	1855	1429	1633		524	703
2424	Soap, cleaning & cosmetic preparations		2899	2946	1417	1536		670	776	328	394		24	96
2429	Other chemical products n.e.c.		3313	3390	2858	3018		768	622	528	695		224	317
2430	Man-made fibres		8718	8360	8297	7577		2015	1336	1253	722		140	417
251	Rubber products		17965	20529	22869	24082		4718	5398	5827	5852		1677	1567
2511	Rubber tyres and tubes		14230	16006	18222	19354		3753	4132	4530	4454		1321	1266
2519	Other rubber products		3736	4522	4651	4728		969	1265	1297	1401		356	301
2520	Plastic products		19058	23881	24994	30713		4239	5568	4743	6600		2093	3200
2610	Glass and glass products		10481	11916	12031	13263		4248	3527	3862	4377		3642	629
269	Non-metallic mineral products n.e.c.		27657	27943	29748	32442		8624	8742	9441	9804		3598	4960
2691	Pottery, china and earthenware		...	...	...	...		...	...	...	...		...	...
2692	Refractory ceramic products		5678	5709	5631	5597		1738	1693	1585	1606		224	363
2693	Struct.non-refractory clay; ceramic products		2826	...	3346	...		1084	...	1329	...		236	...
2694	Cement, lime and plaster		8697	9264	10010	...		3095	2871	2994	...		2285	...
2695	Articles of concrete, cement and plaster		5926	5240	6255	8353		1422	1539	2029	2312		596	892
2696	Cutting, shaping & finishing of stone		444	...	612	378		132	...	240	100		24	39
2699	Other non-metallic mineral products n.e.c.		3061	3099	3178	3362		773	867	965	977		200	154
2710	Basic iron and steel		72289	...	...	100936		16121	...	...	29262		...	6817
2720	Basic precious and non-ferrous metals		17701	15484	17378	18400		2387	2933	4230	3655		436	1042
273	Casting of metals		2130	...	...	4921		534	...	...	1420		...	633
2731	Casting of iron and steel		...	...	...	...		...	...	...	...		...	...
2732	Casting of non-ferrous metals		...	...	...	...		...	...	...	...		...	...
281	Struct.metal products;tanks;steam generators		12560	14106	20179	...		3386	3788	5311	...		1093	...
2811	Structural metal products		8774	9949	15372	16868		2331	2713	4214	4505		504	1583
2812	Tanks, reservoirs and containers of metal		3202	3941	4538	5026		781	1008	1009	1073		588	224
2813	Steam generators		585	216	268	...		273	66	88	...		-	...
289	Other metal products; metal working services		20706	22748	27571	...		6831	7489	8241	...		2521	...
2891	Metal forging/pressing/stamping/roll-forming		1550	1610	2013	...		525	448	564	...		256	...
2892	Treatment & coating of metals		7330	8667	10074	11367		2792	3473	3478	4443		620	1042
2893	Cutlery, hand tools and general hardware		2387	2348	2754	3350		939	755	840	1015		88	289
2899	Other fabricated metal products n.e.c.		9440	10124	12731	14432		2574	2813	3358	3617		1557	1336
291	General purpose machinery		26572	37299	40570	45099		8227	10418	12471	13448		3278	4794
2911	Engines & turbines (not for transport equipment)		845	776	949	1320		102	108	128	185		16	100
2912	Pumps, compressors, taps and valves		5563	6572	7800	8137		1853	1539	2137	1880		929	1069
2913	Bearings, gears, gearing & driving elements		13944	17152	19463	23862		4483	5530	6295	7944		1937	3269
2914	Ovens, furnaces and furnace burners		265	220	92	124		30	41	24	27		-	12
2915	Lifting and handling equipment		2113	2108	2137	2868		524	631	656	764		52	69
2919	Other general purpose machinery		3842	10480	10134	8785		1230	2572	3230	2652		340	278

292	Special purpose machinery	18781	19321	21344	21202	5951	5846	7160	6813	1097	1656
2921	Agricultural and forestry machinery	1968	1589	1885	1988	679	560	684	510	56	131
2922	Machine tools	2929	2796	2962	3416	871	780	965	1100	188	251
2923	Machinery for metallurgy	393	274	276	625	145	178	164	378	4	46
2924	Machinery for mining & construction	2634	2357	3458	3848	743	581	1113	1224	236	247
2925	Food/beverage/tobacco processing machinery	1119	1436	1325	1447	444	469	444	324	80	158
2926	Machinery for textile, apparel and leather	811	892	784	895	209	174	244	313	68	139
2927	Weapons and ammunition	546	456	336	359	188	149	140	127	20	54
2929	Other special purpose machinery	8376	9522	10322	8627	2673	2954	3410	2833	444	629
2930	Domestic appliances n.e.c.	8961	12820	15008	13514	1294	1705	969	-208	872	645
3000	Office, accounting and computing machinery	1588	9027	27071	50862	389	349	-1049	3513	1293	1166
3110	Electric motors, generators and transformers	13927	10766	11935	19365	2455	1962	2581	3833	592	1390
3120	Electricity distribution & control apparatus	3437	4041	4651	5327	1037	1016	1161	1281	140	262
3130	Insulated wire and cable	12138	12467	13187	15459	2651	2900	3758	4508	1141	872
3140	Accumulators, primary cells and batteries	167	87	92	85	43	12	16	15	-	19
3150	Lighting equipment and electric lamps	3484	4327	5727	8241	845	1158	1721	2204	913	1363
3190	Other electrical equipment n.e.c.	7237	15500	19399	22797	2604	4593	5971	6226	1305	1004
3210	Electronic valves, tubes, etc.	9380	13301	14272	12923	1473	2564	2129	1749	1021	575
3220	TV/radio transmitters; line comm. apparatus	3859	3415	2369	2007	798	975	784	513	92	185
3230	TV and radio receivers and associated goods	3189	3137	3390	9302	760	689	804	1096	160	205
331	Medical, measuring, testing appliances, etc.	8808	8879	9105	...	3074	2830	2866	...	336	...
3311	Medical, surgical and orthopaedic equipment	2856	2933	2297	3694	1145	1166	989	1502	168	309
3312	Measuring/testing/navigating appliances,etc.	4094	3896	4026	5334	1315	1054	1141	1718	144	621
3313	Industrial process control equipment	1857	2050	2782	...	615	610	736	...	24	...
3320	Optical instruments & photographic equipment	...	...	...	...	...	...	...	...	...	...
3330	Watches and clocks	...	...	...	...	...	...	...	...	...	...
3410	Motor vehicles	...	...	...	...	...	...	...	...	...	...
3420	Automobile bodies, trailers & semi-trailers	...	...	...	...	...	...	...	...	...	...
3430	Parts/accessories for automobiles	11647	33594	41871	42293	3403	4219	6932	6971	1401	1949
351	Building and repairing of ships and boats	722	867	1617	...	137	195	428	...	16	...
3511	Building and repairing of ships	...	...	...	...	...	...	...	...	...	...
3512	Building/repairing of pleasure/sport. boats	...	...	...	...	...	...	...	...	...	...
3520	Railway/tramway locomotives & rolling stock	8730	9555	9861	8484	1776	1738	2069	1440	364	482
3530	Aircraft and spacecraft	401	361	428	1170	167	141	152	405	20	482
359	Transport equipment n.e.c.	324	278	304	...	73	58	84	...	8	...
3591	Motorcycles	...	...	20	...	...	...	8	...	-	...
3592	Bicycles and invalid carriages	...	...	...	...	...	...	...	...	...	...
3599	Other transport equipment n.e.c.	...	...	...	...	...	...	...	...	...	...
3610	Furniture	22073	30059	28728	30397	3702	3962	5095	6157	840	1803
369	Manufacturing n.e.c.	3048	2311	2477	2934	820	577	672	1050	148	278
3691	Jewellery and related articles	589	444	949	737	77	12	72	205	12	8
3692	Musical instruments	...	17	4	12	...	4	-	4	-	-
3693	Sports goods	...	340	156	127	...	91	20	66	4	73
3694	Games and toys	640	730	644	1173	184	228	252	398	68	131
3699	Other manufacturing n.e.c.	1499	780	724	884	491	241	328	378	64	66
3710	Recycling of metal waste and scrap	794	1178	1245	1606	423	382	392	560	112	351
3720	Recycling of non-metal waste and scrap	299	332	416	610	98	104	192	282	200	39
D	Total manufacturing	788506	941655	1027025	1116642	171547	185808	213153	226495	66156	107757

Slovakia

ISIC Revision 3			Index numbers of industrial production (2000=100)											
ISIC	Industry	Note	1995	1996	1997	1998	1999	2000	2001	2002	2003	2004	2005	2006
15	Food and beverages		...	...	...	97	101	100	103	107	106	108	109	110
16	Tobacco products		...	...	...	85	96	100	85	99	66	24	6	4
17	Textiles		...	...	...	99	90	100	111	117	110	113	106	101
18	Wearing apparel, fur		...	...	...	116	100	100	107	110	103	95	88	122
19	Leather, leather products and footwear		...	...	...	74	86	100	111	127	128	120	130	129
20	Wood products (excl. furniture)		...	...	...	95	88	100	102	99	101	113	128	141
21	Paper and paper products		...	...	...	84	85	100	110	101	99	117	129	135
22	Printing and publishing		...	...	...	91	87	100	131	143	141	140	153	168
23	Coke,refined petroleum products,nuclear fuel		...	...	...	92	90	100	103	114	112	120	114	113
24	Chemicals and chemical products		...	...	...	98	95	100	103	107	101	99	103	109
25	Rubber and plastics products		...	...	...	85	79	100	109	124	145	156	167	183
26	Non-metallic mineral products		...	...	...	115	103	100	110	112	116	119	125	136
27	Basic metals		...	...	...	90	92	100	104	115	121	117	115	121
28	Fabricated metal products		...	...	...	102	93	100	114	122	135	155	179	243
29	Machinery and equipment n.e.c.		...	...	...	105	86	100	109	117	129	149	169	210
30	Office, accounting and computing machinery		...	...	...	56	85	100	131	183	194	208	222	192
31	Electrical machinery and apparatus		...	...	...	94	103	100	133	156	182	206	220	228
32	Radio,television and communication equipment		...	...	...	74	71	100	155	195	205	241	276	361
33	Medical, precision and optical instruments		...	...	...	112	92	100	91	102	112	113	153	175
34	Motor vehicles, trailers, semi-trailers		...	...	...	71	75	100	106	127	166	164	160	206
35	Other transport equipment		...	...	...	136	121	100	167	139	190	173	134	117
36	Furniture; manufacturing n.e.c.		...	...	...	101	94	100	117	135	154	170	199	213
37	Recycling		...	...	...	...	...	...	...	...	...	...	...	...
D	Total manufacturing		86	88	89	95	91	100	110	119	128	134	140	158

Slovenia

Supplier of information:
Statistical Office of the Republic of Slovenia, Ljubljana.

Basic source of data:
Annual census/exhaustive survey; administrative source.

Major deviations from ISIC (Revision 3):
Data presented in ISIC (Revsion3) were originally classified according to NACE (Revision 1.1).

Reference period:
Calendar year.

Scope:
All registered enterprises.

Method of data collection:
Data for gross fixed capital formation are collected through mail questionnaires; all other data come mainly from administrative sources.

Type of enumeration:
Complete enumeration; between 1995 and 2004 final data for gross fixed capital formation were collected from all legal units with 10 or more paid employees; in 2005 data were collected from all reporting units; provisional data for 2006 include all reporting units with 20 or more paid employees.

Adjusted for non-response:
No.

Concepts and definitions of variables:
Wages and salaries excludes housing and family allowances paid directly by the employer and payments in kind.
Output excludes net change between the beginning and end of the year in the value of work in process and stocks and goods to be shipped in the same condition as received. It is valued in current prices.
Gross fixed capital formaiton also includes land.

Related national publications:
None reported.

Slovenia

ISIC Revision 3		Number of enterprises					Number of employees a/					Wages and salaries paid to employees a/				
			(number)					(number)					(millions of Euros)			
ISIC	Industry	Note	2003	2004	2005	2006	Note	2003	2004	2005	2006b/	Note	2003	2004	2005	2006b/
151	Processed meat,fish,fruit,vegetables,fats		212	241	243	232		...	...	...	6562		...	...	...	87
1511	Processing/preserving of meat		131	144	139	141		5798	5667	5374	5058		66	65	67	62
1512	Processing/preserving of fish		5	4	5	7		...	...	...	201		...	...	...	3
1513	Processing/preserving of fruit & vegetables		48	61	69	55		1936	1857	1171	1105		30	33	18	19
1514	Vegetable and animal oils and fats		28	32	30	29		221	...	204	198		3	...	3	3
1520	Dairy products		48	56	54	67		1805	1645	1595	1463		27	26	26	23
153	Grain mill products; starches; animal feeds		56	55	50	46		...	1119	1064	860		13	17	18	14
1531	Grain mill products		44	42	36	33		...	...	...	...		...	...	...	...
1532	Starches and starch products		2	2	2	1		...	...	...	...		...	...	...	...
1533	Prepared animal feeds		10	11	12	12		...	368	376	386		1	6	6	7
154	Other food products		416	425	408	429		7811	7696	7971	6902		101	104	115	120
1541	Bakery products		310	317	317	337		5676	5582	5407	4536		71	71	71	80
1542	Sugar		1	1	1	1		...	...	...	...		...	...	...	...
1543	Cocoa, chocolate and sugar confectionery		10	9	9	12		744	723	679	654		10	...	9	10
1544	Macaroni, noodles & similar products		24	29	22	19		199	...	247	239		2	...	3	3
1549	Other food products n.e.c.		71	69	59	60		...	...	...	...		...	...	...	...
155	Beverages		69	68	71	78		2468	2257	2114	1965		42	41	39	38
1551	Distilling, rectifying & blending of spirits		20	20	19	20		...	...	...	...		...	...	...	...
1552	Wines		20	21	22	29		...	...	...	...		...	...	...	...
1553	Malt liquors and malt		14	12	15	12		969	...	870	820		21	...	21	20
1554	Soft drinks; mineral waters		15	15	15	17		621	...	485	451		11	...	8	9
1600	Tobacco products		1	1	1	-		...	...	...	-		...	...	...	-
171	Spinning, weaving and finishing of textiles		50	44	35	33		3773	...	2030	1874		39	...	24	22
1711	Textile fibre preparation; textile weaving		34	31	22	21		3230	3135	1999	1845		33	33	24	22
1712	Finishing of textiles		16	13	13	12		543	...	31	29		6	...	-	-
172	Other textiles		347	339	329	336		7085	7219	6596	6050		76	...	77	72
1721	Made-up textile articles, except apparel		157	161	158	172		5042	5193	4662	4161		54	56	54	48
1722	Carpets and rugs		7	7	4	3		4	...	8	...		-	-	-	...
1723	Cordage, rope, twine and netting		10	10	12	11		241	...	217	...		2	...	2	...
1729	Other textiles n.e.c.		173	161	155	150		1798	...	1709	1675		19	...	21	21
1730	Knitted and crocheted fabrics and articles		166	147	131	125		2205	...	1910	1599		20	...	19	16
1810	Wearing apparel, except fur apparel		1196	1137	940	857		12996	...	10526	9769		110	...	94	92
1820	Dressing & dyeing of fur; processing of fur		21	20	18	18		26	...	23	20		-	...	-	-
191	Tanning, dressing and processing of leather		147	141	120	110		3786	...	3256	3113		37	...	33	34
1911	Tanning and dressing of leather		6	7	7	7		1347	...	953	904		15	...	12	12
1912	Luggage, handbags, etc.; saddlery & harness		141	134	113	103		2439	...	2303	2209		22	23	21	22
1920	Footwear		130	132	114	108		3600	2574	2358	2481		35	...	27	29
2010	Sawmilling and planing of wood		444	450	439	441		2389	2243	2083	2051		25	25	25	25
202	Products of wood, cork, straw, etc.		1146	1162	1148	1093		8823	8846	8721	8710		91	95	101	104
2021	Veneer sheets, plywood, particle board, etc.		33	31	27	24		1926	1940	1712	1728		22	22	21	22
2022	Builders' carpentry and joinery		504	527	506	485		5176	5166	4728	4570		53	55	55	55
2023	Wooden containers		188	177	179	168		393	373	454	505		3	4	5	5
2029	Other wood products; articles of cork/straw		421	427	436	416		1328	1367	1827	1907		13	14	20	22
210	Paper and paper products		206	206	185	181		5888	5753	5359	5171		82	82	81	81
2101	Pulp, paper and paperboard		12	13	10	10		2452	2382	2077	1940		40	39	36	36
2102	Corrugated paper and paperboard		80	81	78	77		1676	...	1509	1524		21	...	21	21
2109	Other articles of paper and paperboard		114	112	97	94		1760	...	1773	1706		21	...	24	24
221	Publishing		431	453	450	473		3453	...	3360	3427		69	...	78	81
2211	Publishing of books and other publications		138	151	159	162		1265	...	1165	1166		19	...	22	22
2212	Publishing of newspapers, journals, etc.		148	159	160	170		1933	1929	1954	2005		47	50	53	55
2213	Publishing of recorded media		43	47	45	54		79	80	102	105		1	1	2	2
2219	Other publishing		102	96	86	87		177	160	140	151		2	2	2	2

222	Printing and related service activities	1094	1112	1120	1117	5686	5567	5555	5432	75	77	80	81
2221	Printing	436	446	456	466	4411	...	...	...	60	...	...	...
2222	Service activities related to printing	658	666	664	651	1275	...	...	...	15	...	...	...
2230	Reproduction of recorded media	14	17	17	19	14	...	14	16	-	...	-	-
2310	Coke oven products	-	-	-	-	-	-	-	-	-	-	-	-
2320	Refined petroleum products	4	3	3	4	...	93	87	90	...	1	1	2
2330	Processing of nuclear fuel	-	-	-	-	-	-	-	-	-	-	-	-
241	Basic chemicals	44	46	44	45	2804	2580	2612	2581	45	44	47	48
2411	Basic chemicals, except fertilizers	29	32	28	29	...	...	2297	2268	39	...	41	41
2412	Fertilizers and nitrogen compounds	3	3	4	4	...	...	...	...	-	-	...	...
2413	Plastics in primary forms; synthetic rubber	12	11	12	12	377	287	...	...	6	5	...	...
242	Other chemicals	144	145	131	126	...	...	...	...	...	...	...	...
2421	Pesticides and other agro-chemical products	4	4	3	3	...	251	...	...	...	4	...	...
2422	Paints, varnishes, printing ink and mastics	10	11	12	12	1320	1397	1416	1457	22	25	27	29
2423	Pharmaceuticals, medicinal chemicals, etc.	17	15	15	14	5643	4651	4721	5314	197	211	224	218
2424	Soap, cleaning & cosmetic preparations	46	44	39	34	1388	...	1398	1338	20	...	23	22
2429	Other chemical products n.e.c.	67	71	62	63	1994	2162	2143	2023	33	38	38	36
2430	Man-made fibres	1	1	2	2	...	...	...	...	...	...	...	...
251	Rubber products	111	108	106	116	3305	...	3404	3485	52	...	60	62
2511	Rubber tyres and tubes	27	24	25	27	2588	...	...	...	42	...	...	...
2519	Other rubber products	84	84	81	89	718	767	916	968	10	13	15	16
2520	Plastic products	1066	1056	1008	991	9154	...	8970	9361	114	...	125	137
2610	Glass and glass products	68	70	70	65	2964	2895	3081	2371	32	35	38	37
269	Non-metallic mineral products n.e.c.	412	431	419	430	...	...	...	...	...	...	...	...
2691	Pottery, china and earthenware	37	36	35	39	...	...	...	303	...	...	...	...
2692	Refractory ceramic products	7	8	8	10	...	48	45	46	1	1	1	1
2693	Struct.non-refractory clay; ceramic products	39	37	34	29	...	...	...	...	...	...	...	...
2694	Cement, lime and plaster	7	7	7	7	...	...	609	...	15	...	16	14
2695	Articles of concrete, cement and plaster	135	136	135	140	2026	2035	1991	2100	25	27	28	31
2696	Cutting, shaping & finishing of stone	153	171	164	168	810	799	766	774	9	10	10	10
2699	Other non-metallic mineral products n.e.c.	34	36	36	37	2066	2089	2149	2179	29	31	33	37
2710	Basic iron and steel	13	12	16	16	...	...	3225	3350	...	...	56	63
2720	Basic precious and non-ferrous metals	7	5	6	5	...	...	1071	1072	20	...	21	24
273	Casting of metals	88	91	96	100	3861	4043	4281	4640	53	...	64	71
2731	Casting of iron and steel	35	34	33	29	2213	2279	2373	2472	27	30	32	36
2732	Casting of non-ferrous metals	53	57	63	71	1649	1764	1909	2168	25	...	32	35
281	Struct.metal products;tanks;steam generators	551	570	559	581	...	...	6503	7529	67	...	88	108
2811	Structural metal products	505	526	517	533	4760	5284	5627	6572	58	69	77	94
2812	Tanks, reservoirs and containers of metal	42	40	39	45	...	...	869	950	9	...	11	14
2813	Steam generators	4	4	3	3	...	...	7	7	-	...	-	-
289	Other metal products; metal working services	3905	3886	3716	3673	23894	22704	22982	23208	294	297	311	332
2891	Metal forging/pressing/stamping/roll-forming	91	94	98	95	3076	2750	2595	2392	41	40	38	37
2892	Treatment & coating of metals	1986	2041	1958	1935	6155	5506	5679	5861	68	65	68	75
2893	Cutlery, hand tools and general hardware	414	409	386	379	7134	6908	7044	6942	94	98	103	106
2899	Other fabricated metal products n.e.c.	1414	1342	1274	1264	7529	7540	7664	8013	91	94	102	114
291	General purpose machinery	556	578	560	560	6448	6384	6445	6869	88	93	104	113
2911	Engines & turbines (not for transport equipment)	27	22	22	22	444	...	459	469	7	...	8	9
2912	Pumps, compressors, taps and valves	78	81	73	71	1006	...	900	1017	13	...	16	16
2913	Bearings, gears, gearing & driving elements	28	32	30	35	518	589	675	942	6	8	9	14
2914	Ovens, furnaces and furnace burners	37	39	36	36	83	91	101	111	1	1	2	2
2915	Lifting and handling equipment	131	136	136	134	1851	1702	1829	2031	26	27	30	35
2919	Other general purpose machinery	255	268	263	262	2547	2438	2482	2300	35	35	38	37
292	Special purpose machinery	863	870	851	881	...	...	8235	8410	89	...	123	135
2921	Agricultural and forestry machinery	251	246	234	230	...	...	1321	1321	15	16	17	19
2922	Machine tools	286	276	273	281	1872	1912	2309	2390	26	...	35	39
2923	Machinery for metallurgy	11	15	16	18	184	...	229	239	3	...	4	4
2924	Machinery for mining & construction	47	50	46	50	624	1728	1735	1772	8	25	27	28
2925	Food/beverage/tobacco processing machinery	74	93	101	121	770	771	588	650	11	12	10	11
2926	Machinery for textile, apparel and leather	35	34	34	33	154	...	279	290	2	...	4	4
2927	Weapons and ammunition	18	18	19	21	...	...	71	12	1	...	1	-
2929	Other special purpose machinery	141	138	128	127	1701	1717	1703	1736	23	25	26	29

continued

Slovenia

ISIC Revision 3		Number of enterprises					Number of employees a/					Wages and salaries paid to employees a/			
			(number)					(number)					(millions of Euros)		
ISIC	Industry	Note	2003	2004	2005	2006	Note	2003	2004	2005	2006b/	Note	2003	2004	2005	2006b/
2930	Domestic appliances n.e.c.		43	39	38	43		10416	10382	10222	10615		139	146	160	164
3000	Office, accounting and computing machinery		107	112	100	103		818	813	773	726		13	14	14	15
3110	Electric motors, generators and transformers		71	73	77	74		4652	4436	4186	4328		65	65	64	72
3120	Electricity distribution & control apparatus		72	73	69	67		2611	2668	2631	2634		31	35	35	36
3130	Insulated wire and cable		8	10	15	26		...	...	89	50		3	3	1	1
3140	Accumulators, primary cells and batteries		5	6	5	8		...	...	839	755		10	12	14	12
3150	Lighting equipment and electric lamps		69	72	69	67		574	623	598	240		7	8	8	3
3190	Other electrical equipment n.e.c.		558	537	497	477		5349	5459	6055	6349		73	78	92	96
3210	Electronic valves, tubes, etc.		186	173	166	150		3973	4020	3247	3330		44	47	40	45
3220	TV/radio transmitters; line comm. apparatus		78	74	65	58		1617	1555	1392	1063		57	48	42	39
3230	TV and radio receivers and associated goods		78	87	83	83		398	399	425	443		4	5	5	5
331	Medical, measuring, testing appliances, etc.		325	338	338	346		5509	5613	5264	4825		77	79	82	78
3311	Medical, surgical and orthopaedic equipment		109	110	108	114		1059	1110	881	1178		11	12	10	16
3312	Measuring/testing/navigating appliances,etc.		129	129	118	115		3964	3924	3774	3097		58	56	59	50
3313	Industrial process control equipment		87	99	112	117		486	579	609	550		8	11	13	12
3320	Optical instruments & photographic equipment		87	90	81	84		1683	1935	1698	1833		18	22	20	23
3330	Watches and clocks		27	22	20	15		14	11	12	11		-	-	-	-
3410	Motor vehicles		7	8	8	8		2409	2564	2996	2834		36	40	50	48
3420	Automobile bodies, trailers & semi-trailers		23	25	30	29		1292	1380	1477	1515		18	20	23	25
3430	Parts/accessories for automobiles		49	54	56	60		3351	3759	3859	4469		46	54	63	71
351	Building and repairing of ships and boats		67	89	96	115		...	639	635	647		7	8	10	10
3511	Building and repairing of ships		21	25	24	25		...	133	107	95		2	1	2	1
3512	Building/repairing of pleasure/sport. boats		46	64	72	90		425	506	527	552		5	7	8	8
3520	Railway/tramway locomotives & rolling stock		4	4	4	5		...	...	1392	1464		...	...	22	25
3530	Aircraft and spacecraft		9	13	13	14		60	...	...	89		...	...	...	1
359	Transport equipment n.e.c.		14	13	15	15		832	693	...	358		11	...	...	5
3591	Motorcycles		2	3	3	3		...	...	...	...		...	...	...	...
3592	Bicycles and invalid carriages		12	10	10	12		...	...	...	...		...	...	...	...
3599	Other transport equipment n.e.c.		-	-	2	-		-	-	...	-		-	-	...	-
3610	Furniture		1153	1170	1094	1052		12335	12149	11714	11290		129	134	136	136
369	Manufacturing n.e.c.		644	641	586	563		2195	...	2058	2046		23	...	23	24
3691	Jewellery and related articles		201	197	176	176		477	466	411	401		5	...	4	4
3692	Musical instruments		28	29	32	26		46	...	44	46		-	...	-	1
3693	Sports goods		53	56	49	49		554	...	600	626		7	...	8	8
3694	Games and toys		41	44	39	35		582	604	543	486		6	6	6	6
3699	Other manufacturing n.e.c.		321	315	290	277		536	...	460	487		5	5	5	5
3710	Recycling of metal waste and scrap		32	31	32	39		732	777	528	879		12	14	10	17
3720	Recycling of non-metal waste and scrap		24	23	24	27		174	240	314	348		2	3	4	5
D	Total manufacturing		17767	17855	17041	16886		232664	228473	222502	221110		3075	3224	3318	3433

a/ ... refers to suppressed data due to confidentiality rules.
b/ Provisional data.

Slovenia

ISIC Revision 3		Output a/					Value added in factor values a/					Gross fixed capital formation a/	
		(millions of Euros)					(millions of Euros)					(millions of Euros)	
ISIC	Industry	Note	2003	2004	2005	2006b/	Note	2003	2004	2005	2006b/	Note	2005	2006b/
151	Processed meat,fish,fruit,vegetables,fats		...	...	...	609		...	...	...	111		...	...
1511	Processing/preserving of meat		410	407	451	464		98	88	85	76		30	31
1512	Processing/preserving of fish		...	...	...	16		...	...	...	4		...	...
1513	Processing/preserving of fruit & vegetables		189	170	93	101		57	47	23	26		4	6
1514	Vegetable and animal oils and fats		32	...	26	28		7	...	6	5		2	...
1520	Dairy products		248	247	235	228		14	22	22	19		24	8
153	Grain mill products; starches; animal feeds		92	126	111	88		25	28	24	24		10	...
1531	Grain mill products		...	...	...	...		...	...	...	...		...	...
1532	Starches and starch products		...	...	...	...		...	...	...	...		...	...
1533	Prepared animal feeds		20	57	52	55		6	9	10	13		4	1
154	Other food products		436	432	479	550		164	172	184	220		27	25
1541	Bakery products		228	231	227	294		100	102	103	124		...	...
1542	Sugar		...	...	...	...		...	...	...	...		...	...
1543	Cocoa, chocolate and sugar confectionery		43	...	49	49		15	...	14	15		5	4
1544	Macaroni, noodles & similar products		5	...	7	6		3	...	3	3		-	-
1549	Other food products n.e.c.		...	...	...	...		...	...	...	...		...	...
155	Beverages		270	237	237	254		92	79	93	96		20	19
1551	Distilling, rectifying & blending of spirits		...	...	...	...		...	...	...	...		...	...
1552	Wines		...	...	...	...		...	...	...	...		...	...
1553	Malt liquors and malt		163	...	149	160		57	...	65	73		11	13
1554	Soft drinks; mineral waters		57	...	41	45		22	...	15	15		4	3
1600	Tobacco products		...	...	...	-		...	...	...	-		...	-
171	Spinning, weaving and finishing of textiles		183	...	130	132		47	...	30	33		7	...
1711	Textile fibre preparation; textile weaving		121	160	124	126		33	41	29	32		7	6
1712	Finishing of textiles		62	...	6	6		14	...	1	1		-	...
172	Other textiles		427	...	436	427		129	...	132	133		22	10
1721	Made-up textile articles, except apparel		319	311	322	302		87	78	91	87		6	4
1722	Carpets and rugs		-	-	1	...		-	-	-	...		...	...
1723	Cordage, rope, twine and netting		12	...	13	...		4	...	4	...		...	...
1729	Other textiles n.e.c.		96	...	100	107		38	...	37	43		14	5
1730	Knitted and crocheted fabrics and articles		68	...	65	64		25	...	19	19		2	...
1810	Wearing apparel, except fur apparel		242	...	217	218		124	...	111	107		...	4
1820	Dressing & dyeing of fur; processing of fur		1	...	1	1		-	...	-	-		...	-
191	Tanning, dressing and processing of leather		213	...	262	248		44	...	52	41		4	7
1911	Tanning and dressing of leather		70	...	70	70		16	...	16	15		3	4
1912	Luggage, handbags, etc.; saddlery & harness		143	175	192	178		28	16	36	26		1	3
1920	Footwear		116	...	94	109		41	...	36	41		3	5
2010	Sawmilling and planing of wood		123	125	130	151		47	43	44	50		17	21
202	Products of wood, cork, straw, etc.		408	414	462	512		139	137	143	158		36	61
2021	Veneer sheets, plywood, particle board, etc.		116	117	115	124		36	31	31	35		13	48
2022	Builders' carpentry and joinery		217	225	221	246		74	76	74	83		12	7
2023	Wooden containers		16	15	21	24		6	6	7	9		3	2
2029	Other wood products; articles of cork/straw		59	57	105	118		23	24	31	31		8	4
210	Paper and paper products		581	610	620	632		147	156	148	144		34	51
2101	Pulp, paper and paperboard		350	381	378	380		78	86	80	75		11	32
2102	Corrugated paper and paperboard		124	...	120	123		36	...	34	34		7	9
2109	Other articles of paper and paperboard		106	...	123	129		33	...	35	36		17	11
221	Publishing		277	...	321	340		102	...	116	121		12	6
2211	Publishing of books and other publications		76	...	96	97		27	...	34	32		3	1
2212	Publishing of newspapers, journals, etc.		182	203	204	217		68	72	74	78		6	...
2213	Publishing of recorded media		7	9	10	10		2	3	4	4		2	-
2219	Other publishing		12	12	11	17		4	4	4	7		-	...

continued

Slovenia

ISIC Revision 3		Output a/					Value added in factor values a/					Gross fixed capital formation a/		
			(millions of Euros)					(millions of Euros)					(millions of Euros)	
ISIC	Industry	Note	2003	2004	2005	2006b/	Note	2003	2004	2005	2006b/	Note	2005	2006b/
222	Printing and related service activities		348	359	365	397		137	143	139	148		43	39
2221	Printing		262	...	...	...		101	...	...	...		...	...
2222	Service activities related to printing		86	...	...	...		36	...	...	...		...	...
2230	Reproduction of recorded media		1	...	1	1		-	...	-	1		-	-
2310	Coke oven products		-	-	-	-		-	-	-	-		-	-
2320	Refined petroleum products		...	6	6	7		...	1	1	2		1	3
2330	Processing of nuclear fuel		-	-	-	-		-	-	-	-		-	-
241	Basic chemicals		316	294	327	393		92	86	89	101		48	28
2411	Basic chemicals, except fertilizers		274	...	285	345		81	...	79	89		...	...
2412	Fertilizers and nitrogen compounds		-	-	...	...		-	-	...	...		-	-
2413	Plastics in primary forms; synthetic rubber		43	33	...	...		11	9	...	...		...	...
242	Other chemicals		...	...	...	...		...	...	...	...		...	...
2421	Pesticides and other agro-chemical products		...	23	...	...		...	11	...	...		...	2
2422	Paints, varnishes, printing ink and mastics		214	247	267	296		51	60	61	66		18	13
2423	Pharmaceuticals, medicinal chemicals, etc.		1018	1005	1011	1165		573	551	530	648		117	119
2424	Soap, cleaning & cosmetic preparations		144	...	158	169		42	...	44	47		8	...
2429	Other chemical products n.e.c.		182	216	214	226		53	63	59	59		14	17
2430	Man-made fibres		...	...	...	...		...	...	...	...		...	...
251	Rubber products		345	...	402	434		113	...	124	131		31	22
2511	Rubber tyres and tubes		279	...	...	...		86	...	...	...		...	...
2519	Other rubber products		67	82	84	87		28	38	31	34		7	5
2520	Plastic products		685	...	822	947		230	...	249	280		78	54
2610	Glass and glass products		133	141	138	146		53	52	48	59		8	9
269	Non-metallic mineral products n.e.c.		...	...	...	...		...	...	...	...		...	...
2691	Pottery, china and earthenware		...	...	...	...		...	...	...	...		...	...
2692	Refractory ceramic products		3	3	4	4		1	1	2	2		-	...
2693	Struct.non-refractory clay; ceramic products		...	...	...	...		...	...	...	...		...	...
2694	Cement, lime and plaster		98	...	102	120		51	...	48	60		14	17
2695	Articles of concrete, cement and plaster		128	144	163	198		42	49	51	61		9	11
2696	Cutting, shaping & finishing of stone		39	37	36	42		15	13	15	17		6	2
2699	Other non-metallic mineral products n.e.c.		173	193	206	246		62	64	69	79		13	11
2710	Basic iron and steel		...	...	610	710		...	...	142	135		...	...
2720	Basic precious and non-ferrous metals		234	...	278	372		54	...	69	69		...	...
273	Casting of metals		236	...	314	394		83	...	110	131		29	31
2731	Casting of iron and steel		112	136	160	190		39	45	50	59		14	16
2732	Casting of non-ferrous metals		124	...	153	206		43	...	61	72		14	15
281	Struct.metal products;tanks;steam generators		367	...	476	626		109	...	151	196		41	59
2811	Structural metal products		327	380	426	567		96	122	134	175		38	57
2812	Tanks, reservoirs and containers of metal		39	...	50	59		13	...	17	21		3	2
2813	Steam generators		1	...	-	-		-	...	-	-		-	-
289	Other metal products; metal working services		1454	1576	1650	1965		547	594	568	660		155	91
2891	Metal forging/pressing/stamping/roll-forming		320	346	380	471		71	77	81	94		22	16
2892	Treatment & coating of metals		290	310	304	346		132	137	134	154		33	9
2893	Cutlery, hand tools and general hardware		348	361	375	427		161	179	171	185		47	36
2899	Other fabricated metal products n.e.c.		496	559	591	721		183	201	182	227		53	30
291	General purpose machinery		414	460	518	590		144	162	168	191		43	32
2911	Engines & turbines (not for transport equipment)		29	...	38	40		10	...	12	16		4	...
2912	Pumps, compressors, taps and valves		52	...	68	76		20	...	26	33		5	...
2913	Bearings, gears, gearing & driving elements		42	48	58	79		17	18	21	27		10	6
2914	Ovens, furnaces and furnace burners		5	7	10	11		2	2	3	3		-	-
2915	Lifting and handling equipment		133	149	186	221		40	50	54	58		14	12
2919	Other general purpose machinery		153	162	158	162		56	56	53	55		12	7

292	Special purpose machinery	389	...	522	595	143	...	192	215	35	31
2921	Agricultural and forestry machinery	74	81	84	91	25	28	26	28	5	5
2922	Machine tools	120	...	168	201	43	...	59	67	10	4
2923	Machinery for metallurgy	10	...	17	21	4	...	8	9	2	2
2924	Machinery for mining & construction	32	72	77	87	12	32	33	36	6	6
2925	Food/beverage/tobacco processing machinery	42	46	39	51	17	19	16	21	2	3
2926	Machinery for textile, apparel and leather	7	...	15	16	3	...	6	7	1	-
2927	Weapons and ammunition	2	...	4	2	1	...	2	1	1	-
2929	Other special purpose machinery	103	116	117	126	38	44	42	47	7	11
2930	Domestic appliances n.e.c.	923	1010	1077	1134	258	285	293	316	63	52
3000	Office, accounting and computing machinery	66	79	77	73	22	26	22	22	4	1
3110	Electric motors, generators and transformers	333	360	352	442	132	133	116	139	34	30
3120	Electricity distribution & control apparatus	108	127	129	150	46	52	52	57	10	8
3130	Insulated wire and cable	13	15	4	3	5	5	2	1	-	...
3140	Accumulators, primary cells and batteries	58	69	74	83	19	17	17	24	6	4
3150	Lighting equipment and electric lamps	46	53	49	14	13	14	9	6	1	...
3190	Other electrical equipment n.e.c.	351	375	476	542	128	132	168	196	35	22
3210	Electronic valves, tubes, etc.	183	205	165	226	68	81	64	76	10	15
3220	TV/radio transmitters; line comm. apparatus	217	211	146	80	74	72	26	29	13	...
3230	TV and radio receivers and associated goods	22	27	28	34	7	10	9	11	1	...
331	Medical, measuring, testing appliances, etc.	311	336	350	337	130	133	130	120	24	12
3311	Medical, surgical and orthopaedic equipment	46	49	47	70	17	17	17	26	4	2
3312	Measuring/testing/navigating appliances,etc.	213	214	224	185	92	87	84	62	16	8
3313	Industrial process control equipment	52	73	79	82	21	29	29	32	4	2
3320	Optical instruments & photographic equipment	62	67	62	75	32	36	33	39	7	6
3330	Watches and clocks	1	1	1	1	-	-	-	-	-	-
3410	Motor vehicles	777	908	1178	1058	62	83	102	106	...	...
3420	Automobile bodies, trailers & semi-trailers	193	253	270	297	32	38	45	58	...	...
3430	Parts/accessories for automobiles	296	354	408	446	90	117	125	140	46	75
351	Building and repairing of ships and boats	45	54	58	63	11	16	16	20	10	4
3511	Building and repairing of ships	7	4	3	5	-	-	1	2	-	...
3512	Building/repairing of pleasure/sport. boats	38	50	55	59	11	16	16	18	10	...
3520	Railway/tramway locomotives & rolling stock	...	...	58	75	...	...	28	37	3	2
3530	Aircraft and spacecraft	...	...	...	5	...	...	...	2	...	...
359	Transport equipment n.e.c.	55	...	...	19	12	...	...	5	...	...
3591	Motorcycles	...	...	...	...	...	...	...	...	...	...
3592	Bicycles and invalid carriages	...	...	...	...	...	...	...	...	...	...
3599	Other transport equipment n.e.c.	-	-	...	-	-	-	...	-	...	-
3610	Furniture	551	580	562	570	199	205	190	203	38	27
369	Manufacturing n.e.c.	130	...	137	143	46	...	53	49	8	...
3691	Jewellery and related articles	23	...	18	19	9	...	8	9	-	1
3692	Musical instruments	1	...	2	2	1	...	1	1	1	...
3693	Sports goods	42	...	44	55	13	...	14	13	3	...
3694	Games and toys	37	42	45	34	13	16	21	14	2	1
3699	Other manufacturing n.e.c.	27	27	28	33	10	9	9	12	2	1
3710	Recycling of metal waste and scrap	83	135	88	171	26	38	20	42	5	11
3720	Recycling of non-metal waste and scrap	7	15	22	24	3	6	7	9	6	2
D	Total manufacturing	16776	18076	19025	20917	5516	5821	5801	6442	1530	1413

a/ ... refers to suppressed data due to confidentiality rules.
b/ Provisional data.

Slovenia

ISIC Revision 3			Index numbers of industrial production (2000=100)											
ISIC	Industry	Note	1995	1996	1997	1998	1999	2000	2001	2002	2003	2004	2005	2006
15	Food and beverages		94	97	91	93	94	100	102	101	102	91	90	90
16	Tobacco products		...	...	...	...	...	...	...	...	...	...	...	...
17	Textiles		93	98	90	96	92	100	89	87	78	68	62	58
18	Wearing apparel, fur		115	107	115	112	100	100	96	73	64	55	47	46
19	Leather, leather products and footwear		185	165	159	122	96	100	98	84	73	68	73	77
20	Wood products (excl. furniture)		137	138	100	103	98	100	92	94	91	95	101	104
21	Paper and paper products		99	97	96	97	96	100	99	107	101	103	106	106
22	Printing and publishing		177	169	135	102	98	100	94	97	101	98	102	101
23	Coke,refined petroleum products,nuclear fuel		...	...	...	...	...	...	...	...	...	...	...	...
24	Chemicals and chemical products		82	83	86	89	91	100	108	115	128	148	159	179
25	Rubber and plastics products		84	82	89	93	91	100	101	100	104	117	122	130
26	Non-metallic mineral products		81	88	94	100	104	100	100	101	102	85	79	84
27	Basic metals		96	96	83	85	89	100	105	108	115	106	109	131
28	Fabricated metal products		82	81	83	86	89	100	105	109	111	109	120	130
29	Machinery and equipment n.e.c.		105	99	88	95	95	100	116	129	121	139	141	150
30	Office, accounting and computing machinery		...	...	...	365	263	100	106	111	75	78	68	64
31	Electrical machinery and apparatus		93	108	80	83	87	100	110	114	115	178	181	209
32	Radio,television and communication equipment		...	...	...	68	74	100	105	110	132	128	134	165
33	Medical, precision and optical instruments		63	56	65	101	105	100	101	103	144	131	139	146
34	Motor vehicles, trailers, semi-trailers		82	77	71	92	91	100	104	109	114	154	189	174
35	Other transport equipment		...	...	...	78	87	100	90	93	98	145	162	193
36	Furniture; manufacturing n.e.c.		72	74	95	108	102	100	108	106	101	99	106	102
37	Recycling		...	...	...	81	89	100	111	112	123	152	136	176
D	Total manufacturing		89	90	90	94	93	100	103	105	107	112	116	123

South Africa

Supplier of information:
Statistics South Africa, Pretoria.

Basic source of data:
Quarterly employment statistics; periodic censuses.

Major deviations from ISIC (Revision 3):
None reported.

Reference period:
Calendar year.

Scope:
All enterprises.

Method of data collection:
Questionnaires.

Type of enumeration:
Sample survey.

Adjusted for non-response:
Yes.

Concepts and definitions of variables:
Wages and salaries includes employers' contributions paid to social security, pension and insurance schemes as well as the benefits received by employees under these schemes and severance and termination pay.

Related national publications:
Quarterly Employment Statistics, published by Statistics South Africa, Pretoria.

South Africa

ISIC Revision 3		Establishments					Number of employees					Wages and salaries paid to employees				
			(number)					(thousands)					(millions of South African Rand)			
ISIC	Industry	Note	2003	2004	2005	2006	Note	2003	2004	2005	2006	Note	2003	2004	2005	2006
151	Processed meat,fish,fruit,vegetables,fats		...	...	...	...		43.4	53.7	51.3	48.4		1935.6	2716.3	2370.4	...
1511	Processing/preserving of meat		...	...	...	...		...	...	...	...		...	...	...	...
1512	Processing/preserving of fish		...	...	...	...		...	...	...	...		...	...	...	...
1513	Processing/preserving of fruit & vegetables		...	...	...	...		...	...	...	...		...	...	...	...
1514	Vegetable and animal oils and fats		...	...	...	...		...	...	...	...		...	...	...	...
1520	Dairy products		...	...	...	...		18.6	18.7	17.2	16.5		1229.4	1406.4	1330.5	...
153	Grain mill products; starches; animal feeds		...	...	...	...		31.6	16.0	8.3	7.8		1424.2	699.6	377.2	...
1531	Grain mill products		...	...	...	...		...	...	...	...		...	...	...	...
1532	Starches and starch products		...	...	...	...		...	...	...	...		...	...	...	...
1533	Prepared animal feeds		...	...	...	...		...	...	...	...		...	...	...	...
154	Other food products		...	...	...	...		57.0	58.1	73.1	71.8		3376.9	3871.4	5265.6	...
1541	Bakery products		...	...	...	...		...	...	...	...		...	...	...	...
1542	Sugar		...	...	...	...		...	...	...	...		...	...	...	...
1543	Cocoa, chocolate and sugar confectionery		...	...	...	...		...	...	...	...		...	...	...	...
1544	Macaroni, noodles & similar products		...	...	...	...		...	...	...	...		...	...	...	...
1549	Other food products n.e.c.		...	...	...	...		...	...	...	...		...	...	...	...
155	Beverages		...	...	...	...		15.3	15.2	31.4	31.1		1170.2	1333.7	3770.9	...
1551	Distilling, rectifying & blending of spirits		...	...	...	...		...	...	...	...		...	...	...	...
1552	Wines		...	...	...	...		...	...	...	...		...	...	...	...
1553	Malt liquors and malt		...	...	...	...		...	...	...	...		...	...	...	...
1554	Soft drinks; mineral waters		...	...	...	...		...	...	...	...		...	...	...	...
1600	Tobacco products		...	...	...	...		2.9	3.5	2.2	0.8		282.1	291.4	278.6	...
171	Spinning, weaving and finishing of textiles		...	...	...	...		21.5	20.6	15.0	15.4		1019.8	932.5	899.6	...
1711	Textile fibre preparation; textile weaving		...	...	...	...		...	...	...	...		...	...	...	...
1712	Finishing of textiles		...	...	...	...		...	...	...	...		...	...	...	...
172	Other textiles		...	...	...	...		33.7	30.8	31.0	29.3		1567.2	1653.3	1642.9	...
1721	Made-up textile articles, except apparel		...	...	...	...		...	...	...	...		...	...	...	...
1722	Carpets and rugs		...	...	...	...		...	...	...	...		...	...	...	...
1723	Cordage, rope, twine and netting		...	...	...	...		...	...	...	...		...	...	...	...
1729	Other textiles n.e.c.		...	...	...	...		...	...	...	...		...	...	...	...
1730	Knitted and crocheted fabrics and articles		...	...	...	...		12.1	11.2	6.4	6.3		310.3	324.1	257.8	...
1810	Wearing apparel, except fur apparel		...	...	...	...		102.3a/	99.6a/	76.8	72.6		3097.3a/	3319.4a/	3100.8	...
1820	Dressing & dyeing of fur; processing of fur		...	...	...	...		...a/	...a/	0.3	0.3		...a/	...a/	8.2	...
191	Tanning, dressing and processing of leather		...	...	...	...		8.6	9.3	7.6	8.1		457.5	528.0	386.7	...
1911	Tanning and dressing of leather		...	...	...	...		...	...	...	...		...	...	...	...
1912	Luggage, handbags, etc.; saddlery & harness		...	...	...	...		...	...	...	...		...	...	...	...
1920	Footwear		...	...	...	...		15.9	14.0	11.3	10.6		553.3	555.7	514.6	...
2010	Sawmilling and planing of wood		...	...	...	...		18.1	17.5	18.3	18.4		362.3	375.8	469.6	...
202	Products of wood, cork, straw, etc.		...	...	...	...		29.0	30.8	32.3	32.8		1172.2	1395.3	1653.2	...
2021	Veneer sheets, plywood, particle board, etc.		...	...	...	...		...	...	...	...		...	...	...	...
2022	Builders' carpentry and joinery		...	...	...	...		...	...	...	...		...	...	...	...
2023	Wooden containers		...	...	...	...		...	...	...	...		...	...	...	...
2029	Other wood products; articles of cork/straw		...	...	...	...		...	...	...	...		...	...	...	...
210	Paper and paper products		...	...	...	...		48.7	61.1	30.7	37.6		5121.7	5752.4	3334.1	...
2101	Pulp, paper and paperboard		...	...	...	...		...	...	...	...		...	...	...	...
2102	Corrugated paper and paperboard		...	...	...	...		...	...	...	...		...	...	...	...
2109	Other articles of paper and paperboard		...	...	...	...		...	...	...	...		...	...	...	...
221	Publishing		...	...	...	...		23.3	26.1	23.8	22.3		2560.6	3026.0	2768.5	...
2211	Publishing of books and other publications		...	...	...	...		...	...	...	...		...	...	...	...
2212	Publishing of newspapers, journals, etc.		...	...	...	...		...	...	...	...		...	...	...	...
2213	Publishing of recorded media		...	...	...	...		...	...	...	...		...	...	...	...
2219	Other publishing		...	...	...	...		...	...	...	...		...	...	...	...

ISIC	Description												
222	Printing and related service activities	...	...	...	...	23.2	23.9	21.3	23.1	1841.3	1868.3	1730.9	...
2221	Printing	...	...	...	...	...	...	...	...	...	...	...	...
2222	Service activities related to printing	...	...	...	...	...	...	...	...	...	...	...	...
2230	Reproduction of recorded media	...	...	...	...	0.9	0.9	0.5	0.5	151.0	150.5	82.0	...
2310	Coke oven products	...	...	...	...	...b/	...b/	1.7	1.5	...b/	...b/	116.2	...
2320	Refined petroleum products	...	...	...	...	21.0b/	39.7b/	14.3c/	14.6c/	4745.4b/	6913.9b/	3330.9c/	...
2330	Processing of nuclear fuel	...	...	...	...	...b/	...b/	...c/	...c/	...b/	...b/	...c/	...
241	Basic chemicals	...	...	...	...	30.1	27.7	14.6	15.7	3858.0	3954.5	2128.7	...
2411	Basic chemicals, except fertilizers	...	...	...	...	...	...	...	...	...	...	...	...
2412	Fertilizers and nitrogen compounds	...	...	...	...	...	...	...	...	...	...	...	...
2413	Plastics in primary forms; synthetic rubber	...	...	...	...	...	...	...	...	...	...	...	...
242	Other chemicals	...	...	...	...	65.4	63.4	48.7	52.1	6816.4	7195.9	4795.8	...
2421	Pesticides and other agro-chemical products	...	...	...	...	...	...	...	...	...	...	...	...
2422	Paints, varnishes, printing ink and mastics	...	...	...	...	...	...	...	...	...	...	...	...
2423	Pharmaceuticals, medicinal chemicals, etc.	...	...	...	...	...	...	...	...	...	...	...	...
2424	Soap, cleaning & cosmetic preparations	...	...	...	...	...	...	...	...	...	...	...	...
2429	Other chemical products n.e.c.	...	...	...	...	...	...	...	...	...	...	...	...
2430	Man-made fibres	...	...	...	...	...	...	...	...	...	...	...	...
251	Rubber products	...	...	...	...	22.1	22.2	14.3	13.7	1921.5	2015.1	1637.2	...
2511	Rubber tyres and tubes	...	...	...	...	...	...	...	...	...	...	...	...
2519	Other rubber products	...	...	...	...	...	...	...	...	...	...	...	...
2520	Plastic products	...	...	...	...	45.1	44.3	38.5	39.2	2313.1	2476.3	2821.7	...
2610	Glass and glass products	...	...	...	...	5.0	5.6	5.9	6.3	385.2	434.3	467.3	...
269	Non-metallic mineral products n.e.c.	...	...	...	...	51.3	58.1	56.2	56.5	3030.4	3436.3	3168.3	...
2691	Pottery, china and earthenware	...	...	...	...	...	...	...	...	...	...	...	...
2692	Refractory ceramic products	...	...	...	...	...	...	...	...	...	...	...	...
2693	Struct.non-refractory clay; ceramic products	...	...	...	...	...	...	...	...	...	...	...	...
2694	Cement, lime and plaster	...	...	...	...	...	...	...	...	...	...	...	...
2695	Articles of concrete, cement and plaster	...	...	...	...	...	...	...	...	...	...	...	...
2696	Cutting, shaping & finishing of stone	...	...	...	...	...	...	...	...	...	...	...	...
2699	Other non-metallic mineral products n.e.c.	...	...	...	...	...	...	...	...	...	...	...	...
2710	Basic iron and steel	...	...	...	...	24.9	25.1	32.4	31.3	2440.0	2831.9	4838.0	...
2720	Basic precious and non-ferrous metals	...	...	...	...	13.5	13.3	19.4	22.2	1236.8	1318.9	1821.8	...
273	Casting of metals	...	...	...	...	37.1d/	37.1d/	4.7	4.3	2781.8d/	2969.8d/	385.7	...
2731	Casting of iron and steel	...	...	...	...	...	...	...	...	...	...	...	...
2732	Casting of non-ferrous metals	...	...	...	...	...	...	...	...	...	...	...	...
281	Struct.metal products;tanks;steam generators	...	...	...	...	...d/	...d/	32.1	34.8	...d/	...d/	2428.9	...
2811	Structural metal products	...	...	...	...	...	...	...	...	...	...	...	...
2812	Tanks, reservoirs and containers of metal	...	...	...	...	...	...	...	...	...	...	...	...
2813	Steam generators	...	...	...	...	...	...	...	...	...	...	...	...
289	Other metal products; metal working services	...	...	...	...	74.4	74.6	61.2	64.1	4892.1	5049.7	4545.0	...
2891	Metal forging/pressing/stamping/roll-forming	...	...	...	...	...	...	...	...	...	...	...	...
2892	Treatment & coating of metals	...	...	...	...	...	...	...	...	...	...	...	...
2893	Cutlery, hand tools and general hardware	...	...	...	...	...	...	...	...	...	...	...	...
2899	Other fabricated metal products n.e.c.	...	...	...	...	...	...	...	...	...	...	...	...
291	General purpose machinery	...	...	...	...	31.4	33.4	33.4	34.2	2663.0	3154.7	3135.4	...
2911	Engines & turbines (not for transport equipment)	...	...	...	...	...	...	...	...	...	...	...	...
2912	Pumps, compressors, taps and valves	...	...	...	...	...	...	...	...	...	...	...	...
2913	Bearings, gears, gearing & driving elements	...	...	...	...	...	...	...	...	...	...	...	...
2914	Ovens, furnaces and furnace burners	...	...	...	...	...	...	...	...	...	...	...	...
2915	Lifting and handling equipment	...	...	...	...	...	...	...	...	...	...	...	...
2919	Other general purpose machinery	...	...	...	...	...	...	...	...	...	...	...	...
292	Special purpose machinery	...	...	...	...	38.2	39.6	51.3	52.0	3458.9	3853.3	5240.0	...
2921	Agricultural and forestry machinery	...	...	...	...	...	...	...	...	...	...	...	...
2922	Machine tools	...	...	...	...	...	...	...	...	...	...	...	...
2923	Machinery for metallurgy	...	...	...	...	...	...	...	...	...	...	...	...
2924	Machinery for mining & construction	...	...	...	...	...	...	...	...	...	...	...	...
2925	Food/beverage/tobacco processing machinery	...	...	...	...	...	...	...	...	...	...	...	...
2926	Machinery for textile, apparel and leather	...	...	...	...	...	...	...	...	...	...	...	...
2927	Weapons and ammunition	...	...	...	...	...	...	...	...	...	...	...	...
2929	Other special purpose machinery	...	...	...	...	...	...	...	...	...	...	...	...

continued

ISIC Revision 3		Establishments					Number of employees					Wages and salaries paid to employees			
			(number)					(thousands)					(millions of South African Rand)		
ISIC	Industry	Note	2003	2004	2005	2006	Note	2003	2004	2005	2006	Note	2003	2004	2005	2006
2930	Domestic appliances n.e.c.		...	...	...	...		9.5	9.6	8.2	8.9		635.7	705.2	674.9	...
3000	Office, accounting and computing machinery		...	...	...	...		11.0	11.4	10.0	11.0		1518.5	1605.6	1292.1	...
3110	Electric motors, generators and transformers		...	...	...	...		...e/	...e/	9.8	11.5		650.6f/	717.5f/	965.0	...
3120	Electricity distribution & control apparatus		...	...	...	...		7.7e/	7.2e/	5.2	5.4		...f/	...f/	526.7	...
3130	Insulated wire and cable		...	...	...	...		...g/	...g/	6.4	5.7		...f/	...f/	692.9	...
3140	Accumulators, primary cells and batteries		...	...	...	...		...g/	...g/	3.6	4.3		...f/	...f/	345.3	...
3150	Lighting equipment and electric lamps		...	...	...	...		14.0g/	14.6g/	2.1	2.2		1068.7	1148.3	157.1	...
3190	Other electrical equipment n.e.c.		...	...	...	...		11.9	11.4	13.4	13.9		1011.0	1045.2	1123.4	...
3210	Electronic valves, tubes, etc.		...	...	...	...		...h/	...h/	1.1	1.1		...h/	...h/	100.2	...
3220	TV/radio transmitters; line comm. apparatus		...	...	...	...		...h/	...h/	3.1	3.5		...h/	...h/	313.0	...
3230	TV and radio receivers and associated goods		...	...	...	...		8.5h/	7.5h/	2.3	2.4		1193.5h/	1342.3h/	224.3	...
331	Medical, measuring, testing appliances, etc.		...	...	...	...		...i/	...i/	8.4	7.9		...i/	...i/	953.2	...
3311	Medical, surgical and orthopaedic equipment		...	...	...	...		...	...	...	...		...	...	...	...
3312	Measuring/testing/navigating appliances,etc.		...	...	...	...		...	...	...	...		...	...	...	...
3313	Industrial process control equipment		...	...	...	...		...	...	...	...		...	...	...	...
3320	Optical instruments & photographic equipment		...	...	...	...		15.4i/	17.2i/	1.6	1.6		1125.1i/	1269.3i/	147.7	...
3330	Watches and clocks		...	...	...	...		...i/	...i/	0.1	0.1		...i/	...i/	9.5	...
3410	Motor vehicles		...	...	...	...		23.4	23.1	46.0	48.1		1910.7	2158.9	5641.6	...
3420	Automobile bodies, trailers & semi-trailers		...	...	...	...		6.3	6.9	8.9	9.0		373.6	432.5	589.3	...
3430	Parts/accessories for automobiles		...	...	...	...		47.5	48.6	53.6	52.5		3429.3	3934.3	4801.4	...
351	Building and repairing of ships and boats		...	...	...	...		...j/	...j/	4.5	4.5		...j/	...j/	343.1	...
3511	Building and repairing of ships		...	...	...	...		...	...	...	...		...	...	...	...
3512	Building/repairing of pleasure/sport. boats		...	...	...	...		...	...	...	...		...	...	...	...
3520	Railway/tramway locomotives & rolling stock		...	...	...	...		...j/	...j/	1.0	1.0		...j/	...j/	103.5	...
3530	Aircraft and spacecraft		...	...	...	...		...j/	...j/	5.8	6.5		...j/	...j/	1122.9	...
359	Transport equipment n.e.c.		...	...	...	...		15.8j/	17.4j/	3.5	3.9		1252.3j/	1691.9j/	226.1	...
3591	Motorcycles		...	...	...	...		...	...	...	...		...	...	...	...
3592	Bicycles and invalid carriages		...	...	...	...		...	...	...	...		...	...	...	...
3599	Other transport equipment n.e.c.		...	...	...	...		...	...	...	...		...	...	...	...
3610	Furniture		...	...	...	...		40.5	33.2	37.7	36.9		1658.4	1884.2	1800.2	...
369	Manufacturing n.e.c.		...	...	...	...		31.6	32.9	44.7	47.0		2333.0	1766.6	2605.9	...
3691	Jewellery and related articles		...	...	...	...		...	...	...	...		...	...	...	...
3692	Musical instruments		...	...	...	...		...	...	...	...		...	...	...	...
3693	Sports goods		...	...	...	...		...	...	...	...		...	...	...	...
3694	Games and toys		...	...	...	...		...	...	...	...		...	...	...	...
3699	Other manufacturing n.e.c.		...	...	...	...		...	...	...	...		...	...	...	...
3710	Recycling of metal waste and scrap		...	...	...	...		28.5	29.1	13.4	11.0		1717.3	3114.4	1369.6	...
3720	Recycling of non-metal waste and scrap		...	...	...	...		...	...	...	...		...	...	...	...
D	Total manufacturing		...	...	...	...		1237.0	1265.4	1182.1	1196.0		88053.4	98621.2	97231.7	...

a/ 1810 includes 1820.
b/ 2320 includes 2310 and 2330.
c/ 2320 includes 2330.
d/ 273 includes 281.
e/ 3120 includes 3110.
f/ 3110 includes 3120, 3130 and 3140.
g/ 3150 includes 3130 and 3140.
h/ 3230 includes 3220 and 3210.
i/ 3320 includes 331 and 3330.
j/ 359 includes 351, 3520 and 3530.

South Africa

ISIC Revision 3		Output					Value added					Gross fixed capital formation		
		Note	(billions of South African Rand)				Note	(billions of South African Rand)				Note	(billions of South African Rand)	
ISIC	Industry		2003	2004	2005	2006		2003	2004	2005	2006		2005	2006
151	Processed meat,fish,fruit,vegetables,fats	a/	112.5	121.6	129.6	145.4	a/	22.1	24.3	26.1	30.3		...	...
1511	Processing/preserving of meat		...	...	...	...		...	...	...	...		...	...
1512	Processing/preserving of fish		...	...	...	...		...	...	...	...		...	...
1513	Processing/preserving of fruit & vegetables		...	...	...	...		...	...	...	...		...	...
1514	Vegetable and animal oils and fats		...	...	...	...		...	...	...	...		...	...
1520	Dairy products	a/	...	...	...	...	a/	...	...	...	...		...	...
153	Grain mill products; starches; animal feeds	a/	...	...	...	...	a/	...	...	...	...		...	...
1531	Grain mill products		...	...	...	...		...	...	...	...		...	...
1532	Starches and starch products		...	...	...	...		...	...	...	...		...	...
1533	Prepared animal feeds		...	...	...	...		...	...	...	...		...	...
154	Other food products	a/	...	...	...	...	a/	...	...	...	...		...	...
1541	Bakery products		...	...	...	...		...	...	...	...		...	...
1542	Sugar		...	...	...	...		...	...	...	...		...	...
1543	Cocoa, chocolate and sugar confectionery		...	...	...	...		...	...	...	...		...	...
1544	Macaroni, noodles & similar products		...	...	...	...		...	...	...	...		...	...
1549	Other food products n.e.c.		...	...	...	...		...	...	...	...		...	...
155	Beverages	b/	38.6	44.0	48.6	53.7	b/	13.3	15.2	16.5	20.0		...	...
1551	Distilling, rectifying & blending of spirits		...	...	...	...		...	...	...	...		...	...
1552	Wines		...	...	...	...		...	...	...	...		...	...
1553	Malt liquors and malt		...	...	...	...		...	...	...	...		...	...
1554	Soft drinks; mineral waters		...	...	...	...		...	...	...	...		...	...
1600	Tobacco products	b/	...	...	...	...	b/	...	...	...	...		...	...
171	Spinning, weaving and finishing of textiles	c/	19.2	18.4	17.0	17.4	c/	3.9	4.1	3.8	3.9		...	...
1711	Textile fibre preparation; textile weaving		...	...	...	...		...	...	...	...		...	...
1712	Finishing of textiles		...	...	...	...		...	...	...	...		...	...
172	Other textiles	c/	...	...	...	...	c/	...	...	...	...		...	...
1721	Made-up textile articles, except apparel		...	...	...	...		...	...	...	...		...	...
1722	Carpets and rugs		...	...	...	...		...	...	...	...		...	...
1723	Cordage, rope, twine and netting		...	...	...	...		...	...	...	...		...	...
1729	Other textiles n.e.c.		...	...	...	...		...	...	...	...		...	...
1730	Knitted and crocheted fabrics and articles	c/	...	...	...	...	c/	...	...	...	...		...	...
1810	Wearing apparel, except fur apparel	d/	16.2	15.5	14.4	14.7	d/	4.7	4.9	4.6	4.9		...	...
1820	Dressing & dyeing of fur; processing of fur	d/	...	...	...	...	d/	...	...	...	...		...	...
191	Tanning, dressing and processing of leather		4.5	4.5	4.3	4.4		0.7	0.8	0.7	0.8		...	...
1911	Tanning and dressing of leather		...	...	...	...		...	...	...	...		...	...
1912	Luggage, handbags, etc.; saddlery & harness		...	...	...	...		...	...	...	...		...	...
1920	Footwear		3.6	3.5	3.3	3.4		0.9	0.9	0.8	0.9		...	...
2010	Sawmilling and planing of wood	e/	18.5	19.4	20.7	22.0	e/	5.5	5.8	5.9	6.0		...	...
202	Products of wood, cork, straw, etc.	e/	...	...	...	...	e/	...	...	...	...		...	...
2021	Veneer sheets, plywood, particle board, etc.		...	...	...	...		...	...	...	...		...	...
2022	Builders' carpentry and joinery		...	...	...	...		...	...	...	...		...	...
2023	Wooden containers		...	...	...	...		...	...	...	...		...	...
2029	Other wood products; articles of cork/straw		...	...	...	...		...	...	...	...		...	...
210	Paper and paper products		40.0	39.6	43.1	45.7		9.5	9.2	9.7	10.0		...	...
2101	Pulp, paper and paperboard		...	...	...	...		...	...	...	...		...	...
2102	Corrugated paper and paperboard		...	...	...	...		...	...	...	...		...	...
2109	Other articles of paper and paperboard		...	...	...	...		...	...	...	...		...	...
221	Publishing	f/	18.0	19.1	21.4	23.1	f/	6.4	6.7	6.7	7.7		...	...
2211	Publishing of books and other publications		...	...	...	...		...	...	...	...		...	...
2212	Publishing of newspapers, journals, etc.		...	...	...	...		...	...	...	...		...	...
2213	Publishing of recorded media		...	...	...	...		...	...	...	...		...	...
2219	Other publishing		...	...	...	...		...	...	...	...		...	...

continued

South Africa

ISIC Revision 3		Output					Value added					Gross fixed capital formation		
			(billions of South African Rand)					(billions of South African Rand)					(billions of South African Rand)	
ISIC	Industry	Note	2003	2004	2005	2006	Note	2003	2004	2005	2006	Note	2005	2006
222	Printing and related service activities	f/	...	...	...	...	f/	...	...	...	...		...	...
2221	Printing		...	...	...	...		...	...	...	...		...	...
2222	Service activities related to printing		...	...	...	...		...	...	...	...		...	...
2230	Reproduction of recorded media	f/	...	...	...	...	f/	...	...	...	...		...	...
2310	Coke oven products	g/	64.8	70.5	75.0	84.8	g/	15.7	16.9	18.1	19.3		...	...
2320	Refined petroleum products	g/	...	...	...	...	g/	...	...	...	...		...	...
2330	Processing of nuclear fuel	h/	54.4	56.6	60.0	67.5	h/	12.4	12.3	13.5	14.7		...	...
241	Basic chemicals	h/	...	...	...	...	h/	...	...	...	...		...	...
2411	Basic chemicals, except fertilizers		...	...	...	...		...	...	...	...		...	...
2412	Fertilizers and nitrogen compounds		...	...	...	...		...	...	...	...		...	...
2413	Plastics in primary forms; synthetic rubber		...	...	...	...		...	...	...	...		...	...
242	Other chemicals		68.1	71.0	74.4	82.6		14.6	15.7	17.6	19.8		...	...
2421	Pesticides and other agro-chemical products		...	...	...	...		...	...	...	...		...	...
2422	Paints, varnishes, printing ink and mastics		...	...	...	...		...	...	...	...		...	...
2423	Pharmaceuticals, medicinal chemicals, etc.		...	...	...	...		...	...	...	...		...	...
2424	Soap, cleaning & cosmetic preparations		...	...	...	...		...	...	...	...		...	...
2429	Other chemical products n.e.c.		...	...	...	...		...	...	...	...		...	...
2430	Man-made fibres		...	...	...	...		...	...	...	...		...	...
251	Rubber products		8.9	9.3	10.0	10.7		2.3	2.4	2.6	2.6		...	...
2511	Rubber tyres and tubes		...	...	...	...		...	...	...	...		...	...
2519	Other rubber products		...	...	...	...		...	...	...	...		...	...
2520	Plastic products		23.5	24.3	25.5	27.9		7.8	8.3	8.7	9.7		...	...
2610	Glass and glass products		4.9	5.5	6.2	6.1		1.6	1.8	2.1	2.1		...	...
269	Non-metallic mineral products n.e.c.		19.1	21.6	24.7	26.3		6.3	7.1	7.8	8.5		...	...
2691	Pottery, china and earthenware		...	...	...	...		...	...	...	...		...	...
2692	Refractory ceramic products		...	...	...	...		...	...	...	...		...	...
2693	Struct.non-refractory clay; ceramic products		...	...	...	...		...	...	...	...		...	...
2694	Cement, lime and plaster		...	...	...	...		...	...	...	...		...	...
2695	Articles of concrete, cement and plaster		...	...	...	...		...	...	...	...		...	...
2696	Cutting, shaping & finishing of stone		...	...	...	...		...	...	...	...		...	...
2699	Other non-metallic mineral products n.e.c.		...	...	...	...		...	...	...	...		...	...
2710	Basic iron and steel	i/	68.2	74.6	78.5	92.5	i/	13.7	14.9	16.4	21.1		...	...
2720	Basic precious and non-ferrous metals		25.8	26.5	27.8	29.9		8.7	9.1	9.9	11.2		...	...
273	Casting of metals	i/	...	...	...	...	i/	...	...	...	...		...	...
2731	Casting of iron and steel		...	...	...	...		...	...	...	...		...	...
2732	Casting of non-ferrous metals		...	...	...	...		...	...	...	...		...	...
281	Struct.metal products;tanks;steam generators	j/	40.9	44.8	48.4	54.5	j/	11.9	13.3	14.6	16.6		...	...
2811	Structural metal products		...	...	...	...		...	...	...	...		...	...
2812	Tanks, reservoirs and containers of metal		...	...	...	...		...	...	...	...		...	...
2813	Steam generators		...	...	...	...		...	...	...	...		...	...
289	Other metal products; metal working services	j/	...	...	...	...	j/	...	...	...	...		...	...
2891	Metal forging/pressing/stamping/roll-forming		...	...	...	...		...	...	...	...		...	...
2892	Treatment & coating of metals		...	...	...	...		...	...	...	...		...	...
2893	Cutlery, hand tools and general hardware		...	...	...	...		...	...	...	...		...	...
2899	Other fabricated metal products n.e.c.		...	...	...	...		...	...	...	...		...	...
291	General purpose machinery	k/	38.5	41.5	43.7	46.4	k/	9.9	11.0	12.0	13.6		...	...
2911	Engines & turbines (not for transport equipment)		...	...	...	...		...	...	...	...		...	...
2912	Pumps, compressors, taps and valves		...	...	...	...		...	...	...	...		...	...
2913	Bearings, gears, gearing & driving elements		...	...	...	...		...	...	...	...		...	...
2914	Ovens, furnaces and furnace burners		...	...	...	...		...	...	...	...		...	...
2915	Lifting and handling equipment		...	...	...	...		...	...	...	...		...	...
2919	Other general purpose machinery		...	...	...	...		...	...	...	...		...	...

292	Special purpose machinery	k/	...	...	...	...	k/	...	...	...	...		...	...
2921	Agricultural and forestry machinery		...	...	...	...		...	...	...	...		...	...
2922	Machine tools		...	...	...	...		...	...	...	...		...	...
2923	Machinery for metallurgy		...	...	...	...		...	...	...	...		...	...
2924	Machinery for mining & construction		...	...	...	...		...	...	...	...		...	...
2925	Food/beverage/tobacco processing machinery		...	...	...	...		...	...	...	...		...	...
2926	Machinery for textile, apparel and leather		...	...	...	...		...	...	...	...		...	...
2927	Weapons and ammunition		...	...	...	...		...	...	...	...		...	...
2929	Other special purpose machinery		...	...	...	...		...	...	...	...		...	...
2930	Domestic appliances n.e.c.	k/	...	...	...	...	k/	...	...	...	...		...	...
3000	Office, accounting and computing machinery		...	...	...	...		...	...	...	...		...	...
3110	Electric motors, generators and transformers	m/	26.6	27.5	28.2	30.5	m/	6.5	6.4	6.9	7.3		...	...
3120	Electricity distribution & control apparatus	m/	...	...	...	...	m/	...	...	...	...		...	...
3130	Insulated wire and cable	m/	...	...	...	...	m/	...	...	...	...		...	...
3140	Accumulators, primary cells and batteries	m/	...	...	...	...	m/	...	...	...	...		...	...
3150	Lighting equipment and electric lamps	m/	...	...	...	...	m/	...	...	...	...		...	...
3190	Other electrical equipment n.e.c.	m/	...	...	...	...	m/	...	...	...	...		...	...
3210	Electronic valves, tubes, etc.	n/	6.8	7.3	7.6	9.2	n/	2.0	2.2	2.4	2.7		...	...
3220	TV/radio transmitters; line comm. apparatus	n/	...	...	...	...	n/	...	...	...	...		...	...
3230	TV and radio receivers and associated goods	n/	...	...	...	...	n/	...	...	...	...		...	...
331	Medical, measuring, testing appliances, etc.	p/	3.9	4.4	4.6	5.5	p/	1.1	1.2	1.3	1.7		...	...
3311	Medical, surgical and orthopaedic equipment		...	...	...	...		...	...	...	...		...	...
3312	Measuring/testing/navigating appliances,etc.		...	...	...	...		...	...	...	...		...	...
3313	Industrial process control equipment		...	...	...	...		...	...	...	...		...	...
3320	Optical instruments & photographic equipment	p/	...	...	...	...	p/	...	...	...	...		...	...
3330	Watches and clocks	p/	...	...	...	...	p/	...	...	...	...		...	...
3410	Motor vehicles	q/	116.6	127.1	139.3	151.9	q/	17.8	19.3	20.8	21.9		...	...
3420	Automobile bodies, trailers & semi-trailers	q/	...	...	...	...	q/	...	...	...	...		...	...
3430	Parts/accessories for automobiles	q/	...	...	...	...	q/	...	...	...	...		...	...
351	Building and repairing of ships and boats	r/	8.1	7.9	9.0	10.8	r/	1.7	1.7	1.9	2.0		...	...
3511	Building and repairing of ships		...	...	...	...		...	...	...	...		...	...
3512	Building/repairing of pleasure/sport. boats		...	...	...	...		...	...	...	...		...	...
3520	Railway/tramway locomotives & rolling stock	r/	...	...	...	...	r/	...	...	...	...		...	...
3530	Aircraft and spacecraft	r/	...	...	...	...	r/	...	...	...	...		...	...
359	Transport equipment n.e.c.	r/	...	...	...	...	r/	...	...	...	...		...	...
3591	Motorcycles		...	...	...	...		...	...	...	...		...	...
3592	Bicycles and invalid carriages		...	...	...	...		...	...	...	...		...	...
3599	Other transport equipment n.e.c.		...	...	...	...		...	...	...	...		...	...
3610	Furniture		10.9	12.3	12.1	12.9		2.7	3.1	3.1	3.6		...	...
369	Manufacturing n.e.c.	s/	41.1	42.9	44.6	46.0	s/	13.8	14.0	14.5	14.5		...	...
3691	Jewellery and related articles		...	...	...	...		...	...	...	...		...	...
3692	Musical instruments		...	...	...	...		...	...	...	...		...	...
3693	Sports goods		...	...	...	...		...	...	...	...		...	...
3694	Games and toys		...	...	...	...		...	...	...	...		...	...
3699	Other manufacturing n.e.c.		...	...	...	...		...	...	...	...		...	...
3710	Recycling of metal waste and scrap	s/	...	...	...	...	s/	...	...	...	...		...	...
3720	Recycling of non-metal waste and scrap	s/	...	...	...	...	s/	...	...	...	...		...	...
D	Total manufacturing		902.2	961.6	1022.8	1129.4		221.7	237.1	254.4	284.6		...	...

a/ 151 includes 1520, 153 and 154.
b/ 155 includes 1600.
c/ 171 includes 172 and 1730.
d/ 1810 includes 1820.
e/ 2010 includes 202.
f/ 221 includes 222 and 2230.
g/ 2310 includes 2320.
h/ 2330 includes 241.
i/ 2710 includes 273.
j/ 281 includes 289.

k/ 291 includes 292 and 2930.
m/ 3110 includes 3120, 3130, 3140, 3150 and 3190.
n/ 3210 includes 3220 and 3230.
p/ 331 includes 3320 and 3330.
q/ 3410 includes 3420 and 3430.
r/ 351 includes 3520, 3530 and 359.
s/ 369 includes 3710 and 3720.

South Africa

ISIC Revision 3			Index numbers of industrial production											
			(2000=100)											
ISIC	Industry	Note	1995	1996	1997	1998	1999	2000	2001	2002	2003	2004	2005	2006
15	Food and beverages		101	104	103	104	103	100	105	102	104	112	119	120
16	Tobacco products		...	...	...	...	...	...	...	...	...	...	...	...
17	Textiles		106	103	109	100	98	100	103	112	98	101	99	100
18	Wearing apparel, fur		119	108	111	106	107	100	96	102	99	104	101	103
19	Leather, leather products and footwear		...	...	...	...	...	...	...	...	...	...	...	...
20	Wood products (excl. furniture)		85	86	94	91	96	100	101	111	109	113	120	126
21	Paper and paper products		94	83	86	89	93	100	98	103	100	103	104	113
22	Printing and publishing		109	106	109	105	105	100	96	94	98	102	110	116
23	Coke,refined petroleum products,nuclear fuel		92	93	97	96	102	100	100	103	103	105	103	95
24	Chemicals and chemical products		...	...	...	...	...	...	...	...	...	...	...	...
25	Rubber and plastics products		...	...	...	...	...	...	...	...	...	...	...	...
26	Non-metallic mineral products		...	...	...	...	...	...	...	...	...	...	...	...
27	Basic metals		...	...	...	...	...	...	...	...	...	...	...	...
28	Fabricated metal products		97	99	107	103	95	100	107	120	115	117	113	124
29	Machinery and equipment n.e.c.	a/	96	101	107	103	97	100	110	121	117	119	123	127
30	Office, accounting and computing machinery	a/	...	...	...	...	...	...	...	...	...	...	...	...
31	Electrical machinery and apparatus		98	96	101	98	95	100	101	103	101	98	98	105
32	Radio,television and communication equipment		85	71	86	97	103	100	76	77	77	82	93	96
33	Medical, precision and optical instruments		116	112	112	98	96	100	111	121	132	141	134	123
34	Motor vehicles, trailers, semi-trailers		89	85	84	76	86	100	109	109	109	118	133	152
35	Other transport equipment		86	112	107	107	96	100	103	118	99	94	92	96
36	Furniture; manufacturing n.e.c.		...	...	...	...	...	...	...	...	...	...	...	...
37	Recycling		...	...	...	...	...	...	...	...	...	...	...	...
D	Total manufacturing		94	98	100	97	96	100	103	107	105	110	114	119

a/ 29 includes 30.

Spain

Supplier of information:
Instituto Nacional de Estadística (I.N.E.), Ministerio de Economía y Hacienda, Madrid. Industrial statistics for the OECD countries are compiled by the OECD secretariat, which supplies them to UNIDO.

Basic source of data:
Business industrial survey.

Major deviations from ISIC (Revision 3):
The original system used was the National Classification of Economic Activities (CNAE 1993). This classification is equivalent, at the 4-digit level to NACE (Revision 1) and aligns with ISIC (Revision 3).

Reference period:
Calendar year.

Scope:
All units employing one or more persons.

Method of data collection:
Establishments with 20 or more persons engaged are completely enumerated. Smaller establishments are sampled.

Type of enumeration:
Not reported.

Adjusted for non-response:
Not reported.

Concepts and definitions of variables:
Number of employees is calculated as the mean of the number on four dates during the survey (in March, June, October, December) and includes both paid and unpaid staff and office staff as well as operatives.
Output follows the Spanish definition of gross output, this being the aggregate total of: (a) the output of goods and services for sale, including payments received for services and work performed by others and the value of electricity sold; (b) goods resold in the same condition as received; (c) payments for services rendered (rental of machines, technical assistance, etc.); (d) products and work in progress; and (e) capital formation for own account (fixed assets produced for own use and the value of major repairs and improvements to own capital assets using own resources).
Value added is calculated as the difference between the value of gross output and intermediate consumption in purchaser prices. Intermediate consumption includes the cost of: (a) raw materials and consumables; (b) energy consumed for power and heating, steam, electricity, gas, etc.; (c) purchases of industrial and non-industrial services; and (d) goods purchased for resale in the same condition as received.
Gross fixed capital formation is calculated by subtracting the value of sales of own fixed assets from the value of purchases of new and used fixed assets, major repairs and improvements to fixed assets performed by others, construction of assets for own account and major repairs and improvements to fixed assets carried out using own materials and labour.

Related national publications:
Encuesta Industrial Anual de Empresas, published by the Instituto Nacional de Estadística (I.N.E.), Madrid.

Spain

ISIC Revision 3		Number of enterprises					Number of employees					Wages and salaries paid to employees			
			(number)					(thousands)					(millions of Euros)		
ISIC	Industry	Note	2002	2003	2004	2005	Note	2002	2003	2004	2005	Note	2002	2003	2004	2005
151	Processed meat,fish,fruit,vegetables,fats		7262	7448	7577	7755		135.7	141.0	144.7	153.6		2187.6	2389.7	2501.0	2763.0
1511	Processing/preserving of meat		4304	4342	4243	4298		70.8	73.9	76.2	82.2		1160.5	1276.5	1349.0	1521.0
1512	Processing/preserving of fish		683	690	727	745		22.2	22.8	22.3	22.0		288.6	319.4	322.0	335.0
1513	Processing/preserving of fruit & vegetables		634	879	1139	1281		30.7	31.4	34.1	35.6		468.3	516.6	567.0	612.0
1514	Vegetable and animal oils and fats		1641	1537	1468	1431		11.9	12.9	12.1	13.7		270.2	277.1	263.0	295.0
1520	Dairy products		1544	1495	1520	1502		23.9	24.3	25.5	26.0		536.3	561.3	607.0	645.0
153	Grain mill products; starches; animal feeds		1685	1585	1532	1600		20.8	20.5	21.4	20.7		438.3	454.4	497.0	491.0
1531	Grain mill products		770	680	685	699		5.5	5.6	6.0	6.0		106.2	113.6	128.0	128.0
1532	Starches and starch products		15	23	22	21		0.9	0.9	0.9	0.9		36.8	35.5	37.0	37.0
1533	Prepared animal feeds		900	882	825	880		14.4	14.1	14.5	13.7		295.3	305.3	331.0	325.0
154	Other food products		15612	14901	14724	13983		120.1	116.6	116.6	118.2		1973.4	2004.3	2076.0	2204.0
1541	Bakery products		12420	11955	11568	11028		78.4	75.6	74.5	75.7		1076.3	1087.5	1107.0	1181.0
1542	Sugar		61	76	51	55		2.5	2.6	2.3	2.2		63.4	67.0	67.0	68.0
1543	Cocoa, chocolate and sugar confectionery		1119	1000	1094	993		15.3	15.0	15.4	14.8		296.3	294.0	311.0	300.0
1544	Macaroni, noodles & similar products		119	94	118	82		1.2	1.0	1.0	1.1		23.2	23.1	22.0	26.0
1549	Other food products n.e.c.		1893	1776	1893	1825		22.6	22.5	23.4	24.3		514.2	532.8	569.0	629.0
155	Beverages		4741	4605	4444	4513		48.8	49.7	49.2	50.1		1268.8	1333.1	1395.0	1439.0
1551	Distilling, rectifying & blending of spirits		355	344	343	338		5.0	5.3	5.2	5.0		132.6	141.2	151.0	162.0
1552	Wines		...	...	...	...		...	...	...	...		...	...	...	...
1553	Malt liquors and malt		...	...	...	...		...	...	...	...		...	...	...	...
1554	Soft drinks; mineral waters		491	445	434	456		14.5	14.6	14.3	14.9		402.7	436.0	442.0	453.0
1600	Tobacco products		67	60	64	60		6.1	5.4	6.1	5.8		192.7	175.0	204.0	204.0
171	Spinning, weaving and finishing of textiles		2783	2743	2592	2364		45.6	44.7	36.5	34.6		781.7	825.1	700.0	699.0
1711	Textile fibre preparation; textile weaving		1676	1605	1543	1364		31.0	30.3	24.3	22.6		525.3	557.9	460.0	457.0
1712	Finishing of textiles		1107	1138	1049	1000		14.6	14.4	12.1	12.0		256.4	267.2	240.0	241.0
172	Other textiles		5056	4894	4850	4941		36.3	34.4	32.5	33.9		534.7	523.3	507.0	560.0
1721	Made-up textile articles, except apparel		3754	3597	3524	3610		22.5	21.3	20.3	21.3		306.4	297.1	288.0	319.0
1722	Carpets and rugs		214	150	239	112		1.9	1.7	2.0	1.5		35.0	31.7	35.0	28.0
1723	Cordage, rope, twine and netting		435	409	369	472		2.2	1.6	1.5	2.2		30.1	23.0	24.0	36.0
1729	Other textiles n.e.c.		653	738	718	747		9.7	9.8	8.6	9.0		163.2	171.5	160.0	177.0
1730	Knitted and crocheted fabrics and articles		2115	2029	1909	1677		21.5	19.7	17.8	16.2		304.0	300.6	273.0	256.0
1810	Wearing apparel, except fur apparel		15040	14278	13844	12773		103.7	100.3	90.4	84.7		1292.7	1282.4	1270.0	1248.0
1820	Dressing & dyeing of fur; processing of fur		457	446	437	387		2.4	2.3	2.0	2.0		36.7	35.4	31.0	33.0
191	Tanning, dressing and processing of leather		1812	1789	1737	1672		15.5	14.3	13.4	12.7		246.3	231.2	227.0	217.0
1911	Tanning and dressing of leather		377	375	375	341		7.2	6.7	5.9	5.4		135.4	129.8	126.0	113.0
1912	Luggage, handbags, etc.; saddlery & harness		1435	1414	1362	1331		8.3	7.6	7.5	7.2		110.9	101.4	102.0	104.0
1920	Footwear		4675	4418	4556	4389		45.5	43.9	41.3	38.6		525.5	527.2	527.0	495.0
2010	Sawmilling and planing of wood		1598	1562	1500	1427		11.6	11.1	11.5	10.5		158.8	156.2	171.0	166.0
202	Products of wood, cork, straw, etc.		16017	15390	15377	14435		84.1	83.9	81.9	81.7		1222.8	1269.8	1290.0	1371.0
2021	Veneer sheets, plywood, particle board, etc.		520	496	505	471		12.9	13.0	12.9	12.6		224.9	231.1	247.0	257.0
2022	Builders' carpentry and joinery		11316	10847	10938	10316		47.3	47.4	47.0	47.7		656.4	681.3	697.0	750.0
2023	Wooden containers		1057	1033	1047	1022		9.2	8.6	8.5	8.5		135.2	134.9	139.0	148.0
2029	Other wood products; articles of cork/straw		3124	3014	2887	2626		14.6	14.9	13.5	12.9		206.2	222.6	207.0	216.0
210	Paper and paper products		2034	2081	2149	2109		54.3	54.4	54.4	54.4		1254.8	1339.3	1385.0	1431.0
2101	Pulp, paper and paperboard		262	268	330	268		14.2	14.6	14.7	14.5		411.4	445.9	461.0	470.0
2102	Corrugated paper and paperboard		792	841	825	928		22.5	22.7	22.7	23.9		467.7	500.1	530.0	565.0
2109	Other articles of paper and paperboard		980	...	994	...		17.5	...	17.0	...		375.7	...	394.0	...
221	Publishing		6282	6689	7051	6966		46.2	47.5	47.4	51.8		1245.6	1342.5	1361.0	1616.0
2211	Publishing of books and other publications		3526	3332	3208	3629		17.5	15.9	15.5	17.4		420.5	413.1	402.0	492.0
2212	Publishing of newspapers, journals, etc.		1518	1793	1888	1743		26.1	27.9	28.5	30.3		769.8	857.2	884.0	1019.0
2213	Publishing of recorded media		45	67	129	93		0.4	0.7	0.5	0.5		17.5	20.1	15.0	17.0
2219	Other publishing		1193	1497	1826	1501		2.1	3.1	2.9	3.7		37.8	52.1	61.0	88.0

222	Printing and related service activities	14445	13958	15070	14593	84.9	82.9	84.3	85.1	1698.5	1676.5	1775.0	1849.0
2221	Printing	10548	10485	11799	11613	65.2	63.9	66.4	67.2	1323.5	1317.2	1421.0	1476.0
2222	Service activities related to printing	3897	3473	3271	2980	19.7	19.0	17.9	17.9	375.0	359.3	355.0	373.0
2230	Reproduction of recorded media	943	940	1039	1147	2.7	2.5	2.6	2.8	58.1	52.3	54.0	57.0
2310	Coke oven products	...	...	...	...	...	...	...	...	...	...	...	...
2320	Refined petroleum products	...	9	8	8	...	7.3	7.6	7.7	...	327.0	353.0	366.0
2330	Processing of nuclear fuel	...	...	...	...	...	...	...	...	...	...	...	...
241	Basic chemicals	974	973	994	1012	34.2	34.8	33.3	33.2	1107.2	1158.3	1169.0	1159.0
2411	Basic chemicals, except fertilizers	385	345	382	393	16.4	16.6	15.7	16.6	560.6	594.4	559.0	597.0
2412	Fertilizers and nitrogen compounds	229	214	229	172	4.3	4.2	4.2	3.6	101.5	95.5	103.0	99.0
2413	Plastics in primary forms; synthetic rubber	360	414	383	447	13.4	14.0	13.5	13.1	445.1	468.5	507.0	464.0
242	Other chemicals	3200	3145	3138	3158	94.6	98.0	97.2	99.2	2806.1	3028.3	3150.0	3323.0
2421	Pesticides and other agro-chemical products	90	100	96	97	1.9	2.0	2.1	2.1	57.0	62.9	70.0	66.0
2422	Paints, varnishes, printing ink and mastics	617	639	589	600	17.2	17.6	16.7	17.5	459.5	480.0	471.0	508.0
2423	Pharmaceuticals, medicinal chemicals, etc.	399	414	374	390	35.6	37.4	37.4	38.9	1252.9	1377.3	1467.0	1517.0
2424	Soap, cleaning & cosmetic preparations	1240	1164	1223	1249	25.3	26.7	26.3	26.1	628.0	689.0	711.0	751.0
2429	Other chemical products n.e.c.	854	828	856	822	14.7	14.4	14.6	14.6	408.8	419.0	432.0	482.0
2430	Man-made fibres	60	60	59	59	5.0	4.5	4.2	4.1	133.5	124.5	128.0	120.0
251	Rubber products	996	970	891	881	31.6	32.6	31.4	29.9	780.5	852.4	821.0	831.0
2511	Rubber tyres and tubes	194	227	186	204	15.6	16.9	16.3	15.7	459.2	523.6	496.0	510.0
2519	Other rubber products	802	743	705	677	16.0	15.7	15.1	14.1	321.3	328.7	325.0	321.0
2520	Plastic products	4952	4809	4878	4947	89.6	88.7	89.0	90.3	1780.1	1862.4	1944.0	2042.0
2610	Glass and glass products	1366	1410	1372	1422	25.3	25.1	24.6	26.0	532.4	565.2	567.0	613.0
269	Non-metallic mineral products n.e.c.	10448	10514	10332	10468	161.7	162.0	160.4	167.9	3246.0	3430.8	3534.0	3822.0
2691	Pottery, china and earthenware	...	1401	...	1259	...	12.6	...	11.9	...	243.2	...	249.0
2692	Refractory ceramic products	126	166	160	126	3.3	3.2	3.2	3.0	76.1	78.0	76.0	80.0
2693	Struct.non-refractory clay; ceramic products	1067	1043	1050	1041	39.4	39.2	38.5	38.9	821.4	845.7	871.0	904.0
2694	Cement, lime and plaster	194	205	182	180	10.0	10.5	10.2	10.3	363.9	405.0	411.0	406.0
2695	Articles of concrete, cement and plaster	2948	3033	3032	2999	52.1	53.4	55.3	59.3	972.1	1064.2	1120.0	1291.0
2696	Cutting, shaping & finishing of stone	4335	4342	4326	4554	35.4	35.9	34.2	37.6	566.4	597.1	609.0	688.0
2699	Other non-metallic mineral products n.e.c.	308	324	306	309	7.0	7.1	6.6	7.1	182.5	197.6	186.0	204.0
2710	Basic iron and steel	600	584	561	595	38.8	38.9	38.6	37.4	1097.7	1145.6	1171.0	1209.0
2720	Basic precious and non-ferrous metals	309	289	299	291	15.0	15.0	14.3	14.5	413.6	441.9	424.0	424.0
273	Casting of metals	738	699	681	669	21.8	22.0	21.3	20.5	497.1	527.2	534.0	523.0
2731	Casting of iron and steel	304	289	196	232	12.9	13.3	12.3	12.4	299.4	319.1	316.0	321.0
2732	Casting of non-ferrous metals	434	410	485	437	9.0	8.7	8.9	8.1	197.8	208.0	219.0	202.0
281	Struct.metal products;tanks;steam generators	21480	22342	23416	24006	145.5	153.7	158.3	168.6	2430.4	2716.9	2969.0	3136.0
2811	Structural metal products	20260	21174	22248	22799	126.0	134.2	139.2	149.3	2018.7	2295.3	2544.0	2686.0
2812	Tanks, reservoirs and containers of metal	1136	1089	1096	1143	17.2	17.2	16.9	17.3	355.1	366.1	372.0	401.0
2813	Steam generators	84	79	72	64	2.3	2.3	2.2	2.0	56.6	56.0	54.0	49.0
289	Other metal products; metal working services	18909	18362	18957	18890	174.1	177.5	173.5	175.1	3624.3	3809.4	3871.0	4103.0
2891	Metal forging/pressing/stamping/roll-forming	1920	1783	1846	1856	28.8	29.8	29.4	30.2	628.6	675.4	679.0	750.0
2892	Treatment & coating of metals	8987	8942	9005	8969	69.7	72.6	71.4	71.4	1393.0	1505.9	1545.0	1620.0
2893	Cutlery, hand tools and general hardware	3812	3500	3785	3886	28.9	28.3	26.8	27.5	643.1	641.3	623.0	650.0
2899	Other fabricated metal products n.e.c.	4190	4137	4321	4179	46.7	46.9	45.9	46.0	959.7	986.8	1024.0	1083.0
291	General purpose machinery	3318	3231	3256	3205	81.5	83.3	82.7	83.0	1900.2	2030.0	2093.0	2169.0
2911	Engines & turbines (not for transport equipment)	141	122	74	101	2.1	2.2	2.1	2.5	52.3	56.8	57.0	63.0
2912	Pumps, compressors, taps and valves	510	523	412	485	13.8	13.7	12.1	12.7	316.9	344.2	304.0	351.0
2913	Bearings, gears, gearing & driving elements	189	165	309	201	4.5	4.4	5.8	5.0	115.6	117.6	152.0	137.0
2914	Ovens, furnaces and furnace burners	171	46	90	75	2.0	1.0	1.2	1.0	43.6	21.5	32.0	25.0
2915	Lifting and handling equipment	636	960	918	849	26.7	30.8	30.3	31.1	653.5	757.6	782.0	807.0
2919	Other general purpose machinery	1671	1415	1453	1494	32.2	31.2	31.2	30.7	718.3	732.3	766.0	785.0
292	Special purpose machinery	10235	9814	10148	10666	80.5	80.3	81.3	82.7	1784.7	1875.8	1924.0	2010.0
2921	Agricultural and forestry machinery	1279	1114	1225	1192	9.8	10.0	10.5	10.2	177.8	189.2	203.0	213.0
2922	Machine tools	712	649	834	746	13.5	13.2	13.0	12.2	332.8	336.0	338.0	332.0
2923	Machinery for metallurgy	1521	629	852	1320	7.5	5.8	5.9	7.9	170.0	136.2	149.0	174.0
2924	Machinery for mining & construction	1182	1095	1021	966	8.1	7.8	7.5	9.0	170.8	173.4	181.0	215.0
2925	Food/beverage/tobacco processing machinery	1640	1740	1496	1521	11.6	12.5	12.3	10.5	251.1	270.9	294.0	256.0
2926	Machinery for textile, apparel and leather	667	921	734	649	4.5	5.0	3.6	3.4	94.1	110.1	93.0	79.0
2927	Weapons and ammunition	84	81	84	93	3.8	3.7	3.5	3.8	97.8	102.0	95.0	112.0
2929	Other special purpose machinery	3150	3585	3902	4179	21.9	22.2	25.0	25.7	490.3	558.0	573.0	629.0

continued

Spain

ISIC Revision 3		Number of enterprises					Number of employees					Wages and salaries paid to employees				
			(number)					(thousands)					(millions of Euros)			
ISIC	Industry	Note	2002	2003	2004	2005	Note	2002	2003	2004	2005	Note	2002	2003	2004	2005
2930	Domestic appliances n.e.c.		446	377	384	383		22.2	21.7	21.7	21.2		503.2	506.3	539.0	534.0
3000	Office, accounting and computing machinery		969	1071	1091	1131		5.6	5.2	4.2	4.6		124.7	116.8	92.0	111.0
3110	Electric motors, generators and transformers		1005	1172	1077	1018		18.5	20.0	20.2	19.3		494.2	580.6	574.0	558.0
3120	Electricity distribution & control apparatus		280	342	315	314		14.0	14.2	14.2	14.4		327.0	358.5	361.0	383.0
3130	Insulated wire and cable		233	229	255	210		7.9	7.5	7.8	7.4		196.1	190.0	205.0	207.0
3140	Accumulators, primary cells and batteries		38	23	30	19		3.3	3.1	3.0	3.1		77.7	80.2	81.0	84.0
3150	Lighting equipment and electric lamps		898	1001	881	856		12.3	13.2	10.9	11.3		235.3	249.3	237.0	246.0
3190	Other electrical equipment n.e.c.		603	591	557	552		32.8	28.2	27.1	27.1		742.8	703.2	677.0	717.0
3210	Electronic valves, tubes, etc.		618	604	577	586		11.5	11.2	10.5	10.0		241.6	261.3	250.0	224.0
3220	TV/radio transmitters; line comm. apparatus		263	265	247	261		10.5	7.1	6.7	7.4		383.9	190.9	165.0	191.0
3230	TV and radio receivers and associated goods		173	184	172	162		8.1	7.7	7.1	7.0		194.3	203.7	191.0	209.0
331	Medical, measuring, testing appliances, etc.		4978	4970	5120	5342		26.1	26.7	27.1	28.0		556.0	564.6	601.0	644.0
3311	Medical, surgical and orthopaedic equipment		4166	4165	4254	4448		13.0	13.7	13.6	14.6		215.0	241.6	253.0	281.0
3312	Measuring/testing/navigating appliances,etc.		669	671	721	754		9.5	9.4	9.8	9.9		244.9	225.4	245.0	263.0
3313	Industrial process control equipment		143	134	145	140		3.6	3.6	3.7	3.5		96.1	97.5	104.0	101.0
3320	Optical instruments & photographic equipment		96	109	97	98		2.6	2.7	2.5	2.7		56.8	61.7	58.0	66.0
3330	Watches and clocks		97	83	104	90		0.6	0.6	0.6	0.5		11.9	13.4	14.0	10.0
3410	Motor vehicles		180	200	186	156		76.8	77.2	75.0	74.5		2149.6	2126.7	2148.0	2228.0
3420	Automobile bodies, trailers & semi-trailers		892	893	890	939		13.9	13.9	14.1	14.3		249.4	260.0	280.0	300.0
3430	Parts/accessories for automobiles		1064	1009	1026	1042		70.8	72.2	72.7	70.2		1677.7	1768.6	1819.0	1827.0
351	Building and repairing of ships and boats		2040	2013	2131	2132		30.5	29.5	28.7	26.6		715.5	714.0	714.0	700.0
3511	Building and repairing of ships		1584	1548	1755	1608		27.5	26.4	26.3	24.1		667.9	663.3	672.0	649.0
3512	Building/repairing of pleasure/sport. boats		456	465	376	524		3.0	3.2	2.4	2.5		47.6	50.7	41.0	51.0
3520	Railway/tramway locomotives & rolling stock		58	64	66	79		8.5	8.9	9.3	8.9		239.9	263.5	281.0	287.0
3530	Aircraft and spacecraft		110	126	140	153		13.3	13.1	14.4	15.2		429.7	455.6	531.0	533.0
359	Transport equipment n.e.c.		208	209	201	196		4.4	4.3	4.1	4.1		92.6	96.0	96.0	99.0
3591	Motorcycles		93	94	95	83		3.0	2.9	2.8	2.8		66.5	68.9	68.0	73.0
3592	Bicycles and invalid carriages		42	44	42	47		0.9	0.8	0.8	0.9		18.0	18.5	19.0	19.0
3599	Other transport equipment n.e.c.		73	71	64	66		0.5	0.5	0.4	0.4		8.0	8.6	8.0	7.0
3610	Furniture		18906	19884	19707	19432		126.6	127.8	129.1	128.2		1917.5	2000.8	2107.0	2194.0
369	Manufacturing n.e.c.		6160	6132	6227	5905		28.8	29.4	29.4	28.2		487.5	524.6	541.0	531.0
3691	Jewellery and related articles		2901	2817	2876	2750		8.7	8.5	8.8	8.1		136.6	140.7	147.0	143.0
3692	Musical instruments		190	201	198	202		0.8	0.9	0.8	0.9		14.0	15.2	15.0	16.0
3693	Sports goods		192	188	185	172		1.9	1.9	1.9	2.1		34.8	36.9	38.0	40.0
3694	Games and toys		433	438	398	385		5.8	5.7	5.5	4.7		112.0	117.1	118.0	106.0
3699	Other manufacturing n.e.c.		2444	2488	2570	2396		11.5	12.4	12.4	12.5		190.2	214.7	223.0	226.0
3710	Recycling of metal waste and scrap		57	62	58	72		1.2	1.3	1.4	2.9		28.9	35.0	36.0	65.0
3720	Recycling of non-metal waste and scrap		146	144	150	165		2.1	2.1	2.3	2.9		39.7	42.0	45.0	58.0
D	Total manufacturing		222291	220284	222656	219868		2470.0	2472.9	2442.0	2464.5		50610.3	52774.6	54178.0	56637.0

Spain

ISIC Revision 3		Output					Value added in factor values					Gross fixed capital formation		
		Note	(millions of Euros)				Note	(millions of Euros)				Note	(millions of Euros)	
ISIC	Industry		2002	2003	2004	2005		2002	2003	2004	2005		2004	2005
151	Processed meat,fish,fruit,vegetables,fats		27981.7	29399.6	31929.0	35333.0		4875.7	5366.6	5546.0	6472.0		1373.0	1331.0
1511	Processing/preserving of meat		13387.2	14108.6	15173.0	16759.0		2478.0	2795.1	2808.0	3257.0		615.0	642.0
1512	Processing/preserving of fish		3274.5	3509.4	3543.0	3705.0		618.6	677.3	694.0	754.0		173.0	152.0
1513	Processing/preserving of fruit & vegetables		4882.8	5391.4	6051.0	6764.0		1005.7	1116.5	1238.0	1363.0		353.0	318.0
1514	Vegetable and animal oils and fats		6437.2	6390.2	7163.0	8105.0		773.5	777.7	806.0	1099.0		233.0	220.0
1520	Dairy products		7117.6	7265.6	7839.0	8632.0		1421.9	1483.3	1660.0	1672.0		330.0	423.0
153	Grain mill products; starches; animal feeds		8456.8	9145.8	10319.0	9342.0		1096.4	1249.8	1161.0	1225.0		323.0	320.0
1531	Grain mill products		1892.4	1981.1	2406.0	2226.0		250.1	289.6	294.0	276.0		78.0	58.0
1532	Starches and starch products		350.0	349.5	384.0	385.0		111.2	102.8	113.0	106.0		18.0	21.0
1533	Prepared animal feeds		6214.5	6815.3	7530.0	6731.0		735.1	857.4	754.0	843.0		228.0	241.0
154	Other food products		11992.8	12326.3	13147.0	13650.0		4063.5	4223.9	4347.0	4694.0		675.0	740.0
1541	Bakery products		5029.2	4972.0	5330.0	5597.0		2012.6	1980.9	2144.0	2325.0		321.0	311.0
1542	Sugar		981.8	939.8	1021.0	897.0		299.7	350.8	281.0	292.0		63.0	58.0
1543	Cocoa, chocolate and sugar confectionery		2035.6	2022.3	2202.0	2123.0		529.2	542.2	566.0	576.0		104.0	116.0
1544	Macaroni, noodles & similar products		199.2	195.7	203.0	220.0		54.0	54.8	58.0	68.0		18.0	19.0
1549	Other food products n.e.c.		3746.9	4196.6	4391.0	4814.0		1168.1	1295.3	1298.0	1432.0		170.0	236.0
155	Beverages		13585.4	13804.1	15260.0	15810.0		3963.2	4029.5	4245.0	4379.0		1217.0	1233.0
1551	Distilling, rectifying & blending of spirits		1320.5	1471.7	1625.0	1727.0		424.7	409.8	436.0	453.0		69.0	67.0
1552	Wines		...	...	...	...		...	...	...	...		...	...
1553	Malt liquors and malt		...	...	...	...		...	...	...	...		...	...
1554	Soft drinks; mineral waters		4351.6	4799.8	5232.0	5644.0		1062.5	1194.7	1218.0	1263.0		359.0	290.0
1600	Tobacco products		1414.7	1301.4	1372.0	1224.0		517.3	537.7	595.0	580.0		46.0	26.0
171	Spinning, weaving and finishing of textiles		4464.9	4592.9	4016.0	3906.0		1398.8	1448.9	1226.0	1115.0		171.0	134.0
1711	Textile fibre preparation; textile weaving		3400.2	3522.8	3006.0	2969.0		953.4	999.9	821.0	743.0		129.0	93.0
1712	Finishing of textiles		1064.7	1070.1	1010.0	937.0		445.4	448.9	404.0	372.0		43.0	40.0
172	Other textiles		3161.8	3034.0	3061.0	3356.0		975.2	927.5	897.0	992.0		118.0	120.0
1721	Made-up textile articles, except apparel		1904.6	1748.5	1722.0	1852.0		559.6	515.9	506.0	552.0		48.0	36.0
1722	Carpets and rugs		211.0	213.1	238.0	175.0		61.3	61.1	70.0	55.0		10.0	8.0
1723	Cordage, rope, twine and netting		213.1	156.4	185.0	289.0		63.3	51.3	48.0	71.0		4.0	11.0
1729	Other textiles n.e.c.		833.2	916.0	917.0	1041.0		291.0	299.2	273.0	314.0		56.0	65.0
1730	Knitted and crocheted fabrics and articles		1716.6	1634.5	1626.0	1578.0		550.9	529.6	537.0	450.0		70.0	42.0
1810	Wearing apparel, except fur apparel		7223.1	7229.1	6949.0	6814.0		2344.5	2396.2	2298.0	1970.0		167.0	135.0
1820	Dressing & dyeing of fur; processing of fur		274.3	245.9	179.0	186.0		72.9	76.6	52.0	59.0		4.0	4.0
191	Tanning, dressing and processing of leather		1621.2	1398.7	1210.0	1212.0		450.1	375.8	360.0	369.0		25.0	31.0
1911	Tanning and dressing of leather		1069.8	875.4	698.0	645.0		246.8	195.0	171.0	169.0		15.0	20.0
1912	Luggage, handbags, etc.; saddlery & harness		551.4	523.3	512.0	568.0		203.3	180.8	189.0	200.0		10.0	11.0
1920	Footwear		3818.6	3725.8	3663.0	3435.0		904.1	941.2	887.0	849.0		66.0	47.0
2010	Sawmilling and planing of wood		1134.3	1152.1	1260.0	1179.0		321.4	296.3	330.0	340.0		63.0	45.0
202	Products of wood, cork, straw, etc.		8160.6	8366.7	8387.0	8845.0		2408.3	2464.5	2521.0	2643.0		369.0	407.0
2021	Veneer sheets, plywood, particle board, etc.		2089.5	2112.6	2192.0	2386.0		514.0	469.5	535.0	555.0		158.0	129.0
2022	Builders' carpentry and joinery		3828.2	3889.2	3939.0	4180.0		1294.3	1326.2	1345.0	1442.0		137.0	197.0
2023	Wooden containers		940.5	975.3	988.0	1014.0		243.8	242.7	254.0	264.0		33.0	33.0
2029	Other wood products; articles of cork/straw		1302.5	1389.7	1268.0	1266.0		356.2	426.1	388.0	382.0		42.0	48.0
210	Paper and paper products		10843.7	10806.2	10834.0	11170.0		3237.5	3168.5	3206.0	3261.0		711.0	694.0
2101	Pulp, paper and paperboard		3948.3	3985.6	4012.0	4175.0		1202.8	1147.9	1175.0	1169.0		340.0	231.0
2102	Corrugated paper and paperboard		3685.6	3819.5	3876.0	4119.0		1077.1	1059.1	1113.0	1156.0		219.0	312.0
2109	Other articles of paper and paperboard		3209.7	...	2946.0	...		957.6	...	918.0	...		152.0	...
221	Publishing		7340.7	7598.2	8068.0	9378.0		2712.1	2991.3	2930.0	3730.0		145.0	141.0
2211	Publishing of books and other publications		2926.5	2969.2	2986.0	3375.0		1014.6	1129.6	924.0	1236.0		28.0	43.0
2212	Publishing of newspapers, journals, etc.		3908.2	4298.7	4566.0	5332.0		1567.0	1750.6	1880.0	2255.0		111.0	79.0
2213	Publishing of recorded media		254.4	131.0	126.0	165.0		41.6	32.9	23.0	32.0		-	1.0
2219	Other publishing		251.6	199.9	390.0	506.0		89.0	78.1	104.0	206.0		5.0	18.0

continued

Spain

ISIC Revision 3		Output					Value added in factor values					Gross fixed capital formation		
			(millions of Euros)					(millions of Euros)					(millions of Euros)	
ISIC	Industry	Note	2002	2003	2004	2005	Note	2002	2003	2004	2005	Note	2004	2005
222	Printing and related service activities		8230.2	8034.8	8447.0	8550.0		3248.1	3327.2	3471.0	3520.0		436.0	448.0
2221	Printing		6712.2	6665.1	6991.0	7059.0		2569.7	2671.8	2854.0	2870.0		372.0	346.0
2222	Service activities related to printing		1518.0	1369.7	1456.0	1491.0		678.3	655.5	617.0	650.0		65.0	102.0
2230	Reproduction of recorded media		401.5	435.0	429.0	376.0		127.4	131.3	142.0	131.0		33.0	30.0
2310	Coke oven products		...	...	...	...		...	...	...	...		...	...
2320	Refined petroleum products		...	17986.0	21799.0	30121.0		...	3841.0	5014.0	6975.0		746.0	497.0
2330	Processing of nuclear fuel		...	...	...	...		...	...	...	...		...	...
241	Basic chemicals		12156.3	12623.8	13504.0	15213.0		3204.4	3069.8	3192.0	3516.0		742.0	805.0
2411	Basic chemicals, except fertilizers		5392.2	5600.4	5753.0	6905.0		1774.5	1654.7	1566.0	1881.0		330.0	404.0
2412	Fertilizers and nitrogen compounds		807.4	848.4	949.0	979.0		175.5	181.0	225.0	262.0		164.0	42.0
2413	Plastics in primary forms; synthetic rubber		5956.6	6174.9	6803.0	7328.0		1254.4	1234.1	1401.0	1374.0		248.0	359.0
242	Other chemicals		21323.1	22114.0	23406.0	24412.0		6379.2	6570.5	6831.0	7042.0		1005.0	916.0
2421	Pesticides and other agro-chemical products		509.8	557.5	616.0	571.0		171.3	186.4	203.0	135.0		20.0	11.0
2422	Paints, varnishes, printing ink and mastics		3292.0	3265.2	3236.0	3394.0		985.9	979.8	1003.0	982.0		122.0	127.0
2423	Pharmaceuticals, medicinal chemicals, etc.		9305.0	10003.9	10391.0	10429.0		2848.7	3025.3	3038.0	3234.0		511.0	468.0
2424	Soap, cleaning & cosmetic preparations		5176.5	5318.3	5580.0	6014.0		1420.1	1477.4	1584.0	1676.0		235.0	192.0
2429	Other chemical products n.e.c.		3039.8	2969.1	3583.0	4003.0		953.2	901.5	1004.0	1015.0		117.0	119.0
2430	Man-made fibres		906.7	856.5	840.0	795.0		242.4	194.5	231.0	239.0		47.0	50.0
251	Rubber products		4023.4	4215.6	4294.0	4575.0		1595.5	1597.9	1720.0	1621.0		214.0	215.0
2511	Rubber tyres and tubes		2327.2	2555.4	2594.0	2882.0		1012.9	1045.7	1143.0	1089.0		145.0	150.0
2519	Other rubber products		1696.2	1660.2	1700.0	1693.0		582.6	552.2	577.0	531.0		69.0	66.0
2520	Plastic products		11967.4	12277.9	12817.0	14392.0		3763.3	3854.5	3943.0	4174.0		771.0	705.0
2610	Glass and glass products		3160.2	3255.5	3291.0	3525.0		1299.0	1260.1	1337.0	1381.0		232.0	232.0
269	Non-metallic mineral products n.e.c.		23357.3	23804.6	24974.0	28188.0		8174.2	8351.4	8779.0	9799.0		1835.0	1726.0
2691	Pottery, china and earthenware		...	1003.8	...	1080.0		...	510.2	...	510.0		...	53.0
2692	Refractory ceramic products		510.2	434.2	442.0	465.0		160.2	153.3	155.0	155.0		22.0	31.0
2693	Struct.non-refractory clay; ceramic products		4728.1	4578.8	4873.0	5170.0		1931.6	1857.0	1978.0	2044.0		419.0	424.0
2694	Cement, lime and plaster		3412.1	3509.9	3768.0	4171.0		1653.8	1673.2	1730.0	1872.0		409.0	285.0
2695	Articles of concrete, cement and plaster		8639.4	9029.7	9979.0	11886.0		2315.3	2511.9	2673.0	3366.0		587.0	625.0
2696	Cutting, shaping & finishing of stone		3240.5	3388.7	3351.0	3786.0		1140.5	1176.7	1270.0	1388.0		262.0	205.0
2699	Other non-metallic mineral products n.e.c.		1732.8	1859.5	1449.0	1631.0		448.0	469.0	449.0	464.0		74.0	103.0
2710	Basic iron and steel		11288.5	11846.6	15907.0	15975.0		2638.7	2563.0	3611.0	3380.0		662.0	482.0
2720	Basic precious and non-ferrous metals		5933.7	5575.5	5819.0	6987.0		1069.5	915.5	966.0	1202.0		174.0	224.0
273	Casting of metals		2614.9	2794.0	3165.0	3295.0		921.7	968.9	1054.0	1050.0		213.0	184.0
2731	Casting of iron and steel		1576.4	1736.8	2020.0	2187.0		568.6	601.8	660.0	684.0		142.0	110.0
2732	Casting of non-ferrous metals		1038.6	1057.1	1144.0	1108.0		353.1	367.1	394.0	366.0		71.0	74.0
281	Struct.metal products;tanks;steam generators		12915.0	13535.1	15644.0	17382.0		4525.5	4980.9	5276.0	5803.0		608.0	768.0
2811	Structural metal products		11233.7	11879.7	13833.0	15441.0		3843.0	4280.3	4582.0	5089.0		542.0	698.0
2812	Tanks, reservoirs and containers of metal		1451.6	1426.8	1587.0	1719.0		592.6	614.5	612.0	636.0		59.0	59.0
2813	Steam generators		229.7	228.7	224.0	222.0		89.9	86.1	81.0	79.0		8.0	11.0
289	Other metal products; metal working services		18126.5	18878.2	19985.0	21844.0		6987.9	7195.4	7382.0	7872.0		989.0	1160.0
2891	Metal forging/pressing/stamping/roll-forming		3865.9	4185.1	4373.0	5098.0		1286.5	1361.5	1398.0	1490.0		249.0	291.0
2892	Treatment & coating of metals		5553.6	5978.1	6127.0	6860.0		2500.1	2659.9	2699.0	2856.0		361.0	373.0
2893	Cutlery, hand tools and general hardware		2807.2	2769.0	2731.0	2910.0		1211.2	1189.6	1167.0	1242.0		127.0	107.0
2899	Other fabricated metal products n.e.c.		5899.8	5946.1	6754.0	6976.0		1990.1	1984.4	2118.0	2284.0		252.0	389.0
291	General purpose machinery		10205.6	10524.9	11555.0	11638.0		3656.6	3765.0	4076.0	4046.0		328.0	308.0
2911	Engines & turbines (not for transport equipment)		392.6	485.4	681.0	599.0		104.3	116.5	127.0	147.0		19.0	27.0
2912	Pumps, compressors, taps and valves		1702.0	1782.5	1696.0	1798.0		596.0	611.3	615.0	631.0		67.0	57.0
2913	Bearings, gears, gearing & driving elements		573.7	563.7	690.0	677.0		236.6	228.7	279.0	241.0		33.0	41.0
2914	Ovens, furnaces and furnace burners		228.0	83.8	101.0	108.0		81.8	34.4	47.0	32.0		1.0	2.0
2915	Lifting and handling equipment		3506.6	3856.7	4388.0	4291.0		1340.6	1468.8	1620.0	1611.0		78.0	85.0
2919	Other general purpose machinery		3802.8	3752.9	3999.0	4166.0		1297.4	1305.3	1389.0	1384.0		131.0	96.0

292	Special purpose machinery	9119.1	8930.6	9484.0	9672.0	3293.2	3133.1	3266.0	3568.0	322.0	336.0
2921	Agricultural and forestry machinery	1065.2	1033.9	1094.0	1196.0	343.0	345.6	366.0	374.0	39.0	52.0
2922	Machine tools	1624.0	1600.0	1582.0	1583.0	551.2	526.8	533.0	525.0	44.0	40.0
2923	Machinery for metallurgy	744.7	655.2	670.0	830.0	294.0	207.0	258.0	329.0	17.0	39.0
2924	Machinery for mining & construction	1197.8	976.5	1086.0	1321.0	351.4	344.0	337.0	469.0	44.0	45.0
2925	Food/beverage/tobacco processing machinery	1238.8	1417.9	1584.0	1282.0	452.1	489.4	463.0	495.0	45.0	44.0
2926	Machinery for textile, apparel and leather	490.2	474.3	417.0	350.0	184.2	168.5	134.0	128.0	6.0	6.0
2927	Weapons and ammunition	613.4	600.5	622.0	626.0	191.7	149.5	193.0	182.0	37.0	26.0
2929	Other special purpose machinery	2145.6	2172.3	2430.0	2484.0	925.5	902.3	984.0	1067.0	88.0	84.0
2930	Domestic appliances n.e.c.	3357.5	3527.1	3930.0	3927.0	1002.5	1013.9	1164.0	1219.0	135.0	140.0
3000	Office, accounting and computing machinery	962.3	872.2	732.0	902.0	188.6	176.7	139.0	232.0	9.0	14.0
3110	Electric motors, generators and transformers	4216.9	4602.8	5577.0	6099.0	1004.6	1138.1	1192.0	937.0	102.0	114.0
3120	Electricity distribution & control apparatus	1810.8	1845.7	1938.0	2110.0	717.2	765.8	786.0	837.0	47.0	59.0
3130	Insulated wire and cable	1444.4	1390.1	1851.0	2161.0	369.0	337.2	409.0	432.0	60.0	78.0
3140	Accumulators, primary cells and batteries	557.1	545.0	555.0	590.0	157.5	175.0	172.0	171.0	19.0	16.0
3150	Lighting equipment and electric lamps	1322.3	1420.8	1305.0	1352.0	415.2	454.8	439.0	418.0	44.0	70.0
3190	Other electrical equipment n.e.c.	4107.1	4221.9	4352.0	4534.0	1411.5	1427.2	1480.0	1476.0	170.0	149.0
3210	Electronic valves, tubes, etc.	1215.0	1204.1	1217.0	1149.0	368.1	362.1	394.0	381.0	84.0	96.0
3220	TV/radio transmitters; line comm. apparatus	1610.1	1098.3	1026.0	1111.0	449.5	385.5	290.0	330.0	25.0	29.0
3230	TV and radio receivers and associated goods	2557.9	2318.6	2064.0	2185.0	385.3	348.2	322.0	355.0	35.0	56.0
331	Medical, measuring, testing appliances, etc.	2893.3	2807.2	2915.0	3088.0	1059.0	1117.2	1138.0	1192.0	104.0	116.0
3311	Medical, surgical and orthopaedic equipment	1069.5	1121.8	1169.0	1263.0	462.4	540.0	545.0	571.0	54.0	61.0
3312	Measuring/testing/navigating appliances,etc.	1293.8	1244.2	1249.0	1352.0	438.0	432.2	435.0	459.0	43.0	47.0
3313	Industrial process control equipment	530.1	441.2	497.0	474.0	158.6	145.0	158.0	163.0	7.0	8.0
3320	Optical instruments & photographic equipment	294.1	321.6	315.0	364.0	110.1	117.6	121.0	147.0	6.0	13.0
3330	Watches and clocks	80.2	72.9	90.0	58.0	22.7	27.4	38.0	24.0	1.0	1.0
3410	Motor vehicles	30754.1	32964.2	34234.0	33900.0	4218.3	4803.6	4828.0	4567.0	1346.0	1053.0
3420	Automobile bodies, trailers & semi-trailers	1837.4	1937.9	2103.0	2307.0	482.5	517.4	564.0	555.0	42.0	42.0
3430	Parts/accessories for automobiles	12004.8	12987.5	14066.0	13856.0	3249.1	3546.7	3718.0	3571.0	801.0	575.0
351	Building and repairing of ships and boats	3651.9	3633.7	3015.0	3580.0	1025.5	1009.0	852.0	988.0	73.0	66.0
3511	Building and repairing of ships	3389.7	3345.9	2766.0	3260.0	930.1	919.2	772.0	868.0	64.0	57.0
3512	Building/repairing of pleasure/sport. boats	262.2	287.7	249.0	320.0	95.5	89.8	81.0	120.0	9.0	9.0
3520	Railway/tramway locomotives & rolling stock	1234.8	1559.1	1683.0	1953.0	431.3	569.5	579.0	619.0	22.0	44.0
3530	Aircraft and spacecraft	2356.2	2527.9	2617.0	2943.0	846.9	977.5	896.0	943.0	269.0	264.0
359	Transport equipment n.e.c.	1011.5	1051.0	1022.0	1136.0	275.0	238.0	248.0	262.0	25.0	29.0
3591	Motorcycles	824.5	862.5	830.0	937.0	225.9	184.5	195.0	201.0	22.0	23.0
3592	Bicycles and invalid carriages	119.8	118.0	127.0	143.0	33.9	33.8	35.0	47.0	2.0	4.0
3599	Other transport equipment n.e.c.	67.3	71.1	66.0	56.0	15.1	19.7	18.0	14.0	2.0	2.0
3610	Furniture	10007.5	10253.1	11509.0	11760.0	3404.1	3411.0	3745.0	3863.0	440.0	474.0
369	Manufacturing n.e.c.	2776.5	2839.4	2961.0	2986.0	940.1	992.0	1050.0	987.0	215.0	123.0
3691	Jewellery and related articles	774.0	762.0	838.0	797.0	271.0	251.1	268.0	240.0	31.0	42.0
3692	Musical instruments	49.2	55.4	55.0	55.0	24.5	26.5	25.0	26.0	1.0	1.0
3693	Sports goods	193.6	191.2	205.0	244.0	62.5	59.1	69.0	76.0	10.0	11.0
3694	Games and toys	791.1	762.2	799.0	670.0	241.0	259.9	260.0	208.0	117.0	32.0
3699	Other manufacturing n.e.c.	968.6	1068.6	1065.0	1219.0	341.2	395.4	429.0	438.0	55.0	38.0
3710	Recycling of metal waste and scrap	369.4	450.1	614.0	852.0	74.3	89.7	107.0	156.0	24.0	43.0
3720	Recycling of non-metal waste and scrap	291.4	290.1	297.0	358.0	91.6	83.9	92.0	147.0	14.0	27.0
D	Total manufacturing	386628.0	397815.0	426887.0	457602.0	109038.0	112298.0	117954.0	125049.0	19354.0	18671.0

Spain

ISIC Revision 3			Index numbers of industrial production											
			(2000=100)											
ISIC	Industry	Note	1995	1996	1997	1998	1999	2000	2001	2002	2003	2004	2005	2006
15	Food and beverages		92	89	97	101	101	100	102	106	108	111	113	113
16	Tobacco products		100	100	96	105	99	100	83	88	83	70	68	58
17	Textiles		109	103	109	110	101	100	98	96	89	84	74	71
18	Wearing apparel, fur		107	103	105	108	103	100	95	74	71	69	62	63
19	Leather, leather products and footwear		87	82	86	88	102	100	97	93	83	72	62	58
20	Wood products (excl. furniture)		88	81	86	90	100	100	86	86	86	88	86	87
21	Paper and paper products		82	82	88	94	97	100	98	104	108	111	110	113
22	Printing and publishing		84	83	88	92	99	100	98	108	109	113	118	118
23	Coke,refined petroleum products,nuclear fuel		101	95	99	102	100	100	97	101	111	111	113	113
24	Chemicals and chemical products		88	88	94	98	101	100	101	104	108	107	107	111
25	Rubber and plastics products		71	73	78	86	95	100	99	107	109	111	109	112
26	Non-metallic mineral products		82	80	85	92	96	100	101	100	102	103	105	108
27	Basic metals		80	78	83	87	88	100	96	103	104	110	108	114
28	Fabricated metal products		86	88	91	97	99	100	95	96	98	98	103	107
29	Machinery and equipment n.e.c.		80	81	87	93	95	100	101	94	93	96	96	108
30	Office, accounting and computing machinery		104	115	106	118	110	100	67	41	27	21	21	14
31	Electrical machinery and apparatus		73	74	83	92	96	100	100	103	108	114	114	134
32	Radio,television and communication equipment		97	95	96	98	84	100	84	72	64	64	56	57
33	Medical, precision and optical instruments		86	84	91	94	93	100	92	74	78	83	80	91
34	Motor vehicles, trailers, semi-trailers		69	72	79	89	91	100	96	94	97	99	93	98
35	Other transport equipment		68	68	94	99	102	100	99	96	97	98	98	101
36	Furniture; manufacturing n.e.c.		85	83	86	91	98	100	103	96	94	92	90	102
37	Recycling		...	...	...	...	...	...	...	...	...	...	...	...
D	Total manufacturing		84	83	89	95	97	100	98	98	100	101	101	105

Sri Lanka

Supplier of information:
Department of Census & Statistics, Colombo

Basic source of data:
Annual survey of industries; sample survey.

Major deviations from ISIC (Revision 3):
None reported.

Reference period:
Calendar year.

Scope:
Establishments with five or more persons engaged.

Method of data collection:
Direct interview in the field.

Type of enumeration:
Sample survey.

Adjusted for non-response:
Yes.

Concepts and definitions of variables:
Output excludes value of goods shipped in the same condition as received less the amount paid for these goods; net change between the beginning and end of the year in the value of work in process and stocks of goods to be shipped in the same condition as received; revenue from non-industrial activities.
Value added excludes cost of non-industrial activities.
Gross fixed capital formation includes land, other construction and land improvements. It excludes intellectual property products such as products of R&D, computer software, databases, etc.

Related national publications:
Annual Survey of Industries. Published by the Department of Census & Statistics, Colombo.

Sri Lanka

ISIC Revision 3		Number of establishments					Number of employees					Wages and salaries paid to employees				
			(number)					(number)					(millions of Sri Lanka Rupees)			
ISIC	Industry	Note	2003	2004	2005	2006	Note	2003	2004	2005	2006	Note	2003	2004	2005	2006
151	Processed meat,fish,fruit,vegetables,fats		...	...	...	900		...	...	...	36862		...	...	...	3615
1511	Processing/preserving of meat		...	...	...	23		...	...	...	93		...	...	...	8
1512	Processing/preserving of fish		...	...	...	307		...	...	...	16932		...	...	...	1788
1513	Processing/preserving of fruit & vegetables		...	...	...	94		...	...	...	1816		...	...	...	89
1514	Vegetable and animal oils and fats		...	...	...	476		...	...	...	18021		...	...	...	1729
1520	Dairy products		...	...	...	170		...	...	...	12706		...	...	...	1437
153	Grain mill products; starches; animal feeds		...	...	...	963		...	...	...	32894		...	...	...	3121
1531	Grain mill products		...	...	...	961		...	...	...	32629		...	...	...	3068
1532	Starches and starch products		...	...	...	-		...	...	...	-		...	...	...	-
1533	Prepared animal feeds		...	...	...	2		...	...	...	265		...	...	...	53
154	Other food products		...	...	...	2730		...	...	...	207015		...	...	...	15840
1541	Bakery products		...	...	...	682		...	...	...	13626		...	...	...	1132
1542	Sugar		...	...	...	2		...	...	...	1127		...	...	...	151
1543	Cocoa, chocolate and sugar confectionery		...	...	...	187		...	...	...	10641		...	...	...	1303
1544	Macaroni, noodles & similar products		...	...	...	151		...	...	...	5097		...	...	...	315
1549	Other food products n.e.c.		...	...	...	1708		...	...	...	176524		...	...	...	12939
155	Beverages		...	...	...	279		...	...	...	9347		...	...	...	1063
1551	Distilling, rectifying & blending of spirits		...	...	...	74		...	...	...	4916		...	...	...	459
1552	Wines		...	...	...	-		...	...	...	-		...	...	...	-
1553	Malt liquors and malt		...	...	...	-		...	...	...	-		...	...	...	-
1554	Soft drinks; mineral waters		...	...	...	205		...	...	...	4431		...	...	...	604
1600	Tobacco products		...	...	...	244		...	...	...	7787		...	...	...	2595
171	Spinning, weaving and finishing of textiles		...	...	...	1892		...	...	...	32778		...	...	...	2050
1711	Textile fibre preparation; textile weaving		...	...	...	1815		...	...	...	29677		...	...	...	1677
1712	Finishing of textiles		...	...	...	77		...	...	...	3101		...	...	...	373
172	Other textiles		...	...	...	557		...	...	...	28316		...	...	...	2588
1721	Made-up textile articles, except apparel		...	...	...	159		...	...	...	3959		...	...	...	134
1722	Carpets and rugs		...	...	...	63		...	...	...	3424		...	...	...	183
1723	Cordage, rope, twine and netting		...	...	...	149		...	...	...	1877		...	...	...	203
1729	Other textiles n.e.c.		...	...	...	186		...	...	...	19056		...	...	...	2068
1730	Knitted and crocheted fabrics and articles		...	...	...	121		...	...	...	36564		...	...	...	4393
1810	Wearing apparel, except fur apparel		...	...	...	2245		...	...	...	482345		...	...	...	53978
1820	Dressing & dyeing of fur; processing of fur		...	...	...	-		...	...	...	-		...	...	...	-
191	Tanning, dressing and processing of leather		...	...	...	66		...	...	...	2298		...	...	...	220
1911	Tanning and dressing of leather		...	...	...	-		...	...	...	-		...	...	...	-
1912	Luggage, handbags, etc.; saddlery & harness		...	...	...	66		...	...	...	2298		...	...	...	220
1920	Footwear		...	...	...	305		...	...	...	13312		...	...	...	1444
2010	Sawmilling and planing of wood		...	...	...	1052		...	...	...	16884		...	...	...	1924
202	Products of wood, cork, straw, etc.		...	...	...	630		...	...	...	17012		...	...	...	1325
2021	Veneer sheets, plywood, particle board, etc.		...	...	...	70		...	...	...	4540		...	...	...	152
2022	Builders' carpentry and joinery		...	...	...	157		...	...	...	1519		...	...	...	330
2023	Wooden containers		...	...	...	114		...	...	...	5848		...	...	...	663
2029	Other wood products; articles of cork/straw		...	...	...	289		...	...	...	5105		...	...	...	180
210	Paper and paper products		...	...	...	148		...	...	...	21227		...	...	...	3788
2101	Pulp, paper and paperboard		...	...	...	16		...	...	...	886		...	...	...	77
2102	Corrugated paper and paperboard		...	...	...	27		...	...	...	3588		...	...	...	629
2109	Other articles of paper and paperboard		...	...	...	105		...	...	...	16753		...	...	...	3081
221	Publishing		...	...	...	51		...	...	...	597		...	...	...	63
2211	Publishing of books and other publications		...	...	...	51		...	...	...	597		...	...	...	63
2212	Publishing of newspapers, journals, etc.		...	...	...	-		...	...	...	-		...	...	...	-
2213	Publishing of recorded media		...	...	...	-		...	...	...	-		...	...	...	-
2219	Other publishing		...	...	...	-		...	...	...	-		...	...	...	-

222	Printing and related service activities	...	...	...	756	...	...	...	37425	...	...	...	5190
2221	Printing	...	...	...	676	...	...	...	33158	...	...	...	4817
2222	Service activities related to printing	...	...	...	80	...	...	...	4267	...	...	...	372
2230	Reproduction of recorded media	...	...	...	-	...	...	...	-	...	...	...	-
2310	Coke oven products	...	...	...	-	...	...	...	-	...	...	...	-
2320	Refined petroleum products	...	...	...	3	...	...	...	2638	...	...	...	1225
2330	Processing of nuclear fuel	...	...	...	-	...	...	...	-	...	...	...	-
241	Basic chemicals	...	...	...	275	...	...	...	9334	...	...	...	3423
2411	Basic chemicals, except fertilizers	...	...	...	34	...	...	...	451	...	...	...	29
2412	Fertilizers and nitrogen compounds	...	...	...	241	...	...	...	8883	...	...	...	3377
2413	Plastics in primary forms; synthetic rubber	...	...	...	...	...	...	...	...	...	...	...	18
242	Other chemicals	...	...	...	582	...	...	...	51510	...	...	...	11538
2421	Pesticides and other agro-chemical products	...	...	...	-	...	...	...	-	...	...	...	-
2422	Paints, varnishes, printing ink and mastics	...	...	...	30	...	...	...	608	...	...	...	62
2423	Pharmaceuticals, medicinal chemicals, etc.	...	...	...	228	...	...	...	11654	...	...	...	1565
2424	Soap, cleaning & cosmetic preparations	...	...	...	162	...	...	...	37054	...	...	...	9787
2429	Other chemical products n.e.c.	...	...	...	162	...	...	...	2194	...	...	...	124
2430	Man-made fibres	...	...	...	-	...	...	...	-	...	...	...	-
251	Rubber products	...	...	...	481	...	...	...	28744	...	...	...	3050
2511	Rubber tyres and tubes	...	...	...	35	...	...	...	7748	...	...	...	1318
2519	Other rubber products	...	...	...	446	...	...	...	20996	...	...	...	1732
2520	Plastic products	...	...	...	351	...	...	...	29573	...	...	...	4256
2610	Glass and glass products	...	...	...	-	...	...	...	-	...	...	...	-
269	Non-metallic mineral products n.e.c.	...	...	...	3107	...	...	...	86412	...	...	...	11362
2691	Pottery, china and earthenware	...	...	...	200	...	...	...	19006	...	...	...	1514
2692	Refractory ceramic products	...	...	...	-	...	...	...	-	...	...	...	-
2693	Struct.non-refractory clay; ceramic products	...	...	...	1248	...	...	...	31362	...	...	...	4857
2694	Cement, lime and plaster	...	...	...	106	...	...	...	2059	...	...	...	281
2695	Articles of concrete, cement and plaster	...	...	...	647	...	...	...	15783	...	...	...	2261
2696	Cutting, shaping & finishing of stone	...	...	...	891	...	...	...	18070	...	...	...	2444
2699	Other non-metallic mineral products n.e.c.	...	...	...	15	...	...	...	132	...	...	...	6
2710	Basic iron and steel	...	...	...	46	...	...	...	3856	...	...	...	672
2720	Basic precious and non-ferrous metals	...	...	...	64	...	...	...	7067	...	...	...	1407
273	Casting of metals	...	...	...	264	...	...	...	24985	...	...	...	9861
2731	Casting of iron and steel	...	...	...	112	...	...	...	1496	...	...	...	158
2732	Casting of non-ferrous metals	...	...	...	152	...	...	...	23489	...	...	...	9703
281	Struct.metal products;tanks;steam generators	...	...	...	146	...	...	...	1649	...	...	...	124
2811	Structural metal products	...	...	...	146	...	...	...	1649	...	...	...	124
2812	Tanks, reservoirs and containers of metal	...	...	...	-	...	...	...	-	...	...	...	-
2813	Steam generators	...	...	...	-	...	...	...	-	...	...	...	-
289	Other metal products; metal working services	...	...	...	534	...	...	...	16900	...	...	...	1672
2891	Metal forging/pressing/stamping/roll-forming	...	...	...	-	...	...	...	-	...	...	...	-
2892	Treatment & coating of metals	...	...	...	215	...	...	...	3294	...	...	...	235
2893	Cutlery, hand tools and general hardware	...	...	...	18	...	...	...	1625	...	...	...	144
2899	Other fabricated metal products n.e.c.	...	...	...	301	...	...	...	11981	...	...	...	1293
291	General purpose machinery	...	...	...	13	...	...	...	377	...	...	...	25
2911	Engines & turbines (not for transport equipment)	...	...	...	-	...	...	...	-	...	...	...	-
2912	Pumps, compressors, taps and valves	...	...	...	-	...	...	...	-	...	...	...	-
2913	Bearings, gears, gearing & driving elements	...	...	...	-	...	...	...	-	...	...	...	-
2914	Ovens, furnaces and furnace burners	...	...	...	-	...	...	...	-	...	...	...	-
2915	Lifting and handling equipment	...	...	...	-	...	...	...	-	...	...	...	-
2919	Other general purpose machinery	...	...	...	13	...	...	...	377	...	...	...	25
292	Special purpose machinery	...	...	...	18	...	...	...	755	...	...	...	48
2921	Agricultural and forestry machinery	...	...	...	14	...	...	...	191	...	...	...	17
2922	Machine tools	...	...	...	-	...	...	...	-	...	...	...	-
2923	Machinery for metallurgy	...	...	...	-	...	...	...	-	...	...	...	-
2924	Machinery for mining & construction	...	...	...	-	...	...	...	-	...	...	...	-
2925	Food/beverage/tobacco processing machinery	...	...	...	4	...	...	...	564	...	...	...	31
2926	Machinery for textile, apparel and leather	...	...	...	-	...	...	...	-	...	...	...	-
2927	Weapons and ammunition	...	...	...	-	...	...	...	-	...	...	...	-
2929	Other special purpose machinery	...	...	...	-	...	...	...	-	...	...	...	-

continued

ISIC	Industry	Note	Number of establishments (number) 2003	2004	2005	2006	Note	Number of employees (number) 2003	2004	2005	2006	Note	Wages and salaries paid to employees (millions of Sri Lanka Rupees) 2003	2004	2005	2006
2930	Domestic appliances n.e.c.		...	...	...	14		...	...	...	512		...	...	...	61
3000	Office, accounting and computing machinery		...	...	...	2		...	...	...	3777		...	...	...	339
3110	Electric motors, generators and transformers		...	...	...	8		...	...	...	1854		...	...	...	200
3120	Electricity distribution & control apparatus		...	...	...	-		...	...	...	-		...	...	...	-
3130	Insulated wire and cable		...	...	...	-		...	...	...	-		...	...	...	-
3140	Accumulators, primary cells and batteries		...	...	...	-		...	...	...	-		...	...	...	-
3150	Lighting equipment and electric lamps		...	...	...	-		...	...	...	-		...	...	...	-
3190	Other electrical equipment n.e.c.		...	...	...	42		...	...	...	17304		...	...	...	4155
3210	Electronic valves, tubes, etc.		...	...	...	7		...	...	...	1194		...	...	...	106
3220	TV/radio transmitters; line comm. apparatus		...	...	...	-		...	...	...	-		...	...	...	-
3230	TV and radio receivers and associated goods		...	...	...	5		...	...	...	379		...	...	...	41
331	Medical, measuring, testing appliances, etc.		...	...	...	3		...	...	...	105		...	...	...	16
3311	Medical, surgical and orthopaedic equipment		...	...	...	3		...	...	...	105		...	...	...	16
3312	Measuring/testing/navigating appliances,etc.		...	...	...	-		...	...	...	-		...	...	...	-
3313	Industrial process control equipment		...	...	...	-		...	...	...	-		...	...	...	-
3320	Optical instruments & photographic equipment		...	...	...	38		...	...	...	5085		...	...	...	245
3330	Watches and clocks		...	...	...	-		...	...	...	-		...	...	...	-
3410	Motor vehicles		...	...	...	-		...	...	...	-		...	...	...	-
3420	Automobile bodies, trailers & semi-trailers		...	...	...	14		...	...	...	703		...	...	...	112
3430	Parts/accessories for automobiles		...	...	...	17		...	...	...	1355		...	...	...	251
351	Building and repairing of ships and boats		...	...	...	67		...	...	...	605		...	...	...	101
3511	Building and repairing of ships		...	...	...	67		...	...	...	605		...	...	...	101
3512	Building/repairing of pleasure/sport. boats		...	...	...	-		...	...	...	-		...	...	...	-
3520	Railway/tramway locomotives & rolling stock		...	...	...	-		...	...	...	-		...	...	...	-
3530	Aircraft and spacecraft		...	...	...	-		...	...	...	-		...	...	...	-
359	Transport equipment n.e.c.		...	...	...	19		...	...	...	187		...	...	...	14
3591	Motorcycles		...	...	...	4		...	...	...	14		...	...	...	1
3592	Bicycles and invalid carriages		...	...	...	15		...	...	...	173		...	...	...	13
3599	Other transport equipment n.e.c.		...	...	...	-		...	...	...	-		...	...	...	-
3610	Furniture		...	...	...	664		...	...	...	16667		...	...	...	1318
369	Manufacturing n.e.c.		...	...	...	1020		...	...	...	57803		...	...	...	5306
3691	Jewellery and related articles		...	...	...	455		...	...	...	28362		...	...	...	2709
3692	Musical instruments		...	...	...	-		...	...	...	-		...	...	...	-
3693	Sports goods		...	...	...	55		...	...	...	9350		...	...	...	1068
3694	Games and toys		...	...	...	92		...	...	...	7195		...	...	...	646
3699	Other manufacturing n.e.c.		...	...	...	418		...	...	...	12896		...	...	...	883
3710	Recycling of metal waste and scrap		...	...	...	-		...	...	...	-		...	...	...	-
3720	Recycling of non-metal waste and scrap		...	...	...	16		...	...	...	747		...	...	...	99
D	Total manufacturing		...	...	...	20929		...	...	...	1367446		...	...	...	165660

ISIC Revision 3		Output in producers' prices (millions of Sri Lanka Rupees)					Value added in producers' prices (millions of Sri Lanka Rupees)					Gross fixed capital formation (millions of Sri Lanka Rupees)		
ISIC	Industry	Note	2003	2004	2005	2006	Note	2003	2004	2005	2006	Note	2005	2006
151	Processed meat,fish,fruit,vegetables,fats		...	...	...	209091		...	...	...	64556		...	847
1511	Processing/preserving of meat		...	...	...	18		...	...	...	10		...	...
1512	Processing/preserving of fish		...	...	...	109293		...	...	...	40893		...	471
1513	Processing/preserving of fruit & vegetables		...	...	...	371		...	...	...	152		...	48
1514	Vegetable and animal oils and fats		...	...	...	99409		...	...	...	23501		...	328
1520	Dairy products		...	...	...	68550		...	...	...	34074		...	4162
153	Grain mill products; starches; animal feeds		...	...	...	63075		...	...	...	20161		...	3705
1531	Grain mill products		...	...	...	56428		...	...	...	18986		...	3691
1532	Starches and starch products		...	...	...	-		...	...	...	-		...	-
1533	Prepared animal feeds		...	...	...	6648		...	...	...	1176		...	14
154	Other food products		...	...	...	246337		...	...	...	104460		...	5796
1541	Bakery products		...	...	...	8429		...	...	...	2868		...	886
1542	Sugar		...	...	...	2697		...	...	...	1390		...	175
1543	Cocoa, chocolate and sugar confectionery		...	...	...	17080		...	...	...	4832		...	850
1544	Macaroni, noodles & similar products		...	...	...	4004		...	...	...	1242		...	57
1549	Other food products n.e.c.		...	...	...	214127		...	...	...	94128		...	3827
155	Beverages		...	...	...	15592		...	...	...	10749		...	1398
1551	Distilling, rectifying & blending of spirits		...	...	...	10705		...	...	...	8325		...	...
1552	Wines		...	...	...	-		...	...	...	-		...	-
1553	Malt liquors and malt		...	...	...	-		...	...	...	-		...	-
1554	Soft drinks; mineral waters		...	...	...	4888		...	...	...	2425		...	1398
1600	Tobacco products		...	...	...	98382		...	...	...	91189		...	493
171	Spinning, weaving and finishing of textiles		...	...	...	29772		...	...	...	18269		...	810
1711	Textile fibre preparation; textile weaving		...	...	...	14265		...	...	...	7347		...	653
1712	Finishing of textiles		...	...	...	15508		...	...	...	10922		...	156
172	Other textiles		...	...	...	9743		...	...	...	5388		...	849
1721	Made-up textile articles, except apparel		...	...	...	232		...	...	...	161		...	-
1722	Carpets and rugs		...	...	...	575		...	...	...	195		...	...
1723	Cordage, rope, twine and netting		...	...	...	2095		...	...	...	414		...	277
1729	Other textiles n.e.c.		...	...	...	6841		...	...	...	4617		...	572
1730	Knitted and crocheted fabrics and articles		...	...	...	49886		...	...	...	34355		...	5072
1810	Wearing apparel, except fur apparel		...	...	...	460138		...	...	...	262909		...	15634
1820	Dressing & dyeing of fur; processing of fur		...	...	...	-		...	...	...	-		...	-
191	Tanning, dressing and processing of leather		...	...	...	427		...	...	...	357		...	246
1911	Tanning and dressing of leather		...	...	...	-		...	...	...	-		...	-
1912	Luggage, handbags, etc.; saddlery & harness		...	...	...	427		...	...	...	357		...	246
1920	Footwear		...	...	...	10006		...	...	...	4284		...	192
2010	Sawmilling and planing of wood		...	...	...	10641		...	...	...	8047		...	42
202	Products of wood, cork, straw, etc.		...	...	...	5738		...	...	...	3595		...	869
2021	Veneer sheets, plywood, particle board, etc.		...	...	...	596		...	...	...	352		...	322
2022	Builders' carpentry and joinery		...	...	...	1149		...	...	...	810		...	88
2023	Wooden containers		...	...	...	3579		...	...	...	2193		...	324
2029	Other wood products; articles of cork/straw		...	...	...	415		...	...	...	240		...	134
210	Paper and paper products		...	...	...	53497		...	...	...	15660		...	803
2101	Pulp, paper and paperboard		...	...	...	621		...	...	...	288		...	15
2102	Corrugated paper and paperboard		...	...	...	10071		...	...	...	3029		...	445
2109	Other articles of paper and paperboard		...	...	...	42805		...	...	...	12342		...	343
221	Publishing		...	...	...	524		...	...	...	139		...	...
2211	Publishing of books and other publications		...	...	...	524		...	...	...	139		...	...
2212	Publishing of newspapers, journals, etc.		...	...	...	-		...	...	...	-		...	-
2213	Publishing of recorded media		...	...	...	-		...	...	...	-		...	-
2219	Other publishing		...	...	...	-		...	...	...	-		...	-

continued

Sri Lanka

ISIC Revision 3		Output in producers' prices (millions of Sri Lanka Rupees)					Value added in producers' prices (millions of Sri Lanka Rupees)					Gross fixed capital formation (millions of Sri Lanka Rupees)		
ISIC	Industry	Note	2003	2004	2005	2006	Note	2003	2004	2005	2006	Note	2005	2006
222	Printing and related service activities		...	...	...	97969		...	...	...	32463		...	5142
2221	Printing		...	...	...	96740		...	...	...	31473		...	4954
2222	Service activities related to printing		...	...	...	1229		...	...	...	990		...	187
2230	Reproduction of recorded media		...	...	...	-		...	...	...	-		...	-
2310	Coke oven products		...	...	...	-		...	...	...	-		...	-
2320	Refined petroleum products		...	...	...	118843		...	...	...	12792		...	464
2330	Processing of nuclear fuel		...	...	...	-		...	...	...	-		...	-
241	Basic chemicals		...	...	...	58106		...	...	...	29593		...	95
2411	Basic chemicals, except fertilizers		...	...	...	488		...	...	...	280		...	13
2412	Fertilizers and nitrogen compounds		...	...	...	57618		...	...	...	29313		...	82
2413	Plastics in primary forms; synthetic rubber		...	...	...	...		...	...	...	...		...	...
242	Other chemicals		...	...	...	379100		...	...	...	120654		...	8571
2421	Pesticides and other agro-chemical products		...	...	...	-		...	...	...	-		...	-
2422	Paints, varnishes, printing ink and mastics		...	...	...	618		...	...	...	420		...	...
2423	Pharmaceuticals, medicinal chemicals, etc.		...	...	...	17072		...	...	...	8535		...	2045
2424	Soap, cleaning & cosmetic preparations		...	...	...	360746		...	...	...	111393		...	6521
2429	Other chemical products n.e.c.		...	...	...	665		...	...	...	306		...	5
2430	Man-made fibres		...	...	...	-		...	...	...	-		...	-
251	Rubber products		...	...	...	34826		...	...	...	17657		...	1343
2511	Rubber tyres and tubes		...	...	...	14837		...	...	...	6719		...	383
2519	Other rubber products		...	...	...	19989		...	...	...	10938		...	960
2520	Plastic products		...	...	...	84994		...	...	...	52684		...	2559
2610	Glass and glass products		...	...	...	-		...	...	...	-		...	-
269	Non-metallic mineral products n.e.c.		...	...	...	126835		...	...	...	36352		...	4460
2691	Pottery, china and earthenware		...	...	...	7820		...	...	...	4333		...	231
2692	Refractory ceramic products		...	...	...	-		...	...	...	-		...	-
2693	Struct.non-refractory clay; ceramic products		...	...	...	35671		...	...	...	11777		...	1891
2694	Cement, lime and plaster		...	...	...	49141		...	...	...	4124		...	217
2695	Articles of concrete, cement and plaster		...	...	...	17041		...	...	...	7495		...	172
2696	Cutting, shaping & finishing of stone		...	...	...	17105		...	...	...	8610		...	1948
2699	Other non-metallic mineral products n.e.c.		...	...	...	58		...	...	...	13		...	1
2710	Basic iron and steel		...	...	...	...		...	...	...	...		...	...
2720	Basic precious and non-ferrous metals		...	...	...	30792		...	...	...	10173		...	1616
273	Casting of metals		...	...	...	73164		...	...	...	38623		...	...
2731	Casting of iron and steel		...	...	...	5250		...	...	...	357		...	...
2732	Casting of non-ferrous metals		...	...	...	67914		...	...	...	38267		...	...
281	Struct.metal products;tanks;steam generators		...	...	...	703		...	...	...	285		...	...
2811	Structural metal products		...	...	...	703		...	...	...	285		...	...
2812	Tanks, reservoirs and containers of metal		...	...	...	-		...	...	...	-		...	-
2813	Steam generators		...	...	...	-		...	...	...	-		...	-
289	Other metal products; metal working services		...	...	...	6569		...	...	...	3594		...	766
2891	Metal forging/pressing/stamping/roll-forming		...	...	...	-		...	...	...	-		...	-
2892	Treatment & coating of metals		...	...	...	1072		...	...	...	839		...	417
2893	Cutlery, hand tools and general hardware		...	...	...	1029		...	...	...	430		...	145
2899	Other fabricated metal products n.e.c.		...	...	...	4469		...	...	...	2325		...	204
291	General purpose machinery		...	...	...	249		...	...	...	118		...	...
2911	Engines & turbines (not for transport equipment)		...	...	...	-		...	...	...	-		...	-
2912	Pumps, compressors, taps and valves		...	...	...	-		...	...	...	-		...	-
2913	Bearings, gears, gearing & driving elements		...	...	...	-		...	...	...	-		...	-
2914	Ovens, furnaces and furnace burners		...	...	...	-		...	...	...	-		...	-
2915	Lifting and handling equipment		...	...	...	-		...	...	...	-		...	-
2919	Other general purpose machinery		...	...	...	249		...	...	...	118		...	...

292	Special purpose machinery	...	...	...	217	...	...	...	84	...	22
2921	Agricultural and forestry machinery	...	...	...	89	...	...	...	42	...	22
2922	Machine tools	...	...	...	-	...	...	...	-	...	-
2923	Machinery for metallurgy	...	...	...	-	...	...	...	-	...	-
2924	Machinery for mining & construction	...	...	...	-	...	...	...	-	...	-
2925	Food/beverage/tobacco processing machinery	...	...	...	128	...	...	...	41	...	-
2926	Machinery for textile, apparel and leather	...	...	...	-	...	...	...	-	...	-
2927	Weapons and ammunition	...	...	...	-	...	...	...	-	...	-
2929	Other special purpose machinery	...	...	...	-	...	...	...	-	...	-
2930	Domestic appliances n.e.c.	...	...	...	1011	...	...	...	604	...	16
3000	Office, accounting and computing machinery	...	...	...	4812	...	...	...	2015	...	92
3110	Electric motors, generators and transformers	...	...	...	1879	...	...	...	716	...	54
3120	Electricity distribution & control apparatus	...	...	...	-	...	...	...	-	...	-
3130	Insulated wire and cable	...	...	...	-	...	...	...	-	...	-
3140	Accumulators, primary cells and batteries	...	...	...	-	...	...	...	-	...	-
3150	Lighting equipment and electric lamps	...	...	...	-	...	...	...	-	...	-
3190	Other electrical equipment n.e.c.	...	...	...	77378	...	...	...	37414	...	9782
3210	Electronic valves, tubes, etc.	...	...	...	440	...	...	...	315	...	96
3220	TV/radio transmitters; line comm. apparatus	...	...	...	-	...	...	...	-	...	-
3230	TV and radio receivers and associated goods	...	...	...	405	...	...	...	119	...	4
331	Medical, measuring, testing appliances, etc.	...	...	...	16	...	...	...	11	...	-
3311	Medical, surgical and orthopaedic equipment	...	...	...	16	...	...	...	11	...	-
3312	Measuring/testing/navigating appliances,etc.	...	...	...	-	...	...	...	-	...	-
3313	Industrial process control equipment	...	...	...	-	...	...	...	-	...	-
3320	Optical instruments & photographic equipment	...	...	...	1072	...	...	...	962	...	...
3330	Watches and clocks	...	...	...	-	...	...	...	-	...	-
3410	Motor vehicles	...	...	...	-	...	...	...	-	...	-
3420	Automobile bodies, trailers & semi-trailers	...	...	...	138	...	...	...	95	...	...
3430	Parts/accessories for automobiles	...	...	...	1439	...	...	...	640	...	397
351	Building and repairing of ships and boats	...	...	...	235	...	...	...	130	...	10
3511	Building and repairing of ships	...	...	...	235	...	...	...	130	...	10
3512	Building/repairing of pleasure/sport. boats	...	...	...	-	...	...	...	-	...	-
3520	Railway/tramway locomotives & rolling stock	...	...	...	-	...	...	...	-	...	-
3530	Aircraft and spacecraft	...	...	...	-	...	...	...	-	...	-
359	Transport equipment n.e.c.	...	...	...	29	...	...	...	16	...	...
3591	Motorcycles	...	...	...	4	...	...	...	2	...	...
3592	Bicycles and invalid carriages	...	...	...	25	...	...	...	15	...	...
3599	Other transport equipment n.e.c.	...	...	...	-	...	...	...	-	...	-
3610	Furniture	...	...	...	19463	...	...	...	8140	...	508
369	Manufacturing n.e.c.	...	...	...	26758	...	...	...	14395	...	2003
3691	Jewellery and related articles	...	...	...	13231	...	...	...	9071	...	591
3692	Musical instruments	...	...	...	-	...	...	...	-	...	-
3693	Sports goods	...	...	...	5809	...	...	...	1990	...	1223
3694	Games and toys	...	...	...	2899	...	...	...	1668	...	117
3699	Other manufacturing n.e.c.	...	...	...	4820	...	...	...	1667	...	72
3710	Recycling of metal waste and scrap	...	...	...	-	...	...	...	-	...	-
3720	Recycling of non-metal waste and scrap	...	...	...	1028	...	...	...	207	...	17
D	Total manufacturing	...	...	...	2495305	...	...	...	1105357	...	81744

Sri Lanka

ISIC Revision 3			Index numbers of industrial production (2000=100)											
ISIC	Industry	Note	1995	1996	1997	1998	1999	2000	2001	2002	2003	2004	2005	2006
15	Food and beverages	a/	96	86	86	90	95	100	103	107	113	117	123	130
16	Tobacco products	a/	...	...	...	...	...	...	...	...	...	...	...	...
17	Textiles	b/	66	65	77	81	86	100	98	96	93	101	105	109
18	Wearing apparel, fur	b/	...	...	...	...	...	...	...	...	...	...	...	...
19	Leather, leather products and footwear	b/	...	...	...	...	...	...	...	...	...	...	...	...
20	Wood products (excl. furniture)		...	...	...	...	...	...	...	...	...	...	...	...
21	Paper and paper products		79	72	92	93	94	100	101	103	106	107	112	118
22	Printing and publishing		...	...	...	...	...	...	...	...	...	...	...	...
23	Coke,refined petroleum products,nuclear fuel	c/	85	102	81	86	91	100	103	105	109	115	131	141
24	Chemicals and chemical products	c/	...	...	...	...	...	...	...	...	...	...	...	...
25	Rubber and plastics products	c/	...	...	...	...	...	...	...	...	...	...	...	...
26	Non-metallic mineral products		69	68	76	80	85	100	98	97	94	102	108	120
27	Basic metals		93	89	85	91	97	100	102	106	110	119	126	134
28	Fabricated metal products	d/	68	65	82	88	94	100	103	106	108	111	114	119
29	Machinery and equipment n.e.c.	d/	...	...	...	...	...	...	...	...	...	...	...	...
30	Office, accounting and computing machinery	d/	...	...	...	...	...	...	...	...	...	...	...	...
31	Electrical machinery and apparatus	d/	...	...	...	...	...	...	...	...	...	...	...	...
32	Radio,television and communication equipment	d/	...	...	...	...	...	...	...	...	...	...	...	...
33	Medical, precision and optical instruments	d/	...	...	...	...	...	...	...	...	...	...	...	...
34	Motor vehicles, trailers, semi-trailers	d/	...	...	...	...	...	...	...	...	...	...	...	...
35	Other transport equipment	d/	...	...	...	...	...	...	...	...	...	...	...	...
36	Furniture; manufacturing n.e.c.		...	...	...	...	...	...	...	...	...	...	...	...
37	Recycling		...	...	...	...	...	...	...	...	...	...	...	...
D	Total manufacturing		99	93	90	96	98	100	104	108	109	112	116	120

a/ 15 includes 16.
b/ 17 includes 18 and 19.
c/ 23 includes 24 and 25.
d/ 28 includes 29, 30, 31, 32, 33, 34 and 35.

Sweden

Supplier of information:
Statistics Sweden, Stockholm.
Industrial statistics for the OECD countries are compiled by the OECD secretariat, which supplies them to UNIDO.

Basic source of data:
Structural business statistics survey.

Major deviations from ISIC (Revision 3):
The data presented in ISIC (Revision 3) were originally classified according to NACE (Revision 1).

Reference period:
Calendar year.

Scope:
The survey covers all enterprises included in the business register.

Method of data collection:
Large enterprises with 50 or more employees are surveyed by questionnaires, whereas smaller enterprises are covered by administrative data only.

Type of enumeration:
Not reported.

Adjusted for non-response:
Yes.

Concepts and definitions of variables:
Number of employees was computed using the average number of wage earners throughout the year plus the number of salaried employees at a certain date.
Wages and salaries includes regular and overtime cash payments, bonuses and cost-of-living allowances, vacation and sick leave pay, taxes and those social insurance contributions that are payable by employees and deducted by employers and payments in kind. Social security costs are not included.

Related national publications:
Structural Business Statistics; Swedish manufacturing according to Structural Business Statistics, both published by Statistics Sweden, Stockholm.

Sweden

ISIC Revision 3		Number of enterprises					Number of employees					Wages and salaries paid to employees				
			(number)					(number)					(millions of Swedish Kronor)			
ISIC	Industry	Note	2002	2003	2004	2005	Note	2002	2003	2004	2005	Note	2002	2003	2004	2005
151	Processed meat,fish,fruit,vegetables,fats		860	...	976	966		25045	...	...	...		5732	...	...	...
1511	Processing/preserving of meat		498	...	546	525		14955	...	15112	13906		3231	...	3475	3361
1512	Processing/preserving of fish		173	...	207	211		2185	...	...	...		411	...	...	...
1513	Processing/preserving of fruit & vegetables		144	...	175	182		5290	...	4966	4196		1283	...	1224	1108
1514	Vegetable and animal oils and fats		45	...	48	48		2615	...	1327	1291		807	...	422	428
1520	Dairy products		103	...	115	117		12869	...	9145	8661		1965	...	2372	2321
153	Grain mill products; starches; animal feeds		220	...	225	221		2072	...	2317	2599		562	...	653	699
1531	Grain mill products		119	...	117	109		966	...	1205	1400		262	...	326	373
1532	Starches and starch products		13	...	12	12		366	...	279	290		104	...	77	74
1533	Prepared animal feeds		88	...	96	100		740	...	833	909		196	...	251	252
154	Other food products		1707	...	1818	1859		...	...	23261	22810		...	...	5240	5322
1541	Bakery products		1385	...	1460	1488		15807	...	16304	16311		3231	...	3416	3539
1542	Sugar		3	...	4	4		...	...	...	...		...	...	...	...
1543	Cocoa, chocolate and sugar confectionery		163	...	188	195		4380	...	3212	2891		1001	...	815	731
1544	Macaroni, noodles & similar products		11	...	11	11		...	...	...	...		...	...	...	...
1549	Other food products n.e.c.		145	...	155	161		2143	...	2947	2857		569	...	796	846
155	Beverages		90	...	115	125		6553	...	6022	5618		1973	...	1856	1661
1551	Distilling, rectifying & blending of spirits		18	...	25	29		...	...	...	...		...	...	...	...
1552	Wines		15	...	13	14		...	...	...	...		...	...	...	...
1553	Malt liquors and malt		30	...	38	42		...	...	...	...		...	...	...	...
1554	Soft drinks; mineral waters		27	...	39	40		...	...	...	...		...	...	...	...
1600	Tobacco products		9	...	14	17		...	...	...	...		...	...	...	...
171	Spinning, weaving and finishing of textiles		368	...	400	412		1818	...	1648	1761		345	...	386	406
1711	Textile fibre preparation; textile weaving		191	...	192	187		1195	...	1137	1272		224	...	276	291
1712	Finishing of textiles		177	...	208	225		623	...	511	489		122	...	110	115
172	Other textiles		1362	...	1489	1543		5796	...	5183	4470		1272	...	1221	1100
1721	Made-up textile articles, except apparel		717	...	756	780		1970	...	1777	1491		381	...	369	317
1722	Carpets and rugs		44	...	40	39		193	...	176	176		40	...	44	46
1723	Cordage, rope, twine and netting		50	...	47	49		88	...	66	...		17	...	13	...
1729	Other textiles n.e.c.		551	...	646	675		3545	...	3164	...		834	...	797	...
1730	Knitted and crocheted fabrics and articles		136	...	142	133		657	...	508	467		131	...	116	114
1810	Wearing apparel, except fur apparel		1575	...	1623	1650		2070	...	1586	1470		395	...	348	352
1820	Dressing & dyeing of fur; processing of fur		93	...	90	85		63	...	57	61		9	...	9	9
191	Tanning, dressing and processing of leather		281	...	300	305		780	...	799	807		158	...	188	183
1911	Tanning and dressing of leather		31	...	32	32		...	...	...	...		...	...	...	...
1912	Luggage, handbags, etc.; saddlery & harness		250	...	268	273		...	...	...	...		...	...	...	...
1920	Footwear		120	...	105	98		397	...	366	362		77	...	75	75
2010	Sawmilling and planing of wood		1498	...	1576	1575		14648	...	15116	14765		3509	...	3685	3880
202	Products of wood, cork, straw, etc.		4942	...	5206	5264		23352	...	22038	22071		5066	...	5079	5265
2021	Veneer sheets, plywood, particle board, etc.		67	...	76	81		2030	...	1734	1691		507	...	452	465
2022	Builders' carpentry and joinery		3154	...	3406	3465		17292	...	16603	16653		3766	...	3820	3957
2023	Wooden containers		403	...	406	407		2106	...	2014	2070		424	...	458	487
2029	Other wood products; articles of cork/straw		1318	...	1318	1311		1924	...	1687	1657		369	...	349	356
210	Paper and paper products		420	...	497	495		40544	...	40192	38627		11831	...	12428	12488
2101	Pulp, paper and paperboard		104	...	155	159		29414	...	29164	28255		8843	...	9335	9432
2102	Corrugated paper and paperboard		136	...	154	154		5374	...	4775	4705		1342	...	1295	1323
2109	Other articles of paper and paperboard		180	...	188	182		...	...	6253	...		...	...	1798	...
221	Publishing		4677	...	5356	5790		25883	...	24542	23912		6740	...	6636	6778
2211	Publishing of books and other publications		1467	...	1632	1766		4358	...	3922	4012		1063	...	1024	1041
2212	Publishing of newspapers, journals, etc.		1087	...	1227	1298		19271	...	18636	18037		5144	...	5136	5286
2213	Publishing of recorded media		1446	...	1832	2084		1329	...	1173	1101		321	...	270	252
2219	Other publishing		677	...	665	642		925	...	811	762		212	...	206	199

222	Printing and related service activities	3683	...	3673	3704	22606	...	19986	19772	5448	...	5269	5268
2221	Printing	2488	...	2488	2465	17058	...	15378	15036	4245	...	4138	4101
2222	Service activities related to printing	1195	...	1185	1239	5548	...	4608	4736	1204	...	1131	1168
2230	Reproduction of recorded media	219	...	244	251	342	...	271	275	77	...	65	71
2310	Coke oven products	13	...	10	10	12	...	...	...	3	...	...	...
2320	Refined petroleum products	29	...	36	37	...	...	1810	2137	...	...	629	778
2330	Processing of nuclear fuel	4	...	8	8	...	...	...	...	...	...	...	...
241	Basic chemicals	193	...	211	210	13014	...	10939	10953	4248	...	3891	4145
2411	Basic chemicals, except fertilizers	124	...	143	144	...	...	...	...	...	...	...	...
2412	Fertilizers and nitrogen compounds	12	...	15	14	...	...	...	...	...	...	...	...
2413	Plastics in primary forms; synthetic rubber	57	...	53	52	...	...	...	...	...	...	...	...
242	Other chemicals	643	...	729	752	...	...	29214	28335	...	...	10203	10151
2421	Pesticides and other agro-chemical products	14	...	14	16	67	...	60	61	15	...	13	15
2422	Paints, varnishes, printing ink and mastics	119	...	136	138	4178	...	3941	3939	1100	...	1171	1210
2423	Pharmaceuticals, medicinal chemicals, etc.	118	...	139	152	21534	...	19441	18838	7220	...	7361	7221
2424	Soap, cleaning & cosmetic preparations	201	...	222	231	1333	...	1856	1919	301	...	477	482
2429	Other chemical products n.e.c.	191	...	218	215	...	...	3916	3578	...	...	1182	1223
2430	Man-made fibres	6	...	6	5	...	...	14	12	...	...	4	3
251	Rubber products	229	...	254	263	6555	...	5883	5530	1528	...	1554	1549
2511	Rubber tyres and tubes	109	...	111	115	...	...	...	...	...	...	...	...
2519	Other rubber products	120	...	143	148	4590	...	5197	4752	1114	...	1391	1338
2520	Plastic products	1295	...	1399	1384	18008	...	19919	19324	4261	...	5110	5146
2610	Glass and glass products	280	...	332	338	4822	...	4226	4136	1128	...	1121	1121
269	Non-metallic mineral products n.e.c.	1328	...	1474	1547	14500	...	13048	13110	3705	...	3473	3701
2691	Pottery, china and earthenware	619	...	702	767	...	...	...	...	...	...	...	...
2692	Refractory ceramic products	28	...	29	28	...	...	462	487	...	...	131	151
2693	Struct.non-refractory clay; ceramic products	17	...	22	19	...	...	76	...	...	...	17	...
2694	Cement, lime and plaster	37	...	34	29	737	...	884	868	222	...	275	277
2695	Articles of concrete, cement and plaster	274	...	306	311	8430	...	7264	6629	2135	...	1917	1883
2696	Cutting, shaping & finishing of stone	299	...	314	320	1030	...	986	948	214	...	218	215
2699	Other non-metallic mineral products n.e.c.	54	...	67	73	1866	...	1691	2193	525	...	484	666
2710	Basic iron and steel	169	...	208	201	28470	...	24502	24580	7930	...	7173	7539
2720	Basic precious and non-ferrous metals	102	...	111	108	5746	...	7025	6955	1568	...	2017	2121
273	Casting of metals	124	...	148	147	2863	...	3675	3778	658	...	879	948
2731	Casting of iron and steel	49	...	55	50	1209	...	1413	1448	300	...	354	380
2732	Casting of non-ferrous metals	75	...	93	97	1654	...	2262	2330	358	...	525	568
281	Struct.metal products;tanks;steam generators	1150	...	1245	1239	15868	...	15418	15103	3827	...	3991	3810
2811	Structural metal products	984	...	1061	1048	14547	...	13656	13309	3521	...	3537	3328
2812	Tanks, reservoirs and containers of metal	155	...	176	183	1190	...	1637	1672	269	...	416	441
2813	Steam generators	11	...	8	8	131	...	125	122	38	...	38	42
289	Other metal products; metal working services	9247	...	9977	10217	58298	...	60812	60364	13328	...	14910	15542
2891	Metal forging/pressing/stamping/roll-forming	964	...	944	900	2708	...	2605	2784	597	...	614	662
2892	Treatment & coating of metals	5985	...	6624	6885	29208	...	29921	30632	6428	...	6988	7444
2893	Cutlery, hand tools and general hardware	886	...	923	925	9992	...	13027	12457	2462	...	3465	3671
2899	Other fabricated metal products n.e.c.	1412	...	1486	1507	16390	...	15259	14491	3840	...	3842	3765
291	General purpose machinery	2044	...	2284	2312	49079	...	49237	49621	13849	...	14970	15568
2911	Engines & turbines (not for transport equipment)	178	...	197	211	...	...	3881	3973	...	...	1458	1527
2912	Pumps, compressors, taps and valves	248	...	271	276	...	...	9595	9560	...	...	2792	2837
2913	Bearings, gears, gearing & driving elements	77	...	95	102	3887	...	4198	4657	1048	...	1315	1528
2914	Ovens, furnaces and furnace burners	61	...	65	63	895	...	492	485	230	...	138	142
2915	Lifting and handling equipment	487	...	555	560	11891	...	11809	11863	3148	...	3275	3355
2919	Other general purpose machinery	993	...	1101	1100	18178	...	19262	19083	5435	...	5995	6179
292	Special purpose machinery	2992	...	3223	3302	43867	...	40820	40793	12044	...	11996	12356
2921	Agricultural and forestry machinery	528	...	594	612	3976	...	3461	3313	1059	...	911	889
2922	Machine tools	670	...	682	717	10301	...	8471	8508	2731	...	2487	2581
2923	Machinery for metallurgy	22	...	30	32	...	...	1116	998	...	...	345	307
2924	Machinery for mining & construction	376	...	412	432	7925	...	7920	8414	2173	...	2306	2586
2925	Food/beverage/tobacco processing machinery	123	...	135	137	...	...	878	891	...	...	224	231
2926	Machinery for textile, apparel and leather	58	...	64	66	1811	...	1771	1662	469	...	485	468
2927	Weapons and ammunition	86	...	92	92	3539	...	3540	3534	1164	...	1256	1251
2929	Other special purpose machinery	1129	...	1214	1214	14201	...	13663	13473	3918	...	3983	4044

continued

Sweden

ISIC Revision 3		Number of enterprises					Number of employees					Wages and salaries paid to employees				
			(number)					(number)					(millions of Swedish Kronor)			
ISIC	Industry	Note	2002	2003	2004	2005	Note	2002	2003	2004	2005	Note	2002	2003	2004	2005
2930	Domestic appliances n.e.c.		96	...	115	122		8009	...	7558	6937		2006	...	2200	2046
3000	Office, accounting and computing machinery		398	...	397	387		3741	...	3896	3865		1040	...	1138	1157
3110	Electric motors, generators and transformers		246	...	261	266		8849	...	5598	5112		2631	...	1769	1658
3120	Electricity distribution & control apparatus		294	...	321	334		8382	...	7664	7396		2200	...	2373	2229
3130	Insulated wire and cable		64	...	75	76		...	...	3790	3671		...	...	1000	1066
3140	Accumulators, primary cells and batteries		29	...	25	24		...	...	...	...		...	...	...	...
3150	Lighting equipment and electric lamps		232	...	243	240		3048	...	...	...		682	...	...	...
3190	Other electrical equipment n.e.c.		380	...	395	385		4164	...	3475	3227		1102	...	1002	936
3210	Electronic valves, tubes, etc.		389	...	414	411		5636	...	3134	...		1346	...	860	...
3220	TV/radio transmitters; line comm. apparatus		129	...	177	189		33922	...	...	...		10654	...	...	...
3230	TV and radio receivers and associated goods		150	...	166	183		3231	...	...	2130		805	...	...	599
331	Medical, measuring, testing appliances, etc.		1839	...	1967	2008		23109	...	22762	22035		7129	...	7475	7430
3311	Medical, surgical and orthopaedic equipment		1160	...	1225	1243		9287	...	10426	10183		2737	...	3136	3149
3312	Measuring/testing/navigating appliances,etc.		468	...	498	504		10762	...	10672	10095		3549	...	3759	3659
3313	Industrial process control equipment		211	...	244	261		3060	...	1664	1757		843	...	579	622
3320	Optical instruments & photographic equipment		166	...	176	174		1890	...	1580	1552		560	...	489	504
3330	Watches and clocks		19	...	23	24		174	...	175	172		40	...	41	41
3410	Motor vehicles		130	...	166	179		49623	...	46650	48131		14479	...	14418	15287
3420	Automobile bodies, trailers & semi-trailers		209	...	234	241		3518	...	8755	8797		804	...	2346	2457
3430	Parts/accessories for automobiles		415	...	507	513		20092	...	26074	24481		4931	...	6827	6848
351	Building and repairing of ships and boats		1147	...	1249	1296		5241	...	4946	4746		1280	...	1248	1252
3511	Building and repairing of ships		253	...	251	251		2744	...	2382	2218		721	...	666	639
3512	Building/repairing of pleasure/sport. boats		894	...	998	1045		2497	...	2564	2528		559	...	582	613
3520	Railway/tramway locomotives & rolling stock		37	...	52	49		5039	...	4585	4326		1455	...	1426	1442
3530	Aircraft and spacecraft		151	...	166	169		10340	...	10304	10149		3207	...	3285	3560
359	Transport equipment n.e.c.		135	...	155	157		1638	...	1439	1365		395	...	373	369
3591	Motorcycles		24	...	30	32		...	...	...	...		...	...	...	...
3592	Bicycles and invalid carriages		61	...	68	71		...	...	...	...		...	...	...	...
3599	Other transport equipment n.e.c.		50	...	57	54		183	...	211	209		38	...	44	48
3610	Furniture		3121	...	3183	3216		21693	...	19234	18700		4759	...	4396	4340
369	Manufacturing n.e.c.		2422	...	2650	2768		30552	...	26079	25189		4898	...	4597	4627
3691	Jewellery and related articles		626	...	687	730		518	...	452	453		93	...	89	93
3692	Musical instruments		187	...	219	233		...	...	141	149		...	...	32	31
3693	Sports goods		264	...	292	297		915	...	715	854		209	...	172	215
3694	Games and toys		253	...	294	289		...	...	534	536		...	...	141	135
3699	Other manufacturing n.e.c.		1092	...	1158	1219		28191	...	24237	23197		4356	...	4162	4154
3710	Recycling of metal waste and scrap		143	...	176	193		1105	...	1345	1212		246	...	330	281
3720	Recycling of non-metal waste and scrap		64	...	83	85		476	...	696	755		122	...	176	201
D	Total manufacturing		54616	...	58995	60379		760933	...	722469	709486		196832	...	202275	206542

Sweden

ISIC Revision 3		Output					Value added in factor values					Gross fixed capital formation		
			(millions of Swedish Kronor)					(millions of Swedish Kronor)					(millions of Swedish Kronor)	
ISIC	Industry	Note	2002	2003	2004	2005	Note	2002	2003	2004	2005	Note	2004	2005
151	Processed meat,fish,fruit,vegetables,fats		48113	...	...	...		11295	...	...	...		...	...
1511	Processing/preserving of meat		28234	...	28223	29864		5868	...	6097	5550		1123	767
1512	Processing/preserving of fish		3517	...	...	...		920	...	...	...		...	...
1513	Processing/preserving of fruit & vegetables		9648	...	9231	8130		2998	...	2160	2067		433	338
1514	Vegetable and animal oils and fats		6714	...	4452	4779		1510	...	1110	1276		569	164
1520	Dairy products		20887	...	23040	22506		4159	...	4871	4625		1584	1244
153	Grain mill products; starches; animal feeds		6638	...	8905	8510		1438	...	1366	1679		298	323
1531	Grain mill products		2964	...	3414	3472		824	...	1092	1112		151	159
1532	Starches and starch products		1084	...	767	645		195	...	131	101		50	49
1533	Prepared animal feeds		2591	...	4725	4392		420	...	142	467		97	114
154	Other food products		...	...	29144	30610		...	...	10977	10746		1705	1634
1541	Bakery products		12766	...	14105	14590		5505	...	6145	6150		779	835
1542	Sugar		...	...	...	...		...	...	...	...		...	...
1543	Cocoa, chocolate and sugar confectionery		7440	...	5140	5178		2201	...	1755	1748		539	356
1544	Macaroni, noodles & similar products		...	...	...	...		...	...	...	...		...	...
1549	Other food products n.e.c.		4976	...	7187	7887		1266	...	2256	2216		329	413
155	Beverages		15389	...	14967	14968		5597	...	4942	5080		811	509
1551	Distilling, rectifying & blending of spirits		...	...	...	...		...	...	...	...		...	...
1552	Wines		...	...	...	...		...	...	...	...		...	...
1553	Malt liquors and malt		...	...	...	...		...	...	...	...		...	...
1554	Soft drinks; mineral waters		...	...	...	...		...	...	...	...		...	...
1600	Tobacco products		...	...	...	...		...	...	...	...		...	...
171	Spinning, weaving and finishing of textiles		1798	...	2045	2020		578	...	520	621		41	47
1711	Textile fibre preparation; textile weaving		1250	...	1554	1553		373	...	399	476		18	24
1712	Finishing of textiles		548	...	491	467		205	...	121	145		23	23
172	Other textiles		6590	...	5863	5364		2450	...	2381	2097		263	260
1721	Made-up textile articles, except apparel		1917	...	1717	1706		708	...	678	630		57	62
1722	Carpets and rugs		223	...	227	241		81	...	85	81		6	6
1723	Cordage, rope, twine and netting		126	...	75	...		34	...	26	...		5	...
1729	Other textiles n.e.c.		4325	...	3844	...		1627	...	1591	...		194	...
1730	Knitted and crocheted fabrics and articles		839	...	665	637		264	...	223	214		25	37
1810	Wearing apparel, except fur apparel		2839	...	2623	2795		859	...	827	791		31	45
1820	Dressing & dyeing of fur; processing of fur		82	...	76	79		25	...	24	24		1	2
191	Tanning, dressing and processing of leather		1016	...	1144	1070		276	...	378	329		54	43
1911	Tanning and dressing of leather		...	...	...	...		...	...	...	...		...	...
1912	Luggage, handbags, etc.; saddlery & harness		...	...	...	...		...	...	...	...		...	...
1920	Footwear		461	...	370	426		130	...	131	139		7	19
2010	Sawmilling and planing of wood		38008	...	40715	43034		8148	...	7336	7977		1971	2394
202	Products of wood, cork, straw, etc.		29217	...	31211	32069		9483	...	9676	10365		1326	1287
2021	Veneer sheets, plywood, particle board, etc.		3036	...	2965	2967		784	...	557	782		155	175
2022	Builders' carpentry and joinery		21868	...	23618	24422		7198	...	7492	7936		915	866
2023	Wooden containers		2407	...	2851	2852		798	...	930	954		111	100
2029	Other wood products; articles of cork/straw		1906	...	1777	1828		703	...	698	692		144	147
210	Paper and paper products		110254	...	113576	115753		40105	...	34585	31618		7416	11013
2101	Pulp, paper and paperboard		90753	...	93156	95965		33485	...	28034	25475		6692	10063
2102	Corrugated paper and paperboard		7765	...	7622	7500		2670	...	2575	2509		247	257
2109	Other articles of paper and paperboard		...	...	12799	...		...	...	3975	...		478	...
221	Publishing		37136	...	39122	40557		11353	...	12253	12037		760	589
2211	Publishing of books and other publications		7596	...	7668	7983		2353	...	2272	2250		91	100
2212	Publishing of newspapers, journals, etc.		25563	...	27766	28971		7869	...	8939	8783		535	369
2213	Publishing of recorded media		2516	...	2321	2206		737	...	659	615		110	86
2219	Other publishing		1460	...	1366	1396		393	...	383	390		24	35

continued

Sweden

ISIC Revision 3		Output					Value added in factor values					Gross fixed capital formation		
			(millions of Swedish Kronor)					(millions of Swedish Kronor)					(millions of Swedish Kronor)	
ISIC	Industry	Note	2002	2003	2004	2005	Note	2002	2003	2004	2005	Note	2004	2005
222	Printing and related service activities		26051	...	25555	25236		9673	...	9432	9275		1868	1497
2221	Printing		21340	...	20873	20446		7508	...	7285	7174		1693	1265
2222	Service activities related to printing		4712	...	4683	4791		2164	...	2147	2101		175	231
2230	Reproduction of recorded media		516	...	339	691		136	...	120	149		10	14
2310	Coke oven products		22	...	...	...		7	...	...	...		...	...
2320	Refined petroleum products		...	...	8215	8918		...	...	2491	3750		1178	2748
2330	Processing of nuclear fuel		...	...	...	...		...	...	...	...		...	...
241	Basic chemicals		39731	...	38320	40792		12243	...	10875	11258		1622	3220
2411	Basic chemicals, except fertilizers		...	...	...	...		...	...	...	...		...	...
2412	Fertilizers and nitrogen compounds		...	...	...	...		...	...	...	...		...	...
2413	Plastics in primary forms; synthetic rubber		...	...	...	...		...	...	...	...		...	...
242	Other chemicals		...	...	90498	92437		...	...	43659	44712		3725	2991
2421	Pesticides and other agro-chemical products		101	...	65	79		33	...	28	30		4	2
2422	Paints, varnishes, printing ink and mastics		7885	...	8393	9397		2353	...	2404	2597		241	273
2423	Pharmaceuticals, medicinal chemicals, etc.		61812	...	70292	70948		34827	...	36984	37530		2893	2266
2424	Soap, cleaning & cosmetic preparations		1818	...	3307	3304		590	...	1203	1024		109	108
2429	Other chemical products n.e.c.		...	...	8442	8709		...	...	3039	3532		478	343
2430	Man-made fibres		...	...	24	11		...	...	8	7		-	-
251	Rubber products		7935	...	8136	7880		2829	...	2859	2756		338	230
2511	Rubber tyres and tubes		...	...	...	...		...	...	...	...		...	...
2519	Other rubber products		5629	...	7088	6832		2242	...	2623	2440		287	198
2520	Plastic products		23386	...	28052	29677		8443	...	10425	10198		1863	1463
2610	Glass and glass products		5683	...	5616	6461		2163	...	1979	2186		283	312
269	Non-metallic mineral products n.e.c.		21686	...	20689	22391		7765	...	7419	7833		1203	1189
2691	Pottery, china and earthenware		...	...	...	...		...	...	...	...		...	...
2692	Refractory ceramic products		...	...	695	723		...	...	255	262		12	28
2693	Struct.non-refractory clay; ceramic products		...	...	104	...		...	...	36	...		5	...
2694	Cement, lime and plaster		1857	...	2452	2714		726	...	749	814		140	116
2695	Articles of concrete, cement and plaster		12759	...	11435	12042		4334	...	3928	4036		755	724
2696	Cutting, shaping & finishing of stone		1033	...	1153	1024		401	...	529	433		76	54
2699	Other non-metallic mineral products n.e.c.		3018	...	2948	3563		1066	...	1027	1237		121	149
2710	Basic iron and steel		58221	...	79101	89441		18543	...	19410	20685		2251	2208
2720	Basic precious and non-ferrous metals		14124	...	24985	28090		3345	...	5033	5476		650	709
273	Casting of metals		2917	...	3933	4275		1189	...	1571	1649		292	300
2731	Casting of iron and steel		1102	...	1428	1740		445	...	607	683		72	67
2732	Casting of non-ferrous metals		1815	...	2505	2536		744	...	964	966		220	233
281	Struct.metal products;tanks;steam generators		20549	...	21974	22673		6968	...	7307	7147		711	670
2811	Structural metal products		18884	...	19404	19874		6315	...	6405	6295		630	579
2812	Tanks, reservoirs and containers of metal		1425	...	2376	2550		562	...	818	764		73	85
2813	Steam generators		240	...	194	249		90	...	83	88		8	6
289	Other metal products; metal working services		60845	...	72523	78969		25998	...	31177	32522		3699	4200
2891	Metal forging/pressing/stamping/roll-forming		2865	...	3150	3739		1130	...	1169	1258		146	157
2892	Treatment & coating of metals		27449	...	32625	35541		11970	...	13587	14515		1984	2186
2893	Cutlery, hand tools and general hardware		10760	...	16773	17743		5367	...	8459	8991		698	991
2899	Other fabricated metal products n.e.c.		19771	...	19975	21947		7530	...	7962	7759		871	866
291	General purpose machinery		77902	...	87457	94358		28317	...	29366	30743		3070	3229
2911	Engines & turbines (not for transport equipment)		...	...	11902	13996		...	...	2310	3217		220	213
2912	Pumps, compressors, taps and valves		...	...	14070	14773		...	...	5362	5722		476	471
2913	Bearings, gears, gearing & driving elements		5803	...	7698	7416		2725	...	3071	3377		258	218
2914	Ovens, furnaces and furnace burners		1360	...	882	1033		390	...	242	272		12	11
2915	Lifting and handling equipment		18716	...	19634	21824		6271	...	6181	6154		662	801
2919	Other general purpose machinery		30548	...	33271	35315		10937	...	12199	12002		1443	1518

292	Special purpose machinery	68740	...	74289	82019	23339	...	23898	25937	2061	2067
2921	Agricultural and forestry machinery	6587	...	6203	6782	2186	...	2131	2135	183	229
2922	Machine tools	13881	...	15250	17754	6111	...	6605	7280	461	368
2923	Machinery for metallurgy	...	...	1395	1387	...	...	456	467	98	45
2924	Machinery for mining & construction	14991	...	18657	22518	3873	...	3581	4754	576	701
2925	Food/beverage/tobacco processing machinery	...	...	1005	1041	...	...	387	404	36	27
2926	Machinery for textile, apparel and leather	2746	...	2594	2599	1139	...	1103	973	76	46
2927	Weapons and ammunition	5731	...	7193	6622	2386	...	2831	2672	118	124
2929	Other special purpose machinery	22495	...	21991	23316	6725	...	6804	7253	514	526
2930	Domestic appliances n.e.c.	10478	...	10961	10969	3597	...	2913	2988	322	355
3000	Office, accounting and computing machinery	5579	...	5456	6041	1687	...	2017	1981	127	99
3110	Electric motors, generators and transformers	15532	...	10479	11662	3981	...	3222	3019	186	130
3120	Electricity distribution & control apparatus	13647	...	11933	11484	4365	...	4404	4665	196	174
3130	Insulated wire and cable	...	...	7729	8869	...	...	2099	2205	107	116
3140	Accumulators, primary cells and batteries	...	...	...	...	...	...	...	...	...	...
3150	Lighting equipment and electric lamps	3704	...	...	...	1320	...	...	...	...	...
3190	Other electrical equipment n.e.c.	5398	...	5434	5492	1764	...	1891	1800	99	124
3210	Electronic valves, tubes, etc.	4253	...	4526	...	70	...	1247	...	98	...
3220	TV/radio transmitters; line comm. apparatus	101219	...	...	...	2144	...	...	...	...	...
3230	TV and radio receivers and associated goods	4822	...	...	4320	1049	...	...	1123	...	104
331	Medical, measuring, testing appliances, etc.	39426	...	38935	40891	13473	...	16931	17560	1055	961
3311	Medical, surgical and orthopaedic equipment	15481	...	16609	18539	5366	...	7889	8552	709	609
3312	Measuring/testing/navigating appliances,etc.	19621	...	18869	18018	7172	...	7867	7707	285	290
3313	Industrial process control equipment	4324	...	3457	4334	935	...	1175	1301	61	62
3320	Optical instruments & photographic equipment	1908	...	2474	2915	401	...	766	1202	100	60
3330	Watches and clocks	171	...	197	174	60	...	71	64	3	2
3410	Motor vehicles	152131	...	187322	194930	27616	...	36936	32446	5105	9221
3420	Automobile bodies, trailers & semi-trailers	4625	...	15320	16057	1330	...	5027	5410	791	1220
3430	Parts/accessories for automobiles	28161	...	45136	48712	8812	...	13177	12989	1986	1610
351	Building and repairing of ships and boats	6641	...	6286	6222	2226	...	2352	1500	226	357
3511	Building and repairing of ships	3059	...	2804	2520	1119	...	1199	524	65	108
3512	Building/repairing of pleasure/sport. boats	3583	...	3482	3702	1106	...	1152	976	162	250
3520	Railway/tramway locomotives & rolling stock	8844	...	7345	7196	2474	...	2423	2538	119	84
3530	Aircraft and spacecraft	14154	...	15830	19557	6001	...	6420	6540	1221	433
359	Transport equipment n.e.c.	2788	...	3003	2607	763	...	796	722	59	62
3591	Motorcycles	...	...	...	...	...	...	...	...	...	...
3592	Bicycles and invalid carriages	...	...	...	...	...	...	...	...	...	...
3599	Other transport equipment n.e.c.	207	...	217	240	76	...	89	89	6	8
3610	Furniture	26364	...	29025	27435	7689	...	7989	7921	1031	967
369	Manufacturing n.e.c.	9775	...	12783	8437	3503	...	7452	2950	214	223
3691	Jewellery and related articles	746	...	664	651	280	...	268	258	16	26
3692	Musical instruments	...	...	145	145	...	...	58	60	5	5
3693	Sports goods	1152	...	980	1419	541	...	416	496	25	38
3694	Games and toys	...	...	702	683	...	...	256	123	34	23
3699	Other manufacturing n.e.c.	6721	...	10292	5539	2277	...	6453	2012	133	131
3710	Recycling of metal waste and scrap	2544	...	3902	3211	646	...	923	769	220	177
3720	Recycling of non-metal waste and scrap	2467	...	2684	3180	247	...	493	599	107	114
D	Total manufacturing	1335902	...	1481633	1552424	397262	...	463557	463623	58508	66221

Sweden

ISIC Revision 3			Index numbers of industrial production											
			(2000=100)											
ISIC	Industry	Note	1995	1996	1997	1998	1999	2000	2001	2002	2003	2004	2005	2006
15	Food and beverages		96	101	100	101	101	100	103	100	96	96	97	97
16	Tobacco products		...	...	...	...	...	...	...	...	...	...	...	...
17	Textiles		...	...	...	...	...	...	...	...	...	...	...	...
18	Wearing apparel, fur		...	...	...	...	...	...	...	...	...	...	...	...
19	Leather, leather products and footwear		...	...	...	...	...	...	...	...	...	...	...	...
20	Wood products (excl. furniture)		87	84	93	97	98	100	100	99	101	106	109	110
21	Paper and paper products		87	84	91	92	94	100	98	103	105	109	105	109
22	Printing and publishing		95	95	91	99	99	100	91	92	92	88	91	95
23	Coke,refined petroleum products,nuclear fuel		101	103	106	102	98	100	95	93	96	102	99	99
24	Chemicals and chemical products		73	78	83	86	92	100	110	118	130	138	138	151
25	Rubber and plastics products		99	97	104	103	99	100	93	89	86	89	88	91
26	Non-metallic mineral products		97	90	89	95	100	100	104	98	99	102	102	108
27	Basic metals		91	92	96	95	95	100	108	113	111	118	114	109
28	Fabricated metal products		79	78	86	91	92	100	97	92	90	89	91	94
29	Machinery and equipment n.e.c.		108	102	102	100	99	100	96	98	104	107	113	124
30	Office, accounting and computing machinery		...	...	...	...	...	...	...	...	...	...	...	...
31	Electrical machinery and apparatus		70	68	72	78	84	100	97	96	96	96	95	96
32	Radio,television and communication equipment		39	55	61	71	88	100	94	69	68	88	111	121
33	Medical, precision and optical instruments		87	78	80	89	91	100	101	114	105	116	117	120
34	Motor vehicles, trailers, semi-trailers		67	65	74	83	88	100	97	101	114	127	130	135
35	Other transport equipment		93	94	100	101	99	100	95	96	89	96	88	89
36	Furniture; manufacturing n.e.c.		83	86	92	97	97	100	92	91	89	87	89	91
37	Recycling		...	...	...	...	...	...	...	...	...	...	...	...
D	Total manufacturing		82	83	87	91	94	100	99	100	103	107	110	115

Syrian Arab Republic

Supplier of information:
Central Bureau of Statistics, Damascus.

Basic source of data:
Sample survey; administrative source.

Major deviations from ISIC (Revision 3):
None reported.

Reference period:
Fiscal year.

Scope:
All reported establishments.

Method of data collection:
Mail questionnaire for public sector; direct interview in the field for private sector.

Type of enumeration:
Complete enumeration; sample survey.

Adjusted for non-response:
Not reported.

Concepts and definitions of variables:
Wages and salaries excludes housing and family allowance paid directly by the employer and payments in kind; it includes employers' contributions paid to social security, pension and insurance schemes as well as the benefits received by employees under these schemes and severance and termination pay.

Related national publications:
None reported.

Syrian Arab Republic

ISIC Revision 3		Number of establishments					Number of employees					Wages and salaries paid to employees				
			(number)					(number)					(millions of Syrian Pounds)			
ISIC	Industry	Note	2003	2004	2005	2006	Note	2003a/	2004a/	2005	2006	Note	2003a/	2004a/	2005	2006
15	Food and beverages		9575	10973	...	...		23733	23526	...	...		3043	3131	...	...
16	Tobacco products		517	427	...	...		9470	9470	...	...		1374	1320	...	...
17	Textiles		7634	7636	...	...		28958	27794	...	...		3822	3894	...	...
18	Wearing apparel, fur		11237	15340	...	...		2829	2616	...	...		369	392	...	...
19	Leather, leather products and footwear		3658	3082	...	...		1490	1348	...	...		221	524	...	...
20	Wood products (excl. furniture)		7239	10069	...	...		219	179	...	...		39	37	...	...
21	Paper and paper products		194	367	...	...		659	621	...	...		91	98	...	...
22	Printing and publishing		810	1482	...	...		...	...	...	...		...	...	...	...
23	Coke,refined petroleum products,nuclear fuel		38	56	...	...		7701	7896	...	...		1684	1771	...	...
24	Chemicals and chemical products		853	1010	...	...		5550	5576	...	...		1100	1222	...	...
25	Rubber and plastics products		3672	2050	...	...		1786	1699	...	...		324	370	...	...
26	Non-metallic mineral products		9611	8424	...	...		18890	18077	...	...		3278	3501	...	...
27	Basic metals		880	1838	...	...		1704	1684	...	...		292	340	...	...
28	Fabricated metal products		15687	20696	...	...		846	670	...	...		103	111	...	...
29	Machinery and equipment n.e.c.		711	1086	...	...		1971	1811	...	...		395	425	...	...
30	Office, accounting and computing machinery		...	16	...	...		...	...	...	...		...	...	...	...
31	Electrical machinery and apparatus		187	260	...	...		1738	1641	...	...		299	315	...	...
32	Radio,television and communication equipment		11	131	...	...		986	959	...	...		159	165	...	...
33	Medical, precision and optical instruments		413	701	...	...		...	...	...	...		...	...	...	...
34	Motor vehicles, trailers, semi-trailers		307	97	...	...		...	...	...	...		...	...	...	...
35	Other transport equipment		17	39	...	...		...	...	...	...		...	...	...	...
36	Furniture; manufacturing n.e.c.		13378	12696	...	...		288	260	...	...		35	37	...	...
37	Recycling		216	78	...	...		...	...	...	...		...	...	...	...
D	Total manufacturing		86845	98554	...	...		108818	105827	...	...		16628	17653	...	...

a/ For public sector only.

ISIC Revision 3		Output					Value added					Gross fixed capital formation		
			(millions of Syrian Pounds)					(millions of Syrian Pounds)					(millions of Syrian Pounds)	
ISIC	Industry	Note	2003	2004	2005	2006	Note	2003	2004	2005	2006	Note	2005	2006
15	Food and beverages	a/	100285	108259	115667	113243	a/	7494	11832	12970	7636		...	...
16	Tobacco products	a/	...	...	...	...	a/	...	...	...	...		...	...
17	Textiles	b/	83051	90796	102558	107515	b/	24084	41633	36779	38114		...	...
18	Wearing apparel, fur	b/	...	...	...	...	b/	...	...	...	...		...	...
19	Leather, leather products and footwear	b/	...	...	...	...	b/	...	...	...	...		...	...
20	Wood products (excl. furniture)	c/	11837	22226	24564	26258	c/	4107	7585	8375	8958		...	...
21	Paper and paper products	d/	6187	9285	10352	11245	d/	1801	4196	4195	4243		...	...
22	Printing and publishing	d/	...	...	...	...	d/	...	...	...	...		...	...
23	Coke,refined petroleum products,nuclear fuel	e/	114463	129564	35994	25249	e/	-14305	-49167	-54917	-67222		...	...
24	Chemicals and chemical products	e/	...	...	...	...	e/	...	...	...	...		...	...
25	Rubber and plastics products	e/	...	...	...	...	e/	...	...	...	...		...	...
26	Non-metallic mineral products		23128	40145	46747	48402		7490	19998	15642	17167		...	...
27	Basic metals		4692	7853	8918	9345		934	1678	2445	2614		...	...
28	Fabricated metal products	f/	36805	50668	56925	60288	f/	11166	10965	20405	22018		...	...
29	Machinery and equipment n.e.c.	f/	...	...	...	...	f/	...	...	...	...		...	...
30	Office, accounting and computing machinery	f/	...	...	...	...	f/	...	...	...	...		...	...
31	Electrical machinery and apparatus	f/	...	...	...	...	f/	...	...	...	...		...	...
32	Radio,television and communication equipment	f/	...	...	...	...	f/	...	...	...	...		...	...
33	Medical, precision and optical instruments	f/	...	...	...	...	f/	...	...	...	...		...	...
34	Motor vehicles, trailers, semi-trailers	f/	...	...	...	...	f/	...	...	...	...		...	...
35	Other transport equipment	f/	...	...	...	...	f/	...	...	...	...		...	...
36	Furniture; manufacturing n.e.c.	c/	...	...	...	...	c/	...	...	...	...		...	...
37	Recycling		909	1167	1249	1335		419	538	550	588		...	...
D	Total manufacturing		381357	459963	402974	402880		43190	49258	46444	34116		35673	28364

a/ 15 includes 16.
b/ 17 includes 18 and 19.
c/ 20 includes 36.
d/ 21 includes 22.
e/ 23 includes 24 and 25.
f/ 28 includes 29, 30, 31, 32, 33, 34 and 35.

Syrian Arab Republic

ISIC Revision 3			Index numbers of industrial production											
			(2000=100)											
ISIC	Industry	Note	1995	1996	1997	1998	1999	2000	2001	2002	2003	2004	2005	2006
15	Food and beverages		96	102	105	96	102	100	103	114	106	119	135	147
16	Tobacco products		85	75	89	92	97	100	108	118	123	119	108	121
17	Textiles		75	76	86	88	92	100	109	116	120	138	138	141
18	Wearing apparel, fur		110	101	101	92	96	100	101	113	85	67	66	58
19	Leather, leather products and footwear		...	...	...	...	...	...	...	...	...	...	...	...
20	Wood products (excl. furniture)		333	273	193	257	177	100	124	92	108	91	80	103
21	Paper and paper products		111	98	89	78	103	100	89	64	51	51	54	43
22	Printing and publishing		...	...	...	...	...	...	...	...	...	...	...	...
23	Coke,refined petroleum products,nuclear fuel		98	87	101	102	102	100	105	106	87	104	103	107
24	Chemicals and chemical products		76	100	107	125	102	100	104	129	107	113	108	131
25	Rubber and plastics products		130	119	140	129	96	100	146	120	119	138	104	69
26	Non-metallic mineral products		110	104	107	105	109	100	111	109	108	104	111	102
27	Basic metals		72	106	118	115	107	100	109	95	92	84	94	90
28	Fabricated metal products		200	178	166	126	162	100	230	163	120	185	164	177
29	Machinery and equipment n.e.c.		222	238	202	231	218	100	93	113	97	73	93	90
30	Office, accounting and computing machinery		...	...	...	...	...	...	...	...	...	...	...	...
31	Electrical machinery and apparatus		71	77	79	106	99	100	146	150	151	153	149	125
32	Radio,television and communication equipment		46	76	81	85	83	100	80	95	67	34	24	35
33	Medical, precision and optical instruments		...	...	...	...	...	...	...	...	...	...	...	...
34	Motor vehicles, trailers, semi-trailers		...	...	...	...	...	...	...	...	...	...	...	...
35	Other transport equipment		...	...	...	...	...	...	...	...	...	...	...	...
36	Furniture; manufacturing n.e.c.		667	440	413	440	413	100	81	78	56	73	88	130
37	Recycling		...	...	...	...	...	...	...	...	...	...	...	...
D	Total manufacturing		92	93	100	101	101	100	97	101	88	99	100	105

The former Yugoslav Republic of Macedonia

Supplier of information:
State Statistical Office, Skopje.

Basic source of data:
National accounts report.

Major deviations from ISIC (Revision 3):
The data were originally classified according to NACE (Revision 1), and are not fully compatible with ISIC (Revision 3).

Reference period:
Calendar year.

Scope:
All establishments.

Method of data collection:
Not reported.

Type of enumeration:
Not reported.

Adjusted for non-response:
Not reported.

Concepts and definitions of variables:
No deviations from the standard UN concepts and definitions are reported.

Related national publications:
None reported.

The former Yugoslav Republic of Macedonia

ISIC Revision 3		Establishments					Employees					Wages and salaries				
			(number)					(number)					(millions of Macedonia Denars)			
ISIC	Industry	Note	2003	2004	2005	2006	Note	2003	2004	2005	2006	Note	2003	2004	2005	2006
15	Food and beverages		...	...	...	...		...	...	...	...		...	...	...	...
16	Tobacco products		...	...	...	...		...	...	...	...		...	...	...	...
17	Textiles		...	...	...	...		...	...	...	...		...	...	...	...
18	Wearing apparel, fur		...	...	...	...		...	...	...	...		...	...	...	...
19	Leather, leather products and footwear		...	...	...	...		...	...	...	...		...	...	...	...
20	Wood products (excl. furniture)		...	...	...	...		...	...	...	...		...	...	...	...
21	Paper and paper products		...	...	...	...		...	...	...	...		...	...	...	...
22	Printing and publishing		...	...	...	...		...	...	...	...		...	...	...	...
23	Coke,refined petroleum products,nuclear fuel		...	...	...	...		...	...	...	...		...	...	...	...
24	Chemicals and chemical products		...	...	...	...		...	...	...	...		...	...	...	...
25	Rubber and plastics products		...	...	...	...		...	...	...	...		...	...	...	...
26	Non-metallic mineral products		...	...	...	...		...	...	...	...		...	...	...	...
27	Basic metals		...	...	...	...		...	...	...	...		...	...	...	...
28	Fabricated metal products		...	...	...	...		...	...	...	...		...	...	...	...
29	Machinery and equipment n.e.c.		...	...	...	...		...	...	...	...		...	...	...	...
30	Office, accounting and computing machinery		...	...	...	...		...	...	...	...		...	...	...	...
31	Electrical machinery and apparatus		...	...	...	...		...	...	...	...		...	...	...	...
32	Radio,television and communication equipment		...	...	...	...		...	...	...	...		...	...	...	...
33	Medical, precision and optical instruments		...	...	...	...		...	...	...	...		...	...	...	...
34	Motor vehicles, trailers, semi-trailers		...	...	...	...		...	...	...	...		...	...	...	...
35	Other transport equipment		...	...	...	...		...	...	...	...		...	...	...	...
36	Furniture; manufacturing n.e.c.		...	...	...	...		...	...	...	...		...	...	...	...
37	Recycling		...	...	...	...		...	...	...	...		...	...	...	...
D	Total manufacturing		...	...	...	...		...	...	...	...		...	...	...	...

The former Yugoslav Republic of Macedonia

ISIC Revision 3		Output					Value added					Gross fixed capital formation		
			(millions of Macedonia Denars)					(millions of Macedonia Denars)					(millions of Macedonia Denars)	
ISIC	Industry	Note	2003	2004	2005	2006	Note	2003	2004	2005	2006	Note	2005	2006
15	Food and beverages	a/	33216	32148	35749	30332		...	...	...	...		...	...
16	Tobacco products	a/	...	...	...	...		...	...	...	...		...	...
17	Textiles	b/	7031	6555	6384	5626		...	...	...	...		...	...
18	Wearing apparel, fur	b/	...	...	...	...		...	...	...	...		...	...
19	Leather, leather products and footwear		762	797	816	810		...	...	...	...		...	...
20	Wood products (excl. furniture)		480	554	476	583		...	...	...	...		...	...
21	Paper and paper products	c/	2124	1643	2098	2364		...	...	...	...		...	...
22	Printing and publishing	c/	...	...	...	...		...	...	...	...		...	...
23	Coke,refined petroleum products,nuclear fuel		13567	14239	22725	29658		...	...	...	...		...	...
24	Chemicals and chemical products		6702	6563	5837	5776		...	...	...	...		...	...
25	Rubber and plastics products		1587	1739	1744	1221		...	...	...	...		...	...
26	Non-metallic mineral products		10184	7092	8241	6852		...	...	...	...		...	...
27	Basic metals	d/	18390	20591	29348	38347		...	...	...	...		...	...
28	Fabricated metal products	d/	...	...	...	...		...	...	...	...		...	...
29	Machinery and equipment n.e.c.		902	1053	21501	1163		...	...	...	...		...	...
30	Office, accounting and computing machinery	e/	2862	2623	2602	2381		...	...	...	...		...	...
31	Electrical machinery and apparatus	e/	...	...	...	...		...	...	...	...		...	...
32	Radio,television and communication equipment	e/	...	...	...	...		...	...	...	...		...	...
33	Medical, precision and optical instruments	e/	...	...	...	...		...	...	...	...		...	...
34	Motor vehicles, trailers, semi-trailers	f/	1787	1675	2128	1975		...	...	...	...		...	...
35	Other transport equipment	f/	...	...	...	...		...	...	...	...		...	...
36	Furniture; manufacturing n.e.c.		802	700	773	602		...	...	...	...		...	...
37	Recycling		...	...	...	174		...	...	...	...		...	...
D	Total manufacturing		100252	98016	121151	127866		...	...	...	...		...	...

a/ 15 includes 16.
b/ 17 includes 18.
c/ 21 includes 22.
d/ 27 includes 28.
e/ 30 includes 31, 32 and 33.
f/ 34 includes 35.

The former Yugoslav Republic of Macedonia

ISIC Revision 3			Index numbers of industrial production											
			(2000=100)											
ISIC	Industry	Note	1995	1996	1997	1998	1999	2000	2001	2002	2003	2004	2005	2006
15	Food and beverages		...	...	...	...	97	100	97	89	113	109	113	114
16	Tobacco products		...	...	...	...	107	100	100	97	91	75	76	78
17	Textiles		...	...	...	...	110	100	87	95	70	62	62	55
18	Wearing apparel, fur		...	...	...	...	105	100	98	86	69	70	73	79
19	Leather, leather products and footwear		...	...	...	...	137	100	95	62	37	38	33	29
20	Wood products (excl. furniture)		...	...	...	...	104	100	94	118	194	194	154	144
21	Paper and paper products		...	...	...	...	88	100	99	102	81	81	88	108
22	Printing and publishing		...	...	...	...	146	100	99	107	52	54	52	57
23	Coke,refined petroleum products,nuclear fuel		...	...	...	...	82	100	99	67	97	100	117	131
24	Chemicals and chemical products		...	...	...	...	92	100	98	99	72	73	73	73
25	Rubber and plastics products		...	...	...	...	96	100	98	159	123	122	116	94
26	Non-metallic mineral products		...	...	...	...	77	100	94	131	109	112	137	152
27	Basic metals		...	...	...	...	83	100	95	77	92	105	140	152
28	Fabricated metal products		...	...	...	...	122	100	99	113	72	53	63	73
29	Machinery and equipment n.e.c.		...	...	...	...	97	100	90	97	82	76	83	86
30	Office, accounting and computing machinery	a/	...	...	...	...	100	100	100	79	53	44	48	48
31	Electrical machinery and apparatus	a/	...	...	...	...	...	...	...	...	...	...	...	...
32	Radio,television and communication equipment	a/	...	...	...	...	...	...	...	...	...	...	...	...
33	Medical, precision and optical instruments	a/	...	...	...	...	...	...	...	...	...	...	...	...
34	Motor vehicles, trailers, semi-trailers		...	...	...	...	106	100	100	192	137	132	97	68
35	Other transport equipment		...	...	...	...	...	...	...	...	...	...	...	...
36	Furniture; manufacturing n.e.c.		...	...	...	...	80	100	100	88	166	176	155	102
37	Recycling		...	...	...	...	86	100	97	84	108	133	178	229
D	Total manufacturing		...	...	...	...	...	100	97	92	97	95	102	106

a/ 30 includes 31, 32 and 33.

Trinidad and Tobago

Supplier of information:
Central Statistical Office, Port-of-Spain.

Basic source of data:
Annual sample survey on registered establishments.

Major deviations from ISIC (Revision 3):
None reported.

Reference period:
Calendar year.

Scope:
All registered establishments.

Method of data collection:
Mail questionnaires followed-up by direct visits.

Type of enumeration:
Sample survey.

Adjusted for non-response:
Yes.

Concepts and definitions of variables:
Wages and salaries excludes remuneration for time not worked and payments in kind.
Output is reported at basic prices, which excludes taxes on commodity and includes commodity related subsidies.
Value added is reported at basic prices, which equals output at basic prices less value of input (at purchaser's prices).

Related national publications:
National Income Report of Trinidad and Tobago, published by Central Statistical Office, Port-of-Spain.

Trinidad and Tobago

ISIC Revision 3		Number of establishments					Number of employees					Wages and salaries paid to employees				
			(number)					(number)					(millions of Trinidad and Tobago Dollars)			
ISIC	Industry	Note	2003	2004	2005	2006	Note	2003	2004	2005	2006	Note	2003	2004	2005	2006
151	Processed meat,fish,fruit,vegetables,fats		24	26	30	31		2524	...	...	...		113.1	152.0	34.3	38.1
1511	Processing/preserving of meat		11	10	13	10		1146	...	...	...		34.5	57.0	...	...
1512	Processing/preserving of fish		9	12	12	17		624	...	...	...		24.0	30.9	...	...
1513	Processing/preserving of fruit & vegetables		2	2	4	3		449	...	...	...		35.6	39.5	...	...
1514	Vegetable and animal oils and fats		2	2	1	1		305	...	...	...		19.0	24.6	...	...
1520	Dairy products		10	15	16	15		892	...	...	...		79.8	83.8	...	...
153	Grain mill products; starches; animal feeds		16	19	14	14		886	...	...	...		76.8	83.2	...	...
1531	Grain mill products		7	8	8	8		456	...	...	...		44.9	46.9	...	...
1532	Starches and starch products		...	...	...	...		...	...	...	...		...	...	...	...
1533	Prepared animal feeds		9	11	6	6		430	...	...	...		31.9	36.3	...	...
154	Other food products		267	272	278	281		3086	...	...	...		313.8	247.3	...	...
1541	Bakery products		231	231	231	231		508	...	...	...		93.4	87.9	...	...
1542	Sugar		1	1	1	...		...	...	...	...		95.0	4.1	4.7	5.4
1543	Cocoa, chocolate and sugar confectionery		14	14	18	18		1542	...	...	...		69.8	88.2	...	...
1544	Macaroni, noodles & similar products		...	...	...	...		...	...	...	...		...	...	...	...
1549	Other food products n.e.c.		21	26	28	32		1036	...	...	...		55.6	67.1	...	...
155	Beverages		12	12	12	11		2661	...	...	...		191.3	197.4	...	...
1551	Distilling, rectifying & blending of spirits		2	2	2	1		...	...	...	...		27.7	25.5	29.6	32.7
1552	Wines		1	1	1	1		...	...	...	...		...	...	...	...
1553	Malt liquors and malt		1	1	1	1		821	...	...	...		68.9	73.9	...	...
1554	Soft drinks; mineral waters		8	8	8	8		1840	...	...	...		94.7	98.0	...	...
1600	Tobacco products		1	1	1	1		188	...	...	...		27.8	38.4	...	...
171	Spinning, weaving and finishing of textiles		16	16	15	13		155	...	...	...		3.2	7.1	7.8	8.6
1711	Textile fibre preparation; textile weaving		...	...	...	...		...	...	...	...		...	...	...	...
1712	Finishing of textiles		...	...	...	...		...	...	...	...		...	...	...	...
172	Other textiles		5	5	5	4		38	...	...	...		1.6	1.7	1.8	1.9
1721	Made-up textile articles, except apparel		...	...	...	...		...	...	...	...		...	...	...	...
1722	Carpets and rugs		...	...	...	...		...	...	...	...		...	...	...	...
1723	Cordage, rope, twine and netting		...	...	...	...		...	...	...	...		...	...	...	...
1729	Other textiles n.e.c.		5	5	5	4		38	...	...	...		...	...	...	...
1730	Knitted and crocheted fabrics and articles		3	3	5	5		...	...	...	...		...	...	...	...
1810	Wearing apparel, except fur apparel		128	128	107	102		1752	...	...	...		38.5	56.2	57.9	69.6
1820	Dressing & dyeing of fur; processing of fur		...	...	...	...		...	...	...	...		...	...	...	...
191	Tanning, dressing and processing of leather		...	...	...	...		...	...	...	...		...	...	...	...
1911	Tanning and dressing of leather		...	...	...	...		...	...	...	...		...	...	...	...
1912	Luggage, handbags, etc.; saddlery & harness		...	...	...	...		...	...	...	...		...	...	...	...
1920	Footwear		10	9	8	8		53	...	...	...		1.1	1.8	1.7	1.8
2010	Sawmilling and planing of wood		58	60	65	65		541	...	...	...		7.8	10.3	...	...
202	Products of wood, cork, straw, etc.		257	256	256	243		1683	...	...	...		61.9	52.9	...	...
2021	Veneer sheets, plywood, particle board, etc.		...	...	...	...		...	...	...	...		...	...	...	...
2022	Builders' carpentry and joinery		15	14	14	12		404	...	...	...		16.7	15.8	...	...
2023	Wooden containers		...	...	...	...		...	...	...	...		...	...	...	...
2029	Other wood products; articles of cork/straw		242	242	242	231		1279	...	...	...		45.2	37.1	...	...
210	Paper and paper products		32	29	29	30		1644	...	...	...		58.2	60.7	...	...
2101	Pulp, paper and paperboard		...	...	...	...		...	...	...	...		...	...	...	...
2102	Corrugated paper and paperboard		...	...	...	...		...	...	...	...		...	...	...	...
2109	Other articles of paper and paperboard		...	...	...	...		...	...	...	...		...	...	...	...
221	Publishing		19	18	18	17		841	...	...	...		59.5	59.1	...	...
2211	Publishing of books and other publications		...	...	...	...		...	...	...	...		...	...	...	...
2212	Publishing of newspapers, journals, etc.		...	...	...	...		...	...	...	...		...	...	...	...
2213	Publishing of recorded media		...	...	...	...		...	...	...	...		...	...	...	...
2219	Other publishing		...	...	...	...		...	...	...	...		...	...	...	...

222	Printing and related service activities	154	144	144	143	2241	...	...	...	93.1	120.7	...	...
2221	Printing	...	...	...	...	...	...	...	...	...	...	...	...
2222	Service activities related to printing	...	...	...	...	...	...	...	...	...	...	...	...
2230	Reproduction of recorded media	...	...	...	...	...	...	...	...	...	...	...	...
2310	Coke oven products	...	...	...	...	...	...	...	...	...	...	...	...
2320	Refined petroleum products	2	2	2	2	2569	...	...	...	571.7	672.2	...	...
2330	Processing of nuclear fuel	...	...	...	...	...	...	...	...	...	...	...	...
241	Basic chemicals	11	11	13	13	1525	...	...	...	298.4	432.4	378.8	429.0
2411	Basic chemicals, except fertilizers	...	...	...	...	...	...	...	...	...	...	...	...
2412	Fertilizers and nitrogen compounds	...	...	...	...	...	...	...	...	...	...	...	...
2413	Plastics in primary forms; synthetic rubber	...	...	...	...	...	...	...	...	...	...	...	...
242	Other chemicals	89	88	92	85	...	...	...	...	133.0	135.1	...	...
2421	Pesticides and other agro-chemical products	...	...	...	...	...	...	...	...	...	...	...	...
2422	Paints, varnishes, printing ink and mastics	15	15	12	15	...	...	...	...	53.0	38.4	...	...
2423	Pharmaceuticals, medicinal chemicals, etc.	63	63	70	63	...	...	...	...	65.6	81.9	...	...
2424	Soap, cleaning & cosmetic preparations	...	...	...	...	...	...	...	...	...	...	...	...
2429	Other chemical products n.e.c.	11	10	10	7	...	...	...	...	14.4	14.8	...	...
2430	Man-made fibres	...	...	...	...	...	...	...	...	...	...	...	...
251	Rubber products	19	17	15	16	40	...	...	...	19.9	6.2	...	...
2511	Rubber tyres and tubes	14	12	11	12	...	...	...	...	18.9	5.4	...	...
2519	Other rubber products	5	5	4	4	...	...	...	...	1.0	0.8	...	...
2520	Plastic products	44	44	48	48	1463	...	...	...	75.4	81.3	...	...
2610	Glass and glass products	1	1	1	1	...	...	...	...	66.0	30.1	...	...
269	Non-metallic mineral products n.e.c.	53	56	60	50	110	...	...	...	187.9	186.8	...	...
2691	Pottery, china and earthenware	15	15	15	8	...	...	...	...	9.1	9.7	...	...
2692	Refractory ceramic products	...	...	...	...	...	...	...	...	...	...	...	...
2693	Struct.non-refractory clay; ceramic products	5	5	6	7	...	...	...	...	18.8	15.1	...	...
2694	Cement, lime and plaster	1	1	1	1	...	...	...	...	91.5	92.4	...	...
2695	Articles of concrete, cement and plaster	32	35	38	34	...	...	...	...	68.5	69.6	...	...
2696	Cutting, shaping & finishing of stone	...	...	...	...	...	...	...	...	...	...	...	...
2699	Other non-metallic mineral products n.e.c.	...	...	...	...	...	...	...	...	...	...	...	...
2710	Basic iron and steel	16	16	19	19	...	...	...	...	166.9	169.5	...	...
2720	Basic precious and non-ferrous metals	...	...	...	...	...	...	...	...	...	...	...	...
273	Casting of metals	...	...	...	...	...	...	...	...	...	...	...	...
2731	Casting of iron and steel	...	...	...	...	...	...	...	...	...	...	...	...
2732	Casting of non-ferrous metals	...	...	...	...	...	...	...	...	...	...	...	...
281	Struct.metal products;tanks;steam generators	39	42	44	44	...	...	...	...	47.7	27.6	...	...
2811	Structural metal products	...	...	...	...	...	...	...	...	...	...	...	...
2812	Tanks, reservoirs and containers of metal	...	...	...	...	...	...	...	...	...	...	...	...
2813	Steam generators	...	...	...	...	...	...	...	...	...	...	...	...
289	Other metal products; metal working services	118	118	122	122	...	...	...	...	22.5	25.9	...	...
2891	Metal forging/pressing/stamping/roll-forming	...	...	...	...	...	...	...	...	...	...	...	...
2892	Treatment & coating of metals	...	...	...	...	...	...	...	...	...	...	...	...
2893	Cutlery, hand tools and general hardware	...	...	...	...	...	...	...	...	...	...	...	...
2899	Other fabricated metal products n.e.c.	...	...	...	...	...	...	...	...	...	...	...	...
291	General purpose machinery	...	...	...	...	...	...	...	...	...	...	...	...
2911	Engines & turbines (not for transport equipment)	...	...	...	...	...	...	...	...	...	...	...	...
2912	Pumps, compressors, taps and valves	...	...	...	...	...	...	...	...	...	...	...	...
2913	Bearings, gears, gearing & driving elements	...	...	...	...	...	...	...	...	...	...	...	...
2914	Ovens, furnaces and furnace burners	...	...	...	...	...	...	...	...	...	...	...	...
2915	Lifting and handling equipment	...	...	...	...	...	...	...	...	...	...	...	...
2919	Other general purpose machinery	...	...	...	...	...	...	...	...	...	...	...	...
292	Special purpose machinery	...	...	...	...	...	...	...	...	...	...	...	...
2921	Agricultural and forestry machinery	...	...	...	...	...	...	...	...	...	...	...	...
2922	Machine tools	...	...	...	...	...	...	...	...	...	...	...	...
2923	Machinery for metallurgy	...	...	...	...	...	...	...	...	...	...	...	...
2924	Machinery for mining & construction	...	...	...	...	...	...	...	...	...	...	...	...
2925	Food/beverage/tobacco processing machinery	...	...	...	...	...	...	...	...	...	...	...	...
2926	Machinery for textile, apparel and leather	...	...	...	...	...	...	...	...	...	...	...	...
2927	Weapons and ammunition	...	...	...	...	...	...	...	...	...	...	...	...
2929	Other special purpose machinery	...	...	...	...	...	...	...	...	...	...	...	...

continued

Trinidad and Tobago

ISIC Revision 3		Number of establishments					Number of employees					Wages and salaries paid to employees				
			(number)					(number)					(millions of Trinidad and Tobago Dollars)			
ISIC	Industry	Note	2003	2004	2005	2006	Note	2003	2004	2005	2006	Note	2003	2004	2005	2006
2930	Domestic appliances n.e.c.		3	3	3	3		...	...	...	...		2.8	9.0	...	...
3000	Office, accounting and computing machinery		1	1	1	1		...	...	...	...		0.5	0.5	...	...
3110	Electric motors, generators and transformers		...	...	...	...		...	...	...	...		...	...	...	...
3120	Electricity distribution & control apparatus		...	...	...	...		...	...	...	...		...	...	...	...
3130	Insulated wire and cable		13	12	15	12		...	...	...	...		38.0	37.3	...	...
3140	Accumulators, primary cells and batteries		1	1	4	4		...	...	...	...		13.1	6.7	...	...
3150	Lighting equipment and electric lamps		...	...	...	...		...	...	...	...		...	...	...	...
3190	Other electrical equipment n.e.c.		...	...	...	...		...	...	...	...		...	...	...	...
3210	Electronic valves, tubes, etc.		...	...	...	...		...	...	...	...		...	...	...	...
3220	TV/radio transmitters; line comm. apparatus		...	...	...	...		...	...	...	...		...	...	...	...
3230	TV and radio receivers and associated goods		8	8	2	2		...	...	...	...		...	...	...	...
331	Medical, measuring, testing appliances, etc.		...	...	...	...		...	...	...	...		...	...	...	...
3311	Medical, surgical and orthopaedic equipment		...	...	...	...		...	...	...	...		...	...	...	...
3312	Measuring/testing/navigating appliances,etc.		...	...	...	...		...	...	...	...		...	...	...	...
3313	Industrial process control equipment		...	...	...	...		...	...	...	...		...	...	...	...
3320	Optical instruments & photographic equipment		...	...	...	...		...	...	...	...		...	...	...	...
3330	Watches and clocks		...	...	...	...		...	...	...	...		...	...	...	...
3410	Motor vehicles		...	...	...	...		...	...	...	...		...	...	...	...
3420	Automobile bodies, trailers & semi-trailers		3	3	3	3		...	...	...	...		1.1	1.1	...	...
3430	Parts/accessories for automobiles		...	...	...	...		...	...	...	...		...	...	...	...
351	Building and repairing of ships and boats		17	20	20	19		...	...	...	...		3.6	12.6	...	...
3511	Building and repairing of ships		...	...	...	...		...	...	...	...		...	...	...	...
3512	Building/repairing of pleasure/sport. boats		...	...	...	...		...	...	...	...		...	...	...	...
3520	Railway/tramway locomotives & rolling stock		...	...	...	...		...	...	...	...		...	...	...	...
3530	Aircraft and spacecraft		...	...	...	...		...	...	...	...		...	...	...	...
359	Transport equipment n.e.c.		...	...	...	...		...	...	...	...		...	...	...	...
3591	Motorcycles		...	...	...	...		...	...	...	...		...	...	...	...
3592	Bicycles and invalid carriages		...	...	...	...		...	...	...	...		...	...	...	...
3599	Other transport equipment n.e.c.		...	...	...	...		...	...	...	...		...	...	...	...
3610	Furniture		12	12	10	10		...	...	...	...		11.5	...	...	...
369	Manufacturing n.e.c.		110	106	99	99		1290	...	...	...		62.0	38.4	35.5	38.3
3691	Jewellery and related articles		23	23	20	20		265	...	...	...		8.6	10.9	...	...
3692	Musical instruments		...	...	...	...		...	...	...	...		...	...	...	...
3693	Sports goods		...	...	...	...		...	...	...	...		...	...	...	...
3694	Games and toys		...	...	...	...		...	...	...	...		...	...	...	...
3699	Other manufacturing n.e.c.		87	83	79	79		1025	...	...	...		53.4	27.5	...	...
3710	Recycling of metal waste and scrap		...	...	...	...		...	...	...	...		...	...	...	...
3720	Recycling of non-metal waste and scrap		...	...	...	...		...	...	...	...		...	...	...	...
D	Total manufacturing	a/	1572	1574	1576	1536	a/	26182	...	...	...	a/	2849.5	3045.3	517.8	587.3

a/ Sum of available data.

ISIC Revision 3		Output					Value added					Gross fixed capital formation		
			(millions of Trinidad and Tobago Dollars)					(millions of Trinidad and Tobago Dollars)					(millions of Trinidad and Tobago Dollars)	
ISIC	Industry	Note	2003	2004	2005	2006	Note	2003	2004	2005	2006	Note	2003	2004
151	Processed meat,fish,fruit,vegetables,fats		1074.8	1237.9	1389.7	1636.8		156.0	209.1	264.5	303.7		63.6	37.2
1511	Processing/preserving of meat		554.6	606.1	690.7	784.4		51.9	60.7	75.1	55.0		54.3	11.6
1512	Processing/preserving of fish		113.5	170.3	144.7	154.7		25.5	73.0	37.0	27.1		5.7	22.1
1513	Processing/preserving of fruit & vegetables		197.9	219.9	300.5	401.6		53.9	51.5	124.0	192.6		3.5	3.2
1514	Vegetable and animal oils and fats		208.8	241.6	253.8	296.1		24.7	23.9	28.4	29.0		0.1	0.3
1520	Dairy products		391.2	428.9	462.4	507.3		179.7	195.7	203.5	200.4		19.4	13.3
153	Grain mill products; starches; animal feeds		824.3	972.2	991.7	1160.8		206.4	223.9	234.9	264.0		33.3	56.6
1531	Grain mill products		418.8	459.8	503.2	588.4		112.8	101.1	128.4	144.3		31.0	46.6
1532	Starches and starch products		...	...	...	...		...	...	...	...		...	...
1533	Prepared animal feeds		405.5	512.4	488.5	572.4		93.6	122.8	106.5	119.7		2.3	10.0
154	Other food products		1428.7	1606.2	1540.6	1710.3		266.5	431.4	346.6	439.3		36.9	80.7
1541	Bakery products		387.0	397.4	496.5	568.5		142.7	150.4	197.3	213.9		9.6	1.3
1542	Sugar		320.2	278.8	235.0	219.8		-100.0	67.6	-50.2	25.7		2.1	...
1543	Cocoa, chocolate and sugar confectionery		383.7	413.5	429.2	488.5		122.4	121.8	109.1	109.2		14.4	1.3
1544	Macaroni, noodles & similar products		...	...	...	...		...	...	...	...		...	...
1549	Other food products n.e.c.		337.8	516.5	379.9	433.5		101.4	91.6	90.4	90.5		10.8	78.1
155	Beverages		1608.1	1377.2	1790.2	2213.4		778.0	656.3	796.1	1067.9		53.3	107.7
1551	Distilling, rectifying & blending of spirits		352.2	106.2	303.1	297.0		205.2	126.0	145.7	142.8		1.2	...
1552	Wines		...	...	...	...		...	...	...	...		...	...
1553	Malt liquors and malt		600.3	564.5	685.2	953.2		413.7	317.2	456.6	682.4		22.0	54.6
1554	Soft drinks; mineral waters		655.6	706.5	801.9	963.2		159.1	213.1	193.8	242.7		30.1	53.1
1600	Tobacco products		451.2	506.0	616.4	697.5		330.7	376.0	468.9	522.7		35.5	10.9
171	Spinning, weaving and finishing of textiles		32.2	32.8	37.0	18.8		13.7	10.5	11.5	12.6		1.3	1.5
1711	Textile fibre preparation; textile weaving		...	...	...	...		...	...	...	...		...	...
1712	Finishing of textiles		...	...	...	...		...	...	...	...		...	...
172	Other textiles		4.3	5.1	4.1	2.2		2.2	2.2	2.4	2.4		-	...
1721	Made-up textile articles, except apparel		...	...	...	...		...	...	...	...		...	...
1722	Carpets and rugs		...	...	...	...		...	...	...	...		...	...
1723	Cordage, rope, twine and netting		...	...	...	...		...	...	...	...		...	...
1729	Other textiles n.e.c.		4.3	5.1	4.1	2.2		2.2	2.2	2.1	3.0		-	-
1730	Knitted and crocheted fabrics and articles		2.0	1.7	2.0	2.0		0.5	0.4	0.4	0.6		-	-
1810	Wearing apparel, except fur apparel		202.6	193.3	239.4	279.1		81.1	89.3	92.0	110.6		3.7	7.9
1820	Dressing & dyeing of fur; processing of fur		...	...	...	...		...	...	...	...		...	...
191	Tanning, dressing and processing of leather		...	...	...	...		7.3	7.1	7.9	8.4		...	...
1911	Tanning and dressing of leather		...	...	...	...		...	...	...	...		...	...
1912	Luggage, handbags, etc.; saddlery & harness		...	...	...	...		7.3	7.1	7.9	8.4		...	...
1920	Footwear		6.0	9.7	9.2	7.8		3.7	3.5	3.4	3.6		-	-
2010	Sawmilling and planing of wood		45.3	48.0	53.8	56.5		13.3	17.0	17.5	18.4		...	...
202	Products of wood, cork, straw, etc.		86.2	101.2	102.4	107.5		30.1	34.6	38.3	40.2		...	...
2021	Veneer sheets, plywood, particle board, etc.		...	...	...	...		...	...	...	...		...	...
2022	Builders' carpentry and joinery		67.9	63.4	80.6	84.7		19.9	15.8	26.3	27.6		...	...
2023	Wooden containers		...	...	...	...		10.2	10.8	12.0	12.6		...	...
2029	Other wood products; articles of cork/straw		...	...	...	...		...	...	...	...		...	...
210	Paper and paper products		550.0	565.2	696.4	757.0		195.8	187.3	225.8	238.8		25.1	20.2
2101	Pulp, paper and paperboard		...	...	...	...		...	...	...	...		...	...
2102	Corrugated paper and paperboard		...	...	...	...		...	...	...	...		...	...
2109	Other articles of paper and paperboard		...	...	...	...		...	...	...	...		...	...
221	Publishing		258.0	282.4	320.9	320.6		140.2	153.1	188.1	231.6		1.6	7.4
2211	Publishing of books and other publications		...	...	...	...		...	...	...	...		...	...
2212	Publishing of newspapers, journals, etc.		...	...	...	...		...	...	...	...		...	...
2213	Publishing of recorded media		...	...	...	...		...	...	...	...		...	...
2219	Other publishing		...	...	...	...		...	...	...	...		...	...

continued

Trinidad and Tobago

ISIC Revision 3		Output					Value added					Gross fixed capital formation		
			(millions of Trinidad and Tobago Dollars)					(millions of Trinidad and Tobago Dollars)					(millions of Trinidad and Tobago Dollars)	
ISIC	Industry	Note	2003	2004	2005	2006	Note	2003	2004	2005	2006	Note	2003	2004
222	Printing and related service activities		445.9	555.2	524.9	600.1		201.7	225.0	271.4	281.0		22.1	65.7
2221	Printing		...	...	...	...		...	...	...	...		...	...
2222	Service activities related to printing		...	...	...	...		...	...	...	...		...	...
2230	Reproduction of recorded media		...	...	...	...		...	...	...	...		...	...
2310	Coke oven products		...	...	...	...		...	...	...	...		...	...
2320	Refined petroleum products		23816.0	28021.0	41656.2	49180.5		4608.5	5750.8	7294.0	8650.0		4244.7	2871.0
2330	Processing of nuclear fuel		...	...	...	...		...	...	...	...		...	...
241	Basic chemicals		7707.7	11210.7	14840.2	20509.7		3243.9	5165.3	6526.9	8761.7		195.4	831.3
2411	Basic chemicals, except fertilizers		...	...	...	...		...	...	...	...		...	...
2412	Fertilizers and nitrogen compounds		...	...	...	...		...	...	...	...		...	...
2413	Plastics in primary forms; synthetic rubber		...	...	...	...		...	...	...	...		...	...
242	Other chemicals		763.3	912.4	876.2	923.3		292.4	501.2	336.5	357.0		22.2	15.8
2421	Pesticides and other agro-chemical products		...	...	...	...		...	...	...	...		...	...
2422	Paints, varnishes, printing ink and mastics		242.6	231.2	257.3	262.4		87.8	112.3	93.2	95.0		6.9	6.7
2423	Pharmaceuticals, medicinal chemicals, etc.		19.1	11.6	44.9	49.9		4.4	6.3	10.4	11.5		15.3	9.1
2424	Soap, cleaning & cosmetic preparations		203.9	422.7	241.0	242.1		54.1	253.5	64.0	64.3		...	...
2429	Other chemical products n.e.c.		297.7	246.9	333.0	368.9		146.1	129.1	168.9	186.2		...	...
2430	Man-made fibres		...	...	...	...		...	...	...	...		...	...
251	Rubber products		163.2	78.7	31.4	22.4		59.1	19.4	12.8	9.7		...	...
2511	Rubber tyres and tubes		158.9	73.7	25.8	16.4		56.1	16.1	9.1	5.8		...	...
2519	Other rubber products		4.3	5.0	5.6	6.0		3.0	3.3	3.7	3.9		...	...
2520	Plastic products		454.4	534.3	623.5	677.6		130.5	238.1	199.5	217.0		38.1	6.4
2610	Glass and glass products		126.8	141.0	176.4	200.9		74.2	62.5	103.2	117.6		122.8	2.2
269	Non-metallic mineral products n.e.c.		976.8	1083.1	1198.0	1405.7		498.6	656.8	601.9	700.4		43.4	445.6
2691	Pottery, china and earthenware		...	...	...	...		...	...	...	...		0.5	...
2692	Refractory ceramic products		127.4	145.2	161.1	205.1		100.9	117.6	122.4	155.0		...	...
2693	Struct.non-refractory clay; ceramic products		...	...	...	...		...	...	...	...		0.1	3.5
2694	Cement, lime and plaster		453.2	517.1	531.1	578.9		269.5	276.1	315.8	344.3		19.6	420.9
2695	Articles of concrete, cement and plaster		396.1	420.8	505.8	621.7		128.2	263.1	163.7	201.1		23.2	21.2
2696	Cutting, shaping & finishing of stone		...	...	...	...		...	...	...	...		...	...
2699	Other non-metallic mineral products n.e.c.		0.1	...	...	...		...	...	...	...		...	...
2710	Basic iron and steel		2956.4	4003.8	3213.4	4544.1		385.3	1547.1	884.6	728.8		1515.4	101.5
2720	Basic precious and non-ferrous metals		...	...	...	...		...	...	...	...		...	...
273	Casting of metals		...	...	...	...		...	...	...	...		...	...
2731	Casting of iron and steel		...	...	...	...		...	...	...	...		...	...
2732	Casting of non-ferrous metals		...	...	...	...		...	...	...	...		...	...
281	Struct.metal products;tanks;steam generators		137.8	191.0	224.2	239.5		64.1	74.6	104.2	111.3		1.4	11.6
2811	Structural metal products		...	...	...	...		...	...	...	...		...	...
2812	Tanks, reservoirs and containers of metal		...	...	...	...		...	...	...	...		...	...
2813	Steam generators		...	...	...	...		...	...	...	...		...	...
289	Other metal products; metal working services		191.5	235.5	275.3	346.1		88.5	38.4	124.6	159.7		10.9	...
2891	Metal forging/pressing/stamping/roll-forming		...	...	...	...		...	...	...	...		...	...
2892	Treatment & coating of metals		...	...	...	...		...	...	...	...		...	...
2893	Cutlery, hand tools and general hardware		...	...	...	...		...	...	...	...		...	...
2899	Other fabricated metal products n.e.c.		...	...	...	...		...	...	...	...		...	...
291	General purpose machinery		...	...	...	...		...	...	...	...		...	...
2911	Engines & turbines (not for transport equipment)		...	...	...	...		...	...	...	...		...	...
2912	Pumps, compressors, taps and valves		...	...	...	...		...	...	...	...		...	...
2913	Bearings, gears, gearing & driving elements		...	...	...	...		...	...	...	...		...	...
2914	Ovens, furnaces and furnace burners		...	...	...	...		...	...	...	...		...	...
2915	Lifting and handling equipment		...	...	...	...		...	...	...	...		...	...
2919	Other general purpose machinery		...	...	...	...		...	...	...	...		...	...

292	Special purpose machinery		...	...	...	...		...	...	...	...		...	...
2921	Agricultural and forestry machinery		...	...	...	...		...	...	...	...		...	...
2922	Machine tools		...	...	...	...		...	...	...	...		...	...
2923	Machinery for metallurgy		...	...	...	...		...	...	...	...		...	...
2924	Machinery for mining & construction		...	...	...	...		...	...	...	...		...	...
2925	Food/beverage/tobacco processing machinery		...	...	...	...		...	...	...	...		...	...
2926	Machinery for textile, apparel and leather		...	...	...	...		...	...	...	...		...	...
2927	Weapons and ammunition		...	...	...	...		...	...	...	...		...	...
2929	Other special purpose machinery		...	...	...	...		...	...	...	...		...	...
2930	Domestic appliances n.e.c.		31.7	34.7	39.2	43.0		8.4	21.1	10.4	11.4		20.4	2.8
3000	Office, accounting and computing machinery		0.9	1.1	1.1	3.7		0.4	0.4	0.4	1.9		...	...
3110	Electric motors, generators and transformers		...	...	...	...		...	...	...	...		...	...
3120	Electricity distribution & control apparatus		...	...	...	...		...	...	...	...		...	...
3130	Insulated wire and cable		345.1	444.8	487.1	506.5		110.2	197.8	155.5	161.7		11.8	10.9
3140	Accumulators, primary cells and batteries		75.4	94.3	118.1	118.1		19.6	26.5	30.7	30.7		-	0.2
3150	Lighting equipment and electric lamps		...	...	...	...		...	...	...	...		...	...
3190	Other electrical equipment n.e.c.		98.2	97.5	144.9	170.1		36.6	37.2	54.0	63.4		...	...
3210	Electronic valves, tubes, etc.		...	...	...	...		...	...	...	...		...	...
3220	TV/radio transmitters; line comm. apparatus		24.8	24.5	26.7	24.7		...	...	...	...		...	...
3230	TV and radio receivers and associated goods		...	...	...	...		...	...	...	...		...	...
331	Medical, measuring, testing appliances, etc.		...	...	...	...		...	...	...	...		...	...
3311	Medical, surgical and orthopaedic equipment		...	...	...	...		...	...	...	...		...	...
3312	Measuring/testing/navigating appliances,etc.		...	...	...	...		...	...	...	...		...	...
3313	Industrial process control equipment		...	...	...	...		...	...	...	...		...	...
3320	Optical instruments & photographic equipment		...	...	...	...		...	...	...	...		...	...
3330	Watches and clocks		...	...	...	...		...	...	...	...		...	...
3410	Motor vehicles		...	...	...	...		...	...	...	...		...	...
3420	Automobile bodies, trailers & semi-trailers		8.3	9.1	9.2	6.4		1.4	1.7	1.5	1.0		...	...
3430	Parts/accessories for automobiles		46.9	50.5	71.7	68.9		8.6	5.8	13.3	11.8		...	...
351	Building and repairing of ships and boats		43.7	35.1	43.7	50.0		6.2	18.0	19.0	21.7		3.0	0.3
3511	Building and repairing of ships		...	...	...	...		...	...	...	...		...	...
3512	Building/repairing of pleasure/sport. boats		...	...	...	...		...	...	...	...		...	...
3520	Railway/tramway locomotives & rolling stock		...	...	...	...		...	...	...	...		...	...
3530	Aircraft and spacecraft		...	...	...	...		...	...	...	...		...	...
359	Transport equipment n.e.c.		...	...	...	...		...	...	...	...		...	...
3591	Motorcycles		...	...	...	...		...	...	...	...		...	...
3592	Bicycles and invalid carriages		...	...	...	...		...	...	...	...		...	...
3599	Other transport equipment n.e.c.		...	...	...	...		...	...	...	...		...	...
3610	Furniture		340.8	364.8	410.3	424.7		...	...	...	...		1.0	1.1
369	Manufacturing n.e.c.		255.1	296.0	331.6	351.5		93.3	91.3	104.1	100.3		16.7	...
3691	Jewellery and related articles		30.5	35.4	39.7	42.1		8.2	9.5	12.5	13.2		0.8	...
3692	Musical instruments		...	...	...	...		...	...	...	...		...	...
3693	Sports goods		...	...	...	...		...	...	...	...		...	...
3694	Games and toys		...	...	...	...		...	...	...	...		...	...
3699	Other manufacturing n.e.c.		224.6	260.6	291.9	309.4		85.1	81.8	91.6	87.1		15.9	...
3710	Recycling of metal waste and scrap		...	...	...	...		...	...	...	...		...	...
3720	Recycling of non-metal waste and scrap		...	...	...	...		...	...	...	...		...	...
D	Total manufacturing	a/	45975.6	55786.9	72883.1	89895.1	a/	12336.7	17276.4	19750.3	23963.3	a/	6543.0	4709.8

a/ Sum of available data.

Trinidad and Tobago

ISIC Revision 3			Index numbers of industrial production (2000=100)											
ISIC	Industry	Note	1995	1996	1997	1998	1999	2000	2001	2002	2003	2004	2005	2006
15	Food and beverages		...	...	...	...	...	...	...	...	...	...	...	...
16	Tobacco products		45	54	68	82	95	100	106	111	119	124	138	169
17	Textiles		14	14	22	33	77	100	97	103	169	198	234	250
18	Wearing apparel, fur		...	...	...	...	...	...	...	...	...	...	...	...
19	Leather, leather products and footwear		...	...	...	...	...	...	...	...	...	...	...	...
20	Wood products (excl. furniture)		76	102	112	107	114	100	119	65	32	29	35	39
21	Paper and paper products		132	104	83	95	95	100	133	117	88	104	88	64
22	Printing and publishing		59	62	75	95	100	100	172	203	194	238	246	345
23	Coke,refined petroleum products,nuclear fuel		...	...	...	...	...	...	...	...	...	...	...	...
24	Chemicals and chemical products		...	...	...	...	...	...	...	...	...	...	...	...
25	Rubber and plastics products		...	...	...	...	...	...	...	...	...	...	...	...
26	Non-metallic mineral products		...	...	...	...	...	...	...	...	...	...	...	...
27	Basic metals		...	...	...	...	...	...	...	...	...	...	...	...
28	Fabricated metal products		65	69	64	73	85	100	130	121	201	497	687	1136
29	Machinery and equipment n.e.c.		...	...	...	...	...	...	...	...	...	...	...	...
30	Office, accounting and computing machinery		...	...	...	...	...	...	...	...	...	...	...	...
31	Electrical machinery and apparatus	a/	60	85	73	118	109	100	96	144	150	154	123	116
32	Radio,television and communication equipment	a/	...	...	...	...	...	...	...	...	...	...	...	...
33	Medical, precision and optical instruments		...	...	...	...	...	...	...	...	...	...	...	...
34	Motor vehicles, trailers, semi-trailers	b/	120	88	116	109	106	100	119	128	135	136	166	175
35	Other transport equipment	b/	...	...	...	...	...	...	...	...	...	...	...	...
36	Furniture; manufacturing n.e.c.		...	...	...	...	...	...	...	...	...	...	...	...
37	Recycling		...	...	...	...	...	...	...	...	...	...	...	...
D	Total manufacturing		...	...	...	...	...	...	...	...	...	...	...	...

a/ 31 includes 32.
b/ 34 includes 35.

Tunisia

Supplier of information:
Institut National de la Statistique, Ministère du développement économique, Tunis.

Basic source of data:
Industrial survey.

Major deviations from ISIC (Revision 2):
Data collected under the national classification system have been reclassified by the national authorities to achieve the best possible correspondence with ISIC (Revision 2).

Reference period:
Calendar year.

Scope:
Establishments with six or more employees.

Method of data collection:
Enumerators visited individual sites.

Type of enumeration:
Not reported.

Adjusted for non-response:
Yes.

Concepts and definitions of variables:
Number of employees includes full-time, part-time and seasonal workers.
Wages and salaries paid to employees includes employers' contributions (in respect of their employees) paid to social security, pension and insurance schemes as well as the benefits received by employees under these schemes and severance and termination pay.

Related national publications:
Les comptes de la nation, published by the Institut National de la Statistique, Tunis.

ISIC Revision 2		Number of establishments a/					Number of employees a/					Wages and salaries paid to employees			
			(number)					(number)					(millions of Tunisian Dinars)		
ISIC	Industry	Note	2002	2003	2004	2005	Note	2002	2003	2004	2005	Note	2002	2003	2004	2005
311/2	Food products		2962	3069	3383	3482		36852	38161	38986	39615		423.8	452.6	...	...
3111	Slaughtering, preparing and preserving meat		8	8	9	8		979	950	969	1173		...	...	...	...
3112	Dairy products		48	52	58	61		3775	3738	3453	3461		...	...	...	...
3113	Canning, preserving of fruits and vegetables		31	28	32	28		2602	2082	2471	2362		...	...	...	...
3114	Canning, preserving and processing of fish		64	62	73	83		3157	3176	2484	3954		...	...	...	...
3115	Vegetable and animal oils and fats		397	510	607	621		4049	6619	7353	7328		...	...	...	...
3116	Grain mill products		95	94	99	118		2353	2566	2297	2165		...	...	...	...
3117	Bakery products		2116	2115	2287	2347		14008	14366	14826	14677		...	...	...	...
3118	Sugar factories and refineries		16	14	15	5		1265	951	927	753		...	...	...	...
3119	Cocoa, chocolate and sugar confectionery		29	28	30	21		1241	1025	1094	791		...	...	...	...
3121	Other food products		47	47	53	63		1677	1645	1489	1255		...	...	...	...
3122	Prepared animal feeds		111	111	120	127		1746	1043	1623	1696		...	...	...	...
313	Beverages		57	52	54	87		3057	3213	3123	4269		68.6	73.3	...	...
3131	Distilling, rectifying and blending spirits		29	27	28	38		494	460	392	752		...	...	...	...
3132	Wine industries		10	8	8	9		791	739	678	695		...	...	...	...
3133	Malt liquors and malt		2	2	2	2		711	820	834	875		...	...	...	...
3134	Soft drinks and carbonated waters		16	15	16	38		1061	1194	1219	1947		...	...	...	...
314	Tobacco		7	7	7	7		2578	2616	2577	934		51.4	54.9	...	...
321	Textiles		1660	2043	2329	2177		66271	88327	99219	95706		138.5	137.6	...	...
3211	Spinning, weaving and finishing textiles		1474	1861	2135	2014		59639	81927	92182	90301		...	...	...	...
3212	Made-up textile goods excl. wearing apparel		24	18	21	27		986	398	414	669		...	...	...	...
3213	Knitting mills		87	80	85	61		3665	3860	4643	2833		...	...	...	...
3214	Carpets and rugs		17	19	17	16		360	214	118	137		...	...	...	...
3215	Cordage, rope and twine		11	14	15	14		582	672	687	634		...	...	...	...
3219	Other textiles		47	51	56	45		1039	1256	1175	1132		...	...	...	...
322	Wearing apparel, except footwear		1391	1163	1205	957		109839	101266	101667	87825		350.6	348.3	...	...
323	Leather and fur products		87	77	77	59		3041	2871	3077	3553		56.7b/	56.4b/	...	...
3231	Tanneries and leather finishing		17	15	15	10		493	481	472	388		...	...	...	...
3232	Fur dressing and dyeing industries		2	1	1	1		26	23	24	6		...	...	...	...
3233	Leather prods. excl. footwear and wearing		68	61	61	48		2522	2367	2581	3159		...	...	...	...
324	Footwear, except rubber or plastic		225	179	182	146		15312	14595	14181	11710		...b/	...b/	...	...
331	Wood products, except furniture		2266	2293	2473	2491		6629	8517	9181	8643		127.6c/	137.4c/	...	...
3311	Sawmills, planing and other wood mills		2217	2245	2418	2432		6212	8260	8790	7999		...	...	...	...
3312	Wooden and cane containers		3	5	7	6		46	13	24	40		...	...	...	...
3319	Other wood and cork products		46	43	48	53		371	244	367	604		...	...	...	...
332	Furniture and fixtures, excl. metal		277	246	266	314		8665	6762	7106	6013		...c/	...c/	...	...
341	Paper and products		61	72	77	70		3591	3626	3435	3104		83.4d/	89.8d/	...	...
3411	Pulp, paper and paperboard articles		15	17	19	20		1680	1585	1396	1341		...	...	...	...
3412	Containers of paper and paperboard		34	39	42	34		1416	1544	1543	1108		...	...	...	...
3419	Other pulp, paper and paperboard articles		12	16	16	16		495	497	496	655		...	...	...	...
342	Printing and publishing		324	312	355	340		5356	4928	5426	4194		...d/	...d/	...	...
351	Industrial chemicals		60	63	69	80		6241	1926	2896	2193		104.3	107.5	...	...
3511	Basic chemicals excl. fertilizers		47	52	58	67		5991	1681	2675	2014		...	...	...	...
3512	Fertilizers and pesticides		3	3	3	8		61	65	60	98		...	...	...	...
3513	Synthetic resins and plastic materials		10	8	8	5		189	180	161	81		...	...	...	...
352	Other chemicals		366	401	440	405		10123	9996	10205	9936		106.1	109.4	...	...
3521	Paints, varnishes and lacquers		60	70	76	68		1918	1970	1931	1734		...	...	...	...
3522	Drugs and medicines		42	43	47	56		3077	3142	3236	3729		...	...	...	...
3523	Soap, cleaning preps., perfumes, cosmetics		218	244	266	238		4054	3992	4105	3718		...	...	...	...
3529	Other chemical products		46	44	51	43		1074	892	933	755		...	...	...	...
353	Petroleum refineries		7	8	8	6		624	637	633	634		7.5e/	7.5e/	...	...

354	Misc. petroleum and coal products	1	-	-	-	-	-	-	-	...e/	...e/	...	...
355	Rubber products	200	207	233	224	5906	5810	5945	6134	32.7	33.7	...	...
3551	Tyres and tubes	179	182	205	187	4805	4673	4848	4921	...	...	...	...
3559	Other rubber products	21	25	28	37	1101	1137	1097	1213	...	...	...	...
356	Plastic products	120	149	159	172	5061	5272	5403	5598	31.4	32.3	...	...
361	Pottery, china and earthenware	164	156	175	132	6311	6262	6427	6963	100.0	106.7	...	...
362	Glass and products	77	78	87	95	1876	1834	1749	2099	18.9	20.2	...	...
369	Other non-metallic mineral products	553	532	564	626	19582	18820	19181	17387	109.0	116.3	...	...
3691	Structural clay products	57	60	61	47	4511	4769	4859	3121	...	...	...	...
3692	Cement, lime and plaster	19	19	20	22	2973	2900	2954	2637	...	...	...	...
3699	Other non-metallic mineral products	477	453	483	557	12098	11151	11368	11629	...	...	...	...
371	Iron and steel	37	46	48	49	3608	3172	2809	1965	72.5	80.2	...	...
372	Non-ferrous metals	26	29	31	31	748	914	882	854	103.5f/	114.4f/	...	...
381	Fabricated metal products	1771	1786	1924	1562	16022	15661	17353	16061	...f/	...f/	...	...
3811	Cutlery, hand tools and general hardware	30	29	31	36	878	861	926	702	...	...	...	...
3812	Furniture and fixtures primarily of metal	-	-	-	-	-	-	-	-	...	...	...	...
3813	Structural metal products	292	290	327	663	5782	5378	5607	8944	...	...	...	...
3819	Other fabricated metal products	1449	1467	1566	863	9362	9422	10820	6415	...	...	...	...
382	Non-electrical machinery	126	138	149	162	4169	4216	3460	3340	25.8	28.5	...	...
3821	Engines and turbines	1	1	1	1	144	141	141	7	...	...	...	...
3822	Agricultural machinery and equipment	15	14	15	12	732	770	500	299	...	...	...	...
3823	Metal and wood working machinery	4	3	3	2	47	25	32	10	...	...	...	...
3824	Other special industrial machinery	19	18	19	20	172	187	176	152	...	...	...	...
3825	Office, computing and accounting machinery	8	5	7	8	102	54	135	93	...	...	...	...
3829	Other non-electrical machinery and equipment	79	97	104	119	2972	3039	2476	2779	...	...	...	...
383	Electrical machinery	435	459	497	503	32844	39120	42330	44905	131.8	145.7	...	...
3831	Electrical industrial machinery	280	286	303	290	12868	14794	15275	19255	...	...	...	...
3832	Radio, television and communication equipment	41	52	58	69	3769	6256	6624	6990	...	...	...	...
3833	Electrical appliances and housewares	25	23	24	36	1248	1086	1019	1236	...	...	...	...
3839	Other electrical apparatus and supplies	89	98	112	108	14959	16984	19412	17424	...	...	...	...
384	Transport equipment	121	135	157	162	5730	6118	6734	7893	75.1	83.0	...	...
3841	Shipbuilding and repairing	34	44	55	67	966	1083	1185	1643	...	...	...	...
3842	Railroad equipment	1	1	1	-	357	357	336	-	...	...	...	...
3843	Motor vehicles	75	80	91	84	4214	4508	5046	6011	...	...	...	...
3844	Motorcycles and bicycles	8	9	9	9	153	160	159	221	...	...	...	...
3845	Aircraft	1	-	-	2	-	-	-	18	...	...	...	...
3849	Other transport equipment	2	1	1	-	40	10	8	-	...	...	...	...
385	Professional and scientific equipment	60	65	68	116	1482	1562	1466	1676	...	...	...	...
3851	Prof. and scientific equipment n.e.c.	43	46	49	105	1126	1213	1092	1148	...	...	...	...
3852	Photographic and optical goods	13	14	14	9	338	325	294	437	...	...	...	...
3853	Watches and clocks	4	5	5	2	18	24	80	91	...	...	...	...
390	Other manufacturing industries	142	135	147	245	2832	2687	2858	5718	34.2	36.8	...	...
3901	Jewellery and related articles	39	35	36	37	255	253	243	252	...	...	...	...
3902	Musical instruments	2	1	2	6	15	13	12	235	...	...	...	...
3903	Sporting and athletic goods	6	7	7	6	375	241	280	327	...	...	...	...
3909	Manufacturing industries, n.e.c.	95	92	102	196	2187	2180	2323	4904	...	...	...	...
3	Total manufacturing	13583	13900	15164	14700	384350	398889	418309	398922	2253.4	2372.5	...	...

a/ Data derived from social security records.
b/ 323 includes 324.
c/ 331 includes 332.
d/ 341 includes 342.
e/ 353 includes 354.
f/ 372 includes 381.

Tunisia

ISIC Revision 2		Output in producers' prices					Value added in producers' prices					Gross fixed capital formation		
			(millions of Tunisian Dinars)					(millions of Tunisian Dinars)					(millions of Tunisian Dinars)	
ISIC	Industry	Note	2002	2003	2004	2005	Note	2002	2003	2004	2005	Note	2004	2005
311/2	Food products		4426.6	4733.5	...	...		730.7	778.6	...	...		...	...
3111	Slaughtering, preparing and preserving meat		1134.8	1219.5	...	...		119.7	128.6	...	...		...	...
3112	Dairy products		499.8	479.2	...	...		65.4	62.7	...	...		...	...
3113	Canning, preserving of fruits and vegetables		327.3a/	372.6a/	...	...		49.3a/	56.1a/	...	...		...	...
3114	Canning, preserving and processing of fish		...a/	...a/	...	...		...a/	...a/	...	...		...	...
3115	Vegetable and animal oils and fats		256.6	397.9	...	...		36.3	56.3	...	...		...	...
3116	Grain mill products		1234.5b/	1291.5b/	...	...		283.1b/	297.2b/	...	...		...	...
3117	Bakery products		...b/	...b/	...	...		...b/	...b/	...	...		...	...
3118	Sugar factories and refineries		271.1c/	284.0c/	...	...		63.5c/	66.5c/	...	...		...	...
3119	Cocoa, chocolate and sugar confectionery		...c/	...c/	...	...		...c/	...c/	...	...		...	...
3121	Other food products		702.5d/	688.8d/	...	...		113.4d/	111.2d/	...	...		...	...
3122	Prepared animal feeds		...d/	...d/	...	...		...d/	...d/	...	...		...	...
313	Beverages		567.6	563.7	...	...		169.0	167.9	...	...		...	...
3131	Distilling, rectifying and blending spirits		567.6e/	563.7e/	...	...		169.0e/	167.9e/	...	...		...	...
3132	Wine industries		...e/	...e/	...	...		...e/	...e/	...	...		...	...
3133	Malt liquors and malt		...e/	...e/	...	...		...e/	...e/	...	...		...	...
3134	Soft drinks and carbonated waters		...e/	...e/	...	...		...e/	...e/	...	...		...	...
314	Tobacco		722.4	760.8	...	...		41.4	44.6	...	...		...	...
321	Textiles		1062.3	1044.5	...	...		356.3	351.3	...	...		...	...
3211	Spinning, weaving and finishing textiles		949.2f/	928.6f/	...	...		293.3f/	286.9f/	...	...		...	...
3212	Made-up textile goods excl. wearing apparel		...f/	...f/	...	...		...f/	...f/	...	...		...	...
3213	Knitting mills		...	...	...	...		...	...	...	...		...	...
3214	Carpets and rugs		113.1	115.9	...	...		63.0	64.4	...	...		...	...
3215	Cordage, rope and twine		...	...	...	...		...	...	...	...		...	...
3219	Other textiles		...	...	...	...		...	...	...	...		...	...
322	Wearing apparel, except footwear		4173.9	4097.1	...	...		1260.5	1219.5	...	...		...	...
323	Leather and fur products		1030.9g/	1099.9g/	...	...		357.1g/	367.2g/	...	...		...	...
3231	Tanneries and leather finishing		...h/	...h/	...	...		...h/	...h/	...	...		...	...
3232	Fur dressing and dyeing industries		...	...	...	...		...	...	...	...		...	...
3233	Leather prods. excl. footwear and wearing		...	...	...	...		...	...	...	...		...	...
324	Footwear, except rubber or plastic		...g/	...g/	...	...		...g/	...g/	...	...		...	...
331	Wood products, except furniture		886.9i/	944.9i/	...	...		352.0i/	374.9i/	...	...		...	...
3311	Sawmills, planing and other wood mills		...	...	...	...		...	...	...	...		...	...
3312	Wooden and cane containers		...	...	...	...		...	...	...	...		...	...
3319	Other wood and cork products		...	...	...	...		...	...	...	...		...	...
332	Furniture and fixtures, excl. metal		...i/	...i/	...	...		...i/	...i/	...	...		...	...
341	Paper and products		488.2j/	510.3j/	...	...		141.3j/	147.6j/	...	...		...	...
3411	Pulp, paper and paperboard articles		...	...	...	...		...	...	...	...		...	...
3412	Containers of paper and paperboard		...	...	...	...		...	...	...	...		...	...
3419	Other pulp, paper and paperboard articles		...	...	...	...		...	...	...	...		...	...
342	Printing and publishing		...j/	...j/	...	...		...j/	...j/	...	...		...	...
351	Industrial chemicals		1765.6	1742.4	...	...		308.9	305.7	...	...		...	...
3511	Basic chemicals excl. fertilizers		123.6	126.4	...	...		41.2	42.1	...	...		...	...
3512	Fertilizers and pesticides		1642.0	1616.0	...	...		267.7	263.6	...	...		...	...
3513	Synthetic resins and plastic materials		...	...	...	...		...	...	...	...		...	...
352	Other chemicals		741.4	792.1	...	...		240.8	253.8	...	...		...	...
3521	Paints, varnishes and lacquers		570.6k/	608.8k/	...	...		171.1k/	183.2k/	...	...		...	...
3522	Drugs and medicines		170.8	183.3	...	...		69.7	70.6	...	...		...	...
3523	Soap, cleaning preps., perfumes, cosmetics		...k/	...k/	...	...		...k/	...k/	...	...		...	...
3529	Other chemical products		...k/	...k/	...	...		...k/	...k/	...	...		...	...
353	Petroleum refineries		...	...	...	...		...	...	...	...		...	...

354	Misc. petroleum and coal products	...	...	...	...	...	...	...	...	...	...
355	Rubber products	141.0	138.2	...	...	56.4	55.3	...	...	...	...
3551	Tyres and tubes	...	...	...	...	...	...	...	...	...	...
3559	Other rubber products	...	...	...	...	...	...	...	...	...	...
356	Plastic products	380.4	385.9	...	...	105.1	106.1	...	...	...	...
361	Pottery, china and earthenware	429.7	442.9	...	...	159.8	165.4	...	...	...	...
362	Glass and products	102.3	105.1	...	...	32.1	32.2	...	...	...	...
369	Other non-metallic mineral products	1071.5	112.9	...	...	335.4	358.7	...	...	...	...
3691	Structural clay products	...	...	...	...	...	...	...	...	...	...
3692	Cement, lime and plaster	833.3	878.0	...	...	244.5	262.1	...	...	...	...
3699	Other non-metallic mineral products	238.2	251.0	...	...	90.9	96.6	...	...	...	...
371	Iron and steel	422.9	373.1	...	...	63.1	55.7	...	...	...	...
372	Non-ferrous metals	589.4m/	620.9m/	...	...	170.9m/	180.0m/	...	...	...	...
381	Fabricated metal products	...m/	...m/	...	...	...m/	...m/	...	...	...	...
3811	Cutlery, hand tools and general hardware	...	...	...	...	...	...	...	...	...	...
3812	Furniture and fixtures primarily of metal	...	...	...	...	...	...	...	...	...	...
3813	Structural metal products	...	...	...	...	...	...	...	...	...	...
3819	Other fabricated metal products	...	...	...	...	...	...	...	...	...	...
382	Non-electrical machinery	196.7	215.5	...	...	27.5	30.1	...	...	...	...
3821	Engines and turbines	...	...	...	...	...	...	...	...	...	...
3822	Agricultural machinery and equipment	...	...	...	...	...	...	...	...	...	...
3823	Metal and wood working machinery	...	...	...	...	...	...	...	...	...	...
3824	Other special industrial machinery	...	...	...	...	...	...	...	...	...	...
3825	Office, computing and accounting machinery	...	...	...	...	...	...	...	...	...	...
3829	Other non-electrical machinery and equipment	...	...	...	...	...	...	...	...	...	...
383	Electrical machinery	1612.4	1809.3	...	...	397.5	447.9	...	...	...	...
3831	Electrical industrial machinery	1128.0n/	1293.0n/	...	...	317.8n/	363.8n/	...	...	...	...
3832	Radio, television and communication equipment	334.4p/	353.0p/	...	...	45.3p/	47.8p/	...	...	...	...
3833	Electrical appliances and housewares	150.0	163.3	...	...	34.4	36.3	...	...	...	...
3839	Other electrical apparatus and supplies	...n/	...n/	...	...	...n/	...n/	...	...	...	...
384	Transport equipment	681.4	792.3	...	...	185.2	214.6	...	...	...	...
3841	Shipbuilding and repairing	25.1q/	26.7q/	...	...	9.9q/	10.6q/	...	...	...	...
3842	Railroad equipment	...q/	...q/	...	...	...q/	...q/	...	...	...	...
3843	Motor vehicles	656.3r/	765.6r/	...	...	175.3r/	204.0r/	...	...	...	...
3844	Motorcycles and bicycles	...r/	...r/	...	...	...r/	...r/	...	...	...	...
3845	Aircraft	...q/	...q/	...	...	...q/	...q/	...	...	...	...
3849	Other transport equipment	...r/	...r/	...	...	...r/	...r/	...	...	...	...
385	Professional and scientific equipment	...	...	...	...	...	...	...	...	...	...
3851	Prof. and scientific equipment n.e.c.	...p/	...p/	...	...	...p/	...p/	...	...	...	...
3852	Photographic and optical goods	...	...	...	...	...	...	...	...	...	...
3853	Watches and clocks	...	...	...	...	...	...	...	...	...	...
390	Other manufacturing industries	301.8	308.1	...	...	75.2	86.8	...	...	...	...
3901	Jewellery and related articles	...	...	...	...	...	...	...	...	...	...
3902	Musical instruments	...	...	...	...	...	...	...	...	...	...
3903	Sporting and athletic goods	...	...	...	...	...	...	...	...	...	...
3909	Manufacturing industries, n.e.c.	...	...	...	...	...	...	...	...	...	...
3	Total manufacturing	21795.3	21593.4	...	...	5951.3	6161.1	...	...	...	...

a/ 3113 includes 3114.
b/ 3116 includes 3117.
c/ 3118 includes 3119.
d/ 3121 includes 3122.
e/ 3131 includes 3132, 3133 and 3134.
f/ 3211 includes 3212.
g/ 323 includes 324.
h/ 3220 includes 3231.
i/ 331 includes 332.
j/ 341 includes 342.

k/ 3521 includes 3523 and 3529.
m/ 372 includes 381.
n/ 3831 includes 3839.
p/ 3832 includes 3851.
q/ 3841 includes 3842 and 3845.
r/ 3843 includes 3844 and 3849.

Tunisia

ISIC Revision 3			Index numbers of industrial production (2000=100)											
ISIC	Industry	Note	1995	1996	1997	1998	1999	2000	2001	2002	2003	2004	2005	2006
15	Food and beverages		74	78	87	87	95	100	99	101	104	113	113	118
16	Tobacco products		63	61	66	74	88	100	101	107	107	112	110	115
17	Textiles		79	74	76	83	85	100	110	113	108	111	107	105
18	Wearing apparel, fur		77	79	82	89	91	100	111	105	97	94	85	81
19	Leather, leather products and footwear		65	69	77	82	86	100	113	115	115	112	117	124
20	Wood products (excl. furniture)		72	60	80	90	98	100	107	109	107	116	121	128
21	Paper and paper products		105	96	97	98	100	100	103	96	112	119	118	128
22	Printing and publishing		79	77	81	86	100	100	104	103	104	112	105	127
23	Coke,refined petroleum products,nuclear fuel		98	97	102	99	98	100	97	98	99	92	88	86
24	Chemicals and chemical products		82	86	88	95	97	100	104	108	109	112	112	114
25	Rubber and plastics products		65	70	73	87	89	100	109	111	112	122	123	106
26	Non-metallic mineral products		81	80	80	86	89	100	106	109	109	116	117	119
27	Basic metals		80	81	84	81	96	100	96	86	71	70	85	95
28	Fabricated metal products		89	90	86	100	103	100	108	116	113	108	108	131
29	Machinery and equipment n.e.c.		69	64	59	49	72	100	119	128	129	134	151	170
30	Office, accounting and computing machinery		...	...	...	...	...	...	...	...	...	...	...	...
31	Electrical machinery and apparatus		46	51	64	83	90	100	109	114	127	146	169	196
32	Radio,television and communication equipment		70	71	93	97	96	100	113	92	108	114	146	181
33	Medical, precision and optical instruments		60	72	69	75	76	100	104	103	99	107	112	112
34	Motor vehicles, trailers, semi-trailers	a/	57	66	65	75	89	100	123	123	140	152	155	206
35	Other transport equipment	a/	...	...	...	...	...	...	...	...	...	...	...	...
36	Furniture; manufacturing n.e.c.		99	111	95	96	97	100	105	110	112	111	118	119
37	Recycling		...	...	...	...	...	...	...	...	...	...	...	...
D	Total manufacturing		75	77	81	87	92	100	107	107	107	111	112	117

a/ 34 includes 35.

Uganda

Supplier of information:
Uganda Bureau of Statistics, Kampala.

Basic source of data:
Sample survey (every 10 years).

Major deviations from ISIC (Revision 3):
None reported.

Reference period:
Fiscal year.

Scope:
Privately owned establishments only.

Method of data collection:
Direct interview in the field.

Type of enumeration:
Sample survey.

Adjusted for non-response:
Yes.

Concepts and definitions of variables:
Output is the value of total receipts adjusted with stock changes, excluding excise duty and indirect taxes. It is reported at basic prices.
Value added is reported at basic prices, which excludes taxes on commodity and includes commodity related subsidies).

Related national publications:
Uganda Business Inquiry, published by the Uganda Bureau of Statistics, Kampala.

Uganda

ISIC Revision 3		Number of establishments					Number of employees					Wages and salaries paid to employees				
			(number)					(number)					(millions of Uganda Shillings)			
ISIC	Industry	Note	1999	2000	2001	2002	Note	1999	2000	2001	2002	Note	1999	2000	2001	2002
15	Food and beverages		...	...	...	3054		...	...	...	28360		...	...	...	61905.3
16	Tobacco products		...	...	...	2		...	...	...	1171		...	...	...	8404.1
17	Textiles		...	...	...	38		...	...	...	2888		...	...	...	7966.5
18	Wearing apparel, fur		...	...	...	3930a/		...	...	...	6693a/		...	...	...	2749.5a/
19	Leather, leather products and footwear		...	...	...	...a/		...	...	...	...a/		...	...	...	...a/
20	Wood products (excl. furniture)		...	...	...	2766		...	...	...	11124		...	...	...	11235.1
21	Paper and paper products		...	...	...	10		...	...	...	704		...	...	...	2035.1
22	Printing and publishing		...	...	...	317		...	...	...	2365		...	...	...	6553.3
23	Coke,refined petroleum products,nuclear fuel		...	...	...	...		...	...	...	...		...	...	...	...
24	Chemicals and chemical products		...	...	...	296		...	...	...	5247		...	...	...	20861.0
25	Rubber and plastics products		...	...	...	...		...	...	...	...		...	...	...	...
26	Non-metallic mineral products		...	...	...	...		...	...	...	...		...	...	...	...
27	Basic metals		...	...	...	...		...	...	...	...		...	...	...	...
28	Fabricated metal products		...	...	...	1536		...	...	...	6745		...	...	...	9992.7
29	Machinery and equipment n.e.c.		...	...	...	28b/		...	...	...	168b/		...	...	...	379.9b/
30	Office, accounting and computing machinery		...	...	...	...b/		...	...	...	...b/		...	...	...	...b/
31	Electrical machinery and apparatus		...	...	...	5c/		...	...	...	118c/		...	...	...	507.8c/
32	Radio,television and communication equipment		...	...	...	...c/		...	...	...	...c/		...	...	...	...c/
33	Medical, precision and optical instruments		...	...	...	5		...	...	...	...		...	...	...	...
34	Motor vehicles, trailers, semi-trailers		...	...	...	133d/		...	...	...	746d/		...	...	...	1272.7d/
35	Other transport equipment		...	...	...	...d/		...	...	...	...d/		...	...	...	...d/
36	Furniture; manufacturing n.e.c.		...	...	...	...		...	...	...	...		...	...	...	...
37	Recycling		...	...	...	...		...	...	...	...		...	...	...	...
D	Total manufacturing		...	...	...	12120e/		...	...	...	66329e/		...	...	...	133862.9e/

a/ 18 includes 19.
b/ 29 includes 30.
c/ 31 includes 32.
d/ 34 includes 35.
e/ Sum of available data.

Uganda

ISIC Revision 3		Output					Value added					Gross fixed capital formation		
			(millions of Uganda Shillings)					(millions of Uganda Shillings)					(Uganda Shillings)	
ISIC	Industry	Note	1999	2000	2001	2002	Note	1999	2000	2001	2002	Note	2001	2002
15	Food and beverages		...	...	...	834563		...	...	...	289045		...	...
16	Tobacco products		...	...	...	82237		...	...	...	27742		...	...
17	Textiles		...	...	...	52725		...	...	...	18673		...	...
18	Wearing apparel, fur		...	...	...	26828a/		...	...	...	12297a/		...	...
19	Leather, leather products and footwear		...	...	...	...a/		...	...	...	...a/		...	...
20	Wood products (excl. furniture)		...	...	...	68722		...	...	...	25261		...	...
21	Paper and paper products		...	...	...	44293		...	...	...	6398		...	...
22	Printing and publishing		...	...	...	53014		...	...	...	22465		...	...
23	Coke,refined petroleum products,nuclear fuel		...	...	...	...		...	...	...	...		...	...
24	Chemicals and chemical products		...	...	...	299480		...	...	...	105652		...	...
25	Rubber and plastics products		...	...	...	...		...	...	...	...		...	...
26	Non-metallic mineral products		...	...	...	...		...	...	...	...		...	...
27	Basic metals		...	...	...	...		...	...	...	...		...	...
28	Fabricated metal products		...	...	...	87104		...	...	...	31246		...	...
29	Machinery and equipment n.e.c.		...	...	...	3536b/		...	...	...	1008b/		...	...
30	Office, accounting and computing machinery		...	...	...	...b/		...	...	...	...b/		...	...
31	Electrical machinery and apparatus		...	...	...	4340c/		...	...	...	2907c/		...	...
32	Radio,television and communication equipment		...	...	...	...c/		...	...	...	...c/		...	...
33	Medical, precision and optical instruments		...	...	...	...		...	...	...	...		...	...
34	Motor vehicles, trailers, semi-trailers		...	...	...	9928d/		...	...	...	4847d/		...	...
35	Other transport equipment		...	...	...	...d/		...	...	...	...d/		...	...
36	Furniture; manufacturing n.e.c.		...	...	...	...		...	...	...	...		...	...
37	Recycling		...	...	...	...		...	...	...	...		...	...
D	Total manufacturing		...	...	...	1566770e/		...	...	...	457543e/		...	...

a/ 18 includes 19.
b/ 29 includes 30.
c/ 31 includes 32.
d/ 34 includes 35.
e/ Sum of available data.

Uganda

ISIC Revision 3			Index numbers of industrial production (2000=100)											
ISIC	Industry	Note	1995	1996	1997	1998	1999	2000	2001	2002	2003	2004	2005	2006
15	Food and beverages		66	82	82	88	96	100	99	103	112	116	101	119
16	Tobacco products		...	...	...	...	...	...	...	...	...	...	...	...
17	Textiles	a/	98	57	134	125	129	100	67	85	135	162	152	141
18	Wearing apparel, fur	a/	...	...	...	...	...	...	...	...	...	...	...	...
19	Leather, leather products and footwear		71	125	69	102	123	100	115	139	153	169	51	19
20	Wood products (excl. furniture)		76	82	89	96	90	100	...	...	...	...	...	...
21	Paper and paper products	b/	64	30	81	90	105	100	122	141	155	153	147	165
22	Printing and publishing	b/	...	...	...	...	...	...	...	...	...	...	...	...
23	Coke,refined petroleum products,nuclear fuel		...	...	...	...	...	...	...	...	...	...	...	...
24	Chemicals and chemical products		47	47	71	86	95	100	110	95	108	107	131	124
25	Rubber and plastics products		...	...	...	...	...	...	...	...	...	...	...	...
26	Non-metallic mineral products		28	51	81	89	94	100	113	137	129	183	...	...
27	Basic metals		...	...	...	...	...	...	...	...	...	...	...	...
28	Fabricated metal products		...	...	...	...	...	...	...	...	...	...	...	...
29	Machinery and equipment n.e.c.		...	...	...	...	...	...	...	...	...	...	...	...
30	Office, accounting and computing machinery		...	...	...	...	...	...	...	...	...	...	...	...
31	Electrical machinery and apparatus	c/	172	218	180	129	113	100	84	173	98	182	83	...
32	Radio,television and communication equipment	c/	...	...	...	...	...	...	...	...	...	...	...	...
33	Medical, precision and optical instruments		...	...	...	...	...	...	...	...	...	...	...	...
34	Motor vehicles, trailers, semi-trailers	d/	74	101	88	107	105	100	110	98	...	...	...	...
35	Other transport equipment	d/	...	...	...	...	...	...	...	...	...	...	...	...
36	Furniture; manufacturing n.e.c.		...	...	...	...	...	...	...	...	...	...	...	...
37	Recycling		...	...	...	...	...	...	...	...	...	...	...	...
D	Total manufacturing		61	72	84	93	100	100	119	122	127	141	146	150

a/ 17 includes 18.
b/ 21 includes 22.
c/ 31 includes 32.
d/ 34 includes 35.

Ukraine

Supplier of information:
State Statistics Committee of the Ukraine, Kiev.

Basic source of data:
Annual survey on registered enterprises.

Major deviations from ISIC (Revision 3):
None reported.

Reference period:
Calendar year.

Scope:
All registered enterprises.

Method of data collection:
Mail questionnaires.

Type of enumeration:
Not reported.

Adjusted for non-response:
Not reported.

Concepts and definitions of variables:
Wages and salaries was computed by UNIDO from reported monthly wages and salaries per employee. It excludes payment in kind and housing and family allowances paid directly by the employer.

Related national publications:
None reported.

Ukraine

ISIC Revision 3		Number of enterprises					Number of employees					Wages and salaries paid to employees				
			(number)					(thousands)					(millions of Ukrainian Hryvnias)			
ISIC	Industry	Note	2003	2004	2005	2006	Note	2003	2004	2005	2006	Note	2003	2004	2005	2006
151	Processed meat,fish,fruit,vegetables,fats		2676	2536	2552	2538		110.0	108.3	108.2	132.8		492.0	605.2	806.4	1395.6
1511	Processing/preserving of meat		1259	1188	1198	1230		61.3	58.9	55.7	77.8		256.3	286.6	366.6	795.3
1512	Processing/preserving of fish		274	273	293	283		8.4	8.8	10.5	10.4		30.3	48.0	73.7	90.2
1513	Processing/preserving of fruit & vegetables		547	542	543	511		22.4	22.4	23.3	22.9		76.2	109.9	164.4	203.9
1514	Vegetable and animal oils and fats		596	533	518	514		17.9	18.1	18.8	21.7		129.2	160.6	201.2	306.5
1520	Dairy products		819	763	712	640		83.7	89.0	91.4	87.9		411.3	527.4	701.9	814.5
153	Grain mill products; starches; animal feeds		1539	1424	1387	1305		47.8	43.9	43.2	37.4		218.0	261.6	319.2	355.6
1531	Grain mill products		1201	1100	1073	1009		36.4	32.7	31.7	28.0		168.2	196.4	232.0	246.3
1532	Starches and starch products		23	20	20	24		2.4	2.3	2.5	2.5		14.2	17.5	21.1	32.7
1533	Prepared animal feeds		315	304	294	272		8.9	9.0	9.0	6.9		35.6	47.7	66.4	76.6
154	Other food products		2996	2898	2827	2818		203.5	201.4	201.6	222.9		1106.7	1329.9	1795.5	2458.0
1541	Bakery products		2018	1944	1888	1827		108.9	108.6	111.2	106.7		539.2	661.4	955.6	993.4
1542	Sugar		252	219	200	226		44.0	40.3	38.5	53.8		199.8	219.7	288.5	548.5
1543	Cocoa, chocolate and sugar confectionery		149	145	138	146		31.8	33.7	33.2	42.5		252.0	303.5	376.4	695.7
1544	Macaroni, noodles & similar products		213	205	186	186		4.4	3.8	4.1	5.9		23.5	25.6	34.7	63.9
1549	Other food products n.e.c.		364	385	415	433		14.4	15.1	14.6	13.9		92.2	119.6	139.4	157.8
155	Beverages		1108	1130	1104	1057		77.6	78.5	77.6	80.5		565.2	661.5	875.4	1172.1
1551	Distilling, rectifying & blending of spirits		218	221	209	198		26.7	29.3	28.7	28.8		159.0	201.8	297.2	347.8
1552	Wines		138	143	148	147		11.7	11.1	11.5	14.8		67.0	73.3	94.7	148.7
1553	Malt liquors and malt		118	112	111	97		18.3	17.8	16.5	16.4		219.6	248.7	296.4	423.9
1554	Soft drinks; mineral waters		634	654	636	615		20.9	20.4	20.9	20.4		119.6	137.7	186.6	251.6
1600	Tobacco products		29	26	25	21		5.9	5.7	5.7	5.3		163.1	200.2	223.9	253.5
171	Spinning, weaving and finishing of textiles		207	188	181	172		25.8	22.0	19.7	14.6		74.3	100.1	112.3	109.9
1711	Textile fibre preparation; textile weaving		200	177	167	150		25.8	22.0	19.5	14.3		74.2	99.5	111.2	107.7
1712	Finishing of textiles		7	11	14	22		-	0.1	0.1	0.2		0.1	0.5	1.1	2.2
172	Other textiles		579	591	611	638		17.1	15.8	15.9	21.9		58.1	75.1	97.9	186.2
1721	Made-up textile articles, except apparel		479	489	504	518		12.5	11.6	12.2	13.7		39.0	49.6	69.8	107.3
1722	Carpets and rugs		13	16	17	17		0.8	0.7	0.7	0.4		5.6	7.8	9.0	6.0
1723	Cordage, rope, twine and netting		24	19	22	28		0.8	0.8	0.8	1.1		2.6	5.1	4.8	8.3
1729	Other textiles n.e.c.		63	67	68	75		2.9	2.7	2.2	6.7		10.8	12.5	14.2	64.3
1730	Knitted and crocheted fabrics and articles		336	313	309	286		13.1	11.0	9.8	7.7		42.1	44.0	55.0	53.0
1810	Wearing apparel, except fur apparel		2922	2982	2878	2741		121.1	115.6	108.3	95.1		426.4	524.6	612.2	662.0
1820	Dressing & dyeing of fur; processing of fur		70	73	71	69		2.4	2.3	2.1	1.9		10.3	13.2	14.7	16.0
191	Tanning, dressing and processing of leather		195	206	195	186		8.6	8.5	8.4	7.0		45.0	51.0	62.0	64.3
1911	Tanning and dressing of leather		71	79	74	75		4.9	4.9	4.7	3.9		31.8	36.4	43.9	43.0
1912	Luggage, handbags, etc.; saddlery & harness		124	127	121	111		3.7	3.6	3.7	3.0		13.2	14.6	18.2	21.3
1920	Footwear		538	505	501	462		22.7	20.7	19.2	17.9		79.1	88.6	108.1	126.5
2010	Sawmilling and planing of wood		1609	1731	1728	1764		25.3	26.7	22.3	22.5		84.7	111.8	116.4	146.1
202	Products of wood, cork, straw, etc.		2511	2484	2481	2369		39.6	38.7	38.9	35.4		167.1	206.7	273.7	319.0
2021	Veneer sheets, plywood, particle board, etc.		128	120	119	139		10.0	10.7	11.4	13.0		69.0	88.5	124.7	174.3
2022	Builders' carpentry and joinery		2001	1953	1945	1818		23.8	22.5	22.0	17.8		72.7	86.2	108.6	116.7
2023	Wooden containers		125	142	130	146		1.7	1.7	1.5	2.3		4.5	5.6	6.1	16.1
2029	Other wood products; articles of cork/straw		257	269	287	266		4.1	3.8	4.1	2.2		21.0	26.4	34.3	11.9
210	Paper and paper products		512	569	563	598		27.0	27.7	28.8	31.2		173.1	224.2	304.7	386.5
2101	Pulp, paper and paperboard		61	74	72	79		11.1	10.1	9.8	9.0		70.3	80.6	112.0	132.3
2102	Corrugated paper and paperboard		246	267	278	290		7.8	9.0	10.3	12.0		54.4	76.3	113.0	141.2
2109	Other articles of paper and paperboard		205	228	213	229		8.1	8.6	8.6	10.2		48.4	67.4	79.9	113.1
221	Publishing		2560	2809	2988	2933		42.9	45.3	45.6	33.8		307.7	364.4	460.4	422.7
2211	Publishing of books and other publications		532	606	652	676		8.3	8.7	8.2	6.7		49.7	62.6	67.8	68.5
2212	Publishing of newspapers, journals, etc.		1605	1783	1906	1823		28.5	31.3	32.5	23.9		213.7	266.4	351.1	326.6
2213	Publishing of recorded media		10	10	16	29		-	0.1	0.1	0.2		0.1	1.0	0.7	1.5
2219	Other publishing		413	410	414	405		6.1	5.2	4.8	3.0		44.1	34.5	41.2	26.0

222	Printing and related service activities	3003	2994	3075	3068	40.2	40.0	39.4	46.8	180.4	245.3	305.9	536.0
2221	Printing	2610	2633	2693	2698	36.7	37.0	36.5	44.2	165.1	229.8	287.0	514.5
2222	Service activities related to printing	393	361	382	370	3.5	2.9	2.9	2.6	15.3	15.4	19.0	21.6
2230	Reproduction of recorded media	61	59	57	62	0.4	0.6	0.6	0.6	1.6	4.3	6.3	5.9
2310	Coke oven products	24	22	22	23	32.5	32.7	33.2	28.1	295.4	397.6	525.5	496.0
2320	Refined petroleum products	159	168	201	193	20.9	20.2	19.1	35.9	252.3	296.6	348.8	874.7
2330	Processing of nuclear fuel	...	...	...	...	...	...	...	...	...	...	...	...
241	Basic chemicals	393	405	409	430	82.9	79.0	85.6	85.9	607.2	764.5	1131.4	1374.4
2411	Basic chemicals, except fertilizers	287	283	279	280	36.5	35.3	42.4	47.2	212.0	279.6	469.1	652.1
2412	Fertilizers and nitrogen compounds	59	64	62	62	43.0	40.4	40.0	34.2	370.9	456.7	628.2	668.6
2413	Plastics in primary forms; synthetic rubber	47	58	68	88	3.4	3.3	3.2	4.6	24.2	28.2	34.0	53.1
242	Other chemicals	1198	1222	1274	1198	65.4	62.7	62.6	57.0	404.2	485.2	655.4	748.9
2421	Pesticides and other agro-chemical products	29	30	34	28	0.2	0.2	0.2	0.1	1.3	1.7	1.3	1.3
2422	Paints, varnishes, printing ink and mastics	299	298	291	274	7.8	7.7	8.1	8.5	44.2	51.4	72.8	101.8
2423	Pharmaceuticals, medicinal chemicals, etc.	322	331	361	322	21.3	20.9	21.7	20.4	172.8	211.3	278.0	337.9
2424	Soap, cleaning & cosmetic preparations	266	251	269	275	8.5	8.7	7.7	7.6	53.8	67.5	83.3	97.3
2429	Other chemical products n.e.c.	282	312	319	299	27.5	25.2	24.8	20.4	132.1	153.3	219.6	210.8
2430	Man-made fibres	10	14	16	16	9.5	10.1	11.0	0.2	50.1	62.7	89.8	1.4
251	Rubber products	212	219	240	229	22.9	21.4	21.6	20.7	149.9	175.5	222.9	282.0
2511	Rubber tyres and tubes	43	52	55	45	15.0	13.6	13.9	13.1	107.5	122.8	156.9	199.9
2519	Other rubber products	169	167	185	184	7.9	7.8	7.7	7.6	42.3	52.7	66.0	82.0
2520	Plastic products	1476	1559	1733	1931	35.7	40.6	47.1	51.7	172.5	248.3	369.0	500.2
2610	Glass and glass products	278	293	301	320	27.5	27.0	27.6	27.4	170.4	210.7	264.7	320.5
269	Non-metallic mineral products n.e.c.	2886	3027	3119	3211	149.1	152.0	151.3	149.5	786.6	1036.7	1388.9	2048.5
2691	Pottery, china and earthenware	159	154	152	128	19.5	19.6	16.9	14.0	75.3	92.7	101.9	109.1
2692	Refractory ceramic products	73	72	78	75	15.0	15.1	15.4	13.9	88.1	121.8	165.8	179.7
2693	Struct.non-refractory clay; ceramic products	656	711	695	724	31.5	32.0	31.7	32.1	149.0	193.8	254.3	322.4
2694	Cement, lime and plaster	90	99	97	102	18.5	17.9	18.2	17.3	128.1	160.9	229.1	536.1
2695	Articles of concrete, cement and plaster	1209	1289	1357	1426	44.2	47.4	49.8	53.2	248.4	348.5	493.1	708.9
2696	Cutting, shaping & finishing of stone	468	454	500	525	7.7	7.6	7.4	8.3	28.5	33.8	41.4	62.3
2699	Other non-metallic mineral products n.e.c.	231	248	240	231	12.6	12.4	11.9	10.7	69.3	85.3	102.4	129.7
2710	Basic iron and steel	187	223	252	283	329.2	336.2	344.6	341.5	3304.4	4301.7	5702.6	6511.1
2720	Basic precious and non-ferrous metals	65	68	72	83	22.4	23.1	25.6	25.8	226.0	262.3	360.7	459.1
273	Casting of metals	152	162	182	176	17.8	18.7	16.9	15.9	102.4	138.4	162.0	197.1
2731	Casting of iron and steel	102	110	131	116	15.7	17.2	15.2	13.9	95.1	130.6	150.0	178.7
2732	Casting of non-ferrous metals	50	52	51	60	2.0	1.6	1.8	2.0	7.3	7.7	12.0	18.3
281	Struct.metal products;tanks;steam generators	1472	1574	1661	1739	34.2	36.3	40.9	53.2	170.6	232.1	355.1	584.4
2811	Structural metal products	1292	1370	1448	1516	25.6	26.1	28.2	37.2	123.6	160.8	237.9	398.2
2812	Tanks, reservoirs and containers of metal	88	111	121	119	5.4	6.6	8.6	11.3	30.4	46.0	77.9	129.6
2813	Steam generators	92	93	92	104	3.3	3.6	4.0	4.7	16.6	25.3	39.4	56.1
289	Other metal products; metal working services	1469	1545	1650	1798	49.6	50.9	53.3	60.0	226.3	298.2	414.1	590.7
2891	Metal forging/pressing/stamping/roll-forming	97	102	107	108	5.1	4.9	5.3	4.2	20.6	26.6	36.4	36.6
2892	Treatment & coating of metals	299	377	428	537	6.0	7.5	7.7	13.5	29.7	43.8	60.2	137.6
2893	Cutlery, hand tools and general hardware	247	240	241	219	10.4	10.1	10.0	9.8	48.8	58.3	75.9	89.3
2899	Other fabricated metal products n.e.c.	826	826	874	934	28.1	28.5	30.3	32.4	127.2	169.5	241.4	327.0
291	General purpose machinery	2112	2154	2197	2309	134.0	132.3	132.9	136.8	828.2	1010.9	1301.1	1692.7
2911	Engines & turbines (not for transport equipment)	224	219	209	195	33.4	31.4	29.9	25.9	243.9	275.6	321.4	349.8
2912	Pumps, compressors, taps and valves	383	390	425	479	43.1	44.8	46.8	46.8	273.5	333.2	483.9	595.2
2913	Bearings, gears, gearing & driving elements	122	119	112	103	12.9	12.0	11.2	10.4	73.0	94.5	104.9	126.8
2914	Ovens, furnaces and furnace burners	46	43	43	47	2.9	2.8	2.5	1.6	17.5	19.2	19.7	16.5
2915	Lifting and handling equipment	299	343	354	445	17.0	16.9	18.3	27.8	92.3	131.7	177.7	348.8
2919	Other general purpose machinery	1038	1040	1054	1040	24.8	24.5	24.1	24.4	128.0	156.7	194.2	255.3
292	Special purpose machinery	3038	3010	2929	2742	264.7	243.2	226.4	196.6	1390.1	1695.8	2089.2	2354.5
2921	Agricultural and forestry machinery	967	929	902	778	81.1	66.5	58.0	46.0	321.1	345.5	414.6	416.2
2922	Machine tools	511	524	516	450	46.9	42.8	39.3	36.1	237.8	269.3	333.8	398.2
2923	Machinery for metallurgy	180	167	168	164	31.4	31.7	36.1	32.1	305.1	401.9	540.6	637.4
2924	Machinery for mining & construction	394	409	431	438	52.5	55.1	52.9	44.1	276.8	398.7	486.5	501.6
2925	Food/beverage/tobacco processing machinery	411	384	342	314	19.1	17.2	14.0	10.0	86.8	95.6	103.1	89.0
2926	Machinery for textile, apparel and leather	43	44	31	28	1.6	0.9	0.4	0.1	5.5	3.1	2.9	0.7
2927	Weapons and ammunition	...	...	...	...	...	...	...	...	...	...	...	...
2929	Other special purpose machinery	532	553	539	570	32.1	29.0	25.7	28.2	157.1	181.7	208.7	312.1

continued

Ukraine

ISIC Revision 3		Number of enterprises					Number of employees					Wages and salaries paid to employees				
		Note	(number)				Note	(thousands)				Note	(millions of Ukrainian Hryvnias)			
ISIC	Industry		2003	2004	2005	2006		2003	2004	2005	2006		2003	2004	2005	2006
2930	Domestic appliances n.e.c.		136	139	143	124		17.3	17.9	18.1	16.7		124.5	156.6	205.8	229.5
3000	Office, accounting and computing machinery		518	522	522	487		9.1	8.1	8.4	7.8		36.7	47.4	65.8	88.3
3110	Electric motors, generators and transformers		503	493	515	551		34.0	31.9	33.7	36.6		166.9	212.8	302.0	424.9
3120	Electricity distribution & control apparatus		666	705	720	710		39.7	39.2	37.8	28.6		174.0	229.6	292.7	278.9
3130	Insulated wire and cable		110	96	103	102		8.5	8.7	8.8	8.3		58.4	73.4	94.4	110.7
3140	Accumulators, primary cells and batteries		44	52	51	46		2.6	2.4	2.4	3.1		15.5	14.7	20.8	38.9
3150	Lighting equipment and electric lamps		96	103	107	100		7.5	6.8	6.8	6.3		38.6	46.2	53.9	62.0
3190	Other electrical equipment n.e.c.		627	630	676	680		21.1	23.2	24.1	21.3		129.4	175.5	236.3	251.4
3210	Electronic valves, tubes, etc.		219	208	213	184		11.7	9.2	8.2	6.2		48.1	57.6	68.8	91.0
3220	TV/radio transmitters; line comm. apparatus		344	324	352	325		18.0	16.0	14.2	12.9		76.0	93.4	118.9	144.8
3230	TV and radio receivers and associated goods		258	264	250	221		10.6	10.1	9.1	9.3		44.9	77.9	93.3	133.2
331	Medical, measuring, testing appliances, etc.		1234	1289	1324	1332		49.7	49.3	51.0	53.5		251.2	322.7	428.3	550.3
3311	Medical, surgical and orthopaedic equipment		446	468	490	483		10.9	11.2	11.0	9.9		59.3	77.7	99.0	109.9
3312	Measuring/testing/navigating appliances,etc.		681	718	718	751		35.3	35.1	36.2	42.2		175.2	224.4	299.2	426.5
3313	Industrial process control equipment		107	103	116	98		3.5	3.1	3.7	1.4		16.7	20.6	29.8	13.6
3320	Optical instruments & photographic equipment		67	69	64	57		8.9	7.7	5.7	4.3		34.5	36.0	34.4	33.0
3330	Watches and clocks		7	9	8	10		0.1	0.1	0.1	0.1		0.4	0.6	0.7	1.3
3410	Motor vehicles		281	258	279	92		39.3	45.8	44.4	36.2		260.5	414.4	487.2	563.9
3420	Automobile bodies, trailers & semi-trailers		40	42	43	63		2.8	2.1	1.5	3.4		10.5	8.7	8.4	33.7
3430	Parts/accessories for automobiles		191	202	204	192		15.6	17.0	20.3	17.7		72.6	109.2	174.1	191.3
351	Building and repairing of ships and boats		364	388	426	440		43.5	40.4	37.7	31.0		294.7	335.5	379.8	389.5
3511	Building and repairing of ships		328	358	392	394		43.1	40.0	37.2	30.2		292.2	332.9	375.6	382.6
3512	Building/repairing of pleasure/sport. boats		36	30	34	46		0.4	0.4	0.5	0.8		2.4	2.5	3.9	7.0
3520	Railway/tramway locomotives & rolling stock		147	155	171	186		75.2	79.7	79.1	80.4		565.1	721.9	880.3	1160.3
3530	Aircraft and spacecraft		99	107	102	96		86.2	85.7	80.6	73.1		517.7	654.9	748.0	894.0
359	Transport equipment n.e.c.		49	48	49	48		2.2	2.1	2.2	2.4		9.5	12.5	18.4	24.4
3591	Motorcycles		9	7	7	6		0.6	0.5	0.6	0.6		3.0	4.3	7.1	3.5
3592	Bicycles and invalid carriages		21	20	20	20		1.4	1.3	1.2	1.7		5.8	7.3	9.9	19.6
3599	Other transport equipment n.e.c.		19	21	22	22		0.3	0.2	0.3	0.2		0.7	0.9	1.5	1.3
3610	Furniture		1732	1817	1856	1813		48.8	48.2	51.9	51.8		184.5	237.9	339.1	426.5
369	Manufacturing n.e.c.		668	697	725	773		20.7	20.9	20.5	23.0		98.7	129.9	157.5	232.5
3691	Jewellery and related articles		228	245	280	306		8.9	9.6	11.2	11.6		52.6	71.8	102.8	127.4
3692	Musical instruments		21	19	22	18		0.6	0.6	0.5	0.2		1.7	1.8	2.0	1.0
3693	Sports goods		54	47	51	57		1.1	1.2	1.2	2.6		3.8	5.4	7.5	37.5
3694	Games and toys		71	74	79	83		2.3	2.6	2.7	3.1		9.9	13.3	16.2	21.8
3699	Other manufacturing n.e.c.		294	312	293	309		7.7	6.9	4.9	5.4		30.6	37.7	28.9	44.9
3710	Recycling of metal waste and scrap		694	729	755	667		19.8	21.1	17.7	14.0		115.8	164.0	166.1	156.8
3720	Recycling of non-metal waste and scrap		245	292	326	331		4.0	4.9	4.5	4.0		15.5	22.4	29.0	29.5
D	Total manufacturing		48740	49584	50487	50038		2809.3	2786.8	2775.5	2740.9		17086.9	21611.9	28044.1	35062.2

Ukraine

ISIC Revision 3		Output in producers' prices					Value added in producers' prices					Gross fixed capital formation		
			(millions of Ukrainian Hryvnias)					(millions of Ukrainian Hryvnias)					(millions of Ukrainian Hryvnias)	
ISIC	Industry	Note	2003	2004a/	2005	2006	Note	2003	2004	2005	2006	Note	2005	2006
151	Processed meat,fish,fruit,vegetables,fats		12161.1	17425.8	...	...		...	...	...	...		...	...
1511	Processing/preserving of meat		5626.4	8269.2	...	...		...	...	...	...		...	...
1512	Processing/preserving of fish		394.6	645.2	...	...		...	...	...	...		...	...
1513	Processing/preserving of fruit & vegetables		1817.7	2087.4	...	...		...	...	...	...		...	...
1514	Vegetable and animal oils and fats		4322.4	6424.0	...	...		...	...	...	...		...	...
1520	Dairy products		6684.5	8955.3	...	...		...	...	...	...		...	...
153	Grain mill products; starches; animal feeds		4270.4	5049.4	...	...		...	...	...	...		...	...
1531	Grain mill products		2646.8	3465.7	...	...		...	...	...	...		...	...
1532	Starches and starch products		427.6	483.2	...	...		...	...	...	...		...	...
1533	Prepared animal feeds		1196.0	1100.5	...	...		...	...	...	...		...	...
154	Other food products		13799.4	17130.9	...	...		...	...	...	...		...	...
1541	Bakery products		4435.3	5751.3	...	...		...	...	...	...		...	...
1542	Sugar		2979.2	3600.2	...	...		...	...	...	...		...	...
1543	Cocoa, chocolate and sugar confectionery		4134.9	5057.3	...	...		...	...	...	...		...	...
1544	Macaroni, noodles & similar products		423.2	471.8	...	...		...	...	...	...		...	...
1549	Other food products n.e.c.		1826.8	2250.3	...	...		...	...	...	...		...	...
155	Beverages		8275.0	10498.8	...	...		...	...	...	...		...	...
1551	Distilling, rectifying & blending of spirits		2235.6	3563.9	...	...		...	...	...	...		...	...
1552	Wines		1540.5	1631.9	...	...		...	...	...	...		...	...
1553	Malt liquors and malt		2736.8	3279.4	...	...		...	...	...	...		...	...
1554	Soft drinks; mineral waters		1762.1	2023.6	...	...		...	...	...	...		...	...
1600	Tobacco products		3736.3	4327.4	...	...		...	...	...	...		...	...
171	Spinning, weaving and finishing of textiles		469.5	653.4	...	...		...	...	...	...		...	...
1711	Textile fibre preparation; textile weaving		466.8	636.7	...	...		...	...	...	...		...	...
1712	Finishing of textiles		2.7	16.7	...	...		...	...	...	...		...	...
172	Other textiles		539.5	637.7	...	...		...	...	...	...		...	...
1721	Made-up textile articles, except apparel		383.3	419.5	...	...		...	...	...	...		...	...
1722	Carpets and rugs		59.7	88.6	...	...		...	...	...	...		...	...
1723	Cordage, rope, twine and netting		27.8	32.6	...	...		...	...	...	...		...	...
1729	Other textiles n.e.c.		68.7	97.0	...	...		...	...	...	...		...	...
1730	Knitted and crocheted fabrics and articles		184.8	207.5	...	...		...	...	...	...		...	...
1810	Wearing apparel, except fur apparel		1332.0	1704.9	...	...		...	...	...	...		...	...
1820	Dressing & dyeing of fur; processing of fur		96.1	102.0	...	...		...	...	...	...		...	...
191	Tanning, dressing and processing of leather		666.2	776.8	...	...		...	...	...	...		...	...
1911	Tanning and dressing of leather		574.6	698.7	...	...		...	...	...	...		...	...
1912	Luggage, handbags, etc.; saddlery & harness		91.6	78.1	...	...		...	...	...	...		...	...
1920	Footwear		453.7	585.8	...	...		...	...	...	...		...	...
2010	Sawmilling and planing of wood		884.9	1040.8	...	...		...	...	...	...		...	...
202	Products of wood, cork, straw, etc.		1353.6	1957.3	...	...		...	...	...	...		...	...
2021	Veneer sheets, plywood, particle board, etc.		785.0	1245.5	...	...		...	...	...	...		...	...
2022	Builders' carpentry and joinery		425.4	544.7	...	...		...	...	...	...		...	...
2023	Wooden containers		73.0	94.8	...	...		...	...	...	...		...	...
2029	Other wood products; articles of cork/straw		70.2	72.3	...	...		...	...	...	...		...	...
210	Paper and paper products		3143.3	4284.5	...	...		...	...	...	...		...	...
2101	Pulp, paper and paperboard		626.8	912.5	...	...		...	...	...	...		...	...
2102	Corrugated paper and paperboard		1165.1	1783.6	...	...		...	...	...	...		...	...
2109	Other articles of paper and paperboard		1351.4	1588.4	...	...		...	...	...	...		...	...
221	Publishing		1513.5	1795.1	...	...		...	...	...	...		...	...
2211	Publishing of books and other publications		268.4	432.3	...	...		...	...	...	...		...	...
2212	Publishing of newspapers, journals, etc.		1083.3	1182.8	...	...		...	...	...	...		...	...
2213	Publishing of recorded media		20.4	4.6	...	...		...	...	...	...		...	...
2219	Other publishing		141.4	175.4	...	...		...	...	...	...		...	...

continued

Ukraine

ISIC Revision 3		Output in producers' prices (millions of Ukrainian Hryvnias)					Value added in producers' prices (millions of Ukrainian Hryvnias)					Gross fixed capital formation (millions of Ukrainian Hryvnias)		
ISIC	Industry	Note	2003	2004a/	2005	2006	Note	2003	2004	2005	2006	Note	2005	2006
222	Printing and related service activities		2659.0	3764.1	...	...		...	...	...	...		...	...
2221	Printing		2457.2	3500.2	...	...		...	...	...	...		...	...
2222	Service activities related to printing		201.8	263.9	...	...		...	...	...	...		...	...
2230	Reproduction of recorded media		24.3	44.4	...	...		...	...	...	...		...	...
2310	Coke oven products		6491.1	12682.1	...	...		...	...	...	...		...	...
2320	Refined petroleum products		14950.8	23664.0	...	...		...	...	...	...		...	...
2330	Processing of nuclear fuel		...	...	...	...		...	...	...	...		...	...
241	Basic chemicals		8968.1	11914.1	...	...		...	...	...	...		...	...
2411	Basic chemicals, except fertilizers		3083.8	4445.8	...	...		...	...	...	...		...	...
2412	Fertilizers and nitrogen compounds		5182.5	6686.3	...	...		...	...	...	...		...	...
2413	Plastics in primary forms; synthetic rubber		701.8	782.0	...	...		...	...	...	...		...	...
242	Other chemicals		5233.4	6613.5	...	...		...	...	...	...		...	...
2421	Pesticides and other agro-chemical products		22.9	31.0	...	...		...	...	...	...		...	...
2422	Paints, varnishes, printing ink and mastics		867.5	1032.7	...	...		...	...	...	...		...	...
2423	Pharmaceuticals, medicinal chemicals, etc.		2289.2	2194.5	...	...		...	...	...	...		...	...
2424	Soap, cleaning & cosmetic preparations		1015.4	1952.8	...	...		...	...	...	...		...	...
2429	Other chemical products n.e.c.		1038.4	1402.5	...	...		...	...	...	...		...	...
2430	Man-made fibres		291.1	382.3	...	...		...	...	...	...		...	...
251	Rubber products		1269.9	1786.1	...	...		...	...	...	...		...	...
2511	Rubber tyres and tubes		923.4	1342.2	...	...		...	...	...	...		...	...
2519	Other rubber products		346.5	443.9	...	...		...	...	...	...		...	...
2520	Plastic products		2822.1	4252.7	...	...		...	...	...	...		...	...
2610	Glass and glass products		1210.7	1637.4	...	...		...	...	...	...		...	...
269	Non-metallic mineral products n.e.c.		6653.6	8860.8	...	...		...	...	...	...		...	...
2691	Pottery, china and earthenware		330.3	381.8	...	...		...	...	...	...		...	...
2692	Refractory ceramic products		780.5	999.3	...	...		...	...	...	...		...	...
2693	Struct.non-refractory clay; ceramic products		678.4	939.2	...	...		...	...	...	...		...	...
2694	Cement, lime and plaster		1496.1	2251.4	...	...		...	...	...	...		...	...
2695	Articles of concrete, cement and plaster		2350.0	3083.7	...	...		...	...	...	...		...	...
2696	Cutting, shaping & finishing of stone		178.4	234.4	...	...		...	...	...	...		...	...
2699	Other non-metallic mineral products n.e.c.		839.9	971.0	...	...		...	...	...	...		...	...
2710	Basic iron and steel		47401.6	78887.8	...	...		...	...	...	...		...	...
2720	Basic precious and non-ferrous metals		4143.8	4470.2	...	...		...	...	...	...		...	...
273	Casting of metals		1171.9	1477.0	...	...		...	...	...	...		...	...
2731	Casting of iron and steel		986.5	1145.9	...	...		...	...	...	...		...	...
2732	Casting of non-ferrous metals		185.4	331.1	...	...		...	...	...	...		...	...
281	Struct.metal products;tanks;steam generators		1789.6	3105.5	...	...		...	...	...	...		...	...
2811	Structural metal products		1313.6	2237.4	...	...		...	...	...	...		...	...
2812	Tanks, reservoirs and containers of metal		310.0	625.8	...	...		...	...	...	...		...	...
2813	Steam generators		166.0	242.3	...	...		...	...	...	...		...	...
289	Other metal products; metal working services		2806.4	5470.3	...	...		...	...	...	...		...	...
2891	Metal forging/pressing/stamping/roll-forming		275.7	406.0	...	...		...	...	...	...		...	...
2892	Treatment & coating of metals		554.2	2080.2	...	...		...	...	...	...		...	...
2893	Cutlery, hand tools and general hardware		241.5	252.7	...	...		...	...	...	...		...	...
2899	Other fabricated metal products n.e.c.		1735.0	2731.4	...	...		...	...	...	...		...	...
291	General purpose machinery		4802.3	6191.7	...	...		...	...	...	...		...	...
2911	Engines & turbines (not for transport equipment)		1115.6	1080.0	...	...		...	...	...	...		...	...
2912	Pumps, compressors, taps and valves		1548.0	2006.3	...	...		...	...	...	...		...	...
2913	Bearings, gears, gearing & driving elements		487.5	700.2	...	...		...	...	...	...		...	...
2914	Ovens, furnaces and furnace burners		123.9	131.5	...	...		...	...	...	...		...	...
2915	Lifting and handling equipment		494.2	839.1	...	...		...	...	...	...		...	...
2919	Other general purpose machinery		1033.1	1434.6	...	...		...	...	...	...		...	...

292	Special purpose machinery	7148.9	9352.2	...	...	...	...	...	...	...	...
2921	Agricultural and forestry machinery	1704.6	1934.5	...	...	...	...	...	...	...	...
2922	Machine tools	1002.3	1196.2	...	...	...	...	...	...	...	...
2923	Machinery for metallurgy	880.0	1052.6	...	...	...	...	...	...	...	...
2924	Machinery for mining & construction	2351.1	3520.4	...	...	...	...	...	...	...	...
2925	Food/beverage/tobacco processing machinery	364.6	502.2	...	...	...	...	...	...	...	...
2926	Machinery for textile, apparel and leather	18.2	16.6	...	...	...	...	...	...	...	...
2927	Weapons and ammunition	...	...	...	...	...	...	...	...	...	...
2929	Other special purpose machinery	828.1	1129.7	...	...	...	...	...	...	...	...
2930	Domestic appliances n.e.c.	1168.0	1444.6	...	...	...	...	...	...	...	...
3000	Office, accounting and computing machinery	492.5	959.7	...	...	...	...	...	...	...	...
3110	Electric motors, generators and transformers	1293.1	1668.4	...	...	...	...	...	...	...	...
3120	Electricity distribution & control apparatus	1402.0	5502.3	...	...	...	...	...	...	...	...
3130	Insulated wire and cable	919.6	1280.4	...	...	...	...	...	...	...	...
3140	Accumulators, primary cells and batteries	174.3	158.9	...	...	...	...	...	...	...	...
3150	Lighting equipment and electric lamps	230.9	388.3	...	...	...	...	...	...	...	...
3190	Other electrical equipment n.e.c.	670.1	1587.9	...	...	...	...	...	...	...	...
3210	Electronic valves, tubes, etc.	281.9	631.3	...	...	...	...	...	...	...	...
3220	TV/radio transmitters; line comm. apparatus	807.0	865.0	...	...	...	...	...	...	...	...
3230	TV and radio receivers and associated goods	283.4	769.1	...	...	...	...	...	...	...	...
331	Medical, measuring, testing appliances, etc.	1378.4	2523.1	...	...	...	...	...	...	...	...
3311	Medical, surgical and orthopaedic equipment	340.0	547.3	...	...	...	...	...	...	...	...
3312	Measuring/testing/navigating appliances,etc.	909.8	1871.8	...	...	...	...	...	...	...	...
3313	Industrial process control equipment	128.6	104.0	...	...	...	...	...	...	...	...
3320	Optical instruments & photographic equipment	105.8	94.1	...	...	...	...	...	...	...	...
3330	Watches and clocks	5.2	8.4	...	...	...	...	...	...	...	...
3410	Motor vehicles	3816.5	6955.6	...	...	...	...	...	...	...	...
3420	Automobile bodies, trailers & semi-trailers	76.9	210.2	...	...	...	...	...	...	...	...
3430	Parts/accessories for automobiles	491.0	947.1	...	...	...	...	...	...	...	...
351	Building and repairing of ships and boats	1032.5	1313.4	...	...	...	...	...	...	...	...
3511	Building and repairing of ships	1001.8	1276.6	...	...	...	...	...	...	...	...
3512	Building/repairing of pleasure/sport. boats	30.7	36.8	...	...	...	...	...	...	...	...
3520	Railway/tramway locomotives & rolling stock	5618.3	7861.4	...	...	...	...	...	...	...	...
3530	Aircraft and spacecraft	2558.2	2761.1	...	...	...	...	...	...	...	...
359	Transport equipment n.e.c.	72.2	94.9	...	...	...	...	...	...	...	...
3591	Motorcycles	10.1	8.5	...	...	...	...	...	...	...	...
3592	Bicycles and invalid carriages	54.2	73.9	...	...	...	...	...	...	...	...
3599	Other transport equipment n.e.c.	7.9	12.5	...	...	...	...	...	...	...	...
3610	Furniture	1664.5	2203.2	...	...	...	...	...	...	...	...
369	Manufacturing n.e.c.	711.9	881.1	...	...	...	...	...	...	...	...
3691	Jewellery and related articles	289.5	394.9	...	...	...	...	...	...	...	...
3692	Musical instruments	6.8	8.8	...	...	...	...	...	...	...	...
3693	Sports goods	98.5	128.1	...	...	...	...	...	...	...	...
3694	Games and toys	40.2	74.9	...	...	...	...	...	...	...	...
3699	Other manufacturing n.e.c.	276.9	274.4	...	...	...	...	...	...	...	...
3710	Recycling of metal waste and scrap	2252.9	3194.6	...	...	...	...	...	...	...	...
3720	Recycling of non-metal waste and scrap	189.2	274.2	...	...	...	...	...	...	...	...
D	Total manufacturing	207098.7	306267.9	...	...	49702.0	64124.0	...	...	...	...

a/ Output in factor values.

Ukraine

ISIC Revision 3			Index numbers of industrial production											
			(2000=100)											
ISIC	Industry	Note	1995	1996	1997	1998	1999	2000	2001	2002	2003	2004	2005	2006
15	Food and beverages		...	...	...	...	...	100	119	128	155	174	198	217
16	Tobacco products		...	...	...	...	...	...	...	...	...	...	...	...
17	Textiles	a/	...	...	...	...	...	100	116	117	120	138	142	135
18	Wearing apparel, fur	a/	...	...	...	...	...	...	...	...	...	...	...	...
19	Leather, leather products and footwear		...	...	...	...	...	100	112	109	118	132	121	135
20	Wood products (excl. furniture)		...	...	...	...	...	100	128	158	196	246	295	335
21	Paper and paper products	b/	...	...	...	...	...	100	119	129	161	204	230	255
22	Printing and publishing	b/	...	...	...	...	...	...	...	...	...	...	...	...
23	Coke,refined petroleum products,nuclear fuel		...	...	...	...	...	100	154	199	217	226	196	173
24	Chemicals and chemical products		...	...	...	...	...	100	108	117	136	151	162	164
25	Rubber and plastics products		...	...	...	...	...	100	126	126	152	199	234	260
26	Non-metallic mineral products		...	...	...	...	...	100	112	118	138	167	190	214
27	Basic metals	c/	...	...	...	...	...	100	106	110	126	141	139	152
28	Fabricated metal products	c/	...	...	...	...	...	...	...	...	...	...	...	...
29	Machinery and equipment n.e.c.		...	...	...	...	...	100	119	120	145	173	194	200
30	Office, accounting and computing machinery		...	...	...	...	...	100	90	110	145	208	270	263
31	Electrical machinery and apparatus		...	...	...	...	...	100	114	125	147	241	219	244
32	Radio,television and communication equipment		...	...	...	...	...	100	139	138	176	195	248	246
33	Medical, precision and optical instruments		...	...	...	...	...	100	115	124	142	180	165	193
34	Motor vehicles, trailers, semi-trailers	d/	...	...	...	...	...	100	122	159	257	329	371	442
35	Other transport equipment	d/	...	...	...	...	...	...	...	...	...	...	...	...
36	Furniture; manufacturing n.e.c.		...	...	...	...	...	...	...	...	...	...	...	...
37	Recycling		...	...	...	...	...	...	...	...	...	...	...	...
D	Total manufacturing		88	84	83	83	86	100	116	125	148	168	173	183

a/ 17 includes 18.
b/ 21 includes 22.
c/ 27 includes 28.
d/ 34 includes 35.

United Kingdom

Supplier of information:
National Statistics, London.
Industrial statistics for the OECD countries are compiled by the OECD secretariat, which supplies them to UNIDO.

Basic source of data:
Annual employment survey, annual business inquiry.

Major deviations from ISIC (Revision 3):
Data presented in accordance with ISIC (Rev. 3) were originally classified in the Standard Industrial Classification of economic activities 1992 (SIC92), which was compatible with NACE (Revision 1).

Reference period:
Calendar year.

Scope:
All establishments.

Method of data collection:
Questionnaires are distributed by mail.

Type of enumeration:
Not reported.

Adjusted for non-response:
Yes.

Concepts and definitions of variables:
Wages and salaries includes all overtime payments, bonuses, commissions, holiday pay and redundancy payments less any amounts reimbursed from government sources. No deduction is made for income tax, insurance, contributory pensions, etc. Payments in kind, traveling expenses, lodging allowances, etc. are excluded.
Output relates to gross output and is calculated by adjusting the value of total sales, work done and services rendered, by the net changes during the year of work in progress and stocks of finished goods. Total sales represents deliveries on sale of goods produced by establishments and includes sales of goods made from materials given out by them to other organizations or to outworkers. The value of sales is the amount charged to customers. Where products attract excise duty, the value is inclusive of duty if goods are sold "duty-paid", and exclusive of duty if goods are sold in bond or exported. Sales of fixed assets are excluded.
Value added represents gross value added in factor values and is defined as the value of gross output less the cost of purchases of materials for use in production and packaging, fuels, goods for merchanting or factoring and the cost of industrial and non-industrial services received. The value of purchases is adjusted for changes in stocks of materials, stores and fuel.
Gross fixed capital formation is the value of purchases of fixed assets less the value of sales of such assets. Valuation is at full cost incurred, including the cost of installation and certain fees and taxes (namely legal fees, stamp duty, agents' commissions, etc.), and is inclusive of any amounts received or expected to be received in grants and/or allowances from government sources, statutory bodies or local authorities. The value of capital goods produced for own use are included. The value of any assets acquired in taking over an existing business are excluded. The figures include non-deductible VAT but exclude deductible VAT.

Related national publications:
Labour Market Trends, published by National Statistics, London.

United Kingdom

ISIC Revision 3		Number of enterprises					Number of employees					Wages and salaries paid to employees				
			(number)					(thousands)					(millions of British Pounds)			
ISIC	Industry	Note	2002	2003	2004	2005	Note	2002	2003	2004	2005	Note	2002	2003	2004	2005
151	Processed meat,fish,fruit,vegetables,fats		2075	1963	1907	1871		172	177	175	170		2807	2871	2903	2939
1511	Processing/preserving of meat		1113	1028	1013	1009		111	117	117	112		1826	1904	1907	1904
1512	Processing/preserving of fish		393	401	394	388		20	20	18	17		255	269	266	254
1513	Processing/preserving of fruit & vegetables		507	484	461	441		35	39	38	40		580	651	683	724
1514	Vegetable and animal oils and fats		62	50	39	33		5	2	2	2		146	48	47	57
1520	Dairy products		578	574	549	534		31	31	29	29		593	604	613	618
153	Grain mill products; starches; animal feeds		680	657	645	612		28	27	28	27		725	669	770	716
1531	Grain mill products		...	...	...	118		...	...	...	12		...	...	...	...
1532	Starches and starch products		...	...	...	4		...	...	...	1		...	...	...	...
1533	Prepared animal feeds		547	528	518	490		14	13	13	13		348	276	294	305
154	Other food products		3419	3334	3206	3182		197	190	183	181		3280	3399	3250	3435
1541	Bakery products		2137	2066	1975	1939		116	114	107	110		1653	1710	1655	1726
1542	Sugar		...	...	...	...		...	...	...	...		...	...	...	...
1543	Cocoa, chocolate and sugar confectionery		285	288	286	278		29	29	27	25		552	624	554	609
1544	Macaroni, noodles & similar products		...	...	...	...		...	...	...	...		...	...	...	...
1549	Other food products n.e.c.		971	957	922	...		47	42	...	...		941	...	...	...
155	Beverages		768	740	759	795		54	53	51	51		1472	1405	1498	1578
1551	Distilling, rectifying & blending of spirits		90	84	90	89		12	11	10	10		330	288	327	358
1552	Wines		118	59	67	75		3	2	2	2		82	77	45	43
1553	Malt liquors and malt		312	342	346	381		24	23	23	21		660	641	652	683
1554	Soft drinks; mineral waters		248	255	256	250		16	17	17	18		400	399	474	494
1600	Tobacco products		25	11	10	10		6	6	5	5		251	270	231	227
171	Spinning, weaving and finishing of textiles		1239	1118	1035	1074		34	29	26	24		565	498	451	451
1711	Textile fibre preparation; textile weaving		703	611	527	531		24	20	17	16		404	359	308	295
1712	Finishing of textiles		536	507	508	543		10	8	9	8		161	139	143	156
172	Other textiles		3362	3299	3302	3284		65	53	53	49		922	829	860	836
1721	Made-up textile articles, except apparel		1951	1969	2030	2068		33	27	31	28		413	380	428	450
1722	Carpets and rugs		287	263	259	245		12	10	8	8		205	185	172	143
1723	Cordage, rope, twine and netting		96	96	106	103		2	1	1	1		20	18	24	25
1729	Other textiles n.e.c.		1028	971	907	868		18	14	13	11		284	246	236	218
1730	Knitted and crocheted fabrics and articles		685	619	535	492		20	17	15	11		264	211	204	163
1810	Wearing apparel, except fur apparel		5362	...	4444	4204		68	...	45	39		817	...	584	601
1820	Dressing & dyeing of fur; processing of fur		21	...	14	14		-	...	-	-		2	...	1	1
191	Tanning, dressing and processing of leather		548	540	533	525		7	6	5	5		105	84	84	76
1911	Tanning and dressing of leather		151	129	111	95		3	2	2	1		42	44	36	31
1912	Luggage, handbags, etc.; saddlery & harness		397	411	422	430		4	4	4	3		63	40	48	44
1920	Footwear		350	299	273	251		9	7	6	5		142	88	88	70
2010	Sawmilling and planing of wood		973	909	862	825		12	11	9	10		194	157	166	182
202	Products of wood, cork, straw, etc.		7411	7529	7596	7630		75	69	70	67		1261	1135	1320	1198
2021	Veneer sheets, plywood, particle board, etc.		177	164	169	166		7	6	6	6		123	122	129	143
2022	Builders' carpentry and joinery		4979	5216	5408	5519		48	46	47	46		897	769	962	827
2023	Wooden containers		559	537	502	497		8	7	6	6		110	102	82	95
2029	Other wood products; articles of cork/straw		1696	1612	1517	1448		12	11	10	9		131	143	147	133
210	Paper and paper products		2494	2346	2255	2156		91	85	81	75		1939	1950	1893	1777
2101	Pulp, paper and paperboard		436	364	353	331		17	17	16	14		419	431	418	402
2102	Corrugated paper and paperboard		822	757	718	685		40	36	35	34		796	785	761	752
2109	Other articles of paper and paperboard		1236	1225	1184	1140		34	32	30	27		723	734	714	623
221	Publishing		9616	9621	9451	9472		162	159	163	159		4028	4133	4270	4287
2211	Publishing of books and other publications		2743	2738	2719	2739		31	29	29	25		823	820	814	744
2212	Publishing of newspapers, journals, etc.		2642	2546	2626	2725		112	112	114	114		2817	2976	3093	3103
2213	Publishing of recorded media		985	1034	1077	1118		3	2	3	3		92	75	49	131
2219	Other publishing		3246	3303	3029	2890		16	16	17	17		296	262	314	309

222	Printing and related service activities	18777	18283	17433	16906	172	170	157	149	3549	3469	3295	3203
2221	Printing	13694	13432	12943	12700	139	139	128	126	2895	2839	2712	2698
2222	Service activities related to printing	5083	4851	4490	4206	33	31	29	24	654	630	583	505
2230	Reproduction of recorded media	1447	1452	1387	1438	7	6	5	5	120	108	117	123
2310	Coke oven products	11	...	-	-	...	...	-	-	6	...	-	-
2320	Refined petroleum products	198	...	173	...	12	...	...	...	...	...	...	...
2330	Processing of nuclear fuel	7	...	5	...	...	...	...	...	...	...	...	...
241	Basic chemicals	1206	1163	1153	1119	67	62	59	56	2072	1933	1909	1771
2411	Basic chemicals, except fertilizers	469	447	427	398	...	...	...	...	...	...	...	1128
2412	Fertilizers and nitrogen compounds	82	81	81	78	3	3	2	3	68	67	75	77
2413	Plastics in primary forms; synthetic rubber	655	635	645	643	25	20	20	21	628	505	546	566
242	Other chemicals	2588	2556	2567	2643	182	170	163	155	4888	4708	4849	4761
2421	Pesticides and other agro-chemical products	74	71	68	74	5	5	4	3	174	165	116	111
2422	Paints, varnishes, printing ink and mastics	555	534	501	504	23	23	21	20	552	540	537	520
2423	Pharmaceuticals, medicinal chemicals, etc.	477	519	540	564	84	73	73	68	2494	2244	2429	2421
2424	Soap, cleaning & cosmetic preparations	678	675	686	716	38	38	35	34	853	900	855	790
2429	Other chemical products n.e.c.	804	757	772	785	31	31	30	30	815	859	912	919
2430	Man-made fibres	23	23	18	20	2	2	2	2	55	61	58	53
251	Rubber products	750	739	725	707	36	33	31	29	768	739	729	728
2511	Rubber tyres and tubes	166	162	147	132	12	10	9	9	315	313	294	303
2519	Other rubber products	584	577	578	575	24	23	21	20	454	426	435	425
2520	Plastic products	6230	6164	6306	6325	195	183	182	172	3373	3433	3601	3529
2610	Glass and glass products	1629	1443	1280	1258	33	33	30	32	612	644	638	700
269	Non-metallic mineral products n.e.c.	3748	3768	3723	3691	94	91	93	79	1826	1782	1935	1768
2691	Pottery, china and earthenware	...	...	...	...	...	...	...	...	...	...	...	...
2692	Refractory ceramic products	158	168	174	166	5	5	6	4	150	100	109	116
2693	Struct.non-refractory clay; ceramic products	474	477	448	428	12	11	11	11	223	220	224	230
2694	Cement, lime and plaster	53	37	32	29	6	4	5	5	159	130	160	168
2695	Articles of concrete, cement and plaster	1143	1162	1158	1168	34	34	38	32	659	715	869	737
2696	Cutting, shaping & finishing of stone	940	989	1047	1099	6	10	9	6	81	120	126	101
2699	Other non-metallic mineral products n.e.c.	356	341	328	312	10	8	9	7	193	169	184	176
2710	Basic iron and steel	901	879	538	552	48	45	37	38	1094	1092	1017	1088
2720	Basic precious and non-ferrous metals	639	586	546	518	23	20	19	18	525	501	471	466
273	Casting of metals	794	807	749	729	24	24	21	19	462	452	440	396
2731	Casting of iron and steel	418	424	390	387	13	12	11	10	253	238	232	202
2732	Casting of non-ferrous metals	376	383	359	342	12	12	10	9	210	214	208	194
281	Struct.metal products;tanks;steam generators	4497	4611	4717	4899	103	95	93	93	2009	2046	1935	2086
2811	Structural metal products	3901	4004	4105	4256	84	78	75	75	1572	1580	1484	1549
2812	Tanks, reservoirs and containers of metal	419	435	443	458	13	12	12	11	256	276	264	279
2813	Steam generators	177	172	169	185	6	6	6	7	180	190	186	259
289	Other metal products; metal working services	24336	23692	23030	22676	249	243	237	225	4484	4578	4473	4460
2891	Metal forging/pressing/stamping/roll-forming	1258	1250	1224	1175	33	33	30	27	584	764	556	527
2892	Treatment & coating of metals	14946	14482	14044	13929	120	112	113	113	2118	2049	2161	2266
2893	Cutlery, hand tools and general hardware	2324	2278	2273	2264	32	32	31	28	638	617	552	546
2899	Other fabricated metal products n.e.c.	5808	5682	5489	5308	64	66	62	58	1143	1148	1204	1120
291	General purpose machinery	6349	6284	6298	6346	180	164	173	160	3931	3781	3994	3994
2911	Engines & turbines (not for transport equipment)	340	348	333	356	13	11	15	15	360	320	474	469
2912	Pumps, compressors, taps and valves	928	907	901	896	43	40	40	39	993	978	964	991
2913	Bearings, gears, gearing & driving elements	400	408	403	429	12	12	15	12	273	265	251	265
2914	Ovens, furnaces and furnace burners	215	212	218	207	3	3	3	3	69	58	75	87
2915	Lifting and handling equipment	1401	1364	1341	1331	33	33	35	32	763	732	756	757
2919	Other general purpose machinery	3065	3045	3102	3127	76	66	66	59	1472	1428	1474	1425
292	Special purpose machinery	6346	6135	6015	5964	112	103	97	95	2563	2531	2373	2373
2921	Agricultural and forestry machinery	1254	1226	1143	1130	12	10	10	9	225	253	213	185
2922	Machine tools	1737	1625	1565	1478	19	18	15	14	448	348	342	318
2923	Machinery for metallurgy	62	63	31	29	1	1	1	1	36	28	22	30
2924	Machinery for mining & construction	408	388	389	384	20	18	14	15	464	498	391	448
2925	Food/beverage/tobacco processing machinery	489	506	564	604	12	11	11	10	239	283	244	225
2926	Machinery for textile, apparel and leather	260	239	240	227	3	2	2	2	51	49	48	37
2927	Weapons and ammunition	147	149	152	146	14	14	17	16	408	419	486	481
2929	Other special purpose machinery	1989	1939	1931	1966	31	28	27	27	693	653	627	648

continued

United Kingdom

ISIC Revision 3		Number of enterprises					Number of employees					Wages and salaries paid to employees				
			(number)					(thousands)					(millions of British Pounds)			
ISIC	Industry	Note	2002	2003	2004	2005	Note	2002	2003	2004	2005	Note	2002	2003	2004	2005
2930	Domestic appliances n.e.c.		562	575	615	594		30	28	26	25		536	531	542	549
3000	Office, accounting and computing machinery		1776	1764	1718	1652		43	34	30	28		1143	773	753	705
3110	Electric motors, generators and transformers		950	896	872	861		30	23	24	23		628	528	473	471
3120	Electricity distribution & control apparatus		1019	1004	988	1005		46	42	39	39		940	899	852	823
3130	Insulated wire and cable		425	387	354	373		14	11	10	9		278	228	205	182
3140	Accumulators, primary cells and batteries		123	128	132	154		5	5	5	4		95	78	82	82
3150	Lighting equipment and electric lamps		699	710	722	736		21	19	17	17		349	342	282	346
3190	Other electrical equipment n.e.c.		2246	2172	2121	2137		44	41	37	35		854	807	773	770
3210	Electronic valves, tubes, etc.		923	891	839	797		36	29	31	27		707	648	670	642
3220	TV/radio transmitters; line comm. apparatus		821	776	942	903		40	31	26	21		1449	1028	745	673
3230	TV and radio receivers and associated goods		1062	997	1025	1045		25	22	20	18		491	442	420	399
331	Medical, measuring, testing appliances, etc.		5077	5020	5080	5056		108	105	101	102		2605	2491	2471	2410
3311	Medical, surgical and orthopaedic equipment		1725	1702	1727	1751		33	34	31	35		663	687	656	667
3312	Measuring/testing/navigating appliances,etc.		2949	2922	2968	2937		67	63	62	60		1730	1604	1618	1545
3313	Industrial process control equipment		403	396	385	368		8	8	8	8		212	199	196	198
3320	Optical instruments & photographic equipment		691	676	679	649		17	15	15	14		328	309	291	285
3330	Watches and clocks		102	98	103	95		1	1	1	1		17	16	18	16
3410	Motor vehicles		661	657	713	767		95	94	89	86		2627	2484	2572	2597
3420	Automobile bodies, trailers & semi-trailers		800	832	877	911		27	27	26	25		495	535	494	495
3430	Parts/accessories for automobiles		1487	1473	1476	1484		98	94	88	80		2068	2041	2010	1922
351	Building and repairing of ships and boats		1531	1463	1507	1538		35	31	33	32		711	774	829	762
3511	Building and repairing of ships		764	701	700	690		26	22	24	24		559	591	638	575
3512	Building/repairing of pleasure/sport. boats		767	762	807	848		9	10	9	9		152	183	190	186
3520	Railway/tramway locomotives & rolling stock		142	134	151	158		14	14	13	11		351	372	402	392
3530	Aircraft and spacecraft		716	663	626	598		106	101	100	100		3071	3082	3121	3273
359	Transport equipment n.e.c.		313	312	305	299		7	5	5	5		114	100	91	84
3591	Motorcycles		77	81	84	86		1	1	1	1		24	23	20	19
3592	Bicycles and invalid carriages		141	131	129	119		4	3	3	3		67	55	47	43
3599	Other transport equipment n.e.c.		95	100	92	94		2	1	1	1		22	22	24	21
3610	Furniture		7634	7492	7471	7380		134	122	117	109		2261	2114	2058	2057
369	Manufacturing n.e.c.		11035	10763	10174	9640		65	64	58	52		957	934	958	825
3691	Jewellery and related articles		1606	1557	1519	1491		9	7	7	7		132	137	117	98
3692	Musical instruments		243	253	274	277		1	1	1	1		18	18	19	18
3693	Sports goods		479	483	504	521		5	5	5	5		94	85	63	98
3694	Games and toys		723	733	736	737		9	9	6	6		152	134	114	110
3699	Other manufacturing n.e.c.		7984	7737	7141	6614		40	42	39	34		562	560	645	502
3710	Recycling of metal waste and scrap		597	610	656	691		8	6	7	9		145	124	151	188
3720	Recycling of non-metal waste and scrap		723	825	898	1012		9	9	9	9		83	110	117	132
D	Total manufacturing		162197	158477	155083	153445		3641	3422	3294	3138		75924	73655	73320	72358

United Kingdom

ISIC Revision 3		Output					Value added in factor values					Gross fixed capital formation		
			(millions of British Pounds)					(millions of British Pounds)					(millions of British Pounds)	
ISIC	Industry	Note	2002	2003	2004	2005	Note	2002	2003	2004	2005	Note	2004	2005
151	Processed meat,fish,fruit,vegetables,fats		19229	19631	20559	...		5272	5481	5528	...		...	...
1511	Processing/preserving of meat		11540	12565	13043	13273		2947	3331	3232	3356		371	395
1512	Processing/preserving of fish		1818	1874	1810	2157		416	478	473	530		64	...
1513	Processing/preserving of fruit & vegetables		3730	4188	4533	4790		1373	1521	1679	1731		190	192
1514	Vegetable and animal oils and fats		2141	1004	1174	...		536	151	143	...		...	...
1520	Dairy products		5543	6198	5791	5761		1309	1388	1129	1086		235	277
153	Grain mill products; starches; animal feeds		6663	6171	7677	6133		1673	1616	1896	1657		235	185
1531	Grain mill products		...	...	...	2803		...	...	...	929		...	...
1532	Starches and starch products		...	...	...	318		...	...	...	48		...	...
1533	Prepared animal feeds		3528	2988	3125	3012		750	658	671	680		120	95
154	Other food products		17757	18588	18981	19882		7327	8117	8638	9069		640	714
1541	Bakery products		6723	7098	7153	7238		2798	3151	3323	3544		297	332
1542	Sugar		...	...	...	...		...	...	...	...		...	...
1543	Cocoa, chocolate and sugar confectionery		3885	4250	4347	4567		1741	2116	2424	2278		121	133
1544	Macaroni, noodles & similar products		...	...	...	...		...	...	...	...		...	...
1549	Other food products n.e.c.		5712	...	...	...		2344	...	...	...		...	...
155	Beverages		12242	12561	13407	13804		3764	3757	3971	3877		664	743
1551	Distilling, rectifying & blending of spirits		2869	2395	2977	3150		1189	749	1336	1426		105	115
1552	Wines		786	655	560	637		201	183	232	239		...	27
1553	Malt liquors and malt		5600	6165	6409	6307		1537	1795	1211	1088		...	381
1554	Soft drinks; mineral waters		2987	3346	3461	3710		836	1030	1192	1125		211	220
1600	Tobacco products		8925	8595	8915	...		1152	1184	1269	...		...	...
171	Spinning, weaving and finishing of textiles		2277	2032	1909	1852		914	825	681	590		45	61
1711	Textile fibre preparation; textile weaving		1632	1424	1228	1200		614	538	431	388		32	48
1712	Finishing of textiles		645	608	681	652		300	287	250	202		13	14
172	Other textiles		3879	3666	3726	3666		1495	1497	1428	1493		126	89
1721	Made-up textile articles, except apparel		1858	1782	1808	1871		710	778	755	831		70	43
1722	Carpets and rugs		844	801	761	749		313	268	252	286		22	18
1723	Cordage, rope, twine and netting		83	86	108	87		35	37	39	29		...	1
1729	Other textiles n.e.c.		1094	997	1049	959		437	414	383	347		...	27
1730	Knitted and crocheted fabrics and articles		910	830	757	538		401	327	299	210		18	14
1810	Wearing apparel, except fur apparel		4262	...	3372	3294		1579	...	1356	1513		71	72
1820	Dressing & dyeing of fur; processing of fur		8	...	4	6		3	...	2	2		-	-
191	Tanning, dressing and processing of leather		544	496	467	456		217	172	168	172		...	9
1911	Tanning and dressing of leather		297	293	255	218		82	79	71	59		8	6
1912	Luggage, handbags, etc.; saddlery & harness		247	203	212	238		135	93	96	113		...	3
1920	Footwear		652	400	315	290		342	197	146	125		...	5
2010	Sawmilling and planing of wood		1039	991	967	1031		339	352	351	412		60	67
202	Products of wood, cork, straw, etc.		5570	5686	5925	5996		2066	2238	2538	2459		203	192
2021	Veneer sheets, plywood, particle board, etc.		877	880	906	925		231	238	269	246		21	41
2022	Builders' carpentry and joinery		3461	3645	3905	3838		1357	1560	1818	1729		135	115
2023	Wooden containers		539	500	460	506		179	174	166	197		9	16
2029	Other wood products; articles of cork/straw		692	662	654	726		299	266	286	287		38	20
210	Paper and paper products		11102	10504	11362	10755		3696	3416	3268	2785		471	541
2101	Pulp, paper and paperboard		3427	2998	2941	2895		999	854	768	705		186	134
2102	Corrugated paper and paperboard		3743	3620	3512	3450		1255	1239	1265	1279		140	235
2109	Other articles of paper and paperboard		3931	3887	4909	4411		1442	1322	1236	800		...	...
221	Publishing		18719	18560	19227	19254		8261	8539	8949	9232		519	572
2211	Publishing of books and other publications		4121	3990	3915	3732		1657	1693	1669	1845		88	62
2212	Publishing of newspapers, journals, etc.		12395	12883	13494	13754		5557	6123	6427	6544		379	458
2213	Publishing of recorded media		728	709	495	657		314	330	146	174		...	5
2219	Other publishing		1475	978	1323	1111		733	392	708	670		...	48

continued

United Kingdom

ISIC Revision 3		Output					Value added in factor values					Gross fixed capital formation		
			(millions of British Pounds)					(millions of British Pounds)					(millions of British Pounds)	
ISIC	Industry	Note	2002	2003	2004	2005	Note	2002	2003	2004	2005	Note	2004	2005
222	Printing and related service activities		13495	12339	13215	12122		6695	6215	6558	6015		686	1016
2221	Printing		11268	10409	11139	10138		5489	5127	5379	4898		...	...
2222	Service activities related to printing		2227	1930	2076	1984		1206	1088	1179	1117		...	...
2230	Reproduction of recorded media		679	738	717	510		300	352	344	259		35	30
2310	Coke oven products		...	...	-	-		7	...	-	-		-	-
2320	Refined petroleum products		22695	...	26784	...		1816	...	...	...		...	...
2330	Processing of nuclear fuel		...	...	1315	...		762	...	...	...		...	...
241	Basic chemicals		15813	15798	16683	16773		4331	4245	4209	3929		759	912
2411	Basic chemicals, except fertilizers		...	10990	11644	...		...	...	...	...		...	...
2412	Fertilizers and nitrogen compounds		755	824	879	1073		129	170	165	167		18	57
2413	Plastics in primary forms; synthetic rubber		4213	3984	4160	4458		1155	1226	1082	...		...	250
242	Other chemicals		27339	26969	27630	28152		11602	10493	11476	12293		...	1219
2421	Pesticides and other agro-chemical products		974	995	750	736		426	392	306	268		25	23
2422	Paints, varnishes, printing ink and mastics		3097	3088	3196	3191		1114	1107	1204	1192		...	66
2423	Pharmaceuticals, medicinal chemicals, etc.		14145	13336	13693	14551		6621	5580	6241	7239		930	706
2424	Soap, cleaning & cosmetic preparations		5112	5274	5388	5134		1882	1853	1965	1800		221	260
2429	Other chemical products n.e.c.		4011	4275	4604	4540		1558	1560	1761	1794		183	164
2430	Man-made fibres		456	489	404	389		187	212	153	132		...	28
251	Rubber products		3186	3157	3239	3259		1338	1558	1330	1336		87	104
2511	Rubber tyres and tubes		1412	1472	1554	1655		559	759	585	602		39	64
2519	Other rubber products		1774	1685	1685	1604		778	799	745	734		49	40
2520	Plastic products		15438	15694	16491	16897		5963	5945	6360	6326		701	633
2610	Glass and glass products		2758	2920	2913	2931		1137	1317	1264	1278		159	168
269	Non-metallic mineral products n.e.c.		8753	9009	10010	8667		3710	3890	4398	3843		496	572
2691	Pottery, china and earthenware		...	...	...	...		...	...	...	...		...	...
2692	Refractory ceramic products		598	404	407	484		209	149	155	180		9	13
2693	Struct.non-refractory clay; ceramic products		771	829	927	997		377	438	475	483		47	106
2694	Cement, lime and plaster		1245	968	995	908		519	453	424	348		75	99
2695	Articles of concrete, cement and plaster		3854	4672	5432	4168		1479	1777	2232	1781		279	271
2696	Cutting, shaping & finishing of stone		422	443	475	402		241	237	253	220		32	17
2699	Other non-metallic mineral products n.e.c.		941	811	923	940		366	322	364	356		36	47
2710	Basic iron and steel		6594	7018	8558	9173		1035	1096	1649	1569		332	320
2720	Basic precious and non-ferrous metals		3976	3723	4278	4425		938	855	1002	1026		87	91
273	Casting of metals		1630	1562	1511	1454		687	645	646	640		47	57
2731	Casting of iron and steel		802	831	873	788		376	352	366	334		...	24
2732	Casting of non-ferrous metals		828	732	639	666		311	293	280	306		23	32
281	Struct.metal products;tanks;steam generators		8198	8777	8835	9608		3329	3729	3462	3483		...	260
2811	Structural metal products		6715	7174	7071	7633		2673	3034	2708	2602		236	193
2812	Tanks, reservoirs and containers of metal		1031	1100	1142	1264		439	455	461	506		39	60
2813	Steam generators		452	503	622	712		216	240	293	375		...	7
289	Other metal products; metal working services		16428	16095	16524	16720		8345	8098	8119	8346		...	680
2891	Metal forging/pressing/stamping/roll-forming		2118	1633	2018	2044		918	584	810	786		...	88
2892	Treatment & coating of metals		6838	6781	6962	7322		3830	3724	3901	4144		295	330
2893	Cutlery, hand tools and general hardware		2497	2345	1957	1926		1455	1418	1047	1089		76	79
2899	Other fabricated metal products n.e.c.		4974	5335	5588	5429		2142	2372	2361	2327		182	184
291	General purpose machinery		15628	15331	17001	17220		6277	6287	6906	6890		463	507
2911	Engines & turbines (not for transport equipment)		1777	1624	2573	2537		663	543	879	851		...	73
2912	Pumps, compressors, taps and valves		3629	3656	3587	3832		1492	1519	1580	1666		...	119
2913	Bearings, gears, gearing & driving elements		919	900	921	1080		396	406	343	379		34	41
2914	Ovens, furnaces and furnace burners		278	272	302	260		109	110	134	113		2	26
2915	Lifting and handling equipment		3027	3083	3319	3504		1157	1268	1374	1534		86	101
2919	Other general purpose machinery		5999	5796	6299	6008		2461	2441	2596	2346		133	147

292	Special purpose machinery	11000	11555	11037	12505	3947	4244	3950	4342	236	237
2921	Agricultural and forestry machinery	1786	1776	1512	1472	515	490	284	289	27	26
2922	Machine tools	1622	1182	1172	1271	760	573	549	627	...	34
2923	Machinery for metallurgy	98	94	68	124	44	43	38	48	...	2
2924	Machinery for mining & construction	2403	3099	2560	2980	631	1068	755	735	64	54
2925	Food/beverage/tobacco processing machinery	936	899	956	1116	404	433	424	498	13	15
2926	Machinery for textile, apparel and leather	157	143	112	144	82	75	56	75	...	2
2927	Weapons and ammunition	1654	2038	2293	2878	459	629	777	935	...	44
2929	Other special purpose machinery	2344	2323	2364	2519	1053	934	1066	1134	64	59
2930	Domestic appliances n.e.c.	2596	2676	2751	2828	933	998	1070	788	92	99
3000	Office, accounting and computing machinery	10387	6751	5546	4039	2517	2212	2200	1299	103	118
3110	Electric motors, generators and transformers	2438	2461	2701	2953	732	707	820	977	71	45
3120	Electricity distribution & control apparatus	3732	3499	3425	3470	1583	1453	1510	1500	62	81
3130	Insulated wire and cable	1076	1056	1100	1089	343	375	424	315	15	18
3140	Accumulators, primary cells and batteries	392	424	407	369	125	121	124	133	22	15
3150	Lighting equipment and electric lamps	1425	1310	1203	1402	599	532	495	658	27	40
3190	Other electrical equipment n.e.c.	3508	3487	3501	3493	1364	1341	1322	1312	197	117
3210	Electronic valves, tubes, etc.	3676	3515	3674	3396	1277	1145	1240	1193	...	112
3220	TV/radio transmitters; line comm. apparatus	5625	4248	3368	3315	1286	1227	1113	762	...	...
3230	TV and radio receivers and associated goods	3029	2668	2823	2231	873	776	909	620	61	...
331	Medical, measuring, testing appliances, etc.	10551	10033	9927	10692	4708	4948	5092	5484	...	402
3311	Medical, surgical and orthopaedic equipment	2745	2605	2390	2792	1372	1354	1318	1517	...	151
3312	Measuring/testing/navigating appliances,etc.	6977	6617	6683	6844	2988	3293	3417	3496	173	237
3313	Industrial process control equipment	830	811	854	1056	349	301	357	470	15	14
3320	Optical instruments & photographic equipment	966	1063	1158	1214	421	481	560	562	...	63
3330	Watches and clocks	65	71	69	55	32	31	38	33	2	1
3410	Motor vehicles	22977	24143	25077	25992	3701	4015	4973	4213	...	947
3420	Automobile bodies, trailers & semi-trailers	2435	2754	2713	2822	778	827	862	927	...	74
3430	Parts/accessories for automobiles	9876	10145	10322	10248	3080	3026	2981	3041	359	428
351	Building and repairing of ships and boats	2463	2466	2775	2659	943	1001	1214	996	54	90
3511	Building and repairing of ships	1801	1728	2016	1852	701	734	906	731	36	69
3512	Building/repairing of pleasure/sport. boats	663	738	760	807	242	268	307	264	18	21
3520	Railway/tramway locomotives & rolling stock	1660	2104	1952	1508	509	840	354	551	...	30
3530	Aircraft and spacecraft	15098	13987	15009	16528	7062	6407	6409	6955	534	628
359	Transport equipment n.e.c.	520	528	478	523	212	224	159	169	...	20
3591	Motorcycles	153	181	159	185	90	104	42	49	...	9
3592	Bicycles and invalid carriages	282	235	203	208	88	77	75	82	...	8
3599	Other transport equipment n.e.c.	86	112	116	130	33	42	42	38	...	3
3610	Furniture	9265	8630	8814	9116	3580	3324	3447	3549	277	264
369	Manufacturing n.e.c.	4684	4789	4957	4321	2022	2060	2153	1882	156	125
3691	Jewellery and related articles	721	650	809	701	368	368	326	258	19	8
3692	Musical instruments	64	60	72	67	33	32	40	35	3	3
3693	Sports goods	445	385	369	466	192	158	164	241	10	13
3694	Games and toys	653	726	750	677	281	288	287	232	22	18
3699	Other manufacturing n.e.c.	2802	2969	2958	2410	1148	1215	1336	1115	102	83
3710	Recycling of metal waste and scrap	1636	1752	2566	2656	388	350	661	581	88	85
3720	Recycling of non-metal waste and scrap	430	531	690	737	201	237	316	357	57	59
D	Total manufacturing	415460	410700	427512	436013	141483	140966	146458	144090	15019	15475

United Kingdom

ISIC Revision 3			Index numbers of industrial production (2000=100)											
ISIC	Industry	Note	1995	1996	1997	1998	1999	2000	2001	2002	2003	2004	2005	2006
15	Food and beverages		96	98	100	99	100	100	102	104	104	106	107	105
16	Tobacco products		139	147	143	134	112	100	92	92	90	86	79	73
17	Textiles		119	117	117	109	103	100	87	83	85	79	77	74
18	Wearing apparel, fur		131	128	120	112	101	100	88	80	77	69	67	71
19	Leather, leather products and footwear		133	131	138	120	113	100	102	89	73	54	49	55
20	Wood products (excl. furniture)		108	106	103	102	98	100	100	103	104	105	101	96
21	Paper and paper products		113	110	106	102	101	100	97	100	100	102	99	99
22	Printing and publishing		96	94	96	99	99	100	100	100	98	97	91	87
23	Coke,refined petroleum products,nuclear fuel		119	109	113	105	95	100	95	96	89	94	97	90
24	Chemicals and chemical products		88	88	91	92	95	100	106	106	107	110	112	115
25	Rubber and plastics products		98	97	97	100	100	100	96	93	93	92	89	92
26	Non-metallic mineral products		101	97	100	97	97	100	100	99	105	111	110	109
27	Basic metals		106	108	109	108	104	100	98	88	88	90	88	88
28	Fabricated metal products		96	96	98	98	96	100	98	102	99	103	103	106
29	Machinery and equipment n.e.c.		110	108	107	106	100	100	102	96	98	103	107	110
30	Office, accounting and computing machinery		48	52	63	74	89	100	115	91	88	69	68	60
31	Electrical machinery and apparatus		97	101	97	95	98	100	94	85	80	83	79	84
32	Radio,television and communication equipment		49	53	55	60	74	100	72	57	51	57	51	54
33	Medical, precision and optical instruments		104	106	100	98	96	100	107	100	106	110	109	103
34	Motor vehicles, trailers, semi-trailers		94	99	101	105	104	100	95	103	107	109	108	105
35	Other transport equipment		74	81	89	95	104	100	101	85	92	101	101	116
36	Furniture; manufacturing n.e.c.		95	96	97	98	101	100	98	98	99	98	98	93
37	Recycling		76	80	89	99	99	100	116	124	115	111	123	124
D	Total manufacturing		94	95	96	97	98	100	99	96	96	98	97	98

United States of America

Supplier of information:
The Bureau of the Census, Department of Commerce, Washington, D.C.
Industrial statistics for the OECD countries are compiled by the OECD secretariat, which supplies them to UNIDO.

Basic source of data:
Annual survey of manufacturing.

Major deviations from ISIC (Revision 3):
Data presented in accordance with ISIC (Revision 3) were originally classified in the 1997 North American Industry Classification System (NAICS).

Reference period:
Calendar year.

Scope:
All manufacturing establishments with at least one employee.

Method of data collection:
Data are collected by mail and other communication media.

Type of enumeration:
Not reported.

Adjusted for non-response:
Not reported.

Concepts and definitions of variables:
Number of employees refers to all full- and part-time employees on the payrolls of operating establishments. An average of four quarterly observations (taken on 12 March, May, August and November) is taken for production workers (operatives) and combined with the figure for all other employees that is taken on 12 March.
Wages and salaries covers gross earnings, including wages, salaries and employers' contributions to pension funds and social security schemes. Regular and overtime cash payments, bonuses and cost of living allowances are included, as are vacation and sick leave pay, taxes and social insurance contributions payable by employees and deducted by employers, payments in kind and allowances. Also included are payments for health insurance, life insurance, pension plans and stock purchase plans. Wages and salaries are based upon the remuneration minus supplemental labour costs.
Output is measured as deliveries in terms of shipments, fob, adjusted for change in inventory for work-in-process and finished goods. Goods shipped include goods produced in the establishments, those shipped in the same condition as received, and receipts for industrial work done on materials owned by others or industrial services rendered to others. The value of goods shipped is in producer prices. In industries where the product is typically delivered, the value of shipments is in delivered prices.
Value added is based on the census concept and is calculated as output less the cost of materials, fuels and other supplies, goods shipped in the same condition as received, contract and commission work done by others, and electricity purchased. Input estimates are on a consumed basis. Valuation is the same as for output.
Gross fixed capital formation relates to the value of new plant and equipment purchased and constructed by the unit's own labour force for its own use. Used plant and equipment purchases are excluded. Fixed assets are defined as those with a productive life of more than one year. The valuation of new fixed capital formation is at full cost and includes the value of additions, alterations, improvements and repairs to existing assets (if capitalized). Purchased new assets are at delivered prices and include the cost of installation but exclude fees and taxes.

Related national publications:
The Employment Situation, distributed by the U.S. Bureau of Labor Statistics;
Employment and Earnings, distributed by the U.S. Government Printing Office.

United States of America

ISIC Revision 3		Number of enterprises (number)					Number of employees (thousands)					Wages and salaries paid to employees (millions of US Dollars)			
ISIC	Industry	Note	2002	2003	2004	2005	Note	2002	2003	2004	2005	Note	2002	2003	2004	2005
151	Processed meat,fish,fruit,vegetables,fats		4945	...	...	...		662	...	628	622		18302	18317	17684	18050
1511	Processing/preserving of meat		3091	...	...	...		487	...	493	486		12327	12350	13176	13286
1512	Processing/preserving of fish		643	...	...	...		39	...	39	39		1057	1131	1079	1172
1513	Processing/preserving of fruit & vegetables		991	...	...	...		112	...	81	81		3939	3856	2758	2896
1514	Vegetable and animal oils and fats		260	...	...	...		24	...	16	16		979	981	671	696
1520	Dairy products		1190	...	...	...		129	...	126	128		4850	4963	5063	5316
153	Grain mill products; starches; animal feeds		1673	...	...	...		101	...	79	81		4105	4028	3582	3771
1531	Grain mill products		478	...	...	...		45	...	27	29		1839	1739	1343	1425
1532	Starches and starch products		30	...	...	...		9	...	9	9		507	484	498	504
1533	Prepared animal feeds		1183	...	...	...		47	...	43	44		1759	1805	1741	1842
154	Other food products		14245	...	...	...		556	...	615	608		18470	18505	20233	20661
1541	Bakery products		9345	...	...	...		268	...	287	279		8601	8175	8993	8810
1542	Sugar		53	...	...	...		14	...	14	14		563	644	590	609
1543	Cocoa, chocolate and sugar confectionery		1495	...	...	...		67	...	56	54		2177	2143	2086	2090
1544	Macaroni, noodles & similar products		226	...	...	...		5	...	...	...		134	144	...	...
1549	Other food products n.e.c.		3199	...	...	...		202	...	258	261		6995	7398	8564	9152
155	Beverages		2266	...	...	...		137	...	123	124		5461	5440	5589	5771
1551	Distilling, rectifying & blending of spirits		134	...	...	...		8	...	5	5		350	349	254	273
1552	Wines		1175	...	...	...		27	...	23	24		1037	1045	1117	1162
1553	Malt liquors and malt		429	...	...	...		32	...	24	24		1485	1494	1390	1441
1554	Soft drinks; mineral waters		543	...	...	...		70	...	70	70		2588	2551	2828	2895
1600	Tobacco products		107	...	...	...		24	...	22	21		1400	1404	1290	1278
171	Spinning, weaving and finishing of textiles		2365	...	...	...		201	...	157	139		5388	4935	4492	4130
1711	Textile fibre preparation; textile weaving		1023	...	...	...		148	...	112	100		3833	3509	3168	2867
1712	Finishing of textiles		1385	...	...	...		53	...	44	39		1554	1427	1324	1263
172	Other textiles		7683	...	...	...		231	...	206	196		6340	6161	6291	6197
1721	Made-up textile articles, except apparel		6422	...	...	...		136	...	116	110		3130	3011	3092	3022
1722	Carpets and rugs		361	...	...	...		44	...	41	39		1291	1280	1299	1266
1723	Cordage, rope. twine and netting		166	...	...	...		6	...	4	4		155	145	144	140
1729	Other textiles n.e.c.		775	...	...	...		46	...	45	43		1764	1726	1756	1768
1730	Knitted and crocheted fabrics and articles		1139	...	...	...		76	...	55	48		1856	1712	1411	1301
1810	Wearing apparel, except fur apparel		12069	...	...	...		295	...	219	192		6233	5659	5069	4640
1820	Dressing & dyeing of fur; processing of fur		...	...	...	...		...	...	...	...		...	...	...	...
191	Tanning, dressing and processing of leather		1178	...	...	...		27	...	21	22		696	641	633	662
1911	Tanning and dressing of leather		274	...	...	...		9	...	7	6		282	258	236	230
1912	Luggage, handbags, etc.; saddlery & harness		906	...	...	...		17	...	14	16		414	383	397	432
1920	Footwear		307	...	...	...		21	...	17	16		456	471	464	439
2010	Sawmilling and planing of wood		5056	...	...	...		152	...	106	105		4399	4330	3683	3876
202	Products of wood, cork, straw, etc.		10023	...	...	...		331	...	430	434		10126	10040	13356	13956
2021	Veneer sheets, plywood, particle board, etc.		531	...	...	...		67	...	59	115		2255	2114	2191	4112
2022	Builders' carpentry and joinery		5010	...	...	...		180	...	282	231		5688	5780	8839	7453
2023	Wooden containers		2763	...	...	...		48	...	50	50		1155	1116	1203	1258
2029	Other wood products; articles of cork/straw		1760	...	...	...		37	...	39	37		1029	1029	1123	1134
210	Paper and paper products		3473	...	...	...		489	...	538	430		21244	20457	23753	20701
2101	Pulp, paper and paperboard		905	...	...	...		208	...	274	136		10866	10156	13093	8227
2102	Corrugated paper and paperboard		1617	...	...	...		202	...	191	225		7461	7366	7866	9694
2109	Other articles of paper and paperboard		1073	...	...	...		78	...	73	69		2918	2936	2794	2780
221	Publishing		17263	...	...	...		676	...	...	...		...	...	...	...
2211	Publishing of books and other publications		5132	...	...	...		134	...	...	...		...	...	...	...
2212	Publishing of newspapers, journals, etc.		11547	...	...	...		515	...	...	...		...	...	...	...
2213	Publishing of recorded media		600	...	...	...		11	...	...	...		...	...	...	...
2219	Other publishing		88	...	...	...		16	...	...	...		...	...	...	...

222	Printing and related service activities	35174	...	...	...	706	...	659	642	25731	25127	24789	24893
2221	Printing	31999	...	...	...	645	...	608	593	23606	23107	22821	22910
2222	Service activities related to printing	3249	...	...	...	61	...	51	49	2125	2020	1968	1982
2230	Reproduction of recorded media	644	...	...	...	27	...	25	25	1077	1007	923	927
2310	Coke oven products	...	...	...	...	...	...	...	...	...	...	...	...
2320	Refined petroleum products	529	...	...	...	75	...	96	76	5019	5174	6736	6611
2330	Processing of nuclear fuel	...	...	...	...	...	...	...	...	...	...	...	...
241	Basic chemicals	2620	...	...	...	285	...	266	261	16911	16501	16386	16841
2411	Basic chemicals, except fertilizers	1089	...	...	...	171	...	161	156	10622	10432	10430	10593
2412	Fertilizers and nitrogen compounds	511	...	...	...	20	...	18	17	947	926	882	891
2413	Plastics in primary forms; synthetic rubber	1098	...	...	...	93	...	87	87	5342	5144	5074	5357
242	Other chemicals	6952	...	...	...	525	...	494	489	26728	27899	27166	28616
2421	Pesticides and other agro-chemical products	198	...	...	...	14	...	11	10	567	556	609	590
2422	Paints, varnishes, printing ink and mastics	1328	...	...	...	59	...	53	52	2626	2669	2571	2628
2423	Pharmaceuticals, medicinal chemicals, etc.	1411	...	...	...	238	...	231	236	13835	14388	14209	15684
2424	Soap, cleaning & cosmetic preparations	2113	...	...	...	111	...	101	98	4879	5148	4808	4977
2429	Other chemical products n.e.c.	2022	...	...	...	103	...	98	92	4820	5137	4969	4736
2430	Man-made fibres	75	...	...	...	27	...	18	18	922	970	752	813
251	Rubber products	1902	...	...	...	181	...	158	158	6916	6805	6604	6758
2511	Rubber tyres and tubes	494	...	...	...	69	...	62	62	3174	3155	3092	3161
2519	Other rubber products	1420	...	...	...	112	...	96	96	3742	3650	3512	3597
2520	Plastic products	10875	...	...	...	777	...	725	728	26805	26517	25517	26398
2610	Glass and glass products	1879	...	...	...	115	...	103	101	4442	4211	4150	4146
269	Non-metallic mineral products n.e.c.	10089	...	...	...	386	...	378	391	14654	14759	15161	16316
2691	Pottery, china and earthenware	966	...	...	...	34	...	25	23	968	851	824	796
2692	Refractory ceramic products	185	...	...	...	11	...	9	9	384	387	383	419
2693	Struct.non-refractory clay; ceramic products	346	...	...	...	21	...	21	20	688	698	692	724
2694	Cement, lime and plaster	176	...	...	...	21	...	20	21	1070	1066	1070	1172
2695	Articles of concrete, cement and plaster	5432	...	...	...	198	...	207	217	7630	7690	8065	8788
2696	Cutting, shaping & finishing of stone	1498	...	...	...	20	...	22	26	677	718	781	888
2699	Other non-metallic mineral products n.e.c.	1667	...	...	...	81	...	74	74	3237	3348	3345	3531
2710	Basic iron and steel	1792	...	...	...	186	...	178	171	8501	7888	9632	9615
2720	Basic precious and non-ferrous metals	1209	...	...	...	138	...	120	121	6240	5870	5597	5821
273	Casting of metals	2254	...	...	...	183	...	161	161	7020	6661	6789	6842
2731	Casting of iron and steel	936	...	...	...	102	...	91	93	3938	3842	4111	4182
2732	Casting of non-ferrous metals	1346	...	...	...	81	...	70	68	3081	2818	2679	2660
281	Struct.metal products;tanks;steam generators	14167	...	...	...	457	...	429	422	16113	15845	16116	16662
2811	Structural metal products	12012	...	...	...	362	...	362	355	12433	12306	13392	13825
2812	Tanks, reservoirs and containers of metal	1892	...	...	...	74	...	50	49	2876	2747	1981	2033
2813	Steam generators	334	...	...	...	21	...	17	17	804	792	744	803
289	Other metal products; metal working services	47667	...	...	...	1095	...	989	986	39916	38613	38929	40293
2891	Metal forging/pressing/stamping/roll-forming	2668	...	...	...	132	...	120	121	4696	4523	4923	5127
2892	Treatment & coating of metals	28466	...	...	...	398	...	368	375	13734	13269	14047	14863
2893	Cutlery, hand tools and general hardware	7707	...	...	...	223	...	194	187	8473	7971	8153	8225
2899	Other fabricated metal products n.e.c.	9211	...	...	...	342	...	307	302	13013	12851	11807	12078
291	General purpose machinery	8291	...	...	...	650	...	650	652	27100	26370	28702	29650
2911	Engines & turbines (not for transport equipment)	327	...	...	...	66	...	59	65	3184	3013	3086	3283
2912	Pumps, compressors, taps and valves	2067	...	...	...	196	...	183	151	8176	8091	8286	7094
2913	Bearings, gears, gearing & driving elements	562	...	...	...	60	...	54	51	2400	2263	2358	2351
2914	Ovens, furnaces and furnace burners	333	...	...	...	12	...	10	10	475	452	441	476
2915	Lifting and handling equipment	1572	...	...	...	78	...	74	76	3263	3206	3272	3531
2919	Other general purpose machinery	3600	...	...	...	237	...	270	298	9602	9346	11259	12915
292	Special purpose machinery	12642	...	...	...	535	...	481	489	24153	23327	22757	23699
2921	Agricultural and forestry machinery	1265	...	...	...	79	...	74	74	2778	2815	2926	2898
2922	Machine tools	1901	...	...	...	81	...	52	49	3534	3297	2606	2575
2923	Machinery for metallurgy	69	...	...	...	2	...	2	2	138	126	128	143
2924	Machinery for mining & construction	1367	...	...	...	97	...	93	100	4242	4113	4339	4693
2925	Food/beverage/tobacco processing machinery	535	...	...	...	17	...	...	...	756	785	...	...
2926	Machinery for textile, apparel and leather	463	...	...	...	12	...	...	...	414	388	...	...
2927	Weapons and ammunition	417	...	...	...	33	...	34	40	1547	1559	1697	1903
2929	Other special purpose machinery	6738	...	...	...	213	...	225	223	10745	10245	11061	11487

continued

United States of America

ISIC Revision 3		Number of enterprises					Number of employees					Wages and salaries paid to employees				
			(number)					(thousands)					(millions of US Dollars)			
ISIC	Industry	Note	2002	2003	2004	2005	Note	2002	2003	2004	2005	Note	2002	2003	2004	2005
2930	Domestic appliances n.e.c.		334	...	...	...		91	...	83	77		3023	2862	2855	2699
3000	Office, accounting and computing machinery		1584	...	...	...		172	...	126	108		8925	8864	7734	6634
3110	Electric motors, generators and transformers		1103	...	...	...		92	...	77	76		2966	2835	2798	2929
3120	Electricity distribution & control apparatus		2191	...	...	...		162	...	144	143		5807	5636	6070	6378
3130	Insulated wire and cable		307	...	...	...		50	...	35	34		1753	1544	1437	1448
3140	Accumulators, primary cells and batteries		123	...	...	...		26	...	25	25		987	976	1011	1078
3150	Lighting equipment and electric lamps		1122	...	...	...		64	...	140	137		2241	2150	5243	5336
3190	Other electrical equipment n.e.c.		2353	...	...	...		173	...	138	138		7918	7425	6187	6343
3210	Electronic valves, tubes, etc.		4290	...	...	...		412	...	322	316		18779	17366	16602	17058
3220	TV/radio transmitters; line comm. apparatus		1346	...	...	...		182	...	124	111		9103	8238	7514	7188
3230	TV and radio receivers and associated goods		1985	...	...	...		45	...	21	19		951	996	911	834
331	Medical, measuring, testing appliances, etc.		17442	...	...	...		716	...	678	662		36127	37036	37951	38582
3311	Medical, surgical and orthopaedic equipment		13258	...	...	...		346	...	335	282		15162	16012	16259	13825
3312	Measuring/testing/navigating appliances,etc.		3355	...	...	...		332	...	307	343		19141	19291	19832	22695
3313	Industrial process control equipment		929	...	...	...		38	...	36	37		1824	1732	1860	2063
3320	Optical instruments & photographic equipment		1176	...	...	...		58	...	44	43		2179	2129	2038	2125
3330	Watches and clocks		111	...	...	...		4	...	...	2		126	102	...	98
3410	Motor vehicles		2212	...	...	...		359	...	378	366		21276	21186	22360	21688
3420	Automobile bodies, trailers & semi-trailers		1291	...	...	...		110	...	75	79		3450	3385	2508	2692
3430	Parts/accessories for automobiles		2506	...	...	...		447	...	416	394		20767	20308	20617	19366
351	Building and repairing of ships and boats		1612	...	...	...		131	...	142	141		5093	5199	5506	5617
3511	Building and repairing of ships		560	...	...	...		86	...	87	84		3628	3656	3773	3786
3512	Building/repairing of pleasure/sport. boats		1055	...	...	...		45	...	55	56		1465	1543	1734	1832
3520	Railway/tramway locomotives & rolling stock		620	...	...	...		49	...	24	26		1196	1166	1123	1181
3530	Aircraft and spacecraft		3673	...	...	...		450	...	385	383		23208	23101	24550	25989
359	Transport equipment n.e.c.		346	...	...	...		14	...	14	14		633	642	626	632
3591	Motorcycles		346	...	...	...		14	...	14	14		633	642	626	632
3592	Bicycles and invalid carriages		...	...	...	...		...	...	...	...		...	...	...	...
3599	Other transport equipment n.e.c.		...	...	...	...		...	...	...	...		...	...	...	...
3610	Furniture		21002	...	...	...		603	...	589	562		18810	18398	18924	18853
369	Manufacturing n.e.c.		16964	...	...	...		340	...	274	259		12782	12860	9560	9493
3691	Jewellery and related articles		2341	...	...	...		39	...	44	42		1315	1306	1483	1444
3692	Musical instruments		557	...	...	...		14	...	13	13		470	460	463	477
3693	Sports goods		2185	...	...	...		60	...	58	55		2067	2028	2079	2051
3694	Games and toys		865	...	...	...		20	...	15	15		699	609	530	563
3699	Other manufacturing n.e.c.		11041	...	...	...		207	...	143	134		8231	8456	5005	4958
3710	Recycling of metal waste and scrap		...	...	...	...		...	...	...	...		...	...	...	...
3720	Recycling of non-metal waste and scrap		...	...	...	...		...	...	...	...		...	...	...	...
D	Total manufacturing		345926	...	...	...		15201	...	13571	13169		575672	565015	575566	579891

United States of America

ISIC Revision 3		Output					Value added					Gross fixed capital formation		
			(millions of US Dollars)					(millions of US Dollars)					(millions of US Dollars)	
ISIC	Industry	Note	2002	2003	2004	2005	Note	2002	2003	2004	2005	Note	2004	2005
151	Processed meat,fish,fruit,vegetables,fats		192860	208372	212193	220278		70495	74764	73990	79510		3809	3967
1511	Processing/preserving of meat		119761	132154	143147	150437		38505	42983	47811	53632		2192	2378
1512	Processing/preserving of fish		8801	8874	9008	10145		3290	3381	3511	3971		166	161
1513	Processing/preserving of fruit & vegetables		40969	40190	31358	31286		22382	21568	16428	15375		1193	1022
1514	Vegetable and animal oils and fats		23329	27153	28680	28411		6317	6832	6240	6533		258	406
1520	Dairy products		66145	67478	73038	76926		22266	22582	24422	25376		1618	1781
153	Grain mill products; starches; animal feeds		58494	62251	61977	64409		25415	28559	27938	29647		1512	1534
1531	Grain mill products		22267	24990	21434	21778		11571	14062	11940	11793		533	548
1532	Starches and starch products		8234	8231	8676	9291		3278	3352	3523	3864		368	329
1533	Prepared animal feeds		27994	29030	31867	33339		10567	11145	12474	13990		610	658
154	Other food products		140749	144893	164241	173265		85156	86240	97083	101140		4327	4786
1541	Bakery products		42859	41338	51633	53666		29062	27934	34098	35139		1287	1469
1542	Sugar		6524	7506	7073	7244		2065	2519	2303	2521		230	264
1543	Cocoa, chocolate and sugar confectionery		18948	18968	19611	21397		11511	11266	11880	13424		643	480
1544	Macaroni, noodles & similar products		1436	1833	...	...		611	915	...	...		...	...
1549	Other food products n.e.c.		70981	75248	85924	90958		41908	43606	48802	50055		2168	2572
155	Beverages		67338	70194	73457	80922		32496	35979	38259	43436		2535	2992
1551	Distilling, rectifying & blending of spirits		6151	6501	4805	5376		3132	3628	2842	3228		97	143
1552	Wines		9407	9131	10055	10453		5194	5030	5454	6340		381	372
1553	Malt liquors and malt		18086	19780	20369	20795		10950	12573	13349	13417		885	1016
1554	Soft drinks; mineral waters		33695	34781	38228	44299		13220	14749	16614	20450		1171	1461
1600	Tobacco products		39505	39077	38813	42714		33683	33677	33441	37280		349	350
171	Spinning, weaving and finishing of textiles		32413	29942	27992	28197		13157	12221	10796	11463		597	458
1711	Textile fibre preparation; textile weaving		22018	20744	20068	19516		8616	8381	7636	7629		447	341
1712	Finishing of textiles		10395	9198	7924	8681		4541	3840	3160	3834		149	117
172	Other textiles		41627	39856	42551	46841		17574	18210	18724	19767		807	787
1721	Made-up textile articles, except apparel		16380	15584	16311	17421		7919	7678	7729	8157		246	225
1722	Carpets and rugs		13596	13408	14993	17284		4475	5157	6055	5879		215	191
1723	Cordage, rope, twine and netting		786	681	777	816		376	282	373	430		28	30
1729	Other textiles n.e.c.		10865	10183	10470	11320		4804	5093	4568	5301		317	342
1730	Knitted and crocheted fabrics and articles		9906	8656	7330	7550		4469	4073	3384	3599		129	152
1810	Wearing apparel, except fur apparel		38710	35555	29135	26916		18608	17903	14674	13885		269	419
1820	Dressing & dyeing of fur; processing of fur		...	...	...	...		...	...	...	...		...	...
191	Tanning, dressing and processing of leather		4106	3854	3738	3992		1903	1806	1714	1812		51	75
1911	Tanning and dressing of leather		2286	2144	1836	1774		777	770	636	502		22	23
1912	Luggage, handbags, etc.; saddlery & harness		1820	1710	1902	2218		1126	1036	1078	1309		29	52
1920	Footwear		2230	2149	2019	2021		1049	1071	1003	1054		30	27
2010	Sawmilling and planing of wood		31466	32612	30227	32786		9567	10453	10861	10946		897	930
202	Products of wood, cork, straw, etc.		50227	52714	73193	79231		22251	23560	32801	33816		1816	2088
2021	Veneer sheets, plywood, particle board, etc.		13741	14523	16352	26609		5174	5711	7410	11078		507	895
2022	Builders' carpentry and joinery		26728	28449	45942	40422		12177	12805	19768	16648		1015	851
2023	Wooden containers		5064	4933	5378	5955		2413	2352	2505	2717		142	192
2029	Other wood products; articles of cork/straw		4695	4809	5521	6245		2487	2692	3118	3373		153	150
210	Paper and paper products		152375	147135	180097	162848		75415	71198	83008	75889		5876	5598
2101	Pulp, paper and paperboard		85027	80499	109918	75428		45357	41782	52305	38619		4077	3397
2102	Corrugated paper and paperboard		45549	45321	49559	66070		18313	18347	20176	26598		1311	1605
2109	Other articles of paper and paperboard		21799	21315	20619	21350		11744	11069	10527	10672		408	595
221	Publishing		...		...	-		...	...	...	-		...	...
2211	Publishing of books and other publications		...	...	...	...		...	...	...	...		...	...
2212	Publishing of newspapers, journals, etc.		...	...	...	...		...	...	...	...		...	...
2213	Publishing of recorded media		...	...	...	...		...	...	...	...		...	...
2219	Other publishing		...	...	...	...		...	...	...	...		...	...

continued

United States of America

ISIC Revision 3		Output					Value added					Gross fixed capital formation		
			(millions of US Dollars)					(millions of US Dollars)					(millions of US Dollars)	
ISIC	Industry	Note	2002	2003	2004	2005	Note	2002	2003	2004	2005	Note	2004	2005
222	Printing and related service activities		95619	92191	93193	97095		59207	56589	57250	58930		4088	4343
2221	Printing		90224	87168	88046	91899		55014	52677	53314	55025		3941	4178
2222	Service activities related to printing		5395	5022	5147	5195		4194	3912	3936	3905		147	166
2230	Reproduction of recorded media		5156	4521	4736	5151		3302	2895	3022	2927		211	207
2310	Coke oven products		...	...	...	...		...	...	...	...		...	...
2320	Refined petroleum products		202270	222850	302119	458730		30942	40046	58830	110740		6864	10673
2330	Processing of nuclear fuel		...	...	...	...		...	...	...	...		...	...
241	Basic chemicals		177004	189518	226199	274178		69970	71702	91954	113357		7302	8155
2411	Basic chemicals, except fertilizers		105491	114678	139431	169863		43264	44905	58589	75396		4557	5143
2412	Fertilizers and nitrogen compounds		10251	11274	12571	13753		3440	3627	4417	5009		450	368
2413	Plastics in primary forms; synthetic rubber		61262	63567	74197	90562		23265	23169	28948	32952		2295	2644
242	Other chemicals		271405	279432	298422	323913		178146	185475	201813	212068		9922	8704
2421	Pesticides and other agro-chemical products		8919	9858	11357	14074		5706	6503	7482	9496		236	224
2422	Paints, varnishes, printing ink and mastics		23486	23819	26551	28905		11076	11724	13649	14735		313	301
2423	Pharmaceuticals, medicinal chemicals, etc.		141333	148099	157479	165969		102434	110502	120870	124586		7086	5630
2424	Soap, cleaning & cosmetic preparations		62123	60349	66053	77352		39897	36995	40459	43529		1263	1519
2429	Other chemical products n.e.c.		35545	37307	36983	37612		19034	19750	19354	19723		1024	1030
2430	Man-made fibres		7648	8290	6802	8962		3425	3451	2739	3805		115	198
251	Rubber products		33056	33575	34055	36562		17322	17528	17121	17402		1162	1092
2511	Rubber tyres and tubes		14740	15357	15768	16375		7689	8000	7958	7488		549	619
2519	Other rubber products		18316	18219	18287	20187		9632	9528	9163	9914		613	473
2520	Plastic products		144069	146629	148492	163927		76521	76350	74396	78946		5488	5876
2610	Glass and glass products		22402	22227	22609	23221		13036	12594	12852	12582		1265	1091
269	Non-metallic mineral products n.e.c.		85783	88283	94762	108444		46886	47543	51970	58764		4063	4438
2691	Pottery, china and earthenware		3341	3119	3094	3078		2241	2111	2066	2173		114	152
2692	Refractory ceramic products		1985	2007	2027	2297		1084	1072	1134	1350		58	75
2693	Struct.non-refractory clay; ceramic products		3018	3105	3334	3628		2182	2154	2368	2429		175	170
2694	Cement, lime and plaster		8448	8544	9612	11315		5112	5112	6160	7191		650	858
2695	Articles of concrete, cement and plaster		41176	42068	44936	52704		21751	21991	23719	27614		1785	2145
2696	Cutting, shaping & finishing of stone		2202	2344	2424	2861		1501	1595	1612	1920		120	131
2699	Other non-metallic mineral products n.e.c.		25612	27096	29334	32561		13015	13508	14910	16086		1161	907
2710	Basic iron and steel		63029	61175	96577	107232		24151	22660	40514	42558		1997	2258
2720	Basic precious and non-ferrous metals		51574	51554	58210	68924		17758	17728	19015	20633		928	1196
273	Casting of metals		27238	25741	28093	30522		15928	14449	15495	16429		1095	1115
2731	Casting of iron and steel		14966	14653	16828	18739		9047	8187	9192	10081		723	682
2732	Casting of non-ferrous metals		12271	11088	11265	11783		6880	6262	6303	6348		373	433
281	Struct.metal products;tanks;steam generators		72152	71497	76203	87779		37855	37364	38922	43433		1662	1831
2811	Structural metal products		56514	56334	63682	73557		29313	28777	32004	36072		1359	1592
2812	Tanks, reservoirs and containers of metal		11993	11841	9318	10508		6570	6609	5253	5682		169	168
2813	Steam generators		3645	3322	3203	3714		1971	1978	1665	1678		134	71
289	Other metal products; metal working services		162104	158390	163834	179236		94062	90965	93033	99161		5479	5518
2891	Metal forging/pressing/stamping/roll-forming		20570	20855	24892	28181		10439	10516	12128	13119		773	829
2892	Treatment & coating of metals		45577	44412	48777	54577		29055	28047	30030	33310		2002	1914
2893	Cutlery, hand tools and general hardware		33086	30614	31977	33746		21401	19274	19856	20306		990	943
2899	Other fabricated metal products n.e.c.		62871	62509	58188	62731		33167	33129	31020	32427		1714	1831
291	General purpose machinery		152189	151912	162978	184297		78342	76709	80483	87575		3744	4255
2911	Engines & turbines (not for transport equipment)		33737	33985	29759	33935		16086	14383	10737	10869		625	996
2912	Pumps, compressors, taps and valves		39897	40895	43242	41044		21881	22624	24183	22234		924	810
2913	Bearings, gears, gearing & driving elements		10542	10335	10921	11770		6425	6487	6896	7324		322	365
2914	Ovens, furnaces and furnace burners		1636	1580	1561	1901		936	907	904	1069		31	24
2915	Lifting and handling equipment		15438	15552	17929	22207		6867	6925	7718	9285		309	271
2919	Other general purpose machinery		50939	49565	59567	73439		26147	25383	30045	36795		1533	1789

292	Special purpose machinery	117485	119574	130959	143946	62426	58851	67090	69095	2540	2844
2921	Agricultural and forestry machinery	21257	23620	25109	28437	9421	10110	10827	12353	409	458
2922	Machine tools	15790	14485	11318	11821	11349	7482	5895	5962	191	210
2923	Machinery for metallurgy	491	541	479	614	249	287	278	317	15	15
2924	Machinery for mining & construction	26616	27766	35184	41800	11239	10811	16091	16818	554	755
2925	Food/beverage/tobacco processing machinery	2880	3034	...	...	1649	1774	...	...	...	...
2926	Machinery for textile, apparel and leather	1484	1407	...	...	820	819	...	...	...	...
2927	Weapons and ammunition	6483	7437	7905	8914	4321	4878	5335	5717	126	140
2929	Other special purpose machinery	42485	41285	50965	52361	23377	22690	28664	27927	1246	1266
2930	Domestic appliances n.e.c.	22823	23813	23501	24620	10212	10667	10039	10483	451	391
3000	Office, accounting and computing machinery	77083	70722	67068	70681	36045	31561	33586	37711	1428	1400
3110	Electric motors, generators and transformers	14991	14833	15183	16974	7941	7841	7883	8354	441	248
3120	Electricity distribution & control apparatus	28674	27282	32127	33476	16363	16073	18632	18566	523	613
3130	Insulated wire and cable	11660	10418	11534	12855	4858	4357	4716	4434	240	157
3140	Accumulators, primary cells and batteries	6337	6176	5961	6662	3217	3058	2785	3122	164	155
3150	Lighting equipment and electric lamps	12472	11897	22113	23707	7210	6726	12727	13219	455	442
3190	Other electrical equipment n.e.c.	43806	42128	35572	36584	23533	22158	19157	18020	863	1033
3210	Electronic valves, tubes, etc.	107534	108260	111781	114950	68509	69565	74760	78716	6228	8888
3220	TV/radio transmitters; line comm. apparatus	59398	55598	53663	54713	29567	27776	27678	29947	932	988
3230	TV and radio receivers and associated goods	8824	8648	10718	10371	3422	3193	3414	3106	174	114
331	Medical, measuring, testing appliances, etc.	150739	156188	166303	177573	98345	106086	110653	118053	4759	6501
3311	Medical, surgical and orthopaedic equipment	73468	77911	81325	72523	49706	54685	55560	50070	2472	2634
3312	Measuring/testing/navigating appliances,etc.	70105	71784	77868	97304	44246	47402	50794	63395	2154	3201
3313	Industrial process control equipment	7166	6493	7110	7746	4394	3999	4299	4588	133	666
3320	Optical instruments & photographic equipment	9735	10143	10000	10661	5946	6200	6158	6523	386	390
3330	Watches and clocks	700	601	...	641	419	360	...	410	...	9
3410	Motor vehicles	294974	313930	321036	320457	91035	97036	93363	89983	6108	5924
3420	Automobile bodies, trailers & semi-trailers	17313	17039	14099	16477	6878	6893	5092	5746	205	188
3430	Parts/accessories for automobiles	121469	119955	122946	124249	54635	52297	52322	50887	4331	4233
351	Building and repairing of ships and boats	21247	22073	23718	25516	12249	12636	13149	13587	358	437
3511	Building and repairing of ships	12815	13409	13706	14150	8449	8620	8573	8716	177	220
3512	Building/repairing of pleasure/sport. boats	8432	8664	10012	11367	3800	4016	4575	4871	182	218
3520	Railway/tramway locomotives & rolling stock	7798	7514	7566	9205	3744	2907	3217	3311	111	124
3530	Aircraft and spacecraft	124227	124071	126129	137105	62847	65389	67594	71221	2293	3069
359	Transport equipment n.e.c.	4689	5107	5144	5058	2145	2336	2169	1965	100	137
3591	Motorcycles	4689	5107	5144	5058	2145	2336	2169	1965	100	137
3592	Bicycles and invalid carriages	...	...	...	...	...	...	...	...	...	...
3599	Other transport equipment n.e.c.	...	...	...	...	...	...	...	...	...	...
3610	Furniture	90300	90754	93452	99558	47104	47758	48521	49703	1542	1642
369	Manufacturing n.e.c.	60473	60596	48159	52273	33776	34023	26842	30001	1388	1500
3691	Jewellery and related articles	8015	7827	9026	9965	3407	3459	4311	5057	138	139
3692	Musical instruments	1816	1824	1739	1678	1228	1208	1158	1010	40	32
3693	Sports goods	11863	12149	11928	12429	6739	7029	7063	7466	409	459
3694	Games and toys	4847	3937	3541	3751	2697	2120	1967	2033	80	74
3699	Other manufacturing n.e.c.	33931	34859	21925	24450	19706	20206	12344	14435	721	797
3710	Recycling of metal waste and scrap	...	...	...	...	...	...	...	...	...	...
3720	Recycling of non-metal waste and scrap	...	...	...	...	...	...	...	...	...	...
D	Total manufacturing	3915601	3979842	4306647	4735384	1892784	1912093	2049612	2204095	116419	128325

United States of America

ISIC Revision 3			Index numbers of industrial production (2000=100)											
ISIC	Industry	Note	1995	1996	1997	1998	1999	2000	2001	2002	2003	2004	2005	2006
15	Food and beverages		93	92	95	98	99	100	100	102	104	104	108	109
16	Tobacco products		116	118	116	112	99	100	98	82	86	86	89	86
17	Textiles		100	98	103	102	102	100	90	89	86	85	86	79
18	Wearing apparel, fur		121	117	116	110	105	100	86	68	63	54	52	51
19	Leather, leather products and footwear		111	111	117	108	103	100	81	59	57	57	62	63
20	Wood products (excl. furniture)		88	91	93	97	102	100	94	96	97	101	106	106
21	Paper and paper products		102	98	101	101	102	100	94	95	92	93	93	93
22	Printing and publishing		87	87	93	97	99	100	94	88	86	86	87	85
23	Coke,refined petroleum products,nuclear fuel		90	94	104	110	102	100	95	106	107	110	118	112
24	Chemicals and chemical products		88	90	95	97	99	100	98	105	107	111	115	119
25	Rubber and plastics products		83	85	91	94	99	100	94	97	97	99	99	100
26	Non-metallic mineral products		86	91	94	99	100	100	96	96	97	100	104	106
27	Basic metals		95	97	102	103	103	100	89	90	89	99	96	101
28	Fabricated metal products		85	89	93	96	96	100	93	90	89	89	93	99
29	Machinery and equipment n.e.c.		87	90	95	97	95	100	89	85	85	88	94	98
30	Office, accounting and computing machinery		24	33	47	65	86	100	101	97	105	106	126	156
31	Electrical machinery and apparatus		85	87	90	94	95	100	90	82	80	82	83	84
32	Radio,television and communication equipment		16	23	34	47	68	100	104	102	126	148	169	203
33	Medical, precision and optical instruments		77	82	85	93	95	100	104	108	115	113	123	128
34	Motor vehicles, trailers, semi-trailers		79	80	86	91	101	100	91	100	104	104	104	100
35	Other transport equipment		88	91	102	118	114	100	107	101	96	95	106	112
36	Furniture; manufacturing n.e.c.		81	84	88	94	96	100	97	101	102	103	109	111
37	Recycling		...	...	...	...	...	...	...	...	...	...	...	...
D	Total manufacturing		75	79	85	91	96	100	96	96	97	100	104	106

Uruguay

Supplier of information:
Instituto Nacional de Estadística, Montevideo.

Basic source of data:
Annual sample survey.

Major deviations from ISIC (Revision 3):
None reported.

Reference period:
Calendar year.

Scope:
Establishments with five and more persons engaged.

Method of data collection:
Questionnaires are distributed by electronic mail.

Type of enumeration:
Extended sample survey.

Adjusted for non-response:
Yes.

Concepts and definitions of variables:
Number of persons engaged includes home workers.
Output excludes net change between the beginning and end of the year in the value of work in process and stocks of goods to be shipped in the same condition as received.
Value added includes net receipts of non-industrial services.

Related national publications:
Encuesta Anual de Actividades Economicas, published by the Instituto Nacional de Estadística, Montevideo.

Uruguay

ISIC Revision 3		Establishments					Number of persons engaged					Wages and salaries paid to employees				
		Note	(number)				Note	(number)				Note	(millions of Uruguayan Pesos)			
ISIC	Industry		2002	2003	2004	2005		2002	2003	2004	2005		2002	2003	2004	2005
151	Processed meat,fish,fruit,vegetables,fats		...	...	...	...		13465	14684	15072	17637		1226.8	1518.4	1761.3	2219.8
1511	Processing/preserving of meat		...	...	...	...		10218	11105	11094	13107		884.7	1108.4	1289.2	1691.5
1512	Processing/preserving of fish		...	...	...	...		2217	2337	2715	3257		232.2	284.7	332.8	380.1
1513	Processing/preserving of fruit & vegetables		...	...	...	...		808	967	966	960		77.4	84.5	88.9	92.1
1514	Vegetable and animal oils and fats		...	...	...	...		222	275	297	313		32.6	40.8	50.4	56.1
1520	Dairy products		...	...	...	...		3987	4030	4303	5089		743.0	798.8	880.5	1016.0
153	Grain mill products; starches; animal feeds		...	...	...	...		2381	2989	3549	3979		364.2	405.9	485.2	525.9
1531	Grain mill products		...	...	...	...		743	964	1189	1346		325.2	126.8	148.4	178.7
1532	Starches and starch products		...	...	...	...		...	...	...	...		...	...	...	...
1533	Prepared animal feeds		...	...	...	...		411	488	558	533		39.0	52.2	55.7	69.2
154	Other food products		...	...	...	...		11341	12207	12357	13813		986.2	1022.8	1010.2	1147.0
1541	Bakery products		...	...	...	...		7700	8019	8517	9710		550.0	523.0	513.6	621.4
1542	Sugar		...	...	...	...		427	521	721a/	493		52.9	66.5	95.9a/	76.3
1543	Cocoa, chocolate and sugar confectionery		...	...	...	...		191	202	...a/	323		12.1	14.1	...a/	35.1
1544	Macaroni, noodles & similar products		...	...	...	...		1411	1590	1399	1644		91.4	101.0	102.1	124.6
1549	Other food products n.e.c.		...	...	...	...		1612	1875	1720	1643		279.8	318.3	298.6	289.6
155	Beverages		...	...	...	...		2996	2908	2821	2950		553.3	601.1	555.4	738.0
1551	Distilling, rectifying & blending of spirits		...	...	...	...		235	148	169	163		80.3	41.5	51.0	54.8
1552	Wines		...	...	...	...		928	858	934	942		57.5	56.4	70.5	94.9
1553	Malt liquors and malt		...	...	...	...		745	707	600	657		234.2	266.3	245.1	289.4
1554	Soft drinks; mineral waters		...	...	...	...		1088	1195	1118	1188		181.3	236.9	188.9	298.9
1600	Tobacco products		...	...	...	...		598	567	467	456		258.0	275.4	284.2	292.2
171	Spinning, weaving and finishing of textiles		...	...	...	...		3160	3814	3790	4272		412.4	500.0	547.6	613.9
1711	Textile fibre preparation; textile weaving		...	...	...	...		2345	2909	2974	3449		408.9	301.5	340.6	393.0
1712	Finishing of textiles		...	...	...	...		56	107	94	96		3.5	6.2	6.4	7.5
172	Other textiles		...	...	...	...		429	476	617	1119		35.7	42.8	50.9	86.0
1721	Made-up textile articles, except apparel		...	...	...	...		...	...	...	...		...	...	...	...
1722	Carpets and rugs		...	...	...	...		...	...	...	...		...	...	...	...
1723	Cordage, rope, twine and netting		...	...	...	...		...	...	...	...		...	...	...	...
1729	Other textiles n.e.c.		...	...	...	...		...	...	...	...		...	...	...	...
1730	Knitted and crocheted fabrics and articles		...	...	...	...		1416	1687	1913	2358		88.0	115.5	139.1	153.6
1810	Wearing apparel, except fur apparel		...	...	...	...		4032	4705	5331	6747		263.1	346.1	412.3	485.4
1820	Dressing & dyeing of fur; processing of fur		...	...	...	...		...	...	...	...		...	...	...	...
191	Tanning, dressing and processing of leather		...	...	...	...		2730	3299	3433	4087		334.8	445.2	452.8	575.3
1911	Tanning and dressing of leather		...	...	...	...		2532	3023	3138	3608		325.8	430.7	431.3	541.7
1912	Luggage, handbags, etc.; saddlery & harness		...	...	...	...		198	276	295	479		8.9	14.5	21.5	33.6
1920	Footwear		...	...	...	...		477	547	571	756		20.2	26.6	34.1	53.9
2010	Sawmilling and planing of wood		...	...	...	...		710	926	1012	1311		58.3	88.1	107.6	162.5
202	Products of wood, cork, straw, etc.		...	...	...	...		792	884	1139	1326		49.7	57.0	72.9	92.4
2021	Veneer sheets, plywood, particle board, etc.		...	...	...	...	b/	656	748	867	1326	b/	37.8	45.3	55.7	92.4
2022	Builders' carpentry and joinery		...	...	...	...	b/	...	...	...	...	b/	...	...	...	...
2023	Wooden containers		...	...	...	...	b/	...	...	...	...	b/	...	...	...	...
2029	Other wood products; articles of cork/straw		...	...	...	...		136	136	272	...		12.0	11.7	17.2	...
210	Paper and paper products		...	...	...	...		1284	1723	1709	1797		274.2	313.8	299.6	340.6
2101	Pulp, paper and paperboard		...	...	...	...		462	738	740	784		116.2	145.9	123.5	139.4
2102	Corrugated paper and paperboard		...	...	...	...		538	629	594	629		83.3	90.0	87.8	100.3
2109	Other articles of paper and paperboard		...	...	...	...		284	356	375	384		74.7	77.8	88.3	100.9
221	Publishing		...	...	...	...		4154	4315	4832	5345		639.8	609.2	689.5	847.4
2211	Publishing of books and other publications		...	...	...	...	c/	2115	2246	2922	3389	c/	323.0	294.5	375.5	505.7
2212	Publishing of newspapers, journals, etc.		...	...	...	...		2039	2069	1910	1956		316.8	314.8	314.0	341.7
2213	Publishing of recorded media		...	...	...	...	c/	...	...	...	...	c/	...	...	...	...
2219	Other publishing		...	...	...	...	c/	...	...	...	...	c/	...	...	...	...

222	Printing and related service activities	...	...	...	...		...	...	...	...		...	...	...	...
2221	Printing	...	...	...	...	c/	...	...	...	...	c/	...	...	...	...
2222	Service activities related to printing	...	...	...	...	c/	...	...	...	...	c/	...	...	...	...
2230	Reproduction of recorded media	...	...	...	...		28	9	6	6		2.7	1.4	0.8	1.2
2310	Coke oven products	...	...	...	...		-	-	-	-		-	-	-	-
2320	Refined petroleum products	...	...	...	...		890	840	940	865		210.2	275.5	361.1	447.9
2330	Processing of nuclear fuel	...	...	...	...		...	...	...	...		...	...	...	...
241	Basic chemicals	...	...	...	...		912	996	1070	1151		308.9	309.3	383.6	422.0
2411	Basic chemicals, except fertilizers	...	...	...	...		645	711	781	828		191.4	233.8	288.7	315.9
2412	Fertilizers and nitrogen compounds	...	...	...	...		207	217	224	224		109.4	64.4	80.7	80.0
2413	Plastics in primary forms; synthetic rubber	...	...	...	...		60	68	65	99		8.1	11.1	14.2	26.1
242	Other chemicals	...	...	...	...		4441	4796	5326	5828		1010.2	1095.9	1242.5	1407.9
2421	Pesticides and other agro-chemical products	...	...	...	...		130	144	140	149		30.4	40.8	41.6	42.9
2422	Paints, varnishes, printing ink and mastics	...	...	...	...		524	537	595	605		96.9	109.4	152.0	175.3
2423	Pharmaceuticals, medicinal chemicals, etc.	...	...	...	...		2510	2564	2867	3165		658.6	699.0	761.2	852.0
2424	Soap, cleaning & cosmetic preparations	...	...	...	...		1066	1335	1513	1676		179.2	192.7	231.5	266.4
2429	Other chemical products n.e.c.	...	...	...	...		211	216	211	233		45.1	54.0	56.3	71.4
2430	Man-made fibres	...	...	...	...		...	...	...	...		...	...	...	...
251	Rubber products	...	...	...	...		281	258	350	414		25.8	27.4	36.4	33.5
2511	Rubber tyres and tubes	...	...	...	...		108	82	120	135		8.8	8.2	11.4	9.4
2519	Other rubber products	...	...	...	...		173	176	230	279		17.0	19.2	25.0	24.2
2520	Plastic products	...	...	...	...		2688	2687	2974	3351		286.0	329.7	363.9	447.4
2610	Glass and glass products	...	...	...	...		387	418	444	519		27.1	31.6	35.0	59.1
269	Non-metallic mineral products n.e.c.	...	...	...	...		2095	2082	2225	2498		288.1	380.0	400.8	442.3
2691	Pottery, china and earthenware	...	...	...	...		744	784	856	924		72.1	109.3	127.6	142.1
2692	Refractory ceramic products	...	...	...	...		90	92	75	142		5.9	6.9	5.0	10.2
2693	Struct.non-refractory clay; ceramic products	...	...	...	...		...	...	...	...		...	...	...	...
2694	Cement, lime and plaster	...	...	...	...		856	847	795	818		169.7	212.4	193.9	232.5
2695	Articles of concrete, cement and plaster	...	...	...	...		353	311	312	318		34.9	45.5	50.6	34.3
2696	Cutting, shaping & finishing of stone	...	...	...	...	d/	...	...	...	...	d/	...	...	...	...
2699	Other non-metallic mineral products n.e.c.	...	...	...	...	d/	52	48	187	296	d/	103.3	5.8	23.7	23.2
2710	Basic iron and steel	...	...	...	...		547e/	846e/	1020e/	...		...	...	...	...
2720	Basic precious and non-ferrous metals	...	...	...	...		...e/	...e/	...e/	...		...	...	...	...
273	Casting of metals	...	...	...	...		...e/	...e/	...e/	...		...	...	...	...
2731	Casting of iron and steel	...	...	...	...		...	...	...	...		...	...	...	...
2732	Casting of non-ferrous metals	...	...	...	...		...	...	...	...		...	...	...	...
281	Struct.metal products;tanks;steam generators	...	...	...	...		1518	1813	1441	2273		137.3	152.1	167.2	264.0
2811	Structural metal products	...	...	...	...		1287	1588	1200	2016		124.2	139.2	153.2	227.1
2812	Tanks, reservoirs and containers of metal	...	...	...	...	f/	231	225	241	257	f/	13.2	12.9	14.0	36.9
2813	Steam generators	...	...	...	...	f/	...	...	...	...	f/	...	...	...	...
289	Other metal products; metal working services	...	...	...	...		1554	1410	1385	1812		110.2	124.0	147.6	193.6
2891	Metal forging/pressing/stamping/roll-forming	...	...	...	...		...	...	...	...		...	...	...	...
2892	Treatment & coating of metals	...	...	...	...		...	...	...	...		...	...	...	...
2893	Cutlery, hand tools and general hardware	...	...	...	...		...	...	...	...		...	...	...	...
2899	Other fabricated metal products n.e.c.	...	...	...	...		...	...	...	...		...	...	...	...
291	General purpose machinery	...	...	...	...		544	585	694	712		82.2	96.2	112.3	135.9
2911	Engines & turbines (not for transport equipment)	...	...	...	...		...	...	...	...		...	...	...	...
2912	Pumps, compressors, taps and valves	...	...	...	...		...	...	...	...		...	...	...	...
2913	Bearings, gears, gearing & driving elements	...	...	...	...		...	...	...	...		...	...	...	...
2914	Ovens, furnaces and furnace burners	...	...	...	...		...	...	...	...		...	...	...	...
2915	Lifting and handling equipment	...	...	...	...		...	...	...	...		...	...	...	...
2919	Other general purpose machinery	...	...	...	...		...	...	...	...		...	...	...	...
292	Special purpose machinery	...	...	...	...		514	596	477	549		35.3	50.0	56.0	57.2
2921	Agricultural and forestry machinery	...	...	...	...		...	...	...	...		...	...	...	...
2922	Machine tools	...	...	...	...		...	...	...	...		...	...	...	...
2923	Machinery for metallurgy	...	...	...	...		...	...	...	...		...	...	...	...
2924	Machinery for mining & construction	...	...	...	...		...	...	...	...		...	...	...	...
2925	Food/beverage/tobacco processing machinery	...	...	...	...		...	...	...	...		...	...	...	...
2926	Machinery for textile, apparel and leather	...	...	...	...		...	...	...	...		...	...	...	...
2927	Weapons and ammunition	...	...	...	...		...	...	...	...		...	...	...	...
2929	Other special purpose machinery	...	...	...	...		...	...	...	...		...	...	...	...

continued

Uruguay

ISIC Revision 3		Establishments					Number of persons engaged					Wages and salaries paid to employees				
			(number)					(number)					(millions of Uruguayan Pesos)			
ISIC	Industry	Note	2002	2003	2004	2005	Note	2002	2003	2004	2005	Note	2002	2003	2004	2005
2930	Domestic appliances n.e.c.		...	...	...	...		521	425	307	367		62.7	58.1	39.0	49.2
3000	Office, accounting and computing machinery		...	...	...	...		...	...	...	161		0.8	0.7	...	63.6
3110	Electric motors, generators and transformers		...	...	...	...		898g/	931g/	1048g/	...		111.0g/	122.9g/	...	...
3120	Electricity distribution & control apparatus		...	...	...	...		...g/	...g/	...g/	...		...g/	...g/	...	...
3130	Insulated wire and cable		...	...	...	...		...g/	...g/	...g/	...		...g/	...g/	...	...
3140	Accumulators, primary cells and batteries		...	...	...	...		...g/	...g/	...g/	...		...g/	...g/	...	...
3150	Lighting equipment and electric lamps		...	...	...	...		...g/	...g/	...g/	...		...g/	...g/	...	...
3190	Other electrical equipment n.e.c.		...	...	...	...		...g/	...g/	...g/	...		...g/	...g/	...	...
3210	Electronic valves, tubes, etc.		...	...	...	...		72h/	79h/	70h/	...		...	...	...	...
3220	TV/radio transmitters; line comm. apparatus		...	...	...	...		...h/	...h/	...h/	...		...	...	...	...
3230	TV and radio receivers and associated goods		...	...	...	...		...h/	...h/	...h/	...		...	...	...	...
331	Medical, measuring, testing appliances, etc.		...	...	...	...		1085i/	1262i/	1378i/	...		111.8i/	127.9i/	...	...
3311	Medical, surgical and orthopaedic equipment		...	...	...	...		...	...	...	...		...	...	...	...
3312	Measuring/testing/navigating appliances,etc.		...	...	...	...		...	...	...	...		...	...	...	...
3313	Industrial process control equipment		...	...	...	...		...	...	...	...		...	...	...	...
3320	Optical instruments & photographic equipment		...	...	...	...		...i/	...i/	...i/	...		...i/	...i/	...	...
3330	Watches and clocks		...	...	...	...		...i/	...i/	...i/	...		...i/	...i/	...	...
3410	Motor vehicles		...	...	...	...		959j/	919j/	1175j/	...		148.4j/	134.6j/	...	...
3420	Automobile bodies, trailers & semi-trailers		...	...	...	...		...j/	...j/	...j/	...		...j/	...j/	...	...
3430	Parts/accessories for automobiles		...	...	...	...		...j/	...j/	...j/	...		...j/	...j/	...	...
351	Building and repairing of ships and boats		...	...	...	...		412	445	526	490		110.2	67.8	96.7	85.1
3511	Building and repairing of ships		...	...	...	...		...	...	...	...		...	...	...	...
3512	Building/repairing of pleasure/sport. boats		...	...	...	...		...	...	...	...		...	...	...	...
3520	Railway/tramway locomotives & rolling stock		...	...	...	...		...	...	...	...		...	...	...	...
3530	Aircraft and spacecraft		...	...	...	...		4	5	...k/	5		0.3	0.4	...k/	0.4
359	Transport equipment n.e.c.		...	...	...	...		492	418	519k/	593		70.5	53.0	64.4k/	91.6
3591	Motorcycles		...	...	...	...		...	...	...	...		...	...	...	...
3592	Bicycles and invalid carriages		...	...	...	...		...	...	...	...		...	...	...	...
3599	Other transport equipment n.e.c.		...	...	...	...		...	...	...	...		...	...	...	...
3610	Furniture		...	...	...	...		1172	1137	1601	1721		113.9	96.9	132.8	179.4
369	Manufacturing n.e.c.		...	...	...	...		611	609	743	787		46.7	50.5	63.7	64.7
3691	Jewellery and related articles		...	...	...	...		56	62	67	80		5.2	7.8	9.3	13.4
3692	Musical instruments		...	...	...	...	m/	...	...	...	...	m/	...	...	...	...
3693	Sports goods		...	...	...	...	m/	...	...	...	...	m/	...	...	...	...
3694	Games and toys		...	...	...	...	m/	...	...	...	...	m/	...	...	...	...
3699	Other manufacturing n.e.c.		...	...	...	...	m/	555	547	676	707	m/	41.5	42.7	54.4	51.3
3710	Recycling of metal waste and scrap		...	...	...	...		29	29	18n/	...		0.6	4.3	...	...
3720	Recycling of non-metal waste and scrap		...	...	...	...		...	...	...n/	...		...	...	...	...
D	Total manufacturing		...	...	...	...	p/	76606	83356	88653	96551	p/	9608.4	10756.5	11487.0	13796.0

a/ 1542 includes 1543.
b/ 2021 includes 2022 and 2023.
c/ 2211 includes 2213, 2219, 2221 and 2222.
d/ 2699 includes 2696.
e/ 2710 includes 2720 and 273.
f/ 2812 includes 2813.
g/ 3110 includes 3120, 3130, 3140, 3150 and 3190.
h/ 3210 includes 3220 and 3230.
i/ 331 includes 3320 and 3330.
j/ 3410 includes 3420 and 3430.
k/ 359 includes 3530.
m/ 3699 includes 3692, 3693 and 3694.
n/ 3710 includes 3720.
p/ Sum of available data.

Uruguay

ISIC Revision 3		Output in producers' prices					Value added in producers' prices					Gross fixed capital formation		
			(millions of Uruguayan Pesos)					(millions of Uruguayan Pesos)					(millions of Uruguayan Pesos)	
ISIC	Industry	Note	2002	2003	2004	2005	Note	2002	2003	2004	2005	Note	2004	2005
151	Processed meat,fish,fruit,vegetables,fats		17442.3	26151.1	35121.5	35987.2		3655.6	3425.8	4597.6	4708.8		778.9	1011.0
1511	Processing/preserving of meat		14481.3	22355.5	30974.3	31637.6		2629.9	2280.6	3489.6	3566.1		573.0	658.4
1512	Processing/preserving of fish		1782.0	2484.6	2690.9	2973.4		577.9	765.5	789.9	818.3		138.4	233.9
1513	Processing/preserving of fruit & vegetables		719.6	671.2	592.1	693.9		301.8	262.3	202.8	206.2		37.3	100.3
1514	Vegetable and animal oils and fats		459.4	639.8	864.2	682.2		146.0	117.5	115.4	118.1		30.1	18.4
1520	Dairy products		6670.6	8546.9	10492.5	11421.9		1978.6	1889.4	2063.0	2125.7		542.8	120.7
153	Grain mill products; starches; animal feeds		6154.5	8467.9	10387.9	8597.9		1829.3	1549.4	1715.1	1375.7		252.9	276.8
1531	Grain mill products		2487.0	2661.5	2739.7	2338.5		1672.9	456.1	437.4	308.7		35.2	40.4
1532	Starches and starch products		...	...	...	...		...	...	...	...		...	...
1533	Prepared animal feeds		401.1	639.4	926.2	795.8		156.4	227.9	317.5	249.2		15.0	94.6
154	Other food products		8268.4	10161.9	11232.1	12397.5		3435.6	4505.2	5108.7	6191.4		295.2	635.7
1541	Bakery products		2376.3	2370.0	2610.6	3024.2		801.3	739.3	859.5	1047.0		198.9	236.8
1542	Sugar		647.3	831.5	930.2a/	749.9		228.0	259.4	215.6a/	187.2		3.2a/	4.9
1543	Cocoa, chocolate and sugar confectionery		58.5	112.6	...a/	195.6		15.5	27.9	...a/	58.5		...a/	6.1
1544	Macaroni, noodles & similar products		436.1	525.5	550.4	617.7		148.6	179.3	192.5	225.2		-1.2	11.4
1549	Other food products n.e.c.		4750.1	6322.4	7140.9	7810.1		2242.1	3299.4	3841.1	4673.6		94.3	376.4
155	Beverages		5510.0	6347.8	8160.8	8543.8		2660.2	2624.7	3997.7	3934.6		-155.3	1464.4
1551	Distilling, rectifying & blending of spirits		324.4	311.0	369.1	370.8		199.3	185.3	237.7	224.8		1.5	1.8
1552	Wines		615.1	682.3	1145.7	1120.6		288.3	303.0	476.9	500.8		29.2	96.9
1553	Malt liquors and malt		2422.3	2916.1	4180.0	4089.1		1093.0	1140.5	2222.9	1899.8		-41.8	1319.5
1554	Soft drinks; mineral waters		2148.3	2438.4	2465.9	2963.4		1079.5	995.9	1060.3	1309.2		-144.2	46.2
1600	Tobacco products		3355.3	3482.8	4140.9	4075.5		2177.9	2194.1	2820.5	3002.1		33.4	13.0
171	Spinning, weaving and finishing of textiles		5994.4	7225.1	6803.1	5525.6		1447.6	1993.5	1435.5	1212.9		229.0	64.4
1711	Textile fibre preparation; textile weaving		...	2224.4	2432.7	1972.9		...	820.1	847.4	698.5		191.6	44.5
1712	Finishing of textiles		15.6	36.1	39.7	36.6		4.9	14.4	13.1	12.5		0.5	0.9
172	Other textiles		215.6	279.4	400.5	624.7		69.8	104.4	143.0	200.7		37.7	17.3
1721	Made-up textile articles, except apparel		...	...	...	...		...	...	...	...		...	...
1722	Carpets and rugs		...	...	...	...		...	...	...	...		...	...
1723	Cordage, rope, twine and netting		...	...	...	...		...	...	...	...		...	...
1729	Other textiles n.e.c.		...	...	...	...		...	...	...	...		...	...
1730	Knitted and crocheted fabrics and articles		387.0	601.8	741.9	733.4		176.3	264.1	326.8	335.5		21.7	26.8
1810	Wearing apparel, except fur apparel		1619.1	2086.8	2721.0	2633.1		570.9	769.8	1122.7	1079.0		67.3	51.9
1820	Dressing & dyeing of fur; processing of fur		...	...	...	...		...	...	...	...		...	...
191	Tanning, dressing and processing of leather		6846.8	9015.7	9045.6	8204.7		1621.5	1736.8	2101.9	1693.6		490.1	303.1
1911	Tanning and dressing of leather		6806.4	8952.6	8953.7	8071.4		1606.8	1709.5	2057.8	1628.9		487.3	295.6
1912	Luggage, handbags, etc.; saddlery & harness		40.4	63.1	91.9	133.3		14.7	27.3	44.1	64.7		2.9	7.6
1920	Footwear		97.9	176.4	293.6	327.2		41.6	54.6	110.5	111.9		6.3	8.0
2010	Sawmilling and planing of wood		624.8	2322.2	3022.6	3008.1		290.4	842.7	708.9	628.7		865.1	542.0
202	Products of wood, cork, straw, etc.		255.5	297.1	398.8	469.2		108.0	106.6	126.1	160.0		18.5	26.2
2021	Veneer sheets, plywood, particle board, etc.	b/	182.9	245.7	314.0	469.2	b/	73.2	83.7	103.8	160.0		18.4b/	26.2b/
2022	Builders' carpentry and joinery	b/	...	...	...	...	b/	...	...	...	...		...b/	...b/
2023	Wooden containers	b/	...	...	...	...	b/	...	...	...	...		...b/	...b/
2029	Other wood products; articles of cork/straw		72.6	51.4	84.8	...		34.8	22.9	22.3	...		-	...
210	Paper and paper products		2330.0	2964.5	3215.8	3212.0		748.8	1046.8	891.3	903.7		246.8	163.2
2101	Pulp, paper and paperboard		1249.8	1586.4	1431.9	1404.8		460.3	691.6	464.1	433.0		191.1	141.7
2102	Corrugated paper and paperboard		572.7	680.7	829.5	828.3		120.4	160.0	185.7	194.3		38.9	12.6
2109	Other articles of paper and paperboard		507.5	697.4	954.5	978.9		168.1	195.2	241.5	276.4		16.8	8.9
221	Publishing		2990.8	3392.8	4149.9	4434.1		1497.6	1442.2	1669.1	1915.2		256.2	147.0
2211	Publishing of books and other publications	c/	1751.7	2103.5	2657.8	2843.4	c/	847.0	878.2	1026.3	1156.9		248.8c/	125.7c/
2212	Publishing of newspapers, journals, etc.		1239.0	1289.2	1492.1	1590.7		650.6	564.0	642.7	758.3		7.4	21.4
2213	Publishing of recorded media	c/	...	...	...	...	c/	...	...	...	...		...c/	...c/
2219	Other publishing	c/	...	...	...	...	c/	...	...	...	...		...c/	...c/

continued

Uruguay

ISIC Revision 3		Output in producers' prices					Value added in producers' prices					Gross fixed capital formation		
			(millions of Uruguayan Pesos)					(millions of Uruguayan Pesos)					(millions of Uruguayan Pesos)	
ISIC	Industry	Note	2002	2003	2004	2005	Note	2002	2003	2004	2005	Note	2004	2005
222	Printing and related service activities		...	...	...	...		...	...	...	...		...	...
2221	Printing	c/	...	...	...	...	c/	...	...	...	...		...c/	...c/
2222	Service activities related to printing	c/	...	...	...	...	c/	...	...	...	...		...c/	...c/
2230	Reproduction of recorded media		34.4	12.8	8.1	9.8		9.5	3.1	2.0	2.7		-	-
2310	Coke oven products		-	-	-	-		-	-	-	-		-	-
2320	Refined petroleum products		16661.6	20621.2	33235.0	35220.9		10240.5	7353.0	11804.3	11095.6		786.0	-1248.8
2330	Processing of nuclear fuel		...	...	...	...		...	...	...	...		...	...
241	Basic chemicals		4167.9	4418.5	5661.7	5739.1		1429.2	1272.1	1344.1	1248.3		202.6	209.2
2411	Basic chemicals, except fertilizers		1736.3	2278.1	2785.9	3145.8		520.6	631.4	761.8	749.9		133.7	111.3
2412	Fertilizers and nitrogen compounds		1948.9	1424.9	1947.7	1681.1		762.6	484.5	520.5	436.6		60.3	61.8
2413	Plastics in primary forms; synthetic rubber		482.7	715.5	928.1	912.3		146.0	156.2	61.8	61.8		8.7	36.1
242	Other chemicals		5749.2	7443.7	8588.2	8867.9		2351.2	2932.6	3068.4	3220.2		346.1	434.1
2421	Pesticides and other agro-chemical products		360.4	626.2	726.8	639.0		171.4	246.3	277.0	232.9		18.2	12.7
2422	Paints, varnishes, printing ink and mastics		784.0	1134.4	1496.3	1614.2		314.3	410.8	534.3	559.6		14.6	13.9
2423	Pharmaceuticals, medicinal chemicals, etc.		3500.2	4213.5	4544.3	4608.3		1439.3	1752.5	1723.7	1797.2		247.4	337.7
2424	Soap, cleaning & cosmetic preparations		823.9	1083.5	1347.1	1468.0		321.0	397.4	389.2	452.1		17.5	19.2
2429	Other chemical products n.e.c.		280.6	386.0	473.6	538.3		105.1	125.6	144.1	178.4		48.4	50.7
2430	Man-made fibres		...	...	...	...		...	...	...	...		...	...
251	Rubber products		179.6	145.5	140.5	143.4		52.4	44.0	66.7	57.6		17.1	27.2
2511	Rubber tyres and tubes		37.5	36.3	52.4	66.3		16.7	16.4	27.5	17.9		13.5	26.9
2519	Other rubber products		142.1	109.2	88.1	77.1		35.7	27.7	39.1	39.7		3.7	0.2
2520	Plastic products		2553.4	3394.0	4667.6	5279.6		894.3	1089.6	1482.6	1587.0		283.7	994.8
2610	Glass and glass products		184.8	226.3	243.6	313.9		48.2	65.1	74.4	99.9		29.3	16.4
269	Non-metallic mineral products n.e.c.		1378.1	2023.3	2478.9	2696.4		813.6	767.3	990.5	1013.0		96.5	100.0
2691	Pottery, china and earthenware		278.6	362.2	460.7	504.5		114.0	176.3	215.4	230.9		2.0	3.3
2692	Refractory ceramic products		15.7	19.9	20.8	42.4		7.5	9.3	9.8	20.4		0.4	3.4
2693	Struct.non-refractory clay; ceramic products		...	...	...	...		...	...	...	...		...	...
2694	Cement, lime and plaster		800.7	1130.5	1350.3	1620.0		257.7	427.8	552.6	626.3		41.0	53.2
2695	Articles of concrete, cement and plaster		240.0	461.5	442.1	365.2		65.1	137.8	149.0	83.6		51.5	36.2
2696	Cutting, shaping & finishing of stone		...	...d/	...d/	...d/		...	...d/	...d/	...d/		...d/	...d/
2699	Other non-metallic mineral products n.e.c.		...	49.2d/	205.0d/	164.4d/		...	16.1d/	63.7d/	51.9d/		1.5d/	3.9d/
2710	Basic iron and steel		...	...	...	...		...	...	...	...		...	...
2720	Basic precious and non-ferrous metals		...	...	...	...		...	...	...	...		...	...
273	Casting of metals		...	...	...	...		...	...	...	...		...	...
2731	Casting of iron and steel		...	...	...	...		...	...	...	...		...	...
2732	Casting of non-ferrous metals		...	...	...	...		...	...	...	...		...	...
281	Struct.metal products;tanks;steam generators		925.2	1334.8	1917.3	2212.0		293.8	451.5	545.4	697.8		78.6	181.7
2811	Structural metal products		788.3	1235.9	1784.6	2039.2		251.3	419.9	493.0	637.8		67.8	179.9
2812	Tanks, reservoirs and containers of metal	e/	136.9	98.9	132.7	172.9	e/	42.4	31.6	52.4	60.0		10.8e/	1.8e/
2813	Steam generators	e/	...	...	...	...	e/	...	...	...	...		...e/	...e/
289	Other metal products; metal working services		639.7	964.6	1299.3	1521.5		275.7	342.8	435.0	595.8		51.3	24.3
2891	Metal forging/pressing/stamping/roll-forming		...	...	...	...		...	...	...	...		...	...
2892	Treatment & coating of metals		...	...	...	...		...	...	...	...		...	...
2893	Cutlery, hand tools and general hardware		...	...	...	...		...	...	...	...		...	...
2899	Other fabricated metal products n.e.c.		...	...	...	...		...	...	...	...		...	...
291	General purpose machinery		352.3	375.2	427.3	455.4		172.9	193.2	193.0	227.3		2.0	7.2
2911	Engines & turbines (not for transport equipment)		...	...	...	...		...	...	...	...		...	...
2912	Pumps, compressors, taps and valves		...	...	...	...		...	...	...	...		...	...
2913	Bearings, gears, gearing & driving elements		...	...	...	...		...	...	...	...		...	...
2914	Ovens, furnaces and furnace burners		...	...	...	...		...	...	...	...		...	...
2915	Lifting and handling equipment		...	...	...	...		...	...	...	...		...	...
2919	Other general purpose machinery		...	...	...	...		...	...	...	...		...	...

292	Special purpose machinery		271.0	412.9	545.4	506.3		123.9	124.4	198.7	198.7		58.7	38.7
2921	Agricultural and forestry machinery		...	...	...	...		...	...	...	...		...	...
2922	Machine tools		...	...	...	...		...	...	...	...		...	...
2923	Machinery for metallurgy		...	...	...	...		...	...	...	...		...	...
2924	Machinery for mining & construction		...	...	...	...		...	...	...	...		...	...
2925	Food/beverage/tobacco processing machinery		...	...	...	...		...	...	...	...		...	...
2926	Machinery for textile, apparel and leather		...	...	...	...		...	...	...	...		...	...
2927	Weapons and ammunition		...	...	...	...		...	...	...	...		...	...
2929	Other special purpose machinery		...	...	...	...		...	...	...	...		...	...
2930	Domestic appliances n.e.c.		195.7	268.3	279.9	289.4		80.7	99.0	108.3	142.5		0.7	4.0
3000	Office, accounting and computing machinery		4.9	5.7	...	514.8		1.2	0.6	...	89.4		-	2.2
3110	Electric motors, generators and transformers		...	...	...	...		220.9f/	314.9f/	...	...		-42.4f/	...
3120	Electricity distribution & control apparatus		...	...	...	...		...f/	...f/	...	...		...f/	...
3130	Insulated wire and cable		...	...	...	...		...f/	...f/	...	...		...f/	...
3140	Accumulators, primary cells and batteries		...	...	...	...		...f/	...f/	...	...		...f/	...
3150	Lighting equipment and electric lamps		...	...	...	...		...f/	...f/	...	...		...f/	...
3190	Other electrical equipment n.e.c.		...	...	...	...		...f/	...f/	...	...		...f/	...
3210	Electronic valves, tubes, etc.		...	...	...	...		2.7g/	3.9g/	...	...		-g/	...
3220	TV/radio transmitters; line comm. apparatus		...	...	...	...		...g/	...g/	...	...		...g/	...
3230	TV and radio receivers and associated goods		...	...	...	...		...g/	...g/	...	...		...g/	...
331	Medical, measuring, testing appliances, etc.		...	...	...	...		284.1h/	325.9h/	...	...		56.4h/	...
3311	Medical, surgical and orthopaedic equipment		...	...	...	...		...	...	...	...		...	...
3312	Measuring/testing/navigating appliances,etc.		...	...	...	...		...	...	...	...		...	...
3313	Industrial process control equipment		...	...	...	...		...	...	...	...		...	...
3320	Optical instruments & photographic equipment		...	...	...	...		...h/	...h/	...	...		...h/	...
3330	Watches and clocks		...	...	...	...		...h/	...h/	...	...		...h/	...
3410	Motor vehicles		...	...	...	...		506.5i/	447.9i/	...	...		42.1i/	...
3420	Automobile bodies, trailers & semi-trailers		...	...	...	...		...i/	...i/	...	...		...i/	...
3430	Parts/accessories for automobiles		...	...	...	...		...i/	...i/	...	...		...i/	...
351	Building and repairing of ships and boats		427.5	295.8	423.3	381.7		168.5	122.7	183.0	176.3		5.0	9.5
3511	Building and repairing of ships		...	...	...	...		...	...	...	...		...	...
3512	Building/repairing of pleasure/sport. boats		...	...	...	...		...	...	...	...		...	...
3520	Railway/tramway locomotives & rolling stock		...	...	...	...		...	...	...	...		...	...
3530	Aircraft and spacecraft		3.2	2.4	...j/	...j/		0.7	1.2	...j/	...j/		...j/	0.6
359	Transport equipment n.e.c.		420.3	481.0	598.1j/	960.3j/		117.3	125.7	150.2j/	295.9j/		9.1j/	13.6
3591	Motorcycles		...	...	...	...		...	...	...	...		...	...
3592	Bicycles and invalid carriages		...	...	...	...		...	...	...	...		...	...
3599	Other transport equipment n.e.c.		...	...	...	...		...	...	...	...		...	...
3610	Furniture		960.8	1017.8	1496.9	1487.6		316.8	323.5	472.0	363.5		21.1	53.9
369	Manufacturing n.e.c.		139.3	196.2	288.5	294.2		60.5	81.5	122.0	130.7		283.8	375.2
3691	Jewellery and related articles		11.3	27.3	37.3	47.6		5.0	13.2	18.6	20.4		0.1	1.2
3692	Musical instruments	k/	...	...	...	...	k/	...	...	...	...		...k/	...
3693	Sports goods	k/	...	...	...	...	k/	...	...	...	...		...k/	...
3694	Games and toys	k/	...	...	...	...	k/	...	...	...	...		...k/	...
3699	Other manufacturing n.e.c.	k/	128.0	168.9	251.2	246.6	k/	55.5	68.3	103.4	110.3		283.7k/	374.0
3710	Recycling of metal waste and scrap		...	...	...	...		1.6	1.4	...	...		...	...
3720	Recycling of non-metal waste and scrap		...	...	...	...		...	...	...	...		...	...
D	Total manufacturing	m/	104011.6	135160.3	172628.2	177090.3	m/	40776.4	41036.9	50178.8	50821.8	m/	6314.4	6115.2

a/ 1542 includes 1543.
b/ 2021 includes 2022 and 2023.
c/ 2211 includes 2213, 2219, 2221 and 2222.
d/ 2699 includes 2696.
e/ 2812 includes 2813.
f/ 3110 includes 3120, 3130, 3140, 3150 and 3190.
g/ 3210 includes 3220 and 3230.
h/ 331 includes 3320 and 3330.
i/ 3410 includes 3420 and 3430.
j/ 359 includes 3530.
k/ 3699 includes 3692, 3693 and 3694.
m/ Sum of available data.

Uruguay

ISIC Revision 3			Index numbers of industrial production (2000=100)											
ISIC	Industry	Note	1995	1996	1997	1998	1999	2000	2001	2002	2003	2004	2005	2006
15	Food and beverages		88	96	104	107	105	100	92	93	95	115	144	160
16	Tobacco products		74	83	91	103	113	100	102	96	71	85	70	68
17	Textiles		153	151	160	128	95	100	89	74	90	108	109	98
18	Wearing apparel, fur		166	172	194	164	109	100	65	35	42	49	50	52
19	Leather, leather products and footwear		77	96	90	88	83	100	106	114	134	164	177	186
20	Wood products (excl. furniture)		100	100	100	100	100	100	100	100	200	154	144	185
21	Paper and paper products		66	79	89	95	97	100	94	92	96	107	110	118
22	Printing and publishing		101	107	114	131	114	100	97	75	71	81	86	97
23	Coke,refined petroleum products,nuclear fuel		71	83	78	99	84	100	92	92	112	138	133	122
24	Chemicals and chemical products		142	141	114	113	110	100	92	85	94	109	117	126
25	Rubber and plastics products		79	75	89	95	95	100	91	73	64	82	86	94
26	Non-metallic mineral products		144	143	161	157	124	100	98	65	66	80	89	111
27	Basic metals		99	97	106	110	104	100	99	99	121	155	173	204
28	Fabricated metal products		174	163	156	137	119	100	91	71	107	137	165	192
29	Machinery and equipment n.e.c.		...	...	...	...	...	...	...	...	...	...	...	...
30	Office, accounting and computing machinery		...	...	...	...	...	...	...	...	...	...	...	...
31	Electrical machinery and apparatus	a/	92	114	138	149	121	100	146	87	101	132	123	115
32	Radio,television and communication equipment	a/	...	...	...	...	...	...	...	...	...	...	...	...
33	Medical, precision and optical instruments		...	...	...	...	...	...	...	...	...	...	...	...
34	Motor vehicles, trailers, semi-trailers		61	28	45	91	69	100	69	23	...	...	...	...
35	Other transport equipment		...	...	...	...	...	...	...	...	...	...	...	...
36	Furniture; manufacturing n.e.c.		...	...	...	...	...	...	...	...	...	...	...	...
37	Recycling		...	...	...	...	...	...	...	...	...	...	...	...
D	Total manufacturing		78	87	93	98	96	100	102	107	119	146	164	180

a/ 31 includes 32.

Viet Nam

Supplier of information:
General Statistics Office of Viet Nam, Hanoi.

Basic source of data:
Survey.

Major deviations from ISIC (Revision 3):
None reported.

Reference period:
Calendar year.

Scope:
All registered enterprises.

Method of data collection:
Not reported.

Type of enumeration:
Complete enumeration.

Adjusted for non-response:
Not reported.

Concepts and definitions of variables:
No deviations from the standard UN concepts and definitions are reported.

Related national publications:
Statistical Yearbook of Viet Nam, published by the General Statistics Office of Viet Nam, Hanoi.

Viet Nam

ISIC Revision 3		Number of enterprises					Number of employees					Wages and salaries				
			(number)					(thousands)					(thousands of Vietnamese Dongs)			
ISIC	Industry	Note	2003	2004	2005	2006	Note	2003	2004	2005	2006	Note	2003	2004	2005	2006
15	Food and beverages		4114	4484	5076	5437		377.8	410.0	427.8	439.7		...	...	...	...
16	Tobacco products		26	25	25	24		14.2	14.5	14.6	14.1		...	...	...	...
17	Textiles		708	843	1046	1250		165.4	168.2	188.4	203.8		...	...	...	...
18	Wearing apparel, fur		1211	1567	1745	1958		436.3	498.2	511.3	585.4		...	...	...	...
19	Leather, leather products and footwear		396	508	580	565		472.0	517.9	550.9	581.7		...	...	...	...
20	Wood products (excl. furniture)		1186	1478	1710	2032		89.7	108.6	114.0	112.4		...	...	...	...
21	Paper and paper products		680	817	985	1100		52.6	61.0	69.9	70.2		...	...	...	...
22	Printing and publishing		753	1073	1295	1740		33.5	40.2	44.6	48.4		...	...	...	...
23	Coke,refined petroleum products,nuclear fuel		10	17	15	31		0.8	1.0	1.2	3.9		...	...	...	...
24	Chemicals and chemical products		759	901	1071	1237		79.9	87.5	89.2	98.6		...	...	...	...
25	Rubber and plastics products		911	1164	1457	1643		90.4	107.7	114.3	128.0		...	...	...	...
26	Non-metallic mineral products		1385	1633	1788	1885		197.7	216.9	220.0	228.1		...	...	...	...
27	Basic metals		267	324	409	473		37.2	39.7	43.0	45.5		...	...	...	...
28	Fabricated metal products		1573	2126	2608	3056		89.7	114.7	130.0	149.8		...	...	...	...
29	Machinery and equipment n.e.c.		492	593	690	756		49.5	54.7	54.3	59.0		...	...	...	...
30	Office, accounting and computing machinery		17	26	26	30		4.5	6.0	11.2	16.2		...	...	...	...
31	Electrical machinery and apparatus		287	371	421	459		63.1	66.4	80.0	98.0		...	...	...	...
32	Radio,television and communication equipment		149	192	212	226		24.8	30.1	35.3	40.9		...	...	...	...
33	Medical, precision and optical instruments		63	78	94	123		11.6	13.0	11.3	13.9		...	...	...	...
34	Motor vehicles, trailers, semi-trailers		261	311	377	264		29.1	34.2	36.8	42.5		...	...	...	...
35	Other transport equipment		422	475	554	585		70.2	82.2	89.9	99.4		...	...	...	...
36	Furniture; manufacturing n.e.c.		1219	1488	1796	1921		166.6	219.3	260.2	320.1		...	...	...	...
37	Recycling		27	37	37	68		0.7	1.0	1.3	2.0		...	...	...	...
D	Total manufacturing		16916	20531	24017	26863		2557.4	2893.1	3099.4	3401.6		...	...	...	...

Viet Nam

ISIC Revision 3		Output					Value added					Gross fixed capital formation		
			(billions of Vietnamese Dongs)					(billions of Vietnamese Dongs)					(billions of Vietnamese Dongs)	
ISIC	Industry	Note	2003	2004	2005	2006	Note	2003	2004	2005	2006	Note	2005	2006
15	Food and beverages		124282	156097	204028	245848		...	...	...	...		47364	54579
16	Tobacco products		12422	13651	16222	15945		...	...	...	...		1781	2433
17	Textiles		24741	29703	39791	57800		...	...	...	...		28929	31958
18	Wearing apparel, fur		25241	32574	39280	49156		...	...	...	...		13660	17475
19	Leather, leather products and footwear		25646	33480	42424	48235		...	...	...	...		19487	20872
20	Wood products (excl. furniture)		11249	14787	19539	21326		...	...	...	...		5243	5189
21	Paper and paper products		11440	15202	18574	22428		...	...	...	...		10395	11221
22	Printing and publishing		8033	9902	12528	14537		...	...	...	...		4626	5438
23	Coke,refined petroleum products,nuclear fuel		1060	1586	2150	3181		...	...	...	...		457	705
24	Chemicals and chemical products		30793	43855	55302	71254		...	...	...	...		17426	21035
25	Rubber and plastics products		23021	32427	38952	49176		...	...	...	...		15403	19101
26	Non-metallic mineral products		41115	46203	54217	69764		...	...	...	...		44935	62035
27	Basic metals		21874	31010	37303	45372		...	...	...	...		11001	13427
28	Fabricated metal products		25985	35039	46013	59571		...	...	...	...		14488	20731
29	Machinery and equipment n.e.c.		8796	12821	13802	15961		...	...	...	...		5965	5492
30	Office, accounting and computing machinery		6721	7945	14467	17680		...	...	...	...		3283	4713
31	Electrical machinery and apparatus		17206	24155	33209	44520		...	...	...	...		9756	10425
32	Radio,television and communication equipment		14089	17653	20386	23309		...	...	...	...		5818	6973
33	Medical, precision and optical instruments		1825	2554	2474	2976		...	...	...	...		1343	1410
34	Motor vehicles, trailers, semi-trailers		22603	26911	28502	30277		...	...	...	...		8166	9889
35	Other transport equipment		25103	38597	44314	52363		...	...	...	...		17887	20338
36	Furniture; manufacturing n.e.c.		20720	30357	40520	56069		...	...	...	...		12842	17195
37	Recycling		398	608	724	987		...	...	...	...		103	134
D	Total manufacturing		504364	657115	824718	1017733		...	...	...	...		300359	362770

Viet Nam

ISIC Revision 3			Index numbers of industrial production											
			(2000=100)											
ISIC	Industry	Note	1995	1996	1997	1998	1999	2000	2001	2002	2003	2004	2005	2006
15	Food and beverages		...	...	...	...	...	100	114	128	148	171	198	228
16	Tobacco products		...	...	...	...	...	100	117	133	160	177	196	214
17	Textiles		...	...	...	...	...	100	111	123	141	165	190	221
18	Wearing apparel, fur		...	...	...	...	...	100	118	135	173	212	253	306
19	Leather, leather products and footwear		...	...	...	...	...	100	113	125	153	181	214	251
20	Wood products (excl. furniture)		...	...	...	...	...	100	112	125	152	183	226	286
21	Paper and paper products		...	...	...	...	...	100	112	124	144	182	211	240
22	Printing and publishing		...	...	...	...	...	100	113	126	155	166	203	261
23	Coke,refined petroleum products,nuclear fuel		...	...	...	...	...	100	121	142	138	194	261	333
24	Chemicals and chemical products		...	...	...	...	...	100	116	132	147	171	214	256
25	Rubber and plastics products		...	...	...	...	...	100	125	150	175	235	282	340
26	Non-metallic mineral products		...	...	...	...	...	100	121	142	164	183	203	228
27	Basic metals		...	...	...	...	...	100	122	144	176	190	236	285
28	Fabricated metal products		...	...	...	...	...	100	124	147	185	225	305	384
29	Machinery and equipment n.e.c.		...	...	...	...	...	100	117	134	167	195	199	207
30	Office, accounting and computing machinery		...	...	...	...	...	100	89	77	119	143	248	359
31	Electrical machinery and apparatus		...	...	...	...	...	100	140	180	206	250	331	432
32	Radio,television and communication equipment		...	...	...	...	...	100	120	140	163	181	208	242
33	Medical, precision and optical instruments		...	...	...	...	...	100	108	117	135	159	178	198
34	Motor vehicles, trailers, semi-trailers		...	...	...	...	...	100	139	179	257	269	302	372
35	Other transport equipment		...	...	...	...	...	100	117	133	151	190	247	313
36	Furniture; manufacturing n.e.c.		...	...	...	...	...	...	...	...	...	...	...	...
37	Recycling		...	...	...	...	...	100	108	116	136	174	179	192
D	Total manufacturing		...	...	...	...	...	100	118	135	160	187	223	266

Yemen

Supplier of information:
Ministry of Planning and International Co-operation, Central Statistical Organization, Sana'a.

Basic source of data:
Industrial survey.

Major deviations from ISIC (Revision 3):
None reported.

Reference period:
Calendar year.

Scope:
Privately owned units with one or more employees.

Method of data collection:
Direct interview in the field.

Type of enumeration:
Complete enumeration; sample survey.

Adjusted for non-response:
Yes.

Concepts and definitions of variables:
Wages and salaries is compensation of employees.

Related national publications:
Statistical Yearbook; Final Results of Industrial Survey (Annual), both published by the Central Statistical Organization, Sana'a.

Yemen

ISIC Revision 3		Number of establishments					Number of employees					Wages and salaries paid to employees			
			(number)					(number)					(millions of Yemeni Rials)		
ISIC	Industry	Note	2003	2004	2005	2006	Note	2003	2004	2005a/	2006a/	Note	2003	2004	2005a/	2006a/
15	Food and beverages		17346	17619	...	...		24134	57711	62359	77930		6533	9657	12153	15188
16	Tobacco products		176	157	...	...		1234	879	945	1265		521	129	162	217
17	Textiles		1073	689	...	...		4647	2367	2532	3166		734	259	326	408
18	Wearing apparel, fur		3687	5626	...	...		4211	17716	18943	28780		557	1428	1795	2727
19	Leather, leather products and footwear		313	122	...	...		1229	1445	1599	2160		170	213	268	362
20	Wood products (excl. furniture)		1941	2467	...	...		1962	8152	8664	11316		383	516	649	848
21	Paper and paper products		6	13	...	...		496	1953	2161	2615		132	370	465	563
22	Printing and publishing		198	232	...	...		2522	1424	1560	2022		585	181	228	296
23	Coke,refined petroleum products,nuclear fuel		4	40	...	...		3264	953	1059	1059		2334	188	237	237
24	Chemicals and chemical products		18	49	...	...		1775	3221	3585	5052		307	628	791	1115
25	Rubber and plastics products		32	70	...	...		3107	6180	6927	10225		758	1659	2088	3082
26	Non-metallic mineral products		2953	4337	...	...		8036	22599	24532	32142		2745	2724	3422	4484
27	Basic metals		...	...	...	...		...	...	...	...		...	...	...	...
28	Fabricated metal products		4644	6070	...	...		7523	23305	24924	32214		1438	2037	2562	3311
29	Machinery and equipment n.e.c.		18	37	...	...		91	301	331	337		20	39	49	50
30	Office, accounting and computing machinery		...	...	...	...		...	...	...	...		...	...	...	...
31	Electrical machinery and apparatus		3	4	...	...		144	157	176	191		32	33	42	46
32	Radio,television and communication equipment		...	...	...	...		...	...	...	...		...	...	...	...
33	Medical, precision and optical instruments		17	...	...	...		30	...	...	...		3	...	...	...
34	Motor vehicles, trailers, semi-trailers		...	2	...	...		...	10	11	12		...	1	1	1
35	Other transport equipment		30	17	...	...		281	303	335	345		49	60	76	78
36	Furniture; manufacturing n.e.c.		1898	2054	...	...		2272	6325	6700	9755		515	424	533	776
37	Recycling		...	...	...	...		...	...	...	...		...	...	...	...
D	Total manufacturing	b/	34357	39605	...	...	b/	66958	155001	167343	220586	b/	17816	20546	25847	33789

a/ Estimated data.
b/ Sum of available data.

Yemen

ISIC Revision 3		Output					Value added					Gross fixed capital formation		
			(millions of Yemeni Rials)					(millions of Yemeni Rials)					(millions of Yemeni Rials)	
ISIC	Industry	Note	2003	2004	2005a/	2006a/	Note	2003	2004	2005a/	2006a/	Note	2005	2006
15	Food and beverages		139668	205126	287176	358884		34230	82710	96971	121301		...	...
16	Tobacco products		30882	9354	13094	17528		17977	3648	5106	7386		...	...
17	Textiles		5520	4162	5827	7285		2841	1583	2187	2571		...	...
18	Wearing apparel, fur		6500	14028	19642	29844		4133	7397	9782	14242		...	...
19	Leather, leather products and footwear		3237	5254	7354	9934		639	1659	2313	3161		...	...
20	Wood products (excl. furniture)		6424	12049	16870	22034		3088	4895	6580	8139		...	...
21	Paper and paper products		2164	13834	19368	23439		835	4820	4721	5627		...	...
22	Printing and publishing		8692	1667	2334	3026		4740	975	1353	1755		...	...
23	Coke,refined petroleum products,nuclear fuel		296790	6098	8537	9220		9130	1334	1803	1930		...	...
24	Chemicals and chemical products		5324	9717	13601	19168		1307	3666	5233	8052		...	...
25	Rubber and plastics products		9595	26148	36606	54034		2778	6670	7381	10009		...	...
26	Non-metallic mineral products		33447	35690	49966	65465		14602	...	...	...		...	...
27	Basic metals		...	...	...	...		...	...	...	...		...	...
28	Fabricated metal products		22383	28904	40467	52304		8985	13667	18542	23315		...	...
29	Machinery and equipment n.e.c.		311	318	445	454		100	176	168	158		...	...
30	Office, accounting and computing machinery		...	...	...	...		...	...	...	...		...	...
31	Electrical machinery and apparatus		103	177	248	270		29	104	109	117		...	...
32	Radio,television and communication equipment		...	...	...	...		...	...	...	...		...	...
33	Medical, precision and optical instruments		59	...	...	...		41	...	...	...		...	...
34	Motor vehicles, trailers, semi-trailers		...	6	8	9		...	3	4	5		...	...
35	Other transport equipment		205	272	382	393		83	153	175	173		...	...
36	Furniture; manufacturing n.e.c.		5966	8536	11952	17402		2476	3393	4533	6339		...	...
37	Recycling		...	...	...	...		...	...	...	...		...	...
D	Total manufacturing	b/	577270	381340	533877	690693	b/	108014	136853	166961	214280		...	...

a/ Estimated data.
b/ Sum of available data.